Trophies of Victory

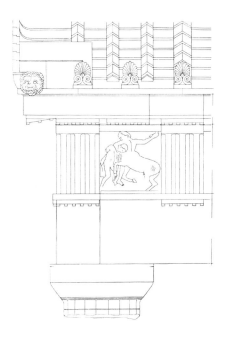

Trophies of Victory

Public Building in Periklean Athens

T. Leslie Shear, Jr.

Department of Art and Archaeology
Princeton University

In Association with Princeton University Press

Published by the Department of Art and Archaeology,
Princeton University, Princeton, New Jersey 08544-1018
in association with Princeton University Press

Distributed by Princeton University Press,
41 William Street, Princeton, New Jersey 08540-5237
press.princeton.edu

ISBN 978-0-691-17057-2

eISBN 978-1-400-88113-0

Library of Congress Control Number 2015946153

British Library Cataloging-in-Publication Data is available

Designer: Pamela Schnitter

Typesetter: Kerri Cox Sullivan

Indexers: Carol Roberts, Nina Roberts

This book was typeset in Adobe Garamond, Odyssea, and New Athena Unicode; the Odyssea fonts are
available from linguistsoftware.com/lgk.htm.

Print-on-demand edition printed by Acme Bookbinding, Charlestown, Massachusetts

Printed on acid-free paper. ∞

THIS BOOK IS DEDICATED TO

THE MEMORY OF NONIE

Table of Contents

ILLUSTRATIONS

PREFACE

My first encounter with the Parthenon came in my teenage years when I held one end of the meter tape as William B. Dinsmoor, Sr., measured the entablature blocks of the north colonnade. Ever since that day, the buildings of Periklean Athens have been a subject of absorbing interest. Some of the ideas expounded in the present volume go back to my doctoral dissertation for Princeton University in the mid-1960s. But the material has been greatly shaped and refined with the help of several dozen Princeton graduate students who, over a period of forty years, participated in my seminars on Athenian architecture of the fifth century. From their discussions and insights on the various buildings have developed many of the ideas incorporated in this book.

During the course of the twentieth century scholars have described the classical buildings, and especially those on the Acropolis, in exhaustive detail. Orlandos, Ἡ ἀρχιτεκτονικὴ τοῦ Παρθενῶνος, the Dinsmoors, *The Propylaia to the Athenian Akropolis* II, *The Classical Building*, and Paton and Stevens, *The Erechtheum* are outstanding examples of the extraordinary expertise that has been lavished upon the Acropolis buildings, each treated individually. The thrust of the present volume, however, has been somewhat different: an attempt to reconstruct the architectural and historical context in which the buildings were built, both those on the Acropolis and elsewhere in Athens and Attica. The goal has been to reconstruct an overarching program to aggrandize the cults and festivals of Athens in response to the Greek military victories in the Persian Wars. Moreover, the recognition that several of the buildings must have been under construction more or less simultaneously has emphasized the revolutionary character of the Parthenon and has enabled some of its unusual features to be observed in the smaller temples.

Many people have helped in the preparation of this book, and it is a pleasure here to express my thanks. Much of the manuscript was written in the Blegen Library of the American School of Classical Studies at Athens, and over the years the staff of the library has been consistently helpful. I am most especially grateful for the support of my colleagues in the Department of Art and Archaeology at Princeton University, in particular its former chair, Thomas Leisten, and current chair, Michael Koortbojian, for undertaking the publication of the book in association with the Princeton University Press. I thank the editor of publications for the department, Christopher Moss, for his patience and expertise. Moreover, the computer files could not have been produced without the invaluable assistance of Julie Angarone. For assistance in acquiring digital images for the illustrations, I note particularly the kindness and efficiency of the archivist of the American School, Natalia Vogeikoff-Brogan, as well as members of the Agora Excavations staff, Craig Mauzy, Jan Jordan, and Anne Hooton, and also the School's administrator, Ioanna Damanaki. I am especially grateful to Ioanna Ninou of the Photographic Archive of the Archaeological Society at Athens for permission to reproduce illustrative material under her control. For similar permissions, I thank Andrew Reinhard, former director of publications for the American School, and Naomi Norman, former editor of *The American Journal of Archaeology*. Without the willing assistance of these many people, the book could not have been published, and I express my warm gratitude to them.

BIBLIOGRAPHIC ABBREVIATIONS

Titles of periodicals and series are abbreviated according to the usage of the *American Journal of Archaeology* (www.ajaonline.org/submissions/abbreviations). Works cited by author and short title or by journal citation are fully listed by author in the bibliography. The following abbreviations are also used.

ABV	J. D. Beazley, *Attic Black-Figure Vase-Painters* (Oxford 1956)
Addenda[2]	T. H. Carpenter, T. Mannack, and M. Mendonça, *Beazley Addenda: Additional References to ABV, ARV*[2] *and Paralipomena,* 2nd ed. (Oxford 1989)
Agora III	R. E. Wycherley, *The Athenian Agora* III: *Literary and Epigraphical Testimonia* (Princeton 1957)
Agora IV	R. H. Howland, *The Athenian Agora* IV: *Greek Lamps and Their Survivals* (Princeton 1958)
Agora XI	E. B. Harrison, *The Athenian Agora* XI: *Archaic and Archaistic Sculpture* (Princeton 1965)
Agora XII	B. A. Sparkes and L. Talcott, *The Athenian Agora* XII: *Black and Plain Pottery of the 6th, 5th and 4th Centuries B.C.* (Princeton 1970)
Agora XIII	S. A. Immerwahr, *The Athenian Agora* XIII: *The Neolithic and Bronze Ages* (Princeton 1971)
Agora XIV	H. A. Thompson and R. E. Wycherley, *The Athenian Agora* XIV: *The Agora of Athens* (Princeton 1972)
Agora XV	B. D. Meritt and J. S. Traill, *The Athenian Agora* XV: *Inscriptions; The Athenian Councillors* (Princeton 1974)
Agora XVI	A. G. Woodhead, *The Athenian Agora* XVI: *Inscriptions; The Decrees* (Princeton 1997)
Agora XIX	G. V. Lalonde, M. K. Langdon, and M. B. Walbank, *The Athenian Agora* XIX: *Inscriptions; Horoi, Poletai Records, Leases of Public Lands* (Princeton 1991)
Agora XXI	M. Lang, *The Athenian Agora* XXI: *Graffiti and Dipinti* (Princeton 1976)
Agora XXIII	M. B. Moore and M. Z. Philippides, *The Athenian Agora* XXIII: *Attic Black-Figured Pottery* (Princeton 1986)

Agora XXV	M. Lang, *The Athenian Agora* XXV: *Ostraka* (Princeton 1990)
Agora XXX	M. B. Moore, *The Athenian Agora* XXX: *Attic Red-Figured and White-Ground Pottery* (Princeton 1997)
Agora XXXI	M. M. Miles, *The Athenian Agora* XXXI: *The City Eleusinion* (Princeton 1998)
*ARV*²	J. D. Beazley, *Attic Red-Figure Vase-Painters*, 2nd ed. (Oxford 1963)
ATL	B. D. Meritt, H. T. Wade-Gery, and M. F. McGregor, *The Athenian Tribute Lists*, 4 vols. (Cambridge, MA, and Princeton 1939–53)
BCSMS	*Bulletin of the Canadian Society for Mesopotamian Studies*
Brommer, *Vasenlisten*³	F. Brommer, *Vasenlisten zur griechischen Heldensage,* 3rd ed. (Marburg 1973)
*CAH*¹	*The Cambridge Ancient History*, 1st ed., 12 vols. (Cambridge 1926–39)
*CAH*²	*The Cambridge Ancient History*, rev. ed., 14 vols. (Cambridge 1970–2005)
CHI	*The Cambridge History of Iran*, 7 vols., ed. W. B. Fisher (Cambridge 1968–91)
CID II	J. Bousquet, *Corpus des inscriptions de Delphes* II: *Les comptes du quatrième et du troisième siècle* (Paris 1989)
Clinton, *Eleusis*	K. Clinton, *Eleusis, the Inscriptions on Stone: Documents of the Sanctuary of the Two Goddesses and Public Documents of the Deme*, vol. 1A (Athens 2005)
Davies, *APF*	J. K. Davies, *Athenian Propertied Families, 600–300 B.C.* (Oxford 1971)
de Ste. Croix, *OPW*	G. E. M. de Ste. Croix, *The Origins of the Peloponnesian War* (London 1972)
Dinsmoor, *AAG*³	W. B. Dinsmoor, *The Architecture of Ancient Greece*, 3rd ed. (London 1950)
EAD	*Exploration archéologique de Délos faite par l'École française d'Athènes*
FdD III.2	*Fouilles de Delphes* III, *Épigraphie*, fasc. 2, *Inscriptions du trésor des Athéniens*, 4 vols., ed. G. Colin (Paris 1909–13)
FdD III.5	*Fouilles de Delphes* III, *Épigraphie*, fasc. 5, *Les comptes du IVᵉ siècle*, ed. E. Bourguet (Paris 1932)
FGrH	F. Jacoby, *Die Fragmente der griechischen Historiker* (Berlin 1923–30; Leiden 1940–58)
FHG	C. Müller, *Fragmenta Historicorum Graecorum*, 4 vols. (Paris 1841–70)
Fraser and Matthews	See under *LGPN* I
Gomme, *HCT*	A. W. Gomme et al., *A Historical Commentary on Thucydides,* 5 vols. (Oxford 1945–81)

Gruben, *Gr. Tempel*[5]	G. Gruben, *Griechische Tempel und Heiligtümer,* 5th ed. (Munich 2001)
Hignett, *HAC*	C. Hignett, *A History of the Athenian Constitution* (Oxford 1952)
IDélos	F. Dürrbach, ed., *Inscriptions de Délos,* 7 vols. (Paris 1926–37)
IG I[3]	*Inscriptiones Graecae: Inscriptiones Atticae Euclidis Anno Anteriores,* 3rd ed. (Berlin 1981)
IG II[2]	*Inscriptiones Graecae: Inscriptiones Atticae Euclidis Anno Posteriores,* 2nd ed. (Berlin 1913–40)
IG IV[2]	*Inscriptiones Graecae: Inscriptiones Epidauri,* 2nd ed. (Berlin 1929)
IG XI.2	*Inscriptiones Graecae: Inscriptiones Deli* (Berlin 1912–14)
I. Priene	F. Hiller von Gaertringen, ed., *Inschriften von Priene* (Berlin 1906)
Jahn and Michaelis, *Arx*	O. Jahn and A. Michaelis, *Arx Athenarum a Pausania Descripta* (Bonn 1901; repr. Chicago 1976)
Jeffery, *LSAG*[2]	L. H. Jeffery, *The Local Scripts of Archaic Greece: A Study of the Origin of the Greek Alphabet and Its Development from the Eighth to the Fifth Centuries B.C.,* rev. ed. (Oxford 1990)
Judeich, *Topographie*[2]	W. Judeich, *Topographie von Athen,* 2nd ed. (Munich 1931)
Kagan, *OPW*	D. Kagan, *The Outbreak of the Peloponnesian War* (Ithaca, NY, 1969)
Kassel-Austin, *PCG*	R. Kassel and C. Austin, *Poetae Comici Graeci,* 8 vols. (Berlin and New York 1983–2001)
Kirchner, *PA*	J. E. Kirchner, *Prosopographia Attica,* 2 vols. (Berlin 1901–1903; repr. Berlin 1966; repr. Chicago 1981)
LGPN I	P. M. Fraser and E. Matthews, *A Lexicon of Greek Personal Names,* vol. 1, *The Aegean Islands, Cyprus, Cyrenaica* (Oxford 1987)
LGPN II	M. J. Osborne and S. G. Byrne, *A Lexicon of Greek Personal Names,* vol. 2, *Attica* (Oxford 1994)
LIMC	*Lexicon Iconographicum Mythologiae Classicae,* 9 vols. (Zurich 1981–94)
LSJ[9]	H. G. Liddell, R. Scott, and H. S. Jones, *A Greek-English Lexicon,* 9th ed., with revised supplement (Oxford 1996)
Marm. Par.	*Marmor Parium, IG* XII.5 444, *FGrH* 239; ed. F. Jacoby, *Das Marmor Parium* (Berlin, 1904)
Mattingly, *AER*	H. B. Mattingly, *The Athenian Empire Restored: Epigraphical and Historical Studies* (Ann Arbor 1996)
Meiggs, *AE*	R. Meiggs, *The Athenian Empire* (Oxford 1972)
Meritt, *AFD*	B. D. Meritt, *Athenian Financial Documents of the Fifth Century* (Ann Arbor 1932)
MittdAI	*Mitteilungen des deutschen archäologischen Instituts* (1948–53)

ML	R. Meiggs and D. M. Lewis, *A Selection of Greek Historical Inscriptions to the End of the Fifth Century B.C.*, rev. ed. (Oxford 1988)
Müller, *FHG*	See under *FHG*
Olympia	E. Curtius and F. Adler, eds., *Olympia: Die Ergebnisse der von dem deutschen Reich veranstalteten Ausgrabung;* vol. 2, *Die Baudenkmäler*, ed. F. Adler et al. (Berlin 1892); vol. 5, *Die Inschriften*, ed. W. Dittenberger and K. Purgold (Berlin 1896)
Orlandos, Παρθ.	A. K. Orlandos, Ἡ ἀρχιτεκτονικὴ τοῦ Παρθενῶνος, 3 vols. (Athens 1976–78)
Osborne and Byrne	See under *LGPN* II
Overbeck, *Schriftquellen*	J. Overbeck, *Die antiken Schriftquellen zur Geschichte der bildenden Künste bei den Griechen* (Leipzig 1868; repr. Hildesheim 1959)
Page, *PMG*	D. L. Page, *Poetae Melici Graeci* (Oxford 1962)
Parthenon-Kongress Basel	*Parthenon-Kongress Basel: Referate und Berichte, 4. bis 8. April 1982*, ed. E. Berger, 2 vols. (Mainz 1984)
Penrose, *Principles*[2]	F. C. Penrose, *An Investigation of the Principles of Athenian Architecture*, 2nd ed. (London 1888)
Paralipomena	J. D. Beazley, *Paralipomena: Additions to Attic Black-Figure Vase-Painters and to Attic Red-Figure Vase-Painters* (Oxford 1971)
Propylaia I	W. B. Dinsmoor, Jr., *The Propylaia to the Athenian Akropolis*, vol. 1, *The Predecessors* (Princeton 1980)
Propylaia II	W. B. Dinsmoor and W. B. Dinsmoor, Jr., *The Propylaia to the Athenian Akropolis*, vol. 2, *The Classical Building* (Princeton 2004)
Radt, ed., *TrGF*	See under *TrGF*
Raubitschek, *DAA*	A. E. Raubitschek, *Dedications from the Athenian Akropolis: A Catalogue of the Inscriptions of the Sixth and Fifth Centuries B.C.* (Cambridge, MA, 1949)
RE	A. Pauly, G. Wissowa, and W. Kroll, *Real-Encyclopädie der classischen Altertumswissenschaft* (Stuttgart 1893–)
Rhodes and Osborne, *GHI*	P. J. Rhodes and R. Osborne, *Greek Historical Inscriptions, 404–323 B.C.* (Oxford 2003)
SEG	*Supplementum Epigraphicum Graecum* (1923–)
SIG[3]	W. Dittenberger, *Sylloge Inscriptionum Graecarum*, 3rd ed. (Leipzig 1915–24)
Sokolowski, *LSCG*	F. Sokolowski, *Lois sacrées des cités grecques* (Paris 1969)
Tod, *GHI*	M. N. Tod, *A Selection of Greek Historical Inscriptions*, 2nd ed., 2 vols. (Oxford 1946–48)
Travlos, *BTA*	J. N. Travlos, *Bildlexikon zur Topographie des antiken Attika* (Tübingen 1988)
Travlos, *PDA*	J. N. Travlos, *Pictorial Dictionary of Ancient Athens* (London 1972)

TrGF	*Tragicorum Graecorum Fragmenta*, ed. B. Snell, 5 vols. (Göttingen 1971–86)
Wade-Gery, *EGH*	H. T. Wade-Gery, *Essays in Greek History* (Oxford 1958)

1

Introduction

The biographer Plutarch, in a few brief paragraphs of the *Life of Perikles* (13), provides the single surviving narrative source that describes one of the most extraordinary cultural and artistic phenomena of classical Athens. That is the construction of sacred buildings and other monuments commonly attributed to the administration of Perikles in antiquity, and often called collectively by modern writers the Periklean building program. Plutarch here speaks of "the works of Perikles," while such phrases as "when Perikles was overseer of the works"[1] or "when Perikles was building a temple on the Acropolis"[2] are to be found elsewhere in Plutarch's writings and in several other ancient authors. It was precisely consistent with the biographer's purpose of displaying his hero's greatness of spirit to dwell at some length on the buildings of Perikles as the most enduring, tangible evidence of the man's *megalophrosyne.* They were monuments which, far more than the ancient history of military victories or of political speeches, could dazzle the visitor of Plutarch's own day; their beauty, as he notes, seemed "untouched by time." There can be no doubt that Plutarch was enormously moved by his visits to the Acropolis and viewed its marble temples as the manifest exemplar of Perikles' towering stature as a statesman.

Despite Plutarch's obvious admiration, however, his account of the Periklean buildings raises almost as many questions as it answers. The biographer mentions specifically the Parthenon, the Telesterion at Eleusis, the Odeion, the Propylaia, the gold and ivory statue of Athena, and the middle Long Wall, which connected Athens to the Peiraieus by means of a fortified corridor. Fundamental questions arise immediately from the very specificity of this group of monuments. We should like to know in the first place what criterion makes them a group, what thread of common purpose can have tied them together. Since the modern term "building program" implies a coherent public policy, its use suggests that investigation might disclose the factors that motivated their choice. Still more perplexing is the attribution of these buildings specifically to the statesman Perikles. In what sense, we ask, are they to be regarded as the "works of Perikles." Phrases that recur repeatedly in the literary tradition—"having appointed Perikles construction overseer,"[3] "he was appointed manager"[4]—clearly imply his appointment to some position of official administrative oversight. Moreover, we shall see in due course that for the administration of public works the Athenians habitually made use of annually elected committees, officially entitled ἐπιστάται (overseers), who managed all aspects of construction and published accounts of their receipts and expenditures, inscribed on stone, during each year of building operations. Even though the inscriptions have come down to us in woefully fragmentary condition, it is plain to see that there is no place in these documents for the insertion of

[1] Strabo 9.1.12 (p. 395).
[2] Plut. *Mor.* 970A.
[3] Aristodemos, *FGrH* 104 F 16.1.
[4] Diodoros 12.39.1 (= Ephoros, *FGrH* 70 F 196).

Figure 1. View of the Acropolis from north

Perikles' name as some sort of construction manager, serving year after year, as the literary references seem to imply.[5]

Then, too, there is the problem of Plutarch's apparent omissions from the list of monuments ascribed to Perikles. In addition to the four buildings named by Plutarch, even the most cursory glance at the archaeological remains of Athens and Attica reveals the existence of no fewer than eight other marble temples, all of which were constructed in the second half of the fifth century. Both the Temple of Athena Nike and the Erechtheion were built at this time and are obviously important parts of the classical embellishment of the Acropolis (Figs. 1, 2). In the Agora below, the Hephaisteion occupied the low hill overlooking the market square, while outside the city walls on the east bank of the Ilissos River stood a small Ionic temple, identified by some scholars as the Temple of Artemis Agrotera. Two temples dedicated respectively to Poseidon and to Athena Sounias dominated the heights of Cape Sounion at the southeastern tip of Attica. At Rhamnous in northeastern Attica was the Temple of Nemesis, and its close contemporary was the Temple of Ares, which in Roman times was moved to the center of the Agora but stood originally in the deme of Pallene as the Temple of Athena Pallenis.[6] Since none of these eight buildings is included among the "works of Perikles," modern commentators have been inclined to remark upon the incompleteness of Plutarch's list of monuments.[7] Plainly, any attempt to describe public building in fifth-century Athens must account for a total of ten temples dedicated to different deities; the Propylaia, the entrance gateway to the city's principal sanctuary; and the Odeion, the venue for musical contests at the city's principal festival, the Panathenaia. We shall see that some of these buildings were being built at the same time, and much of their construction falls in the period from the 450s to the 420s.

Plutarch referred collectively to κατασκευαὶ οἰκοδομημάτων ἐξ ὧν ἐκόσμησεν ὁ Περικλῆς τὰς Ἀθήνας (Per. Comp. 3.7), "construction of buildings with which Perikles adorned Athens," and else-

---

[5] See pp. 43–48 below.

[6] Travlos, PDA, 148–157 (Athena Nike), 213–227 (Erechtheion), 261–273 (Hephaisteion), 112–120 (Artemis Agrotera), 104–108 (Ares); Travlos, BTA, 388–398 (Rhamnous), 404–424 (Sounion). For identification of the Temple of Ares as the classical Temple of Athena Pallenis, see M. Korres, Horos 10–12 (1992–98) 83–104. For recent accounts of the building program, Hurwit, Athenian Acropolis, 87–105; cf. Camp, Archaeology of Athens, 59–117, 248–251.

[7] Boersma, Building Policy, 65–81; Corso, Monumenti Periclei, 24–28; Stadter, Commentary, 144.

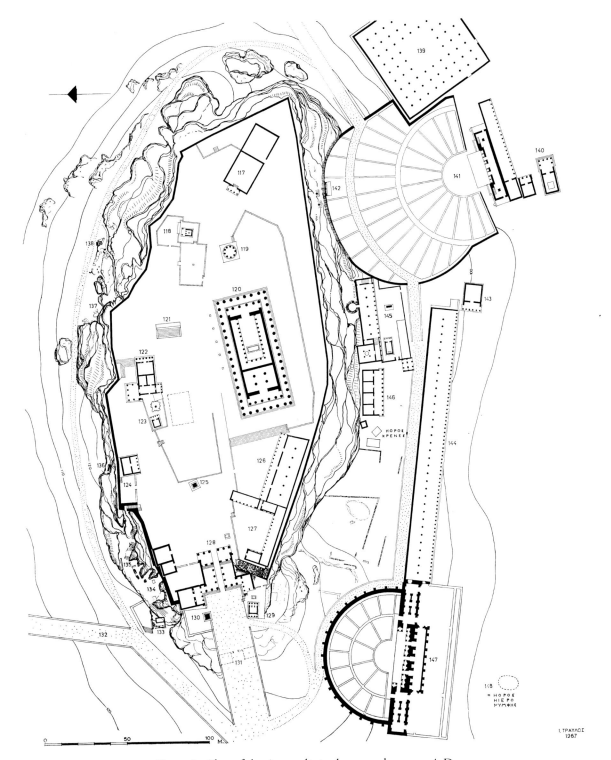

Figure 2. Plan of the Acropolis in the second century A.D.

where he called them more specifically ἀναθήματα (*Per.* 12.1), that is, sacred dedications offered to the gods and set up in their sanctuaries. The notion that the city of Athens was adorned with new sacred buildings during the period of Perikles' political ascendency by no means finds its earliest expression in the writings of Plutarch. Although it suited the biographer's purpose to give a more detailed description of the buildings than has survived elsewhere, it is important to emphasize that he drew upon a long tradition that first appeared in the fifth century, received rhetorical embroidery at the hands of Athenian orators of the fourth century, and was quoted thence in the Greek lexicons and by later scholiasts on classical authors.

Our first surviving reference to the embellishment of Athens comes from the chorus of cavalrymen who gave their name to Aristophanes' *Knights*, a play that was produced in the winter of 424, less than five years after Perikles had passed from the stage of history:

> Let us eulogize our fathers, since they were mighty men
> worthy of their native soil and worthy of Athena's robe,
> who always winning everywhere in battles on dry land
> and in the ship-fenced host beautified this city [τήνδ' ἐκόσμησαν πόλιν].[8]

The aristocratic young horsemen praise a whole generation of Athenians, their fathers who fought the wars of the first half of the century. By their victories on land and sea, they had built up the empire that lesser men were now trying to hold together. Particularly noteworthy is the juxtaposition of military victories and the beautification of the city, although in the poetic ellipsis it may not be obvious that the former enables the latter. As every contemporary spectator knew, however, on the morrow of the battle, the victors amassed the spoils. Those from the battles of Marathon and Salamis, Plataia and the Eurymedon were legendary, and their enormous value at sale was a well-known source of revenue both for the obligatory thank-offerings to the gods and for all manner of public works.[9]

Athenian public speakers of the fourth century liked to berate their less worthy contemporaries by extolling their fifth-century forebears, whose exploits came by the alchemy of oratory to form the mythology of Athens's heroic past. The adornment of Athens with sacred buildings and dedications was a frequently cited example of the virtues of the Athenians' ancestors; but the orators imply that these monuments were thought of almost as trophies erected from the spoils of the Persian Wars. There seems, in fact, to have been a general assumption that the temples of the third quarter of the fifth century were associated in some way with the titanic events of that illustrious decade that began at Marathon and ended at Plataia. Demosthenes, in his *Third Olynthiac* oration, delivered in 349, likened the temples generally to trophies celebrating military victory:

> Many and honorable trophies [τρόπαι] for victories on land and sea did they erect, themselves campaigning in the field; and they alone of mankind left behind them by their exploits a glory too great for envy. Such was their place in the Greek world: as pertains to the city itself, look around you and see what manner of men they were both in public and in private. In public, they built for us so many buildings and monuments of such beauty, temples and votive offerings to the gods, that to none of those who come after is there left a hope of surpassing them.[10]

An ancient scholiast on the passage understood the text of Demosthenes to be a more specific reference to monuments commemorating the victories of the Persian Wars:

> All these they made and dedicated from the Persian spoils, the silver-footed throne of Xerxes, and the scimitar of Mardonios, and they erected the Propylaia of the Acropolis, and the bronze statue of Athena and that of gold and ivory.[11]

Some years earlier, in 355, Demosthenes had given the same theme greater rhetorical development in two passages of his speech *Against Androtion* (22):

---

[8] Aristoph. *Knights* 565–568.

[9] See W. K. Pritchett, *The Greek State at War* (Berkeley 1991) vol. 5, 369–371, 416–425.

[10] Demosth. 3.24–25; and cf. similar praise for the buildings, 23 *Aristokr.* 207; [13] *Organization* 28. For the buildings as trophies of victory, cf. Plut. *Mor.* 349D.

[11] Schol. Demosth. 3.25 (121 Dilts).

One could cite many instances, both ancient and modern, but of those that are most familiar for all to hear, take, if you please, this. The men who built the Propylaia and the Parthenon, and adorned the other temples from the spoils of the barbarians, men in whom we all take natural pride—you know this of course from tradition that after they abandoned the city and shut themselves up in Salamis, it was because they had the triremes that they were victorious in the sea battle and saved the city and all their belongings, and they made themselves authors for the rest of the Greeks of many and great benefits, of which not even time can erase the memory. (13)

For possessing at one time the greatest wealth of all the Greeks, they spent it all for love of honor; they made donation from their private fortunes and shrank from no danger for the sake of glory. Therefore immortal possessions are passed down to the Athenian people, on the one hand the memory of their exploits, on the other the beauty of the votives erected in their honor, yonder Propylaia, the Parthenon, the stoas, the ship-sheds. (76)

In the first of these two passages, Demosthenes' rhetoric gets the better of chronological accuracy, for his syntax makes the builders of the Propylaia and the Parthenon, the grammatical subject of the verb, the same men who saved the city by winning the sea battle at Salamis. Indeed, one ancient commentator on the passage, writing about the time of Plutarch, was at pains to set the record straight. Even though his commentary has come down to us as a mutilated papyrus fragment that preserves only the right half of a column of text, the writer plainly cited a decree moved by Perikles himself to show that Demosthenes had misdated the construction of the Propylaia and the Parthenon by thirty years.[12] Of greater interest, however, than the orator's chronological inexactitude is the fact that he clearly believed the great temples of the fifth century to have been built and adorned with Persian spoils. Moreover, he regarded it as common knowledge, a fact with which every member of the great citizen jury was perfectly familiar. Other ancient scholia on the same passage state that the two famous colossal statues of Athena made by Pheidias, the one of bronze and the other of gold and ivory, were funded from the spoils of the battles of Marathon and Salamis, respectively.[13] Indeed, Demosthenes himself later made an explicit statement to that effect about the bronze Athena, when, in 343, he had occasion to mention an inscribed stele that stood beside that statue:

By Zeus, was the inscription set up just anywhere as it chanced? No. Even though the whole of our Acropolis is a holy place, and although its area is so large, it stands at the right hand beside the great bronze Athena that was dedicated by the city as a meed of valor of the war against the barbarians, with money given by the Greeks.[14]

It was also known to the orators of the fourth century that the embellishment of Athens with sacred buildings was in some way to be attributed to Perikles, and that statesman was said to have been responsible for depositing on the Acropolis large sums of money from which the temples could be financed. A clear statement comes from Isokrates, writing in advanced old age; but he was born in 436, when the sculptures of the Parthenon were still being carved and the Propylaia had just been begun, and he is as close to an eyewitness as our sources will bring us.

---

[12] P. Strassburg 84 verso: Meritt and Wade-Gery, *Hesperia* 26 (1957) 163–197; but see the criticism of the restorations by R. Sealy, *Hermes* 86 (1958) 440–446, and the cautious remarks of Meiggs, *AE,* 515–518; de Ste. Croix, *OPW,* 310–311.

[13] Schol. Demosth. 22.13 (45 Dilts); and cf. schol. VM Aristoph. *Knights* 1169a (Koster).

[14] Demosth. 19 *Embassy* 272; for the dedication of the statue from the spoils of Marathon, cf. Paus. 1.28.1, 9.4.1; chap. 2, pp. 17–21 below.

Finally, Perikles, because he was both a good leader of the people and an excellent orator, so adorned the city [ἐκόσμησε τὴν πόλιν] with temples, sacred dedications, and other monuments, that still to this day visitors who come to Athens think her worthy to rule not only the Greeks, but all the world as well; and in addition he carried up to the Acropolis no less than ten thousand talents.[15]

Still more explicit is a brief quotation that has survived from a speech of Lykourgos against Kephisodotos, and in favor of the honors proposed for the orator Demades: "Perikles, who captured Samos and Euboia and Aigina, who built the Propylaia and the Odeion and the Hekatompedon, and who carried up to the Acropolis ten thousand talents of silver, was crowned with a wreath of olive."[16]

These passages show that well-informed Athenians of the fourth century gave credit to Perikles not only for the beautification of the sanctuaries with sacred dedications in general, but also for the construction of specific buildings. Lykourgos mentioned by name the Propylaia, the Odeion, and the Parthenon, all of which were to appear later in Plutarch's account of the Athenian buildings. Philochoros, in the fourth book of his *Atthis,* named Perikles as overseer of the Lykeion gymnasium, although this notice appears nowhere else.[17] Most notorious of the "works of Perikles," however, that which caught the popular imagination and received the most fanciful embroidery, was his alleged involvement with the gold and ivory statue of Athena in the Parthenon. That notoriety is probably due in large part to Aristophanes, who, in a famous passage of the *Peace* (603–611) written ten years after the fact, joked that Perikles had fanned the flames of war in order to avoid incrimination in the scandalous peculations of the sculptor Pheidias. In the fourth century, Philochoros cited the dates of the eponymous archons to prove that the golden statue was dedicated seven years before the outbreak of the Peloponnesian War, but he simply stated as a well-known fact that Perikles was overseer of the statue.[18] The contemporary historian Ephoros of Kyme gave the incident elaborate and lengthy development, including direct quotation of Aristophanes' lines, in his discussion of the causes of the Peloponnesian War; but he too made Perikles' administrative collaboration with Pheidias the basis for his account. Ephoros's narrative was later quoted at length by Diodoros and abridged by Aristodemos.[19] These references to the dedication of sacred buildings, few and scattered as they may be, indicate that Athenians traditionally thought of these monuments as commemorating the military victories of the Persian Wars and associated their construction with the name of the statesman Perikles.

Comparison of the literary tradition of the fourth century and later with the archaeological record of the temples themselves reveals a striking chronological discrepancy. None of the buildings discussed above began construction much before 450, and some were begun as late as the 420s, whereas the great battles of the Persian Wars that they were thought to commemorate had occurred fully a generation earlier. It would be easy to conclude that the orators were simply poorly informed about Athenian history of the previous century and mistakenly assumed that the dedication of splendid monuments to the gods was a response to the unexpected good fortune of epic military victories. This erroneous assumption was then embroidered and embellished by later writers, who developed the anecdotes about Perikles personal involvement. Finally, Plutarch attributed the temples and sacred dedications to the greatness of Perikles' statesmanship. That this is an overly simplistic re-

[15] Isokr. 15 *Antid.* 234; and cf. the closely similar statements Isokr. 7 *Areop.* 66, 8 *Peace* 126; see also Plut. *Mor.* 343D, 348D, 351A.

[16] Frag. 58 (Conomis) = Glossa Patmia, s.v. Ἑκατόμπεδον (*BCH* 1 [1877] 149). Hekatompedon, the official name of the eastern cella, was sometimes applied to the whole building: Harpokration, s.v. (ε 17 Keaney).

[17] Harpokration, s.v. Λύκειον (λ 30 Keaney) = Philochoros, *FGrH* 328 F 38.

[18] Schol. RVΓ Aristoph. *Peace* 605 (Holwerda) = Philochoros, *FGrH* 328 F 121.

[19] Ephoros, *FGrH* 70 F 196, quoted by Diodoros 12.39.1–41.1; Aristodemos, *FGrH* 104 F 16.1–2; cf. Plut. *Per.* 31.2–5, 32.6; *Suda,* s.v. Φειδίας (φ 246 Adler).

construction will become apparent in detailed discussion of the individual buildings in subsequent chapters, which will attempt to elucidate some of the difficulties that emerge upon first reading the literary references to the Periklean buildings. If, on the other hand, the orators' statements preserve reliable information, then the Parthenon and the other temples are to be interpreted as thank-offerings to the gods for the victories of the Persian Wars. In that case, it will be necessary to explain why more than three decades elapsed between the battles of Salamis and Plataia and the beginning of construction on the Parthenon, while thereafter a flurry of continuous temple building occupied much of the rest of the century.

The lack of building activity in the second quarter of the fifth century is the more surprising because Athens reacted so differently to the victory at Marathon in 490. There is now fairly general agreement that the first great marble temple on the Acropolis, the Older Parthenon, began to be built in the immediate aftermath of that battle.[20] The building was planned as a Doric peristyle temple of huge scale, measuring 23.53 × 66.94 m, with a peristyle of 6 × 16 columns. It was to be the largest temple on the mainland of Greece at the time of its design, and it was to be entirely of Pentelic marble. The new temple would have greatly surpassed in grandeur the Old Temple of Athena Polias that stood on the north side of the Acropolis. It was a perfect expression of the exuberant outpouring of thanks to the goddess Athena for bestowing the victory, and of civic pride in the military achievement of the young democracy. In the early years of the 480s, work began on the poros podium that formed an artificial platform to support the temple.[21] The builders progressed to the setting of the lowest column drums of the peristyle and the orthostates of the cella walls before construction was abruptly disrupted by the Persian destruction of the Acropolis in 480.

At about the same time, the Athenians seem to have built their famous treasury at Delphi and dedicated to Apollo the firstfruits (ἀρχοθίνια) of the battle. Many scholars have now come to accept a date in the 480s for the building's construction, as long espoused by the French excavators.[22] This view has recently found support in Amandry's demonstration that the Marathon base, along the building's south flank, rests in part on a foundation course projecting 0.15–0.30 m from the south wall of the treasury, and obviously so built to support the base.[23] So, in addition to a new temple on the Acropolis, the Athenians celebrated their defeat of the Persians by erecting a marble treasury for Apollo. It was the first Athenian monument dedicated in a Panhellenic sanctuary, prominently located at a turn of the Sacred Way, where every visitor ascending to Apollo's temple would pass its southern flank. There, along the foot of the wall, the inscription on the base proclaimed to all that Athens had dedicated the firstfruits of the Battle of Marathon.

Quite different was Athens's response to the decisive victories at Salamis and Plataia. To be sure, according to Herodotos (9.13.2), both the Acropolis and the entire lower city were reduced to ruins when Mardonios's army withdrew to central Greece. So it is only natural that the returning Athenian refugees would turn first to the repair of their private houses, and then to the city's fortification walls, as Thucydides tells us.[24] But it was a moment when all Greeks could exult in the final repulse of Xerxes' armies, and by long tradition thank-offerings to the gods were obligatory. Indeed, immediately after the Battle of Salamis, the Greeks sent captured Phoenician triremes to Poseidon

---

[20] E.g., Dinsmoor, *AAG*³, 149–150; W. C. West, "Greek Public Monuments of the Persian Wars" (Ph.D. diss., University of North Carolina, 1965) 62–63; Boersma, *Athenian Building Policy,* 39; Travlos, *PDA,* 444: Hurwit, *Athenian Acropolis* (1999) 130–132; Lawrence, *Greek Architecture*⁵, 103; Camp, *Archaeology of Athens,* 52–53; Gruben, *Gr. Tempel*⁵, 171–172; contra R. Tölle-Kastenbein, *JdI* 108 (1993) 43–75.

[21] On the date of the podium, see endnote 2, pp. 395–397 below.

[22] E.g., Neer, *Style and Politics in Athenian Vase Painting,* 197–198; Neer, *ClAnt* 23 (2004) 67, 72–74; Brinkmann, in P. C. Bol, ed., *Geschichte der antiken Bildhauerkunst,* vol. 1, 271–280; Lawrence, *Greek Architecture*⁵, 99. Cf. von den Hoff, in Schultz and von den Hoff, eds., *Structure, Image, Ornament,* 98–104, with bibliography.

[23] P. Amandry, *BCH* 122 (1998) 75–90, especially 86–88.

[24] Thuc. 1.89.5, 90.3, 93.2.

at Sounion and the Isthmus, and another to Ajax at Salamis (Hdt. 8.12.1). In due course, sale of the booty from the battles enabled the dedication of colossal bronze statues of Apollo at Delphi, of Zeus at Olympia, and of Poseidon at the Isthmus.[25] Most famous of all the Greek votive offerings was the gilded tripod dedicated to Apollo at Delphi. The tripod itself was supported by a tall column formed of three intertwined serpents, and on the coils of their bodies were inscribed the names of the thirty-one cities that fought the war for the deliverance of Greece.[26] In all this activity, the gods of the Panhellenic sanctuaries were richly rewarded for their help in the defeat of the barbarians, but Athena at Athens is conspicuously absent. Her temple on the Acropolis suffered heavy damage at the hands of the Persians, and the great new temple, the Older Parthenon, was abandoned in the early stages of construction.

There is no evidence for the dedication of thank-offerings on the Acropolis before the 460s. The only building activity seems to have involved reconstruction of the northern fortification wall, which was carried out in large part with spolia from the ruined temples.[27] Blocks from the entablature of the Old Athena Temple were reassembled in their correct order, with triglyphs and metopes from the frieze resting on architraves and surmounted by parts of the Doric cornice. Another part of the wall consisted of unfinished marble column drums for the Older Parthenon, many of them heavily calcined from the fires that consumed the scaffolding on the building site.[28] Placed in this way, the spolia were clearly intended to be visible, as they are to this day, to all who frequented the Agora below. This was no votive offered to the goddess, but a grim memorial for all time of the destruction wrought by the barbarians. In the years after the defeat of Persia, the Athenians seemingly made no effort to repair the damaged peristyle of the Old Athena Temple. It is obvious, too, that work on the Older Parthenon was indefinitely suspended. Although many of the column drums in the north wall are far too damaged to be used in the building, and so were consigned to reuse as spolia, many others, still lying about the Acropolis in good condition, were abandoned in the early stages of dressing the stone.

Athens's conspicuous failure to rebuild the temples on the Acropolis in the immediate aftermath of the Persian Wars has often encouraged scholars to explain this phenomenon by recourse to the so-called Oath of Plataia. It is well known that a tradition was current in fourth-century Athens of a solemn oath allegedly sworn by the Greek armies before the Battle of Plataia. A version of this oath, swearing to stand firm against the barbarian invaders, was later inscribed on stone in the fourth century.[29] A slightly different version was quoted by the orator Lykourgos about 330 and later repeated almost verbatim by Diodoros, presumably drawing on Ephoros.[30] The literary versions of the oath, but not the text of the inscription, include a pledge not to rebuild the temples burned by the Persians but to allow them to remain as "memorials of the barbarians' impiety." It is, of course, this part of the oath that has been invoked to account for the lack of building activity in Athenian sanctuaries during the second quarter of the fifth century. But the authenticity of the Plataian oath was already impugned in the fourth century by Theopompos of Chios, who regarded it as an Athenian

---

[25] Hdt. 8.21.2; Paus. 10.14.5 (Apollo); Hdt. 9.81; Paus. 5.23.1–2, 6.10.6, 10.14.5 (Zeus); Hdt. 9.81 (Poseidon). See Gauer, *Weihgeschenke aus den Perserkriegen*, 96–98; West, "Public Monuments," 87–90, 92–93.

[26] Hdt. 9.81; Thuc. 1.32.2–3; [Demosth.] 59 *Near.* 97; Diod. 11.33; Paus. 10.13.9; ML 27; Gauer, *Weihgeschenke aus den Perserkriegen*, 75–96; West, "Public Monuments," 74–87.

[27] See M. E. Korres, in M. Stamatopoulou and M. Yerolanou, eds., *Excavating Classical Culture* (Oxford 2002) 179–186.

[28] See A. Tschira, *JdI* 55 (1940) 242–261. A completely different history of the site is proposed by G. Ferrari, *AJA* 106 (2002) 11–35, who attempts to revive the unconvincing theory of Dörpfeld that the ancient Temple of Athena Polias was not destroyed by the Persians and continued standing until the Roman period.

[29] Rhodes and Osborne, *GHI* 88.

[30] Lyk. *Leokr.* 81; Diod. 11.29.3.

fabrication.[31] This, combined with Herodotos's silence about any such oath in his detailed account of the preliminaries leading up to the battle, has caused a majority of modern historians to disbelieve in its historicity.[32] Even if one accepts that religious prohibition exerted its force on Athenians of this period, that sanction would only have exacerbated an underlying problem that has been overlooked in the lengthy debate about the authenticity of the Plataian oath.

That problem was largely inherent in the process of building a Greek temple and was completely obscured by Plutarch's misunderstanding of the economics of public works in the fifth century. In his lively account of the debates on the buildings (*Per.* 12), the biographer ascribed to Perikles the argument that public works were a source of economic power and profit: "They put, as it were, the whole city on the payroll" (σχεδὸν ὅλην ποιοῦσιν ἔμισθον τὴν πόλιν [12.4]). He then goes on to characterize Perikles' social policy in terms that foreshadow the welfare state: "In his desire that the disorganized crowd of common laborers should neither have no share at all in the public receipts, nor take payment for being idle and lazy, he proposed enthusiastically to the people projects for great constructions" (12.5). Plutarch goes on to list the raw materials to be used and the many specialized skills needed to supply and work these materials, which provides the most detailed and accurate picture of the complexities of ancient building operations that has come down to us in literature. Furthermore, most of the details can be verified in the records of actual builders of the fifth and fourth centuries. On the other hand, what is disconcerting in Plutarch's description, and completely anachronistic in the Classical period, is his picture of the Athenian labor force as "τὸν ἀσύντακτον καὶ βάναυσον ὄχλον" (the disorganized crowd of common laborers) that is "ἀργὸν καὶ σχολάζοντα" (idle and lazy). Both language and imagery conjure up a vast urban proletariat, largely unemployed and unskilled, such as confronted successive emperors in the Roman capital of Plutarch's day. But such a picture could hardly be farther from the reality of classical Athens, where, as we shall see, the problem confronting building administrators was almost precisely the opposite. For most of the Classical period the chief difficulty lay in finding and attracting a sufficiently large number of sufficiently skilled workmen to carry out the complex tasks involved in building a marble temple.[33] It is clear that Plutarch has misunderstood the economics and sociology of the Greek city-state in the fifth century, and in so doing has greatly skewed our picture of Athenian temple building.

There is abundant evidence that ancient builders and craftsmen were a migratory lot, who moved readily from place to place as demand for their services changed. Masons and quarrymen, carpenters and gilders, painters and plasterers, architects and sculptors, theirs was a small community of highly skilled and specialized artisans whose livelihood depended on building projects in different cities and sanctuaries. To the administrators of such a project, it was important to attract these craftsmen from all over Greece, and much effort was evidently expended on the search for skilled

---

[31] *FGrH* 115 F 153. See W. R. Connor, *Theopompos and Fifth-Century Athens* (Washington, DC, 1968) 78–89; J. Walsh, *Chiron* 11 (1981) 43–45; E. Badian, *From Plataea to Potidaea* (Baltimore 1993) 26–29.

[32] Among the many who have rejected the historicity of the oath, see F. Koepp, *JdI* 5 (1890) 271–277; J. G. Frazer, *Pausanias* (London 1898) vol. 5, 440, note on 10.35.2; G. Busolt, *Griechische Geschichte*, 2nd ed., vol. 2 (Gotha 1893) 654, note 3; W. Kolbe, *JdI* 51 (1936) 27–28; E. Meyer, *Geschichte des Altertums*, 3rd ed., vol. 4 (Stuttgart 1931) 350, note 1; Robert, *Études epigraphiques*, 307–316; *ATL* III, 105; R. Sealey, *JHS* 80 (1960) 194–195; C. Habicht, *Hermes* 89 (1961) 11–20; C. Hignett, *Xerxes' Invasion of Greece* (Oxford 1963) 460–461; W. K. Pritchett *The Greek State at War* (Berkeley 1979) vol. 3, 232–233, note 8; N. D. Robertson, *AJAH* 5 (1980) 117–119; A. J. Podlecki, *Perikles and His Circle* (London 1998) 70; Rhodes and Osborne, *GHI,* 442–448. Fewer scholars have ventured to accept the authenticity of the oath; see W. N. Bates, *HSCP* 12 (1901) 319–326; W. B. Dinsmoor, *Hesperia* Suppl. 5 (1941) 158 and note 333; A. E. Raubitschek, *TAPA* 91 (1960) 178–183; Raubitschek, *BICS* 8 (1961) 60–61; West, "Public Monuments," 94–104; P. Siewert, *Der Eid von Plataiai;* Meiggs, *AE,* 504–507; Walsh, *Chiron* 11 (1981) 53–54, note 58; M. Ostwald, *Autonomia* (Chico, CA, 1982) 18–21; A. R. Burn, *Persia and the Greeks*, 2nd ed. (London 1984) 512–515; J. P. Barron, *CAH*², vol. 4 (1988) 604; I. S. Mark, *Athena Nike*, 98–104.

[33] See A. M. Burford, "The Economics of Greek Temple Building," *PCPS* 191 (1965) 21–34.

personnel. The available evidence illustrates the practice of the fourth century and later periods, but there is no reason to believe that time-honored procedures of the building trades underwent significant changes with the passage of decades. We learn from the inscribed accounts that representatives from Epidauros let contracts at Corinth, Argos, Megara, Aigina, Tegea, and elsewhere. The overseers of the Tholos at Epidauros dispatched a herald to recruit Athenian labor, and next to his wages in the annual account, they recorded the price of paper on which they wrote the contracts that he offered, and they listed the traveling expenses of two Athenian workmen whom he managed to engage.[34] As a result of these and similar efforts, the building records from the sanctuary of Asklepios list by name no fewer than forty Corinthian contractors, nineteen from Argos, and thirteen from Athens, who worked at Epidauros over the years.[35]

At about the same time, similar heralds from Delphi sought to recruit skilled labor for the new Temple of Apollo, and as a result craftsmen and contractors from Athens, Corinth, Argos, and Tegea journeyed to Delphi to take work in the sanctuary. Among them appears to be Philon, the Athenian architect of the arsenal in the Peiraieus, who took a contract to manage the stoa in the gymnasium.[36] The builders of all periods seem to have formed heterogeneous crews summoned from all the corners of Greece for a single enterprise or a few years' work. The accounts of the fourth century abound in payments to workmen traveling to and from building sites, and in living expenses paid to foreign laborers recruited for the job.[37] The Eleusinian overseers hired men and dealt with retailers from Megara and Troizen for work in the sanctuary,[38] and Thucydides reports (5.82.6) that Athenian carpenters and stonemasons helped build the long walls of Argos in 417. The prominence of resident aliens on the payrolls of the Erechtheion overseers is well known; there are no fewer than 42 metics among the 107 workmen whose names survive, while only 24 are known to have been Athenian citizens.[39]

Fluctuations in the availability of skilled labor were a major factor affecting the conduct and timing of building operations and are no doubt reflected, if only indirectly, in the building accounts. At Epidauros, the accounts show that the Temple of Asklepios was built quickly and efficiently and stood fully complete in four years and eight months. The Tholos, however, was still unfinished after work dragged on for twenty-seven years. In the year of the priest Damopeitheus, the only payment was for inscribing the account on the stele; and in Years 23, 24, and 25 no work at all was done.[40] In her study of the economics of building temples, A. M. Burford has particularly emphasized the remarkable lack of building operations in much of Greece from the end of the Peloponnesian War

[34] Recruitment of Athenian labor, *IG* IV² 103, lines 158–161; the ἐγδοτῆρες who let the contracts in various cities, *IG* IV² 103, lines 4–5, 44–45. The numerous heralds whose missions are recorded in *IG* IV² 102, lines 222–259. See Burford, *Temple Builders,* 103, 132–133, 160–163.

[35] Prosopography of the Epidaurian inscriptions is listed in Burford, *Temple Builders,* 232–245; ethnics are included where known.

[36] For heralds "selling" contracts for work at Delphi in 335, *CID* II 76, col. II, lines 6, 62; col. III, lines 21–22. Foreign contractors at Delphi in 334/3, *CID* II 79A, col. I, lines 23–28: a group of specialized silversmiths from Athens and Corinth undertook the repair of the great silver craters of Kroisos (Hdt. 1.51); cf. later repairs to the same vessels, 81A, lines 5–13. *CID* II 79A, col. I, lines 33–34: Philon the Athenian; lines 34–36: contractors from Tegea and Argos. It is interesting to note that two of the Argives, Chremon and Nikostratos, had worked previously at Epidauros: *IG* IV² 103, lines 12, 44, 53–55.

[37] For traveling expenses (ἐφόδια): *IG* IV² 102, lines 252–300, passim; 103, lines 12, 37, 42, 56; *CID* II 84B, line 8; 87, line 3; 110, lines 27, 30, 31. For living expenses (σιτηρέσιον): *IG* IV² 103, line 168; *CID* II 76, col. III, line 17; 79A, col. I, lines 40–41. See J. K. Davies, in D. J. Mattingly and J. Salmon, eds., *Economics Beyond Agriculture in the Classical World* (London 2001) 209–229.

[38] *IG* II² 1673 = Clinton, *Eleusis,* 159, lines 28, 45, 46, 53, 59.

[39] R. H. Randall, *AJA* 57 (1953) 199–210.

[40] Timing of the Asklepios temple: Burford, *Temple Builders,* 192; of the Tholos, Burford, 220–221. The year of Damopeitheus: *IG* IV² 103, lines 139–141; Years 23–25, lines 146–147.

down through the first quarter of the fourth century. She has argued convincingly that "the only really satisfactory explanation for this widespread building recession is not shortage of money, not war, but a widespread scarcity of skilled labour."[41] It may be suggested that similar conditions affected the building trades in mainland Greece during the period after the Persian Wars. This was a period when the absence of public works under construction in mainland Greece contrasted conspicuously with the situation in contemporary Sicily and South Italy. There, in the wake of the Greek victory over the Carthaginians at Himera in 480, the tyrants of Sicily indulged in an extravagant campaign of temple building. During the period ca. 480 to ca. 460, at least nine Doric peripteral temples began to be built, and work continued on others begun in earlier years.[42] Much the greater number of Greek construction workers was no doubt employed in these operations.

In the chapters that follow, we shall examine in detail the buildings of an equally extravagant program of temple construction. By reviewing the monuments each in turn, it will be possible to observe among the buildings unusual similarities of detail in both design and decoration, which are probably best attributed to teams of skilled craftsmen moving from one building to the next. What will also emerge from this survey is the unusual number of anomalies in the tempo of construction: long delays at various stages of the work, changes in plans as work progressed, removal of personnel from one project to another, and stonework left unfinished. Some of these anomalies may be due in part to the logistics of constructing multiple buildings on different sites at the same time. But others, it will be argued, are best explained by fluctuations in the number and skills of the available labor force. Unfortunately, the copious details preserved in the building accounts from Epidauros, Delphi, and Delos are not found in the Athenian documents until the end of the fifth century. This is partly because the inscriptions themselves are extremely fragmentary, but also because the earlier texts show a much more rudimentary form of accounting. Nevertheless, variations in the pace of work can often be detected in the construction history of the buildings themselves.

A good example of this can be seen on the Acropolis itself in the remains of the Older Parthenon. Construction of that temple seems to have begun in the years just after the Battle of Marathon and was certainly cut short by the destruction of 480. So work continued for eight or nine years at the most, possibly for as few as five. In these years the foundation podium and crepidoma were built, and marble blocks for the colonnade and superstructure began to be prepared. All eighteen examples of bottom column drums show by the dressing of their upper and lower surfaces that they were set in place on the stylobate. Only three of the eight surviving drums of the second tier were set in their columns, while those intended for higher positions in the shafts had barely been roughed out when work was abandoned.[43] So in the five to eight years that the temple was under construction, the builders had barely begun to raise the columns of the peristyle. By striking contrast, the Periklean Parthenon, a slightly larger building on the same foundations and with more columns in its peristyle, was finished to the rooftop, with all of its sculpture in place, except for the pediments, in only ten years.[44] This glaring discrepancy in the speed of construction surely indicates that a substantially

---

[41] Burford, *PCPS* 191 (1965) 32.

[42] At Syracuse, Temple of Athena; at Himera, Temple of Nike; three temples at Akragas: "Hera Licinia," Athena, and Demeter; three temples at Selinous: Hera (ER), A, and O; at Paestum, Temple of Hera II. See Dinsmoor, *AAG*[3], 107–111. Work continued on the colossal temples of Olympian Zeus at Akragas (Dinsmoor, *AAG*[3], 101–105) and of Apollo (Temple GT) at Selinous (Dinsmoor, *AAG*[3], 99–101).

[43] See Tschira, *JdI* 55 (1940) 245–246. All but one of the eighteen bottom drums are in the north wall. Of the drums in course II, only nos. 5, 14, and 25 were set in place. For drums abandoned in the early stages of dressing, course I, no. 32 (fig. 9); course III, no. 44 (fig. 2); course IV, no. 45 (fig. 8). The peristyle columns of the Periklean Parthenon have eleven courses of drums to complete the height of the shaft.

[44] The Periklean building was begun in 447/6 and completed, except for the pediment sculpture, in 438/7. See chap. 3, pp. 67–68 below.

larger, more skillful, and more experienced group of craftsmen had been assembled at Athens by the middle years of the century.[45]

As we pass in review the *anathemata* that arose in the sanctuaries of Attica during the second half of the fifth century, we shall need to observe, where possible, evidence for the timing and tempo of their construction, and in some cases how the construction of one affected or influenced the design of others. Then, too, we shall need to emphasize the extraordinary fact of their sheer numbers, that the city of Athens erected ten marble temples, all of which were at some stage in the process of construction in the period from 450 to 420. We saw earlier how orators of the fourth century spoke of the temples generally as monuments commemorating the victories in the Persian Wars. So it will be important to ask whether individual buildings reveal any evidence to support such an overarching theme, either in the deities to whom they were dedicated or in the design and decoration of their architecture. Taken as a group, the *anathemata* will tell us much about Athens's attitude toward the Persian Wars, and how that attitude developed as the decades lengthened after the deliverance of Greece. In one respect the modern visitor to the Acropolis can agree with Plutarch and the orators that the builders of the fifth century, in the words of Demosthenes, passed down "immortal possessions to the Athenian people."

---

[45] Cf. Burford, *Temple Builders*, 203.

2

The Development
of the Periklean Program

Unlike the Panhellenic sanctuaries, at Athens the first monuments commemorating the victories of Marathon and Salamis were not dedications to Athena on the Acropolis but consisted of marble trophies erected on the battlefield. It was normal practice in Greek warfare for the victorious army to erect a trophy at the spot where its phalanx had turned the enemy to rout; but these battle trophies were temporary affairs consisting of armor and weapons captured from the enemy and hung about a post or tree trunk.[1] Quite different was the permanent memorial that the Athenians erected on the field at Marathon nearly thirty years after the victory. This took the form of a freestanding marble column of the Ionic order that probably supported a marble replica of a battle trophy, possibly decorated by a figure of Nike. Several unfluted drums and the monumental capital of this column were later built into a medieval tower in the northeastern part of the plain of Marathon, where they were seen and mentioned by various early travelers in the nineteenth century, but only received formal study by E. Vanderpool in 1965.[2]

The surviving pieces of the column include three drums, measuring 0.82 m in diameter, and large fragments of several others, together with the Ionic capital itself that measures 1.35 m across the volutes. The abacus of the capital is surmounted by a high plinth that carries a large trapezoidal socket plainly intended to receive a piece of marble sculpture. Also found nearby was a severely damaged fragment of sculpture that preserves a few folds of drapery. The style of the capital conforms to L. S. Meritt's Type I, with ovolo echinus and painted details,[3] presumably originally an egg-and-dart pattern on the echinus and painted palmette leaves at the corners. The proportions of the capital are similar to those of the interior capital from the Stoa Poikile in the Agora, which must be nearly contemporary with the Marathon monument, in the 460s, although the capital from the stoa is much smaller in scale, measuring only 0.92 m across the volutes.[4] E. Vanderpool estimated that the column originally stood about 10 m in height and resembled the well-known Naxian column and sphinx at Delphi, as well as similar column monuments from the Athenian Acropolis.[5] He has argued convincingly that the column should be identified as the "trophy of white marble" that Pausanias (1.32.4–5) saw at Marathon. It is noteworthy that the medieval tower that incorporated the spolia of the column is located just a few meters south of the great marsh, where Pausanias says that

---

[1] On battlefield trophies, see Pritchett, *Greek State at War*, vol. 2, 246–275.
[2] E. Vanderpool, *Hesperia* 35 (1966) 93–106; cf. Vanderpool, *ArchDelt* 24 (1969 [1971]) 1–5.
[3] L. S. Meritt, *Hesperia* 65 (1996) 143–153.
[4] Shear, Jr., *Hesperia* 53 (1984) 9–11.
[5] P. Amandry, *FdD* II, *La colonne des Naxiens et le portique des Athéniens* (Paris 1953) 45–47, 98–101. For other examples of various periods, Dinsmoor, *AAG*³, 121, 143, 326.

the Persians suffered the most casualties. So the monument stood at the point where the rout began, just like a normal battle trophy, but by great exception served as a permanent memorial to Athens's most celebrated military achievement.

The trophy at Marathon is invoked in literature as a proud reminder of Athens's glorious days of old. Aristophanes cites it three times as a measure of Athenian valor and patriotism.[6] Plato's Sokrates, in the *Menexenos* (240D, 245A), says that Athenians were the first to erect trophies over the Persians, and in their subsequent dealings with the Great King could never forget those trophies at Marathon and Salamis. Plutarch (*Arist.* 16.4) has the Athenian soldiers, about to join battle at Plataia, encouraging one another to defend the honor of the trophies at Marathon and Salamis.

The trophy on Salamis was also mentioned by Plato and Plutarch and seen by Pausanias.[7] It was evidently located on the long narrow peninsula called Kynosoura that projects northeastward from the island at the entrance to the straits. Here, among other early travelers, the British architects James Stuart and Nicholas Revett saw the fragments of a column of white marble, which they took to be the remains of the trophy for the sea battle.[8] William Gell, writing in 1827, described it as a column on a circular base, of which many of the marbles were in the sea.[9] But when the site was examined in 1967 by E. Vanderpool and P. W. Wallace, all remains of the column monument had disappeared, and all they found was a cutting in bedrock, 1.80 m square, and a single worked block of its foundation, of course no evidence whatever to restore the monument's appearance or its date.[10] Comparison with the similar column at Marathon may at least give some impression of the original trophy. Placed as it was near the very tip of Kynosoura, the column would have been prominently visible from the opposite shore, as its ruins were to Stuart and Revett in the eighteenth century.

Taken together, the marble trophies at Marathon and Salamis tell us much about the Athenians' attitude to those great military victories, and how they wished to remember and memorialize them for all time. Fascinating, too, is the apparent date of the trophy at Marathon, nearly thirty years after the victory, when the oldest veterans of the battle were beginning to pass away. There is clear evidence also for the Athenians' continued reverence for their ancestors' epic defeats of the Persians on land and sea. Even in the late second century, the corps of ephebes included in their curriculum of military exercises special ceremonies of remembrance: "They marched to the polyandreion at Marathon and offered crowns and sacrifices to those who had died in war in behalf of liberty" (*IG* II[2] 1006, lines 26–27). At another point in their calendar of activities, they sailed to Salamis, where they sacrificed in the festival honoring Ajax, and then "having set sail for the trophy in two ships, they sacrificed to Zeus Tropaios" (*IG* II[2] 1028, lines 27–28).

THE PAINTINGS IN THE STOA POIKILE

About contemporary with the trophy at Marathon was the first great colonnaded stoa in the Agora that flanked the north side of the market square. The stoa was called Peisianakteios, after a certain Peisianax, who seems to have been a relative of Kimon and evidently had something to do with its construction. But the building soon acquired the name Poikile after the four great paintings that hung on its walls. In later antiquity, the Painted Stoa would become one of the most celebrated public

[6] Aristoph. *Knights* 1334; *Wasps* 711; *Lysistrata* 285. For Athenian attitude toward the Marathon trophy, W. C. West, *CP* 64 (1969) 7–19, and *GRBS* 11 (1970) 271–82.
[7] Plato *Menex.* 245A; Plut. *Arist.* 16.4; Paus. 1.36.1. For the topography, P. W. Wallace, *AJA* 73 (1969) 292–303.
[8] J. Stuart and N. Revett, *The Antiquities of Athens* (London 1762) vol. 1, ix, paragraph L, 4.
[9] W. Gell, *The Itinerary of Greece* (London 1827) 303.
[10] P. W. Wallace, *AJA* 73 (1969) 301–302.

buildings in Athens and would give its name to the Stoic school of philosophy.[11] In the fifth century, however, it was unabashedly a war memorial and is specifically so described by orators of the fourth century. Not only were "great deeds" of the Athenians depicted in the paintings, but captured shields from battles of the Peloponnesian War were still hanging in the stoa in the time of Pausanias.[12]

It is the paintings that have the most to tell us about the Athenian response to the victories of the Persian Wars. They presented a provocative correlation of themes. In Pausanias's account, Mikon's Amazonomachy of Theseus hung beside Polygnotos's picture of the Greeks after the capture of Troy; and the two mythological paintings were framed by the Battle of Oinoe and the Battle of Marathon, a pair of true historical paintings which showed Athenians fighting Spartans on the one hand, and Persians on the other.[13] By this visual juxtaposition of myth and history, battles at home and battles abroad, the paintings in their chiastic order suggested mythical archetypes for the historical events. Miltiades and Kallimachos at Marathon repulsed a foreign invasion on Attic soil just as Theseus had done before them. But the painting was not a literal picture of what actually happened on the battlefield, for the figure of Theseus was shown as if rising from the earth. Also present were Herakles, the heroes Marathon and Echetlos, and the goddess Athena herself, all coming to the aid of the Greeks. So the scene was infiltrated by supernatural elements and placed beside the Amazonomachy. Together, the pair of paintings perfectly illustrates a pervasive characteristic of Greek thought—to assimilate human actions and the events of history to the mythical exploits of the heroic past.

This cast of mind was clearly recognized by Herodotos (1.4), for whom the Trojan War formed an ancient archetype of conflict between Greeks and barbarians, which could be cited as precedent and used to justify the Persian invasion of Greece. Thucydides (1.21) criticized both the poets, who embroidered their themes, and the prose chroniclers, whose subject matter had been "won over into the unbelievable realms of the mythical." The daring deeds of mythical heroes were often regarded as paradigms for contemporary events and a source of inspiration for modern men. According to Plato (*Protagoras* 325E–326A), an Athenian schoolboy learned the poets by heart so that he would know "the many tales, and praises, and encomia of ancient famous men in order that he may imitate them or emulate them and desire to become like them." The orator Lykourgos (*Leokr.* 103–104) quoted Hektor's speech from *Iliad* 15 (lines 494–499) in an Athenian law court, and he asserted that such lines and such deeds inspired the victors of Marathon to emulate the hero's prowess. Athenian writers and orators of the fourth century, especially those who spoke at the public funerals for the casualties of war, routinely compared contemporary military actions with a set roster of mythical archetypes:[14] Theseus's defeat of the Amazons, the war of the Seven against Thebes, the Trojan War, the return of the Herakleidai. These are set beside the historical battles of Marathon and Salamis, a juxtaposition that illustrates the generative force of this essentially mythopoeic process, for the specific historical battles, by assimilation to the mythic archetypes, themselves gradually merge with the

[11] For a preliminary account of its remains, Shear, Jr., *Hesperia* 53 (1984) 5–24. The paintings are described by Paus. 1.15.1–16.1. See also the discussion of D. Castriota, *Myth, Ethos, and Actuality* (Madison, WI, 1992) 76–89. For Peisianax, schol. Aischin. 3 *Ktes.* 186 (425b Diltz); Kirchner, *PA* 11775. Stoic philosophy named for the stoa because Zeno of Kition lectured there, Diog Laert. 7.1.5. Full testimonia, Wycherley, *Agora* III, 31–45.

[12] Memorials of "great deeds": Aischin. 3 *Ktes.* 186; [Demosth.] 59 *Neaira* 94. Shields of the Skionians and those of the Lakedaimonians captured at Sphakteria, Paus. 1.16.1.

[13] Paus. 1.15.1–3. Pausanias's account of the two historical battles, Marathon and Oinoe, is certainly to be preferred to the fanciful speculations of E. D. Francis and M. Vickers, *BSA* 80 (1985) 99–113, despite the approving remarks of Castriota, *Myth, Ethos*, 78–79. Meiggs, *AE*, 471–472, was surely correct to assign the otherwise unknown battle at Oinoe to the First Peloponnesian War in the 450s; similarly, L. H. Jeffery, *BSA* 60 (1965) 41–57, although she thought that the painting was depicted in terms of the Seven against Thebes.

[14] See Lysias, 2 *Epitaphios* 4–16, 21–23; Demosth. 60 *Epitaphios* 8, 10–11, 23–31; Hypereides, *Epitaphios* 35, 37–38; Isokr. 4 *Panegyr.* 66–71; Isokr. 12 *Panathen.* 42–44, 49–52, 163–164, 168, 189–195; Plato *Menex.* 239–242. Cf. Hdt. 9.27.

timeless realms of heroic myth. And the glory of myth-making is its power to procreate: where no appropriate archetype stands ready to hand, mythical thought invents one.

This process of mythical creation came to be fully exploited by mural painters of the second quarter of the fifth century, whose works were on prominent display in Athenian public buildings. In the hands of these painters, various familiar exploits of ancient myth underwent a fascinating metamorphosis in order to provide paradigms for the events of the Persian Wars. One of the most familiar, and best-studied, of Athenian myths is the story of the invasion of Attica by the Amazons and their defeat by Theseus in command of the Athenians at the very gates of the Acropolis.[15] Like the cycle of Theseus's other "labors," the invasion of the Amazons is plainly a mutation of Herakles' conquest of the Amazons' city of Themiskyra on the eastern borders of the known world. It is instructive that Herakles' battle appears on no fewer than 376 black-figure vases of the Archaic period,[16] whereas we find not a single example of the Athenian version of the myth before the second quarter of the fifth century. Scenes of the Amazonomachy without Herakles are first seen on red-figure vases of the 460s, and after the middle of the century Theseus is named by inscriptions as the protagonist in the battle on twelve vases, the earliest of which is the calyx-krater from Spina by the Achilles Painter.[17] Our earliest literary reference to Theseus's battle occurs in Aischylos's *Eumenides* (685–689), so the story was current in Athens by 458. About this same time began the splendid series of vases with great battle scenes, of which some seventeen examples are known and from which a small group of figures or duels was excerpted on more than a hundred red-figure vases.[18] Although the combatants are not identified by inscriptions, Herakles is never depicted, and the protagonist is often a beardless Athenian ephebe of heroic stature. In the bold and tumultuous combat of these pictures, often composed on several levels with irregular ground lines and unusual landscape elements, scholars have felt the general influence of some of the most celebrated paintings of Athens.[19] Mikon's first picture of the Amazonomachy was in the Theseion and was painted in the years after 476, when Kimon with great pomp brought back the bones of Theseus and enshrined them in a heroon in the city. The same painter created another version of the battle about a decade later for the Stoa Poikile, a picture particularly renowned for its rendition of Amazons fighting on horseback.[20] Pausanias (1.15.2, 17.2) identified both paintings as the Athenian version of the myth, and he mentions Theseus by name on the panel of the Stoa Poikile. There seems every likelihood that Theseus's defeat of the Amazons in Attica first appeared in art in Mikon's murals for two of the most frequented public buildings of Athens.

The new Athenian version of the Amazonomachy formed a perfect heroic archetype for the Marathon painting and served to elevate the military victory that it depicted; but we notice how in certain details of the paintings myth and history have begun to mutate and to partake each of the other. Despite reports of the more credulous warriors, there was no divine epiphany on the battlefield, and Theseus did not fight in the Athenian phalanx, although Plutarch's anecdote to that effect (*Thes.* 35.5) may be based on the hero's appearance in Mikon's picture. On the other hand, the historical invasion undoubtedly generated the action of the myth and determined its transplanted setting

---

[15] For detailed discussion of the paintings of the Amazonomachy in the Theseion and the Stoa Poikile, see Castriota, *Myth, Ethos,* 43–58 (Theseion), 76–89 (Stoa Poikile). Cf. J. Boardman, in D. Kurtz and B. Sparkes, eds., *The Eye of Greece* (Cambridge 1982) 1–28; J. P. Barron, *JHS* 92 (1972) 20–45.

[16] Brommer, *Vasenlisten*³, 8–22.

[17] Earliest inscription of Theseus: Ferrara T 1052, from Spina: Beazley, *ARV*², 991, no. 53; *Paralipomena* 437; D. von Bothmer, *Amazons in Greek Art* (Oxford 1957) 161, no. 4, 170. The other inscribed vases: von Bothmer, *Amazons,* 234, s.v. Theseus X. Cf. Boardman, in *Eye of Greece,* 11, 20–21.

[18] The large-scale battles are collected and catalogued by von Bothmer, *Amazons,* 161–163, and discussed 163–174; the partial scenes and excerpted figures, von Bothmer, 175–207. Brommer, *Vasenlisten*³, 215.

[19] For the reflection of the great wall paintings in Attic red figure, see generally Barron, *JHS* 92 (1972) 20–45; S. Woodford, *JHS* 94 (1974) 158–165; B. Cohen, in W. G. Moon, ed., *Ancient Greek Art and Iconography* (Madison, WI, 1983) 171–192; Castriota, *Myth, Ethos,* 34–58, 76–89.

[20] Aristoph. *Lysist.* 677–679, schol. 679 (Holwerda).

in Attica. If we may judge from the vase paintings, Mikon depicted those wild oriental women of ancient story so as to emphasize their exotic suits and weapons that Greeks associated with Persians in recent experience. We shall have occasion to see in subsequent chapters that the designers of sculptural decoration for Athenian temples frequently employed a similar strategy of reshaping received mythology to disseminate the message of Athenian victory.

The Great Bronze Athena

About 460, the Athenians commissioned Pheidias to erect on the Acropolis a colossal bronze statue of Athena, which, according to the dedicatory inscription, was a "tithe from the Medes who landed at Marathon."[21] It appears to be the first major new dedication on the Acropolis, for there is no evidence to suggest any restoration of the ruined sanctuary for twenty years following the destruction of 480. The incorporation of spolia from the temples in the reconstructed north wall plainly implies the continued ruinous condition of the buildings themselves. Several ancient writers attribute construction of the southern fortifications of the Acropolis to Kimon's period of ascendancy, and Plutarch tells us that the south wall and other projects in the city were made possible by sale of the rich booty captured by Kimon's forces in the battle at the Eurymedon.[22] To all appearances, however, there was no major dedication of the customary war tithe to Athena throughout this period.

From literary references to it, we know that Pheidias's statue depicted the goddess standing tall upon her base, wearing her aegis and helmet, with her right arm extended forward, and with spear and shield grounded at her left side. The shield was richly adorned in relief with a scene of the Centauromachy executed by a metalsmith called Mys from designs of Parrhasios of Ephesos. The statue became a famous landmark, for the crest of Athena's helmet and the tip of her spear gleamed in the sunlight and flashed a beacon to sailors approaching the Peiraieus from the direction of Sounion.[23] Just such a figure appears on the reverse of certain Athenian bronze coins of the Antonine period. Although these have numerous variations in detail, the statue is generally shown, towering at enormous scale, between the Propylaia and the Erechtheion. The Acropolis is seen from the north, with the statue in three-quarter view or profile to the right. The figure appears to be wearing a belted peplos and crested helmet, and she holds out some attribute in her extended hand. On the best examples, a spear can be seen resting against one shoulder, and a shield on the ground beside her.[24] On the basis of this evidence, it has been possible to recognize the statue's foundation in a great square platform, partly built of poros blocks and partly cut from the bedrock. At the center of the platform is a deep square socket that probably carried a heavy wooden mast that served as a central armature

[21] The inscription is apparently paraphrased by Paus. 1.28.1 and cf. 9.4.1.

[22] For the spolia in the north wall, see chap. 1, p. 8 above. For the south wall as the work of Kimon: Plut. *Kim.* 13.5; Plut. *Comp. Kim.* and *Luc.* 1; Plut. *Mor.* 349D; Paus. 1.21.3, 25.2, 28.3; Nepos *Cim.* 2.5. On the booty from the Eurymedon, Paus. 10.15.4; Diod. 11.62.3. See Pritchett, *Greek State at War,* vol. 5, 371.

[23] Since the spear point and the crest of the helmet were visible from the sea (Paus. 1.28.2), the goddess was shown wearing her helmet, and the spear must have been held vertically at her side. Because of the size of the figure, the Lapiths and Centaurs on the shield would hardly have been recognizable if the shield were not also on the ground at her side, as on the Athena in the Parthenon. Cf. Maximus of Tyre, *Diss.* 8.6: εἰ τοιαύτην ἡγεῖ τὴν Ἀθηνᾶν οἵαν Φειδίας ἐδημιούργησεν, οὐδὲν τῶν Ὁμήρου ἐπῶν φαυλοτέραν, παρθένον καλήν, γλαυκῶπιν, ὑψηλήν, αἰγίδα ἀνεζωσμένην, κόρυν φέρουσαν, δόρυ ἔχουσαν, ἀσπίδα κατέχουσαν. Testimonia conveniently collected: Jahn and Michaelis, *Arx,* 76–77; West, "Greek Public Monuments," 55–59, no. 18. For the statue's extended arm, see note 24 below. Recent discussions: Mattusch, *Greek Bronze Statuary,* 166–172; Harrison, *YCS* 30 (1996) 28–34; B. Lundgreen, *JHS* 117 (1997) 190–197; Davison, *Pheidias,* 277–291.

[24] See Svoronos, *Les monnaies d'Athènes,* pl. 98, nos. 19–43; and detailed discussion of the variations: B. Pick, *AM* 56 (1931) 59–74; A. Linfert, *AM* 97 (1982) 66–71; J. H. Kroll, *Agora* XXVI (1993) no. 280; Lundgreen, *JHS* 117 (1997) 190–197.

for the statue.[25] The siting of the bronze colossus is especially significant, for Athena stood with her back against the terrace wall of the archaic temple that the Persians burned. She beckoned with her outstretched hand to every visitor who entered the Acropolis by the western gates, and with her overwhelming scale she dominated the first view of the sanctuary. Pheidias so placed his statue base that it aligned precisely with the central axis of the ruined temple, but he turned it a few degrees to the south of west so that the base was not parallel with the terrace behind, and thus the goddess's extended right hand pointed directly at the approaching visitor.[26] To Athenians of the Classical period the great bronze Athena[27] embodied the most conspicuous and most familiar image of their city goddess. Unlike the cult statues hidden away in their locked and lightless temples, she was visible from all points in the lower city; she loomed high above the ramparts of her citadel, the perfect epiphany of Athena, guardian of Athens.

Our knowledge of Pheidias's statue is supplemented in some important details by the records of expenditure kept by the officials designated to administer its construction. What survives are eleven fragments of a marble stele on which the accounts were inscribed.[28] That they pertain to the great bronze Athena has been universally accepted, for they show massive purchases of copper and tin over many years, and they record the purchase of silver bullion for the decorative details of what is best restored as "the statue" (ἀ[ργύριον ἄσεμ]ον ἐς ποι[κιλίαν] τõ [ἀγάλματος], lines 79–80). The document covers at least nine years of work on the project, but all were inscribed at the same time, when the statue had been completed. That date can be placed in the years around the middle of the century, according to the letter forms of the inscription, and so the inception of work about 460 agrees with the evidence of the inscription.[29] The accounts of Pheidias's statue are the earliest records of Athenian bookkeeping for sacred construction. They stand at the head of a long series of similar documents that includes the accounts of the Parthenon, of the gold and ivory statue, of the Propylaia, of the statues in the Hephaisteion, and the last years of the Erechtheion.[30] Like the accounts of the Parthenon and Propylaia, which we shall have occasion to examine in due course, the records of the bronze Athena were arranged on the stele in three double columns. To the left were sums of money, and to the right descriptive itemization that indicated the purpose of each expenditure. Each double column apparently contained the accounts for three years, but no fragment preserves the top edge of the stele, and so it is impossible to estimate accurately how much has been lost from the top of each column. No trace of a title or introductory preamble for the whole document has survived, thus we cannot tell whether that common feature of the later building accounts appeared already in this earliest example.

In the accounts of the bronze Athena, we meet for the first time the organizational principle that was regularly employed in all later Athenian public works under the radical democracy. Day-to-day operations for the construction of the statue and the disbursement of funds were entrusted to a committee of epistatai, or overseers, who were annually elected from the demos and worked under

[25] See Stevens and Raubitschek, *Hesperia* 15 (1946) 107–114, attempting to identify three inscribed blocks from the pedestal; but Thompson, in Χαριστήριον Ὀρλάνδος, vol. 1, 314–323, and Dinsmoor, in Χαριστήριον Ὀρλάνδος, vol. 4, 145–155, have shown that the attribution is not possible. Cf. Harrison, *YCS* 30 (1996) 29.

[26] The importance of the siting of the statue is the observation of Michael Djordjevitch and will be presented in detail in a forthcoming study, of which only a brief notice has so far been published, *AJA* 98 (1994) 323.

[27] παρα τὴν χαλκῆν τὴν μεγάλην Ἀθηνᾶν. The locution is that of Demosth. 19 *Embassy* 272, the earliest literary reference. The modern parlance "Promachos" is never attested in the Classical period and appears only once, in a late scholium, schol. Demosth. 22 *Androtion* 13 (45 Dilts); Harrison, *YCS* 30 (1996) 28; Lundgreen, *JHS* 117 (1997) 190; Davison, *Pheidias*, 280–282.

[28] *IG* I³ 435; and for recent discussion, Meiggs, *AE*, 93–94; Mattusch, *Greek Bronze Statuary*, 170–172; Harrison, *YCS* 30 (1996) 30.

[29] Meritt, *Hesperia* 5 (1936) 373–374.

[30] Parthenon, *IG* I³ 436–451; gold and ivory statue, *IG* I³ 453–460; Propylaia, *IG* I³ 462–466; statues in the Hephaisteion, *IG* I³ 472; Erechtheion, *IG* I³ 474–479.

the supervision of the boulē, as we learn from almost contemporary references to the formation of similar boards.[31] Elected along with this committee was a secretary (γραμματεύς) and an assistant who is described as hυπερέτες,[32] and together these officials kept the books, presented their accounts for audit, and eventually published the inscription. Each year's account is introduced by the name and demotic of the secretary to the epistatai, but the names of his colleagues were not inscribed on the stone, as they were in the later accounts of the Parthenon and the Propylaia.[33] Thus there is no evidence to indicate the size of the board, or whether the overseers were always the same number in every year. In such matters there is good reason to believe that the Athenians were not particularly consistent. The nearly contemporary accounts for construction of an unknown building spanned eight years on either side of 450 and listed boards consisting of two, three, four, and five epistatai, in addition to the annual secretary.[34]

The epistatai received funds from only one source, the kolakretai who were the public treasurers of the Athenian state. A specific statement to that effect appeared at the beginning of every annual account: ἐπιστάται ἔλαβον παρὰ κολακρετõν σύνπαν.[35] In addition, they received from their predecessors the unexpended balance available from the previous year, and they in turn would pass on to their successors any unspent funds when they left office. The surviving fragments give us only glimpses of the large sums of money involved. In the second year, for example, the overseers listed total receipts of at least 78,109 drachmas (lines 4–8), an amount just over 13 talents, while the account for the sixth year preserves a figure for total expenditures of at least 12,217 drachmas and an unexpended balance forward that is probably 5,280 drachmas (lines 83–85). It is noteworthy that the treasurers of Athena contributed no money from the goddess's sacred funds toward the construction of her statue. This is in striking contrast to the financial arrangements adopted a few years later to meet the costs of the great sacred buildings. Since the kolakretai alone paid for the bronze Athena, we may believe more readily that the funds came in fact from the sale of booty from the Persian Wars, as Pausanias reports. Although there is no specific evidence concerning the deposit of such profits from the sale of war booty, they are most likely to have been placed in the public treasury in the custody of the kolakretai. There is, at any rate, ample evidence that the Athenian assembly maintained close control over the fate of captured persons and the disposition of captured property.[36] Furthermore, for what it is worth, Plutarch (*Kim.* 13.6) states that the demos itself was responsible for funding various projects from the spoils of the battle of the Eurymedon, and the assumption is that the demos controlled public funds in the treasury of the kolakretai.

On the expense side of the ledger, the epistatai reported the costs of the materials purchased and the wages paid to the craftsmen and other employees; but their expenditures are grouped in general categories without much detail. Moreover, only a few scraps of information have been preserved. The largest items were the purchase of copper and tin, which probably recurred in every year.

[31] For annual election of epistatai, *IG* I³ 32, lines 7–10, 17–20. The epistatai are directed to cooperate with the boulē and the architect in drafting a bill that they are to present to the demos for action: *IG* I³ 64A, lines 16–19. The boulē is to elect a committee of three of their own members who are to cooperate with the architect in preparing specifications: *IG* I³ 35, lines 15–18; see p. 27 below.

[32] See p. 25 and note 65 below.

[33] The introductory formula for the annual accounts is best preserved at *IG* I³ 435, lines 36–37 (Year 5): [hοῖς Κ]αλ[λίστ]ρατος [ἐγραμμάτευε] Α[...⁵...]ς ἐπι[στάται]. The same formula can be restored at lines 4–5 (Year 2), 63–64 (Year 6), 94–95 (Year 8), 120–121 (Year 9).

[34] *IG* I³ 433, with the following variations in the number of epistatai: lines 4–7 (Year 2), at least three; lines 12–13 (Year 3), two; lines 18–20 (Year 4), three; lines 24–28 (Year 5), five; lines 33–36 (Year 6), five listed in tribal order I–V; lines 42–45 (Year 7), five; lines 52–54 (Year 8), four.

[35] The text is best preserved at *IG* I³ 435, lines 95–97 and 121–122 (Years 8 and 9); the same entry can be restored in lines 5–6 (Year 2), 38 (Year 5), 65 (Year 6). On the kolakretai, see L. J. Samons, *Empire of the Owl: Athenian Imperial Finance, Historia* Einzelschriften 142 (Stuttgart 2000) 58–70.

[36] On the sale of war booty at Athens, see Pritchett, *Greek State at War*, vol. 5, 416–425.

The price paid for copper in the second year was 34,852 drachmas, while at the same time more than 6,350 drachmas were spent for tin.[37] Other itemized purchases are for coal and firewood; the price of wax can be restored once; and the cost of constructing casting furnaces appears several times. There are a number of references to the purchase of clay and hair, always together on the same line. The former substance was undoubtedly used to fashion the molds from which the various parts of the statue were cast, and it has been suggested that hair was mixed with the clay to avoid distortion of the mold through shrinkage.[38]

The overseers lumped together in one item the total costs for labor, but the description shows that the personnel of the project was divided into three categories: those who received day wages, those paid by the prytany, and those paid for piecework. The number of people employed in a given year evidently fluctuated considerably; for the total cost of labor in the sixth year was probably 6,602 drachmas, while in the eighth year the same figure was substantially more than 10,100 drachmas.[39] That certain salaries were paid by the prytany (μισθοὶ κατὰ πρυτανείαν) is a point of special interest. In the later accounts of the Parthenon and the Propylaia no salaries are described in this way, but a similar class of personnel is probably indicated by the item there called καταμένια, monthly salaries.[40] This payment by the prytany throughout the accounts of the bronze Athena must take its place among the earliest references to the existence of that institution, whereby the bouleutic year was subdivided into ten segments, during each of which one tribal delegation held the prytany as executive committee of the boulē. There is no unequivocal evidence for the system of rotating prytanies during the first quarter of the fifth century, and this has led some scholars to argue that they were first introduced as a part of the Ephialtic reforms in 462.[41] If this argument is correct, then the references here to wages reckoned by the prytany require that the inception of work on the bronze Athena likewise follow the democratic reforms.

Such a conclusion also agrees well with other indications in the accounts of the statue. In each year, the last item before the total annual expenditure is the salaries for the administrative board (μισθοὶ ἐπιστάτεσι καὶ γραμματει καὶ hυπερέτει), carefully kept separate from the wages of other personnel.[42] In the sixth year of the account, the stone preserves the amount of 1,963 dr. 2 ob. (lines 81–82) as the total payment that they received. That the great statue was supervised by annually rotating boards of epistatai, a practice characteristic of later democratic administration, and, what is more important, that these epistatai were salaried officials of the state is the clearest indication that

---

[37] *IG* I³ 435, lines 10–12. The amounts paid for each metal are preserved, but the text of each item is entirely restored. Raubitschek, *SEG* 10.243, associated the larger figure with the purchase of tin and the smaller with the purchase of copper. But, as Lewis noted in *IG* I³, lines 101–104 (Year 8) show that copper cost more than five times the price of tin, about the same ratio as the figures in lines 10–12.

[38] Coal and firewood: *IG* I³ 435, lines 17, 24, 49, 75, 110; price of wax: line 105; construction of casting furnaces: lines 16, 46–47, 74; clay and hair: lines 20, 27, 53, 78, 86, 113. On the use of clay and hair in the casting process, see Mattusch, *Greek Bronze Statuary,* 170.

[39] One total figure for labor is listed, but the text of the item regularly reads: μισθοὶ κατ᾿ ἐμέραν, μισθοὶ κατὰ πρυτανείαν, μισθοὶ ἀπόπαχς, lines 18–19, 25–26, 51–52, 76–77 with amount restorable, 111–112 with amount partly preserved.

[40] See p. 308 below.

[41] See Rhodes, *Athenian Boule,* 17–19. The earliest certain epigraphical reference to a tribe in prytany is in the Phaselis Decree (*IG* I³ 10 = ML 31, dated 469–450), for which Wade-Gery, *EGH,* 180–200, advocated a date between 469 and 462; but cf. the reservations of R. Sealey, *CP* 59 (1964) 14–18, and Rhodes, *Athenian Boule,* 204, note 1, who would lower the date into the 450s. The bouleutic calendar was certainly not in use in 485/4, for the Hekatompedon Inscription (*IG* I³ 4B, lines 17–21) instructs the treasurers to inspect the *oikemata* three times a month and specifies the days by the lunar calendar and not by the day of the prytany. The singular prytanis mentioned there (*IG* I³ 4A, lines 20–21, 29–30; 4B, lines 23, 24) is the chairman of the treasurers; see Jordan, *Servants of the Gods,* 62–63. Plut. *Mor.* 628E mentions a decree passed in the prytany of Aiantis, as a result of which Miltiades led the army to Marathon, but the reference to the tribe in prytany is best understood as an anachronism; see Habicht, *Hermes* 89 (1961) 17, 20.

[42] *IG* I³ 435, lines 21–22, 28–29, 54–55, 81–82, 87–88, 114–115.

the project should be attributed to the democratic reformers and its beginning should be dated after the ostracism of Kimon.[43] Perikles himself is reported to have been the first to introduce the practice of payment for jurors in the popular courts and for other civic officials. Our sources describe the policy in the context of the young Perikles' political rivalry with Kimon.[44] The great general used his private fortune to spread largesse among the populace and so to win political supporters. Since Perikles' private assets did not run to such prodigious displays of munificence, he conceived the notion of distributing to the demos from its own wealth in the public coffers.[45] Kimon's liberality as a factor in politics can only refer to the period of his greatest popularity, between the Battle of the Eurymedon and his ostracism in 461, for Perikles is still depicted as a politician on the rise. Both Aristotle and Plutarch specifically describe the introduction of pay for civic service in the context of the attack on the Areopagos by Ephialtes and Perikles.[46] One infers that payment for jurors was, in fact, a necessary corollary to Ephialtes' judicial reform, which so broadly increased the jurisdiction of the popular courts at the expense of the Areopagos. The salaried overseers of the bronze Athena will then have been among the first Athenian civic officials to benefit from Perikles' policy and to draw their pay from the funds that the kolakretai put at their disposal. The kolakretai, it should be observed, were also the treasurers who disbursed the stipend of two obols a day to the great juries of the popular courts.[47] In light of this discussion, it seems proper to regard Pheidias's great bronze Athena as the first Athenian sacred dedication in the late 460s. The project was administered and financed in accordance with policies that reflect the Ephialtic reforms of 462. By the time of its completion, plans for the construction of new temples were already under discussion.

Plans for the Acropolis and Eleusis

In 454/3, in the immediate aftermath of the disastrous expedition to Egypt, the decision was made to remove the common treasury of the Delian Confederacy from Delos to Athens. Our literary sources do not make clear the circumstances of the transfer. Thucydides makes no mention of the incident; Plutarch, in the *Life of Perikles,* implies that the money was moved at Athenian instigation out of fear of the Persian menace. Elsewhere, however, on the authority of Theophrastos, Plutarch attributes the proposal to the Samians but dates it to the lifetime of Aristeides.[48] Diodoros mentions it, but not in the proper chronological context. He paraphrases from Ephoros the elaborate series of apocryphal anecdotes purporting to show how Perikles personally caused the Peloponnesian War,

---

[43] So Meiggs, *AE*, 94–95. Harrison, *YCS* 30 (1996) 30, argues for a date for Pheidias's commission shortly after the Battle of Eurymedon, in the mid-460s, but she takes no account of the chronological implications suggested by the salaried epistatai who supervised construction of the statue.

[44] [Aristot.] *Ath. Pol.* 27.3; Plato *Gorg.* 515E; Aristot. *Pol.* 1274a8–9; Plut. *Per.* 9.2–3.

[45] The tradition of Kimon's generosity was famous in antiquity. [Aristot.] *Ath. Pol.* 27.2–4 and Theopompos, *FGrH* 115 F 89, say that his farms were unfenced so that anyone who wished might harvest from his crops. He provided free meals in his house. He was surrounded by a group of young men who passed out alms to the poor, and he would order them to exchange clothes with ill-clothed citizens whom he happened to meet. Cf. Theophrastos ap. Cic. *Off.* 2.64; Nepos *Cim.* 4.1–3; Plut. *Kim.* 10 (citing *Ath. Pol.*, Kratinos, Gorgias, and Kritias). For discussion of the sources, see Rhodes, *Commentary*, 338–344; Connor, *Theopompos and Fifth-Century Athens*, 30–37, 108–110; Wade-Gery, *EGH*, 235–238. Only *Ath. Pol.* 27.3 and Plut. *Per.* 9.2 state that Perikles instituted pay for the jury courts in order to counter the effects of Kimon's largesse.

[46] Aristot. *Pol.* 1274a8–9; Plut. *Per.* 9.2–5. A date for the introduction of jurors' pay before the ostracism of Kimon was argued by Wade-Gery, *EGH*, 197, 235–238; cf. Meiggs, *AE*, 94 and note 4; Connor, *Theopompos*, 33; Podlecki, *Perikles*, 54. Others have preferred to date its inception later in the 450s; see Hignett, *HAC*, 342–343; Rhodes, *Commentary*, 339–340; Podes, *Athenaeum* 82 (1994) 95–110. Only Meiggs, *AE*, 94, has seen the bearing that the accounts of the bronze Athena have on the date of introduction of pay for civic service.

[47] Schol. Aristoph. *Birds* 1541b, c (Holwerda); *Suda*, s.v. κωλακρέται (κ 2234 Adler).

[48] Plut. *Per.* 12.1, *Arist.* 25.3.

among which we hear twice that the treasury was moved from Delos to Athens.[49] Athenian orators
of the fourth century commented on the amount of the treasure (8,000 or 10,000 talents had become traditional), and they attributed to Perikles its deposit on the Acropolis.[50]

That the transfer of the treasury took place in 454/3 is made certain by contemporary epigraphical evidence. In that year the Athenians erected on the Acropolis a marble stele of unusual height,
at the top of which was inscribed a list of the allied cities that paid tribute in that year. Against each
name was a sum of money amounting to one-sixtieth of the city's assessed tribute that was paid to
the goddess Athena as *aparchai* or firstfruits. At the head of the list stands an introductory prescript
preserving the name of the archon Ariston (454/3).[51] This serves as a general title for the fourteen
annual lists inscribed year after year from 454/3 to 440/39, until the stone was completely filled.
Great significance surely attaches to these so-called tribute lists, with their long columns of annual
contributions, many of them small amounts of money, which were given solemn permanence and
public display in Athena's sanctuary. It is undoubtedly correct to infer that by 454/3 the treasury of
the confederacy had been moved from Delos to Athens. Moreover, the exceptional size of the stele
then inscribed for the first time bespeaks the start of a new era in Athens's relations with her allies. It
is as if each city's quota were a sacred dedication stored up like golden phialai as a possession for all
time. Like inscriptions on sacred dedications in sanctuaries throughout the Greek world, the tribute
lists seem to proclaim that all citizens of the allied states worshipped on the Athenian Acropolis. The
symbolic significance of the message is unmistakable: Athena Polias has replaced Delian Apollo as
tutelary deity of the Aegean confederacy.

It needs to be stressed once again that, in the middle years of the fifth century, the Acropolis was
still in ruinous condition. When the treasury of the league was transferred to Athens from Delos, no
temple was standing on the Acropolis in which the monies could be deposited for safekeeping. In
fact, Athena Polias had been bereft of her temple for a quarter century. Throughout this long period,
no reconstruction of the sacred buildings had been undertaken, and the only thank-offering to the
goddess for the victories of the Persian Wars was Pheidias's great bronze Athena, on which work had
just begun a few years earlier. It can hardly be coincidence that the first references to the building
of temples in Athens appear to date to the six-year period between the first payment of the tribute
quota to Athena, in the spring of 453, and the start of work on the Parthenon in the summer of 447.
In these years, with the ascendency of Perikles and the death of Kimon, plans for the restoration of
the city's sanctuaries first came to be publicly debated by the Athenian demos.

The random chance of preservation gives us a few glimpses of this parliamentary process in
the form of documents that are undoubtedly typical representatives of the administrative legislation
that necessarily accompanied the major projects. An inscription of exceptional interest preserves the
amendment proposed by a certain Thespieus to a decree whose text is now almost totally lost.[52] The
amendment, however, orders the establishment and election of a board of five epistatai (overseers),
who are evidently to have charge of important building operations in the sanctuary of Demeter at
Eleusis, and for this purpose they are to administer the finances of the sanctuary. The appointment
of such annual boards of epistatai was, as we have just seen, an invention of the radical democracy,

[49] Diod. 12.38–41.1 = Ephoros, *FGrH* 70 F196; Diod. 13.21.3; cf. Nepos, *Arist.* 3.1; Aristodemos (*FGrH* 104) 7;
Justin 3.6.4.

[50] The amount of money is reported as 8,000 talents by Isokr. 8 *Peace* 126; Diod. 12.38.2. It is said to have been 10,000
talents by Isokr. 8 *Peace* 69, 15 *Antidosis* 234, quoted above, p. 6; Demosth. *Ol.* 3.24; Lykourgos, frag. 58 (Conomis) =
Glossa Patmia, s.v. Ἑκατόμπεδον (*BCH* 1 [1877] 149), quoted above, p. 6; Diod. 12.40 2, 54.3. Cf. Giovannini, *Historia*
46 (1997) 153–155, who believes that the amounts mentioned by the orators have nothing to do with the Delian treasury.

[51] *IG* I³ 259, lines 1–4; *ATL* II, list 1 + Meritt, *Hesperia* 41 (1972) 403–417. See *ATL* III, 19–28, 265–274; Meiggs,
AE, 234–237.

[52] *IG* I³ 32 (appendix, p. 408 below) and, for the most recent text and translation, M. B. Cavanaugh, *Eleusis and Athens*
(Atlanta 1996) 19–21; cf. also Clinton, *Eleusis,* 30. See chap. 6, pp. 163–165 below.

first used a few years earlier for the great bronze Athena,[53] and similar boards were now adopted as the basic instrument of administration for the construction of the new buildings.

It has long been noticed that the elaborate organization envisaged by Thespieus must have been appended to a decree authorizing construction of a large and important building. The great Hall of the Mysteries itself, the central monument of the sanctuary and Temple of Demeter, remains the logical candidate, and it seems quite probable that the missing decree included the original proposal to reconstruct the Telesterion at Eleusis.[54] If this is correct, the document assumes a considerable importance in the history of the building program, for it would then give us not only valuable detail concerning the administration of the program, but also some clue to one of the major building projects. It may be well to note that the main part of this decree was actually drafted by the boulē and introduced into the assembly by the prytaneis.[55] All that is now preserved, however, are tantalizing references to the hieropoioi of the sanctuary and to the spending of funds, and the motion ends with the instruction that the prytaneis are to bring the appointed men before the boulē whenever they request it.

Interpretation of Thespieus's amendment has proved to be a notorious crux in epigraphical studies of the fifth century because the date implied by the letter forms of the inscription seemed to contradict the syntax of the language. From the time of its discovery, scholars generally accepted a date for the inscription about the middle of the century because the three-bar sigma appears throughout the text, whereas other diagnostic letters, such as beta, nu, rho, and phi, have their classical forms.[56] The lettering finds its closest epigraphical parallels in the accounts for the bronze Athena (*IG* I³ 435), in the earlier decree concerning Athena Nike (*IG* I³ 35), and in the third tribute list of 452/1 (*IG* I³ 261). On the other hand, when Thespieus drafted the language of his amendment, he described the work of the new Eleusinian overseers by comparison with another board appointed to oversee work on the Athenian Acropolis: τούτο[ς] δὲ ἐπιστε͂]ναι [τ]οῖς χρέμασι τοῖς τοῖν θ[ε]οῖν καθάπερ hοι ἐπὶ τοῖς ἐμ πό[λ]ει ἔργ[οι]ς ἐπεστ[ά]το[ν] το͂ι νεο͂ι καὶ το͂ι ἀ[γ]άλματι (lines 10–13) (These men are to have charge of the properties of the Two Goddesses just as those who had charge of the works on the Acropolis for the temple and the statue). It has seemed to many natural, even obvious, to understand the words "for the temple and the statue" as a reference to the Parthenon and its gold and ivory statue of Athena. But in that case, the imperfect tense of the verb in the relative clause appeared to present difficulties, for it seemed to imply that the Athenian overseers had finished their work and gone out of office before Thespieus mentioned them in his motion.[57] This difficulty has

[53] See pp. 17–21 above.

[54] This was originally suggested by K. Kourouniotis, Ἐλευσινιακά, vol. 1 (Athens 1932) 173–189. Cf. Mylonas, *Eleusis*, 114; Meritt and Wade-Gery, *JHS* 83 (1963) 113–114. That the amendment of Thespieus anticipates construction of the Telesterion is rejected by A. A. Papaioannou, in *Studies Mylonas*, vol. 3 (Athens 1989) 231–244, who believes that the document deals exclusively with financial administration, despite the specific instructions that the epistatai are to spend whatever amount is necessary in consultation with the priests and the boulē (lines 28–30): ἀναλίσκεν δὲ ὅ τι ἂν [μά]λιστα δέει μετα τῶν hιερέον καὶ τε͂ς β[ολ]ε͂ς βολευομένος τὸ λοιπόν.

[55] *IG* I³ 32, lines 6–7 with the normal formula of amendment: [τὰ μὲν] ἄλλα καθάπερ τε͂[ι β]ο[λ]ε͂ι. Cf. also the new text of Cavanaugh, *Eleusis,* 19, lines 1–6, with some improvements.

[56] R. Vallois, *REA* 35 (1933) 195–200; O. Rubensohn, *Gnomon* 9 (1933) 428–432; C. Picard, *CRAI* (1933) 8–21; M. Segre, *Clara Rhodos* 9 (1938) 167, note 3; S. Accame, *RivFil,* n.s., 13 (1935) 486–488, and *RivFil,* n.s., 33 (1955) 155–157; Raubitschek, *SEG* 10.24; M. N. Tod, *AJP* 77 (1956) 52; Mylonas, *Eleusis,* 114; Meritt and Wade-Gery *JHS* 83 (1963) 113–114; Meiggs, *HSCP* 67 (1963) 26; Meiggs, *JHS* 86 (1966) 96 and note 26. Now that *IG* I³ 11 (the Egesta Decree), with three-bar sigma throughout the text, has been shown to date to 418/7, the old orthodoxy about letter forms carries much less weight. See M. H. Chambers, R. Gollucci, and P. Spanos, *ZPE* 83 (1990) 38–57; Mattingly, *AER,* 551–552; P. J. Rhodes, *CQ* 58 (2008) 500–506.

[57] Advocates of a date after 433/2, the year in which the last account of the Parthenon overseers was filed, follow the lead of H. B. Mattingly, *Historia* 10 (1961) 171–173. Cf. Mattingly, *AJP* 105 (1984) 347; Mattingly, in I. Carradice, ed., *Coinage and Administration in the Athenian and Persian Empires* (Oxford 1987) 69; K. Clinton, in *Studies Mylonas,* vol. 2, 256–257; Clinton, in Πρακτικά του XII Διεθνούς Συνέδριου, vol. 4, 33–36; Papaioannou, in *Studies Mylonas,* vol. 3, 231–244; Cavanaugh, *Eleusis,* 23–27; Samons, *Empire of the Owl,* 133–136; Mattingly, *AER,* 483; Mattingly, *ZPE* 162 (2007) 107; Clinton, *Eleusis,* no. 30; Rhodes, *CQ* 58 (2008) 505.

been explained in two ways. Those who prefer to date the inscription ca. 450 on the basis of the letter forms have sometimes felt constrained to identify the temple and the statue as a reference to the great bronze Athena and to some unidentified temple, possibly the archaic Temple of Athena.[58] The most recent discussions of the problem have understood "the temple and the statue" to refer to the Parthenon and the statue of Athena, but it is argued that the imperfect tense of the verb necessitates a date after 433/2, when the overseers of the Parthenon completed the building. Adherents to this view translate the relative clause "just as those who used to have charge of the works on the Acropolis for the temple and the statue."[59] Neither of these two expedients solves the problem satisfactorily.

It seems inevitable that the Parthenon and its cult statue are meant to be the temple and the statue which the Athenian epistatai were intended to supervise. Throughout the middle decades of the century, there was no other temple under construction on the Acropolis, no other building that all would easily understand as ὁ νεός. The temple par excellence was the Parthenon, and, what is more, there had been no other temple that could be so described since the Persian destruction.[60] Thespieus's reference to the Athenian overseers sounds like the paraphrase of an official title, and he modeled the proposed Eleusinian board on an Athenian board evidently called ἐπιστάται τὸν ἐμ πόλει ἔργον τοῖ νεὸι καὶ τοῖ ἀγάλματι (or something similar), "overseers of the works on the Acropolis for the temple and the statue." One is at once reminded of the phraseology used to describe the boards that supervised later building projects: ἐπιστάται προπυλαίο ἐργασίας (overseers of the Propylaia); ἐπιστάται τõ νεõ τõ ἐμ πόλει ἐν hõι τὸ ἀρχαῖον ἄγαλμα (overseers of the Erechtheion); ἐπιστάται ἀγαλμάτοιν ἐς τὸ Ηεφαίστιον (overseers of the two statues in the Hephaisteion).[61] It seems necessary to postulate a previous decree to which Thespieus here made reference. That decree, very likely debated and voted in the same assembly that Thespieus later addressed, or in the recent past, must have ordered the election of a board entitled the "overseers of the works on the Acropolis for the temple and the statue." It was Thespieus's proposal to create a board of overseers at Eleusis along the lines already set forth for these Athenian officials. His motion came as an amendment to a decree of the boulē and was possibly drafted extemporaneously on the floor of the assembly. It has been acutely noted that such informal composition probably accounts for the abrupt changes in the subjects of the main infinitives in lines 23–30, whereby the logistai are the subject of λογίζεσθαι (line 23) and ἀνακαλẽν (line 30), but the epistatai must be construed as the subject of ἀναλίσκεν (line 28).[62] The speaker probably also found it natural to refer in the imperfect tense to officials who were the subject of previously passed legislation. We should understand the force of the imperfect to mean: "These men are to have charge of the properties of the Two Goddesses just as those who had charge (as we voted earlier) of the works on the Acropolis for the temple and the statue."[63]

[58] So Vallois, *REA* 35 (1933) 195–200; Picard, *CRAI* (1933) 10–12; Meiggs, *HSCP* 67 (1963) 26; Meiggs, *JHS* 86 (1966) 96.

[59] Cavanaugh, *Eleusis*, 20, 25–27, following Clinton, in *Studies Mylonas*, vol. 2, 254–262; Papaioannou, in *Studies Mylonas*, vol. 3, 231–244.

[60] In similar manner, the archaic poros Temple of Athena was called simply ὁ νεός before the Persian destruction: *IG* I³ 4B, lines 9–10; cf. the discussion of Paton and Stevens, *Erechtheum*, 442–445; Dinsmoor, *AJA* 51 (1947) 119–121; but this building had now lain in ruins for nearly thirty years.

[61] Propylaia: *IG* I³ 462, line 1; Erechtheion: *IG* I³ 474, line 1; Hephaisteion: *IG* I³ 472, line 1.

[62] As observed by Meritt and Wade-Gery, *JHS* 83 (1963) 114, followed by Cavanaugh, *Eleusis*, 22 and note 7.

[63] This was the interpretation of Meritt and Wade-Gery, *JHS* 83 (1963) 113–114. They cited the parallel of Plato, *Laws* 9.867D: ὁ δὲ θυμῶ . . . κτείνας, τὰ μὲν ἄλλα κατὰ τὸν πρόσθεν αὖ, τρία δὲ ἔτη, καθάπερ ἄτερος ἔφευγε τὰ δύο, φευγέτω, "he who kills . . . in passion shall be treated in other respects like the former, but he shall be exiled for three years, whereas the other was (as we decided) exiled for two." They described the construction as the "imperfect of points assumed," with reference to B. L. Gildersleeve, *Syntax of Classical Greek* (New York 1900) vol. 1, 96, §218. In this usage, the imperfect expresses something which is the result of a previous discussion, called by others the "philosophical imperfect"; see H. W. Smyth, *Greek Grammar* (Cambridge, MA, 1956) 426, §1903; W. W. Goodwin, *Syntax of the Moods and Tenses of the Greek Verb* (London 1889) 13, §40. Parallels are not infrequent in the philosophical discourse of Plato; cf., e.g., *Crito* 47D: διαφθεροῦμεν ἐκεῖνο, ὃ τῷ μὲν δικαίῳ βέλτιον ἐγίγνετο, τῷ δὲ ἀδίκῳ ἀπώλλυτο, "We shall destroy that which

The argument that Thespieus's wording requires a date for the inscription after the completion of the Parthenon in 433/2 is predicated on the assumption that the Athenian overseers to whom he referred actually held office and actually built the temple, but this assumption is demonstrably incorrect. There is no extant record of any officials entitled "overseers of the works on the Acropolis for the temple and the statue." Moreover, in the event, they were divided into two different boards, the epistatai of the Parthenon, whose full official title is nowhere preserved, and the ἐπιστάται ἀγάλματος χρυσῶ (*IG* I³ 457), "overseers of the golden statue." As we shall see later in detail, the two boards functioned separately, had different funding arrangements, and published separate accounts.[64] The first epistatai of the Parthenon were empaneled in the summer of 447, when they began to keep their accounts, to draw their salaries, and to build the building. Their successors rotated annually for fifteen years until the last pedimental statuary was complete in 433/2.[65] The epistatai of the golden statue seem to be attested first in 446/5, although there was possibly one earlier board, and they went out of office in 438, when the statue was dedicated.[66] That the two boards were composed of different personnel is shown by the accounts of 440/39. In that year Kichesippos of the deme Myrrhinous was secretary to the epistatai of the statue (*IG* I³ 458, lines 1–4), whereas the eighth secretary to the epistatai of the Parthenon came from the deme Probalinthos (*IG* I³ 443, line 203). After 433/2, it is difficult to see how a speaker in the assembly could refer to these two boards in the locution that Thespieus chose, especially since the epistatai of the Propylaia also went out of office in the same year as the epistatai of the Parthenon, whereas the overseers of the golden statue completed their work six years earlier.

The inscription from Eleusis is better dated ca. 450 by analogy with the closest parallels for its style of lettering. This early date for the inscription also agrees better with the architectural history of the site, as we shall see in detail. Another detail of the text also speaks in favor of an early rather than a later date for the document. The five men elected epistatai at Eleusis are to draw daily salaries of four obols each, to be paid by the kolakretai. These public treasurers of Athens had defrayed all the costs of the bronze Athena during the nine years of its construction in the 450s; but the kolakretai

---

(as we proved) becomes better by justice and is ruined by injustice"; *Republic* 4.441C: οὐκοῦν ... ἀναγκαῖον, ὡς πόλις ἦν σοφὴ καὶ ᾧ, οὕτω καὶ τὸν ἰδιώτην καὶ τούτῳ σοφὸν εἶναι, "Is it not necessary that as and whereby the city was [shown to be] wise, so and thereby is the individual wise?"; *Republic* 4.441D: καὶ δίκαιον δὴ φήσομεν ἄνδρα εἶναι τῷ αὐτῷ τρόπῳ ᾧπερ καὶ πόλις ἦν δίκαια, "And now we shall say that a man is just in the same way in which also the city was [shown to be] just"; *Republic* 7.522A: ἀλλ᾽ ἦν ἐκείνη [ἡ μουσικὴ] ... ἀντίστροφος τῆς γυμναστικῆς, εἰ μέμνησαι, "But music was [as we proved] the counterpart of gymnastics, if you remember"; *Republic* 9.587C: ἀπὸ τοῦ ὀλιγαρχικοῦ τρίτος που ὁ τύραννος ἀφειστήκει· ἐν μέσῳ γὰρ αὐτῶν ὁ δημοτικὸς ἦν, "The tyrant, I believe, we found at third remove from the oligarch, for the democrat was in between them"; *Theaetetus* 156A: ἀρχὴ δὲ, ἐξ ἧς καὶ ἃ νῦν δὴ ἐλέγομεν πάντα ἤρηται ἥδε αὐτῶν, ὡς τὸ πᾶν κίνησις ἦν, "The beginning, upon which all the things we were just now discussing depended, is the assumption that everything was [as we saw] real motion." A closely similar usage of the imperfect occurs in the speech of the Korkyraeans, Thuc. 1.35.5: πολλὰ δὲ, ὥσπερ ἐν ἀρχῇ ὑπείπομεν, τὰ ξυμφέροντα ἀποδείκνυμεν, καὶ μέγιστον ὅτι οἵ τε αὐτοὶ πολέμιοι ἡμῖν ἦσαν, "As we suggested in the beginning, we can show you many advantages, and the greatest is this, that the enemies of both of us are [as we saw] the same." The verb was unnecessarily deleted by Classen-Steup, 7th ed. (Berlin 1966), commentary ad loc. The MSS reading was defended by K. von Fritz, in *Thesaurismata: Festschrift für Ida Kapp zum 70. Geburtstag* (Munich 1954) 25–37, and the text is retained by H. S. Jones and J. E. Powell (Oxford 1966), and J. B. Alberti (Rome 1972). This interpretation of the imperfect in *IG* I³ 32 was rejected by Clinton, in *Studies Mylonas*, vol. 2, 256–257, followed by Cavanaugh, *Eleusis*, 26, chiefly on the grounds that the literary passages imply a continuous text to which the past tense refers back. Thus, for the usage to apply, according to Clinton, one would have to postulate that the Acropolis overseers had been appointed in an earlier portion of the same decree. But this is an overly narrow view. Thespieus could just as easily have referred in this way to debate and legislation either earlier at the same meeting or at a recent meeting of the assembly.

[64] See chap. 3, pp. 43–48 below.

[65] See *IG* I³ 436, Year 1 (447/6); 450, Year 15 (archon Apseudes, 433/2).

[66] *IG* I³ 453 probably dates to 446/5 because of the name Exekestos (line 1), who is known to have been secretary of the treasurers of Athena in that year: *IG* I³ 437, line 48 (Parthenon, Year 2). There is no evidence for dating *IG* I³ 454; either 447/6 or 445/4 is possible.

made no contributions to the later projects of the building program, and they are accordingly never mentioned as a source of funds in the accounts of the Parthenon, the golden statue, or the Propylaia. It may then be useful to review what we can deduce about the state of plans for new buildings ca. 450 on the evidence of Thespieus's amendment. Before that speaker arose in the assembly to discuss the management of Eleusinian finances, one infers that plans for the Acropolis project had progressed to the stage where administrative arrangements could be enacted, but not so far that they could not still be changed. The original plan called for the construction of the Parthenon and the gold and ivory statue under the direction of a single board of overseers. Those epistatai on the Acropolis served as a model for the Eleusinian overseers that Thespieus proposed to create. A second amendment[67] (*IG* I³ 32, lines 34–38) requires the Eleusinian epistatai to cooperate with the architect in preparing the audit of the sanctuary's financial resources. Both amendments plainly anticipate the administration of major building operations at Eleusis, and this was the subject of the main decree drafted by the boulē, which probably authorized construction of the Telesterion.

By the time of the Eleusinian inscription, the assembly had approved in principle the construction of temples in the two most important sanctuaries of Attica, and organizational details of the works were under discussion. The date ca. 450 suggests that this was the state of the plans about three years, and possibly even longer, before work on the Parthenon actually began in the summer of 447. But there is no evidence to suggest that the epistatai for the Acropolis project, to whom Thespieus referred, were ever elected as originally provided; and when construction began in 447, new overseers were appointed who had charge only of the temple itself. Clearly, they had not been in office for several years before their published records began. Their annual accounts are numbered in series from 447/6, and the expenses for the first year, which happen to be completely preserved, show no payments for salaries prior to the beginning of that year. We can only conclude that a considerable time elapsed between the decision to build the Parthenon and the beginning of its construction. Moreover, the project for the Telesterion encountered still more serious complications and delays, as will become clear when we consider the archaeology of that building in chapter 6.

To this same period between the removal of the Delian treasury to Athens and the start of work on the Parthenon are to be dated the heated debates in the Athenian assembly concerning the use of the tribute of the allies to fund Athenian public works. Our only source for this parliamentary opposition is the colorful passage in Plutarch's *Life of Perikles* (12) where the assemblies are elaborately embroidered, and the claim is made that the buildings provoked more hostile outcry than all the other public policies of Perikles. In the biographer's account, the argument on both sides of the controversy is predicated on the continued existence of a state of war with Persia. So Plutarch thought the debates occurred before the final cessation of hostilities, which he does not mention. Unfortunately, it is difficult to know how much, if any, of this is reliable history. Since the same passage betrays Plutarch's misunderstanding of the economics of temple building in the Classical period, it is likely that much of the argument between Perikles and his opponents is the biographer's fanciful invention.[68] It is just possible, however, that the delay of several years suggested by the wording of the Eleusinian decree occurred because of political opposition as well as administrative changes.

[67] The name of the speaker of the second amendment is restored as Lysanias, *IG* I³ 32, line 34. Papaioannou, in Φίλια Ἔπη, vol. 3, 231–244, thinks the restoration of the speaker's name is highly unlikely.

[68] A. Andrewes, *JHS* 98 (1978) 1–8, regards Plutarch's account of the debates on the buildings as "worthless"; W. Ameling, *Historia* 34 (1985) 47–63, thinks the chapters on the buildings are rhetorical embroidery of Plutarch's own devising, based on notions culled from Thucydides and Isokrates. Cf. Stadter, *Commentary*, 130, 146, 149–151.

THE DECREES CONCERNING ATHENA NIKE

We turn now to another inscription concerning the cults on the Acropolis. This records the text of a decree whose authorship is not absolutely certain, although it was most likely the motion of a certain Glaukos,[69] who concerned himself with the cult and sanctuary of Athena Nike. The decree also illustrates another aspect of the parliamentary process preparatory to the beginning of building operations: the initial proposal in general terms of an individual building, and the designation of an architect to prepare the plans.

IG I³ 35:

```
      [Λ ε ο ν τ ὶ ς ἐ π ρ υ τ ά ν ε υ ε]
      [ἔδοχσεν τε͂ι βολε͂ι καὶ το͂]ι̣ [δέ]μο]ι· . . .]
      [. . .7. . . ἐπεστάτε, Γλ]αῦκος εἶπε· [τε͂ι]
      ['Αθεναίαι τε͂ι Νί]κει hιέρεαν hὲ ἂγ [κλ]-
  5   [ερομένε λάχε]ι̣ ἐχς 'Αθεναίον hαπα[σο͂]-
      [ν καθίστα]σθαι καὶ τὸ hιερὸν θυρο͂σα-
      ι καθ' ὅ τι ἂν Καλλικράτες χσυγγράφσ-
      ει· ἀπομισθο͂σαι δὲ τὸς πολετὰς ἐπὶ τ-
      ε͂ς Λεοντίδος πρυτανείας. φέρεν δὲ τ-
 10   ὲν hιέρεαν πεντέκοντα δραχμὰς καὶ
      τὰ σκέλε καὶ τὰ δέρματα φέρεν τὸν δε-
      μοσίον· νεὸν δὲ οἰκοδομε͂σαι καθ' ὅ τι
      ἂν Καλλικράτες χσυγγράφσει καὶ βο-
      μὸν λίθινον        vacat
 15   hεστιαῖος εἶπε· τρε͂ς ἄνδρας hελέσθ-
      αι ἐγ βολε͂ς· τούτος δὲ μετ[ὰ] Καλλικρά-
      [το]ς χσυγγράφσαντας ἐπ[ιδεῖχσαι τε͂]-
      [ι βολ]ε͂ι καθ' ὅ τι ἀπομ[ισθοθέσεται . .]
      [. . .6. . .]ει τὸ σ- – – – – – – – –
```

[Leontis held the prytany. Resolved by the boulē and] the [de]mo[s; _____ presided; Gl]aukos made the motion: that there be [established for Athena] Nike a priestess who would be appointed [by lot] from all Athenian women; and that the sanctuary be closed with a gate according as Kallikrates may specify. The poletai are to let the contract during the prytany of Leontis. The priestess is to receive a salary of fifty drachmas and the legs and hides from the public sacrifices. And a temple is to be built according as Kallikrates may specify, together with a stone altar.

Hestiaios made the motion: that three men be chosen from the boulē. These, when they have drawn up the specifications together with Kallikrates, are to [present them to the boulē] just as the contract is to be let. . . .

The decree of Glaukos (lines 1–14) does in fact authorize construction of a temple for Athena Nike and appoints the architect Kallikrates to prepare the specifications. But this is hardly the principal thrust of the speaker's motion, and the brief text actually consists of five separate and distinct clauses, each of which succinctly legislates a different action.[70] (1) A new priestess for Athena Nike is

---

[69] See pp. 29–30 below.
[70] For recent discussion, ML 44; Meiggs, *AE*, 496–503; Mattingly, *AJA* 86 (1982) 381–385 = Mattingly, *AER*, 461–471; Mark, *Athena Nike*, 104–108; Mattingly, *CQ* 50 (2000) 604–606; Mattingly, *CQ* 52 (2002) 337–339; Mattingly, *ZPE* 162 (2007) 107–110; D. W. J. Gill, *Historia* 50 (2001) 257–278; P. J. Rhodes, *CQ* 58 (2008) 500–506.

to be appointed by the democratic procedure of allotment, and all Athenian women are eligible. The position is not to be the private perquisite of some ancient aristocratic family.[71] (2) The sanctuary of Athena Nike on the southwest bastion of the Acropolis is to be closed with gates that are to be designed by Kallikrates. (3) A contract for the construction of the gates is to be let out by the poletai during the prytany of Leontis. This is almost certainly to be understood as the tribe in prytany when the decree was passed, and this provision anticipates the speedy installation of the gates. (4) Glaukos set the salary of the new priestess at fifty drachmas, and she was to receive the additional perquisite of the legs and hides of the sacrificial victims offered to the goddess in the public sacrifices. (5) Finally, a temple and altar of stone are to be constructed, again according to Kallikrates' designs. The inscription continues (lines 15–19) with an amendment to Glaukos's decree proposed by a certain Hestiaios, who made the motion that three members of the boulē be elected as an ad hoc committee. These men are to work with Kallikrates in order to expedite preparation of the specifications, and they are to present them to the boulē just as the contract is to be let. The amendment of Hestiaios seems to be concerned with facilitating the sale of the contract within the time allotted by the third clause of Glaukos's decree. Although the inscription breaks off before the end of the text, it appears likely that the committee of the boulē would involve itself primarily with the design and construction of the gates for the sanctuary.

On the reverse side of the same stone is the text of a second decree pertaining to the priestess of Athena Nike:

IG I³ 36:

> ἔδοχσεν τε̑ι βολε̑ι καὶ το̑ι δέ-
> μοι· Αἰγεὶς ἐπρυτάνευε, Νεοκ-
> λείδες ἐγραμμάτευε, Ἁγνόδε-
> μος ἐπεστάτε, Καλλίας εἶπε· τ-
> 5 ε̑ι hιερέαι τε̑ς Ἀθενάας τε̑ς Νί-
> κες : πεντήκοντα δραχμὰς τὰ-
> ς γεγραμμένας ἐν τῆι στήλ[ηι]
> ἀποδιδόναι τὸς κωλακρ[έτας],
> [ο]ῒ ἂν κωλακρετῶσι τὸ Θ[αργηλ]-
> 10 [ιῶ]νος μηνός, τῆι ἱερ[έαι τῆς Ἀ]-
> [θην]αίας τῆς Νίκη[ς . . . .⁸. . . .]

Resolved by the boulē and the demos, Aigeis held the prytany, Neokleides was secretary, Hagnodemos presided, Kallias made the motion: to the priestess of Athena Nike the kolakretai who hold office in the month of Thargelion are to pay the fifty drachmas inscribed on the stele. To the priestess of Athena Nike....

The two decrees are related to each other not only by their subject matter, in that both concern the priestess of Athena Nike, but also by the specific reference in the second text to the fourth clause of Glaukos's decree, which had stipulated that the priestess receive a salary of fifty drachmas. When Kallias addressed his motion to the assembly, the stone bearing the text of Glaukos's decree was standing on the Acropolis, and so he naturally referred to the salary of fifty drachmas "inscribed on the stele." It is clear from the beginning of the second sentence, with phraseology identical to the first sentence, that Kallias planned some change in status for the priestess. Whether she was to have addi-

---

[71] The lot fell on Myrrhine, daughter of Kallimachos, whose metrical epitaph (ca. 400) boasts proudly, ἡ πρώτη Νίκης ἀμφεπόλευσε νεών. See *SEG* 12.80; J. Papademetriou, *ArchEph* (1948–49) 146–153; D. Lewis, *BSA* 50 (1955) 1–7; C. W. Clairmont, in *Studies von Blanckenhagen,* 103–110; P. Rahn, *BSA* 81 (1986) 195–207; Mark, *Athena Nike,* 111–113. It was no doubt to her position as first priestess that Myrrhine owed her immortal caricature in Aristophanes' *Lysistrata.*

tional responsibilities, or to offer additional sacrifices, or to receive additional emoluments, there is of course no way of knowing; but what would not change was her salary of fifty drachmas that had been specified in Glaukos's decree. Because the second decree orders so specifically that the priestess be paid her salary, scholars have sometimes inferred that she had been paid only irregularly, or perhaps not at all, since the time of her election.[72] But that does not seem to be an inevitable inference from Kallias's language, for it may be that she had previously been paid at a different time of year or by different financial officers.[73] The text does imply that the priestess will receive her entire annual stipend in one lump sum during the month of Thargelion.

Ever since their discovery in 1897,[74] these documents have bulked large in attempts to reconstruct the history of the building program on the Acropolis. In the case of the first decree, for nearly a century after its discovery, the style of the lettering was taken to indicate a date for the inscription near the middle of the fifth century; but that early date presented scholars with the difficult problem of reconciling the architectural history of the Temple of Athena Nike with the epigraphical evidence of the text that seemed to refer to it. For a consensus arose fairly early that construction of the well-known marble temple should be dated as late as the 420s on the strength of its architecture and primarily its sculptural decoration. The inscription, on the other hand, suggested that the building had been authorized and the architect appointed as much as twenty years or more before its construction actually got under way.[75] In the case of the second decree, the date is certain. Mention of Neokleides, the secretary for the prytany of Aigeis, shows that the decree of Kallias was passed during the same prytany of 424/3 as the treaty with Halieis, and in the same year as the decree honoring Herakleides of Klazomenai, on which occasion the same Neokleides presided in the assembly.[76]

The notion of building a temple for Athena Nike and of appointing a priestess for her cult suggested the commemoration of a great military victory. Moreover, scenes depicting the tumult of heroic battle could be seen to run around three sides of the temple's sculptured frieze. That the temple authorized by the inscription was meant to celebrate the victorious campaigns of the Persian Wars, an offering long overdue to the goddess who had conferred those victories, can hardly be doubted. To this extent, most students of Athenian monuments would probably be in agreement.

What called for special explanation, however, was the seemingly awkward chronological gap between the two decrees on two sides of the same stele and their curious insistence upon the payment of the priestess's salary. Furthermore, that same chronological gap appeared to separate the authorization of the temple, around midcentury, from its construction in the 420s. Efforts to explain these circumstances have inevitably stimulated unusual scholarly ingenuity. The occasion for the earlier decree has been found in the final cessation of hostilities with Persia in 449: a temple for Athena Nike was intended to commemorate the conclusion of the notorious Peace of Kallias, or perhaps its renewal, in that year.[77] Early editors of the text dramatically enlivened the story by restoring the bro-

[72] See commentary on Tod, *GHI*, vol. 1, 73; ML 71.

[73] Cf. Meritt and Wade-Gery, *JHS* 83 (1963) 111; Mark, *Athena Nike*, 108.

[74] P. Kavvadias, *ArchEph* (1897) 176–191.

[75] For early bibliography, Judeich, *Topographie*[2], 219, note 3, 220, note 1. See also Dinsmoor, *AAG*[3], 185–186; Meiggs, *AE*, 496–499; Mark, *Athena Nike*, 115–118; D. Giraud, Μελέτη ναού της Αθηνάς Νίκης (Athens 1994) 38–48.

[76] Neokleides as secretary for Aigeis in the treaty with Halieis, *IG* I[3] 75, lines 1, 3. His name is also partly preserved in *IG* I[3] 74, line 5. Neokleides appears as epistates in the decree honoring Herakleides, *IG* I[3] 227, line 7 (= ML 70). As secretary, he was not a member of the tribe in prytany (Rhodes, *Athenian Boule*, 134–135), but as epistates he was (Rhodes, 23–24), thus the decree for Herakleides was passed in a different prytany, but in the same year as *IG* I[3] 36, 74, and 75. For the date in 424/3: Meritt and Davidson, *AJP* 56 (1935) 65–71; Wade-Gery, *EGH*, 207–211.

[77] Cf. A. Körte, *Hermes* 45 (1910) 623–627; Judeich, *Topographie*[2], 218–219, note 1; Dinsmoor, *Hesperia* Suppl. 5 (1941) 156–160; Dinsmoor, *AAG*[3], 185–186; Wade-Gery, *EGH*, 209; Meritt and Wade-Gery, *JHS* 83 (1963) 105–111; ML 44, commentary on pp. 109–110; Boersma, *Building Policy*, 66–67, 71; Meiggs, *AE*, 134–135, 154, 501. That the Peace of Kallias was renewed in 449 after the Cypriot campaign and Kimon's death is the suggestion of Badian, *From Plataea to Potidaea*, 20–23.

ken name of the speaker who proposed the earlier decree as [Ἱππόν]ικος, and by identifying him as Hipponikos son of Kallias, the negotiator of the peace with Persia that bore his name.[78] The Kallias who proposed the later decree on the priestess's salary was then identified as the son of Hipponikos and grandson of Kallias the peacemaker. Support for this identification seemed to come from a co-incidence of date in 424/3, for in that same year the decree for Herakleides of Klazomenai attested a treaty between Athens and Darius II of Persia, which was understood to be a kind of renewal of the Peace of Kallias when the next Persian king came to the throne. That event in turn was appropriately celebrated by the family's renewed interest in the cult of Athena Nike.[79]

In this way the great priestly family of the Kerykes, hereditary torchbearers of the Eleusinian Mysteries, was cast in the role of champion for the cult of Athena Nike. But it appeared from the later decree that the priestess whose election they had proposed was not receiving her proper salary.[80] The question arose whether she had ever been elected, and thus the suspicion of political infighting cast a pall of smoke over the whole episode. The temple that "Hipponikos" proposed to build for the goddess could be seen as the response of the conservative religious establishment to the radical ideas of Perikles and his circle, who planned to enclose the entire western end of the Acropolis in the enormous and grandiose gatehouse of the Propylaia. In consequence of this perceived political dispute, the delay in the temple's construction was attributed to the political opposition of Perikles and his friends. The more imaginative proponents of this theory conceived of a kind of architectural wrestling match between Mnesikles, architect of the Propylaia, supported by Perikles, and Kallikrates, architect of the Nike temple, supported by the Kerykes. Material evidence for this combat was sought in the sundry architectural vicissitudes that truncated Mnesikles' plan for the Propylaia, and the eventual construction of the Nike temple was a victory for the religious establishment.[81] Much of this hypothetical reconstruction, however, had been extrapolated from the speaker's name restored as "Hipponikos" in the earlier decree. But careful reexamination of the inscription revealed that only the last three letters of the name -κος could be read with certainty. Of the letter before kappa, only the bottom of a centered vertical stroke was preserved, so that upsilon was just as likely as iota. More important, the next letter to the left was triangular, the only possible readings being alpha or gamma; thus Hipponikos was excluded, and much the most likely restoration was [Γλ]αῦκος.[82] Realization that the author of the earlier decree was an otherwise unknown Athenian citizen should have been sufficient to demolish much of the speculative mythology that had been spun from the erroneous restoration of Hipponikos's name, but it has taken some decades for that to happen. Seductive theories are something like satellites that orbit on their own momentum long after the ideas that first launched them have fallen to the ground like spent rockets.

Removal of the famous names and the bickering architects from the discussion did nothing, however, to help close the chronological gap between the temple's authorization in the decree of

---

[78] The suggestion of Körte, *Hermes* 45 (1910) 626–627, adopted by Hiller von Gaertringen, *IG* I² 24, line 4 and commentary. The man so identified is Hipponikos (II) son of Kallias (II), Kirchner, *PA* 7658, and see Davies, *APF*, 262–263.

[79] Note 78 above. On the treaty with Darius, Wade-Gery, *EGH*, 207–211; the treaty of 424/3 is mentioned in *IG* I³ 227, lines 15–18. The argument is summarized by Mark, *Athena Nike,* 116–117.

[80] ML 71, commentary p. 204.

[81] On the political dimensions of the controversy, see A. Furtwängler, *Meisterwerke der griechischen Plastik* (Leipzig 1893) 209–210; A. Furtwängler, "Zu den Tempeln der Akropolis von Athen," *SBMünch* 1 (Munich 1898) 380–390; Judeich, *Topographie*², 218–219; Dinsmoor, *AJA* 27 (1923) 321; Dinsmoor, *AAG*³, 185; G. Welter, *AA* (1939) 14; Meritt and Wade-Gery, *JHS* 83 (1963) 109–110; Giraud, Μελέτη Αθηνάς Νίκης, 39–40. For the debate on the altered plans of the Propylaia: Dörpfeld, *AM* 36 (1911) 55–60; Welter, *AM* 48 (1923) 196–201; Wrede, *AM* 57 (1932) 74–91; H. Schleif, *JdI* 48 (1933) 177–184; B. Schweitzer, in *Aus Antike und Orient: Festschrift Wilhelm Schubart* (Leipzig 1950) 116–125. The arguments are summarized by Mark, *Athena Nike,* 117–119; Gruben, *Gr. Tempel*⁵, 203–205.

[82] The reading was first made by Dinsmoor in 1924; see *Hesperia* Suppl. 5 (1941) 159, note 337. Reference to the necessary correction of the text was first published in 1933; see Tod, *GHI*, vol. 1, 40, p. 79. Mattingly, *ZPE* 162 (2007) 109–110, prefers Dinsmoor's less likely alternative and restores the speaker's name as [– Πατ]αικος.

Glaukos and its subsequent construction. More recent writers have therefore directed their efforts to show that the gap is illusory and never existed in fact; and two mutually exclusive lines of argument have been adduced in this attempt. The first maintains that the decree of Glaukos has been wrongly dated to midcentury. The usual date was based solely on the style of the lettering, and the only letter form that is seemingly incompatible with a later date is the three-bar sigma. This, it is argued, is too nebulous a criterion to compel an early date for the inscription, which should be abandoned in favor of a date in the 420s, whereupon the awkward interval between authorization and construction simply disappears. This late date for the decree of Glaukos appeared to gain strong support from the discovery that the Egesta Decree (*IG* I³ 11), which has the three-bar sigma throughout the text, actually dates to the year of the archonship of Antiphon (418/7) and not before the middle of the century, as previously thought.[83]

The second line of argument likewise hinges upon alteration of generally accepted chronology, but in this case it is the chronology of the architecture rather than of the epigraphy that needs to be lowered by the requisite number of years. Proponents of this view accept a date for the decree of Glaukos in the years around the middle of the fifth century, but they maintain that the inscription has nothing to do with the familiar marble Ionic temple that was built in the 420s. The temple and altar that the decree orders Kallikrates to design for Athena Nike are identified as the small poros naiskos and its poros altar that stand at the archaic level of the bastion beneath the northeastern corner of the later building. This same structure has been interpreted by many others as a temporary shelter for the cult statue of Athena Nike erected or restored in the first years after the Persian destruction.[84] In order to bring the poros naiskos into relation with the decree of Glaukos, it becomes necessary to lower its date from the 470s to the early 440s.

Acceptance of either of these two propositions is fraught with difficulties. The demonstration that one inscription with the earlier form of lettering actually dates to the late fifth century does not give license to lower the dates of other such inscriptions at will. It means only that other inscriptions with the three-bar sigma can no longer necessarily be assigned dates before the middle of the century. The fact remains that the dated document with lettering most similar to the decree of Glaukos is the third tribute list of 452/1 (*IG* I³ 261). Moreover, the early date has received strong support from the convincing argument that the same mason carved both the decree of Glaukos and the accounts of the bronze Athena (*IG* I³ 435).[85] The latter inscription, as we have already seen, is the earliest of the building accounts and is clearly to be dated before the accounts of the Parthenon and Propylaia. But acceptance that the same hand inscribed both these accounts and the first Nike temple decree has posed difficulties for proponents of the late date for the latter. Accordingly, some scholars have also ventured to lower the date of the great bronze Athena to the 430s, although neither evidence nor

[83] For the date of the Egesta Decree, see Chambers, Gallucci, and Spanos, *ZPE* 83 (1990) 38–57; and cf. now the remarks of Rhodes, *CQ* 58 (2008) 500, notes 1, 2. The late date for *IG* I³ 35 was originally championed by Mattingly, *Historia* 10 (1961) 169–171 = Mattingly, *AER,* 30–32; Mattingly, *Historia* 14 (1965) 278 = Mattingly, *AER,* 113–114; Mattingly, *AJA* 86 (1982) 381–385 = Mattingly, *AER,* 461–471. His conviction briefly wavered in Carridice, ed., *Coinage and Administration,* 68 = Mattingly, *AER,* 481. But he returned to a date in the 420s, *CQ* 50 (2000) 604–606; suggested 425/4, *CQ* 52 (2002) 337–339; and argued for 424/3, *ZPE* 162 (2007) 109–110. See also Gill, *Historia* 50 (2001) 257–278.

[84] On the date of the poros naiskos beneath the Nike temple, see endnote 1, pp. 393–394 below. Various dates have been proposed, ranging from the late sixth century to the mid-fifth: Welter, *AA* (1939) 11–12 (late sixth century, rebuilt after the Persian Wars); Boersma, *Building Policy,* 178, no. 46 (late archaic and rebuilt after 479); Travlos, *PDA,* 148 (built 490–480, restored after 479); Dinsmoor, *AAG*³, 151 (built after 479); Bundgaard, *Parthenon,* 44–45 (mid-fifth century); followed by Mark, *Athena Nike,* 58–67; and Romano, "Cult Images," 61–62. Bundgaard, in *Mélanges G. Daux,* 43–49, followed by Mark, *Athena Nike,* 115–122, associated the poros naiskos with the Nike temple decree, *IG* I³ 35.

[85] The early date for *IG* I³ 35 is still accepted by Rhodes, *CQ* 58 (2008) 501, 504. On the letter-cutter of *IG* I³ 35 and 435, S. V. Tracy, in K. J. Rigsby, ed., *Studies Presented to Sterling Dow* (Durham, NC, 1984) 281–282; cf. the remarks of Lewis, in Carradice, ed., *Coinage and Administration,* 57. R. S. Stroud, *The Athenian Empire on Stone: David Lewis Memorial Lecture, Oxford, 2006* (Athens 2006) 26–32, expresses doubts about the identification.

Figure 3. View of the Nike bastion showing steps

probability supports this view.[86] Pheidias's statue is better seen as the first major dedication on the Acropolis after the Persian Wars, and the records of the expenses for erecting it provide important corroborating evidence for the date of the early decree for Athena Nike.

With regard to the second solution, the idea that the earlier decree authorized construction of the poros naiskos and its associated altar, whose dates must then be brought down to the early 440s, presents equally difficult problems. The technical architectural evidence marshaled to advocate the later date has been examined in detail elsewhere, and, far from compelling acceptance of that date, the architectural parallels favor a date for the naiskos and its altar in the 470s.[87] The proposition that Kallikrates designed the poros naiskos in response to the decree of Glaukos involves an extraordinary incongruity, for we should then have to suppose that the tiny, nondescript poros box of the naiskos and the marble Parthenon—largest, costliest, and most splendid temple in Greece—were both designed for the same sanctuary, at about the same time, and by the same architect.

Most discussions of the decree of Glaukos have overlooked a critical detail in the architectural history of the stele itself. If the earlier inscription is to be dated ca. 450, as is almost certainly correct, then the stele was first erected in topographical circumstances quite different from those that exist today. In the middle years of the fifth century, the sanctuary of Athena Nike was an isolated protrusion of the Acropolis, its level about 1.35 m below that of the later terrace and several meters lower than the Acropolis proper,[88] from which it was separated by the great mass of the ancient Pelasgian

---

[86] A. Linfert, *AM* 97 (1982) 67, attempted to make the bronze Athena contemporary with the Athena Parthenos; rejected by Lundgreen, *JHS* 117 (1997) 190–197. Gill, *Historia* 50 (2001) 269–274, attempted to revive a date for the statue in the early 430s.

[87] See endnote 1 below.

[88] N. Balanos, *ArchEph* (1937) pt. 3 [1956], followed by Mark, *Athena Nike*, 43, note 4, records the elevation of the naiskos euthynteria as 1.295 m below the euthynteria of the Nike temple at its northeast corner (+142.213 − 1.295 = +140.918). T. Tanoulas, *AM* 107 (1992) 156, says that the "level of the early sanctuary is +140.91." Dinsmoor, Jr., *Propylaia*, plan A, records the naiskos euthynteria at +140.877, in agreement with Giraud, Μελέτη Αθηνάς Νίκης, pl. 9. But Dinsmoor, Jr., shows the northeast corner of the Nike temple euthynteria at +142.223, a difference of 1.346 m between

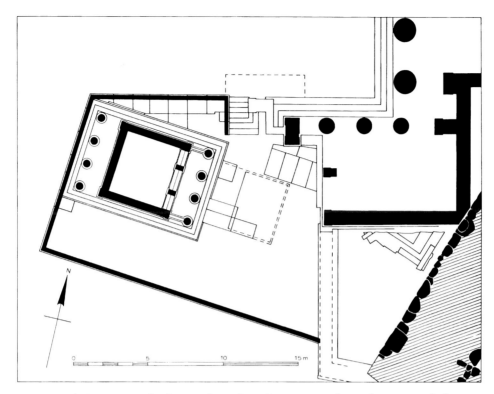

Figure 4. Sanctuary of Athena Nike and southwest wing of Propylaia, restored plan

wall of Mycenaean date. The sanctuary itself occupied a salient bastion of the Bronze Age citadel that was still supported by walls of Cyclopean masonry (Fig. 3). The only access to the shrine was at the northeast corner, where the lowest of the rock-cut steps in front of the Pelasgian wall brought the level down nearly to the top of the bastion (Fig. 4). It was no doubt at this very point that Kallikrates was to erect the gates specified in the inscription. The stele will originally have stood nearby within the sanctuary, its base resting on the archaic ground level. In the 430s, when the Propylaia were under construction, the decision was made to enlarge the bastion by surrounding its Cyclopean walls with a sheathing of ashlar masonry.[89] This construction brought the north face of the bastion into alignment with the lowest step of the southwest wing of the Propylaia and raised the level of its pavement, so that the open porch of the southwest wing could provide the principal means of access to the sanctuary of Athena Nike (Fig. 5). The stele bearing the decree of Glaukos was removed from its original position at this time and placed on the raised terrace of the newly enlarged bastion. Such is the obvious and necessary conclusion to be drawn from the fact that the reverse of the stone was available for the later inscription in 424/3.

It has often escaped notice that the site of the stele's secondary position can be identified. The steps of the Propylaia are enclosed at the southwest by a low Z-shaped parapet, whose northern arm terminates in the gatepost (pier W) beside the stairs leading down to the main approach ramp.[90] The

the two levels. Giraud (p. 32) places the level of the earlier sanctuary 1.80 m below the marble floor of the Propylaia, in agreement with Wrede, *AM* 57 (1932) Beil. 16, but this leaves only 1.208 m between the terrace of the Nike temple and the earlier sanctuary. Stevens, *Hesperia* 15 (1946) 79, recorded the same measurement as 1.395 m between the earlier and the later levels. Recently, Mark, *Hesperia* 64 (1995) 383–388, and J. C. Wright, *Hesperia* 64 (1995) 389, have been disposed to quibble about millimeters, but clearly even the most accurate instruments yield different results in the hands of different investigators.

[89] On the enlargement of the Nike bastion and its date of construction, see chap. 10, pp. 341–346 below.

[90] The gatepost, pier W, is the designation of Wrede, *AM* 57 (1932) 74–91 and fig. 1 (plan), Beil. 16 (sections). For the marble steps leading down from the bastion, see also Welter, *AM* 48 (1923) 190–201; Schleif, *JdI* 48 (1933) 177–184; Bundgaard, *Mnesicles*, 177–180.

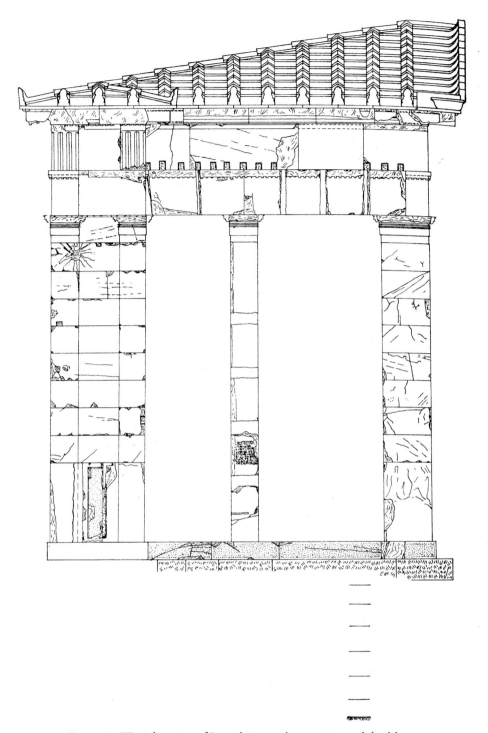

Figure 5. West elevation of Propylaia, southwest wing and double anta

southern arm of this parapet abuts the stylobate of the southwest wing at the midpoint of the great double anta, where the stylobate is dressed with anathyrosis to accommodate the joint (Fig. 5). The block abutting the stylobate preserves a socket for the placement of a stele aligned with the midpoint of the double anta and turned at a right angle to its western face. The socket measures 0.062 m deep and 0.11 m from front to back. Its width is preserved for 0.37 m to the point where the right end of the block is broken away; but if the socket was cut equidistant from the ends of the block, its full original width was just over 0.38 m. That a stele stood in this position, immediately adjacent to the double anta, is certain because the center of the anta's western face still retains a panel of protective surface 0.295 m wide and rising to a height of 1.357 m above the stylobate. We owe to W. B. Dinsmoor, Sr.,[91] the observation, made long ago, that the socket has precisely the correct dimensions to accommodate the stele bearing the two inscriptions concerning Athena Nike. That stone measures 0.38 m in width, and its slight taper from top to bottom enables the thickness at the bottom to be calculated as 0.106 m.

Identification of the site for the stele in its second period allows us to draw more specific inferences concerning the significance and chronology of the monument. Its position is plainly a prominent one. Midway between the northern stairs and the main eastern entrance by way of the Propylaia, the inscriptions would have been immediately visible to every visitor on the bastion. The interrelation between the inscribed stele and the architecture of the Propylaia allows the date of its re-erection on the bastion to be placed within narrow limits. It was the standard practice of Greek stonemasons to erect the marble blocks of a building's superstructure while all their visible surfaces were still protected by a layer of stone several millimeters thick. The final process in completing construction was to dress both the vertical and horizontal surfaces to a smooth finish by polishing away the last few millimeters of stone. The Propylaia themselves provide the clearest evidence that this final dressing was carried out after the blocks were set in place, for the protective surface and lifting bosses were never removed from the exterior walls of the central hall. But the double anta of the southwest wing has been polished to its final finish on all faces except at the midpoint of the west side, where the narrow panel of protective surface is still to be seen. This can only mean that the stele was already in position immediately beside the anta when the final dressing took place. The blocks of the double anta were set in position; then the inscription was placed beside it before the anta received its final polishing. In terms of the five-year construction history of the Propylaia,[92] the inscription was necessarily re-erected before work stopped at the end of 433/2, and thus it was in place by ca. 433 at the very latest.

At this point, having in mind the contents of the decree of Glaukos, one may well inquire why it should be deemed important to display the inscription so prominently on the raised bastion. The priestess whose election it prescribed had presumably held office by that time for nearly seventeen years. Kallikrates' gates were presumably completely obliterated by construction of the southwest wing. If the temple of the inscription refers to the poros naiskos, as the most recent students of the problem maintain, that structure also was by now entombed within the lowest foundation courses of the Ionic temple. The simplest answer to the question is that in the decree of Glaukos the demos of the Athenians gave its formal authorization to build a temple for Athena Nike, whose construction had been delayed and was just then beginning.

In light of the foregoing discussion, it is clear that a new temple and altar for Athena Nike formed an integral part of the building program on the Acropolis. The decree of Glaukos shows that the project received official authorization in the years ca. 450, at about the same time when there is good reason to believe that plans were under discussion for the Parthenon and its statue, and for the Telesterion at Eleusis. A temple for Athena in her special capacity as bringer of victory plainly implies the commemoration of military victories as an important motivating factor and lends credence to the statements of fourth-century public speakers who regarded the Parthenon and other temples as trophies celebrating the victories in the Persian Wars.[93] Moreover, the election of a new priestess of Athena Nike gives tangible evidence for the aggrandizement of Athenian cults and festivals which, we may suggest, was one of the principal desiderata of Periklean religious imperialism.

[91] Dinsmoor, *AJA* 27 (1923) 320–321; see also Giraud, Μελέτη Αθηνᾶς Νίκης, 41; I. M. Shear, *JHS* 119 (1999) 124.
[92] See chap. 9, pp. 300–302 below.
[93] See chap. 1, pp. 4–6 above.

The Ideology of Religious Imperialism

The evidence for the building of new temples both on the Acropolis and in the sanctuary at Eleusis shows that the ideology of the building program had evolved considerably by the middle years of the fifth century. What had begun as the erection of thank-offerings to the gods and war memorials for the military victories over the Persians seems to have become a deliberate effort to aggrandize the most important cults and festivals of Athens. In the pairing of the two sanctuaries, there is a discernible common theme: the glorification of those deities who had bestowed their special gifts on Athens, and the glorification of Athens for sharing those gifts with the Greek world. The Acropolis temples paid homage to Athena, first and foremost the bringer of victory, who had helped her warriors to drive off the Persians at Marathon and conferred the boon of military victory. The cult of Athena Nike would now have its own priestess as well as a new temple and altar.

Still more important was Athena Polias, the guardian of the city and patron of political Athens. Her gifts were government and the rule of law; she was the Athena of Aischylos's *Eumenides* and protector of the Aegean confederacy. In the first flush of victory after the Battle of Marathon, the Athenians had begun to build a great temple as a thank-offering to the goddess, but after the destruction of 480, its wreckage had lain about for thirty years. Construction of that temple was now to be resumed with different plans. Now, too, Athena's ancient citadel would become the seat of empire and a stronghold for the imperial treasury. During the third quarter of the fifth century, her festival, the Great Panathenaia, developed into the festival par excellence of the Athenian Empire. At this quadrennial celebration were held the official assemblies of the allies, which seem to have replaced the original Delian synods as early as 454.[94] The tribute assessments for the next quadrennium were determined then and Athena's portion of the tribute was delivered over to her treasurers. The first evidence for the conversion of the Panathenaia into the festival of the empire comes in the decree of 453/2 (?) specifying regulations for Erythrai. Although the exact wording of the Erythraian obligations is beyond recovery, the city was ordered to contribute a specified amount of wheat, to be presented at the festival.[95] In later years, all Athenian colonies and allied cities were represented at the festival, for it was their duty to sacrifice a cow to the goddess and to dedicate a panoply of arms, in return for which they were accorded the privilege of marching in the Panathenaic procession.[96] Thus the Athenians could be sure that every city of the empire would hear accounts of the great procession, the games, and the sacrifices. This systematic aggrandizement of Athena's festival reached its culmination in the Great Panathenaia of 446 or 442, when Perikles introduced his decree concerning the revival of the musical contests, and himself served as athlothetes.[97] The venue for the

[94] The tribute assessments of the allies were normally reviewed at the Great Panathenaia: *IG* I³ 71, lines 26–33 = ML 69 (425/4); *IG* I³ 61, lines 8–9 = ML 65 (430/29) with *ATL* III, 134–136; [Xen.] *Ath. Pol.* 3.5. From the foundation of the confederacy the synods had met at Delos, Thuc. 1.96.2–97.1. After removal of the treasury to Athens in 454, the meetings at Delos were probably replaced by assemblies held at the Panathenaia; see *ATL* III, 138, 262, note 91.

[95] *IG* I³ 14, lines 3–8 (= ML 40). On the participation of the allies as colonists, J. L. Shear, "Polis and Panathenaia," 139–143.

[96] *IG* I³ 34, lines 41–43 (= ML 46), 425/4; 71, lines 56–58 (= ML 69), 425/4: ηοπόσ[εσι πό]λεσι φόρος [ἐταχ]θ[ε ἐπὶ τ]ἔς [βολἔς ηεἶ Πλειστί]ας πρōτος [ἐγρα]μμάτευε ἐπὶ Στρατοκ[λέος] ἄρχοντος βō[ν καὶ πανηοπ]λ[ίαν ἀπάγεν ἐς Παναθ]ἔναια τὰ με[γάλα] ηαπάσας· πεμπόντων δ[ὲ ἐν] τεῖ πομπεῖ [καθάπερ ἄποι]κ[οι], "All those cities for which tribute [was assessed in the boulē in which Pleistias] was first secretary, in the archonship of Stratokles, [shall bring] a cow and a [panoply of armor] to the Great Panathenaia. They are to take part in the procession [just like colonists]." Cf. also the colony at Brea: *IG* I³ 46, lines 11–13 (= ML 49); schol. Aristoph. *Clouds* 386a (Holwerda); the obligation of the Parians during the Second Athenian Confederacy (372/1), *SEG* 31.67, lines 2–6. Similar panoplies sent to the Great Panathenaia from Priene, *I. Priene* 5, lines 2–6 (shortly before 326/5); and from Colophon, *IG* II² 456B, lines 4–8 (307/6). On the allies' Panathenaic obligations, see Meritt and Wade-Gery, *JHS* 82 (1962) 69–71. On the dedication of armor, J. L. Shear, "Polis and Panathenaia," 187–195.

[97] Plut. *Per.* 13.11; Plut. *Mor.* 1134A; for the date in 442, *ATL* III, 302, note 5, 306; for the date in 446, Davison, *From Archilochus to Pindar*, 63–64; Stadter, *Commentary*, 175–176. In 410/9, when Athenian finances were hardly what they

revived musical contests was to be another new building specifically dedicated to that purpose, the enormous Odeion on the south slope of the Acropolis beside the Theater of Dionysos. This building is attributed to the "works of Perikles" by both Plutarch (*Per.* 13.11) and Lykourgos (Frag. 58). When we examine its remains in detail in chapter 7, we shall see that its construction should most likely be dated to the 440s.

If the Acropolis was to become the principal sanctuary of the Athenian Empire, and the Panathenaia the national festival for Athenians and their allies, the appeal of Eleusis was Panhellenic. An important inscribed stele, dated about 460, whose text is now difficult to read and restore, records detailed regulations for the conduct of the Eleusinian Mysteries.[98] The document is a sacred law no doubt drafted by action of the Athenian demos; the boulē is mentioned by name. The democratic government legislates its own deep involvement in the administration of festival and sanctuary, and exerts its control over the aristocratic priestly families of Eleusis, who by ancient tradition performed the mystic rites. Specific fees are prescribed that the Eumolpidai, the Kerykes, and the other priestly officials may charge each initiate, and from the monies thus collected the priestess of Demeter is to withhold 1,600 drachmas to defray the expenses of the festival. The law regulates initiation into the Mysteries; it states who shall be eligible to conduct the ritual and how and where it is to take place.[99] The clearest indication that the assembly asserted its right to manage the Eleusinian sanctuary comes in a clause providing for disposition of the sacred monies. It specifically states that the Athenians may use the funds, probably from the *aparchai*, as they see fit, just as they use the treasury of Athena on the Acropolis. Furthermore, the Eleusinian hieropoioi are instructed to deposit the money of the Two Goddesses on the Acropolis at Athens.[100] Of special interest, however, are the provisions for the sacred truce. Specific dates are mentioned when the truce was to be in force for the Great Mysteries in the fall and for the Lesser Mysteries in the winter, and this would ensure safe passage to Attica for Eleusinian initiates, both Athenian and foreign alike.[101] Plainly implied is the dispatch of *spondophoroi* to proclaim the truce, to summon the faithful *mystai*, and to invite would-be new initiates to visit Athens from cities all over Greece.

The far-reaching popularity of the Mysteries and the evident prosperity of the Eleusinian sanctuary throughout antiquity testify to the tremendous success that Athens achieved in publicizing her ancient agrarian festival. This success was due in part to the innate religious appeal of the mystery cult itself, for it not only emphasized the rich benefits of Demeter's grain, but it held out to the initiate the irresistible promise of Elysium. "Happy of mortal men is he who has seen these things. Who is uninitiate of the mysteries, who has had no part of them will not have like destiny when consumed by gloomy darkness."[102] This was the hope that Demeter's hymn held out to all people, and the cries of the initiates echo the joy that they found in the cult. "Thrice happy are those of mortals who, hav-

had been in the 440s, the athlothetai received 5 talents, 1,000 drachmas for the Great Panathenaia (*IG* I³ 375, lines 5–6 = ML 84); in 415/4, they had received as much as 9 talents (*IG* I³ 370, lines 66–68 = ML 77). For the athlothetai, [Aristot.] *Ath. Pol.* 60.1; Rhodes, *Commentary*, 668–672; Podlecki, *Perikles*, 77–81; J. L. Shear, "Polis and Panathenaia," 455–463. For the Periklean aggrandizement of the festival, Shear (above), 543–547.

[98] *IG* I³ 6 = Clinton, *Eleusis*, no. 19, and cf. *SEG* 31.2 for a complete re-edition of the text by S. Cataldi, with very extensive restorations, especially on side A. References to line numbers here are cited as in *IG* I³.

[99] *IG* I³ 6C, lines 20–26, fees payable to the Eumolpidai and Kerykes; C, lines 6–14, fees payable to the hieropoioi and the priestess of Demeter; C, lines 15–20, 1,600 drachmas withheld for expenses; C, lines 30–31, 40–50, regulations for conduct of the ritual.

[100] *IG* I³ 6C, lines 32–38 with the restorations of K. Clinton, *The Sacred Officials of the Eleusinian Mysteries*, TAPS 64, pt. 3 (Philadelphia 1974) 10–12 = Clinton, *Eleusis*, no. 19.

[101] *IG* I³ 6B, lines 8–17.

[102] Homeric *Hymn to Demeter* 480–482:

ὄλβιος, ὃς τάδ᾽ ὄπωπεν ἐπιχθονίων ἀνθρώπων·
ὃς δ᾽ ἀτελὴς ἱερῶν ὅς τ᾽ ἄμμορος, οὔ ποθ᾽ ὁμοίων
αἶσαν ἔχει φθίμενός περ ὑπὸ ζόφῳ εὐρώεντι.

ing seen those rites, depart for Hades; for to them alone is it granted to have true life there; to the rest all there is evil," sang Sophokles.[103] But perhaps as much as to the religion of its cult, Eleusis owed its growth to the ingenuities of Athenian propaganda; for the benefits of agriculture and the joys of initiation were represented to the Greek world at large not so much as god-given gifts as the products of Athenian goodwill and enlightenment. The notion was carefully nourished and widely disseminated that the Athenians were a chosen people on whom the gods first lavished the gifts of civilization, and Athenian magnanimity had bestowed these gifts on other Greeks. The most fulsome expression of this idea we owe to Isokrates in the *Panegyricus*:

> In the first place, then, that which was the first necessity of man's nature was provided by our city. Yes, even if the story has become myth, yet it deserves to be told again. When Demeter came to our land in her wanderings after the rape of Kore, she was moved to kindness toward our ancestors by services which may not be told save to her initiates; and she gave these two gifts, the greatest in the world: the fruits of the earth, which have enabled us to rise above the life of beasts, and the holy mysteries, which inspire in those who partake of them sweeter hopes regarding both the end of life and all eternity. Our city was not only so beloved of the gods but so loving of men that, endowed with these great blessings, she did not begrudge them to others, but what she got she shared with all. Even now we continue to reveal the mystic rites each year; and as for the fruits of the earth, our city has, in a word, instructed the world in their uses, their cultivation, and the benefits derived therefrom.[104]

The vehicle for the propagation of these ideas was the venerable medium of myth, and the tale was spread that an Eleusinian aristocrat named Triptolemos had been delegated as the special agent of Demeter to travel to all countries of the world and instruct the peoples in the raising of grain.[105] This story seems first to have been concocted at Athens during the latter part of the sixth century, when Triptolemos began to enjoy some popularity as a subject for the painters of late black-figure and early red-figure vases.[106] But the myth came into special prominence in the arts and letters of the mid-fifth century, inspired no doubt in part by the reorganization of the cult after the Persian Wars. One of the earliest tragic victories of Sophokles, if not the first, was his production of the play *Triptolemos*, whose central theme was Demeter's gift of grain to all the world through the agency of the young hero.[107] At this time, too, Eleusis seems to have made a special effort to cultivate its Panhellenic relations; and, as we have seen, the Athenian law reorganizing the cult about 460 made detailed provision for the sacred truce that enabled all Greeks to journey with impunity on the great pilgrimage.[108] There can be little doubt that the proclamations of the *spondophoroi*, who announced

---

[103] Radt, *TrGF* 10 F 837; and cf. Pindar, frag. 137 (Maehler).

[104] *Panegyr.* 4.28–29; translation adapted from G. Norlin (Loeb). With these sentiments, cf. Plato, *Menex.* 237E–238A.

[105] Paus. 1.14.2–3; Apollodoros 1.5.2; M. P. Nilsson, *Greek Popular Religion* (New York 1940) 55–58; Mylonas, *Eleusis,* 20–21. The recent fabrication of the myth is indicated by the fact that the *Hymn to Demeter* knows nothing of it; cf. lines 149–155, 473–479.

[106] See A. E. Raubitschek and I. K. Raubitschek, "The Mission of Triptolemos," *Hesperia* Suppl. 20 (Princeton 1982) 109–117; H. A. Shapiro, *Art and Cult under the Tyrants in Athens* (Mainz 1989) 76–77; C. Dugas, "La mission de Triptolème d'après l'imagerie athénienne," *MÉFRA* 62 (1950) 6–31. Dugas's catalogue of vases (pp. 23–31) perfectly reflects the growth of the myth from the third quarter of the sixth century through the middle of the fifth. The number of vases, listed by quarter century, is as follows: third quarter sixth: 2 (nos. 1, 2); fourth quarter sixth: 15 (nos. 3–17); first quarter fifth: 18 (nos. 18–35); second quarter fifth: 36 (nos. 36–71).

[107] See Dion. Hal. 1.12.2. For the fragments, Radt, *TrGF* 10 F 596–617; A. C. Pearson, *The Fragments of Sophocles* (Cambridge 1917) vol. 2, 239–253. The date seems to be 468. Pliny, *NH* 18.65, dated its performance about 145 years before the death of Alexander the Great. Cf. *Marm. Par., FGrH* 239 ep. 56 (469/8); Plut. *Kim.* 8.7–8.

[108] *IG* I³ 6B, lines 8–17, 27–36 = Clinton, *Eleusis,* no. 19: [σ]πονδὰς εἶν[αι] τοῖσι μύστ[εσιν] καὶ τοῖς ἐπ]όπτεισιν [καὶ τ]οῖς ἀκολ[ούθ]οισιν καὶ [χρέ]μασιν τὸν [ὀθ]νεῖον καὶ [᾿Αθε]ν[α]ίοισιν [h]άπασιν . . . . τὰς δὲ σπονδὰς εἶναι ἐν τεῖσι πόλεσιν hό[σ]αι χρõνται τõι hιερõι καὶ ᾿Αθεναίοισιν ἐκεῖ ἐν τεῖσιν αὐτεῖσι πόλεσιν. Cf. *SEG* 10.6, 17.2, 31.2.

the truce to the cities, offered perfect opportunities to spread the gospel of Athenian ideology. But the most august spokesmen of Eleusis were the priests themselves, when they served the city in civic capacity as diplomatic envoys to foreign governments. Unfortunately, we have no record of speeches made by Kallias (II) son of Hipponikos, the dadouchos of the Mysteries, who served on foreign missions as an energetic diplomat throughout the middle years of the century and gave his name to the notorious peace with Persia.[109] But his grandson and namesake, likewise dadouchos of the Mysteries, spoke for the Athenian embassy at Sparta during the peace negotiations of 371. His words, as recorded by Xenophon,[110] well illustrate the means by which Athens advanced her national image through the normal channels of international diplomacy:

> We ought never to bear arms against each other since it is said that Triptolemos our ancestor revealed the secret rites of Demeter and Kore first among foreigners to Herakles, your founder, and the Dioskouroi, your fellow-citizens, and gave the seed of Demeter's fruit first to the Peloponnese. How then can it be just, either for you to come and destroy the crops of those from whom you got the seed, or for us to begrudge full abundance of food to those to whom we gave it?

This liberal magnanimity of Athens, her desire to win friends abroad and attract them to Attica, was one of the keynotes of Periklean diplomacy; and the mythological propaganda, though expounded in all its rhetorical detail by writers of the fourth century, finds its roots deep in the Periklean age. In the phrases of the Funeral Oration, Thucydides attributes this line of thought to Perikles himself:[111] "And as regards nobility of spirit, we are the opposite of most men; for it is not by receiving kindness, but by conferring it that we acquire our friends. Now he who confers the favor is the stauncher friend . . . . and, finally, we alone fearlessly bestow our gifts on anyone not with calculation of our own advantage, but with confidence in our own spirit of liberality." We may be confident that the statesman did not fail to appreciate the full potential of Eleusinian mythology and the Eleusinian cult. The civilizing powers that the ministers of Demeter could claim for their cult will have given high priority to the new Telesterion, as the architectural and material realization of the expanded festival. The fifth-century designers characteristically anticipated a broad and successful expansion, for the new Hall of the Mysteries was to be four times the size of its archaic predecessor. The success that they achieved in fact may be measured best not in the physical remains of the sanctuary, but in the total intellectual conquest of Eleusinian propaganda. The Athenian boulē could invite the whole Greek world to send the firstfruits of the crops to Eleusis, and in so doing it had the comfortable sanction of the Delphic oracle. The decree contains the significant clause ἐπαγγέλλεν δὲ τὲν βολὲν καὶ τἔσι ἄλλεσι πόλεσιν [τ]ἔ[σι] hε[λ]λενικἔσιν ἀπάσεσι . . . ἐκέ[νοις] δὲ μὲ ἐπιτάττοντας, κελεύοντας δὲ ἀπάρχεσθαι ἐὰν βόλονται [κ]ατὰ τὰ πάτρια καὶ τὲν μαντείαν τὲν ἐγ Δελφōν, "The boulē shall also send a proclamation to every one of the other Hellenic cities . . . not ordering them but urging them to offer firstfruits, if they wish to do so, in accordance with ancestral custom and the oracle from Delphi."[112]

By the Hellenistic period Delphi had graduated from approving sanction to total acceptance, and in the late second century the Amphictyonic Council itself could draft a decree reiterating all the weary adulations of a bygone day, in phrases that were at home on the Athenian Pnyx, but in other councils cause surprise:

---

[109] Kirchner, *PA* 7825; Davies, *APF*, 258–262; for his position as dadouchos, Plut. *Arist.* 5.5–7, 25.3; schol. Aristoph. *Clouds* 64.

[110] Xen. *Hell.* 6.3.6. For Kallias (III), Kirchner, *PA* 7826; Davies, *APF*, 263–265.

[111] Thuc. 2.40.4–5: καὶ τὰ ἐς ἀρετὴν ἐνηντιώμεθα τοῖς πολλοῖς· οὐ γὰρ πάσχοντες εὖ, ἀλλὰ δρῶντες κτώμεθα τοὺς φίλους. βεβαιότερος δὲ ὁ δράσας τὴν χάριν . . . . καὶ μόνοι οὐ τοῦ ξυμφέροντος μᾶλλον λογισμῷ ἢ τῆς ἐλευθερίας τῷ πιστῷ ἀδεῶς τινα ὠφελοῦμεν.

[112] *IG* I³ 78, lines 30–34 = ML 73.

The demos of the Athenians, having become the originator of all good things among
men, converted men from the life of the beasts to civilization, and became in part the
cause of their mutual association by imparting the tradition of the Mysteries, and through
them proclaiming to all that the greatest good among men is their mutual acquaintance
and good faith. The city imparted also what the gods had given concerning human laws
and education, and likewise the gift of the fruits of the earth, though she had received it
for herself alone, yet she granted the ready use of it to be common to all Greeks.[113]

Demeter's seeds so carefully sown by the diplomats of Periklean Athens had grown and ripened
and borne their fruit. The enrichment of Attic cults and festivals, and dissemination of the idea of
Athenian liberality and magnanimity reveal an important motivation for the building of temples
in the fifth century. To be sure, they were in part thank-offerings for victories on the battlefield, but
more than that they celebrated the civilizing powers, the god-given gifts, bestowed uniquely upon
Athenians, which set them apart from other Greeks.

---

[113] *FdD* III.2 69, lines 11–16 (117/6) = *IG* II² 1134, lines 17–23: ὁ δῆμος (τῶν Ἀθηναίων) ἀ[πάντων τῶν ἐν ἀν-
θρ]ώποις ἀγαθῶν ἀρχη[γὸς κατασταθε]ὶς ἐγ μὲν τοῦ θηριώδους βίου μετήγαγεν τοὺς ἀνθρώπους εἰς ἡμερότη[τα,
παραίτιος δ' ἐγε]νήθη τ[ῆ]ς πρὸς ἀλλήλ[ους κοινωνί]ας – – – εἰσαγαγὼν τὴν τῶν μυστηρίων παράδοσιν, καὶ διὰ τού-
των πα[ρα]γ[γείλας τοῖς ἅπασιν] ὅτι μ[έγι]στον ἀγαθό[ν ἐστιν ἐν] ἀνθρώποις ἡ πρὸς ἑαυτοὺς χρῆσίς τε καὶ πίστις,
ἔτι τε τῶν δοθέντων [ὑπὸ θεῶν περὶ τῶν ἀνθρώ]πων νόμων [καὶ τῆς π]αιδείας· ὁμοίως δὲ καὶ τῆς τοῦ καρποῦ παρα-
δόσεως ἰδίαι μὲν ἐδέξατο [τὸ δῶρον, κοινὴν δὲ] τὴν ἐξ ἑ[α]υτ[οῦ] εὐχρ[ηστίαν τ]οῖς Ἕλλησιν ἀπέδωκεν. Cf. also Diod.
13.26.3–27.1. For Eleusinian propaganda, see W. K. C. Guthrie, *The Greeks and Their Gods* (Boston 1955) 284–287;
Mylonas, *Eleusis*, 21.

3

The Builders of the Parthenon

In the years around 450, the men who organized the Athenian public works were confronted by the same problem that would face the managers of Epidauros and Delphi, and all the other builders of the fourth century and the Hellenistic period. They must seek out the finest artisans, the best architects, the greatest sculptors, who alone had the necessary skills to build great marble peripteral temples. Athenian recruiting agents doubtless visited the building sites of Greece, with news of the complex projects that were under discussion and offering high wages for the work. They would hope to attract foreign craftsmen with their plea of good pay and long employment, but equally they would try to lure home the expatriate Athenians who had gradually wandered abroad in search of work because of the dearth of building activity in the last generation. At this moment, they were fortunate to have present at Athens a man eminently able to translate the matter-of-fact clauses of official decrees into enduring monuments of art. This was Pheidias, the son of Charmides. He was already a sculptor of wide repute in 450, but especially in his native Athens, where shortly before he had completed the colossal bronze statue of Athena that towered above the bastions of the Acropolis. Pheidias, like so many of his fellows in the arts, had accepted commissions in a number of different cities during the years after the Persian invasion. At Delphi, he had made a large monument with multiple statues to commemorate the victory at Marathon. Other commissions were for a gold and ivory statue of Athena at Pellene in Achaia, and for a second statue of Athena for the new Temple of Athena Areia at Plataia.[1]

According to Plutarch, he was Perikles' personal choice to direct the planning of a large and costly project, and the biographer speaks of him (*Per.* 13.4) as general overseer and superintendent of the works: πάντα δὲ διεῖπε καὶ ἐπίσκοπος ἦν αὐτῷ Φειδίας. From this one is evidently meant to infer that the other artists and craftsmen all worked to some extent under his direction. No doubt all who worked beside him felt the deep influence of his towering artistic personality. But we shall see presently that Athenian practice in the administration of public works had no place for an artistic director or construction manager of the kind envisaged by Plutarch. As much as one may wish to see the master's style reflected in the architectural designs or sculptural embellishment of the Parthenon, it is highly unlikely, one must concede, that Pheidias exercised any official administrative authority over the other personnel working on the Acropolis. What is certain, however, is his own personal artistic contribution in the form of another colossal statue of Athena, this time in gold and ivory, to be the cult image of the new temple.[2] The overwhelming majesty of this creation, we

---

[1] For Pheidias's monument at Delphi and the great bronze Athena on the Acropolis, see chap. 2, pp. 17–21 above; the statue at Pellene, Paus. 7.27.2. For the Athena at Plataia: Paus. 9.4.1; Plut. *Arist.* 20.3. See E. Harrison, *YCS* 30 (1996) 34–38. The ancient sources on Pheidias's career are conveniently collected by Overbeck, *Schriftquellen,* 113–144. See Davison, *Pheidias,* 579–617, for his role in the Parthenon.

[2] On Pheidias's commission for the gold and ivory statue, Plut. *Per.* 13.14, where it is called τῆς θεοῦ τὸ χρυσοῦν ἕδος.

may suspect, was itself largely responsible for the unduly exalted position attributed to the sculptor in later antiquity, just as the great statue itself was the cause of the legal and personal difficulties he encountered in his own lifetime.

The building program, as it began to emerge from the debates in the Athenian assembly, was far too great a responsibility for one man to shoulder, even if that had been desirable; and the detailed designs and construction of the individual buildings were duly entrusted to other leading architects. Plutarch (*Per.* 13.4–7) in fact reports the names of six: Kallikrates and Iktinos, who built the Parthenon; Koroibos, who worked on the Telesterion and was succeeded after his death by Metagenes and Xenokles; and Mnesikles, the author of the Propylaia. There were probably other prominent architects as well whose names we no longer know, for there is no evidence to suggest that the architects of the Hephaisteion and the Odeion are to be identified with any of those in Plutarch's list. There is astonishingly little information about this group of men, but it is perhaps noteworthy that some at least appear to have been Athenian citizens. Kallikrates, whose acquaintance we have already made in connection with the Temple of Athena Nike, was almost certainly an Athenian, although there is no specific statement to this effect either in Plutarch or in the inscriptions. Metagenes and Xenokles belonged to the Attic demes of Xypete and Cholargos, respectively; and although the evidence is not so conclusive in the case of Koroibos and Mnesikles, both are good Athenian names.[3] The outstanding exception is Iktinos, who may well have been one of those recruited from abroad. His name is unique in Greek prosopography and yields no clue to his origin or nationality. It is even possible that Iktinos is some kind of nickname, since the word as a common noun describes that species of hawk called a kite.[4] We shall see in due course that he was apparently commissioned at first to design the Telesterion at Eleusis and moved to the Acropolis only with the postponement of that project.[5]

By what process these architects were chosen and commissioned, it is difficult to say with any precision. Athenian procedure in such matters is not likely to have been rigidly uniform, but the final decision will certainly have rested with the assembly itself. In some cases, perhaps for routine building operations or for smaller and less controversial projects than the Parthenon, an orator simply included an architect's name in his original proposal. If the bill passed the assembly as proposed, the architect received the commission. Glaukos's decree proposing the construction of the Temple of Athena Nike is an example of this; the decree states simply that the temple is to be built "as Kallikrates shall prepare the specifications."[6] This is clearly the first time that the subject has been broached in the assembly, and yet the orator already has in mind a particular man to do the job.[7] Alternatively, a speaker might propose that the design be thrown open to public competition. Such a competition was held for some part of the decorative embellishment of the Nike temple. In this case, anyone wishing to enter the competition was ordered to submit his designs, drawn to a specified scale, within ten days; and the boulē was apparently responsible for judging the designs.[8] As was perhaps inevitable at Athens, this process led to heated debate in which architectural knowledge

---

[3] For the name Koroibos in Attica, Kirchner, *PA* 8719–8725; *LGPN* II, 271, where twelve bearers of the name are listed. For Mnesikles, Kirchner, *PA* 10304–10318; *LGPN* II, 317, where the name occurs twenty-nine times.

[4] LSJ⁹, s.v. ἴκτινος.

[5] On Iktinos at Eleusis, see chap. 6, pp. 174–178 below.

[6] *IG* I³ 35, lines 7, 13.

[7] For similar instances in which the architect for a certain piece of work is named in the original decree, cf. *IG* I³ 45, lines 6–8 (repair of the fortifications of the Acropolis), and *IG* I³ 79, lines 16–17 (the bridge across the Rhetoi at Eleusis). Both of these rank as minor public works. For appointment of architects, Francotte, *L'industrie*, vol. 2, 68–71.

[8] *IG* I³ 64, lines 5–9:

> [τὸν δ]-
> ὲ [βο]λόμενον γράφσαντα ἀποδ[εῖχσαι τῆι βολῆι]
> δ[έ]κα ἑμερõν ἐπειδὰν δόχσει [γράμμα μὲ ἔλαττο]-
> ν ὲ πεχ[υ]αῖον. γραφόντον δὲ ἀπ[αγγέλαντες πρὸς]
> τ[ὸ]ς ἐπ[ι]στάτας.

occasionally gave way to forensic skill. Both Iktinos and the sculptors Alkamenes and Nesiotes were counted among artists who lacked the oratorical powers of persuasion, while Philon of Eleusis is said to have delivered a similar speech in stirring oratory when trying to win from the assembly the commission for the arsenal at Peiraieus.[9] We hear of one lively incident when the assembly had summoned two competing architects to question them about certain aspects of their proposed plans for some public work. One of the architects made a deep impression on the assembly by delivering a prepared speech, eloquently extolling the virtues of his design. His competitor, hopelessly outdistanced in rhetorical elegance, retorted with the laconic simplicity of the superior craftsman, "Men of Athens, what this man has said, I will do."[10] We are not told how the assembly decided, and the anecdote may be apocryphal; but it points up the heavy role of articulate persuasion in all aspects of Athenian public life. One can feel confident that the great architectural commissions for the Periklean buildings were awarded only after lengthy discussion.

In the course of nearly two decades, this small group of architects and artists, as the principal personalities that shaped the great buildings, must have worked together in close but unofficial association. Tradition has preserved for us a few anecdotes about the dealings of Perikles with the sculptor Pheidias, whose relationship seems to have flowered into friendship. The artist is even said to have owed his influential position to the favor of Perikles' friendship,[11] though, on the face of it, it is more likely that the friendship was the result of his commission and not the cause of it. The sculptor's growing prominence in the Periklean circle is best attested by the scurrilous assault of the comic poets, that sure barometer of celebrity in ancient Athens—for Pheidias enjoyed the dubious privilege of being vilified at Perikles' side on the comic stage. His eminence aroused the envy of his fellow artisans, and their slanderous gossip made him the abettor of Perikles' alleged degeneracy. But of this intimacy between craftsman and statesman, there is no better indication than Pheidias's trial for embezzling ivory or gold from the chryselephantine statue. In a series of unsavory legal attacks against the Periklean circle, orators of the opposition would arraign Pheidias among the closest friends of Perikles, and the ribald wit of the comic stage would concoct the charge that the statesman drummed up the war with Sparta as a diversion to save his friends.[12]

THE OVERSEERS AND THE ROLE OF PERIKLES

At this point we need to question what exactly was the relation between the statesman Perikles and the construction of temples that later sources uniformly regarded as his "works." Plutarch gives the impression that the statesman maintained not only a vital interest in the buildings, but even had a personal influence of some sort over the operations. On this point the literary tradition appears at first sight fairly explicit. In connection with Pheidias's alleged theft from the statue of Athena in the Parthenon, a scholiast on Aristophanes, citing Philochoros, informs us that Perikles was elected by the assembly to supervise the construction of the project.[13] Furthermore, as we have seen, various an-

---

Cf. also the competition for work on the walls of the Peiraieus in 337/6: *IG* II² 244, lines 6–10; Maier, *Mauerbauinschriften,* 36–48, no. 10.

[9] Iktinos, Alkamenes, and Nesiotes: Plut. *Mor.* 802A. Philon's persuasive speech on the arsenal: Cicero, *De orat.* 1.14.62; Val. Max. 8.12.2; Philodemos, *Rhet.* 4, col. XIa (Sudhans, p. 192).

[10] Plut. *Mor.* 802B.

[11] Plut. *Per.* 13.14–15, 31.2; cf. Dio Chrys. *Orat.* 12.55, where he describes Pheidias as Perikles' ἑταῖρος.

[12] For the envy of Pheidias's associates, Plut. (note 11 above); for the slander of the comic poets, Aristoph. *Peace* 605–611 (and cf. *Clouds* 859); Plut. *Per.* 13.15–16. For the trial of Pheidias and the attacks on the friends of Perikles, see chap. 9, pp. 311–325 below; Plut. *Per.* 31–32; Diod. 12.39.1–2; schol. Aristoph. *Peace* 605 (Holwerda) quoting Philochoros, *FGrH* 328 F 121. For discussion of the role of Perikles see Davison, *Pheidias,* 570–575.

[13] Schol. Aristoph. *Peace* 606 a.β (Holwerda): ἐδόκει γὰρ ὁ Περικλῆς συνεγνωκέναι τῇ κλοπῇ, ἐπεὶ καὶ ἐργεπιστατεῖν ὑπὸ τῶν Ἀθηναίων κεχειροτόνηται.

cient sources speak of Perikles himself as the overseer or epistates of specific constructions. We hear of his serving in this capacity for both the Parthenon itself and the Telesterion at Eleusis; and in this case, as in most of the others, the phrase describing his position reads Περικλέους ἐπιστατοῦντος τῶν ἔργων,[14] or some closely similar locution. Plutarch describes Perikles' construction of the Odeion in much the same way, and Philochoros attributes to him the gymnasium known as the Lykeion in the same words.[15] The most notorious instance in which Perikles is referred to as epistates is the affair of Pheidias. The statesman seems to have been implicated in this because he was in charge of the work on the gold and ivory statue: διὰ τὸ ἐπιστατῆσαι τῇ κατασκευῇ τοῦ ἀγάλματος.[16] Now, this literary testimony is not so clear as it might appear on the surface. If one attempts to reconstruct the organization of the public works as a whole, or even of the Acropolis project, for which more abundant evidence is available, there will emerge at once a certain difficulty in reconciling the literary sources with the official records of the builders themselves.

The routine administration of the buildings, the hiring and firing of workmen, the day-to-day disbursement of funds, the detailed accounts that Athenian officials were required to keep—all this was in the hands of a committee titled the epistatai, or overseers, of a particular project. We have already encountered similar boards of epistatai as the administrative apparatus responsible for erecting the great bronze Athena of Pheidias and for building operations at Eleusis.[17] Before we consider the tangible results of their work—the Parthenon and the other buildings—it might be instructive to review the administrative operation of the project. The officials in charge of construction on the Acropolis seem to have been initially authorized in legislation passed ca. 450 under the title "overseers of the temple and the statue."[18] For whatever reason, they did not formally assume office until the summer of 447, and they functioned thereafter as two separate boards: the epistatai of the Parthenon and the epistatai of the golden statue. Since this board, as originally planned, provided a model for the Eleusinian overseers, it is a natural inference that the board was similarly constituted. If this is correct, the overseers of the Parthenon were originally intended to be five in number, elected annually from all the Athenian citizenry, and they would be instructed to choose one of their number as secretary of the board.[19] This committee rotated annually for fifteen years, from 447/6 to 433/2, changing its personnel and its secretary; and the overseers of each year submitted their accounts to the boulē and inscribed them on a large marble stele on the Acropolis. These accounts, fragmentary as they are today, are still invaluable documents for the historian of the Athenian public works, and we shall need to examine them in detail.

The stele on which the epistatai of the Parthenon published their records survives in twenty-five fragments that preserve parts of its front and back faces, of both lateral edges, and of top and bottom. Although the extant fragments comprise only a small fraction of the original stone, they join each other in such a way that the original dimensions of the stele can be reconstructed within close limits: it measured approximately 1.60 m in height, 1.80 m in width, and 0.20 m in thickness.[20]

---

[14] Strabo 9.1.12 (p. 395); cf. chap. 1, pp. 1–3 above.

[15] Plut. *Per.* 13.9; Harpokration, s.v. Λύκειον (λ 30, Keaney), citing Philochoros, *FGrH* 328 F 37; cf. also the Alphitopolis Stoa in the Peiraieus, schol. Aristoph. *Acharn.* 548a (Wilson), τῆς λεγομένης ἀλφιτοπώλιδος (στοᾶς) ἣν ᾠκοδόμησε Περικλῆς.

[16] Schol. Aristoph. *Peace* 606 a.α (Holwerda). Philochoros, *FGrH* 328 F 121, had said Περικλέους ἐπιστατοῦντος. Cf. Aristodemos (*FGrH* 104) 16.1.4. Diod. 12.39.1 speaks of Perikles as ἐπιμελητής instead of ἐπιστάτης for the statue, while the *Suda*, s.v. Φειδίας (φ 246, Adler), describes him as ἐπὶ τοῖς ἀναλώμασι ταχθείς.

[17] For the board of epistatai in *IG* I³ 435 (the accounts of the bronze statue), see chap. 2, pp. 17–21 above; *IG* I³ 32 (at Eleusis), see chap. 2, pp. 23–26 above. See also *IG* I³ 433 (project unknown).

[18] They are so named in *IG* I³ 32, lines 12–13; see chap. 2, p. 23 above.

[19] For the two separate boards, see chap. 2, p. 26 above. Provisions for their election and salaries, *IG* I³ 32, lines 7–10.

[20] For reconstruction of the stele and its dimensions, see Dinsmoor, *AJA* 25 (1921) 233–240; earlier discussion of the fragments: E. Cavaignac, *Études sur l'histoire financière*, l–lxix; Dinsmoor, *AJA* 17 (1913) 53–80; small fragments added by Meritt, *AJA* 36 (1932) 472–473. The texts of the Parthenon accounts are reproduced in the appendix, pp. 410–418 below.

The annual accounts were arranged in three double columns of inscribed text on both front and back, and in one double column on the two lateral edges. Like the earlier accounts for Pheidias's bronze Athena, figures for receipts and expenditures appear on the left-hand side of the double column, while entries describing the source of the receipts or the purpose of the expenditures are listed on the right. The introductory heading for each year spans the full width of the double column. Arranged in this way, the accounts for the first six years of construction occupied the obverse of the stele. The reverse of the stone displayed the seventh through the thirteenth annual accounts, and the shorter statements covering Years 14 and 15 were inscribed on the right and left edges, respectively. That the documents thus inscribed pertain to the construction of the Parthenon can be stated with certainty, even though the general heading for the first year, together with the official title of the overseers, has perished almost completely from the top of the stele. The twelfth account preserves an item of expenditure that reads: [ἀγαλ]ματοποιοῖς ἐναιετίο[ν μισθός], "salaries for the sculptors of the pediments"; and the same item can be restored in Years 10, 11, 13, and 14.[21] Moreover, it is apparent from the eleventh account that all blocks of marble extracted from the Pentelic quarries during the last six years of the project were specifically designated ἐς τὰ ἐναιέτια, "for the pediments."[22] In the third quarter of the fifth century—the period to which, as we shall see, the accounts must be dated—the Parthenon alone of the buildings on the Acropolis was adorned with such elaborate pedimental statuary.

The overseers of the Parthenon began their annual statements with a heading that gave the number of the account in series from the first year of construction. It included also a formula of date using the name of the first secretary of the boulē. In the last five years, and possibly also in the first year of construction, the name of the eponymous archon was added as well. The epistatai of the first ten boards had their names inscribed in the annual prescript in addition to the name of their secretary, but this practice was abandoned for the sake of brevity in the last five accounts. Only the prescripts for Years 14 and 15 have survived in complete form, and the text of the former illustrates the more abbreviated formula adopted during the last five years of construction.[23]

τοῖς ἐπιστάτεσι, hοῖς
Ἀντικλε̃ς ἐγαμμάτευ[ε],
ἐπὶ τε̃ς τετάρτες καὶ δε-
κάτες βολε̃ς, hε̃ι Μετα-
γένες προ̃τος ἐγραμμ-
άτευε, ἐπὶ Κράτετος ἄρχ-
οντος Ἀθεναίοισιν,
λέμματα το̃ ἐνιαυτο̃
τούτο τάδε·

To the overseers for whom Antikles was secretary, in the fourteenth boulē for which Metagenes was first secretary, when Krates was archon for the Athenians, the receipts of this year were as follows.

The names of the eponymous archons Krates and Apseudes are preserved in these two accounts, and they serve to fix the date for the completion of work on the Parthenon in 434/3 and 433/2, respectively. The first board of overseers thus commenced construction of the temple fifteen years earlier, in 447/6.

[21] Reference to the sculptors of the pediments is best preserved in *IG* I³ 447, line 360 (Year 12). The same formula can be restored in *IG* I³ 445, line 310; 446, line 338; 448, line 368; 449, lines 401–402.
[22] *IG* I³ 446, lines 332, 334.
[23] *IG* I³ 449, lines 369–377; 450, lines 410–418.

Although it is possible to reconstruct the formulas of the prescripts for the first ten accounts, or at least their principal components, none has been completely preserved. Comparison of the prescripts for Years 2, 5, and 10 make it clear that each annual statement began with the serial number of the board, followed by the name of the secretary of the overseers and his demotic, e.g., ἐπι τε͂[ς δευτέρας ἀρχε͂ς] ἐι Ε[....ₛ.... ἐγραμμάτευε] ℎαλαι[εύς. The second element of the formula is the date expressed in terms of the first secretary of the boulē for the given year, e.g., [τε͂ι βολε͂ι Ἀντ]ίδο[ρος προ͂τος ἐγραμμάτευε].[24] There follow the names and demotics of the overseers in the nominative and the word ἐπιστάται. All prescripts conclude with the statement that the receipts for the year were as follows. As chance would have it, the names of the individual overseers, with the exception of Salaminokles in 446/5 and of Timotheos, the secretary of 443/2, have survived only in truncated fragments which are not susceptible of restoration. As a result, the personnel of the Parthenon project must remain almost wholly anonymous. But if the names are lost to us, the space that they occupied on the stone can be determined fairly accurately in six of the first ten years, and it seems likely that the size of the committee varied somewhat from year to year. If the prescribed number of overseers was intended to be five, the Athenians characteristically permitted themselves a certain freedom in applying the regulations. In the fifth and seventh years (443/2 and 441/0) there is space for only three names and their demotics, in addition to their secretary, which suggests that one fewer than the proper number of overseers was elected. In the ninth year (439/8), a board of six men and a secretary was probably chosen, while only the committees of the eighth and tenth years (440/39 and 438/7) appear to have consisted of the canonical four overseers and a secretary.[25] The second prescript, longer by one line than the normal formula, allows room for as many as six or seven names after the secretary and the date, if only the names and the demes of the overseers are to be restored, as elsewhere in the inscription. But on the analogy of the early accounts of the gold and ivory statue, it might be preferable to suppose that the overseers of the first two years were listed with their fathers' names as well as their demotics.[26] Inclusion of the fathers' names would probably reduce the size of the second board to the prescribed four men and a secretary.

The administration of the Parthenon project was in one respect unique among the building operations of the fifth century. Perhaps because of the size and complexity of the building and the anticipated long duration of the work, a permanent assistant secretary was attached to the board of overseers. This appointment was a realistic concession that a committee of ordinary citizens, changing its membership from year to year, could scarcely supervise with utmost efficiency the vast amount of technical architectural and structural detail that is so prominent a feature of the Parthenon. The assistant secretary would give continuity and efficient stability to the rotating boards, and in time he doubtless came to assume considerable responsibility for the administration of the project. During the late 430s, when the work was drawing rapidly to a close and the administration seems to have been curtailed, this assistant secretary served as permanent secretary to the overseers for the last four years.[27] The accounts of the two final years (434/3 and 433/2) indicate that it was a certain Antikles who held this important post. The first line of the eleventh account (437/6) must almost necessar-

---

[24] *IG* I³ 437, lines 33–34, Year 2 (446/5).

[25] It is perhaps just possible that there were two short names in *IG* I³ 445, line 285 or 286, before -ΓΕΣΙΑΣ or before -ΥΔΕΣ, since ca. twenty-three letters are missing from the left end of both lines. This would increase the number of overseers in Year 10 from four to five, in addition to the secretary. The same fluctuation in the size of the board is to be noted in the accounts of the Propylaia; see chap. 9, pp. 300–311 below. Cf. Dinsmoor, *AJA* 17 (1913) 384.

[26] The accounts of the statue are reproduced in the appendix, pp. 405–407 below. The treasurers of Athena are listed with patronymics and demotics in *IG* I³ 455 (445/4 or 444/3). See Meritt, *AFD*, 30–41; Dinsmoor, *HSCP* Suppl. 1 (1940) 158–165; G. Donnay, *BCH* 91 (1967) 56–61. That the overseers of the first year appeared with patronymics is, of course, purely conjectural, but it may help to explain the abnormal length of the first annual prescript, which covered five lines of approximately ninety letters in length.

[27] *IG* I³ 447, line 344; 448, line 366; 449, line 370; 450, lines 410–412.

ily be restored [τοῖς ἐπιστάτεσι h]οῖς Ἀντ[ικλῆς χσυ]νεγραμμάτευ[ε], "to the epistatai for whom Antikles was assistant secretary." This prescript thus yields the information that Antikles served as assistant secretary of the overseers before becoming secretary in 436/5.[28] It is apparent that the position of assistant secretary likewise existed during the first ten years of construction, although in the longer formulas of the heading the assistant secretary followed the list of epistatai. Comparison of the fifth and tenth prescripts makes possible the reconstruction of the formula ἐπιστάται καὶ hοῖς – – – – χσυνεγραμμάτευε,[29] while the beginning of the name Ἀν[τικλῆς] is preserved in the fifth year, which suggests that Antikles was already assistant secretary in 443/2 and that his name should be restored in each account thereafter.

The second prescript shows a variant formula after the list of epistatai, ΚΑΙΗΟ[- and ΡΟΙΣΙ[- at the beginning of two consecutive lines. Since the formula begins in the normal manner, this phrase probably refers to the assistant secretary whose name was here appended to the list of epistatai. The two lines should then be restored to read: ἐπιστάται] καὶ hο[ῖς Ἀντικλῆς χσυνεγραμμάτευε καὶ τοῖς προτέ]ροισι[ν ἐπιστάτεσι], "epistatai to whom also Antikles was assistant secretary as also for the former epistatai."[30] The phrase may then be understood to mean that the assistant secretary of the second year had previously served the overseers of the first year in the same capacity. The longer formula was used to indicate his first reappointment, but this was deemed unnecessary in succeeding years.

If it is correct to restore the name of Antikles as permanent assistant secretary of the Parthenon overseers from the first year onward, then we may learn something more of the man. The fifth line of the first prescript preserves, at the extreme right edge of the stele, the letters -]ΝΑΙΟΣ, which undoubtedly terminated the demotic of the last named official.[31] The following line probably contained only the short formula regularly used to introduce the column of receipts: τούτοις λέμματα τὸ ἐνιαυτὸ τούτο τάδε, "For these men the receipts of this year were the following." The phrase immediately preceding this, as in the rest of the first ten accounts, will have designated the assistant secretary; and it will thus be his demotic that is partially preserved in the letters -]ΝΑΙΟΣ.[32] Now, there are only two possible restorations for this demotic: [Ἀφιδ]ναῖος and [Οἰ]ναῖος, of which the former has already been proposed,[33] while the latter may in fact be preferable. Elsewhere in the inscription the demotic of the assistant secretary was normally omitted, so that the other accounts offer us no parallel. The only exception is the fifth year, where the demotic was almost certainly included and, if our assumptions are correct, where the same demotic that appears in the first prescript ought now

---

[28] Dinsmoor, *AJA* 17 (1913) 61. The same Antikles is undoubtedly to be restored in the prescripts of Years 12 and 13, *IG* I³ 447, line 344; 448, line 366. Both lines require a name of eight letters in the nominative, and the final -ΕΣ is preserved in the prescript for Year 13. The tribute quota lists 12 and 13, for 443/2 and 442/1, provide a close parallel. In both years Satyros of Leukonoe is named as assistant secretary to the hellenotamiai: *IG* I³ 269, line 36; 270, line 2.

[29] *IG* I³ 440, line 115; 445, line 287. It is preferable to restore line 115 as [– – ἐπιστάται κ]αι hοῖς Ἀν[τικλῆς χσυνε-γραμμάτευε] in order to reduce the length of the third overseer's name.

[30] *IG* I³ 437, lines 38–39. So Dinsmoor, *AJA* 17 (1913) 63, and *AJA* 25 (1921) 243, note 2. While the name Antikles fits the space well and is probably the correct restoration, any name of eight letters is possible epigraphically. It is still possible that Antikles did not become permanent assistant secretary until 443/2, as Dinsmoor at first suggested, *AJA* 17 (1913) 78.

[31] The letters at the end of lines 1–5 on the obverse of fragment D, at the extreme right edge of the stele, stand immediately above the last lines of receipts for Year 5, at the top of column III. The greater height of these letters (0.0135 m, as compared with 0.012 m in Year 5) and their wider spacing (0.019 m on centers, as opposed to 0.0125 m in Year 5) make it easy to distinguish the receipts in column III from the first annual prescript, which extended across the entire width of the stele.

[32] As first proposed by Dinsmoor, *AJA* 17 (1913) pl. II, line 5. Although the demotic of the assistant secretary was regularly omitted elsewhere, except in the fifth year, on which see below, the great length of the first heading suggests that it was written with the fullest possible formulas, and among these the demotic of the assistant secretary would not be out of place.

[33] By Dinsmoor, *AJA* 17 (1913) 78; Hiller, *IG* I² 343, col. III, line 5.

to be restored. While it might just be possible to restore the longer demotic Aphidnaios in the fifth prescript, the spacing of the letters is such that the shorter name is definitely preferable.[34] We may suggest, then, that the permanent assistant secretary, who coordinated the work of the successive boards of overseers for fifteen years, was Antikles of the deme Oinoe.

This discussion may serve to emphasize the elaborate nature of the administrative apparatus that had charge of the construction of the Acropolis buildings. But what is difficult to understand is the precise relation of Perikles—whom, as we have seen, the literary sources describe as ἐπιστατῶν τῶν ἔργων—to the duly elected epistatai who filed their annual accounts with the boulē. Perikles was almost certainly not himself a regular member of the boards of overseers, annually reappointed like Antikles, the assistant secretary. In fact, his name can have appeared nowhere in the inscriptions, except possibly in the general heading of the first prescript, now almost totally lost. In 409, the overseers of the Erechtheion compiled their report on the unfinished state of that temple in response to a decree of the demos moved by Epigenes, which they cited in the prescript of the document.[35] On this analogy, it is conceivable that the Parthenon overseers may have mentioned a similar decree of Perikles that authorized their administration of the project. But Perikles' name can have appeared nowhere else in the records of the builders, and the overseers do not seem to have had any official responsibility to him. Although the statesman is said to have been epistates of the Telesterion (Strabo 9.1.12), the inscription authorizing the election of the Eleusinian epistatai makes no mention of him, and the overseers are to report directly to the boulē.[36] It seems likely that the authors of the literary tradition, which can in fact be traced no earlier than Ephoros and Philochoros in the fourth century, attributed to Perikles an official responsibility for the buildings commensurate with the fame that had made them his forever. As possible author and likely political sponsor for the building program, he was preeminently the epistates of the buildings, but always no doubt in an unofficial capacity. Some of them he may possibly have proposed in council or assembly; some of the ideas for the designs and some of the details may reflect his taste. Without his unflagging support in the assembly the buildings are not likely to have been built. But his was the trusteeship of personal influence and political power, not the authority of an appointed office. The actual management of the building operations and, most important of all, the audit of the accounts the assembly jealously reserved for itself, through the administrative committees of the boulē.

PAYING FOR THE PARTHENON

The builders of the Parthenon initially seem to have faced problems of politics and personnel. Skilled craftsmen had to be assembled in sufficient numbers, and the Athenian assembly had to be persuaded to support the enterprise, as has already been suggested. The architects, Iktinos and Kallikrates, may have begun work on the plans and specifications as early as 450 or 449, for they would certainly have been ordered to present formal specifications to the assembly, probably through the agency of a committee of the boulē,[37] before final action on the Parthenon project could be taken. In any event, all was in readiness to begin construction of the great temple by midsummer of 447, in the archon-

[34] The restorations indicated by the stoichedon order of the letters on fragment I leave space for a demotic in seven letters at the beginning of *IG* I³ 440, line 116. A demotic in nine letters, Ἀφιδναῖος, appears too long for the space available.
[35] *IG* I³ 474, lines 4–5: [τά]δε ἀνέγραφσαν ἔργα τō νεō hος κατέλαβον ἔχοντα κατὰ τὸ φσέ[φισ]μα τō δέμο hὸ Ἐπιγένες εἶπεν, "(the epistatai) recorded as follows the state of the work on the temple in obedience to a decree of the demos which Epigenes moved."
[36] *IG* I³ 32, lines 14–15.
[37] Cf. the procedure stipulated by Hestiaios for Kallikrates' work in the sanctuary of Athena Nike, *IG* I³ 35, lines 15–19.

ship of Timarchides; and, accordingly, in the spring of that year, the first board of overseers had been officially empaneled and the architects received their formal commissions.

It was this first board of overseers which began to compile the long series of building accounts and was itself responsible for the publication of the first annual statement.[38] They prefaced their account with a general heading, carved in slightly larger letters than the accounts themselves and extending across the full width of the great marble stele.[39] This served as an introduction, beneath which would be arranged the receipts and expenditures for the first six years. Of this general heading only twelve letters out of several hundred have survived, and it is obviously impossible to reconstruct any of its actual wording. But we may surmise what information it contained by comparing the preserved annual prescripts with similar general headings on other building inscriptions. Without question the prescript will have included the date, and it probably mentioned both the eponymous archon Timarchides and the secretary for the first prytany of the boulē, whose name is unknown in this year.[40] Equally without doubt, the overseers will have listed their own names, together with those of their secretary and the assistant secretary, Antikles of Oinoe. Another feature of some building inscriptions was the name of the designing or supervising architect, and Kallikrates and Iktinos possibly had their names inscribed in the heading of the Parthenon stele.[41] In addition, the prescript will certainly have opened with the official title of the board of overseers and the name of the temple that they were appointed to supervise, but the exact wording of their title has not survived and cannot be restored.

The published accounts of the Parthenon reveal at once that the overseers received contributions from a variety of sources to help finance the building operations. In this respect their project differed sharply from Pheidias's bronze Athena; for the colossal statue, recently completed, had been financed exclusively by the kolakretai from funds in the public treasury of the Athenian state.[42] In striking contrast, the kolakretai contributed nothing to the new buildings on the Acropolis, and by 447 completely different financial arrangements were in place. The principal funding for the Parthenon came from the sacred treasury of Athena, and the treasurers of the goddess appropriated funds annually for the first nine years, from 447/6 to 439/8. Their entry in the accounts is sufficiently well preserved in a number of years that the formula can be restored with certainty; that for the second year reads: παρὰ ταμιõν hοὶ τὰ τες θεõ ἐταμίευον, hοῖς Ἐχσέκεστος ἐγραμμάτευε Ἀθμο-νεύς, "From the treasurers who stewarded the funds of the goddess, to whom Exekestos of Athmone

[38] The actual date of publication of the inscriptions cannot be precisely fixed, for it is not clear whether the accounts were inscribed on stone at the end of each year, like the tribute quota lists, or whether they were published only after the work had been in progress for several years, like the accounts of the bronze Athena. An examination of the lettering of the inscription, carried out in company with R. Meiggs, revealed the fact that the first five accounts were in all probability carved by the same mason. (Years 1, 2, 4, and 5 are fairly certain, while too little remains of Year 3 to be sure.) Thereafter, the sixth, seventh, and eighth accounts were each carved by a different hand and probably at the close of the year in question. Still another mason produced the inscriptions for Years 9, 10, probably 11, and 12. Year 13 is too mutilated to permit any statement concerning its engraver; but the last two years, 14 and 15, were carved by a sixth mason, different from all the others. It is a possible conclusion, though not necessarily the most likely, that the first five accounts were not published and the stele was not erected until the end of the fifth year, in the summer of 442. But regardless of the date of the inscription, the overseers naturally will have had to prepare their accounts annually and present them to the logistai and the boulē for approval upon the expiration of their term of office.

[39] See p. 47, note 31 above.

[40] Cf. the formulas of date in *IG* I³ 462, lines 3–4 (Propylaia); 472, lines 5–6 (statues in the Hephaisteion); 474, lines 5–7 (Erechtheion). All list the eponymous archon as well as the secretary for the first prytany of the boulē.

[41] Cf. *IG* I³ 474, lines 2–3, where the supervising architect is named together with the epistatai of the Erechtheion. Mnesikles, the architect of the Propylaia, was probably also included in the first annual account of that building, for his name still appears the most likely restoration for *IG* I³ 462, line 2, as proposed by Dinsmoor, *AJA* 17 (1913) 383.

[42] See chap. 2, pp. 17–21 above.

was secretary."[43] The same formula recurs in the fourth, fifth, ninth, and fourteenth years, the only change being the name of their annual secretary. It can be restored with certainty in the seventh year, and undoubtedly stood originally among the missing receipts for the third, sixth, and eighth years. In Year 2 (446/5), for some unexplained reason, the treasurers made two separate contributions to the building fund; that they also paid a generous sum to the overseers in the first year of construction is suggested by the huge balance of more than 200,000 drachmas (33⅓ talents) that was carried forward unspent from the first year to the second.[44] There can be little doubt that the goddess Athena herself was the largest steady contributor to the Acropolis buildings. Her treasurers seem normally to have been listed first among the annual donors, directly after the previous balance was recorded, and in the four years from 438/7 to 435/4, when they are not found in the accounts of the Parthenon, the treasurers probably transferred their deposits each year to the overseers of the Propylaia. The identical formula appears in the second and fourth years of the Propylaia accounts for 436/5 and 434/3, and it is a safe assumption that the treasurers of Athena contributed to that building in the other three years as well.[45]

Since almost all the actual figures are lost, it is impossible to estimate the size of the treasurers' contributions or the total receipts. In Year 4 (444/3), where four numerals are missing at the beginning of the figure, restoration of the minimum amount yields a contribution from the treasurers of 95,822 drachmas, or just under 16 talents, but the figure may have been considerably larger.[46] In both Years 2 and 7 (446/5 and 441/0), there was an unexpended balance of more than 200,000 drachmas (33⅓ talents) carried forward from the previous overseers.[47] In Year 14 (434/3), the only year for which the figure is completely preserved, the treasurers contributed 25,000 drachmas (4⅙ talents).[48] But the mere recitation of these random figures shows that the accounts of the Parthenon, in their present fragmentary state, yield virtually no information concerning the amount of money that the sacred treasury actually spent on the building.

It is clear from other evidence that all of these annual appropriations from the treasurers of Athena were charged against the capital reserve fund on the Acropolis. Thucydides (2.13.3), in summarizing Athenian financial assets available in 431, was careful to distinguish the current annual revenue of 600 talents on average from the accumulated reserve, which he describes as follows: ὑπαρχόντων δὲ ἐν τῇ ἀκροπόλει ἔτι τότε ἀργυρίου ἐπισήμου ἑξακισχιλίων ταλάντων (τὰ γὰρ πλεῖστα τριακοσίων ἀποδέοντα μύρια ἐγένετο, ἀφ' ὧν ἔς τε τὰ προπύλαια τῆς ἀκροπόλεως καὶ τἆλλα οἰκοδομήματα καὶ ἐς Ποτείδαιαν ἀπανηλώθη), "and there were at this time still on hand on the Acropolis six thousand talents of coined silver (the maximum amount had been nine thousand seven hundred talents, from which funds had been expended for the construction of the Propylaia of the Acropolis and the other buildings, as well as for the campaign at Poteidaia)."[49] The bearing of this statement on

---

[43] The formula is best preserved in Years 4 and 14 (*IG* I³ 439, lines 69–71; 449, lines 385–388), which between them give all parts of the wording. The same wording is to be restored in *IG* I³ 440, lines 122–123; 442, lines 176–178; 444, lines 245–246.

[44] *IG* I³ 437, lines 40–41.

[45] In five of the six years in which the treasurers appear in the extant Parthenon accounts, their payment is listed first among the receipts, the exception being in 443/2, *IG* I³ 440, lines 120–124. For their appearance in the Propylaia accounts, *IG* I³ 463, lines 69–70; 465, lines 121–122. They are possibly to be restored in *IG* I³ 464, lines 99–100.

[46] *IG* I³ 439, line 70. Restoration of the minimum figure yields [ΓΜΜΜ]ΜΓΡΗΗΗΔΔΗⱵ.

[47] *IG* I³ 437, lines 40–41 (Year 2); 442, line 173 (Year 7).

[48] *IG* I³ 449, line 386.

[49] The text of the passage is quoted here as it appears in the manuscripts of Thucydides. In the middle years of the twentieth century, great effort was expended in support of a different version of the text as quoted by schol. RV Aristoph. *Plout.* 1193 (Dindorf). See *ATL* III, 118–132. The principal differences from the received text of Thucydides are αἰεί ποτε for ἔτι τότε and περιεγένετο for μύρια ἐγένετο. With these alterations by the scholiast, the passage was translated in *ATL* III, 131: ". . . there was, he said, a regular standing amount of 6,000 talents on the Acropolis. The greater part of this, actually 5,700 talents, was in fact still there. . . ." This reading, if correct, obviously has important implications for the

the financing of the Acropolis buildings needs to be underscored, for it shows that the costs of constructing "the Propylaia and the other buildings" and the costs of preventing the secession of tributary allies were charged to the same account. Both were deemed legitimate expenses of the empire, and the costs of both were met by disbursements from the accumulated reserve.[50] This is borne out by contemporary records of military expenditures. In the Samian War of 440 and 439, the treasurers (ταμίαι ἐκ πόλεος) handed over large sums of money belonging to Athena Polias to the generals at Samos.[51] When naval squadrons were dispatched to Korkyra in 433, the treasurers of Athena (ταμίαι hιερõν χρεμάτον τε̃ς Ἀθεναίας) paid out money to the generals appointed to command the forces.[52] In 432/1, the treasurers disbursed funds for the war chest by way of the hellenotamiai to the armies in Macedonia and at Poteidaia.[53] On the other hand, direct evidence for the use of tribute to fund Athenian public works comes from the fragmentary decree approving construction of a fountain house and its aqueduct. The last sentence of the document provides funding for the project: [ἀπαναλίσκεν δὲ ἀπὸ τõν χρεμάτον] hόσα ἐς τὸν φόρον τõν Ἀθεναίον τελ[ε̃ται, ἐπειδὰν hε θεὸς ἐχς αὐτõν λαμ]βάνει τὰ νομιζόμενα, "[expenditures shall be made from the monies] that are paid into the tribute of the Athenians, [after the goddess has] received from them her accustomed share."[54]

Thucydides' description of Athens's resources (2.13.3) was closely paraphrased in a similar passage of Ephoros's *History* that is specifically attributed to him by Diodoros (12.40.1–3). On the basis of Thucydides, Ephoros distinguished the reserve fund from current annual income, and, like Thucydides, he included an evaluation of the sacred processional vessels, the Persian spoils, the dedications in the sanctuaries, and the gold and ivory statue. In light of these obvious similarities, Ephoros's description of the reserve fund takes on special interest. He refers to: τὸ πλῆθος τῶν μετακεκομισμένων ἐκ Δήλου χρημάτων εἰς τὰς Ἀθήνας, ἃ συνέβαινεν ἐκ τῶν φόρων ταῖς πόλεσι κοινῇ συνηθροῖσθαι· κοινῶν δ' ὄντων τῶν μυρίων ταλάντων ἀπανήλωτο πρὸς τὴν κατασκευὴν τῶν προπυλαίων καὶ τὴν Ποτιδαίας πολιορκίαν τετρακισχίλια τάλαντα, "the large amount of money transferred from Delos to Athens, which happened actually to have been collected from the tribute into one fund for the common use of the cities; from the ten thousand talents in the common fund, four thousand had been expended on the construction of the Propylaia and the siege of Poteidaia."[55]

financial history of Athens. Vigorous objections, however, both to the reading of the text in *ATL* and to its reconstruction of Athenian finance, were raised by Gomme, *Historia* 2 (1953–54) 1–21, *Historia* 3 (1954–55) 333–338, and *HCT*, vol. 2, 26–33, who retains the MSS text of Thucydides. In this he is followed by S. Hornblower, *A Commentary on Thucydides*, vol. 1 (Oxford 1991) 253–254. See now schol. Aristoph. *Plout.* 1193c (Chantry, p. 190) with critical apparatus. For recent discussion, L. J. Samons, *Historia* 42 (1993) 131–133.

[50] There have been recent attempts to argue that the building program and the Parthenon in particular were funded entirely without recourse to the tribute of the allies, except for the *aparchai*; see L. Kallet-Marx, *ClAnt* 8 (1989) 252–266; A. Giovannini, *Historia* 39 (1990) 129–148; Giovannini, *Historia* 46 (1997) 145–157. Their arguments have been refuted by Samons, *Historia* 42 (1993) 129–138. Significantly, Kallet-Marx offers no discussion of Thucydides 2.13.3. Giovannini (1990) 143–144 believes that no substantial reserve ever accumulated at Delos, and (p. 131 and note 7) that what little was brought to Athens in 454/3 did not become the property of Athena but was merely managed by her treasurers. The epigraphical records of the treasurers, however, never distinguish different accounts as the sources of their payments. References to the many scholars who believe that the Parthenon was financed largely by tribute are conveniently collected by Kallet-Marx (above) 252, note 1.

[51] *IG* I³ 363 = ML 55.

[52] *IG* I³ 364 = ML 61.

[53] *IG* I³ 365, lines 1–28. The accounts record nine separate payments by the treasurers to the hellenotamiai for dispatch to the armies in Macedonia and at Poteidaia. The year is 432/1, at the end of which Thucydides 2.13.3 says that the balance of the reserve fund stood at 6,000 talents. This evidence is plainly incompatible with the statement of Kallet-Marx, *ClAnt* 8 (1989) 259: "it seems best rather to suppose that the Hellenotamiai had charge of the year's tribute *in toto* except for the annual *aparche* to Athena, as well as the entire tribute reserve."

[54] *IG* I³ 49, lines 14–16. Neither Kallet-Marx, *ClAnt* 8 (1989), nor Giovannini, *Historia* 39 (1990) and *Historia* 46 (1997), comment on this inscription.

[55] Diodoros 12.40.1–2, quoting Ephoros, *FGrH* 70 F 196.

In reporting the amount of the reserve fund as 10,000 talents, Ephoros followed the oratorical tradition of the fourth century preserved by Isokrates, Demosthenes, and Lykourgos, who had attributed to Perikles the conveyance of this money to the Acropolis.[56] From Thucydides, Ephoros stated, somewhat imprecisely, that expenditures had been made for the construction of the Propylaia and the siege of Poteidaia; and it is noticeable that the fourth-century historian attempted to reconcile with Thucydides' figures his amount of 10,000 talents by increasing the expenditures to 4,000 talents, so that the funds available in 431 are still the 6,000 talents that Thucydides reports. Also according to Ephoros, on the basis of what source we cannot say, the reserve fund on the Acropolis had as a principal component the surplus accumulated from the tribute of the allies and removed from Delos to Athens in 454, a transaction for which the tribute quota lists provide important indirect evidence. There is no good reason, then, to disparage the evidential value of Ephoros's statement because we can no longer identify its source, and because Thucydides, writing of the year 431, failed to mention a financial transaction that took place twenty-three years earlier.

The crucial financial operation that lay in the background was, of course, the transfer of the common treasury from Delos to Athens and its deposit on the Acropolis, where the accumulated surplus of the tribute had been commingled with the sacred monies of Athena's personal assets to form the capital reserve fund that both Thucydides and Ephoros described.[57] From this source the overseers of the Parthenon undoubtedly received a substantial portion of their annual funding. The treasurers of Athena in their turn charged their contributions to the Parthenon as debits against the reserve; they reckoned the costs of constructing a temple as nonrecurring capital expenditures in the same way that they met the costs of fighting the wars of the empire.

The treasurers of Athena were probably also responsible for another receipt that came to the overseers of the Parthenon in 447/6. This consisted of two small groups of electrum staters of Lampsakos and Kyzikos, which were carried forward by each successive board and remained unspent at the end of every year throughout the construction of the building. Together they did not represent a very considerable sum of money, for the 74 Lampsakene and 27⅙ Kyzikene staters amounted to only 2,428 drachmas in Attic silver, at a rate of exchange of 24:1.[58] Now, electrum staters of Kyzikos at least are known to have been paid into the imperial treasury as part of the tribute.[59] The currency of these two cities probably circulated freely and was always acceptable in payment of tribute. It is notable that the decree imposing Attic coinage on the empire, whatever its date may be, makes no mention of the electrum issues, and Kyzikene staters appear to have been in plentiful supply throughout the period in question.[60] In any event, by 447 the sacred treasury will have accumulated many of the coins, and more likely large numbers of them, a few of which were deposited to the account of the Parthenon overseers in that year. That the electrum staters remained unspent for fifteen years suggests that the overseers found them an inconvenient form of currency. The coins were too valuable to defray the costs of the daily payroll or the purchase of normal goods and services.[61] In

[56] Isokr. 8 *Peace* 69, 15 *Antidosis* 234 (10,000 T.), 8 *Peace* 126 (8,000 T.); Lykourgos, frag. 58 (Conomis) = Glossa Patmia, s.v. Ἑκατόμπεδον (*BCH* 1 [1877] 149); cf. Demosth. *Olynth.* 3.24, quoted above, chap. 1, p. 4.

[57] See the useful discussion of Samons, *Historia* 42 (1993) 132–136.

[58] Estimates of the value of Kyzikene electrum staters in Attic drachmas have varied considerably. *ATL* III, 266 (24 drachmas), with earlier references; W. E. Thompson, *NC* 3 (1963) 1–4 (almost 25 drachmas); R. Bogaert, *AntCl* 32 (1963) 85–119 (around 28 drachmas); his conclusions attacked by J. Guépin, *AntCl* 34 (1965) 199–203; Meiggs, *AE*, 442–443 (27 drachmas). The most detailed discussion is by S. K. Eddy, *ANSMN* 16 (1970) 13–22, who concludes (pp. 21–22) that the valuation was 24 drachmas, 5 obols, when staters were disbursed, but 24 drachmas when staters were accepted in payment, an exchange premium of 5 obols per stater.

[59] *IG* I³ 259, postscript, lines 10–13 = *ATL* II, list 1.

[60] For the Coinage Decree, ML 45 and commentary, pp. 113–117. Kyzikene staters continued to circulate unaffected by the provisions of the decree: E. S. G. Robinson, *Hesperia* Suppl. 8 (1949) 332–333.

[61] In the time of Xenophon, one Kyzikene stater was a month's pay for a mercenary soldier, Xen. *Anab.* 5.6.23.

fact, they are likely to have been held in reserve for possible conversion into bullion when the extensive gilded decoration was being added to the temple in the final stages of construction.

The only other constant contributors to the building fund of whom we can be sure were the hellenotamiai, who appear among the donors in five of the first ten years and almost certainly stood among the missing receipts of the other five years. The formula is best preserved in Year 4 (444/3): παρὰ hελλε[νοταμιõν, hοῖς] Στρόμβιχο[ς ἐγραμμάτευε] Χολλείδε[ς], "from the hellenotamiai to whom Strombichos of Cholleidai was secretary." Comparison of the receipts for the fifth, seventh, ninth, and tenth years shows that the same formula, with the necessary changes in the secretary's name, is also to be restored in those four accounts.[62] After the dedication of the Parthenon in 438, the hellenotamiai, like the treasurers of Athena, made their contributions to the Propylaia, in four of whose five accounts their name may still be read.[63] But unlike the sacred treasurers, they contributed a fixed item of the budget, the *aparchai* of ¹⁄₆₀ of the annual tribute, whose fluctuations in size were governed solely by the changing assessments in the tribute itself or by the failure of some cities to meet their commitments. This fixed nature of their annual payments is most explicitly expressed by the entry describing their donations to the Propylaia: τõ χσυμμαχικõ φόρο μνᾶ ἀπὸ τõ ταλάντο, "of the tribute of the allies, a mina in the talent."[64] In the fourth account of the Parthenon, the figure is preserved except for the first four numerals. Although the restoration is not quite certain, by far the most likely amount is 37,675 drachmas, 5 obols, which would represent the *aparchai* due to Athena on a total annual tribute collection of 376 talents, 4,550 drachmas.[65] There is thus established a specific cross-reference between the tribute quota lists and the accounts of the Acropolis buildings. In each year, it was the responsibility of the hellenotamiai to receive the tribute payments from the cities of the empire and to report to the assembly which cities had met their assessments and which were in arrears. They then calculated the *aparchai* of ¹⁄₆₀ of each payment and presented their accounts to the thirty logistai for audit, whereupon the duly audited quota lists were inscribed on the great stele on the Acropolis as a permanent record of each city's contribution to Athena.[66] Beginning in 447/6, assuredly in response to specific legislation, the hellenotamiai then handed over the amount of the *aparchai* to the overseers of the Parthenon, who recorded the transaction among the receipts for the building fund and in due course published it in their annual accounts. During the seven years from 454/3 to 448/7, the hellenotamiai had undoubtedly paid the *aparchai* directly to the treasurers of Athena for deposit in the goddess's sacred treasury.

[62] *IG* I³ 439, lines 72–74, Year 4 (444/3). Cf. *IG* I³ 440, lines 124–125 (Year 5); 442, lines 179–181 (Year 7); 444, lines 247–248 (Year 9); 445, lines 292–293 (Year 10).

[63] Payments from the hellenotamiai in the Propylaia accounts: *IG* I³ 462, lines 15–17, Year 1 (437/6); 463, lines 71–73; 464, lines 109–111; 465, lines 123–125.

[64] See chap. 9, note 100 below.

[65] *IG* I³ 439, line 73. The figure on the stone is best restored as: [ΜΜΜℾ]ΧΧℙΗℙΔΔℾΙΙΙΙ. *ATL* II 17; ML 39, p. 88. Dinsmoor, *AJA* 17 (1913) 65, originally tried to restore higher figures.

[66] On the duties of the hellenotamiai, Meiggs, *AE*, 234–238; ML 39, pp. 83–88. The attempt of A. Giovannini, *Historia* 46 (1997) 149–151, to argue that the board identified by its secretary in the prescripts of the tribute quota lists was not the hellenotamiai but some otherwise unattested financial officials is shown to be wrong by comparison of the tribute lists with payments by the hellenotamiai to the Parthenon and Propylaia. In 444/3, Strombichos of Cholleidai was secretary of the hellenotamiai; Parthenon, Year 4 (*IG* I³ 439, lines 72–74): παρὰ hελλε[νοταμιõν, hοῖς] Στρόμβιχο[ς ἐγραμμάτευε] Χολλείδε[ς]. Cf. list 11 (*IG* I³ 268, line 1): [ἐπὶ τẽς ἀρχẽς τẽς hεν]δεκάτες hẽι Στρόμ[βιχος Χο]λλείδες ἐγ[ραμ]μάτευε. In 443/2, Sophias of Eleusis was secretary of the hellenotamiai; Parthenon, Year 5 (*IG* I³ 440, lines 124–125): [παρ]ὰ hελλ[ενοταμιõν, hοῖς Σοφίας Ἐλ]ευσίνι[ος ἐγραμμάτευε]. Cf. list 12 (*IG* I³ 269, line 1): [ἐπὶ τẽς ἀρχẽς τẽς δο]δεκα[τ]ες hẽι [Σ]οφίας ἐγρα[μμάτ]ευε Ἐλευσίνι. In 435/4, Thoinilos of Acharnai was secretary of the hellenotamiai; Propylaia, Year 3 (*IG* I³ 464, lines 109–110): παρὰ hελλενοτα]μιõν, hοῖς Θοινίλος [ἐγραμμάτευεν Ἀ]χαρνεύς. Cf. list 20 (*IG* I³ 277, line 1): ἐπὶ [τẽς ε]ἰ[κοστẽς ἀρχẽς hẽ]ι Θ[οινίλος . . . 7 . . .] Ἀχαρνε[ὺς ἐγραμμάτευε. In 434/3, Protonichos of Kerameis was secretary of the hellenotamiai; Propylaia, Year 4 (*IG* I³ 465, lines 123–124): [π]αρὰ hελλενοταμι[õν, h]οῖς Προτόν[ιχος ἐγραμ]μάτευε Κερ[αμε]ύς. Cf. list 21 (*IG* I³ 278, line 1): [ἐπὶ τẽς μιᾶς καὶ εἰκοστẽς ἀρχẽς hẽι Προτ]όνιχος ἐκ Κεραμέον Ἐπιχάρος [ἐγραμμάτευε].

During the fourth and fifth years (444/3 and 443/2), still other funds found their way into the hands of the Parthenon overseers, evidently from other boards of Athenian public officials. These occasional contributions, which appear only once or twice during the fifteen years of construction, are probably best understood as unallocated funds that remained unspent in the accounts of these boards at the end of the previous year and were earmarked for the Parthenon by special vote of the demos. All three items in the accounts are in need of restoration, but in each case the first few letters of the name are highly suggestive. Of these, the most curious are the two payments that appear in Year 4 as παρὰ χσεν[οδικõν, hοῖς – – –] ἐγγραμμά[τευε – – –], and in Year 5 as [π]αρὰ χσεν[οδικõν].[67] This is by far the earliest reference to magistrates called xenodikai, who are mentioned in one or two very fragmentary inscriptions of the fourth century as having jurisdiction in contract disputes involving foreigners.[68] There are no other literary or epigraphical references to them at the time of the Parthenon; they appear suddenly in 444/3 in possession of a considerable amount of money and disappear just as suddenly after 443/2. The fact that they are listed with their secretary in the first year and with no secretary in the second has suggested to some that they may have completed their work,[69] in other words, that they were a special board of magistrates empaneled to meet the needs of a particular situation. In that case, the striking chronological coincidence that their contributions appear only in 444/3 and 443/2 makes it possible to postulate their identification as the officials charged with adjudicating the hundreds of prosecutions for illegal citizenship (γράφαι ξενίας) which arose at just this time as a result of Perikles' citizenship law of 451/0. During a severe shortage of grain in Attica in 445/4, Psammetichos, the king of Libya, had alleviated the crisis with a princely gift of thirty (or forty) thousand medimnoi to the state, but efforts to distribute this grain among the populace precipitated charges that hundreds of foreigners had managed to enroll themselves in Athenian demes and phratries in the interval since 451. As a result of the prolonged prosecutions that followed, 4,760 resident aliens were disenfranchised, according to Philochoros, and thus lost the right to own property in Attica.[70] If fourth-century procedures were in force at this time, those who appealed the decision unsuccessfully were sold into slavery.[71] On the Parthenon stele, the figure donated by the xenodikai in 444/3 is missing its first four numerals, but the smallest amount that properly fills the space is 19,148 drachmas. If the source of their funds is correctly identified, their two payments to the Parthenon will represent at least a portion of the state's profits from the sale of the real estate confiscated from the disenfranchised or of the persons who failed on appeal.[72]

The overseers of 444/3 also recorded among their receipts an item that should probably be restored to read: παρὰ τρ[ιεροποιõν], "from the trieropoioi."[73] The entry is unique in the building

[67] *IG* I³ 439, lines 75–76; 440, line 126. The restoration and identification of the xenodikai were first proposed by Cavaignac, *Études,* lxvii. For more recent discussion of the xenodikai, see E. E. Cohen, *Ancient Athenian Maritime Courts* (Princeton 1973) 166–176. Cf. also A. Körte, *Hermes* 68 (1933) 238–242.

[68] *IG* II² 46; *IG* II²144; cf. *SEG* 18.10.

[69] So Cavaignac, *Études,* lxviii. Cf. Cohen, *Maritime Courts,* 171; *ATL* III, 10.

[70] Philochoros, *FGrH* 328 F 119, quoted by schol. Aristoph. *Wasps* 718a (Koster): the gift was 30,000 bushels, five for each Athenian, and it was distributed to 14,240 persons, while 4,760 were deprived of citizenship. Plut. *Per.* 37.3–4: the gift was 40,000 bushels, and as a result of much litigation 14,040 people were judged Athenian citizens, while a little fewer than 5,000 were sold into slavery. Cf. [Aristot.] *Ath. Pol.* 26.4, 42.1. See Hignett, *HAC,* 343–347; J. Labarbe, "La distribution de blé de 445–444 à Athènes et ses incidences démographiques," in H. J. Diesner, ed., *Sozialökonomische Verhältnisse im alten Orient und in klassischen Altertum* (Berlin 1961) 191–207; Cohen, *Maritime Courts,* 169–171; C. Patterson, *Pericles' Citizenship Law of 451–50 B.C.* (New York 1981) 94–115; A. L. Boegehold, in A. L. Boegehold and A. Scafuro, eds., *Athenian Identity and Civic Ideology* (Baltimore 1994) 57–66.

[71] The procedure is described by [Aristot.] *Ath. Pol.* 42.1.

[72] The payment from the xenodikai, *IG* I³ 439, lines 75–76, is missing four numerals at the left end of the figure. The smallest amount that can be restored is [ΜϜΧΧ]ΧΧΗΔΔΔΔΠΗΗ. For the suggestion that the source of the money was the sale of confiscated real estate, Cohen, *Maritime Courts,* 172.

[73] *IG* I³ 439, line 77. They are restored as recipients of state funds in *IG* I³ 366, line 13 (431/0).

accounts of the fifth century, but it would be difficult to find another group of public officials whose title begins with tau and rho. The trieropoioi are known to us from the fourth century as a subcommittee consisting of ten members of the boulē who administered the funds appropriated for ship-building and supervised the work of the shipwrights in the dockyards. If their fifth-century counterparts had the same duties in the days of the naval empire, it was the trieropoioi who managed the maintenance of the Athenian fleet and oversaw construction of new triremes.[74] To this end, we meet them in a fragmentary inscription of 431/0 which records disbursements from the sacred treasury for military expenditures. The lines pertaining to the naval commissioners cannot be restored with any degree of certainty, but it appears that in this year they received at least 50 talents and perhaps twice that amount from the treasurers of Athena.[75] The number of new ships to be built in a given year was in all likelihood determined by vote of the assembly,[76] and sufficient funds to complete the task would be allocated at the same time. In this light, the money from the naval board among the receipts for the Parthenon should be understood as a special one-time appropriation, undoubtedly voted by the assembly, and not merely the balance of their account after completion of some new triremes. This is suggested also by the large round number of 10,000 drachmas, which is the only numeral that survives of the original figure in the left-hand column. But there are four numerals missing from the beginning of the figure, and so the smallest amount that can be restored is 90,000 drachmas (an even 15 talents), which makes the payment from the trieropoioi a very substantial one indeed.[77]

There is some slight evidence to suggest the transfer of surplus funds from other public works to the overseers of the Parthenon. An item among the receipts for the fifth year (443/2) is generally restored to read: [π]αρὰ τειχ[οποιõν], "from the wall commissioners."[78] These officials are at once reminiscent of the teichopoioi appointed by tribe to supervise the reconstruction of the fortification walls in about 337/6. According to the law ordering that reconstruction, the tribal officers are to cooperate with the epistatai elected by the demos; the teichopoioi appear also on the series of inscriptions marking individual segments of the walls that were completed each year.[79] It has generally been assumed that their namesakes in the accounts of the Parthenon were in charge of building the so-called middle Long Wall. This was the third and latest of the Long Walls, built parallel to the northernmost wall, and its completion connected the city of Athens to the Peiraieus by means of a narrow fortified corridor.[80] The project was certainly under construction in the 440s; but it is impossible to tell whether the laconic entry in the accounts of the Parthenon signals its completion

[74] [Aristot.] *Ath. Pol.* 46.1, describes the duties of the trieropoioi and their election from the membership of the boulē. In the fourth century, their funds were handled by a special treasurer of the trieropoeic fund. Cf. Demosth. 22 *Andro.* 17–20. See Rhodes, *Athenian Boule,* 115–122; B. Jordan, *The Athenian Navy in the Classical Period* (Berkeley 1975) 46–50.

[75] *IG* I³ 366, lines 13–15; and cf. *SEG* 10.226 with fuller restorations.

[76] This seems to be the meaning of [Aristot.] *Ath. Pol.* 46.1, but some editors have read the text as providing for a fixed quota of four or ten new ships per year; see Rhodes, *Commentary,* 546, and *Athenian Boule,* 115, note 3.

[77] *IG* I³ 439, line 77, should be restored [ΓΜΜΜ]Μ. The single preserved Μ is almost aligned with the first preserved numeral Χ in line 76, and there is not room for more than four numerals to the left of Μ. See *ATL* III, 341, note 63, for the assumption that this payment was merely an unexpended balance in the account of the trieropoioi.

[78] *IG* I³ 440, line 127. The restoration proposed by Cavaignac, *Études,* lxviii; cf. Dinsmoor, *AJA* 17 (1913) 78, *AJA* 25 (1921) 243.

[79] The teichopoioi appointed by tribe, *IG* II² 1658, line 1; 1660, lines 1–3; cf. Aischin. 3 *Ktes.* 30. The law directing cooperation of the teichopoioi and elected epistatai, *IG* II² 244, lines 28–40. Records of individual portions of the walls, *IG* II² 1658–1661; Maier, *Mauerbauinschriften,* nos. 1–9, pp. 21–36. On their supervision by the boulē, Rhodes, *Athenian Boule,* 123–125, 220. For discussion of the law, Maier, no. 10, pp. 36–48.

[80] The wall was called τὸ διὰ μέσου τεῖχος: Plato, *Gorg.* 455E; Harpokration, s.v. (δ 44 Keaney), citing Plato. See the detailed discussion of D. H. Conwell, "The Athenian Long Walls" (Ph.D. diss., University of Pennsylvania, 1992) 58–79, and, for the topography and remains, 270–290, 310–341.

in that year, or whether the teichopoioi simply finished the year with an unexpended surplus in their account that was redirected to the Parthenon.[81]

A similar policy may have guided the transfer of surplus funds from nonstrategic public works to the overseers of the Parthenon. The first item in the receipts of 443/2 should probably be interpreted in this way, and the text has been restored to read: [π]αρὰ ταμ[ιõν ἐκ – – – – κ]αὶ ἐγ βα[λανείον.[82] This seems possibly to refer to surplus funds paid to the Parthenon in this year by those responsible for construction of public baths, if the restoration is correct; but even if it is not, the surplus from some other project was evidently combined to form this item. There is, of course, no way of guessing the identity of the building whose name stood first in the entry and was paired with the baths; but the two buildings will have been juxtaposed in this way because their funds were originally allocated by the same board of tamiai, possibly the treasurers of Athena, since their regular annual appropriation stands next in the order of receipts. The tamiai are mentioned to indicate the primary source of the money which passed to the Parthenon from the overseers of these two projects.

Still another source of revenue apparently came to the overseers of the Parthenon from the state's interests in the silver mines of Laureion. In Year 9 (439/8), the last preserved receipt can be restored to read in part [παρὰ ταμιõν hεφαιστικõ] ἀπὸ Λαυρε[ίο . . . . . .[12] . . . . . τõμ π]έντε μερ[õν]. The wording of the formula is somewhat better preserved in Year 10 (438/7) and in the fourth year of the Propylaia accounts, for 434/3. Comparison of these three passages makes the text of the first line certain, but there is no way to restore the missing words at the beginning of the second line.[83] The entry seems to record a contribution from the treasurers of the Hephaisti(a)kon mine in the Laureion district for two years only, but it is possible that this was a recurring item which has simply not been preserved in the accounts of the earlier years. The name of the mine, Hephaistiakon, is attested in the fourth century among the records of the poletai, who at that time were in charge of leasing the mining rights on behalf of the state; but there is no reason to believe that the mine in the Parthenon accounts was still being worked a century later, since the names were often duplicated.[84] The true nature of the revenue is unknown, since it is by no means clear whether the tamiai named here are state officials or private entrepreneurs who had leased the mining concession from the city, in accordance with fourth-century practice.[85] Nor is there any way of knowing what part of the state's profits from the mine could be described as "five shares" in the genitive case. Like so many other funds that came to the Parthenon, the mining revenues were also paid to the Propylaia for the last years, during the mid-430s.

As will be seen shortly, the Parthenon was formally dedicated and the gold and ivory statue was formally unveiled at the Great Panathenaia of 438.[86] This signal event in the cultural history of Athens marked the virtual completion of the new temple. The architectural work and most of the decoration had been finished, and only the sculptured figures destined to adorn the pediments of the building had yet to be carved. In consequence, it is perfectly natural that most of the sources of

[81] For the assumption that the wall was completed in 443/2, Dinsmoor, *AJA* 17 (1913) 78, *AJA* 25 (1921) 243; *ATL* III, 341, note 64. Plato, *Gorg.* 455D–E, provides a terminus post quem of 452 for the beginning of construction, since Sokrates was in the assembly when it was proposed; cf. Plut. *Per.* 13.7. For discussion, Conwell, "Athenian Long Walls," 69–71. From Thucydides 2.13.7, one infers that the Middle Wall was certainly completed by 431 (Conwell, 76).

[82] *IG* I³ 440, lines 120–121. The restoration of Hiller, *IG* I² 343, line 121, on the analogy of *IG* I³ 402, line 10.

[83] *IG* I³ 444, lines 249–250 (Year 9). Cf. *IG* I³ 445, lines 294–295 (Year 10); 465, lines 126–127 (Propylaia, Year 4). The restoration is due to Dinsmoor, *AJA* 25 (1921) 239.

[84] Langdon, *Agora* XIX P 15, line 14 (= *IG* II² 1584); P 18, line 9; P 43, line 7. Cf. the earlier publication of M. Crosby, *Hesperia* 19 (1950) 189–312.

[85] On the administration of the Laureion mines, see R. J. Hopper, *BSA* 48 (1953) 200–254; Hopper, *G&R* 8 (1961) 138–151; for an account of the physical remains, J. E. Jones, *G&R* 29 (1982) 169–183.

[86] Philochoros, *FGrH* 328 F 121, quoted by schol. Aristoph. *Peace* 605 (Holwerda), quoted below, p. 72.

revenue which had been at the disposal of the epistatai for ten years past were now redirected to the next phase of construction on the Acropolis. In 438/7, the year of the dedication, the hellenotamiai and the treasurers of the Hephaistiakon mine made their last payments to the Parthenon, while the treasurers of Athena had already withdrawn their support. The principal sources of new income during these final years were the profits that the overseers realized from the sale of surplus materials. In the account of 438/7, they recorded the sale of gold bullion, and in the following year a similar sale of surplus ivory. The formulas for both transactions are fully preserved in Year 14 (434/3): χρυ-σίο πραθέ[ντος] σταθμὸν ⊢ΔΔΔ[Δ]Γ[⊢⊢⊢] τιμὲ τούτο, "98 dr. weight of gold sold, price of this." Both precious materials were sold by weight, given in talents and drachmas as part of the description, while the left column showed the price they fetched in silver.[87] While it is true that the overseers had purchased some ivory the previous year and probably had some small amounts of gold on hand for the final decorative detail, it has been suggested that these sales of gold and ivory in Years 10, 11, and 14 may represent surplus materials that had been turned over to the Parthenon overseers when the overseers of the golden statue liquidated their accounts and closed their books in 438.[88] This would in fact have been the most efficient way for the overseers to dispose of the excess gold and ivory from the statue and at the same time to account for the surplus in their final report.

Aside from the substantial sums of money that the gold and ivory would fetch, smaller receipts came from the sale, in both 438/7 and 437/6, of lumber from the scaffolding and the wood from the heavy wheels on which the marble blocks had been rolled from the Pentelic quarries to the foot of the Acropolis. Excess supplies of tin, and probably also of copper and other materials used to fashion the hardware and fittings of the temple, likewise went on the market in 437/6.[89] In addition to these various sales, the only item of income that can plausibly be reconstructed is an entry in Year 10 bearing the names of three private individuals. The laconic description reads: παρ' Εὐφέρ[ο, παρὰ Πλε]ισ[τίο], παρὰ Σαύρονο[ς – –], "from Eupheros, from Pleistias, from Sauron." In the complete absence of any evidence, we can only suppose that the item records voluntary donations from three public-spirited Athenians. Lastly, in Year 14 (434/3), we note a final payment of 25,000 drachmas from the treasurers of Athena, who in the four previous years had lent their financial support to the overseers of the Propylaia.[90]

THE EXPENSE ACCOUNTS OF THE BUILDERS

When we come to consider the building on which the overseers spent their money, the scene shifts at first from Athena's citadel on the Acropolis to the pine-clad slopes of Mount Pentelikon, whose great pyramidal peak guards the Attic plain on the northeast about sixteen kilometers distant from the center of Athens. Here, in the folds and ridges of the mountain, difficult of access and rising in places to more than a thousand meters above the sea, run the finest veins of architectural marble in the eastern Mediterranean. Fine of grain and milky white, the opaque purity of the stone is touched only with the slightest tincture of iron, causing it to weather in that golden hue that has evoked the praise of ages.[91] Today the ancient quarries, some twenty in number, can be seen for miles descending from the heights of the ridge along its southwestern flank, a thin chain of white scars that flash in the light. But in the summer of 447, when the quarrymen and foremen and architects of the Parthenon,

---

[87] Sale of gold, *IG* I³ 445, lines 296–297; sale of ivory, *IG* I³ 446, lines 320–321; restored on the basis of fully preserved entries, *IG* I³ 449, lines 389–394.
[88] So Dinsmoor, *AJA* 17 (1913) 70–71.
[89] Sale of wood, *IG* I³ 445, line 298; sale of wooden wheels, *IG* I³ 446, lines 324–325; sale of tin, *IG* I³ 446, line 327.
[90] Private contributions, *IG* I³ 445, lines 299–300; final payment from the treasurers, *IG* I³ 449, lines 385–388.
[91] See G. R. Lepsius, *Griechische Marmorstudien* (Berlin 1890) 11–23.

perhaps even the overseers themselves, toiled up from the village of Pentele, which nestled on the lower slopes and gave its name to the mountain, they will have found that there had been few comers before them in their search for a spot to cut their stone. For the Athenians had begun to extract marble from this rich resource only a generation earlier; and, except for the blocks of the Older Parthenon, some recent deliveries of stone for the Hephaisteion, and possibly one or two earlier buildings, the mountain was still an unexploited treasure.[92]

The finest of the Pentelic marble runs in two parallel veins along the crest of the ridge that scores the southwest flank of the mountain. Here, at an altitude of about 700 meters above sea level, the quarrymen of the Parthenon began to cut their stone. Today this is the point of entry into an enormous roughly rectangular trench that measures about 140 meters in length, with an average width of 80 meters. At the northeast corner, the ancient quarry face towers for more than 37 meters above the accumulated debris of marble waste that fills the lowest part of the quarry cutting to a depth of another 10 meters and more.[93] The Spelia Quarry, as it has been called since medieval times, takes its name from the natural cave that runs deep into the core of the mountain from its northeast corner. Already known in the Classical period, the cave may have been sacred to the nymphs, like another smaller one 100 meters higher up the slope.[94] To these rustic spirits the ancient quarrymen directed their prayers, and with their benevolent blessing thousands upon thousands of blocks have been prised from the living marble of the mountain. To this day one contemplates with awe the vast artificial chasm which produced the marble buildings of classical Athens.

On these rocky slopes above Pentele, the builders of the Parthenon began their work. That much of the activity of the first year took place here, the accounts of the overseers will suffice to demonstrate. The chance of survival enables us to reconstruct the entire list of expenditures for 447/6, and it is clear that there were no payments to stonemasons, either for working stone or for construction on the Acropolis. There is only one payment to quarrymen recorded, and this is surely to the men at Pentele.[95] The first item of expenditure can be restored to read: λιθοτ[όμοις Πεντελῆθεν], "To quarrymen from Pentele," by comparison with similar entries for Years 9 and 10, which preserve the full formula.[96]

A fact of some importance emerges at once from the expenses of the first year: the overseers did not have to purchase the marble for the building. Like the silver in the mines at Laureion, it was the property of the Athenian state, and they had only to hire the labor to cut it and carry it across the plain to Athens. But this labor for the quarrying and transportation of marble probably accounted for a large part of the total cost of a building. Furthermore, this stage of the work was exceedingly time consuming, and it apparently took a full year to quarry and transport sufficient quantities of marble

[92] The earliest use of Pentelic marble for sculpture occurred about 570, e.g., Acropolis kore 593 (Brouskari, *Acropolis Museum*, 43–44; Schrader, *Marmorbildwerke*, 43–44) and the "Lyons" kore 269 (Brouskari, 60–61; Schrader, 66–67). Dedications of Pentelic marble became more frequent by the end of the sixth century, e.g., Acropolis 6503 (Brouskari, 31; Raubitschek, *DAA*, no. 290), Acropolis 6505 (Brouskari, 48; Raubitschek, *DAA*, no. 40). The earliest architectural marbles may be the metopes of the early archaic temple on the Acropolis, although they are perhaps more likely Hymettian than Pentelic; see Butz, "Hekatompedon Inscription," 4–20, 295–299.

[93] On the topography of the Pentelic quarries, Strabo 9.1.23 (p. 399); Paus. 1.32.1–2. See M. Korres, *From Pentelicon to the Parthenon* (Athens 1995) 78–87, 94–100, with earlier bibliography; M. Korres, in Y. Maniatis, N. Herz, and Y. Basiakos, eds., *The Study of Marble and Other Stones Used in Antiquity* (London 1995) 1–5. For the use of the Attic quarries, R. Osborne, *Demos: The Discovery of Classical Attika* (Cambridge 1985) 93–110. For ancient quarries generally, A. Dworakowska, *Quarries in Ancient Greece* (Wrocław 1975).

[94] On the caves of the nymphs at Pentele: P. Zorides, *ArchEph* (1977) Χρον., 4–11; J. M. Wickens, "The Archaeology and History of Cave Use in Attica" (Ph.D. diss., Indiana University, 1986) 194–211.

[95] Expenses Year 1, *IG* I³ 436, lines 22–32. By contrast, the Propylaia accounts record payments each year to several groups of quarrymen at the different quarries that provided stone for the building: *IG* I³ 462, lines 35–40; 463, lines 84–86; 466, lines 150–155.

[96] *IG* I³ 436, line 23; cf. 444, line 27 (Year 9); 445, line 304 (Year 10).

to the Acropolis so that the masons could begin their work. Something of the methods of the quarrymen may still be observed, for the marble walls of the ancient quarry surfaces preserve indelibly the neat sure strokes of the heavy stone hammers and the slots for the iron wedges, descending row upon row like the courses of masonry.[97] They removed the stone in roughly rectangular masses as a matter of course and tried wherever possible to exploit natural fissures to facilitate separating the building block from the parent mass of rock. At appropriate points along these natural strata of the marble, sockets would be cut for the insertion of iron wedges and heavy iron levers with which to split off the desired block from the living marble of the mountain. Where the block to be quarried was not bounded by natural joints, or these could not be observed, the masons had to resort to a much more laborious method. In that event, they had to free the perimeter of the block by opening narrow channels around all four sides to a depth equal to the desired thickness, before the slots for the wedges could be cut. This system of wedging the marble from the natural mass of rock, which is indicated by the traces left on the quarry surface, finds corroboration in the ancient sources. A fragment of a book titled *Mechanics* by Heron of Alexandria describes the process specifically: "The next power is that through the wedge and that is of great service . . . when it comes to splitting off the stones from the quarries from their attachment on the underside."[98] After the rough mass of marble had been extracted from the quarry, excess stone would be removed from all its surfaces, and the block would slowly be reduced in bulk and trimmed to the required shape and dimensions. In this process the guiding principle was to reduce the weight of the block as much as possible to facilitate its transportation, but at the same time to minimize the chance of damage by leaving a protective layer of stone about 0.02 m thick on all its surfaces. It has been estimated that it would require two months of work in the quarry to extract the stone and prepare the preliminary carving for a Doric column capital of the Parthenon, and the half-finished block to be transported would weigh about twelve tons.[99]

Extraction of the marble was only the first part of the job, for all the evidence suggests that the handling and transportation of the stone was a difficult and complex operation. At this point we may recall that Plutarch (*Per.* 12.6–7), in his list of trades and industries which Perikles claimed would benefit most from the public works, placed special emphasis on the carters and teamsters who would transport the building materials, "by land wagon makers, keepers of draught animals, and muleteers. There were also rope-makers, linen-weavers, leatherworkers, road builders, and quarrymen."[100] The accuracy of Plutarch's picture is amply borne out by the records of the builders themselves; and in fact all the expenses in the first account of the Parthenon, except the wages for the quarrymen at Pentele and the monthly salaries of the overseers, secretaries, and architects (καταμένια), probably went to pay for one process or another in the transportation of stone. First and most critical was the task of moving the heavy blocks down the precipitous slopes of the mountain, when the least miscalculation might send a huge architrave hurtling hundreds of meters toward the village below. To facilitate handling of the large quantities of marble, the ancient builders constructed a quarry road or slipway, portions of which can still be seen, climbing steeply up the rugged slope from just above the site of Pentele to the highest quarries on the ridge. The surviving section can be traced for about 850 m to the entrance of the Spelia Quarry. It rises in a nearly straight line at a gradient of between 25% and

[97] On the techniques of ancient quarrying, Korres, *Pentelicon*, 74–75; R. Martin, *Manuel d'architecture grecque* (Paris 1965) 146–155; A. K. Orlandos, Τὰ ὑλικὰ δομῆς τῶν ἀρχαίων Ἑλλήνων (Athens 1958) vol. 2, 83–88.

[98] Heron of Alexandria, *Mechanicorum Fragmenta* 2.4 (Nix and Schmidt, vol. 2, pt. 1, p. 280): ἡ δὲ ἑξῆς δύναμις ἡ διὰ τοῦ σφηνὸς καὶ αὐτὴ μεγάλας χρείας παρεχομένη . . . ὅταν τοὺς ἐκ τῶν λατομιῶν λίθους ἀποσπᾶν δέη τῆς κατὰ τὰ κάτω μέρος συνεχείας. The Greek text as excerpted by Pappos, p. 1122 (Hultsch); the translation, A. G. Drachmann, *The Mechanical Technology of Greek and Roman Antiquity* (Copenhagen 1963) 55. Cf. mention of wedges of olive wood, *IG* II² 463, line 44; 1672, line 9; and iron wedges at Delos, *IG* XI.2 161A, lines 87–88; 199B, line 89.

[99] Korres, *Pentelicon*, 28.

[100] Plut. *Per.* 12.6.

30% and is laid out almost exactly parallel to the long axis of the quarries.[101] The road is narrow and steep, paved with rough stones of marble waste, long since worn smooth in places by the traffic that they bore. Down this rough track would have come the raw blocks of stone. They were maneuvered upon wooden sleds in the quarries above and hauled with the aid of winches to the slipway, down which they scraped and slid, the smaller loads on rollers, the larger without lest they gather too much speed on their descent. Their own momentum bore them, guided with the leverage of crowbars; but at intervals in the rock beside the road are square cuttings for the posts on which were anchored ropes and tackle to brake the downward progress of the stone.[102] Here and there in the rough terrain along the slipway, an occasional block of marble, damaged and discarded in handling, may still be found; and of special interest is a pair of great column drums, still sheathed in the rough-picked coat of their quarry surface.

The builders of this and similar quarry roads have left frequent records in the expense accounts of the overseers. During the 430s, when the accounts of the Parthenon are more fully preserved, we find payments to the road builders (ϊοδοποιοί) in Years 10, 11, and 12; and again in the first account of the Propylaia there is an entry that begins: ϊυποργ[οῖς Πεντελε̃θεν ϊοδο]ποιο̃[σι]; "For assistants building roads at Pentele." On the analogy of this item, we may restore precisely the same formula in the first account of the Parthenon, where only part of the first word is actually preserved.[103] For the road builders, who saw so much action in the later years of the building program, must surely have been at work on the slopes of Mount Pentelikon from the very beginning of operations. Without them no marble could have been delivered to the building site on the Acropolis.

The teamsters who were responsible for the actual deliveries of marble figure in the accounts only in the short phrase λιθαγογίας Πεντελε̃θεν, "for transportation of stone from Pentele," which appears in every year in which marble was quarried.[104] But behind this laconic entry lies a complex process that can be elucidated to some extent from various ancient sources. The first stage was the construction of vehicles of sufficient strength to carry the great loads across the plain to Athens. We hear of these vehicles at first only indirectly, when the wood from some of the heavy wheels was sold off in 437/6: [χσύλον πραθέντον τρ]οχο̃ν κυκλιαίον, "sale of wood from round wheels." Also in the later years, payments are recorded to workmen: λίθος ἀνατιθε̃σι ἐπι τὰ κύκλα Πεντελε̃σι, "putting up the blocks on wheels at Pentele."[105] We may surmise that the carpenters employed in the first year were actually engaged in the construction of these wheels and of the vehicles to which they were attached.[106] Now, it will be noted that there is no mention of carts or wagons but only of the wheels themselves. On this point the accounts of the Parthenon can be usefully supplemented by the detailed inventories kept by the Eleusinian overseers at the end of the fifth century and especially in

---

[101] For the quarry roads, see Korres, *Pentelicon*, 92–93, 100–102; Martin, *Manuel*, 164–167; Orlandos, Ῠλικὰ δομῆς, 88–93.

[102] The use of wooden sleds or "tortoises" (χελῶναι), as they are called in the ancient accounts, is fully described by Heron, *Mech. Frag.* 3.1 (Nix and Schmidt, vol. 2, pt. 1, 294): "Things which are to be carried along the ground are dragged on tortoises, he says. The tortoise is a frame fitted together of squared timbers, whose ends have been turned up like snub noses. On these, then, the loads are placed, and to their ends are tied either compound pulleys or the ends of ropes. These are either drawn by hand or attached to capstans, and when they are turned the tortoise slides along the ground with rollers or boards placed under it. For if the load is small, it is necessary to use rollers, if it is larger, boards, because these do not slide so easily. For the turning rollers can be dangerous if the load gains momentum. Some people use neither rollers nor boards, but they put solid wheels on the tortoises and drag them that way." For discussion of the passage, see Drachman, *Mechanical Technology,* 94–97. For the rock-cut postholes, Korres, *Pentelicon,* 102–103.

[103] *IG* I³ 436, line 28 (Year 1). Cf. *IG* I³ 445, line 306; 446, line 333; 447, line 357 (Years 10, 11, 12); *IG* I³ 462, line 49 (Propylaia, Year 1).

[104] *IG* I³ 436, line 24; 444, line 271; 445, line 308; 446, line 335; 447, line 356.

[105] Sale of wooden wheels: *IG* I³ 446, line 324; mounting blocks on wheels: *IG* I³ 445, lines 306–307; 446, lines 333–334; 447, lines 357–358; 449, lines 398–400.

[106] Carpenters in Year 1: *IG* I³ 436, line 26.

the fourth. These documents include frequent references to the equipment used for the transportation of stone from the quarries to the building site. The vehicles themselves were called τετράκυκλα ("four-wheelers") or the more generic term hάμαχσαι ("wagons"). But it is noticeable that the overseers more often than not listed their various component parts separately, evidently because these parts could be assembled in different configurations to accommodate blocks of different shapes and dimensions. Thus the inventory for 407/6 includes such items as fifty-one iron-clad wagon poles, a pair of large axles, a pair of small axles, and wood for the wheels of a "four-wheeler": thirteen pieces of elm, eight iron wheel rims.[107]

From another Eleusinian account, of the late 330s, there emerges a clearer image of the great stone-hauling rigs. The framework that carried the marble blocks and the ropes that drew or lifted them had to be exceptionally strong, and the builders took equipment from the dockyards for this purpose. Surplus timber was moved from Peiraieus to Eleusis, and the heavy twisted cables (ὑποζώματα) that served as undergirding for the hulls of the triremes were used as harness or cut up to make suspension ropes.[108] Even so, the great weight of the marbles and roughness of the roads combined to exact their toll, for in this same year the Eleusinian overseers had to repair no fewer than seventeen broken axles, at a cost of 119 drachmas.[109] Other expenses recorded in the account help us to visualize the appearance of the vehicles. One purchase reads: δοκοὶ εἰς μεσόμνας τέτταρες παρ᾽ Ἑρμαίου ξυλοπώ[λου], "four roof beams for long timbers from the woodseller Hermaios"; and the next item is a payment to a carpenter for drilling and joining the beams.[110] The long timbers were probably mounted in pairs lengthwise, directly on top of the heavy wooden axles and thus gave the carriage sufficient length to accommodate such extra-long blocks as architraves, lintels, or doorjambs. Another item of particular interest records the purchase of ἐπώτιδες εἰς τὴν λιθαγωγίαν : HΓ : παρὰ Ἀρίστωνος Χολλῃΐδου, "150 epotides for the transportation of stone from Ariston of Cholleidai."[111] In naval architecture, epotides were the earlike projecting beams that protruded from either side at the bow of a trireme. The word is probably used in this context to describe short wooden timbers placed crosswise at intervals on top of the long beams as needed, and upon which the marble blocks would be seated for transport.[112] The relative size of the epotides is indicated by the payment to the same Ariston for sawing some of them from the fragments of broken axles.

The detailed expense accounts of these building operations at Eleusis give us a vivid picture of the transportation of stone from the Pentelic quarries. The largest marbles—the column drums and architraves, slabs for the stylobates and orthostates, the lintels and doorjambs—were of necessity moved individually, mounted on their improvised conveyances and dragged by the brute strength of many teams of oxen or mules. The inscription just mentioned records in twenty-seven lines, and

---

[107] *IG* I³ 386, line 24 (τετράκυκλον), line 113 (hάμαχσαι), line 21 (wagon poles), line 25 (axles), lines 26–27 (wheels of a "four-wheeler"), line 36 (iron wheel rims). Cf. the commentary of Cavanaugh, *Eleusis*, 135–143. Literary references to four-wheeled wagons: Diod. 4.80; Athenaeus 2.45B; cf. Orlandos, Ὑλικὰ δομῆς, vol. 2, 93–97.

[108] *IG* II² 1673, line 10, surplus timber from the Peiraieus; lines 12–15, *hypozomata* cut to specified lengths and other naval equipment from the dockyards. Cf. the commentary of Clinton, *ArchEph* (1971) 89–90. The *hypozoma* ("undergirdle") was the heavy twisted cable that "ran stern to stem and back again within the hull, where alone it can be structurally significant": J. S. Morrison and J. F. Coates, *The Athenian Trireme* (Cambridge 1986) 171.

[109] *IG* II² 1673, lines 31–33 = Clinton, *ArchEph* (1971) 83, with new fragment of the text; commentary, 93–94.

[110] Clinton, *ArchEph* (1971) 83, lines 35–36.

[111] Clinton, *ArchEph* (1971) 83, lines 34–35.

[112] For *epotides* in naval architecture as bow timbers (literally, "ear-timbers"), Morrison and Coates, *Athenian Trireme*, 166–168. For the likely appearance of the stone-hauling vehicles, see Korres, *Pentelicon*, 36–39, 104; for a variation using the same component parts, Orlandos, Ὑλικὰ δομῆς, 97; see also A. Burford, *Economic History Review* 13 (1960) 1–18. A far less likely reconstruction, using the evidence of the same inscription, is the impractical contraption proposed by G. Raepsaet, *AntCl* 53 (1984) 101–136; D. Vanhove, *AntCl* 56 (1987) 284–289. The Eleusinian overseers affectionately refer to this ungainly carriage as ἁμαξίς, "little cart," *IG* II² 1673, lines 11–12, 40.

in minute detail, the transportation of twenty-three column drums for the porch of the Telesterion. Since the columns of that building have almost exactly the same dimensions as those of the Parthenon, the details of the Eleusinian record illustrate the magnitude of the task that confronted the builders of the Parthenon. It took two and a half to three days for the trek across the plain to Eleusis, and the teamsters needed thirty to thirty-three teams of mules to pull the vehicle on which each drum traveled. One daring driver began the journey with only twenty-eight teams and had to add three more on the second day. The total cost of moving each drum is carefully recorded, and the fully preserved figures range from 318 to 402 drachmas.[113] Although Athens is much nearer the quarries than Eleusis, it will have taken two days and 200 to 250 drachmas each to move the comparable column drums of the peristyle. We can conjure up the scene in our mind's eye: the endless trains of mules, goaded by the whips and lashed by the tongues of the loquacious teamsters; and behind them, their progress measured by the creaking cadence of the slowly turning wheels, would come the blocks of the Parthenon, like gigantic floats in some ritual procession. Across the dry fields of summer, when there was no danger of bogging down in muddy roads, through the deme of Phlya, to the eastern suburbs at the foot of Lykabettos, along the banks of the Ilissos and into the city at one of the eastern gates near the site of the Olympieion, the procession would thread its way to the foot of the Acropolis.

A third and final process in the delivery of stone appears as a separate item of expense whenever marble for the Parthenon was quarried and moved to Athens. Comparison of this item in Years 9, 10, 11, and 12 shows that the full text read λιθολκίας πρὸς τὰ ἐργαστέρια, "for haulage of stone to the workshops," and this wording is plainly to be restored among the expenses of the first year.[114] The word λιθολκία, which occurs in this form only in the Parthenon accounts, is evidently used to describe a difficult and laborious operation that has confronted all who would build on the Athenian Acropolis from earliest antiquity to the present day, that is, the task of moving building stone from the lowest slopes to the top of the great rock. In this task, the builders of the Parthenon benefited greatly from their predecessors who had built the archaic temples in the sixth century and started the Older Parthenon in the 480s. In the middle of the fifth century, the western approach to the Acropolis was by way of a broad sloping ramp that extended straight westward from the front of the Old Propylon for a distance of at least 84 meters and had a width of about 12 meters as it ascended beside the Nike bastion. The ramp is supported by retaining walls of archaic polygonal masonry, and it had been constructed in the second quarter of the sixth century, undoubtedly for the purpose of hauling up the poros blocks for the first monumental stone temple of Athena Polias.[115] The process described as λιθολκία probably refers to the method of rolling the stone wagons up the slope of this ramp with their marble loads intact. The teams of mules would be released from the arriving wagon at the bottom of the slope and harnessed again to another wagon at the top. The two wagons were then connected by a heavy cable that passed through an enormous pulley anchored at the head of the ramp. As the mule teams dragged the upper wagon downward, the loaded wagon slowly ascended; and the process was subject to fine adjustment because the upper wagon could be hauled down empty, or it could be loaded with marble waste from the stone yards to provide just the necessary

---

[113] *IG* II² 1673, lines 64–89 = Clinton, *ArchEph* (1971) 86–87 and commentary on 102–107; for the driver who hired three more teams the second day, Clinton, line 70; cf. the payments to drivers and muleteers, lines 18, 20, 90. We hear also of special horse troughs placed at intervals along the road to water the teams, line 21. Note that the transport of column drums took place in Metageitnion (August–September), the driest time of the year, line 64.

[114] *IG* I³ 436, line 25 (Year 1); 444, line 272 (Year 9); 445, line 309 (Year 10); 446, line 336 (Year 11); 447, line 359 (Year 12).

[115] Portions of the northward-facing retaining wall are still visible, oriented almost exactly on the central axis of the Mnesiklean Propylaia: Travlos, *PDA*, 482, figs. 608, 614; E. Vanderpool, in Bradeen and McGregor, eds., Φόρος, 157–159, fig. 1; I. M. Shear, *JHS* 119 (1999) 105–107.

counterweight.[116] In this way, at their journey's end the marble blocks of the Parthenon would roll up the slope of the archaic ramp to the stone yards and workshops above, there to be maneuvered on sleds and rollers, and made ready for the masons to dress.

Regrettably, our understanding of the construction of the Parthenon cannot be greatly enhanced by the building accounts; for, as chance would have it, the lists of expenses for the principal years of construction have perished without trace, and we have no detailed information until the last year before the dedication. Enough survives, however, of the account of 446/5 to suggest that the overseers made heavy expenditures in the second year. They had received from their predecessors a surplus of more than 200,000 drachmas, in addition to two separate contributions from the treasurers of Athena, and yet at the conclusion of their term there was no balance to carry forward except the electrum staters of Lampsakos and Kyzikos. It is possible to make a very rough and conservative estimate of the funds spent in this year, for a column of seven figures from the expense account has been preserved.[117] A reconstruction of six of these figures yields a sum in excess of 63 talents (378,670 drachmas) for the year's work, and the amount may have been much larger, since in five of the six lines the lowest possible figure has been restored. Although the items describing the nature of these expenditures have perished entirely from the right side of the account, we may conjecture that the first three preserved figures (*IG* I³ 437, lines 52–54) refer to quarrying and transportation of stone, as in the account of Year 1. Line 52 evidently contained a very large amount, since a minimum restoration yields the reading [Ꜳ℞ΜΜ]ΜΜ[– – (190,000). The next figure was considerably smaller [ΜΜ℞ΧΧ]ΧΧ[– – (29,000), while the third was smaller still, too small in fact to offer any plausible restoration. These three figures arranged in descending order are reminiscent of the first three expenses of the preceding year (*IG* I³ 436, lines 23–25), and they may likewise record payments for the quarrymen at Pentele, for the transportation of stone, and for hauling the blocks up to the workshops on the Acropolis. The four remaining figures are all of considerable size, ranging from about 3 to 11 talents. These no doubt covered various operations in the construction of the foundations and laying the blocks of the crepidoma; it is also possible that this year saw the first payments to sculptors for work on the temple's sculptured metopes. But unfortunately we cannot safely assign any of these operations to the preserved figures in the second year's account.

Despite the loss of the actual lists of expenses from the building accounts, the space that these occupied on the stele can be calculated with some accuracy. Now, if the years of most varied and abundant building activities may reasonably be supposed to have produced the longest expense accounts, then the heaviest construction came between 444/3 and 442/1. The expenses for the fourth year (444/3) covered twenty-four lines on the stele; those of the fifth and sixth years about twenty-six lines each. During the first three years of construction, however, the expenses were only about half this length: ten lines in the first year, at least ten and not more than twelve lines in the second, and probably about fourteen lines in the third. The last three years just before the dedication also

---

[116] The procedure is described in exact detail by Heron, *Mech. Frag.* 3.9 (Nix and Schmidt, vol. 2, pt. 1, 220–221), preserved only in the Arabic translation. For translation of the Arabic text, Drachmann, *Mechanical Technology*, 106–107. Heron describes the process as a means of controlling the downward momentum of a block to be brought down a mountainside, but the method would obviously work just as effectively in reverse; so Korres, *Pentelicon*, 48–49, 107. Cf. the square socket "suitable for anchoring a tackle for hauling materials up the incline" that was identified by Stevens, *Hesperia* 5 (1936) 449, note 1. Since this socket is located on the axis of the central passage of the Propylaia, it is too far north to have functioned with the archaic ramp. The width of the ramp, ca. 10–12 m, allows plenty of space for two wagons to pass each other. The paved quarry road on Mount Pentelikon varies in width from 2.60 m to 3.30 m, and that was sufficient for the wooden sledges to descend; see Orlandos, Ὑλικὰ δομῆς, 91, note 1.

[117] *IG* I³ 437, lines 52–58. Not more than two lines of figures are missing from the expenses, for there is a lacuna of only six lines between the bottom of fragment S (receipts Year 2) and the top of fragments N + W (expenses Year 2). Three of these lines almost certainly contained the receipt of the *aparchai* from the hellenotamiai, and one was the heading line of the expenses, thus leaving only two possible additions to the expenses.

showed much shorter accounts, the expenses of the ninth year covering not much more than sixteen lines, while those of the seventh and eighth years were shorter still, probably not much more than fourteen or fifteen lines each. We have already seen that the first year was devoted solely to the quarrying and transportation of marble. The second and third years doubtless saw work on the substructure of the temple and the cutting of countless blocks for its superstructure. But if the length of the overseers' accounts is any indication, the bulk of the superstructure was actually erected during the fourth, fifth, and sixth years. Of all the activity of these three years, we have only the single mutilated notice, in the sixth account, of work on the columns and on some kind of wooden construction.

The expense account of the ninth year (439/8), on the other hand, is almost completely preserved, and it yields some interesting information about the final ornamental detail of the temple. The account will have been closed about midsummer of 438, only a few weeks before the dedication of the temple at the Great Panathenaia of that year. Thus it is not surprising to find no record of major architectural work; the marble quarried in this year and carried to the Acropolis was almost certainly intended for the pedimental figures, the carving of which had not as yet commenced.[118] The stonemasons, however, were still at work, as an entry for their wages shows; but by now they were probably employed exclusively for the smoothing and polishing of the floor and wall surfaces, for removing the rough lifting bosses from the masonry, and especially for the channeling of columns. It is evident that a second item was combined with the wages for stonework (line 273), and the text should probably be restored to read: λιθοργ[ί]ας καὶ [ῥαβδόσεος τõν κιόνον], "for stonework and fluting of the columns." The very detailed accounts of the Erechtheion for 408/7 show that fluting the columns was a long and slow process. This would almost certainly have extended into the last year of construction.[119]

The most interesting expenditures of this year were those for the decorative details of the building. The overseers recorded the purchase of ivory, the wages for goldsmiths, and a payment for silver ornament, together with a statement that possibly recorded the weight of silver used in this decoration.[120] Probably the most elaborate piece of work that yet remained for the gilders and metalsmiths was the ornamentation of the great doors leading into the cella and the western chamber of the building. These doors were very likely hung during the previous year, for a mutilated entry in the eighth account refers to the great doorways (τοῖς θυρόμασι) in which the doors themselves would have been installed;[121] but undoubtedly much of the final decoration in gold and ivory would have been applied after the doors were in place. The extant cuttings for the door pivots of the western door and the circular arcs of wear still visible on the marble pavement indicate that each doorway of the Parthenon was closed by two great valves, built of heavy wooden frames and undoubtedly clad with bronze paneling. Traces for the valves of the western door, which are still measurable, show that the wooden frames were 0.31 m thick and were further strengthened with ten vertical rods of bronze within the thickness of the door. Each of the valves opened inward, swinging through a half circle with the aid of small metal wheels that helped them pivot smoothly despite their great weight.[122]

---

[118] *IG* I³ 444, lines 270–272.

[119] The Erechtheion accounts show that fluting the six columns of the east porch continued through at least four prytanies of the year: *IG* I³ 476, lines 72–103, 192–248, 304–327.

[120] *IG* I³ 444, lines 266–267, 274–276. It should be noted that the overseers had to purchase the ivory, so that they had evidently not yet received the surplus materials from the overseers of the statue at the time this purchase was made. The silver bullion, however, was apparently on hand, and they simply recorded the amount that they used. No mention was made of the gold bullion for the gilders, and yet the sale of surplus gold was recorded in the following year (*IG* I³ 445, lines 296–297). Perhaps the surplus from the statue was turned over to the Parthenon later in this same year and appeared among the missing receipts of the ninth account. If so, no mention of the gold would be expected in the list of expenses.

[121] *IG* I³ 443, line 228.

[122] For the details of the evidence and likely reconstruction of the doors, see G. P. Stevens, *Hesperia* Suppl. 3 (1940) 74–77 and fig. 58; Orlandos, *Παρθ.*, 332–339 (east door), 425–430 (west door), and especially fig. 230. That the doors

We can reconstruct the general appearance of these valves on the basis of the marble doors that have occasionally survived in Macedonian tombs of the Hellenistic period.[123] Thus a broad vertical stile will have masked the point of contact where the valves swung together at the center, while a series of horizontal rails will have articulated the surface of the valves themselves, dividing each of them into large panels. In the Hellenistic examples, the panels of each valve were normally two in number, the upper one being smaller than the lower. The stiles and rails of such doors were regularly decorated with a row of studs or bosses in imitation of the nails that served a functional purpose on wooden doors. In addition, ornamental medallions of bronze or precious metal frequently adorned the centers of the panels.[124]

In the case of the Parthenon, there is evidence that the doors received an unusually rich embellishment. We learn a few details of this decoration because during the fourth century some pieces of the goldwork became detached from the doors and were kept with the other treasures in the cella, where they were regularly catalogued by the treasurers of Athena. Thus our picture of the richly decorated doors has to be drawn from the bits of ornamental detail that the treasurers reported as missing. The inventory for 341/0 and a better-preserved text of the late fourth century have left a detailed report on the condition of the eastern doors.

IG II[2] 1457, lines 9–20:

αἱ θύραι αἱ ἐν τῶι Ἑκατομπέδωι τῶνδε δέοντ[αι μ]-
[ὴ ἐ]ντε[λ]εῖς [ε]ἶ͂ναι· περὶ τὴν τοῦ λέοντος κεφαλὴν ἐλλείπε[ι τῶ]-
[ν φύλ]λων ἑνός, περὶ δὲ τὴν τοῦ κριοῦ προτομὴν φύλλων ἐλλ[είπ]-
[ει] τῶν ἐλ[α]ττόνων · Γ :, περὶ δὲ τὴν τοῦ γορ[γ]ονέου ἐλλείπε[ι το]-
[ῦ κ]υματ[ί]ο[υ] ὅσ[ον] ἐπὶ ὀκτὼ δακτύλους· οἱ ἧλοι οἱ ἐν τοῖς κ[ατωτ]-
ά[τω] ζυγοῖ[ς τ]ῶν θυρῶν δέονται κωδυῶν : ΙΙΙ :, ἐμ μὲν τῶι [· ΙΙ · ἐ]-
[ν δ]ὲ τῶι : Ι : αὗταί εἰσιν παρὰ τοῖς ταμίαις ἐν τῆι παρα[δόσει·]
ἀ[πὸ] τοῦ πρώτου ἥλου τῆς δεξιᾶς θύρας τοῦ χρυσίου [ἀ]πο[πέπτω]
[κε μῆκ]ος οἷον ἐπὶ δέκα δακτύλους, πλάτος δακ[τύλους] ἔ[νδεκἄ,]
κάτ[ω]θ[εν] ἐπὶ δύο δακτύλους· ἡ δεξιὰ παραστὰς [......12......]
δεῖται : ΔΔΔΓΙΙΙ :, ἡ ἀριστερὰ παραστὰς πο[μφολύγων δεῖτα]-
ι : ΔΔΔΔΙΙΙΙ : ἐν τῶι Ἑκατομπέδωι.

The doors of the Hekatompedon are lacking these parts and are not complete: Around the lion's head one of the leaves is missing, and around the ram's head 5 of the smaller leaves are missing. Around the gorgon's head a strip of the molding is missing as much as eight daktyls long. The large bosses on the lowest rails of the doors are lacking 3 poppy heads, 2 on one side and 1 on the other. These are in the custody of the treasurers in the transfer. Starting from the first large boss of the right door, some gold has fallen off for a length of ten daktyls, a width of eleven daktyls, and two daktyls from below. The right doorjamb lacks 48 [– – – – –], the left door-jamb lacks 44 small bosses. In the Hekatompedon.[125]

---

were regarded as a very special operation is indicated by three tiny fragments of an inscription that seems to be a separate expense account of the doors, *IG* I[3] 461, and Lewis's commentary.

[123] See especially the tomb at Langada, T. Macridy, *JdI* 26 (1911) 193–215 and pl. 6; and the tombs at Vergina: K. A. Rhomaios, Ὁ Μακεδόνικος τάφος τῆς Βεργίνας (Athens 1951) 25, figs. 9, 10, and pl. I; M. Andronicos, *Vergina* (Athens 1984) 31–35, 76, 101, 106, 198–199.

[124] Macridy, *JdI* 26 (1911) 202–205.

[125] The date of the inventory is after 316/5, but substantially the same text, although much less well preserved, appears as early as 341/0, *IG* II[2] 1455, lines 36–49; for the dates, D. Harris, *The Treasures of the Parthenon and Erechtheion* (Oxford 1995) 56.

This inventory of the treasurers vividly illustrates the richness of ornament that adorned the great eastern doors. The stiles and rails (ζυγά) of the paneling were studded with large gilded nail heads or bosses (ἧλοι), some of which were fashioned into elaborate floral ornaments of poppy heads (κωδύα) surrounded by a cluster of foliage.[126] Among extant Greek architectural ornaments, the lavish rosettes mounted in the ceiling coffers from the interior ambulatory of the Tholos at Epidauros can perhaps best convey the effect of these gilded poppies from the Parthenon. Not only the bosses, but the stiles and rails themselves seem to have been covered with gold plates. The piece that was missing from the right door, starting at the first large boss, measured 0.19 × 0.21 m, and it bent around the bottom edge of the rail for nearly 0.02 m. Further decoration was applied, probably to the steps of the panels, in the form of a molding with the profile of egg-and-dart or leaf-and-tongue (κυμάτιον), of which a strip eight daktyls (0.15 m) long was missing from one panel.[127] Perhaps the most prominent part of the decorative scheme was the series of animal protomes, of which the treasurers mentioned the lion's head, the ram's head, and the gorgoneion. These seem to have been encircled with some variety of foliate ornament that consisted of at least two sizes of leaves, since the five "smaller leaves" missing from the ram's head are carefully distinguished from the single leaf that had been lost from the lion's head. In the case of the gorgoneion, however, it was not any of the leaves but a strip of molding from the surrounding panel that the treasurers catalogued. From this we may conclude that the animal protomes were mounted as the central ornaments of the panels, probably a different type in each of the four panels of the door. Of course, the treasurers described only the three that happened to be defective, and their use of the definite article in each case makes it obvious that every protome was of a different type, without duplication.[128] Finally, the jambs (παραστάδες) on either side of the valves were also decorated, probably with bosses and rosettes, giving a general appearance similar to the northern doorway of the Erechtheion.[129] Although we must form our impression of the doors only from the negative evidence of the missing parts, the magnificence of the originals emerges clearly from the treasurers' inventory. The bronze of their paneling polished to a brilliant sheen, their gilded ornament etched and chased with masterly precision, and punctuated here and there with the soft luster of ivory, they will have been rare specimens of the goldsmith's art and fully commensurate with the splendid temple whose entrance they were to guard.

That the goldsmiths were employed in 439/8 primarily to complete the embellishment of the doors can hardly be doubted. This task will also account for much of the silver trim and ivory that appear among the expenses of that year. Still another group of craftsmen was likewise engaged on the final details of the woodwork.[130] The major woodwork of a Greek temple was, of course, in the coffered ceilings of the interior and in the beams and rafters of the roof. But the woodwork of 439/8 can have nothing to do with this, since the roof of the building must have been completed a year or more earlier. We are concerned here with detail, not with extensive construction; nevertheless, the carpenters seem to have left traces of their work which can still be detected in the blocks of the Parthenon. These traces consist of a series of cuttings, which are best preserved in the opisthodomos,

---

[126] This we learn from the fact that three of the poppy heads and at least one of the leaves had broken off; cf. *IG* II² 1414, line 4; 1425, lines 41–42. For κωδύα, see Theophrastos, *Hist. pl.* 9.12.4; Damocrates apud Galen 13.40. These ornaments were far more elaborate than the simple bosses described by Macridy, *JdI* 26 (1911) 204 and fig. 16.

[127] Orlandos, *Παρθ.*, 333–334. For the molding described in inscriptions as κυμάτιον, see Paton, *Erechtheum*, 366; Shoe, *Greek Mouldings*, 8.

[128] For similar bronze medallions of a lion's head and gorgoneion, cf. the fittings for the marble doors from Langada, Macridy, *JdI* 26 (1911) 205, fig. 17, 207, fig. 19, 210, fig. 23. Those from the Parthenon were clearly far more elaborate.

[129] The variety of small bosses called πομφόλυγες in the Erechtheion accounts (*IG* I³ 475, line 259) provides the most likely restoration for *IG* II² 1457, line 19, and probably describes the ornaments missing from the left doorjamb. These ornaments are not thought of as decorating the marble trim of the doorjambs themselves, but rather bronze-clad pilasters framing the valves within the marble jambs. Cf. Stevens, *Hesperia* Suppl. 3 (1940) 77; Orlandos, *Παρθ.*, 336, fig. 230, where no such decoration is shown.

[130] *IG* I³ 444, line 269.

on opposite sides of every column. At the foot of the shaft, the fluting on each side has been cut back to receive the ends of marble sills which originally occupied all fourteen bays between the columns and antae of both pronaos and opisthodomos. Aligned with the cuttings for the sills are three dowel holes, spaced at intervals running up the height of the column, and shallow rectangular cuttings at the necking of the column capitals. Similar rectangular cuttings have also been identified in two surviving fragments of the marble sills. This series of cuttings unmistakably held in place the jambs and lintels of wooden grilles that enclosed the temple at either end.[131] Now, it was no small piece of carpentry to build the fourteen grilles, six of which had to be fitted with swinging gates to permit entry into the building; and yet the installation of these grilles must have been one of the very last operations before the completion of the temple. The flow of workmen, materials, and equipment through the great doors of the cella must have come entirely to a halt; the colossal cult statue must already have been in place; the final dressing of the marble floors and walls, the last channeling of the columns in the pronaos and opisthodomos must have been finished before the carpenters could erect the wooden grilles in the intercolumniations. On the other hand, the grilles were almost certainly installed before the dedication of the temple in 438. There is, in any event, no record of woodwork in the completely preserved expense accounts for the years just after 438; and the pronaos was already in use as a treasury, and thus necessarily enclosed by the grilles, in 434/3, when the treasurers began their series of sacred inventories.[132] We can, then , with some confidence identify the wooden grilles of the pronaos and opisthodomos with the record of woodwork in the ninth account, for 439/8.

A perceptible change sets apart the records of the last five years from those of the first ten. The simplified phrases of the annual prescripts reflect the diminishing administrative organization. One suspects that most of the work of the overseers devolved upon Antikles, the permanent secretary, who alone is mentioned by name in the final accounts of the Parthenon. This in itself suggests the slackening pace of the work after the building's dedication. We have already seen that the overseers' receipts were gradually reduced to nothing, while the major funds of the sacred treasury were diverted in these years to the Propylaia. Along with the money went also the workmen—the masons and quarrymen, carters and carpenters—who for a decade had found work with the overseers of the Parthenon and now hired out their services to the builders of the Propylaia. It is no coincidence that the new building commenced just a year after the dedication of the Parthenon, when the overseers had laid off their men in large numbers.

That the Parthenon was drawing to completion is made explicit, however, in the expense accounts of the last years, four of which have chanced to survive almost entirely. What strikes us at once is the brevity and uniformity of the preserved accounts. The items of expenditure, their arrangement, and the forms of their expression are virtually identical in the three years from 438/7 to 436/5.[133] The same was probably true of 435/4, but this account is largely missing. Furthermore, it is apparent that the expenses for these years arose from but one piece of work, the creation of the sculpture for the two pediments. All the marble quarried in these years and carted from Pentele to the Acropolis is specifically designated as λίθος τὸς ἐς τὰ ἐναιέτια, "stone for the pedimental statuary."[134] Also in every year from 438/7 to 434/3 were recorded the salaries paid to the sculptors of the

---

[131] The evidence for the wooden grilles has been collected by Stevens, *Hesperia* Suppl. 3 (1940) 69–73, and restored drawings, 70, fig. 56; Orlandos, Παρθ., 318–327. The lintels of the grilles were doweled into the cuttings in the necking of the capitals. The part of the grilles projecting above the lintels fitted into smaller cuttings in the echinus. For the marble sills with similar cuttings for the wooden jambs, see Stevens, *Hesperia* 11 (1942) 354–364. The overseers of the Erechtheion in 409/8 paid for the installation of similar wooden grilles in the western colonnade, *IG* I³ 475, lines 256–258. That they were of wood emerges from the fact that they were installed by a carpenter, *IG* I³ 475, line 250.

[132] For the inventories of the treasures in the pronaos, see *IG* I³ 292–316; Harris, *Treasures,* 64–80.

[133] *IG* I³ 445–447, Years 10, 11, 12.

[134] *IG* I³ 445, lines 305, 307; 446, lines 332, 334; 447, line 358.

pedimental figures, ἀγαλματοποιοῖς ἐναιετίον μισθός.[135] Clearly, the decoration of the pediments was the one task that remained to be finished after the dedication of the building. This goes far to explain the apparently odd fact that the Parthenon was not finally completed for a full six years after the temple was formally opened. The work on the sculpture will have been slower and more painstaking than the construction of the building itself, and it progressed only as fast as the sculptors could carve the stone. With regard to the chronology of these famous sculptures, the inscriptions offer unequivocal evidence. First, it must be emphasized that in 439/8 there were no sculptors of any description on the payroll of the Parthenon overseers. But for five years thereafter the overseers employed sculptors explicitly to carve the pedimental statuary. The necessary conclusion is that no sculptors worked on the Parthenon in 439/8 because all the other sculptural adornment of the temple, including the ninety-two metopes and the entire length of the Ionic frieze, must have been completed before the summer of 439, and no work on the pedimental sculptures can have started before midsummer of 438. Any chronological scheme that proposes to date portions of the frieze later than the east pediment, solely on the basis of a subtle appreciation of sculptural style, must therefore be abandoned.[136]

In general, the quarrying and handling of marble for the sculpture seems to have been closely analogous to the cutting of stone for the architecture. But the accounts reveal a few interesting variations in procedure. The payments to the quarrymen seem to have been described during the first nine years with the simple formula λιθοτόμοις Πεντελῆθεν, but in the tenth and eleventh accounts the same item reads: λιθοτόμοις Πεντελῆθεν καὶ πελεκητέσι τὸν λίθον τὸν ἐς τὰ ἐναιέτια.[137] The word πελεκητής signifies one who hews or cuts, and this designation suggests that their task was to trim down the rough masses of marble as they came out of the mountain. These artisans took their name from the tool with which they chiefly worked, the pointed stone hammer used to produce the characteristic rough dressing that was applied to all blocks before shipment to the building site. But the question arises why the πελεκηταί are here distinguished from the regular quarrymen (λιθοτόμοι) for the first time when their work was necessarily performed from the time when the first marble was extracted from the quarry. The blocks cut for architectural construction had only to be trimmed into rough rectangles of specified dimensions or rounded off for column drums and capitals, and this elementary bit of stonecutting was, we may safely suppose, entrusted to the quarrymen themselves. In the case of the sculptural marbles, however, the preliminary trimming was not so simple. The blocks had originally to be of immense size and of irregular shapes in order to make possible the carving of the huge pedimental figures, larger than life and of great projection in their animated poses. But often half or two-thirds of the block would be cut away and left for waste in the initial stages of the carving. Obviously much labor and expense could be saved if the sculpture was roughly blocked out at the quarry. This called for a hand far more skilled and experienced than the ordinary quarryman's, and it called for an artist who knew the intended design of the statue. The πελεκηταί of the Parthenon inscription were probably men of this sort, assistant sculptors and apprentices, who journeyed out to Pentele from the sculptors' studios to trim off the excess stone and block out the sculptures

[135] IG I³ 445, line 310; 446, line 338; 447, line 360; 449, lines 401–402.
[136] E.g., the chronology of B. Schweitzer, JdI 53 (1938) 29, 41, and JdI 55 (1940) 238–241, where he argues that the eastern and western friezes are contemporary with the east pediment, while the northern and southern friezes are later and contemporary with the west pediment. Cf. Koch, Theseustempel, 145; M. I. Wienke, AJA 67 (1963) 219. On the date of the frieze, see F. Brommer, Der Parthenonfries (Mainz 1977) 171–172. What the epigraphical evidence certainly precludes is the position adopted by I. Jenkins, The Parthenon Frieze (London 1994) 19–20: "The carving could have been done in time for the dedication ceremony of 438 B.C., but it could equally have been carried out after the main building was finished.... Assuming that it was begun after 438 B.C., the frieze was probably completed by 432 B.C." Harrison, YCS 30 (1996) 39, allows the same possibility.
[137] IG I³ 445, lines 304–305; 446, lines 331–332. Comparison of the two passages yields the complete text of the entry.

before their long, slow trek to the Acropolis.[138] These craftsmen did not figure in the earlier years of the accounts because the nature of the work did not demand their presence. They were concerned only with facilitating the handling of the colossal statues that were to be carved in the round for the pediments. The sculptors had previously worked only on the reliefs for the metopes and frieze, and these relatively smaller and simpler slabs will have been trimmed by the quarrymen and shipped to the workshops like any other architectural block.[139]

One further detail of the expense accounts calls for notice. This is the curious and, one had thought, inordinately frequent record of payments to road builders just in these final years. We found good reason to suspect the employment of these road builders in the very first years of construction, but it is difficult at first to imagine why it suddenly became necessary to employ them each year from 438/7 to 436/5, when most of the marble for the Parthenon had long since been carried down the slipway beside the Spelia Quarry and the building was virtually complete. Stranger still is the fact that in 437/6 the overseers of the Propylaia hired their own crew of road builders to enable them to move their marbles from the quarries by a different route.[140] As many as twenty ancient quarries are known on the ridges of Mount Pentelikon, and the Periklean builders were evidently using more than one at this time for their supply of stone. It is important to remember, however, that the marble quarried in these years for the Parthenon was intended for sculpture, not for architecture, and in all likelihood the sculptors were far more particular than the architects about the stones they carved. They will have demanded for the pediments marbles of the very highest quality, pure of color, fine of grain, without flaw or blemish; and they doubtless searched the gullies and crevices of the trackless mountain for just those outcroppings which promised to yield the finest stone, without thought or care for the difficulties of transporting it to the plain below. We should not hesitate to suppose that the overseers were now forced to open up new quarries only to extract a block or two before moving on to another spot that appeared to offer still better stone.

THE OVERSEERS OF THE GOLDEN STATUE

The surviving records that pertain to Pheidias's gold and ivory statue of Athena could hardly present a more conspicuous contrast when set beside the accounts of the building in which the statue stood, or for that matter beside any other building accounts of the fifth century. The annual statements of the overseers were published on a series of narrow marble stelai, measuring only 0.284 m in width, of which the upper parts of three have come down to us. Each of these inscriptions has a cutting for a double-T clamp in its top surface; thus they were plainly intended to be displayed side by side and set as revetment against a low wall or parapet. One of them, preserved in two pieces, carried the reports of two years' work, and it is just possible that all three inscriptions originally bore two of the annual accounts. Three other shattered fragments evidently refer to the statue, although their texts are too

[138] For preliminary carving of statuary in the quarries, see C. Blümel, *Griechische Bildhauerarbeit* (Berlin 1927) 48–51, nos. 1–5; Blümel, *Greek Sculptors at Work* (London 1969) 14–18; J. Wiseman, *AJA* 72 (1968) 75–76; R. Carpenter, *AJA* 72 (1968) 279–280; Korres, *Pentelicon,* 88–89.

[139] Evidently, in the Periklean period the term πελέκησις was not applied to the preliminary trimming of architectural blocks. Nowhere in the accounts of the Parthenon and Propylaia can reference to this process be restored in a context where it would apply to ordinary building blocks. Salaries were paid only to λιθοτόμοι, and the inference is that they did both the quarrying and the trimming. The only mention of πελεκηταί (*IG* I³ 445, lines 304–305; 446, lines 331–332) refers specifically to sculptural marbles. In the fourth century and Hellenistic period, the term was applied to any stone fresh from the quarry. Cf. the specifications for blocks at Eleusis, *IG* II² 1666, lines 30, 32: λίθους τεμε͂ν Π[ε]ν[τελη ικους εἰς μετόπια . . .] καὶ ἐκπελεκῆ[σαι ὀρθ]ὸ[ς πανταχεῖ], "cut blocks of Pentelic marble for metopes . . . and trim them true on all sides."

[140] Road builders for the Parthenon, *IG* I³ 445, line 306; 446, line 333; 447, line 357; for the Propylaia, Year 1, *IG* I³ 462, line 49.

mutilated to allow restoration; but the wording that has survived seems to call for longer lines and thus wider stelai than the three better-preserved examples. Unique among the records of Athenian buildings is another stele, larger than the others and inscribed in the most beautiful lettering of any fifth-century inscription. This document appears to be a general summary of total receipts and expenditures which the overseers prepared upon completion of their work on the statue.[141]

The chronology of the inscriptions relative to each other is difficult to establish since they are not numbered in series, like the accounts of the Parthenon and Propylaia. The large stele with the general summary is presumably to be dated in 438, the year of the dedication. For the dating of the other accounts, the only information at our disposal is the personnel of the board of treasurers of Athena, and, most importantly, the names of their secretaries in several years. It has long been recognized that in the period from 443/2 to 429/8 the secretaries of the treasurers were appointed according to a cycle that rotated among the ten tribes in the reverse of their official order. From the accounts of the Parthenon, we learn that one of these ten-year cycles ended in 434/3, when Krates of Lamptrai was secretary, representing the tribe Erechtheis (I). Accordingly, five years earlier, in 439/8, the secretary came from Lakiadai, a deme of the tribe Oineis (VI). On this principle, Demostratos of Xypete from the tribe Kekropis (VII) has been placed one year earlier, in 440/39; and since he is known to us from one of the accounts of the statue, the inscription bearing his name is to be dated to that year.[142] Another account of the statue pertains to a year when the secretary of the treasurers came from Aphidna in the tribe Aiantis (IX), and so this document must be dated in 442/1, two years before Demostratos.[143] One of the smallest fragments appears to preserve the name Exekestos, a man who is known from Year 2 of the Parthenon to have been secretary of the treasurers in 446/5; this would then stand earliest in the sequence of inscriptions concerning the statue.[144] One other account preserves the name of the secretary Deinias of Philaidai, and since this deme belonged to the tribe Aigeis (II), the inscription should be dated before the beginning of the reverse cycle of secretaries, and thus in 445/4 or, more likely, 444/3.[145]

Not only in the epigraphy but also in the content of the documents do the accounts of the golden statue differ from the accounts of the Parthenon. On the three narrow stelai the text is set out in a single column to the right, and the figures for receipts and expenditures are inscribed along the left margin of the stone. The annually rotating boards of overseers are identified only by the names of their secretaries and dated by citation of the secretary for the first prytany of the boulē. The other elected epistatai for each year, however, are not named individually, as they were in the first ten accounts of the Parthenon and in those of the Propylaia. Among the three extant documents, two different formulas are preserved: ἐπὶ Ἀρρε[νεί]δο [γρ]αμματεύον[τ]ο[ς ἐπ]ιστάτεσι ἀ[γάλμα]τος χρυσõ, "In the secretaryship of Arreneides to the overseers of the golden statue" (*IG* I³ 457, lines 2–5); and Κιχέσιππος ἐγρ[α]μμάτευε ἀγάλ[μ]ατος ἐπιστάτε(σ)ι Μυρρινόσιος, "Kichesippos of Myrrhinous was secretary to the overseers of the statue" (*IG* I³ 458, lines 1–4). Although these two secretaries are the only epistatai known to us by name, they provide sufficient evidence to demonstrate that the

---

[141] The narrow stelai, *IG* I³ 455, 457, 458 (with the accounts of two years); Donnay, *BCH* 91 (1967) 50–86, nos. 1, 3–5. Small mutilated fragments, *IG* I³ 453, 454, 456. Stele with the final summary account, *IG* I³ 460; Donnay, no. 6. For recent accounts of the statue, see G. Nik, in Hoepfner, ed., *Kult und Kultbauten*, 22–26; B. Schmaltz, in *Kult und Kultbauten*, 25–30. For discussion of the statue itself, see Davison, *Pheidias*, 69–140.

[142] For the reverse rotation of the secretaries to the treasurers of Athena, Meritt, *AFD*, 26–29; Dinsmoor, *HSCP* Suppl. 1 (1940) 157–182. Krates of Lamptrai, *IG* I³ 449, lines 387–388 (Parthenon, Year 14); 465, line 122 (Propylaia, Year 4); 317, lines 2–3. The secretary from Lakiadai, *IG* I³ 444, line 246 (Parthenon, Year 9). Demostratos of Xypete, *IG* I³ 458, lines 6–8.

[143] *IG* I³ 457, lines 10–11, names the secretary Φιλο[...⁶...Ἀφιδν]αῖο[ς].

[144] *IG* I³ 453, line 1. Exekestos of Athmone (Kekropis VII) is named as secretary of the treasurers for 446/5, *IG* I³ 437, lines 45–46, 48–49 (Parthenon, Year 2).

[145] *IG* I³ 455, lines 8–9; Donnay, *BCH* 91 (1967) 56–61, no. 1.

overseers of the statue formed a different board, separate and distinct from those of the Parthenon, as argued in chapter 2.[146] One of the narrow stelai (*IG* I³ 458) is securely dated to 440/39 by the reverse rotation of the secretaries of the treasurers. The overseers of that year are identified by their secretary Kichesippos, who came from the deme Myrrhinous. In that same year, the eighth board of overseers of the Parthenon held office. On the Parthenon stele, the prescript for the eighth account preserves just enough at the left edge of the stone to be certain that the secretary of the overseers came from the deme Probalinthos.[147] Accordingly, the epistatai for the two projects must necessarily have been composed of different personnel, since the boards are identified by different secretaries.

In each account, after the secretary of the overseers there follows a statement of the receipts from the treasurers of Athena, and then the bulk of the extant text consists of a complete list of the treasurers for that year together with their secretary. In 444/3, the treasurers were ten in number, one chosen from each tribe, and after the secretary their names are listed, along with their fathers and demes, in the correct order of the tribes. The board of 442/1 consisted of eight members and a secretary whose names and demotics were inscribed, apparently in random order, while the seven treasurers of 440/39 are identified only by their own names, except for their secretary, whose deme is also inscribed.[148] One gains the impression that the documents show extraordinary deference to the sacred treasurers, who figure far more prominently than the overseers responsible for transacting the business and publishing the accounts. The overseers of the Parthenon and the Propylaia simply entered the treasurers' annual appropriation among their other receipts, but the accounts published by the overseers of the statue make it obvious that they received funds from no other source except the sacred treasury. The treasurers of Athena bore the entire cost of the chryselephantine statue. Moreover, their prominence in the inscriptions suggests that they may have exercised much closer control over the administration of the statue than they did over the Acropolis buildings.

Several other peculiar features in the accounts of the golden statue are worth noting. The total annual payment to the overseers from the sacred treasury is preserved for four years, and the figures show enormous variation: 34 T. 2,858 dr. 2 ob. (444/3), 26 T. (442/1), 100 T. (440/39), and 160 T. (undated fragment from an earlier year). Items of expenditure are also preserved in part for four years, but the only disbursements that have survived are payments for the purchase of gold and ivory. Although it may simply be due to the chance of preservation, our inscriptions record no outlays for miscellaneous purchases, for wages of sculptors and craftsmen, nor for administrative expenses, all of which are regular components both of the contemporary building accounts and of the accounts for Pheidias's earlier colossal statue, the bronze Athena. The text for one year (440/39) appears to be completely preserved, and the only expenses listed are purchases of gold and ivory. In that year the overseers spent a total of 89 T. 5,395 dr. 5 ob. on the two precious materials, but since they received 100 talents from the sacred treasury, the amount of 10 T. 604 dr. 1 ob. remains unaccounted for in the overseers' report.[149] Moreover, there is no indication that they had an unexpended balance to hand down to their successors at the end of their term of office, another regular occurrence in each year of the building accounts. In 444/3, when the sacred treasury paid out to the overseers a total of 34 T. 2,858 dr. 2 ob., they recorded the cost of gold as 34 T. 1,800 dr.;[150] thus only the small sum of 1,058 dr. 2 ob. remained to be accounted for in the missing lines of the inscription. In this connection, it is instructive to recall that the accounts for Pheidias's bronze Athena recorded administrative expenses alone for one year as a considerably higher amount, 1,963 dr. 2 ob., which covered only

[146] See pp. 24–26 above.
[147] *IG* I³ 443, line 203 (Parthenon, Year 8).
[148] *IG* I³ 455, lines 8–22 (444/3); 457, lines 9–20 (442/1); 458, lines 5–13 (440/39).
[149] *IG* I³ 458, lines 15–22.
[150] *IG* I³ 455, lines 27–29. The figure requires restoration, and that proposed by Donnay, *BCH* 91 (1967) 61, seems almost certain: ΔΔΔΤΤΤΤ[Χ⊢]ΗΗ[Η]. On the ratio of gold to silver, see pp. 73–74 below.

salaries for the epistatai, the secretary, and the assistant.[151] While the contemporary accounts of the Parthenon and the Propylaia, and most especially the later accounts of the Erechtheion, represent genuine examples of official bookkeeping, in which the overseers were concerned to record every obol that passed through their hands, the documents published by the overseers of the golden statue seem more like statements for display, as if their purpose was to memorialize the funds spent by the sacred treasury on precious materials in a given year.

The peculiarities of the documents are perhaps best explained by the extraordinary character of the statue itself, for the colossal cult image was not merely a pious expression of Athenian megalomania. The golden robe and helmet and shield of Athena were the repositories of a very considerable amount of treasure. The *Atthis* of Philochoros specifically mentions the dedication of the statue in the archonship of Theodoros (438/7): καὶ τὸ ἄγαλμα τὸ χρυσοῦν τῆς Ἀθηνᾶς ἐστάθη εἰς τὸν νεὼν τὸν μέγαν, ἔχον χρυσίου σταθμὸν ταλάντων μδ', Περικλέους ἐπιστατοῦντος, Φειδίου δὲ ποιήσαντος, "and the golden statue of Athena was set up in the great temple, having 44 talents' weight of gold; Perikles was epistates and Pheidias the maker."[152] Gold bullion weighing 44 talents had a monetary value of 616 talents in Attic silver (3,696,000 drachmas). This is a sum considerably larger than all the uncoined gold and silver in all the public and private dedications on the Acropolis in 431, which Thucydides (2.13.4) evaluated at 500 talents; it is also more than a year's income from the entire empire, which the historian (2.13.3) estimated at 600 talents. In addition to the cost of the gold, the overseers had large expenditures for ivory, wood, and other materials, as well as wages for the sculptors and other craftsmen, and monthly salaries for the administrative personnel. Even if their annual statements did not include these costs, the final summary report showed a total expenditure that was considerably in excess of 700 talents but certainly less than 1,000 talents, which made the chryselephantine statue very likely the most costly single project of the building program.[153]

Among the surviving accounts, the purchase of gold is preserved in three years. The overseers recorded the transaction in the formula: χρυσίον ἐονέθε σταθμόν – – – – – – – τιμὲ τούτο – – – – – –, "gold was purchased, weight – – – – –, price of this – – – – – –." The weight of the gold is stated in the description, and its value in Attic silver currency is recorded as an expenditure in the left column. In 440/39 the overseers paid 87 T. 4,652 dr. 5 ob. for gold weighing 6 T. 1,618 dr. 1 ob. The ratio of gold to silver was as close to 14:1 as Greek numerical notation could achieve.[154] The account for 444/3 preserves only part of the amount in silver paid for the gold; but the most likely restoration of the figure, 34 T. 1,800 dr., is a precise multiple of 14 and would have purchased gold weighing 2 T. 2,700 dr.[155] Moreover, in both years the overseers managed to acquire the gold from a single source. Ten years later, in 434/3, the overseers of the Parthenon needed to raise cash by selling a small amount of surplus gold. On that occasion they received 1,372 dr. in silver currency for gold weighing 98 dr.; once again, the price was reckoned at a ratio of precisely 14:1.[156] Now, sources of

---

[151] Cf. *IG* I³ 435, lines 81–82, and chap. 2, p. 20 above.

[152] Philochoros, *FGrH* 328 F 121, with the necessary emendation of the archon's name to Θεοδώρου (438/7) from Πυθοδώρου (432/1) of the MSS; the passage quoted by schol. Aristoph. *Peace* 605 (Holwerda). Thucydides 2.13.5 gives the weight of the gold as 40 talents, which is probably a rounding of the number; cf. Gomme, *HCT*, vol. 2, 25. Ephoros, quoted by Diod. 12.40.3, rounded off the figure in the other direction, to 50 talents.

[153] *IG* I³ 460, lines 4–5, appear to give the total amount received by the overseers from the sacred treasury. The stone preserves ⋔ΗΗ[...⁸....]ͰΔΔ and thus more than 700 and less than 1,000 talents. Dinsmoor, *ArchEph* (1937) pt. 2, 507–511, restored ⋔ΗΗ[ΗΔΔΔΔΓΤΤ]ͰΔΔ (847 T. 520+ dr.), which is admittedly the mean between the two epigraphically possible extremes and thus quite arbitrary. Gomme, *HCT*, vol. 2, 25, favored the lowest possible figure, ⋔ΗΗ[ΔΔΔΔΤΤΤΤ]ͰΔΔ (744 T. 520+ dr.), which is no less arbitrary. Cf. also Donnay, *BCH* 91 (1967) 73–74; ML 54, pp. 148–149.

[154] *IG* I³ 458, lines 15–18. The actual arithmetic ratio is 13.99996:1.

[155] See Donnay, *BCH* 91 (1967) 61, and note 156 below.

[156] *IG* I³ 449, lines 389–391 (Year 14). Restoration of the figure for the weight of the gold, ͰΔΔΔ[ΔΓͰͰ] (98 dr.), is due to Dinsmoor, *AJA* 17 (1913) 74–75.

gold bullion were notoriously few in the Greek world, and their product was relatively small. The-opompos described the difficulties encountered by Hieron of Syracuse in his search for enough gold to dedicate a tripod and Nike at Delphi in the years after the Persian Wars. According to Herodotos, the island of Thasos derived a rich annual income of 80 talents from the gold mines at Skaptesyle, but 80 talents was the monetary yield of just over 6 talents' weight of bullion. The overseers of the statue bought more gold than that in the single year of 440/39.[157] It has been acutely observed that Athens's attempt to buy 44 talents' weight of bullion within the space of eight years on the open market should have driven the price of gold to vastly inflated levels, but the law of supply and de-mand plainly did not exert its inescapable logic upon these transactions on the Acropolis. The most likely explanation is that the overseers recorded a controlled official price that governed the transfer of precious metal from one department of the Athenian treasury to another, and they did not quote the market price of new bullion purchased from a private dealer.[158] A possible indication that such transfers took place comes from a tantalizing entry in the final summary account. This appears to record an unused amount of gold left over from a dedication by a certain Kallaischros which had been melted for bullion.[159] In this case, the treasurers of Athena would have handed the gold vessel, if such it was, to the overseers of the statue for consignment to the melting pot, and the overseers duly entered its monetary value as a debit against their annual appropriation.

The huge amount of gold needed to create the colossal cult statue came almost inevitably from a variety of sources. Clear evidence of this is found in the account of 439/8, where the overseers listed the acquisition of precious metal in two different lots, one consisting of uncoined gold bullion, and the other of more than 110 Lydian staters of Kroisos.[160] This record of a relatively small group of antique gold coins, originally struck in the mid-sixth century, is a vivid reminder that one of the most plentiful sources of the metal was the currency of those states that minted gold and electrum coinage. There can be no doubt that a very considerable supply of this foreign coinage had accumu-lated on the Acropolis by the 440s. We have already seen that small groups of electrum staters of Lampsakos and Kyzikos were in the possession of the Parthenon overseers throughout the period. These coins and many more like them had originally been received on the Acropolis in payment of tribute, as we learn from a postscript appended to the first tribute quota list. Here the hellenotamiai of 454/3 summarized the total *aparchai* from the tribute of that year in Attic silver talents and in electrum staters of Kyzikos. Although the number of Kyzikene staters is only partly preserved, a likely restoration is 66, which represents the *aparchai* on 3,960 staters, or a little under 16 T. in Attic silver.[161] There is no way of knowing whether this was the normal amount of tribute remitted in elec-trum because none of the later quota lists have similar summaries. But if 454/3 was a typical year, it is readily apparent that, during the thirty-year period between the beginning of the Delian League and the beginning of work on the gold and ivory statue, electrum staters will have been paid into the confederate treasury in substantial quantities. The 3,960 Kyzikene staters restored as the payment in

---

[157] On the sources of gold, see R. J. Forbes, *Studies in Ancient Technology*, vol. 8 (Leiden 1971) 167; on its scarcity in antiquity, Athenaeus 6.231B, 231E–232B, quoting Theopompos, *FGrH* 115 F 191, on Hieron of Syracuse. On income from gold mines at Thasos, Hdt. 6.46.7.

[158] On the gold for the statue, see S. K. Eddy, *AJA* 81 (1977) 107–111; on the gold-silver ratio, W. E. Thompson, *NC* 24 (1964) 103–123. D. M. Lewis, in C. M. Kraay and G. K. Jenkins, eds., *Essays in Greek Coinage, Presented to Stanley Robinson* (Oxford 1968) 105–110, has argued that the market price of gold at Athens fluctuated between 13.51:1 and 16.66:1 during the period from 434 to 420, as indicated by the prices paid for gold crowns dedicated in the Parthenon. The exchange rate was 13.3:1 in the bimetallic monetary system used throughout the Persian Empire: E. S. G. Robinson, *NC* 18 (1958) 191. By the first half of the fourth century, the ratio had decreased to 12:1: Plato, *Hipparchos* 231D.

[159] *IG* I³ 460, lines 6–9, and cf. the suggested restorations of Dinsmoor, *ArchEph* (1937) pt. 2, 507–511.

[160] *IG* I³ 458, lines 24–33; cf. Donnay, *BCH* 91 (1967) 84–85, for an attempt to calculate the missing figures for the weight of the bullion and the number of staters, and to restore the silver ratio.

[161] *IG* I³ 259, lines 10–13 = *ATL* II, list 1, and, on the restoration of 66 staters, *ATL* III, 266–267, with notes 6, 8; cf. Meritt, *Hesperia* 41 (1972) 416. The minimum that can be restored is 56 staters *aparchai* (tribute of 3,360 staters). The maxi-mum is 96 staters *aparchai* (tribute of 5,760 staters). On the exchange rate for Kyzikene staters, see p. 52, note 58 above.

454/3 would have yielded refined pure gold weighing 1 T. 715 dr.;[162] thus, if payments in electrum remained anywhere near constant from 454/3 to 439/8, refined gold weighing 16⅔ T., more than one-third of the total amount needed for the statue, could have been derived from monies paid into the treasury as tribute in the normal course of events.[163]

That many, if not most, of the electrum staters paid as tribute went to fashion the golden robe and arms of Athena is also suggested by other considerations. Despite the certain evidence that the treasurers most probably received the coins in payment every year, there is no evidence at all either for their use as currency to defray the expenses of the sacred treasury, or for their collection as treasure to be stored for safekeeping on the Acropolis. The records of military expenditures, from the Samian War in 440 through the early years of the Archidamian War, show payments to Athenian armed forces exclusively in Attic silver.[164] Similarly, from 433/2 to 423/2 the sacred treasuries made loans to the Athenian state totaling more than 5,599⅔ talents, of which every payment was in Attic silver.[165] At the same time, the evidence is equally unequivocal that no large hoards of electrum were kept in the sacred treasury. In 434/3, the treasurers began to compile their annual inventories of the precious objects stored in the Parthenon, and among the long lists of golden crowns and sacred vessels there is no mention of coined money.[166] In the same year, the first financial decree of Kallias refers to a large capital payment to Athena of 3,000 talents νομίσματος hεμεδαπō, "of native coin," that is, Attic silver, which was evidently deposited in the reserve fund. Thucydides was just as explicit when he described the same capital reserve a few years later as consisting of 6,000 talents ἀργυρίου ἐπισήμου, "of coined silver."[167] To all appearances, the electrum staters of the Hellespontine cities have disappeared from the records of the sacred treasury, but the most likely eventuality is that they were transformed by Pheidias's art and added their golden luster to the great statue, which, according to Thucydides' specific statement, was composed entirely of "refined" gold.[168]

The preserved accounts of the golden statue show the acquisition of precious metal in three years, 444/3, 440/39, and 439/8; but the total weight of the bullion recorded in these years was a little under 11 talents, and so not quite 25% of the 44 talents' weight that Philochoros reported.[169] This means that the overseers acquired three-quarters of the gold for the statue in years for which the accounts have been lost, and no doubt the largest amounts were acquired in the first two years at

---

[162] A Kyzikene electrum stater weighs ±16.00 grams and contains 46.3% gold, and thus 7.41 grams of gold: Eddy, *ANSMN* 16 (1970) 14: 3,960 × 7.41 = 29,344 grams of pure gold. The weight of an Attic drachma is ±4.37 grams: P. Gardner, *A History of Ancient Coinage* (Oxford 1918) 224. The weight of one talent is ±4.37 × 6,000 = 26,220 grams. 29,344 grams − 26,220 = 3,124 grams ÷ ±4.37 grams = 715 drachmas. Therefore, 3,960 Kyzikene staters yield 1 T. 715 dr. of refined gold.

[163] Some payments that were probably made in electrum staters can be recognized among the partial and irregular amounts remitted occasionally by cities of the Hellespontine district. Although the payments are shown on the tribute quota lists in Attic drachmas, the figures are exactly divisible by 24, the most likely exchange rate for Kyzikene and Lampsakene staters; see p. 52, note 58 above. E.g., Kyzikos: *ATL* II, list 8, I, line 95; list 25, III, line 45. Tenedos: list 5, V, line 15; list 8, I, lines 5, 102, II, lines 108–109; list 14, II, line 24; list 15, II, line 27. Dardanos: list 5, III, line 33; list 7, IV, line 17; list 8, I, line 99. Alopokonessos: list 5, V, line 14. Lampsakos: list 7, IV, line 3; list 8, II, line 59. See S. K. Eddy, *AJP* 94 (1973) 47–70, especially 50–54. Meiggs, *AE*, 442–443, also analyzed the partial payments, but using an exchange rate of 27 drachmas = 1 stater, he produced fewer satisfactory results.

[164] Samian War, *IG* I³ 363, line 19; Korkyra, *IG* I³ 364, lines 12, 33; Macedonia and Poteidaia, *IG* I³ 365, lines 17, 19, 21, 23, 25, 27; Archidamian War (431/0), *IG* I³ 366, line 9. See the discussion of Eddy, *AJA* 81 (1977) 110–111.

[165] *IG* I³ 369, passim, and the total loans for the eleven-year period, line 122.

[166] For the treasurers' inventories of the Parthenon, see *IG* I³ 292–362; Harris, *Treasures,* 64–200.

[167] The amount of 3,000 T. deposited on the Acropolis, *IG* I³ 52A, lines 3–4 = ML 58. In 431, 6,000 T. remained in the reserve fund out of a total of 9,700 T. of coined silver: Thuc. 2.13.3.

[168] Thuc. 2.13.5: ἀπέφαινε δ' ἔχον τὸ ἄγαλμα τεσσαράκοντα τάλαντα σταθμὸν χρυσίου ἀπέφθου καὶ περιαιρετὸν εἶναι ἅπαν, "He pointed out that the statue had forty talents' weight of refined gold, and all of it was removable."

[169] *IG* I³ 455, lines 25–28: 2 T. 2,700 dr. weight of gold (see Donnay, *BCH* 91 [1967] 61); *IG* I³ 458, lines 15–17: 6 T. 1,618 dr. 1 ob.; lines 24–32: ca. 2 T. 1,339 dr. (see Donnay, 84–86).

the beginning of the project. In these complex financial transactions involving large sums of money and elaborate transfers of gold coin and other objects from the sacred treasury, the overseers of the statue were confronted with a very real problem of security. Unlike the Pentelic marble blocks of the Parthenon, their materials were of high intrinsic value and easily portable; and, unlike the overseers of the Parthenon, who probably paid out only a few drachmas at a time to any one man, they had, in the last analysis, to turn over the huge stores of precious metal to Pheidias and his personal assistants. Moreover, all of the gold had to be subjected to the tricky technical process of refinement at the hands of expert goldsmiths. In all these operations, the opportunities for graft were legion, and one cannot be wholly unsympathetic with the anxiety that may have vexed the assembly.

There are several bits of evidence that are perhaps best construed as precautionary measures in the direction of greater security. We have already observed the extraordinary prominence accorded to the treasurers of Athena in documents published by the overseers of the statue. This should possibly be recognized as a deliberate effort to demonstrate to an apprehensive assembly that the purchases of gold and ivory would be conducted with the utmost security and subjected to close scrutiny by the highest financial officers of the state. Indeed, it seems highly likely that concerns about security also dictated the reorganization of administrative arrangements for the projects on the Acropolis. As we saw in chapter 2, early plans for the new temple had called for the creation of an administrative board entitled the "epistatai of the temple and the statue."[170] But no such officers were ever empaneled, and, in the event, authority was divided between two separate committees having charge, respectively, of the Parthenon and the cult statue. The concept that the gold of imperial tribute should be displayed in the goddess's robes and arms was the statue's most famous innovation. At the same time, it remained an important financial reserve of the Athenian treasury by virtue of the detachable pieces in which the drapery was fashioned.[171]

A concern for security certainly guided the decision that the overseers should prepare detailed documentation of the statue's component parts in a permanent catalogue. From the beginning, its most notorious feature had been those very removable plates which permitted the gold to be detached in small sections either for financial use in case of emergency or for verification of its weight in case of controversy. The exact weight in drachmas of each section was inscribed on a bronze stele which stood beside the completed statue in the "hundred-foot cella" of the Parthenon. This stele served as a control with which the weight of each section was compared whenever the treasurers of Athena inspected the statue, as happened on several occasions during the fourth century.[172] The same arrangement of removable plates was adopted for the golden statues of Nike, several of which were dedicated before 430, two others in 426/5, and several more later in the century;[173] the pro-

---

[170] See chap. 2, pp. 23–25 above.

[171] That the gold plates were removable is stated by Thuc. 2.13.5; Diod. 12.40.3, quoting Ephoros, *FGrH* 70 F 196. Plut. *Per.* 31.3 attributes the idea to Perikles himself, allegedly to protect his friend Pheidias from accusations of malfeasance. What Perikles most likely contributed was the innovative notion that the gold reserve of the Athenian treasury could be molded into a statue of the goddess and could be displayed as a great work of art in her new temple. Even during the most troubled years of the Peloponnesian War, this last reserve was left unviolated.

[172] The extant inventories of the fourth century attest the inspection of the statue at least five times: in 385/4 (*IG* II² 1407, lines 5–6), 377/6 (*IG* II² 1410, line 7), 344/3 (*IG* II² 1443, lines 10–11), 321/0 (*IG* II² 1468, lines 6–8 = *SEG* 38.136), and 304/3 (*SEG* 38.143). A decree of 365/4 also orders inspection of the statue, evidently after some kind of irregularities: *SEG* 14.47, lines 13–15; cf. D. M. Lewis, *BSA* 49 (1954) 39–49. Such inspections were clearly major undertakings, for the treasurers are instructed to cooperate with the architect (line 14) and the sculptors, in the plural (line 15). All references to inspections mention the bronze stele that served as a control and no doubt listed the various gold plates by weight, as in the case of the golden Nikai.

[173] The golden Nikai are first mentioned in 434/3, in the plural, *IG* I³ 52B, line 3. Two more are described ca. 430/29 in *IG* I³ 467; another pair in 426/5, *IG* I³ 468; and several are referred to in the last decade of the century, *IG* I³ 469–471. See A. W. Woodward, *ArchEph* (1937) pt. 1, 159–170; D. B. Thompson, *Hesperia* 13 (1944) 173–209; W. E. Thompson, *AJP* 86 (1965) 170–173, *NC* 10 (1970) 1–6.

cedure for these statues was doubtless modeled on Pheidias's gold and ivory statue of Athena. In the case of the golden Nikai, parts of the inscriptions describing the statues are preserved, and they illustrate the format of the bronze stele describing the cult statue of the Parthenon. The inscriptions regularly refer to the Nikai by the name of the maker, list the weight of each section, and give the total combined weight of all the component parts.[174] The stele of 426/5 dates the dedication of the two statues by the eponymous archon and the first secretary of the boulē and then names all members of the board of treasurers responsible for the dedication.[175] Much the same information will have appeared on the bronze stele beside the gold and ivory statue. That inscription stood in place until the Roman period, when Plutarch (*Per.* 13.14) saw it in the Parthenon and cited it as proof that Pheidias had made the statue. The stele also undoubtedly provided Philochoros with the date for its dedication in the archonship of Theodoros (438/7) and with the total weight for the gold of 44 talents. It was possibly something in the wording of the text that made Philochoros identify Perikles as epistates of the statue, and that caused Plutarch to attribute the idea of the removable plates to Perikles' invention (*Per.* 31.3).

A more fundamental problem of security was the physical safety of the precious metals once they had been deposited in the sculptors' workshops on the Acropolis. The already large amounts of gold bullion would assume astronomical proportions in the popular imagination, and to the less law-abiding elements of Athens, it would pose an irresistible temptation to scramble up the Acropolis in the dead of night and make off with a few bars of gold. The assembly will have been quickly advised of the danger, and a partially extant decree may well record the action it voted to take.

IG I³ 45:

    [. . .]πε[. . . . .¹⁰. . . . .]
    [τ]ὲν πόλιν [.] ΑΟ [. . .]
    οἰκο[δ]ομῆσαι : hόπ[ο]-
    [ς] ἄν : δραπέτες μὲ ἐ[σ]-
    [ί]ει : μεδὲ λοποδύτ[ε]-
    [ς] : ταῦτα δὲ χσυνγρά-
    φσαι μὲν Καλλικρά-
    [τ]ε : hόπος ἄριστα κα-
    (ὶ) εὐτελέστατα σκε-
    υάσαι : ἀπομισθῶσα-
    [ι] δὲ τὸ[ς] πολετὰς hό-
    [π]ος ἄν : ἐντὸς heχσέ-
    [κ]οντα : ἐμερῶν : ἐπισκ-
    [ε]υασθῆι : φύλακας δὲ
    ἔναι τρῆς μὲν τοχσό-
    [τ]ας : ἐκ τῆς φυλῆς τῆς
    [π]ρυτανευόσες.
       vacat

---

[174] The Nikai referred to by maker, *IG* I³ 467, lines 3–4: hὲ Νίκε hὲν Δεινοκρ[άτες ἐπ]οίεσεν, "the Nike which Deinokrates made." Cf. *IG* I³ 469, lines 22, 29, 33. Total weight of the gold in the statue, *IG* I³ 467, lines 2–3; 469, lines 26, 33, 36; 470, lines 5, 10.

[175] *IG* I³ 468, lines 2–5: Megakleides of Leukonoe, first secretary of the boulē; lines 5–6: archon Euthynos (426/5); lines 7–15: names of the treasurers of Athena; lines 16–30: the detachable parts of the statue and the weight of each section in drachmas.

> ... [The fortifications?] are to be built on the Acropolis so that neither a runaway slave nor a thief can gain entrance. Kallikrates is to prepare the specifications for these so as to construct them as well and as economically as possible, and the poletai are to let the contracts so that they may be repaired within sixty days. There are also to be three guards, bowmen, drawn from the tribe in prytany.[176]

Although we have only the closing lines of the decree, and the critical phrases are missing, it seems possible to reconstruct the situation. The assembly has become concerned that thieves or runaway slaves might be able to get into the Acropolis, and it has decided to repair the walls and post sentries. Time is plainly of the essence, and the poletai are ordered to let the contracts so as to get the job finished in two months. Kallikrates was the logical man to design the structure, since he was already working on the Acropolis, as one of the architects of the Parthenon, and in these same years he had experience with fortifications when he was building the middle Long Wall.[177] The evidence suggests the recent arrival on the Acropolis of some articles of great value that could nevertheless be carried off with comparative ease and required the presence of soldiers to guard them. We may with good reason suppose that this decree followed very shortly upon the transfer to the sculptors' workshops of the first large quantity of gold bullion for the statue of Athena in 446/5.

It may still be possible to identify with some degree of plausibility that section of the Acropolis fortifications which was repaired by order of this decree. The rock of the Acropolis is extremely precipitous on all sides except the west, where the Propylaia stand, and, in any case, the north and south walls had been reconstructed in the second quarter of the fifth century to a height sufficient to preclude access from these directions.[178] On the west, the refurbished structure of the Old Propylon was still in use until the 440s and, as long as it stood, would be closed and barred at night; but the Nike bastion and the old Mycenaean wall just south of the Propylon might yield access to a determined marauder. Now, it happens that the corner of the southwest wing of the later Mnesiklean Propylaia was beveled off at an angle to fit against the face of the Mycenaean wall. For a height of 4.85 m above the floor of the Propylaia, the bevel was roughly cut to join as closely as possible with the irregular Cyclopean masonry of the prehistoric wall. From this point, 4.85 m above the floor, upward to at least as high as the cornice, the bevel is cut smooth as if it abutted a well-dressed ashlar wall; and it is apparent from the eastward projection of the bevel that this upper section of the wall was set 0.25 m back from the west face of the Mycenaean wall.[179] What has been chiseled into the blocks of the Propylaia is the negative impression of a wall that was standing on the site when the southwest wing was built. The lower part of this existing wall was composed of the irregular stonework of the old Mycenaean fortification, but the upper part had the smooth face of fine classical masonry. This raised section was a repair added to the Mycenaean wall; it increased the height of the old wall at least 5 m, and it extended about 18 m from the Old Propylon to the southwest corner of the Acropolis. As a small repair, it could easily have been completed in the sixty days specified in the decree (*IG* I³ 45), and yet it would have rendered impossible any access to the Acropolis from the terrace of the Nike bastion.

---

[176] The commentary of Dittenberger, *SIG*³ 62, is still useful. Cf. P. Graindor, *RA* 19 (1924) 174–178. The lettering of the inscription, which has the four-bar sigma throughout but still retains the sloping nu, would favor a date ca. 445. Characteristically, Mattingly, *BCH* 92 (1968) 469, prefers a date between 434 and 431 and argues that the decree concerns preparations for war. But the text is plainly concerned with individual malefactors, not enemy invasion, and the three bowmen are night watchmen, not a military garrison.

[177] Plut. *Per.* 13.7 and cf. Plato, *Gorg.* 455E. See p. 56 and note 81 above for the dates of construction.

[178] See chap. 9, Fig. 90 below.

[179] See Stevens, *Hesperia* 15 (1946) 78–79; and cf. Stevens, *Hesperia* 5 (1936) 468. There is no evidence to support his attribution of this repair to the "Kimonian" period. All we know of its date is the fixed terminus ante quem of 437, when the Propylaia were begun.

The foregoing discussion has sought to explore the activities of the people who were most closely involved in the construction of the Parthenon and the gold and ivory statue. They represented a broad spectrum of Greek society—Athenian, foreigner, and metic alike—and the work that they contributed to the project ranged just as widely. They were quarrymen and stonemasons, teamsters and carpenters, sculptors and goldsmiths, architects and overseers, a disparate group of people from all walks of life; but what they shared in common was the astonishing level of technical expertise that each man brought to his appointed task. When we come to consider the product of their labors in the next chapter, what will emerge most strikingly is the extraordinary brilliance not only of the temple's conception, but equally of its design and execution. The medium through which we learn about the builders of the Parthenon is an unsatisfactory one, for the records kept by the overseers have come down to us in fragments so shattered that they are now unintelligible at many points. Taken together, however, the accounts of the Parthenon and the golden statue reveal an aspect that is quintessential to democratic Athens. The city set out to build a great marble temple and a colossal golden cult statue in precisely the same way as it governed a far-flung empire. Ultimate responsibility for the construction of the Parthenon rested with upward of a hundred ordinary Athenian citizens, elected by the demos to serve as overseers, who rotated in boards of four to seven men throughout the fifteen years that the building was under construction. It may well be that Perikles' conceptions fired their imaginations, but it is to these anonymous Athenians that we owe the most profound expression of Greek religious architecture.

4

The Parthenon

We set aside the records of the overseers' bookkeeping and confront the temple that they built. However informative the accounts of the overseers may be, however important for our knowledge of the building's chronology, its finances, and the procedures of construction, it will be obvious from even the most cursory reading of the texts that they leave us with no visual impression of the building whatever. In fact, we would not have the remotest idea of what kind of building the accounts describe had we not the Parthenon's indelible image in our mind's eye. The inscriptions convey nothing of the architecture, the design, or even the plan of the temple. For that, the building must be called upon to speak for itself. There is perhaps no other Greek building so familiar as the Parthenon. It illustrates every textbook on Western art; it leaps to mind as a paradigm of classical architecture, a canon of Doric style. But close examination reveals nothing typical about the Parthenon. Its architects achieved a revolution in the design of the Doric peripteral temple. In their hands the standard grammar of the Doric order itself was significantly altered, and we can detect echoes of their innovations in various of the contemporary temples of Periklean Athens.

THE TEMPLE'S DEBT TO THE OLDER PARTHENON

Various sources have preserved for us the names of its designers, the architects Kallikrates and Iktinos, and the sculptor Pheidias, who himself created the gold and ivory statue of Athena, as we have seen.[1] That the inspiration of these three men produced the Parthenon there can be no doubt; but if we tried to distinguish the hand of any one of them in some novel aspect of the design, or in any particular detail of plan or method or decoration, we should be forced to the conclusion that the personalities of the individual artists had blended together to form a style unique to their creation. And yet one senses the powerful genius of this remarkable triumvirate in the building's every line.

The designers were not, however, allowed to develop their plans with entirely free scope, for the sanctuary of Athena Polias on the Acropolis had developed certain architectural traditions in the design of temples that stretched back more than a century. The two archaic temples of Athena, which seem to have stood successively on the Dörpfeld Foundation, were remarkable among Doric buildings for the design of their interiors. Both temples had double cellas, the larger of which faced east, while the other, its plan subdivided into three compartments, opened toward the west. In this

---

[1] Plut. *Per.* 13.6–7 names all three men and is the only source to mention Kallikrates in connection with the Parthenon. Iktinos is named as architect of the Parthenon by Paus. 8.41.9; Vitruvius 7 praef. 12; Strabo 9.1.12 (p. 395), 16 (p. 396). Pheidias is mentioned as author of the gold and ivory statue by Aischin. 3 *Ktes.* 150; Plato, *Hp. mai.* 290B; Strabo 9.1.16 (p. 396); Plut. *Per.* 13.14, 31.2; Diog. Laert. 2.116; Pollux 7.92; schol. Aristoph. *Peace* 605α (Holwerda). For recent accounts of the temple: Camp, *Archaeology of Athens*, 74–82, 252; Hurwit, *Athenian Acropolis*, 106–154.

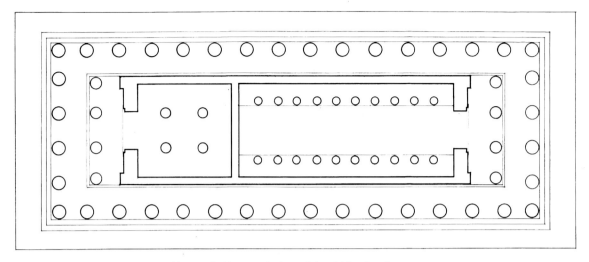

Figure 6. Restored plan of the Older Parthenon

unusual arrangement, the architecture undoubtedly conformed to some requirement of cult or ritual whose nature is unknown to us. Also unusual was the plan adopted for the interior porches of the pronaos and opisthodomos, for in both cases the foundations for the columns are set so close to the cella wall that the porches are best restored with four columns in prostyle arrangement rather than the normal distyle in antis of the Doric temple.[2] Both architectural features, the double cella and the prostyle porches, were borrowed from the archaic temples by the designers of the Older Parthenon, although in the latter building the western cella was planned as a simple square chamber without the tripartite subdivision of its predecessors (Fig. 6). The Periklean architects adhered to the traditions of the Acropolis sanctuary; fundamental to their design was the decision to maintain the two interior compartments planned for the earlier building. As in the Older Parthenon, the principal eastern cella would have more than twice the length of the western chamber, and both would have been approached through the prostyle porches of the pronaos and opisthodomos at either end of the building (Fig. 7).

The Periklean designers also adopted at once another fundamental decision to utilize in the new building as many as possible of the unfinished marble blocks that had been quarried for the Older Parthenon and had lain about the Acropolis for more than thirty years. Some of these blocks were damaged by the Persian fire and were built into the northern wall of the Acropolis.[3] Still others lie about today in the same unfinished state as they were in 447; but enough were available for reuse so that the Periklean building was indebted to its predecessor for some of its guiding dimensions, as well as the basic features of its plan. When the architects first surveyed the site in the early 440s, they will have found it useful to borrow much from the ruins of the earlier temple. Obviously, the new building must be set on the great podium erected as a foundation for its predecessor, and that decision alone determined in general its size and scale. When it came time to calculate the dimensions of the new temple, many were adopted from the corresponding parts of the older building. Most important for the overall proportions, the architects of the Parthenon borrowed the lower diameter of the exterior Doric columns. This dimension in the Periklean building varies from 1.905

[2] For the earlier archaic temple, whose fragmentary blocks are often referred to as the "H-architecture," see Wiegand, *Poros-Architectur*, 1–68; Plommer, *JHS* 80 (1960) 127–159; Bancroft, "Archaic Acropolis," 26–46. For the late archaic temple, see Wiegand, 155–148; H. Riemann, "Der peisistratische Athenatempel auf der Akropolis zu Athen," *MittdAI* 3 (1950) 7–39. For the prostyle porches, Judeich, *Topographie²*, 265; Dinsmoor, *AJA* 36 (1932) 316; Plommer, 130 and note 9.

[3] See A. Tschira, *JdI* 55 (1940) 242–261, who argues for a date after the Persian destruction. On the date of the Older Parthenon, see endnote 2, pp. 395–399 below.

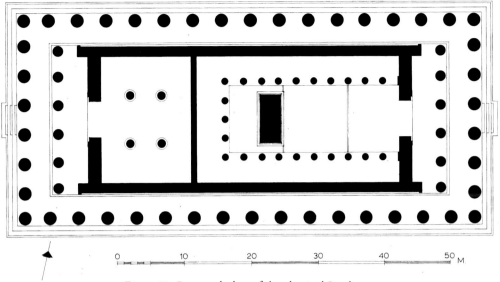

Figure 7. Restored plan of the classical Parthenon

to 1.920 m, measured between the arrises of the flutes. Fourteen bottom drums from the Older Parthenon are still extant in unfinished condition, most of them built into the north wall of the Acropolis. Although the arrises are badly chipped and spalled at their bottom edges, their diameters have been recorded as varying from 1.90 to 1.915 m. In addition, two stylobate blocks from the old temple bear scratched circular arcs to guide the mason in setting the lowest column drum, and they show that the intended finished diameter of the columns was 1.903 m.[4] This coincidence of dimensions reveals the clear intent of the builders to make use of as many of the drums as were in good enough condition to reuse. The surviving bottom drums of the Older Parthenon were all set in position on the platform of that temple, as indicated by the smooth polish of their resting surfaces. Since several drums of the second course were also set,[5] one infers that all forty bottom drums had been prepared before work was disrupted by the Persian War. In that case, the Periklean architects would have found twenty-six bottom drums of the old temple lying ready to hand, and since that is more than half of the forty-six required for the peristyle of the new temple, their reuse represented a substantial saving in labor, time, and expense. There are probably dozens of other column drums originally worked for the Older Parthenon and now reused as second-hand material in the outer peristyle of the Periklean temple, but there is no way of identifying them with certainty.

In similar fashion, the blocks originally cut for the lower step of the cella in the Older Parthenon are now seen to occupy that position in the present building. As is the case throughout the fabric of the Parthenon, the blocks of that course are joined to each other by double-T clamps; but wherever these are visible on the step of the cella, there are found to be two sets of cuttings, one of which served to clamp the blocks in their present positions, while the second has no matching cutting in the adjacent blocks and must therefore have been used when the block was set in a previous position in the Older Parthenon. The blocks that exhibit such disused clamp cuttings measure on average ±1.77 m, that is to say, they are six-foot blocks measured with a foot unit of 0.296 m, which was standard for the Older Parthenon but not for its Periklean successor. Moreover, ±1.77 m is the

---

[4] Variation in the lower diameter in the Periklean Parthenon, Orlandos, Παρθ., 148. For the fourteen bottom drums of the Older Parthenon, Tschira, *JdI* 55 (1940) 247. Details of all fifty-eight extant drums and fragments with dimensions are conveniently assembled in tabular form, Tschira, 245–246; cf. Orlandos, Παρθ., 77–84. The stylobate blocks with circular arcs, Hill, *AJA* 16 (1912) 540–541, 544, fig. 11; cf. Orlandos, Παρθ., 67–68.

[5] Column drums of the second course that were set in place are numbers 5, 14, and 25: Tschira (note 4 above).

average length of twenty out of twenty-nine blocks in the lower step on the northern side and of at least nine blocks on the southern side.[6]

The steps of the crepidoma and the stylobate of the peristyle were also of closely similar height in both buildings. From the earlier temple come several marble blocks of the middle step that were intended to have finished risers 0.521 m high, whereas on the present Parthenon the measurable height of the second marble step varies from 0.514 m to 0.519 m. The dimensions are close enough to suggest reuse of some earlier blocks, but if so, they were finished with a slightly wider tread in the Periklean building.[7] The unfinished stylobate blocks of the old building were intended to be 0.554 m high with their final dressing, and their visible dimensions on the pavement of the platform were ±1.50 m wide by 2.025 m deep. The existing stylobate varies in height from 0.550 m to 0.556 m, depending on the amount of wear, and many of its blocks are 1.50 m wide or slightly less.[8] Although some of the blocks may have been cut for the Older Parthenon, the arrangement of the colonnades differed in the two temples. The peristyle of the Older Parthenon was designed so that the columns were to be centered on every third block of the stylobate, but in the Periklean building the axis of the column conversely falls on every third joint.[9] Nevertheless, the close congruence of dimensions between the two buildings shows that surviving blocks of steps and stylobate and drums from the older columns were actually incorporated into the fabric of the new structure. It is obvious that one purpose that was served by this considerable reuse of old material was that of economy, for the most costly and time-consuming process in ancient construction was the quarrying and transportation of the stone, as we have seen. But it is possible that the reuse of material was also in part a programmatic decision. The great temple had been conceived and begun in the 480s as a thank-offering to Athena for the victory at Marathon. To be sure, work had been disrupted by the destruction of 480, but now was the time to resume the project as the most extravagant way to memorialize the multiple victories over the Persians that ensured the deliverance of Greece.

DESIGN OF THE PERISTYLE

Let us make no mistake, however. The Parthenon was indeed an extravagant building. It was extravagant in the money that it cost to build, in the skill and ingenuity of its architects and the precision that they demanded of the masons, and above all in the intricate mathematics of its proportions, in its richness of architectural ornament, in the magnificence of its sculptures. Even the building's most obvious feature, which we are inclined to take for granted, was unprecedented in the mid-fifth century. It was to be built entirely of Pentelic marble, a plan, to be sure, that had been projected for the Older Parthenon, but the fact remained nonetheless that on the Greek mainland no Doric peripteral temple had been made of marble throughout its fabric before the Periklean period.[10] In one other important respect, the Parthenon had no precedent: the architects plainly intended to build the largest Doric temple in Greece, and in fact its overall dimensions, 33.69 × 72.32 m

[6] See Hill, *AJA* 16 (1912) 549–551; Orlandos, Παρθ., 70–71.

[7] Middle step of the Older Parthenon: Hill, *AJA* 16 (1912) 540; Orlandos, Παρθ., 66–67. For the steps of the existing building, Orlandos, Παρθ., 111–113. Setting lines on a fragment from the earlier building show the finished width of the tread as 0.667 m on the ends and 0.679 m on the sides. The same step on the existing temple has a width of 0.702 m: Hill, 540; Orlandos, 66–67.

[8] Stylobate of the Older Parthenon: Hill, *AJA* 16 (1912) 544, fig. 11; Orlandos, Παρθ., 67. The dimensions on the existing building, Orlandos, Παρθ., 112–113, note 4.

[9] Hill, *AJA* 16 (1912) 549.

[10] In the latter part of the sixth century it was a matter of great note that the Athenian contractors for the Temple of Apollo at Delphi had erected one facade of Parian marble when the plans called for poros stone throughout: Hdt. 5.62.2–3.

measured on the lowest step,[11] were never surpassed among the Doric temples of mainland Greece. Here we may suspect that Iktinos and Kallikrates were responding to the goad of competition, that all-pervading leaven of life in Greece. In this case, just over ten years before the work began on the Acropolis, the new Temple of Zeus had been completed at Olympia and now formed a magnificent centerpiece for the Panhellenic sanctuary. At the time of its construction, that building, too, with dimensions of 30.20 × 66.64 m, surpassed in size all earlier temples in Greece.[12] But there was at work here more than the ordinary challenge that biggest was best and Athenians could out-build Peloponnesians, for the new temple at Olympia pricked Athenian pride with a special irritant. At the apex of its pediment stood a golden Nike, and below the statue a golden shield emblazoned with a gorgon's head, which the Spartans had given as a war tithe for military victory in the Battle of Tanagra. But the dedicatory inscription proclaimed to the whole Greek world that Athens and her allies had gone down to humiliating defeat at Spartan hands in that battle of 457.[13] Such was the message that greeted every visitor to one of the central shrines of Hellenism. Whether or not it was a specific charge to the architects in Athens that they should outstrip the Peloponnesian builders in the dimensions of their temple, the existing platform erected for the Older Parthenon would accommodate a building that exceeded the dimensions of the Temple of Zeus in both width and length. Although the abortive plan for the early temple had called for a broad esplanade on all four sides, the podium itself actually measured 31.39 × 76.816 m on the topmost course of the foundation.[14] That the Periklean architects possessed detailed knowledge of the Temple of Zeus and consciously vied to surpass it is also suggested by a curious detail that the two buildings share in common. We shall see that they were designed with completely different proportions both in plan and elevation, and in the details of their columnar orders, but the actual height of their Doric columns is precisely the same. The exterior columns in the peristyle of the Temple of Zeus measured 10.43 m to the top of the abacus, and the same dimension in the Parthenon is 10.433 m, a virtually identical measurement that can hardly have occurred by coincidence.[15]

Nowhere did the architects of the Parthenon display their ingenuity in design more clearly than in their treatment of the scale and proportions of the temple (Figs. 7, 8). Now, the long tradition of Doric design heavily favored a facade of six columns and coupled this with a flank peristyle which usually had about twice as many columns as the facade, or a few more. While the archaic architects tended to be somewhat free in their use of proportions, toward the middle of the fifth century, owing probably to the influence of the Temple of Zeus at Olympia,[16] there occurred a noticeable crystallization toward a canonical ratio which decreed that the flank colonnades of a Doric temple should contain one more than twice as many columns as the facades. The Older Parthenon would have deviated considerably from this norm because the requirements of the cults and rituals on the Athenian

---

[11] Unless otherwise documented, dimensions of the Periklean Parthenon are those that appear on the dimensioned drawings, Orlandos, Παρθ., pls. 94–98.

[12] Dimensions from *Olympia,* vol. 2, *Baudenkmäler,* pls. VIII, IX.

[13] Paus. 5.10.4 describes the Spartan dedication and quotes the text of the dedicatory inscription on the shield (ἐπὶ τῇ ἀσπίδι). Fragments of a marble stele written in Corinthian letters preserve part of the same text that Pausanias saw and may have stood beside the temple; see ML 36; Jeffery, *LSAG*[2], 132, no. 38; *Olympia,* vol. 5, *Inschriften,* no. 253. The dedication from Tanagra provides a terminus ante quem for completion of the temple.

[14] Orlandos, Παρθ., pl. 3.

[15] Dimensions in Dinsmoor, *AAG*[3], 338; cf. Dörpfeld, in *Olympia,* vol. 2, *Baudenkmäler,* 6; Orlandos, Παρθ., 148 and note 1.

[16] Dinsmoor, *AAG*[3], 151–153. The immediate influence of this temple is perhaps to be seen in the Temple of Poseidon at Isthmia (O. Broneer, *Isthmia* I, 101–103) and in the original plan for the Temple of Apollo at Delos (F. Courby, *Délos* XII, *Les temples d'Apollon,* 4–7). Both of these had peristyles of 6 × 13 columns and were closely contemporary with the temple at Olympia in the 460s. It is significant that prior to these buildings the only Doric temple on the Greek mainland with 6 × 13 columns was the Old Temple of Poseidon at Sounion; see Dinsmoor, *AAG*[3], 107.

Figure 8. The Parthenon, view from northwest

Acropolis demanded by exception an additional rear chamber behind the main cella, and entered from the opposite direction. As a result, the temple had been planned originally with a peristyle of six by sixteen columns, giving it excessively long and narrow proportions. But this plan, with its eastern cella and additional western chamber, was, as we have seen, one of the basic elements that the older building bequeathed to the Periklean Parthenon. Since the arrangement had a still longer history on the site, going back to both of the archaic temples of Athena, it was evidently a traditional feature in the religious architecture of the Acropolis. Thus the great length of the cella was a more or less fixed factor in the design, and the architects were not at liberty to reduce the length appreciably in order to make their plan conform to the increasing preference for more compact proportions that we have just noted.

It is at this point that we witness the architects' first major leap of originality in Doric design: their elegant resolution of the problem posed by the disproportionate length of the Older Parthenon. They resolved the difficulty by abandoning the hexastyle facade in favor of one with eight columns. In that way, they could bring the excessive length of the earlier building into perfect harmony with the width; for the existing foundations, with their great length of 76.816 m, would easily support a flank portico of seventeen columns, one more than twice the number on the front. That awkward dimension, which might have bound lesser architects to an old-fashioned and ungainly plan, became a stimulus to Iktinos and Kallikrates, and the result was a revolution. Their octostyle facade had no forbears in Greece and almost no precedent in Doric architecture.[17] It enormously enlarged the scale of the building, as well as its actual size, and its effect was to introduce a number of striking irregularities in the standard grammar of Doric design. Moreover, the decision to employ a facade of eight columns instead of six at once enabled the architects of the Parthenon to surpass the Temple of Zeus not only in the actual dimensions of the building's width and length, but more strikingly in the

[17] The only other Doric temples to employ an octostyle facade were the early archaic Temple of Artemis on the island of Korkyra (Dinsmoor, *AAG*³, 73–75; Gruben, *Gr. Tempel*⁵, 112–116) and the Temple of Apollo ("Temple GT") at Selinous in Sicily (Dinsmoor, *AAG*³, 99–101; Gruben, 310–314). There are no examples from mainland Greece. The octostyle facade was, however, a common feature of the colossal Ionic temples of East Greece and had been used at Ephesos (Gruben, 382–388), Samos (Gruben, 355–365), and Didyma (Gruben, 396–400) before the time of the Parthenon.

visual scale of the architecture (Fig. 8). The great length imposed by the double cella was evidently a required feature in the design of the temple, and the architects developed the eight-column front deliberately to harmonize the proportions of the facade to the flanks. Of this there is certain evidence in the construction of the foundations, for the platform of the Older Parthenon was widened by the addition of a strip of masonry measuring 3.956 m along its north side and visible at the northwest corner in four courses. The crepidoma of the Periklean temple is aligned with this new foundation on the north, and on the west end it is aligned with the westernmost edge of the old podium; but the east end of the crepidoma falls short of the platform by 4.258 m, and along the south side the Periklean steps are set back 1.656 m from the south edge of the podium.[18]

On the exterior of the temple the problem of its visual scale assumed critical importance. Here, in calculating the proportions of plan and elevation, the architects gave evidence of their mathematical subtlety. We have just seen that they developed the unusual octostyle facade in order to harmonize the width of the temple with its great length. It should not be surprising, then, that a desire to create the ideal proportions for a Doric temple guided the fundamental design of the Parthenon. Iktinos and Kallikrates did not, however, construct their plans from a basic measured unit, using the lower diameter of the columns or the interaxial spacing as a module that could be multiplied or divided to yield all the building's dimensions by simple arithmetic process. Such a clear and rational system had been perfected by Libon of Elis in his designs for the Temple of Zeus at Olympia.[19] But the architects of the Parthenon were not satisfied to derive their plans from the measurement of a single part. They felt more keenly that intangible balance in the interrelationship of part to part, and they based their design not upon a modular dimension but on a dominant mathematical ratio. Now, the critical factors in the design of a Doric peristyle are to determine the width and length of the stylobate so as to carry the desired number of columns on fronts and flanks, and to develop a proportional relation between width and length so that the axial intercolumniation can be uniform on all sides, except at the four corners. Early Greek architects had actually experienced some difficulty in determining such an appropriate proportional relation, and the fronts and flanks of early Doric temples often exhibit wide discrepancies in the spacing of the columns.[20] In order to determine the proportions of the stylobate, the architects of the Parthenon appear to have resorted to a surprisingly simple rule of thumb that had been developed by architects in Sicily and South Italy from the late sixth century onward. According to this formula, the width of the stylobate should be related to the length of the stylobate as the number of columns across the fronts is related to the number of columns along the flanks, plus one.[21] Since the desired number of columns was 8 × 17, application of the Sicilian rule would yield dimensions of the stylobate related to each other as 8:18. That this formula was actually used in the plan of the Parthenon emerges from calculation of the proportion of width to length in its simplest terms:[22] 69.503 ÷ 30.880 = 2.25074 × 8 = 18.006. Thus the width of the temple on the stylobate was related to its length almost exactly as 8:18 = 4:9 = 1:2.25.

[18] The widening of the old podium toward the north and the alignment of the Periklean building with the new construction appears clearly on the plans of Hill, *AJA* 16 (1912) pl. 9; Orlandos, Παρθ., pl. 3. For the four courses of added blocks visible at the northwest corner, see also the discussion in Orlandos, Παρθ., 51 and 47, fig. 30.

[19] See Dörpfeld, in *Olympia Ergebnisse,* text vol. 2, 19; Mallwitz, *Olympia,* 231–233.

[20] For detailed discussion of the problems in laying out the peristyle of a Doric temple, see J. J. Coulton, *BSA* 69 (1974) 61–86. Of the twenty-seven Doric temples listed in his table 1, before the Temple of Zeus at Olympia, sixteen show discrepancies of more than 0.05 m between the axial intercolumniation of the fronts and flanks, and six more have discrepancies of less than 0.05 m.

[21] This rule of thumb is the important observation of Coulton, *BSA* 69 (1974) 71–72; its application to the Parthenon, Coulton, 76.

[22] In the calculation, the actual length of the north stylobate is divided by the actual width of the east stylobate. There are slight differences on the west and south because the platform is not laid out as a perfect rectangle: 69.609 m (south), 30.961 m (west).

Architects working on the Greek mainland had developed another useful rule of thumb to express the relationship between width and length of the stylobate and the axial spacing of the columns. According to this rule, the width of the stylobate equaled the axial intercolumniation multiplied by the number of axial spacings across the front plus a fraction that allowed the correct amount of angle contraction required by the triglyph frieze above; thus the rule might be expressed by the formulas[23] $W = I (N_w + k)$ and $L = I (N_l + k)$. The fraction k was usually ⅓ or ¼ and occasionally ³⁄₁₀, but the smaller the fraction, the greater the effect of contraction at the corners. By the mid-fifth century, it seems clear that the dimensions of stylobates were often calculated in this way from a predetermined axial intercolumniation;[24] but the formula could, of course, be worked in reverse to calculate the appropriate intercolumniation from the length or breadth of the stylobate. Before we turn to analyzing the dimensions of the Parthenon in order to test the applicability of such formulas, it is necessary to distinguish between a theoretical dimension calculated by an architect and an actual, measurable dimension that resulted from the way in which the builders executed the design. The difference emerges starkly when we examine the axial spacing of the columns in the peristyle. The thirty-eight normal intercolumniations on the four sides of the colonnade vary in width from 4.266 m to 4.309 m, a total variation of 0.043 m; and the actual average intercolumniation on the fronts is 4.279 m, and on the flanks 4.2971 m. No single measurable intercolumniation, and neither of the averages, will yield precisely the measurable dimensions of the stylobate by means of the formulas set out above. This suggests that the architects used the formulas in reverse and derived a theoretical intercolumniation from the predetermined dimensions of the stylobate in their proportion 4:9. Moreover, since the Parthenon is notable for its excessive contraction at the corners, the formulas should be applied with a smaller fraction than normal.

The great length of the temple imposed by the double cella was, as we have seen, the traditional element in the architecture of the Acropolis. If, accordingly, we attempt to derive both the width of the stylobate and the axial intercolumniation from the length by the formula $I = L ÷ (N_l + ⅓)$ and $W = I (N_w + ⅓)$, there are some interesting results: $69.503 ÷ 16⅓ = 4.2903$ (theoretical intercolumniation), a figure that deviates from the actual average by 0.0068 m and is much smaller than the measurable variation in the axial spacing (0.043 m). Moreover, the theoretical intercolumniation thus derived is recognizably in the same proportion to the lower diameter of the columns as the length of the stylobate is to its width: $4.2903 ÷ 2.25 = 1.9068$. Although the lower diameter of the Doric columns actually varies from 1.905 m to 1.920 m, the theoretical proportion derived from the theoretical intercolumniation falls well within the actual range; thus $1.9068:4.2903 = 4:9 = 1:2.25$. The spacing of the columns, then, was designed to reflect the same proportion that informed the overall dimensions of the stylobate. Although the lower diameter of the columns came with the second-hand drums from the Older Parthenon, the interaxial spacing planned for the old temple (4.413 m fronts, 4.359 m flanks)[25] was deliberately narrowed to yield the ratio 4:9 for the relation between the lower diameter and intercolumniation of the new building. Now, according to the rule of thumb employed by contemporary architects working on the Greek mainland, it should

[23] The rule for calculating the stylobate size from the intercolumniation is discussed by Coulton, *BSA* 69 (1974) 74–75. The formulas are Coulton's (p. 63, note 20), with the following abbreviations: W = width of stylobate, L = length of stylobate, I = axial intercolumniation, N_w = number of intercolumniations on fronts, N_l = number of intercolumniations on flanks.

[24] The intercolumniation of the Temple of Zeus at Olympia, 16 Doric feet, seems to have resulted from deliberate choice, not from calculation. Cf., however, the Old Temple of Poseidon at Sounion: W = ca. 13.06, I_w = 2.449; 2.449 × 5⅓ = 13.061. The Temple of Nemesis at Rhamnous: W = 9.996, I_w = 1.904; 1.904 × 5¼ = 9.996. See Coulton, *BSA* 69 (1974) table 2, cols. 8–10.

[25] The axial intercolumniations of the Older Parthenon can be determined only approximately. The dimensions given above are those calculated by Dinsmoor, *AAG*³, 338. Hill, *AJA* 16 (1912) 548, calculated slightly wider column spacing: 4.53 m fronts, 4.40 m flanks.

Figure 9. East facade of the Parthenon from east

have been possible to calculate the width of the stylobate from the theoretical intercolumniation by the formula $W = I (N_w + \frac{1}{3})$, hence $4.2903 \times 7\frac{1}{3} = 30.8902$. This calculation produces a width for the stylobate that is greater by 0.010 m than the eastern stylobate of the Parthenon (30.880 m). But it is noticeable that the dimension based on the theoretical intercolumniation is more exactly in the proportion 4:9 with respect to the length as measured along the northern stylobate: $69.503 \div 2.25 = 30.8902$. From this it is probably correct to infer that the architects actually calculated the width of the facade in this way, but an error of 0.010 m occurred when the builders laid out the eastern stylobate on the crepidoma.[26]

The elevation of the temple on its facades had to be studied with special care, for here the novelty of the octostyle front at once obtruded itself (Figs. 9, 10). The Greek eye was long accustomed to the normally rather stout proportions of the Doric hexastyle facade, with its thick and stocky columns spaced rather far apart and surmounted by a heavy entablature. But the addition of two more columns to the width of the facade, with the necessary proportional increase in height, would have created an architectural composition contrasting sharply with familiar Doric style, and chiefly remarkable for its overpowering heaviness. It was this that the architects of the Parthenon particularly eschewed. Once again they chose as the guiding principle of their design the theoretical ratio 4:9, which was now expressed in the relationship of the height of the order, as far as the horizontal cornice, to the width of the stylobate: 10.433 (column) + 1.35 (architrave) + 1.345 (frieze) + 0.60 (cornice) = $13.728 \times 2.25 = 30.888$. From this calculation, it is interesting to observe that the theoretical relation between the height of the order and the width of the stylobate is only 0.008 m greater than the actual width of the eastern stylobate, while it is only 0.002 m less than the width of the stylobate as calculated by formula from the theoretical axial spacing (30.890). Thus 13.728:30.888

---

[26] It should be noted that the same calculations using the measurable dimensions of the south and west stylobates yield less satisfactory results: $69.609 \div 16\frac{1}{3} = 4.2969$ (theoretical intercolumniation from south stylobate); $4.2969 \times 7\frac{1}{3} = 30.938$ (theoretical width of west stylobate). But the actual width of the west stylobate is 30.961 m.

Figure 10. West facade of the Parthenon from west

= 4:9 = 1:2.25. The mathematical structure of the temple thus gained a third dimension, and the facade grew organically from the ground plan in perfect proportion.

The same theoretical proportion 4:9 also appears to have generated dimensions for some of the smaller constituent parts of the facades. In the above calculation of the overall height of the Doric order, it is observable that that same proportion informs the tripartite division of the entablature (Figs. 11, 12). The height of the horizontal cornice (0.60 m) is related to the height of the architrave (1.35 m) as 4:9 (60 × 2.25 = 1.35), and the height of the triglyph frieze (1.345 m) is virtually identical to the architrave. In similar fashion, the width of the triglyphs seems to have been derived theoretically from the lower diameter of the columns: 1.905 ÷ 2.25 = 0.8466, although the actual average is slightly less, 0.8445. Once again, the height of the Doric capitals (0.866 m) is related to the slightly larger lower diameter employed for the four corner columns (1.948 m) in the same proportion: 0.866 × 2.25 = 1.9485.[27]

An even more important development is to be seen in the profile and proportions of the Doric capitals compared with examples earlier in the Classical period. On shafts of nearly identical height, the Doric capitals of the Parthenon are 0.866 m high; those of the Temple of Zeus at Olympia measure 1.447 m (a difference of 0.581 m). On the capitals at Olympia, the echinus (0.420 m) is almost equal to the height of the abacus (0.425 m), but on the Parthenon capitals the echinus is distinctly lower than the abacus (0.275 m to 0.347 m). Not only are the Athenian capitals lower than their predecessors but more compact and less spreading. This change in appearance is the result of a marked decrease in the width of the abacus in relation to the lower diameter of the shaft. At Olympia, the abaci of the capitals are 2.650 m wide and thus project well beyond the lower diameter of the col-

---

[27] The figure 1.948 is Dinsmoor's measurement (*AAG*³, 338) for the lower diameter of the corner columns. Orlandos, Παρθ., 148, gives the dimension as 1.942 to 1.944; for the height of the Doric capitals, 183–184.

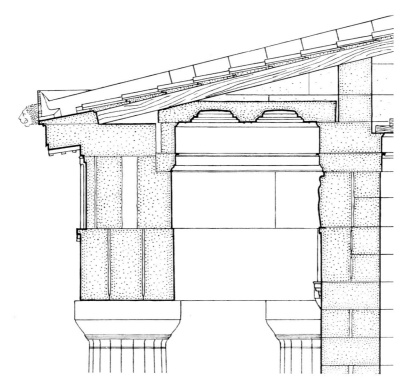

Figure 11. Restored section of entablature and peristyle ceiling

umn (2.25 m fronts) to create the characteristic spreading profile of early classical Doric. The normal abaci of the Parthenon capitals have a slight variation in width between 2.002 m and 2.059 m; but in relation to the lower diameter (1.905 m), the projection of the abaci is barely noticeable, varying between 0.048 m and 0.077 m on each side. These changes in the proportions thus create the narrow, tight profile that is one of the hallmarks of fifth-century Athenian Doric.[28]

Every effort was made to curtail the apparent width of the octostyle front and to give it at the same time the illusion of greater height. The columns were set extraordinarily close together, since the notion of relating the lower diameter of the columns to the axial intercolumniation as 4:9 created proportionately the narrowest axial spacing of any Doric temple on the Greek mainland.[29] This compactness of the colonnade was given special emphasis at the corners, where the intervals were made 0.616 m less than the normal intercolumniations on the fronts (0.604 m less on the flanks), a reduction that was 33% greater than the normal contractions at the corners required by the triglyph frieze. Greek architects had long recognized the notorious problem of placing a Doric triglyph frieze on a peripteral temple if the triglyphs and metopes were to be uniform in size and spacing, and triglyphs were to stand at the four corners. The most effective method of achieving this was

[28] See J. J. Coulton, in *Parthenon-Kongress Basel*, 41. The proportions of Doric capitals have been studied in extensive detail by Coulton, *BSA* 74 (1979) 81–153. The Temple of Zeus falls into his Group 4/5 and the Parthenon into his Group 6, pp. 89–91, 101. For the capitals of the Parthenon, Orlandos, Παρθ., 181–194. There is some evidence that might be taken to indicate that the architects of the Parthenon were experimenting with the proportions of the Doric capitals. The abaci of the east facade (2.059 m) are consistently wider than those of the west facade (2.002 m). The abacus width on the east is almost exactly 1/15 the width of the east stylobate (30.880 ÷ 15 = 2.059). This looks like a planned dimension, but it is difficult to understand why the western abaci should be slightly reduced in width (2.002 m) except as a result of experimentation. See Orlandos, Παρθ., 192–193.

[29] The interaxial spacings, reduced 0.123 m from those of the Older Parthenon, are 2.25 lower diameters in width. In all previous Doric colonnades the columns had been set proportionately wider apart, e.g., the spacing at Olympia (in terms of lower diameters) is 2.32; Old Athena Temple on the Acropolis, ca. 2.48; Athena Pronaia at Delphi, 2.47; Aigina, 2.65; Corinth, 2.31.

Figure 12. Detail of entablature at northeast corner

to reduce the interaxial spacing of the columns adjacent to each corner. Modern students of Doric architecture generally describe the necessary reduction as half the difference between the width of the triglyph and the depth of the architrave from front to back (A – T ÷ 2), although it is doubtful if this formula was used by ancient architects. Thus, for example, on the Temple of Zeus at Olympia: 2.00 (architrave depth) – 1.060 (triglyph width) ÷ 2 = 0.47 m; interaxial spacing of the flanks 5.221 (normal) – 4.748 (angles) = 0.473 m. But a similar calculation for the Doric frieze of the Parthenon emphasizes the striking increase in the contraction at the corners: 1.77 (architrave depth) – 0.8445 (triglyph width) ÷ 2 = 0.463; interaxial spacing of the fronts 4.2979 (normal average) – 3.682 (angles) = 0.616 m.[30]

[30] For angle contraction, see Coulton, *BSA* 69 (1974) 72–74; Gruben, *Gr. Tempel*[5], 41–43. Dimensions of the temple at Olympia, *Olympia Ergebnisse*, text vol. 1, pls. 13, 14; Dinsmoor, *AAG*[3], 338. Dimensions of the Parthenon entablature, Orlandos, *Παρθ.*, 201 (architrave), 224 (triglyphs).

On the other hand, the columns rose to new heights of slenderness, for at the time of construction the peristyle columns of the Parthenon employed unprecedented proportions for the Doric order. The exterior columns measure 10.433 m in height, with a lower diameter 1.905 m, making its proportion to the height 5.48 lower diameters. Once again the comparison with the Temple of Zeus is revealing because the actual height of its columns is almost identical, and in fact, as noted earlier, that dimension appears to have been deliberately borrowed by the architects of the Parthenon. At Olympia, columns measuring 10.43 m in height had a lower diameter of 2.25 m on the fronts (2.21 m on the flanks) and thus a proportion of 4.64 lower diameters (4.72 on the flanks).[31] The effect of this difference in proportion on the appearance of the facade was considerable, for it made the columns of the Temple of Zeus substantially stouter and heavier than those of the Parthenon. An even more significant break with Doric tradition on the Greek mainland has been observed in the relation of the column height to the intercolumniation. All earlier Doric temples had columns about twice as tall as the intercolumniation or a little less. That ratio in the Temple of Zeus was 2.0. The same ratio in the Parthenon was 2.43 intercolumniations to the height of the columns.[32]

The specifically borrowed column height, if so it was, when combined with the theoretical notion that the overall height of the order should relate to the width of the stylobate as 4:9, produced a thoroughgoing reevaluation in the proportions of the entablature. Now for the first time the architrave, heretofore normally the higher member, divided the height almost exactly equally with the triglyph frieze. More important, the whole entablature has been greatly reduced in height in relation to the height of the columns. Above columns of equal height in the two temples, the entablature at Olympia rose 4.09 m, while that of Parthenon rises 3.295 m, a reduction of 0.795 m. In Doric architecture the entablature provides the load that the columns support, and its height determines the apparent weight of that load. In earlier Doric buildings the height of the entablature was normally about two-fifths the height of the columns. But in the Parthenon that dimension has been reduced to less than one-third.[33] The lower entablature of the Parthenon works together with the slenderer proportions of its columns to alter significantly the visual structure of load and support that is fundamental to all design in trabeated architecture. It is this narrower band of the entablature which contributes most to the lightness of the facade, for in the visual logic of the architecture it appears to deliver a far lighter load to the tall columns beneath it. The total effect is of equipoise, a candor of line and dimension that creates perfect balance of weight and support.

Above the entablature rose the temple's double-pitch roof terminating in a triangular pediment at each end; like all other parts of the building, the roof was made entirely of Pentelic marble. As was normal in Greek temple architecture, the roof was composed of flat pan tiles ascending in rows from the eaves to the ridge (Fig. 13). The individual tiles turned up slightly at the sides to meet beneath triangular cover tiles that protected the joint between two rows of pan tiles. On the flanks of the temple the rows of cover tiles usually terminated in decorative antefixes at the edge of the eaves. The roof of the Parthenon was a rather more complex variation of this scheme (Fig. 14). On the long flanks, broad eaves tiles rested directly on the horizontal cornice, their sides aligned with the axes of the triglyphs in the frieze below. From the upper edge of the eaves tiles, the normal pan tiles rose to the ridge of the roof in ninety-six rows, spaced three rows from triglyph to triglyph, and six rows to

---

[31] Cf. the proportion of lower diameter to column height at Corinth, 4.15 (4.40 flanks); Athena Pronaia, Delphi, 4.58 (4.72 flanks); Aigina, 5.32. But the tendency to taller and more attenuated Doric columns is an invariable hallmark of Periklean buildings, no doubt influenced in part by the Parthenon, e.g., the columns of the contemporary Hephaisteion are 5.61 lower diameters in height; Sounion, 5.78; Temple of Ares, 5.70; Propylaia, central hall, 5.65 (west), 5.47 (east); Rhamnous, 5.74; Athenian temple at Delos, 5.71. See Dinsmoor, *AAG*³, table after p. 340.

[32] The observation is due to Coulton, in *Parthenon-Kongress Basel*, 40–44. Cf. the column height to intercolumniation at Olympia (Hera), 1.47; Corinth, 1.80; Athens (Old Athena Temple), 1.83; Delphi (Athena Pronaia), 1.85; Aigina, 2.01.

[33] See Coulton, in *Parthenon-Kongress Basel*, 41.

Figure 13. Restored view of roof at southwest corner

each axial intercolumniation of the columns. The joints centered on the triglyphs were covered by
a series of triangular cover tiles measuring 0.355 × 0.775 m, and these terminated at the edge of the
eaves in carved floral antefixes consisting of palmettes with thirteen leaves above antithetical spirals.
The two joints between these rows of cover tiles were covered by a narrower series of triangular tiles
measuring 0.242 × 0.77 m. These intermediate rows of tiles did not extend all the way to the eaves,
but stopped against solid marble plugs placed 0.75 m back from the edge of the roof. Exactly centered on the eaves tiles, and thus above the midpoint of each metope and between the two narrower
rows of cover tiles, were what can only be called false antefixes. These consisted of carved palmettes
exactly like those to either side of them, but with no triangular cover tiles behind them.[34]

 At the ends of the temple, the treatment of the roof over the facades differed from that on the
flanks. Above the raking cornice of the triangular pediments were placed sima tiles that curved upward at the outside to form gutters for rainwater. The sima tiles corresponded in width to the normal
pan tiles of the roof (±0.695 m), but they measured 1.173 m in depth from front to back. The high
outer face (0.422 m high) took the form of a high ovolo molding above a fascia and crowned by a

[34] The details of the roof tiles are discussed by Orlandos, *Παρθ.*, 600–603 (pan tiles), 603–609 (cover tiles), 609–613
(antefixes and false antefixes), 615–631 (palmettes of the antefixes).

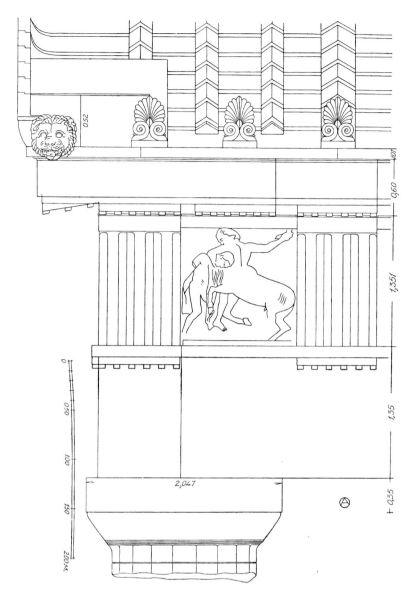

Figure 14. Restored elevation of entablature and roof at southwest corner

fillet. The ovolo of the sima carried painted decoration in gold paint, alternating lotus blossoms and palmettes (Fig. 15). The palmettes of eleven petals rise from antithetical spiral tendrils that surround the blossoms and spiral in the opposite direction to join them to the lotus on either side. At the four corners of the roof, the sima turned the corner for a short distance, and the return carried splendid sculpted lion's heads facing north and south, respectively.[35]

At the four corners of the roof were the bases for acroteria (Fig. 13). These consisted of specially elongated blocks of enormous size (overall dimensions 2.506 × 1.43 × 0.52 m high) and weighing some four tons each. At the outer corners of the bases were large square sockets (0.71 × 0.78 m) fitted with four deep cuttings for iron anchors to retain the statuary.[36] With the acroteria placed at the exact corners of the roof, the greater part of the bases would have served as a counterweight to prevent the statues from falling. On the basis of the shape and dimensions of the plinths, and the depth and placement of the cuttings for the anchors, Korres and Bouras have suggested that the cor-

[35] For the details of the sima, Orlandos, Παρθ., 547–549, 550–554 (lion's heads), 555–557 (painted decoration of the sima).
[36] For the details of the acroterion bases, Orlandos, Παρθ., 558–567.

Figure 15. Raking sima, profile, and ornament

ner acroteria should be restored as marble winged Nikai moving outward as if about to take flight.[37] Since no fragment of such sculpture has ever been identified, the suggestion must remain a very attractive speculation. But if figures of Nike indeed adorned the four corners of the roof, it would be the clearest sign that the whole temple was conceived as a victory monument, begun in the years after Marathon as a thank-offering to Athena for the victory in that battle and now finally brought to completion nearly half a century later.[38]

OPTICAL REFINEMENTS OF THE PERISTYLE

Perhaps none of the building's architectural detail has attracted more wondering comment from historians of architecture than the deliberate deviations from normal dimensions which are often described as optical refinements. These consist of subtle curves and inclinations of supposedly straight lines, which work their effects upon the observer's subconscious and only submit to analysis when they are tested with the most precise measurement of tape and plumb line. Here again we are inclined to regard the Parthenon as a textbook of Greek architectural practice and thus to lose sight

[37] M. Korres and Ch. Bouras, Μελέτη ἀποκαταστάσεως τοῦ Παρθενῶνος, vol. 1 (Athens 1983) 41; see also A. Delivorrias, in *Parthenon-Kongress Basel*, 289–292.

[38] Fragments have survived of two floral acroteria that occupied the apex of the pediment at each end of the temple. These took the form of great acanthus leaves and cauliculi springing from a bed of acanthus. The fragments have been variously restored by earlier scholars, summarized by Orlandos, Παρθ., 558–577. But the style of the fragments has suggested that they are later additions to be dated in the late fifth century. See H. Gropengiesser, *Die pflanzlichen Akrotere klassischer Tempel* (Mainz 1961) 43; H. Möbius, *Die Ornamente der griechischen Grabstelen klassischer und nachklassischer Zeit* (Munich 1968) 15, 24; P. Danner, *ÖJh* 58 (1988) 41–51.

of its supreme position.[39] In no other ancient building was the complexity of optical refinement carried to such an intricate extreme. Although earlier architects had experimented with many of the individual adjustments, Iktinos and Kallikrates were the first to combine all of them in a comprehensive system embracing every part of the temple. The architects achieved the desired effect first by inclining the axes of the columns of the peristyle inward, so that they leaned slightly toward the cella wall. On the four sides of the temple, the axes of the columns were made to incline 0.074 m from the vertical, whereas at the four corners the inclination is proportionately greater, as the diagonal of a square is greater than its sides, a proportion of $1:\sqrt{2}$. The inclination was introduced in the working of the resting and bearing surfaces of the lowest drum so that they deviated from the horizontal. The nine upper drums were made precisely cylindrical, with horizontal surfaces, and the process was reversed in the topmost drum so that the inward-sloping line of the shaft was punctuated by the slight outward inclination of the capital.[40] This inclination of the columns was not, of course, an invention of Iktinos and Kallikrates, for it had been planned in the Older Parthenon and had appeared in one or two other temples of the early fifth century.[41] In the Parthenon, however, the principle was pushed to its logical extreme; thus the lateral walls of the cella were also inclined in sympathy with the peristyle. The northern flank of the cella exhibits a slope of 0.103 m, while the southern wall deviates from the vertical by 0.113 m.[42] The inclination of the walls and column shafts was reflected in almost every vertical plane of the superstructure above. The face of the architrave leans inward 0.015 to 0.020 m, as does the frieze above it, until the perspective is arrested by the contrary movement of the cornice, which leans outward 0.015 m from the vertical to enframe the elevation with a stronger horizontal line at the top (Fig. 15). It was perhaps a similar desire to counterbalance the movement of the perspective which led the architects to incline the face of the antae forward toward the prostyle colonnades of the porches by as much as 0.141 m.[43] Other refinements help to create the illusion of compactness in the colonnades of the facades. Especially effective for this purpose is the unusually narrow axial intercolumniation and the excessive contraction at the corners, which we have already noted in connection with the proportions of the elevation. But again the effect is curtailed, and the composition of the facade is enclosed at each end by the counterweight of the two angle columns, which were made 0.043 m thicker than the others.[44]

The other half of the Parthenon's system of refinements is still subtler of conception and more intricate of execution. This is the delicate curvature that was applied to apparently straight lines so that every surface of the building is in fact slightly convex. Most evident of these curves is the entasis or swelling of the column shaft as it rises. In the earliest examples, such as the archaic temples at Paestum in south Italy, the entasis was so exaggerated as to be easily visible to the eye. By the time of the Parthenon, however, it has become a taut and subtle curve, swelling with almost imperceptible delicacy, whose presence was to be felt but not observed. On the column shafts of the Parthenon, the entasis was applied to the channels and arrises of the flutes so that the diameter of the column decreased very gradually to a point one-third the height of the shaft and then more sharply on the upper two-thirds. The greatest swelling of the curve ranges from 0.017 m to 0.021 m at a height of

[39] On optical refinements in general, see Dinsmoor, *AAG*³, 164–169; Lawrence, *Greek Architecture*⁵, 125–128; Coulton, *Greek Architects at Work*, 108–113; W. H. Goodyear, *Greek Refinements* (New Haven 1912).
[40] The most detailed account of inclination in the Parthenon is Orlandos, Παρθ., 167–175; cf. Penrose, *Principles*², 36–38.
[41] Dinsmoor, *AAG*³, 110, 150, 165. Inclination was first applied to the peristyle columns at Aigina (E. R. Fiechter, in A. Furtwängler, *Aegina*, 27) and at Olympia on the flanks only (Dörpfeld, in *Olympia Ergebnisse,* text vol. 2, 7). About the same time, the refinement appeared also in the Temple of Hera Lacinia at Croton (G. Abatino, *La colonna del tempio di Hera Lacinia* [Naples 1901]).
[42] Orlandos, Παρθ., 274–278.
[43] Orlandos, Παρθ., 216–217 (architrave), 230 (frieze), 241 (cornice), 284 (anta).
[44] The refinement of thicker corner columns seems to have been used first at Aigina and was intended for the Older Parthenon: Dinsmoor, *AAG*³, 165, 328.

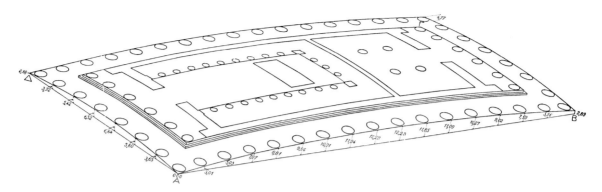

Figure 16. Plan showing curvature of stylobate and steps

about 4 m above the stylobate, but no two flutes exhibit exactly the same degree of entasis.[45] Still more delicate is the upward curvature that inflects the surface of steps and stylobate and in fact the entire floor surface of the temple (Fig. 16). On the fronts, the point of greatest convexity is at the central axis, where the rise, measured on the second step, is 0.065 m (east) and 0.062 m (west) above the level of the corners. On the long flanks the highest rise is beneath the ninth column, where the curvature reaches 0.1025 m (north) and 0.112 m (south) above the corners (Fig. 17).[46] On the interior of the temple, the stylobate of the pronaos has a maximum curvature of 0.033 m at the central axis, and the opisthodomos 0.027 m. Even in the narrow flank peristyles, the pavement rises 0.036 m (south) and 0.029 m (north) from the exterior edge of the stylobate to the first riser of the cella steps.[47] Like so many of the refinements, horizontal curvature was not new to the Parthenon;[48] and yet here the architects came to the logical conclusion that, if an upward curve was desirable in the crepidoma, it was much more desirable in the long horizontal lines of the superstructure. Thus the slight convexity of the stylobate is projected upward through the columns to the architrave, frieze, and cornice, and even the raking cornice of the pediment is curved in harmony with the entablature below.

It is only natural that one should question the motivation for these intricate refinements which so greatly increased the technical complexities of constructing the building. The principle that generated the refinements was known to later classical authors, and several such adjustments are specifically recommended by Vitruvius in his architectural treatise.[49] In general, it was the ancient view that the use of curvature and inclination compensated for optical illusions that deceived the eye of the viewer. On this point the ancient statements on the subject are quite explicit.

> The angle columns also must be made thicker by the fiftieth part of their diameter, because they are cut into by the air and appear more slender to the spectators. Therefore what the eye cheats us of must be made up by calculation.[50]

[45] Detailed discussion of the entasis of the columns, Orlandos, Παρθ., 159–167; cf. Penrose, *Principles*[2], 39–42.

[46] Detailed measurements of the curvature, Orlandos, Παρθ., 124; general discussion, 121–140. Cf. Penrose, *Principles*[2], 22–24, 27–35; Stevens, *AJA* 38 (1934) 533–542; Stevens, *Hesperia* 12 (1943) 135–143; K. Karatheodori, *ArchEph* (1937) 120–124; Dinsmoor, *AAG*[3], 166–169; M. Koch, *ActaArch* 34 (1963) 231; A. D. Mavrikios, *AJA* 69 (1965) 264–268.

[47] Stylobate curvature of the pronaos and opisthodomos, Orlandos, Παρθ., 264; pavement of the peristyle, 144.

[48] It appeared first in the archaic Temple of Apollo at Corinth, probably in the late archaic Temple of Athena on the Acropolis, and certainly in the platform of the Older Parthenon: Dinsmoor, *AAG*[3], 90, 150, 166.

[49] In addition to the passages quoted below, Vitruvius 3.3.13 describes the entasis of the columns; 3.5.4 recommends the inclination of the flank columns; 3.5.13 explains that forward inclination of the entablature and superstructure will make the facade look vertical.

[50] Vitruv. *De arch.* 3.3.11, trans. F. Granger (Loeb).

Figure 17. Elevation showing curvature of colonnade

The stylobate must be so leveled that it increases toward the middle with unequal risers; for if it is set out to a level it will seem to the eye to be hollowed.[51]

The progress to proper building was not the result of one chance experiment. Some of the individual parts, which were equally thick and straight seemed not to be equally thick and straight, because the sight is deceived in such objects, taking no account of perspective. By experimentally adding to the bulk here and subtracting there, by tapering, and by conducting every possible test, they made them appear regular to the sight and quite symmetrical, for this was the aim in that craft.[52]

The goal of the architect is to give his work a satisfying shape using appearance as his standard, and insofar as is possible, to discover compensations for the deceptions of the vision, aiming not at balance or shapeliness based on reality, but at these qualities as they appear to the vision.[53]

To be sure, Vitruvius was writing four centuries after the completion of the Parthenon, at a time when the use of optical refinements had mostly gone out of fashion. Philon's more generalized statement appears to adopt the same position, however, and shows that the theoretical basis for the refinements was current in the late third century B.C., while the much later passage, which has come down to us in the manuscripts of Damianos and is sometimes attributed to Heron, agrees closely that the purpose of the refinements was to correct the deficiencies of human vision. Moreover, among the bibliographical sources cited by Vitruvius was a treatise on the Parthenon written by Iktinos, so there

[51] Vitruv. *De arch.* 3.4.5, trans. F. Granger (Loeb).
[52] Philon, *Belopoeica* 51.1–7; text and translation, E. W. Marsden, *Greek and Roman Artillery: Technical Treatises* (Oxford 1971) 108–109.
[53] Damianos, *Optica* (ed. Schöne, 28–30) = Heron, *Definitiones* 135.13; translation, J. J. Pollitt, *The Ancient View of Greek Art* (New Haven 1974) 239–240.

is every likelihood that the Roman architect's explanation correctly conveys what the Periklean architects intended the refinements to do.[54]

Whatever may have been the precise notion that motivated the system of inclinations and curvature of the Parthenon, there can be no doubt about its effect on the building. It was by means of these refinements that the architects implanted in the marble a personality of its own, as if the whole building had inhaled the breath of life. As in the human personality that created it, one senses in the Parthenon a streak of temperament. The surface of the stone appears to be stretched tight against the swelling of the stylobate and the distended line of the columns; it seems almost to restrain with effort some turbulence that pulses within the stone. We are accustomed to think of architecture as the most precise and rational of the arts; we know from experience that a building's floor is level, its walls vertical and assembled in regular courses of masonry. The human eye is accustomed to look for a regular mechanical paradigm; but there is something supremely illogical—one had almost said perverse—in a straight line that bulges and a vertical that leans. There is here at work an irrational force that threatens the logical physics of trabeated architecture. The columns and stylobate do not bear their load but seem to thrust it up; the entablature does not rest on its supports but is seemingly pushed upward by some force from below. The result is a tension as the observer struggles to reconcile what the mind thinks it knows with what the eye unmistakably sees. It was this dialectic of rational expectation and actual observation that Iktinos and Kallikrates expressed in terms of architecture. They sensed instinctively that mechanical precision was not the sole ingredient of a great design. When they made use of all the subtleties of curvature and inclination, they were harnessing together incompatible forces of static precision and restless movement; and they exploited the dichotomy between expected appearance and reality of form. From this conflict of opposites there arises the peculiar elastic quality of the Parthenon that makes it one of antiquity's most remarkable buildings.

Design of the Cella

The revolutionary octostyle facades of the Parthenon affected the design of the interior just as much as that of the external peristyle. Most importantly, they caused the width of the cella building to be expanded because that dimension was customarily derived from the columnar facades. Here the Athenian architects adhered strictly to Doric tradition in that they aligned the lateral walls of the cella with the axis of the second column from each corner of the facades (see Fig. 7). In a temple with hexastyle fronts, this practice determined a width for the cella equivalent to the three normal axial intercolumniations of the facade, but in the Parthenon this dimension was enlarged to five interaxials. Thus the novel octostyle front produced within the temple a cella of unexampled magnitude for the Greek mainland (Fig. 18).[55] In similar fashion, the architects aligned the first step of the pronaos and opisthodomos with the axis of the second column from each corner of the flanks; but in this they broke with tradition, for Doric custom preferred to align the internal porches with the midpoint of the second intercolumniation of the flanks. Another break with normal Doric design, the shallow prostyle porches at either end of the cella, should likely be attributed to longstanding Athe-

---

[54] See the discussion of Coulton, *Greek Architects at Work*, 108–112. Vitruvius 7 praef. 12 cites a treatise on the Parthenon by Iktinos and a certain Carpion, a name that is otherwise unknown. In view of the fact that refinements were not often employed by Greek architects after the fifth century, Iktinos's book was probably Vitruvius's main source of knowledge on the subject.

[55] A comparison of the Parthenon and the Temple of Zeus at Olympia is revealing because, as we have seen, the two temples are not far apart in overall dimensions: Parthenon 30.88 × 69.503 m on the stylobate, and Olympia 27.68 × 64.12 m. But the interior width of the cella of the Parthenon is 19.065 m, while the same dimension at Olympia is 13.26 m.

Figure 18. View of interior looking west

nian tradition. These replaced the deep pronaos and opisthodomos, whose two columns between projecting antae were so characteristic a feature of the Doric temple. Unusual as the prostyle porches were, however, they found good precedent on the Athenian Acropolis, where, as we have seen, they had been planned for the Older Parthenon and had probably been used in both archaic temples of Athena.[56] All three of the earlier temples had standard hexastyle fronts, and the use of prostyle porches for their cellas thus represents a deliberate preference on the part of the architects, who could just as well have built the pronaos and opisthodomos distyle in antis. In the Periklean Parthenon, however, the prostyle porches were virtually required on the pronaos and opisthodomos since the great width of the cella precluded the canonical distyle plan. Moreover, the expanded width of the cella is emphasized by the six-column porches of the Periklean temple, whereas all the predecessors had been tetrastyle. On the internal porches of the cella, the Periklean architects stretched the already attenuated proportions of the peristyle columns to even greater extremes of slenderness. The columns of the opisthodomos measure 1.712 m in lower diameter and rise to an average height of 10.056 m, which gives them a proportional height of 5.87 lower diameters. Even more exaggerated were the columns of the pronaos: with a lower diameter of 1.651 m and an average height of 10.07 m, they have proportions of 6.10 lower diameters.[57]

[56] Prostyle porches in the archaic temples: Judeich, *Topographie*², 265; Dinsmoor, *AJA* 36 (1932) 316; Dinsmoor, *AAG*³, 90; Plommer, *JHS* 80 (1960) 130. Prostyle porches planned for the Older Parthenon: Hill *AJA* 16 (1912) 551–553; Orlandos, Παρθ., 72–73.

[57] Detailed description of the columns of the opisthodomos, Orlandos, Παρθ., 433; columns of the pronaos, 299, 303.

It was, of course, the columns of the prostyle porches that would carry the two ends of the sculptured Ionic frieze, one of the great glories of the temple's decorative program. In light of this, a curious feature of their architectural design calls for comment. In many Doric temples outside of Athens, the pronaos and opisthodomos, arranged distyle in antis, supported a normal architrave surmounted by a frieze of triglyphs and metopes. In such examples the axial spacing between columns and antae was always smaller than the axial spacing between the two columns in order to maintain metopes of uniform size and to bring the triglyphs to the two corners of the frieze; for the problem of constructing a triglyph frieze on a distyle porch is no different from that encountered in the peristyle of a temple. Since, however, the internal frieze of the Parthenon was to be a continuous band of sculpture, in the manner of Ionic buildings, this plan obviated the necessity of calculating reduced corner spacing for the hexastyle porches; the columns at both ends of the cella could have been set out with uniform intercolumniations. It is therefore a source of some surprise to discover that the prostyle porches exhibit the same exaggerated corner contraction as the outer peristyle. In the opisthodomos, the average normal interaxial spacing measures 4.189 m, reduced at the corners to 3.716 m, to effect corner contraction of 0.473 m. An even greater contraction was introduced in the spacing of the pronaos, where the average normal interaxial spacing is 4.187 m and the spacing at the corners is narrowed to 3.66 m, a reduction of 0.52 m.[58] From the interaxial spacing of the columns, thus contracted at the corners, it seems necessary to infer that the architects had originally contemplated a standard Doric entablature with triglyphs and metopes in the frieze.[59] When the bottom drums were set in place, probably as early as the second or third year of construction, final decisions had apparently not yet been made concerning the extent of the temple's sculptural program. This detail offers an interesting glimpse of the rule-of-thumb methods of design as practiced by even the most sophisticated of classical architects. Decisions affecting the design of the building were made only as necessary to permit the next stage of construction to proceed. When the time came for the architects to mark out the setting lines for the columns of the prostyle porches, it seemed perfectly natural to reduce the axial intercolumniations at the corners of a Doric facade; and in fact this decision in no way precluded the final disposition of the entablature with its continuous sculptural frieze. In the event, the contracted spacing at the corners enabled adoption of a curious amalgam of the two orders of a kind rarely encountered before the Hellenistic period: the columns of the porches carry a normal Doric architrave, crowned by a taenia and with regulae centered correctly on both the columns and intercolumniations; but this architrave in turn supports the continuous band of the extraordinary Ionic frieze (see Fig. 29).

The most fruitful effect of the cella's increased width was upon the interior of the temple, where now for the first time Greek architects attempted to design interior space instead of merely enclosing it with four walls and a roof. Consistent with the whole of Greek religious tradition, the focal point of the interior was, of course, the colossal cult statue of Athena. She it was who dominated the eastern compartment that was officially the hundred-foot cella (ἑκατόμπεδος νεώς). And yet the goddess was not backed against the rear wall of a long tunnel-like nave. Rather, she was set well forward, with a third of the cella behind her, and there was thus a free play of space all around the great image. To this space the architects gave movement and direction; they channeled it into the side aisles with two long colonnades and forced it to run around the back of the cella by joining together the lateral porticoes with a third shorter row of columns. The result was a unique interior peristyle that articulated three sides of the great chamber (see Fig. 7). Its colonnades were ranged in two stories of superimposed Doric columns, ten in number for the lateral porticoes and five across the

[58] Axial spacings of the opisthodomos columns, Orlandos, Παρθ., 437; of the pronaos columns, 299.

[59] So also Orlandos, Παρθ., 449. But this inference has been challenged by B. A. Barletta, *AJA* 113 (2009) 547–568, who argues that the Ionic frieze was designed from the beginning.

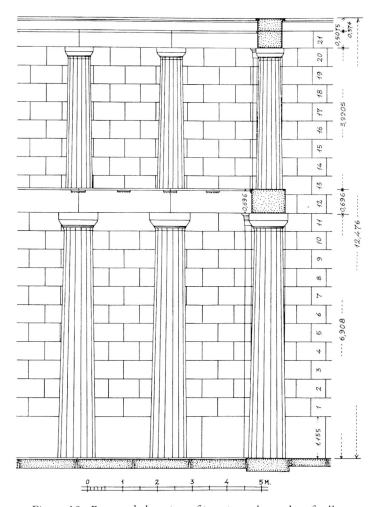

Figure 19. Restored elevation of interior colonnades of cella

end, counting the corner columns twice (Fig. 19).[60] Such superimposed porticoes were, of course, a common feature of Doric interiors, though normally they ran lengthwise from end to end of the cella and were set close to the walls. But in the Parthenon they served a new function in the molding of interior space. No longer was there a cramped and awkward aisle behind the colonnades, as in the temples at Aigina and Olympia; now there opened instead a broad ambulatory encircling the cella on three sides and causing a certain centripetal movement of space which set the great statue in still sharper focus. In fact, the ambulatories measured 4.635 m and 4.615 m, respectively, from the edge of the stylobate to the lateral wall, with the result that their combined width on both sides occupied nearly half of the total interior width of the cella. The architects took pains to increase still further

[60] The number of interior columns was so reported by Dinsmoor, *AAG*[3], 163, followed by Travlos, *PDA*, 446, and Gruben, *Gr. Tempel*[5], 164, fig. 143, because circular traces of the southwest corner column were seen and measured by C. Cockerell and J. Woods at the beginning of the nineteenth century; see Penrose, *Principles*[2], 9–10, note 4. Cockerell measured the diameter as 3' 3⅔" = 1.008 m; Woods reported the same dimension as 3.75' = 1.143 m, one slightly smaller and one slightly larger than Penrose's measurement for the lateral columns, 3.656' = 1.114 m. Orlandos, *Παρθ.*, 359–361, retains the restoration of L-shaped piers at the angles of the peristyle, as advocated by Dörpfeld, *AM* 6 (1881) 291–293 and pl. XII; M. Collignon, *Le Parthénon* (Paris 1914) 122. In favor of the piers, it is argued that they allow restoration of a uniform dimension (2.119 m) from the face of each anta to the axis of the column next to it at both ends of the colonnades, the normal interaxial spacing being 2.605 m with minute variations. The restoration of columns requires an interaxial spacing at the corners considerably wider than normal, 2.904 m. But the observations and measurements of the early travelers plainly have greater evidential value than this admittedly elegant solution.

Figure 20. Restored view of Parthenon chamber showing Ionic columns

the visual scale of this already large interior. To achieve this, they designed the interior columns with extremely slender proportions. Those in the lower order have a bottom diameter of 1.114 m and a height of 6.898 m, dimensions that yield a proportional height of 6.19 lower diameters. The smaller columns of the upper colonnade measured 0.833 m in diameter and rose to a height of 4.394 m, a proportional height of 5.27 lower diameters. Because of their small dimensions and slender proportions, both sets of interior columns were given by exception sixteen flutes instead of the twenty that was canonical for Doric columns of the Classical period.[61] The slender shafts will have lent an unusual feeling of lightness and delicacy to the normally stout Doric colonnades, and it was thus possible to use as many as ten columns in the lateral porticoes. Once again, the Temple of Zeus at Olympia offers an instructive contrast. Its interior colonnades were actually longer than those of the Parthenon, 28.74 m along the edge of the internal stylobate, while the same dimension in the Parthenon was 25.452 m; but because of the heavier proportions of the columns and the considerably larger lower diameters (1.52 m), there was space for only seven columns. The architects of the Parthenon, on the other hand, by their dexterous manipulation of proportions, had achieved in their shorter interior porticoes the impression of immensely greater size.

The interior of the western chamber, properly known to the contemporary Athenian as the Parthenon, offered much less scope for architectural ingenuity than did the great hundred-foot cella. The room was a nearly square rectangle measuring 19.20 m in width and 13.37 m in depth from east to west. Since there was no communication with the eastern cella, its only access was by way of the great door in the opisthodomos that was closely analogous to the door of the Hekatompedon at the other end of the building. Here too, however, the same feeling of lightness, the same slender proportion prevailed, for the roof was almost certainly supported on four Ionic columns reaching from

[61] The detailed dimensions of the interior order are those given by Dinsmoor, Jr., *Hesperia* 43 (1974) 142–146 and fig. 9, based on the fragments found in the Agora excavations. Orlandos, *Παρθ.*, 359–369, calculated the heights of the interior orders slightly differently.

floor to ceiling (Fig. 20). The naturally taller and thinner proportions of the Ionic order allowed a single shaft to reach this great height, which in stockier Doric proportions would have required a superimposed portico or else a considerably larger lower diameter, if a single column of such height were used. The architects evidently felt that the two-story Doric colonnade would appear bulky and unnecessary in so much smaller a room, and they preferred the uncluttered freedom of the single Ionic shafts.

Although not a single fragment of the Ionic columns has survived, their original existence is to be inferred from several pieces of evidence. The floor of the western chamber is paved with rows of rectangular marble slabs measuring 1.20 × 1.75 m and oriented with the longer dimension north-to-south. At the center of the room, the pattern of the pavement is interrupted by four square slabs that are larger and thicker than the others (1.70 × 1.75 m) and so placed that they define a rectangle measuring 6.90 m north-to-south and 4.80 m east-to-west, exactly aligned with the jambs of the western doorway. These four larger slabs evidently served as bases for four interior columns.[62] The columns cannot be restored as superimposed Doric colonnades on the analogy of the eastern cella because the intervening architrave between the upper and lower orders must then have bonded into the western wall in the twelfth course above the orthostates, where no sockets exist to accommodate such a bond. On the other hand, single Doric shafts rising from floor to ceiling would have required a lower diameter greater than that of the columns of the exterior peristyle (1.905 m) and hence impossibly large to stand on the four bases of the western chamber. It is thus generally accepted that the interior columns of the Parthenon chamber were Ionic, with their volutes facing the central aisle and their epistyles running from east to west just beneath the ceiling. The disposition of the interior columns was closely analogous to Mnesikles' later design for the west half of the Propylaia and might well have been the source of inspiration for that building.

EMBELLISHMENT OF THE DORIC ORDER

Iktinos and Kallikrates were designers for whom every detail of a building assumed importance, and they were as ready to express their interest in innovation in the profile of a molding or a decorative ornament as in the overall concept of plan or elevation. But to insist that the Parthenon was unique in the rich detail of its ornament will seem at first a contradiction in terms; for when we speak of richness in architectural decoration, we call to mind at once the sumptuous ornament of the early Ionic treasuries at Delphi or of the later Erechtheion. The decorative detail of the Doric order is sparing and frugal by comparison with these, and the novelty of the Parthenon in this department is not such as would impress itself upon the casual observer.

From the Archaic period onward, Doric architects had used painted decoration to articulate the details of the entablature and ornamental patterns appropriate to the various profiles of their moldings. By the early fifth century, a conventionalized polychromy had developed, according to which the regulae, triglyphs, and mutules of the Doric entablature were painted a rich, deep blue; this contrasted strikingly with bright red for the taenia of the architrave and for the soffit and vias of the geison. The face of the architrave and the corona of the geison always retained the natural color of the stone.[63] The architects of the Parthenon made use of this standard color scheme, but they greatly enriched the ornament on the regulae and taenia of the architrave and the band of the geison soffit. On all four sides of the temple these two continuous red bands above and below the triglyph

---

[62] Orlandos, Παρθ., 404–407 and fig. 262.

[63] See generally L. V. Solon, *Polychromy* (New York 1924); for the architectural decoration of the Parthenon, Orlandos, Παρθ., 642–648.

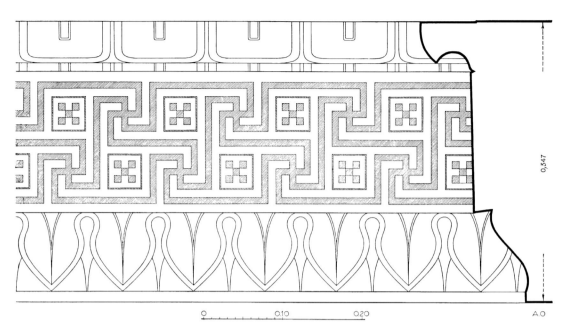

Figure 21. Profile and ornament of epicranitis of peristyle

frieze carried a gilded meander in which the key of the pattern alternated with square saltires composed of five tiny squares (Fig. 21). Against the blue ground of the regulae was a gilded floral pattern
consisting of alternating palmettes and lotus blossoms, while a more elaborate version of this pattern
adorned the raking simas above the pediments (see Fig. 15). At the four corners of the building,
where the geison soffit was exposed in an open square between adjacent corner mutules, there was a
rich and fanciful gilded ornament composed of eight interlocking palmettes and tendrils, a form of
decoration more at home in the repertory of red-figure vase painters than of Doric architects. The
crowning hawksbeak moldings of the cornices were articulated with the normal stylized Doric leaf
pattern alternating red and blue, while the palmette antefixes of the lateral roof had alternating red
and blue petals. In one other detail the architects of the Parthenon added a unique enrichment to the
canonical Doric elevation, one that was scarcely visible from the ground. A tiny half-round molding,
carved with bead and reel, crowned the fascia above the triglyphs and metopes of the Doric frieze. It
is only a slight embellishment, but it appears on no other Doric building.[64]

On the interior of the temple the architects borrowed freely from Ionic design in order to aug-
ment the ornamental vocabulary of the Parthenon. Most striking, of course, is the sculptured Ionic
frieze which encircled the whole of the cella building at the top of the wall and actually replaced
the triglyph frieze over the Doric columns of the pronaos and opisthodomos. Such extraordinary
liberty in the grafting of one order onto the other is unexampled before the Parthenon and rare at
any period. In the same spirit, but rather less radical a departure, was the use of the Ionic order for
the interior columns of the western chamber. The flair for invention that we have noted repeatedly
in the architects of the Parthenon permeates the most minute details of its decoration. The moldings
of the anta capitals show a special elaboration (Fig. 22). The normal Doric hawksbeak was painted
with alternating red and blue stylized leaves. The molding projects more deeply than heretofore, and
its crowning fascia is inclined forward and sharply undercut to deepen the line of shadow which it
casts. Again the architects borrowed boldly from the Ionic ornamental vocabulary, for immediately
below the hawksbeak is a unique Ionic ovolo carved with egg-and-dart ornament. An Ionic cyma

[64] Detailed description of the painted decoration on the taenia and regulae, Orlandos, *Παρθ.*, 206–207; geison soffit
and triglyph crown, 226–227; raking simas, 555; geison soffit at the four corners, 250–252; antefixes of the roof, 609–631.

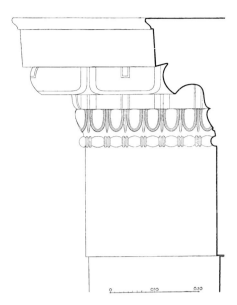

Figure 22. Profile and ornament of anta capital

reversa also crowns the upper fascia, while an astragal carved with bead and reel marks the division between capital and shaft, adding another extra touch of elaboration.[65] In another instance the architects combined a number of elements to form a complex of moldings that crowned the Ionic frieze of the cella, and an identical molding at the same level crowned the Doric frieze backer on the inside of the exterior peristyle (Fig. 21). These two moldings, which faced each other across the peristyle on all four sides, have a combined length of 345.27 m.[66] A cyma reversa with an unusual narrow fillet at its base rested directly above the sculptured figures as the appropriate crowning molding for an Ionic frieze. But this was surmounted by a broad fascia which was crowned in turn by a Doric hawksbeak serving as an epicranitis just beneath the ceiling beams.[67] As elsewhere, the moldings were greatly enriched with painted ornament. The hawksbeak had the Doric leaf pattern, alternately red and blue, and edged with gold. The cyma reversa was decorated with leaf and tongue, or Lesbian leaf, in which alternating white leaves and red tongues were both edged in gold and set against a blue ground. The broad fascia between the two moldings displayed once again the leitmotif of the Parthenon, a gold meander closely related to those which adorned the entablature of the peristyle, but here the pattern was double, with alternating keys and saltire squares in two zones.

An upward glance would have rewarded the visitor with a view of the magnificent marble ceiling of the peristyle (Fig. 23). Here rows of stepped and molded coffers marched in pairs for the full length and breadth of the temple, and every surface of the marble bore sumptuous painted ornament. On the long flanks, two large square coffers spanned the width of the peristyle in fifty-three rows, and six groups of six smaller coffers rested between the ceiling beams across the short ends. Above the pronaos and opisthodomos, coffers of still smaller size, arranged in eight groups of ten, composed the ceiling (Fig. 24), so that altogether the total number of coffers in the ceilings of the peristyle and porches came to 444. Only the fragments of the large flank coffers preserve enough traces to restore the painted decoration, but careful examination of these suggests the true splendor of the original

[65] For the anta capitals of the opisthodomos, preserved in situ, Shoe, *Greek Mouldings*, 116, 119 and pl. LVII:7; Orlandos, Παρθ., 439–443 and pls. 64, 99:5.

[66] Length of sculptured Ionic frieze: 159.74 m. Length of crowning molding of Doric frieze backer: 27.025 (E) + 27.106 (W) + 65.648 (N) + 65.754 (S) = 185.533 + 159.74 (frieze) = 345.273 m.

[67] Shoe, *Greek Mouldings*, 57–58, 173 and pls. XXVIL:16, LX:21; cf. Orlandos, Παρθ., 461–464, pl. 38 (Ionic frieze crown), 253–256 (Doric frieze backer crown).

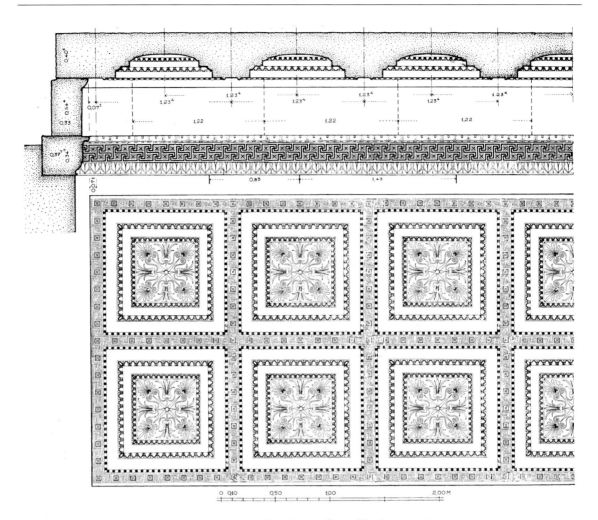

Figure 23. Restored ceiling coffers of flank peristyle

building.[68] Each coffer was surrounded by a carved half-round molding consisting of gold beads between blue reels. On all four sides, the bands between the half-round moldings of adjacent coffers were entirely filled with a gilded meander identical in pattern with those which decorated the exterior entablature. The coffers themselves rose in two steps, with an ovolo marking the transition from vertical to horizontal surfaces. As was appropriate for the ovolo profile, the painted ornament consisted of white eggs alternating with red darts against a blue ground. The square coffer lid carried an elaborate floral pattern in gold on a blue ground. At its center was an eight-pointed star whose points became the stems of palmettes and lotus blossoms arranged so that the lotuses pointed at the four sides of the square, the palmettes at the four corners, and the tendrils of the lotuses curved to become the spirals beneath the palmettes.

In the innovative juxtaposition of Doric and Ionic moldings, in the richness of the polychromy, in the extraordinary elaboration of gilded ornament—just under fourteen hundred meters of gilded meander adorned the moldings and ceilings of the peristyle[69]—in all these we glimpse again the wedding together of the orders, a process which would tauten Ionic with a delicate astringency of line and proportion and would at the same time soften the old harshness of the Doric rigor. The

[68] For reconstruction of the coffered ceiling and its painted decoration: Penrose, *Principles*², 55–57; Dinsmoor, Jr., *Hesperia* 43 (1974) 133–142, 152–154; Orlandos, Παρθ., 471–508, pls. 79–86.
[69] Length of gilded meander: 200.485 (exterior taenia) + 199.877 (exterior geison soffit) + 185.533 (frieze backer crown) + 159.74 (Ionic frieze crown) + 636.996 (coffered ceilings, flanks) = 1,382.631 m.

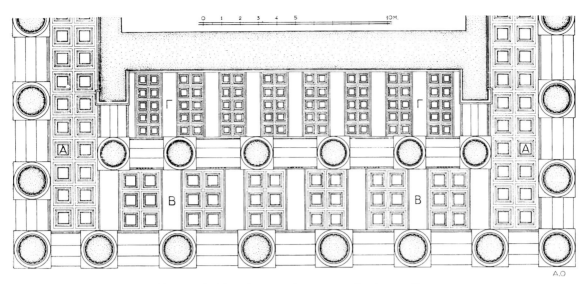

Figure 24. Plan showing three types of ceiling coffers

working out of this process in the hands of the Periklean architects is their enduring achievement and their most significant contribution to the development of Greek architecture.

The Sculptural Program

If the builders of the Parthenon achieved unprecedented subtlety in the design of Doric architecture, still more does the temple deserve its unique position in the history of art for the extensive program of sculptural decoration that enriched the architecture. Although most of the extant sculptures are sadly shattered or cruelly defaced, just enough still survives to let us glimpse their original magnificence, and more than enough to provide the archaeologist with almost insolvable problems concerning their interpretation. So extensively have these problems been studied and so fully have the artistic qualities of the sculpture been appreciated that detailed description of the individual pieces is hardly necessary. What is particularly germane to this study, however, is the overarching thematic unity of the subject matter and its special pertinence to the goddess Athena. Here again it is necessary to emphasize the singular position of the Parthenon. No other Doric temple, throughout the Greek world, was so lavishly embellished with sculptural decoration. Both in its amount and its quality the sculpture of the Parthenon was without parallel. Not only were its great pediments filled completely with figures of larger than life size, but all ninety-two metopes of the Doric frieze were adorned with sculpture, as well as the entire length of the Ionic frieze on all four sides of the cella, which formed a continuous band of sculptured relief measuring 159.74 m in length.[70] This vast sculptural program obviously resulted from the deliberate decision of the builders to utilize to the fullest extent possible the medium of artistic representation to proclaim a specific message. Here, if ever, in the choice of narrative themes and in the overall conception of their design, we feel the creative power of a single artistic personality. For it is one thing to decorate a building with carved and painted moldings, with gilded doors or delicate refinements; but it is quite another to enrich it with hundreds of sculptural figures. Unlike architectural ornament, which is purely abstract, sculptured scenes depicting figures in action or repose narrate a story or illustrate an event, and by the juxtaposition of their subjects a specific ideation is created. We have already examined enough of the planning of the Periklean buildings to suspect that the designers would not fail to exploit so splendid

[70] See Smith, *Sculptures of the Parthenon*, 51; and cf. F. Brommer, *Der Parthenonfries* (Mainz 1977) 158.

a medium for the expression of ideas. Indeed, we shall have occasion to see shortly that the subjects were chosen with care to depict certain characteristically Periklean themes.

The Metopes

On the eastern facade of the temple, all fourteen metopes remain in their original position, but they have been so grievously defaced by zealous Christians that at many points the compositions are exceptionally difficult to decipher. Enough is preserved, however, to be sure that all the decoration of the east frieze was devoted to the gods, and here they are depicted in mortal combat with the earthborn giants of earliest Greek myth.[71] Ten of the scenes depict a single god and giant locked in battle; and in all of them the gods are overwhelmingly victorious, while the giants are represented in various attitudes of ignominious defeat. The panels have been arranged with balanced symmetry. In the three southernmost metopes (E 1–3) the action moves from left to right, whereas in the two northernmost (E 13, 14) the figures move from right to left. The fourth metope from each corner (E 4, 11) has by exception three figures, and the action of the scenes moves outward. The fifth metope from each corner (E 5, 10) depicts chariots moving toward the center. All the Olympians appear to have been represented, with the possible exception of Demeter, if E 5 shows Amphitrite driving the chariot of Poseidon, who does battle in E 6.[72] But other figures have been added to their number: the sun god Helios in his rising chariot (E 14), Herakles (E 9, 11, or 13), and the boy Eros (E 11).[73] Athena's conquest of her adversary is particularly emphasized (E 4), since a small winged Nike seems to hover at her shoulder with her arm raised to crown the victor. Appropriately, the two central metopes are reserved for Zeus and Hera. The king and father of the gods prepares to hurl the thunderbolt at his kneeling enemy (E 8), while his consort hastens to his aid in a chariot drawn by once-splendid winged horses (E 7).

The fourteen metopes of the west frieze are likewise preserved on the temple, but their condition is even more ruinous than those on the east front. Three of them (W 6–8) are so destroyed that little or nothing of their sculptural decoration can be made out. The others make it clear that yet another battle raged across the western facade, balancing the celestial combat of the eastern metopes.[74] On one side the combatants are Greeks, who are armed with shields and helmets and attack with swords. Their adversaries wear Oriental dress, and some ride horseback and fight with spears (W 1, 3, 5, 9, 13), while others wield swords and curved eastern shields (W 10, 12). Most scholars identify the battle as a mythical one deeply rooted in local Attic legend: the war of Theseus and his Athenians against the Amazons, those female warriors from the distant east.[75] Local tradition placed the battle in the western part of the city. The lines were said to have extended from the Mouseion to the Pnyx, and the fighting raged as far as the shrine of the Eumenides on the Areopagos.[76] Thus the story was appropriately depicted on that side of the temple which overlooked the legendary battlefield. On

[71] Basic publications of the metope sculptures are: F. Brommer, *Die Metopen des Parthenon* (Mainz 1967), with full earlier bibliography; E. Berger, *Der Parthenon in Basel: Dokumentation zu den Metopen* (Mainz 1986), with bibliography from 1967 to 1986. See also generally F. Brommer, *The Sculptures of the Parthenon* (London 1979); J. Boardman and D. Finn, *The Parthenon and Its Sculptures* (London 1985); H. Knell, *Mythos und Polis: Bildprogramme griechisches Bauskulptur* (Darmstadt 1990) 95–126 (east metopes), 106–108.
[72] See Berger, *Metopen*, 61–62. Brommer, *Metopen*, 201–203, identified E 5 as Demeter and E 6 as a male god. The various identifications proposed by different scholars are conveniently set out in tabular form by Berger, *Metopen*, 56–57.
[73] So Brommer, *Metopen*, 203–204, 207, 208.
[74] Detailed description of the extant remains: Brommer, *Metopen*, 3–21; Berger, *Metopen*, 99–107; C. Praschniker, *ÖJh* 41 (1954) 5–54. See also Knell, *Mythos und Polis*, 101–102.
[75] So Berger, *Metopen*, 99. Brommer, *Metopen*, 192, lists the great number of earlier scholars who have accepted the west metopes as the Amazonomachy; but he argues at length against the identification (191–195) and prefers to call the subject Greeks fighting Persians. Cf. also Brommer, *Sculptures of the Parthenon*, 21–22.
[76] Aisch. *Eumen.* 685–690; Plut. *Thes.* 27, citing Hellanikos.

the Parthenon the battle was apparently represented with scenes of single combat alternating with unequal duels between horseman and foot soldier. The exact representations cannot be certainly understood, however, because the metopes are so badly defaced; and there are few clear traces of female anatomy to indicate the disposition of the Amazons. Nonetheless, one gains the impression that the battle was not as one-sided as the Gigantomachy of the eastern facade. Five of the Amazon cavalry gallop victoriously over fallen Greeks (W 3, 5, 9, 11, 13), while only three scenes show the Greeks clearly prevailing (W 4, 10, 14). In two of the duels on foot (W 2, 12), the outcome still hangs in the balance, but the equestrian Amazon of W 1 is poised to hurl her spear at the Greek of W 2. Some scholars have seen in the shattered remains of W 8 a Greek hero, possibly Theseus, locked in even combat with a mounted Amazon.[77]

The metopes of the southern flank portray one of the favorite subjects of the Greek artistic repertory. To be sure, it involved violent combat, but this time more of a brawl than a battle: the fight between the Lapiths and Centaurs, when those crude denizens of the mountains, besotted with lust and drink, attempted to rape the Lapith women at the wedding feast of Peirithoos and Deidameia. The various episodes of the fray unfolded on twenty-four metopes ranged in two symmetrical groups on either end of the south side, and curiously separated from each other by eight central metopes.[78] The scenes of the Centauromachy are the best preserved of the metopes, for they miraculously escaped the iconoclastic vandalism which so destroyed the sculptures on the other three sides of the Doric frieze. As a result, the southern metopes still enable us to glimpse the extraordinary vigor and variety with which the sculptors treated their subject. As in the battles on the eastern and western fronts, the square format of the metope panel once again lent itself to scenes of single combat, but now the equestrian Amazons of the west front are replaced by the equine bodies of the hybrid monsters. This is no military engagement like the Amazonomachy, however, for the Lapiths are not properly armed for battle. Only two (S 4, 11) may manage to grab shields to fend off their attackers, and only one (S 32) may originally have been shown with a helmet.[79] In fact, many of the men fight in the stylish mantles that they wore to the wedding, although for the most part their drapery is in advanced stages of disarray.[80] Several details of iconography make it plain that the brawl erupted in the aftermath of the wedding banquet. In the violence of the onset, great jars that once held the wine for the feast have been thrown to the floor and roll about among the feet of the combatants (S 9, 23), while a Centaur has seized another vessel and is about to smash it on the head of his fallen foe (S 4). Two of the Greeks (S 1, 26) wield roasting spits as if they were spears, and the attacking Centaurs rear up in pain. On both metopes the spits were added to the sculpture as bronze rods for the attachment of which small round holes, still visible today, were drilled in the Centaurs' left rear flanks.[81] The sculptors took pains to depict the outrageous disruption of the wedding ceremony, for five metopes (S 10, 12, 22, 25, 29) show Centaurs attacking women whose clothes are torn and disheveled to reveal their naked breasts. One woman is being physically abducted by her assailant (S 29), and two others who narrowly escaped the assault cling in terror to the statue of a goddess (S 21) in the hope that this act of sacred asylum will be left inviolate.

---

[77] Praschniker, *ÖJh* 41 (1954) 48; Berger, *Metopen,* 103 and pl. 114. Brommer, *Metopen,* 12–13, is much less optimistic in his reading of the scant remains.

[78] Detailed descriptions of the south metopes, Brommer, *Metopen,* 71–129; Berger, *Metopen,* 82–98. On the subject matter as the familiar Thessalian Centauromachy, Berger, *Metopen,* 77–79. Brommer (*Metopen,* 230–238) has found few followers in his attempt to argue that the subject is an otherwise unknown local Attic Centauromachy in order to explain the eight central metopes, S 13–20, which are known only from the Carrey drawings. The number of scenes in the Centauromachy depends upon the disposition of S 21, which most scholars interpret as two Lapith women taking refuge from the Centaurs at a cult statue. See also Knell, *Mythos und Polis,* 98–102.

[79] For S 32, see Brommer, *Metopen,* 128; Berger, *Metopen,* 98.

[80] Disheveled male drapery forms a prominent part of the composition in S 1, 2, 3, 6, 7, 8, 9, 11, 23, 26, 27, 30.

[81] Brommer, *Metopen,* 74, 115–116.

The eight central metopes of the south flank are known only from the drawings of Carrey, made in 1674 before the explosion that destroyed the central section of the building. Accordingly, their interpretation has been long and heatedly debated, and some scholars have even despaired of finding a uniform theme embracing the whole south side of the temple.[82] In view of the fact that the Centauromachy rages on either side of the central scenes to the ends of the frieze, it seems preferable to think that they were closely related to the same cycle of myth. A most attractive suggestion would understand the central metopes as alluding to the monstrous ancestry of the race of Centaurs, that is, the story of the hubris and punishment of Ixion, the father of Peirithoos.[83] The myth told how Ixion, at his own wedding, had murdered his father-in-law-to-be, an act that may have been depicted on metope S 16.[84] Thereafter, in his hubris he conceived an overweening infatuation for the goddess Hera herself and attempted to seduce her on Olympos. Before consigning Ixion to perpetual punishment, Zeus drove him mad with lust and fashioned a cloud-phantom in the likeness of Hera which he allowed Ixion to embrace. The unnatural offspring of this strange union was Kentauros, who consorted with the Magnesian mares of Mount Pelion and so sired the race of monsters that bore his name.[85] If this is the correct reading of the metopes S 13 to 20, this cycle of myth greatly enriches our understanding of the way the Centauromachy was depicted on the Parthenon, for it exposes a dark substratum of violent hubris which had spawned the hybrid monsters in the first place and endowed them with an inherited propensity to attack the very underpinnings of civilized society.[86]

On the northern flank of the temple we find ourselves once again in the realm of heroic legend and of brutal conflict. Nineteen of the original thirty-two metopes are lost, and totally unrecorded even in the drawings of the early travelers. Eleven of the surviving metopes are still in their positions on the temple, but all of these except one have been severely and deliberately mutilated. Nevertheless, the preserved pieces seem to fall in a recognizable cycle of myth. The general subject is the sack of Troy at the hands of the Greeks.[87] It has long been recognized that metopes N 24 and N 25 represent the recovery of Helen by Menelaos because an Attic red-figure oinochoe depicts that scene, with the two figures disposed in identical positions as on the Parthenon and identified by appropriate inscriptions.[88] Menelaos rushes to the right (N 24), armed with shield and sword and no doubt originally wearing a helmet. Behind him to the left follows another armed Greek. Helen flees in terror to a sacred shrine and clutches the statue of the Palladion as her only hope of safety (N 25). But the stately figure of Aphrodite intervenes between outraged husband and faithless wife, while the tiny winged figure of Eros flies toward Menelaos and rekindles the old flame of love that ten years of war had snuffed out. In the vase painting, Menelaos drops his sword in surprise. In metope N 28, it has been possible to recognize the figure of Aineas armed with a shield and escaping the

[82] The diverse and often wildly disparate interpretations that have been proposed for S 13–21 are summarized in tabular form by Berger, *Metopen,* 92–93.

[83] This interpretation, expounded by E. Simon, *JdI* 90 (1975) 100–120, represents a radical departure from the local Attic myths that most scholars have proposed to decipher in the central metopes. Her ideas have been fruitfully developed by Castriota, *Myth, Ethos,* 157–165.

[84] So Simon, *JdI* 90 (1975) 112. In this interpretation she is followed by E. Harrison, in G. Kopke and M. B. Moore, eds., *Studies von Blanckenhagen,* 92; but Harrison (pp. 97–98) reads S 17–20 as illustrating different scenes from the wedding ceremony of Perithoos.

[85] The myth had been recounted in detail in the 470s by Pindar, *Pyth.* 2.21–48, and had formed the subject matter for drama in the Athenian theater during the second quarter of the century, for the titles *Ixion* and *Perraibides* are listed among the lost plays of Aischylos. See Radt, *TrGF* 5 T 78, 7a, 13b; for the fragments of *Ixion, TrGF* 5 F 89–93; of *Perraibides, TrGF* 5 F 184–186.

[86] Castriota, *Myth, Ethos,* 159–162.

[87] Detailed descriptions of the surviving metopes: Brommer, *Metopen,* 39–70; Berger, *Metopen,* 11–50.

[88] Red-figure oinochoe, Vatican H 525: *ARV²* 1173; *Paralipomena* 460. See L. Kahil, *Les enlèvements et le retour d'Hélène* (Paris 1955) 90–91, no. 72, pl. 66; Simon, *AntK* 7 (1964) 91–95, pl. 30; Berger, *Metopen,* 38–39; G. Ferrari Pinney, *HSCP* 100 (2000) 119–150; Knell, *Mythos und Polis,* 103–105.

ruins of his homeland with his son Askanios, his aging father, and his household gods.[89] In metope
N 2, traces of a curved ship's stern are barely discernible, along with two figures moving right who
are better interpreted as disembarking rather than preparing to depart. Two more warriors can be
made out in N 3. One thinks of Odysseus and Neoptolemos bringing from the island of Lemnos the
wounded Philoktetes, last of the Greek heroes to reach the Trojan shores, but without whose arms
and presence it was ordained that Troy could not be captured.[90]

The selection of scenes is highly significant because it reveals the manner in which the sculptors of the Parthenon chose to portray the myth of the Ilioupersis. Unlike the battles on the east,
west, and south metopes, no scenes of actual combat survive among the Trojan cycle metopes.
Missing too are the scenes of rape and pillage and violent killing; and this is the more remarkable
because the vase painters of the early fifth century had depicted with morbid delight such brutal
carnage at the sack of Troy.[91] Although it may be due to the chance of survival, the sculptors seem
rather to have concentrated on incidents of ominous import, of high drama and pathos, and of
reconciliation. The Trojan scenes are enclosed at either end by two celestial deities to give the action a place in time. A goddess on horseback (N 29) is securely identified as Selene, goddess of the
moon, since part of the lunar crescent survives in the upper right-hand corner of the metope. Her
counterpart in metope N 1 is a figure of indeterminate gender driving a horse-drawn chariot. The
deity has often been called Helios, but there is no suggestion that the chariot emerges from the
depth of the ocean at the dawn of morning, as it is so clearly shown on metope E 14 and in the east
pediment. It is better, then, to recognize the charioteer as Nyx, goddess of night;[92] so the nocturnal
goddesses frame the Trojan scenes and time the action in agreement with the literary versions of the
fall of Troy. It is midnight, then, in the streets of Troy when Menelaos confronts Helen and Aineas
departs for the west.

The sculptors of the Parthenon have set their special stamp on the interpretation of the Ilioduper-
sis by including in the three westernmost metopes (N 30–32) an assembly of the Olympian gods. In
the center (N 31), Zeus is seated on a rocky outcrop, presumably on the slopes of Mount Ida, and
before him stands a winged figure usually identified as Iris. To the left, in N 30, are two standing
male gods who have been variously identified, while to the right are two female deities (N 32). The
matronly goddess seated on an outcrop of rock is better recognized as Hera, rather then Athena, since
there is no trace of an aegis covering her chiton and himation; before her stands a second goddess
gesticulating in animated conversation.[93] An attractive recent interpretation of the three metopes has
proposed that they represent the council of the gods in which Zeus, through the mediation of Themis,
persuaded the supporters of the Greeks and the supporters of the Trojans to stop their bickering and

---

[89] The departure of Aineas was reconstructed in metopes N 27 and N 28 by Praschniker, *Parthenonstudien,* 107–114,
followed by Brommer, *Metopen,* 54, 212–216, and others; see the summary of opinion, Berger, *Metopen,* 16–17, and cf.
44–45.

[90] Reconstruction of N 3, Praschniker, *Parthenonstudien,* 114–122. Interpreted as the arrival of Philoktetes: F. Studniczka, *Neue Jahrbücher für Wissenschaft und Jugendbildung* 5 (1929) 642–647; and cf. B. Schweitzer, *JdI* 55 (1940) 185–
187. For various readings of the remains, see the survey of Berger, *Metopen,* 14–15, 20–22; Brommer, *Metopen,* 219.

[91] For depiction of the Ilioupersis in earlier Greek art, see the discussion of Castriota, *Myth, Ethos,* 96–101, 168–169;
cf. K. Schefold, *Myth and Legend in Early Greek Art* (New York 1966) 46–47; K. Schefold, *Gods and Heroes in Late Archaic
Greek Art* (Cambridge 1992) 283–290.

[92] The identification of N 29 as Selene, by Praschniker, *Parthenonstudien,* 89–93, has been generally accepted by all
subsequent scholars; cf. the survey of Berger, *Metopen,* 14. There has been greater diversity of opinion as to whether N 1
represents Helios or Nyx or some other deity; cf. Brommer, *Metopen,* 218–219; Berger, *Metopen,* 22–24. But the arguments
in favor of Nyx seem more compelling; so Schweitzer, *JdI* 55 (1940) 185–186; Simon, *JdI* 90 (1975) 109–110; Castriota,
Myth, Ethos, 171–173.

[93] For interpretation of N 30–32 as a council of the gods, Praschniker, *Parthenonstudien,* 132–141. His identification
of Zeus and Iris on N 31 has been universally accepted; cf. Brommer, *Metopen,* 48, 221; Berger, *Metopen,* 50–53. For the
seated goddess as Hera: Praschniker, *Parthenonstudien,* 136–139; Brommer, *Metopen,* 59–60.

Figure 25. South half of east pediment, drawing by Carrey, 1674

allow the preordained destruction of Troy to go forward.[94] The inclusion of the Olympians materially affects our reading of the familiar myth, for their presence as approving witnesses confers a special status upon the Greeks who are sacking Troy. They have become the instruments of divine justice; they are the special agents of Zeus who implement the sacred ordinance of the gods. In this light, the destruction of Troy emerges as the inevitable punishment meted out by Zeus for the sins of Paris. By his abduction of Helen, he had flouted the sacred laws of marriage and guest-friendship which lay at the roots of social order in a civilized state. For these intolerable acts of hubris, not only Paris but the whole race of Trojans were doomed to utter destruction by divine will ordained.

The Pediments

Above the metopes the place of honor was reserved for Athena, and she it was who dominated the two pediments of the Parthenon. Happily, the subjects of these immense compositions are not in doubt, thanks to the specific statement of Pausanias (1.24.5) that the east pediment showed the birth of Athena, while in the western the goddess strove with Poseidon for possession of the land of Attica. The statement is most fortunate, for without it we should doubtless have no inkling whatever as to the subject of the east pediment; and the struggle of Athena and Poseidon could perhaps have been only tentatively deciphered with the aid of Carrey's drawings (Figs. 25–28). But pass beyond the fact of Pausanias's statement and one enters a no-man's-land of scholarly disputation; for beyond this there is little agreement as to the precise disposition of the surviving fragments or the details of reconstruction and identification of the figures.[95] For our immediate purpose the broad lines of composition are sufficient, and these seem clear enough. The east pediment is conceived on a cosmic scale. The action takes place on Mount Olympos, but its scene has been expanded to encompass the whole firmament, spreading from the sun's arising to the setting moon. The moment is the break of day, when horses of Helios first rear their heads above the waves of Ocean, and Selene's chariot descends the western sky. The horses of these two deities toss their great heads in the angles of the gable, their bodies together

[94] Castriota, *Myth, Ethos*, 172–174; and cf. Simon, *JdI* 90 (1975) 110–111.
[95] Comprehensive studies of the pedimental sculptures with full bibliography up to the date of publication are F. Brommer, *Die Skulpturen der Parthenon-Giebel* (Mainz 1963), and O. Palagia, *The Pediments of the Parthenon* (Leiden 1993). For studies specifically concerned with reconstruction of the east pediment, see Harrison, *AJA* 71 (1967) 27–58; I. Beyer, *AM* 89 (1974) 123–149; E. Berger, *Die Geburt der Athena im Ostgiebel des Parthenon* (Basel 1974); E. Berger, *AntK* 20 (1977) 124–141; K. Jeppesen, in *Parthenon-Kongress Basel*, 267–277; Knell, *Mythos und Polis*, 115–119.

Figure 26. North half of east pediment, drawing by Carrey, 1674

with the chariots they draw invisible, as it were, beneath the pediment floor.[96] In the left angle, the horses of Helios breast the waves, snorting with fiery energy at the dawn of morning, while opposite them the horses of Selene are weary from the long night's drive. No image has ever caught more perfectly the animals' exhausted expressions. The lead horse pants with nostrils flared; with bulging eyes and laid-back ears his noble head sinks beneath the surface of the sea. Within this setting, the gods were assembled to witness the miracle of Athena's birth. But unfortunately all the figures from the central part of the pediment have been destroyed except for a few fragments, and thus the main action of the scene can only be restored conjecturally. Almost certainly all twelve Olympians were present together with their closest friends and relations with whom they were so often depicted in other media of art. Zeus, in all likelihood, occupied the center, a truly formidable figure gazing in imperturbable majesty at his daughter, newly sprung from his own brow without the mediation of a female mother. On one side of him would stand Athena, full grown and fully armed. Already in the moment of birth she was the goddess of war, and a winged Victory possibly reached out to crown her head. Behind Athena would have stood Hephaistos still brandishing the double axe with which he had brought to pass the miraculous birth. Several pieces of a standing female deity should probably be identified as Hera, and the scale is appropriate for her to stand beside Zeus next to the center. Groups of standing or seated gods numbering three or four each need to be restored to the left and right of the central group, but there is no way of recovering the actual composition of the scene.[97]

On the analogy of the west pediment, we may suppose that the momentous event of the goddess's birth was expressed by an explosive outward movement of the figures, and certainly a centrifugal ripple of excitement animates the surviving figures from the two angles of the pediment. We feel this most strongly in the sharply striding movement of Artemis (G), who clutches her wind-blown mantle with both raised hands. Although the other figures are seated or reclining at ease in the

[96] Chariot of Helios (A, B, C): Brommer, *Giebel*, 3–7; Palagia, *Pediments*, 18–19. Chariot of Selene (N, O, P): Brommer, *Giebel*, 22–26; Palagia, *Pediments*, 22–23.

[97] Earlier attempts to restore the lost central group tried to make use of a representation of the birth of Athena, supposedly copied from the Parthenon, on a Roman altar in Madrid (later remade into a wellhead and thus known as the Madrid puteal). See R. Carpenter, *Hesperia* 2 (1933) 1–88. On the basis of this evidence, Zeus was usually restored as enthroned at the center of the pediment. More recently, scholars have come to recognize that the prototype of the puteal was fourth-century in date, and, moreover, that restoration of an enthroned marble statue ca. 3.50 m high at the center of the pediment would present formidable technical difficulties. Accordingly, Zeus has gradually come to be restored as a standing figure like his counterpart in the east pediment of the Temple of Zeus at Olympia. Cf. Brommer, *Giebel*, 143; Beyer, *AM* 89 (1974) 134; Berger, *Geburt*, 15–16; Palagia, *Pediments*, 27, 29.

Figure 27. North half of west pediment, drawing by Carrey, 1674

narrowing angles of the gable, the wind rustles the drapery over their bodies, and their attention is riveted on the central action, except for Aphrodite (M), who gazes languidly at the departing Moon, and Dionysos (D), if so he be, who turns to greet the rising Sun.[98] From an unlikely source, it is possible to get some feeling for the powerful animation of the figures that the artist caught in his design. The source is a short poem, the *Homeric Hymn to Athena* (28.4–16):

> From his awful head wise Zeus himself bare her arrayed in warlike arms of flashing gold, and awe seized all the gods as they gazed. But Athena sprang quickly from the immortal head and stood before Zeus who holds the aegis, shaking a sharp spear. Great Olympus began to reel horribly at the might of the bright-eyed goddess, and earth round about cried fearfully, and the sea was moved and tossed with dark waves, while foam burst forth suddenly. The bright son of Hyperion stopped his swift-footed horses a long while, until the maiden Pallas Athena had stripped the heavenly armor from her immortal shoulders. And wise Zeus was glad.[99]

The vivid description of Athena and the inclusion of the sun god Helios, son of Hyperion, indicates a close relationship between poem and pediment. The mention of Helios is the more remarkable because no other artistic version of the birth of Athena includes the sun god among the attending divinities. Moreover, the appearance of Helios and his chariot in the east pediment of the Parthenon is the god's earliest representation in sculpture. There is no indication of the date at which the poem was composed, and so we are left to wonder whether the artist took the inspiration from the vivid lines of the poem, or whether the poet responded to the splendid sculptures of the pediment.[100]

Although more of the original sculptures have now been lost from the west pediment than from the east, the whole composition was in remarkably good state of preservation when Carrey drew the figures in 1674 (Figs. 27, 28). His drawings thus enable us to get a clear sense of the overall design,

---

[98] For variations of opinion concerning the identification of individual figures, see the chart assembled by Palagia, *Pediments*, 60.

[99] Trans. H. G. Evelyn-White (Loeb).

[100] On the relation of poem and pediment, cf. Harrison, *AJA* 71 (1967) 38.

Figure 28. South half of west pediment, drawing by Carrey, 1674

and they provide an accurate record of the poses of the individual figures, but the increase in visual detail has by no means served to reduce the number of conflicting opinions concerning interpretation of the scene.[101] From Pausanias's specific statement, we know that the myth depicted was the contest between Athena and Poseidon for the land of Attica. It is a most unusual subject of which there is no artistic representation earlier than the Parthenon, and in fact there is no literary reference to the myth before Herodotos's *Histories*.[102] The designer of the pediment was thus in no way constrained by any iconographical tradition and could indulge in free invention. He chose to show the two deities, their escorts, and the chariots in which they traveled occupying the center of the scene, while ranged on either side were groups of spectators crowding the angles of the pediment. They balance the Olympic pantheon that celebrated the birth of Athena on the east pediment, but here it was the autochthonous heroes and heroines of Attica who gathered to observe the fierce struggle, as a result of which Athena would become guardian of the city of Athens. In the center, god and goddess confront each other, Poseidon recoiling to the right and Athena striding left, their legs crossing, their eyes aglare in an attitude of tense conflict.[103] Behind them, their great horses and chariots create a striking visual image that translates the Olympian duel into a familiar and specifically Athenian contest. Like *apobatai* at the Panathenaia, they have raced their chariots from Olympos with the Acropolis as the goal. We see them at the moment when the two gods have leapt from their speeding cars as if they were hoplites in the Athenian games. They rush to plant their tokens first on the sacred rock, and thus to win the race and gain possession of the land. Poseidon braces his feet wide apart and lifts the trident in his right hand. Every muscle of his great torso ripples with the taut energy of his titanic strength. In the next instant he will drive his trident down into the rock and cause the salt seawater to gush forth.[104] But in that very instant a miracle occurs. With the effortless legerdemain that characterizes all her victories, Athena conjures from the sacred rock her special gift to men which won the day, "a growth uncon-

[101] On reconstruction of the west pediment: Brommer, *Giebel,* 158–170; Palagia, *Pediments,* 40–52. Cf. also Harrison, in D. Fraser et al., eds., *Essays in the History of Art Presented to Rudolf Wittkower* (London 1967) 1–9; Simon, in H. A. Cahn and E. Simon, eds., *Tainia: Roland Hampe zum 70. Geburtstag* (Mainz 1980) 238–255; L. Weidauer, *AA* (1985) 195–210; B. S. Spaeth, *Hesperia* 60 (1991) 331–362.

[102] Hdt. 8.55.

[103] For the surviving fragments of Athena (L) and Poseidon (M): Brommer, *Giebel,* 39–40, 42–43; Palagia, *Pediments,* 45–47.

[104] On the nature of the contest and the moment depicted in the pediment, see J. Binder, in K. J. Rigsby, ed., *Studies Dow,* 15–22.

quered, self-renewing, causing fear to foemen's spears, which flourishes greatly in the land—leaf of the gray olive, nourisher of children."[105] It is the moment when the sacred olive of Attica has just sprung from the rock of the Acropolis. The tree stood between the gods at the exact center of the composition with Athena's sacred serpent coiling up its trunk, a palpable token of her victory in the contest.[106]

Athena's olive tree bursts forth with explosive energy that only divine power can produce. The gods' horses rear up on either side at the sight, while the charioteers rein them in with all their strength. A strong gust of wind whips the drapery of the assembled spectators, and they react with astonishment when they see what it is that the goddess has bestowed upon the land. The two groups of spectators at the angles of the pediment play a vital role in the myth. Although there is considerable disagreement about the identification of individual figures, they are generally recognized as early heroes and heroines of Attica, the autochthonous ancestors of classical Athenians.[107] Most readily identifiable is the seated male figure at the far left (B), who is almost certainly Kekrops, first king of Attica, as is indicated by the snake that coils at his feet. In Carrey's drawing his right arm is raised level with his chest, and it probably held a scepter. One of his daughters (C) kneels beside him, her arms flung around his shoulders. Next to the seated pair, the group of two women and a young child (D, E, F) are best interpreted as the other two daughters of Kekrops and his foster son, the boy Erichthonios, with whose upbringing Athena herself had entrusted him.[108] The great reclining figure in the extreme left angle (A) was another Attic hero, but there is little agreement concerning his identity, and the empty space between him and Kekrops will have held another figure of the same type.[109] The royal family of the Acropolis was balanced by another group of early Athenians in the right angle of the pediment. Behind Poseidon's chariot were three seated women, one carrying two small children (P, Q, R), a second with an older boy on her knee (S, T), and a third leaning toward the empty space to the right (U), who evidently formed a pair with the missing figure. In the right angle were a reclining male and female (V, W).

In Carrey's drawings, it is noticeable that the spectators around Kekrops are stirred with greater excitement than those behind Poseidon's chariot. Accordingly, it has been plausibly suggested that the two groups were arrayed behind the deity of their choice, supporters of Athena to the left and supporters of Poseidon to the right.[110] The critical importance of the spectators emerges from some of the earliest references to the myth: Kekrops and his Athenians judged the contest of the gods. In the *Memorabilia* of Xenophon (3.5.9–10), Sokrates tells the son of Perikles that one can inspire men to greatness by reminding them of their earliest ancestors' greatness, to which the young man

---

[105] Soph. *OC* 698–701, trans. R. C. Jebb.

[106] On the fragments of the tree, Brommer, *Giebel*, 41, 80, nos. 148 and 149, 96, no. 4, 101, no. 11. The marble pieces are now taken to be Roman in date and have been dissociated from the pediment. The original was probably of bronze: Palagia, *Pediments*, 46–47. Simon, in Cahn and Simon, eds., *Tainia*, 243–244, has reinterpreted the moment depicted. She argues that the pediment showed a later stage in the myth when Poseidon, enraged by his loss, attacked Attica with floods until forced to desist by the intervention of Zeus; followed by Spaeth, *Hesperia* 60 (1991) 333, note 3. But cf. the critical remarks of Castriota, *Myth, Ethos*, 147–148. It is preferable to understand the pediment as celebrating the moment of Athena's victory, a reading that accords much better with the overarching theme of the sculptural program.

[107] For the various identifications proposed for individual figures, see the chart, Palagia, *Pediments*, 61.

[108] Figure B has been almost universally identified as Kekrops; see Brommer, *Giebel*, 166–167, 182. A majority of scholars has recognized his three daughters, Pandrosos, Herse, and Aglauros, in C, D, and F: Jeppesen, *ActaArch* 34 (1963) 75; Harrison, in *Essays Wittkower*, 9, note 55; Binder, in *Studies Dow*, 20; Spaeth, *Hesperia* 60 (1991) 347; Castriota, *Myth, Ethos*, 145–146; Palagia, *Pediments*, 43. The young boy (E) has more often been called Erysichthon, the natural son of Kekrops: Brommer, *Giebel*, 167; Palagia, *Pediments*, 44; but the arguments in favor of Erichthonios make a stronger case; see Jeppesen, *ActaArch* 34 (1963) 76–77; Spaeth, *Hesperia* 60 (1991) 350; and cf. Harrison (above); Castriota, *Myth, Ethos*, 145, 149.

[109] Others prefer to see A and his counterpart in the right angle, the pair V and W, as personifications of Attic rivers: Palagia, *Pediments*, 41.

[110] For the idea that the spectators were opposing partisans of the two gods, Weidauer, *AA* (1985) 206–207; Spaeth, *Hesperia* 60 (1991) 345. But their identification as Eleusinian heroes in the right half of the pediment is unconvincing.

replies, "Do you mean the judgment of the gods which Kekrops and his people rendered because of their virtue?" To classical Athenians, the underlying message of the myth was that Athens occupied a special place in the affections of the gods because of the excellent virtue of their autochthonous ancestors. In a well-known passage of the *Menexenos* (237C), Sokrates cites the myth as evidence of that special relationship: "The country is worthy to be praised, not only by us, but by all mankind; first, and above all, because it happens that she is beloved of the gods. This is proved by the strife and judgment of the gods who contended for her possession. And ought not the country that the gods praise to be praised by all mankind?" The contest of Athena and Poseidon sets Attica apart from all other countries and marks her as a prized possession for which immortal gods compete. Moreover, the contest takes the form of a singularly Athenian chariot race in which the gods alight from their speeding vehicles and mark their tokens upon the rock of the Acropolis. Most important of all is the way the contest is decided: mortal Athenians, a king and his people, are trusted to pass fair judgment on immortal contestants.[111]

Mythical Victories

The various myths and legends that were selected for the decorative program of the Parthenon seem at first glance to yield little in the way of a common denominator. We should not suppose, however, that they were chosen purely for the possibilities of their pictorial development, for Pheidias deliberately repeated several of the same myths in the subordinate decoration of the gold and ivory statue. On the edges of the goddess's sandals the myth of the Lapiths and Centaurs was repeated from the southern metopes. The battle of Athenians and Amazons on Athena's great shield reiterated the subject of the western metopes, while the warring gods and giants of the eastern metopes appeared again on the concave inner surface of the shield. The serpent that coiled between the shield and Athena's foot was thought to represent the earthborn Erichthonios, who may well have appeared also on the west pediment among the family of Kekrops.[112] Of these, the battle of the gods and giants was a subject especially dear to Athena. That scene had adorned the pediment of her archaic temple destroyed by the Persians, and immemorial tradition required that this theme, and this alone, should be woven into the decoration of the Panathenaic peplos.[113] So great a tribute was this myth to Athena's special prowess in war. Similarly, on the eastern metopes of the Parthenon, Athena's role in the battle was specially celebrated; for she it is who brings the victory, and a Nike crowns her even as she dispatches her foe (metope E 4).

It may be well to recall at this point the circumstances surrounding the beginning of the building program. We found reason to believe that the Parthenon was originally proposed as a thankoffering to Athena for the victories of the Persian Wars, and originally begun for that purpose in the first flush of victory after the Battle of Marathon. The attitude of later Athenians themselves toward the building is illuminating. We have seen that, within a century of its construction, Demosthenes, speaking on the Pnyx, could refer with a wave of the hand to the buildings on the Acropolis as "im-

---

[111] Binder, in *Studies Dow,* 15–22, has rightly emphasized the importance of interpreting both the pediment and the myth in terms of the earliest literary testimonia. The discussion of Castriota, *Myth, Ethos,* 145–151, is greatly flawed by his preference for the later and Latin sources. The heavily embroidered anecdote in Augustine, *City of God* 18.9 (purportedly based on Varro, but to what extent is by no means clear), should plainly not be given the same evidential value as two Athenian authors of the Classical period.

[112] On the decoration of the statue, see Pliny, *NH* 36.18; Paus. 1.17.2, 24.5; and cf. Plut. *Per.* 31.4. See W.-H. Schuchardt, *AntP* 2 (1963) 31–53; N. Leipen, *Athena Parthenos: A Reconstruction* (Toronto 1971) 29–30 (sandals), 41–50 (shield), 50 (serpent); Harrison, *YCS* 30 (1996) 38–52; and specifically on the shield, Harrison, *Hesperia* 35 (1966) 107–133, and *AJA* 85 (1981) 281–317.

[113] Eur. *Hec.* 466–474, schol. 467, 468 (Schwartz); Eur. *IT* 222–224; schol. Aristoph. *Knights* 566a (II), 566c (Koster); Plato, *Euthphr.* 6B–C.

mortal possessions."[114] The Athenian orator swelled with civic pride as he regarded the great temple. It reminded him of the wealth which had once been Athens's; it evoked memories of the proudest hours of Athenian history; and he cited it together with the Propylaia, with the stoas and ship sheds, and all the other sacred monuments to a greater Athens of a bygone day. Without a doubt, the Periklean temple commemorated military battles, and those were the most momentous that had ever been fought on the soil of Greece. The feelings that the building inspired were patriotic, and the heroic victories that it commemorated were as much human as divine. Far more than a mere war tithe, however, the Parthenon was a glittering trophy to the totality of Athenian achievement—military, political, religious, and cultural. The sculptural cycle of the Parthenon encapsulated the Athenian claim to primacy in the Hellenic world of the fifth century. The long tradition of decorating Greek religious architecture, however, naturally required that such a message be expressed in the symbolism of myth, but the Periklean designers selected their subject matter so skillfully that the observer could read in the building's sculptural decoration the full scope of Athenian triumph. The sculptors of the Parthenon adopted the narrative strategy introduced by Mikon and Polygnotos in the paintings of the Stoa Poikile. In their paintings, military engagements of the recent past were assimilated to mythical exploits of ancient story, altered and reshaped as needed in order to elevate the action to heroic status.

On the western metopes of the Parthenon, the narrative of the Amazonomachy has become greatly abstracted, partly as a result of the iconic nature of the metope compositions with their repeated scenes of single combat. To be sure, no protagonist stands out among the Greeks to claim identification as Theseus, but the sculpture has been completely obliterated from two of the central metopes (W 6, 7), where Theseus would surely have had his place.[115] Moreover, the depiction of equestrian Amazons in six of the surviving metopes and the details of their exotic oriental dress plainly refer to the famous paintings of Mikon. To the Athenian of the mid-fifth century, they proclaimed a specifically Athenian victory, won by the hero Theseus and his people over a barbarian race of easterners who had invaded the land of Attica. The parallel with the Persian invasion at Marathon lies scarcely beneath the surface, and the connection between myth and history would have been drawn by every contemporary observer, since it had been so specifically enunciated by the juxtaposition of the Amazonomachy and the Battle of Marathon in the paintings of the Stoa Poikile.

In the scene of the Fall of Troy on the northern metopes, the metabolism of mythical invention has once again begun to work its way. We have seen that the sculptors of the Parthenon seem to have avoided the savage rampage and the slaughter of women and children so vividly immortalized by epic poetry and earlier artistic tradition. Once again they had the precedent of Polygnotos's painting in the Stoa Poikile. That painter had adopted a somewhat similar iconographic strategy for representing the Ilioupersis in a remarkably unorthodox manner. According to Pausanias, the picture showed the Greek leaders consulting about Ajax's outrage in dragging Kassandra from the altar of Athena. Ajax and Kassandra were both depicted, as well as other captive Trojan women.[116] On the Parthenon, the scenes of the capture of Troy unfold under the watchful eyes of the Olympic deities who by their very presence proclaim that the inexorable destruction of Troy fulfills the will of heaven. But Zeus's avengers are a united host of Greek heroes under the command of Agamemnon who triumph over an eastern enemy on Asian soil. Here also the process of mythical analogy suggests a still wider victory in contemporary history, the triumph of a united Greek league under the hegemony of Athens over the Asiatic empire of Persia. Already before the time of the Parthenon, Athenians had begun to think of Troy in terms of Persia, and the painting of the Ilioupersis in the

---

[114] Demosth. 22 *Andro.* 76, quoted above, chap. 1, p. 5.

[115] Unless Theseus is to be recognized in the terribly mutilated remains of W 8; see p. 109, note 77 above.

[116] Paus. 1.15.3. On Polygnotos's treatment of the Ilioupersis, Castriota, *Myth, Ethos*, 102–118, 127–133; for the north metopes of the Parthenon, 165–174.

Stoa Poikile had made the comparison explicit. At about the same time, the chorus of Aischylos's *Agamemnon* attributed to the Trojans all the excessive wealth, arrogance, and decadence of oriental barbarians, while the victorious Greek king reacted with disgust at the thought of returning home, like an eastern potentate, to prostrate sycophants and tapestries spread in his path.[117] Moreover, in the hands of Athenian artists, the mythical archetype perfectly prefigured the military successes of the recent past, for the greatest exploit of the united allies of the Delian League had been Kimon's victory at the Eurymedon River in Asia Minor. In that celebrated engagement, the armed forces of the king of Persia had gone down to ignominious defeat on both land and sea in a single day.[118] To be sure, the destruction of Troy did not afford a particularly apt military parallel for the battles at the Eurymedon. Whereas the Bronze Age heroes had eradicated the Trojan race, the Athenians and their allies had inflicted on the Persian king an important but isolated defeat. But it is the beauty of myth that it slides imperceptibly from legend to propaganda. It had no doubt been every Athenian's hope for a generation past to sack the barbarian kingdom on Asian soil, as their ancestors had done at Troy. For this the Delian League had been founded; but by the middle years of the fifth century this dream had not yet been realized. The best that the united forces of the Athenian allies could achieve was the stalemate in the Aegean which resulted in peace on the basis of the status quo. But the intricacies of international politics are no stuff for the sculptor, and we can forgive the boast implicit in the Trojan metopes of the Parthenon.

In the Centauromachy of the southern metopes, the designers of the Parthenon chose to depict another familiar myth which had been greatly transformed in the second quarter of the fifth century. In the new version of the myth, the wedding feast of Perithoos and Deidameia was disrupted by the brawling Centaurs, who were beaten off by the Lapiths led by the Athenian Theseus. Like the battle with the Amazons, this story too served to aggrandize the career of Theseus and was similarly embroidered from Herakles' various earlier adventures with Centaurs in the wild mountains of Thessaly and Arcadia. Some 144 black-figure vases and 27 red-figure vases show Herakles with Centaurs.[119] Once again, the Athenian version of Theseus's Centauromachy at the wedding of Perithoos appeared first in the 460s. The earliest of twenty-two examples in red-figure vase painting is a column-krater by the Florence Painter[120] that must be nearly contemporary with the most famous treatment of the story, in the west pediment of the Temple of Zeus at Olympia. In the Theseion at Athens, besides Mikon's picture of the Amazonomachy of Theseus, Pausanias (1.17.2) saw and described a painting of the battle of Lapiths and Centaurs in which Theseus was a protagonist and was depicted killing a Centaur. It has been convincingly suggested that the new version of the myth first appeared in Athenian art in that painting for the Theseion.[121]

In Athenian ideology of the second quarter of the fifth century, we have seen that three mythological exploits came to be compared with the titanic events of the Persian Wars: the war against the Amazons, the capture of Troy, and the battle of the Lapiths and Centaurs. In two cases, the mythology itself was adapted to give prominence to the Athenian Theseus, and splendid narrative paintings of all these stories were created for Athenian public buildings. The designers of the Parthenon chose the same three myths for positions of special importance in the sculptural decoration of the

[117] Aisch. *Ag.* 385–402 (the chorus describes the evil hubris of Paris), 918–925 (Agamemnon on barbarian decadence), 935–936 (Priam's decadence).
[118] On the battles at the Eurymedon, Thuc. 1.100.1; Diod. 11.60.3–62; Plut. *Kim.* 12–13.3. Meiggs, *AE*, 73–83.
[119] Black figure, Brommer, *Vasenlisten*³, 84–87, 178–181; red figure, *Vasenlisten*³, 88, 181.
[120] Examples collected by B. Shefton, *Hesperia* 31 (1962) 365–366. The earliest is Florence 3997, column-krater by the Florence Painter, *ARV*² 541, no. 1. For the date "a little earlier than the Olympia pediment," Shefton, 355, note 103.
[121] See Shefton, *Hesperia* 31 (1962) 355; Barron, *JHS* 92 (1972) 28. The new iconography may well have influenced scenes such as that by the Painter of the Woolly Satyrs on the volute-krater in New York, 07.286.84, *ARV*² 613, no. 1. It is particularly suggestive that the Centauromachy at the wedding feast should be combined with the great Amazonomachy in the decoration of a single vase, just as the myths appeared side by side on the walls of the Theseion.

temple: in the metopes of the exterior Doric frieze and on various decorated elements of Pheidias's cult statue. Significantly, the three heroic exploits were combined with a fourth myth, the battle of the gods and giants, in the eastern metopes. The latter provides a divine and celestial archetype for the heroic battles and was, moreover, a myth central to Athena's cult on the Acropolis. The eastern metopes carry the cycle of victory to its logical conclusion. They show the divine counterpart of the wars of men, in which, as we have seen, Athena plays a leading role. But here the warring forces will have become almost abstract principles to the fifth-century observer—the struggle of civilization and law against the rash insolence of primordial chaos, the punishment of mortal hubris by divine *sophrosyne*.[122] This was, of course, the most characteristic moral concept of classical thought; and in terms of this morality, the Athenians of the fifth century interpreted their ancestral myth and understood the current history of the age in which they lived. This same idea they will have found in the east metopes of the Parthenon, and they will have seen in them the ultimate victory of divine justice.

Thus grouped together, the four wars of ancient fable have become abstracted into mythic symbols of combat and victory. The abstraction of the narrative is greatly emphasized by the individual duels of the metope composition, icons which stand for battle, where nude heroic Greeks conquer invading Amazons at home, foreign Trojans in Asia, and raucous, raping Centaurs who disrupt the most sacred rites of marriage and guest-friendship, the unwritten laws of civilized life. Fascinating, too, is the metamorphosis in the enemy. In the juxtaposition of images, the historical invaders are seen now as decadent overweening foreigners, now as exotic women on horses, now as hybrid horse-man monsters. The sculptors expended endless ingenuity to model in vivid lines the cruel insolence and uncontrollable barbarity of the beasts, so that the victory became all the more remarkable. The Medes who came to Marathon and fought for Xerxes at Thermopylai, Salamis, and Plataia have become transmogrified into barbarians. *Hoi barbaroi* signified to Greeks a generalized enemy of monstrous and uncouth foreigners, who wore funny clothes and lacked Hellenic speech and gods and culture. In literature the term was first used extensively in the *Persians* of Aischylos in 472, and then by Herodotos in the next generation; but in art the idea is most perfectly expressed by the mythic images of the Parthenon metopes.[123]

The sculptures of the west pediment proclaim the victory of the goddess herself over Poseidon, her rival for possession of Attica. The token of victory was the creation of the olive tree, Athena's great gift to the people of Attica. This staple of Greek life had indeed been a primary source of Athenian agricultural prosperity during the Archaic period. But the rare subject of the west pediment, its first known representation in art, hints also at wider significance, based not upon idle boast but political reality. Athena's conquest of the sea god Poseidon inevitably brings to mind the fleets of Athenian triremes which had in fact made Athens mistress of the sea. It was the triremes that had won the day at Salamis; it was they that had turned the Aegean into an Attic lake, in the words of Thucydides (2.41.4), "forcing every sea and every land to give access to our daring." Everywhere on the temple, Athena herself appears in close association with victory. She is in the act of conquest on the west pediment and in the Gigantomachy of the eastern metopes, and she may have been crowned by a Nike in the east pediment, as she was again on metope E 4, while Nike was her charioteer on the west pediment.[124] Furthermore, the iconography of the cult statue itself particularly stressed Athena's power to give or withhold victory on the battlefield. She held a golden Nike in the palm of her hand, outstretched to the beholder at her feet. To the patriotic Athenian, it was a gesture of pride

[122] That the Gigantomachy was already interpreted in allegorical terms in the fourth century is suggested by Plato, *Rep.* 2.378B–E. This interpretation of the eastern metopes is expounded fully by C. J. Herington, *Athena Parthenos and Athena Polias* (Manchester 1955) 59–62.

[123] See chap. 2, pp. 14–17 above. The development of the concept of the barbarian in literature has been explored in detail by Hall, *Inventing the Barbarian*, 62–100. Interpretation of the Parthenon metopes, Castriota, *Myth, Ethos*, 134–174.

[124] Figure G of the west pediment is known only from Carrey's drawing, but it is generally identified as Nike: Brommer, *Giebel*, 36, 167; Palagia, *Pediments*, 44, 61.

Figure 29. View of west frieze, seen between columns of peristyle

and promise; it called to mind victories of the past and gave hope of more to come. But here the artist was subtler than the propagandist. He was aware of the fickle woman beneath the divine aegis, and he portrayed in that outstretched hand the gentle threat that it might one day be withdrawn, as it had been in Egypt, at Tanagra and Koroneia.[125]

When the observer's eye traveled upward from the cult statue within to the east pediment, it would alight first upon the huge figure of Zeus in the center with the newborn Athena beside him. The assembly of gods at the birth of Athena formed a magnificent subject with which to crown the entrance of the Parthenon. As a myth it expressed the peculiarly close relation of Athena to the chief godhead of the Olympic pantheon; and this in religious and mythological terms was Athena's principal claim to greatness.[126] It is also well to recall the time at which the scene is set. A new and powerful goddess is born at the dawning of a new and brighter day. With her is Hephaistos, her colleague in the civilizing arts, who would share with her the contemporary temple on the Kolonos Agoraios. In Athenian terms, the east pediment delivers a message of hope for the future. The morrow of the military victories brings a renaissance in the arts of Athenian culture.

The Frieze

The most unusual, and arguably the most spectacular, element of the sculptural program was the continuous Ionic frieze which ran around the top of the cella wall on all four sides of the temple (Fig. 29). The designers of the Parthenon determined to adorn this part of the building with a unified sculptural composition measuring 159.74 m in length.[127] The subject matter of the frieze was unique in the repertory of Greek architectural decoration because the designers departed radically from the tradition that prescribed mythological scenes as the only appropriate sculptural embellishment for Greek temples. Instead of traditional mythology, the artists of the Parthenon chose to depict scenes

[125] On the iconography of the Nike: Schuchhardt, *AntP* 2 (1963) 36; Leipen, *Athena Parthenos*, 34–36; Harrison, *YCS* 30 (1996) 51–52.

[126] The importance of Zeus in the east pediment has been well argued by Herington, *Athena Parthenos*, 57–58, 62; cf. Herington, *G&R* 10 Suppl. (1963) 61–73.

[127] See p. 105, note 66 above.

Figure 30. Cavalry of north frieze (N 113–116)

of the Panathenaic festival itself, and the enormous length of the available space naturally suggested that the composition take the form of the great procession which preceded the culminating rituals on the Acropolis.[128] It would be a mistake to expect the ancient artist to document religious ceremonial in detail or to cramp the scope of his composition by portraying the entire procession at any given moment of its progress. Time is deliberately left ambiguous in the structure of the narrative, and there is no attempt whatsoever to show the physical environment in which the scenes are set.[129] The designer gives us rather an impression of the whole. He shows us part of the procession forming up along the western side; he has caught the drama and excitement of the march as two parallel columns move from west to east along the long flanks; and he depicts the solemn dignity of the religious ritual as the two columns converge on the center of the eastern front. As originally placed on the building, the sculptured parade would unfold in a series of vignettes animated by the movement of the spectator himself as he walked about the temple, and each scene framed by the Doric columns of the peristyle which defined one's view of the frieze from below (Fig. 29).[130]

The longest and most dramatic section of the procession on the Parthenon is the splendid cavalry that brought up the rear (Fig. 30). The horsemen occupy the whole of the western end, fully half the southern flank, and only slightly less of the northern side. On the west frieze, we see them mustering. Some attempt to control their spirited horses prior to mounting (W 15, 23, 27), two horsemen lace their boots (W 12, 29), a groom holds a horse while his master ties the festal wreath upon his head (W 4, 6), still others move off to join the procession (W 2, 3, 7, 8, 10, 11, 13, 14, 16–21).[131] On the south flank, the cavalry is drawn up in ten ranks of six horsemen riding abreast. Each

[128] The many alternative and mutually exclusive approaches to interpreting the subject of the Parthenon frieze are summarized in endnote 4, pp. 401–404 below, with recent bibliography. See especially the discussion of J. Neils, *The Parthenon Frieze* (Cambridge 2001); Knell, *Mythos und Polis*, 108–115.

[129] P. Fehl, *JWarb* 24 (1961) 1–44, suggested that the different episodes of the frieze were punctuated by rocky landscape elements at intervals along the ground line, which would have been almost impossible to decipher from below. There is no element of the iconography to alert the viewer that the scene is supposed to be set in the Agora, as Boardman has repeatedly argued: in *Festschrift Brommer*, 39–49; in *Parthenon-Kongress Basel*, 210–215; and *RA* (1999) 325–326. Cf. W. Gauer, in *Parthenon-Kongress Basel*, 220–229. In the absence of any such indication, one infers that the designer did not attach importance to specificity of setting.

[130] See R. Stillwell, *Hesperia* 38 (1969) 231–241; R. Osborne, *JHS* 107 (1987) 99–100; and cf. Fehl, *JWarb* 24 (1961) 9.

[131] The numbers of the frieze slabs and individual figures follow the rearrangement and renumbering of the figures by I. Jenkins, *The Parthenon Frieze* (London 1994) 51, 54–111.

Figure 30 (*cont.*). Cavalry of north frieze (N 117–122)

group wears a distinctive uniform, and they all advance in disciplined formation at a full gallop. Assuredly, the scene is intended to recall the ten tribal contingents that participated in the *anthippasia*,
or sham cavalry battle, which was a contest among the ten Athenian tribes at the Great Panathenaia.[132] The horsemen of the north frieze are likewise sixty in number, and they too are shown in over-
lapping ranks, but the ranks are irregular, varying in number from four to eight riding abreast. Greek
gatherings are noisy and disorderly, and here the pace varies from a walk at the western end (N 131–
136) to a full gallop at the midpoint (N 91–98, 103–108), while the leading rank of cavalry (N 75–
80) rein in their mounts so as not to run down the last of the chariots in the next section of the procession. At intervals a marshal beckons to the men to close ranks (N 90), and the proud knights of
Athens sweep by in wave upon wave of cavalcade.[133]

   In front of the cavalry went the charioteers, each with a four-horse team and a passenger, or
apobates, a foot soldier armed with shield and helmet, who leapt from the chariot in full career and
remounted again in bold exercise of skill and daring (Fig. 31). According to the recent reconstructions of the missing portions of the frieze, the chariots on the south flank were ten in number, like
the squadrons of the cavalry, while the chariotry of the north frieze numbered eleven groups.[134]
The latter illustrated all phases of this exciting contest. The first group is ready at the starting line; a
groom holds the horses' halters, and the foot soldier is posed beside the car (N 72–74). In the next
three groups, the *apobates* swings aboard the chariot as the horses move off at a canter (N 63–71).
There are some wild moments when a marshal leaps from the path of an oncoming team, his cloak
in disarray, his arm flung up in angry gesticulation (N 65). The remaining chariots charge forward at
full gallop, most probably with the foot soldier riding beside the driver (N 52–62). But the leading

---

[132] On the dress and tenfold division of the south horsemen, Harrison, in *Parthenon-Kongress Basel*, 230–232; Jenkins,
Frieze, 5–63. On the *anthippasia*, D. Kyle, *Athletics in Ancient Athens* (Leiden 1987) 189–190; G. R. Bugh, *The Horsemen
of Athens* (Princeton 1988) 59–60; E. Vanderpool, *Hesperia* 43 (1974) 311–313. The event was a tribal contest at both the
Great Panathenaia and the Olympieia, *IG* II² 3079 (282/1), but no viewer of the Parthenon frieze will have confused it
with the latter festival.
   [133] On the horsemen of the north frieze, Jenkins, *Frieze,* 99–101.
   [134] Jenkins, *Frieze,* 64–68 (south), 88–95 (north); E. Berger and M. Gisler-Huwiler, *Der Parthenon in Basel: Dokumentation zum Fries* (Mainz 1996) 70–72 (north), 124–125 (south). On the nature of the apobatic contest, Dion. Hal.
Ant. Rom. 7.73.3; Demosth. 61 *Erotikos* 23–29 (see N. B. Crowther, *JHS* 111 [1991] 174–176); Photios, *Lex.,* s.v. ἀπο-
βατῶν ἀγών (α 2450, Theodoridis); Kyle, *Athletics in Ancient Athens*, 188–189.

Figure 31. Chariots of north frieze (N 56–61)

team shows the culminating moment of action. A marshal leaps forward to signal the end of the race (N 44), and the horses rear up as the charioteer (N 46) pulls back sharply on the reins. At just this moment, the armored soldier springs down from the car, looks back at the next team speeding up behind him, and prepares to dash for the goal (N 47).

In contrast, the chariots of the south frieze present a picture of the processional far more than of the contest itself. Again, the two rearmost teams are stationary and the soldiers stand at rest beside the chariots (S 62–66), while the two leading chariots (S 83–88), known to us mostly from the Carrey drawings, had come to a full halt so as not to run over the pedestrians moving slowly in the next section of the parade. The intervening teams all advance at speed, but in each case the soldier seems to have been mounted beside the driver. The message of the chariotry taken together is unmistakable, for the apobatic contest was practiced only in Athens and Boiotia; and at this period it was unique to the Great Panathenaia. Moreover, it was a contest in which only Athenians competed with their fellow citizens, and whose invention Attic legend attributed to Athena's own foster son, the earthborn Erichthonios.[135] Thus, even to the most casual observer, and even in the less than perfect conditions in which the frieze was to be viewed, the chariot scenes provided the exact specificity to enable identification of the subject as the procession of the Great Panathenaia.

Farther up in the line of march come groups of older male citizens, eighteen on the south side (S 89–106) and sixteen on the north (N 28–43). All the preserved faces are bearded, and the figures wear the voluminous mantles of Athenian gentlemen. The pedestrian marchers shuffle slowly along, for the procession has come nearly to a halt. There is a palpable ripple of conversation. A man adjusts his wreath; another looks back at the approaching chariots behind (N 38, 43). Scholars have often identified these figures as *thallophoroi*,[136] bearers of the victors' olive branches awarded to those who

[135] Apobatic contest only in Athens and Boiotia, Harpokr., s.v. ἀποβάτης (α 182 Keaney). Erichthonios inventor of chariot, first *apobates*, and founder of Panathenaia, *Marm. Par., FGrH* 239, ep. 10; pseudo-Eratosthenes, *Catasterismi* 13 (ed. A. Olivieri, *Mythographi Graeci*, vol. 3, fasc. 1 [Leipzig 1897] p. 16), quoted below, chap. 5, note 59. The contest was celebrated only in honor of Athena (Photios, note 134 above). G. van Hoorn, *Choes and Anthesteria* (Leiden 1951) 34, suggests that the apobatic contest was held at the Anthesteria solely on the basis of one red-figure chous depicting an apobatic chariot (van Hoorn, no. 611 and fig. 127) and one small fragment (van Hoorn, no. 248 sept., fig. 388f). But there is no literary or epigraphical evidence to support this view, and Kyle, *Athletics in Ancient Athens*, 45–46, is rightly dubious. Harpokration's mention of apobatic contests in Boiotia undoubtedly refers to the Amphiareia at Oropos; see Brommer, *Parthenonfries*, 221–224. See now the interesting discussion of the apobatic race, J. Neils and P. Schultz, *AJA* 116 (2012) 195–207.

[136] E.g., Berger and Gisler-Huwiler, *Fries*, 67–69; Brommer, *Parthenonfries*, 32–33, 217, with bibliography.

Figure 32. Hydria-bearers of north frieze (N 16–19)

had won the beauty contest at the Panathenaia. But there is no trace of such hand props, and it is surely a desperate expedient to suppose that they were painted over the exquisite carving of the relief, especially when many of the figures have their hands in inappropriate positions. It is preferable to think that these elderly men represent some of the many Athenian officials who are known to have shared in the administration and sacrifices of the festival. The athlothetai and the hieropoioi managed the games and the sacrifices, respectively, while numerous members of the government had a part in the distribution of sacrifices at the Lesser Panathenaia, and almost certainly at the quadrennial festival as well—the fifty prytaneis, the nine archons, the ten generals and taxiarchs, and the treasurers of Athena. The undifferentiated older men on both flanks of the temple may well be intended to depict these dignitaries participating in the procession.[137]

Ahead of the elders on the north frieze come the musicians, a group of four pipers followed by four kithara-players, all dressed in sumptuous ceremonial robes (N 20–27). These are indispensable participants in any ritual procession, for together they set the cadence for the march and provide the accompaniment for the hymns and songs of the festival. On the south frieze, in a position analogous to the four *kitharistai* of the north frieze, Carrey drew four figures carrying large, flat tablets (S 107–110). Here it seems probable that he misinterpreted the poorly preserved remains of musical instruments and that the figures were playing kitharas like those of the north frieze.[138] The procession appears to move forward again as the spectator walks eastward along the north flank. In front of the musicians, a youth picks up the heavy hydria that he had set down to rest, while three companions have already lifted similar water jars to their shoulders and rejoined the line of march (N 16–19) (Fig. 32). We pass next a group of three young men bearing trays on their shoulders (N 13–15); only one fragment of similar figures is preserved from the south frieze (S 120). The late lexicons call them *skaphephoroi* and identify them as resident aliens who carry trays filled with offerings of honeycombs

[137] So E. Simon, *Festivals of Attica* (Madison, WI, 1983) 62. On the athlothetai, [Aristot.] *Ath. Pol.* 60.1–3. The other officials are named in the Law on the Lesser Panathenaia, *IG* II² 334, lines 10–15 = *Agora* XVI 75, lines 35–40. Boardman, *RA* (1999) 328–330, has attempted to argue that the old men are the elderly veterans of the Battle of Marathon. His earlier attempts to identify the horsemen of the cavalry as the 192 Athenian dead at Marathon (*Festschrift Brommer,* 39–49; *Parthenon-Kongress Basel,* 210–215) failed to convince because the count could be arrived at only by the arbitrary inclusion and exclusion of certain figures. The metamorphosis of heroized dead into senile veterans is equally unconvincing.

[138] For the drawings, Bowie and Thimme, *Carrey Drawings of the Parthenon Sculptures,* pl. 23. For interpretation of the drawings as musicians: Jenkins, *Frieze,* 69; Berger and Gisler-Huwiler, *Fries,* 135. For interpretation as "pinax-bearers," Brommer, *Parthenonfries,* 98, 220. Simon, *Festivals of Attica,* 62, calls them secretaries.

Figure 33. Sacrificial cattle of north frieze (N 3–5)

and cakes.[139] Before them, at the eastern end of each flank, come the cattle for public sacrifices. On
the north frieze there are four cows followed by four sheep, each led forward by youthful handlers
who respond to directions from the marshal at the northeast corner (N 1). On the south side we see
only cows, ten in number; all are bound for the great altar of Athena and for the hecatomb to Athena
Polias, which will ultimately be distributed as meat to the populace in the Kerameikos. The animals
shamble slowly to a halt at the corners of the frieze, where they wait patiently for their numerous
handlers to prod them forward to the altar (N 2–11, S 122–148). Suddenly, for a moment all is in
confusion as the cries of the crowd frighten some of the beasts. The third cow from the corner on
the north side tugs violently at her tether with raised head and both forelegs in the air (Fig. 33).
An animal on the south frieze abruptly strains its neck upward to low forlornly, and the cow next
behind her threatens to do likewise. The handlers jerk back on the halters with all their strength
(S 130–133), and it is only with difficulty that order is restored.[140]

   The north and south friezes are extraordinarily similar in their constituent parts and in their
arrangement, and this similarity is more pronounced than heretofore in the most recent rearrangement of the slabs in the British Museum. It has become increasingly difficult to distinguish two separate parts of the procession, that on the north frieze being the more sacred, as some scholars have
attempted to do.[141] And yet other interpreters of the frieze seem rightly to have drawn attention to
recurring numbers as distinctive elements of each side. On the south frieze, there are ten ranks of
horsemen, ten chariots, ten cows, while on the north we count four cows, four sheep, four bearers of
hydriai, four pipers, and four kithara players. Such repetition can hardly be due to coincidence, and
indeed the numbers themselves are surely meaningful. In fifth-century Athens, the number ten refers
unmistakably to the ten Kleisthenic tribes into which the whole citizen body was divided, and which
in fact was reflected in most of the boards and committees of the democratic government. Equally,
the number four recalls the four ancient Ionic tribes that encompassed the population of the archaic
city and supported Athens's claim to be the mother city of all Ionian Greeks of the Aegean and Asia

---

[139] The male hydria-bearers N 16–19 have caused much consternation because the late literary testimonia describe
hydriaphoroi as metic girls. For testimonia on *hydriaphoroi* and *skaphephoroi*, Berger and Gisler-Huwiler, *Fries*, 195–196. As
a result, Simon, *Festivals of Attica*, 63–64, identifies them as victors in the torch race because the prize for that contest was
a hydria. But in fact there is no evidence whatever to inform us who may have carried hydrias at the time of the Parthenon.

[140] For the sacrificial animals, Brommer, *Parthenonfries*, 24–28 (north), 99–105 (south), 215–216. Cf. Berger and
Gisler-Huwiler, *Fries*, 59–63 (north) 138–145 (south); Jenkins, *Frieze*, 71–74 (south), 84–85 (north).

[141] Simon, *Festivals of Attica*, 61, 65; cf. S. I. Rotroff, *AJA* 81 (1977) 379–382, and the criticism of Jenkins, *Frieze*,
28–29.

Figure 34. Maidens of east frieze (E 49–56)

Minor.[142] But such a mechanical count of heads should not be thought to reveal some secret cipher that enables us to decode the single hidden message of the composition. If anything, the significant numbers should warn us that this is no photographic snapshot that documents the celebration of a particular festival in the mid-fifth century. All Athenians of every generation marched in the Parthenon frieze, those of the distant past no less than those of the Periklean present. All are highly idealized, their faces solemnly expressionless and undifferentiated one from another, but together they celebrate the goddess's festival at recurring intervals from remote antiquity to the time of the Parthenon.

When the spectator turns the corner to view the eastern side of the frieze, the scene has changed dramatically. The participants leading the procession have entered the Acropolis and approach the doors of the temple.[143] Here the loud tumult of the march gives way to an atmosphere of hushed solemnity. A marshal (E 1) turns backward and beckons to the procession on the south frieze, a gesture that plainly links together the different parts of the composition. The front ranks of the procession are composed entirely of young women, in striking contrast to the other three sides of the temple, where not a single female figure appears. The women converge toward the center in two lines from either corner, sixteen on the south and thirteen at the north. At the head of each file are pairs of *kanephoroi*, maiden daughters chosen from the finest families of Athens to bear the sacred baskets containing barleycorns and the sacrificial knife (E 16 and 17, 50 and 51, 53 and 54). The girls stand quietly with all the poise and grace of their aristocratic breeding, but one toys surreptitiously with a fold of her gown, and we sense the slight stiffening, the shy nervousness of young girls making their first appearance at a great public event (Fig. 34). They are richly draped in peplos and mantle, and they wear their hair long in loose curling locks, as was customary for maidens. The *kanephoroi* of the northern file (E 50, 51) have just handed their baskets to an official, possibly one of the hieropoioi (E 49), and they await further instructions from an approaching marshal (E 48).[144] Another marshal (E 47) beckons with his raised arm to their opposite numbers at the head of the southern column, a clear signal that the two branches are one procession.

[142] Simon, *Festivals of Attica*, 65; Harrison, in *Parthenon-Kongress Basel*, 230–234; but her conclusion (p. 234) that the recurring numbers signify different epochs in the history of the festival is less convincing; cf. Jenkins, *Frieze*, 29–30.

[143] So Rotroff, *AJA* 81 (1977) 379–382.

[144] On the *kanephoroi*, see Harpokr., s.v. κανηφόροι (κ 14 Keaney); Aristoph. *Peace* 948 and schol. 948b (Holwerda), *Birds* 1549–1552 and schol. 1551a (Holwerda). See J. Schelp, *Das Kanoun* (Würzburg 1975) 15–21, and, on the *kanephoroi* of the east frieze, 55–56; Brommer, *Parthenonfries,* 121–122; Simon, *Festivals of Attica*, 60. On their costume and coiffure, Harrison, in S. J. Barnes and W. S. Melion, eds., *Cultural Differentiation and Cultural Identity in the Visual Arts* (Washington, DC, 1989) 53.

Figure 35. Gods and heroes of east frieze (E 20–24)

The groups of women behind the *kanephoroi* carry ritual vessels of silver or gold, shallow phi-alai and ewers for pouring the libations that preceded the sacrifice (E 2–11, 55, 58–63). Other pairs of girls share the weight of tall stands for burning incense (thymiateria) (E 12 and 13, 14 and 15, 55 and 56). Among the female ranks, both maidens and a few married women can be distinguished. The former emulate the *kanephoroi* in both dress and coiffure, but the latter wear their hair pinned up in kerchiefs and are dressed in chiton and wrapped himation (E 8, 9, 11, 57, 61). Here and there among the women are girls with the long locks of maidens who also wear the chiton and himation of the matrons (E 6, 60).[145]

Now the artist ceases to give us a precise account of the visible proceedings, but he draws instead upon his imagination. Beyond the head of the procession on either side there stand two groups of elderly men garbed as befits their age and station, in simple himatia that for the most part leave their upper torsos bare (Fig. 35). They loiter about at ease, most of them leaning on wooden staves. At the north four men nod companionably to each other, engrossed in serious conversation (E 43–46), while the six men of the southern group chat with each other in facing pairs (E 18–23). Both groups studi-ously ignore the columns of women who have drawn up beside them, and one gains the impression that they are supposed to be invisible to the mortal worshippers in the procession, who likewise ignore the men gathered before them. Once again, the number ten is surely meant to be significant, and most scholars identify them as the eponymous heroes of the ten Kleisthenic tribes. These heroes were chosen at random by the Delphic oracle to give names to quite arbitrary divisions of the Attic popula-tion; but it so happened that four of the ten chanced to be legendary early kings of Athens: Kekrops, Erechtheus, Aigeus, and Pandion. This distinction may have guided their division into groups of six and four on the east frieze; and the four at the north, who are plainly men of great age and high no-bility, may be thought to represent the early kings.[146] The presence of the eponymous heroes is vital to the democratic ideology that pervades the iconography of the Parthenon frieze. Although their

[145] On the different dress and hairstyle of the maidens and married women, Harrison (note 144 above).

[146] For identification of the northern group of four heroes as the early kings, see Harrison, in O. Mørkholm and N. M. Waggoner, eds., *Greek Numismatics and Archaeology* (Wetteren 1979) 71, 79–81; U. Kron, in *Parthenon-Kongress Basel*, 235–244. For variations in the identification of the ten figures on the frieze, Berger and Gisler-Huwiler, *Fries*, 175. On Kleisthenes' formation of the tribes and the selection of the Eponymoi by the Delphic oracle, [Aristot.] *Ath. Pol.* 21.6. For attempts to identify the figures on the frieze as Athenian officials, either archons or athlothetai, I. Jenkins, *AJA* 89 (1985) 121–127; B. Nagy, *AJA* 96 (1992) 55–69.

Figure 35 (*cont.*). Gods and heroes of east frieze (E 25–27)

initial selection was quite artificial, the Eponymoi had in fact become the political ancestors of every citizen of democratic Athens. Grouped together as they are on the east frieze of the Parthenon, they symbolize the total population of Attica—past, present, and future—and they perpetuate the myth of autochthony that was always the linchpin of Athenian notions of their own identity.

Placed as they are on the east frieze, the Eponymoi mediate between the human worshippers of the procession and the immortal world of the divine; for next, after the standing heroes, we are made to see a great assembly of deities ranged on either side of the central scene (Figs. 35–37). Here the twelve Olympian gods have gathered to bless Athena's festival with their presence, just as they assembled to witness her birth on the east pediment above. But they have been carefully distinguished from both the mortal participants and the standing heroes by the happy contrivance of their larger scale: although they are seated on stools, they nonetheless fill the full height of the frieze. They sit in easy and expansive postures, talking among themselves and waiting for the ceremonies to begin. Two symmetrical groups of six face the northern and southern branches of the procession, respectively.[147] At the southern end, Hermes is recognizable by his traveler's hat (petasos) and short boots (E 24). Beside him is seated Dionysos, who rests one arm companionably on Hermes' shoulder and evidently grasped an upraised thyrsos in the other hand (E 25). Next to him Demeter sits with sorrowful demeanor, holding her habitual attribute, the torch (E 26). Ares waits impatiently, his body coiled tight with nervous tension, as he clasps his upraised knee in both hands and rests his left foot on the end of his spear (E 27).[148] The four deities are separated from the last two members of the group by a winged female figure (E 28) who stands somewhat behind the seated gods and is therefore smaller in scale (Fig. 36). She arranges her windblown hair and seems about to tie it up with a ribbon. Although she is frequently called Iris, an identification as Nike better coheres with the pervasive theme of victory that so dominates the imagery of the Parthenon sculptures.[149] In the artistic composition, she serves to set apart from the other gods the figures of Hera and Zeus

[147] On the gods of the east frieze, see generally E. Pemberton, *AJA* 80 (1976) 113–124; A. Linfert, *AM* 94 (1979) 41–47; I. S. Mark, *Hesperia* 53 (1984) 289–342.

[148] There is general consensus on the identification of the individual figures of the gods. On Hermes, Dionysos, Demeter, and Ares, see Brommer, *Parthenonfries*, 258–259; Jenkins, *Frieze*, 78; Berger and Gisler-Huwiler, *Fries*, 154.

[149] So Pemberton, *AJA* 80 (1976) 121; the identification argued in detail by Mark, *Hesperia* 53 (1984) 304–312. The figure is called Nike or Iris by Berger and Gisler-Huwiler, *Fries*, 156. Brommer, *Parthenonfries*, 259–260, and Jenkins, *Frieze*, 78, name the figure Iris.

Figure 36. Hera and Zeus of east frieze (E 28–31)

(E 29, 30). Hera, the goddess of marriage, and Zeus, the father of the gods, are portrayed as divine exemplars of the marriage union.[150] Hera holds out her veil in a gesture appropriate to the blushing bride, while Zeus leans back languidly at ease, one arm resting on the back of his throne. Oblivious to all around them, the divine couple have eyes only for each other, and they exchange a gaze that smolders with conjugal desire.

Significantly, Hera and Zeus are balanced in the northern group of gods by a couple whose relations were of a different sort—Athena and Hephaistos, seated side by side (E 36, 37) (Fig. 37). The goddess has spread the protective aegis across her lap, and drill holes on her right side indicate the position in which she held her spear. For his part, Hephaistos exhibits the muscular arms and torso of the blacksmith, but the wooden crutch beneath his right arm shows that the god was forever lame as a result of his fall from heaven.[151] In a different context, we shall see that the two Olympians collaborated as patrons of the civilizing arts, and as such were celebrated together in the Hephaisteion;[152] but here their pairing conveys a different meaning. The artist has placed the two divine couples in answering positions on either side of the central scene deliberately to remind us that Hephaistos had been the would-be consort of the virgin goddess. Like Zeus, he looks with longing into Athena's eyes, but his attention elicits no response. She sits stiffly, wary of his lustful gaze, and stares back coldly; the unusual placement of the aegis across her lap provides the kind of protection most needed at the moment. But the charged glance that they exchange foretells the whole myth of Athenian autochthony. From the unnaturally consummated union of Hephaistos and Athena the baby Erichthonios was born from the earth, the mythical ancestor of every autochthonous Athenian, whom the goddess herself raised in her temple, who dedicated the ancient image on the Acropolis, and who founded her festival, the Panathenaia.[153]

Farther north, a final group of four divinities rounds out the Olympian assembly. All are seated facing the procession, the arrival of which they eagerly anticipate. First is Poseidon (E 38), Athena's erstwhile antagonist, who makes a remark and gestures to Apollo seated beside him (E 39). In re-

[150] Pemberton, *AJA* 80 (1976) 115–116; cf. Brommer, *Parthenonfries,* 260; Berger and Gisler-Huwiler, *Fries,* 156; Mark, *Hesperia* 53 (1984) 302–304.

[151] Brommer, *Parthenonfries,* 260–261; Mark, *Hesperia* 53 (1984) 313–314; Jenkins, *Frieze,* 79; Berger and Gisler-Huwiler, *Fries,* 160–161.

[152] See chap. 5, pp. 159–160 below.

[153] References cited chap. 5, p. 160, notes 63 and 64.

Figure 37. Athena and Hephaistos of east frieze (E 35–37)

sponse, the youthful god looks back over his shoulder and raises his left hand in acknowledgment. His sister Artemis (E 40) adjusts the folds of her drapery with her right hand and links her left through the arm of her neighbor Aphrodite, who points excitedly at the approaching procession (E 41). At her side stands the boy Eros (E 42), shaded from the morning sun beneath a parasol. He clings affectionately to his mother's knee as his eyes follow the direction of her pointing hand that rests lightly on her son's shoulder.[154]

The full assembly of the twelve Olympian gods marks the procession of the Panathenaic frieze as an event of special solemnity and majesty worthy of such divine attention. Their inclusion here is the more striking because an equally full assembly gathered to celebrate the birth of Athena in the east pediment of the temple, while a smaller group of deities had witnessed with approval the capture of Troy in the northern metopes. Greek art, both in vase painting and in architectural sculpture, had a rich tradition of depicting gatherings of the gods to add luster and dignity to the exploits of heroes and even of mortal men. The birth of Athena was regularly attended by other gods, and they turned out to welcome the introduction of Herakles to Olympos. Important weddings like that of Peleus and Thetis attracted the gods in large numbers, and they are seen arriving in elaborate processions of chariots.[155] Companies of gods viewed the battles of the Trojan War on the Siphnian Treasury at Delphi, an exploit of Theseus on the east frieze of the Hephaisteion, and later both heroic and historical battles on the Temple of Athena Nike.[156] Of all these, however, the divine assembly on the east frieze of the Parthenon is the fullest, most detailed, and most richly portrayed. An excellent recent discussion of the frieze has laid particular emphasis on the notion that such gatherings of the gods imply apotheosis, as for example, quite explicitly in the case of Herakles' introduction into

[154] For Poseidon and Apollo, Brommer, *Parthenonfries,* 260; Berger and Gisler-Huwiler, *Fries,* 162–163. For Artemis, Aphrodite, and Eros: Brommer, *Parthenonfries,* 262–263; Mark, *Hesperia* 53 (1984) 295–302; Berger and Gisler-Huwiler, *Fries,* 163–164.

[155] Gods at the birth of Athena, H. Knell, *Die Darstellung der Götterversammlung in der attischen Kunst des VI. u. V. Jahrhunderts v. Chr.* (Diss. Freiburg 1965) 5–22. Gods at the introduction of Herakles, Knell, 23–27; Brommer, *Vasenlisten*³, 159–174. Gods at the wedding of Peleus and Thetis, *Vasenlisten*³, 318–320; cf. especially the dinos by Sophilos, London BM GR 1971.11–1.1: *Paralipomena* 19.16bis; *Beazley Addenda*² (1989) 10–11.40.16bis; and the François Vase by Kleitias, Florence 4209, *ABV* 76, no. 1.

[156] East frieze of the Siphnian Treasury: P. de la Coste-Messelière, *BCH* 68–69 (1944–45) 8–27; L. V. Watrous, *AJA* 86 (1982) 171–172; cf. Knell, *Darstellung der Götterversammlung,* 55–61. Pronaos frieze of the Hephaisteion, see chap. 5, pp. 153–155 and notes 198, 201 below. East frieze of the Nike temple, chap. 10, p. 352 below.

Olympos.[157] The idea is an attractive one, and wholly characteristic of the art of Periklean Athens, that the presence of the Olympian gods subtly suggests, but does not assert too boldly, the apotheosis of all Athenians by virtue of their faithful worship at Athena's festival.

The Peplos Scene

In the precise center of the eastern side, above the great doors of the Hekatompedon, is a scene which should be the climactic episode of the entire frieze (Fig. 38).[158] But to the uninitiated modern viewer it seems curiously banal and enigmatic. We are shown a ritual of preparation antecedent to the main event. A man and a child are in the act of folding or unfolding a large piece of cloth which in the context of the Panathenaia can only be the peplos of Athena, the robe presented to the goddess in every fourth year and draped about the ancient wooden image. The man is dressed like no other figure on the Parthenon: he wears a long ungirt tunic with short sleeves that was made of sheer material and was called *kretikon*. This garment was the specific ritual vestment of the basileus, the archon who had charge of all aspects of the state religion. The king also wears soft leather shoes that were specific to his official dress.[159] Identification of the child is more difficult since there is not even consensus as to whether the figure represents a boy or a girl, and obviously determination of the gender materially affects the figure's interpretation.[160] Next to the king and back to back with him stands an older woman who is most likely to be the priestess of Athena Polias, the principal priestly official of the Acropolis and custodian of the goddess's temple. She directs two young women who approach from the left carrying cushioned stools on their heads; the second girl also holds a low footstool in her left hand. They have frequently been called *arrhephoroi*, but the scale of the figures suggests that they are older than eleven years, the maximum age of the *arrhephoroi*, and, moreover, they are dressed in chiton and himation like the women in the procession. It is best to regard them as female acolytes who assist the priestess in her preparations. The stools that the girls carry closely resemble those on which the gods are seated, and it is natural to suppose that at some point in the ceremony two people will take their seats upon them. In the action of the liturgy, it is easy to imagine that the basileus and the priestess of Athena Polias become the ritual surrogates for the first royal family of Athens who presided at the first dedication of the peplos.[161]

---

[157] See Castriota, *Myth, Ethos,* 213–218. Cf. Boardman, in *Festschrift Brommer,* 46, who comments on the implied apotheosis in the juxtaposition of the procession and the seated gods.

[158] For discussion of the peplos scene, see generally Brommer, *Parthenonfries,* 114–116, 263–270; Simon, *AM* 97 (1982) 127–144; T. Schäfer, *AM* 102 (1987) 85–122; Jenkins, *Frieze,* 35–42; Berger and Gisler-Huwiler, *Fries,* 157–160, 171–174; Harrison, in J. Neils, ed., *Worshipping Athena,* 198–214; Boardman, *RA* (1999) 307–321. For alternative interpretations, see endnote 4, pp. 401–404 below.

[159] The dress of E 34 is generally described as priestly, but it is defined more specifically by Pollux 7.77: ἐκαλεῖτο δέ τι καὶ Κρητικόν, ᾧ Ἀθήνησιν ὁ βασιλεὺς ἐχρῆτο, "there was also a garment called Kretikon which the king used at Athens." Similarly, the shoes are mentioned in Pollux 7.85: ὑποδημάτων δὲ εἴδη βασιλίδες· ἐφόρει δὲ αὐτὰς ὁ βασιλεὺς Ἀθήνησιν, "A kind of shoes is called royal; the king used to wear these at Athens." Cf. Cook, *Zeus,* vol. 2, pt. 2, 1135–1136.

[160] By far the majority of scholars call E 35 a boy; see the table of identifications in Berger and Gisler-Huwiler, *Fries,* 172–174. Boardman has argued long and consistently in favor of identifying the child as a girl and an *arrhephoros: Festschrift Brommer,* 41; *Parthenon-Kongress Basel,* 214; and Schmidt, ed., *Kanon,* 9–10. Objections from C. Clairmont, *AA* (1989) 496–497; and Boardman's reply, *OJA* 10 (1991) 119–121, and *RA* (1999) 314–321, the most detailed argumentation. The child is often said to be a "temple boy" like Ion in the play of Euripides (Jenkins, *Frieze,* 79), but Ion served the Temple of Apollo at Delphi. No such male children are attested as serving the cult of Athena on the Acropolis. Brommer, *Parthenonfries,* 269, cites a passage of Eudocia, *De S. Cypriano* 2.20–21 (ed. A. Ludwich), which claims that the saint himself performed the "snaky rites of Athena" on the Acropolis. Since the saint lived ca. A.D. 200–258, and his life was written in the fifth century, this is surely a desperate measure to document an image of the fifth century B.C. In this debate probability seems to favor Boardman.

[161] On the stools carried by the two girls, see Boardman, *RA* (1999) 309–314, rebutting B. Wesenberg, *JdI* 110 (1995) 149–178, who thinks that they carry trays and torches. On the function of the stools as seats for the priestess and the

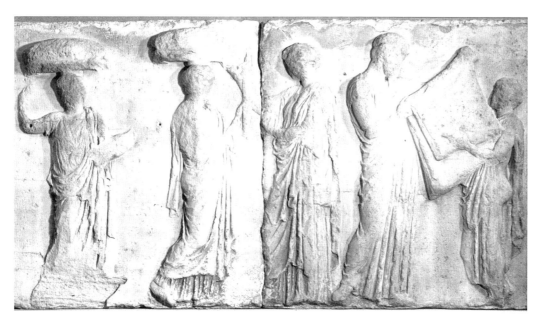

Figure 38. Peplos scene of east frieze (E 31–35)

A remarkable aspect of the Parthenon frieze and equally of the festival that it depicts is the priority given to young women of marriageable age. Up to this point, the entire sculptural program of the temple celebrated the fierce goddess who brings victory on the battlefield, and the mythological subject matter has been subtly shaped to prefigure the military victories of the Persian Wars. Even the religious procession of the frieze is dominated on three sides of the temple by a display of those martial arts which were Athena's special province. In striking contrast, all who marched at the head of the procession on the east frieze were Athenian women and their maiden daughters. They represent the other half of the polis who worshipped the other side of Athena's character, her patronage of the civilizing crafts that created the infrastructure of human culture. The women's offering to the goddess was of her own creation—the sacred peplos, newly woven in each quadrennium to clothe her ancient statue. It was very likely one of the most ancient elements of the festival, and its manufacture and dedication were deeply symbolic of the female role in Athenian life. Throughout Greek society, the working of wool and the weaving of cloth were regarded as women's work. From the earliest days of the Bronze Age, the production of textiles had been one of the most characteristic activities of Greek home life; and the making of clothing was just as central to civilized culture as the preparation of food or the nurturing of children.[162]

Weaving of the peplos brought the domestic craft of women out of the household and to the religious center of the polis, for the robe was made by women of marriageable age who worked the wool and wove the cloth on the Acropolis. At the festival of the Chalkeia, exactly nine months before the Great Panathenaia, the priestess of Athena, with the help of the *arrhephoroi,* set the warp upon the loom and began the work.[163] The participation of the *arrhephoroi* was significant. They

basileus: Brommer, *Parthenonfries,* 267; Boardman, in *Parthenon-Kongress Basel,* 213–214; cf. Jenkins, *Frieze,* 36. Variations of opinion summarized, Berger and Gisler-Huwiler, *Fries,* 171.

[162] On the early importance of textiles in the Greek household, see E. J. W. Barber, in Neils, ed., *Goddess and Polis,* 103–106; E. J. W. Barber, *Women's Work: The First 20,000 Years* (New York 1994) 29–41. Cf. Jenkins, *Arethusa* 18 (1985) 109–112; D. M. Schaps, *Economic Rights of Women in Ancient Greece* (Edinburgh 1979) 18–20.

[163] The women who wove the peplos were called ἐργαστῖναι, Hesych. s.v. (ε 5669 Schmidt); cf. schol. Eurip. *Hec.* 467 (Schwartz); *IG* II² 1036, lines 11–13, where they are called "the maidens who worked the wool for Athena for the peplos." The festival of the Chalkeia on Pyanepsion 30, *Suda,* s.v. Χαλκεῖα (χ 36 Adler) = Harpokr., s.v. Χαλκεῖα (χ 2 Keaney). The day the priestesses began to weave, *Suda,* s.v. Χαλκεῖα (χ 35 Adler).

were two girls between the ages of seven and eleven, born of noble families and chosen by the basileus to spend a year in the service of the goddess. Their sojourn on the Acropolis was a rite of passage in which they represented all Athenian girls as they approached the onset of puberty.[164] In the weaving of the peplos, Athena herself, through the mediation of her priestess, revealed the skills and secrets of the female craft to yet another generation of girls. In this ancient ceremonial of the city's foremost festival, the women of Athens clothed the image of their goddess in a garment of their own manufacture. That ritual act acknowledged symbolically that the female role was indispensable in creating the comforts of home life—the warmth of clothing, the nourishment of food, and the nurturing care that had always been Athena's special gifts to women. But in the democratic ideology of fifth-century Athens, the women's priority reminds us that they are just as indispensable to the propagation of the polis as are the gallant groups of warriors who display their horsemanship at the other end of the frieze.

The peplos scene undoubtedly depicts a preliminary ceremony that was immediately recognizable to every fifth-century Athenian. Even though its precise meaning eludes the modern student, it still seems possible to understand some aspects of its significance. That the preparations are indeed preliminary is made certain by the attitude of the gods seated on either side. They ignore the central scene and focus their attention wholly on each other or on the arriving procession, whose leading elements are just reaching the Acropolis. In fact, it will be observed that the anticipatory character of the iconography is all-pervasive on the Parthenon frieze, and no action has been definitively completed. At the west, horsemen are still joining the procession; the cavalry and chariots advance at full speed; the marchers and musicians move slowly forward on foot; the sacrificial cattle plod toward the altar but never reach their goal. As in many votive reliefs and dedicatory statues, the incomplete ritual serves to perpetuate the sacrificial act; the calf-bearer forever brings his victim to the goddess, and his statue stands in for the dedicator himself. Similarly, the forever-advancing marchers of the Parthenon frieze guarantee that Athenians will celebrate the goddess's festival in perpetuity. Moreover, we have seen that the never-ending procession of horsemen and chariots, musicians and cattle is arrayed in significant numbers, some of which appear to evoke the celebrants of the distant past and to distinguish them from contemporary worshippers. When this is taken together with the naturally introductory character of the processional act itself and the preparatory atmosphere of the peplos scene, one message of the frieze is unmistakable: Athenians of every generation have worshipped Athena from remotest antiquity and will continue to do so to the end of time. The two most important religious acts of the festival were the sacrifices at the great altar and the dedication of the peplos in the temple. It is surely the ritual preparation for the latter that we see in the central scene of the east frieze. Since, however, the leaders of the procession are just now arriving and the sacrificial victims are still making their way toward the Acropolis, the narrative logic of the episode suggests that the robe we see cannot be the newly woven peplos, as one purpose of the procession was to convey it to the Acropolis. For in that case the robe must be thought to have arrived magically in advance of those who bore it. On the contrary, the peplos that we see has clothed the ancient image for the past four years, and, now removed from the statue, it is carefully folded at the hands of the basileus and the young child for storage as a permanent possession of the goddess's wardrobe.[165]

---

[164] *Arrhephoroi*, two girls selected from four elected, Harpokr., s.v. ἀρρηφορεῖν (α 239 Keaney); chosen by the basileus, *Suda*, s.v. ἐπιώψατο (ε 2504 Adler); between the ages of seven and eleven, I. Bekker, *Anecdota Graeca* (Berlin, 1814), s.v. ἀρρηφορεῖν (p. 202, 3). For interpretation of the rituals as a rite of passage, Jenkins, *Frieze*, 38–39.

[165] On the preparatory character of the frieze, see M. Robertson and A. Frantz, *The Parthenon Frieze* (London 1975) 11. Harrison, in Neils, ed., *Worshipping Athena*, 202–203, has analyzed in precise detail exactly how the peplos is being folded by the basileus with the child's help. That they are folding the old peplos rather than unfolding the new was first suggested more than a century ago by G. Hill, *CR* 8 (1894) 225–226, followed by Robertson and Frantz (above): "The folded cloth will then be the *old* robe, its four-year service finished, implying the timeless repetition of the ritual."

In one important respect the meaning of the peplos scene appears to have escaped notice, and that is what it tells us about the intended purpose of the Parthenon, of whose frieze it is the focal point. The robe that the king and his acolyte are in the act of folding has been the clothing of the wooden xoanon of Athena Polias. A new peplos will arrive shortly with the procession, and by long tradition members of the *genos* of the Praxiergidai will drape it around the image of the goddess.[166] From the late years of the fifth century to the time of Pausanias and beyond, the goddess's wooden image stood in the building we call the Erechtheion on the north side of the Acropolis. Fifth-century Athenians referred to it specifically as "the temple for the Ancient Image," and later literary and epigraphical sources called it the Ancient Temple of Athena Polias or, more simply, the Ancient Temple (Archaios Neos).[167] After the completion of the marble Ionic temple, there can be no doubt whatever that the dedication of the peplos and the robing of the statue took place within its walls. How, then, are we to interpret the appearance, centered above the doors of the Parthenon, of a scene that plainly depicts the preparations for this very ceremony? It seems necessary to emphasize that the Parthenon frieze was designed in the middle years of the 440s, some twenty years before the decision was taken to construct the Erechtheion, and nearly half a century before that building's completion. There is no evidence to suggest that the builders of the Parthenon anticipated the construction of the Erechtheion at that early date, nor is there reason to regard the later temple as part of the Periklean program at all. Moreover, the archaeological record of the Acropolis has produced not the slightest trace of a putative archaic predecessor for the Erechtheion, whose frequent invention has so confounded modern understanding of the Acropolis temples.[168] When work began on the Parthenon, the only temple of Athena on the Acropolis was the wreckage of the archaic temple burned by the Persians, and the Periklean architects doubtless assumed that their new "hundred-foot" Doric temple would replace its ruined predecessor in every aspect of Athena's cult. The presence of the peplos scene at the midpoint of the east frieze encourages this inference, since it depicts preparations for the ceremony that will be performed within the temple itself,[169] and, moreover, one that implies that the goddess's ancient image had found a new home beside the gold and ivory statue in the east cella of the Parthenon. Why this disposition of the wooden relic was afterward deemed unsatisfactory, and why the Erechtheion came later to be built, are questions that call for investigation in a subsequent chapter.[170]

[166] Hesych., s.v. Πραξιεργίδαι (π 3205 Schmidt): οἱ τὸ ἕδος τὸ ἀρχαῖον τῆς Ἀθηνᾶς ἀμφιεννύντες, "those who clothe the ancient statue of Athena." The ritual is specified in *IG* I³ 7, lines 10–12, 24 (460–450). Cf. Plut. *Alkib.* 34.1–2 and the discussion of Mansfield, "Robe of Athena," 366–379; R. Parker, *Athenian Religion: A History* (Oxford 1996) 307–308.

[167] The term "Erechtheion" appears only twice in extant Greek literature: Paus. 1.26.5; [Plut.] *Mor.* 843E. "The temple for the Ancient Image" appears in the overseers' report of 409, *IG* I³ 474, line 1. For the title "the Ancient Temple of Athena Polias," see *IG* II² 983, lines 4–6; *IG* II² 1036 + 1060 = *SEG* 28.90, lines 23–25 (S. B. Aleshire and S. D. Lambert, *ZPE* 142 [2003] 68–69); *IG* II² 687, lines 42–44; Strabo 9.1.16 (p. 396). The title was shortened to "Ancient Temple" (Archaios Neos) in the fragmentary inventories of the treasurers of Athena: *IG* II² 1445, line 43; 1447, line 6; 1424A, line 346; 1425, line 283; 1487, line 31.

[168] The architectural difficulty of postulating an early predecessor on the site of the later Erechtheion is well illustrated by Bundgaard, *Parthenon,* 103–111 and fig. 733a, where he attempts to show plans of both the "pre-Erechtheion" and the Old Athena Temple. Robertson, in Neils, ed., *Worshipping Athena,* 29–37, and Hurwit, *Athenian Acropolis,* 167–168, are modern proponents of a primordial predecessor for the Ionic temple. On the lack of archaic remains, see Dinsmoor, *AJA* 36 (1932) 313–314, *AJA* 51 (1947) 109–110 and note 4, 118–119; I. T. Hill, *The Ancient City of Athens* (London 1953) 135–140.

[169] So Brommer, *Parthenonfries,* 269; Harrison, in Neils, ed., *Worshipping Athena,* 203; Fehl, *JWarb* 24 (1961) 15. Gauer, in *Parthenon-Kongress Basel,* 223, 226, argues that the whole scene takes place in the Agora, where the basileus is inspecting the robe. For different opinions on the location of the scene, Berger and Gisler-Huwiler, *Fries,* 171.

[170] See chap. 11, pp. 360–366 below.

5

The Hephaisteion

The most important contribution that the monuments themselves can make to our knowledge of Athenian temple building in the fifth century is the Hephaisteion, located on the brow of the Kolonos Agoraios overlooking the civic buildings of the Agora (Fig. 39).[1] This temple, best preserved of all Greek temples, housed the uniquely Athenian double cult of Hephaistos and Athena Hephaisteia. A scattering of literary references to the building record its location; and some information about its principal festival, the Hephaisteia, and a few dedications to its deities are preserved in the epigraphical record.[2] But no ancient reference attributes it specifically to the "works of Perikles," and the literary tradition as a whole is silent about its architectural history. Nevertheless, both in the details of its architecture and in the chronology of its construction, the temple forms a fascinating foil to the Parthenon.

ARCHITECTURE

In many ways the Hephaisteion conforms more closely to the normal design of Doric peripteral temples than does the Parthenon. Its peristyle has six columns on the facades combined with thirteen on the flanks, and the pronaos and opisthodomos of the cella are configured in the distyle in antis arrangement the was traditional for Doric temples (Fig. 40). Overall, the building is less than a quarter the size of the Parthenon, but we shall see that many features of its architecture plainly show

---

[1] That the temple above the Agora, popularly known as the "Theseion," should be identified as the Hephaisteion still needs to be emphasized. The arguments against that identification advanced by H. Koch, *Studien zum Theseustempel in Athen* (Berlin 1955) 9–15, were rebutted by Wycherley, *JHS* 79 (1959) 153–156; Thompson and Wycherley, *Agora* XIV, 140–142. The literary testimonia are virtually decisive. Hired men were called *kolonetai*: ἐπειδὴ παρὰ τῷ Κολωνῷ εἱστήκεσαν, ὅς ἐστι πλησίον τῆς ἀγορᾶς, ἔνθα τὸ Ἡφαιστεῖον καὶ τὸ Εὐρυσάκειόν ἐστιν· ἐκαλεῖτο δὲ ὁ Κολωνὸς οὗτος ἀγοραῖος, Harpokration, s.v. Κολωνέτας (κ 72 Keaney); cf. *Suda*, s.v. Κολωνέτας (κ 1961 Adler). The Hephaisteion was on a hill *near* the Agora that was called the Market Hill. Cf. Paus. 1.14.6: ὑπὲρ δὲ τὸν Κεραμεικὸν καὶ στοὰν τὴν καλουμένην βασίλειον ναός ἐστιν Ἡφαίστου . . . πλησίον δὲ ἱερόν ἐστιν Ἀφροδίτης Οὐρανίας. Now that excavation has clarified the topography at the northwest corner of the Agora, the marble temple is seen to stand on the hill immediately above the Stoa Basileios, which stands beside the Stoa of Zeus. The sanctuary of Aphrodite Ourania lies directly across the street from the Stoa Basileios, on the north side of the Panathenaic Way. See Shear, Jr., *Hesperia* 40 (1971) 243–255, *Hesperia* 53 (1984) 24–40. It is also highly significant that ten of the twenty-five foundry deposits from the excavations were found on the Kolonos nearly encircling the temple; see C. Mattusch, "Bronze and Ironworking in the Area of the Athenian Agora," *Hesperia* 46 (1977) 340–379. E. B. Harrison was one of the few scholars who remained unpersuaded: *AJA* 81 (1977) 137, 411. But see J. McK. Camp, *The Athenian Agora: Excavations in the Heart of Classical Athens* (London 1986) 82–87; Camp, *Archaeology of Athens,* 102–104; Knell, *Mythos und Polis,* 127–139.

[2] That the cult honored Hephaistos and Athena jointly is indicated by *IG* I³ 82, line 15 (421/0); *IG* II² 223B, lines 3–4 (343/2). For the two cult statues, *IG* I³ 472 (421/0).

Chapter 5

Figure 39. View of the Hephaisteion from northeast

the influence of the great temple on the Acropolis. Neither the overall dimensions of its crepidoma (15.42 × 33.48 m)[3] nor the width and length of the stylobate (13.708 × 31.769 m) show the simple proportional relationship that is fundamental to the design of the Parthenon. This suggests that the Hephaisteion was one of those temples for which the actual dimensions of the stylobate were calculated from a predetermined intercolumniation. According to this rule of thumb, the width of the stylobate was equal to the intercolumniation multiplied by the number of intercolumniations across the width of the facade plus a fraction that allowed for contraction at the corners; and the length of the stylobate equals the intercolumniation multiplied by the number of intercolumniations along the flank plus the same fraction for corner contraction.[4] The calculation may be expressed in formulas: $W = I(N_w + k)$ and $L = I(N_l + k)$. If we assume that the normal axial spacing of the facades (2.583 m) was the predetermined dimension, then the length of the stylobate may be calculated as 2.583 × 12³⁄₁₀ = 31.7709, while the measurable length of the stylobate as built is barely two millimeters shorter (13.769 m). Similarly, the width of the stylobate may be calculated from the predetermined dimension: 2.583 × 5³⁄₁₀ = 13.6899, and the theoretical width is actually 18 millimeters less than the measurable width of the stylobate (13.708 m). Obviously such minute deviations from the calculated dimensions could well have come about in the final dressing of the stonework, long after the columns of the peristyle were in place.

---

[3] The dimensions are from Dinsmoor, *AAG*³, unless otherwise noted.

[4] For discussion of this method of calculating the dimensions of the stylobate, see Coulton, *BSA* 69 (1974) 74–76, and chap. 4, pp. 85–87 above.

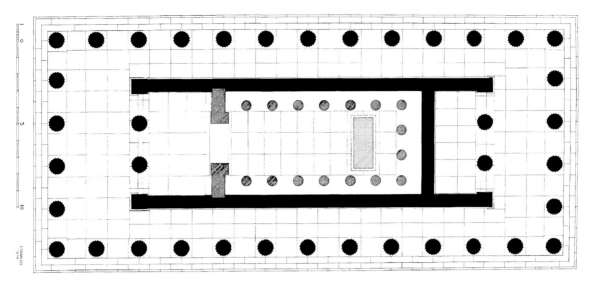

Figure 40. Plan of the Hephaisteion with interior columns restored

The colonnades of the peristyle exhibit a number of the proportional relationships that appear to have been innovative in the Parthenon and form a clear break with earlier Doric tradition (Figs. 41, 42). The columns measure 5.713 m in height, with a lower diameter of 1.018 m, and thus a proportion of diameter to height of 5.61, which makes them even slenderer than the columns of the Parthenon. Also like the Parthenon, their height is well over twice the axial spacing. The actual ratio is 2.21, which exceeds all other Doric temples on the Greek mainland except those in Periklean Athens.[5] The Doric capitals also have the lower, more compact, less spreading profile that was favored by the architects of the Parthenon; and the width of the abaci (1.14 m) allows them to extend beyond the lower diameter by only 0.061 m on each side.[6] That the architect of the Hephaisteion adopted proportions more closely related to the Parthenon than to earlier Doric temples can also be seen in the relation of the entablature height to the column height. The architrave and triglyph frieze are almost equal in height, and the entablature to the horizontal cornice is just over one-third the column height, whereas in earlier temples in mainland Greece that proportion is more nearly two-fifths.[7]

Another feature of the design may also be attributed to the Parthenon but is barely detectable without the most precise measurement. That is the upward vertical curvature that is applied to the stylobate and projected upward to the horizontal cornice. The architects of the Parthenon made such extensive use of this refinement that nearly every straight line in the building is slightly curved. Because the Hephaisteion is so much smaller a building, the architect applied curvature to the horizontal lines more timidly and less systematically. The maximum vertical rise in the stylobate is only 0.044 m along the western half of the north flank, while the maximum curvature in the cornice above is 0.036 m.[8] So slight are the deviations from the horizontal that they do not even engage the observer's perception as do the more comprehensive refinements of the Parthenon.

Above the columns and entablature of the peristyle, the entire roof of the temple was composed of marble tiles (Fig. 43). Only a few fragments of these have been recovered in the excavations; and no parts of the roof remain on the building today, since the entire cella was covered with a con-

[5] For the innovative characteristics common to Periklean Doric architecture, see Coulton, in *Parthenon-Kongress Basel,* 40–41.

[6] The proportions of Doric capitals have been extensively studied by Coulton, *BSA* 74 (1979) 81–103; the Periklean temples form his Group 6 (pp. 89–91, 101).

[7] Coulton, in *Parthenon-Kongress Basel,* 41.

[8] Dinsmoor, Jr., *AJA* 80 (1976) 224 and note 5.

Figure 41. View of east facade of the Hephaisteion from southeast

Figure 42. View of south flank of the Hephaisteion from southwest

crete barrel vault in the medieval period. All blocks of the horizontal and raking cornices, however, remain in their original positions, except for the northern slope of the east pediment. The tops of the cornice blocks preserve a regularly repeated pattern of dowel holes to anchor the marble sima tiles to the edge of the roof. Careful recording and study of these cuttings together with the surviving pieces of the tiles themselves have enabled the entire scheme of the roof structure to be reconstructed with

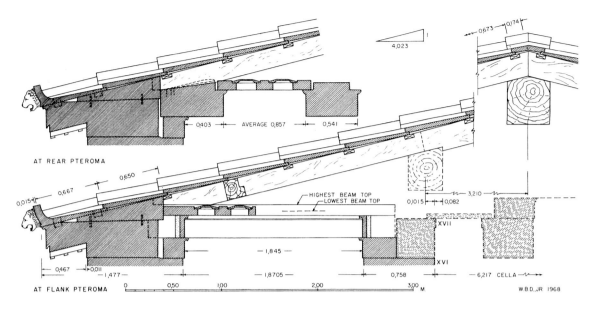

Figure 43. Sections of roof at west end and center of flank peristyle

accuracy.[9] On all four sides of the building, the edges of the roof were lined with a sima, which on the flanks was pierced at intervals by rainwater spouts in the form of lion heads (Fig. 45). Both the flank and raking simas had the profile of a tall, nearly flat ovolo terminating in a fillet at the bottom and an astragal at the top. The ovolo itself carried a painted pattern consisting of palmettes joined to each other by S-shaped tendrils and alternating with spindly, three-leaf lotus blossoms.[10] The dowel holes in the top of the cornice blocks show that the normal flank sima tiles measured 1.2995 m in width, almost exactly half the interaxial spacing. Since the lion-head spouts were presumably centered on the tiles, their spacing would have been equal to the width of the tiles, and they would have aligned with the metopes of the frieze below.[11] Two of the extant fragments can be assigned to the northeast corner and southwest pedimental slope, respectively, and give evidence for the way the sima turned the corner. Taken together with the dowel holes on the raking sima blocks, they show that the blocks of the raking sima were half the width of the flank simas (0.650 m); more importantly, the two fragments incorporate parts of the plinths for acroteria at the corners and apex of the roof.[12]

Even more fragmentary than the simas are the remains of the normal pan tiles and cover tiles that ascended in rows to the apex of the roof. A few tiny fragments of marble pan tiles may possibly have come from the Hephaisteion; and two triangular cover tiles, 0.23 m wide, match the weather marks left by cover tiles on the back of the sima. Although not a single marble roof tile has survived intact, the size and spacing of the simas allows the dimensions of the individual roof tiles to be calculated. The flat pan tiles would have been square, measuring 0.65 m on each side, and the joints between them would have been covered by triangular cover tiles equal in length to the side of the pan tile and about 0.23 m wide.[13]

[9] The roof has been studied in detail by Dinsmoor, Jr., *AJA* 80 (1976) 223–246. All dimensions pertaining to the roof, simas, and roof tiles are cited from this article.

[10] Dinsmoor, Jr., *AJA* 80 (1976) 235–238. For the profile of the sima, Shoe, *Greek Mouldings*, 35 and pl. LXXVI:2, where sima fragment Agora inv. A 394 was attributed in 1936 to the Stoa Poikile; later assigned to the Temple of Ares, Dinsmoor, *Hesperia* 9 (1940) 36; now assigned to the Hephaisteion, Dinsmoor, Jr., *AJA* 80 (1976) 233–234 and note 29. The painted design is illustrated by Travlos, *PDA*, fig. 344.

[11] Dinsmoor, Jr., *AJA* 80 (1976) 236–237.

[12] Dinsmoor, Jr., *AJA* 80 (1976) 232–239.

[13] Dinsmoor, Jr., *AJA* 80 (1976) 242–245.

Figure 44. Ceiling of south peristyle with coffer frame in place

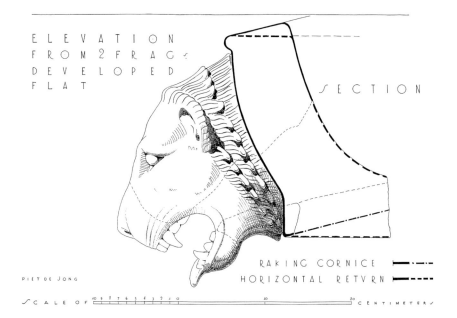

Figure 45. Sima profile and ornament

Within the peristyle, the entire pteroma was covered with a marble coffered ceiling on all four sides of the temple, but the design and structure of the ceiling were extremely unusual (Fig. 44). In order to reduce the thickness and weight of the ceiling as much as possible, the masons carved the coffer frames from thin slabs of marble in which they cut two rows of square openings that pierced the full thickness of the slab and formed the lower part of the coffers. Each of the square openings was then fitted with a coffer cover fashioned from a separate piece of extremely thin marble. The coffers are of uniform size, and the frames of uniform width, but they have alternately four or six coffers cut in two rows. These were combined in different ways. One frame of six coffers and one frame of four spanned the flank pteroma on each side in sixteen bays. At the west end, where the pteroma is wider, two frames of six and one of four were set parallel to the long axis of the building in eight bays. The still wider space in front of the pronaos required two frames of each type set in eight bays, as at the west.[14]

CHRONOLOGY

When we turn to consider the chronology of the building's construction, its complicated relationship to the Parthenon becomes especially interesting. The design and proportions of its peristyle exhibit many of the features that have been described as particular hallmarks of "Periklean Doric" and recur in other Athenian temples of the fifth century.[15] One infers that various architects were responding to the revolutionary features of the building that was rising on the Acropolis during the 440s. Therefore, it is a source of some surprise that various details of the architecture suggest a date ca. 450 for the foundation of the Hephaisteion, several years before the beginning of work on the Parthenon. Such an early date finds some corroboration in the external evidence of pottery found in the excavation of the temenos around the temple. Particularly indicative also is the extensive use of Parian marble for the sculptural decoration. This imported stone was used for the eighteen sculptured metopes of the exterior order, for both of the interior Ionic friezes, and for some of the fragmentary pieces assigned to the pediments. Parian and Pentelic marble appear to have been used indiscriminately for the coffered ceilings and the sima of the roof.[16] In contrast, the buildings on the Acropolis, beginning with the Parthenon, employed only local Pentelic marble throughout their fabric. Other architectural features that suggest an early date for the temple are the use of poros limestone instead of marble for the euthynteria and lowest step of the crepidoma and the molded Ionic toichobate with cyma reversa profile along the foot of the cella wall. Both these details hark back directly to the stunted podium of the Older Parthenon on the Acropolis, but they are conspicuously lacking in all later Athenian buildings of the Doric order.[17]

More specific evidence comes from the unusual design of the coffered ceilings over the peristyle, with their separate coffer frames and individual coffer covers. To facilitate assembly of the ceiling, the coffer covers were marked with letters of the alphabet that corresponded to another set of letters inscribed beside the square openings of the coffer frames.[18] The forms of these masons' marks

---

[14] Cf. the actual-state plan of the ceiling, Dinsmoor, Jr., *AJA* 80 (1976) ill. 2.

[15] The relationship of the Hephaisteion to the Parthenon is discussed by Coulton, in *Parthenon-Kongress Basel,* 41–43.

[16] On the use of Parian marble for the metopes and friezes: Morgan, *Hesperia* 31 (1962) 211, 221, 222; Dinsmoor, *Hesperia* Suppl. 5 (1941) 117. For the simas, Dinsmoor, *Hesperia* Suppl. 5 (1941) 112–113. For the ceiling coffers, Dinsmoor, Jr., *AJA* 80 (1976) 223, 243, 245; Wyatt and Edmonson, *AJA* 88 (1984) 135, 143–148, 152.

[17] Dinsmoor, *Hesperia* Suppl. 5 (1941) 36–37, 151; and for the parallel of the Older Parthenon, Hill, *AJA* 16 (1912) 553; Orlandos, Παρθ., 64–65, 71–72.

[18] Design of the coffered ceiling, Wyatt and Edmonson, *AJA* 88 (1984) 135–141; description of the masons' marks, 141–156.

provide one indication of the temple's chronological position. To be sure, the dating of letter forms even in official inscriptions is notoriously precarious, whereas the letters on the ceiling of the Hephaisteion were informal guides intended to aid the builders, and no one else would read or even see them. Thus these letter forms might seem to be even less reliable as a criterion for chronology than is the case in formal epigraphy. Nevertheless, the masons' marks exhibit noticeable characteristics that are comparable to the lettering of inscriptions dated before the middle of the century. Beta and rho have angular profiles. Nu has one vertical shorter than the other and slopes to the right. Upsilon has an early tailless form. Gamma and lambda appear in their characteristic Attic forms, the former like alpha without the cross-bar and the latter with left vertical stroke and a short diagonal to the right. Three-bar sigma appears once. All these characteristics find parallels in the first five tribute lists, dated between 454/3 and 450/49; and, taken together, the masons' marks speak in favor of a date for the beginning of work earlier rather than later in the century.[19] On the basis of the mason's marks, a date as early as 460 has been proposed, and one scholar has attributed construction of the Hephaisteion to "Kimon or one of his circle."[20]

The early date for the beginning of construction appears to be confirmed by the ceramic evidence from the excavations, much of which was found in conjunction with marble chips and other debris from the masons' stone yards around the building site. Particularly useful was the fill dumped into a square rock-cut pit 33 meters to the southwest of the building. This consisted of masses of working chips of Pentelic marble dumped together with fine sand of the kind used as an abrasive in the final polishing of marble. The pit was evidently filled in an effort to clean up the accumulated debris on the building site when construction was still in progress, and so the pottery found in it provides welcome external evidence for the date at which that happened. Some of the pottery is red figure of fine quality dating to the 470s and 460s, while a few of the black-figure pieces belong much earlier, in the sixth century. Of the thirty-eight pots and fragments in the group, seven are datable to the second quarter of the fifth century, seven others belong in the decade 470–460, and the six latest pieces are to be dated ca. 450. In addition to these, there is an ostrakon of Dieitrephes and two ostraka of Menon Gargettios, all of which were probably cast in the 460s.[21] Thus the evidence of the pottery agrees closely with the evidence of the masons' marks on the coffered ceiling, and together they suggest that the temple was already under construction in ca. 450.

What calls for explanation is how the architect of the Hephaisteion can have borrowed innovative features of Doric design from the Parthenon when that building was not begun until three years later and continued construction throughout the 440s. A possible explanation may lie in the difficulty of assembling a sufficiently large and skilled labor force when there had been so little construction in Athens during the previous quarter century. Undoubtedly, work started at a slow pace. The foundations for the peristyle may have been laid, and debris from the stone yards found with

[19] Discussion of the letter forms, Wyatt and Edmonson, *AJA* 88 (1984) 158–160. For closely similar letter forms in the early tribute lists: angular beta and rho, *IG* I³ 263 III, lines 14–17, 20–22 (list 5, 450/49); *ATL* I, 28 fig. 29. Sloping nu, *IG* I³ 262 IV, line 6 (list 4, 451/0); *ATL* I, 19, fig. 17. Tailless upsilon, *IG* I³ 261 I, lines 2, 5, 10 (list 3, 452/1); *ATL* I, 11, fig. 8. Wyatt and Edmonson date the beginning of work ca. 460 on the basis of the same letter forms, but the parallels of the tribute lists make it preferable to bring the date down to the latter half of the 450s. H. R. Immerwahr, *Attic Script: A Survey* (Oxford 1990) 140, regards Wyatt's dates as "perhaps somewhat extreme."

[20] J. S. Boersma, *BABesch* 39 (1964) 101–106; Boersma, *Building Policy*, 59–61, proposes to attribute construction of the Hephaisteion to "Kimon or one of his circle." But all references to Kimon's interest in public works fall in the period from 476/5 (founding of the Theseion, Plut. *Thes.* 36.1) to 461/0 (Kimon's ostracism). Whether or not one believes in Kimon's early recall from ostracism (see Meiggs, *AE*, 422–423; Badian, *From Plataea to Potidaea*, 17–19), there is no trace of Kimon's presence in Athenian domestic affairs in the historical record of the 450s before the five-years' truce with Sparta in 451 (Thuc. 1.112.1) and the last expedition to Cyprus in 450 (Thuc. 1.112.2–4). Boersma suggests that the Hephaisteion was proposed by Kimon after the truce with Sparta, but by that time planning for the Periklean program had already begun to gather momentum.

[21] The pottery from Deposit C 9:6 was first studied by L. Talcott, in Dinsmoor, *Hesperia* Suppl. 5 (1941) 130–149. See endnote 3, pp. 399–401 below, for later publication references.

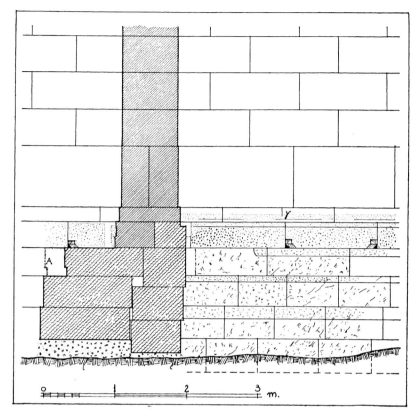

Figure 46. Section of west cross-wall foundation looking north

the pottery shows that marble workers had begun to cut building blocks. But that did not prevent the alteration of the specifications as plans for the Parthenon became generally known, and in fact that is exactly what happened. Moreover, in 447, when the overseers began to recruit labor for the Parthenon, many workmen from the Hephaisteion may have sought jobs on the larger project.

Both the architecture and the sculptural decoration of the Hephaisteion also show unequivocal signs that construction languished at a slow pace over many years. Indeed, the work probably stopped altogether for a considerable period of time before the temple reached completion and its cult statues were commissioned in 421/0.[22]

Greek builders often preferred to erect the exterior peristyle of a temple before laying the foundations for the cella walls, and this was the order of construction in the Hephaisteion. The lateral foundations for the cella were set down in trenches excavated through stratified layers of building debris that had accumulated during construction in the open rectangle of the peristyle.[23] But as work proceeded, the architect made several adjustments to the proportions of the cella so as to increase its width as much as possible and to reduce its interior length. Before the lateral walls of the cella were raised on the foundation, a secondary foundation was laid for the door wall of the pronaos, with the intention of setting that wall 0.877 m farther west than the original plan; but when it came time to erect the wall itself, the westward shift was increased by 0.328 m. Similarly, the foundation for the western cross-wall was widened by the addition of three extra courses of masonry laid along its inner face 0.761 m farther to the east than had first been planned (Fig. 46). When the wall of the opisthodomos was finally erected, it was built at the easternmost edge of the newly widened foundation. The effect of these changes was to reduce the clear interior length of the cella by 1.966 m, but at the

---

[22] The surviving accounts of the cult statues show that work on them commenced in the fifth prytany of 421/0 (archon Aristion) and the statues were dedicated in 416/5 (archon Arimnestos): *IG* I³ 472, lines 5, 20.

[23] Dinsmoor, *Hesperia* Suppl. 5 (1941) 30–31.

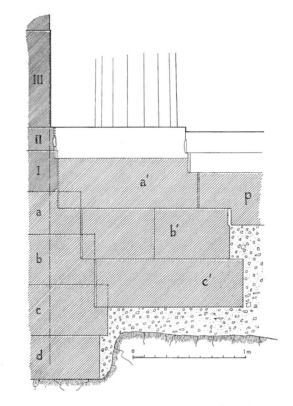

Figure 47. Section detail of interior column foundation at south

same time the builders placed the flank walls of the cella not centered on the foundation as normal practice dictated but at the extreme outer limits of their foundations.[24] The reason for these adjustments that both shortened and widened the interior dimensions of the cella was almost certainly the architect's decision to introduce a three-sided interior peristyle inside the cella, which had originally been planned without interior columns. There can be no doubt that this decision came late in the planning process. In order to provide foundations for the newly planned interior colonnades, it was necessary to trim back the projecting edges on the top three foundation courses of the cella walls and thus to accommodate the foundations for the interior columns, which actually rest in part on the lateral foundations for the cella walls (Fig. 47).[25]

Three-sided interior colonnades, such as that built in the Hephaisteion, were extremely rare in Greek temple architecture. The design was first invented for the Parthenon, where the excessive width of the great eastern cella allowed proper ambulatories behind the colonnades on all three sides.[26] But the cella of the Parthenon has an interior width of 19.065 m, more than three times the interior width of the Hephaisteion (6.217 m), and only by means of difficult adjustments to the cella walls was the architect able to insert such a peristyle inside the building (Fig. 48). The interior appearance was no doubt overcrowded, and in fact the interior columns stood scarcely 0.40 m away from the walls. All these circumstances suggest that the cella of the Hephaisteion was designed in imitation of the Parthenon and cannot have been built before the late 440s, or even later, when the plans for the Parthenon were widely known. But more important, this extraordinary effort to reproduce one of the most innovative features of the Parthenon in a building that was already under

[24] Alteration of the east cross-wall, Dinsmoor, *Hesperia* Suppl. 5 (1941) 49–57; west cross-wall, 45–46; flank walls of the cella, 37–39.

[25] Dinsmoor, *Hesperia* Suppl. 5 (1941) 40–44, 65–73.

[26] See chap. 4, pp. 98–102 above.

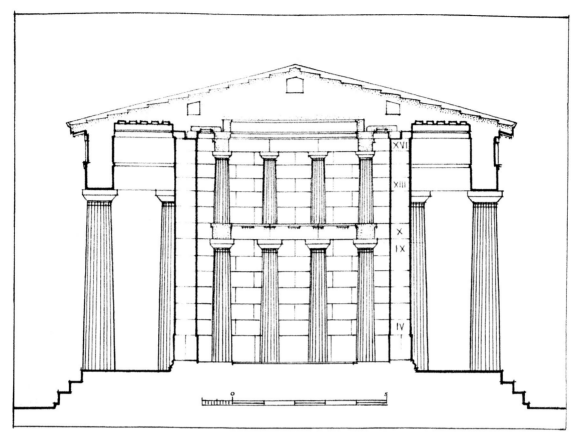

Figure 48. Restored section showing interior colonnade

construction, and, moreover, that was too small to contain it properly, shows how great a revolution the Parthenon wrought in Doric design.

That the temple was completed only after considerable delay emerges from examination of several pieces of evidence. Students of its sculptural program have long observed a curious stylistic discrepancy between the metopes of the exterior order and the Ionic friezes of the pronaos and opisthodomos. The metopes, although severely damaged, still exhibit a style that is not inconsistent with a date about the middle of the century; they recall the sculptures of the Temple of Zeus at Olympia more than those of the Parthenon.[27] By contrast, the Centauromachy of the west frieze betrays the heavy influence of the Parthenon. Several of the battling pairs of Lapiths and Centaurs are almost literal quotations from its southern metopes and must surely be later in date.[28] The scenes of fierce combat on the frieze of the pronaos find their closest parallels in the Ionic frieze of the Temple of Athena Nike and so point to a date in the 420s for completion of the uppermost parts of the temple.[29] A similar discrepancy has also been noted in the development of the building's

[27] On the style of the metopes, Morgan, *Hesperia* 31 (1962) 214–218; cf. Koch, *Theseustempel*, 117–125, with different identifications of the Theseus metopes; H. A. Thompson, *AJA* 66 (1962) 339–347; Knell, *Mythos und Polis*, 129–132.
[28] Cf. the Lapith and Centaur, Hephaisteion, west frieze 1, 2 (Morgan, *Hesperia* 31 [1962] pl. 80:a) with the similar pair on Parthenon, south metope 4 (F. Brommer, *Die Metopen des Parthenon* [Mainz 1967] 80–82, pl. 173). Cf. the Centaurs, Hephaisteion, west frieze 17, 19 (Morgan, pl. 81:b), with the Centaurs on Parthenon south metopes 28, 30 (Brommer, *Metopen,* 120–121, pl. 221; 124–125, pl. 229). See also the discussion of the west frieze, S. von Bockelberg, "Die Friese des Hephaisteions," *AntP* 18 (1979) 32–40.
[29] Morgan, *Hesperia* 31 (1962) 26–31; Bockelberg, *AntP* 18 (1979) 42–48. J. Dörig, *Le frise est de l'Héphaisteion* (Mainz 1985) 74–79, argues for a date in the decade 450–440, but this is incompatible with evidence of the masons' marks and the architectural details on the upper parts of the superstructure.

Figure 49. Entablature of east facade showing sculptured metopes

Figure 50. Restored elevation of east facade

architectural moldings (Figs. 49, 50). The moldings that articulate the exterior order to the level of the horizontal cornice exhibit less developed profiles than those on the upper parts of the cella building. Particularly striking also is the difference between the Doric hawksbeak moldings that crown the exterior cornices. The crowning molding on the horizontal cornice is closely similar to that on the corresponding member of the Parthenon. The upper curve has rather little projection, and the lower curve is shallow and slopes back gently to the face of the corona.[30] In contrast, the hawksbeak on the raking cornice of the pediments has a deeply rounded upper curve and deeply undercut lower curve that springs sharply from the vertical junction with the corona. Significantly, the epicranitis moldings at the top of the cella walls are closer in profile to the hawksbeak of the raking cornice than to that on the horizontal cornice.[31] The conspicuously greater development of moldings on the upper and inner parts of the building tells the same story as the sculptural decoration. Beginning ca. 450, the first campaign of construction carried up the exterior peristyle as far as the horizontal cornice, but this may not have been completed before the late 440s. Also at this time, down in the stone yards, sculptors were carving the metopes of the exterior order, while other masons began working the coffered ceiling of the peristyle and marked the frames and lids with letters appropriate to the period. After construction of the Parthenon had advanced sufficiently so that its interior colonnades were available for imitation, the builders of the Hephaisteion erected their cella building with a similar three-sided peristyle of columns inside. But the sculptured friezes of the pronaos and opisthodomos, the pediments, and the raking cornices of the roof remained unfinished until the 420s. As part of the last phase of construction, the coffered slabs of the marble ceiling were set in place above the peristyle. It is interesting to observe that some of the frames and lids were inscribed at this time with a second series of masons' marks in letters of the Ionic alphabet contemporary with the latest sculpture and architectural details.[32]

SCULPTURAL DECORATION

When we turn to consider the sculptural decoration of the temple, we at once encounter still more anomalies. The exterior order includes eighteen sculptured metopes, ten of which are displayed across the east facade (Figs. 49, 50), while on the north and south flanks the first four metopes beginning at the eastern corner likewise have sculptured scenes. This disposition of sculptural decoration has no parallel among Greek temples of the Classical period; and it has been suggested that the original scheme may have called for sculpture in all the exterior metopes, but that plan had to be altered when the building encountered long delays in construction.[33] A technical detail of the Hephaisteion frieze adds strength to this suggestion. Sculptured metopes were carved separately and slid into slots in the sides of the adjacent triglyphs. But on the Hephaisteion not only the eighteen sculptured metopes but all sixty-eight metopes on the four sides of the temple were made of separate pieces of marble mounted between the adjacent triglyphs. The idea of sculptured scenes in all the exterior metopes is a decorative scheme already used forty years earlier on the Athenian Treasury at Delphi, and it was adopted again for the Parthenon in the very years when the metopes of the Hephaisteion were being carved. In fact, during the decade of the 440s, sculptors were at work on all ninety-two metopes and the entire Ionic frieze of the Parthenon, as well as the Ionic frieze slabs for the temple of Poseidon at Sounion. It is easy to see that the temple on the Acropolis got priority, and why the Hephaisteion encountered long delays in construction.

[30] For the horizontal geison of the Hephaisteion, Shoe, *Greek Mouldings,* 108, pl. LIII:21, and cf. the closely similar hawksbeak from the geison crown of the Parthenon, pl. LIII:20.
[31] For the raking geison of the Hephaisteion, Shoe, *Greek Mouldings,* 108, pl. LIII:22. Note the considerably greater development in contrast to Shoe, 20, 21; but cf. the comparable profiles of the epicranitis in the pronaos and opisthodomos, 128, pl. LXI:1, 2.
[32] The later series of masons' marks is described by Wyatt and Edmonson, *AJA* 88 (1984) 158–161.
[33] Morgan, *Hesperia* 31 (1962) 215–216, 218–219.

No matter the original intention, the metopes now in place on the front of the temple depict nine of the traditional twelve labors of Herakles. But here again is an anomaly. The twelve labors had been canonized in art a decade earlier in the Temple of Zeus at Olympia, where they occupied the twelve metopes of the pronaos and opisthodomos. On the frieze of the Hephaisteion, however, three of the labors are omitted altogether, and one has been spread curiously across two adjacent metopes. The eight metopes on the flanks illustrate the deeds of Theseus, with each metope allotted to a separate adventure. It was not the first time that the exploits of these two heroes had shared the decorative program of an Athenian building. They had lent their mythical iconography to the builders of the Athenian Treasury at Delphi, where, accompanied by scenes from the war with the Amazons, they had helped to commemorate the Athenian victory over the Persians at Marathon. It is quite likely, in fact, that the treasury at Delphi served as a source of inspiration for the Periklean designers; and it clearly shows that the heroic adventures of Herakles and Theseus were deemed appropriate subjects to adorn a war memorial.[34]

As often in the decoration of Greek temples, the sculptural program is not drawn from traditional mythology specific to the particular deity to whom the temple was dedicated. Rather, the subject matter illustrates how the special powers of that deity are made manifest in ways that affect the actuality of human life. Here we see Herakles, greatest and most ubiquitous of the heroes of early Greece, and in each scene he conquers wild beasts and frightful monsters, all the bogeys of the mythopoeic mind. The cycle is well known, although in this case incomplete. The first four metopes from the south show Peloponnesian labors: the Nemean lion, the Lernaean hydra, the Kerynian stag, the wild boar of Erymanthos. Then follow five labors that took the hero to the limits of the known world: the man-eating Thracian mares; Kerberos, guardian of the gates of hell; Hippolyte the Amazon, warrior woman of the distant east; and, spread across two metopes (8 and 9), the recovery of the cattle of Geryon, that creature of nightmare who lurked on an island of the distant west. Only the recovery of the belt of Hippolyte did not involve the slaughter of some evil being.[35] Significantly, the cycle culminates in the northernmost metope, where the hero, at the end of his labors, retrieves the apples of the Hesperides, accompanied by Athena, in a scene that is meant to foreshadow Herakles' eventual introduction into Olympos.

Set beside the labors of Herakles, the deeds of Theseus form a fascinating foil. Mythical archetype of the Athenian ephebe, Theseus and his mythology were largely an invention of democratic Athens; and Athenian arts and letters had fleshed him out with *res gestae* so closely imitative of the exploits of the older hero that ἄλλος οὗτος Ἡρακλῆς, "this other Herakles," became a popular proverb.[36] Accordingly, in each of his eight metopes, Theseus is shown in single combat with one of a group of mythical ruffians. Most notorious is the Minotaur in his Cretan labyrinth (S 1), but other vicious beasts that roil the good order of their neighborhoods are the Krommyonian sow (N 4) and the bull of Marathon (S 2). All his other adversaries are brigands and highwaymen who skulk by the roadside and waylay the unwary traveler: Periphetes, who wields a club (N 1); Sinis the pine-bender (S 3); Kerkyon the Eleusinian wrestler (N 2); Prokroustes, who lops off parts of his guests so they match the length of his bed (S 4); and Skeiron, who flings his victims down the cliffs that bear his name to the waters of the Saronic Gulf (N 3).[37] On the temple of those two gods whose special

[34] For the treasury at Delphi, P. de la Coste-Messelière, *FdD* IV.4, *Sculptures du trésor des Athéniens* (Paris 1957) 37–81 (Theseus), 104–153 (Herakles). For discussion of the metopes of the Hephaisteion: Koch, *Theseustempel*, 117–125; Morgan, *Hesperia* 31 (1962) 210–219; Thompson, *AJA* 66 (1962) 339–341. On the date of the treasury, Amandry, *BCH* 122 (1998) 75–90; cf. chap. 1, pp. 7–8 above.

[35] Of the canonical twelve, the Stymphalian birds, the Augean stables, and the Cretan bull have been omitted. Cf. the literary versions of the myths: Diod. 4.11–28; Apollod. *Bibl.* 2.5.

[36] Plut. *Thes.* 29.3; and cf. Isokr. 10 *Helen* 23.

[37] For identification of the Theseus metopes, Morgan, *Hesperia* 31 (1962) 212–214: north (E–W), Periphetes, Ker-

gifts were the civilizing arts, the cycle of myth proclaims the gradual evolution of civilization itself. As always, the heroes mediate between the Olympians and humankind, and by their actions the divine will is fulfilled on earth. In the mythic narrative, the development of culture passes through two distinct stages. Herakles rids the world of fantastic creatures and hideous ogres who dwell at the ends of the earth. In contrast, the beasts that Theseus tames are unruly cattle: the sow of Krommyon was named Phaia, and some said she was a murderous woman called "pig" for her porcine habits; the Marathonian bull is led by the hero through the city alive and sacrificed on the altar of Apollo. But for the most part Theseus, the noble sheriff, apprehends felons and malefactors who infest the countryside and menace the peace of civilized life.[38]

Even more interesting are the two Ionic friezes above the pronaos and opisthodomos, both of which show by the style of the sculpture that they must belong to a late phase of the temple's construction. They have been compared to the friezes of the Athena Nike temple on the Acropolis and dated to the 420s.[39] But they must have been planned from the beginning because the antae of the pronaos are perfectly aligned with the third column on the flanks, a most unusual arrangement for the inner porch of a Doric temple. This plan was adopted so that the frieze could extend across the flank pteroma on either side to abut the frieze of the external peristyle. The antae of the opisthodomos, on the other hand, align with the midpoint of the second intercolumniation in the normal Doric manner, and the frieze is confined to the width of the cella.

Both friezes depict tumultuous scenes of pitched battle. That at the west end is one of the most popular myths in the repertory of Athenian artists, the battle of the Lapiths and Centaurs (Figs. 51–53). This is not, however, the battle that broke out when the raucous Centaurs disrupted the wedding feast of the Lapith king Perithoos and Hippodameia. That version of the myth was shown in the west pediment of the Temple of Zeus at Olympia and in the southern metopes of the Parthenon. Here, at the center of the frieze, two rearing Centaurs raise an enormous boulder above the figure of Kaineus (W 8–10), who is already half buried in the earth (Fig. 52); so we have the Thessalian version of the Centauromachy.[40] No women are present; there are no accouterments of the feast; and the Lapiths are armed warriors, not wedding guests. The central group is an exact replica of a scene on the frieze of the Temple of Poseidon at Sounion that was probably carved as early as the 440s. If the Centauromachy at Sounion were better preserved, it might prove to have been the principal source of inspiration for the sculptor of the Hephaisteion frieze. But there is one interloper in the Thessalian version of the myth. At the center of the frieze, an isolated heroic warrior (W 11) attacks the rearing Centaur group (Fig. 53). He strides forward with his right leg and raises his sword above his head for a swift cutting blow to the Centaur. The traveler's hat that has slipped down to his shoulder marks him as a visitor from abroad, and we shall see presently that he must be identified as the Athenian Theseus.

Identification of the battle in the eastern frieze is by no means so obvious and has been the subject of much scholarly debate (Figs. 54–59). A specifically local Attic myth is most probable, and one that has found favor with many investigators is the story in which Theseus leads his Athenians against the fifty sons of Pallas, the primitive giants who inhabited the eastern slopes of Mount

---

kyon, Skeiron, sow; south (W–E): Prokroustes, Sinis, bull, Minotaur. Koch, *Theseustempel*, 121–122, 125, exchanges Prokroustes and Periphetes, following B. Saur, *Das sogenannte Theseion* (Berlin 1899) 94–95; cf. also Thompson, *AJA* 66 (1962) 341. Cf. Plut. *Thes.* 8–14. For development of the myth after ca. 510, H. J. Walker, "The Early Development of the Theseus Myth," *RhM* 138 (1995) 1–33.

[38] The sow named Phaia, Plut. *Thes.* 9.1; sacrifice of the bull, 14.1. For a similar interpretation of the Hephaisteion sculptures, see E. C. Olsen, *AJA* 42 (1938) 276–287.

[39] See Morgan, *Hesperia* 31 (1962) 226–231.

[40] The Thessalian version of the Centauromachy is discussed below in connection with the frieze of the Temple of Poseidon at Sounion, chap. 8, pp. 240–243. See Knell, *Mythos und Polis,* 133–136.

Figure 51. West frieze, Lapiths and Centaurs (W 1–5)

Figure 52. West frieze, Centaurs and Kaineus (W 6–10)

Figure 53. West frieze, detail of Theseus (W 11)

Figure 54. East frieze, warriors (E 1–5)

Hymettos.[41] In both friezes the protagonist and central figure can be none other than Theseus himself, but now the democratic hero of Athens assumes a stance that is certainly to be read as a political statement. By a kind of visual alchemy, the two figures of Theseus take on the appearance of the most celebrated statuary group in Athens, the Tyrant Slayers by Kritias and Nesiotes, which stood in the midst of the Agora below the temple.[42] The figure in the east frieze poses as Aristogeiton, lunging forward with his left leg; over his outstretched left arm his cloak falls away in long, loose folds (Fig. 57, E 15). On the west frieze, he strides with his right leg forward in the guise of Harmodios, his right arm cocked above his head, his sword poised to deliver a downward slashing blow (Fig. 53, W 11).[43] The message is unmistakable: Theseus impersonates the historic foes of tyranny whose murder of Hipparchos had been canonized as a courageous blow for liberty in the popular mythology of democratic Athens. In like manner, the democratic hero strikes out against the tyranny of barbaric savagery and uncouth otherness which the riotous Centaurs always represented in the iconography of the fifth century.

If the subject of the pronaos frieze is correctly interpreted as Theseus's battle against the Pallantidai, the political message of the sculptural narrative is still more trenchant. The stature of the engagement is enhanced by the presence of Olympian spectators who sit on rocks, as if perched on Attic hilltops, above each anta of the cella walls. At the south are Athena, Hera, and Zeus (Fig. 55, E 6–8); and they are balanced at the north end by another divine couple that should probably be identified as Poseidon and Amphitrite, while Hephaistos himself occupies the northernmost position and nods to Athena at the far south end (Fig. 58, E 22–24).[44] Like the gods of the *Iliad*, they observe

---

[41] For the subject of the east frieze, Thompson, *AJA* 66 (1962) 341–344, and, for earlier bibliography on the identification, 343, note 18. Morgan, *Hesperia* 31 (1962) 232, also accepts the subject as Theseus battling the Pallantidai. For interpretation of the friezes along the lines adopted here, see now K. Reber, *JdI* 113 (1998) 31–48, especially 37–46 for the east frieze. Koch, *Theseustempel*, 126–137, calls it simply a mythical battle. Cf. Bockelberg, *AntP* 18 (1979) 23–48, who also avoids identification of a specific incident. Dörig, *Frise est de l'Héphaisteion*, 71–73, prefers Athenians against Eumolpos and the Thracians. Cf. Knell, *Mythos und Polis*, 136–139.

[42] See Morgan, *Hesperia* 31(1962) 226.

[43] The two central figures are East 15 (Bockelberg, *AntP* 18 [1979] 27) and West 11 (Bockelberg, 35).

[44] The seated gods are East 6, 7, 8 and 22, 23, 24: Bockelberg, *AntP* 18 (1979) 25, 28–29; see also Thompson, *AJA* 66 (1962) 344. Morgan identified East 22 and 23 as Apollo and Aphrodite: *Hesperia* 31 (1962) 222. Dörig, *Frise est de l'Héphaisteion*, 53, following Koch, *Theseustempel*, 135, calls E 23 Aphrodite.

Figure 55. East frieze, deities (E 6–9)

Figure 56. East frieze, warriors (E 10–14)

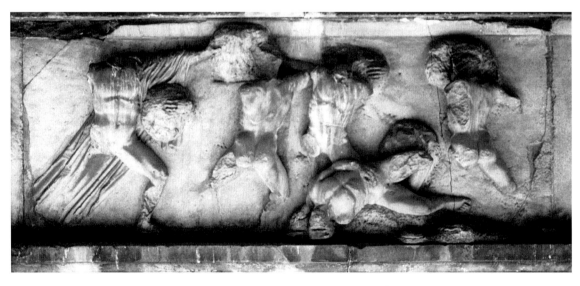

Figure 57. East frieze, Theseus and opponents (E 15–19)

Figure 58. East frieze, deities (E 20–24)

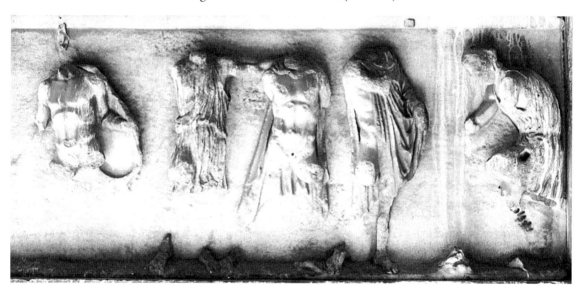

Figure 59. East frieze, warriors (E 25–29)

with cool aloofness the desperate struggle that rages on the human plane. Theseus's Athenians are armed with shields and helmets, and they fight with swords and spears, those very weapons that the blacksmith god had fashioned for Achilles and made to be invincible with his cunning craft. Ranged against them are fierce and brutish giants of superhuman strength who lob enormous boulders as their chosen weapons, but they know nothing of the martial skills in which Athena drills her people. As the myth has come down to us in literature, however, the sons of Pallas rose up in armed insurrection in order to drive Theseus from the kingdom because he was an immigrant and stranger, and his father Aigeus only an adopted son of Pandion.[45] The myth is a tale of political revolt against the ruling royal power, but on the frieze of the Hephaisteion, the democratic warrior king has become a tyrannicide who fights for the freedom of his people. He reacts to armed rebellion just as democratic Athens handled revolution among her tributary allies. The sculptor has injected yet another new

[45] Plut. *Thes.* 3.5, 13.1–3; Apollod. *Epit.* 1.11; schol. Eurip. *Hipp.* 35, quoting Philochoros, *FGrH* 328 F 108; cf. Soph. *Aigeus, TrGF* 10 F 24 (Radt); Paus. 1.22.1, 28.10.

element into the iconography of the story, for nothing in the literary version of the myth suggests the vivid dichotomy between the armed Athenian hoplites and the naked savages hurling stones. To all appearances, civilized Athenians of the fifth century are locked in mortal and heroic combat not with legitimate descendants of Erechtheus, but with a race of boorish aborigines who inhabit the wilderness untouched by the arts of civilization. A persistent refrain rings through this cycle of myth, which comprises the preserved sculptural program of the temple: the unending struggle of the human community against the beasts of the forest and of civilization against the anarchy of primordial chaos; and it is just here that the arts of Hephaistos and Athena were thought most potent to win the day for mankind.[46]

THE DOUBLE CULT

It was particularly appropriate to site the Temple of Hephaistos and Athena Hephaisteia in the midst of the industrial area west of the Agora, where all manner of craftsmen and artisans plied their trades, for these two were preeminently the guardian deities of the arts and crafts. Their double cult, unparalleled elsewhere in Greece, appears to have enjoyed considerable antiquity at Athens, where it was mentioned already by Solon at the beginning of the sixth century and probably dates from the earliest development of Athenian industry.[47] An early locus of the cult in Attica seems to have been at the Academy, where, in a temenos sacred to Athena, there stood an altar and dedicatory relief shared jointly by Hephaistos and Prometheus. Both relief and altar are described as archaic by writers of the Hellenistic period. From this altar, according to Pausanias, runners lit torches that would bear the sacred fire to Athens in one or another of the famous Athenian torch races. At the festivals of the Hephaisteia and the Prometheia, the torch races would most appropriately begin at this spot, although at the Panathenaia the torch race is said specifically to have begun at the altar of Eros, which Pausanias saw outside the entrance to the Academy.[48]

In later times, Hephaistos had an altar in a sanctuary far more central to Athenian religion, which he also shared with Athena; for one of the three altars seen by Pausanias in the Erechtheion was sacred to Hephaistos. A marble throne for the priest of the god, inscribed ἱερέως Ἡφαίστου, was probably one of the interior appointments of that temple by the fourth century, if we may judge from the lettering of the inscription.[49] There is fair consensus that the existing marble temple, which we call the Erechtheion, replicated the functions and the interior plan of the archaic temple de-

[46] The sculptural fragments that have been attributed to the pediments are too few and too broken to permit any but the most speculative identification of the subject. For attempts, see Thompson, *Hesperia* 18 (1949) 230–268; Thompson, *AJA* 66 (1962) 344–347; Morgan, *Hesperia* 32 (1963) 91–108.

[47] Solon 12.49–50 (West, *IE* 2). For Hephaistos, see generally L. Malten, "Hephaistos," *JdI* 27 (1912) 232–264; M. Delcourt, *Héphaistos ou la légende du magicien* (Paris 1957); F. Brommer, *Hephaistos* (Mainz 1978). Evidence for the cult at Athens has been studied by E. Reisch, "Athena Hephaisteia," *ÖJh* 1 (1898) 55–93; A. B. Cook, *Zeus*, vol. 3 (Cambridge 1940) 181–237; Delcourt, *Héphaistos,* 194–203; H. A. Shapiro, *Art and Cult under the Tyrants in Athens: Supplement* (Mainz 1995) 1–14. For the uniqueness of the Athenian double cult, Malten, 243.

[48] The altar and relief in the temenos of Athena at the Academy, schol. Soph. *OC* 56, quoting Apollodoros, *FGrH* 244 F 147, and citing Lysimachides, *FGrH* 366 F 4. Torch races run from the altar of Prometheus, Paus 1.30.1; three torch races at the Panathenaia, Hephaisteia, and Prometheia, Harpokr., s.v. λαμπάς (λ 3 Keaney), citing Polemon (Müller, *FHG* III, 117 F 6); schol. Aristoph. *Frogs* 129c (Chantry). Altar of Eros dedicated by Charmos, Paus. 1.30.1; by Peisistratos, Plut. *Sol.* 1.7; start for the torch race of the Panathenaia, schol. Plato, *Phaedr.* 231E.

[49] Altar of Hephaistos in the Erechtheion, Paus. 1.26.5; the inscribed throne, *IG* II² 4982. The throne of his priest is one of a pair carved from a single block of marble, closely similar to the priestly thrones in the proedria of the Theater of Dionysos. The second throne is inscribed ἱερέως Βούτου, *IG* II² 5166. The thrones are described and illustrated by Paton and Stevens, *Erechtheum,* 484–485, fig. 201.

stroyed by the Persians; and, if that is correct, there is reason to believe that an altar of Hephaistos
may have stood in the Temple of Athena Polias already in the Archaic period. In any event, much of
the mythology that associates Hephaistos and Athena is clearly located on the Acropolis. The mythical aition for the double cult told of the abortive union between Hephaistos and the virgin goddess
that resulted in the birth of Erichthonios from the earth itself. Wishing to make him immortal, the
goddess took the newborn babe to her own temple on the Acropolis, where she hid him in a chest,
set her own serpent to be his guardian, and entrusted him to the care of the daughters of Kekrops.
When the girls violated the goddess's command and opened the chest, it was from the cliffs of the
Acropolis that they hurled themselves to their deaths, driven mad by Athena's wrath.[50] Raised to
manhood in the temple on the Acropolis, Erichthonios dedicated the ancient xoanan to the goddess
and founded the Panathenaia in thanks for her nurturing care. With the cunning craft of Hephaistos, he invented the chariot and instituted the athletic contests; and upon his death his tomb was
established in the Temple of Athena Polias on the Acropolis, where the goddess herself had reared
him.[51] This story of Erichthonios's birth from the earth is first known from its appearance in Athenian vase painting at the beginning of the fifth century, and it appears fairly frequently by the second
quarter of the century.[52] In literature the earliest reference to the autochthonous birth seems to have
been made by Pindar and the poet of the *Danais*, but the earliest narrative version of the myth is a
fragment from an *Atthis* by Amelesagoras.[53]

There appears to be some recollection in the later Classical period that the double cult of Athena and Hephaistos was localized on the Acropolis in early times, and this is reflected in Plato's fanciful description of the antediluvian Acropolis in the *Kritias*. In describing the areas occupied by the
different classes of his primeval city of Athens, Plato (*Kritias* 112A–B) says of the Acropolis, "but on
its highest part only the military class by itself had its dwellings around about the Temple of Athena

[50] See Apollodoros 3.14.6; cf. Eurip. *Ion* 20–26, 266–275; Paus. 1.2.6, 14.6, 18.2; Amelesagoras, *FGrH* 330 F 1; schol. Hom. *Il.* 2.547 (Dindorf).

[51] Dedicated the xoanon and established the Panathenaia, Apollod. 3.14.6. For the Panathenaia, cf. *Marm. Par., FGrH* 239, ep. 10, under the year 1505/4; Harpokr., s.v. Παναθήναια (π 14 Keaney), who cites the *Atthides* of Hellanikos (*FGrH* 323a F 2) and Androtion (*FGrH* 324 F 2). He invented the chariot (or the four-horse chariot) and instituted the contests: *Marm. Par.* (above); Hyginus, *Astronom.* 2.13; pseudo-Eratosthenes, *Catasterismi* 13, of which the last says that he estab-lished the apobatic contest. His tomb in the temenos of Athena: Apollod. 3.14.7; Clem. Alex. *Protr.* 3.45 (p. 39, Potter).

[52] See the vases catalogued by U. Kron, *LIMC*, vol. 4, 928–929, nos. 1–7; and U. Kron, *Die zehn attischen Phylenhe-roen, AM-BH* 5 (Berlin 1976) 249–250, nos. 1–5, with discussion on pp. 55–64; cf. E. Kearns, *The Heroes of Attica, BICS* Suppl. 57 (London 1989) 160–161. Both authors treat Erechtheus and Erichthonios as one individual whose mythology has become confused (Kron, *Phylenheroen*, 37–39), and perhaps there was confusion in the later sources. In the earliest sources, however, the only thing they have in common is their autochthonous birth. Hom. *Il.* 2.548 says of Erechtheus, τέκε δὲ ζείδωρος ἄρουρα; Hdt. 8.55 calls him γηγενής; Eurip. *Ion* 20 uses the same adjective to describe Erichthonios, but Soph. *Ajax* 202 speaks of Athenians generally as χθονίων ἀπ' Ἐρεχθειδῶν; all descendants of Erechtheus are "earthborn." In fifth-century Athens, the two were plainly regarded as separate individuals of different generations. In Euripides' *Ion*, Kreousa says she is the daughter of Erechtheus (260); at line 267, Ion asks, ἐκ γῆς πατρός σου πρόγονος ἔβλαστεν πατήρ, "Was your father's ancestor sprung from the earth?" to which she answers, "Yes, Erichthonios" (268). There follows the story (269–274) of Erichthonios, Athena, and the daughters of Kekrops. Whereupon Ion asks (277), πατὴρ Ἐρεχθεὺς σὰς ἔθυσε συγγόνους, "Did your father Erechtheus sacrifice your sisters?" Then comes the story (278–284) of Erechtheus's sacrifice of his daughters and his subsequent death by the stroke of Poseidon's trident. Similarly, on the red-figure cup by the Kodros Painter (ca. 440–430), on which all figures are identified by inscriptions, side A shows Kekrops, Ge, Erichthonios, Athena, Herse; side B shows Aglauros, Erechtheus, Pandrosos, Aigeus, Pallas (Berlin F 2537: *ARV²* 1268, no. 2; *LIMC*, vol. 1, 287, s.v. Aglauros 7; *LIMC*, vol. 4, 929, s.v. Erechtheus 7; Kron, *Phylenheroen*, 250, E 5). Erichthonios is the babe in arms handed to Athena; Erechtheus is a mature adult. Euripides reversed the generations, but both he and the vase painter thought the two heroes were different figures of different ages.

[53] Harpokration, s.v. αὐτόχθονες (α 272 Keaney), mentions both Pindar and the poet of the *Danais* as referring to Erichthonios's autochthonous birth. For the *Atthis* of Amelesagoras, *FGrH* 330 F 1. Dion. Hal. *Thuc.* 5 lists Amelesagoras among authors who wrote before the Peloponnesian War (*FGrH* 330 T 1), but Jacoby in *FGrH* considers the name spurious and dates the fragment ca. 300.

and Hephaistos where they had surrounded themselves with a single enclosure wall like the garden of a single dwelling." The general tone of the passage is one of imaginative invention, and clearly no one would espouse Plato's explanation for the geomorphology of the Acropolis; but the topographical references, on the contrary, conform accurately to the familiar physical landmarks of the city that everyone knew. The rivers Ilissos and Eridanos form its boundaries in two opposite directions, while it included the Pnyx Hill to the west and Lykabettos set over against it to the east. There is, then, no reason to think that Plato's contemporary readers would have found fault with his passing reference to a Temple of Athena and Hephaistos at the highest point of the Acropolis in earliest antiquity.

Against this background, the choice of the Kolonos Agoraios as the site for the new Hephaisteion appears to break sharply with religious tradition. The Market Hill lay in the midst of that district of the city which took its name from the potter's craft, the Kerameikos. Here, from Early Archaic times and especially after the Persian Wars, the potters had fashioned their wares. It was a section of Athens that teemed with the manifold activities of small industry. The foundries of the braziers and ironmongers lay around about the site itself, while the kilns and workshops of the potters, the stone yards of the masons and sculptors crowded the slopes of the Kolonos Agoraios.[54] These craftsmen approached their gods with simple, homely prayers, beseeching Athena to hold her protecting hand over the potter's kiln, that the vessels might fire well and fetch a good price at market. The poet prays that the potters may gain great wealth; but if they are shameless, he invokes the evil spirits that haunt the potters' craft and cause the pots to shatter and warp and misfire in the kiln.[55] The cries of the local coppersmiths still ring in the verses of Sophokles as they call their fellows to the festival of the Chalkeia. This ancient rite, especially dear to workers of bronze and craftsmen of all sorts, was plainly a major celebration of the double cult. Learned Hellenistic scholars argued over which deity had the more important share. Some said the festival honored Hephaistos because he first worked bronze in Attica; others claimed it for Athena. In the third century, the prytaneis of the boulē offered special sacrifices to Athena "the founder" at the Chalkeia; and on this day, Pyanepsion 30, in every fourth year, the priestesses on the Acropolis, assisted by the *arrhephoroi,* began to weave the peplos for the next Panathenaic festival.[56]

The foundation of the Hephaisteion on the Kolonos presents several interesting anomalies in the building's architectural history, some of which have already been discussed. Not the least of these is the temple's initial priority over the Parthenon in the order of projects. As we have seen, a date for the beginning of its construction in ca. 450, and perhaps as much as three or four years before the Parthenon, is based on reliable evidence.[57] In this connection, it is perhaps highly significant that no earlier building had occupied the site. Excavation beneath the floor of the temple and over the whole surface of the hill has brought to light no trace of earlier architectural remains.[58] To the Periklean designers of the midcentury, the Kolonos Agoraios offered a piece of virgin soil unencumbered by

[54] For industrial establishments around the Hephaisteion: Shear, *Hesperia* 6 (1937) 342–344; Thompson, *Hesperia* 6 (1937) 14–21; Dinsmoor, *Hesperia* Suppl. 5 (1941) 1; Mattusch, *Hesperia* 46 (1977) 340–379.

[55] For the potters' prayer, *Homeric Epigrams* 14, preserved in the pseudo-Herodotean *Life of Homer* 32 (U. von Wilamowitz, *Vitae Homeri et Hesiodi* [Bonn 1916] 17–18); M. J. Milne, in J. V. Noble, *The Techniques of Painted Attic Pottery* (London 1988) 186–196.

[56] For the coppersmiths, Sophokles, *TrGF* 10 F 844 (Radt). Special festival for craftsmen and coppersmiths, Harpokr., s.v. Χαλκεία (χ 2 Keaney) = *Suda,* s.v. Χαλκεία (χ 36 Adler), with the date Pyanepsion 30, citing Apollonios of Acharnai, *FGrH* 356 F 3 (festival for Athena), and Phanodemos, *FGrH* 325 F 18 (festival for Hephaistos). Cf. Pollux 7.105; *Suda,* s.v. Χαλκεία (χ 35 Adler) (the day the priestesses began to weave the peplos). The prytaneis sacrifice at the Chalkeia, *IG* II² 674, lines 16–19 = *Agora* XV 78; *Agora* XV 70, lines 6–8. See Parker, *Polytheism and Society,* 464–465.

[57] See p. 144 and note 19 above, and endnote 3, pp. 399–401 below.

[58] On the absence of earlier architectural remains, Dinsmoor, *Hesperia* Suppl. 5 (1941) 125–127. Broken pottery of a quality that might suggest dedication was found scattered over the rock surface west of the temple, but if it came from an earlier sanctuary, it must have been a simple affair.

the ruins of an archaic temple, unlike the Acropolis and particularly the site of the Parthenon. But the double cult is plainly older than the Periklean temple, for its mythical aition, the autochthonous birth of Erichthonios, was known and depicted by Attic vase painters from the beginning of the century. Furthermore, the apparently earlier associations of Hephaistos and Athena with the Academy and the Acropolis suggest that in the marble temple on the Market Hill an older, preexisting cult was to receive refoundation on a new and different site. Some support for this notion comes from an interesting variant of the foundation myth in which the familiar story of Erichthonios's birth was retold by Euripides in an unknown play:

> Concerning the birth of Erichthonios, Euripides tells this tale. Hephaistos, having fallen in love with Athena, wished to unite with her. But she turned her back on him and, choosing rather to keep her virginity, hid herself in a certain place of Attica, which they say was called after him Hephaisteion. He, thinking to overpower her by assault, was struck by her spear and let drop his desire, so that the seed fell to earth. From this, they say, was born a child who for this reason was called Erichthonios.[59]

This version of the story attributed to Euripides differs from all other accounts of the myth in that it defines precisely the place where Erichthonios was born from the earth. Pursued by Hephaistos, Athena sought a hiding place somewhere in Attica. The god found and attacked her, whereupon the spot was named Hephaisteion. The addition of this detail to the traditional myth is the more striking because it derives ultimately from an author of the fifth century who was already writing at the time when construction began on the marble temple, and who was himself much given to manipulating his mythological sources. We may readily believe that Euripides' telling of the story preserved the variant mythical aition which explained the foundation of the Periklean temple on the Kolonos Agoraios.

The decision to house the double cult in a splendid marble temple set in the midst of the Kerameikos displays a shrewd understanding of the Athenian populace on the part of the Periklean planners. The dedication of this building to Hephaistos and Athena will have earned at once the support of all the artisans and craftsmen who put their trust in these deities and celebrated their festivals. For Hephaistos and Athena were not merely the spirits of kiln and foundry, but rather protectors of all δημιουργοί in all the crafts; even Sokrates, a stonemason by profession, could claim Hephaistos as his ancestor.[60] For all these artisans of the working classes, the Hephaisteion would assume a special role as a seemly and propitious offering to the very deities who could bless with their benign protection the sundry operations of the building program, for these were the gods of the builders themselves.[61] It will come as no surprise, however, to learn that these homely guardians of Athenian industry acquired a new and loftier stature in the course of the fifth century, for the ideals of the Periklean age left their indelible stamp upon the cult. Hephaistos and Athena came now to be regarded specifically as the educators and civilizers of mankind, since their mechanical arts gave men the knowledge to lead a civilized life.[62] They underwent an intellectual transformation closely

---

[59] Pseudo-Eratosthenes, *Catasterismi* 13 (ed. A. Olivieri, *Mythographi Graeci*, vol. 3, fasc. 1 [Leipzig 1897] p. 16) = Eurip. frag. 925 (Nauk2): λέγει δὲ καὶ Εὐριπίδης περὶ τῆς γενέσεως αὐτοῦ (Erichthonios) τὸν τρόπον τοῦτον· Ἥφαιστον ἐρασθέντα Ἀθηνᾶς βούλεσθαι αὐτῇ μιγῆναι, τῆς δὲ ἀποστρεφομένης καὶ τὴν παρθενίαν μᾶλλον αἱρουμένης ἔν τινι τόπῳ τῆς Ἀττικῆς κρύπτεσθαι, ὃν λέγουσι καὶ ἀπ' ἐκείνου προσαγορευθῆναι Ἡφαιστεῖον· ὃς δόξας αὐτὴν κρατήσειν καὶ ἐπιθέμενος πληγεὶς ὑπ' αὐτῆς τῷ δόρατι ἀφῆκε τὴν ἐπιθυμίαν, φερομένης εἰς τὴν γῆν τῆς σπορᾶς· ἐξ ἧς γεγενῆσθαι λέγουσι παῖδα, ὃς ἐκ τούτου Ἐριχθόνιος ἐκλήθη.

[60] Plato, *Laws* 11.920D–E; for Sokrates' "ancestry," Plato, *Alcibiades* I, 121A.

[61] Cf. the monthly sacrifice to Athena made by the overseers and workmen of the Erechtheion, *IG* I³ 476, lines 285–287 (408/7).

[62] Plato, *Prot.* 321C–E, *Polit.* 274C.

analogous to that of Demeter, and from this they emerged no longer as patrons of simple craftsmen but as lovers of philosophy and the fine arts:

> Hephaistos and Athena, since they shared in common a like nature, being at once kindred born of the same father and, moreover, agreeing in their love of wisdom and in their love of fine craftsmanship, they both took for their joint portion this land of ours as being naturally congenial and well adapted for virtue and for wisdom; and they created men of virtue, sprung from the land itself, and they inspired in their mind the form of government.[63]

In poetry this notion finds its most explicit and succinct expression in the *Homeric Hymn to Hephaistos*, where the god has shed all the old mythology of the lame blacksmith and in partnership with Athena teaches mankind the arts of civilized life:

> Sing, clear-voiced Muse, of Hephaistos famed for his skill. With bright-eyed Athena he taught glorious crafts to men on earth—men who before used to dwell in caves in the mountains like wild beasts. But now having learned crafts through Hephaistos the famous artisan, they live life easily in their own homes free from care the whole year round. Be gracious, Hephaistos, and grant me excellence and bliss.[64]

It remains to be noticed that the decision to build the Hephaisteion on the Kolonos Agoraios commended itself to the fifth-century temple builders for another reason beyond the cult's popularity with the artisans of the Kerameikos. We can scarcely doubt that some of its appeal lay in the splendid location of the site itself. In all the lower city of Athens, there is no more commanding site than the Market Hill, and the temple on its brow would have drawn the constant gaze of every merchant in the market and every councilor and magistrate doing business among the civic buildings at its foot. It will have been a daily reminder to every citizen and every visitor of the material splendor which Athens had reaped from the empire.

---

[63] Plato, *Kritias* 109C: Ἥφαιστος δὲ κοινὴν καὶ Ἀθηνᾶ φύσιν ἔχοντες, ἅμα μὲν ἀδελφὴν ἐκ ταὐτοῦ πατρός, ἅμα δὲ φιλοσοφίᾳ φιλοτεχνίᾳ τε ἐπὶ τὰ αὐτὰ ἐλθόντες, οὕτω μίαν ἄμφω λῆξιν τήνδε τὴν χώραν εἰλήχατον ὡς οἰκείαν καὶ πρόσφορον ἀρετῇ καὶ φρονήσει πεφυκυῖαν, ἄνδρας δὲ ἀγαθοὺς ἐμποιήσαντες αὐτόχθονας ἐπὶ νοῦν ἔθεσαν τὴν τῆς πολιτείας τάξιν.

[64] *Homeric Hymn to Hephaistos* (20):
> Ἥφαιστον κλυτόμητιν ἀείσεο, Μοῦσα λίγεια,
> ὃς μετ' Ἀθηναίης γλαυκώπιδος ἀγλαὰ ἔργα
> ἀνθρώπους ἐδίδαξεν ἐπὶ χθονός, οἳ τὸ πάρος περ
> ἄντροις ναιετάασκον ἐν οὔρεσιν, ἠΰτε θῆρες.
> νῦν δὲ δι' Ἥφαιστον κλυτοτέχνην ἔργα δαέντες
> ῥηϊδίως αἰῶνα τελεσφόρον εἰς ἐνιαυτὸν
> εὔκηλοι διάγουσιν ἐνὶ σφετέροισι δόμοισιν.
> Ἀλλ' ἵληθ' Ἥφαιστε· δίδου δ' ἀρετήν τε καὶ ὄλβον.

This short poem, undoubtedly of Athenian origin since it mentions the double cult, is strikingly imbued with the fifth-century concept of civilization. One is tempted to suggest that it might be a product of this very period. Cf. T. W. Allen and E. E. Sikes, *Homeric Hymns* (London 1904) 271. It was, however, reserved for Sophokles to pen the most exalted picture of human achievements in civilization, and, significantly, in a document dating from the greatest years of Periklean culture (ca. 442). The chorus of *Antigone* 332–375 exudes precisely the same spirit that we have been tracing elsewhere and is the clearest indication that these ideas were current in the 440s.

6

The Telesterion at Eleusis

In the middle years of the fifth century, the sanctuary of Demeter at Eleusis would have struck the visitor in much the same way as the Athenian Acropolis or any one of a number of Attic sanctuaries, all of which had felt the flames of the Persian invaders a generation before, and all of which still displayed the shattered remains of their former temples. From the court of the sanctuary, the Eleusinians still looked out to the bay and the straits of Salamis from behind the ramparts of the old archaic fortifications (Fig. 61). The breach in the mud-brick wall left by Persian battering rams will have been patched in the intervening years, and the circuit was somewhat enlarged by the addition to the northeast of a new service area for the sanctuary.[1] But the central terrace would have looked much the same in 450 as it had in 478. The Persian invasion seems to have caught the Eleusinian shrine in the midst of reconstruction, at a time when the archaic Telesterion had been largely dismantled and its successor was only in the earliest stages of construction.[2] Thus the Telesterion will have remained, like the Older Parthenon, in a state of stunted dilapidation for thirty years.

The great hall of the mysteries itself was in fact the Temple of Demeter at Eleusis,[3] although among Greek temples the building was unique in its architecture, for its design had more in common with the Odeion in Athens than with the Parthenon or the Hephaisteion. The name Telesterion derives from Plutarch (*Per.* 13.7) and is very generally used by modern scholars, but in fact the word is attested only rarely in antiquity. In the fifth century the building was called the Eleusinion (τὸ Ἐλευσίνιον) in the usage of official inscriptions, as we learn from the decree concerning the dedication of the firstfruits of the grain. This document directs the Eleusinian priests:

---

[1] The peribolos wall was breached at a point just east of the Philonian porch of the Telesterion, where a section of the original mud brick has been replaced with fine pseudo-isodomic masonry founded on the early polygonal socle. On the location, see F. Noack, *Eleusis, die baugeschichtliche Entwicklung des Heiligtumes* (Berlin 1927) 30–33, 90–92; G. E. Mylonas, *Eleusis and the Eleusinian Mysteries* (Princeton 1961) 107–108. The northeast extension of the peribolos was erroneously dated to the Early Archaic period by Noack, *Eleusis,* 32–39, and was subsequently restudied by K. Kourouniotes, *ArchDelt* 15 (1933–35) parart., 33–36; Mylonas, *Eleusis,* 108–111.

[2] This so-called Kimonian Telesterion has been almost universally attributed to reconstruction in the 470s and 460s. See most recently Travlos, *BTA,* 94. For evidence for its pre-Persian date, see Shear, Jr., *Hesperia* Suppl. 20 (1982) 128–140. For the early stage at which the project was abandoned, see Noack, *Eleusis,* 102–105.

[3] That the Telesterion was identical with the Temple of Demeter has been conclusively demonstrated by Kourouniotes and Travlos, *ArchDelt* 15 (1933–35) 54–114. Noack, *Eleusis,* 48, 85, 218, argued that the small Roman building—which he called Temple F, high on the rock just above the northeast side of the Telesterion—was actually archaic and the Temple of Demeter. All the archaic blocks found in this building come, however, from the superstructure of the archaic Telesterion itself, and there was in fact no temple on this site before Roman times. Noack's thesis has now to be rejected despite the efforts of O. Rubensohn, *JdI* 70 (1955) 29–34, to revive it.

IG I³ 78, lines 26–30:

ἀναγράφσαντες δὲ ἐ[μ]

πινακίοι τὸ μέτρον τõ καρπõ . . .

[κ]αταθέντον ἔν τε τõι Ἐλευσινίοι Ἐλευσῖνι καὶ ἐν τõι βολ[ευτ]ε-

[ρ]ίοι.

Having recorded the measure of the crop on a wooden tablet . . . they are to deposit it in the Eleusinion at Eleusis and in the Bouleuterion.[4]

The mystery cult of Demeter undoubtedly felt the loss of its temple far more than any of the other Attic sanctuaries. The other temples, although they housed sacred images which demanded ritual attention, were fundamentally elaborate repositories of sacred treasure. The gods were expected to take a keener interest in the sacrifices at their outdoor altars. At Eleusis, however, the ceremonial of the Mysteries functioned primarily within the shrouded secrecy of the Telesterion. Here the ritual pageant of Demeter's search for her daughter Persephone was annually reenacted. Here, too, were performed the secret rites of initiation, and the hierophantes revealed to the initiates the holiest relics of the cult, which since the beginning of the shrine had resided in the same hallowed spot, the Anaktoron, the sanctum sanctorum of Demeter's temple.[5] Use of the name is first attested by Herodotos (9.65) in describing the Persian destruction of the sanctuary. Occasionally in poetic passages, more frequently in the sophists and rhetors of the later Roman period, and especially in the late verse inscriptions, the name of the part came to be applied to the whole, and the building itself was sometimes called Anaktoron.[6] The word means the dwelling or palace of a king and derives from the *wanax* (ϝάναξ) of Mycenaean Greek, the ἄναξ ἀνδρῶν (king of men) of the Homeric heroes, and titles of gods and kings on the tragic stage. In the *Homeric Hymn to Demeter* (lines 270–274, 296–298) the goddess visits Keleos, the king of Eleusis, in his palace, and at her command he bids his people build her a great temple and altar. Thus did the ancient royal dwelling become a part of the topography of the Eleusinian sanctuary.

In view of the nature of the Mysteries and the venerable tradition associated with the particular site on which the Anaktoron stood, there can be little doubt that some sort of temporary structure was erected amid the ruins of the archaic building.[7] This will have been of very light construction which has left no trace in the physical remains of the building. But we may surmise that it occupied

[4] That τὸ Ἐλευσίνιον was the correct classical nomenclature for the building we call the Telesterion was demonstrated in detailed argument by Rubensohn, *JdI* 70 (1955) 1–20. Since the Firstfruits Decree provides for the keeping of records on wooden tablets, their deposit "in the Eleusinion at Eleusis" cannot simply refer to the sanctuary generally, where perishable documents would be exposed to the weather. Similarly, the Athenian copies of the wooden tablets are to be deposited in the Bouleuterion. For discussion of similar wooden tablets deposited in the Bouleuterion, see Shear, Jr., in M. H. Hansen and K. Raaflaub, eds., *Studies in the Greek Polis, Historia* Suppl. 95 (1995) 185–187. The inscribed stele bearing the text of *IG* I³ 78 was to be set up Ἐλευσῖνι ἐν τõι hιερõι, "at Eleusis in the sanctuary" (line 50). This is the proper classical locution for the sanctuary as a whole: Rubensohn, 2–4. For the attempt of K. Clinton, *Myth and Cult: The Iconography of the Eleusinian Mysteries* (Stockholm 1992) 126–132, to argue that the name of the Telesterion was τὸ Ἀνάκτορον, see note 6 below. For other references to the Telesterion as τὸ Ἐλευσίνιον: *IG* II² 1672, line 6; 1666A, line 1; 1673, line 81; 1363, line a1.

[5] For the Anaktoron, see Travlos, *ArchEph* (1950–51) 1–16. Recent general accounts of the Mysteries: Mylonas, *Eleusis*, 224–285; C. Kerényi, *Eleusis* (London 1967); W. Burkert, *Homo Necans* (Berkeley 1983) 248–297; D. Lauenstein, *Die Mysterien von Eleusis* (Stuttgart 1987); R. Parker, *Polytheism and Society* (Oxford 2005) 327–368.

[6] Clinton, *Myth and Cult,* 128–132, assembles testimonia on the use of the term Anaktoron. Those passages dating to the Classical period are all poetic except for Herodotos 9.65. The great majority of authors there cited is of Roman date. Of the inscriptions, *IG* II² 3709, 3764, 3811 4077, 4218, and *IDélos* 2552 are all late votive dedications in verse. What these testimonia show is that in later antiquity the name of the inner sanctum was sometimes given to the temple as a whole, most frequently to accommodate the exigencies of poetic meter. They offer no evidence bearing on the classical nomenclature of the temple.

[7] Noack, *Eleusis,* 105–106. Themistokles' reconstruction of the Telesterion of the Lykomedai at Phlya (Plut. *Them.* 1.4) may have been guided by similar exigencies of cult.

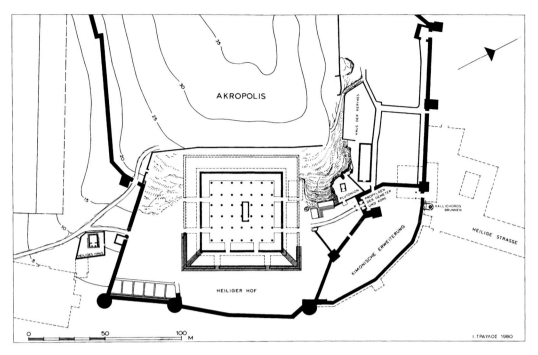

Figure 60. Restored plan of sanctuary at Eleusis in the late fifth century

the northeastern half of the present structure, since both phases of the Periklean building began on the southwest side behind the Anaktoron, where there had been no previous construction of any sort. Whatever these temporary arrangements may have been, the Eleusinian sanctuary was clearly in a sad state not long before the middle of the fifth century. In fact, the shrine probably had no building of suitable security to house the sacred treasury, for the money of the Two Goddesses seems to have been deposited for safekeeping on the Acropolis beside the treasury of Athena.[8]

The Eleusinian Epistatai

This situation was soon to be rectified, for we have already seen that the Eleusinian cult assumed a special place in the Panhellenic aspirations of Athens; and it seems highly probable that the original plans for the building program included the reconstruction and enlargement of the Hall of the Mysteries at Eleusis. This project was in itself scarcely less grand than the plan for the Parthenon, although it never enjoyed the special renown that has been accorded to the Acropolis, and its history, as we shall see, was far more checkered. Any attempt to reconstruct the history of the fifth-century building operations at Eleusis must begin with the Athenian decree reorganizing the administration of the sanctuary. This is the amendment of Thespieus,[9] which provides for the establishment of a new committee of overseers for the sanctuary and outlines broad administrative powers for the new officials. The new epistatai were to be five in number, of whom one was to be chosen secretary, and they were to serve a term of one year (lines 7–10, 17). We have already seen that Thespieus based his plan on a similar board of overseers that had already been voted for the Acropolis buildings.

The Eleusinian epistatai were intended to assume control of τὰ χρέματα τα τοῖν θεοῖν, that is, the whole corpus of sacred property, money, dedications, and real estate belonging to the Two

---

[8] *IG* I³ 6 (face C), lines 32–38, cited above, chap. 3, p. 37, note 100.
[9] *IG* I³ 32, chap. 2, pp. 23–26 above, p. 408 below; cf. the discussion of Cavanaugh, *Eleusis and Athens*, 19–27.

Goddesses, including their other shrines in the city of Athens and in Phaleron (lines 10–12). They were to report to the boulē any outstanding debts payable to the sanctuary, and these they were empowered to collect (lines 14–17). If they learned that any part of the property in their charge was lost, they, as the proper custodians, were to recover it. Finally, and most important, they were entrusted with the annual income of the goddesses, and it was in their power to spend this on "whatever was most necessary," with the advice of the priests and the boulē (lines 20–22, 28–30). Now, most of these powers had probably resided up to this time with the hieropoioi of Eleusis, who were now to transfer control of the property to the new board. Thus, Thespieus provided for the logistai, the state auditors, to prepare a complete audit of all expenditures in the three sanctuaries at Eleusis, Athens, and Phaleron since the deposit of the sacred treasury on the Acropolis (lines 22–28, 30–32).

Thespieus's description of the audit is of considerable interest for the chronology of the building operations at Eleusis. The logistai were instructed to audit τὰ ἀνελομένα, and the tense of the participle indicates that these are all past expenditures made prior to the decree itself (lines 24–25, 28). Furthermore, in connection with the audit of the City Eleusinion, the logistai are to call upon the architect Koroibos and a certain Lysanias, λογίζεσθαι ... ἐν ἄστει δὲ τὰ ἐν ἄστει ἀνελομένα ἀνακαλõντας τὸν ἀρχιτέκτονα Κόροιβον καὶ Λυσανίαν ἐν τõι Ἐλευσινίοι, "to audit in the city money that had been spent in the city consulting the architect Koroibos and Lysanias in the Eleusinion." The phraseology leaves no doubt that Koroibos is expected to give information concerning only his activities in the city of Athens, and not at Eleusis or Phaleron. But it is important to note that no specialized consultants were thought necessary in order to prepare the audit at Eleusis and Phaleron. The logistai would presumably get all the information they needed from the archives of the hieropoioi. The inference is clear that certain building operations had been carried out in the City Eleusinian under Koroibos's direction.[10] But the opposite is equally clear: that no building had yet taken place at Eleusis or Phaleron,[11] or else we should have expected the logistai to interview the architects in charge. The audit at Eleusis and Phaleron would involve only the routine operating expenses of the sanctuaries.

On the other hand, the elaborate reorganization of Demeter's financial management presupposes a momentous change in the sanctuary itself. Since it will be possible to show that work began on the Telesterion very shortly after the passage of Thespieus's amendment, there is no reason to doubt that the first major undertaking of the new overseers was the construction of the Telesterion itself. This, indeed, will almost surely have been the main subject of the lost decree to which Thespieus attached his amendment on the administration of the sanctuary. Thespieus was concerned that the epistatai should gather together all the money that was legitimately theirs, hence the careful audit and the specific injunction to collect payable debts and recover lost property. The vague clause instructing the overseers to spend "whatever is most necessary" after consultation with the priests and the boulē reads almost like a blank check. All the indications suggest that Thespieus anticipated large expenditures in the near future.

The new board proposed by Thespieus was destined to become the permanent administrative arm of the sanctuary, and as such it lasted for well over a century, unlike its model, the overseers of

---

[10] There is, of course, no reason to suppose that Koroibos's work in Athens was connected in any way with the reconstruction of a sacred building, for it may just as well have been repairs to the temenos wall that he had supervised. Cf. Kallikrates' slightly later repair of the Acropolis walls, *IG* I³ 45 and chap. 3, p. 76 above.

[11] The period within which no construction had taken place at Eleusis is defined by *IG* I³ 32, lines 30–32, 35–38. The audit was to begin from the time when Eleusinian funds had been handed over to the treasurer, presumably the Ktesias whose name appears in line 31, and the accounting was to come down to the date of the inscription. Repairs to the peribolos walls and any temporary structure to accommodate the Mysteries would have been carried out earlier. In fact, no reconstruction of the sanctuary of Demeter at Phaleron was ever undertaken, for Pausanias (10.35.2) saw the shrine still in ruins more than six centuries later.

the Acropolis buildings. The committee's official title was the ἐπιστάται Ἐλευσινόθεν,[12] and many of their later activities may be followed in detail in the documents that survive from their archives. Evidently, as one might expect, the organization of the committee was altered on several occasions during its long history. While they were originally intended to be an annually rotating board with an annual secretary (*IG* I³ 32, lines 9–10, 17), the secretary of 420/19, Philostratos of Kydathenaion, seems to have held office for the whole Panathenaic quadrennium 422/1 to 419/8.[13] In the fourth century also the Eleusinian epistatai regularly served a four-year term of office,[14] but for the years 409/8 to 407/6 we find a different board and secretary each year, as originally provided.[15] The number of overseers in any given year probably also varied considerably, but this should not occasion surprise since the Athenians habitually tolerated irregularity in this regard.[16] Of greater interest than this, however, is the fact that the epistatai, as far as we can trace their activities, seem to have exercised the same broad administrative responsibilities originally set out for them in Thespieus's amendment. It has been justly noted that the Eleusinian overseers bore in some ways a closer resemblance to the treasurers of Athena than to the overseers of the Parthenon, on whom they had been modeled.[17] Indeed, we find among their published documents numerous inventories of sacred treasure and dedications closely analogous to the inventories of the Acropolis treasures;[18] and these are supplemented with statements recording the transfer of the firstfruits from the hieropoioi to the epistatai for deposit in the treasury of the goddesses.[19] Unlike the treasurers of Athena, however, the Eleusinian overseers regularly supervised all building operations in the sanctuaries under their jurisdiction. It was they who published the architects' specifications for new buildings,[20] and it was their responsibility to pay for the construction. Thus, we also find a series of detailed accounts recording all their expenditures for various constructions: walls and gates at Eleusis, a new entrance to the City Eleusinion, and the prostoon of the Telesterion.[21] From this brief review of the overseers' manifold activities, it will be obvious that they are the men who stand always in the background, who let the contracts, pay the expenses, and publish the accounts for the construction of the Telesterion. It was undoubtedly for this purpose that Thespieus proposed their original appointment.

[12] *IG* I³ 391, lines 32–38; *IG* II² 1544, line 1; 1672, lines 1, 37, 137. The variant title ἐπιστάται Ἐλευσῖνι occurs in *IG* I³ 386, line 2, and in one document the board of 356/5–353/2 called itself ἐπιστάται Ἐλευσινίο, *IG* II² 1666A, line 1. See Cavanaugh, *Eleusis,* 16.

[13] He was certainly in office for two years, from 421/0 to 420/19: *IG* I³ 391, lines 9, 16; Cavanaugh, *Eleusis,* 5–6.

[14] *IG* II² 1541, lines 1–7, and cf. the remarks of Dittenberger, in *SIG*² 587, note 5; Cavanaugh, *Eleusis,* 9–10.

[15] *IG* I³ 386, lines 2–4; 387, lines 2–3; Cavanaugh, *Eleusis,* 7–8.

[16] There were only three in 408/7: note 15 above. From 356/5 to 353/2 they numbered at least seven: *IG* II² 1666A, lines 1–6. During the two quadrennia 336/5–329/8, they were eight: *IG* II² 1544, lines 1–11. Cf. the similar variation in the number of the Parthenon overseers, chap. 3, pp. 45–48 above.

[17] Meritt and Wade-Gery, *JHS* 83 (1963) 114.

[18] *IG* I³ 384–390, 400; *IG* II² 1540–1552.

[19] *IG* I³ 391, and cf. *IG* II² 1672, lines 263–288. The hieropoioi, as the managers of all sacred aspects of the sanctuary, were the officials authorized to receive the firstfruits of the grain on behalf of the goddesses (cf. *IG* I³ 78, lines 9–10, 17–18). The proceeds of the firstfruits would then be transferred to the epistatai for purposes of bookkeeping.

[20] *IG* II² 1666, which gives the specifications for the letting of contracts for one of the phases of the prostoon, based on the designs of the architect Philagros; for interpretation of the inscription, see J. A. Bundgaard, *Mnesicles* (Copenhagen 1957) 111–116; K. Jeppesen, *Paradeigmata* (Aarhus 1958) 109–138. It is to be noted that these specifications were published by the same board that published the treasure list, *IG* II² 1541 (356/5–353/2), of which Nikodemos of Athmone was chairman. Various other documents concerning the specifications and contracts for Eleusinian buildings were not put out explicitly under the docket of the epistatai, but were probably published by them, e.g., *IG* II² 1671, 1675–1677, 1679–1683. From one of these (1675, lines 27–28) we learn that one member of the board of overseers was to be present on the building site during operations.

[21] Expenses for the walls and gates, *IG* II² 1672, lines 1–78; cf. F. G. Maier, *Griechische Mauerbauinschriften* (Heidelberg 1959) vol. 1, 92–103, no. 20. For the entrance to the City Eleusinion, *IG* II² 1672, lines 129–134, 162–168, 170–171, 183, 194; transportation of column drums for the prostoon, *IG* II² 1673 + K. Clinton, *ArchEph* (1971) 83–113 = Clinton, *Eleusis,* 159.

ARCHAEOLOGICAL REMAINS: PHASE I

We should turn now to the remains of the sanctuary itself in order to see just what it was that these new epistatai had to administer in the late fifties of the fifth century. The early architectural history of the Telesterion is a story of rapid and massive expansion. Because of the secret nature of the cult and the pageantry of its ritual, all the worshippers at the festival had to be accommodated within the Hall of the Mysteries itself or be excluded from the mystic rites. Thus, the growing popularity of Demeter's cult in the fifth century necessitated the enlargement of the building. As Demeter's mysteries flourished, her temple doubtless grew in direct proportion. Although the temple itself was of an architectural type quite extraordinary among Greek religious buildings, its plan adhered to a rigid tradition that dictated the architectural development of the site throughout antiquity. This tradition was the location and architectural prominence of the Anaktoron, for that small rectangular structure became the focal point of every building ever designed to enclose it. Furthermore, experience had shown that a large columnar hall was the most successful design for the performance of the Mysteries. The Telesterion of the late sixth century had set the type, with its square hall ranged with five parallel rows of columns, its walls lined with banks of steps for the initiates, and its facade decorated with a large prostyle portico. In its western corner had stood the Anaktoron.[22] Early in the fifth century, the plan was to enlarge the building to twice its original length so that the Anaktoron would then be located symmetrically in the middle of the southwest wall. The columns were then rearranged in three rows of seven, and the front wall was advanced to the stylobate of its predecessor, thus sacrificing the portico in the interest of increased capacity within.[23]

It was the ruins of these two buildings that confronted the Periklean architects and the traditions of their plans that had to be molded into a new and still larger Telesterion (Fig. 61). The physical remains on the site have revealed clear evidence of two different plans for the enlargement of the building, both of which date to the fifth century. Since one was completed, while the other was abandoned very early in its construction, the latter is evidently the first attempt to restore the building. The early excavations brought to light a pair of large square foundations for columns outside the southwest wall of the archaic temple, and obviously no part of the later Periklean and Roman phases. The poros foundation piers also align with two square beddings of equal size cut in the rock floor of the western corner. These foundations are arranged in two rows of four each, in such a way that they fall in the intercolumniations between rows I, II, and III of the Roman column bases, and, if completed, the foundations would have supported four columns in each row. They are clearly designed for a building equal in depth to the later Periklean structure; and if extended to the northeast in five rows of four each, they would have filled a hall of precisely the same width as the surviving Telesterion. The original plan, then, seems to have called for a great, nearly square hall whose roof was to be carried on twenty interior columns arranged in five rows of four columns each.[24] The building would have retained the depth of the unfinished earlier structure of the early fifth century while exactly doubling its width, and the resulting plan was just four times the size of the old archaic temple. Like its abandoned predecessor, the new building would have used the stylobate of the ar-

[22] On the archaic Telesterion, see Noack, *Eleusis*, 48–70, with the corrections of Kourouniotes and Travlos, *ArchDelt* 15 (1933–35) 74–82; cf. Mylonas, *Eleusis*, 78–88; Shear, Jr., *Hesperia* Suppl. 20 (1982) 128–140. On the sanctuary generally, see Camp, *Archaeology of Athens*, 106–108, 283–284.

[23] On the so-called Kimonian Telesterion, see Noack, *Eleusis,* 93–106; Mylonas, *Eleusis,* 111–112; Travlos, *BTA,* 94. On its abandonment before completion, Shear, Jr., *Hesperia* Suppl. 20 (1982) 139–140.

[24] See D. Philios, *Prakt* (1884) 78, who was the first to note the two fifth-century building periods. The existing building measures 51.968 m in depth (southeast to northwest) and 51.562 m in width (southwest to northeast), interior dimensions; but the Periklean building was 2.15 m shorter in depth than the Roman reconstruction. For the evidence of the building's depth, see p. 181 and note 72 below. For the arrangement of columns in the early Periklean plan, Noack, *Eleusis,* 143, 149–150, 292; Mylonas, *Eleusis,* 113–117.

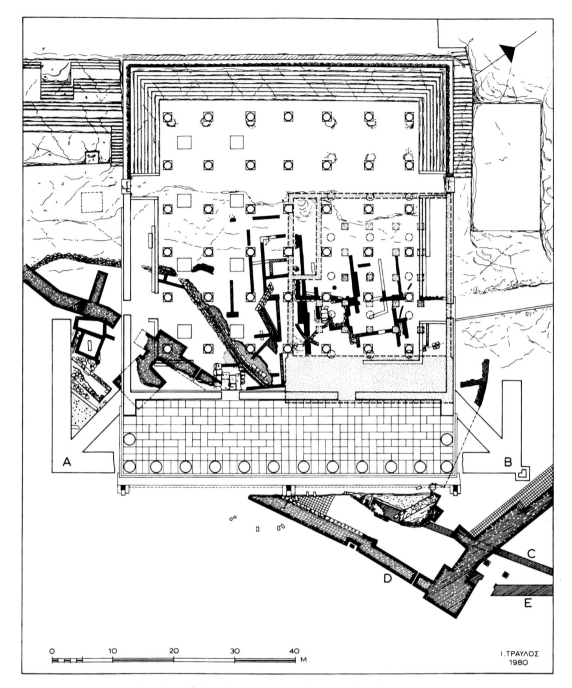

Figure 61. Plan of the Telesterion, actual state with earlier archaic remains

chaic Telesterion, now extended to the southwest, as a foundation for its front wall. Its northeast side would have rested on the foundations of both its predecessors, while its back wall would be quarried deep into the natural rock of the hill.[25] In the center of the hall would have been the Anaktoron,

[25] The southwestward extension of the line of the earlier stylobate is easily distinguishable from the archaic foundations in its material and the working of the blocks. At the south corner, the new foundations had to descend 8.725 m to the rock, and here they survive in seventeen courses of poros masonry with a step and toichobate of blue Eleusinian limestone. The side walls of the Periklean building were 0.45 m thicker than those of the old temple, and thus the top two courses of the archaic foundations for the northeast wall were worked down to receive the wider step and toichobate on which the Periklean orthostates rest. The euthynteria for the Periklean wall was simply placed flush against the third course of the archaic foundation. See Noack, *Eleusis,* 139–141 and pl. 2, section 11.

reconstructed on the same foundations that it had occupied since Archaic times, its rear wall now on the central axis of the building.[26]

While the Periklean architects revived the square hypostyle hall originally designed in the late sixth century, they introduced a number of innovations in the plan (Fig. 62). The new Telesterion was to have six broad doorways, two on each side, except in the rock-cut northwest wall. On the interior, eight rows of steps were designed to be carried around all four walls of the building, so that every available space between the entrances would be filled and the building could accommodate about three thousand standing initiates on the steps during a celebration of the Mysteries.[27] The most daring departure was the spacing of the internal supports for the roof. The new Telesterion was to have had only twenty interior columns, while its immediate predecessor, a building just half its size, had one more column, and the archaic temple, one quarter the size of the new building, had two more columns in the interior. This meant that the architects were attempting spans of enormous length in the interior superstructure. The axes of the columns in the individual rows were spaced as much as 10.06 m apart, and the axial spacing from row to row was 8.41 m. The architects can hardly have hoped to span these great distances with stone architraves, and we may suppose that a good deal of woodwork was projected for the upper parts of the temple.[28]

The existing remains leave no doubt that this bold design was never carried to completion but was in fact halted with only a small part of the substructure in place. It is difficult to determine, however, at just what point the work was abandoned, because the later Periklean plan was almost identical, except for the arrangement of the interior columns. Certainly the later architects incorporated in their foundations whatever had been built of the original plan. Many blocks cut for the foundations or superstructure of the first building were no doubt also eventually laid in the walls of the second without our being able to distinguish them. Nevertheless, it is evident that most, if not all, of the work was limited to the southwestern half of the building. Only here did the construction progress as far as the laying of foundations for the interior columns. Since this preliminary construction was not even begun in the northeastern half, one infers that it was the intention of the builders to leave the temporary "Telesterion" in the ruins of the archaic temple until the new section could be at least partially completed. Only then would the builders have progressed with the reconstruction of the ruined building to the northeast.[29]

The first major operation undertaken by the Periklean builders must have been the quarrying of the living rock of the hill. For it must be borne in mind that the natural slope of the rock originally rose abruptly behind the back wall of the archaic Telesterion. Since the back wall of the new building was intended to lie 17.70 m farther to the northwest, great masses of rock had to be cut away. On the line of the new northwest wall, the natural surface of rock before construction probably rose between seven and eight meters at the highest point above the level of the present floor, so that nearly 1,600

---

[26] Travlos, *ArchEph* (1950–51) 1–16.

[27] All eight rows of steps from the later Periklean building are preserved in the north corner. Only three rows are preserved on the southwest side, and parts of a single step are in situ along the front. The first Periklean step on the front rested on the poros toichobate for the archaic front wall: Noack, *Eleusis,* 142.

[28] For the calculations of the dimensions of the interior columns and spans, Noack, *Eleusis,* 149–150. Since the square foundations for the columns measure 1.96 m with slight variations, the lower diameter of these interior columns was probably intended to be ca. 1.90 m. It is instructive to compare this dimension with the later columns, of which the diameters varied from 1.27 m to 1.325 m. Cf. also the interior lower diameter of the Parthenon, 1.114 m, and of the Temple of Zeus at Olympia, 1.52 m. That the architraves cannot have been stone is indicated by comparison with the famous marble ceiling beams over the lateral aisles of the Propylaia, which were 5.489 m clear span, only a little over half the longest spans planned for the Telesterion. There is, however, no reason to believe, with Dinsmoor, *AAG*[3], 196, and Mylonas, *Eleusis,* 115, that these long spans caused the abandonment of the plan, for they could certainly have been carried by architraves of timber.

[29] Noack, *Eleusis,* 139–146, assumed that all the Periklean foundations and orthostates for the northeast wall, together with the interior steps built along it, were laid during the first phase of Periklean construction. The total absence of foundations for the twenty-column plan in the north half of the building is strong evidence against this.

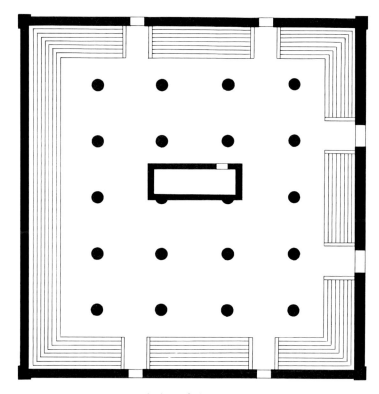

Figure 62. Restored plan of phase I, the project of Iktinos

cubic meters of blue Eleusinian stone had to be removed. Thus the lower part of the walls at the western corner, as well as the steps along part of the southwest side and all of the northwest, would have been cut from the rock itself, just as their Roman successors are today. That all this quarrying was completed before the abandonment of the project is clear because the foundation for the last column in each of the two rows is simply a square bedding let down a few centimeters into the rock-cut floor. When work stopped on the first phase of the building, the floor in the western corner was therefore exactly as we see it today (see Fig. 64).

Farther east, the hill falls off sharply so that the foundations for the front and side walls had to be extremely deep.[30] Here the first Periklean builders did not progress very far, for the square foundations of the interior columns were left with only four courses of masonry finished, and their top surfaces lie 3.17 m below the Periklean floor.[31] Despite their incomplete state, these foundations exhibit all the characteristic excellence of Periklean workmanship. They are everywhere lowered to the rock itself, and the rock had been cut down to make a smooth and level bedding for the lowest course. The square piers are built of almost uniform rectangular blocks of poros stone, whose surfaces have been carefully smoothed; and they are laid in regular courses in header and stretcher fashion. Since the architects were able to lay out the arrangement of the interior columns, we can safely assume that they had already surveyed the general lines of the exterior walls. They will have begun construction in the southern corner, where the foundations had to be deepest, and we may suppose that several of the lowest courses along the front and the southwest side were in place before the work was interrupted. But in any event, the exterior foundations can hardly have risen appreciably higher than the internal piers for the columns. It is impossible to estimate how far the masons had progressed with the cutting of blocks for the superstructure. A larger number had probably been roughly worked, for in the later Periklean building the steps and orthostates, and

---

[30] See note 25 above.
[31] For detailed description of the square column foundations, see Noack, *Eleusis,* 292.

the blocks of the exterior walls, were all made of local Eleusinian limestone. We have seen that large quantities of this stone had already been quarried from the building site itself and were ready to be worked in the stone yards from the very beginning of construction. Now, since this local stone was not used for the foundations, which were of poros, it is a reasonable assumption that it was intended for the superstructure of the first phase, just as it was in fact used for the superstructure of the later. The steps and orthostates still visible in the ruins of the Telesterion will actually have been quarried in the west corner of the present building.

Expense Account of Phase I

The information derived from this examination of the actual remains enables us to associate with this early construction a hitherto unidentified inscription found in the early years of the excavations.[32] The fragment records the receipts and expenditures for one year of a building operation. The last five lines of the receipt column are preserved; the items of expenditure appear to be virtually complete. This account, like those of the Parthenon and the Propylaia, was arranged in a double column, with the amounts of the expenditure recorded to the left and the descriptive itemization to the right. The left-hand column with its sums of money has perished entirely. Line 3 indicates the agency responsible for paying the expenses and publishing the account: παρὰ τῶν προτέρο[ν] ἐπ[ιστατῶν].[33] These are the ἐπιστάται Ἐλευσινόθεν whose acquaintance we have already made in connection with the amendment of Thespieus. In fact, as we shall see, this must have been one of the earliest accounts published by the overseers after their formation. The most likely restoration of line 18 corroborates the identification: for here we read [μισθὸς ℎιερ]οποιοῖς. If this is correct, the hieropoioi draw their salaries from the epistatai, which indicates that Thespieus's financial reorganization of the sacred properties has already taken effect.

Since the column of expenses is probably complete for the year, except for the balance forward, it gives us a fairly clear picture of the work which the overseers had in progress. The account conveys the impression that the building was not very far along, for there is no mention of extensive construction.[34] Payments were made for the quarrying and working of poros stone from the island of Aigina and from Steiria on the east coast of Attica (lines 8, 11). The soft Aiginetan poros was used especially for columns, entablature, or wall blocks, and in this capacity it is well attested at Eleusis both by the inscriptions[35] and by the monuments themselves. In fact, there are extant a Doric cornice block and fragments of three triglyphs, all of Aiginetan poros, which in all likelihood belonged to the external Doric frieze of the later Periklean Telesterion. As we shall see shortly, there is good reason to believe that a similar Doric frieze had also been designed for the earlier building.[36] The overseers will have ordered the Aiginetan poros for this purpose, and the blocks that were cut from it (line 11) may well be those used for the frieze and cornice of the later building. From the deme of

---

[32] *IG* I[3] 395 = Clinton, *Eleusis,* 23; text, p. 409 below. The inscription was found built into Late Roman or Byzantine construction near the church of Saint Zacharias at Eleusis; see Philios, *ArchEph* (1890) 117–118, no. 58.

[33] The N and unmistakable traces of ΕΠ are visible on the stone. The reading of Raubitschek in *SEG* 10.245 should be accepted as certain. Clinton, *Eleusis,* 23, brackets E but accepts the restoration.

[34] This account is quite similar to that for the first year of the Parthenon (*IG* I[3] 436, lines 23–32) both in its brevity and in the nature of the expenses, though here payments are recorded for working stone, whereas there are no such expenses in the first year of the Parthenon.

[35] Old column drums of Aiginetan poros, *IG* II[2] 1672, line 310; poros for triglyphs of the prostoon, *IG* II[2] 1666A, lines 24–25, and cf. line 16; poros for the walls of the sanctuary, *IG* II[2] 1672, line 52. On the Aiginetan quarries, see A. Orlandos, *Τὰ ὑλικὰ δομῆς τῶν ἀρχαίων Ἑλλήνων* (Athens 1959–60) vol. 2, 69.

[36] See p. 175 below.

Steiria, the modern Porto Raphti,[37] there came a different kind of poros, harder than the Aiginetan stone and more suitable for foundations than for superstructure.[38] This reminds us at once of the fine poros foundations for the columns and the exterior walls of the Telesterion. The soft Aiginetan stone is not practical for foundations, and the foundations of the Periklean Telesterion are not built of it. The poros from Steiria that was quarried, transported, and worked in the year of our account was perhaps intended for the foundations of the first Periklean building. For it is a curious coincidence, if coincidence it be, that the architect of the Telesterion required two different types of poros for his building and the inscription records the use of the same two materials.

More interesting still is the record of a third building material in lines 12–13 of the account: [λίθο]ν τομὲ τõμ μελάνον, [λιθορ]γοῖς τõμ μελάνον, "quarrying of black stone, for masons working black stone." These items clearly record the quarrying and working of local blue Eleusinian limestone of the kind used for the steps, toichobate, orthostates and walls of the Telesterion, and for which the inscription uses the locution "black stone."[39] But it is important to notice the juxtaposition of the two entries. Although the overseers paid for the quarrying of the stone and for the carving of blocks on the building site, they made no expenditure for the transportation of the stone from quarry to sanctuary. The transportation of building material was, however, a slow and costly process that normally figures prominently in the accounts.[40] In fact, just three lines before, the overseers had entered two separate expenditures for the transportation of poros stone from Aigina and Steiria: [να]υσὶ λιθαγογοῖς, [λιθ]οκομικόν (lines 9–10). The first was a payment for the ships which carried the stone by sea, from Steiria around the Attic peninsula and from Aigina across the Saronic Gulf to the harbor of Eleusis. The second entry doubtless refers to the moving of stone from the waterfront to the sanctuary.[41] Furthermore, when the secretary of the overseers drew up the account, he arranged all the items pertaining to the handling of poros in businesslike order: quarrying, transportation by sea and land, stonework—the order in which the work had been done.[42] We may assume that

[37] The deme of Steiria lay on the east coast of Attica between Prasiai and Brauron (Strabo 9.1.22 [p. 399]). It is probably to be located on the north side of the fine natural harbor called today Porto Raphti, and just at the foot of the hills of the Perati promontory: A. Milchhoefer, *Untersuchungen über die Demenordnung des Kleisthenes* (Berlin 1892) 18; E. Meyer, *RE*, 3rd ser. (1929) cols. 2305–2306, s.v. Steiria; J. S. Traill, *The Political Organization of Attica, Hesperia* Suppl. 14 (Princeton 1975) 43.

[38] The stone described as Στεριãθεν in *IG* I³ 395, line 8, probably came from an ancient quarry cutting on the southern slopes of the hilly promontory of Perati, just behind the deme site of Steiria. The quarry is located about 300 m inland from the shore of Erotospilia Bay, the small cove to the northeast of Porto Raphti harbor, and it lies just about 50 m east of the Mycenaean cemetery of Perati, at an elevation of roughly 20 to 30 m above sea level. A streambed at the foot of the slope below the quarry would give easy and direct access to the beach for shipment of the stone. The quarry itself is a relatively small cut, approximately 70 × 20 m, and for the most part only about 1 m deep. Not more than about 1,500 cubic meters of stone can have been cut from it, which may explain the fact that we know of it from only one ancient reference. The stone is hard but rather coarse, poros of the kind ideally suited for foundations and not practical for superstructure. I am greatly indebted to S. Iakovidis for drawing my attention to the existence of the quarry and for providing me with detailed measurements of its size and location.

[39] The Eleusinian stone of the Erechtheion frieze is described as "black stone," *IG* I³ 474, lines 199–200. The stone is more frequently called Ἐλευσινιακὸς λίθος in the Erechtheion accounts (*IG* I³ 474, lines 1, 234, 236; 475, line 2) and in the fourth-century Eleusinian inscriptions (*IG* II² 1666B, lines 69, 72, 75, 81; 1672, line 53). It was also used for the top step against the interior gate wall of the Propylaia, for the lowest step of the Pinakotheke, and for the benches and orthostates behind the Ionic colonnades of its central hall. The transportation of the stone from Eleusis is probably mentioned in *IG* I³ 462, line 36. On the use of Eleusinian stone generally, see L. T. Shoe, *Hesperia* Suppl. 8 (1949) 341–352.

[40] See the expenses for moving the column drums of the prostoon of Philon from the Pentelic quarries to Eleusis, *IG* II² 1673, lines 64–89 + K. Clinton, *ArchEph* (1971) 83–113 = Clinton, *Eleusis,* 159. Cf. chap. 3, pp. 60–62 above.

[41] The word λιθοκομικόν is not found elsewhere, but cf. the process described as λιθολκίας in the Parthenon accounts (*IG* I³ 444, line 272), which is regularly distinguished from the transportation itself and must refer to dragging the blocks up the slope of the Acropolis.

[42] Cf. the same invariable order in the Parthenon accounts: *IG* I³ 436, lines 23–25; 444, lines 270–273; 445, lines 304–309; 446, lines 331–336; 447, lines 355–359.

he exercised the same clerical precision on the records of the Eleusinian stone. If any money had been spent for the transportation of "black stone," it would have been duly entered into the account between the cutting of the stone in line 12 and the carving of it in line 13.[43] We are forced, then, to draw the obvious inference that, if no money was paid for transportation, the stone was not in fact transported, but it was rather quarried on the building site within the sanctuary of Demeter itself. If this fact be admitted, then the inscription can hardly refer to any building except the Telesterion, for during the fifth century the only extensive quarrying of the hillside within the sanctuary was carried out in connection with the westward expansion of that building.[44]

Lines 14, 16, and 17 of the inscription are very fragmentary, and any attempt to restore them is accordingly hazardous and necessarily conjectural. The text of *IG* I³ 395 reads:

   . . .⁶. . . ΑΤΑ
     vacat
   . . . .⁸. . . . ΟΝ
   . . . .⁹. . . . ΟΝ

Line 14 is most easily understood as [μισθόμ]ατα, the payment of the numerous miscellaneous contracts let out in the course of any building operation. The entry occurs in the accounts of the Parthenon and Propylaia in very year for which the expenses survive. It was evidently a standard item on the books of building overseers, and we should expect to find it here.[45] In the case of lines 16–17, it is not certain whether they should be taken together as one item, on the analogy of the two lines immediately following, or rather as two separate items. Since, however, the whole column of expenses seems to be preserved, except for any unexpended balance carried forward, and there is nowhere else any reference to construction of any kind, we might expect these lines to refer in some way to the actual process of laying the worked stones. Again, the unfinished foundations of the early Periklean Telesterion come to mind. Surely most, if not all, of the surviving foundations would have been laid in the final year before that project was abandoned. With this in mind, we may propose to read lines 16–17: [θέσις λίθ]ον [τõν θεμελί]ον, "laying of foundation stones."[46] The identification of *IG* I³ 395 as one of the building accounts of the early Periklean Telesterion finds some confirmation in the items of expenditure. Since almost all the expenses concern the quarrying, handling, and working of stone, it is obvious that construction of the building had not advanced very far when our account was recorded.[47] It is even possible that we possess the overseers' last account of a building whose con-

[43] R. Vallois, *REA* 35 (1933) 199–200, attempted to restore an entry for the transportation of Eleusinian stone in lines 16–17, [τõμ μελάν]ον, [λιθοκομικ]όν (cf. *SEG* 10.245); but this does violence both to the order of the account and to the normal phraseology of the other entries. For an alternate reading of the lines, see below.

[44] Vallois (note 43 above) tried to relate this account to the construction carried out by Koroibos in the City Eleusinion (*IG* I³ 32, lines 24–27; p. 164 above). This possibility, highly unlikely in any event, is now excluded by the proper reading of line 3 of the account, which shows that it was a record of the epistatai, and naturally was published after they took office. Koroibos's activities in the City Eleusinion are placed among the ἀνελομένα, the expenses before the epistatai had been appointed, and subject to audit by the logistai. Noack, *Eleusis,* 153, associated the "black stone" of the inscription with a known stone quarry on the north side of the acropolis of Eleusis (see G. R. Lepsius, *Griechische Marmorstudien* [Berlin 1890] 119), but this would also involve the transportation of stone. An exact parallel to the procedure proposed here is to be found in the so-called Kimonian Telesterion. Here the southeastern columns were set on foundations of rough Eleusinian limestone blocks whose side surfaces are left entirely unworked and show traces of the wedges used to pry them out of the hill. They undoubtedly came from the western extension of the building. See Noack, *Eleusis,* 272–273; Mylonas, *Eleusis,* 112.

[45] Vallois, *REA* 35 (1933) 200 (= *SEG* 10.245), proposed [χσυλόμ]ατα, which is epigraphically possible though not otherwise attested in the building inscriptions.

[46] Θέσις was the standard term for the laying of blocks; cf. the Erechtheion accounts, *IG* I³ 475, lines 1, 50, and the participial form -θέντι (passim); and Caskey's commentary, in Paton and Stevens, *Erechtheum,* 344, 346–347; A. K. Orlandos and J. N. Travlos, Λεξικὸν ἀρχαίων ἀρχιτεκτονικῶν ὅρων (Athens 1986) 128, s.v. θέσις.

[47] In the case of the Parthenon, quarrying had stopped by 434, two years before the completion of the pedimental statuary, and in the next-to-last account the last stones were moved from Pentele to the Acropolis, *IG* I³ 449, lines 399–400.

struction they abandoned at an early stage. We have also the abortive remains of a building which suffered a similar abandonment before even its foundations were complete. It is an economical interpretation of the evidence to suppose that the account describes the building and that both show signs of the same abandonment.

This account of the overseers now enables us to date within close limits the interruption of work of the initial plan of the Telesterion—for there can be little doubt about the chronological position of *IG* I³ 395 in relation to the other Attic building accounts. These inscriptions form a particularly well-dated series of documents spanning two-thirds of the fifth century. They begin with the accounts of the great bronze Athena (*IG* I³ 435: ca. 460–450) and include those of the Parthenon (447/6–433/2), the Athena Parthenos (446–438), the Propylaia (*IG* I³ 462–466: 437/6–433/2), the statues in the Hephaisteion (*IG* I³ 472: 421/0–416/5), and the last years of the Erechtheion (*IG* I³ 474–479: 409/8–405/4). The system of accounting employed in these documents shows a clear and marked development. The early accounts of the bronze Athena, the Parthenon, and the Propylaia are extremely simple and brief, summarizing the expenses under a few general headings.[48] But the system develops detail; the general headings are broken down into small categories, until in the accounts of the Erechtheion the name of every workman is listed together with the sum of money he received from the overseers. Within this series the Eleusinian account finds its closest parallel in the accounts of the Parthenon and the earlier bronze Athena. Both in format and in detail our inscription closely resembles the Parthenon stele. It is arranged in the same double columns: sums of money on the left and items on the right, receipts and expenses grouped together under separate headings. Similar also are the types of entries, the listing of expenses in roughly the order in which the work was done, and even the vocabulary used to describe the work.[49]

There are, however, a few details in which the Eleusinian account more closely resembles the earlier accounts of the bronze Athena. Most interesting is the receipt from the kolakretai in line 4, which reminds us that those treasurers had paid for the entire construction of Pheidias's statue.[50] After the beginning of the Parthenon, however, they seem never to have contributed funds for public works, and their name does not appear in any of the later building accounts. Also noteworthy is the frequent use of the nominative case in the phrases describing items of expenditure.[51] This was the regular form of expression in the accounts of the bronze Athena, but the authors of the Parthenon accounts preferred to use the genitive of a particular operation or category of expense,[52] and they normally listed payments to types of workmen using the dative of their profession or a participle describing the job they had done.[53] In the later documents this becomes standard usage, but in the Eleusinian account we see only the beginnings of it.[54] All of these details combine to suggest that our inscription was engraved before the first year of the Parthenon, though not necessarily very long before.

It will be appropriate at this point to mention the style of the lettering that fully corroborates a date before the start of work on the Parthenon. The most characteristic letters of the Eleusinian

---

[48] Even more cursory are the unidentified accounts published as *IG* I³ 433. These show no itemization at all, but simply the total receipt, the total expenditure, and any surplus left over at the end of the year.

[49] One cannot help noting that the Eleusinian epistatai were, after all, modeled on those of the Parthenon (*IG* I³ 32, lines 12–13). Their earliest publications and activities seem to betray a closer similarity to their model than one would have expected from their later documents.

[50] *IG* I³ 435, lines 6, 38, 65, 96, 121–122; cf. Raubitschek, *Hesperia* 12 (1943) 12–17. On the kolakretai, see chap. 2, p. 19 above. It is, of course, just possible that their contribution to the Eleusinian epistatai merely covered the salaries of the overseers themselves (cf. *IG* I³ 32, lines 8–9).

[51] Lines 8, 12: λίθον τομέ; line 10: λιθοκομικόν; line 14: [μισθόμ]ατα.

[52] See, e.g., *IG* I³ 436, line 27: ὀνεμάτον, line 29: καταμενίον; *IG* I³ 444, line 269: χουλοργίας, lines 271–273: λιθαγογίας, λιθολκίας, λιθοργίας, line 277: μισθομάτον.

[53] See, e.g., *IG* I³ 445, lines 304–307: λιθοτόμοις, πελεκετε̄σι, ηοδοποιοῖς καὶ λίθος ἀνατιθε̄σι.

[54] Line 9: ναυσὶ λιθαγογοῖς, lines 11, 13: λιθοργοῖς.

account are the sigma, which consistently has three bars, and the nu, whose final stroke rises sharply higher than its first. In general appearance the lettering is close to that of the seventh and eighth tribute quota lists, for 448/7 and 447/6. It should not be later than list 8, since this shows the last securely dated appearance of the three-bar sigma throughout the text of an Athenian public document. On the other hand, it can hardly be much earlier, for *IG* I³ 395 lacks the pointed beta and rho, the sloping nu, and other early features of lists 3, 4, and 5.[55] A date between 450 and 448 for the interruption of work on the Telesterion will fit well with the other evidence. This will allow for at least one previous account and perhaps more, as indicated by line 3 of the Eleusinian inscription, and it will confirm a date before 450 for the foundation of the college of epistatai, according to the provisions of Thespieus's amendment. The two or three years around 450 would have been ample time for the construction that has been associated with the initial phase of the Telesterion. Such a date would place the abandonment of the first plan in close chronological relation to the beginning of the Parthenon. We shall have occasion to see that this relation was not only close in time, but also probably a relation of cause and effect.

THE ARCHITECT OF PHASE I

The last two items of the expense account record anonymously the salaries of the hieropoioi and the architect, and we are now in a position to inquire just who this architect may have been. The writers of later antiquity were variously informed on the subject, and they appear to provide two different traditions. The Roman architect Vitruvius, writing in the reign of Augustus, gives the following brief account of the Telesterion:

> At Eleusis, Iktinos built the temple of Ceres and Proserpina of immense size and in the Doric style without exterior columns; and he roofed it over as a broad room for the customary sacrifices. Afterward, however, when Demetrius of Phaleron was master of Athens, Philo erected columns on the facade before the temple and made it prostyle. Thus, by adding an entrance hall he gave the initiates more space, and imparted the greatest dignity to the building.[56]

Vitruvius's version finds corroboration in the still briefer statement of his contemporary, the geographer Strabo (9.1.12 [p. 395]):

> Then one comes to the city of Eleusis in which is the sanctuary of Eleusinian Demeter, and the mystic shrine which was built by Iktinos, a temple capable of accommodating a crowd of spectators. This Iktinos also built the Parthenon on the Acropolis for Athena, when Perikles was superintending the works.

---

[55] For the lettering of list 7, see *ATL* I 30, fig. 31, 31, fig. 32, 37, figs. 45 and 46, 38, figs. 47 and 48. Particularly comparable are the nu and the very small circle of the omicron and theta. For the three-bar sigma of list 8, see *ATL* I 14, fig. 11, 29, fig. 30, 39, fig. 50 (*IG* I³ 264, 265). Cf. Raubitschek, *AJP* 61 (1940) 477–478 and note 11. It would serve no purpose to enter here into the discussions concerning the dating of Attic inscriptions with three-bar sigmas. H. B. Mattingly, *Historia* 10 (1961) 148–188, attempted a radical revision of the standard system of dating, but his arguments have been countered by Meritt and Wade-Gery, *JHS* 82 (1962) 67–74, and *JHS* 83 (1963) 100–117; R. Meiggs, *HSCP* 67 (1963) 24–30, and *JHS* 86 (1966) 86–98. For a convenient summary of the epigraphical problems, ML, pp. 133–136. See chap. 2, pp. 23–25 above, for discussion.

[56] Vitruv. 7 praef. 16–17: "Eleusine Cereris et Proserpinae cellam inmani magnitudine Ictinos dorico more sine exterioribus columnis ad laxamentum usus sacrificiorum pertexit. Eam autem postea, cum Demetrius Phalereus Athenis rerum potiretur, Philo ante templum in fronte columnis constitutis prostylon fecit; ita aucto vestibulo laxamentum initiantibus operique summam adfecit auctoritatem."

A completely different version is offered by Plutarch, writing nearly a century later, in the time of the Flavians and Trajan. In his famous account of the Periklean building program, the biographer wrote of Eleusis (*Per.* 13.7):

> It was Koroibos who began to build the Telesterion at Eleusis, and he set the columns on the floor and joined together their capitals with the architraves. But on his death Metagenes of Xypete carried up the frieze and the upper columns; while Xenokles of Cholargos roofed over the lantern above the Anaktoron.

At first sight these two accounts, of Plutarch on the one side and of Vitruvius and Strabo on the other, appear to be in irresolvable conflict. Both Vitruvius and Strabo speak of a building completed by Iktinos (*pertexit*, κατεσκεύασεν). Plutarch, on the other hand, having mentioned Iktinos's work on the Parthenon in the first half of the same sentence, seemingly knows nothing whatever of his activities at Eleusis, which he attributes to three architects of whom Vitruvius and Strabo make no mention. This crux might be resolved most easily, and least satisfactorily, by supposing that Strabo and Vitruvius were simply ill-informed on Eleusinian matters, and, knowing nothing of Koroibos and his fellows, they simply associated the famous name of Iktinos with the famous site of Eleusis.

The archaeological evidence from the remains of the Telesterion is in its way equally unequivocal, and it tells a story not wholly compatible with Plutarch's. The biographer reports that the building was completed in three stages, and the first, that of Koroibos, got as high as the columns and architraves. Obviously, this can have nothing to do with the abandoned early structure of phase I, of which not even the foundations were completed, let alone its columns and architraves. Furthermore, the phraseology of Thespieus (*IG* I³ 32, lines 24–27) suggests that Koroibos's services were engaged at this time exclusively in the City Eleusinion. There are, then, but two alternatives: either the architect of the early Periklean plan is unknown, or else it was Iktinos, and Vitruvius and Strabo mistakenly assumed that he finished a project which they knew him to have begun.[57] Upon closer examination, it will emerge that Vitruvius knew quite as much about the building as Plutarch, and his account ought not to be lightly dismissed. The two authors were clearly in possession of different kinds of information, derived from evidently independent sources. Plutarch stressed the building's structural history but was not interested in its architectural detail. Without a plan of the Telesterion before us, his description of the building is incomprehensible. Vitruvius, as an architect, naturally emphasizes the building itself. He reports that it was originally built in the Doric order, but without exterior columns, and he knows that the front portico was added in the late fourth century.

Once again, the archaeological remains suggest that Vitruvius's information was not only detailed but accurate. His statement that the Telesterion was designed *dorico more sine exterioribus columnis* implies a building whose plain exterior walls were crowned with a Doric triglyph frieze and cornice, and whose facade was not adorned with a portico.[58] It is now well known that the Telesterion had, in fact, no exterior portico until the prostoon of Philon was erected at the end of the fourth century, just as Vitruvius says. A prostyle porch was evidently planned and actually begun in connection with the later Periklean building, while another project for a prostoon was certainly undertaken in the mid-fourth century.[59] Neither plan, however, was carried very far, and Vitruvius's account of

---

[57] Iktinos's association with the early, unfinished plan has long been assumed. Cf. Noack, *Eleusis,* 143–144, 167–175, 198–199; D. S. Robertson, *Greek and Roman Architecture,* 2nd ed. (Cambridge 1945) 171–174; Dinsmoor, *AAG*³, 195–196; C. Weickert, Ἔργα Περικλέους, *AbhBerl* (1950) no. 1, 10–12; Mylonas, *Eleusis,* 113–114; Knell, *Perikleische Baukunst,* 72–73; Corso, *Monumenti Periclei,* 52–54; Travlos, *BTA,* 94.

[58] Cf., e.g., the Peiraieus arsenal, which, according to Philon's specifications (*IG* II² 1668, lines 26–30), was to have a triglyph frieze on all four sides of the building, but no exterior columns.

[59] On the portico designed for the later Periklean building, see pp. 182–183 below. Between 356/5 and 353/2, specifications for another columnar porch, officially called the prostoon, were prepared by the architect Philagros (*IG* II² 1666,

the history of the portico is correct. Furthermore, it is now also evident that the Periklean building was equipped with an exterior Doric frieze from the time of its construction in the fifth century. The frieze survives in fragments of three triglyphs and a Doric geison of corresponding scale.[60] The blocks are easily distinguishable from those of Philon's portico or the later Roman reconstruction because the material is Aiginetan poros, whereas the later entablature was of Pentelic marble. Nor can the surviving fragments come from blocks that were ordered in the mid-fourth century according to the specifications of Philagros, because the entablature of his projected plan likewise had a cornice of Pentelic marble, while in the frieze marble metopes were to alternate with poros triglyphs.[61] The preserved pieces of Doric entablature must, then, have belonged to the Periklean building, and they add weight to Vitruvius's statement about the architecture of the Telesterion.

If the Roman architect enjoyed so precise a knowledge about the temple at Eleusis, it is legitimate to inquire whence he derived his information. His source is obviously different from Plutarch's, which may just possibly be documentary or monumental evidence in the sanctuary. Vitruvius, on the other hand, was notoriously a reader of books on architecture, and he filled his pages with titles and epitomes gleaned from his bibliographical researches. Now, Vitruvius described the Telesterion as one of a group of four temples, of which the other three were the Artemision at Ephesos, the Didymaion near Miletos, and the Olympieion in Athens. Four paragraphs earlier in the same preface (7 praef. 12), he lists some of his sources for the seventh book. Among them is a book by the architects Chersiphron and Metagenes about the Artemision at Ephesos, and this is evidently the chief source for his knowledge of that temple. In the same list, he cites a book by Philon of Eleusis, *De aedium sacrarum symmetriis et de armamentario, quod fuerat Piraei portu,* "On the Proportions of Temples and the Arsenal Which Was in the Harbor at Piraeus." It was no doubt to this volume that Vitruvius owed his knowledge of Philon's prostoon for the Telesterion. Furthermore, in his discussion of the Olympieion in Athens, immediately following his description of the Telesterion (7 praef. 17), we sense the wail of the scholar deserted by his sources, for he says of Cossutius, architect of the Olympieion, *cuius commentarium nullum est inventum,* "no commentaries by him are extant."

Thus Vitruvius evidently relied heavily, if not wholly, on primary literary sources for his information about this group of temples. It is a fair guess that he also had literary authority for his statements about the Telesterion of Iktinos. Philon's book on the proportions of temples would seem a natural source, but this appears to be excluded, for if Philon had mentioned the plan of Iktinos, he would have also mentioned Koroibos and his colleagues. Since, however, Vitruvius knew nothing of Koroibos, one infers that Philon had made no reference to the work of any of his predecessors at Eleusis. The Roman architect may well have learned of Iktinos's plans from a far better source in-

---

face B, line 53). This document should be brought into relation with the L-shaped foundations (A and B on the plan, Fig. 61) which project from the east and south corners of the Telesterion: Jeppesen, *Paradeigmata,* 103–139. The foundations were surely not designed to carry a peristyle around three sides of the building, as argued by Noack, *Eleusis,* 149–151 (with incorrect fifth-century date; see note 62 below), and Dinsmoor, *AAG*[3], 233. The L-shaped foundations almost certainly anticipated a plan to double the capacity of Telesterion, as proposed by Jeppesen, *Paradeigmata,* 105–106; see now Travlos, *BTA,* 95, 142, fig. 170. They are too massive to have supported merely a crepidoma and terrace, as argued earlier by Kourouniotes and Travlos, *ArchDelt* 16 (1935–36) 1–42.

[60] The cornice block, consisting of one mutule and one via, is well enough preserved so that the spacing of the guttae indicates a width for the mutule of ca. 0.97 m. The height of the block from the soffit of the mutule is ca. 0.45 m. The triglyph fragments, though cut down for later reuse, also came from blocks measuring ca. 0.97 m in width. These dimensions are so close to those of the colossal marble entablature, both of Philon's prostoon and of the later Roman repair of the cella, that they can only come from an earlier phase of the same building. The great marble triglyphs measure 0.987 to 1.008 m in width. The mutule of the later geison has a width of 1.01 m, and the height from the soffit of the mutule is 0.464 m: Noack, *Eleusis,* 130–131. The poros fragments have not been published except for brief mention and illustration in Jeppesen, *Paradeigmata,* 107, figs. 71, 72, 108; Travlos, *BTA,* 94, 138, figs. 162, 163.

[61] *IG* II[2] 1666, face A, lines 24–25, 39, 54–55. If these blocks were ever carved, they were certainly never set on the building, while the preserved fragments show clear signs of reuse.

deed—none other than Iktinos himself. For in the same list of sources for book 7 (praef. 12), Vitruvius made his only citation of a treatise on the Parthenon by Iktinos and a certain Carpion. It is, of course, hazardous to guess at the contents or format of this work, but it seems not only plausible but highly likely that Iktinos might have referred, perhaps in detail, to other designs of his. If this was Vitruvius's source, we can also more readily understand his error in supposing that the building was finished; for Iktinos would have referred only to his plans and not to an unfinished and abandoned foundation. If this conclusion is not far wide of the mark, we should look upon Vitruvius's statement as thoroughly reliable testimony not only for the architect of the early Periklean phase of the Telesterion, but also for the projected appearance of the building itself.[62]

From the foregoing discussion we may conclude that Iktinos was indeed the first Periklean architect to work at Eleusis. He will have received his authorization to do so in the lost decree to which the amendment of Thespieus was appended. He will have started operations promptly, only to find that his work was to be interrupted and his plan abandoned a few years later, perhaps in the very year in which work began on the Parthenon.[63] It has sometimes been suggested that the plan was abandoned at so early a stage because of the difficulty of spanning the tremendous intercolumniations that Iktinos had projected.[64] This is a reconstruction of events that is hardly complimentary to the architect of the Parthenon, and the chronology proposed above seems to suggest a rather different story. It would, of course, be idle to speculate in detail on the causes for the interruption of the work at Eleusis, when the possibilities are so manifold and the only evidence to guide us is the fact itself. The best that we can do is to set the fact of the abandonment in the context of its contemporary events.

The years around 450 were, as we have already seen, a time of ferment in Athenian cultural circles. For it was in these few years that the designs and specifications for the first of the Periklean temples were being drafted and debated in the assembly. It seems virtually certain that the Parthenon with its colossal cult statue and the Telesterion at Eleusis were being discussed together at this time. Such is the implication of Thespieus's reference to the original board of epistatai for the works on the Acropolis. Are we to infer that Iktinos was intended from the beginning to design both buildings? His colleague Kallikrates was commissioned to prepare the specifications for the Temple of Athena Nike at just this time, but he was also evidently at work on the Long Wall and the walls of the Acropolis at the same time that plans for the Parthenon were under discussion. There cannot have been very many experienced architects in Athens at this time, after a generation of evident idleness in the building trades; and it should not be surprising that the major architectural commissions were in the hands of only a few men. What needs to be emphasized, however, is the apparent synchronism

---

[62] With regard to the facade designed for Iktinos's Telesterion, we should take Vitruvius at his word and assume that no portico was planned for the building. Iktinos's plan will have closely resembled the exactly contemporary design for the Odeion in Athens. Noack, *Eleusis,* 146–149, 167–169, based his restoration of Iktinos's plan on a great three-sided peristyle, founded on the L-shaped foundations A and B, on the two flights of rock-cut steps at the north and west corners, and on the rock-cut terrace behind the building. Knell, *Perikleische Baukunst,* 72–75, figs. 21, 22, still follows Noack's scheme and shows no awareness of the work of the Greek excavators. The L-shaped foundations in question have now been shown to date to the fourth century: Kourouniotes and Travlos, *ArchDelt* 16 (1935–36) 1–42; Travlos, *BTA,* 95. The south wing is constructed entirely of materials obviously reused from the southern section of the Periklean fortification wall, which was demolished in the fourth century in order to enlarge the court of the sanctuary toward the south and southwest. So systematic was the transfer of material from the Periklean peribolos to foundation A that the courses of Eleusinian limestone which formed a socle for the wall appear only in the two uppermost courses of foundation A. The lower part of the foundation was built of the rusticated poros blocks removed first from the higher courses of the fortification wall (Travlos, *BTA,* 142, fig. 171). The rock-cut steps and terrace are clearly Roman: Kourouniotes and Travlos, *ArchDelt* 15 (1933–35) 54–114. Cf. Mylonas, *Eleusis,* 115–117, 121–123.

[63] If Iktinos was still engaged at Eleusis as late as 447, as might be inferred from the date of *IG* I³ 395 (pp. 173– 174), this may help to account for the fact that no actual construction was begun on the Parthenon until a year later. The account of 447/6 (*IG* I³ 436) records only expenditure for the quarrying and hauling of marble.

[64] Cf. Dinsmoor, *AAG*³, 196; Mylonas, *Eleusis,* 115.

between the interruption of work on the Telesterion and the inception of work on the Parthenon. It seems to reflect a deliberate decision, undoubtedly by vote of the demos, to give clear priority to the great temple on the Acropolis in the expertise of its architects, in the allocation of skilled labor, in the distribution of building materials. Moreover, a pattern emerges among these various contemporary projects. Construction of the Hephaisteion began first, but work advanced so slowly that the architect could borrow the proportions of the Doric order and the design of the cella from the Parthenon, and the building was not completed until the 420s. No work at all was done on the Temple of Athena Nike for fifteen years or more. Construction of the Telesterion was interrupted when Iktinos was called to the Acropolis. We shall see presently that, after work resumed, the second phase of the temple remained unfinished in the last decade of the fifth century. But the Parthenon was completed, except for its pedimental sculpture, in the space of ten years.

ARCHAEOLOGICAL REMAINS: PHASE II

The abandonment of Iktinos's plan was by no means final and irrevocable. Although Iktinos himself was never again to work at Eleusis, the influence of the Eleusinian priesthood was such that the construction that he had begun was not long to be interrupted. With the resumption of work, the design of the building was somewhat altered from the original plan, but its general lines remained the same (Fig. 63). The resulting structure is fundamentally that which we still see today, although it was extensively restored and the superstructure rebuilt in the late second century A.D.[65] This second phase of the Periklean Telesterion is almost certainly to be associated with the three architects named by Plutarch (*Per.* 13.7), and accordingly his account gives us a brief but invaluable history of the building. Plutarch informs us that the work was begun by the architect Koroibos. He is, of course, the same architect to whom Thespieus had referred (*IG* I[3] 32, line 26) when he directed the logistai to audit the accounts of the City Eleusinion with the architect's advice. Koroibos had therefore rendered previous service to the cult of Demeter, although to our knowledge only in one of its subsidiary sanctuaries. He was an architect of some experience and perhaps enjoyed the confidence of the Eleusinian officials by virtue of his former association with the works of the sanctuary. Other than this meager information, we know nothing about him; but it is possible that he was of an Eleusinian family and perhaps the grandfather of another Eleusinian Koroibos, who was active about the middle of the fourth century.[66] In any event, he it was who received the commission to continue Iktinos's work.

One senses a feeling for caution and economy in Koroibos's earliest work, for the foundations and superstructure of his cella were built according to Iktinos's specifications, doubtless in order to make use of materials which had been prepared for the earlier plan and were lying ready for use on the site. Thus the toichobate and orthostates, which had been quarried from the western extension of the hall, were now laid in their proper positions on the foundations. Thus the eight interior steps of Aiginetan poros were laid in place along the northeast wall, where they now covered the steps of the archaic and early-fifth-century temples. Thus too the poros blocks of the exterior Doric frieze,

---

[65] For the Roman repair, see Noack, *Eleusis,* 107–112, 275–283; Mylonas, *Eleusis,* 160–162; R. F. Townsend, "Aspects of Athenian Architectural Activity in the Second Half of the Fourth Century B.C." (Ph.D. diss., University of North Carolina, 1982) 147–159. For the date of the Kostovok destruction (A.D. 170), see A. von Premerstein, *Klio* 12 (1912) 145–164.

[66] This is the Koroibos son of Antiphon of Eleusis whose son Antiphon was secretary of the boulē in 325/4: *IG* II[2] 360, line 2; 361, line 2; Kirchner, *PA* 8722. His brother was Philoxenos son of Antiphon, mentioned in a dedicatory inscription before the middle of the fourth century: *IG* II[2] 2814; Kirchner, *PA* 14708. For the association of the fifth-century architect with this fourth-century family, see E. Cavaignac, *Le trésor sacré d'Éleusis* (Versailles 1908) 40.

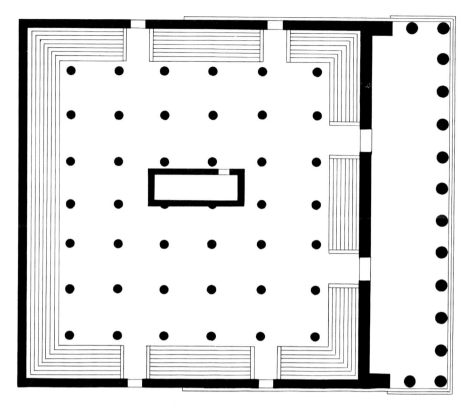

Figure 63. Restored plan of phase II, work of Koroibos with later stoa of Philon

designed for Iktinos's building, were carved and eventually hoisted into place atop the gray walls of the cella. But radical changes are now evident in the new plan for the interior. Koroibos had not the adventurous spirit nor the structural genius of Iktinos, and he evidently had little taste for the problems of roofing the immense hall with only the twenty internal supports projected by Iktinos. The 2,528.5 square meters of roof were more safely disposed, or so he thought, upon a forest of columns which would relieve the structural problems but would also remove the open spaciousness of the great interior designed by Iktinos. Koroibos was evidently concerned also to incorporate in the fabric of his building as much as possible the unfinished remains of the early-fifth-century structure; for he would thus save labor and expense in the construction of the northeastern half of the new Telesterion. Accordingly, his first scheme sought to take advantage of the foundations prepared long ago for the twenty-one columns of the early-fifth-century temple; and he seems to have proposed simply to double that plan by reproducing its arrangement of columns (three rows of seven) in the southwestern half of the hall, and by adding a middle row of seven columns along the line of the old southwestern wall.

The evidence for this plan with seven rows of seven columns consists solely of three circular beddings let down into the rock floor of the western corner and intended to carry the first column in each of the three new rows (Fig. 61).[67] These cuttings were laid out in relation to the axial spacing of

[67] The beddings were first noticed by Noack, *Eleusis,* 101–103, who considered them contemporary with his so-called Kimonian plan. He accordingly proposed that the great square of the final Telesterion was laid out, with the necessary quarrying of the hillside, before the Periklean period. Dinsmoor, *AAG*³, 195–196, assigned the 7 × 7 column plan to Koroibos but dated it in the mid-fifth century, influenced no doubt by the appearance of Koroibos's name in *IG* I³ 32, line 26. Since, however, it is impossible to associate with this plan any work other than the three column beddings, and since the foundations for the great hall now seem to have been built around 450 according to the plan of Iktinos, it seems easier to regard the 7 × 7 column plan as a first abortive scheme of Koroibos, altered immediately into his final arrangement, as presented above. It is difficult to see how this plan could be part of the Roman repair, as suggested by Mylonas, *Eleusis,* 117, note 19.

the old columns at the northeastern end of the same back row. But it is interesting that no bedding was cut for the first column of the central row. This suggests that the same temporary structure, of whatever nature, still occupied the ruins of the archaic temple, and Koroibos, like Iktinos before him, commenced work in the new southwestern half of the building. So little remains to tell us of this abortive plan that the architect evidently changed it almost at once. Koroibos's initial forty-nine-column interior, with all its structural advantages, raised unforeseen problems when it came time to adjust it to the existing dimensions of Iktinos's square cella. In the first place, the new plan called for four lateral entrances in order to permit more direct access to the great hall. But the revised plan, with its forty-nine interior columns, was ill adapted to this arrangement of exterior doorways; for now the second column from the front of each row was awkwardly aligned with the opening of the eastern door on either side. Still more important was the problem of roofing above the Anaktoron. One of Iktinos's greatest innovations in the traditional architecture of the Telesterion was his design for a clerestory lantern, or opaion, to be set in the roof over the Anaktoron and supported on the oblong group of six central columns.[68] But if seven rows of seven columns had actually been constructed on the interior, no central lantern would have been possible because one column would have fallen in the exact center of the hall.

These difficulties probably led Koroibos to restudy his interior plan almost at once. His solution was to retain the seven rows of columns, but to set the individual columns more widely apart, thereby eliminating from each row the column that would have partially obstructed the side entrances (Fig. 63). The result was the present plan, with seven rows of six columns arranged so that the doorways correspond with the aisles and no column falls in the exact center to prevent the erection of a lantern.[69] Signs of this adjustment from forty-nine to forty-two columns are still to be detected in the wide variation among the axial spacings. The axial spacing between rows 5 and 6[70] measures 8.25 m, considerably larger than all the others; but this results because row 5 was now aligned as closely as possible with the northwestern jambs of the side doors. It is instructive, however, to notice that this alignment was carried out precisely only at the eastern corner door, where the Sacred Way enters the Telesterion. At this most important of all the entrances Koroibos had to resort to drastic means in order to align the doorway with an open aisle, and, having extended the axial spacing as far as he dared, he shifted the whole doorway 0.52 m toward the corner. The corresponding doorway on the southwest side was not redesigned accordingly. It thus betrays a slight asymmetry in the placement of the doors and gives evidence of that alteration in plan which brought it about. In a similar manner, the axial spacing between rows 3 and 4 was reduced as much as possible, to 7.04 m,[71] because it was over this intercolumniation that the lantern was to be set above the Anaktoron, and the shorter span would facilitate its construction.

It was this plan, then, that Koroibos began to build, with its forty-two columns arranged in ranks and files within the great square cella of Iktinos (Fig. 63). Unlike his predecessor, the new architect did not have to begin by quarrying back the rock face of the rear wall: that part of the work Iktinos must have virtually completed, as we have already seen, and Koroibos was content to retain

[68] For the opaion, see p. 187 below. That it was a part of Iktinos's plan, as well as of the later plan, is indicated by the arrangement of columns with only four in a row, so as to form two concentric rings, of which the innermost just enframes the Anaktoron; furthermore, no column falls in the exact center.

[69] For detailed description of this final plan of the Periklean building, see Noack, *Eleusis,* 175–183; Mylonas, *Eleusis,* 117–124. The existing remains of columns and doorways date from the Roman repair (see Noack, *Eleusis,* 275–283), but the restoration was faithfully executed so that both plan and dimensions are identical except for the increase of 2.15 m in the depth of the hall.

[70] For convenience of reference the rows of columns are numbered from southwest to northeast with Roman numerals I–VII, and from northwest to southeast (back to front) with Arabic numerals 1–6.

[71] This is not, however, the shortest span of all. No two axial spacings are the same: rows 1–2 = 7.24 m; rows 2–3 = 6.91 m; rows 3–4 = 7.04 m; rows 4–5 = 7.43 m; rows 5–6 = 8.25 m.

Figure 64. Rear steps of the Telesterion, looking southwest

the line of the rock-cut wall laid out for the earlier building (Fig. 64). We have noted that this rock-cut wall and steps were, however, cut back into the hill an additional 2.15 at some later time in the building's history. The evidence for this further quarrying is unmistakable. At the northern corner all eight tiers of the Periklean poros steps have been preserved in situ; but the poros blocks terminate, and the steps are hewn from the rock for a distance of 2.93 m from the end of the last poros block to the present corner of the building (Fig. 65). The poros steps, however, do not all stop at the same point. Each step receded a few centimeters farther to the southeast than the end of the step next to it, so that a line connecting the ends of the steps forms an angle of 45 degrees with the northeastern wall of the building.[72] This line obviously bisected the northern angle of the building's earlier phase, and it thus gives the precise location of the earlier rear wall: 2.93 – 0.78 (to complete the turning of the step at the angle) = 2.15 m farther to the southeast than the existing rock face.[73] Noack assumed that the preserved poros steps were the work of Iktinos, and he accordingly attributed the northwestward

[72] See Noack, *Eleusis*, 98, 145, and the plan pl. 3 (with incorrect fifth-century date; see below).

[73] This calculation is corroborated by the remains at the adjacent western corner. Here the steps are all rock-cut, but the topmost step abuts an uncut projection of rock in the later corner at a point 2.92 m southeast of the present angle: Noack, *Eleusis*, 145, 181, and fig. 73. Furthermore, the masonry of the southwest wall was stepped up to bond with the rock-cut rear wall at the corner, and each higher course was fastened by means of a double-T clamp to ledges cut from the rock for the purpose. The rock face behind the next to highest of these clamps is 2.16 m from the existing corner. The highest ledge informs us that a masonry facing 0.50 m in thickness was built along the upper part of the original rock wall. Noack (above) calculated the angles slightly differently, allowing only 0.41 m to complete the turning of the angle from the end of the last step, and he thus placed the original rear wall 2.52 m southeast of the existing rock face.

Figure 65. North corner of the Telesterion, looking north

extension of the Telesterion to the later Periklean architects. This can hardly be the case, for there is no trace of the earlier abandoned plan in the northwestern half of the building. The square foundations for Iktinos's columns were never even begun on this side of the temple, and it is difficult to see how a complete section of steps could have been constructed here when the pattern of the interior columns had not yet been laid out. The poros steps in the northern corner are clearly the work of Koroibos, and the additional quarrying of the rear wall will then be part of the Roman restoration.

Most of the gray limestone orthostates, the interior steps, and the walls of the great cella will probably have been laid on their foundations under the direction of Koroibos. But we are told specifically that he did not live to see the building finished, and Plutarch (*Per.* 13.7) adds some information on the state of the work at his death. The forty-two interior columns of the lower story he had evidently set in place and had joined their capitals with architraves. Since the excavations have produced no fragments of interior stone architraves, it is a reasonable guess that they were of wood, like those of the archaic temple.[74] The length of the spans would certainly favor this type of construction. The exact arrangement of the architraves cannot, of course, be determined; but they probably formed three concentric squares around the Anaktoron and were surely not laid in a network that linked every capital to every other.

Plutarch neglects to mention a most important feature of Koroibos's design, which, however, had not progressed very far at the time of his death. This was the prostyle portico evidently planned for the southeastern facade of the temple (see Fig. 63). The idea was not original with Koroibos but was simply revived from the plan of the archaic Telesterion, since the prostoon had apparently been

[74] These were stored in the sanctuary along with other material removed from the archaic temple and were listed by the overseers in *IG* I³ 386, line 106; 387, line 116; see Shear, Jr., *Hesperia* Suppl. 20 (1982) 128–140. Undoubtedly, Iktinos had also intended wooden architraves for the tremendous spans of his plan; see p. 168 and note 28 above.

omitted from the designs of Iktinos and his predecessors, the early-fifth-century architects. The evidence of Koroibos's intentions can be read easily in the foundations at the eastern corner. Here the masonry of the Periklean substructure projects 6.73 m beyond the corner of the building. But this section of foundation was not completed to a uniform height, so that its courses appear today in a series of descending steps beneath the later foundations for the northeast end of Philon's stoa.[75] Nearer the corner, the first step of the crepidoma can still be seen in place, with the lifting bosses protruding from its still unsmoothed surface as silent witnesses of its unfinished state. Koroibos's plan was probably similar to the later one of Philon, for the great projection of the fifth-century substructure suggests that it was intended for a pseudodipteral portico with a return of one column at each end.

Now, Koroibos's addition of a prostyle portico to the plan probably demanded some alterations in the detail of the superstructure. It has been argued above that Iktinos had conceived the Telesterion with great expanses of blue-gray wall, whose blank austerity was to be unrelieved except for the narrow ribbon of a Doric frieze running around the entire building at the top of the wall. Koroibos would naturally have wished to extend the Doric frieze around the exterior of his Doric porch, and he would accordingly have had to design some kind of molded epicranitis to take the place of the frieze as the crowing member of the southeast facade behind the colonnade. Several blocks of this molded course have been preserved, and they should all be assigned to the epicranitis of the facade; for the other three walls carried the Doric frieze of the porch around the portico. The poros blocks of the epicranitis are decorated with a colossal hawksbeak molding, surmounted by a fascia and a small projecting fillet.[76] The blocks themselves are of such a height (0.61 m) that, together with two additional courses of ashlar wall blocks (0.41 m high), they would probably equal the height of the Doric frieze that they were designed to replace.[77] This molded epicranitis must assume considerable importance in the history of the Telesterion because it is our only tangible clue to the dating of Koroibos's work on the temple. Because of its size and its crowning fascia, the hawksbeak has been instructively compared to the moldings of anta and pier capitals, rather than to those of the normal epicranitis.[78] Indeed, it seems to find its closest neighbors in the hawksbeaks on the antae and piers of the Propylaia and the Temple of Nemesis at Rhamnous.[79] A general date during the decade of the 430s will not be far wrong, and there is of course greater likelihood that construction was resumed earlier rather than later in that decade.

THE CHRONOLOGY OF PHASE II

This brings us to the important question of the chronology of the building that Plutarch describes. His statement, though exasperatingly brief, as we have seen, nevertheless accounts for the whole construction of the Telesterion. After Koroibos left the structure unfinished at his death, "Metagenes of Xypete carried up the frieze and the upper columns; while Xenokles of Cholargos roofed over the lantern above the Anaktoron" (*Per.* 13.7). Metagenes' contribution to the building is fairly clear. He

[75] Noack, *Eleusis,* 117–118 with fig. 51 and pls. 39:d, 40:b.

[76] See Shoe, *Greek Mouldings,* 128, pl. LXI:3; Noack, *Eleusis,* 182, fig. 74. The hawksbeak is 0.145 m high. The hawksbeak in the corresponding position atop the cella wall of the Parthenon measures 0.063 m in height, though it is, to be sure, a multiple molding with a fascia and cyma reversa beneath it; see chap. 4, p. 104 and Fig. 21 above.

[77] On the wall courses, Noack, *Eleusis,* 136–137, 182.

[78] Shoe (note 76 above), with date ca. 440.

[79] Shoe, *Greek Mouldings,* 120, pl. LVII:11–14; R. Bohn, *Die Propylaeen der Akropolis zu Athen* (Berlin 1882) pls. 11, 13, 14. These moldings, being anta capitals, are naturally more complex, but the profiles of the hawksbeaks themselves and their combination with a fascia and crowning molding (at Eleusis a simple fillet, on the Propylaia a cyma reversa) are strikingly similar.

added a frieze above the architraves[80] of Koroibos and built the second story of interior columns. Since his successor, Xenokles, was concerned only with the construction of the lantern itself, one infers that Metagenes also succeeded in roofing a portion of the hall, so that it was probably partially enclosed and in use by the time Xenokles inherited the task of completing it. Now, it is not unnatural for death to overtake a man in midcareer, and for his work to pass on to a successor. That Metagenes succeeded Koroibos when the building was still incomplete should thus occasion no surprise. But when we are informed that it took three architects in succession to finish the job, we are naturally predisposed to believe that the Telesterion was building for a long time.

There is evidence to suggest that the Eleusinian overseers were still deeply involved in building operations in the late 420s. This is suggested by a very fragmentary series of accounts (*IG* I³ 392–394), of which three small pieces have been discovered at Eleusis and a fourth in the Athenian Agora, probably from the Athenian copy of the same inscription. The document of which these fragments are a part can almost certainly be identified as a publication of the Eleusinian epistatai, for there appear to be several entries recording sums of money received from the hieropoioi, and only the epistatai of Eleusis are likely to have received sacred monies directly from the hands of the hieropoioi.[81] But this is clearly not an inventory of sacred properties like those preserved for the year 408/7 (*IG* I³ 386–387). All four fragments contain records of receipts from various sources, and one preserves the beginning of a column of expenses (*IG* I³ 394, line 14). The texts are so fragmentary that there can be little certainty about many of the items, and in most cases restoration seems impossible. The individual receipts are not listed on separate lines with money and items in separate columns, as in the accounts of the Parthenon and Propylaia, or the early account of the Telesterion. Instead, the entries are written continuously, the sum of money following directly upon the description of its source and separated from the next item by a punctuation mark. The parallel with the later accounts of the Erechtheion is close indeed.[82] The receipts were collected from widely divergent sources. In addition to those from the hieropoioi, we find a large payment—more than 12,670 drachmas—apparently from the *mystai* at one of the celebrations of the Mysteries (*IG* I³ 392, lines 1–2), together with contributions from a prytany of the boulē (line 13), from some other board of magistrates (lines 15–16), and from several private individuals.[83] The overseers also drew upon rents from sacred properties (*IG* I³ 394, lines 7, 10), while a number of items may record contributions from religious societies of unknown character.[84] The clue to the identification of the documents comes, however, from the entries recording receipts from the sales of building materials. One indicates the sale of unspecified equipment: [πραθέντον σ]κευôν τι[μέ]; other items account for the sale of building blocks, of rope, and of hides, probably from the public sacrifices.[85] These transactions

[80] Plutarch's term is τὸ διάζωμα, which has been variously interpreted to mean: a second story over the whole building (Philios, *JIAN* 7 [1904] 11–59; D. Philios, Ἐλευσίς [Athens 1906] 90; denied by J. N. Svoronos, *JIAN* 8 [1905] 131–160); balconies over the tiers of steps (Frazer, *Pausanias's Description of Greece*, vol. 2, 508; Noack, *Eleusis*, 153–156; Kourouniotes, Ἐλευσίς, ὁδηγὸς τῶν ἀνασκαφῶν, 40); a frieze over the architraves laid by Koroibos (P. Foucart, *Les mystères d'Éleusis* [Paris 1914] 352; E. Fabricius, *RE* 9 [1914] 996, s.v. Iktinos; Mylonas, *Eleusis*, 117–119; Stadter, *Commentary*, 170). Since there appears to be no possible means of access to upper balconies, and there is no independent architectural evidence to suggest that they ever existed, it seems most probable that Plutarch referred to the frieze. The same word was used to describe the frieze of Ptolemy's barge: Athen. 5.205C.

[81] See *IG* I³ 393, lines 7–8: παρὰ hιεροποι[ôν Ἐλευσῖνι . . .ᶜᵃ⁷. .] Χουπεται[όνος καὶ χουναρχόντον . . .ᶜᵃ⁷. .]; perhaps also *IG* I³ 394, lines 3–4; 392, lines 4–5; cf. Raubitschek, *Hesperia* 12 (1943) 36.

[82] Cf. the format of *IG* I³ 475 and 476.

[83] *IG* I³ 394, lines 5, 6; 392, line 14; and cf. the similar contributions of private individuals to the Parthenon and Propylaia: *IG* I³ 445, lines 299–300; 462, lines 25, 27.

[84] *IG* I³ 392, lines 8, 10, 11, 12; 394, lines 7–8, but the reading is by no means certain.

[85] *IG* I³ 392, line 17 (for the restoration, W. Bannier, *PhilWoch* 47 [1927] 670); *IG* I³ 393, lines 2, 4–6; 394, lines 12–13. Cf., e.g., in the Parthenon accounts the sale of gold and lumber (*IG* I³ 445, lines 296–298); of ivory, wooden wheels,

are typical of Athenian building administrators, and they give strong evidence that we have here to do with the accounts of building operations. The entries on the expense side of the ledger are too fragmentary to afford precise understanding, but they seem to corroborate the identification.

All these receipts cannot, however, pertain to the account of a single year. It seems preferable to suppose that the fragments come from one or more large stelai arranged in several columns, again like the accounts of the Erechtheion.[86] They will then represent a series of accounts covering the operations of several years. The internal chronological indications of the inscriptions themselves suggest precisely this. It has been thought that line 6 of *IG* I³ 392 should be understood to refer to a tithe paid to the goddesses from the ransom of prisoners of war: [δεκατὲ] λύτρον ΗΗΔ–. A likely occasion for this has been found in Thucydides' statement that the Athenians ransomed certain Megarian prisoners for a specified sum of money in 424.[87] This restoration, if correct, would provide an exact date for the account. On the other hand, a different date, but equally exact, is indicated by *IG* I³ 394, line 15, where the first preserved item of expenditure reads: ἐς τὸν Ῥε[τὸν – – – –]. This is, in all probability, a reference to the famous twin lakes that guarded the end of the pass leading from Athens into the Thriasian plain of Eleusis.[88] Since the item is in the expense column, it naturally indicates some activity at the Rheitoi which cost the overseers money. Now, it happens that in 421/0 a decree of the Athenian assembly had ordered the construction of a new bridge across the Rheitoi;[89] and it seems difficult to avoid the conclusion that the expenditure in the account refers likewise to this construction. This identification would suggest a firm terminus post quem of 421/0 for *IG* I³ 394 and a span of at least four years for the preserved fragments of the building accounts.

It should, of course, be emphasized that too little survives of the inscriptions to be sure that they pertain to the Telesterion. The large number of receipts does, however, indicate a long and expensive operation. They cannot account solely for the Rheitoi bridge, since they begin at least four years before that project was even proposed; but the reference to the Rheitoi suggests that the epistatai grouped together in one series of accounts the expenses for all the work currently under their management in order to facilitate their bookkeeping.[90] On the other hand, the Telesterion was the largest building project undertaken by the Eleusinian sanctuary in the fifth century. We shall see in a moment that it was still under construction many years later. Thus, a series of Eleusinian building accounts extending over a period of at least four years would be likely to belong at least in part to the construction of this great temple. The preponderance of probability supports the identification of the inscription as the accounts of the Telesterion, among other projects, and we should perhaps relate this activity to the second of Plutarch's three architects, Metagenes of Xypete.[91]

---

and tin (*IG* I³ 446, lines 320–321, 324–326); of gold and ivory (*IG* I³ 449, lines 389–394). Similarly, in the Propylaia accounts we find sales of tiles, lumber, plaques, and hides from sacrifices (*IG* I³ 462, lines 18–23, 26), and of *kyanos* (*IG* I³ 466, line 147).

[86] *IG* I³ 393 preserves the top line of one column. Since there is no heading of any kind, this cannot be the beginning of the inscription or even the first receipt of the account. This fact also suggests a document engraved in several columns.

[87] Thuc. 4.69.3: οἱ ἐν τῇ Νισαίᾳ . . . ξυνέβησαν τοῖς Ἀθηναίοις ῥητοῦ μὲν ἕκαστον ἀργυρίου ἀπολυθῆναι ὅπλα παραδόντας, "The people in Nisaia . . . capitulated to the Athenians on condition that each man be released for a fixed ransom and surrender his arms." See J. J. E. Hondius, *Novae Inscriptiones Atticae* (Leiden 1925) 101–105.

[88] On the Rheitoi, Paus. 1.38.1; Hesych., s.v. Ῥειτοί (ρ 202 Schmidt); and cf. Thuc. 2.19.2.

[89] *IG* I³ 79, lines 5–8: τὸν Ῥετὸν τὸμ παρὰ τὸ ἄστεος γεφυρῶσαι λίθοις χρομέ[ν]ος Ἐλευσινόθεν, "to bridge over the Rheitos on the side toward the city, making use of the blocks at Eleusis." Cf. Raubitschek, *Hesperia* 12 (1943) 35; Shear, Jr., *Hesperia* Suppl. 20 (1982) 128–140.

[90] As was regularly the case in the fourth century; cf. *IG* II² 1672, 1673.

[91] Mention may be made at this point of another piece of construction of great importance to the sanctuary. This was the extension to the south of the peribolos, without which the new temple would have had no forecourt, and no defenses at all on the south, southeast, and southwest. Sometime during the Periklean period, a heavy fortification wall was

Fortunately, however, we are not forced to conclude our study of the Periklean Telesterion with the tantalizing but somewhat unsatisfactory evidence of these badly mutilated accounts from the 420s. Chance has preserved for us the almost complete inventory of sacred properties prepared by the epistatai of 408/7 (*IG* I³ 386 and 387). This document provides an exhaustive catalogue of all movable property, cash, and plate belonging to the Two Goddesses at that time, and it reveals in embarrassing detail the appalling depletion of Demeter's treasury and the forlorn state of her buildings during the final years of the Peloponnesian War. The presence in the inventory of an inordinately large amount of building materials has long been noticed,[92] but it has not been generally recognized that the inscription yields an exceedingly accurate picture of the progress of Eleusinian building operations. The secretary of the overseers devoted thirty-two lines[93] to an orderly description of building stone and lumber which were stored in the sanctuary. This was an effort analogous in some ways, though on a much smaller scale, to the detailed survey published just a year earlier by the overseers of the Erechtheion (*IG* I³ 474). A lacuna of several lines in our text just at the critical point somewhat obscures the detail of the passage. But around the edges of this gap, the picture emerges in clear focus, and it is unmistakably the picture of an unfinished building.

The building stones seem to have been grouped together according to their material. Most striking is a considerable body of Pentelic marble blocks (lines 78–91; *IG* I³ 387, line 87). The overseers counted four stylobates; fifteen steps of the crepidoma, of which at least one measured eight feet in length; twelve orthostates; and a variety of other pieces, one of which was represented by as many as forty blocks. Three items—a step block, a corner block, and a column capital—are specifically designated as ἐργασμένον, "worked." Since it was necessary to single out these blocks, the inference is inescapable that the others were not as yet completely worked. Farther up in the column, in a particularly fragmentary section (lines 70–78), we read of six foundation blocks and an unspecified number of column drums that were probably cut from a different kind of stone. Five of the foundation blocks are now restored as measuring eight feet in length.[94] The character of the architectural members here represented—the steps and stylobate, capitals and orthostates—suggests at once that the pieces were intended for an exterior colonnade, while the Pentelic marble of which they were made and the tremendous length (eight feet) of the steps and foundation blocks both point to the Telesterion as the only building of suitable scale in the sanctuary.[95] We have already seen that the plan of Koroibos called for a portico on the southeast facade of the temple, and indeed the foundations for this structure were partially laid. It is now reasonable to suppose that the stones so carefully

constructed, beginning in a great round tower (see Fig. 60) at the south corner of the Kimonian extension and running southwest for some 70 m to a matching round tower. From here it turned almost due west for about 43 m until it was breached by the south gate of the sanctuary, protected by its great square tower. Just beyond the gate, the Periklean wall joined the old archaic fortifications which still enclosed the rest of the acropolis. See Noack, *Eleusis,* 183–189; Mylonas, *Eleusis,* 124–125; Travlos, *BTA,* 135, fig. 157. In view of the fact that the south corner of the Periklean Telesterion extends beyond the archaic peribolos, the sanctuary would have been undefended during the whole period of construction of the Telesterion. The Periklean wall was thus almost certainly designed and probably begun in the early 440s. It too was still under construction in the 420s, as we learn from a fragment of its building account, *IG* I³ 398, which is to be dated to that decade. See Maier, *Griechische Mauerbauinschriften,* 86–88, no. 18.

[92] See Cavaignac, *Trésor,* 26–51; W. Sardemann, *Eleusinische Übergabeurkunden aus dem V. Jahrhundert* (Marburg 1914) no. 7, Beil. I–IV; Cavanaugh, *Eleusis,* 157–168, commentary on *IG* I³ 386, col. II.

[93] *IG* I³ 386, lines 70–102; 387, lines 80–112. Reference will henceforth be made only to the line numbers of *IG* I³ 386, except in the few instances where the items preserved on the reverse of the stele were clearly absent from the obverse.

[94] Cavanaugh, *Eleusis,* 162–163.

[95] Cf. Cavaignac, *Trésor,* 38–39. Commentary on these lines, Cavanaugh, *Eleusis,* 164–165. That the steps and foundation blocks were intended for a building on the scale of the Telesterion is indicated by the blocks specified for the fourth-century portico: stylobate blocks measuring 6 × 4 ft. were to be placed on euthynteria blocks measuring 12 × 3½ ft. (*IG* II² 1666, lines 68–71, stylobate; lines 43–45, euthynteria).

listed by the overseers were relics of this abandoned project, just as much as were those that chanced to be laid in the foundations of the building.[96]

The overseers also found in the sanctuary, and duly measured and recorded, a group of Aiginetan poros blocks, of which the most interesting are described as στυλίδες : ΓΙ : δίποδε ἀμφοτ[έραι : ΙΙ], "six small columns; two measuring 2 × 2 ft." (line 95; *IG* I³ 387, line 105). They are evidently a series of six small monolithic columns, two of which had not yet been worked into cylindrical shafts but were still in their rough quarry state, square in section and measuring two feet along each face. Cavaignac proposed long ago to assign these small columns to the upper story of the Telesterion, to which Noack rightly objected that their size was far too small for the upper order of the interior Doric columns.[97] In their unfinished state the shafts measured 2 ft. = 0.654 m on a side, and their finished lower diameter could thus hardly be more than about 0.60 m. Now, the lower diameter of the interior columns of the Telesterion varies from 1.27 m to 1.325 m, and, according to the prevailing proportions of the late fifth century, their diameter at the top of the shaft would be about 1.00 to 1.05 m. The lower diameter of the next tier of columns would then be just slightly less than this figure. But it will be observed that a column with a lower diameter of ca. 0.60 m would be just about the right scale to stand on top of the upper columns as a third tier.

Let us now recall that the small monolithic shafts recorded in the inscription were six in number. A glance at a plan of the Telesterion will further acquaint us with the fact that the innermost ring of columns, surrounding the Anaktoron in an oblong rectangle, is likewise precisely six in number. It was above these six central columns that the lantern of Xenokles was surely intended to be set. To be sure, the exact nature of this structure, which Plutarch called τὸ ὀπαῖον (*Per.* 13.7), has consistently defied archaeological investigation, but general probability would favor a low clerestory carried above the line of the main roof on a series of columns or piers.[98] The στυλίδες of *IG* I³ 386 and 387 would be of the appropriate size and of the correct number to support just such a clerestory; and we may with good reason suppose that they were ordered from the Aiginetan quarries to serve this very function.

This identification of the columns for the lantern gains considerable support from other entries in the inventory, which strongly suggest that the roof of the Telesterion was far from complete in 408/7. After his visit to the stone yards, the secretary of the epistatai came to the lumber pile, which he also described systematically (lines 96–101). The most striking items in his list are forty-five great square beams imported from Thouria. These he designated as so large that they had to be transported on a wagon. Also catalogued were six timbers of pine and thirty of fir, together with 138 pieces of

[96] It was evidently Koroibos's plan to construct his great frontispiece of Pentelic marble, which would stand out in bold contrast to the somber gray wall of Eleusinian stone behind it. This experimentation with different materials to achieve special effects of color is reminiscent of Mnesikles' Eleusinian orthostates, benches, and steps in the Propylaia. We may find in this perhaps one more hint that the work of Koroibos belongs in the 430s rather than the 440s, *pace* K. Clinton, "The Date of the Classical Telesterion," in Φίλια Ἔπη, vol. 2 (Athens 1987) 254–262; followed by Cavanaugh, *Eleusis,* 160. Noack, *Eleusis,* 201, assigned the marble blocks of *IG* I³ 386 to his "Iktinian peristyle." Since, however, the foundations of this structure have now been shown to be of the fourth century (note 62 above), the marble colonnade of the inscription has necessarily to be attributed to the later Periklean portico.

[97] Noack, *Eleusis,* 201; cf. Cavaignac, *Trésor,* 37–38. These small columns were evidently monolithic, whereas the second-story columns would surely have been constructed in drums, like those at Aigina and Paestum.

[98] Cf. Dinsmoor, *AAG*³, 196; Mylonas, *Eleusis,* 120. The clerestory over the Hellenistic hypostyle hall at Delos will form a close parallel, and it is interesting to note that it was carried above the interior columns on a series of small stone piers: R. Vallois and G. Poulsen, *EAD: Nouvelles récherches sur la salle hypostyle* (Paris 1914) 3–13 and pl. II (cf. also G. Leroux, *EAD* II: *La salle hypostyle* [Paris 1909] 52–53). Plutarch's term τὸ ὀπαῖον will then refer to the window openings of the clerestory. Cf. the iron muntins from a window (σιδήρια ἐξ ὀπῆς) mentioned in a fifth-century inscription from Aigina (*IG* IV 39, line 2). Noack, *Eleusis,* 156–167, took the word to refer to a pierced roof tile and restored the opaion of Xenokles simply as dozens of pierced tiles, which can hardly be the case.

smaller lumber in various sizes. Stored with the lumber were the roof terracottas, purchased and
ready for use but not yet laid in place; the overseers enumerated 400 pairs of new tiles (κεράμο καινõ
ζεύγε, line 102). An additional 42 pairs of new tiles had already been carried into the Telesterion
before work was suspended, and there they remained, still unlaid, for the overseers to catalogue in
408/7.[99] Such a recitation of unused materials certainly suggests that the Telesterion had not yet
been finished. Moreover, we can hardly suppose that the roof timbers and terracottas had already
been ordered for the columnar porch when even its foundations were not entirely laid. The heavy
timbers were very likely intended for the wooden superstructure of the opaion, while the smaller
lumber would have formed its rafters. The tiles, however, seem too numerous for the lantern itself,
and we should perhaps suppose that a considerable area around the clerestory had been left unroofed
to facilitate the erection of scaffolding, the hoisting of materials, and the movement of workmen.
Similarly, one of the six great doorways seems to have been left open in order to carry equipment in
and out of the building more easily, for we find listed in the inventory a single pair of double doors,
θυρõν ζεῦγος καινόν (line 123).

    We are led inexorably to the same conclusion, that the construction of the Telesterion dragged
on to the closing years of the fifth century, and that the work of Plutarch's third architect, Xenokles
of Cholargos, should be placed at least in part after 408/7. But with all this Noack took serious
issue.[100] He asserted that the building materials of the inventory were in part left over from the
abandoned building of Iktinos, and in part salvaged from the archaic temple. Since, however, the
overseers headed the list of stored materials in lines 103–110 with the specific rubric ἀπὸ τõ νεὸ
καθειρεμένα, "taken down from the temple," it is a reasonable supposition that they would have
similarly titled the other lists of building materials, had they come from the same source. Noack[101]
thought that the Telesterion had been completed by Plutarch's three architects sometime during the
late 420s. More recently, Clinton has sought to date the work of all three of Plutarch's architects to
the 440s or the 430s at the latest.[102] Both scholars have failed to account for the extraordinary condition in which the overseers of 408/7 found the building.

    Greek sacred buildings habitually acquired dedications of considerable value—gold and silver
vessels, ivory furniture, and spoils dedicated to the gods from victorious battles. These it was the task
of the sacred treasurers to weigh and record, and to pass on to the custody of their successors. The
long series of inventories of the treasures stored on the Acropolis is the most conspicuous example,[103]
but the Eleusinian epistatai prepared similar catalogues of plate and other dedications belonging to
Demeter and Kore. The inventory of 408/7 begins with just such a listing of treasure.[104] The possessions of the goddesses were grouped together according to their location in one of four places: ἐμ
πόλει, ἐν τõι Ἐλευσινίοι τõι ἐν ἄστει, ἐν τõι Ἐλευσινίοι, Ἐλευσῖνι. The valuables on the Acropolis
(lines 5–13), in the City Eleusinion (lines 14–19), and at Eleusis (lines 39–69) were typical of all
temple treasures: gold and silver plate, bullion, cash, jewelry, and a few miscellaneous dedications.
But the material described as σκεύε ἐν τõι Ἐλευσινίοι (lines 20–38) commands our attention at
once, for this was stored in the Telesterion itself, the most sacred building of the sanctuary.[105] So

[99] Line 23; on the location of these tiles inside the Telesterion itself, see pp. 189–190 below.
[100] *Eleusis,* 200–201; the outlines of this chronology were originally proposed by Cavaignac, *Trésor,* 36–40, 49–51.
[101] *Eleusis,* 143–144, 198–199.
[102] Clinton, in Φίλια Ἔπη, vol. 2, 254–262. His statement that the Telesterion must have been "of the highest priority
in any general political and architectural plan for Athens" (p. 259) is no doubt true, but that is no argument for the actual
chronology of the building's construction. Cavanaugh, *Eleusis,* 159–160, cites Clinton but equivocates on the date.
[103] *IG* I³ 292–362, covering the last third of the fifth century.
[104] *IG* I³ 386 (408/7), 387 (407/6). Fragments of other lists are preserved: *IG* I³ 384, 385, 388–390; *IG* II² 1540–1552.
[105] Cavanaugh, *Eleusis,* 131, claims that the materials listed in lines 21–38 were located in the City Eleusinion, but the
rubric σκεύε ἐν τõι Ἐλευσινίοι (line 20) clearly sets this section of the inventory apart from the immediately preceding
lines, which are located by the rubric ἐν τõι Ἐλευσινίοι τõι ἐν ἄστει (line 14). If the objects in lines 21–38 had been in

remarkably does this list of "equipment" (σκεύε) contrast with the treasures in the other repositories that it is worth quoting in full:

ρρυμοὶ : σεσιδερομέ[νοι : ⊢Ι]
ρρυμοὶ : ἀσιδέροτοι : [ΔΙ]
κεράμο ζεύγε καινὰ : [ΔΔΔΔΙΙ]
ἄμπρον : Ι : τετρακύκλ[ο καινὸ : ΙΙ]
ἄχσονε μεγ[ά]λο : ΙΙ ἄχσ[ονε σμικρὸ : ΙΙ]
χσύλα ἐς τροχὸς τε[τρακύκλο]
πτελέϊνα : ΔΙΙΙ : μ– –
ρρυμὸς δίκρο[ς σεσιδερομένος]
ἀσιδέρο[τος δίκρος : Ι]
[. . . . .ˮ. . . . . ἴα : Ι]
[σερὰ καινὲ πέχεον : ⊢ΔΔ]
[σερὰ καινὲ πέχεον : ⊢Δ]
[ἀρτέματα ρρυμοῖς : ΔΔΔΔΙ]
[βύρσαι Σικελικαί : ΔΓΙΙΙ]
[ηιχσõ : Τ : καὶ στατῆρες : ΓΙΙΙ]
[κατάδεσμα σιδερᾶ : ΓΙΙΙ]
[χάλικες σιδεραῖ : ΓΙΙΙ]
[κόφινος καὶ ἄμε : Ι]

51 iron-clad wagon poles; 11 wagon poles without iron; 42 new pairs of tiles; 1 heavy cable; 2 new four-wheeled wagons; 2 large axles; 2 small axles; wood for the wheels of a four-wheeled wagon; 13 pieces of elm; ? – – –; 1 forked pole, iron clad; 1 forked pole without iron; – – –; new tackle 70 cubits long; new tackle 60 cubits long; 41 chains for wagon poles; 18 Sicilian hides; 1 talent and 8 staters' weight of oak gum; 8 iron bands; 8 iron lumps; 1 basket and shovel.[106]

This list represents everything that the epistatai found in the Telesterion during their tour of inspection in 408/7. It is difficult to imagine more peculiar appointments in a temple that had been completed and was functioning for more than a decade. These are the accoutrements of construction workers, not of priests and *mystai*, and their presence in the otherwise empty temple admits of no other explanation, except that the building was not in fact complete. Indeed, the overseers found elsewhere on the premises a complete line of builders' tools and equipment, left in the workshops and stone yards in the expectation that work would be resumed shortly. The inventory mentions (lines 111–116, 125–133):

κλίμακε μεγάλο : ΙΙ : σμικ[ρ]ὰ : Ι
τροχιλεία μεγάλο : ΙΙ : σ[μ]ικρὸ : Ι
ηάμαχσαι : ΙΙΙ : κανόνε [λι]θίνο : ΙΙ
ηυπερτερία τετρακ[ύ]κλο : Ι
[η]υπερτερία μονοκ[ύ]κλο : Ι
[τροχο]ὶ τετρακύκλο : ΙΙΙΙ : ηύσπλεχς : Ι

---

the City Eleusinion, there was no need to locate them by means of a special rubric, which does not in fact *say* that they are in the City Eleusinion. Nowhere in the epigraphical documents of the two sanctuaries does τὸ Ἐλευσίνιον, standing alone, mean the City Eleusinion. In the Classical period, the Eleusinion, without further qualification, means the Telesterion at Eleusis; see p. 162 and note 4 above.

[106] See the useful commentary of Cavanaugh, *Eleusis*, 135–144.

[μοχλοὶ σιδ]εροῖ : ΔΙΙΙ : σταθμὸν ΓΔΣΣΣ
μοχλοὶ : ΙΙΙΙ : σταθμὸν ΤΤΤ
χοίνικε σιδερᾶ : ΙΙ : τέρετρα : ΙΙΙ : χοάνα : ΙΙ
σμινύαι : ΙΙΙΙ : σιδερίο ℎυπάμπρο : ΙΙ
κλεῖθρα : ΙΙΙ : σταθμὸν : Τ : πρίον λιθοπρίστες [: Ι]
πρίστις : Ι : καρκίνος : Ι
σιδέρο παλινℎαιρέτο : ΤΤΓ
σφυροπέλεκυς : Ι : κόφινοι : Γ
σανὶς πτελείνε : Ι

(Lines 111–116): 2 large ladders, 1 small one; blocks and tackle, 2 large, 2 small; 3 wagons; 2 stone rules; 1 body of a four-wheeled wagon; 1 wheelbarrow body; 4 wheels for a four-wheeled wagon; 1 – – –?

(Lines 125–133): 13 iron crowbars (weight 5 talents, 13 staters); 4 crowbars (weight 3 talents); 2 iron axle boxes; 3 drills; 2 melting pots; 4 hoes; 2 – – –?; 3 door bars (weight 1 talent); 1 stone saw; 1 saw; 1 pair of lifting tongs; reused iron (weight 2 talents, 5 staters); 1 hammer-axe; 5 baskets; 1 elm plank.[107]

The inventory makes it abundantly clear that the building operations at Eleusis had been suspended in midcourse before they were complete. This conclusion is corroborated by the remains of the building itself, for the ashlar wall blocks, steps, and toichobate still retain their protective quarry surfaces and lifting bosses.[108] The year, we should recall, is 408/7, and the parallel of the Erechtheion once more obtrudes itself. After the beginning of the Dekeleian War, the celebrations of the Mysteries had been sharply curtailed, and the splendid processions had to be conducted by sea.[109] It was no doubt at that time, in 413, that the construction of the Telesterion stopped, with the crowning lantern not yet in place. The corollary to the depredations of war was, of course, the slackening off of attendance at the Mysteries, with its concomitant financial crisis for the Eleusinian sanctuary.

The Source of the Hypostyle Hall

The Telesterion at Eleusis as designed and built by the Periklean architects made use of an architectural form, the square hypostyle hall, of which there were very few examples among Greek buildings of the Archaic and Classical periods. But comparison of its plan with that of the Odeion in Athens reveals some striking similarities between the two buildings. We will see in chapter 7 that the columnar hall of the Odeion was unique in both size and form at the time of its construction in the 440s. Likewise, the Telesterion also was unique among Greek temples, which by the mid-fifth century had developed canonical characteristics far different from the architecture of the Telesterion. Although the building was the principal temple of Demeter at Eleusis,[110] unlike all other Greek temples it had to accommodate within its walls the large congregation of initiates because of the secret ceremonial of the Great Mysteries.

In the years after 450, Athenian builders were at work on these two extraordinary buildings at roughly the same time. The innovative design of Iktinos for the Telesterion, and perhaps even more the building begun by Koroibos, show obviously close affinities with the design of the Odeion. Both

---

[107] Cavanaugh, *Eleusis,* 174–181.

[108] They are clearly visible in Noack, *Eleusis,* pls. 35:c, 40:a, 40:b.

[109] Plut. *Alkib.* 34.3.

[110] See note 3 above.

were enormous square halls: the internal dimensions of the Telesterion were 51.56 m from north-east to southwest and 51.96 m from back to front; the Odeion measured 62.40 m on a side. In both buildings a forest of internal columns supported the superstructure of the roof: seven rows of six columns in the Telesterion, and nine rows of ten in the Odeion. The principal southern facade of the Odeion was quite possibly simply an open colonnade, while a deep colonnaded portico was planned for the Telesterion by Koroibos, although it was not actually built until the late fourth century.[111] Indeed, the close similarity of concept in the two buildings has led one scholar to speculate that the design of the Odeion might be attributed to Iktinos himself.[112] Now, we will see presently that the plans for the Odeion seem likely to have been inspired by direct observation of the royal Persian campaign tent captured by the Greeks at Plataia. But that model can hardly have influenced the columnar hall that Iktinos designed for the Telesterion because at Eleusis the concept of the hypostyle hall with prostyle porch was first introduced in the archaic predecessor of the Periklean building.

The archaic temple, as the building is called in fifth-century inscriptions,[113] exhibited a plan closely similar to the Periklean Telesterion but roughly one-quarter the size. Its foundations have survived beneath the eastern corner of the classical building, whose front and side walls rest directly on the earlier structure (see Fig. 61). The hall itself was nearly square (25.30 × 27.10 m); its internal columns were laid out as a square grid, five rows of five, interrupted at the western corner by the wall of the Anaktoron, which aligned with the first row of columns and reduced the number by three. The Anaktoron itself was a small rectangular room (12.40 × 3.60 m) occupying the western corner of the hall. That this structure enclosed the most sacred spot in the sanctuary is clear from its archaeological history; for the small chamber of the archaic temple rested upon the remains of a still earlier building which, significantly, did not have the form of a square columnar hall. Moreover, the Anaktoron of the archaic temple retained precisely the same position in each successive reconstruction of the Telesterion throughout antiquity.[114] Along the side and rear walls beyond the Anaktoron, there rose banks of nine stone steps, and the steps were carried down the full length of the northeast wall. Three doorways in the southeast wall gave access to the hall from the front portico. The columnar prostyle porch was the one element of the design that conformed to the standard syntax of Greek temple architecture. It should probably be restored with ten columns on the facade and one on the return and was certainly of the Doric order, as we learn from fragments of its triglyphs and metopes and numerous blocks of the horizontal mutular cornice. A triangular pediment crowned the columnar facade and reflected the double-pitched roof of the normal Doric temple. All elements of the roof were of Parian marble: on the sides the rows of cover tiles terminated at the eaves in brightly painted palmette antefixes; on the facade the raking sima, painted with alternating palmettes and lotus blossoms, sloped down to ornamental ram's heads at the corners.

There can be no doubt that the design of this building was totally revolutionary in sixth-century Greece. Moreover, the excellent quality of its stonework and the lavish use of imported marble for its roof mark the archaic Telesterion as an architectural monument of the first importance. Unfortunately, proper understanding of the source of its design and appreciation of the meaning of its form have eluded modern interpreters because of the early date that has very generally been accepted for the building. The excavators attributed its construction either to the tyrant Peisistratos or to his

[111] See pp. 182–183 above.
[112] Weickert, Ἔργα Περικλέους, no. 1, 12.
[113] *IG* I³ 79, line 8; cf. *IG* I³ 386, line 103; 387, line 113. For the architecture of the building, see Noack, *Eleusis,* 48–70; Kourouniotes and Travlos, *ArchDelt* 15 (1933–35) 74–82; Mylonas, *Eleusis,* 78–88.
[114] For the Anaktoron, see Travlos, *ArchEph* (1950–51) 1–16.

sons and dated it to the thirties or teens of the sixth century.[115] In this chronology they have been followed by subsequent investigators almost without exception. But it is important to emphasize that the date depends entirely upon stylistic comparison of the building's architectural ornament with closely similar details of the archaic poros temple on the Acropolis, commonly called the Old Athena Temple. Particularly striking is the similarity between the ram's head finial at the corner of the raking sima and a pair of ram's heads, less well preserved, which occupied similar positions on the Old Athena Temple. So close is the shaping of the heads, the details of the eyes and hair, and the sweeping curves of the horns that the finials from the two buildings have seemed to be the products of the same workshop; but it was also observed long ago that the ram's heads from the Acropolis are slightly less developed and therefore slightly older than the example from Eleusis.[116] This relationship between the two buildings has critical consequences for the date of the archaic Telesterion. If the Old Athena Temple should be dated in the last decade of the sixth century on the basis of the style of its sculptures, as some scholars now think,[117] then the date of the archaic Telesterion should also be brought down to the last years of the century. Other details of the building's architecture also fit more comfortably at the end of the century. The marble raking sima that carries the ram's head at the corner of the roof is an ovolo sima of Corinthian type crowned by a small rounded ovolo instead of the normal astragal. The profile finds its closest parallel in the terracotta sima of the Megarian treasury at Olympia, which is now dated to the first decade of the fifth century.[118] The poros anta capital from the columnar portico exhibits a well-developed Doric hawksbeak crowned by a fascia and is closely similar to one from the Heraion on Delos, which has likewise been dated to the end of the century.[119]

There have occasionally been suggestions that the hypostyle hall of the archaic Telesterion should be compared with the royal audience halls, the apadanas, of the Persian palaces.[120] But the most recent investigation of the matter has sought to disparage such attempts, largely because the Telesterion was thought to be contemporary with the earlier buildings of Cyrus at Pasargadae,[121] which, with their rectangular plans, multiple columnar facades, and almost certainly flat roofs, admittedly do not offer a close parallel for the Eleusinian building. We will see in chapter 7, however, that students of Persian architecture now date the construction of the Apadana at Susa to the first years of Darius's reign (ca. 521 or ca. 518).[122] At the same time, careful comparison with the Old Athena Temple suggests a date for the archaic Telesterion around 500. In light of this chronological

---

[115] Dated to Peisistratos: Kourouniotes and Travlos, *ArchDelt* 15 (1933–35) 74–82; Mylonas, *Eleusis,* 78–79. Dated Peisistratid: Noack, *Eleusis,* 68–69. Cf. Dinsmoor, *AAG*³, 113; Gruben, *Gr. Tempel*⁵, 241–242; Lawrence, *Greek Architecture*⁵, 191; Boersma, *Building Policy,* 24–25.

[116] Detailed discussion of the roof and ornamental ram's head, Orlandos, in Noack, *Eleusis,* 63–68, who compares the ram's head from the Old Athena Temple. See Wiegand, *Poros-Architektur,* 125, figs. 121a, b. The second ram's head (Wiegand, fig. 122) was built into a fountain in the monastery at Kaisariani when Wiegand wrote, but it is now known to be from the Old Athena Temple as well. He describes the Acropolis pieces as "sehen etwas altertümlicher aus als der herrliche Widderkopf der Sima des vorpersischen eleusinischen Haupttempels." Noack, *Eleusis,* 69, quotes the opinion of H. Winnefeld, *BWPr* 59 (1899) 19ff., that the ram's head at Eleusis was made in the same workshop as the heads from the Acropolis.

[117] K. Stähler, in *Festschrift Hans Erich Stier* (Münster 1972) 88–112; Stähler, *Boreas* 1 (1978) 28–31; W. A. P. Childs, in Coulson et al., eds., *Athens under the Democracy,* 1–6; Childs, *JdI* 108 (1993) 404–406.

[118] The raking sima from Eleusis, Shoe, *Greek Mouldings,* 34, pl. XVIII:10 (there dated ca. 525); cf. Noack, *Eleusis,* 67, fig. 31. The sima of the Megarian treasury, Shoe, pl. XVIII:11 (there dated ca. 520). The pedimental sculptures of the treasury are now dated 500–490: P. C. Bol, *AM* 89 (1974) 73–74; cf. Childs, in *Athens under the Democracy,* 3.

[119] The anta capital, Noack, *Eleusis,* 87, fig. 41. Cf. Shoe, *Greek Mouldings,* 119, pl. LVII:5 (dated to the end of the sixth century).

[120] K. Schefold, *AMIran* 1 (1968) 56; Meinel, *Odeion,* 141–142.

[121] Miller, *Athens and Persia,* 230–231.

[122] See Stronach, in *Recueil Deshayes,* 438–439, 444, with date ca. 521. M. W. Stolper, in P. O. Harper et al., eds., *The Royal City of Susa* (New York 1992) 271, dates the "Foundation Charter" of the Apadana ca. 518.

relationship, the question needs to be asked yet again whether in fact the Telesterion's apparent similarity of plan to the Persian apadana is merely fortuitous coincidence. If that appearance of similarity is thought not to be illusory, then the further question arises why it seemed appropriate to use so unusual a plan for the Temple of Demeter at Eleusis at the end of the sixth century.

It has generally been assumed that the architect's primary desideratum was to produce a roofed hall of great size capable of accommodating a large crowd of initiates for the secret rites, and in order to roof so large a space multiple rows of interior columns provided the only possible structural solution.[123] But the square hypostyle hall with prostyle columnar portico was by no means the inevitable choice of plan for the Telesterion. On three prior occasions in the sixth century, the builders of East Greece had erected temples of colossal size: that by Rhoikos for the Heraion on Samos, its successor at the same site begun by the tyrant Polykrates, and the archaic Temple of Artemis at Ephesos. All three temples had dipteral peristyles in the mainstream tradition of Ionic architecture, and all three had significantly more space within their cella walls than was available in the archaic Telesterion at Eleusis.[124] Moreover, sheer size does not appear to have been the only consideration. The site chosen for the building was an unusually difficult one, a steeply sloping hillside which required deep artificial foundations for the front wall and deep quarrying of the natural hill for the back. But the history of the chamber called the Anaktoron shows that it was of utmost importance for that inner sanctum to maintain physical contact with the most sacred spot in the sanctuary. Excavations beneath the sixth-century building have revealed not only an earlier archaic predecessor on the same site, but also the remains of still older structures receding as far back as the fifteenth century, which have led some scholars to argue that the cult itself was active in the Bronze Age.[125]

In light of this history of the site, it seems worth considering the possibility that the architectural form of the Telesterion was specifically chosen to express the special imagery of the Eleusinian myth and sanctuary. The most sacred chamber of the temple was the Anaktoron, the king's palace, a name sometimes applied later to the whole building, and possibly even as early as Herodotos's use of the term (9.65). The name reflects directly the foundation myth of the Mysteries, according to which King Keleos received Demeter in his palace hall, and there the goddess first revealed the secret rites and commanded him to build her a temple.[126] The archaic Telesterion was the lineal descendant of that mythical Anaktoron in which Demeter had initiated the Eleusinians into her Mysteries. Now, at the end of the sixth century, every Athenian knew what a Doric temple should look like. They were in fact just at that time completing a new one on the Acropolis for Athena Polias, but at Eleusis they chose to build a temple for Demeter, the like of which no Greek had ever seen. It seems possible that the architect's notion was to design a building that looked like an anaktoron and so proclaimed in the language of architectural form the idea of the king's palace which the goddess had blessed with the Mysteries. Since Greek architecture offered the builders no precedent for the appearance of a royal palace, they turned to the audience hall of the Great King of Persia as the quintessential architectural expression of royal power in the Late Archaic age.

---

[123] Miller, *Athens and Persia*, 230–231, explains the plan of the Telesterion "as a result of functional need." See also G. Leroux, *Les origines de l'édifice hypostyle en Grèce, en orient et chez les romains* (Paris 1913) 204.

[124] The dimensions of the archaic Telesterion (25.30 × 27.10 m) should be compared to the dimensions of the cella building, without the pronaos, in the Ionian temples: Samos, Rhoikos's temple, ca. 25 × 52.50 m (Gruben, *Gr. Tempel*⁵, 356; D. Ohly, *AM* 68 [1953] Beil. 1); Samos, Polykrates' temple, ca. 27 × 58 m (Ohly, Beil. 1); Ephesos, archaic Artemision, 21 × ca. 44.21 m (A. Bammer and U. Muss, *Das Artemision von Ephesos* [Mainz 1996] 54, fig. 61).

[125] For the so-called Solonian Telesterion, see Mylonas, *Eleusis,* 67–70. The Mycenaean structures beneath and the possibility that the cult dates from the fifteenth century are discussed in G. Mylonas, *The Hymn to Demeter and Her Sanctuary at Eleusis* (Saint Louis 1942) 51–55; Mylonas, *Eleusis,* 31–49; cf. N. J. Richardson, *The Homeric Hymn to Demeter* (Oxford 1974) 18. The early remains, Fig. 61 above.

[126] Demeter received in the house of Keleos, *Homeric Hymn to Demeter* 184–189; Demeter demands a temple and reveals her rites, 270–274.

Before dismissing as totally fanciful the notion that the Apadana of Darius I at Susa inspired the design of the hypostyle hall at Eleusis, we might inquire by what means Greek builders would have acquired any knowledge at all of the Persian capital and its palatial architecture. As it happens, detailed study of the limestone masonry at Pasargadae has convinced historians of Persian architecture that much of the stonework for Cyrus's palaces was executed by Ionian Greek masons.[127] At Pasargadae the introduction of stone columns, pavements, and masonry platforms is itself noteworthy in a land that for centuries had built exclusively with mud brick. More specifically, the techniques for working and setting the blocks—the use of clamps and dowels, pry holes and pour channels, the dressing of joints with anathyrosis—all conform precisely with standard Greek practice.[128] Then there are the subtle touches that reveal the Hellenic instinct for architectural ornament. A cyma reversa molding crowns the walls of Cyrus's tomb and marks the transition from the vertical plane to the horizontal cornice above. So closely does the profile resemble contemporary examples from Greece that it must be the product of Greek craftsmanship. The upper curve of the cyma is longer than the lower curve, which is tangent to the chord, and the profile finds a close parallel in the anta capital from the Massiliote treasury at Delphi (ca. 535).[129]

The most convincing evidence that Ionian Greek masons were at work in Pasargadae comes from the column bases of Palace P. The bases of both the exterior porticoes and those within the great hall consisted of a square plinth surmounted by a half-round torus with horizontal fluting. Such horizontally fluted tori are the characteristic hallmark of the Ionic order as it developed on the western coast of Asia Minor, and a few scattered examples are known from the Aegean islands and the Greek mainland.[130] Beyond Greek lands, however, they have been found on no site of the Near East except Pasargadae.[131] Among the bases of Palace P are examples on which the greatest diameter has been transferred below the midpoint of the torus, a detail which finds exact parallel at the archaic Temple of Artemis at Ephesos.[132] Other bases from Palace P show the greatest diameter of the torus transferred above the midpoint in precisely the same way as tori from the Rhoikos temple on Samos,[133] while still others are carved with elaborately molded patterns that closely resemble those from the East Greek sites. Taken together, the evidence of the stonework at Pasargadae strongly suggests the presence of Ionian craftsmen working at the site and shows, of course, that East Greek builders were familiar with Persian royal architecture from the 530s onward. In Greek the technical term for the Ionic column base is σπεῖρα, a word whose root meaning is "a twisted coil," doubtless because the horizontal fluting of the torus was reminiscent of a coiled rope or the coils of a snake.[134] Now, it is fascinating to discover that the archaic Telesterion at Eleusis had bases of just this type for its interior columns, as we learn from the inventory of building materials salvaged from the demolition of the temple, which includes sixteen σπεῖραι.[135] This constitutes the earliest evidence for the

---

[127] For this conclusion, see C. Nylander, *Ionians in Pasargadae* (Uppsala 1970) 144–147; D. Stronach, "Pasargadae," in *The Cambridge History of Iran*, vol. 2 (1985) 840.

[128] For setting procedures, Nylander, *Ionians*, 38–42; clamps and dowels, 42–45, 63–67; pry holes and pour channels, 62–63; joints with anathyrosis, 35–38, 58–62. Also noteworthy is the later use of the claw chisel (Nylander, 53–56), a tool that seems to have been used first by Greek masons about the middle of the sixth century and was possibly invented on the coast of Asia Minor. See S. Casson, *The Technique of Early Greek Sculpture* (Oxford 1933) 126–128.

[129] The cyma reversa on the tomb of Cyrus: Nylander, *Ionians*, 95–98; D. Stronach, *Pasargadae* (Oxford 1978) 34–35, fig. 18b. Cf. the anta capital of the Massiliote treasury: Shoe, *Greek Mouldings*, 56, pl. XXV:17.

[130] For the distribution of examples, Shoe, *Greek Mouldings*, 180.

[131] The bases from Palace P: Nylander, *Ionians*, 103–109; Stronach, *Pasargadae*, 83–85.

[132] Cf. Stronach, *Pasargadae*, 84, fig. 46b (Palace P); Nylander, *Ionians*, 108, fig. 37c (Ephesos).

[133] Cf. Stronach, *Pasargadae,* 84, fig. 46c (Palace P); Nylander, *Ionians*, 108, fig. 37b (Samos).

[134] LSJ⁹, s.v. σπεῖρα 1, 8.

[135] *IG* I³ 386, line 105 (408/7); 387, line 115 (407/6). Cf. the commentary of Cavanaugh, *Eleusis*, 171–172. For identification of the stored materials from the archaic Telesterion, Shear, Jr., *Hesperia* Suppl. 20 (1982) 128–140.

use of the Ionic order in an Athenian building and suggests the influence, if not the actual participation, of East Greek builders at Eleusis.

At Pasargadae the presence of Ionian artisans has been inferred from the remnants of their handiwork, but at Susa their participation is documented epigraphically. The text of DSf, often referred to as the "Foundation Charter" of Susa, is among the earliest inscriptions of Darius I and commemorates in three languages the construction of his new royal palace, and particularly the great audience hall called the Apadana. The document was inscribed in multiple exemplars on baked clay tablets, large stone blocks, and glazed bricks, some of which were buried in the mud-brick walls of the palace, while others formed part of the visible decoration of the hall.[136] The text emphasizes the rare and precious materials that went into the construction of the palace and enumerates the craftsmen who came from the far-flung limits of the empire to contribute their labor to the Great King. For our present purpose, several passages are worth quoting in full from the Old Persian text of the inscription.[137]

> §3e (lines 22–23): This palace which I built at Susa, from afar its ornamentation was brought. . . .

> §3g (lines 30–34): The cedar timber, this—a mountain by the name Lebanon—from there was brought. The Assyrian people, it brought it to Babylon; from Babylon the Carians and the Ionians brought it to Susa. . . .

> §3i (lines 41–43): The ornamentation with which the wall was adorned, that from Ionia was brought. . . .

> §3j (lines 45–49): The stone columns which were here wrought, a village by name Abiradu, in Elam—from there were brought. The stone-cutters who wrought the stone, those were Ionians and Sardians.

Students of Persian royal inscriptions have cautioned that Darius's purpose in drafting this document was more propagandistic than archival. Indeed, there is no mistaking its political message: that the palace was the center of the empire to which all lands should bear the richest of their commodities and the tribute of their labor.[138] But that does not mean that its statements are factually incorrect, and there is no reason to doubt that Ionian Greek stonemasons were working at Susa in the years around 520, just as they are thought to have been working at Pasargadae some fifteen years earlier.

The evidence from the Persian royal capitals shows that East Greek builders would have been intimately familiar with the rapid and impressive developments in Iranian palatial architecture during the second half of the sixth century. The overpowering scale and soaring height of Darius's audience hall would have made an indelible impression on the Ionians, who were themselves particularly receptive to the effects of colossal architecture, as their temples at Ephesos, Samos, and Didyma plainly reveal. In their hands, it is easy to see how the concept of the hypostyle hall came to be transmitted to Attica by the end of the sixth century, and why Darius's Apadana provided a suitable model for Demeter's Anaktoron at Eleusis.

---

[136] On the inscriptions, Stolper, in Harper et al., eds., *Royal City of Susa*, 271–272, no. 190. For editions of the trilingual texts, see chap. 7, note 89 below.

[137] The translation of R. G. Kent, *Old Persian: Grammar, Texts, Lexicon,* 2nd ed. (New Haven 1953) 144.

[138] See C. Nylander, "Foreign Craftsmen in Achaemenian Persia," in *The Memorial Volume of the Vth International Congress of Iranian Art and Archaeology* (Tehran 1972) vol. 1, 311–318; Nylander, "Anatolians in Susa—and Persepolis (?)," in *Monumentum H. S. Nyberg,* vol. 3 (Tehran and Leiden 1975) 317–323; Stolper, in Harper et al., eds., *Royal City of Susa*, 272.

7

The Odeion

The sanctuary of Athena on the Acropolis was the site of an extraordinary campaign of building activity for fully fifteen years, during which the Parthenon and its gold and ivory statue as well as the gate building of the Propylaia were under construction. While the reconstruction of the Acropolis was a major goal of Athenian building operations in these years, the picture is greatly clarified by examination of almost exactly contemporary construction elsewhere in the city. From this there emerges in sharp focus the twofold purpose of the great new temples and public buildings. On the one hand was the desire to celebrate to the fullest extent that architecture and its sculptural adornment made possible the military victories of the Persian Wars,[1] and, on the other hand, the systematic aggrandizement of the Attic sanctuaries and the festivals of their cults which helped to promulgate the notion of Athenian cultural and religious primacy in the Greek world.[2] These twin aims, the commemoration of victory and the ideology of religious imperialism, find perfect expression in two extremely unusual Athenian buildings, the Telesterion at Eleusis, which we have already examined, and the Odeion in Athens. Both buildings were associated in antiquity with the name of the statesman Perikles. Both buildings also served as the locale for parts of major Athenian festivals: the Odeion for the musical contests of the Great Panathenaia and the Proagon of the City Dionysia, and the Telesterion for the Eleusinian Mysteries. The two buildings are mentioned together in the famous chapter of Plutarch's *Life of Perikles* (13.7, 9–11).

The Odeion is specifically described in the literary testimonia as a monument for which the architectural model was not even another building. Although it was originally erected in the third quarter of the fifth century, all but a few stones of its fabric belong to a late Hellenistic reconstruction that apparently replicated the original structure in every detail. Even the few surviving blocks of its walls and its foundations stand on a site that has been only partially excavated, and in fact the vastly greater part of its interior area is still covered by some six meters of accumulated fill. According to the later Greek lexicons, the structure took its name from the singing of the musical contests, and Athenians called it "the Odeion," invariably in the singular and usually accompanied by the definite article.[3] The name first appears within a few years of the building's construction and was plainly attached to it from the very beginning.[4] Already in the fourth century the orator Lykourgos had occasion to name the Odeion together with the Parthenon and the Propylaia as buildings with which Perikles was reputed to have beautified the city, and for whose construction he had carried up to the

---

[1] See chap. 4, pp. 117–121 above.

[2] See chap. 2, pp. 36–40 above.

[3] *Suda*, s.v. ᾠδεῖον (ω 18 Adler): Ἀθήνησιν ὥσπερ θέατρον, ὃ πεποίηκεν, ὥς φασι, Περικλῆς εἰς τὸ ἐπιδείκνυσθαι τοὺς μουσικοὺς διὰ τοῦτο γὰρ καὶ ᾠδεῖον ἐκλήθη, ἀπὸ τῆς ᾠδῆς, "At Athens, like a theater, which they say Perikles built to display musicians. It was called Odeion from the singing." Cf. Photius, s.v. ᾠδεῖον.

[4] Kratinos, Kassel-Austin, *PCG* IV, *Thrattai* frag. 73, quoted by Plut. *Per.* 13.10.

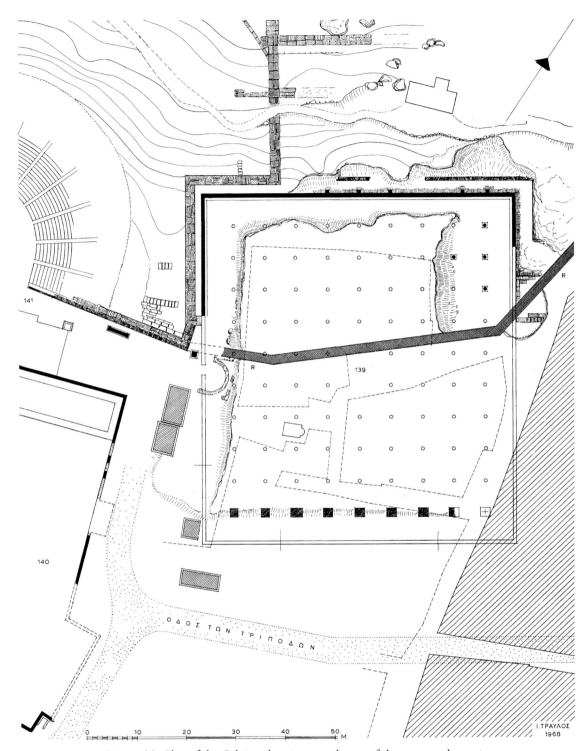

Figure 66. Plan of the Odeion showing actual state of the excavated remains

Acropolis ten thousand talents of silver.[5] At the time of its construction, the Odeion was unique in Greece. Its interior dimensions, almost exactly twice the size of the Parthenon, made it the largest roofed structure ever erected by Greek builders, and as a concert hall it remained without parallel for several centuries.[6] In fact, so unusual was its architectural form, and so apparently ill-suited to its function as a concert hall in the opinion of some commentators, that a tendency has developed

[5] Lykourgos, frag. 58 (Conomis) = Glossa Patmia, s.v. Ἑκατόμπεδον (*BCH* 1 [1877] 149) quoted above, chap. 1, p. 6.
[6] See R. Meinel, *Das Odeion* (Frankfurt am Main 1980) 135; A. H. L. Robkin, *AncW* 2 (1979) 3.

to disparage the explicit statements of our ancient sources concerning the building's design and purpose.[7] Nevertheless, despite these efforts, and even with the appallingly fragmentary state of our evidence, it will be suggested here that the building provides a fascinating glimpse at the often totally capricious interrelationship of form, function, symbol, and meaning in architectural design.

ARCHAEOLOGICAL REMAINS

The excavated remains of the building lie on the southeastern slope of the Acropolis immediately east of the Theater of Dionysos. Here sporadic campaigns of excavation, conducted by P. Kastriotes from 1914 to 1927 and by A. Orlandos from 1928 to 1931, have brought to light the north side of an enormous square structure whose north–south axis is oriented 31 degrees to the west of north (Fig. 66). The early excavations were carried out in the available spaces between modern houses high above the classical remains and so were able to reveal only the northern wall and two corners of the building, together with sections of foundation for its east and west walls.[8] During the 1960s, the remaining modern houses overlying the classical building were demolished preparatory to systematic excavation of the whole site, which has unfortunately never been carried out. The process of demolition, however, uncovered a row of isolated foundations of poros limestone that almost certainly carried the southernmost row of columns and thus enables the position of the southern facade to be estimated within close limits.[9] But most of the vast interior space of the building still lies buried beneath the earth fill that reaches a depth of six meters toward the north (Fig. 68).

A glance at the plan reveals a close interrelation between the Odeion and the neighboring Theater of Dionysos. The heavy conglomerate retaining wall that supported the cavea of the theater on its east side makes a right-angled jog around the northwest corner of the Odeion (Figs. 66, 70). The retaining wall is parallel to the building's west wall for a distance of 25.50 m and parallel to its north wall for a distance of 17.00 m, whereupon it turns northward again and proceeds uphill to the cliff face of the Acropolis. Although the conglomerate retaining wall is separated from the walls of the Odeion by 1.50 m, its outer face was not intended to be visible because the decorative facing of poros ashlar masonry was applied to its southern end for only a length of 5.30 m from the entrance to the parados. The peculiar manner in which the corner of the Odeion impinges upon the semicircular seating of the cavea makes it absolutely certain that the square building occupied the site before the Lykourgan cavea was built between 336 and 326. This in itself is an important conclusion because it is almost equally certain that most of the existing masonry must date to the Hellenistic restoration of the Odeion, as we shall see presently.

The early excavations exposed the entire length of the north wall, measuring 62.40 m between the exterior corners and preserved for much of its length in several courses of masonry that reached its greatest height (3.41 m) at the northwest corner. In contrast, the returns of the east and west walls survived only at foundation level and were uncovered for a distance of 17 m and 15 m, respectively.[10] The

---

[7] So A. L. H. Robkin, "The Odeion of Perikles: Some Observations on Its History, Form, and Functions" (Ph.D. diss., University of Washington, 1976) 41–45; Robkin, *AncW* 2 (1979) 10; Meinel, *Odeion*, 155; H. Kotsidu, *Die musischen Agone der Panathenäen in archaischer und klassischer Zeit* (Munich 1991) 146–149; M. C. Miller, *Athens and Persia* (Cambridge 1997) 232–235.

[8] Preliminary reports on the progress of the early excavations: P. Kastriotes, *ArchEph* (1914) 141, 143–166, (1915) 145–155, (1918) 109–110, (1922) 25–38; Kastriotes, *ArchDelt* 5 (1919) parart., 1–14; Kastriotes, *Prakt* (1914) 81–124, (1915) 55–58, (1919) 27–31, (1925) 21–24, (1926) 98–103, (1927) 23–27, (1928) 34–40, (1929) 52–57; A. K. Orlandos, *Prakt* (1931) 25–36. For orientation of the building, Orlandos, in Kastriotes, *ArchEph* (1922) 36.

[9] See Travlos, *PDA*, 387, figs. 501, 502; briefly reported by G. Dontas, *ArchDelt* 25 (1970) B′ 1, 30. See also Camp, *Archaeology of Athens*, 100–101.

[10] Discussion of the preserved fabric of the north wall, Orlandos, in Kastriotes, *ArchEph* (1922) 36–37, and cf. 25–28. Preserved remains summarized, Robkin, "Odeion of Perikles," 11–18, 31; more briefly, Miller, *Athens and Persia*, 224–227.

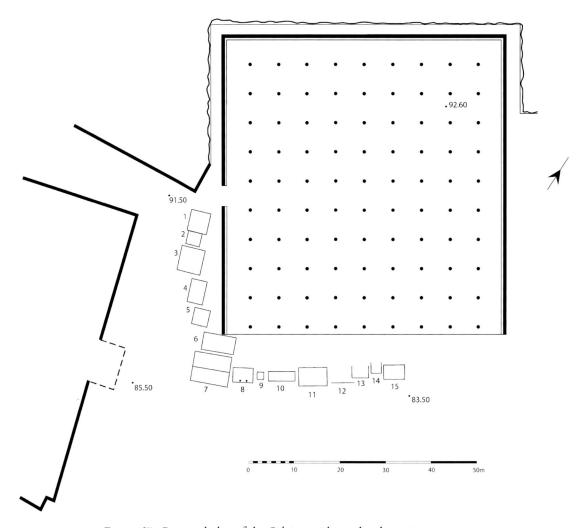

Figure 67. Restored plan of the Odeion with nearby choregic monuments

fabric of the wall is composed of several courses and different kinds of stone (Fig. 69). A euthynteria of poros limestone projects 0.63 m from the face of the wall above and probably carried a bench around the perimeter of the building (Fig. 67).[11] Above this a poros toichobate 0.405 m in height formed the wall base and carried the orthostate course, which consisted of facing slabs of Hymettian marble 0.905 m high and 0.19 m thick, set in front of poros backing blocks 0.44 m thick.[12] A string course of Pentelic marble 0.225 m in height crowns the orthostates and projects slightly from their face. Above the string course began the poros wall blocks, 0.63 m high and set in regular isodomic masonry; two courses are preserved for much of the wall and three at the northwest corner. At the time of excavation, the poros wall courses preserved traces of stucco and painted decoration.[13] Because the north wall is set back deeply into the slope of the Acropolis and a great weight of fill would have accumulated against its upper reaches, it was equipped with supporting buttresses of poros spaced at intervals of about six meters and extending more than a meter into the rock of the hillside. For much the same reason,

[11] To this bench the excavator assigned a number of marble bench supports decorated with carved owls: Kastriotes, *ArchEph* (1914) 160–161, figs. 18, 19, 19a; Kastriotes, *ArchDelt* 5 (1919) 4. Orlandos, in Kastriotes, *ArchEph* (1922) 37, rejected their assignment to the Odeion and associated them correctly with the stadium. Cf. C. Gasparri, *ASAtene* 52–53 (1974–75) 313–392, figs. 25, 27–32; Korres, *ArchDelt* 35 (1980) B′ 1, 18.

[12] The orthostate slabs of Hymettian marble are separated from the poros backing blocks by a space 0.07 m wide, so that the total thickness of the wall at the orthostate course is 0.70 m.

[13] Orlandos, *Prakt* (1931) 25–27 and figs. 1, 2. See p. 224 below.

Figure 68. Site of the Odeion from the Acropolis

Figure 69. North wall of the Odeion

Figure 70. Northwest corner of the Odeion

a subsidiary retaining wall was set parallel to the north wall at a distance of 3.20 m and higher on the hill, so that its lowest blocks are 2.45 m above the toichobate of the Odeion.[14] The combination of materials in the stonework of the north wall is noteworthy. The use of Hymettian marble orthostates together with Pentelic marble string course and poros wall blocks finds close parallels in other Athenian buildings of the Hellenistic period, most particularly in the Stoas of Attalos II and Eumenes II, and in the Hellenistic Metroon in the Agora. Thus the fabric of the wall alone gives clear indication that the surviving remains do not belong to the original Periklean building.

At the northeast corner of the building, enough of the rock-cut floor was exposed to reveal the disposition of the interior columns that supported the superstructure and roof of the great hall. Preserved in situ were four square plinths of Hymettian marble measuring 0.90 m on each side and 0.30 m in thickness. Three of these were aligned parallel to the east wall, and the fourth plinth occupied the second position from the north in the next row to the west. In addition, the excavators found four more square cuttings in the bedrock from which the marble bases had been removed. These rock-cut beddings verified the positions of the fourth column from the north in the easternmost row and the first, third, and fourth columns in the second row. Taken together, the evidence for these eight columns showed that the interior supports were arranged in a regular grid pattern, with the columns spaced 6.15 m on centers in each direction and with the first column set in 5.00 m from each wall, measured from its axis to the edge of the euthynteria.[15] The upper surface of the marble bases was level with the poros euthynteria beneath the walls, but both were 0.05 m to 0.07 m higher

[14] Kastriotes, *ArchEph* (1918) 109–110; Kastriotes, *ArchDelt* 5 (1919) parart., 12 and fig. 14; Orlandos, in Kastriotes, *ArchEph* (1922) 36–37.

[15] For details of the interior column bases, Kastriotes, *ArchEph* (1922) 27, fig. 2, 33; Orlandos, in Kastriotes, *ArchEph* (1922) 37; and cf. the plan, Kastriotes, *Prakt* (1926) 99.

than the leveled bedrock at the northeast corner. This suggests that in the Hellenistic restoration the floor may have been paved with marble slabs that were subsequently removed.[16] Of the columns themselves, the excavations yielded some fragments of unfluted shafts with a lower diameter of about 0.60 m; these undoubtedly stood directly on the marble plinths without intervening bases.[17]

Further clearing of the southern part of the site in the 1960s enabled the disposition of the interior columns to be fully corroborated. This work exposed a row of isolated foundation piers running west to east across nearly the entire width of the building. The piers were composed of three courses of soft yellow poros blocks, laid three blocks to a course as alternating headers and stretchers, and forming roughly square foundations that measure 1.80 m on a side. Seven poros piers and half of an eighth are preserved, and, like the column bases at the northeast corner, they are spaced 6.15 m on centers, whereas the center line of the row is almost exactly 62.40 m from the exterior northwest corner of the building.[18] Thus the architectural remains reveal a great square hypostyle hall measuring 62.40 m from east to west and only a little more than that from north to south.[19] The superstructure of its enormous roof was supported by nine rows of ten columns arranged in a regular grid pattern. Moreover, the foundations for the southernmost row of columns were made of soft yellow poros, a material that is consistent with fifth-century building practice, whereas in the Late Hellenistic period similar foundation piers would almost certainly have used conglomerate. This is very likely the only stonework of the original Periklean building that has yet come to light.

More recent investigations, carried out from 1978 to 1980, have greatly clarified the eastern approaches to the Theater and sanctuary of Dionysos along the Street of the Tripods.[20] One of the principal thoroughfares of eastern Athens, this street encircled the east end of the Acropolis at approximately 84 m above sea level and undoubtedly provided the main route of access to both the sanctuary and theater. The street took its name from the choregic monuments erected to display the bronze tripods awarded to victorious choruses in the dithyrambic contests, of which the best known example is the Monument of Lysikrates, a little farther to the northeast along its route.[21] The Street of the Tripods passed a few meters south of the Odeion at an elevation of 83.50 m sloping up to 85.50 m at the propylon to the sanctuary of Dionysos,[22] whereupon it turned at a right angle and ascended a steep ramp to the entrance of the eastern parodos of the theater at an elevation of 91.50 m. The investigations of the later 1970s located the foundations of no fewer than fifteen choregic monuments, built side by side along the street and completely enclosing the southwest corner of the Odeion from the midpoint of its west side to well beyond the middle of its south facade (see Fig. 67).[23] The topography of the site now makes it obvious why the monuments

---

[16] Kastriotes, *ArchEph* (1918) 109.

[17] Orlandos, in Kastriotes, *ArchEph* (1922) 37. One of the two inscriptions honoring King Ariobarzanes of Cappadocia (*IG* II[2] 3427; see pp. 206–207 below) was carved on an unfluted column shaft of the series that the excavator assigned to the interior of the Odeion: Kastriotes, *Prakt* (1914) 109–110.

[18] Travlos, *PDA*, 387, figs. 501, 502; cf. Dontas, *ArchDelt* 25 (1970) B´ 1, 30; Robkin, "Odeion of Perikles," 11–12, 15.

[19] The north–south dimension of 68.60 m reported by Travlos, *PDA*, 387, and restored on his plan, fig. 502, is shown to be too long by the subsequent clearing of the full foundation for Choregic Monument 6 (see p. 204, note 26, and Fig. 67 below), which must have nearly abutted the southwest corner of the Odeion.

[20] For work in the area of the sanctuary of Dionysos, Korres, *ArchDelt* 35 (1980) B´ 1, 9–21; for the route of the Street of the Tripods around the east end of the Acropolis, A. Choremi-Spetsieri, in Coulson et al., eds., *Athens under the Democracy*, 31–42, and especially the survey plan 33, fig. 2.

[21] The name of the street, Paus. 1.20.1: ἔστι δὲ ὁδὸς ἀπὸ τοῦ πρυτανείου καλουμένη Τρίποδες· ἀφ᾽ οὗ καλοῦσι τὸ χωρίον, ναοὶ ὅσον ἐς τοῦτο μεγάλοι, καί σφισιν ἐφεστήκασι τρίποδες, χαλκοῖ μέν, μνήμης δὲ ἄξια μάλιστα περιέχοντες εἰργασμένα, "Leading from the Prytaneion is a street called Tripods. The place takes its name from the shrines, large enough to hold the tripods which stand upon them, of bronze, but containing very remarkable works of art." The monument dedicated by the choregos Lysikrates in 335/4 (*IG* II[2] 3042): Travlos, *PDA*, 348–351.

[22] Elevations above sea level in the area of the Odeion and the Theater of Dionysos are shown on the plan in Korres, *ArchDelt* 35 (1980) B´ 1, 12, fig. 1.

[23] Choregic Monuments 7 through 15 south of the Odeion are discussed by Korres, *ArchDelt* 35 (1980) B´ 1, 16–17.

came to be built in just this area, where, on a plan, they seem to obstruct access so completely to the great hall. The floor level of the Odeion, as indicated by the column bases in the northeast corner, lay at 92.60 m above sea level. Thus the whole southern half of the building stood on an enormous artificial terrace supported by a great masonry retaining wall that rose some eight or nine meters above the Street of the Tripods at the south.[24] There was never any possibility of gaining access to the Odeion from this side; and, with its odd number of nine columns, there is little likelihood that the building's south facade was treated architecturally as a normal prostoon on the analogy of the porch that was added to the Telesterion at Eleusis in the fourth century.[25] It is noticeable that the foundation piers for the columns of the south facade lie just north of Choregic Monument 6, and it is likely that that structure stood immediately beside the southwestern corner of the Odeion terrace. Thus, in the absence of further excavation, the preserved foundation of that monument gives the best evidence for the southern limit of the Odeion, whose west side would nearly have abutted the north wall of Monument 6.[26] It is likely that the east and west walls of the Odeion were carried straight southward along the edges of the terrace until they terminated in antae on either end of the southernmost row of columns. In that case, the south facade may simply have been an open colonnade enclosed, if at all, by grilles between columns.[27] What is certain about the restoration is the means of access: a great doorway at the midpoint of the west wall must have aligned with the parodos of the theater, and another, presumably the principal entrance, stood opposite on the unexplored eastern side of the building.[28]

EVIDENCE FOR IDENTIFICATION

The architectural remains of the great hypostyle hall beside the theater can be identified with certainty on the basis of several literary references to both the theater itself and to the neighboring building. These passages describe quite precisely the topographical interrelationship that we have already observed in the ruins of the monuments themselves. In the year 400/399, Andokides was prosecuted by a group of his enemies on the charge that he had been involved in the profanation of the Eleusinian Mysteries and the mutilation of the Herms.[29] That infamous scandal had caused panic in Athens just before the departure of the ill-fated Sicilian expedition in 415, and many prominent Athenians had become engulfed in the avalanche of charges and denunciations that it spawned. As a part of his defense, Andokides had occasion to recount to the court the statements of a certain Diokleides, who claimed to be an eyewitness to some of the events of 415 (Andok. 1.38):

---

[24] So Korres, *ArchDelt* 35 (1980) B′ 1, 18.

[25] For the prostoon at Eleusis, see chap. 6, p. 183 above.

[26] Korres, *ArchDelt* 35 (1980) B′ 1, 12, shows the north–south dimension of the Odeion terrace the same as Travlos, *PDA*, fig. 502, but he reduces the east–west dimension in order to avoid Choregic Monument 6, which is now known to extend farther east than Travlos thought. As a result, Korres shows the south half of the Odeion narrower than the north half. He then suggests (p. 18) that the building might best be restored simply as columns and roof without exterior walls. It seems preferable, however, to locate the southwest corner of the Odeion terrace just north of Choregic Monument 6. This allows a uniform east–west dimension of 62.40 m for both north and south halves of the building and reduces the north–south dimension so as to clear the foundations of Choregic Monument 6. The east and west walls, which are well documented in the northern part of the Odeion, can then be restored as in a normal Greek building. Without systematic excavation of the site, there can be no certainty about the architectural restoration.

[27] An open colonnade enclosed only by grilles might explain the curious reference to Ὠδείου πύλας, "the gates of the Odeion," in the same line as the Lykeion and the Academy, as favorite haunts of the philosophers: Alexis, Kassel-Austin, *PCG* II, *Asotodidaskalos* frag. 25, quoted by Athenaeus 8.336E–F.

[28] The early excavators uncovered conglomerate foundations that appeared to be for some sort of propylon on the east side of the building, 15 m south of the northeast corner and more or less aligned with the third interior intercolumniation: Orlandos, in Kastriotes, *ArchEph* (1922) 38 and the plan, 27, fig. 2; cf. Travlos, *PDA*, fig. 502.

[29] On the date of the trial, see D. MacDowell, ed., *Andokides: On the Mysteries* (Oxford 1962) 204–205.

ἀναστὰς δὲ πρῷ ψευσθεὶς τῆς ὥρας βαδίζειν· εἶναι δὲ πανσέληνον. ἐπεὶ δὲ παρὰ τὸ προ-
πύλαιον τοῦ Διονύσου ἦν, ὁρᾶν ἀνθρώπους πολλοὺς ἀπὸ τοῦ ᾠδείου καταβαίνοντας εἰς
τὴν ὀρχήστραν· δείσας δὲ αὐτούς, εἰσελθὼν ὑπὸ τὴν σκιὰν καθέζεσθαι μεταξὺ τοῦ κίο-
νος καὶ τῆς στήλης ἐφ' ᾗ ὁ στρατηγός ἐστιν ὁ χαλκοῦς.

Diokleides stated that he had arisen very early and begun his walk, having mistaken the
hour; for it was full moon. When he was beside the propylon of Dionysos, he saw a large
group of men coming down from the Odeion into the orchestra. Being afraid of them, he
withdrew into the shadow and sat down between the column and the pedestal on which
is the bronze statue of the general.

Andokides' phraseology attests the close proximity of the Odeion to the sanctuary and the Theater
of Dionysos, and the participle καταβαίνοντας accurately describes the sloping descent of the eastern parodos from the Odeion to the lower level of the orchestra. To be sure, the actual remains of
a propylon forming the main entrance to the sanctuary have never been found, but it was probably
located on the east side of the precinct, where the Street of the Tripods turns northward and rises
sharply toward the theater. It is easy to picture Diokleides stopping here when he got an unob-
structed view of men moving, under the cover of darkness, from the Odeion to the theater, and here
too he could have taken cover in the shadowed space between a column of the porch and an adjacent
statue base.[30]

We read of these same monuments in a completely different context when the Roman architect
Vitruvius recommends construction of porticoes beside theaters as places of refuge for the audience
in case of sudden rainstorms. Among other examples he cites the Athenian buildings (Vitruv. 5.9.1):

> itemque Athenis porticus Eumenicae Patrisque Liberi fanum et exeuntibus e theatro sinis-
> tra parte odeum, quod Themistocles columnis lapideis dispositis navium malis et antem-
> nis e spoliis Persicis pertexit, ideo autem etiam incensum Mithridatico bello rex Ariobar-
> zanes restituit.

> At Athens there are the Colonnade of Eumenes, the Sanctuary of Father Liber, and as
> you leave the theater on the left-hand side is the Odeum. This Themistokles planned with
> stone columns and completed with ships' masts and yards from the Persian spoils. It was
> burned, however, in the Mithradatic War and King Ariobarzanes restored it.

Vitruvius gives an accurate account of the topography on the southeast slope of the Acropolis as
it is revealed by the archaeological remains. He knows that the theater is part of the sanctuary of
Dionysos and that next to it is the great Hellenistic stoa given to the city by King Eumenes II of Per-
gamon.[31] He records correctly that spectators leaving the theater by the left-hand or eastern parodos
would have direct access to the Odeion. That building had stone columns, and there was a tradition
at Athens that the elaborate woodwork of its roof had been salvaged from the Persian ships captured
in the Battle of Salamis. The reuse of spoils from the famous sea battle naturally reminded him of the
great Athenian general who was the architect of that victory, and he attributed construction of the
Odeion to Themistokles. It must be a simple error; no other ancient source mentions Themistokles in

---

[30] On the probable location of the propylon to the sanctuary, see Korres, *ArchDelt* 35 (1980) Β′ 1, 12, fig. 1. Andokides
appears to have reported the topography accurately, but whether he correctly reports the testimony of Diokleides there is
no way of knowing. Plut. *Alkib.* 20.8 says that Diokleides' mention of the full moon vitiated his testimony because the mutilation of the Herms took place on the last night of the month, when there was no moon. Bronze statues of Miltiades and
Themistokles stood near the entrances to the theater, the former on the east side, and the latter on the west: schol. Aristeides
46.161 (Dindorf, vol. 3, pp. 535–536). Andokides' other topographical indications suggest that he thought of Diokleides
as taking cover beside the statue of Miltiades to the east. So Judeich, *Topographie*², 314, note 4; but cf. M. Bieber, *AJA* 58
(1954) 282–284, who places him beside Themistokles on the west side of the orchestra.
[31] On the Stoa of Eumenes II, Travlos, *PDA*, 523–526.

connection with the Odeion, while a number of testimonia ranging in date from the fifth century to
the Roman period associate construction of the building with the name of Perikles.[32] Scholars have
worried unnecessarily about an earlier phase of construction or about reuse of salvaged wood after
a lapse of more than thirty years.[33] Large timbers have always been precious commodities in Greece
and were carefully preserved for eventual reuse. Wooden epistyles, rafters, and doors dismantled
from the archaic Telesterion at Eleusis before the Persian Wars were still stored in the sanctuary and
recorded by the overseers in 408/7.[34] Timbers salvaged from the Persian wrecks at Salamis would
have had an extra cachet and would have been specially prized, not least for their symbolic value.

Vitruvius was also accurately informed about the peculiar architectural history of the building
beside the theater, which he says was burned in the Mithradatic War and restored by King Ariobarzanes. The burning of the building is corroborated by Appian, whose history of the Mithradatic War
includes a long and detailed account of the siege of Athens by Lucius Cornelius Sulla. As the Roman
legions overran the lower city in March of 86, a few Athenians, and with them the tyrant Aristion,
took refuge on the Acropolis, but first they set fire to the Odeion so that Sulla would not have a
supply of timber ready to hand to besiege the Acropolis.[35] This deliberate destruction of the building
helps to explain why most of the excavated remains appear to date to a reconstruction of the Late
Hellenistic period, when a great hall on this site was plainly known and mentioned from the fifth
century onward. Restoration of the building by the munificence of Ariobarzanes is documented by
two inscriptions, both of which were found in the vicinity, dedicating honorary statues to the donor
(*IG* II² 3426):

βασιλέα Ἀριοβαρζάνην Φιλοπάτορα τὸν ἐκ βασιλέως
Ἀριοβαρζάνου Φιλορωμαίου καὶ βασιλίσσης
Ἀθηναίδος Φιλοστόργου οἱ κατασταθέντες
ὑπ' αὐτοῦ ἐπὶ τὴν τοῦ ὠιδείου κατασκευὴν
Γάιος καὶ Μᾶρκος Στάλλιοι Γαΐου υἱοὶ καὶ
Μενάλιππος ἑαυτῶν εὐεργέτην.

King Ariobarzanes Philopator, son of King Ariobarzanes Philoromaios and Queen Athe-
nais Philostorgos, the men appointed by him for the construction of the Odeion set up as
their benefactor, Gaius and Marcus Stallios, sons of Gaius, and Menalippos.

The statue honored Ariobarzanes II Philopator, who was king of Cappadocia from his father's abdi-
cation in 63 or 62 until his own assassination in 52 or 51.[36] The monument was set up by the builders whom the king had commissioned to restore the Odeion, whose construction was presumably

[32] The Odeion associated with Perikles: Kratinos, Kassel-Austin, *PCG* IV, *Thrattai* frag. 73; Lykourgos, frag. 58 (Conomis) = Glossa Patmia, s.v. Ἑκατόμπεδον (*BCH* 1 [1877] 149); Plut. *Per.* 13.9–11; Photius, s.v. ᾠδεῖον (Naber); *Suda*, s.v.
ᾠδεῖον (ω 18 Adler). Vitruvius, 5.9.1 in error, Robkin, "Odeion of Perikles," 158; Boersma, *Building Policy*, 72.
[33] So Davison, *JHS* 78 (1958) 33–36; Robkin, *AncW* 3 (1980) 44–46; Meinel, *Odeion*, 148–149; Corso, *Monumenti
Periclei*, 61–63; Kotsidu, *Musischen Agone*, 143–144.
[34] *IG* I³ 386, lines 103–110 (408/7); 387, lines 113–120 (407/6). See Shear, Jr., *Hesperia* Suppl. 20 (1982) 128–140;
Cavanaugh, *Eleusis and Athens*, 169–173, for commentary on the texts of the inscriptions.
[35] Appian, *Mithradatic Wars* 6.38: ὀλίγων δ' ἦν ἀσθενὴς ἐς τὴν ἀκρόπολιν δρόμος· καὶ Ἀριστίων αὐτοῖς συνέφευ-
γεν, ἐμπρήσας τὸ ᾠδεῖον, ἵνα μὴ ἑτοίμοις ξύλοις αὐτίκα ὁ Σύλλας ἔχοι τὴν ἀκρόπολιν ἐνοχλεῖν, "A few had taken their
feeble course to the Acropolis, among them Aristion, who had burned the Odeion, so that Sulla might not have the timber
in it at hand for storming the Acropolis" (trans. H. White, Loeb). Plut. *Sulla* 14.10, citing Sulla's own memoirs, dated the
capture of Athens to the Calends of March, which he equated with the new moon of Anthesterion.
[36] Ariobarzanes I Philoromaios was appointed king of Cappadocia ca. 95 by the Roman senate and abdicated in 63 or
62 in favor of his son: Strabo 12.2.11 (p. 540); Justin 38.2.8. Appian, *Mithr.* 15.105, 17.114, mentions the father's abdica-
tion and the succession of Ariobarzanes II; cf. Val. Max. 5.7, ext. 2. The assassination of Ariobarzanes II took place shortly
before Cicero's arrival in the Province of Cilicia; the plot against him mentioned, Cic. *Fam.* 15.4.6. Cicero (*Fam.* 15.2.5)
warned his son, Ariobarzanes III, to beware lest he suffer his father's calamitous fate.

completed before the end of his reign. An exactly contemporary inscription records the gift of an honorary statue of the same monarch by the demos of the Athenians, which must commemorate the same occasion, although it does not mention the Odeion by name.[37]

The topography of the southeastern slope of the Acropolis is mentioned again in Pausanias's description of Athens. The Roman traveler visited the Prytaneion below the east end of the Acropolis and then strolled through the eastern reaches of the city. He then walked along the Street of the Tripods from the Prytaneion to the sanctuary of Dionysos and the theater (Paus. 1.20.4):[38]

> ἔστι δὲ πλησίον τοῦ τε ἱεροῦ τοῦ Διονύσου καὶ τοῦ θεάτρου κατασκεύασμα, ποιηθῆναι δὲ τῆς σκηνῆς αὐτὸ ἐς μίμησιν τῆς Ξέρξου λέγεται· ἐποιήθη δὲ καὶ δεύτερον, τὸ γὰρ ἀρχαῖον στρατηγὸς ῥωμαίων ἐνέπρησε Σύλλας Ἀθήνας ἑλών.

> Near the sanctuary of Dionysos and the theater is a structure said to have been made in imitation of the tent of Xerxes. It was rebuilt, for the old edifice was burned by the Roman general Sulla when he captured Athens.

That Pausanias described the building in question as adjacent to the sanctuary of Dionysos and the theater leaves no doubt that he refers to the same building as Vitruvius. Moreover, he knew that the original had been burned at the time of the Roman conquest and had later been restored. It is natural enough that he attributed the destruction to the conquering Roman general rather than to the Athenians themselves. From the time of the first excavations beside the theater, scholars have made much of the fact that Pausanias calls the building κατασκεύασμα (a structure). The inference has been drawn that by his time the name Odeion had been forgotten and the building had ceased to function as a concert hall;[39] but Pausanias's locution by no means justifies that conclusion. He knew that the building was not original, and his antiquarian tastes caused him to take no further interest in it. In like manner, he made no mention whatever of the great Hellenistic stoas that enclosed two sides of the Agora. But he did record one quaint bit of antiquarian lore about the building: that it was built "in imitation of the tent of Xerxes." This statement, of course, makes it clear that he referred to the same building that finds its most detailed description in Plutarch's *Life of Perikles*.

Plutarch included the Odeion, along with the Parthenon, the Propylaia, and the Telesterion at Eleusis, among the public works that he attributed to Perikles (*Per.* 13.9–11):

> τὸ δ' Ὠιδεῖον, τῇ μὲν ἐντὸς διαθέσει πολύεδρον καὶ πολύστυλον, τῇ δ' ἐρέψει περικλι-
> νὲς καὶ κάταντες ἐκ μιᾶς κορυφῆς πεποιημένον, εἰκόνα λέγουσι γενέσθαι καὶ μίμημα
> τῆς βασιλέως σκηνῆς, ἐπιστατοῦντος καὶ τούτῳ Περικλέους. διὸ καὶ πάλιν Κρατῖνος ἐν
> Θρᾴτταις παίζει πρὸς αὐτόν·
>
> > ὁ σχινοκέφαλος Ζεὺς ὅδε προσέρχεται
> > Περικλέης τᾠδεῖον ἐπὶ τοῦ κρανίου
> > ἔχων, ἐπειδὴ τοὔστρακον παροίχεται.
>
> φιλοτιμούμενος δ' ὁ Περικλῆς τότε πρῶτον ἐψηφίσατο μουσικῆς ἀγῶνα τοῖς Παν-
> αθηναίοις ἄγεσθαι, καὶ διέταξεν αὐτὸς ἀθλοθέτης αἱρεθείς, καθότι χρὴ τοὺς ἀγωνι-

---

[37] *IG* II² 3427.

[38] Pausanias 1.20.1 mentions the Street of the Tripods leading from the Prytaneion (note 21 above). He next describes the sanctuary and Theater of Dionysos (1.20.3) and finally the Odeion (1.20.4). The order of the narrative has seemed strange, since Pausanias was approaching from the northeast and the Odeion lies to the east of the theater. Pausanias's movements were undoubtedly governed by the topography of the site. Since the Odeion is now known to have stood on a high artificial terrace without access from the south facade, and the Street of the Tripods passed some eight meters lower on the slope, it was perfectly natural for Pausanias to follow the street to the gate of the sanctuary, to visit the temples and theater, and then, having gained the higher level of the orchestra, to approach the Odeion through the east parodos.

[39] Kastriotes, *ArchEph* (1914) 145–146; Kastriotes, *Prakt* (1914) 83; Robkin, "Odeion of Perikles," 167; Miller, *Athens and Persia*, 223.

ζομένους αὐλεῖν ἢ ᾄδειν ἢ κιθαρίζειν. ἐθεῶντο δὲ καὶ τότε καὶ τὸν ἄλλον χρόνον ἐν
Ὠιδείῳ τοὺς μουσικοὺς ἀγῶνας.

The Odeion, which was built in its interior arrangement many-sided and with many columns and with its roof sloping downward on all sides from a single peak, they say was an
exact imitation of the Great King's tent, and this too was built under the superintendence
of Perikles. Therefore Kratinos in his *Thracian Women* pokes fun at him again:

> "Here comes the squill-headed Zeus
> Perikles, wearing the Odeion on his head
> now that the ostrakon is past."

Then first did Perikles, so zealous for the honor was he, get a decree passed that a musical
contest be held at the Panathenaia. He himself was elected athlothetes and prescribed
how the contestants should play the flute, or sing, or play the kithara. These musical contests they used to watch, both then and thereafter, in the Odeion.

The biographer's description of the Odeion is considerably more detailed and conveys the
appearance of the building more successfully than his references to any of the other Periklean buildings. He did not bother to say, for example, that the Parthenon was a Doric temple or that the Propylaia was a Doric gate building with wings, but he described the essential architectural features of
both the interior and exterior of the Odeion. Nevertheless, prior to excavation on the site, a number
of early scholars had formulated the notion that the building ought to have been round.[40] The fact
that Perikles was lampooned as wearing it like a cap evidently encouraged this belief. Both Plutarch
and Pausanias emphasized that its model was the king's tent, and campaign tents should be round,
while Plutarch's description of its roof seemed consistent with a conical roof on a circular structure,
not unlike the Tholos in the Agora. It was then suggested that the building might even be illustrated
on a lead theater ticket and two small bronze coins which depicted a columnar building, apparently circular and with its roof rising steeply to a point.[41] There was, of course, no evidence at all to
indicate that the coins and the token actually showed the Odeion, and their association with the
building was nothing more than the merest speculation. Furthermore, the discovery that the building was in fact a great square hypostyle hall ought to have dispelled any notion either that it was
circular or that it was depicted on the coins.[42] Even some of those who have restored the building
as the square hall that it in fact was have nevertheless persisted in retaining a circular or polygonal
lantern at the midpoint of its roof, a restoration that is inconsistent with Plutarch's description of
the superstructure.[43]

The roof of the Odeion is described by Plutarch as περικλινές, "sloping on all sides," a word he
uses elsewhere to describe the strategic characteristics of the terrain in theaters of military operations.
The fact that hills or wooded glens are περικλινεῖς is what makes them desirable positions for infantry about to engage from high ground, or for strategic lookout posts, or for a hidden ambush in the

---

[40] Miller, *Athens and Persia*, 225 and note 38, rightly rejects the idea but cites earlier bibliography of scholars who
espoused this view. P. Kalligas, in Coulson et al., eds., *Athens under the Democracy*, 25–27, attempted to revive the idea that
the building was round.

[41] Kastriotes, *ArchEph* (1914) 147 and note 2, who attributes the original suggestion to A. Rhoussopoulos, Ἐγχει-
ρίδιον τῆς Ἑλληνικῆς ἀρχαιολογίας, 3rd ed. (Athens 1875) 271, note 219. Detailed discussion of the coins, J. N. Svoronos,
NZ 55 (1922) 119–122; the lead token added by A. L. Oikonomides, in F. W. Imhoof-Blumer and P. Gardner, *Ancient
Coins Illustrating Lost Masterpieces of Greek Art* (Chicago 1964) lxvi, lxxviii, 3.

[42] So, rightly, Miller, *Athens and Persia*, 225. The coins are adduced as evidence for the appearance of the Odeion by
Judeich, *Topographie*², 307; Robkin, "Odcion of Perikles," 34, 104, note 50; H. von Gall, in U. Höchmann and A. Krug, eds.,
Festschrift Brommer, 125; von Gall, *Gymnasium* 86 (1979) 447; Meinel, *Odeion*, 136.

[43] E.g., Dinsmoor, *AAG*³, 211; Dinsmoor, in Mylonas, ed., *Studies Robinson*, 313, note 6 and fig. 2.

enemy's rear. What is important is that they slope all around and not just in one direction.[44] Similarly, Plutarch emphasizes this characteristic of the roof of the Odeion by adding the phrase κάταντες ἐκ μιᾶς κορυφῆς, "downward from a single peak." The roof of the Odeion was not a normal gable roof sloping down on two sides with triangular pediments at the ends. It was a pyramidal or hipped roof sloping down on all four sides from a single peak, a roof of just the kind that has long been restored on the Old Bouleuterion in the Agora and other buildings similarly square in plan.[45] It would have been difficult for Plutarch to describe it more precisely. With regard to the building's interior arrangements, two adjectives convey its appearance with great accuracy. It is πολύστυλον, "with many columns," and even in the ruinous state of its architectural remains and the incomplete state of their excavation, one of the few known facts about the building is its many interior columns. The woodwork of the roof was supported by nine rows of ten columns, the largest number of columns ever used in the interior of a Greek building. Moreover, the unusual number was plainly recognized in classical Athens, where it was considered a fatuous cliché to remark on how many columns there were in the Odeion, one of the empty conversational gambits that Theophrastos attributed to his garrulous man (*Characters* 3.4). The second adjective that Plutarch uses to describe the interior is πολύεδρον, which has universally been translated as "with many seats," although the word is found nowhere else in classical Greek with that meaning, and the remains have revealed no installation for seats beyond the foundation for a single bench along the walls. It has recently been suggested that the word should be translated "many-sided" and should bear the same meaning that it had in the technical vocabulary of Euclidian geometry, where it described a solid defined by many planes, that is, a polyhedron.[46] From the point of view of the spectator gazing upward from within the building at the exposed timbers and rafters, "the geometric polyhedron precisely describes the unusual space created by a pyramidal roof over a rectilinear structure."[47] So we learn from Plutarch's brief description that the Odeion had a low pyramidal roof whose slope was unbroken by a central lantern or clerestory. Its superstructure was supported by a forest of interior columns, and the visible soffit of the woodwork for the roof gave the interior the appearance of being many-sided. In all respects, this description agrees with what little we know about the building from its excavated architectural remains.

Evidence for the Date of Construction

Excavation of the Odeion has never been carried out systematically enough to isolate the construction filling for the classical phase of the building from its later restoration. There is, as a result, no material evidence bearing on the building's original date of construction.[48] Its chronology must be inferred from references to it in the literary record, and most especially from the description in Plutarch's *Life of Perikles*. This last passage includes a quotation from the comedy *Thracian Women* by Kratinos which has the earliest reference to the Odeion by name and must have been written

---

[44] Plut. *Pelopidas* 32.3; *Marcellus* 29.4; *Marius* 20.5. Stadter, *Commentary*, 173, translates the word "steep" in these passages and Plut. *Per.* 13.9, but this does not in fact seem required in the first three or desirable in the last. Cf. also Miller, *Athens and Persia*, 227–228. The roofs of Greek buildings were regularly constructed with an unusually low pitch.

[45] The Old Bouleuterion in the Agora: Shear, Jr., in Coulson et al., eds., *Athens under the Democracy*, 231, 235, fig. 10. Cf. the bouleuterion at Assos: J. T. Clarke, F. H. Bacon, and R. Koldewey, *Investigations at Assos* (Cambridge, MA, 1902) 53–55.

[46] Euclid, *Elementa* 12.17–18, passim. These passages are not cited in LSJ⁹, s.v. πολύεδρον.

[47] Miller, *Athens and Persia*, 227, with useful discussion of the meaning of words in Plut. *Per.* 13.9.

[48] The excavators describe a thick layer of destruction debris extending over the whole excavated area and containing ash, burned wood, iron nails, and great numbers of half-burned roof tiles: Kastriotes, *Prakt* (1914) 117, *ArchEph* (1915) 150–152, and *ArchDelt* 5 (1919) parart., 5. Although the debris is attributed to the burning of the Odeion in the time of Sulla, it must in fact represent the final destruction of the restored Odeion in the Late Roman period.

within a few years of the building's completion.[49] Historians of Attic comedy have associated the theme of the play with the introduction of the Thracian goddess Bendis, whose worship in Athens is attested epigraphically before 429/8.[50] Another fragment of the same play preserves mention of an orator named Euathlos, who is described by Aristophanes as a young man in 425.[51] These considerations have suggested a date for Kratinos's *Thracian Women* between 435 and 430, and probably nearer the later date.[52] Kratinos's reference to the Odeion in this context thus provides a terminus ante quem for the construction of the building.

According to Plutarch, Perikles' association with the Odeion caused Kratinos to poke fun at him, and in the three lines quoted from the play we get a tantalizing glimpse of a marvelously comic scene. An actor on stage introduces the entrance of another character who is evidently supposed to be recognizable at once as Perikles in the guise of Zeus and wearing a funny hat. As often among the contemporary comic poets, it was Perikles' disproportionately large and apparently completely bald head that caused amusement, and here as elsewhere he is called "squill-head" (σχινοκέφαλος). In order to conceal this feature of his physiognomy, the statesman's later portraits all showed him wearing a helmet.[53] Accordingly, Kratinos has fitted out his character with outlandish headgear, and Perikles came on stage with the Odeion on his head. The joke was no doubt partly in the sheer size itself: the largest building in Athens made a good hat for the biggest Athenian head. But the reference seems more pointed, and Perikles' involvement with the Odeion more personal. Indeed, the third line of the quotation is a temporal clause that seems to explain why it is now all right for him to have the Odeion on his head: since the ostracism is over, Perikles can flaunt the great new building with impunity. Plutarch ends his discussion of the building program by recounting the continuous disputes between Thoukydides son of Melesias and his followers and Perikles and his supporters over the costs of the buildings; in that context he says that the two great political opponents underwent the contest of ostracism, which resulted in Thoukydides' removal from Athens.[54] After the political demise of Thoukydides, Perikles enjoyed continuous and unbroken rule for fifteen years by virtue of his annual reelection to the office of general.[55] Since he died in that office in the autumn of 429/8, the first of his fifteen consecutive elections would have been for the year 443/2, and the ostracism

[49] Kassel-Austin, *PCG* IV, *Thrattai* frag. 73 = Plut. *Per.* 13.10, quoted above, pp. 207–208.
[50] See P. Geissler, *Chronologie der altattischen Komödie* (Zurich 1969) 21–22. On the introduction of the cult of Bendis at Athens, Strabo 10.3.18 (p. 471). In the inventory of the property of the Other Gods for 429/8, the name Bendis was listed, the first two letters of which are still preserved on the stone, *IG* I³ 383, line 143. Cf. R. Garland, *Introducing New Gods* (London 1992) 111–114; Parker, *Athenian Religion*, 170–175.
[51] Kassel-Austin, *PCG* IV, *Thrattai* frag. 82 = schol. Aristoph. *Wasps* 592b (Koster-Holwerda). In Aristoph. *Acharn.* 710 with schol. 710b–c (Wilson), Euathlos is depicted as the troublesome young prosecutor of the aged Thoukydides son of Melesias. He was a pupil and protégé of Protagoras: Gellius, *Noct. att.* 5.10; Quintilian 3.1.10; and he is said to have subsequently prosecuted his teacher, Diog. Laert. 9.54. *LGPN* II, 162, s.v. Εὔαθλος (1).
[52] Geissler (note 50 above) dated the play 435 to 430. Kassel-Austin, *PCG* IV, 159, prefer ca. 430.
[53] Plut. *Per.* 3.3–5. That Perikles' head was unusually large is suggested by the image that Plut. *Per.* 3.6 paraphrases from the comic poet Telekleides (= Kassel-Austin, *PCG* VII, frag. 47), who speaks of "the eleven-couched dining chamber of his head" (with reference to a dining room large enough to accommodate eleven couches). Cf. also the line quoted from Hermippos (Kassel-Austin, *PCG* V, frag. 69): τὴν κεφαλὴν ὅσην ἔχει· ὅσην κολοκύτην, "What a big head he's got, as big as a pumpkin." That the comic word σχινοκέφαλος, "squill-head," was applied to Perikles because his head was also completely bald is suggested by Podlecki, *Perikles*, 172, and cf. 177–178.
[54] Plut. *Per.* 14.3: τέλος δὲ πρὸς τὸν Θουκυδίδην εἰς ἀγῶνα περὶ τοῦ ὀστράκου καταστὰς καὶ διακινδυνεύσας, ἐκεῖνον μὲν ἐξέβαλε, κατέλυσε δὲ τὴν ἀντιτεταγμένην ἑταιρείαν, "and finally he ventured to undergo with Thoukydides the contest of ostracism, wherein he secured his rival's banishment, and the dissolution of the faction which had been arrayed against him" (trans. B. Perrin, Loeb). Cf. Stadter, *Commentary*, 183–184.
[55] Plut. *Per.* 16.3: μετὰ δὲ τὴν Θουκυδίδου κατάλυσιν καὶ τὸν ὀστρακισμὸν οὐκ ἐλάττω τῶν πεντεκαίδεκα ἐτῶν διηνεκῆ καὶ μίαν οὖσαν ἐν ταῖς ἐνιαυσίοις στρατηγίαις ἀρχὴν καὶ δυναστείαν κτησάμενος..., "and after the deposition of Thoukydides and his ostracism, for no less than fifteen of these years did he secure an imperial sway that was continuous and unbroken, by means of his annual tenure of the office of general..." (trans. B. Perrin, Loeb). Cf. Stadter, *Commentary*, 183–184, 196; Wade-Gery, *EGH*, 240.

would fall before the eighth prytany in the spring of 443.[56] Between that date and the ostracism of Hyperbolos in 417, when the law was invoked for the last time, there is no hint in our sources of any other ostrakophoria being held.[57] It thus seems virtually certain that the reference in Kratinos's *Thracian Women* was to the ostracism of 443,[58] and that event should have followed shortly upon the completion of the Odeion, hence their juxtaposition in the playwright's description of Perikles. Lest it be thought that ten-year-old events were insufficiently topical for reference in Attic comedy, it needs to be emphasized that Perikles' continuing tenure as general became the more remarkable with each passing year and his was an era that began when the ostracism was over.[59]

Plutarch's narrative contains one other statement that helps to establish the date: he associates with the completion of the Odeion and the passing of the ostracism a decree of Perikles concerning the organization of musical contests at the Great Panathenaic festival. Mention of the decree is included almost parenthetically in Plutarch's discussion, seemingly to explain the purpose of the Odeion, for that building, he says, was the venue for the musical contests both in Perikles' day and in later times. Plutarch is likely to have known of the decree from a documentary source. Possibly he found the text along with the other Periklean decrees in the *Collection of Decrees* by Krateros of Macedon, which he elsewhere cites as a source.[60] Even from the brief summary of its contents, it is plain that the decree sought to introduce major changes into the program of the Panathenaic festival, for it "prescribes how the contestants should play the flute, and sing, and play the kithara." The three infinitives anticipate all four of the major musical competitions that are later attested as part of the program: instrumentalists on the double flute (*aulos*) and lyre (*kithara*), vocalists who sang to the music of the flute (*auloidoi*), and singers who accompanied themselves on the kithara (*kitharoidoi*).[61] It is a striking fact that winners of these contests, alone of all the games, received golden crowns and silver coin instead of the traditional prize amphoras of olive oil.[62] Most prestigious of the competitions was that for the *kitharoidoi*, in which the first prize was a golden crown worth one thousand drachmas, and five hundred silver drachmas in addition; but prizes of descending

---

[56] Thuc. 2.65.6 dates Perikles' death two years and six months after the outbreak of the war. Diod. 12.46.1 and Athenaeus 5.217E say only in the third year of the war, in the archonship of Epameinon (429/8). Cf. Plut. *Per.* 38.1–3 and Stadter, *Commentary*, 341–342. P. Krentz, *Historia* 33 (1984) 499–504, has sought to identify Thoukydides son of Melesias as the general of that name in 440/39 and has accordingly tried to lower the date of the ostracism to 438/7 or 437/6. His arguments have been convincingly refuted, however, by D. J. Phillips, *Historia* 40 (1991) 385–395. Philochoros, *FGrH* 328 F 30, places the annual vote whether or not to hold an ostrakophoria before the eighth prytany; cf. schol. Aristoph. *Knights* 885b (Koster). [Aristot.] *Ath. Pol.* 43.5 says the annual vote took place in the sixth prytany.

[57] The ostraka themselves and the actual known instances in which the law was invoked fall into three distinct and separate periods, the 480s, 461–443, and 417–415. See M. Lang, *Agora* XXV, 3–6, and, on the date of the ostracism of Hyperbolos, 64.

[58] Scholars who wish to dislodge the Odeion from the ostracism of 443 observe that there was an annual vote whether or not to hold an ostrakophoria: Robkin, "Odeion of Perikles," 39; M. Hose, *Philologus* 137 (1993) 7; Miller, *Athens and Persia*, 223. Kratinos's locution τοὔστρακον παροίχεται can therefore mean anytime after the sixth prytany of any year. This seems most unlikely in view of the way Philochoros (*FGrH* 328 F 30) describes the annual procedure: προεχειροτόνει μὲν ὁ δῆμος πρὸ τῆς ὀγδόης πρυτανείας, εἰ δοκεῖ τὸ ὄστρακον εἰσφέρειν, "the demos used to vote before the eighth prytany if it seemed best to introduce the ostrakon." This phraseology suggests that Kratinos's phrase should mean that the actual ostracism had taken place and not merely the annual vote.

[59] The ostracism of 443 was the great crisis of Athenian domestic politics of this period, and it is perfectly natural that Kratinos should refer to it thirteen years after the fact. Cf. Aristoph. *Peace* 603–606, which refers to the trial of Pheidias in 438 and alleges that Perikles fomented the war in 431 to avoid incrimination. These events took place ten and seventeen years, respectively, before the production of the play in 421. Cf. also Aristoph. *Lysistr.* 1137–1144, which refers to the great earthquake at Sparta and Kimon's expedition to bring military aid in 468/7, more than half a century before the date of the play in 411.

[60] Plut. *Per.* 8.7 says that no written works of Perikles survive except his decrees, which implies their collection as documents. Cf. Plut. *Kim.* 13.5; Plut. *Arist.* 26.1–4, where he cites Krateros as his source.

[61] The four musical competitions are attested in *IG* II² 2311, lines 4–20 (400–350), which lists all the prizes that were awarded in the games at the Great Panathenaia. See J. L. Shear, *ZPE* 142 (2003) 90–96.

[62] [Aristot.] *Ath. Pol.* 60.3.

value were awarded also to *kitharoidoi* who finished in second through fifth place.[63] To be sure, the inscription that lists these prizes in the Panathenaic games dates to the early fourth century, but the prizes in music may well go back to the Periklean reorganization of the contests.[64] Plutarch got the impression that Perikles' decree instituted musical contests at the Panathenaia for the very first time, no doubt because the speaker's language in some way conveyed that notion. Nevertheless, modern scholars have been quick to chastise the biographer for his error. In fact, a considerable corpus of Attic vases depicts flourishing musical contests from the mid-sixth century certainly down to the time of the Persian Wars, although it still seems likely that they were suspended thereafter until the time of Perikles' decree.[65]

The true significance of the decree, however, lies in what it tells us of Athens's deliberate aggrandizement of her religious festivals and cultural institutions as an instrument of Periklean policy. Perikles plainly hoped to attract to the Panathenaia the greatest professional musicians from all over the Greek world; and if the rich monetary prizes are contemporary, there was sweet inducement for them to come. Two pieces of evidence allow us to gauge the response of the musical world to the new contests at Athens, and both bear on the date of the Periklean decree and the completion of the Odeion. The first is a red-figure pelike by the Epimedes Painter datable to the years about 440.[66] A kithara player garbed in his festal robes stands on a three-stepped podium. The musician's name, Alkimachos, is inscribed beside the figure, and the quality of his work is proclaimed by another inscription on the second step of the podium: καλός. Four winged Nikai fly toward Alkimachos, two on each side, to symbolize professional victories that he has won with his music. Each is carefully labeled to commemorate the specific occasion: Παναθεναόι[ς] νίκη, Νεμέαι νίκη, Μαραθῶνι, Ἰσθμοῖ. The vase was obviously a special commission, made to order, no doubt, for a symposium to celebrate his most recent triumph. Before the date of its manufacture, ca. 440, he had won at two of the Panhellenic festivals, the Nemean and Isthmian games, and twice in Attica, at the Herakleia at Marathon and at the Great Panathenaia; thus Alkimachos's pelike provides a terminus ante quem for Perikles' decree and the new musical contests at the Panathenaia. If Alkimachos was an Athenian, he evidently traveled far and wide, like most of the great practitioners of his profession, for his pelike was found at Bresovo in Bulgaria.

The second piece of evidence concerns one of the most influential singers of the Classical period, a certain Phrynis who came from Mytilene on the island of Lesbos. A brief notice about his career has come down to us in the scholia on Aristophanes' *Clouds*, and in a slightly different version

[63] *IG* II² 2311, lines 4–7, first prize for *kitharoidoi;* lines 8–11, prizes in silver drachmas for second place 1,200, third place 600, fourth place 400, fifth place 300. Lines 12–14: first prize for *auloidoi* a crown worth 300 drachmas, second prize 100 drachmas. Lines 15–19: first prize for kithara players a crown worth 300 drachmas plus 200 in cash, second prize 200 (?), third prize 100. Lines 20–22: first prize for flute players a crown of unknown value, second prize not preserved.

[64] A gold crown for a victorious *kitharoidos* was dedicated in the Parthenon as early as 402/1 and listed in the treasurers' inventories: *SEG* 23.82, lines 30–31; *IG* II² 1385, lines 18–20 (400/399); 1388, lines 36–37 (398/7); see Harris, *Treasures*, V.416; J. L. Shear, *ZPE* 142 (2003) 95, note 33.

[65] Davison, *JHS* 78 (1958) 36–41 and *JHS* 82 (1962) 141–142, reviewed the ceramic material illustrating the musical contests of the sixth century and postulated a suspension in the contests from the Persian Wars to midcentury. This view has now been challenged by scholars who prefer to see a continuous sequence of vases documenting musical contests; argued most extensively by Kotsidu, *Musischen Agone*, 119–128, with detailed catalogue of vases, 293–300, 301–317. Cf. D. Schafter, *AJA* 95 (1991) 333–334; H. A. Shapiro, in Neils, ed., *Goddess and Polis*, 57, followed by Miller, *Athens and Persia*, 222. This argument is seriously flawed because the red-figure vases that are supposed to document the Panathenaic contests during the second quarter of the century are completely lacking in specific Panathenaic imagery; listed by Kotsidu, 307–309, 312–315, nos. V 52–73, V 103–131. Most recent discussion of the musical contests, J. L. Shear, "Polis and Panathenaia," 352–365.

[66] Plovdiv (no inv.): *ARV*² 1044, no. 9; Kotsidu, *Musischen Agone*, 118, 120, 309, no. V 81; T. Hölscher, *Victoria Romana* (Mainz 1967) 176, pl. 16:8. Cf. J. L. Shear, "Polis and Panathenaia," 359.

in the later *Suda* lexicon, which quotes in part from a book *Lyric Poets* attributed to the Hellenistic historian Istros (*FGrH* 334 F 56):[67]

ὁ Φρῦνις κιθαρωιδός, Μιτυληναῖος· οὗτος δὲ δοκεῖ πρῶτος κιθαρίσαι παρ᾽ Ἀθηναίοις καὶ νικῆσαι Παναθήναια ἐπὶ Καλλίου ἄρχοντος. ἦν δὲ Ἀριστοκλείδου μαθητής, ὁ δὲ Ἀριστοκλείδης κιθαρωιδὸς ἦν ἄριστος. τὸ γένος ἦν ἀπὸ Τερπάνδρου, ἤκμασε δ᾽ ἐν τῆι Ἑλλάδι κατὰ τὰ Μηδικά. παραλαβὼν δὲ τὸν Φρῦνιν αὐλωιδοῦντα κιθαρίζειν ἐδίδαξεν. Ἴστρος δὲ ἐν τοῖς ἐπιγραφομένοις Μελοποιοῖς τὸν Φρῦνιν Λέσβιόν φησιν, Κάμωμος υἱόν· τοῦτον δὲ Ἱέρωνος τοῦ τυράννου μάγειρον ὄντα δοθῆναι σὺν ἄλλοις πολλοῖς Ἀριστοκλείδηι. ταῦτα δὲ σχεδιάσαι ἔοικεν· εἰ γὰρ ἦν γεγονὼς δοῦλος καὶ μάγειρος Ἱέρωνος, οὐκ ἂν ἀπέκρυψαν οἱ κωμικοί, πολλάκις αὐτοῦ μεμνημένοι ἐφ᾽ οἷς ἐκαινούργησε, κλάσας τὴν ὠιδὴν παρὰ τὸ ἀρχαῖον ἔθος, ὡς Ἀριστοφάνης φησὶ καὶ Ἀριστοκράτης.

Phrynis, the Mytilenean *kitharoidos:*[68] He seems to have played the kithara for the first time at Athens and to have won the Panathenaia in the archonship of Kallias. He was a pupil of Aristokleides, who was the greatest of the *kitharoidoi*. The family was descended from Terpander, and he himself flourished in Greece at the time of the Persian Wars. Having taken on Phrynis as an *auloidos*, he taught him to play the kithara. In the book entitled *Lyric Poets*, Istros says that Phrynis was from Lesbos and the son of Kamon; that he was a cook for the tyrant Hieron and was given to Aristokleides along with a number of other slaves. This is likely to be a spurious tale, for if he had actually been a slave and cook for Hieron, the comic poets would not have concealed the fact, considering the many times they mentioned him for his musical innovations and for modulating the style of singing contrary to the ancient mode, as Aristophanes and Aristokrates say.

Phrynis came from a long and distinguished line of Lesbian *kitharoidoi* going back to Terpander in the seventh century. According to the scholia, he visited Athens for the first time in the archonship of Kallias and won a victory at the Great Panathenaia. This statement appears to provide an exact date before which the Periklean reorganization of the musical contests must have taken place, since Phrynis won a Panathenaic victory; but unfortunately the date is not entirely free of problems. The Athenian archon list shows that three men named Kallias held the office of eponymous archon during the fifth century, in 456/5, 412/11, and 406/5.[69] The musical contests were, of course, a part of the international festival and would only have been held at the Great Panathenaia, which was celebrated in the third year of each Olympiad. Since 456/5 and 412/11 both fall in the first year of the Olympiad, the international games were not a part of either festival, and Phrynis's first victory at Athens cannot be dated to either of those years. Since scholars have generally regarded 406/5 as impossibly late in the century for Phrynis's first victory at Athens, the best solution to the problem has been found in an easy emendation of the text. Where the manuscripts have the words ἐπὶ Καλλίου ἄρχοντος, the name should actually be read as ἐπὶ Καλλι<μάχ>ου ἄρχοντος.[70] Kallimachos was the eponymous archon of 446/5,[71] and, that being the third year of an Olympiad, he presided at a

---

[67] Schol. RV Aristoph. *Clouds* 971a, β (Koster); a fuller version of the notice quoting Istros, *FGrH* 334 F 56, appears in schol. EMA Aristoph. *Clouds* 97a, α (Koster) = *Suda*, s.v. Φρῦνις (φ 761 Adler), whence Jacoby's text quoted here.

[68] Phrynis son of Kamon: *LGPN* I, s.vv. Φρῦνις, 476; Κάμων (2) 251. The *Suda*, s.v. Φρῦνις, gives the patronymic as Κάνωπος, but for the correct form of the name, Page, *PMG*, 802, Timotheus.

[69] Archon of 456/5: Diod. 11.84.1; Dion. Hal. *Ant. Rom.* 10.26.1. Archon of 412/11: Diod. 13.34.1; [Aristot.] *Ath. Pol.* 32.1; *IG* I³ 97, line 5. Archon of 406/5: Diod. 13.80.1; Xen. *Hell.* 1.6.1; [Aristot.] *Ath. Pol.* 34.1; *IG* I³ 124, line 3.

[70] So Jacoby, *FGrH* 334 F 56, and cf. 3 B suppl. 655; M. L. West, *Ancient Greek Music* (Oxford 1992) 360 and note 15. Cf. Robkin, *AncW* 2 (1979) 3–6, with references; Robkin, "Odeion of Perikles," 38.

[71] Diod. 12.7.1, 10.3.

celebration of the Great Panathenaia. This year has accordingly been widely accepted as the occasion for Phrynis's visit to Athens and his musical victory.

Other chronological indications in the scholia agree well with a date in the mid-440s for Phrynis's Panathenaic victory. His music teacher was Aristokleides, who claimed descent from Terpander, and he is specifically said to have been in his prime at the time of the Persian Wars, that is to say, between thirty and thirty-five years of age.[72] Whether or not Phrynis was ever in the service of Hieron of Syracuse, the period of his tyranny from 478 to 467 could be associated with Phrynis's youthful years by later writers.[73] He can hardly have been much younger than fifteen in about 470, for he had been trained to sing to the flute before he came under the tutelage of Aristokleides and learned to accompany himself on the kithara. He was presumably working with Aristokleides before 467 or there would be no reason to associate his name in any way with the tyrant Hieron, who died in that year. In 446/5, Phrynis would have been approaching the height of his powers, at thirty-nine years of age, when he visited Athens and won at the Panathenaia. Despite these indications, there have been recent attempts to lower the dates of Phrynis's career, to identify the Kallias of the scholia as the archon of 406/5, and to date the famous *kitharoidos*'s first victory to the Great Panathenaia of that year.[74] But it is important to emphasize that the scholia exist because they were thought to elucidate Aristophanes' casual reference to the great singer in the *Clouds*, where he speaks of his music as τὰς κατὰ Φρῦνιν ταύτας τὰς δυσκολοκάμπτους, "those annoying twists in the style of Phrynis."[75] Plainly, in 423, when the *Clouds* was produced, Phrynis was well known in Athens and the style of his music already notorious.[76] It makes no sense to comment on this line that "he first played the kithara at Athens and won at the Panathenaia in 406/5." Moreover, if the age of his teacher and the dates of his own career as suggested above are anywhere near correct, in 406/5 Phrynis would no longer have been the powerful operatic virtuoso that one expects of a Panathenaic victor, but in fact a quavering octogenarian.

Our evidence for the date of construction of the Odeion can hardly be called satisfactory. At most it can be said that musical contests were a part of the Great Panathenaic festival in the 440s, when two different victories are attested, that of Phrynis the *kitharoidos* apparently in 446/5, and that of Alkimachos the kithara player at some time before ca. 440. The decree of Perikles described by Plutarch ought to antedate both these events. It is possible that both musicians performed before the ostracism of 443, as Kratinos seems to imply; but this is about as much as we can infer from the available evidence.

---

[72] Aristot. *Rhet.* 2.14.4, 1390b9, says that the body is at its prime (ἀκμάζει) between thirty and thirty-five, and the mind at forty-nine.

[73] Date of Hieron's accession, Diod. 11.38.7; date of his death, Diod. 11.66.4.

[74] Hose, *Philologus* 137 (1993) 3–11, followed by Miller, *Athens and Persia*, 222. Cf. West, *Ancient Greek Music*, 63–64, who dates Phrynis's career ca. 490–420, which would make him forty-four in 446/5. It should be observed that both Hose (p. 5) and Miller (p. 222) quote only the first sentence of the notice about Phrynis quoted in full above. This enables them to omit all reference to Phrynis's teacher, Aristokleides, to the implied dates for his career and to the quotation attributed to Istros concerning his service for Hieron of Syracuse. These earlier chronological indications cohere badly with their proposed date of 406/5 for Phrynis's first Panathenaic victory.

[75] Aristoph. *Clouds* 971, trans. Sommerstein.

[76] The point was well emphasized by Davison, *JHS* 78 (1958) 40. There can be no doubt that Phrynis's style was new and notorious: [Plut.] *De musica, Mor.* 1133B, 1141C–D, especially Pherekrates, Kassel-Austin, *PCG* 7 F 155 = [Plut.] *Mor.* 1141E–F. See West, *Ancient Greek Music*, 194–196; W. D. Anderson, *Music and Musicians in Ancient Greece* (Ithaca, NY, 1994) 127–132.

THE TENT OF XERXES

By far the most curious and surprising piece of information about the Odeion is the tradition preserved by both Plutarch and Pausanias[77] that the building was built in imitation (μίμημα, ἐς μίμησιν) of the tent of Xerxes. Modern writers about the Odeion have tended to regard that tradition as an invention of the Roman period because this is the date of the ancient authors who preserve the information. Since the Odeion did not conform to the standard Roman architectural type of the roofed theater, people thought it looked odd and hence Persian.[78] It is difficult to imagine, however, who in Roman Athens was sufficiently knowledgeable about Persian architecture to make the comparison, especially in view of the fact that Alexander had torched Persepolis, and the old Persian homeland, as part of the Parthian kingdom, was inaccessible even to the Roman legions. One scholar has recently found it preferable simply to reject the statements of Plutarch and Pausanias and then to invent possible occasions when Athenian diplomats of the fifth century might have viewed Persian architecture with their own eyes.[79] In order to disparage further the evidence of Pausanias, it is observed that he did not call the building the Odeion but merely a "structure" (κατασκεύασμα), from which his ignorance is to be inferred. It is interesting to notice, however, that Herodotos used a closely similar locution to describe the tent captured by the Greeks after the Battle of Plataia, which he calls a κατασκευή (9.82), but the same establishment is called a σκήνη (tent) at 7.119. The identical word κατασκευὴ ἡ βασιλική was used by Arrian (*Anab.* 3.15.5) to describe another Persian royal tent that Alexander the Great captured from Darius III at Arbela after the battle at Gaugamela in 331.

Before dismissing the statements of Plutarch and Pausanias as anachronistic misunderstanding, we might with profit inquire how exactly the campaign tent of the Great King of Persia might have looked, and what Plutarch and Pausanias, or their sources, meant when they said that the Odeion was an exact reproduction of one. When Xerxes fled from Greece upon defeat of his navy at Salamis, Herodotos says (9.82) that he left behind his campaign tent for Mardonios's use and that it was later captured by the Greek forces in the Persian camp at Plataia.[80] The tent is mentioned on several occasions during the expedition of 480 and 479. Herodotos described the hardships that befell the towns of Macedonia and Thrace which had been ordered to provision the Persian army when the great expeditionary force was outside Akanthos in the Chalkidike (Hdt. 7.119):

> ὅκως δὲ ἀπίκοιτο ἡ στρατιή, σκηνὴ μὲν ἔσκε πεπηγυῖα ἑτοίμη ἐς τὴν αὐτὸς σταθμὸν ποιεέσκετο Ξέρξης, ἡ δὲ ἄλλη στρατιὴ ἔσκε ὑπαίθριος. ὡς δὲ δείπνου ἐγίνετο ὥρη, οἱ μὲν δεκόμενοι ἔχεσκον πόνον, οἳ δὲ ὅκως πλησθέντες νύκτα αὐτοῦ ἀγάγοιεν, τῇ ὑστεραίῃ τήν τε σκηνὴν ἀνασπάσαντες καὶ τὰ ἔπιπλα πάντα λαβόντες οὕτω ἀπελαύνεσκον, λείποντες οὐδὲν ἀλλὰ φερόμενοι.

When the army arrived, there was always a tent set up and ready in which Xerxes himself made his lodging, but the rest of the army camped in the open air. When the hour came for dinner, their hosts had a laborious task, while they themselves, having eaten their fill,

---

[77] Quoted above, pp. 207, 208.

[78] Meinel, *Odeion*, 154; B. K. Lambrinoudakis, Ὀικοδομικά προγράμματα στην ἀρχαία Ἀθήνα ἀπὸ το 479 ἕως το 431 π. X. (Athens 1986) 132; Miller, *Athens and Persia*, 223–224.

[79] Miller, *Athens and Persia*, 223–224, 236, 238; cf. Robkin, "Odeion of Perikles," 167.

[80] Miller, *Athens and Persia*, 236, misconstrues Hdt. 9.82 when she implies that Mardonios's tent was not Xerxes': Herodotos "adds that 'it was said' that Xerxes gave his kataskeue to Mardonios." Λέγεται δὲ καὶ τάδε γενέσθαι, "it is said that the following incident happened." These words introduce the entire anecdote about Pausanias's dinner, and the whole of 9.82 is written in indirect discourse with accusative and infinitive construction. That Xerxes left behind his *kataskeue* for Mardonios is stated as a fact in a subordinate clause.

would pass the night in the place. On the next morning, having pulled down the tent and packed up the utensils and all the furnishings, they would march on, leaving nothing behind but carrying off everything.

We next hear of the royal tent on the night before the Battle of Thermopylai, when Diodoros (11.9.4–10.4) recounts an altogether incredible night assault on the Persian camp by the Spartan forces under Leonidas. According to Diodoros, the Greeks broke into the king's tent and killed many of his retainers but failed to find Xerxes himself. Then, a little over a year later, in the aftermath of the Battle of Plataia, the tent was captured and plundered by the victorious Greeks. The contingent from Tegea was the first of the Greeks to reach the royal tent, and they made off with a remarkable bronze manger from the stables that they later dedicated in the Temple of Athena Alea (Hdt. 9.70). Finally, Herodotos describes briefly the extraordinary opulence of the furnishings, fitted out with gold and silver and richly colored tapestries (9.82). He mentions the many cooks and bakers who prepared a banquet for the Spartan general Pausanias, and he depicts the frugal Greek as struck with amazement at the splendor of the gold and silver dining couches and tables, and the magnificent plate of the banquet service. Herodotos's description conveys the impression of a large and complex structure that included stables for horses and accommodated a retinue of many retainers. His account dwells particularly on the lavish display of prodigious wealth in the fittings and furnishing of the tent, but there is no sense of the shape and actual appearance of the structure.

By long tradition, the Great King of Persia traveled on military campaign with his household and harem and displays of truly extravagant luxury. Even in times of peace, the king's household and entire royal court perambulated seasonally among the four capitals of the empire, wintering in Susa, summering in Ecbatana, passing the autumn months in Persepolis, and then spending the remainder of the year in Babylon.[81] The trip from Susa to Babylon along the royal road was a twenty-day march, whereas the journey from Persepolis to Susa was a twenty-four-day march, and farthest of all was the trip from Susa to Ecbatana, which took forty days.[82] We may be sure that the Great King lodged amid the luxury of the royal tent on these regular seasonal journeys. On several occasions the royal tent chanced to be mentioned in the Greek literary tradition in such a way as to allow us to understand more clearly what it was that the Greeks captured after the Battle of Plataia. Xenophon (*Cyrop.* 5.5.2) writes of Cyrus the Great in the mid-sixth century that he ordered a tent captured from the Assyrian king to be set up for Cyaxares and selected the women to be installed in the women's quarters (γυναικῶν τῆς σκηνῆς). A similar tent was captured by Alexander the Great from Darius III after the Battle of Issos in 333, and among the occupants of its women's quarters were the mother, wife, and unmarried daughters of the Persian king. But according to Plutarch, what really astonished the Macedonian was the luxury of the bath (*Alex.* 20.13):

ὡς δ' εἶδε μὲν ὅλκια καὶ κρωσσοὺς καὶ πυέλους καὶ ἀλαβάστρους, πάντα χρυσοῦ, δι-ηρσκημένα περιττῶς, ὠδώδει δὲ θεσπέσιον οἷον ὑπ' ἀρωμάτων καὶ μύρων ὁ οἶκος, ἐκ δὲ τούτου παρῆλθεν εἰς σκηνὴν ὕψει τε καὶ μεγέθει καὶ τῷ περὶ τὴν στρωμνὴν καὶ <τὰς> τραπέζας καὶ τὸ δεῖπνον αὐτὸ κόσμῳ θαύματος ἀξίαν, διαβλέψας πρὸς τοὺς ἑταίρους, "τοῦτ' ἦν ὡς ἔοικεν" ἔφη "τὸ βασιλεύειν."

When he saw the basins and ewers and bathing tubs and perfume flasks, all of gold, and marvelously wrought, while the apartment was divinely fragrant from spices and unguents, and when from this he passed into a tent that was worthy of wonder for its height

---

[81] The seasonal movements of the royal court are described by Athenaeus 12.513F; cf. Xen. *Cyrop.* 8.6.22, who places the court in the capitals in different seasons. On the significance of these movements, P. Briant, *IrAnt* 23 (1988) 253–272.

[82] Distance from Susa to Babylon, Arrian, *Anab.* 3.16.7; Susa to Persepolis, Diod. 19.21.2; Susa to Ecbatana, Diod. 19.19.2.

and size and for the luxury of the couch and tables and the dinner prepared for him, turning his glance upon his companions, he said, "This, it would seem, is to be a king."

Before the battle, Darius had dispatched most of his baggage and retinue to Damascus, where it was later captured by Parmenion, who prepared an inventory of the household staff in a *Letter to Alexander* preserved by Athenaeus (13.608A):

παλλακίδας εὗρον μουσουργοὺς τοῦ βασιλέως τριακοσίας εἴκοσι ἐννέα, ἄνδρας στεφανοπλόκους ἓξ καὶ τεσσαράκοντα, ὀψοποιοὺς διακοσίους ἑβδομήκοντα ἑπτά, χυτρεψοὺς εἴκοσι ἐννέα, γαλακτουργοὺς τρεισκαίδεκα, ποτηματοποιοὺς ἑπτακαίδεκα, οἰνοηθητὰς ἑβδομήκοντα, μυροποιοὺς τεσσαράκοντα.

I discovered concubines of the king who played musical instruments, to the number of 329; men employed to weave crowns, 46; caterers, 277; kettle tenders, 29; pudding makers, 13; bartenders, 17; wine strainers, 70; perfume makers, 40.

Parmenion's list conveys some inkling of the extraordinary numbers of specialized retainers who regularly traveled with the king and required accommodations in the royal tent.

The luxury of the king's tent may at first have been a source of wonder and surprise to Alexander, but it was a style of living for which he quickly acquired a taste. In the years after his conquest of Persia and the East, Alexander's court became notorious for its level of extravagant luxury. Several accounts have come down to us of the great tent that was erected at Susa in 324 for the multiple weddings of Alexander and his companions to women of the Persian aristocracy.[83] All surviving descriptions of this remarkable structure undoubtedly derive from the tenth book of the *Histories of Alexander* by Chares of Mytilene, who was a royal usher at Alexander's court and therefore wrote from first-hand knowledge (Athenaeus 12.538B–D):[84]

ὅτε εἷλε Δαρεῖον, γάμους συνετέλεσεν ἑαυτοῦ τε καὶ τῶν ἄλλων φίλων, ἐνενήκοντα καὶ δύο θαλάμους κατασκευασάμενος ἐν τῷ αὐτῷ τόπῳ. ἦν δὲ ὁ οἶκος ἑκατοντάκλινος, ἐν ᾧ ἑκάστη ἦν κλίνη κεκοσμημένη στολῇ γαμικῇ εἴκοσι μνῶν ἀργυρᾶ· ἡ δὲ αὐτοῦ χρυσόπους ἦν. . . . κατεσκεύαστο δὲ ὁ οἶκος πολυτελῶς καὶ μεγαλοπρεπῶς ἱματίοις τε καὶ ὀθονίοις πολυτελέσιν, ὑπὸ δὲ ταῦτα πορφυροῖς καὶ φοινικοῖς χρυσουφέσιν. τοῦ δὲ μένειν τὴν σκηνὴν ὑπέκειντο κίονες εἰκοσαπήχεις περίχρυσοι καὶ διάλιθοι καὶ περιάργυροι. περιεβέβληντο δὲ ἐν τῷ περιβόλῳ πολυτελεῖς αὐλαῖαι ζωωτοὶ καὶ διάχρυσοι, κανόνας ἔχουσαι περιχρύσους καὶ περιαργύρους. τῆς δ' αὐλῆς ἦν τὸ περίμετρον στάδιοι τέσσαρες.

When he had defeated Darius, he arranged marriages of himself and of his friends as well and erected ninety-two bridal chambers in the same place. The hall was large enough for a hundred couches, and every couch in it was adorned with nuptial bedclothes and was made of silver worth twenty minae; but his own had feet of gold. . . . Moreover, the apartment was fitted out sumptuously and magnificently with costly draperies and fine linens, and underfoot with carpets of purple and crimson interwoven with gold. To keep it firmly in place, the tent was supported by columns twenty cubits high, overlaid with gold and silver and set with precious stones. The entire enclosure was surrounded with rich curtains decorated with animal patterns embroidered in gold, and having rods plated with gold and silver. The perimeter of the courtyard measured four stadia.

---

[83] Plut. *Alex.* 20.11–13, 21.1; Arrian, *Anab.* 2.11.9–10; Diod. 17.36.2–4.

[84] Chares, *FGrH* 125 F 4 = Athenaeus 12.538B–F (B–D quoted here). Plut. *Alex.* 46 calls him a royal usher. Aelian, *Var. Hist.* 8.7, and Polyainos 4.3.24 both describe the same tent, but the wording is so close to Athenaeus 12.538B–F that they must have used his text as a source.

The same pavilion was described again by the third-century historian Phylarchos, who had occasion to refer to it in his discussion of the extravagant luxuries of Alexander's court:[85]

> ἦν γὰρ αὐτοῦ ἡ σκηνὴ κλινῶν ρ', χρυσοῖς δὲ κίονες ν' κατεῖχον αὐτήν. οἱ δὲ ὑπερτείνον-
> τες οὐρανίσκοι διάχρυσοι ποικίλμασιν ἐκπεπονημένοι πολυτελέσιν ἐσκέπαζον τὸν ἄνω
> τόπον.

> His tent had a hundred couches and was supported by fifty columns. The canopies
> stretched over the upper part to cover the whole were elaborately worked with gold in
> sumptuous embroideries.

Phylarchos went on to enumerate the elements of the army that were stationed in and around the tent when Alexander held court, seated on a golden throne at the center of the pavilion. Within the audience chamber itself were five hundred Persian guards, one thousand bowmen, five hundred Macedonians from the special contingent called Silver Shields, and an unspecified number of bodyguards drawn up in close order around the king. Outside, presumably in the courtyard, the elephant division stood guard with full equipment; in addition, there were a thousand Macedonians, ten thousand Persians, and five hundred more who had been granted the privilege of wearing the purple mantle. The figures, of course, are probably rounded and may well be exaggerated, but they serve to convey some impression of the enormous scale and complexity of these extraordinary portable palaces with which the Achaemenid kings moved around their empire.

These ancient descriptions of royal campaign tents help us to form a general picture of their appearance and appurtenances. They were equipped with stables for horses, bathing facilities, and private quarters for the royal women and harem. The pavilion used for the weddings at Susa had ninety-two bridal chambers provided for the occasion, and one infers that such private quarters could be reconfigured as needed without great difficulty. What most attracted the wondering gaze of Greeks, however, were the great open tents, notable for their size and height, that could accommodate more than two thousand people for a royal audience, or a hundred couches around the perimeter for a royal banquet. The tent in which Alexander entertained was supported by fifty columns that were 20 cubits (ca. 36 feet) high, and it opened onto a square courtyard measuring some six hundred feet on a side (the περίμετρον was four stades). The particular emphasis on the great size of the apartment and its many columns calls to mind a large hypostyle hall with multiple rows of columns, an architectural arrangement not unlike the plan of the Odeion in Athens. But the royal tents evidently had a variety of subsidiary installations in addition to the principal pavilion. Description of the courtyard as having a perimeter of four stades implies that it was enclosed on its other three sides with additional tents, probably of less imposing height. These provided space for the private quarters of the king and his women, for baths and stables, and for service facilities for the large retinue of cooks and stewards who served the king.

The most essential requirement of a campaign tent, no matter its size and complexity, is that its components be easily transportable. It must be possible to erect it at the end of a day's march and pull it down the next morning, as Herodotos (7.119) specifically reports about the tent of Xerxes. In this light it is particularly interesting to observe how sumptuously decorated textiles dominate the descriptions of the Persian royal tents. We hear of draperies and fine linens, and carpets spread on the ground. Chares described the richly embroidered curtains that hung around the whole enclosure (περιεβέβληντο δὲ ἐν τῷ περιβόλῳ [Athenaeus 538D]), while other writers commented on the canopies stretched out to cover the upper part, forming, as it were, the roof of the tent (οἱ δὲ ὑπερτεί-νοντες οὐρανίσκοι ... ἐσκέπαζον τὸν ἄνω τόπον [539E]). Tents, of course, do not have rooms and

---

[85] Phylarchos, *FGrH* 81 F 41, from book 23 of the *Histories* = Athenaeus 12.539C–F (D–E quoted here). Cf. Polyainos 4.3.24, where the same pavilion is said to have served as a courtroom.

walls and a roof; thus the descriptions seem curiously imprecise because these structural elements must all be fashioned of cloth or other material to enable them to be folded for transport. The only other essential structural elements are the poles that stretch and support the material of the tent and are themselves held fast by ropes attached to pegs driven into the ground. On the scale of Alexander's pavilion, the tent poles have become columns twenty cubits high, fifty in number, and doubtless arranged in multiple rows, which were fixed beneath the tent to hold it fast in position (τοῦ δὲ μένειν τὴν σκήνην ὑπέκειντο κίονες [538D]).

Another important detail of the tent's outward appearance emerges from the description of the one captured from Darius III, as reported in the Latin *History of Alexander* by Quintus Curtius Rufus:

> Die iam illustri signum e tabernaculo regis bucina debatur; super tabernaculum, unde ob omnibus conspici posset, imago solis crystallo inclusa fulgebat.

> When the day was already bright, the signal was given from the king's tent with the horn; above the tent, from which it might be seen by all, there gleamed an image of the sun enclosed in crystal.[86]

The Latin locution implies that the decorative "image of the sun" could be seen by the whole army because it adorned the central peak of the tent, from which the uppermost textile canopies descended on all sides to form a structure of pyramidal shape. It was precisely this same pyramidal shape of the roof, "sloping on all sides, downward from a single peak," that Plutarch (*Per.* 13.9) particularly emphasized as a most distinctive feature of the Odeion at Athens. Thus the few references to Persian royal tents afforded by the classical literary tradition suggest that their most important element was a lofty open pavilion whose structural components were arranged in multiple rows like the columns of a great hypostyle hall. If the cloth canopies and wooden poles of such a structure were translated into the stone walls and columns of permanent architecture, there would emerge a building closely resembling the Odeion at Athens.

Persian Architectural Sources

It is also apparent from the literary descriptions that the principal pavilions of the royal tents must have resembled portable versions of the most characteristic unit of all Achaemenid royal architecture, the apadana. That term, found in Old Persian royal inscriptions, specifically designated the enormous square hypostyle halls, with stone columns of great height, that served as the audience halls of the Great King.[87] The architectural type was canonized by Darius I (r. 522–486) early in his reign, and in its majestic form and overpowering scale came to symbolize the imperial ideology of Persian rule. The earliest such palatial audience hall was the Apadana at Susa, which dominates the northern end of a great terrace 32 acres in extent and rising 18 m above the surrounding city. The building's external dimensions measured 109 m on each side and enclosed a single vast hall (58 × 58 m) whose roof was supported by thirty-six columns, arranged in six rows of six, with square bases, fluted shafts, and composite capitals. The mud-brick walls of the hall, originally 5.20 m thick and more than 20 m high,

---

[86] Curtius 3.3.9, trans. J. C. Rolfe (Loeb).

[87] The word "apadana" occurs in a text of Artaxerxes II (r. 405–359) inscribed on stone column bases from the Apadana at Susa (A2Sa): R. G. Kent, *Old Persian*, 154. The king states that the apadana built by his great-great-grandfather, Darius I, and burned in the reign of his grandfather, Artaxerxes I, was restored by himself. The term appears also in an inscription of Darius II (r. 425–405) from Susa (D2Sa) and two others of Artaxerxes II from Hamadān (A2Ha, A2Hb), Kent, 154–155. On the significance of the architectural term, see D. Stronach, in J.-L. Huot et al., eds., *De l'Indus aux Balkans: Recueil à la mémoire de Jean Deshayes* (Paris 1985) 433–437.

were flanked by square towers at the four corners which framed deep columnar porticoes on the north, east, and west sides. The porticoes consisted of two rows of six stone columns aligned with the columns of the main hall within. On the south side, a court gave direct access to the residential complex of the palace.[88] Construction of the Apadana was given priority over the residential parts of the palace, as can be deduced from the trilingual inscriptions known as the "Foundation Charter."[89] These documents for the Apadana were drawn up when Darius's father, Hystaspes, was still alive, and thus near the beginning of the reign, whereas the closely similar texts found in the residential palace offer no prayer for Hystaspes' welfare and were presumably inscribed after his death.[90]

On the monumental terrace at Persepolis, Darius began construction of another audience hall almost identical in plan and even more imposing in its siting because it stands on a platform 2.60 m above the surrounding courtyards; it is thus approached on the north and east by monumental stairways whose facades are adorned with magnificent sculptural reliefs. The building's exterior dimensions were 112 m on each side, while the main hall within measured 60.50 m on a side. Its three external porticoes on the north, east, and west sides, and its thirty-six interior columns, spaced 8.50 m on centers, exactly replicate the arrangement of the Apadana at Susa.[91] The foundation of the Apadana at Persepolis was memorialized by inscribed tablets of gold and silver found buried beneath the fabric of its mud-brick walls.[92] Deposited together with the inscribed tablets was a handful of gold and silver coins, the latest of which was a stater of Cypriote Paphos that has been dated to the early fifth century.[93] If the great hall was begun at the beginning of the fifth century, it was not completed before Darius's death in 486; for inscriptions of Xerxes (r. 486–465/4) on glazed bricks set high in the walls of the corner towers refer to that king's completion of a building begun by his father, Darius.[94]

Largest of all such columnar halls was the Hall of One Hundred Columns, or Throne Hall, erected beside the Apadana on the eastern half of the terrace at Persepolis. The vast square of its

[88] For the excavated remains on the Apadana mound, see R. Ghirshman, *IrAnt* 3 (1963) 148–154; J. Perrot, *Iran* 8 (1970) 190–194, *Iran* 9 (1971) 178–181, *Iran* 10 (1972) 181–183; Perrot et al., *Cahiers de la DAFI* 4 (1974); R. Boucharlat, in *Centre and Periphery: Proceedings of the Groningen 1986 Achaemenid History Workshop* (Leiden 1990) 149–175, with earlier references; and the useful summary of O. W. Muscarella, in P. O. Harper et al., eds., *The Royal City of Susa* (New York 1992) 216–219.

[89] The inscription DSf. For text and translation of the Old Persian version, Kent, *Old Persian*, 142–144, with additions from M.-J. Stève, *StIr* 3 (1974) 145–147; for the Elamite text and translation, F. Vallat, *StIr* 1 (1972) 8–11; for the Akkadian text and translation, Stève (above), 155–161. Cf. the useful summary of M. W. Stolper, in Harper et al., eds., *Royal City of Susa*, 271–272.

[90] For the Elamite and Akkadian inscriptions found in the residential palace (DSz and DSaa), Vallat, *Syria* 48 (1971) 57–59; the Elamite text and translation revised, Vallat, *StIr* 1 (1972) 10–13. DSz omits the opening invocation of Ahuramazda found in DSf, lines 1–4. The latter text concludes, lines 56–58: "Me may Ahuramazda protect, and Hystaspes my father, and my country" (Kent, *Old Persian*, 144). The text of DSz ends, lines 55–56: "Me may Ahuramazda protect, and also my country" (Vallat, *StIr* 1 [1972] 13), from which Vallat (pp. 4–5) concludes that DSf was inscribed before DSz. Cf. Stronach, in *Recueil Deshayes*, 438–439, with a date for the foundation of the Apadana ca. 521 (444). Stolper, in Harper et al., eds., *Royal City of Susa*, 271, dates DSf ca. 518.

[91] For detailed description of the Apadana at Persepolis, E. Schmidt, *Persepolis*, vol. 1 (Chicago 1953) 70–90; cf. the architectural restorations by F. Krefter, *Persepolis Rekonstruktionen* (Berlin 1971) Beil. 3–5, 25–29. Stronach, in *Recueil Deshayes*, 439–445, compares the architecture of the halls at Persepolis and Susa. For development of the architectural type, W. Kleiss, *IrAnt* 15 (1980) 199–211.

[92] The metal plates bore identical trilingual inscriptions (DPh): Kent, *Old Persian*, 136–137; cf. Schmidt, *Persepolis*, vol. 1, 70, 79. Since the texts make no mention of Thrace as the western limit of the empire, Schmidt concluded that they were deposited before the campaign against the European Scythians, probably in 513, but no later than 511 (*Persepolis*, vol. 1, 39, 70; *Persepolis*, vol. 2, 110).

[93] For the coins from the foundation deposits, Schmidt, *Persepolis*, vol. 2, 110; for the stater of Paphos, 114 and pl. 84:38. Dated to the early fifth century, M. Price and N. Waggoner, *Archaic Greek Coinage: The Asyut Hoard* (London 1975) 16. Stronach, in *Recueil Deshayes*, 442–445, argues rightly that the date of the latest coin must lower accordingly the date at which construction of the Apadana began. Cf. also M. D. Roaf, *Iran* 21 (1983) 138–139, 157.

[94] Inscriptions from the corner towers (XPg), Kent, *Old Persian*, 150. Inscriptions of Xerxes are also engraved on panels next to the reliefs on the northern and eastern stairways (XPb): Kent, 148.

interior measured 68.40 m on a side, and its roof was supported by ten rows of ten columns spaced 6.20 m on centers. Unlike the Apadana, it has towers only at its two northern corners and was approached on this side only, by way of a portico consisting of sixteen columns arranged in two rows aligned with the rows of interior columns.[95] The building has usually been dated to the second quarter of the fifth century. It is thought to have been planned and begun by Xerxes and completed by Artaxerxes I sometime between his accession in 465/4 and the middle of the century, as is stated on an inscribed tablet of the latter king that was found in the southeast corner of the hall.[96]

The great columnar halls called the apadana at Susa and Persepolis came to be the distinguishing hallmark of Achaemenid architecture. From the time of their foundation by Darius I, they expressed in the symbolic language of architecture the very essence of the Persian ruling power, for their form was at once and ever afterward specifically associated with the conduct of royal business and the administration of the empire. Although Darius's architects achieved the classic statement of the architectural form, it is important to recognize that the columnar hall has deep roots in the archaeological history of western Iran and long association with political power.[97] At the site of Hasanlu in Azerbaijan, the fortified citadel was crowned by a complex of buildings, at least five of which have columnar halls as their principal apartment. All date to the Iron Age II period (Hasanlu IV, ca. 1150–800). The grandest of these structures, called Burned Building II by its excavators, had a main hall (18 × 24 m) with two rows of four wooden columns. Approached by an open portico and narrow vestibule, the hall was equipped with a raised central hearth, mud-brick benches on its long walls, and an elaborate platform like a dais for a throne centered on the wall opposite the entrance. The buildings of level IV at Hasanlu were sacked and burned by enemy assault about 800.[98]

The fortified site of Nush-i Jan near modern Hamadān, Iran, dates from the middle of the eighth century to the end of the seventh. Here four principal buildings in close proximity to each other have been explored: a fortress with large storage magazines, two temples, and a columned hall. The last structure was an irregular rectangle measuring approximately 15 × 20 m, with entrances at its northeast and northwest corners but no subsidiary rooms. The roof of the hall was supported by three rows of four wooden columns that stood on flat stones embedded in the mud floor. In other respects the hall of Nush-i Jan differed from that at Hasanlu in that it lacked a fixed hearth and other interior appointments. According to the excavators, the columned hall at Nush-i Jan was introduced to the site ca. 700 and continued in use until ca. 615, when the building was subdivided and occupied by squatters.[99]

A more direct descendant of the buildings at Hasanlu was the fortified Median palace on the mound of Godin Tepe (level II, ca. 750–550). Although this establishment expanded greatly over time, its main apartments, the original component, took the form of a great hypostyle hall measuring 25 × 27 m and entered from the south by way of a narrow vestibule spanning the full width of the hall. Five rows of six flat stone bases gave evidence of the thirty wooden columns that once supported the roof. Three walls of the room were lined with benches, and roughly centered on the north wall was an elaborate mud-brick throne seat aligned with a raised hearth and facing the entrance. Equipped with such furnishings, the great hall in all likelihood served as the residence of some local

[95] Detailed description of the Hall of One Hundred Columns, Schmidt, *Persepolis*, vol. 1, 129–137.
[96] The inscription, A1Pa, states that Artaxerxes I completed a building begun by Xerxes: Kent, *Old Persian*, 153. Cf. Schmidt, *Persepolis*, vol. 1, 129 and figs. 60:A, 60:B; Roaf, *Iran* 21 (1983) 158.
[97] For a brief survey of the development of columnar halls, T. C. Young, *BCSMS* 27 (1994) 25–32.
[98] The architecture of Burned Buildings I–V is briefly described by: R. H. Dyson, *AJA* 81 (1977) 550–552; Dyson, in K. DeVries, ed., *From Athens to Gordion* (Philadelphia 1980) 149–151; T. C. Young, *IrAnt* 6 (1966) 48–55. For discussion of the chronology of Period IV and the date of destruction, Dyson, *JNES* 24 (1965) 198–203. For a restored drawing of all five buildings, P. Amiet, *Art of the Ancient Near East* (New York 1980) 550–552, fig. 992.
[99] See Stronach and Roaf, *Iran* 16 (1978) 1–28, with earlier references, especially 6–9 for the Columned Hall, 9–10 for the chronology; Stronach, in *CHI*, vol. 2, 832–837.

chieftain, who here gave audience to clients and petitioners and received and entertained his friends. Moreover, a small square chamber at the southeast corner of the hall likewise had benches around the walls and a throne seat centered on the north side, as if the big man might here hold private audience or confer with his closest lieutenants.[100]

The columnar throne hall of Godin Tepe (level II) and probably similar structures elsewhere in Media form the immediate predecessors of the architecture of Cyrus the Great (ca. 558–529), and the fortified palace at Godin may still have been in use during Cyrus's early years.[101] That ruler, at any rate, adopted the columnar hall that was indigenous to the architectural tradition of western Iran and made it the centerpiece of his new palatial buildings at Pasargadae. Moreover, his builders were the first to introduce stone columns and pavements, and doorjambs decorated with sculptural relief to an architectural form that for centuries had used mud-brick walls and wooden posts. In the hands of Cyrus's architects the hypostyle hall took on monumental scale. Palace S at Pasargadae, probably Cyrus's audience hall, has overall dimensions of 56 × 44 m, with double colonnades on all four sides around a rectangular central hall measuring 32.35 × 22.14 m whose roof was carried by two rows of four columns. At the west and south corners, the walls of the hall project in both directions to form square subsidiary chambers which are the precursors of the corner towers in the apadanas at both Susa and Persepolis.[102] Grander still is the residential Palace P, whose central hall had internal dimensions of 31.10 × 22.10 m, with six rows of five columns to support the roof. The main facade toward the southeast is a deep portico 72.50 m in length, with double rows of twenty columns. Only slightly shorter is the rear portico, with two rows of twelve columns enclosed at either end by small rectangular rooms similar to the rear corner chambers of Palace S.[103]

The greatest innovation at Pasargadae is the careful orientation of the palatial structures with relation to a large and formally laid out royal garden. The central rectangle of the garden was bordered by paths 25 m wide defined by stone-built water channels on either side that served to irrigate the beds of flowers and shrubs. The walkways were approached from the south and east corners by way of pavilions that took the form of miniature versions of the palaces themselves. These buildings gave access to the garden's main feature, a great parterre, 112.50 × 145 m, precisely aligned with the columnar portico of Palace P and separated from it by an esplanade 40 m wide. At the exact center of that portico and placed on the axis of the garden rectangle was a throne from which the king might enjoy the lush foliage and cool waterways of his private paradise.[104] In the palaces of Pasargadae, the hypostyle hall not only achieved monumental scale, but it was the type of building specifically chosen by the first Achaemenid king as his private residence. The buildings of Cyrus thus link the earlier columnar halls of western Iran directly to the Apadanas of Susa and Persepolis in which the architects of Darius I canonized the form of the royal audience hall for the duration of the empire.[105]

---

[100] Excavations at the site: T. C. Young, *Excavations at Godin Tepe: First Progress Report* (Toronto 1969); Young, *Iran* 12 (1974) 207–211; T. C. Young and L. D. Levine, *Excavations of the Godin Project: Second Progress Report* (Toronto 1974) 30–35, for the architecture of Period II, and 120–121, figs. 40, 41, for phases of expansion. Brief summary and updated plan, Young, *BCSMS* 27 (1994) 28–30 and fig. 5. Restored drawing of the fortified palace, Amiet, *Art of the Ancient Near East*, 549–550, fig. 991.

[101] Young, *BCSMS* 27 (1994) 29.

[102] For Palace S, D. Stronach, *Pasargadae* (Oxford 1978) 56–77. For a brief summary of the site, Stronach, in *CHI*, vol. 2, 838–855. For its position in the development of Achaemenid palatial architecture, W. Kleiss, *IrAnt* 15 (1980) 201–204. For the stonework, C. Nylander, *Ionians in Pasargadae* (Uppsala 1970).

[103] For Palace P, Stronach, *Pasargadae*, 78–106; cf. also Young, *BCSMS* 27 (1994) 30–32.

[104] For the royal garden: Stronach, *Pasargadae*, 107–112; Stronach, in L. de Meyer and E. Haerinck, eds., *Archaeologia Iranica et Orientalis: Miscellanea in Honorem Louis Vanden Berghe* (Gent 1989) 475–502; Stronach, *Bulletin of the Asia Institute*, n.s., 4 (1990) 171–182.

[105] Cf. Kleiss, *IrAnt* 15 (1980) 207–211.

Comparison of the Persian halls with the archaeological remains of the Odeion in Athens reveals buildings of closely similar type. Both are square in plan, set on high artificial platforms, and with multiple rows of interior columns to support the roof. But more than that, the Odeion appears to be related to the audience halls at Susa and Persepolis by a striking similarity of dimensions, which can be set out most graphically in tabular form.

	Width of Hall	*Columns*	*Porch*	*Spacing*
Odeion	62.40 m	9 rows of 10	?	6.15 m
Susa, Apadana	58.00 m	6 rows of 6	2 rows of 6	8.50 m
Persepolis, Apadana	60.50 m	6 rows of 6	2 rows of 6	8.50 m
Persepolis, Throne Hall	68.40 m	10 rows of 10	2 rows of 8	6.20 m

Several scholars have observed these similarities and have given them various degrees of significance in their interpretation of the buildings.[106] It is difficult to believe, however, that the coincidence of overall scale and actual dimensions can have arisen by the merest accident. The hypostyle hall was native to the Iranian plateau but quite foreign to the Greek architectural tradition. On the other hand, the literary descriptions discussed above suggest that the central pavilion of the Persian royal tent was a kind of prefabricated, movable version of the apadana itself. Since, then, Plutarch and Pausanias report that the Odeion was a replica of Xerxes' tent, the similarity of plan and dimensions suggests that the Odeion did in fact copy the tent directly.[107]

Form Versus Function

Recent writers about the Odeion have stressed especially the inappropriateness of the building's architectural form to serve its stated function as a concert hall. When the enclosed, roofed auditorium eventually evolved in the Late Hellenistic period as a distinctive architectural type, its model was the bouleuterion, not the hypostyle hall. The odeions of later antiquity bore no relation to the famous Athenian building, which had been the unique exemplar of the type for centuries.[108] This perceived mismatch between form and function has caused some scholars to resort to desperate measures. According to one suggestion, the Odeion was built to accommodate the Panhellenic congress for which Perikles had called in his Congress Decree, and, when that failed to take place, the building was later pressed into service as a concert hall.[109] Another discussion of the building's architectural design "suggests that the Odeion, uniquely in Greek architecture, was built to be rather than to do: to look Persian rather than to accommodate a specific activity (for which it was singularly ill designed)."[110] A more radical approach to the dilemma has been to argue that musical competitions

---

[106] H. Luschey, *AMIran* 1 (1968) 21–22; von Gall, in *Festschrift Brommer*, 123–132; von Gall, *Gymnasium* 86 (1979) 448; Meinel, *Odeion*, 154; Miller, *Athens and Persia*, 237, but she finds it "unwise to join their ranks," 238.

[107] Miller, *Athens and Persia*, 236, 238, considers the tradition that the Odeion copied the tent to be spurious. She prefers to think that the apadana-like plan was transmitted by the personal observation of Athenian diplomats and others who saw actual Persian palaces. Such a source for the Odeion in real architecture is shown to be wrong by Plutarch's precise description of the building's pyramidal roof (quoted above, pp. 207–208). A pyramidal shape is likewise attested for the royal tent of Darius III by the description of Curtius (3.3.8, quoted above, p. 219). Cf. von Gall, *Gymnasium* 86 (1979) 447. But the actual audience halls of the Persian palaces are restored uniformly with flat terrace roofs. See, e.g., Krefter, *Persepolis Rekonstruktionen*, passim. Cf. Stronach, *Pasargadae*, 66, foldout 4a, b. It is difficult to see how anyone viewing the Apadana at Susa or Persepolis would have conceived of a roof such as Plutarch describes.

[108] Meinel, *Odeion*, 36–43, 155.

[109] Robkin, "Odeion of Perikles," 54, 61–67, 71–86, 92–95; Robkin, *AncW* 2 (1979) 10–12.

[110] Miller, *Athens and Persia*, 235.

normally took place out of doors in classical Greece, and therefore Plutarch's statement that the Athenian contests were held in the Odeion should simply be rejected. The musical competitions at the Panathenaia were probably held in the Agora, and Perikles may have built the Odeion as a music school where the musical theories of Damon could be disseminated.[111]

The last of these interpretive strategies plainly hits wide of the mark, for several pieces of evidence attest the association of the building with both the Great Panathenaia and the Dionysia. At the time of excavation, the preserved masonry of the north wall bore traces of painted decoration. Above the marble orthostates and string course, the poros wall blocks had originally been covered with white stucco, and the lowest course was divided into square panels by horizontal and vertical bands of red paint. A single panel of this decorative frieze was well preserved on the third block from the northwest corner; it displayed a victor's wreath of laurel and beside it a small Panathenaic amphora with a palm branch.[112] That the decorative scheme included such overtly Panathenaic imagery leaves no doubt that the Odeion, as restored in the first century, housed part of the festival, as Plutarch reports.

Its predecessor, the older Periklean building, is likewise mentioned in the context of the festival. An inscription of the mid-second century B.C. honors Miltiades son of Zoilos of Marathon for many benefactions to Athens, among them his service as agonothetes of the Great Panathenaia of 142. In that year the revenues budgeted for the festival had fallen short and Miltiades had come forward with interest-free loans and lavish out-of-pocket expenditures to ensure the appropriate preparations (*IG* II² 968, lines 47–52):

> [καὶ] τά τε ἐν ἀκροπόλει προσδεόμε[να ἐργασία]ς καὶ τὰ ἐν τῶι ὠιδείωι
> [καὶ τῶι ᾿Αν]ακεί[ω]ι ἐπεσκεύασεν προσηκ[όντως, ἔδωκ]εν δὲ καὶ ὅπλα στύπ-
> [πινα καὶ] τὰ λοιπὰ τὰ ἐλλείποντα πρ[ὸς τὴν κομιδὴ]ν τοῦ πέπλου
> [καὶ πάντ]α τὰ πρὸς τὴν πομπὴν καὶ τ[ὰς θυσίας τὰς ὀφειλ]ομένας τοῖς
> [θεοῖς ἐπο]ίησεν μεγαλομερῶς καὶ τ[ὸν ἀγῶνα ἔθηκε]ν ἀξίως τῆς τε
> [ἀρχῆς κα]ὶ τοῦ χειροτονήσαντος [αὐτὸν δήμου.]

> and those parts of the Acropolis that were in need [of work] and those of the Odeion [and the An]akion he fittingly repaired; and he [gave] the ropes of tow and the other items that were lacking for the [conveyance] of the peplos; [and everything] for the procession and the [sacrifices ow]ed to the [gods] he prepared magnificently; and [he put on the games] in a manner worthy of the office and of the [demos] that elected [him].

Reference to repair of the Odeion among other preparations for the Great Panathenaia reveals clearly that the building functioned in connection with the festival. There is thus no reason to disbelieve Plutarch's statement that the great hall served from the time of its construction as the venue for the musical competitions, which had been reorganized by a decree of Perikles in the 440s.

We learn also that part of the ceremonial of the festivals of Dionysos likewise took place in the Odeion. Twice each year, a few days before the Lenaia in January and the City Dionysia in March, crowds of spectators gathered in the Odeion to watch the Proagon, a ceremony preliminary to the dramatic contests in tragedy and comedy that took place in the theater a few days later.[113] The

---

[111] Kotsidu, *Musischen Agone*, 148–149, 150–154. The sheer size of the building militates strongly against this theory. According to Xenophon, *Hell.* 2.4.24, the entire Athenian cavalry, one thousand strong, together with their horses and their shields, passed the night in the Odeion in 403. One cannot imagine either that there were so many aspiring musicians in fifth-century Athens, or that the Athenian demos would build so large a building to accommodate them.

[112] Orlandos, *Prakt* (1931) 25–27, figs. 1, 2.

[113] Aischines, 3 Ktes. 67, says that the Proagon took place on Elaphebolion 8 (in 346); schol. ad loc. (145 Dilts): ἐγίγνοντο πρὸ τῶν μεγάλων Διονυσίων ἡμέραις ὀλίγαις ἔμπροσθεν ἐν τῷ ᾿Ωιδείῳ καλουμένῳ τῶν τραγῳδῶν ἀγὼν καὶ ἐπίδειξις ὧν μέλλουσι δραμάτων ἀγωνίζεσθαι ἐν τῷ θεάτρῳ, δι᾿ ὃ ἐτύμως προαγὼν καλεῖται. εἰσίασι δὲ δίχα προσωπείων οἱ ὑποκριταὶ γυμνοί, "There took place a few days before the Great Dionysia in the so-called Odeion a

Proagon was a kind of preview of coming attractions at which the playwrights appeared with their actors and choruses and announced the subjects of their plays. Some vivid glimpses of the ceremony have come down to us. At the Proagon of 406, just after the news of Euripides' death in Macedonia had reached Athens, the aged Sophokles, dressed in mourning, introduced his actors and chorus without the customary crowns, and the whole demos burst into tears.[114] In Plato's *Symposion*, Sokrates compliments the poet Agathon on his performance at the Proagon:

ἐπιλήσμων μεντᾶν εἴην, ὦ Ἀγάθων, εἰπεῖν τὸν Σωκράτη, εἰ ἰδὼν τὴν σὴν ἀνδρείαν καὶ μεγαλοφροσύνην ἀναβαίνοντος ἐπὶ τὸν ὀκρίβαντα μετὰ τῶν ὑποκριτῶν, καὶ βλέψαντος ἐναντία τοσούτῳ θεάτρῳ, μέλλοντος ἐπιδείξεσθαι σαυτοῦ λόγους, καὶ οὐδ᾽ ὁπωστιοῦν ἐκπλαγέντος, νῦν οἰηθείην σε θορυβηθήσεσθαι ἕνεκα ἡμῶν ὀλίγων ἀνθρώπων.

I should be strangely forgetful, Agathon, replied Sokrates, of the courage and magnanimity which you showed when the subjects of your own plays were about to be exhibited, and you mounted the platform with the actors and faced such a vast theater altogether undismayed, if I thought that your nerves could be fluttered at a small party of friends.[115]

The evidence clearly points to the use of the Odeion in connection with major Athenian festivals because the vast area of the hall could accommodate a huge crowd of spectators. The question, then, is not whether the building served this function, for it assuredly did, but rather why it seemed appropriate. The musicians at the Great Panathenaia played in a covered hall, but the dithyrambic choruses sang in the open air; the Proagon of the Dionysia was set in the Odeion, but the plays themselves were produced in the theater next door. To observe that the architectural design of the hall was ill-suited to its function as a concert hall is to miss the point. What the various ceremonies in the Odeion had in common was the enormous audience; and it is important to understand who they were, whence they came, and how Athens hoped they would perceive the architecture of the building in which they gathered.

The evidence for the chronology of the Odeion discussed above suggests that construction of the building was completed in the middle years of the 440s and before the ostracism of 443. It is precisely in this period that one senses a growing rigidity in Athenian relations with the allied cities, and a spirit of ever-increasing imperialism permeates the contemporary documents. In these years the allies of the Delian Confederacy against Persia became the subjects whom Athens ruled, not, however, without considerable demonstrations of discontent, as the records of the tribute payments reveal.[116] On the occasion of the Great Panathenaia, all the allied cities were required to bring a cow and a panoply of armor for dedication to Athena, and their representatives marched in the procession just as Athenian colonists did. The obligation is mentioned in the decree of Kleinias of 425/4 and was specifically restated in the Reassessment Decree of 425/4. The decree authorizing dispatch of an Athenian colony to Brea in Thrace around 445 imposes the same requirement on the colonists and stipulates in addition that they are to bring a *phallos* at the Dionysia.[117] This latter con-

contest and display of the tragic dramas with which they intended to compete in the theater. For this reason it was truly called the Proagon. The actors came in without costumes and masks." Schol. Aristoph. *Wasps* 1109a (Koster) says of the Odeion: τόπος ἐστὶ θεατροειδής, ἐν ᾧ εἰώθεσαν τὰ ποιήματα ἀπαγγέλλειν, πρὶν τῆς εἰς τὸ θέατρον ἀπαγγελίας, "The place is theater-like, in which they were accustomed to announce the plays before their performance in the theater." On the Proagon, see A. W. Pickard-Cambridge, *The Dramatic Festivals of Athens*, 2nd ed. (Oxford 1968) 67–68.

[114] *Vit. Eurip.*, p. 3, lines 11–14 (Schwartz).
[115] Plato, *Symposium* 194A, translation adapted from Jowett.
[116] See Meiggs, *AE*, 163–173. The allies are called πόλες ὁπόσον Ἀθεναῖοι κρατῶσι, "cities which Athens rules," in two contemporary decrees, *IG* I³ 19, lines 8–9; 27, lines 14–15. Cf. Meiggs, *AE*, 171, 425–427; Meiggs, *CR* 63 (1949) 9–12.
[117] Decree of Kleinias, *IG* I³ 34, lines 41–43 (= ML 46); Reassessment Decree, *IG* I³ 71, lines 56–58 (= ML 69). Decree for Brea, *IG* I³ 46, lines 11–13 (= ML 49).

tribution may have been demanded of Athenian colonies and klerouchies generally. Also at the time of the Dionysia, the cities of the empire brought their annual tribute payments to Athens. Isokrates describes how the money was divided into talents and carried by hired porters, who must have numbered in the hundreds, and paraded through the orchestra when the theater was full.[118] No date is attached to this blatant display of raw wealth and heavy-handed power. It is thought to have been a practice of the Archidamian War, but it would not be surprising if this too had begun in the 440s. The crowds that gathered in the Odeion at the great festivals included delegates from all the allied cities, ambassadors and competitors from other states, visitors and tourists from all over Greece. Aischines (3 *Ktesiphon* 43) speaks of proclamations at the Dionysia being made "in the presence of all the Greeks," and Demosthenes (21 *Meidias* 74) attacks Meidias for insulting him "in the presence of many men both foreigners and citizens." At each of the major festivals, this huge international audience packed the great hall of the Odeion for a characteristically Athenian ceremony. In the architecture of the building, they saw an unusual columnar hall that closely resembled the palaces of the Great King of Persia in scale, plan, and actual dimensions. The massive woodwork supporting the pyramidal roof was actually built of royal spolia, the masts and spars of the Persian ships captured in the Battle of Salamis. Moreover, the architectural design was said to replicate the tent of Xerxes captured by the Greeks after the Battle of Plataia.

What has escaped notice in discussions of the Odeion is the true political significance which attached to the capture of the royal campaign tent at Plataia. The peripatetic character of the royal court conferred important symbolic value on the royal tent itself. In peacetime it became a portable palace, a substitute for the apadana, where the king exercised the royal power during his seasonal peregrinations among the four capitals of the empire. In wartime the tent was the military headquarters, the centerpiece of the Persian camp, from which the king directed the movements of the royal armies.[119] From the time of Cyrus the Great, after victory on the battlefield the conqueror took possession of the royal tent of his vanquished enemy to mark symbolically his accession to power:

Κῦρος εἰς τὴν σκηνὴν παρελθὼν καθίζει εἰς τοῦ Ἀστυάγου θρόνον καὶ σκῆπτρον αὐτοῦ λαμβάνει. ἐπευφήμησαν δὲ Πέρσαι, καὶ Οἰβάρας αὐτῶι τὴν κίδαριν ἐπιτίθησιν εἰπών· "ἀξιώτερος σύ γε εἶ Ἀστυάγου φορεῖν θεοῦ σοι διδόντος δι' ἀρετήν, καὶ Πέρσαι Μήδων βασιλεύειν."

Entering the tent, Cyrus sat on the throne of Astyages and took up his scepter, whereupon the Persians cheered and Oibaras placed the royal tiara on his head saying, "You are worthier than Astyages to wear this, since the god gave it to you for your excellence, and the Persians are worthier to rule than the Medes."[120]

That the political significance of this symbolic passage of power from conquered to conqueror was well understood in the Classical period emerges from two accounts of the aftermath of the Battle of Issos. Defeated on the battlefield, Darius III fled on horseback through the countryside of northern Syria with Alexander and the companion cavalry in hot pursuit.

οἱ δὲ τοῦ βασιλέως παῖδες καταλαβόμενοι τὴν τοῦ Δαρείου σκηνὴν τἀκείνου λουτρὰ καὶ δεῖπνα παρεσκευάζοντο καὶ λαμπάδων πολλὴν πυρὰν ἅψαντες προσεδέχοντο τὸν Ἀ-

[118] Tribute payments due at the Dionysia, *IG* I³ 34, lines 18–22 (= ML 46); 68, lines 12–14 (= ML 68); Aristoph. *Acharn.* 504–506 with schol. 504a, b and 378 (Wilson). Display in the theater, Isokr. 8 *Peace* 82.

[119] For discussion of the royal tent and its symbolic importance, P. Briant, *IrAnt* 23 (1988) 267–269: "Bref, pour la durée du déplacement, la tente royale est bien le véritable lieu où s'exerce le pouvoir de l'État, qui se confond avec la personne du roi. Dès lors, la prise de possession, par le vainqueur, de la tente royale marque elle aussi symboliquement le passage d'un pouvoir à l'autre" (p. 269).

[120] Nikolaos of Damascus, *FGrH* 90 F 66 45.

λέξανδρον, ὅπως ἀπὸ του διωγμοῦ γενόμενος καὶ καταλαβὼν ἑτοίμην πᾶσαν τὴν παρα-
σκευὴν τοῦ Δαρείου οἰωνίσηται τὴν ὅλην τῆς Ἀσίας ἡγεμονίαν.

The royal pages now took over the tent of Darius and prepared Alexander's bath and
dinner and, lighting a great blaze of torches, waited for him, that he might return from
his pursuit and, finding ready for him all the riches of Darius, take it as an omen for his
conquest of the empire of all Asia.[121]

An even more explicit statement of the ceremonial reception accorded to the victorious king by the
household staff of his conquered opponent comes from Curtius's report of the same events:

> cum ii qui Dareo tabernaculum exornaverant, omni luxu et opulentia instructum, eadem
> illa Alexandro, quasi veteri domino, reservabant. Namque id solum intactum omiserant
> milites, ita tradito more, ut victorem victi regis tabernaculo exciperent.

> Those who had lavishly adorned Darius's tent and supplied it with every luxury and form
> of wealth were now guarding those same treasures for Alexander, as if for their original
> owner. For these alone the soldiers had left untouched, since it was an established custom
> that they should receive the victor in the conquered king's tent.[122]

These texts document a ritualized passage of political power from vanquished to victor that
confirmed the military reality decided on the battlefield. Curtius calls it an "established custom"
for the retainers of the defeated king to receive the victorious successor in the royal tent with all
the luxurious ceremony that had been accorded to its previous owner. Moreover, the occasions described embrace the full history of the Achaemenid dynasty, from the founding of the empire by
Cyrus the Great to the defeat of Darius III at the hands of Alexander and the Macedonian Greeks
more than two centuries later. In the light of these passages, we can understand the full significance
of Herodotos's anecdote (9.82) concerning the tent of Xerxes after the Battle of Plataia. The Spartan
king Pausanias was received in the royal tent abandoned by the defeated Persian general Mardonios.
Herodotos dwells on the extravagant luxury of the tent, the gold and silver furnishings and dinner
service, and the great disparity between the lavish Persian banquet and the frugal Spartan fare. But
behind the amusing story we can see at work the same "established custom" whereby possession of
the royal tent and entertainment in its luxuries were deeply symbolic acts that signified the acceptance of military defeat and the transfer of political power.

Against this background we can understand the reports that the Odeion at Athens was an
exact reproduction of Xerxes' royal tent. It is hardly relevant whether the original tent, or its principal pavilion, was set up in Athens, as some scholars have thought; whether it went to Pausanias as
senior commander of the Greek forces, as others have suggested; or whether its component parts
were scattered among the Greek cities. (It is hard to imagine that so spectacular a piece of captured
booty would not be put on public display.[123]) What is important is the tent's replication at Athens
in the architectural design of the Odeion, wherein that building became the quintessential trophy

---

[121] Diod. 17.36.5, trans. C. B. Welles (Loeb).

[122] Curtius 3.11.23, trans. J. C. Rolfe (Loeb).

[123] The tent was set up in Athens: O. Broneer, *CPCA*, vol. 1, no. 12 (1944) 305–311. The tent ought to have been
allotted to Pausanias: von Gall, *Gymnasium* 86 (1979) 444; H. Kenner, *ÖJh* 57 (1986–87) 57. The tent was probably
scattered among the Greek cities: Kenner, 58; Miller, *Athens and Persia*, 236. Miller (p. 235) correctly observes that "royal
campaign tents were complex 'palace-tents,' not just 'audience-tents,' and contained a variety of spaces for different uses."
It is, of course, obvious that the Odeion copied only the great central pavilion of the tent, analogous to the one described
by Chares, *FGrH* 125 F 4 = Athenaeus 12.538B–F (quoted above, p. 217), and Phylarchos, *FGrH* 81 F 41 = Athenaeus
12.539C–F (quoted above, p. 218). No doubt the subsidiary components that housed the harem, baths, service quarters,
and stables were indeed dispersed among the other cities.

of victory. In these same years, the builders of the Parthenon drew upon the language of Greek mythology to memorialize the victories of the Persian Wars by comparing them to the conquest of Trojans, Amazons, Centaurs, and Giants in the sculptural program of the temple. The builders of the Odeion drew upon the language of Persian architecture to convey a similar message: they chose as the model for their building a structure whose possession specifically symbolized the legitimate transfer of royal power by right of conquest. Here was a building that unabashedly proclaimed Athens's right to hegemony of the whole Greek world. As an architectural type, its remote ancestors had sheltered the exercise of political power in Iran for four hundred years. The design of the Odeion was closely reminiscent of the enormous hypostyle halls in which the Great King of Persia held court and where, as the extraordinary sculptural reliefs of the Apadana at Persepolis remind us, the tremendous processions of soldiers, courtiers, and all the subject peoples of the empire[124] came to prostrate themselves at the feet of their lord and master. So too in the Odeion at Athens, the Athenian demos would gather, as it were, in a new democratic audience hall to conduct the ceremonial of their greatest festivals. To them also and to this spot would process the subject peoples of imperial Athens, together with guests and visitors from all over Greece. They would see in the architecture of the building the most overt expression of Athenian democratic imperialism that so characterized the Periklean age.

[124] For the sculptural reliefs from the facades of the Apadana at Persepolis, see Schmidt, *Persepolis*, vol. 1, 82–90, pls. 19–61. See also G. Walser, *Die Völkerschaften auf den Reliefs von Persepolis* (Berlin 1966); G. Walser, *Persepolis: Die Königspfalz des Darius* (Tübingen 1980).

8

Temples in the Countryside

The period that began with the construction of the Parthenon and ended with the abandonment of the Propylaia witnessed a remarkable expansion in building activity, not only on the Athenian Acropolis but also in a number of the country sanctuaries of Attica which came at this time to be adorned with new marble temples. In these years the Parthenon itself was dedicated together with its gold and ivory statue. Immediately thereafter, construction of the Propylaia commenced, the southwestern bastion of the Acropolis was raised and enlarged, and foundations were laid for the Temple of Athena Nike. In the lower city, the Hephaisteion continued to rise on the Market Hill, and even if its exterior peristyle was already substantially complete, the interior of its cella could be redesigned to reflect the plan of the Parthenon.[1] At Eleusis the project for the new Telesterion, begun and abandoned in the years around 450, now resumed under the direction of a new architect.[2] In previous chapters we have found reason to believe that all these buildings had been conceived as part of a coordinated program to celebrate Athens's claim to religious as well as political hegemony in the Greek world, and thus their completion in due course served to fulfill the original intentions of the Periklean planners.

But in these same years new temples arose also at several places in Attica. On the banks of the Ilissos River in the city's eastern suburbs was built a little Ionic temple. A new peripteral Temple of Poseidon now crowned the heights of Cape Sounion, and nearby in a separate temenos was the smaller Temple of Athena Sounias. The ancient cult of Athena Pallenis, whose shrine was located in the pass between Hymettos and the lower slopes of Pentelikon, likewise received a peripteral Doric temple, which Pausanias later saw in its Roman reincarnation as the Temple of Ares in the middle of the Agora. A little later, another peripteral temple, dedicated to the goddess Nemesis, began construction in the deme of Rhamnous on the northeast coast of Attica. To be sure, the five country temples are nowhere associated with the "works of Perikles" by any literary source, nor is there independent epigraphical evidence to elucidate the circumstances in which they were built. But it can hardly be coincidental either that they are so numerous or that their construction was so closely contemporary with the great buildings of the Acropolis, and it seems best to regard them as parts of the systematic aggrandizement of Athenian cults and sanctuaries that so characterized the Periklean age. So it is to the period of the Thirty Years' Peace, when in Thucydides' view[3] Athens attained the height of its greatness under Perikles' leadership, that we must now turn our attention.

---

[1] For the Hephaisteion, see chap. 5, pp. 137–150 above.
[2] For the Telesterion, see chap. 6, pp. 161–195 above.
[3] Thuc. 2.65.4.

THE TEMPLE OF POSEIDON AT SOUNION

The heights of Cape Sounion guard the southernmost tip of the Attic peninsula, where precipitous cliffs fall away some seventy meters to the waves below. For ancient mariners, these were the first landfall that proclaimed the calm haven of the Saronic Gulf, where a fragile craft could finally escape the howling north winds of the open Aegean. The chorus of Salaminian seamen in Sophokles' *Ajax* longed for their sight: "Oh to be where the wooded cape, pounded by the surf, looms above the sea, beneath the flat summit of Sounion, so that we might greet sacred Athens" (lines 1216–1222). As one stands on the windswept cliffs, above the pounding of the waves, the sea god is a palpable presence, and it was inevitable that early sailors would come to this spot to appease his wrath and to offer thanks for a safe voyage home. The promontory was already a holy spot in Early Archaic times: by the end of the seventh century, Athenians had begun to erect enormous marble statues of young men, some of them nearly twice life-size. For more than a century, these dour kouroi stood watch above the rolling deep, silent sentinels who sought to placate Poseidon's capricious moods.[4]

In the early years of the fifth century, retaining walls were erected to form a level temenos at the summit; at its southern edge a rectangular terrace supported the foundations for the first Doric peripteral temple on the site. Although a close contemporary of both the Temple of Aphaia at Aigina and the Older Parthenon on the Athenian Acropolis, the Old Temple of Poseidon was designed with a plan well in advance of its time (Fig. 71). Its peristyle, of poros limestone, was laid out with proportions that came to be favored toward the middle of the century, that is, the flank colonnades had one more than twice the number of columns as the facades (6 × 13), whereas the Temple of Aphaia was shorter (6 × 12) and the Older Parthenon considerably longer (6 × 16) than the normal peristyle of the Classical period. At Sounion, the colonnades were laid out with uniform spacing, the axial intercolumniation being 2.449 m on both fronts and flanks except at the corners, where the normal corner contraction occurred. The temple was the earliest example on the mainland of Greece in which the plan of the peristyle was apparently developed from a predetermined interaxial dimension, and this was combined with a lower diameter of 0.98 m for the Doric columns to produce a ratio of 5:2. During the first two decades of the century, the Old Temple of Poseidon was under construction. Its crepidoma of three steps and much of its peristyle were erected. Numerous column drums of hard gray poros limestone and blocks of its architrave and frieze are still visible on the site today and attest the advanced state of the building operations. Within the poros peristyle, the foundations for the cella walls and the lowest course of masonry to support a planned interior colonnade were in place before work on the temple was interrupted by the Persian invasion of 480.[5] There can be no doubt that the sanctuary at Sounion shared the fate of the temples on the Athenian Acropolis and elsewhere in central Greece, all of which succumbed to the vengeful wrath of the Persians. The surviving drums of its Doric columns are without exception unfluted, a certain indication that work on the temple was never carried to completion. Moreover, damaged column drums and capitals, as well as other blocks of the superstructure, were built into the foundations of the later temple or reused in other buildings of the sanctuary.

---

[4] On the sanctuary of Poseidon in the Archaic period, H. R. Goette, Ὁ ἀξιόλογος δῆμος Σούνιον: *Landeskundliche Studien in Südost-Attika* (Rahden/Westf. 2000) 18–21. Kouroi: Athens, NM inv. 2720 (Kouros A) + 3645a (Base B): G. M. A. Richter, *Kouroi*, 3rd ed. (New York 1970) 42–44, no. 2; V. G. Kallipolitis, *AntW* 4.2 (1973) 47–51; G. Papathanasopoulos, "Σούνιον Ἱρόν" (Ph.D. diss., University of Athens, 1983) 48–50. Athens, NM inv. 3645 (Kouros B) + 2720a (Base A): Richter, *Kouroi*, 44–45, no. 3; Papathanasopoulos, 51–53. Papathanasopoulos (pp. 54–78) catalogues fragmentary arms and legs from eleven more statues.

[5] For the old poros temple, see Dörpfeld, *AM* 9 (1884) 329–337; W. B. Dinsmoor, Jr., *Sounion* (Athens 1971) 12–16; Goette, *Sounion*, 21–23; Dinsmoor, *AAG*³, 107, 338 (dimensions); Gruben, *Gr. Tempel*⁵, 230. The dimensions of the stylobate calculated from the interaxial, Coulton, *BSA* 69 (1974) 74–75.

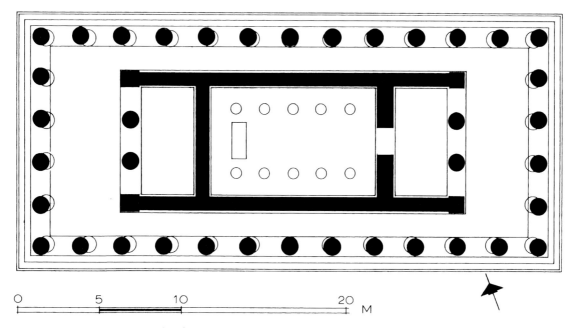

Figure 71. Temple of Poseidon, restored plan showing the archaic temple in outline,
the classical temple in black

In the crisis of 480, the sea god had brought the full fury of his native element to the defense of
the little Greek navies at Artemision. Poseidon had teamed up with Boreas, the north wind, to drive
the Persian armada against the cliffs of Pelion, and no fewer than four hundred ships were lost in
that wild summer storm. Not long thereafter, a second Persian squadron of two hundred ships was
attempting to block the Greek retreat through the Euripos when it was caught by night in the open
sea. In torrential rains and crashing waves, the entire fleet blundered onto the rocks in the Hollows
of Euboia, and Herodotos attributed the disaster to the work of divine power.[6] The tumult of that
summer culminated in the shattering defeat of the Persian navy in the straits of Salamis. Within
days of the battle the victorious Greeks gave thanks to Poseidon by dedicating captured Phoenician triremes in his sanctuaries at Sounion and the Isthmus. When the Athenians returned to their
homeland, they also founded a shrine for Boreas on the banks of the river Ilissos.[7] So the cliff-top
temenos at Sounion displayed a proud trophy of the victory that Poseidon had helped the Greeks
to win, but in other respects the sanctuary fared no better than the Acropolis of Athens during the
second quarter of the fifth century: the ancient kouroi lay smashed upon the ground, and their shattered fragments were dumped into a deep pit in a modest effort to clean up the debris. The blocks of
the half-built temple, like those of the Older Parthenon, had been reduced to wreckage, and by the
middle years of the century the site cried out for the attention of Athenian temple builders. It was a
perfect spot to celebrate the naval victories of the Persian Wars, and equally to proclaim to all who
sailed past that Athens had won total dominion of Poseidon's realm.

    Not long after the beginning of work on the Parthenon, the new marble temple of Poseidon at
Sounion seems to have got under way in the later part of the 440s.[8] Happily for its builders, a con-

[6] Destruction of the Persian fleet off Pelion, Hdt. 7.188–190; the squadron sailing around Euboia, Hdt. 8.7; destroyed
in the Euboian Hollows, Hdt. 8.13; a work of divine power, Hdt. 8.14.
    [7] Trireme dedicated at Sounion, Hdt. 8.121; shrine of Boreas, Hdt. 7.189.
    [8] For discussion of the date, Dinsmoor, *Hesperia* 9 (1940) 44–47. A date in the 440s seems warranted on the basis of
the building's proportions and architectural style, but Dinsmoor's precise date, 444–440 (p. 47), is quite arbitrary; followed
by Dinsmoor, Jr., *Sounion*, 17. Gruben, *Gr. Tempel*[5], 230, dates the temple "soon after 449." Cf. Camp, *Archaeology of Athens*, 108–112, 305–309.

venient local source of building stone existed in the Agrileza quarries just four kilometers north of the sanctuary.[9] The local stone was a good grade of marble, slightly striated and absolutely flat white in color, and it provided by far the greater part of the material needed for the temple. The proximity of the quarries to the building site greatly facilitated construction, for it obviated the laborious and expensive trek across the plain of Athens with which all building operations in the city itself had to begin. Another boon to the Periklean builders was the unusually advanced plan of the old poros temple, for this permitted the new building to follow its layout closely (Fig. 71).[10] The poros crepidoma, as originally built, could be made to serve as foundations for the new marble steps and stylobate that were superimposed directly upon it (see Fig. 73). The overall width of the platform was enlarged by 0.70 m and its length by ca. 1.00 m, the increase being effected by laying some of the disused poros architrave blocks upside down along the earlier foundations, where they could support the marble euthynteria. The marble stylobate was set down directly on its poros predecessor, thus raising the floor level of the temple by one course. Since the height of the risers was increased to 0.361 m from 0.32 m in the poros temple, and the marble euthynteria was placed level with the lowest poros step, the tops of the old steps had to be shaved down slightly to accommodate the marble blocks of the two new steps. In this way the finished dimensions of the marble stylobate were 13.47 × 31.124 m, which makes the temple at Sounion just slightly smaller than the contemporary Hephaisteion in Athens (13.708 × 31.769 m).[11] Within the crepidoma for the peristyle, the walls of the cella were likewise built directly on the preexisting foundations that had been prepared for the old building. So the new Temple of Poseidon arose on precisely the same spot that had been previously consecrated for its predecessor, and by erecting the new building on the same foundations as the old, the builders effected a major economy in its construction.

The marble peristyle was designed to duplicate the earlier plan as closely as possible, the number of columns being identical, arranged with six on the facades and thirteen on the flanks (Fig. 72). The small increase in the width and length of the marble stylobate enabled similar fractional increments in the lower diameter of the shafts (1.043 m) and in the axial intercolumniations (2.522 m).[12] The temple at Sounion is one of the fifth-century Doric buildings whose stylobate dimensions appear to have been calculated from a predetermined axial intercolumniation that was uniform on both fronts and flanks, like its predecessor. In the course of actual construction, however, the finished stylobate very slightly exceeded the theoretical calculation in both width and length by 0.019 m. For an attempt to calculate the width and length of the stylobate from the theoretical interaxial (2.522 m) by application of the formulas $W = I_W (N_w + \frac{1}{3})$ and $L = I_L (N_l + \frac{1}{3})$ yields dimensions that both fall short by exactly 19 millimeters ($2.522 \times 5\frac{1}{3} = 13.451$ m and $2.522 \times 12\frac{1}{3} = 31.105$ m).[13] As a result, the columns were erected with minute variations in spacing to conceal the discrepancy, as almost always happened in Greek marble buildings. In fact, among the nine columns still

[9] For the Agrileza quarries, see Goette, *AM* 106 (1991) 201–222; Goette, *Sounion*, 90–91. Cf. Osborne, *Demos*, 95, 101–102; Langdon and Watrous, *Hesperia* 46 (1977) 172.

[10] The later Temple of Poseidon: Dörpfeld, *AM* 9 (1884) 324–337; Stais, *ArchEph* (1900) 122–131; Stais, *ArchEph* (1917) 168–172; Orlandos, *ArchDelt* 1 (1915) 1–27; Orlandos, *ArchEph* (1917) 213–226; Dinsmoor, *AAG*[3], 181–182; Plommer, *BSA* 45 (1950) 78–94; Plommer, *BSA* 55 (1960) 218–233; Plommer, *BSA* 71 (1976) 113–115; Dinsmoor, Jr., *Sounion,* 17–24; Dinsmoor, Jr., *AJA* 78 (1974) 211–238; Travlos, *BTA,* 404–407; Goette, *Sounion,* 26–31; Gruben, *Gr. Tempel*[5], 229–232.

[11] Dimensions: Dinsmoor, *AAG*[3], 338; slightly different in Plommer, *BSA* 45 (1950) 79.

[12] Dinsmoor (note 11 above); again slightly different in Plommer (note 11 above).

[13] W = width of stylobate, L = length of stylobate, I_W = axial intercolumniation (fronts), I_L = axial intercolumniation (flanks), N_w = number of intercolumniations (fronts), N_l = number of intercolumniations (flanks). For discussion of these formulas and their application in calculating the width and length of the stylobate, see Coulton, *BSA* 69 (1974) 74–76; for their application to the Temple of Poseidon, Coulton, table 2, cols. 8–10. For application of the formulas to the Parthenon, see chap. 4, pp. 85–87 above.

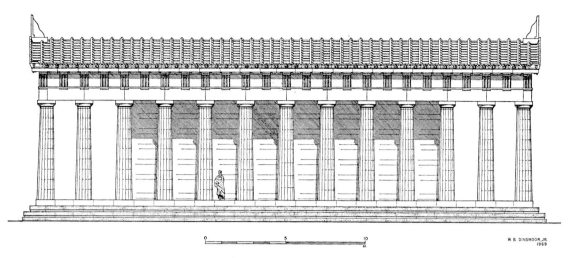

Figure 72. Restored elevation, south flank of Temple of Poseidon

standing in their original positions on the southern flank, three interaxials have been measured as 2.53 m, and the actual average spacing is 2.5238 m.[14]

While the plan of the temple owed much to its late archaic predecessor, its treatment of the Doric order introduced startling innovations. The more attenuated proportions recently developed for the columns of the Parthenon and the Hephaisteion were now adopted by the architect at Sounion, who seemed to stretch the Doric order to new extremes of slenderness (Figs. 76, 77). The marble shafts at Sounion are 6.024 m in height with lower diameter of 1.043 m, which yields a proportion of 5.78. When this is compared to the exterior columns of the Parthenon, which measure 5.48 lower diameters, and those of the Hephaisteion, which measure 5.61,[15] it is clear that the Periklean architects were determined to reinterpret the proportional syntax of the order. In fact, the Temple of Poseidon was nearly a century ahead of its time; not until the temples at Delphi, Tegea, and Nemea in the mid-fourth century would the proportions of height to lower diameter in Doric columns surpass that at Sounion. On the other hand, the designer combined the strikingly modern proportions with a curiously archaic feature: the shafts were finished with only sixteen flutes instead of the normal twenty of the Classical period,[16] a detail that doubtless escaped the notice of all observers except the most painstaking student of architecture.

From the very beginning of the Doric order, Greek architects had seemingly engaged in a quest for some kind of ideal relationship between the visual strength of the supporting members and the visual weight of the load that they carried. This was expressed in the height of the entablature relative to the stoutness of the columns because it was the essence of the trabeated system to make manifest the actual structure in the outward forms of the architecture. The architects of the Parthenon sought to emphasize the lightness of the entablature by reducing its height to 1.73 lower diameters above columns that were 5.48 lower diameters high. In contrast, the Temple of Zeus at Olympia displayed the visual strength of its columns by increasing the lower diameter so as to create a proportion of 4.64 relative to the height and combined this with a height of 1.81 lower diameters for the entablature. In the two smaller temples, of Poseidon and Hephaistos, less than half the size of the Parthenon, it is interesting to observe that the architects evidently felt the need for greater visual weight in the entablature. At Sounion the relative proportions, expressed in lower diameters, are 1.93 for the entablature and 5.78 for the columns, while in the Hephaisteion the same proportions are 1.98 and 5.61.

[14] See Dörpfeld, *AM* 9 (1884) pl. XV, where actual dimensions are shown on the plan.
[15] All proportions in lower column diameters from Dinsmoor, *AAG*³, table opposite p. 340.
[16] Dinsmoor, Jr., *Sounion*, 21.

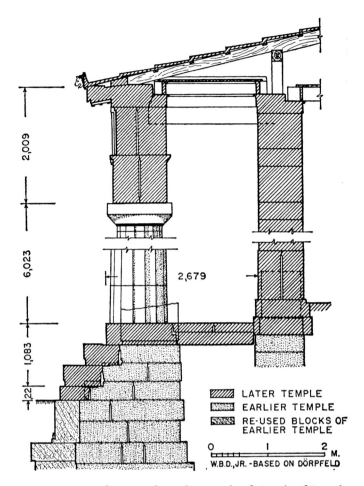

Figure 73. Restored section through peristyle of Temple of Poseidon

A somewhat similar attempt to strengthen the visual appearance of the crepidoma probably best explains the unusual decorative treatment of the stepped platform of the Temple of Poseidon at Sounion (Fig. 73). The first two steps have a recessed rebate crowned with a cavetto molding on the lower part of their risers, while lightly stippled panels decorate the upper faces of the steps and add visual strength to the supporting courses with a kind of subtle rustication. Similar panels of slightly smaller dimensions were worked into the faces of the euthynteria blocks at the bottom of the crepidoma, but, in contrast, the face of the stylobate beneath the colonnade is polished smooth in the usual manner.[17] This difference in treatment gives great visual emphasis to the uppermost course of the temple platform.

The architect also implanted his individual personality in the design of the temple in other ways, especially his predilection for experiment within the constraining syntax of the Doric order. Thus he kept the exterior entablature rigorously devoid of embellishments, except for the necessary component parts of the order, and no sculpture adorned the plain panels of the metopes. On the contrary, his treatment of the sima of the roof was both unusually elaborate and highly decorative (Figs. 74, 75). Above the pediments, the raking sima had an archaizing ovolo profile of Corinthian type, almost identical to that used on the Temple of Aphaia at Aigina more than forty years earlier. The painted ornament on its face consisted of stylized palmettes alternating with lotus blossoms in a double row pointing both upward and downward.[18] Far more unusual was the flank sima in

[17] The rebates and stippled panels on the crepidoma: Plommer, *BSA* 45 (1950) 81–82; Dinsmoor, Jr., *Sounion*, 18. The cavetto molding: Shoe, *Greek Mouldings,* 145, pl. LXIII:10; Dörpfeld, *AM* 9 (1884) 328, pl. XVI.
[18] Orlandos, *ArchDelt* 1 (1915) 14–22; Dinsmoor, Jr., *AJA* 78 (1974) 221–226.

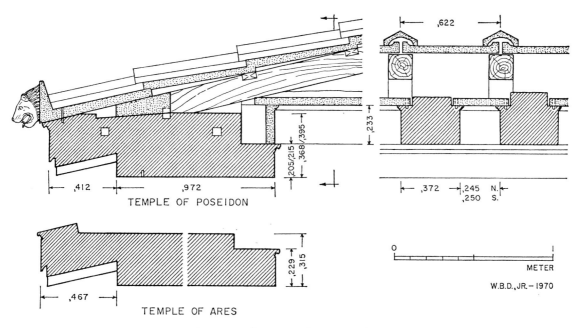

Figure 74. Restored sections through roof and ceiling

Figure 75. Restored view of sima

island marble that crowned both long sides of the roof. Above a vertical fascia, alternating palmettes and lotuses were carved in high relief and linked together by running spirals. Around the petals of the palmettes and the upper parts of the blossoms, the field of the sima was entirely cut away, so that viewed from below the ornaments would have appeared to be freestanding with an undulating upper profile. In place of every third palmette, a lion-head spout projected forward from the face of the sima and allowed rainwater to drain from the roof through its open mouth.[19] In addition to the sima, floral acroteria in marble also sprouted from the corners and apex of each pediment. That from the western end of the temple has survived almost intact and measures 1.14 m in height. It exhibits a complex composition of vigorously spiraling tendrils that turn alternately inward and outward and support a large central palmette and two smaller palmettes on each side.[20]

Within the peristyle, the design of the cella reveals some features that appear to reflect the influence of the slightly earlier Hephaisteion in Athens, similarities which have sometimes encouraged

[19] Dinsmoor, Jr., *AJA* 78 (1974) 226–237, pl. 43, fig. 18.

[20] The western acroterion, Athens, NM inv. 1112: Orlandos, *ArchDelt* 1 (1915) 22–24; Travlos, *BTA*, 411, fig. 513; Goette, *Sounion*, 29.

Figure 76. Temple of Poseidon from northeast

the belief that both temples were designed by the same architect.[21] But at the same time there are some noticeable deviations from the standard grammar of Doric design. In many, if not most, hexastyle temples, the lateral walls of the cella were laid out within the peristyle so that their outer faces aligned with the axes of the second column from each corner of the facades. Thus in this arrangement the exterior width of the cella building was equal to the three normal axial intercolumniations of the facade. The temples at Aigina and Olympia, the Hephaisteion, and even the Parthenon all adhere precisely to this rule. At Sounion, however, the architect aligned the sides of the cella only approximately tangent with the outer face of the second column from each corner, so that the overall width at the wall base was 8.32 m (8.13 m between the outer faces of the walls), whereas the three normal interaxials of the facade yield a considerably narrower dimension ($2.522 \times 3 = 7.566$ m).[22] On the other hand, the pronaos of the cella replicated the same anomalous design that appeared in the Hephaisteion. The front of the porch was aligned with the peristyle in such a way that a line projected laterally from the face of the anta would be tangent to the third column from each front corner. As in the Hephaisteion, the architrave and frieze of the pronaos extended across the pteromata on either side to abut against the entablature of the peristyle. In fact, the architrave blocks extending from the antas to the exterior entablature are still in place (Fig. 76). Thus the broad compartment between the pronaos and the columns of the east facade received its own interior entablature framing all four

[21] The attribution to a single architect of the four temples—the Hephaisteion, Poseidon at Sounion, Ares, and Nemesis at Rhamnous—was argued by Dinsmoor, *Hesperia* 9 (1940) 43–47, who named him the "Theseum architect"; also Dinsmoor, *Hesperia* Suppl. 5 (1941) 153–155; Dinsmoor, *AAG*³, 181–182. The attribution has frequently been accepted: Plommer, *BSA* 45 (1950) 109–112; H. Knell, *AA* (1973) 94–114; Travlos, *BTA*, 404; Korres, *Horos* 10–12 (1992–98) 91–95. Against the attribution to one architect, see M. M. Miles, *Hesperia* 58 (1989) 221–226. She adduces cogent arguments that all of Dinsmoor's eight "characteristics," which he thought indicated the hand of one architect, should "be more accurately described as stylistic trends characteristic of 5th-century temples in general" (p. 226).

[22] Dimensions from Dörpfeld, *AM* 9 (1884) pl. XV. In contrast, the cella of the Hephaisteion is 7.76 m (outer faces of walls), compared to three normal interaxials: $2.58 \times 3 = 7.74$ m. Dimensions from Koch, *Theseustempel*, pl. 41.

Figure 77. Temple of Poseidon, view of south flank

sides of the space. At the west end of the temple, however, the opisthodomos was aligned with the axis of the third column from each corner, so that the space before the rear porch was deeper by half a column diameter than the space before the pronaos. This unique treatment differs considerably from the Hephaisteion, where the opisthodomos aligned with the midpoint of the second intercolumniation. Also unlike the Hephaisteion, the two distyle porches at Sounion were planned with equal depth, whereas in the Athenian temple the depth of the pronaos exceeds that of the opisthodomos by almost half an interaxial.

The construction of the cella walls also departed from standard practice in Athenian temples. Above the high orthostates (0.842 m), the architect adopted the pseudo-isodomic style of masonry and carried up the walls in marble courses that alternated between 0.30 m and 0.60 m in height.[23] At the base of the walls was a molded toichobate with cyma reversa profile, evidently borrowed from the similar decorative feature of the Hephaisteion. At Sounion the molding was smaller than that in the Hephaisteion, but it had greater depth and a larger projecting curve, details that betray the slightly later date of the temple.[24] The epicranitis crowning the cella walls took the form of the standard Doric hawksbeak decorated with stylized leaves painted alternately red and blue, but beneath the molding was a fascia that carried a painted double meander plainly influenced by the same pattern which so dominated the decorative detail of the Parthenon and would later be copied exactly for the interior epicranitis of the Propylaia.[25] Since the interior frieze of the pronaos bore

[23] For the orthostates and wall blocks of alternating dimensions, see Orlandos, *ArchEph* (1917) 215–219; Dinsmoor, Jr., *Sounion*, 21.

[24] Cyma reversa toichobate, Shoe, *Greek Mouldings*, 87, pls. XXXVII:3 (Sounion), XXXVII:2 (Hephaisteion); cf. Orlandos, *ArchEph* (1917) 222, fig. 15.

[25] For the hawksbeak of the epicranitis: Shoe, *Greek Mouldings*, 128, pl. LXI:5; Orlandos, *ArchEph* (1917) 223, figs. 16, 17. For the fascia with double meander, Orlandos, *ArchEph* (1953–54) pt. 3, 9–11; Dinsmoor, Jr., *AJA* 78 (1974) 220–221.

sculptural compositions in a position similar to that of the later frieze of the Hephaisteion, the face
of the architrave beneath it also reflected the Ionic mode of decoration. In place of the taenia and
regulae of the Doric vocabulary was an Ionic epistyle crown consisting of a cyma reversa with base
fillet surmounted by a fascia, and with an astragal below it.[26]

The design of the interior presents two other features that are extraordinarily abnormal for a
Doric temple constructed in the 440s. The marble ceilings of the flank colonnades dispensed entirely
with the usual decorative coffers and were composed instead of beams measuring 0.372 m in width
and set so close to each other that they were themselves wider than the spaces between them (0.245
to 0.250 m), which were covered with thin slabs of marble (see Fig. 74). It was the type of ceiling
sometimes fashioned in wood to span the interior of a cella but was almost without parallel among
the marble ceilings of temple peristyles, and certainly radically different from the coffered ceilings of
the Hephaisteion. In contrast, the ceilings on the two ends of the temple and above the porches of the
pronaos and opisthodomos seem to have been of the usual coffered type.[27] The second interior anomaly concerned the cella itself, which was planned as a single unified chamber uninterrupted by internal
columns, and this despite the fact that foundations for such colonnades had already been prepared for
the temple's poros predecessor.[28] Most Doric temples of the Late Archaic and Classical periods had
two rows of superimposed columns with reduced dimensions to support the ceiling of the cella. We
have seen that the architects of the Parthenon exploited the extra width of the cella, created by the
octostyle facades of that temple, to design a three-sided internal peristyle with central nave and surrounding ambulatories.[29] It is fascinating to observe how differently the builders of the Temples of Poseidon and Hephaistos reacted to that revolutionary innovation in the design of Doric interiors. The
architect of the Hephaisteion drastically altered the interior of the cella at a late stage of construction
and introduced foundations for a three-sided internal peristyle, obviously modeled directly on that of
the Parthenon.[30] But in a space only a fraction the size of the Parthenon, the internal colonnades must
have appeared crowded and out of scale. At Sounion, on the other hand, the architect eliminated the
interior columns entirely in order to display the uncluttered spaciousness of the cella, although the
clear span between the flank walls was almost precisely the same as in the Hephaisteion.[31]

Like other Athenian temples of the fifth century, the Temple of Poseidon was originally embellished with sculptural pediments and Ionic friezes within the peristyle that bore close resemblance
to those installed later in the Hephaisteion. At the east end of the temple, as in the Hephaisteion,
the frieze extended across the pteromata on either side, as indicated by the blocks of the architrave
preserved in situ. Of the sculptured frieze that rested on the interior architrave, fifteen slabs are still
extant, along with a few fragments,[32] but all have suffered grievous damage, while some are so heavily

[26] The Ionic epistyle crown of the pronaos: Shoe, *Greek Mouldings*, 59, pl. XXVII:3; Dörpfeld, *AM* (1884) 328, pl.
XVI.

[27] The ceilings of the flank colonnades, Dinsmoor, Jr., *AJA* 78 (1974) 218–220, coffered ceilings over ends and
porches, 220; Dinsmoor, Jr., *Sounion,* 21. Cf. Orlandos, *ArchEph* (1917) 224–226; Plommer, *BSA* 55 (1960) 224–226,
but the flank ceilings would certainly not have had wooden planks between the marble beams as there suggested (p. 224).

[28] The foundations for the interior colonnades of the Old Temple appear on the actual-state plan, Stais, *ArchEph*
(1900) pl. 6.

[29] For the interior colonnades of the Parthenon, see chap. 4, pp. 98–102 above.

[30] The architect of the Hephaisteion seems initially to have designed a temple without interior colonnades at all, like
the plan adopted slightly later for the Temple of Poseidon. The foundations for the three-sided internal colonnade would
not have been introduced into the cella of the Hephaisteion until after the cella of the Parthenon was built, or at least until
after its design had become generally known. For the alterations to the foundations of the Hephaisteion, Dinsmoor, *Hesperia* Suppl. 5 (1941) 40–44, 65–73. See chap. 5, pp. 145–146 above.

[31] Interior width between flank walls of cella at Sounion: 6.35 m, Dörpfeld, *AM* 9 (1884) pl. XV; in the Hephaisteion:
6.24 m, Koch, *Theseustempel,* pls. 41, 52.

[32] Thirteen frieze slabs were published by E. Fabricius, *AM* 9 (1884) 338–353. A single slab was recovered in the
excavations of Stais, *ArchEph* (1900) 115–116. Five small fragments were added by A. Delivorrias, *AM* 84 (1969) 127–
142. The whole corpus has received a comprehensive republication by I. Leventi, *AntP* 30 (2008) 7–53. In the following

defaced that the original disposition of the carving can be deciphered only by means of the most imaginative conjecture. All the extant slabs came to light around the east end of the temple, several within the peristyle itself. The find spots of the frieze slabs combined with the Ionic epistyle crown on the inner architrave at the east end suggested that the two Ionic features belonged together. Thus early attempts to interpret the sculptures restored a continuous band of relief, not only above the columns of the pronaos, but around all four sides of the internal rectangle between the porch and the east facade.[33] According to this arrangement, the temple at Sounion, unlike the Hephaisteion, had no sculptural decoration in the opisthodomos, but rather an innovative internal frieze at the east end which foreshadowed the interior friezes in the Temple of Apollo at Bassai later in the century. This disposition of the frieze slabs has been upheld in the most recent and most detailed study of the sculptures. This work has demonstrated convincingly that at least three different subjects are represented: (A) Gigantomachy, (B) Centauromachy, and (C) deeds of Theseus. But four of the surviving slabs are so damaged that identification of the subject matter is quite impossible.[34]

Scenes of the Gigantomachy have been recognized on several slabs since the nineteenth century. Slab A2 shows a female figure rushing to right, probably Athena battling a giant.[35] On slab A4 an archer at left is about to shoot an arrow at a figure at the right, while another figure, who appears to be winged, crouches beside the archer. The combatants have been identified as Herakles and Eros fighting a giant, on the analogy of east metope XI on the Parthenon.[36] Slabs A3 + A6 show a four-horse chariot moving to the left, evidently driven by a female deity, who may be Artemis or Hekate.[37] An armed deity with a huge round shield may be Ares charging into battle (A1), and a giant armed with helmet and shield falls to the ground on slab A5. Also to be associated with the Gigantomachy scenes is a slab drawn by A. Blouet in 1838 and now lost (A7). This shows the nude figure of a god, probably Poseidon, lunging to the right against a giant who raises his arms above his head to strike back.[38]

The subject matter of the second group of frieze slabs has never been in doubt: the Centauromachy. The block most likely to have occupied the central position in the narrative sequence (B1) shows the figure of Kaineus already buried to the waist, and he is flanked on either side by two rearing Centaurs who pound him into the earth.[39] An exact replica of this scene would later be included in the Centauromachy on the western frieze of the Hephaisteion. Three other slabs (B2, B3, B4) preserve the unmistakable figures of Centaurs, each of whom is almost certainly to be restored

paragraphs the slabs are referred to by the numbers of her catalogue. See also Leventi, in P. Schultz and R. von den Hoff, eds., *Structure, Image, Ornament: Architectural Sculpture in the Greek World* (Oxford 2009) 121–132. The account of the sculpture here is based on her reconstruction. For the extremely fragmentary remains of the pedimental sculpture, see A. Delivorrias, *Attische Giebelskulpturen* (Tübingen 1974) 61–86; cf. Goette, *Sounion*, 29.

[33] The positions in which the frieze blocks were found are shown by Dörpfeld, *AM* 9 (1884) pl. XVI. The frieze restored on all four sides of the space in front of the pronaos: Fabricius (note 32 above); Stais (note 32 above); R. Herbig, *AM* 66 (1941) 87–133; J. Dörig, *AM* 73 (1958) 88–93; Delivorrias, *AM* 84 (1969) 127–142; Dinsmoor, Jr., *Sounion*, 22–23; A. B. Tataki, *Sounion* (Athens 1994); Leventi, *AntP* 30 (2008) 7–53.

[34] Leventi, *AntP* 30 (2008) 12–23 (Gigantomachy), 23–28 (Centauromachy), 28–33 (deeds of Theseus); the subjects of D1–D4 (pp. 33–34) cannot be determined. Felten, *Tektonische Friese*, 45–69; Felten and Hoffelner, *AM* 102 (1987) 169–184, attempted to place the frieze slabs over the pronaos and opisthodomos, exactly as in the Hephaisteion. They recognized the Centauromachy as the subject of the east frieze, but they proposed to identify their putative west frieze as the Kalydonian Boar Hunt by arguing that the animal on slab C1 is a wild boar instead of a bull. This is a subject never represented in the extant corpus of Greek temple sculpture (but cf. Paus. 8.45.6–7 on the Temple of Athena Alea at Tegea). It is also a subject totally inappropriate for the decoration of an Athenian temple. Their reconstruction is rebutted by Leventi (above) 28–31 and passim; also Leventi, in Schultz and von den Hoff, eds., *Structure, Image, Ornament,* 122–125.

[35] So identified by Furtwängler, *AM* 7 (1882) 397; Fabricius, *AM* 9 (1884) 349–350.

[36] Leventi, *AntP* 30 (2008) 16–20. Similar composition on Parthenon metope E XI, Brommer, *Metopen*, 207–208, pl. 71, where Brommer identifies Apollo and Eros.

[37] See Delivorrias, *AM* 84 (1969) 133, no. 4.

[38] A. Blouet, *Expédition scientifique de Morée*, vol. 3 (Paris 1838) 19, pl. 33. Cf. Furtwängler, *AM* 7 (1882) 396–397; Fabricius, *AM* 9 (1884) 338, 351–352.

[39] Leventi, *AntP* 30 (2008) pl. 6.

grappling with Lapith men. Fierce duals rage across two of the slabs, and the male combatants attack symmetrically to left and right, respectively. On slab B2 a partially draped figure lunges to the right to grab the hair of a Centaur, while slab B3 shows a figure moving to the left to confront a galloping Centaur. On none of the four slabs is there evidence that female figures were included in the scenes, or that the battle takes place at the wedding feast of Peirithoos and Hippodameia, although it is possible that Lapith women appeared on some of the most defaced slabs. So the frieze at Sounion may have been more closely similar to the western frieze of the Hephaisteion than to the southern metopes of the Parthenon or the western pediment of the Temple of Zeus at Olympia.

The third subject that has been generally recognized among the Sounion frieze slabs, the deeds of Theseus, is best represented by two joining fragments that form one slab (C1). The figure of an enormous bull fills almost the entire length of the slab. The animal is seen facing left with its head down and its tail raised high. Behind its forepart is a male figure who appears to grasp at the animal with both hands in order to control it. The scene has long been interpreted as Theseus in the act of roping the Marathonian bull to lead it to the Acropolis for sacrifice.[40] One other exploit of Theseus has been identified on a fragmentary slab published in the nineteenth century and now lost (C3). This appears to show the upper body and head of a bearded figure in a falling or upside down position, and it has been suggested that it might represent Skeiron being hurled down the cliffs of the Saronic Gulf by the young hero.[41]

That the battle of the gods and giants was juxtaposed with the Centauromachy and the deeds of Theseus on the friezes of the Temple of Poseidon articulates once again an important message about the way Athenians commemorated the victories in the Persian Wars. The two mythical battles were among the subjects chosen to decorate the metopes of the Parthenon.[42] Those metopes were almost certainly being carved in the same years of the 440s as the sculptures at Sounion, and the stories they told became one of the most popular ways to illustrate in pictorial narrative the power of the gods to impose order on human affairs. The common theme between the myths was the punishment of hubris on a cosmic scale. The terrible earthborn giants rose up against the gods and launched an assault on Olympus itself, only to be beaten back and crushed for their hubris by the vengeful wrath of the gods. It is easy to see how this myth, which was of fundamental importance to the cult of Athena on the Acropolis[43] and had decorated temples and dedications there since Archaic times, became the archetype to explain by mythical analogy the Greek defeat of the Persian hordes.

The version of the Centauromachy depicted on the Sounion frieze forms a particularly appropriate pendant to the Gigantomachy. It emphasizes the same message, that men who recklessly aspire to the power of the gods will be mercilessly crushed and consigned to oblivion. Moreover, it graphically illustrates the special powers of Poseidon from which the story unfolds. But what made the sculptural program at Sounion specifically Athenian was the participation of the Attic hero Theseus. His deeds formed the subject of the third group of frieze slabs (C1, C3), and he was probably a protagonist in the battle with the Centaurs, as he has been so identified on the western frieze of the Hephaisteion. By the second quarter of the fifth century, Athenian myth-makers and their counterparts in the visual arts had grafted the figure of Theseus onto some of the most venerable legends of early Greece as a means of enhancing the glamour and prestige of the local hero.[44] Moreover, they had

---

[40] See K. Lange, *AM* 6 (1881) 234; Fabricius, *AM* 9 (1884) 347–348; cf. the reconstruction of the scene, Dörig, *AM* 73 (1958) 88–93 with pl. 66:2.

[41] Leventi, *AntP* 30 (2008) 32.

[42] Brommer, *Metopen*, 22–38 (east, Gigantomachy), 71–129 (south, Centauromachy), 174–175 (dating).

[43] For the giants, Apollodoros 1.6.1–2. On the Gigantomachy as the foundation *aition* for the Panathenaic festival, see J. L. Shear, "Polis and Panathenaia," 31–38; on the importance of the myth, F. Vian, *La guerre des géants* (Paris 1952) 246–259.

[44] The process is most vividly illustrated by the description of the mural paintings in the Theseion (Paus. 1.17.2–3) and their reflection in contemporary vase painting. See especially J. P. Barron, *JHS* 92 (1972) 20–45; S. Woodford, *JHS*

added luster to his family tree by inventing for him the special cachet of divine paternity. Theseus was the son of Poseidon. His descent from the sea god was implied already in the 470s by Mikon's painting in the Theseion, which depicted his recovery of Minos's signet ring and his emergence from the depths of the ocean crowned by Amphitrite.[45] At about the same time, the poet Bacchylides treated the Cretan adventure in a dithyramb that specifically mentions Poseidon as Theseus's father.[46] So it was eminently appropriate that the hero's exploits should adorn the friezes of a temple dedicated to his divine father. Now, the Athenian version of the Centauromachy, as a brawl that erupted at the wedding feast of Peirithoos and Hippodameia, presented a different and novel interpretation of the ancient story. In this version, Theseus went to the aid of his friend Peirithoos and helped him defeat the monstrous Centaurs when they disrupted the feast and tried to abduct the Lapith bride and other women. This version of the myth was given monumental form in the western pediment of the Temple of Zeus at Olympia and the southern metopes of the Parthenon. It has been convincingly argued that it first entered the artistic repertory in another painting in the Theseion at Athens.[47] Pausanias (1.17.2) specifically states that the painting showed Theseus in the act of killing a Centaur. The frieze at Sounion, however, showed no sign of the Centauromachy at the wedding feast, as is made clear by the absence of female figures; but it seems likely that the hero Theseus was seen coming to the aid of the Lapith warriors as he did likewise on the frieze of the Hephaisteion.

In this way, the Centauromachy at Sounion presents an interesting amalgam of the brawl at the wedding with a much older Thessalian version of the battle of Lapiths and Centaurs, of which there is no trace in either the pediment at Olympia or the metopes of the Parthenon. The central scene of the frieze depicted two Centaurs rearing symmetrically on either side of the Lapith king Kaineus, of whom only the upper torso is visible, as the Centaurs pound him into the earth with logs and boulders (B1). The motif of the armed Kaineus attacked by Centaurs from both sides had appeared as early as the seventh century on a bronze relief found at Olympia.[48] Similarly, the Centauromachy of the François Vase (ca. 570) showed Kaineus, so named by an inscription, already buried to his waist and surrounded by rearing Centaurs.[49] In this version of the story, the Lapiths are armed hoplites, the Centaurs fight with rocks and uprooted trees, and there is no trace of Peirithoos and the wedding feast. In literature the earlier form of the mythical battle is known already to Homer, who mentions Peirithoos, Kaineus, and others by name, while the pseudo-Hesiodic *Shield of Herakles* describes a picture of the battle worked in gold and silver relief.[50] The myth told how the maiden Kainis lay with Poseidon and afterward asked as a love gift to be transformed into an invulnerable warrior, whereupon the god changed her sex and she became Kaineus, an invincible fighter whose body was

---

94 (1974) 158–165; also D. Castriota, *Myth, Ethos, and Actuality* (Madison, WI, 1992) 33–63; cf. chap. 2, pp. 151–152 above.

[45] Paus. 1.17.3 does not actually describe Mikon's painting, but he is content rather to recount the myth itself because in his view the painting did not illustrate the entire story.

[46] Bacchylides 17.33–38. The poet's floruit is given as 468/7 (Eusebius, *Chronicle*, Ol. 78.1 [II 103 Schöne]), a year in which he wrote an epinician ode (3) to honor the victory in the chariot race at Olympia by Hieron of Syracuse. Later literary references to Poseidon as Theseus's father: Apollodoros 3.15.7; Plut. *Thes.* 6.1.

[47] See Barron, *JHS* 92 (1972) 25–28; Castriota, *Myth, Ethos,* 34–43.

[48] See R. Hampe and U. Jantzen, *Bericht über die Ausgrabungen in Olympia* 1 (1936/37) 85–86, pl. 28; Hampe, *Die Antike* 15 (1939) 39–44; K. Schefold, *Myth and Legend in Early Greek Art* (New York 1966) 40–41, pl. 27:c.

[49] Volute-krater by Kleitias, Florence, Museo Archeologico 4209: Beazley, *ABV* 76, no. 1; Beazley, *Development of Attic Black Figure*, 26–37; Schefold, *Myth and Legend in Early Greek Art,* 60–63, pl. 51:b.

[50] Homer, *Il.* 2.740–746, mentions Peirithoos, Kaineus, Hippodameia, and the Centaurs; *Il.* 1.262–268 calls Peirithoos and Kaineus mighty warriors and refers to the Centaurs as Pheres. [Hes.] *Shield* 178–190 describes the battle worked on the shield of Herakles; cf. Hom. *Od.* 21.295–303. *Il.* 1.265 = [Hes.] *Shield* 182 and introduces the name of Theseus to both poems. Jacoby, *FGrH* III B Suppl. II, 342, note 7, has demonstrated that the identical verse was interpolated into both texts and has argued that the interpolation took place before ca. 400 because Herodoros, *FGrH* 31 F 26, cited by Plut. *Thes.* 29.3, accepted Theseus's participation only in the Centauromachy, while he stripped the hero of his other *res gestae*, which Herodoros regarded as later accretions.

impervious to the blows of any weapons. Exalted by his new military prowess, Kaineus set up his spear in the marketplace and commanded the Lapiths to offer it sacrifice as to a god. Zeus responded to this act of hubris by arranging Kaineus's murder at the hands of the Centaurs, who beat him over the head with fir logs until they drove him beneath the earth. This story had already been recounted in all its peculiar detail by the early prose writer Akousilaos of Argos in the Archaic period; and in two fragments from separate poems Pindar mentions both the punishment of Kaineus and the arrival of the Centaurs at a feast where they became drunk on wine for the first time.[51] It is possible that Mikon's mural painting in the Theseion amalgamated the brawl at the wedding feast with the earlier armed combat in which Kaineus was buried,[52] and in that case the sculptor at Sounion may have drawn inspiration from the Athenian painting. Even though the episode of Kaineus's burial had been omitted from the Centauromachies at Olympia and on the Parthenon, it was highly appropriate that the sculptor at Sounion made it the centerpiece of his frieze, for Kaineus, the invincible warrior, had been the creation of Poseidon himself. But the god's extraordinary gift of power led the Lapith king to commit unspeakable sacrilege, and his punishment was a trenchant reminder that the wrath of the gods was quick to strike down a man who overstepped the limits of human mortality.

The pairing of the Gigantomachy and the Thessalian Centauromachy drives home a fascinating message about the way Athenians interpreted the Greek victories in the Persian Wars. To Greeks, the Great King of Persia—with his storied wealth and vast dominions, with all of Asia at his disposal and all of its men at his command—was the quintessential embodiment of human prosperity gone to excess. Xerxes' invasion of Greece, which had hewn a path of destruction from the Hellespont to Attica, seemed to be just the sort of wanton violence that human excess always bred.[53] But in the mythical analogue, the invincible king has become a transsexual monster, and even Zeus must enlist the brutish Centaurs of the mountains to pound him to oblivion beneath the earth. When the Gigantomachy is placed beside this, we see that here too the combatants have been similarly transmogrified. The Medes of recent history have become terrifying monsters, with hairy bodies and snaky tails, who dare in their hubris to assault the abodes of the gods and are beaten back only by the power and guile of all the Olympians. In the pictorial narrative we can see gradually evolving in the Athenian consciousness a cultural and ethical polarity between Greek and Persian which quite literally invented the barbarian.[54]

The appearance of Theseus partaking in such mythical adventures of ancient story is rather like the interpolation of his name in early poetry and betrays a specifically Athenian form of myth-making. His only real claim to be included in the sculptural program of the temple was as Poseidon's offspring. But in the ideology of the fifth century, he is the democratic warrior king who personifies the magnanimous benevolence of Athens. As it happens, the best-preserved scene of his deeds at Sounion (slab C1) shows the hero subduing the huge bull of Marathon in order to lead it to the Acropolis for sacrifice. By this exploit, he not only rid the countryside of a dangerous and marauding beast, but also by its sacrifice went on to reveal himself as the legitimate son and heir of Aigeus, the king of Athens. The awkward duality of his paternal descent seemed no cause for embarrassment.

---

[51] Akousilaos, *FGrH* 2 F 22; cf. P. Oxy. XIII, 1611, frag. 1, col. II, 38. For his date before the Persian Wars, *FGrH* 2 T 3 = Eusebius, *Praep. evang.* 10.7. Cf. also schol. Hom. *Il.* 1.264; schol. Apollonios Rhodios, *Argonautika* 1.57. Pindar, frag. 128f = Threnos 6 (Race, Loeb), speaks of Kaineus splitting the earth with his upright foot; frag. 166 describes the banquet at the wedding of Peirithoos, but the extant text mentions only the Centaurs (Pheres).

[52] As tentatively suggested by Barron, *JHS* 92 (1972) 32–33.

[53] Cf. the speech that Herodotos (8.109.3) attributes to Themistokles the day after the Battle of Salamis, in which the notion that the gods have punished the hubris of Xerxes is explicitly expressed.

[54] On the Greek interpretation of the Persian Wars in terms of divine punishment of hubris, see E. Hall, *Inventing the Barbarian* (Oxford 1989) 56–76, where she discusses the process by which the polarity of Greek and barbarian came into being. See also Castriota, *Myth, Ethos,* 19–28. For hubris as a principal characteristic of those who exercise despotic power, see F. Hartog, *The Mirror of Herodotos* (Berkeley 1988) 330–334. For Herodotos's belief in divine retribution upon Xerxes and other eastern rulers, see H. Lloyd-Jones, *The Justice of Zeus* (Berkeley 1983) 62–64.

Theseus's participation in the Thessalian Centauromachy also shows him willingly going to the aid of friends at home and abroad, and campaigning to save the oppressed from unjust destruction.

It is greatly to be regretted that the pedimental sculptures of the temple at Sounion have perished almost entirely. A single draped female figure in seated position can be assigned to the east pediment, since it was found at the east end of the building.[55] The figure has appropriate dimensions for the pediment of the temple, but unfortunately preserves no attribute that might signal its identification. Among the few scraps of sculpture that may have come from the pediment, a helmeted head of Athena has suggested to one scholar that the scene might have depicted the confrontation of Athena and Poseidon,[56] like the western pediment of the Parthenon. Although this would seem to be eminently inappropriate subject matter for the decoration of Poseidon's temple, since he was the loser, the sculpture is far too fragmentary to make the suggestion any more than mere conjecture.

THE TEMPLE OF ATHENA SOUNIAS

About 300 meters north of the sanctuary of Poseidon lies the precinct of Athena Sounias, situated on a low saddle with clear vistas to the eastern and western bays of the promontory. This site also had attracted religious activity from remote antiquity, and the early excavations brought to light votive offerings of the eighth, seventh, and sixth centuries that had been dumped into a deep rock-cut shaft in an effort to dispose of debris from the Persian destruction of 480.[57] The earliest literary reference to "holy Sounion," in Homer's *Odyssey* (3.276–285), mentioned the death and burial there of Phrontis, the legendary helmsman of Menelaos, who was struck down by Apollo while sailing home from the Trojan War. Quite possibly the archaic votives give evidence of a cult to the mariner hero on this site from early times.[58] Certainly the walls of the classical temenos were made to abut a roughly oval enclosure of earlier date at the northwest corner of the sanctuary, but nothing is known about its function.

In the fifth century, retaining walls were erected on all sides of the hill so as to create a level terrace measuring roughly 46 m from north to south and 44 m from east to west, but irregularly trapezoidal in shape (Fig. 78). On the central part of the terrace, the classical builders laid out the foundations for a small temple, with its west and south sides set parallel to the precinct walls. Since the temple was to stand directly on the leveled surface of the natural bedrock, the builders cut only shallow trenches to carry a single course of masonry foundations beneath the colonnades and the cella walls, and these lowest substructures are the only parts of the building still visible on the site today. But a glance at the foundations reveals at once the extraordinary and uncanonical form of the temple (Fig. 79).[59] A rectangular cella, measuring 15.582 × 11.14 m, was surrounded on the south and east sides by an L-shaped colonnade forming a deep peristyle that returned in two bays at the northeast and southwest corners. The foundations for the cella walls consist of rough masses hewn from the local bedrock interspersed with bits of poros and rough pieces of Agrileza marble. Two slabs of the latter material in the eastern foundation trench have been taken to indicate the position

[55] Athens, NM 3410: Stais, *ArchEph* (1917) 198–199; A. Delivorrias, *Attische Giebelskulpturen* (Tübingen 1974) 66–70, pls. 19, 20.

[56] Delivorrias, *Attische Giebelskulpturen*, 76–82, Falttaf. 5; on the chronology (before 440), 82–86. But the draped torso of Athena with aegis is now shown to be a Roman copy: G. Despinis, *AA* (1999) 173–181; cf. Goette, *Sounion*, 29.

[57] Stais, *ArchEph* (1917) 201–213; Dinsmoor, Jr., *Sounion*, 2–5; Travlos, *BTA*, 404; Goette, *Sounion*, 32–35.

[58] See H. Abramson, *CSCA* 12 (1979) 1–19; E. Kearns, *The Heroes of Attica* (London 1989) 41–42, 205; C. Antonaccio, *An Archaeology of Ancestors* (Lanham, MD, 1995) 166–169.

[59] Temple of Athena: Stais, *ArchEph* (1900) 122–131; Stais, *ArchEph* (1917) 179–187; Boersma, *Building Policy*, 184; Dinsmoor, Jr., *Sounion*, 40–49; Dinsmoor, Jr., *Hesperia* 51 (1982) 429–433; Travlos, *BTA*, 405; Tataki, *Sounion*, 40–42; Goette, *Sounion*, 37–41; Gruben, *Gr. Tempel*⁵, 233–235.

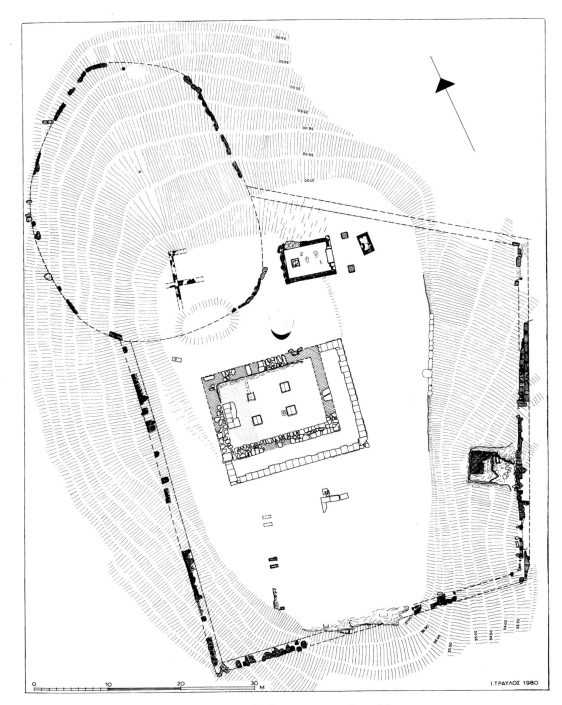

Figure 78. Sanctuary of Athena Sounias, plan of the remains

of the threshold for an eastern door, but it is only convention that suggests that reconstruction. A single course of well-dressed poros slabs formed the foundation for the colonnades and carried the marble stylobate directly, without the stepped crepidoma of the normal Greek temple, so that the building's overall dimensions on the stylobate were 19.175 m on the south flank and 14.62 m on the east facade.[60]

Within the cella the foundations for four interior columns are disposed symmetrically so as to divide the space into three almost equal parts both laterally and longitudinally. Isolated square

[60] Dimensions from Dinsmoor, Jr., *Sounion,* 42–43. The two marble slabs that he takes to indicate the position of the threshold in the east foundation of the cella appear on the actual-state plan, p. 41.

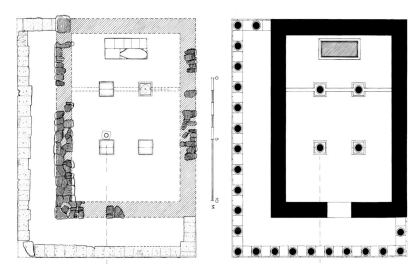

Figure 79. Temple of Athena Sounias, actual-state and restored plans

bases composed of two poros blocks and measuring 1.10 m on a side were set down into the surface of the bedrock. These carried individual square plinths that projected a few centimeters above the floor, and the one surviving example preserves a circular incision 0.716 m in diameter and the cutting for a central empolion for the setting of an Ionic column base. The western third of the cella was originally separated from the rest by a bronze grille running from wall to wall in line with the western pair of columns. Several marble sill blocks found in place at the time of excavation had rectangular sockets at intervals to anchor the fence posts. Against the western wall of the cella, the lowest marble course for the base of the cult statue still remains in place. The area around the statue base bounded by the grille preserves traces of a cement pavement laid over a packing of fine gravel, but in the remainder of the cella and the exterior colonnades as well, the floor consisted of clay or tamped earth laid directly on the dressed surface of the bedrock.[61] The interior of the cella was arranged so that the southern pair of columns fell on the center line of the east facade and supported the ridgepole of the roof; the ceiling of the temple was divided into four nearly equal spans on either side of this line.[62] Triangular pediments on the east and west ends of the building would have lent the semblance of normalcy to this otherwise peculiar structure if one viewed the temple from the southeast angle of the precinct.

Only a few fragmentary blocks remain on the site today because the entire superstructure was dismantled sometime in the first century A.D. and was transported into the heart of Athens, where twelve of the temple's columns were re-erected as a prostyle porch for the Southeast Temple in the Agora. Fifteen column drums, two complete Ionic capitals, a fragmentary base, and a cornice block have been recovered from the excavations in the Agora. These pieces—together with a matching capital, four mutilated architrave blocks, and two ceiling coffers found in the excavations at Sounion—now enable the columnar order of the temple to be reconstructed with assurance (Fig. 80).[63] All the architectural members were fashioned from a rather poor grade of Agrileza marble

[61] The plinth for the northwest column was preserved in place with the circular incision for the placement of the column, and marble sill blocks enclosed the space between that base and the north wall of the cella. See Stais, *ArchEph* (1900) pl. 9; Stais, *ArchEph* (1917) 182; Goette, *Sounion,* 37–38, fig. 78; Dinsmoor, Jr., *Sounion,* 42–43. The pavement around the statue base, Dinsmoor, Jr., *Sounion,* 44.

[62] See the restored section, Dinsmoor, Jr., *Sounion,* 45.

[63] In addition to the larger pieces from the Agora, excavators also found eleven fragments of the series of Ionic capitals, part of the molded epicranitis, and a small fragment of the crowning molding of an architrave block: Dinsmoor, Jr., *Hesperia* 51 (1982) 429. For the Ionic capitals, see note 65 below. Still on the site at Sounion are a few marble blocks from the cella walls whose outer faces are decoratively rusticated with grooves and drafted edges: Dinsmoor, Jr., *Sounion,* 47–49.

Figure 80. Temple of Athena Sounias, restored elevation of facade

characteristic of the buildings at Sounion. The column shafts rose in four tall, unfluted drums from a simple disc base that had not yet developed the canonical Attic profile used for the Ionic order on the Acropolis. Their proportions were extremely tall and slender even for the Ionic order: the shafts had a lower diameter of 0.599 m above the apophage (0.716 m at the base) and a height of ±6.20 m, which yields a proportion of 10.35 lower diameters. Comparison of the foundations at Sounion with the dimensions of the surviving architrave blocks shows that the east facade originally consisted of ten columns with an average spacing of 1.531 m on centers, while the south flank had twelve columns with a slightly wider axial spacing of 1.667 m. Both colonnades returned in one additional column at the northeast and southwest corners of the building.[64]

The Ionic capitals are of highly unusual design and exquisite workmanship, with broad spiraling volutes set close together, their central eyes marked by large bulging bosses (Fig. 81). In the angles with the echinus, the palmettes are solid triangles bearing painted petals. The echinus is carved in the cyma reversa profile crowned by a fascia and with a flat band receding beneath the lower edge of the volute. All the details are executed in painted polychromy, and the patterns varied slightly from one capital to another. The cyma reversa of the echinus was sometimes decorated with the normal Lesbian leaf and a meander above it on the fascia, but on one fragment the cyma carried the egg-and-dart pattern, with a scale pattern on the receding band above the meander. The egg-and-dart pattern also decorated the abacus of the capitals carved in the normal ovolo profile.[65] Above the columns,

On the basis of these pieces, the early notion that the cella walls were of mud brick and the marble peristyle added later is demonstrably untenable. A corner architrave block (with mitred joint), a flank cornice block, and a few sima tiles found at Sounion were published by Orlandos, in Stais, *ArchEph* (1917) 184–186. For the ceiling coffers, see p. 250 below.

[64] For the dimensions and spacing of the columns at Sounion, Dinsmoor, Jr., *Hesperia* 51 (1982) 431. South flank: twelve columns spaced 1.667 m on centers, 1.667 × 11 = 18.337 + 0.716 (diameter of one base) + 0.122 (edge of base to edge of stylobate at each end) = 19.175 m. East facade: ten columns spaced 1.531 m on centers, 1.531 × 9 = 13.779 + 0.716 + 0.122 = 14.617 m. Cf. measurable dimensions on foundations, 19.425 × 14.84 m, with restored dimensions of stylobate, 19.175 × 14.62 m. See plans, Dinsmoor, Jr., *Sounion,* 41, 43.

[65] Three complete Ionic capitals are known: (1) Agora inv. A 1595 (found reused in the Post-Herulian Fortification Wall): L. S. Meritt, *Hesperia* 65 (1996) 134–135, 158–163, fig. 25, no. 17A; cf. Travlos, *PDA,* 104, 111, fig. 151; Dinsmoor,

Figure 81. Ionic column capital, later removed to the Agora (Agora inv. A 1595)

the blocks of the architrave also deviated from the normal form of the Ionic order in that they lack the three superimposed horizontal fascias. Instead, both inside and outside faces of the architrave were left plain, with a single narrow fascia at the top that terminated in a cyma reversa as a crowning molding. No blocks attributable to the frieze course have ever been found either at Sounion or in the Agora. It is possible that the frieze bore continuous sculptural compositions, like the later Ionic buildings in Athens, and in that case it may have been reused elsewhere in Roman times along with the other half of the building's Ionic columns. A block of the horizontal cornice reused in the Agora and another at Sounion show that that part of the order conformed to normal Ionic usage, except that the cyma reversa of its soffit molding was decorated with egg-and-dart pattern.[66]

The discovery that the columns and superstructure of the temple had been dismantled in the early Roman period and reused as spolia in Athens now helps to explain the otherwise curiously erroneous statement of Pausanias about Sounion. The Roman traveler commenced his description of Attica with brief mention of the promontory (1.1.1):

> Cape Sounion, in the land of Attica, juts out from that part of the Greek mainland which faces the Cyclades and the Aegean Sea. When you have sailed past the cape you come to a harbor, and there is a Temple of Athena Sounias on the summit of the cape.

On the strength of this seemingly unequivocal assertion, early writers identified the familiar standing columns of the temple on the summit as the Temple of Athena. Not until the discovery, in that temple itself, of an inscription specifying that it be erected in the sanctuary of Poseidon could the temple on the heights of the cape be correctly attributed to the sea god.[67] But confirmation that the promontory belonged to Poseidon merely served to make Pausanias's statement the more baffling, especially since the foundations of the smaller temple came to light in the same campaign of excavations. We now realize, however, that those foundations had been stripped of their superstructure more than a century and a half before Pausanias's time, and when he visited Attica sometime in the

---

Jr., *Hesperia* 51 (1982) 429, fig. 13; (2) Athens, NM 4478 (found near the Stoa of Attalos): A. Kokkou, *ArchEph* (1974) 102–112, pls. 34, 36:3; (3) Athens, NM 4479 (found at Sounion): Orlandos, in Stais, *ArchEph* (1917) 183–184; Kokkou, 102–112, pls. 33, 35. The capital in the Agora (A 1595) has the normal Lesbian leaf on the echinus. Both capitals in the National Museum have the egg-and-dart with a scale pattern on the band above the meander. Cf. also similar decoration on one of the fragments from the Agora, Meritt, *Hesperia* 65 (1996) 162–163, fig. 26, no. 17B.

[66] Architrave and cornice blocks found at Sounion, Orlandos, in Stais, *ArchEph* (1917) 184–185; cf. Dinsmoor, Jr., *Sounion,* 47.

[67] *IG* II² 1270, lines 16–19 (298/7): ἀ[ναγ]ράψαι δὲ τόδε τὸ ψήφισμα ἐν στήλε[ι λι]θίνει καὶ στῆσαι ἐν τῶι ἱερῶι τοῦ Πο[σε]ιδῶνος, "This decree is to be inscribed on a marble stele and set up in the sanctuary of Poseidon." The inscription was found in a cistern built into the north side of the temple platform: Stais, *ArchEph* (1900) 118. The name of Poseidon is also a certain restoration in *IG* II² 1300, line 9 (ca. 230), also found in the vicinity of the temple.

150s A.D. there was indeed only one temple standing on the cape. It is perhaps just possible that the cult of Athena Sounias had been removed to the Temple of Poseidon and continued to be housed there until the mid-second century. But on the whole, it seems more likely that Pausanias saw the temple on the cliffs only from the spectacular shipboard view and was simply misinformed concerning its identification by a fellow traveler as they sailed around the cape.[68]

One other reference to the Temple of Athena calls for comment, and this is the more interesting because it concerns the building's uncanonical plan for a classical Greek temple. The Roman architect Vitruvius (4.8.4), writing in the time of Augustus, included the temple in a small group of other buildings that were notable for the irregularity of their design:

> Further, temples of other orders are laid out and built with the same symmetries, yet having the arrangements of another type, such as the Temple of Castor in the Circus Flaminius, of Veiovis between the Two Groves, and, with more subtle proportions, the Temple of Diana Nemorensis with the columns added right and left of the sides of the pronaos. The first temples built in the manner of that of Castor in the Circus were those of Pallas Minerva on the Acropolis at Athens and at Sunium in Attica, of the same and not different proportions. For, like the others, the cellas are double in length compared to the breadth. In these temples also, all the features which are customary on the fronts are transferred to the flanks.

Vitruvius is here concerned with a group of unusual temples of Republican Rome in which the long flanks received greater architectural embellishment than the short fronts. The plans of two of his examples are known archaeologically, so that we can understand exactly what features their designers had transferred from fronts to flanks. The plan of the Temple of Castor and Pollux in the Circus Flaminius is preserved on a fragment of the ancient marble plan of Rome, the Forma Urbis Romae.[69] Its rectangular cella is almost exactly twice as long as it is wide, but its columnar porch and only entrance, which Vitruvius calls the pronaos, occupy almost three-quarters of the long side of the cella. With six columns in front and a return of two columns on the sides, the porch projects deeply at right angles to the cella. Since the marble plan shows the building surrounded on three sides by other structures that crowd close to its walls, the long side of the cella has become the facade of the temple. Similarly, the Temple of Veiovis had a columnar porch of four columns, and its only entrance was centered on the long flank and turned at 90 degrees to the rectangular cella.[70] In keeping with the eclectic and classicizing tastes of the late Republican period, Vitruvius attempted to find a classical Greek precedent for the unusual features of these Roman temples, and he cites as appropriate antecedents the temples of Athena at Sounion and on the Acropolis. The latter monument, "Athenis in arce Palladis Minervae," which we know as the Erechtheion after the nomenclature of Pausanias, is, of course, the most uncanonical of all Greek temples.[71] It is difficult to know whether the Ionic temple on the Acropolis actually influenced the designs of the later Roman builders, for there is really only one point of comparison between them; but that is plainly what attracted Vitruvius's attention. The deep north porch of the Erechtheion, arranged in prostyle plan with a return of one column on each side, resembles the Roman columnar porch that Vitruvius calls the pronaos more closely than it does the normal Greek colonnade. Moreover, the north porch has been turned at 90 degrees to the long flank of the temple, and it shelters the main entrance into the western cella.[72]

---

[68] Cf. Goette, *Sounion*, 39.

[69] See M. Conticello de' Spagnolis, *Il tempio dei Dioscuri nel Circo Flaminio* (Rome 1984) 33–42; E. Rodríguez-Almeida, *JRA* 1 (1988) 120–131.

[70] See A. M. Colini, *BullComm* 70 (1942) 5–56 and plan pl. I.

[71] For discussion of Vitruvius's treatment of earlier Athenian monuments, A. Corso, *BSA* 92 (1997) 373–400 and especially 383–389 on the Erechtheion and the Temple of Athena Sounias.

[72] So also Goette, *Sounion,* 39–40.

At first sight, Vitruvius's citation of the Temple of Athena Sounias seems wide of the mark because its peculiar L-shaped colonnade, on one facade and one flank, appears to have nothing in common with either the Erechtheion or the Roman temples. It is difficult to understand what elements Vitruvius thought had here been transferred to the long flank that in normal temples were customary on the fronts. Possibly our interpretation of Vitruvius has been impeded in part by the manner in which the plan of the building has been restored from the exiguous remains of the foundations. All published restorations of the plan have placed its only entrance at the center of the short eastern wall of the cella,[73] where two coarse slabs of Agrileza marble chance to be the only stonework preserved in a foundation trench that has otherwise been almost completely stripped to bedrock. These slabs are said to be the underpinning on which the threshold of the doorway rested directly,[74] but there is no physical evidence for this, and the stones may just as well be part of the socle for the eastern wall. Indeed, it has recently been suggested that the entrance of the temple should be restored at the midpoint of the south flank, and that Vitruvius mentioned it together with the Erechtheion precisely because its principal doorway was on the long side flank behind the colonnade, not unlike the north porch and door of the Athenian temple.[75] Support for this suggestion may come from the large rectangular area immediately south of the temple, which seems to have been used for cult festivities. Here, several large blocks preserved in situ probably formed part of the altar of Athena, and farther west two pairs of stone bases with cuttings in their upper surfaces evidently supported stone cult tables.[76] To worshippers gathered for sacrifices in the southern part of the precinct, the long south colonnade of the temple may well have seemed to be its principal facade.

A final question needs to be addressed: at what date the Temple of Athena Sounias was built and whether it should be included among the temple-building activities in the third quarter of the fifth century. Unfortunately, there is no independent archaeological evidence bearing on the chronology of the building, and earlier writers have tended to follow the opinion of the original excavator that the Ionic colonnades were added to a preexisting structure with mud-brick walls, about 460.[77] More recent investigations of the remains at Sounion have shown this reconstruction to be incorrect. Fragmentary blocks of the same marble as the colonnade are now recognized as belonging to the cella walls, and these exhibit a decorative dressing that was more common on wall blocks of the fourth century.[78] An early date for the temple, ca. 460, seems to find support in the unusual design of the Ionic capitals, which are more closely related to the capitals from the Stoa of the Athenians at Delphi than to the Ionic orders of the Athenian Acropolis.[79] While there can be no doubt that the capitals from Sounion are of markedly different type from those on the Acropolis, there is no certainty that the stylistic difference also signals a necessary chronological difference. The most recent discussion of the capitals in the context of the development of the Ionic order in Attica places them in the mid-fifth century, but the latest studies of the remains at Sounion date the temple more generally to the second half of the fifth century.[80]

[73] See, e.g., Stais, *ArchEph* (1917) pl. 5; Boersma, *Building Policy,* 184; Dinsmoor, Jr., *Sounion,* 43; Travlos, *BTA,* 422; Tataki, *Sounion,* 37; Corso, *BSA* 92 (1997) 389.

[74] Dinsmoor, Jr., *Sounion,* 42.

[75] Goette, *Sounion,* 39–40 and fig. 88, where he also convincingly rebuts the arguments advanced by U. Sinn, *AntW* 23 (1992) 175–190, that the building was not a temple at all but should be interpreted as a banqueting hall.

[76] Dinsmoor, Jr., *Sounion,* 49–50; Goette, *Sounion,* 40 and figs. 81, 82, 90.

[77] Stais, *ArchEph* (1900) 127–130, *ArchEph* (1917) 181; Shoe, *Greek Mouldings* 59, 69, 98; Dinsmoor, *AAG*³, 184; P. Amandry, *FdD* II.1, *La colonne des Naxiens et le portique des Athéniens* (Paris 1953) 100; Boersma, *Building Policy,* 184; Gruben, *Gr. Tempel*⁵, 233–235.

[78] Dinsmoor, Jr., *Sounion,* 47–49; Goette, *Sounion,* 38; Travlos, *BTA,* 405. Cf. note 64 above.

[79] Amandry, *FdD* (note 77 above).

[80] Date in the mid-fifth century: Meritt, *Hesperia* 65 (1996) 163; date in the second half of the fifth century: Dinsmoor, Jr., *Sounion,* 42; Travlos, *BTA,* 405.

An important indication that the Temple of Athena should be dated considerably after the middle of the century comes from the decorated coffer slabs of the marble ceilings in the colonnades. Fragments of two types of coffers are preserved, with slightly different dimensions.[81] The larger, measuring 0.61 m on a side, is of highly unusual design: a square border painted with the bead-and-reel pattern is set in 0.07 m from the edges of the slab. Within the border, the small square coffer itself, surrounded by a broad painted band, is turned at 45 degrees. An ovolo molding, painted with an egg-and-dart pattern, articulates the steps of the coffer, and an eight-pointed star decorates the lid. In the four triangles at the corners of the border, palmettes spring outward from S-shaped spiraling tendrils, while the calyxes of lotus blossoms point toward the center. The second type of coffer, whose ornamentation cannot be fully restored, originally measured 0.50 m on a side and had a painted bead-and-reel around the edges of the slab. The step of the coffer had an ovolo molding painted with the egg-and-dart pattern. On the coffer lid itself, palmettes pointed outward toward the four corners and marked the center of each side, and these alternated with lotus blossoms, all the ornaments being linked together by similar S-shaped spirals. The painted bead-and-reel of the borders, the ovolos on the steps of the coffers, and the star pattern on the lids closely resemble the coffered ceilings of the Propylaia and the Temple of Ares in the Agora and should not be appreciably earlier in date.[82] The palmettes pointing outward at the four corners of the coffer show a variation on the similar pattern developed for the marble coffers of the Parthenon.[83] There is an interesting difference, however: the palmettes of the Parthenon have nine plump petals springing from the central heart, whereas the petals of the palmettes at Sounion are seven in number. Furthermore, they are slender, sharply pointed, and bear closer resemblance to the calyxes of the lotus blossoms that decorated the regulae on the Doric architrave of the Parthenon.[84] It seems clear that the coffered ceilings at Sounion were directly influenced by those of the Parthenon and cannot have been designed earlier than the great temple on the Acropolis.

THE TEMPLE OF ATHENA PALLENIS

When Pausanias visited the Agora of Athens in the second century A.D., he saw among the monuments in the middle of the square a building which he identified as a Temple of Ares. Like many of the older buildings of Greece at that time, the temple had come to house a collection of statuary of different periods. Pausanias mentions two statues of Aphrodite, an image of Ares by Alkamenes, an Athena by a Parian sculptor called Lokros, and a statue of Enyo by the sons of Praxiteles.[85] Around about the temple outside, a number of other sculptures caught his attention, but he says nothing whatever about the building itself. Systematic excavation of the market square in the 1930s brought to light the remains of a building that conformed to the topography of Pausanias's description, but those remains are among the most ruinous of any monument in the excavated area. The building's

[81] Stais, *ArchEph* (1900) 128, with both types of coffers illustrated on pl. 9. Compare also the similar coffers from Pallene reused in the Temple of Ares (see Fig. 84).

[82] Similar patterns and polychromy on the ceilings of the Propylaia, Penrose, *Principles*², pl. XXV, no. 6 (for the star pattern), no. 2 (for the palmettes pointing to the corners of the coffer). Cf. the similar borders and star pattern, but no palmettes, on the ceilings of the Temple of Ares, McAllister, *Hesperia* 28 (1959) 41–45, pl. 6, and the ceilings of the Hephaisteion, Koch, *Theseustempel*, 62–64, pl. 56:5. Note, however, that all these Athenian buildings have sixteen-pointed stars on the coffer lids, whereas the coffer from Sounion had an eight-pointed star like the central motif in the coffers of the flank ceilings of the Parthenon; see Orlandos, Παρθ., 489, opposite 645; cf. Dinsmoor, Jr., *Hesperia* 43 (1974) 133–142, pl. 24.

[83] See Orlandos, Παρθ., 471–495, especially figs. 318–323.

[84] Orlandos, Παρθ., 206, fig. 130.

[85] Paus. 1.8.4, virtually the only reference to the temple itself. What little is known about the cult is summarized by Dinsmoor, *Hesperia* 9 (1940) 1; and Wycherley, *Agora* III, 54–55.

foundations had been reduced to a great rectangular pit from which most of the blocks of a solid masonry platform had been pillaged in late antiquity.[86] The excavations also produced a few pieces of marble superstructure and several hundred shattered fragments, but these yielded enough evidence to enable the excavators to recognize the parts of a Doric peripteral temple. Careful study of the surviving blocks, the profiles of a few moldings, and a single nearly complete Doric capital revealed classical stonework of the finest quality, and, moreover, a building that was closely similar in scale and date to the Hephaisteion on the neighboring Market Hill.[87]

For a Doric temple of the fifth century, however, the remains of the building in the Agora presented two startling anomalies. The foundations, of which somewhat less than a third actually survived, were composed largely of poros blocks reused from earlier structures and erected on their present site in the early Roman period. The marble blocks of the superstructure, although the workmanship betrayed their origin in the Periklean age, all bore mason's marks in letter forms of the Augustan period. In addition, the one complete step block and two blocks belonging to the euthynteria all show that their original double-T clamps were carefully removed and replaced by secondary clamps of later type.[88] The evidence is unmistakable that Pausanias's Temple of Ares was first built on a different site, elsewhere in Attica, and subsequently removed to the Agora some four centuries later. In this respect its later history resembles the Temple of Athena Sounias, except that in that case only half of the columns and entablature were transported to Athens and re-erected as a prostyle porch on a temple of Roman podium type.[89] There can be no doubt, however, that the Temple of Ares was transplanted in its entirety, as is indicated by the size and proportions of the foundations, and by the elaborate code that was marked on the blocks to facilitate reassembly.

The clear evidence that the Temple of Ares was reconstructed in the time of Augustus naturally generated scholarly speculation concerning its original site. The dedication to Ares called to mind the famous hill that took its name from the same god, the Areopagos; but nowhere on that denuded rock were there any traces of the existence of a peripteral temple. The likely association of the rebuilt Roman temple with the imperial cult suggested that the original building might have been moved to make way for the great Market of Caesar and Augustus in the first century.[90] But the analogy of the columns from the Temple of Athena Sounias, and similar spolia from elsewhere in Attica, made it more probable that the temple originated in one of the country sanctuaries, which had fallen into disuse by the Roman period. An attractive candidate appeared to be the sanctuary of Ares and Athena Areia, known from inscriptions to have existed at the deme of Acharnai, thirteen kilometers north of the city center. Although no appropriate remains have ever come to light at the probable site of Acharnai, this theory seemed to gain some support from Pausanias's report that statues of both Ares and Athena stood in the Roman temple. In the absence of any evidence to the contrary, this solution to the problem of the temple's provenience seemed satisfactory and prevailed for several decades.[91] It was therefore a source of considerable surprise when fresh evidence was brought to

[86] H. A. Thompson, in Dinsmoor, *Hesperia* 9 (1940) 5–8.

[87] Studies of the surviving blocks, Dinsmoor, *Hesperia* 9 (1940) 9–42; M. H. McAllister, *Hesperia* 28 (1959) 1–64, with detailed drawings of the principal pieces; for all that is preserved of the foundations, pl. A. The nearly complete Doric capital, Agora inv. A 4805, as yet unpublished: found in 1991 built into the west foundation for the narthex of the church of Agios Nikolaos, shown on the actual-state plan, Shear, Jr., *Hesperia* 66 (1997) 538, fig. 11.

[88] Augustan mason's marks: Dinsmoor, *Hesperia* 9 (1940) 15–18; McAllister, *Hesperia* 28 (1959) 47–54. Original clamps pried out: McAllister, 10, fig. 3; Dinsmoor, 49.

[89] For the transference of the Temple of Ares, the Temple of Athena Sounias, and spolia from other early buildings to the Agora and their reuse in temples honoring members of the imperial family: Thompson, *AJA* 66 (1962) 200; Thompson and Wycherley, *Agora* XIV, 162–165; Shear, Jr., *Hesperia* 50 (1981) 361–365.

[90] As suggested by Dinsmoor, *Hesperia* 9 (1940) 50–51.

[91] That the temple originated at Acharnai was proposed by Thompson, *AJA* 66 (1962) 200; *Agora* XIV, 165. For the sanctuary of Ares and Athena Areia at Acharnai, G. Daux, in Χαριστήριον Ὀρλάνδος, vol. 1, 78–90. The dedication of Dion, priest of Ares and Athena Areia, Rhodes and Osborne, *GHI* 88; the altars of the two deities, *SEG* 21.519.

bear on the problem from a totally unexpected quarter, and with it came the certainty that Pausanias's Temple of Ares originally had nothing to do with that deity but was dedicated anew at the time of its reconstruction in the Agora. Our understanding of the early history of that temple has now been completely changed by the discovery and excavation of its original fifth-century foundation on a site that is known to have accommodated the venerable cult of Athena Pallenis.[92]

The ancient deme of Pallene was located on the low saddle between the steep northern foot of Mount Hymettos and the lowest southern slopes of Mount Pentelikon. Throughout this area sporadic finds since the nineteenth century have yielded inscriptions, tombstones, and some architectural blocks, most of which were built into the oldest of the Byzantine churches; together these make certain the identity of the classical deme.[93] In modern times, the district has become the thickly populated suburb of Aghia Paraskeve and is now bisected from east to west by Mesogheion Boulevard, and from north to south by Lavriou Boulevard. Near the intersection of these thoroughfares, and a little north of the Stavros Bridge, rescue excavations conducted in 1994 and 1995 uncovered the foundations of an ancient peripteral temple. The remains were explored beneath building lots on both sides of Androutsou Street and across the full width of the street itself. Although the existence of modern buildings on neighboring lots prevented the excavators from exposing the full rectangle of the foundation, enough was uncovered to ascertain the exact dimensions and most of the interior plan of the ancient building (Fig. 82).[94] The foundations were composed everywhere of beautifully dressed poros blocks finished to uniform dimensions (0.65 m wide, 1.30 m long, 0.51 m high), and these were laid in perfectly leveled courses with perfectly squared angles, so that the overall dimensions of the foundation rectangle could be measured with great accuracy as 16.40 m in width and 35.20 m in length. In plan, the remains conformed to the normal type for Greek temples of the Classical period, in which two concentric rectangles supported the exterior colonnade and the walls and porches of the cella, respectively. The builders laid the modular blocks in various combinations of headers and stretchers to achieve the appropriate thickness for each part of the foundations. All were multiples of 0.65 m, the standard width of the blocks: exterior crepidoma, $4 \times 0.65 = 2.60$; porches of pronaos and opisthodomos, and door wall of cella, $3 \times 0.65 = 1.95$; side walls of pronaos and opisthodomos, $2 \times 0.65 = 1.30$; side walls of cella, $4 \times 0.65 = 2.60$; rear wall of cella, $6 \times 0.65 = 3.90$. So regular are the dimensions of the blocks and so precisely have they been laid that the damaged or unexcavated portions of the foundations can be restored with complete certainty.[95]

The size and proportions of the foundations, and particularly the disposition of the inner rectangle for the cella and internal porches, suggested at once a building similar in scale and type to the Hephaisteion and the Temple of Poseidon at Sounion, and thus a hexastyle temple of the

[92] The excavations of 1994 and 1995, which uncovered the foundations of the temple, were first reported, except for brief notices in the public press, by the excavator, M. Platonos-Giota, *Archaiologia* 65 (Dec. 1997) 92–97.

[93] The finds from the area of the ancient deme have been collected and catalogued by H. R. Goette, in Hoepfner, ed., *Kult und Kultbauten,* 116–131. The map (fig. 2) locates the early churches and indicates the provenience of inscriptions, gravestones, and architectural blocks. See also Goette, *Horos* 10–12 (1992–98) 105–118; J. S. Traill, *The Political Organization of Attica, Hesperia* Suppl. 14 (Princeton 1975) 54 and map 1, where Pallene is between Gargettos to the east and Phlya to the west.

[94] This account of the newly excavated foundations follows closely the detailed study of M. Korres, *Horos* 10–12 (1992–98) 83–104. Description of the remains and dimensions are based on his measurements. Korres (pp. 91–94) believes in Dinsmoor's "Theseum architect," who is supposed to have designed the Hephaisteion, the Temple of Poseidon at Sounion, and the Temple of Nemesis at Rhamnous, as well as the Temple of Ares. He also follows Dinsmoor's chronology for the four temples (p. 93). This view of the building's authorship does not affect his reconstruction of the superstructure that stood on the foundations at Pallene. See note 21 above for doubts about Dinsmoor's theory. For brief mention of the recent excavations, Camp, *Archaeology of Athens,* 116–117.

[95] Korres, *Horos* 10–12 (1992–98) 88–89, for dimensions and details of the foundations; overall dimensions, 85, where the width is given as 16.50 m. This must be a typographical error, since a width of 16.40 m is used for the calculation (p. 90).

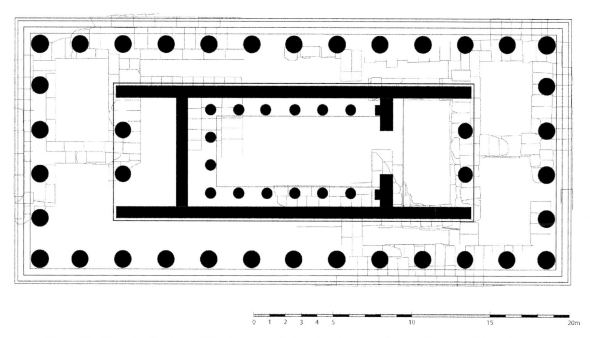

Figure 82. Temple of Athena Pallenis, restored plan showing actual state of excavated foundations

Doric order. On the basis of the foundations alone, without the aid of measurable elements of the superstructure, it is impossible to reconstruct accurately the peristyle of such a building. But Doric hexastyle temples conformed to certain rules of thumb which enable one to estimate the number and spacing of the columns that a given foundation could accommodate. The outer lateral faces of the cella walls normally aligned with the axis of the second column from each corner of the facades, so the width of the cella was equal to the three normal axial intercolumniations. The foundations at Pallene can have carried a cella no wider than ca. 8.40 m and probably a little less, and that yields an approximation of ca. 2.80 m for the normal axial spacing. Another rule of thumb applies to canonical hexastyle temples and provides a more accurate way to estimate the spacing of the columns. The difference between the length and width of the crepidoma, divided by the difference between the number of columns on the flanks and fronts, equals the normal axial intercolumniation. The difference between the length and the width of the preserved foundations is 35.20 − 16.40 = 18.80. If we assume that the flank columns numbered thirteen, as was canonical for the mid-fifth century (13 − 6 = 7), then we can calculate an approximate dimension for the normal axial spacing, 18.80 ÷ 7 = 2.686. This figure is appropriately somewhat smaller than the rough estimate of ca. 2.80 m deduced from the width of the cella building, and the calculation suggests that the excavated foundations supported a Doric hexastyle temple with thirteen columns on its flanks, spaced at intervals of ca. 2.686 m.[96] Not much more than this can be inferred about the peristyle of the temple from the foundations alone.

At the time of excavation, it was obvious that the two uppermost courses of stonework had undergone severe disruption. Many of the blocks were found displaced from their original positions, overturned, or broken into fragments; and, as so often, most of the damage had resulted from scavenging for usable building material in late antiquity and the Middle Ages. Although the excavations produced abundant material from the foundations, and the lower courses were found to be in an

[96] Korres, *Horos* 10–12 (1992–98) 89–90, for the calculations. Dinsmoor, *Hesperia* 9 (1940) 9, used a similar calculation for the superstructure in the Agora. For general rules of thumb governing the design of Doric peristyles, see H. Riemann, *Zum griechischen Peripteraltempel* (Düren 1935) 16–19. For application of the same rule to the Hephaisteion, Koch, *Theseustempel,* 54. For Sounion, p. 232 and note 13 above.

excellent state of preservation, the excavators recovered not one fragment that could be attributed to the superstructure of the temple. This was a most peculiar circumstance, for when ancient buildings fell to wrack and ruin and gradually gave up their stonework for second-hand use, or even when they succumbed to deliberate and violent destruction, there are always telltale signs, albeit shattered fragments, to reveal their existence to the observant investigator. The same situation was true of the whole surrounding district, where some half dozen early churches, those voracious consumers of ancient building blocks, produced no architectural members from the superstructure of this temple.[97] But, significantly, the ruined twelfth-century church of Aghios Ioannes o Theologos, located about 300 meters east of the temple site, utilized in the construction of its walls great squared blocks that were obviously pillaged from the foundation itself. These circumstances led the excavators to conclude that the temple at Pallene had been systematically dismantled, transported to a new site, and reassembled in antiquity, an architectural reincarnation that was not an unknown phenomenon in Roman Athens.[98] Thus it transpired that a classical foundation in the Attic countryside was in need of a superstructure, while a fifth-century temple in the Athenian Agora was in search of its foundation, and it seemed natural to ask whether the two could be joined together in compatible wedlock.

Beginning as early as 1940, several studies have attempted to reconstruct the peristyle of the Temple of Ares in exact detail on the basis of some pieces of the stepped platform, three triglyphs, and fragments of the architrave and cornice.[99] The task was rendered more difficult both by the rough construction of the Roman foundation and by the irregular dimensions of the pit from which two-thirds of the masonry had been pillaged. But a rough estimate from the overall size of the foundation suggested the likelihood that the building was hexastyle with thirteen columns on the flanks. Fortunately, three complete marble blocks of the crepidoma survive, two belonging to the euthynteria course and one to the bottom step. The three blocks have a uniform length of 1.345 m, and, moreover, the dowel holes and pry cuttings in their upper surfaces show that in every case the joints of the next higher course fell at their precise centers. From this evidence, one infers that the temple platform had a regular jointing system based on a modular unit of 1.345 m in each course, except at the four corners.[100] In such a system the vertical joints between the blocks aligned precisely in alternate courses, and every second joint of the euthynteria fell exactly beneath the axis of a column. The axial intercolumniation was thus a simple multiple of the modular unit: 1.345 × 2 = 2.690 m. The blocks of the stylobate then had the same modular dimensions, and a column was centered on every other one.[101] Close comparison with the proportions and dimensions of other Athenian temples, particularly the Hephaisteion and the Temple of Poseidon at Sounion, enabled approximate dimensions to be estimated for the contracted axial spacing at the four corners and for the lower diameter of the Doric columns.[102] In this way it was possible to calculate the total width and length

[97] Goette, in Hoepfner, ed., *Kult und Kultbauten*, 126–131 and fig. 2, for the early churches in the area and the antiquities built into them or found in their vicinity; also Goette, *Horos* 10–12 (1992–98) 106–107, 115–118.

[98] Korres, *Horos* 10–12 (1992–98) 84–88, for disturbance of the foundations and systematic dismantling and removal of the superstructure.

[99] Bibliography, notes 94 and 96 above. Three preserved triglyphs, Agora inv. A 64, A 1375, and A 2277: McAllister, *Hesperia* 28 (1959) 18–21; corner cornice block, inv. A 238, restored from many fragments: McAllister, 23–24; architrave fragments: McAllister, 16–17.

[100] Estimate of overall dimensions, Dinsmoor, *Hesperia* 9 (1940) 9. Two euthynteria blocks: Agora inv. A 146, A 215; bottom step block: inv. A 248. The modular unit of 1.345 m represents the actual average length of the three blocks, which Dinsmoor (pp. 12–13) gives as 1.349 m, 1.343 m, and 1.343 m, respectively. McAllister, *Hesperia* 28 (1959) 9–12 and note 28, gives slight variations in the lengths: 1.339 m, 1.344 m, and 1.3455 m. Dinsmoor's observation that they were "obviously intended to be uniform" is still correct.

[101] See Dinsmoor, *Hesperia* 9 (1940) 26 and fig. 10.

[102] The lower diameter of Doric columns should be very close to twice the width of the triglyph, measurable at 0.554 × 2 = 1.108 m, Dinsmoor, *Hesperia* 9 (1940) 20–21; *AAG*³, 338, gives the lower diameter as ca. 1.10 m. Cf. the Hephaisteion, triglyph 0.519 × 2 = 1.038 m (actual lower diameter 1.018 m, thickened to 1.038 m at the corners). In the Temple of Ares,

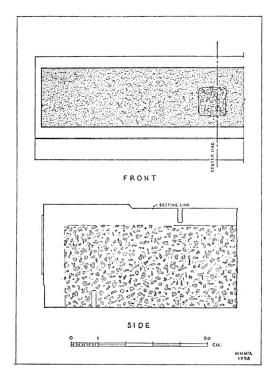

Figure 83. Restored typical step block, later reused in Temple of Ares

of the temple on the stylobate as ca. 14.344 × ca. 33.174 m.[103] To these estimates can be added the projection of the stepped platform beyond the stylobate to yield the building's overall dimensions. The single surviving step block preserves an engraved line 0.395 m behind the finished face, and this indicates the position of the next step (Fig. 83). Similar engraved lines on the euthynteria blocks show that this lowest course of the crepidoma projected 0.157 beyond the first step on all four sides of the temple. When the width of the four step treads and twice the projection of the euthynteria are added in each direction, the overall size of the building on the foundations comes to ca. 16.238 × ca. 35.068 m.[104]

 These calculations reveal an astonishing congruence of dimensions between the foundation at Pallene and the marble superstructure in the Agora (Figs. 83, 85). Two different methods of approximation, conducted quite independently by different scholars—one based on the standard syntax of Doric design, the other on precise measurements of preserved architectural members—have arrived

---

the lower diameter of the corner columns should be increased by 0.02 m, on the analogy of the Hephaisteion, to ca. 1.12 m. The contracted spacing at the corners equals the normal axial spacing minus the contraction of approximately ¹⁄₁₅ of the normal spacing and minus the increment in diameter of the corner column: Dinsmoor (above) 14–15; McAllister, *Hesperia* 28 (1959) 59, note 146. Ares: ¹⁄₁₅ × 2.69 = 0.1793 – 0.02 = 0.1593 m contraction; 2.69 – 0.1593 = 2.531 m corner spacing. Cf. Sounion: ¹⁄₁₅ × 2.522 = 0.1681 – 0.02 = 0.1481 m contraction; 2.522 – 0.1481 = 2.374 m corner spacing. The Hephaisteion used slightly more contraction: ¹⁄₁₅ × 2.581 (flanks), 2.583 (fronts) = 0.172 contraction; 2.581 – 0.172 = 2.409 (flanks), 2.583 – 0.172 = 2.411 (fronts). Dinsmoor, *AAG*³, 338, gives the corner spacing as Ares ca. 2.53 m, Sounion ca. 2.374 m, Hephaisteion 2.413 m.

 [103] Dimensions from Dinsmoor, *AAG*³, 338, and Korres, *Horos* 10–12 (1992–98). Slightly smaller totals calculated earlier: Dinsmoor, *Hesperia* 9 (1940) 24; McAllister, *Hesperia* 28 (1959) 60. Three normal axial spacings (2.69 × 3 = 8.07); two corner axial spacings (2.53 × 2 = 5.06); two corner radii (0.56 × 2 = 1.12); two stylobate projections (0.047 × 2 = 0.094). 8.07 + 5.06 + 1.12 + 0.094 = 14.344 m width of stylobate. Seven normal axial spacings (2.69 × 7 = 18.83); 14.344 + 18.83 = 33.174 m length of stylobate.

 [104] Engraved setting lines on step and euthynteria, Dinsmoor, *Hesperia* 9 (1940) 24. Width of four step treads (0.395 × 4 = 1.580); width of two euthynteria projections (0.157 × 2 = 0.314). 14.344 + 1.580 + 0.314 = 16.238 m overall width of crepidoma; 33.174 + 1.580 + 0.314 = 35.068 m overall length of crepidoma.

Figure 84. Restored ceiling coffer, later reused in Temple of Ares

at the same number of columns and have estimated their axial spacing as 2.686 m at Pallene and 2.69 m in Athens. Furthermore, the overall size of the marble crepidoma, as calculated above, would fit perfectly on the excavated foundations, which measure 16.40 × 35.20 m. The top course of the poros stonework would project beyond the marble enthynteria by approximately 0.081 m along each flank and 0.066 m at the two ends of the temple. One could hardly ask for a more convincing demonstration that the temple in Athens was built for the foundation at Pallene. Only the discovery of identical architectural members on both sites, as for example the Ionic capitals of the same series from Sounion and the Agora, could provide more conclusive proof. We should then proceed to restore the temple in the Agora to its original foundation, at least for purposes of discussion, and revive its classical form as the Temple of Athena Pallenis.

When we attempt to reconstruct the marble superstructure of the peristyle on the excavated foundation, several features of the architectural design at once command our attention. If columns measuring ca. 1.10 m in lower diameter are arranged with axial spacings of 2.69 m on both fronts and flanks (reduced to ca. 2.53 m at the corners), an interesting and unusual relationship between the cella building and its surrounding colonnades is immediately observable. The columns and antae of the pronaos align perfectly with the third column from each corner of the flanks, an arrangement common to both the Hephaisteion in Athens and the Temple of Poseidon at Sounion. In the two latter temples, this alignment enabled the entablature of the pronaos, with its sculptured frieze, to extend across the pteromata on either side, and this feature was undoubtedly replicated in the temple at Pallene. It is interesting to note that the builders anticipated the lateral extension of the entablature in the construction of the foundations. At both ends of the cella, the foundations for the porches are carried across the full interior width to abut the outer foundations. In fact, the inner rectangle is also connected to the outer rectangle at the middle of the fronts and at two intermediate points on each flank. But the architect at Pallene also adopted the same plan at the west end of the temple, where the porch of the opisthodomos is likewise perfectly aligned with the third column from the corner.[105] This represents a significant departure from the design of the other two temples. At Sounion the rear porch aligned with the axis of the third column, while in the Hephaisteion the

[105] Korres, *Horos* 10–12 (1992–98) 93–97.

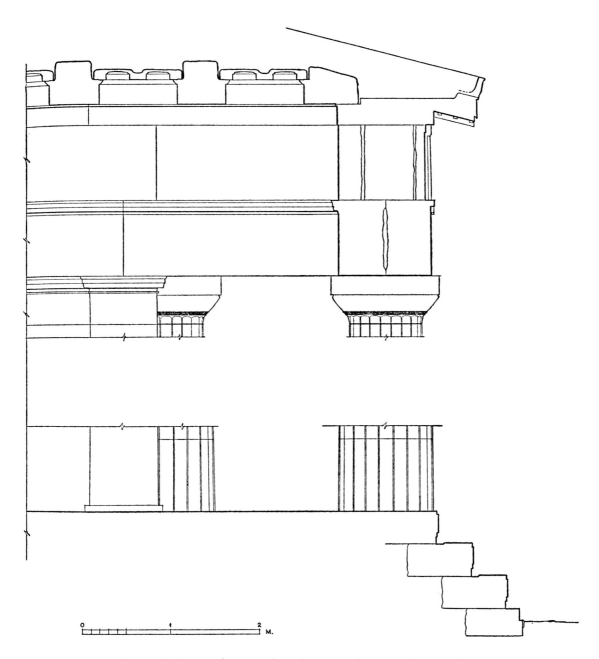

Figure 85. Restored section through east porch, as later Temple of Ares

cella extends to the midpoint of the second intercolumniation. In both temples the result, as we have seen, was to limit the sculptured frieze of the opisthodomos to the width of the cella building. The unusual placement of the pronaos in relation to the outer peristyle has frequently been viewed as one of the distinguishing hallmarks in the style of a single architect, who is supposed to have designed all three temples. In each case, however, the arrangement of the opisthodomos betrays substantial differences, and these are best explained as the work of three closely contemporary architects who were intimately familiar with each other's ideas and influenced by each other's designs.

Examination of the interior plan of the cella building at Pallene leads to the same conclusion. Now for the first time the newly excavated foundation provides firm evidence for the architect's treatment of the cella, which had always been a matter of conjecture for the reconstituted building in Athens. The lateral foundations for the pronaos and opisthodomos measure 1.30 m, an appropriate width for walls ca. 0.70 m thick, which allows for the projection of the wall base and bearings for floor slabs on either side. But the same lateral foundations for the cella itself have been widened to 2.60 m, the same dimension as the outer foundations for the peristyle. This increased width was plainly intended to provide a uniform underpinning for side walls ca. 0.70 m thick and for interior colonnades composed of shafts ca. 0.60 m in lower diameter and set ca. 0.50 m in front of the walls. Exceptional interest, moreover, attaches to the western foundation, which carried the rear cross-wall of the cella. This consisted of a solid masonry platform 3.90 m in width, and the extraordinary enlargement of the foundation shows how the architect provided support not only for the rear wall but for a return of the colonnade across the back of the cella and for the base of the cult statue as well.[106] So the Temple of Athena Pallenis had a three-sided internal peristyle supporting the ceiling within the cella. This feature of Doric design we have already encountered in other temples of the Periklean period. It was invented for the great eastern cella of the Parthenon, where the enormous volume of the interior allowed the colonnades not only to support the ceiling but to mold and articulate the space itself.[107] The stimulus of that revolutionary innovation elicited differing responses from contemporary Athenian architects. In the Hephaisteion, whose construction was already well advanced, the architect inserted extra interior foundations with some difficulty and adjusted the position of the cross-walls in order to replicate the interior of the Parthenon on a small scale. On the contrary, the architect at Sounion reacted to the vast interior of the Parthenon by omitting the internal colonnades altogether in order to emphasize the uncluttered spaciousness of the cella.[108] The architect at Pallene likewise took inspiration from the Parthenon, but for him the internal three-sided peristyle was integral to the design of the temple. The structural unity of the cella foundations and their physical connection with the outer rectangle of the peristyle show that the interior colonnades were part of the plan from the beginning. In this respect the temple contrasts strikingly with the protracted structural history of the Hephaisteion, and the differences between them are best attributed to the work of different architects. Furthermore, we may suspect that the temple at Pallene was not designed until after the completion of the Parthenon, and so its construction should be dated in the 430s rather than earlier.[109]

A few scraps of information have come down to us concerning the cult that the new marble temple was built to serve. The sanctuary at Pallene was the center of a league of neighboring demes that shared the perquisites and responsibilities of conducting the worship of Athena Pallenis.[110] The

---

[106] Korres, *Horos* 10–12 (1992–98) 88–89, dimensions of the foundations; 90, thickness of the walls; 96–97, arrangement of the interior colonnades.

[107] For the interior colonnades in the Parthenon, see chap. 4, pp. 100–102 above.

[108] For the cella of the Temple of Poseidon, pp. 236–237 above. For the interior of the Hephaisteion, Dinsmoor, *Hesperia* Suppl. 5 (1941) 45–46, alterations to the west cross-wall; 49–57, to the east cross-wall; 40–44, 65–73, foundations for the interior colonnades. Cf. chap. 5, pp. 145–146 above.

[109] Dinsmoor, *Hesperia* 9 (1940) 47, dated the Temple of Ares to 440–436, and although this is a quite arbitrary four-year period in his scheme for the career of his "Theseum architect," the actual dates are probably nearly correct. On the basis of the foundations for the cella and interior colonnades at Pallene, one would prefer to think that the temple was not designed until after the completion of the Parthenon in 438. Moreover, it should be emphasized that the step block (A 248) retains the protective surface, 0.008 m thick, on its tread and riser, which means that the stepped platform of the temple never received its final dressing. In this respect it invites comparison with the Propylaia on the Acropolis and the Temple of Nemesis at Rhamnous; see Miles, *Hesperia* 58 (1989) 155–156, pls. 34, 35. Further on the date, see p. 260 below.

[110] The name of the goddess varies in the fifth-century sources between Athena Pallenis, a cult epithet, and Athena at Pallenis, the location of the sanctuary. For the former: *IG* I³ 383, lines 121–122 (429/8), Ἀθεναίας Παλληνίδος; also Hdt. 1.62; Eur. *Heraclid.* 849, 1031. The latter form of the name: *IG* I³ 369, line 88 (426/5), Ἀθε[ναίας ἐπὶ Παλλ]ενίδι; cf. line 71. Pallenis is also used as a place name in [Aristot.] *Ath. Pol.* 15.3, νικήσας τὴν ἐπὶ Παλληνίδι μάχην, "(Peisistratos) having won the battle at Pallenis"; cf. *Ath. Pol.* 17.4; Hesych., s.v. Παρθένου Παλληνίδος (π 926 Schmidt) [ἱέρεια] Ἀθηνᾶς. ἔστι γὰρ ἱερὸν Ἀθηνᾶς ἐν Παλληνίδι, "Athena. For there is a sanctuary of Athena at Pallenis." This form is different from the name of the deme Παλλήνη; see schol. Aristoph. *Acharn.* 234a (Wilson) = Androtion, *FGrH* 324 F 35. It has been suggested that Pallenis may be a more precise locution then the deme name, possibly referring to a hill or other natural feature; see R. Schlaifer, *HSCP* 54 (1943) 39, note 7. In fact, the temple is now known to have stood on the flank of a low hill which

league appears to be extremely old, for already in Archaic times it had come under the control of the Athenian state and its operations were regulated by the sacred laws of the basileus, the king archon of Athens. A few extracts of these texts are quoted by Athenaeus and give the impression that they were early archaic documents reworked in the fifth century.[111] Some tantalizing details of the cult's administration emerge. It was the responsibility of the basileus to appoint officials of the cult called "archons," who in turn chose a number of "parasites," or participants in the sacred feast, from the demes belonging to the league.[112] All of these were joined in some aspect of the ritual by the "old men" of the league and "women married to first husbands."[113] An inscription of the mid-fourth century found near the site of the temple lists the "archons" and "parasites," presumably of a particular year. From this we learn that four "archons" were recruited from the demes of Gargettos, Acharnai, Pallene, and Paiania, which are likely to have formed the original nucleus of the league. Below these officials are the names of twenty-eight "parasites" representing at least twelve other demes widely scattered around the Attic countryside. This somewhat surprising spread of participating demes suggests the possibility that by the mid-fourth century the league had expanded beyond its archaic nexus.[114] In preparation for the festival, the "parasites" selected a sacrificial victim, possibly a cow, from a herd probably belonging to the goddess. They also collected a portion of barley, perhaps from the newly harvested crop likewise raised on sacred property, and the quota brought in by the representatives of Acharnai was to be offered to Apollo in the form of "cakes." After sacrificing the victim to Athena, the whole company "feasted in the temple precinct according to ancestral custom."[115]

One other abstract from the king's laws is of interest because it provides some information about the sanctuary itself: εἰς <δὲ> τὴν ἐπισκευὴν τοῦ νεὼ καὶ τοῦ παρασιτίου καὶ τῆς οἰκίας τῆς ἱερᾶς διδόναι ... τὸ ἀργύριον ὁπόσου ἂν οἱ τῶν ἱερῶν ἐπισκευασταὶ μισθώσωσιν, "For the repair of the temple, the parasites' building, and the sacred house funds are to be provided at whatever price the repairers of sacred buildings shall let the contract."[116] From this clause of the law, we learn of three different structures within the precinct of Athena: the temple itself; the parasition, which was probably a banqueting hall where the "parasites" feasted; and the sacred house, which was probably the dwelling of the priestess[117] or other cult officials. Maintenance of these sacred buildings was assigned to a board of Athenian officials who were authorized to negotiate the price of work with private contractors, just like the overseers of the Periklean buildings. In the time of Aristotle, the repairers of sacred buildings were ten in number, chosen by lot; they operated on a fixed annual bud-

---

is one of the most prominent features of the district; see Goette, in Hoepfner, ed., *Kult und Kultbauten,* 119–122, figs. 2, 3; Goette, *Horos* 10–12 (1992–98) 112.

[111] Athen. 6.235A–D. The quotations in Athenaeus have acquired a number of corruptions in their transmission to us. The most detailed study of the texts and their interpretation is R. Schlaifer, *HSCP* 54 (1943) 35–67; for the date of the laws, 43. See also the brief account of the league, Parker, *Athenian Religion,* 330–331.

[112] Athen. 6.235C, quoting Krates, *Attic Dialect, FGrH* 362 F 7; Schlaifer, *HSCP* 54 (1943) 47–51, 60. For the functions of cult parasites, see P. Schmitt Pantel, *La cité au banquet* (Rome 1992) 100–104.

[113] Athen. 6.235A, quoting Themison, *FGrH* 374 F 1. An author by the name of Themison is otherwise unknown, but the quotation is attributed to a book apparently devoted specifically to describing the Temple of Athena Pallenis, so the sanctuary must have been well appointed with votive offerings and other monuments of interest. See Schlaifer, *HSCP* 54 (1943) 40, note 11. The rare word πρωτοπόσις also attributed to the king's laws, Pollux 3.39.

[114] See G. R. Stanton, *BSA* 79 (1984) 292–298; Stanton, *BSA* 80 (1985) 259, pl. 23, re-editing the inscription first published by W. Peek, *AM* 67 (1942 [1951]) 24–29, no. 26. The stone was built into the church of Aghia Triada located about half a kilometer distant from the temple site; see Goette, in Hoepfner, ed., *Kult und Kultbauten,* 128, no. 3; Goette, *Horos* 10–12 (1992–98) 106. Possible expansion of the league by the fourth century, Parker, *Athenian Religion,* 331.

[115] Athen. 6.235C, quoting Krates, *Attic Dialect, FGrH* 362 F 7; with the discussion of Schlaifer, *HSCP* 54 (1943) 51–59.

[116] Athen. 6.235D, quoting Krates, *FGrH* 362 F 7; text as Schlaifer, *HSCP* 54 (1943) 61, who postulates a lacuna after the infinitive διδόναι. The subject of the infinitive in the original text would presumably have been the official or board providing the funds, e.g., τοὺς κωλακρέτας or τοὺς ταμίας, which was simply omitted in Krates' quotation.

[117] One priestess of Athena Pallenis was a certain Diphile, whose name was copied from an inscription in the sanctuary, where it served as a dating formula for a list of "parasites": Athen. 6.234F.

get of thirty minas, and they carried out only the most necessary repairs. The board described by the king's law seems to have been responsible for more substantial repairs than the routine maintenance handled by their fourth-century successors. But if they were similarly constituted, the board itself was surely a product of democratic administrative procedures, and their appearance here suggests a later redaction of the archaic text, possibly at the end of the fifth century.[118] In any case, the temple mentioned in the law is likely to be the building that stood on the excavated foundation at Pallene.

Another fascinating shred of evidence may possibly have some bearing on the history of the sanctuary in the fifth century. This is the inscribed text of a dedication that was recorded by the Hellenistic antiquarian Polemon of Ilion: ἐν δὲ Παλληνίδι τοῖς ἀναθήμασιν ἐπιγέγραπται τάδε· "ἄρχοντες καὶ παράσιτοι ἀνέθεσαν οἱ ἐπὶ Πυθοδώρου ἄρχοντος στεφανωθέντες χρυσῷ στεφάνῳ," "And at Pallenis there is inscribed on the votive offerings: 'Dedicated by the archons and parasites who were awarded a golden crown in the archonship of Pythodoros.'"[119] The reference must be to the archon of 432/1, and at this early date the award of a golden crown by the Athenian state to local cult officials at a rural sanctuary represents a very significant honor indeed. The grant is the more striking because, as far as our fragmentary evidence goes, the cult managed by these officials catered only to a limited segment of the population from certain participating demes. One infers that the year 432/1 must have marked an important milestone in the history of the sanctuary, and the "archons" and "parasites" of that year memorialized the occasion by staging an especially splendid celebration of the festival. It is tempting to think that what they celebrated was the completion and dedication of the new Temple of Athena Pallenis. If the building was designed just after 438, as the plan of the cella gives reason to believe, the interval of six years provides sufficient time for construction to reach its final stage in 432/1.

Shortly thereafter, the sanctuary at Pallene became the locus for some Athenian political myth-making of the kind that seems to have proliferated as propaganda on both sides on the eve of the Peloponnesian War. Since the Temple of Athena was situated in the narrow gap between Hymettos and Pentelikon, anyone traveling from the Plain of Athens to the Mesogeia or to the Marathonian Tetrapolis in northeastern Attica had of necessity to pass it by, just as do the modern highways that give access to the same districts. On more than one occasion in the past, its strategic location had made it the site of military operations both historical and mythical.[120] Peisistratos, seeking to return as tyrant of Athens, encamped his forces within view of the sanctuary and there fought and defeated the Athenian defenders, who had marched out from the city.[121] Near this same spot, Attic myth placed the battle in which Theseus slaughtered the fifty sons of Pallas, who rebelled against his royal power and sought to trap him from ambush in neighboring Gargettos.[122] By this route, Eurys-

[118] The only information about the repairers of sacred buildings is [Aristot.] *Ath. Pol.* 50.1. For their operations at Pallene, Schlaifer, *HSCP* 54 (1943) 56–57; later editing of the king's law, Schlaifer, 43.

[119] Athen. 6.234F, quoting Polemon; Müller, *FHG* III, p. 138, fr. 78; cf. Schlaifer, *HSCP* 54 (1943) 42.

[120] For Pallene as the site of military operations, see Vian, *Guerre des géants*, 276; Robertson, *Festivals and Legends*, 52–53, but Pallene, the Attic deme, was not the locus of the battle of the gods and giants, as there stated. That mythical engagement is frequently sited on Pallene, the western peninsula of the Chalkidike, but never in Attica; see Vian, 261.

[121] Hdt. 1.62; [Aristot.] *Ath. Pol.* 15.3, 17.4; and Rhodes, *Commentary*, 208–209. Cf. schol. Aristoph. *Acharn.* 234a (Wilson), citing Androtion, *FGrH* 324 F 35. Andok. 1 *Myst.* 106 claims that his great-grandfather Leogoras was victorious against the tyrants in a battle fought ἐπὶ Παλληνίῳ. It is not clear whether Andokides has confused his history or whether he is referring to an otherwise unrecorded engagement at the time of the expulsion of Hippias in 511/10. See MacDowell, ed., *Andokides on the Mysteries,* 212–213; Davies, *APF*, 27–28. When the exiled Hippias guided the Persian forces to Marathon in 490 (Hdt. 6.107), he presumably hoped to repeat his father's successful return by force of arms. Had the Athenian army not met the Persians at Marathon, the invaders would assuredly have marched by the sanctuary at Pallene.

[122] Pallas, from whom the deme took its name, one of four sons of Pandion, who ruled the Mesogeia and southeastern Attica: Apollod. 3.15.5; Strabo 9 1 6 (p. 392), quoting Philochoros, *FGrH* 328 F 107; cf. schol. Aristoph. *Wasps* 1223 (Koster), *Lysist.* 58 (Hangard). Because of his fifty sons, the Pallantidai, Pallas called "breeder of giants," Sophokles, *TrGF* 4.24 (Radt), quoted by Strabo (above). They set out to capture Athens and drive Theseus out, and lay in ambush at Gargettos but were betrayed by a herald of Pallas and slaughtered by Theseus and the Athenians: Schol. Eur. *Hippol.* 35, quoting

theus, the king of Argos, marched his invading army toward Marathon in order to lay hands on the children of Herakles and drive them out from their refuge in the Attic Tetrapolis. But Demophon, the son of Theseus, marshaled the Athenians in defense of the Herakleidai and routed the invaders in battle, while Eurystheus died in the fighting. This latter story of the reception and protection of the Herakleidai was already recounted earlier in the fifth century by Pherekydes and was known to Herodotos.[123] By the fourth century it had become one of the standard ingredients of Athenian panegyric, particularly favored by orators of funeral eulogy.[124]

At the very beginning of the Peloponnesian War, the story received especially striking embroidery in Euripides' dramatic version, *Heraclidae,* a play that historians of the theater date to the spring of 430.[125] Some of the innovative elements by which that playwright manipulated the original myth are specifically associated with the Temple of Athena Pallenis. In Euripides' account of the battle, Eurystheus was not killed but fled from the field in his chariot with the aged and doddering Iolaos in hot pursuit. "As he was passing the sacred hill of divine Athena Pallenis,"[126] a miracle transpired: in answer to his fervent prayers, the old man is rejuvenated for a single day to exact vengeance from his enemies. It is at the sanctuary itself that his chariot is shrouded in cloud and the transformation occurs. Thence begins the long chase across Attica and the Megarid to the Skironian cliffs, whereupon Iolaos returns with Eurystheus as a prisoner of war.[127] At the end of the play, the sanctuary is the scene of an even more profound and enduring transformation. Alkmene, guardian and grandmother of Herakles' children, insists that the helpless prisoner be put to death, contrary to the law of Athens and the customs of all Greeks.[128] In response, the Argive king, who began the play as a brutal and cowardly tyrant, now proclaims himself the future benefactor of Athens.

> For when I die, you Athenians will bury me where fate foretold, before the shrine of the divine maiden, Athena Pallenis. I shall lie for all time beneath the earth, a resident foreigner who is kindly to you and a protector of the city, but most hostile to the descendants of Herakles' children, when they come here with a great army, betraying the kindness you showed them.[129]

The descendants of the Herakleidai are, of course, the Spartans of the fifth century, and it is against aggression from this quarter that Eurystheus will protect Athens. In the finale of the drama, the enemy general stays behind forever and is translated into a local hero whose benign numen will ward off hostile invasion from the land. Euripides places the tomb of Eurystheus in the sanctuary of Pallene; although his is the earliest reference to it, both the location and the existence of the hero cult

Philochoros, *FGrH* 328 F 108; Plut. *Thes.* 3.5, 13.1–3; Apollod. *Ep.* 1.11. See A. Brückner, *AM* 16 (1891) 200–234; Vian, *Guerre des géants,* 274–276.

[123] Pherekydes, *FGrH* 3 F 84, cited by Antoninus Liberalis, *Met.* 33.1–2; Hdt. 9.27.2. On the sources for the myth, see J. Wilkins, ed., *Euripides Heraclidae* (Oxford 1993) xiv–xv.

[124] See Lys. 2.11–16; Xen. *Mem.* 3.5.10; [Plat.] *Menex.* 239B; cf. Isokr. 4 *Panagyr.* 56–60; and the discussion of N. Loraux, *The Invention of Athens* (Cambridge, MA, 1986) 64–76; Gomme, *HCT,* vol. 2, 106–107.

[125] See G. Zuntz, *The Political Plays of Euripides* (Manchester 1955) 81–88; Wilkins, *Heraclidae,* xxxiii–xxxv, is less certain. He dates it after *Medea* (431) and before or after *Hippolytus* (428) but is inclined to follow Zuntz.

[126] Eur. *Heraclid.* 849–850; Wilkins, *Heraclidae,* 164. For the hill as a feature of the topography, Goette, in Hoepfner, ed., *Kult und Kultbauten,* 119–122, figs. 2, 3.

[127] Iolaos rejuvenated in answer to his prayers, Eur. *Heraclid.* 851–853. Shrouded in cloud and transformed into a young man, 854–858. Eurystheus captured near the Skironian cliffs, 859–863. The rejuvenation of Iolaos is also known in the Theban tradition, schol. Pind. *Pyth.* 9.137a (Drachmann). Within Euripides' text Eurystheus is not killed, but in other sources he is. Pind. *Pyth.* 9.79–83: Iolaos kills Eurystheus at Thebes. Apollod. 2.8.1: Hyllos kills him beyond the Skironian cliffs. Paus. 1.44.10: Iolaos kills him as he flees from Attica. Strabo 8.6.19 (p. 377): Eurystheus fell in battle at Marathon. Diod. 4.57: Hyllos kills him. See Wilkins, *Heraclidae,* xvi–xviii.

[128] Eur. *Heraclid.* 958–980.

[129] Eur. *Heraclid.* 1030–1036. On Eurystheus as the enemy who becomes a local hero: Wilkins, *Heraclidae,* xxiv–xxv, 177–178; Kearns, *Heroes of Attica,* 48–50, 164.

are unfortunately unique to this play. According to Strabo and the late lexicons, Eurystheus's body was buried at Gargettos and his severed head at the deme of Trikorynthos near Marathon, while Pausanias saw a tomb that was purportedly that of Eurystheus beyond the Skironion cliffs, near the Isthmus of Corinth.[130] So we cannot say with any confidence why the playwright put special emphasis on the sanctuary of Athena Pallenis as the scene of Iolaos's miraculous rejuvenation and the site of Eurystheus's burial and future cult. The ancient shrine may have been prominent in people's minds at the time simply because the new marble temple had recently been completed. With the hindsight of history, however, we can see the terrible irony of Euripides' telling of the tale. In the spring of 430, Athens had survived the initial Spartan invasion of the previous year relatively unscathed and spent the winter preparing industriously for the forthcoming campaign.[131] At this very moment, the poet issued a clarion call of hope and patriotic confidence, for Eurystheus's prophecy plainly presages the failure of any future Spartan invasion. But we know from Thucydides that the second invasion of Attica was the most devastating of all.[132]

THE TEMPLE OF NEMESIS AT RHAMNOUS

The site of Rhamnous was the northernmost deme on the east coast of Attica, with a clear view across the Euboian Narrows to the mountainous island beyond. The town itself, with its fortified acropolis, was by the seashore; but above, in a saddle of the surrounding hills, was a sanctuary of the goddess Nemesis. Here was built the smallest and latest of the peripteral temples of Attica, but one which has special relevance to the Athenian building program of the fifth century.[133] As her cult developed at Rhamnous in the Classical period, this strange deity was little more than the personification of retribution and righteous indignation, particularly invoked for the punishment of human acts of hubris. When Pausanias (1.33.2–3) visited her temple he heard from the local inhabitants of the goddess's involvement in the Battle of Marathon. The legend told how the Persians who landed at Marathon had brought with them Parian marble to make a trophy of victory, so easily did they think they would conquer the Athenians. From that very piece of marble was later fashioned the cult statue of Nemesis.

The statue was famous in antiquity and brought great renown to the deme of Rhamnous. But ancient writers disagreed about the identity of the sculptor. Pausanias and others attributed it to Pheidias, while according to Pliny and Strabo the image was by Agorakritos of Paros, a favorite pupil

---

[130] Euripides is likely to have invented Eurystheus's tomb at Pallene (Wilkins, *Heraclidae*, 191) or alternatively grafted the story of Eurystheus onto a local hero cult (Kearns, *Heroes of Attica*, 49). The local tradition about the burial was quite precise: Strabo 8.6.19 (p. 377) placed the tomb at Gargettos, which is confirmed by Hesych., s.v. Γαργηττός (γ 177 Latte), and Steph. Byz., s.v. Γαργηττός (p. 199 Meineke); but the severed head was buried at Trikorynthos, "near the spring Makaria below the carriage-road," Strabo (above). Paus. 1.44.10, for the tomb near the Isthmus that was shown to him.

[131] During the invasion of summer 431, the Spartans wasted time besieging Oinoe (Thuc. 2.18.2), did some damage to the Thriasian plain and the district around Acharnai, where they encamped, "ravaged some of the demes between Mount Parnes and Mount Brilessos" (Thuc. 2.23.1), and then withdrew through Boiotia by way of Oropos (Thuc. 2.23.3). Athenian preparations during winter 431/0, Thuc. 2.24. For the bearing of these events on the production of Euripides' *Heraclidae*, Zuntz, *Political Plays of Euripides*, 85–87.

[132] Thuc. 3.26.3 writes of the invasion of 427: "And this invasion proved most grievous to the Athenians after the second," i.e., the invasion of 430 (cf. Thuc. 2.47.2). After ravaging the plain of Athens, they advanced into the Mesogeia as far as Laureion (Thuc. 2.55.1, and see Gomme, *HCT*, vol. 2, 162–163); and in summer 430, "they laid waste the whole land" (Thuc. 2.57.2).

[133] On the site generally, see B. K. Petrakos, Ὁ Δῆμος τοῦ Ῥαμνοῦντος (Athens 1999) vol. 1, Τοπογραφία; B. K. Petrakos, *A Concise Guide to Rhamnous* (Athens 1983). On the Temple of Nemesis: Dinsmoor, *AAG*³, 181–183; Dinsmoor, *Hesperia* 30 (1961) 179–204. For a detailed reconstruction of the architecture, M. M. Miles, *Hesperia* 58 (1989) 133–249, hereafter Miles, "Temple"; Camp, *Archaeology of Athens*, 112–114, 301–305.

of Pheidias.[134] The nice irony of the statue's material and origin was a fine example of the goddess's retribution at work and caught the imagination of later poets. An epigram by Parmenion preserved in the *Greek Anthology* perfectly encapsulates the legend: "I, the stone of whom the Medes hoped to make a trophy, was changed opportunely to the form of Nemesis, the goddess justly planted on the shore of Rhamnous to be a witness to the Attic land of victory and the skill of her artist."[135] It is, of course, impossible to know how much, if not all, of this legend is apocryphal. But it is interesting to note that Georgios Despinis, in a brilliant reconstruction of the statue's shattered fragments, has shown that it was indeed carved from a single piece of Parian marble.[136] It is quite clear, however, that the temple and the statue were made expressly for each other during the decade from 430 to 420. This has much to tell us about the Athenians' motivation for the massive campaign of temple building. They were still prepared to build temples to memorialize the victory at Marathon seventy years after the fact.

Today the Temple of Nemesis is relatively well preserved, although it does not appear so at first sight on the ground. Much of the steps and crepidoma and several drums of Doric columns are still in situ. It has been estimated that approximately 85% of the marble blocks of the peristyle are still extant, though many of them are in fragmentary condition.[137] The temple was still better preserved when the site was first explored by an expedition of the Society of Dilettanti in 1813. At that time the architect John Peter Gandy took measurements and made restored drawings of all parts of the temple.[138] What first strikes the visitor to the ruins today, and even more so in Gandy's restored elevations, is the unfinished state of the building. The risers of the steps still retain a roughly stippled band of protective surface. Similar rough rectangular panels remain on the surface of the stylobate between the columns of the peristyle. The shafts of the columns never received their fluting, and one of the few surviving orthostates of the cella wall has not only the rough stippled panel but the visible remains of two lifting bosses, like the exterior walls of the Propylaia on the Acropolis. Although some scholars have attempted to argue that the rough stippled panels at Rhamnous and at some other Attic temples are deliberate rustication, left for decorative effect, it seems far more likely that the final dressing of the stonework was simply never completed.[139] So we encounter once again a phenomenon that recurred in the construction history of several of the Periklean buildings: work that was delayed, postponed, altered or, in this case, left unfinished. Whether this happened for financial or political reasons, or because of a shortage of skilled marble workers, there is no point in speculating. But construction of the Temple of Nemesis was, as we shall see, almost exactly contemporary with the final phases of the Hephaisteion and the Temple of Athena Nike on the Acropolis, both of which were finally completed in every detail.

The Temple of Nemesis is built of white marble from quarries at Aghia Marina about two kilometers distant from the sanctuary, and it shared with other Athenian buildings—the Older Parthenon, the Hephaisteion, and the Propylaia—the peculiarity that a different stone was used for its euthynteria and lowest step, in this case gray marble quarried even nearer the building site. The

---

[134] Attributed to Pheidias: Paus. 1.33.2–3; Zenobios 5.82; Mela 2.46; Tzetzes (quoted by Overbeck, *Schriftquellen*, nos. 838, 839); and the lexicographers (Hesych., *Suda*, Phot., s.v. Ῥαμνουσία Νέμεσις). Attributed to Agorakritos: Pliny, *NH* 36.17; Strabo 9.1.17 (p. 396).

[135] *Anthologia Graeca* 16.222, trans. W. R. Paton, *The Greek Anthology*, vol. 5 (Loeb). For the date ca. A.D. 40, see A. S. F. Gow and D. L. Page, *The Greek Anthology*, vol. 2, 327.

[136] G. Despinis, Συμβολὴ στὴ μελέτη τοῦ ἔργου τοῦ Ἀγορακρίτου (Athens 1971) pt. 1.

[137] Miles, "Temple," 138.

[138] *The Unedited Antiquities of Attica*, Society of Dilettanti (London 1817) chaps. 6 and 7.

[139] A. T. Hodge and R. A. Tomlinson, *AJA* 73 (1969) 185–192, have argued for deliberate rustication, but cf. the discussion of T. Kalpaxis, *Hemiteles: Akzidentelle Unfertigkeit und "Bossen-Stil" in der griechischen Baukunst* (Mainz 1986) 135–137, 142. Miles, "Temple," 156, regards the stonework as unfinished.

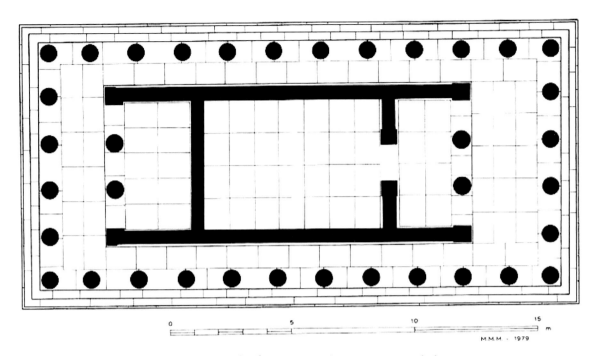

Figure 86. Temple of Nemesis at Rhamnous, restored plan

proximity of the quarries, of course, greatly reduced the cost of transporting the stone and facilitated building operations.

On the platform thus formed, the builders laid out a stylobate measuring 9.996 × 21.420 m[140] to accommodate a peristyle of six columns on the fronts and twelve columns on the flanks (Fig. 86). As was the case with other contemporary temples, the actual dimensions of the stylobate at Rhamnous seem to have been calculated from a predetermined axial intercolumniation of 1.904 m. This dimension was multiplied by the number of intercolumniations in the width and length of the peristyle plus a fraction to allow for the necessary corner contraction. Thus 1.904 × 5¼ = 9.996 and 1.904 × 11¼ = 21.420.[141]

The elevations of the peristyle exhibit a number of the proportional relationships that have now come to be recognized as hallmarks of Periklean Doric architecture (Fig. 87).[142] These innovative alterations to the standard syntax of the Doric order were probably first introduced by the architects of the Parthenon, and borrowed thence by other Athenian architects for the smaller temples. At Rhamnous the columns have a lower diameter of 0.714 m and a height of 4.10 m, which makes the proportion of lower diameter to height 5.74, among the slenderest Doric columns of the Classical period, surpassed in Attica only by the Temple of Poseidon at Sounion. The shafts of the columns incline slightly inward, and the entablature above has been slightly contracted to adjust for the inclination. But the building shows no other refinements, and there is no curvature of the stylobate or crepidoma.[143] Moreover, like other contemporary temples in Attica, the height of the columns was well over twice their axial spacing. The actual ratio is 2.15. The Doric capitals have a compact profile, reduced in height from earlier examples, and the abacus is so narrow (width 0.754 m) that it barely projects at all (0.02 m) beyond the lower diameter on either side.[144] Above the columns, the architrave (0.567 m) and frieze (0.576 m) are almost exactly equal in height, and the

---

[140] Basic dimensions from Dinsmoor, *AAG³*, 339; detailed dimensions from Miles, "Temple," passim.
[141] See Coulton, *BSA* 69 (1974) 76–77 and table 2.
[142] See Coulton, in *Parthenon-Kongress Basel*, 40–44.
[143] Miles, "Temple," 150.
[144] For discussion of the proportions of the capitals, Miles, "Temple," 159–162.

Figure 87. Temple of Nemesis, restored east elevation. Dilettanti, 1817

overall height of the entablature to the horizontal cornice (1.356 m) is just over one-third the height of the columns. In all these respects the temple conforms to the new fifth-century trend in Athenian Doric architecture.

Although the ruins of the temple today appear to be little more than the denuded platform, the entablature is actually the best-preserved part of the superstructure (Fig. 88). Of the original thirty-five blocks that composed the triglyph frieze, twenty-three are still extant, as well as five of the Roman period, when the entire east front of the frieze was replaced. The horizontal cornice that rested on the frieze originally consisted of sixty blocks, of which forty-three and sixteen fragments still survive. The architrave is not so well represented, with only two complete blocks and several large fragments.[145] Undoubtedly the architrave blocks were more extensively pillaged because their regular shape made them more convenient for later reuse. The small size of the temple made it convenient for the masons to carve the blocks of the triglyph frieze with two triglyphs and two metopes on a single block. Most of the extant frieze blocks conform to this pattern, but two shorter blocks have one metope between two triglyphs, one has a triglyph between two metopes, and one has a single triglyph and metope. The tops of the frieze blocks have cuttings for T-clamps at each end to attach them to the adjacent blocks, and cuttings for vertical dowels to anchor the horizontal cornice above. As was standard in the Doric order, the horizontal cornice projected forward of the frieze below it, and the soffit had a mutule centered above each triglyph and each metope of the frieze with a via between the mutules. Each block of the cornice has two mutules and two vias, except at the corners. Like the frieze blocks, the adjacent blocks of the cornice were attached by T-clamps, and they have dowel holes in their tops to fasten the sima of the roof. Exact measurement and careful recording of these cuttings for T-clamps and dowels has made it possible to reconstruct both courses of the entablature with all extant blocks assigned to their precise original positions. It is well to emphasize

---

[145] The preserved blocks of the frieze, Miles, "Temple," 172–181; the horizontal cornice, 185–199; the architrave, 167–168.

Figure 88. Temple of Nemesis, restored elevation of northwest corner. Dilettanti, 1817

that the decision to carve triglyphs and metopes on the same blocks of the frieze shows that the temple had no sculptured metopes. Likewise, the cornice blocks for the east and west fronts have no cuttings in their tops for the installation of pedimental statuary.

Above the horizontal and raking cornices, the edges of the roof were lined with marble sima tiles (Fig. 89). On the flanks, the individual tiles, with the molded sima at the lower edge, were carved in one block with the lowest pan tile. The blocks were wedge shaped to conform to the slope of the roof and had a stop for the cover tiles centered on the upper side of the block. Each tile had a spout for rainwater in the shape of a lion's head, and spaced so that one was above every metope.[146] The profile of the sima consists of an ovolo above a fascia and crowned by an astragal, the same combination of moldings as the sima of the Hephaisteion, but now more developed. The ovolo has greater lower depth and the beginning of a definite upper depth, and the fascia is sharply offset from the curve of the ovolo.[147] The same molded sima turns the corners and ascends to the apex of the pediments. As on the flanks, the individual tiles are carved in one block with the outermost row of

[146] Miles, "Temple," 209–212.
[147] See Shoe, *Greek Mouldings,* 35 and pl. XIX:6; Miles, "Temple," 211, fig. 28. For the sima of the Hephaisteion, see chap. 5, pp. 147–149 and note 10 above; discussed by Dinsmoor, Jr., *AJA* 80 (1976) 233–234 and note 29; cf. Shoe, 35 and pl. LXXVI:2.

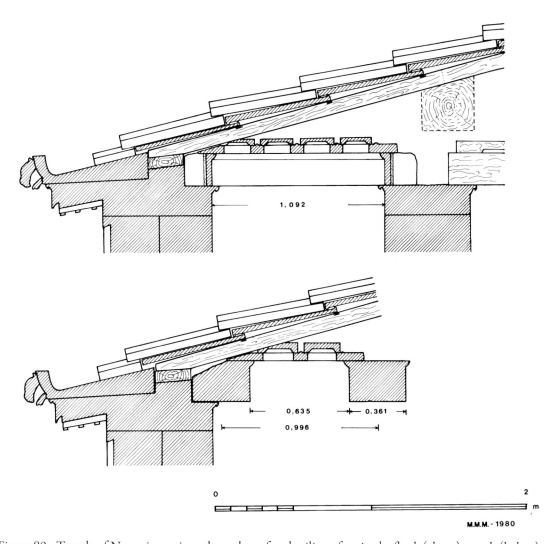

Figure 89. Temple of Nemesis, sections through roof and ceiling of peristyle: flank (above), porch (below)

pan tiles. Between these two ends of the roof, pan tiles measuring 0.476 m wide and 0.686 m long rose to the ridge in forty-four rows, and the joints between them were closed by low triangular cover tiles 0.155 m wide and 0.609 m long. Along the ridge of the roof there was originally a row of palmette antefixes.[148] The only other decorative elements on the exterior of the temple were both corner and central acroteria. A fragmentary corner sima tile preserves part of the base for the southwest corner acroterion, and part of the base for a central acroterion probably also belongs to the west end of the temple. Gandy's restored elevation of the temple shows two corner acroteria, each consisting of a griffin attacking a stag, but these have disappeared from the site since the early nineteenth century.[149]

Within the peristyle, the design of the cella conformed to the normal Doric practice for hexastyle temples. The cella consisted of a single chamber approached by a single door from the east, and at the two ends the pronaos and opisthodomos were arranged with two columns in antis. The col-

[148] Miles, "Temple," 212.
[149] S. Karusu, *AM* 77 (1962) 178–190, attempted to associate with the Temple of Nemesis a fragmentary lower part of a sculptural acroterion consisting of a plinth with feet, which she restores as a central acroterion showing Boreas and Oreithyia. Miles, "Temple," 212–214, rejects the assignment on the grounds that the scale of the sculpture is too big for the temple. The griffin acroteria illustrated by Gandy in *Unedited Antiquities,* pls. 2, 30a, would be inappropriate companions for Boreas and Oreithyia, and it has been suggested by Despinis, Συμβολὴ Ἀγορακρίτου, 163, that they may have been replacements of the Roman period.

umns and antae of the pronaos were aligned with the third exterior flank column so that the pronaos frieze could be carried across the pteromata on either side to abut against the inside of the peristyle frieze. The columns and antae of the opisthodomos, however, were aligned with the midpoint of the second flank intercolumniation, an arrangement which made the opisthodomos rather deeper than the pronaos. The same basic description applies to all four of the Doric hexastyle temples that we have examined, but each temple differs from the others in certain details of the cella. In the Hephaisteion the pronaos and opisthodomos are aligned with the exterior peristyle in the same way as in the Temple of Nemesis, but the pronaos is considerably deeper than the opisthodomos, and the interior was altered in the middle of construction to accommodate a three-sided colonnade, a feature borrowed from the Parthenon. In the cella of the Temple of Nemesis there were no interior columns. In the Temple of Poseidon at Sounion, pronaos and opisthodomos are of equal depth, and the columns and antae of the pronaos are aligned with the third flank column. But the opisthodomos was aligned with the axis of third flank column, so that the frieze was limited to the width of the cella, as in the Hephaisteion. Like the Temple of Nemesis, the Temple of Poseidon had no interior columns. Still another variation of this scheme occurs in the Temple of Athena Pallenis, where the antae at both ends of the cella aligned with the third flank column of the peristyle. The pronaos was deeper than the opisthodomos, and the extant foundations show that a three-sided interior colonnade was planned from the beginning. These variations in the details of the design appear to strengthen the argument put forth by M. M. Miles that the four temples could not have been planned by the same architect, as W. B. Dinsmoor always maintained.[150]

In the four hexastyle temples, it is fascinating to observe how the innovative features of the Parthenon permeated all contemporary Doric designs, often in unexpected details. Plainly the three-sided interior colonnades in the Hephaisteion and the Temple of Athena Pallenis are based directly on the cella of the Parthenon, and the altered proportions of columns and entablature are common to all four temples. At Rhamnous we encounter a detail which shows how thoroughly the Periklean architects studied each others' designs. The anta capitals of the pronaos and opisthodomos have an exceedingly unusual combination of moldings. The normal Doric hawksbeak has a fascia above, but the crowning molding of the fascia has the cyma reversa profile. Below the hawksbeak is an ovolo deeply carved with the egg-and-dart pattern and below that an astragal carved with the bead-and-reel pattern. This same combination of moldings appears elsewhere only on the anta capitals of the Parthenon. Moreover, the height of the moldings in the Temple of Nemesis (0.131 m) is almost exactly a reduction by 50 percent of the moldings in the Parthenon.[151]

Within the peristyle of the Temple of Nemesis, the colonnades had marble coffered ceilings whose construction was closely similar to the coffered ceilings of the Hephaisteion. Along each flank were fourteen ceiling beams spaced 0.960 m on centers and fitted into slots at the back of the cornice blocks. The beams carried coffer frames fashioned from extremely thin slabs of marble (0.054 m thick) that had two rows of four square coffers cut through the full thickness of the frame. Each coffer had a separate lid cut from a separate piece of marble. The coffer frames had a clear span 1.092 m and a visible width between the beams of 0.517 m. At the two ends of the temple, where the ceiling beams were set parallel to the axis of the building, nine beams and eight coffer frames would have had slightly wider and considerably longer dimensions in order to span the deeper porches before the pronaos and opisthodomos.[152]

---

[150] See Miles, "Temple," 223–226.

[151] For the anta capitals at Rhamnous: Shoe, *Greek Mouldings*, 120 and pl. LVII:10; illustrated by Gandy in *Unedited Antiquities*, pls. 6, 9; Miles, "Temple," 217. For the identical molding at larger scale on the Parthenon, cf. Orlandos, Παρθ., 316; Shoe, 119 and pl. LVII:7.

[152] For the ceilings, Miles, "Temple," 218–221.

When we turn to consider the date of construction of the temple, there is no independent archaeological evidence, such as deposits of context pottery, which bear directly on its chronology. The date has rather to be based on an assessment of the building's architectural style in relation to contemporary Doric architecture. Just such a study led W. B. Dinsmoor to propose that the four hexastyle temples were all designed by the same architect whom he called the "Theseum architect." He also proposed the following dates for the buildings:[153]

449–444: Hephaisteion
444–440: Temple of Poseidon
440–436: Temple of Athena Pallenis (Ares)
436–432: Temple of Nemesis

Dinsmoor's attribution of the temples to the same architect and his sequence of dating have been widely accepted, even though it appears suspiciously arbitrary. Each building is allotted the same amount of time, and each is completed before the next is begun. In the case of the Hephaisteion, however, we have already seen that the temple had a long and complicated construction history. Its roof and sculptural friezes were not completed until the 420s, and the cult statues were made between 421 and 415. This alone is sufficient to show that Dinsmoor's dates cannot be correct, even though the temples were probably begun in the order that he assigned to them.

In his publication of the Doric Stoa at Brauron, Ch. Bouras undertook an exhaustive analysis of the proportions of Doric columns, capitals, and entablatures in buildings of the fifth century. His tables of ratios were later augmented in some respects and reproduced by M. M. Miles.[154] Both scholars were able to identify a group of buildings that should be stylistically later in date than the Propylaia of the Acropolis (abandoned in 432). This includes the stoa at Brauron, which Bouras dated ca. 420, the Temple of the Athenians on Delos (ca. 425–417), and the Temple of Nemesis at Rhamnous, which Miles dates ca. 430–420.[155] The columnar orders of the three buildings are similar in size and dimensions. More importantly, the proportional relation of the different parts of capital and column to each other is remarkably consistent among them. On this basis, Miles has argued persuasively that the Temple of Nemesis should be regarded as a slightly earlier contemporary of the stoa at Brauron and the Temple of the Athenians on Delos.

✦

The foregoing discussion has sought to review the evidence for the construction of four temples at various sanctuaries outside the city of Athens itself. These buildings have been considered within the context of the Periklean program of temple building during the third quarter of the fifth century. Taken together, the four seem at first sight to present a sort of random collection of Attic cults, and one may wonder if it is indeed correct to study them beside the great monuments of the Athenian Acropolis. Even though there is no ancient authority for placing these temples together with the Parthenon, the Propylaia, and the Telesterion at Eleusis, there are excellent reasons for doing so, and in closing it may be useful to emphasize them. Despite the appalling wreckage to which the buildings have been reduced, it is obvious that all originally exhibited stonework of exquisite quality, and, moreover, some of the most sophisticated designs in classical architecture. All four temples seem to

---

[153] For the dates, Dinsmoor, *PAPS* 80 (1939) 152, 163–165; cf. also Dinsmoor, *Hesperia* 9 (1940) 47; Dinsmoor, *Hesperia* Suppl. 5 (1941) 153–155; Dinsmoor, *AAG*³, 181–182.
[154] Ch. Bouras, Ἡ ἀναστήλωσις τῆς στοᾶς τῆς Βραυρῶνος (Athens 1967) 149–153, tables 1–8. The same information is shown also in Miles, "Temple," 160–162.
[155] Miles, "Temple," 226–227.

have been erected from the 440s to the 420s, although evidence for their exact chronology is lacking or in dispute, and they are thus closely contemporary with the buildings of the Acropolis. The architects also reveal the immediate and direct influence of the Parthenon itself in various ways: in the more slender proportions of the orders, in the mingling of Doric and Ionic decorative elements, and especially in the interior plan of the cella. There can be no doubt that some of the leading masters of Athenian architecture were dispatched to the country sanctuaries.

It is important to emphasize that the cults in question were administered under the control of the Athenian state and their financial assets were managed by government officials. The inventory of the treasurers of the Other Gods for 429/8 lists property belonging to Poseidon at Sounion and Athena Pallenis.[156] The treasuries of these deities were thus among those removed to the Acropolis in 434 by order of the decrees of Kallias, when the treasurers of the Other Gods were first empaneled. It is interesting to notice that our preserved inscription of these important financial documents was found near the site of Pallene, where it was undoubtedly erected in the sanctuary.[157] Between 426/5 and 423/2, the sacred treasuries of Poseidon and Athena also loaned their funds to the Athenian state in support of the war effort.[158] Evidence is lacking concerning the finances of Athena Sounias and Nemesis, whose names do not appear in the preserved portions of the inscriptions. The cult of Poseidon at Sounion celebrated a penteteric festival to which an official delegation, or *theoria,* sailed in a sacred ship; and we hear of a regatta in which Athenian triremes competed.[159] We have just seen that the laws of the basileus provided the administrative framework for the cult of Athena Pallenis, which shows that the cult was part of the state religion of Athens. Furthermore, a board of public officials was responsible for repairs and maintenance of the temple itself and other buildings in the sanctuary.[160] The assignment of these duties gives the clearest indication that ultimate authority for the sanctuaries lay with the Athenian demos itself, and construction of the country temples resulted from its legislative decree, just as much as on the Acropolis and at Eleusis.

A more difficult question concerns the choice of sanctuaries at Sounion, Pallene, and Rhamnous[161] as sites for the construction of new marble temples at just this time. In the absence of any definitive evidence, the answer to this question must necessarily be speculative; but it is possible to suggest that each of these sites was appropriately included in a program to dedicate thank-offerings to the gods for the military victories of the Persian Wars. At Sounion, Poseidon's old temple had been wrecked by the Persian invaders before completion, so its situation was exactly similar to the Parthenon itself. When the new marble building arose on the same foundations as the old, that act affirmed the city's lasting gratitude for the god's divine assistance in time of need. Unfortunately, there is no evidence at all concerning the neighboring Temple of Athena at Sounion. But it is possible that the Temple of Athena Pallenis also replaced an archaic temple destroyed by the Persians.

[156] *IG* I³ 383, lines 106–107, 319, 330 (Poseidon at Sounion); lines 121–122 (Athena Pallenis). Another temple that has been frequently compared in the foregoing pages to the temples of these three deities is the Hephaisteion in Athens. It is of interest that the property of Hephaistos was also administered by the treasurers of the Other Gods: *IG* I³ 383, line 57. No property belonging to Athena Sounias appears in the preserved fragments of the stele. See T. Linders, *Treasurers of the Other Gods in Athens and Their Functions* (Meisenheim am Glan 1975) 19–32.

[157] Removal of the treasuries to the Acropolis, *IG* I³ 52A, lines 15–18; 52B, lines 22–25 = ML 58. The inscriptions discussed below, chap. 9, pp. 319–322, with bibliography. For their bearing on the treasurers of the Other Gods, Linders, *Treasurers of the Other Gods,* 38–57. Provenience of the stele: Goette, in Hoepfner, ed., *Kult und Kultbauten,* 127 no. 1; Goette, *Horos* 10–12 (1992–98) 106, no. 1.

[158] *IG* I³ 369 = ML 72, lines 62, 82 (Poseidon at Sounion); lines 71, 88 (Athena Pallenis); line 85 (Hephaistos).

[159] The penteteric festival, Hdt. 6.87, evidently describing a time before the Persian Wars. The regatta, Lys. 21.5.

[160] Athen. 6.235A–D, with the readings of Schlaifer, *HSCP* 54 (1943) 60–61.

[161] A fourth temple is often grouped together with the Temple of Poseidon at Sounion, the Hephaisteion, and the Temple of Ares (Athena Pallenis), that is, the Temple of Nemesis at Rhamnous: Dinsmoor, *Hesperia* 9 (1940) 47; Dinsmoor, *Hesperia* Suppl. 5 (1941) 153–155; Plommer, *BSA* 45 (1950) 66–112; Knell, *AA* (1973) 94–114; Korres, *Horos* 10–12 (1992–98) 91–94.

In this case, the recently excavated foundation produced no evidence for an earlier structure in that part of the sanctuary. Long ago, however, early investigators identified several poros column drums, many wall blocks, and two triglyphs of large scale reused in the walls of early churches nearby, and these are almost certainly the membra disjecta of an archaic Doric temple in the immediate vicinity of the classical sanctuary. Whether or not this building was actually destroyed by the Persians, we have no way of knowing, although it can hardly have survived the onslaught unscathed. On the whole, it seems a reasonable conjecture that the same ideology which had motivated the construction of the temples on the Acropolis and at Eleusis was now extended to the rural shrines of Attica.

9

The Propylaia

An integral part of the planned embellishment of the Acropolis was an entrance gatehouse that would provide the western approaches to the sanctuary with a monumental frontispiece. The site was a critical one, at exactly the point where the principal ascent of the hillside led the visitor onto the plateau of the sacred rock itself. On this spot, from the days of the Bronze Age, a heavily fortified gate had defended the approach to the Mycenaean citadel, and in the mid-fifth century a massive section of Cyclopean masonry was still visible at the southwestern angle,[1] while the cult of Athena Nike had occupied the westward salient bastion of the Mycenaean fortress for a hundred years. To this point of entry, the archaic Athenians had built a broad, sloping ramp that began its ascent more than 80 meters due west of the gates and rose nearly 31 meters in height by the time it reached the Acropolis plateau. The northward-facing retaining wall of this ramp may still be seen, almost exactly aligned with the central axis of the Periklean Propylaia. The polygonal style of its masonry, taken together with pottery found in association with its construction, indicates a date in the second quarter of the sixth century.[2] It has been rightly emphasized that the introduction of the ramp marked an important point of transition in the history of the Acropolis, from a fortified castle to a purely religious precinct, and there can be no doubt that it had greatly facilitated the dignified passage of religious processions from the lower city to Athena's sanctuary.[3] But more importantly, the ramp was a vital means of access for the builders of Athena's temples, and it can be no coincidence that its construction was exactly contemporaneous with the beginning of the first monumental stone temple on the Acropolis. Since that time, the building blocks of four Doric peripteral temples had been laboriously hauled up its steep incline to the masons' stone yards above. Most recently, of course, the marbles of the Parthenon had made that precipitous journey on their ungainly four-wheeled rigs. Indeed, without the ramp it was unthinkable to transport that temple's great Doric capitals, which measured 2.25 m in each direction and, with their protective jackets of stone, weighed twelve tons each.[4]

It has frequently escaped notice, however, that the logistical importance of the archaic ramp to all building operations on the Acropolis has directly impinged on the history of successive gatehouses at its top. That is to say, it is unimaginable that construction of a gatehouse of any period can have proceeded simultaneously with the delivery of stone blocks for one of the temples within the

---

[1] For the Mycenaean gate and the west Cyclopean wall, see S. E. Iakovidis, Ἡ Μυκηναϊκὴ Ἀκρόπολις τῶν Ἀθηνῶν (Athens 1962) 166–173; J. C. Wright, *Hesperia* 63 (1994) 323–360; I. M. Shear, *JHS* 119 (1999) 86–104.

[2] Bohn, *Propylaeen,* pl. XXI, shows the elevations from the beginning of the ramp, ca. 46.50 m west of the Beulé Gate. From that point to the east stylobate of the Propylaia, a distance of 101 m, the ramp rises 30.68 m. For the polygonal retaining wall: Travlos, *PDA,* 482, fig. 608; Vanderpool, in Bradeen and McGregor, eds., Φόρος, 156–160; I. M. Shear, *JHS* 119 (1999) 105–107. For the date of the pottery, Vanderpool, 159.

[3] Vanderpool , in Bradeen and McGregor, eds., Φόρος, 159–160, observed that the ramp "de-militarized" the Acropolis.

[4] Weight and dimensions, Korres, *Pentelicon,* 114.

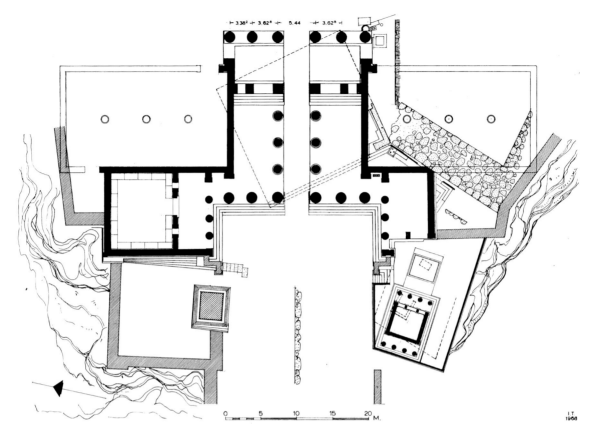

Figure 90. Plan of the Propylaia and sanctuary of Athena Nike;
the Old Propylon in broken lines, the projected east wings in outline

Acropolis. For the erection of scaffolding, the half-built walls and columns of a construction site, the inevitable debris of the masons' stone yards would have impeded impossibly the passage of materials at the point of entry.[5] No doubt for this very reason construction of the Propylaia was postponed until after the completion and dedication of the Parthenon, although plans for the two buildings must have been studied together.

Similarly, the need to use the archaic ramp must have affected the predecessor of the Periklean gatehouse, the building known to modern writers as the Old Propylon (Fig. 90). Only a small portion of this building's southern corner and flank wall survives today, but generations of investigators have observed the fire-damaged surface of its orthostates, the patched fabric of its walls, and the use of second-hand blocks in its anta and pavement.[6] All these are certain indications of a building that sustained serious damage in the Persian destruction of 480 and was afterward heavily repaired; but in this refurbished condition the Old Propylon secured the entrance of the Acropolis for some thirty years. It is necessary to postulate, however, that the building was substantially dismantled in 447, when transportation of marble blocks for the Parthenon began. To be sure, scholars have disagreed on the size and shape of the gatehouse, and on the complexity of its plan.[7] But no matter which res-

[5] The logistical importance of the ramp has been emphasized by I. M. Shear, *JHS* 119 (1999) 105–106.

[6] Detailed description of the remains: Dinsmoor, Jr., *Propylaia* I, 35–64; H. Eiteljorg, *The Entrance to the Athenian Acropolis before Mnesikles* (Boston 1995) 17–44. Repairs to the pavement and flank wall, Dinsmoor, Jr., *Propylaia* I, 54–55; replacement of original anta with one of reduced width, 58; earlier bibliography commenting on the repairs, 54, note 56.

[7] Earlier investigations of the Old Propylon and various restorations advocated by different scholars are reviewed by Dinsmoor, Jr., in *Propylaia* I, 7–15 and pl. 5. His own restoration (pp. 48–52, pl. 16), following the lead of Bundgaard, *Mnesicles,* 30–46, is of an enormous structure closely similar in plan and dimensions to the central hall of Mnesikles' later

Figure 91. Distant view of the Acropolis from west

toration is adopted, at the very least its columns and gate wall, if it had one, must have been removed, and its marble steps and crepidoma, which remain to this day in pristine condition, must have been buried beneath a deep protective filling of earth in order to permit the great stone-hauling wagons to roll onto the Acropolis.[8] From this necessary inference, we can conclude that the plan to build a new gatehouse for the Acropolis was part of the original program. But more than that, it then becomes clear that priority of construction—Parthenon, Propylaia, Nike temple, in that order—was determined not by quarrelsome architects or cantankerous priests but by the logistics of moving building stone onto an exceedingly difficult site. In any event, certainly in 437, preparatory to the beginning of work on the new Periklean building, the remaining sections of the Old Propylon were demolished to clear the site for its successor, and once again the archaic ramp provided the vital artery that enabled the builders to move the blocks of the Propylaia up to the stone yards on the Acropolis.

Mnesikles' Original Plan

Just one year after the dedication of the Parthenon in the summer of 438, the demos of the Athenians voted its final approval for the commencement of work on the Propylaia and commissioned the architect Mnesikles to begin construction (Fig. 91). Both the architect's name and the date in the archonship of Euthymenes (437/6) were recorded by Philochoros, who undoubtedly derived his information from the preamble to the first annual account of the overseers, where, as we shall see,

building. Both Dinsmoor, Jr., and Bundgaard lay great emphasis on cuttings in bedrock beneath the north aisle of the later Propylaia that were originally discovered by Dinsmoor, Sr., in 1910. They interpret these cuttings as evidence that a gate wall, closely modeled on that of Mnesikles, continued at least that far to the northwest of the later central passage and terminated still farther. Plommer, *JHS* 80 (1960) 148–150, questioned the enormous scale of the building proposed by Bundgaard and advocated returning to the smaller distyle plan postulated by C. H. Weller, *AJA* 8 (1904) 35–70. That same conclusion has been convincingly argued more recently by I. M. Shear, *JHS* 119 (1999) 110–118.

[8] So I. M. Shear, *JHS* 119 (1999) 118.

Figure 92. Propylaia, view of the east facade

the archon's name can still be read on the inscription.[9] There is no real evidence to indicate when the idea for the gate building may first have been conceived, but as we have just observed, it would not be surprising if the project had been proposed in principle in the years around 450, when plans for the Parthenon and for the Temple of Athena Nike were under discussion. At any rate, Mnesikles was intimately familiar with the architectural details of the temple and certainly designed his building to complement it in every way. In all likelihood, moreover, he inherited from Iktinos and Kallikrates many of the quarrymen and stonemasons who had been honing their skills for ten years past in the employ of the Parthenon overseers.

About Mnesikles himself nothing whatever is known beyond the single fact that he was architect of the Propylaia,[10] but those monumental remains reveal by far the most imaginative practitioner who ever set his hand to the design of a Doric building. He conceived of a structure the like of which no contemporary Greek had ever seen. Indeed, in all of Greek architecture there is nothing remotely similar before the great architectural complexes of the High Hellenistic period. But at the same time the remains of the building make it devastatingly obvious that the whole project became mired in controversy, with the result that only a little more than half of the brilliant plan was ever achieved. It must be accounted one of the great losses that classical antiquity has inflicted on the history of architecture that Mnesikles' original plans for the Propylaia were never fully executed, for what he created was a total revolution in Doric design. Not only was the sheer size of the gatehouse without parallel, but equally unprecedented was the manipulation of two different scales for the order within a single building. More surprising still is the masterly skill with which the building was implanted on the very brink of its precipitous site. Never before had a Greek architect contrived to

---

[9] Philochoros, *FGrH* 328 F 36, cited by Harpokration, s.v. προπύλαια ταῦτα (π 101 Keaney), quoted below, p. 301. The archon's name is preserved in *IG* I³ 462, line 3. Cf. also Heliodoros, *FGrH* 373 F 1 (also cited by Harpokration), who likewise derived from the documentary source the fact that the building was built in five years; cf. the same information in Plut. *Per.* 13.12. For the fragments of the building accounts, see pp. 300–311 below.

[10] Mnesikles: Kirchner, *PA* 10304. The name is not uncommon in Athenian prosopography: *LGPN* II, 317, cites twenty-nine bearers of it in all periods.

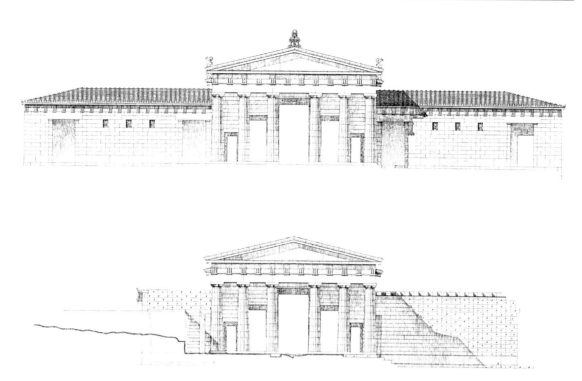

Figure 93. Restored elevation of east facade of the Propylaia , as projected and as built

shape the intractable forms of trabeated architecture so as to express perfectly the building's function as the principal entrance to the sanctuary.

The original scheme for the Propylaia seems to have been just as extravagant in its way as the Parthenon itself. Mnesikles' plan would have enclosed the approach to the Acropolis with one tremendous building spanning the entire width of the citadel at its western end. He conceived of five separate halls of descending size, arranged in symmetrical cruciform plan around a colonnaded central hall whose east–west axis marked the route of the processional entrance. On the outside, the central hall was to be flanked by two matching wings projecting westward, with columnar porches of reduced scale turned at 90 degrees to the main facade; and behind the porches the plan called for nearly square matching chambers. On the inside of the Acropolis there were to be two symmetrical eastern halls whose low hipped roofs and solid masonry walls would focus attention on the projecting columnar facade of the central hall when viewed from within the sanctuary (Figs. 92, 93). The eastern halls were to be so arranged that their long north–south axis aligned with that of the central hall; the tripartite eastern front of the building would thus have formed a single unified facade that approximated the length of the Parthenon itself.[11]

It was the standard practice of Greek builders to prepare in advance the masonry of a wall for the bonding of adjacent walls, the bedding of roof timbers, or the abutment of other architectural features, even if these were not to be undertaken until a subsequent phase of construction. It is from just such preparations to the fabric of the standing walls that we learn of the original plans for the eastern halls that were never built (Figs. 94, 95). The reentrant angle formed by the north wall of the central

[11] On the original plans for the building, see generally Dinsmoor, *AAG*[3], 199–205; Gruben, *Gr. Tempel*[5], 191–203. More detailed discussion: Bundgaard, *Mnesicles,* 47–92, 157–175; Dinsmoor, Jr., *Hesperia* Suppl. 20 (1982) 22–24; P. Hellström, *OpAth* 17 (1988) 107–121; J. de Waele, *The Propylaia of the Akropolis in Athens* (Amsterdam 1990); Camp, *Archaeology of Athens*, 82–90, 252–253; Hurwit, *Athenian Acropolis*, 155–163; Dinsmoor and Dinsmoor, Jr., *Propylaia* II, 1–57, 313–355 (northeast hall), 357–366 (southeast hall), with restored length of the east halls as 24.135 m (north) and 24.145 m (south), pl. II. The stylobate of the east facade measures 21.125 m, 24.135 + 24.145 + 21.125 = 67.405 m. The north stylobate of the Parthenon measures 69.503 m.

Figure 94. Restored elevation, north face of north wall, central building

hall and the east wall of the northwest wing, commonly called the Pinakotheke, was prepared to be the interior of a hall, as is shown by the molded epicranitis in the fifteenth course above the orthostates. This terminal molding was intended to decorate the wall crown of what were to be the back and side walls of the hall. In the uppermost course of the back wall, above the epicranitis, deep sockets (0.615 m wide × 0.49 m high × 0.36 m deep) were cut to receive the ends of wooden rafters for the roof.[12] A similar socket with even larger dimensions (0.762 m wide × 0.645 m high × 0.38 m deep) was let into the side wall of the central hall at an appropriate height, level with the top of the eighteenth course above the orthostates, to carry the ridgepole of the roof.[13] In addition, the projecting console bearing the lateral entablature of the east colonnade has been chamfered on its underside at an angle that conforms with a roof sloping down from the socket of the ridgepole to the top of the epicranitis.[14] These various indications give evidence for the roofline of the northeast hall, while it is clear from the low position of the orthostates that its floor was to be level with the stylobate of the west colonnade. It is most probable that every fifth rafter was intended to align with an interior column supporting the ridgepole. This emerges from special rectangular cuttings let into the upper surface of the epicranitis course along the back wall. These cuttings fall beneath every fifth rafter socket and must have been intended to provide more secure anchorage for the rafters that aligned with the interior columns. Since the cuttings are spaced 5.89 m on centers, and that is the equivalent of five ashlar wall blocks measuring 1.178 m in length, the eastern halls were probably originally planned with three interior columns and an overall length of 23.56 m, or the equivalent of four axial intercolumniations. It is also possible that the length of the ashlar wall blocks (1.178 m) was planned as the module for the triglyph frieze consisting of twenty triglyphs and twenty metopes (1.178 × 20 = 23.56 m).[15]

[12] For the epicranitis molding of the northeast hall and rafter sockets for the roof: Bundgaard, *Mnesicles,* 86–91; *Propylaia* II, 329–336. The dimensions cited here are from a variety of sources: *Propylaia* II, supplemented by Dinsmoor, Jr., *Hesperia* Suppl. 20 (1982) 18–23, and Bundgaard (above). The very detailed older drawings of Bohn, *Propylaeen,* and de Waele, *Propylaia,* show many slight discrepancies between them.

[13] *Propylaia* II, 333–334; Bundgaard, *Mnesicles,* 81–83.

[14] Bundgaard, *Mnesicles,* 83–86.

[15] For restoration of the northeast hall, see Dinsmoor, Jr., *Hesperia* Suppl. 20 (1982) 23–24, where dimensions are cited in Doric feet with the metric equivalent of 0.32723 m = 1 D.F. See now *Propylaia* II, 336, for the interior columns, and, with slightly different calculations for the length of the northeast hall, 342–344.

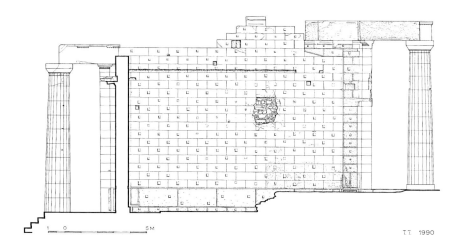

Figure 95. Elevation, actual state, south face of south wall, central building

Significantly, the preparations to accommodate the roof timbers were more fully carried out for the northeast hall than for its counterpart to the southeast. The southern side wall of the central hall also has a deep socket in the eighteenth course above the orthostates, and placed in the proper position to carry the ridgepole of the roof, but it has somewhat smaller dimensions than the similar socket on the north side (0.572 m wide × 0.49 m high × 0.28–0.29 m deep). Likewise, the console beneath the entablature of the east colonnade has been cut away to fit against the sloping roof of the hall.[16] But the fifteenth course above the orthostates consists of standard ashlar wall blocks with no epicranitis molding, while the sixteenth course of the adjacent east wall of the southwest wing has no bedding sockets for rafters like the equivalent course on the north side of the building. In due course, we shall need to consider how to interpret these differing indications for two halls that were plainly conceived at first as matching and symmetrical, but neither of which was ever built.

One other architectural feature that was planned for the eastern halls can be deciphered from the standing masonry of the Propylaia, and that is the doorways that were to give access to the halls from the inside of the Acropolis. On both sides of the eastern colonnade, short spur walls project from behind the antae for a length of one ashlar wall block (see Fig. 90). These are precisely in the intended line of the east facade, and they conform in thickness with the other masonry walls of the building (0.887 m north and 0.892 m south). In their present incomplete state, the spur walls consist of an orthostate and eight ashlar courses with a fillet on the outside face but plain on the inside.[17] They are to be interpreted as the jambs of doorways, even though they are vertical and do not incline northward and southward, respectively, toward the opening of the doors, as was standard in classical doorways, possibly because the side walls of the Propylaia incline inward in the opposite direction. The thresholds of the doorways were to be level with the floor of the eastern colonnade, and the original plans must have included a series of steps on the inside to make good the difference between the threshold and the lower floor level intended for the northeast hall. Preparations for yet another doorway can be discerned in the back wall of the northeast hall, where the existing masonry projects

[16] *Propylaia* II, 362–364; Bundgaard, *Mnesicles,* 81–83 (ridgepole socket), 83–86 (cutting away of entablature console).

[17] Bundgaard, *Mnesicles,* 79–81; *Propylaia* II, 344–347 (north), 365 (south).

beyond the end of the Pinakotheke. Here too are eight courses of ashlar masonry rising above the orthostates, and their outer surface inclines northward toward the empty void beyond, unlike the spur
walls on either side of the eastern colonnade. The ninth and tenth courses have been cut to receive
the lintel of the doorway, which, like every other lintel in the building, would have projected half the
length of a wall block beyond the jambs and had a height equal to two ashlar courses. Two blocks
of the doorway's threshold are still in place ranging with the toichobate of the northeast hall. In this
curious position the door can only have provided access to the tiny terrace behind the Pinakotheke
at the extreme northwest corner of the Acropolis.

On the western side of the Propylaia, it is easier to visualize the architect's original intentions
because actual construction of the northwest wing, or Pinakotheke, more nearly approximated what
Mnesikles had planned (see Figs. 102, 103). Both western wings have columns of smaller size set
between antae, and they share the steps and stylobate of the principal colonnade, which are carried around three sides of the forecourt. Since the two columnar facades have been made as nearly
symmetrical as was practicable, it is surely correct to infer that Mnesikles originally contemplated
wings of identical plan, each with a Doric porch in antis that gave access to a square chamber like
that which was actually built for the Pinakotheke. When we come to consider in detail the vicissitudes that plagued the design of the two wings, however,[18] it will be possible to show that the initial
scheme for the western wings had four columns instead of three, and that the door and windows
were placed symmetrically in the wall behind. Such are the indications for the architect's original
plan that can be deciphered from the standing walls of the Propylaia.

PROBLEMS CONFRONTING THE ARCHITECT

The assembly's charge to the architect was undoubtedly to design and build an entrance gateway to
the sanctuary. In light of this commission, the enormous scale and lavish complexity of the projected
building might strike the observer at once as excessive and certainly without parallel anywhere in
Greece. The discrepancy in grandeur emerges starkly if we compare Mnesikles' plan with the typical
Greek propylon that formed the entrance to other sanctuaries. The notion of protecting an open
gateway in an encircling wall with a projecting roof on either side recedes back to some of the earliest architectural complexes of the prehistoric Aegean.[19] Already in the Bronze Age, such structures
had evolved a plan shaped like the letter H, with the open doorway in the middle of the crossbar
and with one or two columns between the projecting wall ends to support the roof. All three of the
great palaces of Mycenaean Greece—at Pylos, Tiryns, and Mycenae—had a building of this type as
a principal entrance;[20] and between that time and the sanctuaries of the Late Archaic period there
was little evolution in plan except in the forms of the columnar order. In the early years of the fifth
century, just such a propylon was built for the sanctuary of Aphaia at Aigina, replacing a smaller and
simpler structure of earlier date. It consisted of the H-shaped plan, measuring 7.33 m in width and

[18] *Propylaia* II, 23–28. For discussion of the northwest wing, see pp. 292–297 below; for the southwest wing, pp. 297–300 below.

[19] See, e.g., the H-shaped propyla serving as gates to the citadel of Troy IIc, and also giving access to the inner court before the megaron complex: C. W. Blegen, *Troy and the Trojans* (London 1963) 63–66, fig. 15; B. Brandau, *Troia: Eine Stadt und ihr Mythos* (Bergisch Gladbach 1997) 147–150; and cf. Lawrence, *Greek Architecture*[5], 6–7.

[20] Pylos: C. W. Blegen and M. Rawson, *The Palace of Nestor at Pylos in Western Messenia*, vol. 1, *The Buildings and Their Contents* (Princeton 1966) 54–62. Tiryns: K. Müller, *Tiryns*, vol. 3, *Die Architektur der Burg und des Palastes* (Augsburg 1930) 127–134. Mycenae: A. J. B. Wace, *Mycenae* (Princeton 1949) 70; G. E. Mylonas, *Mycenae and the Mycenaean Age* (Princeton 1966) 66–67; and cf. J. R. Carpenter, "The Propylon in Greek and Hellenistic Architecture" (Ph.D. diss., University of Pennsylvania, 1970) 9–37.

6.26 m between the ends of the antae, with a single opening in the gate wall; in each porch were two
Doric columns of peculiar faceted design.[21] A few years earlier, around the turn of the century, the
sanctuary of Apollo at Delos had likewise received a new gatehouse built on the foundations of a
still earlier archaic predecessor. The Delian propylon had the same simple H-shaped plan, with the
gate wall shifted off center toward the inside porch and pierced by three doorways. In keeping with
the traditions of island architecture, the columns were Ionic, distyle in antis for the inside porch and
four columns in prostyle plan for the front facade. But the building had the unpretentious dimensions appropriate to a gatehouse: 9.60 m in width across the front stylobate and 9.45 m from front
to back between the stylobates.[22] Thus the Delian building had smaller overall dimensions than the
Pinakotheke of the Propylaia, while the propylon at Aigina would have fit comfortably in the inner
chamber of that same wing.

No one will seriously doubt that Mnesikles was trying to achieve something much more elaborate than the typical classical propylon. He envisioned a building that would make a grandiose architectural statement about the process of ascending the rock of the Acropolis and of penetrating the
sacred space of Athena's sanctuary. The architect also plainly intended that his building should have
priority over any earlier structures that happened to exist at the western end of the Acropolis or any
part of the site that was as yet architecturally undeveloped. In order to carry out the original design,
the fortification walls of the Acropolis would require extension or, at the very least, buttressing since
the immense width of the east halls would seemingly have extended to the edges of the rock. Several
minor cult places associated with the entrance to the sanctuary would have been completely covered
by the new building. Pausanias mentions Hermes Propylaios, and he knew a triple-bodied statue of
Artemis Hekate that was called Epipyrgidia (on the bastion) and stood near the Temple of Athena
Nike.[23] Property belonging jointly to Hermes and Artemis Hekate was listed by the treasurers of
the Other Gods in their inventory for 429/8.[24] The cult was certainly in existence long before work
began on the Propylaia and probably goes back to Archaic times. Likewise, before the entrance of
the Acropolis was a shrine sacred to the three Graces, who were depicted in a dedication that local
legend attributed to the hand of the philosopher Sokrates.[25] Pausanias says that they were honored
of old, and if the well-known archaic "Graces relief" actually depicts them, the shrine must date to
the end of the sixth century.[26] Venerable too was the sanctuary of Athena Nike that had certainly
occupied the old Mycenaean tower since the middle years of the sixth century, when the first altar

[21] For the early-fifth-century propylon at Aigina: A. Furtwängler, *Aegina* (Munich 1906) 75–85, pls. 56–58; G. Welter, *Aigina* (Berlin 1938) 64–65; cf. Carpenter, "Propylon," 42–46. Its earlier predecessor is smaller and much less well
preserved: Carpenter, "Propylon," 39–42; Furtwängler, *Aegina,* 151–154.

[22] The late archaic propylon II, G. Gruben, *JdI* 112 (1997) 356–372, figs. 48, 53, 54; for chronology and restored
plans, 308–309. The earlier building on the same site, propylon I, is dated to the second quarter of the sixth century: Gruben, 350–356.

[23] Hermes Propylaios at the actual entrance of the Acropolis, Paus. 1.22.8. Artemis Hekate called Epipyrgidia, near
the Nike temple, was by the sculptor Alkamenes: Paus. 2.30.2. The cult has been located in the small walled precinct at the
foot of the Mycenaean wall, behind the southwest wing of the Propylaia: Travlos, *PDA,* 148 and fig. 200; Giraud, Μελέτη
Αθηνάς Νίκης, 44, pls. 6, 7. By the first century B.C., the "fire-bearing" priest, which Artemis Epipyrgidia shared jointly
with the Graces, was assigned a marble throne in the front row at the Theater of Dionysos, *IG* II² 5050; see M. Maaß, *Die
Prohedrie des Dionysostheaters in Athen* (Munich 1972) 122.

[24] *IG* I³ 383, lines 125–130.

[25] Paus. 1.22.8, 9.35.7, describes the figures of the Graces as before the entrance of the Acropolis. Cf. schol. Aristoph.
Clouds 773 b (Holwerda), where they are said to be on the wall behind the Athena. For their proximity to Athena Nike, see
L. Beschi, *ASAtene,* n.s., 29–30 (1967–68) 535–536 and fig. 17.

[26] Honored of old, Paus. 9. 35. 2–3. The "Graces relief," Acropolis Museum 702: H. Schrader, *Die archaischen Marmorbildwerke der Akropolis* (Frankfurt am Main 1939) 311–312, no. 430; M. S. Brouskari, *The Acropolis Museum* (Athens
1974) 58–59, dated to the last decade of the sixth century. Harrison, in *LIMC,* vol. 3, 195, s.v. Charites 20, considers it
impossible to tell whether the three female figures represent Graces or Aglaurids.

was dedicated.[27] Moreover, the assembly had already adopted a plan to enrich that sanctuary with a new marble temple that had been approved more than ten years earlier.[28] But if the original scheme for symmetrical wings of matching dimensions had actually been constructed, the southwest wing of the Propylaia would have encroached on almost half of the bastion.

Within the Acropolis, Mnesikles encountered still more serious impediments that militated against construction of the eastern halls. Here, work was already in progress on a site against the north fortification wall that conflicted directly with the projected northeast wing of the Propylaia. The building in question consisted of two small rooms behind a colonnaded porch, and although it is not quite clear how high the superstructure of the rooms had risen, the portico was abandoned before the foundations had been fully laid.[29] By far the most intractable obstacles, however, occupied the site of the planned southeast hall: the massive section of Cyclopean masonry and the higher rock-cut terrace to the east of it that formed the temenos of Artemis Brauronia. The first of these, the last relic of the Mycenaean fortress, enclosed the entire space between the corner of the Old Propylon and the southwest angle of the citadel, a distance of about 18 m. The Cyclopean wall had a thickness of 6 m and still stood to a height of 4.85 m above the projected floor level of the Propylaia;[30] all of its masonry would need to be demolished before construction could begin on the southeast hall.

The state of architectural development on the Brauronion terrace at this time cannot be accurately ascertained. This Athenian branch of the sanctuary at Brauron is thought to have been founded by Peisistratos, who came from that part of Attica, but the only evidence consists of krater-iskoi that are typical dedications at sanctuaries of Artemis; a few fragments of these, datable to the late sixth century, have been found on the Acropolis.[31] The stoa along the south side of the sanctuary was once thought to have bonded into the masonry of the Kimonian fortification wall, thus providing a date for the building in the 460s; but more recent investigations have shown that no such bond ever existed.[32] The earliest evidence for the removal of treasures from Brauron to the

[27] *IG* I³ 596, dated ca. 550? Cf. Mark, *Athena Nike,* 32–35, dated 580–530, with incorrect reading of the dedicator's name.

[28] See the discussion of the inscriptions for Athena Nike, chap. 2, pp. 27–35 above.

[29] The so-called Northwest Building, whose remains have been studied by T. Tanoulas, *AM* 107 (1992) 129–160, 199–215. He concludes (pp. 210, 214) that the foundations of that building together with those of the Pinakotheke and the northeast hall of the Propylaia, as well as the north fortification wall of the Acropolis, were all constructed by Mnesikles in the period 437–432; followed by Hurwit, *Athenian Acropolis,* 198. Tanoulas's interpretation of the building's construction history has been directly contradicted by Korres, in Hoepfner, ed., *Kult und Kultbauten,* 244–245. Both agree that the foundation for the columnar porch was never completed. In view of the fact that the abortive foundation for the east wall of the northeast hall directly obstructs the south end of the porch, it is difficult to believe that the Northwest Building was not begun earlier and suspended when construction of the Propylaia started. It is impossible to imagine that the same architect was responsible for both projects. The same structure is called the "Portico Building" by Bundgaard, *Mnesicles,* 80, who likewise favors an earlier date, but both he and Hellström, *OpAth* 17 (1988) 111–113, write as if the building were completed and functioning before the Propylaia.

[30] On the Cyclopean wall, see chap. 3, pp. 76–77 above.

[31] Founded by Peisistratos, Hurwit, *Athenian Acropolis,* 197, following L. Kahil, *Hesperia* 50 (1981) 253–263, who publishes the few fragments of krateriskoi from the Acropolis. Cf. the reservations of R. Osborne, *Demos: The Discovery of Classical Attika* (Cambridge 1985) 154–156, emphasizing that krateriskoi are typical dedications at shrines of Artemis. Osborne also points out the lack of evidence for cult activity in the Acropolis precinct. Cf. G. Despinis, in Hoepfner, ed., *Kult und Kultbauten,* 209–217, who restores a temple for which architectural evidence is totally lacking.

[32] The alleged bond and Kimonian date argued by Stevens, *Hesperia* 5 (1936) 459–470, followed by Travlos, *PDA,* 124–125. The bond thought to be with masonry dating 440–430, Dinsmoor, *AJA* 51 (1947) 136–137, followed by J. J. Coulton, *The Architectural Development of the Greek Stoa* (Oxford 1976) 41, 222. More recent work showing that there was no bond with classical masonry of either Kimonian or Periklean date, R. F. Rhodes and J. J. Dobbins, *Hesperia* 48 (1979) 325–341. Despite their evidence, Hurwit, *Athenian Acropolis,* 197, accepts a date in the 430s because the rock-cut north wall of the Brauronion is exactly parallel to the south wall of the Propylaia, but surely this provides no more than a terminus post quem for the precinct. A date as late as the early fourth century for the founding of the Acropolis sanctuary was proposed by C. N. Edmonson, *AJA* 72 (1968) 164–165.

Acropolis comes from an inscription of 416/5 found at Brauron, and the earliest Athenian duplicate copy of the Brauron inventories dates to about the same time.[33] The extant remains of buildings
on the Acropolis are not likely to be much older than this; so it was not a question that Mnesikles
sought to demolish preexisting monuments. The precinct had doubtless already been apportioned to
Artemis, however, and it is fair to say that construction of the southeast hall would have altered drastically the topography of the sanctuary. In view of the various difficulties confronting the architect,
it is not altogether surprising that the building was not erected according to plan. Indeed, the design
was sharply curtailed in the course of construction, and not only by omission of the great eastern
halls; for we shall see that the building shows signs of other alterations and compromises that taxed
the ingenuity of its architect.

THE CENTRAL HALL

As visitors slowly toil up the steep western slope of the Acropolis and confront the building that
Mnesikles actually built, the sheer innovative power of the architecture is quite sufficient to over-
whelm them, despite its asymmetries of plan and unfinished condition.[34] The building's principal
function was to provide a monumental processional approach to the sanctuary and to its central
monument, the newly completed Parthenon, so it is important to emphasize the specific ways in
which the gatehouse was designed to harmonize with the great temple. The axis of the processional
ramp that bisects the Propylaia has been made precisely parallel to the axis of the Parthenon, but
offset toward the north by some thirty meters (see Fig. 2). In order to effect this exact alignment,
Mnesikles changed the orientation of his building from that of the Old Propylon by rotating the axis
twenty degrees farther to the east of north (see Fig. 90). This change in siting had the happy result
that the visitor standing at the midpoint of the eastern colonnade viewed the Parthenon at an angle
of 45 degrees to its northwest corner. This angle of view was seemingly much admired and was often
contrived by Greek architects because it enabled the spectator to grasp both front and flank of a
peripteral temple, in all their articulating detail, from a single vantage point.[35]

Mnesikles was also keenly aware that the Propylaia would be seen most often from afar and in
direct relation to the temple (see Fig. 91). Thus he chose hexastyle facades for the principal colonnades in order to subordinate his building to the octostyle fronts of the Parthenon, and he reduced
the height of the elevation by almost one-fifth, although the proportions of the Doric columns
themselves are closely similar (Figs. 96, 97).[36] The stylobate of the western facade lies 12.06 m below

[33] For the inscription of 416/5 found at Brauron: *Ergon* (1958) 37; Vanderpool, *AJA* 63 (1959) 280, the text unpublished. The earliest Brauronion inventory from the Acropolis, *IG* I³ 403 (ca. 416). That the inventories from the Acropolis
record dedications at Brauron and refer to places for the storage of treasures in the country sanctuary, T. Linders, *Studies
in the Treasure Records of Artemis Brauronia Found at Athens* (Stockholm 1972) 70–73. The earliest records of dedications
belonging to Artemis Brauronia on the Acropolis: *IG* II² 1402, add. p. 799, lines 7–8 (402/1); 1381 + 1386, add. p. 798,
lines 24–26 (401/0), see Harris, *Treasures*, V.138 (a piece of gold with a golden chain); *IG* II² 1386, lines 4–5 (401/0), see
Harris, *Treasures*, II.82 (golden phialai). Cf. the discussion of Osborne, *Demos*, 155–156.

[34] The principal descriptions of the architecture are: Bohn, *Propylaeen*; Dinsmoor, *AAG*³, 198–205; Bundgaard, *Mnesicles*; Gruben, *Gr. Tempel*⁵, 191–203; *Propylaia* II, 59–311. Full bibliography to 1990 in de Waele, *Propylaia*, xiii–xviii;
more recent bibliography to 2001 in Gruben, *Gr. Tempel*⁵, 503–504; *Propylaia* II, xix–xxv.

[35] See the plan, *Propylaia* II, 46. Cf. the similar siting of the propylon in relation to the temple in the sanctuary of
Aphaia at Aigina, Welter, *Aigina*, 70, fig. 59 (early sixth cent.); 65, fig. 56 (early fifth cent.); in the sanctuary of Poseidon at
Sounion, Travlos, *BTA*, 408, fig. 508; H. R. Goette, Ὁ ἀξιόλογος δῆμος Σούνιον: *Landeskundliche Studien in Südost-Attika*
(Rahden/Westf. 2000) pl. 12 (late fifth cent.). On siting for the oblique view, see R. Stillwell, *JSAH* 13 (1954) 3–8; Car-
penter, "Propylon," 198–199.

[36] Parthenon, height of elevation to horizontal cornice: 13.731 × ⅘ = 10.985 m. Propylaia, height of east elevation to
horizontal cornice: 11.253 m.

Figure 96. Propylaia, view of west facade

the euthynteria of the Parthenon, and the height of the western elevation to the horizontal cornice is 11.549 m.[37] The strong horizontal line formed by the entablature of the Propylaia would thus be seen to underscore the crepidoma of the Parthenon, and the building's northward offset would ensure that no part of its superstructure obstructed the view of the temple's facade. The relationship of the two buildings is actually viewed to best advantage from the assembly place on the Pnyx Hill due west of the Acropolis, the spot from which many a classical Athenian probably saw the Acropolis most frequently.

The central hall of the Propylaia exhibits all the familiar features of the normal classical propylon of H-shaped plan, but all have been greatly enlarged and elaborated (see Fig. 90). The basic rectangle of the plan measures 21.125 m across the eastern stylobate and 23.836 m between the stylobates of the two facades, dimensions which give the building a scale far larger than many peripteral temples. The gate wall, which is functionally the most important architectural feature of any gatehouse, has been set far off center to form a deep and spacious outer vestibule behind the western columns. Both facades have six Doric columns arranged in prostyle plan and were surmounted by triangular pediments. The more slender Doric proportions developed for the peristyle of the Parthenon were also adopted by Mnesikles for the Propylaia, doubtless as a subtle way of relating the two buildings to each other. Thus the height of the eastern columns expressed as multiple of their lower diameter is 5.47, a figure that almost exactly replicates the proportion of 5.48 lower diameters used for the columns of the Parthenon.[38] Still more slender are the western columns (5.65 lower diameters), which in fact stand slightly taller than those on the east in order to compensate for the effect of foreshortening, since they would always be seen from below by those ascending the hill. There can be no doubt what the

[37] Bohn, *Propylaeen*, pl. XXI, shows the west stylobate of the Propylaia 13.945 m below the west stylobate of the Parthenon. The west crepidoma of the Parthenon is 1.885 m high (dimensions: Orlandos, Παρθ., pl. 18). 13.945 – 1.885 = 12.06 m. The west elevation of the Propylaia is 11.549 m to the horizontal cornice (dimension: Dinsmoor, *AAG*³, 339).

[38] East: 8.528 (column height) ÷ 1.558 (lower diameter) = 5.474. West: 8.8075 (column height) ÷ 1.558 (lower diameter) = 5.653. Cf. the proportions of the Parthenon columns, chap. 4, p. 91 above. By contrast, the Doric columns of the Propylaia are given slightly stronger entasis than those of the Parthenon, a deviation of 0.019 m from the straight line: Dinsmoor, *AAG*³, 168.

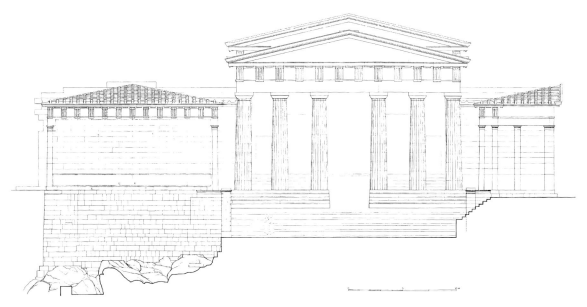

Figure 97. Restored elevation, west facade

contemporary Greek would see in these porches of the Propylaia: the hexastyle facade with crowning pediment was the most characteristic and ubiquitous hallmark of Doric architecture, although heretofore employed almost exclusively in the design of sacred buildings. Mnesikles had appropriated the facade of the temple itself, and by increasing the scale of his building far beyond anything seen in the normal propylon, he presented the entrance to the Acropolis in the form of a temple as the most novel way of proclaiming that the worshipper had reached the boundary of the sacred space.

The Doric peripteral temple, however, although surrounded by a peristyle of open colonnades, in fact creates a visual wall of columns by the uniform spacing of the shafts, articulated by the uniform size and exact placement of triglyphs and metopes. The effects of the architecture are best appreciated in the distant view, and the hexastyle facade in fact offers no visual indication of the point where the spectator might enter the building. It is just here that we witness the powerful originality of Mnesikles' design. The most striking feature of the Propylaia is the wide open passage that ascends through the building as a continuously sloping ramp, uninterrupted by steps or stylobate (Figs. 97, 98). On one level, of course, the ramp was purely functional in that it permitted the thronging crowds of the Panathenaic procession, with their dozens of sacrificial animals, to gain easier access. But in the symbolic language of architectural form, the ramp expresses the fundamental idea of the processional ritual that is so necessary a preparation for most acts of religious worship. It focuses attention on the central axis of the facade as the point of entry, and this is emphasized in a number of specific ways. Not only is the crepidoma entirely omitted from the central intercolumniation of both porches, but the processional passage has been made wider than the normal axial spacing of the columns. This means that the five axial intercolumniations of the facades decrease in width symmetrically toward the corners,[39] and the increased spacing at the center is particularly stressed by the need to introduce an extra triglyph and metope in the frieze above. In similar fashion, the gate wall establishes a hierarchy of entrances: the wall is pierced by five great doorways that correspond roughly to the intercolumniations of the porches, and these decrease symmetrically in height and width from the enormous processional gate at the center to more human-sized doors at the outside.[40]

---

[39] Axial spacings (averaged) of facade columns: 5.436 m (central), 3.628 m (normal), 3.382 m (corners): *Propylaia* II, pl. II.

[40] Doorways of the gate wall: 7.383 m high × 4.189 m wide (central), 5.401 m high × 2.927 m wide (middle pair), 3.437 m high × 1.473 m wide (outside pair): *Propylaia* II, 138–139, fig. 10.9.

Omission of the crepidoma at both ends of the central passage affected the use of optical refinements in the building in curious ways. To be sure, Mnesikles employed some of these subtle curves and inclinations that so permeated the structure of the Parthenon. The columns and walls incline inward, for example, and the face of the antae inclines outward.[41] But the steps and stylobate of both facades are set perfectly level. To construct curvature on a crepidoma with a wide gap at its midpoint was evidently thought to be counterproductive. On the other hand, Mnesikles went to great pains to inflect the entire entablature of both facades with just the slightest curvature. To this end, the columns themselves rise ever so slightly in height from the outside corners to the central intercolumniation, a total increment of only 0.0165 m on each colonnade.[42]

The processional ramp gives force and direction to the actions of ascent and entry by which the approaching visitor participates in the architecture. From lower on the slope, the viewer's gaze is directed to the center of the facade by the juxtaposition of the western wings. These have been carefully subordinated to the hexastyle colonnade. The dimensions of the order have been reduced by one-third.[43] The low hipped roofs rose no higher than the bottom of the central entablature. The solid masonry wall of the Pinakotheke contrasts sharply with the open colonnade of the western porch, its openness further enhanced by the lighted rectangles of the five doorways beyond; and that contrast would have been greatly heightened if the southwest wing had matched the design of the Pinakotheke. As one nears the front of the Propylaia, the porches of the western wings are seen to project forward at right angles to the main facade, and a three-sided forecourt is formed by the steps and stylobate that they share with the hexastyle colonnade. It is as if the building's marble arms reached out to embrace the visitor lest his steps falter at the top of the steep upward climb.

Every line of the architecture reflects the precipitous hillside of the building's site. The floor of the central hall is four steps higher than the approach ramp; the floor of the eastern porch is five steps higher than the western, and its stylobate is one step higher than the floor behind it.[44] This difficult rise in floor level (1.753 m) within the building was logically expressed in the exterior superstructure. The roof of the eastern porch rose above that of western hall and a third westward-facing pediment stood on the line of the gate wall, where it would have been partially visible to the approaching visitor above the pediment of the west facade (Fig. 97). Within the western hall, the orthostates of the side walls measure the same difference in floor level, and they are made of dark gray Eleusinian limestone to give visual emphasis to the eastward rise. The topmost of the five steps before the gate wall, which forms the actual threshold of the doorways, ranges with the top of the orthostates and marks the change in level by the use of the same dark stone. Along both sides of the hall, low benches of the same Eleusinian stone invite the newly arrived visitors to rest their feet after the long ascent and to await the opening of the gates. Thus Mnesikles made the sloping hillside central to the design of his building. It was a site on which a defensible gate had stood for centuries to debar the unwelcome visitor from entry, but his was a building that proclaimed to all comers an invitation to enter the sanctuary. More than that, the architecture itself seems to pull the worshipper upward and inward into the sacred space of the Acropolis.

---

[41] The columns of the facades incline inward 0.0857 m, Dinsmoor, *AAG*[3], 165; inward inclination of the walls and outward inclination of the antae, 165–166.

[42] On curvature of the entablature above a level stylobate, Dinsmoor, *AAG*[3], 167–168, 199–201. Column height, west facade: 8.824 (central) – 8.8075 (corners) = 0.0165 m; column height, east facade: 8.5445 (central) – 8.528 (corners) = 0.0165 m. Cf. *Propylaia* II, 98–100, figs. 10.1, 10.3.

[43] On the reduction in scale, see p. 294 below.

[44] Height of four steps of the western crepidoma, 1.22 m (floor of west porch); height of five steps at gate wall, 1.433 (floor of east porch) + 0.32 (height of east stylobate) = 1.753 m rise from west to east.

THE IONIC INTERIOR

Behind the western portico, the great space of the outer vestibule spreads out in all directions. The notion, first realized by the builders of the Parthenon, that architecture could be used to enhance the feeling of interior space, now motivated the design of Mnesikles' central hall. The interior depth of the vestibule from the columns to the face of the gate wall is 13.548 m, while its width between the side walls measures 18.129 m, dimensions which closely approximate those of the western cella of the Parthenon.[45] But unlike that closed interior chamber, the western hall of the Propylaia is bisected by the processional way; it is lighted by the open colonnade to the west and by the great doorways of the gate wall to the east. The enormous span of the hall demanded interior support sufficient to carry the weight of the ceiling, and here Mnesikles made use of the Ionic order, probably inspired by its earlier use in the Parthenon chamber.[46] But he boldly set the Ionic columns immediately adjacent to the Doric facade, without the mediation of an intervening wall. On either side of the central passage was a row of three, their axes aligned with the central pair of the facades, and their capitals turned frontally toward the sloping ramp. In the rhythm of their spacing they reinforced the cadence of the processional march.

The choice of the Ionic order provided an especially elegant solution to the problem of interior support for the roof. The taller and more slender proportions of Ionic columns, which had characterized the order from its earliest invention in the temples of East Greece,[47] now permitted single Ionic shafts to carry the ceiling beams high above the tops of the shorter exterior Doric columns (Fig. 98). The normal Doric solution to the same problem—two superimposed orders of reduced scale separated by a standard Doric architrave[48]—would have been impossibly awkward in this situation. Such an architrave would have abutted directly against the fluted shafts of the external columns, thus destroying the integrity of the Doric syntax. The soaring height of the Ionic order, on the other hand, imbued the entire interior with a sense of open space and seeming immaterial lightness. The lower diameter of the shafts above the bases (1.036 m) was more than a third smaller than the Doric columns (1.558 m), and they rose to a height of 10.287 m, thus creating a ratio of diameter to height of 9.98.[49] The columns carried an Ionic epistyle with three fascias crowned by an ovolo molding; it was a type that had been used in the great archaic temples of Asia Minor but here made its first known appearance in Attica.[50] The extra height gained by using Ionic columns allowed the epistyle to bond directly into the back of the exterior triglyph frieze, thus knitting together the two orders with satisfying logic.

In the Ionic capitals and bases of the Propylaia we see the beginning of the process by which the architects of the Acropolis set their indelible stamp upon the forms of the order and canonized its development for all future time. The capital has developed significantly from the smaller Ionic capitals of rather different type designed in the 460s for the interior of the Stoa Poikile in the Agora.[51] Now the spiraling volutes are spread wide apart, and the eyes are set well beyond the lines of the shaft (Fig. 99). The moldings at the edge of the volutes are more complex in profile, and they spiral half

[45] The western cella of the Parthenon measures 13.220 m (east to west) and 19.040 m (north to south); dimensions from Orlandos, Παρθ., pl. 94.

[46] See chap. 4, pp. 102–103 above.

[47] On proportions of Ionic columns in East Greek temples, Gruben, *Gr. Tempel*[5], 341–348.

[48] Cf., e.g., the interior colonnades of the Temple of Zeus at Olympia: Mallwitz, *Olympia*, 228 and fig. 177; Gruben, *Gr. Tempel*[5], 60 and fig. 40.

[49] *Propylaia* II, 229–235. The Ionic columns of the Propylaia exhibit some of the most delicate entasis ever applied to marble columns, the deviation from a straight line being 0.0064 m: *Propylaia* II, 233.

[50] *Propylaia* II, 237–239; Shoe, *Greek Mouldings*, 27. Cf. the use of the epistyle with three fascias in Asia Minor during the sixth century: at Ephesos, Gruben, *Gr. Tempel*[5], 380–381, fig. 287; at Didyma, Gruben, 397, fig. 301, 400–402.

[51] For the Ionic capitals of the Stoa Poikile, see Shear, Jr., *Hesperia* 53 (1984) 9–12, fig. 6.

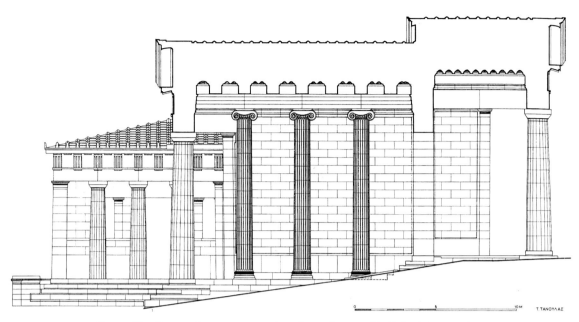

Figure 98. Restored east–west section through central hall, looking north

a turn more than those of the earlier capital. The egg-and-dart on the ovolo of the echinus is richly carved, while the pattern on the stoa capital was added in paint. The half palmettes at the point of junction, where the spirals meet the volute cushion, have six petals instead of four; but in like manner they barely touch the top of the echinus.[52] On the other hand, close proximity in the same building to the more restrained elements of Doric architecture has given the Ionic capitals of the Propylaia a cleaner and more disciplined sense of line and stronger tectonic form. The sumptuously ornamented capitals of the later Erechtheion, with their richly varied moldings and decorative anthemion, are the true descendants of the Ionic tradition; the capitals of the Propylaia are quintessentially Attic. It is likely that Mnesikles' design for the Ionic capitals was influenced by the earlier Ionic order in the west chamber of the Parthenon, as were so many decorative features of the Propylaia, but since these have perished without trace, there is no way to be sure.

In similar fashion, Mnesikles designed the Ionic bases with a profile that would become thereafter the standard form of the order. Whether he invented the design, it is impossible to know, but the bases of the Propylaia are the earliest extant examples; once again, he may have been inspired by the Ionic columns of the Parthenon. In place of the decorative, horizontally fluted *speirai* of the Asiatic order, Mnesikles used a strong tripartite structure that clearly articulates the function of support. The bold half-round of the lower torus projects well beyond the circumference of the shaft above. Its projection is emphasized by the deeply concave scotia above it, while the upper torus, scored with three horizontal flutes, protrudes only slightly beyond the fillets of the scotia.[53] The bases stand directly on the pavement of the hall without the raised step of a formal stylobate, and for this reason they are placed on low circular plinths to articulate the distinction between the colonnades and the surrounding floor.

---

[52] For the Ionic capitals of the Propylaia, see Bohn, *Propylaeen*, 21, pl. XII; O. Puchstein, *Das ionische Capitell* (Berlin 1887) 14–19. For discussion of the Propylaia capitals in relation to those of similar type from the Athena Nike temple and the Erechtheion, I. M. Shear, *Hesperia* 32 (1963) 380–383, pl. 88. The type of capital seems to have been developed on the Acropolis and differs considerably from the Ionic capitals of the Temple of Athena at Sounion and elsewhere in Attica; see chap. 8, pp. 245–246 above.

[53] For the Ionic bases of the Propylaia: Bohn, *Propylaeen,* 21 and pl. XII; Penrose, *Principles*², 70–71 and pl. 32; Shoe, *Greek Mouldings,* 147 and pl. LXVI:1; I. M. Shear, *Hesperia* 32 (1963) 380, pl. 89:b; *Propylaia* II, 231, fig. 15.3.

Figure 99. Ionic column, interior of central hall

One of the chief glories of the Propylaia was the marble coffered ceiling that spanned the entire interior of both the western hall and the eastern porch and was supported by the Ionic colonnades. Even the frequently laconic Pausanias, who saw the building nearly six centuries after its construction, remarked on it especially: "The Propylaia have a ceiling of white marble, and down to my time it is unsurpassed for the beauty and size of its stones" (1.22.4). What particularly caught Pausanias's attention was the enormous spans of the great beams that carried the actual coffer slabs. In the western hall seven marble beams reached from the side walls to the Ionic epistyles and across the central passage; a beam aligned with each Ionic column and with the midpoint of each intercolumniation (Fig. 100). The marble blocks that composed the beams measured 0.847 m in width and 0.617 m in height; those above the side aisles had a clear span of 5.48 m, and those over the central passage 4.35 m, while the eight smaller beams supporting the ceiling of the eastern porch had a clear span of only slightly less. The boldness of Mnesikles' structural daring emerges clearly when we compare these dimensions with those of the marble ceiling over the peristyle of the Parthenon. On the long flanks of the temple the clear span of the ceiling was 2.61 m, whereas the beams over the pronaos and opisthodomos had a span of 3.803 m.[54] In peripteral temples the marble ceiling was limited to the narrow peristyle around the exterior and the porches of pronaos and opisthodomos, whereas the interior of the cella was always roofed by a ceiling of wood. What was truly remarkable about the ceiling of the Propylaia was the way it covered the entire expanse of the interior with a canopy of marble that appeared to float high above the pavement, and for which the slender shafts of the Ionic columns provided seemingly effortless support. In the western hall, the ceiling itself consisted of eight rows of thirty-six coffer slabs, all but two rows of which had a pair of identical square coffers carved in the undersurface of each block (Fig. 101).[55] The ceiling of the eastern porch was arranged in nine rows

[54] Marble ceiling of the Propylaia: Bohn, *Propylaeen,* 21–22, pl. VIII; *Propylaia* II, 245–263. Ceiling in the peristyle of the Parthenon, Orlandos, Παρθ., 471–475. See chap. 4, pp. 105–106 above.

[55] Bohn, *Propylaeen,* 22 and pl. XII; *Propylaia* II, 253–258 and fig. 16.3, give the details of three different types of coffer slabs from the western ceiling. Most numerous originally were the slabs of Type 2 (6 rows × 36 blocks = 216): the visible soffit, 0.911 × 0.403 m, had two square coffers, 0.385–0.386 m on a side and spaced 0.14 m apart. Slabs of Type 1

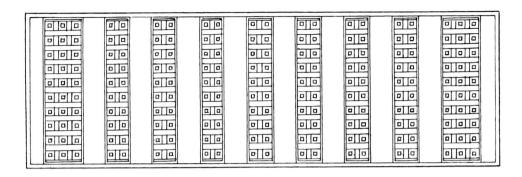

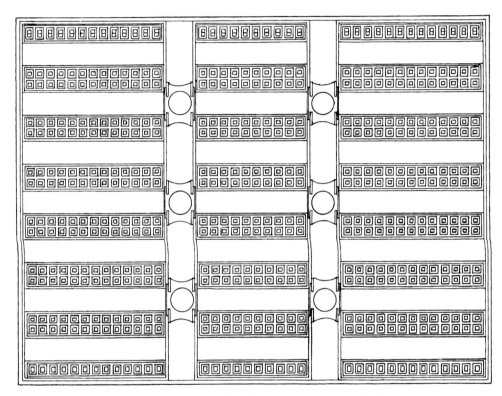

Figure 100. Plan of coffered ceiling of central hall

of ten slabs between the beams, which ran east to west across the narrower depth of the porch. The coffers were smaller and spaced farther apart: in the wider outermost rows there were three coffers on each slab, and in the intervening rows there were two coffers each.[56]

Structural support for the ceiling of the western hall was a matter that plainly worried the architect, as we learn from the ingenious device that he improvised to allay his concerns about the bearing strength of marble. The main ceiling beams weighed more than eleven tons each, and these rested on the Ionic epistyle, not only above each column but above the midpoint of each intercolumnar span. It was the beams in the latter positions that called for special handling. The Ionic epistyle itself was composed of two blocks placed back to back and corresponding in length to the interaxial

_____

(originally one row of thirty-six) came from the easternmost row beside the gate wall. Blocks 0.403 m wide had a single rectangular coffer, 0.302 × 0.363 m, within which were two smaller square coffers, 0.134 m on a side and spaced 0.034 m apart. Slabs of Type 3 (originally one row of thirty-six) came from the westernmost row just behind the Doric colonnade. Each block had a single rectangular coffer measuring 0.450 × 0.404 m.

[56] Bohn (note 55 above), Type 4, from the eastern ceiling, has coffers measuring 0.311 × 0.313 m and spaced 0.208 m apart. Cf. *Propylaia* II, 248, fig. 16.2.

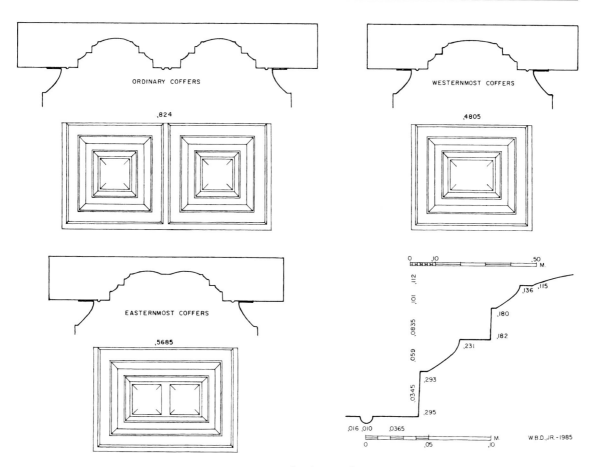

Figure 101. Three types of ceiling coffers in central hall

spacing between the Ionic columns. In the upper surface of each block, Mnesikles embedded a solid iron bar, rectangular in section and just half the length of the epistyle itself. These bars slipped into specially cut channels, where they rested on narrow shelves of marble at each end, the floor of the channels being cut slightly deeper than the bars, so that they were free to deflect under the weight of the marble ceiling beams. Two bronze plates about 0.06 m square were placed near the middle of each bar in order to ensure that the weight of the central ceiling beam transferred directly to the iron bars, and thence toward the ends of the epistyle, which found support in the columns beneath. All sixteen epistyle blocks of the interior colonnades were fitted with such iron bars, but of course Mnesikles' structural caution was entirely invisible to passersby in the hall below.[57]

In its original condition, the ceiling of the Propylaia would have caught the eye of the observer chiefly because of its rich polychrome decoration, which is closely similar to the embellishment of the Parthenon. The details of the ornament were painstakingly recorded by early investigators from surviving fragments of the ceiling, but in the course of the last century almost all traces have been obliterated. All three walls of the western hall terminated at the top in an elaborately ornamented epicranitis molding that continued on the backing blocks of the Doric architrave at the level of the Ionic capitals. The epicranitis of the Propylaia was a direct quotation of the unusually elaborate combination of moldings that crowned the Panathenaic frieze of the Parthenon. In both buildings

---

[57] The grooves cut in the tops of the Ionic epistyle blocks are 1.829 m long, 0.076 m wide, and 0.14 m deep. At each end is a shelf 0.083 m long and rising 0.025 m above the floor of the channel. Nothing is preserved of the iron bars themselves. Their existence was detected from the rust stains on the marble sides of the cuttings. The details described by Dinsmoor, *AJA* 26 (1922) 152–154; cf. Dinsmoor, *AAG*[3], 176, 203 and fig. 66; *Propylaia* II, 238–239 and fig. 15.7.

the moldings are almost identical in height, and the profiles and painted decoration of the Propylaia have been so closely studied from those of the Parthenon that it must be a deliberate attempt to relate the gatehouse to its temple. The lowest member of the epicranitis was a cyma reversa painted with a Lesbian leaf, or leaf-and-tongue, pattern. The leaves were white, edged in gold and with central spines of gold, and they alternated with golden tongues against a dark blue ground, while the narrow fillet at the bottom was painted green. Above the cyma reversa, a broad fascia carried a gilded double meander in which the keys of the pattern alternated with saltire squares that exactly replicated the meanders of the Parthenon. A hawksbeak crowned the fascia and was decorated with the standard conventionalized Doric leaves, alternating bright red and dark blue, edged in gold.[58] Above the epicranitis, crowning moldings of ovolo profile terminated the Ionic epistyle, its equivalent course around the walls,[59] and the main ceiling beams, while similar ovolos articulated the steps of the coffers.[60] All carried identical painted ornament in which white eggs edged in gold alternated with golden darts against a blue ground. In each case, the narrow horizontal fillet beneath the curve of the ovolo was picked out with a band of bright red. On the soffit of the ceiling slabs, the square of each coffer was surrounded by a tiny bead molding painted with a pearl ornament, instead of being carved with the elaborate bead-and-reel of the similar molding in the ceiling of the Parthenon. Bands of color edged the bead molding: a narrow one of green on the outside, a wider one of blue on the inside. The coffer covers themselves were colored deep blue and splashed with sixteen-pointed stars of gold.[61] As seen from below by the passing observer, the ceiling of the Propylaia would have presented contrasting bands of color: crystalline white marble for the beams, brightly painted ornament for the coffers, which marched in alternating rhythm up and down the aisles of the central hall.

THE NORTHWEST WING (PINAKOTHEKE)

We have seen that the projecting western wings of the Propylaia served a vital aesthetic function in the architectural composition of Mnesikles' gatehouse. But when we turn to examine in detail what the architect actually built to north and south of the approach ramp, the true extent of the adjustments in dimension and changes in plan begins to emerge (Figs. 102, 103). Of the two sides, the design of the northwest wing approaches more closely the architect's initial conception of a colonnaded portico in front of a nearly square chamber, enclosed on three sides by solid masonry walls and covered by a low hipped roof. In the time of Pausanias, the inner compartment was used to display paintings dedicated on the Acropolis; he calls it οἴκημα ἔχον γραφάς, "a chamber with paintings,"[62] and describes a number by famous old masters of the fifth century. By that time the picture

[58] The epicranitis of the Propylaia, 0.350 m high: details of the ornament, Penrose, *Principles*², 28, pl. 24; cf. L. V. Solon, *Polychromy* (New York 1924) pl. VIII; position and profile, Bohn, *Propylaeen*, 20, pls. XI, XII; Shoe, *Greek Mouldings*, 58, pl. XXVI:17. The frieze crown of the Parthenon, 0.347 m high: details of the ornament, Penrose, *Principles*², 52, 56, pl. 23; Orlandos, Παρθ., 253–256, pl. 38; profiles, Penrose, *Principles*², pl. 20, figs. 27, 27a; Shoe, *Greek Mouldings*, 58, 127, pls. XXVI:16, LX:21; see chap. 4, pp. 103–104 above.

[59] The Ionic epistyle of the interior order, complete with three fascias and crowning ovolo, was duplicated at the top of the gate wall, along both side walls, and as a frieze backer for the Doric triglyph frieze: Penrose, *Principles*², pl. 24; Bohn, *Propylaeen*, pls. VIII, XI.

[60] Profiles of the ovolo moldings: on the Ionic epistyle, Shoe, *Greek Mouldings*, 27, pl. XV:14; on the ceiling beams, Shoe, 45, pl. XXI:26; on the coffers, Shoe, 43, pl. XXI:5–7.

[61] The painted ornament described, Penrose, *Principles*², 58–59, pl. 24; for variations in the decorative scheme of the coffer covers, pl. 25. Most numerous (note 55 above, Type 2) were the sixteen-pointed stars, or sixteen-pointed stars with intervening rays forming a sunburst, pl. 25:5, 6. The rectangular coffers (note 55 above, Type 3) were decorated with palmettes and tendrils, Penrose, pl. 25:3, 4. The smaller square coffers from the east porch (note 55 above, Type 4) likewise had patterns of palmettes and tendrils, Penrose, pl. 25:1, 2.

[62] Paus. 1.22.6.

Figure 102. View of northwest wing facade from south

gallery had been in existence for several centuries, for the Hellenistic historian Polemon of Ilion wrote a book entitled Περὶ τῶν ἐν τοῖς Προπυλαίοις πινάκων (*On the Panel Paintings in the Propylaia*).[63] Satyros, writing in the third century, described two panels dedicated by the illustrious Alkibiades after his victories in the chariot race at Olympia and Nemea,[64] but there is no indication when the paintings found their way into the northwest wing of the Propylaia. On the basis of these references, modern writers have frequently called the building the Pinakotheke, but there is no ancient authority for the locution and no likelihood that the structure was designed with that purpose in mind. The only evidence for the intended function of the northwest wing is suggested by the architecture itself, but for this there is no confirmation in the written record.

One of the thorniest problems that has haunted interpreters of the Propylaia since the nineteenth century has been to explain the asymmetric placement of the doorway and windows in the front wall behind the colonnade (Fig. 104).[65] We shall need to return to the architectural problem in more detail below, but its bearing on the intended function of the room is what concerns us here. It was John Travlos who first observed that in the eccentric placement of its door the chamber re-

[63] Harpokr., s.v. λαμπάς (λ 3 Keaney), citing Polemon, Müller, *FHG* III, p. 117.

[64] Athenaeus 12.534D, citing Satyros, Müller, *FHG* III, p. 160; the same paintings apparently known also to Plut. *Alkib.* 16.7–8.

[65] Various explanations of the irregular design: Bohn, *Propylaeen,* 23; G. W. Elderkin, *Problems in Periklean Buildings* (Princeton 1912) 1–12; F. Franco, *ASAtene* 13–14 (1930–31) 9–25; Stevens, *Hesperia* 15 (1946) 87–89; Dinsmoor, *AAG*³, 203; Bundgaard, *Mnesicles,* 63–66; C. Tiberi, *Mnesicle, l'architetto dei Propilei* (Rome 1964) 74–79; P. Hellström, *OpAth* 11 (1975) 87–92; Dinsmoor, Jr., *Hesperia* Suppl. 20 (1982) 18–33; Hellström, *OpAth* 17 (1988) 107–121; *Propylaia* II, 382–384.

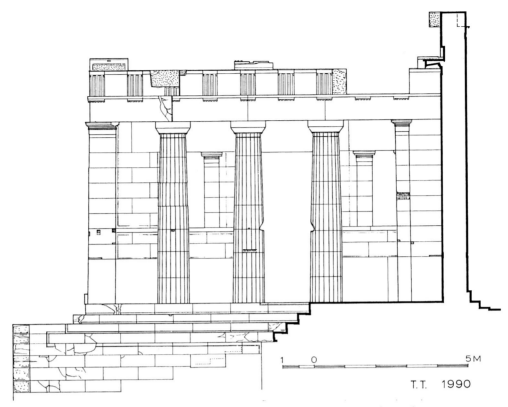

Figure 103. Elevation, actual state, northwest wing colonnade

sembled Greek banqueting rooms,[66] both the androns of private houses and the larger dining halls associated with sanctuaries. His demonstration that seventeen dining couches could be placed end to end around the four walls of the room has won wide acceptance,[67] and the idea has been developed further to explain the intended function of the four subsidiary halls of the Propylaia in the original plan as banqueting facilities for the city's high officials after the sacrifices at the Panathenaic festival.[68] There is no way of knowing whether the northwest wing ever functioned in that capacity, but it is an attractive notion that such an intention may have motivated its design.

The architect's guiding principle was to reduce the scale of the Doric order to about two-thirds of that which he had used for the facades of the central hall. The colonnades of the wings were turned at 90 degrees to the western facade, with the first column aligned with those of the larger order so that the inside corner of the wings adjoined the outside corner of the main building. Accordingly, the height of the western columns (8.808 m) was reduced by one-third, to 5.872 m, and this was adjusted to 5.847 m in order to align the abaci of the capitals with the ninth ashlar course above the orthostates. The architect then adopted the proportion 3:7 to determine the axial intercolumniation (2.506 m) from the height of the columns, and the lower diameter (1.074 m) from the spacing of the columns. The intercolumniation also inevitably determined the spacing of the triglyphs in the frieze (2.506 ÷ 2 = 1.253 m), and this dimension became the module for the ashlar wall blocks of the west and north walls, since their joints had to conform to those of the frieze that rested directly above them. The module for the triglyph frieze (1.253 m) was divided into triglyphs with a width of 0.491 m and metopes of 0.762 m. Using these dimensions, the architect planned to erect the long

[66] Travlos, *PDA*, 482.

[67] See, e.g., Lawrence, *Greek Architecture*⁵, 117–118; Hurwit, *Athenian Acropolis*, 195–196 and fig. 166; Gruben, *Gr. Tempel*⁵, 200 and fig. 149.

[68] See Hellström, *OpAth* 17 (1988) 107–121.

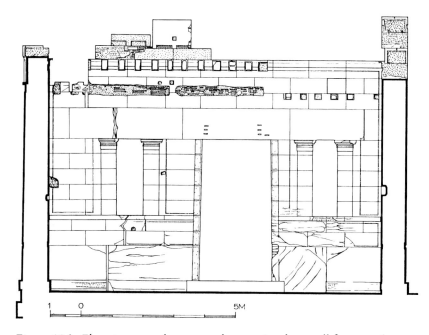

Figure 104. Elevation, actual state, northwest wing door wall from south

western wall of the wing with a frieze composed of twelve metopes and thirteen triglyphs. But by the time construction reached the level of the frieze, it was found necessary to increase the width of the two metopes adjacent to each corner by 0.020 m in order to bring the frieze into agreement with the length of the wall at floor level without overly exaggerating the inward inclination of the walls.[69]

As it stands today, the portico of the northwest wing consists of three columns between antae, of which that to the west is formed by the end of the long western side wall, in the normal fashion for a Doric building (Figs. 102, 103). The eastern anta of the portico, however, is the end of a spur wall aligned with the columns and turned at 90 degrees to the long eastern wall of the building. Thus the point of junction, where the side porch meets the central hall, is marked by the immediate juxtaposition of two antae of different forms, one of which is necessarily only two-thirds the height of the other. This awkward arrangement resulted from an adjustment in plan to the whole western facade of the Propylaia. Careful observation of the triglyph friezes on the central building has revealed a curious anomaly: on the side return of the eastern frieze, the third triglyph is precisely centered above the anta, as was proper in Greek architecture, whereas the third flank triglyph of the western frieze is not correctly aligned with the corresponding anta but is set off center by 0.491 m. Similarly, the columns of the western portico stand 0.491 m closer to the antae than those of the eastern porch. This discrepancy shows that, in the original plan for the Propylaia, Mnesikles had intended the western facade of the building to be placed 0.491 m farther to the west than it was eventually built.[70] Accordingly, the colonnade of the Pinakotheke was initially meant to be wider from east to west by that same amount. That increment in the width of the porch would have allowed exactly the space for a colonnade of four columns instead of three, with equal intercolumniations, and it would

[69] For the details of the design and derivation of the dimensions, see Dinsmoor, Jr., *Hesperia* Suppl. 20 (1982) 24; *Propylaia* II, 373–378.

[70] The original observation of Dinsmoor discussed by Dinsmoor, Jr., *Hesperia* Suppl. 20 (1982) 26–27 and note 25, followed by Hellström, *OpAth* 17 (1988) 115, who prefers to think that the north–south dividing wall between the western wings and the eastern halls, including the antae, was shifted 0.491 m to the west, whereas Dinsmoor, Jr., argued that the western colonnade, together with its frieze, was shifted eastward from a planned position farther west. Cf. W. Hoepfner, in Hoepfner, ed., *Kult und Kultbauten*, 160–163 and fig. 1.

have obviated the need for the awkward spur wall at the east end.[71] Such a four-column porch could
then have carried a more regular frieze composed of ten triglyphs and nine metopes. The reason for
the alteration in the plan of the west facade is undoubtedly to be sought among the difficult problems that the architect encountered in trying to accommodate the opposite southwest wing to the
sanctuary of Athena Nike. A change in one necessitated a change in the other, since the two porches
were intended to be identical. But the altered dimension introduced a number of anomalies in the
portico of the Pinakotheke as well. The colonnade was reduced to the unusual number of three columns placed asymmetrically between their framing antae. The frieze above them consisted of eight
metopes and nine triglyphs, with the easternmost triglyph centered over the anta of the spur wall;
but this left the frieze to terminate at the east in an outsize metope panel, measuring 0.994 m, that
reflected the remaining projection of the spur wall itself.

The change in plan that reduced the westward projection of the side wings also undoubtedly
accounts for the curious asymmetry of the window wall whose explanation has so perplexed successive investigators. As the wall behind the colonnade was eventually built, the central doorway
and two flanking windows are separated by four segments of masonry wall, all four of which have
different dimensions (Fig. 104).[72] Weathering marks on the marble pavement show that below the
windows low benches were carried around the three walls of the porch on either side of the doorway.
It has now been demonstrated that the actual dimensions of the windows themselves were studied
from the triglyph frieze of the portico. The window opening on the sill was equal to the width of one
metope, and the window jambs on either side, in the form of miniature antae, were given the width
of one triglyph. It is also observable that they were so placed in the wall that the jambs of the western window, as seen in elevation, align perfectly with the third and fourth triglyphs from the west
end of the frieze, while the jambs of the other window are centered beneath the two easternmost
triglyphs.[73] Now, if we imagine a putative original form of the plan in which 0.491 m is added to the
east end of the wall and a fourth column, instead of the existing spur wall and anta, is placed in front
of it, the disposition of the two windows would become almost exactly symmetrical.

There is still disagreement about the dislocation of the doorway, which in the extant building
is off center with respect to the windows by 0.245 m. It has been argued that in the initial plan for
the four-column porch the doorway was correctly centered between the windows, but the decrease
in length, by 0.491 m, created an unsatisfactory jointing system for the wall blocks and caused the
doorway to be shifted to the right for aesthetic reasons.[74] Plainly, if aesthetic considerations had
prevailed, the doorway could have been positioned equidistant from each window, and the overall
asymmetry of the wall would have been far less jarring. But that did not happen, evidently because
it did not serve the architect's purpose to center the doorway between the windows. So one infers
that the placement of the doorway depended not on aesthetic considerations, but was determined
rather by the intended function of the room to which it gave access. This line of reasoning, of course,
gave rise to the suggestion that the room was designed as a banqueting hall, and the dislocation of
the doorway enabled it to be properly furnished with dining couches.[75] In this matter, Greek custom
required the couches, preferably of equal length, to be arranged end to end along the walls, so that
the length of a given number plus the width of one exactly filled the available space, except for the

[71] So Dinsmoor, Jr., *Hesperia* Suppl. 20 (1982) 25 and fig. 3; Hellström, *OpAth* 17 (1988) 116–117.
[72] Lengths of the wall segments separating windows and door, from west to east: 2.184 m, 1.855 m, 1.334 m, 1.448 m.
[73] Dinsmoor, Jr. (note 70 above); Hellström (note 70 above); and cf. Hellström, *OpAth* 11 (1975) 91.
[74] So Dinsmoor, Jr., *Hesperia* Suppl 20 (1982) 31–32. Dinsmoor's argument that the existing jointing system im-
proved the aesthetic appearance of the window wall has been rightly criticized by Hellström, *OpAth* 17 (1988) 116, who
finds no need to introduce Dinsmoor's putative intermediate stage into the already complex sequence of adjustments that
resulted in the plan as built.
[75] See p. 294 and note 66 above.

opening of the door itself. It has been acutely observed that the addition of 0.491 m to the width of the chamber, as originally planned, would make the section of wall to the right of the door 4.06 m and that to the left 4.82 m, exactly the space needed for four couches 2.03 m in length and one measuring 0.76 m in width. The same number would fit comfortably along the side walls, with five couches across the back of the room.[76] In the form in which the building was actually built, however, it is impossible to say whether the room was ever so furnished with couches. The one certainty is that it never received a marble pavement like all other parts of the Propylaia. To this day, the toichobate course, against which the pavement slabs would have abutted, reveals that it was never dressed to its finished surface; in fact, many of the blocks still retain their rough lifting bosses, the sure sign of incomplete marble work.[77]

THE SOUTHWEST WING

It seems highly likely that Mnesikles' initial conception of the Propylaia called for two matching western wings facing each other, with identical facades on either side of the approach ramp. The plans for the northwest wing, as we have seen, were carried out with fairly minor adjustments, but a glance at the plan of the building reveals at once that its southern counterpart has been substantially redesigned. Indeed, it is obvious that a building with the overall dimensions of the Pinakotheke (15.73 × 11.59 m) could not have been erected south of the ramp without drastically altering the topography of the site. A structure of that length would have extended beyond the southern fortification wall of the Acropolis, whereas the ancient Cyclopean wall to the east and the sanctuary of Athena Nike to the west served to curtail the width of the available space between them. If the architect had first visualized the southwest wing as a square chamber fronted by a columnar porch, what had changed by the time construction began was the fundamental concept of the building's function. The idea of an enclosed room has been completely abandoned, and in its final form the southern colonnade serves only to provide a monumental entrance to the sanctuary of Athena Nike; but that, after all, is entirely consistent with the basic purpose of the Greek propylon. The various stages in the evolution of the architect's thinking about the design have left clear traces in the architecture, and we shall need to consider this evidence below, not least because of its bearing on the chronology of the Nike sanctuary next door.

Essential to the monumental forecourt of the Acropolis were the identical columnar porches of the wings projecting westward of the main facade. This degree of symmetry Mnesikles managed to achieve. Accordingly, the facade of the southwest wing consists of three columns between antae, of which the dimensions and spacing duplicate the northern porch as perfectly as is possible in marble architecture.[78] Like the portico of the Pinakotheke, the colonnade terminates in a spur wall at right angles to the east wall of the wing; and in like manner it carries a frieze composed of nine triglyphs and eight metopes, of which the first triglyph is centered above the eastern anta, while an elongated metope closes the frieze above the spur wall. Here, however, the symmetry ends, for the colonnade is a full intercolumniation wider than the porch behind it and ends on the west in an extraordi-

[76] As observed by Hellström, *OpAth* 17 (1988) 117.

[77] See Dinsmoor, Jr., *Hesperia* Suppl. 20 (1982) 19, note 14, who thought that the fact of the unfinished toichobate served to refute Travlos's original suggestion (*PDA*, 482) that the room was designed for dining couches. See also Hellström, *OpAth* 11 (1975) 87–89. But the lack of dressing on the toichobate tells us only that the marble pavement was never laid, and it gives no information about the architect's original intentions, concerning which the off-center doorway provides more eloquent testimony. See *Propylaia* II, 372 and fig. 20.4, for lifting bosses on the toichobate.

[78] For the southwest wing, see generally Penrose, *Principles*², 60–70; Bohn, *Propylaeen*, 25–29; Dörpfeld, *AM* 10 (1885) 131–144; Bundgaard, *Mnesicles*, 66–75; Gruben, *Gr. Tempel*⁵, 200–207; *Propylaia* II, 399–445.

nary double anta. This structure, designed expressly for this peculiar situation, took the form of two Doric antae placed back to back with a narrow pier between them. Seen from the north, the anta agrees in width with the corresponding anta of the Pinakotheke and terminates the facade properly. Seen from the south, it aligns with nothing and faces the open northeast corner of the neighboring sanctuary. The dimensions of the double anta were determined by the triglyph frieze that it carried; thus the western return on each side was made equal to the width of one triglyph, and the pier between the antae equaled the width of one metope.[79]

As eventually erected, the porch behind the colonnade was enclosed to east and south by solid masonry walls that bore no architectural adornment except for the terminal anta at the southwest corner. The arrangement of the marble paving slabs within the porch indicates that low benches lined both walls, as was also the case in both the central hall and the portico of the northwest wing. The architect clearly designed the porch with the greatest depth behind the columns that the site could accommodate, as is suggested by the curious beveled angle where the southeast corner abuts the Cyclopean masonry of the Mycenaean wall. The depth of the southwest wing, from the edge of the stylobate to the south wall, is 1.27 m greater than the same dimension in the portico of the Pinakotheke;[80] but the need to bevel off the corner of the building would have been entirely eliminated if the architect had adopted the same depth for both columnar porches. Even that seemingly desperate solution did not widen the building sufficiently to allow the colonnade to return along the west facade of the wing with symmetrical intercolumniations. So Mnesikles abandoned the formal vocabulary of the columnar order and placed at the midpoint of the western stylobate a single slender pier, rectangular in plan, deeper than it is wide, and crowned by the normal moldings of the Doric anta capital.[81] Because the front colonnade projects beyond the porch behind it, the central pier and the southwest anta of the wing align with the last column, not with the double anta; the entablature that they carry also necessarily centers on the westernmost column. Here too Mnesikles' design was unique in Doric architecture. At the top of the architrave, below the taenia, a single band, undifferentiated as regulae, carries a continuous row of guttae across the whole width of the facade. The plain band of the frieze, completely lacking triglyphs and metopes, is adorned only by a crowning fascia and a small half-round molding. Similarly, the horizontal mutular cornice that was standard to the Doric order also seemed illogical without a triglyph frieze, and so the normal raking cornice of the pediment was pressed into service in a horizontal position under the eaves of the curiously truncated hipped roof.[82] We shall see, however, that even this unusual superstructure of the west facade did not arise without further vicissitudes in the course of construction.

Such was the structure that actually stood on the site when building operations halted in 432. But there is evidence for several alterations in the design of the southwest wing, some of which must have been undertaken after work had begun, and all of which concerned either the adjacent Mycenaean wall or the architectural relationship between the Propylaia and the sanctuary of Athena Nike (Fig. 105). When the masons commenced building in the summer of 437, their first task was to raise the foundations on the steepest part of the slope in order to establish a uniform level for the common crepidoma of the main west facade and the projecting wings. To this end, they erected great

[79] Details of the double anta: Penrose, *Principles*², 59, pl. 26; Bohn, *Propylaeen*, 28, pl. XVI:3; Dörpfeld, *AM* 10 (1885) 134–135, pl. V:1, 2; *Propylaia* II, 408–411. For the molding of the capital, Shoe, *Greek Mouldings*, 120, pl. LVII:13.

[80] Depth of the southwest wing, 6.248 m; depth of the porch of the Pinakotheke, 4.978 m.

[81] For the pier of the west facade, Bohn, *Propylaeen*, 27, pl. XVI:4; Bundgaard, *Mnesicles*, 73–75; *Propylaia* II, 411–414. For the hawksbeak molding of the capital, Shoe, *Greek Mouldings*, 120, pl. LVII:14.

[82] Details of the west entablature: Bohn, *Propylaeen*, 27–28, pl. XVI; Bundgaard (note 81 above); *Propylaia* II, 414–418 (architrave), 419–423 (frieze), 423–426 (cornice). For the half-round molding of the frieze crown, Shoe, *Greek Mouldings*, 154, pl. LXXI:19; for the cyma reversa of the geison soffit, 69, pls. XXX:6, LXXV:5; for the hipped roof, Dörpfeld, *AM* 10 (1885) 131–144.

Figure 105. General view of the Athena Nike bastion and Propylaia from northwest

masonry podiums for the two wings, which at their western extremities rose in ten courses of marble above four courses of poros underpinnings. The podiums terminate at the west in matching piers, framing the steps of the crepidoma, and their uppermost molded course ranging with the stylobate. The poros foundations for the podiums step down steeply from east to west in a line that conforms roughly to the slope of the approach ramp, and this makes clear the builders' principle that in general all visible stonework was to be of marble, whereas the poros foundations were to be concealed below grade level.[83]

The podium for the columnar porch of the southwestern wing includes several courses of foundations specifically designed to support the unusual double anta at the western end of the colonnade.[84] This shows that by the beginning of actual construction the original notion of identical projecting wings had already been discarded. Whatever may have been the intended function of the chamber that was supposed to duplicate the Pinakotheke, this had now been set aside, and Mnesikles had redesigned the building to provide a ceremonial entrance to the sanctuary of Athena Nike. Moreover, the new plan invented the double anta at the end of the colonnade and aligned the western facade of the porch with the last column on the front instead of the anta, for the obvious purpose of encroaching as little as possible on the already cramped space of the Nike bastion. But the foundations for the west facade consist of several courses of roughly worked poros blocks that extend southward for a distance of 16.40 m, until they return in a right-angled jog against the fortification wall of the Acropolis. The actual corner extends 2.10 m beyond the southern edge of the Nike bastion and is

[83] For the masonry podium of the northwest wing, see Bundgaard, *Mnesicles,* 167–170; for the southwest wing, see *Propylaia* II, 400–404 and fig. 21.1; also the bibliography cited below, p. 300, note 85.
[84] On the foundations for the double anta, see Wrede, *AM* 57 (1932) 76–77, 81, Beil. 15; Schleif, *JdI* 48 (1933) 177–178; Mark, *Athena Nike,* 80 and note 59.

supported by a special buttress built against the south face of the wall.[85] The laying of this foundation plainly anticipated construction of a building that exactly replicated the north–south length of the Pinakotheke, 15.73 m. With this change of plan, the wing of the Propylaia was probably intended to take the form of an open stoa spanning the full width of the bastion from north to south.[86] The length of the stylobate would exactly accommodate five axial intercolumniations and a terminating anta; so we may suppose that the architect's initial idea was to reproduce the order and dimensions of the northern columns along the west facade.

Such an open colonnaded portico was an attractive modification to the original plan. Not only would it have created a convenient formal entry onto the bastion, but with benches along its walls it would become a spacious lobby where spectators could gather to witness the sacrifices at the altar of Athena Nike. Construction of the western foundations and their extension beyond the existing southern limit of the bastion clearly demonstrates the intentions of the builders. The work was carried out in the full expectation that the massive masonry of the Cyclopean wall would be demolished to make way for the southern halls of the new Propylaia. Alas, we know from the sequel that the old Mycenaean wall proved to be an immovable obstacle that would utterly frustrate Mnesikles' hopes of achieving a symmetrical plan and would force him to truncate the southern portico still further, until it assumed its final extant form, with its eastern corner beveled off to abut the rough boulders of the prehistoric masonry.

THE ACCOUNTS OF THE OVERSEERS

In accordance with normal administrative procedures, responsibility for construction of the Propylaia was vested in a board of epistatai. The election of such boards for the management of public works had become standard practice following the democratic reforms of the late 460s, and we have already observed their operations in connection with the great bronze Athena of Pheidias, the Parthenon and its golden statue, and the Telesterion at Eleusis.[87] As in the case of their predecessors, the epistatai of the Propylaia were charged with the regular oversight of building procedures, and, more important, with the day-to-day disbursement of payments for goods and services. Like all Athenian officials who handled public funds, the overseers of the Propylaia submitted their accounts for audit at the end of each year of service and published them on an inscribed marble stele set up on the Acropolis. The board that administered construction of the new gatehouse was evidently closely modeled on the contemporary epistatai of the Parthenon and, like them, rotated annually until the project was abandoned, with the individual members and their secretary being elected in each year. As it happens, the stele bearing their inscribed accounts has chanced to survive in twenty-three shat-

---

[85] On the foundations for the western facade, see A. Köster, *JdI* 21 (1906) 139, fig. 4; Wrede, *AM* 57 (1932) 86; and cf. M. Miles, *Hesperia* 49 (1980) 324; Mark (note 84 above). The southward extension of the poros foundations beyond the corner of the southwest wing, and projecting beyond the southern limit of the bastion, is shown on the plan of P. Kavvadias and G. Kawerau, Ἡ ἀνασκαφὴ τῆς Ἀκροπόλεως ἀπὸ τοῦ 1885 μέχρι τοῦ 1890 (Athens 1906) pl. Η′ and 137–138.

[86] So also Hoepfner, in Hoepfner, ed., *Kult und Kultbauten*, 164–165 and 161, fig. 1, with the stylobate correctly aligned with the third column and not the double anta. Hoepfner prefers to restore a row of rectangular piers like the single one that was actually erected, but one imagines that the architect's initial idea was to reproduce the columnar order of the north facade with a normal Doric entablature. The four phases in the design of the southwest wing, drawn by Korres, in R. Economakis, ed., *Acropolis Restoration* (London 1994) 46, followed by Gruben, *Gr. Tempel*⁵, 204–206, fig. 156, need to be adjusted. The dressing of the foundations for the double anta (see note 84 above) shows that it was part of the plan from the beginning of construction, whereas the foundations for the west facade were built in alignment with the third column of the porch. If Korres's phase b was ever conceived, it was certainly never built. His phase c should show the west facade restored as a stoa with the full north–south length, as phase b, but aligned with the third column and not the double anta.

[87] For the epistatai of the bronze Athena, chap. 2, pp. 17–21 above; of the Parthenon, chap. 3, pp. 43–48 above; of the golden statue, chap. 3, pp. 69–78 above; of the Telesterion, chap. 6, pp. 163–165 above.

tered fragments, which in fact preserve only a small fraction of the original text. Nevertheless, the inscriptions add a few pieces of valuable information to our knowledge of the building.

Basic to the correct reconstruction of the accounts is the fact, preserved in two apparently independent literary references, that the building was under construction for five years.

> Concerning the Propylaia of the Acropolis, others have recorded and especially Philochoros, in the fourth book, that the Athenians began to build in the archonship of Euthymenes with Mnesikles as architect. Heliodoros in his first book *On the Acropolis at Athens* says, among other things, as follows: "In five years they were completely finished; two thousand talents were expended; and they made five gates, through which they entered the Acropolis."[88]

The duration of the building period is corroborated by Plutarch (*Per.* 13.12), who likewise states that the Propylaia were completed in five years. This information then made it possible to divide the inscribed fragments into five annual accounts, of which only a small part of each is preserved.[89] Two of the largest fragments make a physical join, and together they preserve the top edge of the stone; on their obverse is part of the general heading for the first year, and on the reverse the fourth annual prescript.[90] These pieces also show that the accounts were laid out on the stone in a format closely similar to the contemporary accounts for the Parthenon. The general heading spanned the full width of the stele at the top of the obverse, and beneath it were two double columns, sums of money listed in the left-hand column, and the purpose of the expenditure itemized in the right-hand column. The prescripts for subsequent years after the first filled the width of one of the two double columns; thus the accounts for Years 1–3 were inscribed on the obverse of the stele, while Years 4–5 occupied the reverse. Since the stone tapered from a thickness of 0.186 m near the bottom to 0.111 m at the top, it was possible to locate individual fragments accurately within its vertical height. Likewise, the spacing and width of the columns could be calculated, and hence the original width of the stele has been estimated at 1.23 m; but the height of the stone cannot be determined.[91]

The first annual prescript opens with the official title of the administrative board, [ἐπιστάτ]αι π[ρο]πυλαίο ἐργασ[ίας], "overseers of the construction of the Propylaia," followed by the name and demotic of their secretary. The account is dated by reference to the eponymous archon and to the secretary for the first prytany of the boulē, both of whose names are still preserved: ἐπ' Ε[ὐ]θυμένος ἄρχο[ντος] Ἀθεναίοισιν ἐπὶ τῆς βολῆς ἧι Πε]ιθ[ι]άδε[ς] πρῶτος ἐγραμ[μάτευε].[92] After the word *epistatai*, the name and demotic of each overseer were listed; the spacing indicates that there were five in the first year. The prescript ends with the standard formula that introduces the receipts for the year: τούτοις λέμματα τὸ ἐνιαυτὸ τούτο τάδε, "For these men the receipts for this year were the following." The wording is best preserved in Year 4 of the Propylaia, but the same formula certainly appeared in every prescript, as also in the Parthenon accounts, where it is fully preserved in Years 14

---

[88] Harpokr., s.v. προπύλαια ταῦτα (π 101 Keaney), citing Philochoros, *FGrH* 328 F 36; Heliodoros, *FGrH* 373 F 1.

[89] Correct reconstruction of the stele is due primarily to Dinsmoor, *AJA* 17 (1913) 371–398, with some rearrangement of fragments noted, Dinsmoor, *AJA* 51 (1947) 134, note 134. A few fragments added by Meritt, *Hesperia* 7 (1938) 79–80; R. E. Wycherley, *BSA* 70 (1975) 188–189; *IG* I³ 462–466.

[90] The large opisthographic fragments C + D + L preserve, on the obverse, the right end of the prescript for Year 1 and below that the top of the double column II with the last lines of the receipts and the first lines of the expenses for Year 2: Dinsmoor, *AJA* 17 (1913) 381–382, 389–391. On the reverse, the same fragments have the prescript and receipts for Year 4: Dinsmoor, *AJA* 17 (1913) 392–397.

[91] For the taper, Dinsmoor, *AJA* 17 (1913) 376–377; for the calculation of the width of the stele, 382.

[92] *IG* I³ 462, lines 2–4, Year 1 (437/6). To fill the twenty-two letter spaces to the left of the official title of the epistatai, Dinsmoor, *AJA* 17 (1913) 383, proposed to restore ἀρχιτέκτον Μνεσικλῆς καὶ in the important lacuna at the beginning of line 2. This still seems the most likely restoration of the text. The names of both the secretary of the boulē and the archon appeared also in *IG* I³ 446, lines 313–314, Parthenon Year 11, where only the former is still preserved.

and 15.[93] Much the same information was contained in the prescript for subsequent years, although only that for the fourth year is well preserved. It shows, however, that each annual account was introduced by a serial number and by reference to the name of the overseers' secretary, in a manner similar to the accounts of the Parthenon: [ἐπὶ τῆς τετ]άρτες ἀρχῆς hῆι Διογέ[νες ἐ]γρ[αμμάτευε], "In the year of the fourth board for which Diogenes was secretary."[94] The accounts were dated only by the name of the first prytany secretary, the eponymous archon being limited to Year 1. There followed a list of the individual members of the board and the formula introducing the receipts. As in the case of the Parthenon, the size of the board appears to have fluctuated,[95] if we can judge the spacing accurately from the fragmentary inscriptions. In Years 1 and 4 there were certainly five overseers and a secretary, but the more fragmentary prescript for Year 2 appears to require six names, while that for Year 3 seems limited to four names in addition to the secretary. Not a single fragment is attributable to the prescript of Year 5.

Examination of the sources of revenue that came to the overseers of the Propylaia reveals the strikingly close relationship between their project and the administration of the Parthenon. Not only did the principal contributors to the temple likewise fund the Propylaia, but because there is a parallel series of accounts for the two projects during the five years from 437/6 to 433/2, we can see that donors to the Propylaia accounts normally withheld payments from the Parthenon in the same year. Although the actual sums of money have perished almost completely from the inscription, there is no reason to doubt Thucydides' explicit statement that the capital reserve fund on the Acropolis paid for the "Propylaia and the other buildings."[96] That fund was managed by the treasurers of Athena, who had made large payments for the Parthenon over a period of nine years. Records of their contributions for the Propylaia accounts are preserved in the second and fourth years, the text of the latter being the more complete: παρὰ ταμιῶν ho[ὶ τα τῆ]ς θεῶ ἐτα[μίευον] hοῖς Κράτες ἐγρα[μμά]τε[υ]ε Λαμπ[τρεύς], "From the treasurers who stewarded the funds of the goddess, to whom Krates of Lamptrai was secretary."[97] The same formula, word for word, appeared in the first nine accounts of the Parthenon overseers, the only change being in the name of the secretary. It is interesting to observe that in 438/7, the year of the dedication of the temple, the treasurers made no payment to its overseers; no doubt they anticipated the need for large contributions to the Propylaia, whose construction was scheduled to begin in the following year. Although the record of the treasurers' payments has survived in only two of the five accounts, they almost certainly provided funds in every year. It is to be noted that in Year 1 (437/6) the first seven lines of receipts are entirely missing, while there is a lacuna of at least five lines at the beginning of the receipts for Year 3 (435/4). The payments from the treasurers of Athena were probably recorded in these positions, and it is even possible that the treasurers made two separate contributions to the Propylaia in the first year, as they had to the overseers of the Parthenon in Year 2 (446/5).[98]

The second regular source of income for the building fund came from the hellenotamiai, the officers whose task it was to receive tribute payments from the cities of the empire and to report them to the logistai for audit. This board, like the sacred treasurers, had made regular payments to the Parthenon during the ten years of that building's construction;[99] but beginning in 437/6 they

[93] IG I³ 465, line 118 (Year 4); cf. the restored formula in IG I³ 462, line 7 (Year 1); 463, line 66 (Year 2); 464, line 96 (Year 3). A similar formula appeared in each annual account of the Parthenon and is best preserved in the slightly shortened form in IG I³ 447, line 346 (Year 12); 449, lines 376–377 (Year 14); 450, lines 417–418 (Year 15).
[94] IG I³ 465, line 114 (Year 4). For the annual prescripts of the Parthenon accounts, see chap. 3, pp. 43–47 above.
[95] For the number of epistatai on the board of the Parthenon, see chap. 3, p. 46 above.
[96] Thuc. 2.13.3; for quotation and discussion of the passage, see chap. 3, pp. 50–51 above.
[97] IG I³ 465, lines 121–122 (Year 4); the formula restored, IG I³ 463, lines 69–70 (Year 2). For contributions from the treasurers of Athena to the Parthenon, see chap. 3, p. 49 and note 49 above.
[98] Cf. IG I³ 437, lines 44–49.
[99] See chap. 3, p. 53 above.

had diverted their contributions to the overseers of the Propylaia. The record of their payments is partly preserved in each of the first four years, and the formula of the text can be reconstructed with certainty. The wording of the entry is best preserved for Year 4 (434/3): [π]αρὰ ℎελλενοταμ[ιõν ℎ]οῖς Προτόν[ικος ἐγραμ]μάτευε Κερ[αμε]ύς, τõ χσυμ[μαχικõ φόρο μ]νᾶ ἀπὸ τõ [τα]λάντο, "From the hellenotamiai to whom Protonikos of Kerameis was secretary, of the tribute of the allies, a mina in the talent."[100] This locution specifically designates the payment of the hellenotamiai as comprising the *aparchai,* the firstfruits of ¹⁄₆₀ of the tribute, which were due to the goddess each year. It has been possible to restore the same description of the *aparchai,* a mina in the talent of the allied tribute, in the general heading for the first tribute quota list of 454/3.[101] From that venerable monument, the first overseers of the Propylaia quoted the exact wording of the entry in their accounts, as if to memorialize the fact that every city of the empire had made its contribution, however small, to the beautification of the Acropolis.

It is to be noted that the overseers of the Parthenon had recorded similar payments of Athena's *aparchai* over a ten-year period and never felt the need to list them in their accounts with the specific descriptive phrase τõ χσυμμαχικõ φόρο μνᾶ ἀπὸ τõ ταλάντο, which the overseers of the Propylaia regularly used. The reason for this seeming lack of precision in the Parthenon accounts is that the hellenotamiai paid no moneys to the Parthenon except the *aparchai,* as far as we can tell from the fragmentary state of the inscriptions. The overseers of the Propylaia, on the other hand, were careful to distinguish the *aparchai* of the tribute from other imperial funds that also came to them by way of the hellenotamiai. Among the fragmentary receipts for the last three years, the following three passages can be reconstructed, evidently recording items of similar type:[102]

Year 3 (435/4), *IG* I³ 464, lines 105–108:

> [ἀπὸ τῆς στρατι]ᾶς τῆς με[τ]ὰ Γ[λαύκονος]
> [παρὰ ℎελλενοτ]αμιõν ἀπὸ στ[ρατ]ιᾶς·
> [τῆς μετὰ Προ]τέο παρὰ Δεμ[ο]χάρος
> [. . . . .ᶜ¹¹. . . . .]ασίππο Φλυέος

> [From the arm]y with G[laukon]
> [From the hellenot]amiai, from the a[rm]y
> [with Pro]teas, from Dem[o]chares
> [. . . . .]assippos of Phlya

Year 4 (434/3), *IG* I³ 465, lines 128–130:

> [παρὰ ℎελλενοταμιõν ἀ]πὸ στρατιᾶς τε[ς]
> [μετὰ . . .⁶. . . παρὰ . .⁴. .]σίππο Ἀγρυλῆθε[ν]
> [– – – – – – – – – – – – – – – πα]ρὰ Τιμοσθένο[ς]

[100] *IG* I³ 465, lines 123–125 (Year 4); cf. 462, lines 15–17 (Year 2); and for the restoration, see *ATL* I, 187, II, 125; *IG* I³ 464, lines 71–73 (Year 2); 464, lines 109–111 (Year 3). The meaning of the descriptive phrase could hardly be expressed more accurately or more succinctly, and yet Kallet-Marx, *ClAnt* 8 (1989) 263–264, writes that the phrase "in the Propylaia accounts need only mean ¹⁄₆₀ of the annual tribute, another *aparche,* if one wishes to call it that. There is no evidence that it was Athena's *aparche.*" She postulates this dubious "second" *aparche,* for which of course there is no evidence whatsoever, because she claims that the *aparche* that appears in the tribute lists is not the same money that was handed over to the epistatai of the Propylaia. The payments appear in the tribute lists because the annual audit showed that the cities of the empire had contributed their due assessments to the sacred treasury. The hellenotamiai no doubt paid over the *aparche* to the epistatai of the Propylaia, as they had to the epistatai of the Parthenon, in response to specific legislation by the demos ordering them to do so. All officials who handled the funds had to account for them. See p. 305 below.
[101] *IG* I³ 259, lines 1–4; *ATL* II, list 1 + Meritt, *Hesperia* 41 (1972) 403–417.
[102] For restoration and discussion of the following passages, see *ATL* III, 329–332.

[From the hellenotamiai, f]rom the army
[with . . . . . ., from . . . .]sippos of Agryle
[– – – – – – – – – – – – – – – –, fr]om Timosthenes

Year 5 (433/2), *IG* I³ 466, lines 144–145:

παρὰ hελλε[νοταμιον ἀπὸ στρατιᾶς τες]
μετ' Ἀρχενα[ύτο – – – – – – – – – –]

From the helle[notamiai, from the army]
with Archena[utes – – – – – – – – – – –]

In all three cases, the hellenotamiai appear to have paid over to the building fund of the Propylaia money that was originally appropriated for military expeditions and had been sent out to generals commanding in the field.[103] Thus the overseers entered on their books the origin of the funds
"from the army with Glaukon" (line 105), "from the army with Proteas" (lines 106–107), "from the
army with Archenautes" (lines 144–145). In each instance, they identified the source by citing the
name of the general in command of the forces, to whom the funds would have been issued during the
course of the campaign. The other persons listed by name in these entries—Demochares (line 107),
. . .asippos of Phlya (line 108), ...sippos of Agryle (line 129), and Timosthenes (line 130)—are
to be identified as those members of the board of hellenotamiai who actually carried out the financial transactions.[104] The names of the two generals are probably correctly restored in the account of
435/4, and both men are known to have been elected strategoi in several years during this period.
Glaukon son of Leagros of Kerameis commanded Athenian forces in the Samian War and swore
the oath that sealed the treaty with Samos in 439/8. Later he was one of three generals who sailed
to Korkyra with the second naval squadron in the summer of 433.[105] This is the earliest evidence
for the election of Proteas son of Epikles of Aixone to the board of generals. Two years later he was
dispatched to Korkyra with the first naval squadron. At the beginning of the Archidamian War, he
and two others mounted a naval expedition that harried the coast of the Peloponnese and the Ionian
Islands, and subsequently invaded the Megarid.[106] There is no evidence concerning the theater of operations for either general in 435/4, and nothing whatever is known about Archenautes in 433/2.[107]
It seems likely, however, that their activities in the middle years of the 430s had to do with some kind
of routine police patrols in various parts of the empire that have left no other record in our historical
sources. In that case, the money paid to the overseers of the Propylaia was probably surplus funds
that remained unexpended in the generals' war chest at the end of the campaigning season.

---

[103] The interpretation of *ATL* III, 329–332. W. E. Thompson, *CQ*, n.s., 20 (1970) 39–40, has suggested alternatively
that the ultimate source of the funds may have been booty captured by Athenian expeditions from which the commanding
generals consigned a tithe to the Acropolis as a dedication to Athena. During wartime this would be an attractive possibility—great amounts of booty were generated by great military victories—but in the middle years of the 430s our sources are
silent about any military campaigns that are likely to have yielded such rich spoils.

[104] So *ATL* II, 125; *ATL* III, 331; followed by R. Develin, *Athenian Officials, 684–321 B.C.* (Cambridge 1989) 97, 98.

[105] Restoration of the generals' names, *ATL* III, 330, followed by Develin, *Athenian Officials*, 96–97. Glaukon: Kirchner, *PA* 3027; Davies, *APF*, 91; *LGPN* II, 94, s.v. 22. His command at Samos in 441/0: Androtion, *FGrH* 324 F 38, cited by
schol. Aristeid. 3.74 (vol. 3, p. 485, Dindorf); cf. C. W. Fornara, *The Athenian Board of Generals from 501–404* (Wiesbaden
1971) 49; Develin, 89. Signatory to the Samian treaty in 439/8: *IG* I³ 48, line 44; cf. Develin, 92. His command at Korkyra
in 433: *IG* I³ 364, line 19; Thuc. 1.51.4; cf. Fornara, 51; Develin, 99.

[106] Proteas: Kirchner, *PA* 12298; *LGPN* II, 383, s.v. 6. His command at Korkyra in 433: *IG* I³ 364, line 9; Thuc. 1.45.2;
cf. Develin, *Athenian Officials*, 99. His expedition around the Peloponnese with Karkinos son of Xenotimos of Thorikos
(Kirchner, *PA* 8254) and Sokrates son of Antigenes of Halai (Kirchner, *PA* 13099): Thuc. 2.23.2, 25.1, 30; cf. Diod. 12.42.7.
Funds appropriated for the army: *IG* I³ 365, lines 31, 36, 38–39. Invasion of the Megarid in 431: Thuc. 2.31.1; cf. Fornara,
Athenian Generals, 53; Develin, 102, 117. Proteas's name punned ten years after his death: Aristoph. *Thesmo.* 876, 883.

[107] The restoration Archenautes proposed, *ATL* III, 331, followed by Develin, *Athenian Officials*, 100. Cf. *LGPN* II,
68, s.v. 2.

The payments from Athenian commanders to the overseers of the Propylaia represent the final transfer in a series of financial transactions that would have left a distinctive trail in the public records of Athens. In just these years we can observe the beginning of such a financial trail on the great stele on which the treasurers of Athena published their outlays from the reserve fund for military campaigns. In 432/1, their accounts show expenditures for the armies that sailed to Macedonia, Poteidaia, and the Peloponnese during the first campaigning season of the war.[108] The commanding generals are listed by name (lines 5, 31, 36, 38–39), and the treasurers state that they handed over an amount of money to the hellenotamiai, who are likewise named in the inscription. The transfer of funds is dated by the day of the prytany, and the formula concludes, e.g., ταῦ[τα ἐ]δόθε τεῖ στρ[ατιᾶι τẼι ἐς Ποτείδαιαν] (line 23), "These funds were given to the army at Poteidaia." In this year, nine separate payments were recorded for the Macedonian operations (line 26), and in each case the money was handed over by the treasurers to the hellenotamiai, who conveyed it to the armies in the field. In a year of open hostilities, when Athens enforced her demands by force of arms upon a recalcitrant city of the empire, we may be sure that the generals' war chest was fully expended. In 435/4, the sacred treasurers no doubt published a similar accounting of funds paid out to the hellenotamiai for the armies with Glaukon and Proteas. As a result of their operations, whatever they were, these generals had an unexpended balance at the end of the campaigning season, which they duly handed over to Demochares and another member of the hellenotamiai for payment to the overseers of the Propylaia. Thus everyone who actually handled the funds is named in the various accounts. If our epigraphical record were completely preserved, we would find the same transaction entered on the books of each board of officials because everyone involved—the treasurers, the hellenotamiai, the generals, and the overseers—had to make an official accounting of the proper receipt and authorize disposition of all moneys that passed through their hands.[109]

Among other sources of funding that came to the overseers of the Propylaia, it is interesting to note yet another one that had previously been contributed to the Parthenon. One of the receipts from Year 4 (434/3) can be reconstructed to read: [παρὰ ταμ]ιõν hεφα[ισ]τικõ ἀπο Λ[αυ]ρ[είο ...⁸....]ο[.]το [..τ]õμ πέντε μ[ε]ρõ[ν], "[From the treasur]ers of the Hephaistikon from L[au]r[eion – – – –] of five shares."[110] The same item stood among the receipts for Year 3 (435/4) and, as we saw earlier, can also be restored in the accounts of the Parthenon for 439/8 and 438/7.[111] Funds possibly came to the Propylaia from the same source in each year, for there is certainly space available for the two-line formula in Years 1 and 2, and it was not contributed to the Parthenon in either 437/6 or 436/5. All four entries in the building accounts appear to describe the same source of funding, which seems to have been contributed by the treasurers of the Hephaisti(a)kon mine in the Laureion mining district of southeastern Attica. It is by no means clear who these treasurers were, and whether the money represents a portion of the state's profits from leasing the mining rights to private contractors. Unfortunately, there is also no way of reconstructing the wording of the second line, and so the significance of the "five shares" must remain unexplained.

One other item of income for the overseers is preserved in three of the five accounts for Years 1, 2, and 5, and so very likely recurred in the intervening years where the last lines of the column of

---

[108] *IG* I³ 365. The account was published by the treasurers, identified by their chairman and secretary, whose names appear in the nominative. They made payments to the hellenotamiai, [hελλενοταμίασι]παρέδομ[εν τάδε] (line 7), and the names and demotics of the full board are listed in the dative (lines 7–9).

[109] On the requirement that all public officials present their accounts for audit at εὔθυναι, see [Aristot.] *Ath. Pol.* 48.3–5; Aischin. 3 *Ktes.* 21–23. For modern discussion, R. Bonner and G. Smith, *The Administration of Justice from Homer to Aristotle* (Chicago 1938) vol. 2, 34–36, 256–269; Hignett, *Athenian Constitution,* 203–205; M. Piéart, *AntCl* 40 (1971) 526–573; M. H. Hansen, *Eisangelia* (Odense 1975) 45–47; D. MacDowell, *The Law in Classical Athens* (Ithaca, NY, 1978) 170–172; J. T. Roberts, *Accountability in Athenian Government* (Madison, WI, 1982) 17–18, 24–26.

[110] *IG* I³ 465, lines 126–127; restored also in *IG* I³ 464, lines 103–104. For restoration of the text, Dinsmoor, *AJA* 25 (1921) 239.

[111] See chap. 3, p. 56 and note 83 above.

receipts are lost. In each instance the description reads: οἰκίας ἱερᾶς μίσθοσις, "lease of a sacred house," and in the second account the figure of 132 drachmas is preserved.[112] The leasing of real estate belonging to various deities was a lucrative source of ordinary income for the managers of ancient sanctuaries. Records of the Delian amphictyons for 434/3 refer to the rental of sacred lands, gardens, and houses that were the property of Delian Apollo.[113] More detailed accounts from the first half of the fourth century record the income that the sanctuary derived from such leases, and they list properties on both Delos and Rheneia that had already been rented out or were still available.[114] The Eleusinian epistatai included leases of stables and other buildings among the receipts from which they funded the abortive first phase of the Telesterion, as we saw in chapter 6.[115] Such leases of sacred *temene* and other real estate belonging to sanctuaries came under the purview of the basileus, who together with the poletai arranged the terms of the contract and handled its sale. In the ninth prytany of each year, the annual rent was payable to the apodektai, who in turn handed over the payment to the appropriate sacred treasurers.[116] The rent from the sacred house in the Propylaia accounts was no doubt an item of income that had been allotted to the epistatai by the treasurers of Athena for the duration of the project. There is no indication where the particular sacred house might have been located. Such rental properties owned by Athena Polias and several other deities were widely scattered throughout the city and the country demes of Attica, as we learn from a fragmentary inscription of 343/2 that preserves the official record of at least forty-nine leases.[117] It is suggestive, however, that excavations in the Agora have produced the boundary marker of just such a piece of sacred property, which bears the inscription [Ηό]ρος [οἰκ]ίας ἱερᾶς Ἀθηνᾶς Πολιάδος, "boundary of a sacred house of Athena Polias."[118]

In addition to the items of income already discussed, the accounts show receipts from a variety of miscellaneous sources that seem to have been listed in the closing lines of the receipt column and probably did not bring in large amounts of money. Most of these were received only in the first year of construction. A group of four broken lines, whose wording can be only partially restored,

[112] *IG* I³ 462, line 24 (Year 1, 437/6); 463, line 74 (Year 2, 436/5); 466, line 146 (Year 5, 433/2). The annual rent is preserved for Year 2 as ΗΔΔΔΙΗ; see Dinsmoor, *AJA* 17 (1913) 389–390. The rent is given as 82 drachmas instead of 132 drachmas, M. B. Walbank, *ZPE* 116 (1997) 39, but the stone preserves the right vertical stroke of Η, not the left (Dinsmoor, above), and the first figure cannot be read as Ͱ.

[113] *IG* I³ 402, lines 15–16.

[114] Rental of houses on Delos yielded 297 drachmas in 375/4 and 374/3, *IG* II² 1635, lines 29–31, 66. In the latter year, rents from *temene* on Rheneia brought in 6,305 drachmas, and from *temene* on Delos 1,522 drachmas: *IG* II² 1635, lines 65–66. *IG* II² 1638 appears to be a list of leases already contracted on Rheneia (lines 8–15) and on Delos (lines 15–21). Other sections of these documents record catalogues of houses sacred to Delian Apollo that are apparently available for rent: *IG* II² 1635, lines 140–150 (376/5); 1638, lines 22–23. In the fourth century such rents seem to have varied from about 8 % to 12 % of what the owner deemed to be the resale value of the property. In Peiraieus, a workshop with an adjacent dwelling and privy, having a total value of 700 drachmas, rented for 54 drachmas (7⅔ %), *IG* II² 2496, lines 12, 27–28. A house in Melite, purchased for 3,000 drachmas, and a house in Eleusis, purchased for 500 drachmas, together rented for a total of 300 drachmas (8⅔ %): Isaios 11 *Hagnias* 42. *IG* II² 1241 (300/299) records the terms of lease of a plot of land evaluated at 5,000 drachmas (lines 42–44) that brought in rent of 600 drachmas a year (12 %). See the discussion of Walbank, *Hesperia* 52 (1983) 215–216.

[115] *IG* I³ 395, line 1 (stables), line 5 (other buildings); for discussion of the inscription, see chap. 6, pp. 170–174 above.

[116] The procedures to be followed by the basileus and regulations governing payment of rents to the apodektai in the ninth prytany are outlined by [Aristot.] *Ath. Pol.* 47.4–48.1. Virtually the same procedures are set forth in the decree authorizing the lease of the *temenos* of Kodros, Neleus, and Basile in 418/7, *IG* I³ 84. For discussion of leases of sacred properties, see Walbank, *Hesperia* 52 (1983) 207–231; *Agora* XIX (1991) 152–169.

[117] *Agora* XIX L6 = *Hesperia* 52 (1983) 103–109 = *SEG* 33.167. The analytical table of the leases, Walbank, *Hesperia* 52 (1983) 207–209, shows rental properties located in city demes (Kydathenion and Kollytos), in areas around Athens (Agrai, Alopeke, Kephissia, and Phaleron), from Thria near Eleusis to Philaidai in eastern Attica, one on the island of Salamis, and possibly one at Sounion.

[118] *Agora* XIX H21 = *SEG* 10.364. The sacred house of which the rent appears as a receipt in the Propylaia accounts was assuredly not located on the Acropolis, as Walbank speculates, *ZPE* 116 (1997) 39.

evidently belongs together as the description of a single item. There is a reference to roof tiles that may have been dismantled from the Old Propylon and were sold off as useless building materials.[119] Entries of similar type are the proceeds from the sale of wooden timbers and *pinakes* (boards or panels). The last item recurred in Year 2 (436/5) when the sale of the *pinakes,* whatever they were, yielded total income of 6 drachmas 1½ obols for the building fund. Similarly, the next to last item in the receipts for Year 5 (433/2) appears to record the price fetched by the sale of some sort of coloring matter, but the wording of the text is not susceptible to restoration.[120] Finally, we may note here, again only in Year 1 (437/6), what appear to be two private donations from a certain Pleistias and Sauron, neither of whom can be identified. It is interesting that both men made similar donations to the overseers of the Parthenon project in the previous year (438/7), possibly as a way of celebrating the dedication of the great temple.[121]

Of quite a different character is the entry that appears only once, in Year 1 (437/6), where the text can be restored to read: σκυτῶν [π]εριτμ[εμάτον τιμέ], "price of the trimmings of hides." It has been suggested that the reference is to the hides of sacrificial cattle that had been clipped, dressed, and tanned preparatory to their sale as raw leather.[122] In the time of Lykourgos, moneys that accrued from these sales were called the δερματικόν, or hide account, and the treasurers of Athena recorded in detail the proceeds from every sacrifice at which meat was distributed to the populace. The fullest information comes from their accounts for the quadrennium 334/3 to 331/0, which list the sacrifices in calendric order and show the amount of money raised from each festival.[123] The reference to such a sale in the Propylaia accounts of a century earlier appears to represent a distant precursor in practice of the fourth-century procedure that has left no other trace in the records of the fifth century.[124] It is natural to think that the hides sold by the overseers of the Propylaia came from the cattle of the Panathenaic hecatomb, either at the penteteric festival of 438, or the annual festival of 437, or possibly both. In the preserved accounts of the δερματικόν for 333/2, the amount of 1,233 drachmas 3 obols can be restored as the income from the Panathenaic hecatomb.[125] To be sure, the price of such hides may have been substantially different in the fifth century, but the allocation of this sale to the overseers of the Propylaia seems to have more than a symbolic value.

---

[119] *IG* I³ 462, lines 18–21 (Year 1); cf. Dinsmoor, *AJA* 17 (1913) 385.

[120] *IG* I³ 462, lines 22–23, sale of wooden timbers and *pinakes;* the latter repeated with the price preserved, *IG* I³ 463, line 75. A similar item possibly sold off in Year 5, *IG* I³ 466, line 147; cf. the interpretation of Dinsmoor, *AJA* 17 (1913) 384.

[121] Pleistias: *IG* I³ 462, line 25; see *LGPN* II, 369, s.v. 14. His contribution to the Parthenon, *IG* I³ 445, line 299. The rarity of the name suggests the possibility that he is to be identified with the Pleistias who was active in Athenian public affairs during the 420s: Kirchner, *PA* 11864; *LGPN* II, 369, s.v. 1 = ?2 = ?3; ambassador to Perdikkas of Macedon in 426/5, *IG* I³ 61, line 51; first secretary of the boulē in 425/4, *IG* I³ 71, line 56; 369, line 17. Sauron: *IG* I³ 462, line 27; his contribution to the Parthenon, *IG* I³ 445, line 300; see *LGPN* II, 395, s.v. 1. The name appears only in the two building accounts and nowhere else in Athenian prosopography. It is likely that he was not an Athenian citizen, although the name is just as unusual in other parts of the Greek world.

[122] For the restoration and interpretation, Dinsmoor, *AJA* 17 (1913) 386.

[123] The *dermatikon* defined as moneys accruing from the sales of the hides, Harpokr., s.v. δερματικόν (δ 22 Keaney); cf. the fragmentary law proposed by Lykourgos, *IG* II² 333, line 23. The treasurers' accounts of 334/3–331/0, *IG* II² 1496; see the detailed discussion of V. J. Rosivach, *The System of Public Sacrifice in Fourth-Century Athens* (Atlanta 1994) 48–67.

[124] There is evidence in the fifth century that the hides of the sacrificial victims were sometimes perquisites of priests or other officials. The priestess of Athena Nike received "the legs and hides from the public sacrifices," *IG* I³ 35, line 11 (chap. 2, p. 27 above). The law of the deme Skambonidai awards the hides to the demarch, *IG* I³ 244A, lines 13–14 (ca. 460). In fragmentary regulations for sacrifices, ca. 430, a priest receives the hides: *IG* I³ 255B, lines 6–7, and cf. 15–19. Presumably the officials involved sold the hides for their private profit.

[125] *IG* II² 1496, lines 100–101. Three figures are missing from the beginning of the amount for the Panathenaic hecatomb, which can be restored as [ͰΗΗ]ΔΔΔΗΗΙΙΙ = 733 dr. 3 ob. or more likely as [ΧΗΗ]ΔΔΔΗΗΙΙΙ = 1,233 dr. 3 ob. See Rosivach, *System of Public Sacrifice,* 50–51, note 104. In the fourth century, the prices brought in from such sales seem to have ranged from 4 to 10 drachmas per hide: Rosivach, 62–63, 155.

In the accounts of the Propylaia, the column itemizing the overseer's receipts for each year was followed directly by the list of expenditures, which was introduced by the rubric ἀναλόματα (expenses), inscribed in slightly larger and more widely spaced letters. Once again the format was closely similar to the contemporary accounts of the Parthenon. As chance would have it, the extant fragments of the stele preserve a significantly smaller portion of the expenses than the receipts. From the account of Year 1 parts of some twenty-four broken lines have survived; Years 2, 4, and 5 are represented by tiny scraps; the expenses for Year 3 are entirely lost; and a few fragments preserving only figures cannot be assigned to specific positions. As in the Parthenon account, the expenses were grouped together in general categories without much specificity, and, not surprisingly, the descriptive itemization made use of some of the same formulas. We read of wages for quarrymen (λιθοτόμοι) at the various quarries and transportation of stone to the Acropolis (λιθαγωγία); miscellaneous purchases are subsumed under the heading ὀνέματα; and the item described simply as καταμενίον, "for monthly salaries," probably included all payments to administrative personnel.[126] Among the expenses for 437/6, the wording of one item can be restored with assurance because parts of closely analogous formulations are preserved in five accounts of the Parthenon: hυποργ[οῖς Πεντελε̄θεν hοδο]ποιο͂[σι] καὶ λίθ[ος ἀνατιθε͂σι ἐπὶ τὰ] κύκ[λα], "For workmen building roads at Pentele and putting up blocks on the wheels."[127] The significance of these laconic entries we have already examined in detail when the overseers of the Parthenon made payment for the same processes. Here again the payment was for the construction of a quarry road that allowed the marble blocks to be lowered down the mountainside at Pentele. It may have been necessary to repair the roads that had been built earlier for the blocks of the Parthenon, or possibly the builders of the Propylaia were opening up new sections of the quarries. At the bottom of the slipway, other workmen mounted the blocks on the great stone-hauling wagons for the journey to Athens.

In general it is fair to say that the surviving fragments of the expense accounts advance only marginally our knowledge of the Propylaia. Virtually nothing about the building's architecture and little enough about the history of its construction can be gleaned from these sadly mutilated stones. It is still possible, however, to draw one or two interesting inferences from the fragments of the expenses as they are preserved for us. A piece that can be assigned to Year 1 (437/6) names on consecutive lines the three principal sources of stone for the building. Ἐλευσ[ινό]θεν (line 36) refers to the quarry at Eleusis that produced a characteristic dark gray limestone, called "black stone" by the earlier overseers of the Eleusinian sanctuary. Πεντε[λε͂θ]εν (line 37) is the standard designation for the marble quarries of Mount Pentelikon and appeared throughout the contemporary accounts of the Parthenon. [ἐ]χς Ἀκτε͂[ς] (line 38) describes the quarries on the Akte peninsula of the Peiraieus that yielded a particular kind of fine poros limestone frequently employed by Athenian builders for foundations and wall facings.[128] It is possible that [ἀ]πὸ Σκιρ[άδ]ος (line 39) may refer to another source of poros stone somewhere near the sanctuary of Athena Skiras in Phaleron.[129] It cannot be de-

---

[126] Quarrymen: *IG* I³ 463, lines 84–86; 466, lines 150, 152. Transportation: *IG* I³ 463, line 88; 466, lines 151, 153. Purchases: *IG* I³ 463, line 77. Monthly salaries: *IG* I³ 462, line 51.

[127] *IG* I³ 462, lines 49–50. Cf. similar items of expenditure in the Parthenon accounts: *IG* I³ 436, line 28; 445, lines 306–307; 446, lines 333–334; 447, lines 357–358; 449, lines 398–400. See chap. 3, pp. 60–61 above.

[128] *IG* I³ 462, lines 36–38. For quarries at Eleusis, Travlos, *Hesperia* 18 (1949) 144–145 and note 18; cf. Shoe, *Hesperia* Suppl. 8 (1949) 341 and note 2. For the locution "black stone" used by the Eleusinian overseers, *IG* I³ 395, lines 12–13; chap. 6, pp. 170–174 above. For the Pentelic quarries, see chap. 3, pp. 58–60 above. For quarries at Peiraieus: W. K. Pritchett, *Studies in Ancient Greek Topography,* vol. 1 (Berkeley 1965) 97, 99; I. Papachristodoulou, *ArchDelt* 28 (1973) B′ 1, 46–48; O. Alexandri, *ArchDelt* 29 (1974) B′ 1, 99, 101, fig. 11, 149. See generally Osborne, *Demos,* 96, 103–105.

[129] The words can be restored twice in the expenses for Year 1, *IG* I³ 462, lines 32, 39, but there is no way of reconstructing the beginning of the entry, and the number of missing letters differs at the left end of the two lines. Paus. 1.1.4, 36.4, refers to the ancient Temple of Athena Skiras at Phaleron, which according to legend was founded by the hero Skiros. This is perhaps the more likely reference than the similarly named temple on the island of Salamis: Hdt. 8.94; Strabo 9.1.9 (p. 393).

termined whether these payments were for quarrymen who cut the stone at these four places or for teamsters who hauled it from the quarries to the Acropolis. Similar payments appear to have been recorded in Year 2 (436/5), where three and possibly four consecutive lines of expenses began with the word λιθοτόμοις ("for the quarrymen") and doubtless named the same three or four quarries listed in the first account.[130] The stone from Peiraieus was used only in the foundations of the Propylaia and so would naturally be ordered from the first days of work. Vastly the greatest amount of building material was Pentelic marble, used for every part of the superstructure, and thus we would expect the quarrymen at Pentele to be operating throughout the building's construction. More interesting is the order for Eleusinian stone in the first year. We have already seen that this stone was used to articulate certain details of the architecture—thresholds, string courses, the benches and orthostates of the central hall—where its dark color contrasted strikingly with the white marble. Significantly, however, Eleusinian stone was also used for some of the first visible stonework to be laid in the building, that is, the lowest step of the crepidoma for the two western wings. Thus the epigraphical evidence of the accounts may be thought to corroborate the architectural evidence of the podiums for the western wings that we examined earlier, and both suggest that construction of the wings and central building commenced at the same time in 437/6.[131]

The overseers' payments for quarrying and transportation of stone also have a curious bearing on the final abandonment of the Propylaia project. There can be no doubt that in Year 5 (433/2) they filed their last report. The accounts of this year were inscribed at the top of the fourth double column on the reverse of the stele, where they occupied only the upper part of the stone. The lower part of that column was left roughly picked and unprepared for the inscription of later accounts, as we learn from a portion of the protective surface still visible on the reverse of one fragment.[132] Moreover, the final account does not give the impression of a project that was winding down. The receipts for the year occupied twenty-one lines of text, exactly the same number as the receipts for the first year of the project.[133] The year's expenses began with wages paid to two different groups of quarrymen and two different groups of teamsters for transportation of stone to Athens, obviously from two different quarries. This is in striking contrast to the accounts of the Parthenon, which show that the overseers placed their last order for building stone in 439/8, a year before the dedication.[134] In 438/7 and thereafter, all the marble is specifically described as blocks for the pedimental statuary, and the last of these was cut from the quarries a full two years before completion of the pediments,[135] for the fully preserved expenses of Year 14 (434/3) show no wages paid to quarrymen at Pentele.[136] In the case of the last account of the Propylaia overseers, one gets the distinct impression that the sudden cessation of building activity at the end of the year had not been anticipated at its beginning.

---

[130] See note 128 above.

[131] For construction of the podiums of the western wings, see pp. 298–299 above. R. A. Tomlinson, *BSA* 85 (1990) 405–413 (followed by Hurwit, *Athenian Acropolis*, 211), entertains the possibility that the wings were added to the central hall afterward, "later in the 420s or during the peace of Nikias" (411). Although he is fully aware of the "black stone" in the lowest step, and of the Eleusinian stone ordered in Year 1 (437/6), he has not drawn the inference that the stone delivered in the first year was most probably laid in the first year. He is not troubled by the notion that the builders might store the black stone on the building site for some ten or fifteen years.

[132] See Dinsmoor, *AJA* 17 (1913) 397–398.

[133] The rubric ἀναλόματα for the expenses of Year 5 falls in line 27 of column IV (Dinsmoor, *AJA* 17 [1913] 397–398). The prescript for the year will have occupied five lines at the top of the column, as in Year 4, and that leaves twenty-one lines for the year's receipts. Cf. the receipts of Year 1, *IG* I³ 462, lines 8–28.

[134] *IG* I³ 444, lines 270–271 (Year 9, 439/8).

[135] The accounts record wages for quarrymen, τὸν λίθον τον ἐς τὰ ἐναιέτια (of blocks for the pediments): *IG* I³ 445, lines 304–305 (Year 10, 438/7); 446, lines 331–332 (Year 11, 437/6); or for workmen mounting the blocks on wheels: *IG* I³ 447, lines 357–358 (Year 12, 436/5). The receipts for Year 13 (435/4) are lost. See chap. 3, pp. 67–68 above.

[136] In 434/3 there were still a few marbles awaiting transport from the quarries to Athens (*IG* I³ 449, lines 398–400), but no quarrymen were employed that year.

One other item of expenditure can be restored in three of the extant accounts and possibly appeared originally in every year. In each case, the payment in question was the last entry before the unexpended balance, with which the overseers closed the accounts by means of the formula παρέδο-μεν τοῖς νέοις ἐπιστάτεσι, "We handed over to the new epistatai."[137] The wording of the text is preserved as follows in the inscription:[138]

Year 1 (437/6), *IG* I³ 462, lines 52–53:

> μισθομά[τον ἐς τὲν ἀκρόπολιν]
> ἄνευ τῶν [ἐς τὰ Προπύλαια]

Year 2 (436/5), *IG* I³ 463, lines 90–91:

> [μι]σθομά[τον ἐς τὲν ἀκρόπολιν]
> [ἄνευ τῶν ἐς τὰ Προπύλαια]

Year 4 (434/3), *IG* I³ 465, lines 135–136:

> [μισθομάτο]ν
> [ἐς τὲν ἀκρό]πολιν ἄνευ τ[ῶν ἐς τὰ Π]ροπύλαια

All three items may be translated: "For contracts for work on the Acropolis apart from those for the work on the Propylaia." It has been suggested that these payments were for general landscaping of the Acropolis around the newly completed Parthenon—construction of the stepped terrace wall to the west of the temple, earth filling and grading of levels to its south, dressing of the rock surface to the northeast, and demolition of the ruinous east cella of the Old Athena Temple.[139] It is certain that all these jobs were carried out, and probably in just these years, as part of the necessary tidying up of the construction site around the temple. But the administration of this work can hardly have come under the purview of the Propylaia overseers since their colleagues who oversaw the Parthenon were still an active administrative board throughout these years. Moreover, beginning in 439/8, every account of the Parthenon shows an expenditure recorded simply as μισθομάτον ("for contracts") without further specification.[140] It is much more likely that the work of grading and landscaping around the temple was subsumed under this rubric and charged, as it should have been, to the overseers of the Parthenon.

   If this is correct, the expenses itemized in the Propylaia accounts still call for satisfactory explanation. In light of what we have already seen of Athenian administrative practice in the construction of public buildings and in the operations of their epistatai, this situation must be thought exceedingly odd. The officers responsible for the building of the Propylaia record payments for work on the Acropolis, to be sure, but for work that is specifically described as outside the Propylaia. If this work pertained to another building, we naturally ask why a regular board of epistatai was not empaneled to oversee its construction, and why it seemed appropriate for the epistatai of the Propylaia to defray its costs. The answer may lie in the peculiar relationship between the project for the new gatehouse and the plan for the new Temple of Athena Nike. In chapter 10 we shall examine in detail the archi-

---

[137] The formula for the unexpended balance forward can be restored by comparison of *IG* I³ 462, line 54 (Year 1), with 465, line 137 (Year 4). The position of the closing formula for Year 2 is given by the preserved figure of more than 20,000 drachmas (*IG* I³ 463, line 92), which also appears in the first line after the prescript of Year 3, 464, line 97.

[138] The restorations and translation are those of Wade-Gery and Meritt, *Hesperia* 16 (1947) 281–282, improving on the suggested text of Dinsmoor, *AJA* 51 (1947) 134.

[139] Dinsmoor, *AJA* 51 (1947) 135–136. Dinsmoor's landscaping projects around the Parthenon accepted by Wade-Gery and Meritt, *Hesperia* 16 (1947).

[140] *IG* I³ 444, line 277 (Year 9, 439/8); 445, line 303 (Year 10, 438/7); 446, line 330, restored (Year 11, 437/6); 447, line 354, restored (Year 12, 436/5); 449, line 397 (Year 14, 434/3).

tectural relation of the two monuments, and we shall find that construction of the Propylaia commenced first, but shortly thereafter it was decided to enlarge the bastion of Athena Nike and to raise its level, so that the southwest wing of the Propylaia could provide primary access to the sanctuary.[141] Enlargement of the bastion called for construction of a sheathing of ashlar masonry around the three sides of the old Mycenaean tower, and that sheathing had to rise for twenty courses along the south side and for fourteen at the northwest corner before the lowest foundations of the temple could be set in place, ranging with the fourth ashlar course below the extant bastion crown.[142] Until the walls of the bastion had reached that point, construction of the Nike temple could not begin, and so there was no need to elect its administrative board. On the other hand, enlargement of the bastion greatly affected the overseers of the Propylaia, just as it impinged directly on the shape and purpose of the building for which they were responsible. They could easily supervise the early stages of construction, since the site was immediately adjacent to the future southwest wing; and we may suggest that the payments recorded in their accounts satisfactorily describe work on the bastion of Athena Nike as "on the Acropolis" but "apart from the Propylaia." This identification of the expenditures "apart from the Propylaia" agrees well with the architectural evidence, to be examined presently, that only a short time elapsed between the start of work on the Propylaia and the decision to raise and enlarge the Nike bastion—not a year or more, but a matter of a few months at the most.[143] If our interpretation of the accounts is correct, the first payments for work on the bastion were completed before the summer of 436 and reported by the overseers in the first year of construction.

THE ABANDONMENT OF THE PROPYLAIA PROJECT

From the architecture of the Propylaia, it has been possible to discuss various alterations in the plan of the building. Some of these affected the appearance and dimensions of the colonnades, such as the change from four columns to three columns in the porches of the western wings, which must have been redesigned before the masons ever set hammer to stone. Other changes seem to have occurred after the foundations had already been laid, such as the reduced length of the western facade of the southwest wing and its awkward alignment with the front colonnade. Still other modifications were more radical in nature and represent the curtailment of an overly grandiose original scheme, such as the great eastern halls that were never built.[144] Now, it is readily understandable that an architect might alter certain elements of his design as construction progressed. That major sections of a complicated building might be postponed for a later campaign of construction is also perfectly conceivable. What calls for special explanation in the case of the Propylaia, however, is the unfinished state of the stonework in those parts of the building for which construction had been completed. To this day, the observant visitor feels the sudden cessation of work, as if on the last day of 433/2 the masons walked off the job when the foreman's whistle blew and never returned.

The walls and floors, the steps and columns of Greek stone buildings were always erected with a few millimeters of protective stone still adhering to all visible surfaces, lest the blocks suffer damage in the process of construction. The masons' last task in the finishing process was to chisel away this

---

[141] See pp. 31–35 above.

[142] The courses of the ashlar facing are numbered on the drawings from Balanos's archives published by Mark, *Athena Nike*, pl. 9 (from the south), pl. 10 (from the west).

[143] The decision to raise the Nike bastion intervened between construction of the podium for the southwest wing of the Propylaia and the beginning of work on the steps and superstructure, "stages of construction that may conceivably have been separated by months or even a year or more," Mark, *Athena Nike*, 81; this guesswork is in accord with his wish to date the beginning of the Nike temple as late as possible.

[144] See above, pp. 294–296 (colonnades of wings), pp. 298–300 (west facade of southwest wing), pp. 277–280 (eastern halls).

protective stone, to apply fluting to the columns, and to polish the surfaces of walls and floors. The stonework of the Propylaia was manifestly abandoned when the job was half done. The outside walls of the central hall and the east walls of the wings were left with rough square lifting bosses on every block, although these had been almost completely removed from those walls that were visible from outside the Acropolis. But here and there, even on the highly conspicuous western wall of the Pinakotheke, a few tell-tale lifting bosses give evidence that the masons left before the work was finished. To be sure, the columns of the facades were fluted and polished, but all surfaces of walls and floors throughout the entire building, including the interior of the central hall, still bear the last millimeters of protective stone that has never been chiseled away.

Efforts to explain the unfinished state of the Propylaia have stimulated the imagination of scholarly investigators for more than a century. The building's architectural vicissitudes have been seen as tangible evidence for a kind of territorial imperative on the part of competing religious interests to which Mnesikles' great plan was forced to succumb. On the one hand, supporters of the cult of Athena Nike brought pressure to bear on the southwest wing and succeeded in reducing it to a shallow, truncated porch that served only as an entrance to the sanctuary on the bastion. Similarly, the eastern neighbor, the priesthood of Artemis Brauronia, is thought to have opposed construction of the southeast hall on the grounds that it would have encroached on a large part of their sacred precinct. Alternatively, the surviving masonry of the Mycenaean wall is supposed somehow to have acquired the status of a religious relic so that its demolition could not be tolerated.[145] Even in contemporary accounts of the Propylaia, the obstructive priests still occasionally rear their heads, although the historians of Athenian religion have clearly shown that priests and priestesses had no voice in deliberations concerning the management and financing of their sanctuaries. Power to authorize construction of sacred buildings, or to alter and curtail their plans, resided with the demos alone, and at all times the demos responded to those who could persuade it to their views.[146]

More recent attempts to explain the interruption of work on the Propylaia have sought to avoid the colorful, but imaginary, scenes of conflict between clergy and architects. The abandonment of the eastern halls and the failure to complete the final dressing of the stonework are attributed to the need for economy.[147] With the thunderheads of war looming ominously on the horizon, it was essential for Athens to husband her resources and curtail the expense of the building program. No doubt cautious orators in the assembly eloquently advocated the wisdom of fiscal austerity in anticipation of the incalculable costs of war; but the desire to prepare the city for war cannot be the whole story. The year, to be sure, was 433/2, a critical year in the history of Athens, when the city teetered unwittingly on the edge of the abyss. In the first days of summer, Athens concluded the defensive alliance with Korkyra, and by September of 433, Athenian ships had already skirmished with Corinthian in Korkyrian waters.[148] The spring of 432 saw the revolt of Poteidaia, the spark that would ignite the Greek world for a generation of more or less continuous hostilities. As work stopped on the Propylaia, the fateful congress at Sparta, when the members of the Peloponnesian League would assemble and persuade each other to vote for war, was but a few months off.[149] In such inauspicious circumstances, suspension of further building activities very likely seemed to many the only prudent policy. While the imminence of the Peloponnesian War probably did encourage the demos to reduce expenses and conserve existing funds, this alone cannot explain satisfactorily the sudden and

[145] Cf. Dinsmoor, *AAG*[3], 204–205; Hellström, *OpAth* 17 (1988) 107; Gruben, *Gr. Tempel*[5], 200–201.

[146] On the authority of priests, R. S. J. Garland, *BSA* 79 (1984) 75–76; on the power of the demos with regard to sanctuaries, 78–79. Cf. D. D. Feaver, *YCS* 15 (1957) 123–158; Parker, *Athenian Religion*, 125–127.

[147] See Tomlinson, *BSA* 85 (1990) 405–406, 412; Hurwit, *Athenian Acropolis*, 194–195.

[148] The background of the Korkyrian alliance and subsequent campaign: Thuc. 1.24–55; Diod. 12.30–33. For the chronology, Gomme, *HCT*, vol. 1, 196–199. Cf. Kagan, *OPW*, 222–250; Meiggs, *AE*, 306–309.

[149] The revolt of Poteidaia: Thuc. 1.67–88; Kagan, *OPW*, 286–316. On the chronology: de Ste. Croix, *OPW*, 319–320; Lewis, *CAH*[2] V, 502–503; against the argument for earlier dates, Gomme, *HCT*, vol.1, 222–224, 421–425.

total abandonment of the Propylaia project. The Athenian zeal for building was not conspicuously blunted by long years of war, so we may suspect that in the case of the Propylaia domestic politics played their part as much as did foreign affairs.

There is good reason to believe that the overseers of the Propylaia for Year 5 (433/2) still anticipated major building operations as late as the fall or winter of that year. Their expense accounts show orders for quarrying and transportation of stone from at least two of the principal quarries that provided material for the building.[150] Since by this time the superstructure of the central hall and western wings was probably in place to the rooftops, it appears to have been the overseers' plan to proceed with construction of the eastern halls. The remains on the site reveal that three courses of poros foundations were actually laid for the east front of the northeast hall, but of course there is no way to determine whether they were built in 433/2 or an earlier year.[151] No work at all was even begun on the southeast hall since everything depended on removal of the Cyclopean wall. In any event, all construction was suspended, apparently quite suddenly, a few months later, in the summer of 432, and the overseers filed their final account at the end of their year of office.

Calls for economy there may have been in the expectation that war with the Peloponnese was inevitable, but the hindsight of history illuminates a rather more complex situation. It reveals that major building operations were in progress in virtually every year of the war from about 427 to the last decade of the fifth century; the construction of sacred buildings in the sanctuaries of Attica moved forward in unbroken succession. In these years, the Temple of Athena Nike and the Hephaisteion were completed, the Erechtheion was begun and largely built, the Telesterion at Eleusis continued.[152] The Temple of Nemesis at Rhamnous and the stoas of Artemis at Brauron were under construction.[153] The Temple of the Athenians on the island of Delos was dedicated, and the sanctuary of Asklepios on the south slope of the Acropolis was founded.[154] Funds appropriated by the treasury of the Athenian state paid for many if not most of these projects, and at the same time that the treasury incurred enormous expenditures for the conduct of the war. In the eleven years from 433/2 to 423/2, the sacred treasuries on the Acropolis made loans to the war effort totaling just under 5,600 talents, a figure which includes no contributions at all for the construction of temples.[155] The money expended for any one of these buildings would have been more than adequate to finish the marble work on the Propylaia, to smooth away the lifting bosses and to polish its walls and floors. Only a modest investment of funds was necessary, and a few months' time, but the job was never again taken in hand for the obvious reason that the demos never authorized the work to proceed. So we need to inquire under what circumstances the Propylaia were left forever unfinished, while the Temple of Athena Nike, the Erechtheion, and other buildings were subsequently carried to completion.

Plutarch's account claims that Perikles' initial proposals to rebuild the temples of Attica with funds drawn from the accumulated tribute of the Delian League aroused fierce opposition in the as-

[150] *IG* I³ 466, lines 150–154; see pp. 308–309 above.
[151] For discussion of the foundation, Tanoulas, *AM* 107 (1992) 203–206, pl. 50:2, plan 12.
[152] For construction in the sanctuaries of Attica, see the discussion of Miles, *Hesperia* 58 (1989) 227–235. Athena Nike temple: Mattingly, *AJA* 86 (1982) 381–385; B. Wesenberg, *JdI* 96 (1981) 28–54; Childs, *AM* 100 (1985) 208–210, 249–251; Mark, *Athena Nike,* 82–92. Hephaisteion: the festival was reorganized in 421/0, *IG* I³ 82, line 3; the cult statues were made between 421/0 and 416/5, *IG* I³ 472, lines 5–20. Erechtheion: Paton and Stevens, *Erechtheum,* 452–456; cf. also chap. 11, pp. 376–381 below. Telesterion: see chap. 6, pp. 183–190 above.
[153] Temple of Nemesis: Miles, *Hesperia* 58 (1989) 226–227. Stoas at Brauron: C. Bouras, Ἡ ἀναστήλωσις τῆς στοᾶς τῆς Βραυρῶνος (Athens 1967) 149–159.
[154] Delos: F. Courby, *EAD* XII, *Les temples d'Apollon,* 205, 220–225. Asklepieion: Travlos, *PDA,* 127–128; L. Beschi, *ASAtene,* n.s., 29–30 (1967–68) 381–436; cf. *SEG* 32.266.
[155] *IG* I³ 369, lines 121–122 (= ML 72). The document preserves the audited accounts of loans from the sacred treasuries to the Athenian state, as well as the interest that was owing on the loans. The overall total from all the gods for the period of eleven years is restored as 5,599 T. 4,900 (?) dr. For the scale of the expenditure, cf. Thuc. 2.13.3, where in 431 Perikles reckons the reserve fund available in the treasury of Athena at 6,000 talents.

sembly.[156] He portrays the building program as the most controversial of Perikles' domestic policies. He describes acrimonious debates and a struggle for power between Perikles and Thoukydides that became the most divisive political issue of the 440s and culminated in the ostracism of Thoukydides in 443. Although it is impossible to know how much of this colorful narrative is rhetorical embroidery of Plutarch's invention, the ostracism of Thoukydides in 443 is undoubtedly historical fact. Thereafter, Plutarch characterizes Perikles' position as "a rule and dominating power that was singular and continuous for a period of fifteen years";[157] and in these same years, according to Thucydides' judgment, Athens reached the zenith of her greatness. But we should badly misconstrue the temper of Athenian politics if we suppose that Perikles' undeniable primacy provided any antidote against the poisoned arrows of political attack. On the contrary, the great weight and enduring character of his personal imperium became itself the target of his enemies' invective. It is difficult to gauge the true tenor of these attacks because what has survived for us is a few snatches of comic poetry quoted out of context, but these portray Perikles as an absolute and arbitrary tyrant thinly veiled in the costume of the comic Zeus, while his consort Aspasia appeared on stage as Hera or Omphale.[158] His friends and associates were the "new Peisistratidai,"[159] and to the whole lot of them the poets attributed all the ethical and behavioral excesses that Old Comedy could invent.

    More sinister incidents occurred in the arena of real politics during these same years, when our sources first mention the events that one modern author has labeled "the plot against Perikles and his associates."[160] Athenian politicians frequently conspired to attack an opponent by means of politically motivated litigation; and if the opponent's behavior offered no grounds for impeachment, witnesses could easily be suborned to invent them. This was a time-honored tactic that Perikles himself, together with Ephialtes, had exploited to good effect at the beginning of his career.[161] With Perikles now at the pinnacle of his achievement as a statesman, his enemies sought to turn the tables on him, and to ensnare the great man in the alleged misconduct of various members of his inner circle. Once again it was the embellishment of the Acropolis that came under attack by Perikles' political opponents; for the first of the statesman's friends to feel their wrath was none other than the most prominent artistic personality of the whole building program, the sculptor Pheidias, author of the colossal gold and ivory statue of Athena in the Parthenon. Pheidias's eminence as an artist, the reputation of his works, and his personal influence with Perikles made him a prime target for attack. If he could be successfully convicted in a court of law of malfeasance in the execution of his commission, it would serve to discredit the whole of the building program.

    The circumstances surrounding the attacks on Perikles' friends, and Pheidias in particular, have been the subject of prolonged controversy because the ancient sources are contradictory, difficult to date, and embroidered with anecdote.[162] But these events are plainly central to our understanding of

---

[156] Plut. *Per.* 12–14.

[157] Plut. *Per.* 16.3: οὐκ ἐλάττω τῶν πεντεκαίδεκα ἐτῶν διηνεκῆ καὶ μίαν οὖσαν ἐν ταῖς ἐνιαυσίοις στρατηγίαις ἀρχὴν καὶ δυναστείαν κτησάμενος. Cf. Thuc. 2.65.5 for his judgment of Athens during the ascendancy of Perikles.

[158] For Perikles as tyrant-Zeus: Kratinos, *Cheirones,* Kassel-Austin, *PCG* IV, fr. 258; J. Schwarze, *Die Beurteilung des Perikles durch die attische Komödie* (Munich 1971) 57–60. Kratinos, *Ploutoi,* Kassel-Austin, *PCG* IV, fr. 171, lines 11–28; Schwarze, 43–46, 51–54. Kratinos, *Nemesis,* Kassel-Austin, *PCG* IV, fr. 118; Schwarze, 28–34. Kratinos, *Thrattai,* Kassel-Austin, *PCG* IV, fr. 73; Schwarze, 66–71. For Aspasia as Hera-Omphale: Kratinos, *Cheirones,* Kassel-Austin, *PCG* IV, fr. 259; Schwarze, 57–60. See also A. J. Podlecki, *Perikles and His Circle* (London 1998) 169–170.

[159] Kassel-Austin, *PCG* VIII, fr. 703, from Plut. *Per.* 16.1; cf. P. A. Stadter, *A Commentary on Plutarch's Pericles* (Chapel Hill, NC, 1989) 194; Schwarze, *Beurteilung des Perikles,* 165–166.

[160] The quotation is the subtitle for the second part of the study by J. Mansfeld, *Mnemosyne* 33 (1980) 17–95.

[161] For attacks by Ephialtes and Perikles on Kimon's pro-Spartan policy and personal slander, Plut. *Kim.* 15.2–16.4. Kimon's ostracism: Plut. *Kim.* 17.3; Plut. *Per.* 9.5; Nepos, *Cim.* 3.1; Plato, *Gorg.* 516D.

[162] For bibliography on the trials of Perikles' associates, see Gomme, *HCT,* vol. 2, 184–189; Jacoby, *FGrH* III B (Supplement) 484–496; D. Kienast, *Gymnasium* 60 (1953) 210–229; F. Frost, *JHS* 84 (1964) 69–72; Frost, *Historia* 13 (1964) 385–399; G. Donnay, *AntCl* 37 (1968) 19–36; Kagan, *OPW,* 194–201; L. Prandi, *Aevum* 51 (1977) 10–26; R. Klein, in G. Wirth, ed., *Perikles und seine Zeit* (Darmstadt 1979) 494–533; J. Mansfeld, *Mnemosyne* 33 (1980) 17–95; Roberts,

Athenian domestic politics in the 430s, and of the ultimate demise of the building program. The difficulty is compounded because the accounts that have come down to us depend on a virulently anti-Periklean source that has been heavily influenced by the farcical exuberance of comic invention.[163] Aristophanes, in a wild flight of imagination, claimed that Pheidias was actually to blame for the Peloponnesian War because Perikles, fearing that he might become embroiled in his friend's misdemeanors, concocted the Megarian Decree and whipped up the war to distract people's attention.[164] These famous lines from the *Peace* present a ludicrous fantasy, but one that has worked untold mischief in the later historiography of Periklean Athens. Fortunately, an alert commentator on the passage thought to consult the *Atthis* of Philochoros about the chronology and reports as follows:

> Philochoros under the archonship of Theodoros [438/7] says, "The golden statue of Athena was erected in the great temple, having a weight of 44 talents of gold; Perikles was overseer and Pheidias the maker. And Pheidias who made it, and who was suspected of cheating on the accounts with respect to the ivory in the plaques, was put on trial. Having fled in exile to Elis, he is said to have accepted the contract for the statue of Zeus at Olympia, and after completing it, to have died at the hands of the Elians."[165]

The scholiast goes on to quote Philochoros's comments on the Megarian Decree which he found under the archonship of Pythodoros (432/1), who, as he notes, was seven years later, counting inclusively. It is in the context of that infamous piece of legislation that both Plutarch and Diodoros report the trial of Pheidias, but both authors have based their chronology on nothing more substantial than the fanciful poetry of Aristophanes, whom Diodoros, citing Ephoros, quotes verbatim.[166] Plutarch, who is characteristically vague about the chronology, recounts the attacks on Perikles' friends in order to explain the statesman's adamant refusal to rescind the Megarian Decree. Diodoros dates these legal attacks to the archonship of Euthydemos (431/0), and, accordingly, many modern interpreters have followed their chronology and placed the trials among the events that immediately preceded the outbreak of the Peloponnesian War.[167]

Detailed analysis of the scholia to Aristophanes' *Peace* has shown that Philochoros's account of the Pheidias affair is to be preferred to the poetry of Aristophanes,[168] on which Ephoros, and ultimately both Diodoros and Plutarch, based their versions of the story. As a result, several scholars have argued compellingly that the trial took place in 438/7, as Philochoros stated, and the charges arose in the final auditing of accounts for the gold and ivory statue.[169] We are told that one of Pheidias's assistants, a certain Menon, was persuaded by Perikles' enemies to bring an accusation against

Accountability in Athenian Government, 59–62; W. Ameling, *Klio* 68 (1986) 63–66; Stadter, *Commentary*, 284–289; Podlecki, *Perikles*, 31–34, 101–117, 151–152; Davison, *Pheidias*, 623–628.

[163] Ephoros, *FGrH* 70 F 196, from Diod. 12.38–40, with specific attribution at 12.41.1 and with direct quotation of Aristoph. *Peace* 603–611.

[164] Aristoph. *Peace* 603–625.

[165] Schol. RV Aristoph. *Peace* 605 = Philochoros, *FGrH* 328 F 121 (Jacoby's text). Plut. *Per.* 31.5 says that Pheidias died in prison at Athens after his trial, whereas Philochoros has him put to death in Elis. Both accounts seem to be fictitious invention; see Stadter, *Commentary*, 294–295. Philochoros's statement is belied by Paus. 5.14.5, who reports that the descendants of Pheidias were honored at Elis with the position of cleansers (φαιδρυνταί) of the statue of Zeus. Cf. the honorary statue base, found at Olympia, of one Titus Flavius Herakleitus, who is described as τὸν ἀπὸ Φειδίου, φαιδρυντὴν τοῦ Διὸς τοῦ Ὀλυμπίου: *Olympia* V, *Inschriften*, no. 466.

[166] For Diodoros's version, note 163 above. Plut. *Per.* 31–32 recounts the Pheidias affair as the "worst reason" that Perikles refused to countenance rescinding the Megarian Decree so that, once embroiled in war, the city would turn to him for leadership, since his prestige had been damaged by the attacks on Pheidias and others.

[167] See F. E. Adcock, *CAH*[1] V, 477–480; Gomme, *HCT*, vol. 2, 184–189; Wade-Gery, *EGH*, 260; Hansen, *Eisangelia*, 71–73; Podlecki, *Perikles*, 103–108, 151–152.

[168] Jacoby, *FGrH* III B (Suppl.) 484–496.

[169] Frost, *JHS* 84 (1964) 69–72; Frost, *Historia* 13 (1964) 392–399; Donnay, *AntCl* 37 (1968) 34; Kagan, *OPW*, 194–198; Mansfeld, *Mnemosyne* 33 (1980) 69–70, 76–80.

the sculptor, whereupon a formal prosecution was conducted in the assembly; but, says Plutarch, the charge of embezzlement was not proven.[170] At this point we lose the thread of the story in a welter of conflicting anecdotes from which only two facts emerge with any degree of certainty. Plutarch knew a decree of the assembly, on the motion of Glaukon, that granted Menon freedom from taxation and enjoined the generals to ensure his safety.[171] That Plutarch could cite the author's name and paraphrase the honorific formulas suggests a genuine documentary source for the decree. But if this is the case, we are forced to the conclusion that Pheidias was condemned at trial, for otherwise the demos would not have bestowed public honors upon his accuser. It is possible that the sculptor was found guilty in absentia after his flight to Elis reported by Philochoros. For the second certain fact is Pheidias's subsequent career at Olympia. Excavations within the sanctuary have brought to light the remains of a building specifically erected to serve as the sculptor's workshop for the gold and ivory statue of Zeus. Associated with the construction of the workshop were deposits of pottery that included, among the latest pieces, fragments of an Attic red-figure krater by the Kleophon Painter, dated by the excavators ca. 435. An even more striking piece of evidence was the lower part of a black-glazed mug, with ribbed wall, which bore on its bottom the graffito ΦΕΙΔΙΟ϶ ΕΙΜΙ. Pheidias's mug is to be dated shortly after 440 and provides formal proof that the sculptor was present at Olympia from the middle years of the 430s, when his workshop was being built.[172]

Plutarch's most interesting contribution to our knowledge of these events is another decree of the assembly that was passed on the motion of a certain Drakontides.[173] This document enjoined Perikles to present his accounts of public moneys to the prytaneis, and if any indictment should arise from their scrutiny, the jurors were to cast their votes with ballots that had lain on the altar of Athena on the Acropolis. Diodoros probably refers indirectly to the same occasion when he says that Perikles' enemies accused the statesman himself of stealing sacred property.[174] The purport of Drakontides' decree was to launch a vicious ad hominem attack on Perikles himself. The trial was to take place on the Acropolis, and the exceptional proceedings were to be shrouded about with quasi-religious ritual in order to intimidate the jurors to vote for condemnation. Clearly, the decree responded to extraordinary circumstances which Perikles' enemies hoped to turn to their advantage. For this reason, it has very frequently been associated with the one known occasion, in the summer of 430, when Perikles was fined and deposed from the office of general.[175] But this conclusion is contradicted by the statement of Thucydides, who is explicit about the motivation for the attack:

[170] Plut. *Per.* 31.2–3; cf. Diod. 12.39.1, who speaks of several assistants but gives no names. In order to enlarge on the melodrama, Menon sought asylum by sitting at the Altar of the Twelve Gods in the Agora, where his charges would attract the utmost attention.

[171] The MSS of Plut. *Per.* 31.5 give the speaker's name as Glykon (γράψαντος Γλύκωνος), a name that is unknown in Athenian prosopography. Glaukon (γράψαντος Γλαύκωνος) is the emendation of L. Pareti, *RM* 24 (1909) 274, adopted by modern editors, e.g., the Teubner edition of K. Ziegler, *Plutarchi Vitae Parallelae*, vol. 1, pt. 2 (Leipzig 1964); cf. Stadter, *Commentary*, 296. The grant of *atelia* was normally given to foreign benefactors and suggests that Menon was not an Athenian, perhaps an itinerant craftsman. See A. S. Henry, *Honours and Privileges in Athenian Decrees* (Hildesheim 1983) 241–246; Stadter, *Commentary*, 296. For Glaukon, cf. pp. 322–323 below. For official phraseology of such grants, cf. *IG* I³ 24, lines 4–5; 227, line 21.

[172] The workshop of Pheidias has been studied in detail, with complete architectural restoration, by A. Mallwitz and W. Schiering, *Die Werkstatt des Pheidias in Olympia*, OlForsch 5 (Berlin 1964); for the red-figure krater by the Kleophon Painter, 251–254, no. 5, pls. 82, 83; for Pheidias's mug, 169, no. 1, pl. 64; for the excavators' conclusions on the date, 140, 187, 276.

[173] Plut. *Per.* 32.3–4. For Drakontides, see p. 324, note 208 below.

[174] Diod. 12.39.2. The various anecdotes about the boy Alkibiades advising Perikles how not to render his accounts probably grew out of this incident in the popular history: Diod. 12.38.3–4; Aristodemos 16.4; Val. Max. 3.1, ext. 1 (transferring the story to the Propylaia). Both Diodoros and Plutarch speak generally of Perikles' enemies. For discussion of their personal identity, see Frost, *Historia* 13 (1964) 392–399; Kagan, *OPW,* 194 202.

[175] Adcock, in *CAH*¹ V, 478; Gomme, *HCT*, vol. 2, 187; Schwarze, *Beurteilung des Perikles,* 48; Hansen, *Eisangelia,* 71–73; Podlecki, *Perikles,* 151–152. Earlier bibliography cited by Mansfeld, *Mnemosyne* 33 (1980) 48, note 188.

people were angry with Perikles' conduct of the war and distressed by the hardships of the wartime conditions which his policies as general had inflicted on them. There is not the slightest suggestion that he was charged with misuse of public funds or stealing sacred property.[176]

A far more likely occasion for the decree of Drakontides is the immediate aftermath of the trial of Pheidias in 438.[177] Whether or not the enemies of Perikles managed to get the sculptor condemned, the man had slipped through their fingers and was safely resident in Olympia. Now Drankontides sought to turn the attack against Perikles himself. The moment was opportune, for the great new temple was complete except for the pedimental sculptures, and the gold and ivory statue had almost certainly just been dedicated at the Great Panathenaia of that year. All that remained was to settle the final audit of the statue's accounts, and it was doubtless in the course of these proceedings that Pheidias was denounced by his assistant. Curiously, those scholars who have argued most persuasively for a date in 438 have emphasized Philochoros's statement that Perikles was epistates of the statue[178] and therefore legally responsible for Pheidias's alleged misconduct. If indeed Perikles had been a member, or perhaps chairman, of the board of overseers, as Philochoros states, his involvement in the audit of accounts was a matter of annual routine. No special legislation was necessary to ensure that Athenian public officials accounted for funds that they had spent when they stood for the εὔθυναι at the end of their service.[179] On the contrary, Drakontides' decree indicates precisely the opposite, that Perikles himself was not one of the official overseers and had no legal responsibility to account for the expenditures on the statue. Drakontides' intent was to obfuscate the issue of legal responsibility and generally to besmirch the administration of Perikles with the smoke of corruption and the bogy of stealing sacred treasures, hence the religious rigmarole on the Acropolis. But Plutarch goes on to say that Hagnon[180] managed to carry an amendment to Drakontides' bill, presumably at the same meeting of the assembly. His motion provided that any case against Perikles be tried in an ordinary court of fifteen hundred jurors, whether the prosecution was for embezzlement and bribery or malversation.

It seems likely that Hagnon's amendment successfully negated the thrust of Drakontides' decree. There is no indication in our sources of whether Perikles managed to satisfy the auditors that his accounts were in order, or if his enemies simply abandoned the prosecution. At this time, however, nothing came of the attack on Perikles himself, and his enemies may have turned upon others of his associates. According to Plutarch, at about the same time scandalous charges were filed against Perikles' consort Aspasia, whose acquittal he just managed to secure by shedding copious tears in court. Since, however, her accuser was Hermippos, the comic poet, there is suspicion that the charges against her were in fact the slanders of Old Comedy, and the weeping Perikles was a conceit of the comic theater.[181] More serious was a decree, on the motion of Diopeithes,[182] providing for the impeachment of people who did not believe in gods or who taught theories about the heavens. As Plutarch correctly saw, this was an attempt to direct charges of impiety against Perikles' old friend

[176] Thuc. 2.65.3; cf. Plut. *Per.* 35.4–5; Diod. 12.45.4; Plato, *Gorg.* 515E–516A.

[177] As argued by Frost, *JHS* 84 (1964) 72; Frost, *Historia* 13 (1964) 392–396; Donnay, *AntCl* 37 (1968) 22, 32–34; Mansfeld, *Mnemosyne* 33 (1980) 47–51, 69–70; Roberts, *Accountability in Athenian Government,* 59–62.

[178] Note 162 above.

[179] See the references cited in note 169 above.

[180] For Hagnon, see p. 318 and note 184 below.

[181] Plut. *Per.* 32.1, 5. For the view that Plutarch's account of Aspasia is based on a trial scene in comedy, see Gomme, *HCT,* vol. 2, 187; Donnay, *AntCl* 37 (1968) 29; K. J. Dover, *Talanta* 7 (1975) 28; M. M. Henry, *Prisoner of History: Aspasia of Miletus and Her Biographical Tradition* (Oxford 1995) 15–16; Podlecki, *Perikles,* 116–117. Others have supported the historicity of the trial of Aspasia: Frost, *Historia* 13 (1964) 395–396; Schwarze, *Beurteilung des Perikles,* 110–113; Mansfeld, *Mnemosyne* 33 (1980) 76–80; and cf. the remarks of Stadter, *Commentary,* 297–298.

[182] Diopeithes: Kirchner, *PA* 4309, a seer named in jokes by Aristophanes. He is described as mad and crippled, schol. *Birds* 988b–c (Holwerda); a rhetor with mad inspiration, schol. *Wasps* 380a–c (Koster); and a thief, schol. *Knights* 1085a, c (Jones). He was possibly the speaker who moved the first decree for Methone, *IG* I³ 61, lines 4–5 (430/29) = ML 65.

and mentor, the philosopher Anaxagoras, and thus to cast aspersions on Perikles himself. Elsewhere there is mention of an actual trial, but nothing reliable is said of its outcome, and we are told only that Perikles feared for his friend and sent him out of the city.[183]

Our sources suggest that the dedication of the Parthenon and its gold and ivory statue triggered a nasty round of political infighting to which both Pheidias and Anaxagoras fell victim. Both men abruptly departed Athens under a cloud of criminal charges and no doubt owed their escape to the personal influence of their great patron. If the prosecutions are correctly dated in 438, then there are several indications that Perikles contrived to extricate himself unscathed from the trap that his enemies had laid. Plutarch's report of his continuous reelection as general for fifteen years shows that there were no irregularities or outstanding charges against him, and he was duly returned to office for 437/6. That year also saw the founding of the Athenian colony at Amphipolis in Thrace under the leadership of the same Hagnon who had successfully derailed the decree of Drakontides in the assembly. Hagnon derived great honor and prestige from his position as founder, and scholars have been inclined to see his appointment as a political favor bestowed upon him in return for his parliamentary support of Perikles at a critical moment.[184] But nothing demonstrates more clearly that Perikles had regained control of the demos than the beginning of work on the Propylaia, likewise in 437/6. Although the only surviving records are the accounts of the overseers, these are sufficient to prove that the assembly had passed formal legislation authorizing the election of epistatai and the start of construction.[185] Moreover, that decree of the demos flew squarely in the face of those who had attacked the building program just a few months earlier and forced Pheidias to seek safety in flight.

Whatever may have been the political climate in the assembly, Mnesikles and his overseers began construction of the great frontispiece of the Acropolis in 437/6. Prior to the start of work, however, debate had no doubt raged over the architect's original plan for the project. In the rhetoric of opposing speakers, the magnificence of the architecture became profligate extravagance, the sheer size and scale of the building were branded hubristic, and the costs were deemed exorbitant beyond all proportion for a mere gatehouse. This line of argument was plainly influential, and its effects can be observed in the remains of the building. The assembly approved a compromise whereby the central hall and western wings would go forward, but the colonnades of the wings would have three columns instead of four, and the southwest wing would be redesigned as an entrance portico for the Nike bastion. The great eastern halls were postponed for the time being, pending completion of the gatehouse itself, although the builders clearly anticipated their eventual construction and made preparations accordingly.

From the beginning of the building program, the costs of the Acropolis project and the use of the reserve fund to defray them seems to have been a source of controversy and a subject of increasingly vitriolic debate until the ostracism of Thoukydides, if Plutarch is to be believed. There is reason to believe that the issue may have arisen again over the construction of the Propylaia. Examination

---

[183] Plut. *Per.* 32.2, 5–6; *Nik.* 23.4; Diod. 12.39.2. The actual trial is mentioned at Plut. *Mor.* 169F. Four different and mutually exclusive accounts of the trial are given by Diog. Laert. 2.12–14, each with a different prosecutor and different outcome. From these, Dover, *Talanta* 7 (1975) 27–32, concludes that "no one of them actually knew what happened to Anaxagoras." Conclusions about the chronology of Anaxagoras's career and the date of his trial have varied from the 450s to 430; see Meiggs, *AE*, 435–436. For argument in favor of 438/7: Frost, *Historia* 13 (1964) 396–399; Mansfeld, *Mnemosyne* 33 (1980) 17–95 and especially 80–84 on the trial itself. Stadter, *Commentary*, 298–299, is inclined to be more flexible about the date.

[184] Hagnon son of Nikias of Steiria: Kirchner, *PA* 171; *LGPN* II, 8, s.v. 22; Davies, *APF*, 227–228. General at Samos 440/39: Thuc. 1.117.2–3. Founder of Amphipolis 437/6: Thuc. 4.102.3–4; 5.1.1; schol. Aischin. 2 *Embassy* 31; Diod. 12.68.2. General at Poteidaia 431/0: Thuc. 2.58.1, 6.31.2. General in the Chalkidike 429/8, Thuc. 2.95.3. Swore oath for the Peace of Nikias 422/1, Thuc. 5.19.2, 24.1. His appointment at Amphipolis as a political favor: Frost, *JHS* 84 (1964) 72; Kagan *OPW*, 201; Roberts, *Accountability in Athenian Government*, 61. On Hagnon's career, see also G. E. Pesely, *Athenaeum*, n.s., 67 (1989) 191–209.

[185] See pp. 275–277 above.

of the overseers' accounts earlier in this chapter revealed that the building was financed in much the same way as the Parthenon. The major funds came from the sacred treasury of Athena, that is to say, from the reserve fund on the Acropolis, to which were added the annual *aparchai* of the tribute paid over by the hellenotamiai. Supplementary contributions came from the state's mining revenues, rental of sacred real estate, sales of scrap materials, and a few private benefactions. Then, in the extant accounts for Year 3 (435/4) and again for Year 4 (434/3) and Year 5 (433/2), we observed contributions to the building fund from various Athenian generals commanding in the field. Evidently the generals were donating to the Propylaia their unexpended surplus funds at the conclusion of a campaign instead of returning them to the reserve fund that had originally disbursed the money.[186] Assuredly the demos had voted authorization for these transactions; but that did not prevent those speakers who disapproved from claiming that money budgeted for defense of the empire was being siphoned off from the war chest to help pay for public works, and not even for a temple, but for the entrance gate of a sanctuary. Among those who disapproved, we should not be surprised to find the enemies of Perikles who had earlier attacked his friends and sought to incriminate him, and who by now were likely to be enemies of the Propylaia as well. When the overseers of the Propylaia for 435/4 presented their accounts for audit, we may suspect that these enemies of Perikles were on their feet once again with a bitter protest of misappropriation of funds, and that the whole dispute about the finances and the extravagance of the building program was renewed.

The resurgent controversy over expenditures for the Acropolis buildings appears to be reflected in one of the most important epigraphical documents that has survived from the Periklean period. The inscription preserves two decrees, possibly moved by the same man, a certain Kallias, both of which are concerned with Athens's financial arrangements prior to the Peloponnesian War. Every aspect of their interpretation—date, interrelation, restoration of the text, and historical setting—has provoked continuous and contentious debate, but they provide evidence that bears directly on our present discussion.[187] The text of the first decree (A), on the obverse, is well preserved, and the details of its content are clear. It provides for the repayment of public debts owed to the gods and goddesses of Attica, other than Athena. A board of treasurers for these gods is to be appointed, modeled on the treasurers of Athena. They are to collect the funds from the rural sanctuaries, manage them on the Acropolis, and publish annual accounts of their holdings and transactions.

The opening clauses of the second decree (B), on the reverse, deal directly with the ongoing projects on the Acropolis, but unfortunately many of the crucial words have been lost from the text, and the resulting gaps are such that no compelling restorations have been found. Accordingly, there has been no consensus on the exact wording of the text, and recent studies have not attempted to make use of what evidence can be gleaned from these fragmentary lines. The middle lines of the inscription (12–17) can be restored with a greater degree of certainty so that from these lines there emerges clearly the basic purport of the decree: to set stringent limits on expenditure from the sacred treasury of Athena.

[186] See pp. 302–306 above.

[187] *IG* I³ 52A, B. The orthodox interpretation of the two decrees argues that they were moved by the same orator, Kallias, at the same meeting of the assembly, when a certain Eupeithes was chairman, in 434/3. This position is most succinctly defended by Meiggs and Lewis, ML 58, pp. 154–161; Meiggs, *AE*, 519–523, 601, who responds in detail to the earliest attempts by H. B. Mattingly to lower the date of the decrees to 422/1. More recently, a considerable bibliography has accumulated that argues in favor of dating the decrees later than 434/3 and prefers either 422/1 or 418/7. See Fornara, *GRBS* 11 (1970) 185–196; Mattingly, *AJP* 105 (1984) 355–357; Kallet-Marx, *CQ* 39 (1989) 94–113; Mattingly, *ZPE* 83 (1990) 118–122; L. Kallet-Marx, *Money, Expense, and Naval Power in Thucydides' History 1–5.24* (Berkeley 1993) 105–107; C. W. Fornara and L. J. Samons II, *Athens from Cleisthenes to Pericles* (Berkeley 1991); Samons, *CQ* 46 (1996) 91–102. Careful study of the remaining traces of letters at the beginning of decree B by Kallet-Marx, *CQ* 39 (1989) 97–100, has shown how very doubtful are the chairman's and speaker's names. That Kallias moved both decrees is slightly more likely, but it is probably better to suppose that the chairman was not the same for both. For discussion of the date, see pp. 321–322 below.

IG I³ 52B, lines 12–17:

[. . . .τοῖς δ]ὲ ἄλλοις χρέμα[σιν τοῖ]ς τῆς Ἀθεναίας το[ῖς τε νῦν ὄσι]-
[ν ἐμ πόλει κ]αὶ hάττ' ἀν τ[ὸ] λο[ιπὸν ἀν]αφέρεται μὲ χρε͂σ[θ]α[ι μεδὲ δαν]-
[είζεσθαι ἀ]π' αὐτο͂ν ε[ς] ἄλλο μ[εδὲν ἒ] ἐς ταῦτα hυπὲρ μυ[ρ]ί[ας δραχμὰ]-
[ς ἒ ἐς ἐπισκ]ευὲν ἐάν τι δέε[ι· ἐς ἄλλ]ο δὲ μεδὲν χρε͂σ[θ]α[ι τοῖς χρέμα]-
[σιν ἐὰμ μὲ τ]ὲν ἄδειαν φσεφ[ίσεται] ὁ δῆμος καθάπερ ἐ[ὰμ φσεφίσετ]-
[αι περὶ ἐσφ]ορᾶς·

The other money of Athena which [is now on the Acropolis] and whatever is carried up in the future shall not be used, [nor shall borrowings be made] from it for any purpose other [than] this, above ten thousand [drachmas, except for] restoration if any is needed. But [for] no [other] purpose shall use be made [of the money unless] the demos [pass a] vote of immunity just as [when a vote is passed about] property taxes.

A note of stern fiscal austerity rings through these lines: there is to be no expenditure from Athena's reserves above ten thousand drachmas without a special vote granting license to bring forward an otherwise illegal proposal. To appreciate what strict economy this measure imposed, let us recall that on at least two occasions in the 440s the overseers of the Parthenon recorded an unexpended balance forward of more than two hundred thousand drachmas.[188] In contrast, the opening lines of the decree (2–5) designate various works on the Acropolis that seem to be exempt from the limit on spending. First, in line 3, three specific projects can be recognized: [– – τὰ λί]θινα καὶ τὰς Νί[κας τὰς χ]ρυσᾶς καὶ τὰ Προ[πύλαια – –]. The last two, the golden statues of Nike and the Propylaia, may be regarded as certain. The objects of marble listed first have been plausibly thought to refer to the marble pedimental statuary of the Parthenon.[189] Exactly what Kallias had to say about the three projects can no longer be ascertained because the principal verbs are missing from the sentence. In line 4 is preserved the word παντελο͂ς ("completely") and in line 5 κατὰ τὰ ἐφσεφι[σμένα] ("according to the things voted"), so the sense of the lines was possibly that the marble statuary, the golden Nikai, and the Propylaia should be fully completed in accordance with the decrees previously voted by the demos.

The second principal clause of the decree (lines 5–12) concerns another class of building operations that was also set apart from the general prohibition on spending quoted above. This did not consist of specifically named works already in progress, like the first three projects, but rather it anticipated construction, perhaps chiefly repair work, involving the Acropolis as a whole, which would need to be carried out in the immediate future.

IG I³ 52B, lines 5–12:

καὶ τὲν ἀκρόπολιν [. . . . .¹⁰. . . . .]
[. . . . .⁹. . . . .]ργμένα καὶ ἐπι[σκευά]ζεν δέκα τάλαντα ἀ[ναλίσκοντα]-
[ς τὸ ἐνιαυτ]ο͂ hεκάστο hέος [ἂν . . . .]θει καὶ ἐπισκευα[σθε͂ι hος κάλ]-
[λιστα· συνε]πιστατόντ[ο]ν δ[ὲ το͂ι ἔρ]γ[ο]ι [ο]ἱ ταμίαι καὶ [οἱ ἐπιστάτα]-
[ι· τὸ δὲ γράμ]μα τὸν ἀρχιτέκ[τονα ποιε͂ν ὅ]σπερ τὸμ Προ[πυλαίον· hοῦ]-
[τος δὲ ἐπιμ]ελέσ[θο] μετὰ το͂[ν ἐπιστ]ατο͂ν hόπος ἄριστ[α καὶ εὐτελέ]-
[στατα . . .⁵. .]έσεται hε ἀκρ[όπολις] καὶ ἐπισκευασθέ[σεται τὰ δεό]-
[μενα· – – –]

---

[188] *IG* I³ 437, lines 40–41, Year 2 (446/5); 442, line 173, Year 7 (441/0).
[189] Cf. the suggested restoration for lines 2–3 in *ATL* I, 161: [ἐκποε͂ν τὰ ἐναιέτια τὰ λί]θινα; and the revised version in *ATL* II, 47: [ἐκποε͂ν τἀγάλματα τὰ λί]θινα.

And the Acropolis [they shall – – – –] and they shall restore [by spending] ten talents in each [year] until [it has been – – –] and has been restored [most splendidly.] The treasurers and [the overseers] are [jointly] to supervise the [work]; the architect is [to prepare] the plan just as for the Propylaia. [He is to] see to it together with the overseers that the Acropolis is [– – –] in the best [and most economical way] and is restored [as necessary.]

Admittedly, interpretation of the decree relies heavily on restoration, which in the opening lines is beyond reasonable conjecture, but the speaker appears to be concerned with establishing priorities for funding construction on the Acropolis. Three major projects, including the golden Nikai and the Propylaia, are apparently to be carried to completion as authorized by decrees previously voted. Other work on the Acropolis, perhaps including restoration and landscaping, is projected with an annual budgetary ceiling of ten talents. Beyond that there is to be no expenditure greater than ten thousand drachmas for any project without special legislation.

Our understanding of the historical circumstances to which the decrees of Kallias responded necessarily depends largely on the determination of their date. There are fortunately a number of chronological indicators within the texts of the decrees. Mention of the Propylaia (B, lines 3, 9) establishes a fixed terminus post quem of 437/6.[190] The date is bracketed in the other direction by the instructions to the treasurers of the Other Gods, as yet to be elected, that they publish each year inventories of their assets, income, and expenditures (A, lines 13–18, 24–29). Their earliest extant inventory is dated in the archonship of Epameinon (429/8); and the board in office that year states that they received the listed treasures from their predecessors, so that 430/29 becomes a fixed terminus ante quem for the Kallias inscription.[191] The second decree orders the treasurers of Athena currently in office to catalogue the money in their charge with the cooperation of "the four boards who gave the account from Panathenaia to Panathenaia" (B, lines 26–29), a formulation indicating that the decree was passed in a year in which the Great Panathenaic festival was celebrated.[192] Thus within the period of nine years enclosed by the bracketing dates, the decrees of Kallias can be assigned only to 434/3 or 430/29. But the instructions for the design and supervision of the supplementary works (B, lines 8–10) leave no possible doubt that the architect of the Propylaia was still working on the Acropolis and the overseers in charge of that building were still in office when the

[190] The name of the archon Euthymenes is preserved in Year 1 of the overseers accounts, *IG* I³ 462, line 3, and is given by Harpokration, s.v. προπύλαια ταῦτα (π 101 Keaney), citing Philochoros, *FGrH* 328 F 36.

[191] *IG* I³ 383, lines 1–8. On the date, see T. Linders, *The Treasurers of the Other Gods* (Meisenheim am Glan 1975) 55–57. Lines 4–8 list the names of five treasurers and their secretary. Mattingly, in *Atti del I Convegno del Centro Internazionale di Studi Numismatici* (Naples 1967) 201–222, and *BCH* 92 (1968) 458–468, has expressed the view that the treasurers who published the inventory of 429/8 were a provisional board and not the normal board established by decree A. This, of course, is an attempt to support his argument that the Kallias decrees should be dated in 422/1. The argument turns partly on the small number of treasurers listed, whereas A, lines 14–15, model the treasurers of the Other Gods on the treasurers of Athena, who were ten in number, chosen by lot, one from each tribe: [Aristot.] *Ath. Pol.* 47.1. But the argument from number is fallacious, for there are many instances when Athenian boards appear to have operated with fewer than the prescribed number of personnel. Cf. treasurers of Athena: (444/3) ten names plus secretary (the prescribed number), *IG* I³ 455, lines 8–22; (442/1) eight names plus secretary, *IG* I³ 457, lines 10–20; (440/39) seven names plus secretary, *IG* I³ 458, lines 6–13. Epistatai of public works: *IG* I³ 433 records accounts over a period of eight years in which the number of epistatai varies from two to five.

[192] On the specific meaning of the formula, see R. Develin, *ZPE* 57 (1984) 137–138. According to the orthodox interpretation, decree B, lines 26–29, ordered the treasurers of Athena to prepare and publish inventories of the sacred treasures. Since the long sequence of inventories of treasures stored in the Parthenon began in 434/3 (*IG* I³ 292, Pronaos; 317, Hekatompedon; 343, Parthenon), these inscriptions were thought to support a date for the Kallias decrees in that year; see *ATL* III, 320, 326; ML, 158. It has now been argued that decree B, lines 26–29, refer to the counting and weighing of money, not dedications and sacred vessels in the Parthenon; see L. J. Samons, *CQ* 46 (1996) 91–102, and *ZPE* 188 (1997) 179–182. Indeed, the phraseology of the text suggests that the process of counting and weighing has already been at least partly completed. It may well be that these lines do not order the extant Parthenon inventories, but they were still drafted in a Panathenaic year.

decree was drafted.[193] So the date of the second decree must be earlier than 433/2, the year in which work was suspended and the overseers filed their last accounts. The necessity of attributing the documents to a Great Panathenaic year thus makes it virtually certain that they should be dated to 434/3.

In the context of that year, the two decrees seem to be a curiously mismatched pair. The first decree (A) sets out in orderly fashion how the debts will be repaid to the gods of Attica, and, more important, how the treasures belonging to individual sanctuaries will be centralized on the Acropolis for safekeeping. There the accumulated assets are to be managed by a new board of treasurers, whose duties and responsibilities are described in detail. The document has been cited as evidence of Athens's foresight in securing its financial arrangements before a war that was more than two years in the offing.[194] In contrast, the second decree (B) seems oddly miscellaneous. After dealing with the building operations on the Acropolis (lines 2–12), the speaker severely limits further expenditure from the sacred treasury (lines 12–17); then he turns briefly to the repayment of debts to the Other Gods and allocates space for their treasury within the opisthodomos (lines 19–25). Finally, he orders the treasurers of Athena for the past Panathenaic quadrennium to weigh and count any moneys that remain unweighed and uncounted, a motion that appears to attend to unfinished business (lines 26–29). One wonders if the text of the decree may not have been drafted in response to freewheeling debate on the floor of the assembly. Unless we are seriously misled by the poorly preserved state of the opening lines, the motion to complete the golden Nikai and the Propylaia according to the previously voted decrees appears to be stated so forcefully (lines 3–5) that the clause reads like a blunt retort to a motion that proposed exactly the opposite. On the other hand, there is some measure of compromise, for the treasurers of Athena themselves, together with the overseers, are to supervise the supplementary work jointly (lines 8–9). This provision may well acknowledge the fact that some members of the assembly had expressed skeptical views of the overseers' administration of the Propylaia. Whatever works of restoration the speaker had in mind, they were plainly to be carried out in the future, for the decree directs the architect to prepare the plans as he had for the Propylaia (line 9). Moreover, the work in question is certainly expected to take two years at least, if not more, since a budget of ten talents is authorized [τō ἐνιαυτ]ō hεκάστο, "in each year," until the job is finished (lines 6–7). There can be no doubt that Kallias was chiefly concerned to husband Athens's financial resources and to provide for their security. At the same time, there is a clear intent to curtail expenditure from the sacred treasury for further construction on the Acropolis, which in the recent past had consumed large outlays of cash. But nowhere is there the slightest indication that one year later construction of the Propylaia would be completely abandoned and its overseers' tenure of office would terminate. In fact, Kallias's language appears to have anticipated exactly the reverse.

It is in the area of Athenian domestic politics that we feel the tide of opposition beginning to rise and swell against Perikles once again. The first inkling comes with the election of public officials in the spring of 433.[195] On that occasion the first board of treasurers of the Other Gods was empaneled in accordance with the decree of Kallias passed earlier in the year. Likewise, the last overseers of the Propylaia came into office, although they probably did not realize until later that they would be

[193] Recent writers (see note 187 above) have simply ignored the references in decree B to the Propylaia. Where the text cannot be restored with certainty, no need is apparently felt to offer an interpretation of what is preserved. But the building was mentioned by name twice (lines 3, 9); its architect and epistatai are certain restorations (lines 8–10), and both were clearly still active on the Acropolis. The building is known to have been under construction for five years, and work was suspended in 433/2 (see p. 301 above). It is impossible to understand how a decree describing these matters can be dated eleven or fifteen years after we know that the project terminated. Nevertheless, Kallet-Marx, *CQ* 39 (1989) 113, note 84, and *Money, Expense, and Naval Power,* 137, regards the references to the Propylaia as irrelevant to the date of the decree because the building was left unfinished. She dates the decree in 418/7.

[194] See Meiggs, *AE,* 200–201.

[195] The annual election of generals was held in the first prytany after the sixth in which the omens were favorable, [Aristot.] *Ath. Pol.* 44.4. Election by allotment of the archons and other officials was possibly held at about the same time, although the precise date is not recorded.

ordered to suspend construction of the building at the end of their term. Greater interest attaches to the board of generals elected to serve in 433/2. Nine of its ten members are known, but, aside from Perikles himself, only two had any previous experience in the office of general: Glaukon son of Leagros of Kerameis and Proteas son of Epikles of Aixone.[196] Glaukon was a veteran of the Samian War, and both men had probably held command in 435/4, when they were authorized to contribute their surplus funds to the building account for the Propylaia. The other six men were elected to the strategia only in 433/2. None is reported to have held the office prior to that year, although, to be sure, the membership of the board during the mid-430s is almost entirely unknown to us. More significantly, none was ever reelected during the early years of the Archidamian War, when the generals commanding Athenian forces are much more fully documented. This is the more remarkable at a time when Athens's foreign relations were rapidly deteriorating. If Thucydides knew that Corinth had been building ships for nearly two years and was already mobilizing for war in 433, many Athenian voters must also have known it.[197] And yet that year the electorate passed over some of Athens's most seasoned military commanders—Hagnon son of Nikias of Steiria,[198] Phormion son of Asopios of Paiania,[199] Xenophon son of Euripides of Melite[200]—all three of whom held multiple commands both before and after 433/2. Then there were Sokrates son of Antigenes of Halai[201] and Karkinos son of Xenotimos of Thorikos,[202] both of whom would be elected in each of the next two years; Lamachos son of Xenophanes of Oe had already served with Perikles on the Pontic expedition and would become one of Athens's most illustrious warriors of the late fifth century.[203] All were available for election in 433, but none was chosen.

Instead of such experienced military leaders, the Athenians elected to the board of generals that year six men whose careers have made virtually no impact on the history of Athens. Diotimos son of Strombichos of Euonymon sailed with the first squadron to Korkyra. He is otherwise reported to have gone on missions to Neapolis and Susa, both of which were diplomatic and not military.[204] Archestratos son of Lykomedes of Phlya was one of several generals dispatched to the Chalkidike in an unsuccessful effort to forestall the revolt of Poteidaia, and he later fought in Macedonia. The

[196] Glaukon: see note 105 above; Proteas: see note 106 above. That Perikles was general in 433/2 is nowhere specifically recorded, but is based on Plut. *Per.* 16.3, where it is stated that Perikles was general continuously for fifteen years after the ostracism of Thoukydides. On the membership of the board of generals for 433/2, see Fornara, *Athenian Generals,* 51; Develin, *Athenian Officials,* 99–100.

[197] Thuc. 1.31.1. For discussion of the events immediately preceding the outbreak of the war, Kagan, *OPW,* 222–285; Meiggs, *AE,* 306–310; de Ste. Croix, *OPW,* 64–88.

[198] See note 184 above.

[199] Phormion: Kirchner, *PA* 14958; *LGPN* II, 468, s.v. 21. General at Samos, 440/39, 439/8: Thuc. 1.117.2–3; restored *IG* I³ 48, line 28. General at Poteidaia, 432/1: Thuc. 1.64.2–3; Isokr. 16 *Team of Horses* 29; Diod. 12.37. General in the Chalkidike, 431/0: Thuc. 2.31.1, 58.2. General in the Corinthian Gulf and Naupaktos, 430/29, 429/8: Thuc. 2.69.1, 80ff., 88.1ff., 102.1–2, 103.1; Diod. 12.47.1, 48.

[200] Xenophon: Kirchner, *PA* 11313; Davies, *APF,* 199–200; *LGPN* II, 347, s.v. 35. Hipparch in the 440s: *IG* I³ 511. General at Samos, 441/0, 439/8: Androtion, *FGrH* 324 F 38, cited by schol. Aristeid. 3.74 (vol. 3, p. 485 Dindorf); *IG* I³ 48, line 31. General at Poteidaia, 430/29: Thuc. 2.70.3, 79; Diod. 12.47.3; Plut. *Nik.* 6.3.

[201] Sokrates: Kirchner, *PA* 13099; *LGPN* II, 413, s.v. 59. General around the Peloponnese and Megarid, 432/1, 431/0: Thuc. 2.23.2, 25.1ff., 30; Diod. 12.42.7; *IG* I³ 365, lines 31, 36, 38–39. For his strategia in 431/0, Fornara, *Athenian Generals,* 53.

[202] Karkinos: Kirchner, *PA* 8254; Davies, *APF,* 283; *LGPN* II, 255, s.v. 1. General around the Peloponnese and Megarid 432/1, 431/0: Thuc. 2.32.2, 25.1ff.; Diod. 12.42.7; *IG* I³ 365, lines 31, 36, 38–39.

[203] Lamachos: Kirchner, *PA* 8981; *LGPN* II, 278, s.v. 7. General with Perikles on the Pontic expedition, ca. 436/5: Plut. *Per.* 20.1; cf. Develin, *Athenian Officials,* 96. General in the Hellespont and Pontus, 425/4, 424/3: Thuc. 4.75.1; Diod. 12.72.3–4; Aristoph. *Acharn.* 593–619; cf. Fornara, *Athenian Generals,* 59–61. Swore oath for Peace of Nikias, 422/1: Thuc. 5.19.2, 24.1. General in Sicily, 416/5, 415/4, 414/3: Thuc. 6.8.2, 49.1, 101.6; *IG* I³ 370, lines 50, 52, 54, 56; see Fornara, *Athenian Generals,* 63–65; Develin, *Athenian Officials,* 148, 150, 152.

[204] Diotimos: Kirchner, *PA* 4386; Davies, *APF,* 161; *LGPN* II, 131, s.v. 40. General at Korkyra, 433/2: Thuc. 1.45.2; *IG* I³ 364, line 9. Mission to Italy: Timaios, *FGrH* 566 F 98. Mission to Susa: Strabo 1.3.1 (p. 47); cf. Polyain. 5.22. Nicknamed "the Funnel" because of his drinking habits, Athenaeus 10.436E.

same man is likely to have been the author of at least two decrees in the assembly, and his name is associated with the framing of laws, so he was possibly more of a politician than a soldier.[205] Metagenes of Koile is named as one of the generals commanding the second naval squadron to Korkyra, but that is his only act of public service on record.[206] Archenautes is known to us only because the surplus funds from his war chest were redirected to the overseers of the Propylaia; the area of his command is unrecorded.[207] It may be possible to deduce something of the politics of this curiously lackluster group of men who joined with Perikles in the strategia of 433/2, because their remaining colleagues are recognizable for their anti-Periklean political persuasion. We have already encountered Drakontides son of Leogoras of Thorai, who together with Glaukon and Metagenes commanded the second fleet sent out to Korkyra.[208] He it was who had spearheaded the personal attack on Perikles in the aftermath of the Pheidias affair. His decree had ordered an extraordinary special audit of Perikles' public expenditures in the hope that any irregularity might enable the statesman to be impeached for the sacrilege of temple robbery. In 438, Drakontides' malevolent designs had been adroitly outmaneuvered by the amendment of Hagnon, and that loyal Periklean supporter had been dispatched the following year as founder of the colony at Amphipolis.[209] In light of Drakontides' earlier attempt to incriminate Perikles, his election to the board of generals four years later must be seen as an exceedingly sinister development. Whether his quarrel was with Perikles' person or his policies, he had attracted enough adherents to his anti-Periklean views that they elected him to stand at the great statesman's side in the highest office of Athenian government.

Beside Drakontides, still another conspirator in the plot against Pheidias may be recognized among the generals of 433/2. Plutarch cites a decree of the assembly, on the motion of Glaukon, that provided public honors for Menon, Pheidias's accuser; and it has been suggested that the proposer of the decree should be identified as Glaukon son of Leagros of Kerameis, who in 433/2 was general for the fourth time when he joined Drakontides and Metagenes in command of the second squadron sent to Korkyra.[210] Now, it happens that Glaukon was a fellow tribesman of Perikles, that is to say, both men came from demes—Kerameis and Cholargos, respectively—that belonged to the same tribe, Akamantis (V). Thus in the four years when Glaukon served as general, that tribe enjoyed double representation in the strategia. Moreover, in 433/2 Glaukon was the most experienced military commander on the board aside from Perikles himself. Therefore it is of some interest to observe that he was never reelected thereafter, as far as our records go. In both 432/1 and 431/0 he was replaced by another fellow tribesman, Karkinos son of Xenotimos of Thorikos, who was elected at Perikles' side as a second general from Akamantis (V).[211]

This brings us to the last member of the board, Lakedaimonios son of Kimon of Lakiadai, who together with Diotimos and Proteas sailed for Korkyra in command of the first naval squadron

[205] Archestratos: Kirchner, *PA* 2411; *LGPN* II, 69, s.v. 7; for his deme, Fornara, *Athenian Generals*, 78. General at Poteidaia and in Macedonia: Thuc. 1.57.6. Speaker of decrees, 446/5, 424/3: *IG* I³ 40, line 70; 73, lines 39–40; cf. 48bis, line 11. Author of laws on the Areopagos, [Aristot.] *Ath. Pol.* 35.2.

[206] Metagenes: Kirchner, *PA* 10088; *LGPN* II, 309, s.v. 8. General at Korkyra, 433/2: *IG* I³ 364, line 20.

[207] Archenautes: *LGPN* II, 68, s.v. 2; see p. 304 and note 107 above. General in 433/2: *IG* I³ 466, line 145; cf. 205, line 4?.

[208] Drakontides: Kirchner, *PA* 4551; Davies, *APF*, 173; *LGPN* II, 135, s.v. 14. Epistates of the assembly, 446/5: *IG* I³ 40, line 2. Speaker of decree on audit of Perikles' expenditures, 438/7: Plut. *Per.* 32.3. General at Korkyra, 433/2: *IG* I³ 364, lines 20–21; Thuc. 1.51.4 (where Drakontides' name is emended from MSS Andokides; as also [Plut.] *Mor.* 834B–C); see Gomme, *HCT*, vol. 1, 188–190; Fornara, *Athenian Generals*, 51.

[209] See pp. 317–318 above.

[210] Glaukon: see p. 316 and note 171 above. For the suggestion that the proposer of the decree for Menon (Plut. *Per.* 31.5) be identified as Glaukon son of Leagros of Kerameis (Kirchner, *PA* 3027): Pareti, *RM* 24 (1909) 274; Donnay, *AntCl* 37 (1968) 22; cf. Stadter, *Commentary*, 296; Podlecki, *Perikles*, 138.

[211] On the tribal affiliation of the demes Kerameis, Cholargos, and Thorikos, see J. S. Traill, *The Political Organization of Attica, Hesperia* Suppl. 14 (Princeton 1975) 8–9, 47–48, and table V. On double representation on the board, see Lewis, *JHS* 81 (1961) 118–123.

in the summer of 433.[212] He was a scion of one of Athens's most distinguished aristocratic families. His father was the brilliant general and charismatic statesman of the previous generation, and Perikles' erstwhile rival for political leadership; his grandfather was Miltiades, the victor of Marathon. Lakedaimonios himself had served as a cavalry commander in the mid-440s and together with his two colleagues had dedicated an equestrian statue on the Acropolis from the captured spoils of the enemy. His only other public office was his strategia in 433/2, and thereafter nothing whatever is known of him. Plutarch's account of the Korkyra campaign preserves a vivid glimpse of the popular slanders and propaganda that muddied the political waters of that fateful summer. His anecdote is the more interesting because it probably comes from Stesimbrotos of Thasos, a contemporary but violently anti-Athenian source.[213] The generals were dispatched on a difficult and politically sensitive mission, with orders to help the Korkyrians if necessary but not to engage the Corinthians unless the enemy attacked them first. Only ten ships were assigned to the fleet, a number too small to achieve any military success, and which an inexperienced commander might easily lead into disaster. Plutarch says that Perikles was trying to make a fool of Lakedaimonios and sent him out against his will in the hope that, after accomplishing nothing, he might be the more criticized for his family's historically pro-Spartan sympathies. In immediate response, his political opponents attacked Perikles harshly for the paltry number of ships and forced him to send out a reinforcing fleet that sailed just twenty-three days after the first squadron.[214]

Stesimbrotos's account, on which Plutarch relied, has preserved for us a rare, if ugly, view of Perikles the political infighter who could stoop to personal slander to gain the advantage of an opponent. He was said to malign continually the sons of Kimon—the twins Lakedaimonios and Eleios, and their younger brother Thessalos—and jeered especially at their peculiar names. With such names, these men were not genuine Athenians, but aliens and born of a woman from Arkadia.[215] The point of the attack was to call attention to Kimon's choice of strange foreign names for his sons, and thereby to suggest the opprobrium of illegitimacy. In this light, it is a fascinating detail that the name of the second twin, Eleios, which appears in this form in every literary text, is actually a corruption for Oulios, as the name is written in the official inventories of dedications in the Parthenon.[216] Plutarch probably found the corrupted form in the text of Stesimbrotos and thought nothing of it, so it may even go back to the fifth century. It is possibly a deliberate invention designed to extend the slur of foreign sympathizers to the entire family. Could the invention have been Perikles' own? Elsewhere Plutarch attributes to Diodoros the Periegete the statement that all three men were the sons of Isodike, Kimon's wife and a daughter of the great Alkmeonid family.[217] So Perikles' assertions stand exposed for the base slanders that they were. The whole episode is illuminating, however, for what

[212] Lakedaimonios: Kirchner, *PA* 8965; Davies, *APF,* 305–306; *LGPN* II, 278, s.v. 3. Hipparch in the 440s: *IG* I³ 511, line 2. General at Korkyra, 433/2: Thuc. 1.45.2–3; *IG* I³ 364, line 8; Plut. *Kim.* 16.1, *Per.* 29.1. Cf. *IG* I³ 48bis, line 12.

[213] Plut. *Per.* 29 describes the Korkyra campaign and mentions the sons of Kimon to whom he also refers at *Kim.* 16.1, with specific attribution of the anecdote to Stesimbrotos, *FGrH* 107 F 6. On the anti-Athenian character of his pamphlet *On Themistokles, Thoukydides, and Perikles:* Jacoby, *FGrH* II B, Commentary, 343–349; Stadter, *Commentary,* lxii.

[214] Plut. *Per.* 29.1–3. The three generals named and their orders given, Thuc. 1.45.1–3. The ensuing maneuvers and eventual battle around the Sybota islands, Thuc. 1.46–54. Cf. Gomme, *HCT,* vol. 1, 177–178. *IG* I³ 364 records the funds paid out to the generals in command of the two squadrons. The first group received payment on the thirteenth day of the first prytany (lines 11–12); the second group on the thirty-sixth and last day of the same prytany (lines 21–23). For a somewhat different and rather friendlier interpretation of the sources for these events, Kagan, *OPW,* 242–250; Podlecki, *Perikles,* 136–138.

[215] Plut. *Per.* 29.2, *Kim.* 16.1. The latter passage, specifically attributed to Stesimbrotos, mentions that Lakedaimonios and Eleios were twins born to an Arkadian woman from Kleitor, and therefore Perikles maligned their maternal lineage.

[216] Oulios: Kirchner, *PA* 11496; Davies, *APF,* 306–307; *LGPN* II, 355, s.v. 1. Listed repeatedly in the Acropolis inventories is a painted box dedicated by Kleito, wife of Aristokrates, son of Oulios, son of Kimon: *IG* II² 1388, lines 81–82 (398/7); 1400, line 66 (390/89); 1447, line 16 (before 371/0); 1451, line 16 (after 365/4). See Harris, *Treasures,* 51–52, II.37; Stadter, *Commentary,* 267–268.

[217] Plut. *Kim.* 16.1, citing Diodoros the Periegete, *FGrH* 372 F 37.

it tells us about the political opposition in 433/2 not only in the assembly but also on the board of generals. More revealing still is Perikles' less-than-Olympian reaction, which may measure accurately his perception of the political forces that were beginning to mass against him. In any case, all three of the generals who to our knowledge were most likely to oppose Perikles politically—Drakontides, Glaukon, and Lakedaimonios—found themselves campaigning in Korkyraian waters within the first prytany of the year, and that is probably not coincidence.

The foregoing discussion has sought to reveal something of the political climate in the year that saw the final abandonment of the Propylaia project. Our sources are unanimous that Perikles was able to command the unswerving loyalty of the demos in support of his conduct of foreign affairs.[218] But ancient authors, for the most part, were not concerned to record the internal rivalries and animosities that so proliferate in the political arena, and these can only be inferred from the bare skeleton of available facts. It is evident, however, that Perikles, like all politicians, had enemies among the demos, some of whom had sufficient following to elect them to the board of generals and sufficient hostility to attack the statesman personally. In this context, it will not be wholly fanciful to suppose that such men sought out areas of Periklean policy that might succumb to frontal assault, and to such efforts the Propylaia were eminently vulnerable. In 433/2 the gatehouse proper and its western wings were nearing completion, while construction of the eastern halls had scarcely begun. The building's extravagant scale and the costs of funding it were probably the source of continuing debates in the assembly, which had already imposed architectural changes on the builders. More-over, the decree of Kallias had sought to curtail the open-ended expenditure of sacred funds for the further embellishment of the Acropolis and had set strict limits on future construction.

One other event of ominous portent may have presaged the demise of the Propylaia, and that was the likely return to Athens of Thoukydides son of Melesias of Alopeke, whose ten-year term of ostracism had expired in the spring of 433. No ancient source verifies his arrival in the city at that time, and his activity is not attested before the 420s; but there is no likelihood that he would remain in exile beyond the appointed time.[219] To be sure that he was no friend of the Periklean buildings, we have only to recall the forensic fireworks with which, according to Plutarch, Thoukydides and his associates had assaulted the Parthenon throughout its construction. It was, after all, his opposition to the building program that had been in large measure the cause of his ostracism.[220] So upon his return, there is a strong presumption that the embittered exile would not have greeted with equa-nimity the great new gatehouse of the Acropolis which had sprung up so rapidly in his absence. We shall have no doubt on which side he would align himself in any debate about whether construc-tion of the Propylaia should be completed as planned or summarily abandoned. More influential were Perikles' enemies on the board of generals, who, we may perhaps suppose, had likewise become opponents of the Propylaia and found in that enterprise a place where Periklean policy was most vulnerable to attack. The catalyst for action was probably the revolt of Poteidaia in the spring of 432, which occurred not long before the end of the official year at Athens.[221] Now, with war plainly

---

[218] Cf. Thuc. 2.65.4; Plut. *Per.* 15.1, 16.1–2, quoting Teleklewides, Kassel-Austin, *PCG* VII, fr. 45.

[219] The only reference to Thoukydides' presence in Athens after his term of ostracism is a prosecution brought against him by a certain Euathlos, in which the old man seems to have been treated unfairly: Aristoph. *Acharn.* 685–718 and schol. 703c–d (Wilson); *Wasps* 947–949 and schol. 947b (Koster). See Kagan, *OPW,* 238, 242–243; Podlecki, *Perikles,* 88. Others have attributed to Thoukydides a much more active role after his return by dating the prosecutions of Pheidias and Perikles' friends to 433/2: Wade-Gery, *EGH,* 258–260; O. Lendle, *Hermes* 83 (1955) 284–303; D. Kienast, *Gymnasium* 60 (1953) 210–229.

[220] Plut. *Per.* 12.1–2, 14.

[221] The revolt was synchronous with the arrival of the Athenian forces under Archestratos: Thuc. 1.59.1. Adcock, in *CAH*[1] V, 185, dated it to "the end of June or the beginning of July." About June 1, 432, according to W. E. Thompson, *Hermes* 96 (1968) 216–232; de Ste. Croix, *OPW,* 319, whereas the "prytany year" at Athens probably began as a rule soon after the summer solstice, de Ste. Croix, 318.

in the wind, the opponents of the building program could move with assurance. A bill was surely brought before the demos that ordered the epistatai to terminate construction and close their books. In light of the decree of Kallias a year earlier, supporters of such legislation could now argue that a vote against the Propylaia, no matter how spiteful its motivation, was a vote for fiscal prudence and sensible preparedness for war. We need not ask how the demos voted; the answer is plain to see, for even to this day the silent ruins eloquently proclaim to all their unfinished state.

In the rhetoric of the controversy, construction of the Propylaia became linked with the campaign at Poteidaia, two examples that showed how the Periklean regime had squandered as much money on public buildings as on the defense of the empire. The comparison was doubtless a slogan of the day, for even Thucydides named the two as a pair, which, together with the other buildings, had consumed 3,700 talents of the reserve fund.[222] In another passage he records that the Athenians had spent 2,000 talents on the siege at Poteidaia alone by the time that city was on the point of surrender.[223] Writing in the fourth century, Ephoros paraphrased Thucydides and again linked Poteidaia to the Propylaia, but he neglected to mention the other buildings and increased the total expenditure to 4,000 talents.[224] Isokrates chastised the imperialists of the fifth century for spending 2,400 talents on the siege at Poteidaia, while the Propylaia was the target of Demetrios of Phaleron, who excoriated Perikles for wasting vast sums on its construction.[225] Those sums, according to Heliodoros, came to 2,000 talents, a figure which enormously inflates the actual cost of the building.[226] The sober Cicero cites the wisdom of Demetrios with regard to public works and recommends construction of "walls, docks, harbors, and aqueducts" as worthier investments of public money.[227] But all acknowledged the building's glorious architecture that gave it far-flung fame, a notoriety beyond the Parthenon itself. Athenian orators of the fourth century exhorted their listeners to gaze upon the Propylaia in order to understand the achievements of their ancestors, and they named the building first among the works of Perikles as the perfect exemplar of the greater Athens of a bygone age.[228] When in the fourth century Thebes surpassed Athens as the leading power of Greece, the Boiotian general Epameinandos boasted to his fellow citizens that they should remove the Propylaia from the Acropolis of Athens to the Kadmeia of Thebes.[229] Thus had the gatehouse of Athena's shrine become the iconic image of imperial Athens, and, more than that, the symbol of political hegemony in the Greek world.

---

[222] Thuc. 2.13.3.

[223] Thuc. 2.70.2.

[224] Ephoros, *FGrH* 70 F 196, quoted by Diod. 12.40.2.

[225] Isokr. 15 *Antid.* 113. Demetrios of Phaleron, *FGrH* 228 F 8, cited by Cicero, *Off.* 2.60.

[226] Heliodoros, *FGrH* 373 F 1, quoted by Harpokr., *Suda*, s.v. προπύλαια ταῦτα (π 101 Keaney; π 2579 Adler). Heliodoros probably read in Ephoros that "4,000 talents had been expended on the construction of the Propylaia and the siege of Poteidaia" (Diod. 12.40.2), and he read in Thucydides (2.70.2) that the siege of Poteidaia cost 2,000 talents. Subtracting one sum from the other, he reckoned that 2,000 talents were spent on the Propylaia. For a different explanation of the arithmetic, see *ATL* III, 124 and notes 15, 16; but Heliodoros's source can hardly have been documentary.

[227] Cicero, *Off.* 2.60.

[228] Demosth. 22 *Androt.* 13, 76; 23 *Aristokr.* 207; [Demosth.] 13 *Organization* 28; Aischin. 2 *Embassy* 74; Lykourg. fr. 58, IX. 2 (Conomis).

[229] Aischin. 2 *Embassy* 105.

10

Two Ionic Temples

During the decade of the 430s, while the pediments of the Parthenon were nearing completion and the Propylaia arose at the west end of the Acropolis, Athenian builders turned their attention to two other temples, both of which specifically commemorated Athenian military victories and bore out the overarching theme of the building program. Both temples share the Ionic order and, as we shall see, were closely related to each other in their architectural details. Both buildings have been subjected to long and continuing scholarly debate with respect to their histories, chronologies, and most especially the interpretation of their sculptural programs. We shall consider first the temple on the Ilissos River. Even the deity to whom it belonged has been disputed since the eighteenth century, and its sculptural decoration has been reduced to a few battered slabs. The temple's architecture is known only from drawings made by the British architects James Stuart and Nicholas Revett and published in *The Antiquities of Athens* (1762). But the building has been described as "almost a twin of the Temple of Athena Nike"[1] on the Acropolis and so brings us to the second Ionic temple of this chapter, one of the best-preserved and most familiar monuments of classical Athens. Examination of the two Ionic temples side by side is instructive because the juxtaposition will bring out not only the extraordinary similarities of their architecture but also the close chronological relationship of the two designs.

The Temple on the Ilissos River

We begin in the suburbs of the city, in the district called Agrai, situated among the low hills along the southeastern banks of the Ilissos River just outside the city walls of the Classical period. The lovely spot was immortalized by Plato as the dramatic setting of the *Phaidros*. Here his characters waded in the cool waters of the brook, reclined on the verdant lawn shaded by plane trees and flowering willows, and listened to the summer chorus of the cicadas, as they beguiled the heat of the day with conversation.[2] So vividly does Plato paint the scene that for students of Greek literature the great plane tree still seems to tower above the pure spring waters, undefiled by the traffic-choked boulevards of modern Athens, beneath which the river itself long ago disappeared. In antiquity the district comprised the small suburban villages of Diomeia and Lower Agryle, and it extended from the Ardettos Hill, above the site of the later Panathenaic Stadium, down to the Ilissos crossing and

---

[1] Miles, *Hesperia* 49 (1980) 309.

[2] Plato, *Phaidros* 229A–C, 230B–C (setting of the scene: waters of the Ilissos, grass shaded by plane trees and flowering willows), 242A (the noonday heat), 258E–259A, 262D (chirping of the cicadas, called "prophets of the muses"), 229A, 230A–B (the great plane tree). See Wycherley, *Phoenix* 17 (1963) 88–98.

the nearby gymnasium of Kynosarges, a distance, as Plato tells us, of two or three stadia.[3] Along both banks of the river, the number of sacred places had proliferated. These varied greatly in importance, from the rustic shrine of Pan, Acheloos, and the Nymphs, from simple altars to Boreas and to the Ilissian Muses to the sanctuaries of principal deities like Artemis Agrotera or the Metroon in Agrai, both of which celebrated major festivals in the annual religious calendar.[4]

High on the hill slope just east of the river crossing, there stood until the latter part of the eighteenth century a small marble temple of the Ionic order. This building was the subject of detailed study and measurement by Stuart and Revett during their visit to Athens between 1751 and 1753. To their exquisite drawings of the temple we owe almost everything we know about the building today. The entire superstructure of the temple was dismantled about 1780, apparently on the order of the Turkish authorities, and has subsequently disappeared almost without trace. Four slabs of the building's sculptural frieze found their way to Berlin and Vienna, two more were recovered in the Greek excavations of the area at the end of the nineteenth century, and a few architectural fragments have been dubiously attributed from time to time.[5] But for the student of classical architecture, the information recorded by Stuart and Revett is indispensable.[6] Their drawings reveal a temple of diminutive size and most unusual plan, but there is a jewel-like quality to its architectural details that sets the building at once beside the supreme examples of Athenian architecture. Regardless of how one estimates its date of construction—and we shall return to this controversial subject in due course—the temple on the Ilissos must have been among the earliest Athenian buildings to employ the Ionic order externally. Its facade consisted of four Ionic columns arranged in prostyle plan, and the front porch was exactly duplicated on the rear facade of the building, thus creating the unusual amphiprostyle arrangement that was always extremely rare in temple architecture (Fig. 106). Moreover, the scale of the building was exceptionally small for a Greek temple, the overall dimensions being 5.849 × 12.686 m on the stylobate.[7]

Just as unusual as the amphiprostyle plan was the design of the cella between the two columnar porches, for the interior consisted of one almost exactly square compartment (4.682 m in length by

[3] Paus. 1.19.6: διαβᾶσι δὲ τὸν Ἰλισὸν χωρίον Ἄγραι καλούμενον καὶ ναὸς Ἀγροτέρας ἐστὶν Ἀρτέμιδος, "Across the Ilissos is a district called Agrai and a Temple of Artemis Agrotera." Strabo 9.1.24 (p. 400): ὁ Ἰλισσός, ἐκ θατέρου μέρους τοῦ ἄστεος ῥέων εἰς τὴν αὐτὴν παραλίαν, ἐκ τῶν ὑπὲρ τῆς Ἄγρας καὶ τοῦ Λυκείου μερῶν, καὶ τῆς πηγῆς, ἣν ὕμνηκεν ἐν Φαίδρῳ Πλάτων, "The Ilissos, flowing from the other part of the city to the same coast, from the district of Agrai and the Lykeion, and from the spring which Plato praised in the Phaidros." Kleidemos, FGrH 323 F 1: Ἄγραι· χωρίον ἔξω τῆς πόλεως Ἀθηνῶν, οὗ τὰ μικρὰ τῆς Δήμετρος ἄγεται μυστήρια, ἃ λέγεται τὰ ἐν Ἄγρας . . . καὶ Ἀρτέμιδος τῆς Ἀγραίας αὐτόθι τὸ ἱερόν, "Agrai: a place outside the city of Athens where the Lesser Mysteries of Demeter are performed, that are called in Agrai . . . and there also is the Temple of Artemis Agraia." Harpokr., s.v. Ἀρδηττός (α 229 Keaney): τόπος Ἀθήνησιν ὑπὲρ τὸ στάδιον τὸ Παναθηναϊκόν, πρὸς τῷ δήμῳ τῷ ὑπένερθεν Ἀγρυλέων, "Ardettos: a place at Athens above the Panathenaic stadium, near the deme of Lower Agryle." Stephanus of Byzantium, s.v. Κυνόσαργες (pp. 393–394 Meineke): γυμνάσιον ἐν τῇ Ἀττικῇ καὶ δῆμος, ἀπὸ Διόμου, ἀφ᾽ οὗ ὁ χῶρος Ἀθήνησι Διόμεια καλεῖται, "Kynosarges: a gymnasium in Attica and a deme, from Diomos, from whom the district at Athens is called Diomeia." For the gymnasium, Travlos, AAA 3 (1970) 6–14. Distance downstream to the Ilissos crossing, Plato, Phaidros 229C.

[4] Pan, Acheloos, and the Nymphs, Plato, Phaidros 230B; altar of Boreas, Phaidros 229C; the Ilissian Muses, Paus. 1.19.5. For Artemis Agrotera and the Metroon in Agrai, see note 3 above. See Travlos, PDA, 289–291 and especially the plan, fig. 379.

[5] For modern history of the site and remains, C. A. Picón, AJA 82 (1978) 47–51.

[6] J. Stuart and N. Revett, The Antiquities of Athens, vol. 1 (London 1762) chap. 2, 7–11, pls. I–VIII. For modern bibliography on the temple: A. N. Skias, Prakt (1897) 73–85; F. Studniczka, JdI 31 (1916) 169–230; Judeich, Topographie², 416, 420–421; H. Möbius, AM 60–61 (1935–36) 234–268; Dinsmoor, AAG³, 185–187; A. Rumpf and A. Mallwitz, AM 76 (1961) 15–20; I. M. Shear, Hesperia 32 (1963) 388–399; Travlos, PDA, 112–120; Picón, AJA 82 (1978) 47–81; A. Krug, AntP 18 (1979) 7–21; M. M. Miles, Hesperia 49 (1980) 309–325; Felten, Tektonische Friese, 70–79; W. A. P. Childs, AM 100 (1985) 207–251; M. Krumme, AA (1993) 213–227; Gruben, Gr. Tempel⁵, 205–208; Palagia, in Barringer and Hurwit, eds., Periklean Athens, 177–192; Camp, Archaeology of Athens, 105–106.

[7] All metric dimensions are converted from the dimensions in feet and inches on the drawings of Stuart and Revett, with the equations 1 ft. = 0.3048 m and 1 in. = 0.0254 m, as Dinsmoor, AAG³, 339.

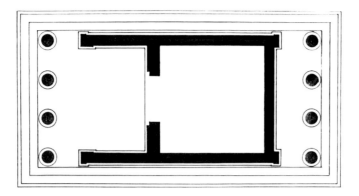

Figure 106. Temple on the Ilissos River, restored plan

4.680 m in width) approached by way of a deep pronaos that measured more than half the length of the cella from the face of the antae to the doorway (2.977 m). The great depth of the pronaos caused the architect to omit an answering opisthodomos behind the rear porch, and there was no access to the building from this direction, so that the western colonnade was purely decorative, like that of the Nike temple. When Stuart and Revett studied the remains, the temple had long since been converted into a Christian church, with the result that the eastern facade had been rebuilt to form the obligatory apse.[8] As a part of this process, the two central Ionic columns of the east facade had been removed, but the British architects were able to determine their exact position because the circular incisions remained on the original stylobate to guide the setting of their bases, and these agreed precisely in diameter with the bases of the surviving corner columns. It is therefore surprising that they apparently found no such traces a few feet away on the same pavement, between the antae of the pronaos. Nevertheless, scholars have sought to fill out this lacuna in the plans: some have restored the pronaos distyle in antis in the normal way; others have suggested the restoration of rectangular piers on the analogy of the Nike temple.[9] But there is no real evidence to make one solution less speculative than the other.

In its treatment of the Ionic order, the Ilissos temple exhibits striking differences from the Ionic Temple of Athena Sounias, and a glance at the facade reveals at once that the forms and details of the columns are more closely related to those developed on the Athenian Acropolis (Fig. 107). Despite the pleasing harmony of the tetrastyle facade, the architect actually employed unusually stout proportions for the Ionic columns. The overall height of the columns was 4.478 m, or 8.254 times the lower diameter of 0.543 m, whereas the same proportion at Sounion was 10.35 lower diameters. This proportion of the columns finds its closest parallel in the Temple of Athena Nike, where the slightly shorter columns (4.049 m) were 7.82 lower diameters in height (Fig. 108). Another curious feature was the spacing of the Ionic columns, which normal practice would have made uniform. Here, however, the axial intercolumniation at the center was slightly reduced from those at the sides, a detail unique in Ionic design before the north porch of the Erechtheion later in the century.[10]

---

[8] The 1762 edition of Stuart and Revett (p. 7) records the name of the church as Panagia sten Petra (the Virgin on the Rock), which at the time of their visit was totally deserted, having "also gone to decay." The 1825 edition adds the information (pp. 29–30, note 3) that the church had been deconsecrated in 1674 after a Roman Catholic mass had been celebrated in it for the Marquis de Nointel; see chap. 2, pl. I. Cf. Picón, *AJA* 82 (1978) 48; I. M. Shear, *Hesperia* 32 (1963) 391, note 115.

[9] Stuart and Revett (1762 edition), 9, for the incised circles on the stylobate. The pronaos is restored with columns as distyle in antis by Judeich, *Topographie*[2], 420; Dinsmoor, *AAG*[3], 185; Gruben, *Gr. Tempel*[5], 202, fig. 155; A. A. Barrett and M. Vickers, *BSA* 70 (1975) 11–16. It is restored with two rectangular piers like the Nike temple by Travlos, *PDA*, 116, fig. 156; Giraud, Μελέτη Αθηνάς Νίκης, pl. 6; Delivorrias, *AntP* 9 (1969) 11.

[10] Proportions of the columns: I. M. Shear, *Hesperia* 32 (1963) 392; axial spacing, 391.

Figure 107. East elevation of temple on the Ilissos River, restored by Stuart and Revett

We have seen in an earlier chapter that the Ionic order used architecturally was probably first introduced on the Periklean Acropolis in the western chamber of the Parthenon. Although no fragment
of those interior columns has chanced to survive, they may well have exerted considerable influence
on the designs adopted by Mnesikles for the interior columns of the Propylaia. These latter, at any
rate, which must have been erected by the mid-430s, are the first closely dated examples of the developed Attic type, and for that reason it is instructive to compare them with the columns of the Ilissos
temple on the one hand (Fig. 108) and with those of the Nike temple on the other (Fig. 114). What
emerges from the comparison is the close interrelationship of the three orders, and how radically they
differ from the nearly contemporary temple at Sounion (see Fig. 73). The three Athenian buildings
exhibit the fully developed form of the Attic Ionic base, composed of a concave scotia between two
half-round tori, of which the upper one is horizontally fluted. The three elements of the base are not
quite equal in height, the lower torus being slightly greater than the other two in the Propylaia, and
slightly less in the Ilissos temple. On both bases three horizontal channels serve to articulate the convex surface of the upper torus. Beside these two examples, the Ionic base of the Nike temple seems
slightly more developed. Although its height corresponds precisely to the Ilissos base, the lower torus
has been reduced by nearly half and the other members increased accordingly, while the upper torus
carries four horizontal flutes, like the later bases on the east porch of the Erectheion.[11]

Among extant Athenian Ionic capitals, those of the Propylaia are clearly more developed than
the interior columns made for the Stoa Poikile in the Agora about 460. The capitals from the two
buildings share the wide-spaced spiral of the volutes and the ovolo molding of the echinus, but the
latter is richly carved with the egg-and-dart pattern that occurs on the Propylaia capitals, while the
echinus in the stoa had the details of the pattern added in paint, like the capitals from Sounion and
other Athenian examples.[12] Closely similar, however, are the carved corner palmettes: both have flat

[11] Ilissos temple, Ionic base: 0.0813 m (lower torus), 0.0914 m (scotia), 0.0927 m (upper torus), 0.271 m (overall
height). Athena Nike temple, Ionic base: 0.048 m (lower torus), 0.113 m (scotia), 0.111 m (upper torus), 0.272 m (overall
height). Cf. I. M. Shear, *Hesperia* 32 (1963) note 127.
[12] For the Ionic capitals from the Stoa Poikile, Agora inv. A 4662: Shear, Jr., *Hesperia* 53 (1984) 9–12, fig. 6, pl.
3:d. Another fragment from the same series, Agora inv. A 661: L. S. Meritt, *Hesperia* 65 (1996) 147, 150, no. 7. Among

Figure 108. Detail of Ionic order, restored by Stuart and Revett

petals with rounded tips, six in number on the Propylaia capital and four in the Stoa Poikile. On both capitals, the petals of the palmettes barely touch the upper edge of the echinus and are treated as separate and distinct parts of the order. Comparison of the Propylaia capitals with those from the Ilissos temple reveals that temple's further development in the richness of the carved detail. The egg-and-dart of the echinus has more rounded forms and is more deeply carved. The corner palmettes are more naturalistic, each petal now being articulated with a central spine; and though their tips are still rounded, they turn upward ever so slightly in clear anticipation of the "flame" palmettes later in the century. What is more, on the Ilissos capitals the corner palmettes have begun to encroach on the carved ovolo of the echinus, so that the clean horizontal line that separated the echinus from the volutes on the Propylaia capitals has now been broken.[13]

The plain exterior walls of the Ilissos temple were enriched with decorative moldings (Fig. 109). The profile of the Ionic column base, with its lower torus somewhat reduced in height, was repeated in the anta base and in the toichobate along the foot of the side walls. Particularly innovative was the molded anta capital of the Ilissos temple, which consisted of an ovolo, cyma reversa, and cavetto, separated by astragals and crowned by a smaller ovolo. The capital terminates at the bottom in a small projecting fillet below the Ionic moldings. This rich complex of moldings was used as an anta capital on only two other Athenian buildings, the Temple of Athena Nike and the Erechtheion.[14]

Athenian examples the most striking variants are Meritt's Type II, painted details with fascia over ovolo echinus: Meritt (above), 154–158, nos. 14A, 14B.

[13] Detailed drawing of the palmettes of the Ilissos capitals, Stuart and Revett (1762 edition), chap. 2, pl. VII, fig. 5. Comparison of the Propylaia capitals with those of the Ilissos and Nike temples: I. M. Shear, *Hesperia* 32 (1963) 380–383, 393–394; Miles, *Hesperia* 49 (1980) 318–320.

[14] I. M. Shear, *Hesperia* 32 (1963) 394–395, pls. 89:a, 90:b.

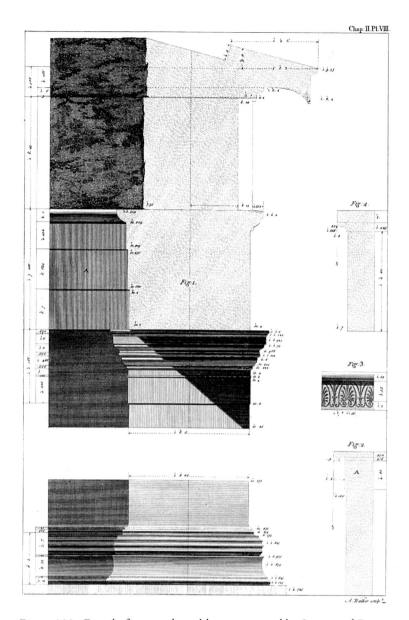

Figure 109. Detail of anta and entablature, restored by Stuart and Revett

A few other decorative anomalies of the Ilissos temple need to be mentioned because some of these have been adduced as evidence in the arguments concerning the temple's date. The exterior entablature differed from the canonical treatment of the Ionic order in that the epistyle was left plain, without the normal three fascias, and its crowning molding consisted of an ovolo with base astragal and a fascia above.[15] Above the epistyle, a sculptured frieze probably extended around all four sides of the temple. Six of its slabs survive today, all of which are reported to be made of Parian marble, but none were seen in place on the building at the time of Stuart and Revett. In the interior of the Ilissos temple the architect designed the decoration of the course corresponding to the epistyle in three distinctive ways. Behind the front columns of the east facade, he used the canonical triple fascias crowned by a simple ovolo. In the same position behind the western columns, the face of the epistyle was plain, and its crowning molding consisted of a cyma reversa surmounted by a fascia. Most interesting of all was his treatment of the corresponding course around the inside of the

[15] Stuart and Revett (1762 edition), chap. 2, pl. VI.

pronaos. The face of the blocks was divided into two fascias of unequal height crowned by a Doric hawksbeak: that most characteristic element in the decorative vocabulary of the Doric order here made a unique appearance in an Ionic building. The fascia beneath the hawksbeak carried a painted anthemion pattern of lotus blossoms alternating with palmettes, surrounded by tendrils that began as antithetical spirals under the palmettes. As recorded by Stuart and Revett, the petals of the palmettes have rounded tips, but, like those of the Ionic capitals, they turn slightly outward as if they were the immediate predecessors of true "flame" palmettes.[16]

All that survives today of the Ilissos temple are four complete slabs of the sculptured frieze and parts of two others. As early as 1910 the sculptures were attributed to the little temple recorded by Stuart and Revett, and their identification has never been questioned.[17] But interpretation of the scenes depicted in the reliefs and attempts to establish their date have provided students of classical sculpture with a most intractable problem. After nearly a century of discussion there is still wide disagreement. Two of the frieze blocks show three draped male figures spaced wide apart. On slab B two men are seated on high rocky outcrops while another stands at ease to the left; the left figure of slab C is also perched on a rocky seat, and the others stand apart to the right. The other two scenes depict violent action in which men are in the act of assaulting women and children with obvious intent to abduct them. In the center of slab D, a draped woman flees in terror from her lunging attacker, while at left another woman is lifted bodily from the ground as a small girl stands watching at the far right. On slab E, a male assailant at left flings his arms around a seated woman, and the pair is balanced at the right by a kneeling woman who clutches a column or altar in hopes of warding off her attacker's grasp. In the center of the scene, another kneeling woman is dragged resisting to her feet by a man who carries a child on his shoulder and pulls violently on her arm and probably also her hair. On one side of the corner slab F, a female figure flees to the left and another at right sits on a high rocky outcrop, while on the adjacent face of the block two armed hoplites run to the right. The better-preserved figure on the left carries a round shield and wears a crested helmet.

Faced with such fragmentary evidence, scholars have understandably advanced wide-ranging suggestions to identify the subject matter of the frieze. In slabs A–C, some have identified a scene of heroes in the underworld similar to Polygnotos's painting of the Nekyia at Delphi.[18] Others have favored an Eleusinian scene depicting the initiation of Herakles into the Mysteries.[19] Alternatively, the same figures have been interpreted as Odysseus's encounter with Aiolos from the Odyssey[20] or a local myth in which the Athenians obtained possession of the Trojan Palladion from the Argives returning from the Trojan War.[21] The violent assaults on women and children shown on slabs D–F have spawned equally divergent opinions. That this section of the frieze showed the capture of Troy

[16] Stuart and Revett (1762 edition), pl. V, shows the interior treatment of the epistyle in all three positions; pl. VIII, fig. 1, detail of architrave of east colonnade; fig. 4, detail of epistyle of west colonnade; fig. 2, detail of architrave of pronaos; fig. 3, detail of painted anthemion.

[17] The preserved pieces of the frieze are as follows: (A) Fragmentary slab, Athens, NM 1780. (B) Complete slab, Berlin, Staatliche Museen inv. Sk 1483-b. (C-1 + C-2) Joining pieces form complete slab: C-1, Vienna, Kunsthistorisches Museum inv. 1094; C-2, Berlin, Staatliche Museen inv. 1483-c. (D) Complete slab, Berlin, Staatliche Museen inv. Sk 1483-a. (E) Complete slab, Vienna, Kunsthistorisches Museum inv. 1093. (F) Partial slab carved on two adjacent faces, Athens, NM 3941. For recent detailed catalogue and description: Picón, *AJA* 82 (1978) 51–67; Krug, *AntP* 18 (1979) 7–21; Felten, *Tektonische Friese*, 70–79; M. Krumme, *AA* (1993) 213–227; Beschi, *RivIstArch* 57 (2002) 7–36; Palagia, in Barringer and Hurwit, eds., *Periklean Athens*, 177–184. The frieze slabs were attributed to the temple as early as 1910 by F. Studniczka, *Leipziger Winckelmannsblatt* (1910), and fully published by Studniczka in *JdI* 31 (1916) 169–230. Cf. H. Möbius, *AM* 60–61 (1935–36) 234–268. There is no need for more than a brief summary of the sculptures here.

[18] Bruckner, *ÖJh* 13 (1910) 50–62; Studniczka, *JdI* 31 (1916) 170–197; Palagia, in Barringer and Hurwit, eds., *Periklean Athens*, 181, 184.

[19] Möbius, *AM* 60–61 (1935–36) 243–253.

[20] Felten, *Tektonische Friese*, 78.

[21] Krumme, *AA* (1993) 221–227.

has often been suggested.[22] An earlier notion that the myth depicted was the rape of the daughters of Leukippos by the Dioskouroi has recently been revived,[23] while others have preferred a more recondite interpretation in which the attackers are exiled Pelasgians in the act of abducting Athenian women from the sanctuary at Brauron to the island of Lemnos.[24] Despite these many theories, the sculptures of the Ilissos temple have repeatedly resisted attempts to explain their subject matter, with the result that no consensus has emerged concerning the correct identification of the myths represented.[25] There is thus the unfortunate corollary that the subject of the frieze offers no assistance whatever to those who would name the deity whose temple it adorned. Only on the basis of other evidence can one propose to identify the deity of the little Ionic temple.

Appreciation of the sculptural style, however, has weighed heavily in efforts to date the frieze and the temple itself, despite the fact that all the preserved pieces are heavily weathered and much of the surface detail has been worn away. Nevertheless, the perceived stylistic date of the sculptures combined with the obviously close architectural relationship between the Ilissos temple and its "twin" on the Acropolis to suggest an interesting sequence of events. Franz Studniczka, who originally assigned the frieze blocks to the temple, was the first to propose this reconstruction, and his hypothesis has until recently won wide acceptance.[26] According to this view, the Temple of Athena Nike was commissioned about 450 by order of the decree of Glaukos,[27] and the architect Kallikrates set to work at once preparing the plans and specifications. But at that time actual construction of the temple was postponed indefinitely, whereupon Kallikrates' unusual plans could be pressed into service for the temple on the Ilissos, which got under way between 450 and 448 and was completed shortly thereafter. When the project for the Nike temple was finally undertaken many years later, its original plans had to be altered somewhat to harmonize with the southwest wing of the Propylaia, which had arisen on the site in the meantime, and a few architectural details were given a more "modern" styling. In our earlier discussion of the decrees concerning Athena Nike, we saw that this hypothetical reconstruction of events received further embroidery at the hands of scholars who sought to explain the postponement of the Nike temple by conjuring up exciting confrontations between national political leaders, or else between competing architects and recalcitrant priests. But all these scenes were extrapolated from the chronological gap between the commissioning of the temple and the construction of the building, and accordingly many students of the problem were content to espouse the temple on the Ilissos as a part of the explanation to help fill the gap.

Comparison of the two Ionic temples reveals, as we shall see presently, their remarkable similarities not only in plan, elevation, and the design of the orders, but also in the proportions of the parts, the profiles of the moldings, and the dimensions of the architectural details. Indeed, the more rigorously they have been subjected to scrutiny by architectural historians, the closer their relationship seems to have grown. In this connection, it is especially interesting to observe that the earliest investigators of the Temple of Athena Nike regarded the Ilissos temple as a contemporary copy of the Acropolis building.[28] Other early students of the Ionic order, as yet undistracted by the style of

[22] Felten, *Tektonische Friese*, 76–77; Palagia, in Barringer and Hurwit, eds., *Periklean Athens*, 183–184.

[23] Proposed by R. von Schneider, *JdI* 18 (1903) 91–93; and revived by K.-V. von Eickstedt, in Coulson et al., eds., *Archaeology of Athens under the Democracy*, 105–111.

[24] Recently Beschi, *RivIstArch* 57 (2002) 23–26; cf. earlier discussion: Studniczka, *JdI* 31 (1916) 191–197; Möbius, *AM* 60–61 (1935–36) 241–242.

[25] For further summary of the conjectures and different scholars' approaches to the iconography: Picón, *AJA* 82 (1978) 61–67; Palagia, in Barringer and Hurwit, eds., *Periklean Athens*, 177–184.

[26] Studniczka, *JdI* 31 (1916) 198–202, 229–230, whose basic hypothesis was followed by, e.g., Dinsmoor, *AAG³*, 185; I. M. Shear, *Hesperia* 32 (1963) 397–398; Travlos, *PDA*, 112–113; E. Pemberton, *AJA* 76 (1972) 307–310; Giraud, Μελέτη Ἀθηνᾶς Νίκης, 40 and pl. 6.

[27] *IG* I³ 35; see chap. 2, pp. 27–35 above, for the text and full discussion.

[28] L. Ross, E. Schaubert, and C. Hansen, *Die Akropolis von Athen nach den neuesten Ausgrabungen*, pt. 1, *Der Tempel der Nike Apteros* (Berlin 1839) 10–11.

the sculptures, placed the Ilissos temple chronologically together with the Propylaia and the Nike temple on the basis of the design of the three Ionic capitals.[29] But dating the sculptural frieze ca. 449–445 necessarily postulates a period of nearly a quarter century between the construction, if not the design, of the two buildings. Moreover, that same quarter century witnessed extraordinary creative ferment in the design of Athenian buildings. In the hands of the Periklean architects, the Doric temple underwent revolutionary developments that affected the plans, proportions, refinements, and decorations of the buildings. No comparable period in the history of Greek architecture produced such variations on the Doric order as we see in the Parthenon and Propylaia, the Temples of Hephaistos and Poseidon, and others elsewhere in Attica. Contemporary treatments of the Ionic order conform even less to a standard type. No doubt this is partly because the Ionic order was not native to Attic soil, and there are fewer examples of its use. Recent studies of the order, however, have emphasized the variety and freewheeling experiment in the design of the Ionic capitals; and in this the Ilissos and Nike temples differ markedly from the capitals of Athena Sounias and those from an unknown building found in the Agora. But all are probably to be dated in the third quarter of the fifth century.[30] Against this background, it is impossible to believe that design of our "twin" temples was separated by twenty-five years, or that the Temple of Athena Nike was built from plans that were nearly a generation out of date. It is true that expert students of Greek sculpture have recently brought to bear all the subtleties of stylistic analysis upon the reliefs from the Ilissos temple; but the same comparative methods, applied with scrupulous care by different practitioners, have yielded estimates of date that range from the early 440s to the mid-430s to the mid-420s.[31] Confronted by such divergence of opinion on the part of those most qualified to judge, one concludes sadly that the date is in the eye of the beholder.

The site of the temple studied by Stuart and Revett was identified archaeologically in 1897 and is located, in terms of the modern city, at the northeast corner of Ardettos Boulevard and D. Koutoula Street. A. N. Skias cleared the rectangular outline of the foundations (7.80 × 14.60 m) that consisted mostly of beddings cut in the natural surface of the rock from which the poros blocks themselves had been stripped. Only a few blocks of the lowest course remained in the line of the east colonnade, the pronaos, and the door wall.[32] Further exploration of the site was carried out by J. N. Travlos when the Ardettos Boulevard was under construction in 1962. This work greatly clarified our understanding of the ancient topography and contributed some new evidence bearing on the chronology of the temple. Travlos's excavations brought to light the remains of a retaining wall composed of massive poros blocks aligned precisely parallel to the flank of the temple and 8.20 m farther north.[33] The retaining wall plainly supported a high artificial terrace forming a broad esplanade around the temple that overlooked the riverbank and afforded a pleasant view of the valley. At the time of its construction, the builders dumped in behind the retaining wall a deep fill of earth mixed with large quantities of both poros and marble working chips, the masons' refuse from dressing the

[29] O. Puchstein, *Das ionische Capitell* (Berlin 1887) 14–19; W. R. Lethaby, *Greek Buildings Represented by Fragments in the British Museum* (London 1908) 154–157.

[30] For variations in the design of Ionic capitals, L. S. Meritt, *Hesperia* 65 (1996) 125–141. The columns from an unknown building found in the Agora are her Type II, 154–158, nos. 14A, 14B, 14C.

[31] The date between 449 and 445, originally proposed by Studniczka, *JdI* 31 (1916) 169–230, has been somewhat lowered by Childs, *AM* 100 (1985) 210, 250–251, who argues for ca. 445–440. Felten, *Tektonische Friese*, 70–79, avoids detailed discussion of the date but seems to prefer the 440s (see p. 154, note 194). Dates between ca. 440 and 430 have been proposed by Möbius, *AM* 53 (1928) 5; Delivorrias, *AntP* 9 (1969) 10. Miles, *Hesperia* 49 (1980) 325, suggests ca. 435–430 after consideration of both the sculpture and the architecture. Dates between ca. 430 and 420 have been argued by T. Dohrn, *Attische Plastik* (Krefeld 1957) 23; Picón, *AJA* 82 (1978) 72–81; Krug, *AntP* 18 (1979) 7–21; B. S. Ridgway, *Fifth Century Styles in Greek Sculpture* (Princeton 1981) 88–89. On the basis of his consideration of the architecture, a date in the 420s is also supported by Boersma, *Building Policy*, 75–76.

[32] Skias, *Prakt* (1897) 73–85; cf. the plan of the excavated remains, Travlos, *PDA*, 116, fig. 156.

[33] Travlos, *PDA*, 112–113, figs. 156 (the retaining wall is marked B), 157.

blocks of the temple. The pottery recovered from this filling was surely discarded by the builders and should provide a terminus post quem for construction of the temple. Unfortunately, the most numerous pieces were miniature votive cups of a kind frequently encountered in sanctuary deposits but not susceptible to close dating. More diagnostic were fragments of a fine black-gloss kantharos with stamped decoration, certainly manufactured in the decade of the 440s.[34] This piece precludes a date as high as 450 for construction of the temple, and by the time one allows for the vessel's use, breakage, and discard, the dispersal of its fragments probably occurred well into the third quarter of the century. Accordingly, a date in the 430s for design and construction of the Ilissos temple seems entirely compatible with the available evidence.

In the course of his investigations in the area of the ancient river, Travlos was able to identify the site of the Ilissos crossing, just above the springs of Kallirrhoe, and about 90 meters west of the rock knoll on which the Ionic temple once stood. Nearby was a gate in the city wall giving egress to traffic from southeastern Athens that would cross the river at this point into the district of Agrai on the south bank.[35] The actual site of the crossing lies at an elevation of roughly 65 meters above sea level, but the terrain slopes sharply upward to the east. The base of the retaining wall for the temple terrace had an elevation of 78 meters, and the excavator calculated the level of the terrace itself at 83 meters above sea level.[36] These topographical details of the temple's siting are pertinent because they undoubtedly motivated the most revolutionary feature of its architecture, the amphiprostyle plan, of which the temple on the Ilissos was apparently the first exemplar. The building was viewed first, most often, and to best advantage by pedestrians crossing the river, who approached the sanctuary from the rear and saw the chased details of its Ionic facade rising high above the valley on its artificial terrace. The temple's most prominent aspect was its northwestern corner, and for spectators from the river crossing the angle of view was almost exactly 45 degrees to the rear colonnade. The main entrance to the shrine was possibly from the westerly direction. Certainly to worshippers approaching in procession the little temple flashed from on high its deity's welcoming beacon in the glistening marble of its fabric. Centuries of worshippers responded to its dramatic siting, for in its final transfiguration as a Christian church the temple became the Παναγία στὴν Πέτρα, the Virgin on the Rock.[37]

Considered in the context of its original topographical setting, the temple on the Ilissos will be seen to bear even more remarkable resemblance to the Nike temple on the Acropolis. That familiar monument so dominates the western approach to the citadel because it looms high above the ascending visitor, who has eyes only for the Ionic columns of its rear facade. It is important to emphasize that the Ilissos temple would have affected the spectator in much the same way. In fact the change in elevation from the river crossing to the temple terrace closely approximates the vertical

[34] The pottery from the deposit is catalogued by Miles, *Hesperia* 49 (1980) 316–317, pl. 96. The kantharos with stamped decoration is no. 1. It was rightly observed by Childs, *AM* 100 (1985) 207, note 4, but needs to be emphasized, that none of the pottery supports a date for the temple as late as the 420s. None of the datable pieces is demonstrably later than ca. 440. The fragmentary kantharos published by Miles is not the same as that mentioned by B. A. Sparkes and L. Talcott, *Agora* XII, 116, note 22a, as suggested by Childs (above).

[35] The Ilissos crossing, Travlos, *PDA*, 112 and figs. 154 (the crossing is marked no. 156 on the plan), 155; cf. also 289. The city gate nearby is the Diomeian Gate (X), *PDA*, 160, and cf. the plans figs. 154 and 380. Mentioned by Alkiphron 1.13.3, 3.15.4; Hesych., s.v. Δημίαισι πύλαις (δ 837 Schmidt). It is probably the unnamed city gate near the Kynosarges Gymnasium, Diog. Laert. 6.13. Plut. *Mor.* 601B refers to the neighboring deme of Diomeia from which the gate took its name. This southeastern section of the Themistoklean wall of Athens was entirely demolished after the Roman conquest in 86 B.C., but the later Roman fortification wall, erected in the reign of Valerian, followed more or less the same line and had a gate in the same position, shown on the plan, *PDA*, 154.

[36] Judeich, *Topographie²*, plan I; on the city plan the 65 m contour line closely follows the south bank of the river and crosses at the springs of Kallirrhoe. On the north side the 65 m contour line returns downstream slightly farther from the riverbank, which here lies at approximately 60 m. The southeast corner of the foundation identified as the Temple of Kronos and Rhea (Travlos, *PDA*, fig. 154, no. 159), ca. 31 m north of the riverbank, had an elevation of 68.10 m (Travlos, *PDA*, fig. 440). Elevations at the Ilissos temple terrace shown, Travlos, *PDA*, fig. 156.

[37] Travlos, *ArchEph* (1953–54) B′, 313–314.

rise from the Beulé Gate to the Nike bastion.[38] Thus the analogous physical siting of the two temples helps to explain many of their similarities, but architectural details, such as the proportions of the columns and the greater length of the Ilissos temple, with its unusually deep pronaos, make it clear that neither building was built from plans designed for the other. Both temples were closely contemporary designs, possibly by the same master architect.[39] In his innovative hands, the Ionic order took on a specifically Athenian character, and the Ionic temple underwent revolutionary changes in scale and plan. The differences between the two temples merely reveal that architect's consummate ability to adjust his designs to the specific site on which each building stood.

Clarification of the topography on the south bank of the Ilissos now makes it possible to identify with more assurance the deity worshipped in the Ionic temple. Ancient writers refer to two important sanctuaries in the district of Agrai: Pausanias saw a temple of Artemis Agrotera near the Ilissos, while other sources mention a sanctuary of Demeter, called the Metroon in Agrai, where the Lesser Mysteries were celebrated in the winter of each year.[40] Already in the time of Stuart and Revett both possibilities were recognized and controversy concerning the identification had surfaced. Since that time both goddesses have had their energetic advocates, until the supporters of Demeter came generally to prevail during the first half of the twentieth century.[41] Important new evidence bearing on the identification of the two shrines came to light in Travlos's excavations along the riverbank. This consisted of a heavy foundation of poros blocks that fixed the northeast corner of a major building. The remains were discovered in the medieval course of the river itself at the level of its bed, and they lay as close to the south bank of the ancient watercourse as it was practical to build a large building. That structure stood at the bottom of the hill, 45 meters due north of the terrace wall for the Ionic temple.[42]

In the Classical period, then, two important buildings stood in close proximity to each other in this area of Agrai: one was high on the hillside, and the other on the riverbank at water level. The topographical distinction helps to interpret the literary references to the two sanctuaries more precisely. To be sure, the late lexicographical sources all define the district of Agrai simply as a sanctuary of Demeter, or a place where the Lesser Mysteries were celebrated, but the references are not specific enough to identify a particular site.[43] Little information is available concerning the content of the Lesser Mysteries, but we are told that part of the ritual included ablutions and purifications preliminary to initiation into the Great Mysteries.[44] These purification ceremonies are said to have been performed in the river,[45] and one author says that he "encamped beside the mystic banks of

[38] R. Bohn, *Die Propylaeen der Akropolis zu Athen* (Berlin and Stuttgart 1882) pl. XXI, measures elevations downward from the stylobate of the Parthenon (167.23 m above sea level at the northwest corner): ground level outside the Beulé Gate, – 33.030 m; top of the Nike bastion, – 4.545 m = 18.485 m vertical rise in a distance of ca. 28 m. Ilissos temple terrace, 83 m; river crossing, 65 m = 18 m vertical rise over a distance of ca. 90 m.

[39] As argued by I. M. Shear, *Hesperia* 32 (1963) 388–399.

[40] Paus. 1.19.6; Kleidemos, *FGrH* 323 F 1, quoted above, note 3.

[41] Stuart and Revett (1762 edition) 7 and note c. In favor of Artemis Agrotera: W. Dörpfeld, *AM* 22 (1897) 227–228; Studniczka, *JdI* 31 (1916) 196; Travlos, *PDA*, 112; Pemberton, *AJA* 76 (1972) 307; Camp, *Archaeology of Athens*, 105–106. In favor of Demeter: Möbius, *AM* 53 (1928) 4, and *AM* 60–61 (1935–36) 244–245; Judeich, *Topographie*[2], 416; Dinsmoor, *AAG*[3], 185 (Metroum in Agrai?); Mylonas, *Eleusis*, 220; Kerényi, *Eleusis*, 45–52; Delivorrias, *AntP* 9 (1969) 12–13. Felten, *Tektonische Friese*, 70–71, and Gruben, *Gr. Tempel*[5], 205–208, both mention both identifications but do not choose between them.

[42] Travlos, *PDA*, 112 and fig. 154 (the poros foundation is no. 152 on the plan).

[43] Hesych., s.v. Ἄγραι (α 746 Schmidt); Stephanus of Byzantium, s.v. Ἄγρα καὶ Ἄγραι (p. 20 Meinecke); *Suda*, s.v. Ἄγρα (α 399 Adler); Eustath. ad *Il.* 2.852 (361.36–39 Van der Valk); Bekker, *Anec. Gr.*, vol. 1, 334.11.

[44] Schol. Aristoph. *Plut.* 845f (Chantry): μυστήρια δύο τελεῖται τοῦ ἐνιαυτοῦ Δήμητρι καὶ Κόρῃ, τὰ μικρὰ καὶ τὰ μεγάλα· καὶ ἔστι τὰ μικρὰ ὥσπερ προκάθαρσις καὶ προάγνευσις τῶν μεγάλων, "Two mysteries are celebrated during the year for Demeter and Kore, the Lesser and the Great; and the Lesser serve as a preparatory cleansing and purification in advance for the Great Mysteries."

[45] Polyainos 5.17.1: ταῦτα μὲν δὴ συνέθεντο παρὰ τὸν Ἰλισσόν, οὗ τὸν καθαρμὸν τελοῦσι τοῖς ἐλάττοσι μυστηρίοις, "They made this agreement beside the Ilissos, where they perform the purification for the Lesser Mysteries."

the Ilissos." In another passage, we read that the clear waters of the river itself foretell the coming Mysteries, and the cries of the waterfowl fill the banks with music.[46] These descriptions are not at all appropriate for a hillside sanctuary raised on a high artificial terrace, but they apply admirably to a building in a low-lying precinct that came ultimately to be engulfed by the changing course of the river itself. Accordingly, the remains on the riverbank should indicate the site of the sanctuary of Demeter, where the Mysteries in Agrai were celebrated, and the Ionic temple on the hillside should be assigned to Artemis Agrotera.

Identification of the Temple of Artemis Agrotera enables us to understand more closely Pausanias's visit to this part of Athens. Having described the buildings and monuments around the Olympieion as far north as the Lykeion, the intrepid sightseer first mentions the Ilissos River and its tributary, the Eridanos (1.19.5). Next he recounts the abduction of the maiden Oreithyia by Boreas, the north wind; he sees the altar of the Ilissian Muses and the spot where King Kodros fell fighting at the hands of the Peloponnesians, whereupon he crosses the river to Agrai (1.19.6). Pausanias was no doubt reminded of the story of Boreas and Oreithyia because he saw the altar of Boreas, which Plato (*Phaidr.* 229C) placed at the river crossing "about two or three stadia" downstream from the pleasant glade where Sokrates and Phaidros passed a summer's afternoon. The river crossing is linked to the springs of Kallirrhoe by the opening sentences of another dialogue in the Platonic corpus which has Sokrates strolling from the city gate in the direction of Kynosarges.[47] At this same spot Pausanias would have made his way to Agrai, and the first sight that met his eyes was the Temple of Artemis Agrotera. It is easy to imagine that the little temple on the hillside worked its effects upon the visitor, with its splendid Ionic facade and cunning siting, and the Roman tourist responded in just the way the architect had intended. He climbed up to the temple, learned the lore of the cult, and viewed the statue of the goddess. Pausanias then continued his walk, following unwittingly in the footsteps of Sokrates and Phaidros up the south bank of the river. But the idyllic spot that Plato knew had long since given way to the Panathenaic Stadium, and when Pausanias saw it that great arena had recently been rebuilt in Pentelic marble by Herodes Atticus.

Artemis Agrotera was the recipient of magnificent sacrifices, and her annual festival provided the Athenian populace with a sumptuous banquet. In the depths of Asia, Xenophon exhorted his despairing troops by recalling the resolute vows by which the Athenians sought to placate the gods in the days before Marathon: "While they had vowed to Artemis that for every man they might slay of the enemy they would sacrifice a goat to the goddess, they were unable to find goats enough; so they resolved to offer five hundred each year, and this sacrifice they are paying even to this day."[48] In this feast of Artemis, on Boedromion 6, the city celebrated the victory at Marathon with its official thank-offering. Aristophanes likened the sacrifice to those for Athena Polias at the Panathenaia. The polemarch himself personally conducted the ritual and offered the victims to both Artemis Agrotera and Enyalios.[49] A particularly colorful part of the festival was the great procession that escorted

[46] The quotation from Himerios, *Or.* 10.20 (Colonna): παρ' Ἰλισσοῦ μυστικαῖς ὄχθαις ἐσκήνημαι. Cf. Himer. *Or.* 47.4 (Colonna): νῦν πλούσια μὲν Ἰλισσοῦ καὶ διαφανῆ τὰ νάματα, καὶ τάχα Δηοῦς μαντεύεται πάλιν ὁ ποταμὸς τὰ μυστήρια· κύκνοι δὲ, εἰ μὲν ἀμφὶ τὰς ὄχθας Ἰλισσοῦ μετὰ Ζεφύρου ποτὲ μέλος εἰργάσαντο ... νῦν πλέον ἢ πρότερον μουσικῆς τὰς ὄχθας ἐπλήσουσιν, "Now are the streams of Ilissos rich and clear, and soon the river will again foretell the Mysteries of Demeter; and the swans, if ever they plied their song about the banks of Ilissos when the west wind blows, ... now more than before will they fill those banks with music."

[47] [Plato], *Axiochos* 364A: Ἐξιόντι μοι ἐς Κυνόσαργες καὶ γενομένῳ κατὰ τὸν Ἰλισσὸν διῆξε φωνὴ βοῶντός του, Σώκρατες, Σώκρατες. ὡς δὲ ἐπιστραφεὶς περιεσκόπουν ὁπόθεν εἴη, Κλεινίαν ὁρῶ τὸν Ἀξιόχου θέοντα ἐπὶ Καλλιρρόην, "As I was going out toward Kynosarges and was down by the Ilissos, a voice came to me of someone calling, 'Sokrates, Sokrates.' When I turned to find out whence it came, I saw Kleinias son of Axiochos running above Kallirrhoe."

[48] Xen. *Anab.* 3.2.12; and cf. Aelian, *Var. Hist.* 2.25; schol. Aristoph. *Knights* 660.

[49] The celebration of Marathon on Boedromion 6, Plut. *Mor.* 349E; and cf. Plut. *Camil.* 19.3, *Thes.* 27.3. Sacrifices for Artemis compared to those for Athena, Aristoph. *Knights* 654–662. Conducted by the Polemarch, [Aristot.] *Ath. Pol.* 58.1; Pollux, 8.91. Cf. Aelian, *Var. Hist.* 2.25.

the hundreds of sacrificial victims to the temple in Agrai. Throughout the Hellenistic period, the ephebic corps marched in full armor to accompany this parade.[50] The procession to Agrai doubtless left the city by the same eastern gate that Pausanias, and Sokrates before him, had used and thence crossed the river at once above the springs of Kallirrhoe. In long lines of marchers, the crowds of worshippers with their military escort, the great flocks of victims with their many handlers, slowly made their way uphill to the sanctuary. Throughout their ceremonial ascent, all would view to best advantage the little Ionic temple because of the happy contrivance of its rear colonnade and its high artificial terrace. The sacrifices to Artemis were ritual acts of central importance in Athens's celebration of the victories in the Persian Wars, for they specifically commemorated the single military exploit that most caused Athenians to swell with pride. The site of these festivities was a natural candidate for architectural embellishment as part of a major program of religious construction. If we have correctly identified the temple on the Ilissos as dedicated to Artemis Agrotera, it will be clear at once why this suburban hillside was subjected to the expert ministrations of one of Athens's leading architects.

THE TEMPLE OF ATHENA NIKE

At this point we return to the central citadel of the Acropolis to examine the temple that celebrated most specifically the goddess who bestowed victory on the battlefield, Athena Nike (Figs. 110, 111). From the middle years of the sixth century, her precinct had occupied the projecting western bastion of the Acropolis. This heavily fortified tower had commanded the western approaches to the citadel since Mycenaean times and was still, in the mid-fifth century, supported by its original Cyclopean masonry. When in 437 work commenced on the Propylaia, the neighboring sanctuary of Athena Nike consisted of a small naiskos that had probably been erected after the Persian Wars to shelter the goddess's archaic cult statue. This diminutive structure, together with the cult's two archaic altars, stood on a ground level that the sanctuary had used since the beginning of the cult, about 1.35 m below the marble pavement of the Classical period.[51] At some time after construction of the Propylaia had already begun, the decision was made to enlarge the bastion and to raise its level. In order to effect this plan, walls of poros limestone from Peiraieus were built as a sheathing around the three outside faces of the Cyclopean masonry. In this way the area available for the goddess's precinct was considerably enlarged. Along the south flank the width increased by nearly two meters; the sheathing of the west wall was set at right angles to the south, and that added more than four meters to the length at the northwest corner, while the north face of the bastion was brought into alignment with the lowest step of the southwest wing of the Propylaia. The project involved a major piece of construction, for the new masonry arose in eighteen courses of ashlar blocks at the northwest corner, and twenty-four courses at the southwest. In its final form the level of the terrace pavement came within two steps of the Propylaia floor.[52] The masonry sheathing brought about a drastic change in

---

[50] The procession to Agrai, Plut. *Mor.* 862A; conducted by the ephebic corps in armor, *IG* II² 1028, line 8. The procession was a regular part of the ceremonial program of the ephebes in the Hellenistic period and is often mentioned in the decrees honoring the corps; *IG* II² 1006, lines 8–9, 58; 1008, line 7; 1011, line 7; 1029, line 6; 1030, line 5; 1040, line 5; 2119, col. III, lines 127–128.

[51] For the archaic configuration of the bastion and the poros naiskos of Athena Nike, see Mark, *Athena Nike*, 42–67; I. M. Shear, *JHS* 119 (1999) 110–125; Giraud, Μελέτη Αθηνάς Νίκης, 34–38; *Propylaia* I. For the earlier Mycenaean remains, Iakovidis, Μυκηναϊκὴ ἀκρόπολις, 106–117; J. C. Wright, *Hesperia* 63 (1994) 323–360; Shear (above) 86–104. For the date of the naiskos, endnote 1, pp. 393–394 below.

[52] For the sheathing of the Nike bastion, see Bohn, *Propylaeen*, 29–31; N. Balanos, *ArchEph* (1937) pt. 3, 789–795; Bundgaard, *Mnesicles*, 177–183; Miles, *Hesperia* 49 (1980) 323; Mark, *Athena Nike*, 69–70; Giraud, Μελέτη Αθηνάς Νίκης, 43–46. The courses of masonry are numbered on Balanos's drawings published by Mark, *Athena Nike*, pls. 9, 10.

Figure 110. Temple of Athena Nike, view of east facade

the old prehistoric tower, and its only purpose can have been to create an artificial site of sufficient size for the new Temple of Athena Nike and to provide direct and convenient access to the site by way of the new gatehouse. For the first time in the long centuries of its history the bastion became an integral part of the Acropolis.

In order to understand the architectural history and chronology of the Nike temple and its bastion, it is necessary to examine in detail the relationship between it and the southwest wing of the Propylaia. Evidence for the sequence of construction comes from the marble stairway that still ascends the north side of the bastion between the podium for the southwest wing of the Propylaia and the corner of the Nike temple (see Fig. 4). The podium for the southwest wing ends in one of two matching marble piers, which students of the site have come to know as pier "W." It was dressed to be visible for its full height on all three exposed faces, and its fillets incline slightly to the west. This indicates that the pier was designed as a gatepost and anticipated the installation of an answering gatepost farther to the west that was never built.[53] When the eight extant steps were placed in position, however, the lowest was set not at the bottom of the pier, but nearly level with the top of the

---

[53] Pier "W" is the designation of Wrede, *AM* 57 (1932) 75, Abb. 1. For discussion of the gatepost and flanking steps: Wrede, 74–91; Schleif, *JdI* 48 (1933) 177–184; Bundgaard (note 52 above), followed by Mark, *Athena Nike*, 80; Miles (note 52 above); and Giraud (note 52 above). For earlier views on the stairway, Dörpfeld, *AM* 36 (1911) 57–58; G. Welter, *AM* 48 (1923) 190–201.

Figure 111. Temple of Athena Nike, east elevation, restored by Hansen

third course above its foot,[54] and a small ramp at right angle to the stairway sloped down eastward so that the steps were accessible from the main approach ramp of the Propylaia. It has been acutely observed that the eight steps of the stairway were designed to communicate not with the higher classical terrace of the bastion but with the lower archaic level that was still in use in 437. That is to say, if the lowest step had been set at the bottom of pier "W," as indicated by the dressing of the marble, the top step would have agreed perfectly with the old level of the bastion.[55] From this evidence one infers correctly that the decision to raise the level was made after the podium for the southwest wing of the Propylaia had already been built. Accordingly, it has often been assumed that the stairway was installed to give access to the Nike sanctuary during the construction of the Propylaia, and the steps were subsequently raised at some later date to conform to the higher classical terrace. But this conclusion is very doubtful, because the rough lifting bosses still visible on the lowest three courses of pier "W" would have obstructed proper joints between the marble step blocks and the

---

[54] Figures from Wrede, *AM* 57 (1932) Abb. 1, Beil. 16: top of lowest step "e" 2.085 m below Propylaia floor + height of step "e" 0.225 = 2.310 m below Propylaia floor. Height of three lowest courses of pier "W" 0.529 + 0.360 + 0.397 = 1.286 m. Foot of pier "W" 3.663 m below Propylaia floor − 1.286 (lowest three courses) = 2.377 m top of third course below Propylaia floor.

[55] See Bundgaard, *Mnesicles*, 180–181 and note 363; Iakovidis, Μυκηναϊκὴ ἀκρόπολις, 166–173. Figures from Wrede (note 54 above): bottom of step "e" 2.310 m below Propylaia floor − 0.601 pavement of raised bastion (below Propylaia floor) = 1.709 m. Height of eight steps + 0.10 m cut down from top step = 1.809 m. Foot of pier "W" 3.663 m below Propylaia floor − 1.809 m level of old bastion (below Propylaia floor) = 1.854 m. Height from foot of pier "W" to level of old bastion.

gatepost.[56] It is preferable to think, therefore, that the stairway was designed to serve the earlier level of the sanctuary but was never set in that position, and it follows that the interval between the construction of pier "W" and the decision to remodel the bastion of Athena Nike was very short indeed.

Further examination of the substructures for the southwest wing of the Propylaia leads to the same conclusion. We saw in an earlier chapter that a low Z-shaped parapet connects pier "W" to the Propylaia steps at the double anta of the southwest wing, and in one arm of this parapet stood the stele bearing the decrees for Athena Nike. The foundations for this structure, and for the double anta itself, consist of poros blocks that are beautifully smoothed and jointed; the top three courses, down to the early level of the bastion, were clearly intended to be visible.[57] In striking contrast, the foundations for the west facade of the wing, spanning the entire north–south width of the bastion in line with the last column, are built of coarsely worked poros blocks.[58] Plainly the builders did not intend this rough masonry to be exposed to view. From this we can conclude that an important change of plan occurred between construction of the podium for the front colonnade of the southwest wing and laying of the foundation for its west facade; and that change resulted from the decision to raise and enlarge the Nike bastion. Moreover, the decision was promptly implemented, as we learn from the filling that the workmen dumped in to raise the bastion to its new level. Beneath the paving slabs of the classical terrace were found masses of marble working chips forming a layer more than twice as thick as the pavement itself. All of this was the masons' waste from the stone yards within the Acropolis where the marble blocks of the Propylaia were in the process of being dressed; it shows that work on the bastion of Athena Nike began shortly after the start of construction of the Propylaia and that the two projects were closely contemporary.[59]

There appears to have been a misunderstanding, however, with respect to the exact level to which the new terrace of the bastion would be raised. On the west facade of the southwest wing, only the stylobate was made of marble, seemingly in the expectation that the pavement of the Nike precinct would be brought level with the floor of the Propylaia or at most one step lower. In the event, of course, the paving slabs of the bastion were laid 0.601 m below the stylobate of the southwest wing, and that difference required two steps along the west facade to enable easy access from the Propylaia. Mnesikles rose to the occasion with characteristic ingenuity. He had the stylobate slabs of the west facade set 0.295 m behind the original intended line in order to reveal the edge of the poros foundation, which was then dressed down to form the tread and riser of the necessary second step. But this alteration at the level of the crepidoma created considerable difficulty in the superstructure, for the change in the position of the stylobate caused the central pier and the southwest anta to be

[56] For the lifting bosses on the lowest three courses of pier "W," Wrede, *AM* 57 (1932) Abb. 2, 3, Beil. 16. Their existence controverts the observation of Bohn, *Propylaeen*, 15, that the archaic bastion crown shows signs of foot wear opposite pier "W." Mark, *Athena Nike*, 80, note 59, adduces this as evidence that the steps were originally set at the lower level, but no marble blocks can ever have been set against the existing surface of the two lowest courses of pier "W." It is interesting to note also that just enough of the lifting boss on the third course has been cut away to allow the backing block for the lowest step (now missing) to be set in place against the northern half of the pier face.

[57] See references cited in chap. 9, note 84 above.

[58] See references cited in chap. 9, note 85 above.

[59] See Welter, *AM* 48 (1923) 194: "Über dem alten Temenosniveau liegt eine gleichmässige Schicht Marmorabfälle, darauf die Porosquadern des Fundaments für den Plattenbelag des Nikebezirks"; his pl. V:7 shows a cross section of the layer of marble chips. Cf. R. Bohn, *AM* 5 (1880) 264: "jedoch fand sich c. 0.60–0.70 M. unter der jetzigen Oberfläche eine durchgehende Schicht kleiner Marmorsplitter, welche also offenbar von dem Abfällen des Propylaeenbaues herrührten." See also Bundgaard, *Mnesicles*, 70 and note 120; Miles, *Hesperia* 49 (1980) 323–324. Masses of the same filling of marble waste were found above the remains of the Old Propylon, Weller, *AJA* 8 (1904) 37; and in the area of the approach ramp to the Propylaia, Dinsmoor, *AJA* 33 (1929) 101–102. For a cross section of the fill in the approach ramp, W. B. Dinsmoor, *The Archons of Athens in the Hellenistic Age* (Cambridge, MA, 1931) 4, fig. 2; Bundgaard, *Mnesicles*, 24, fig. 18. Mark, *Athena Nike*, 86 and note 86, 138 and note 50, simply asserts that the marble-chip waste came from the Nike temple and not the Propylaia because he wishes to date the construction of the building to the late 420s on the basis of the style of its sculptural frieze rather than on the evidence of the stratigraphy of its foundations.

placed 0.20 m behind the last column of the front portico, with which they were supposed to be in perfect alignment. This in turn necessitated a redesign of the entablature, and once again Mnesikles departed from standard Doric structural practice. The front colonnade of the wing has a normal Doric entablature, in which the architrave and its backer have a combined thickness of 1.01 m. On the west facade, however, he omitted the backer altogether and used a single architrave, 0.503 m in thickness, in order to center the course properly on the third column. In the next higher course, he retained both the frieze and frieze backer, with a combined thickness of 0.87 m, but the backer had almost no bearing and projected beyond the inner face of the architrave by 0.37 m.[60]

These sundry adjustments go far to explain how the southwest wing of the Propylaia evolved into the curiously stunted appendage that remains on the site today, but they also help to illuminate the history of construction in the sanctuary of Athena Nike. When Mnesikles' workmen began to build the podiums for the side wings, it was assumed that the neighboring precinct would retain its archaic level, and accordingly they dressed smooth the top three poros foundation courses that would support the double anta of the southwest wing. On the other hand, the poros foundations for the west facade were finished with rough irregular surfaces that were obviously not meant to remain visible. The inference is clear that between construction of the podium for the colonnade and laying of the western foundation, the decision was made to raise and enlarge the Nike bastion. There was uncertainty at first as to exactly how high the level would rise. The architect expected the pavement of the new terrace to range with the stylobate of the west facade and thus to conceal the rough stonework of the foundations. But before the first marble block of the western stylobate was set in place, the height of the bastion had been determined precisely, if it had not already been reached in actual construction, and so the stylobate was shifted backward and the foundation refashioned into a makeshift step.

Construction of the ashlar masonry for the bastion was linked inextricably with the laying of foundations for the Temple of Athena Nike. Along the north flank and at the west end, the foundations of the temple are perfectly leveled with the corresponding courses of the bastion facing, and the foundations and facing are so bonded together by the system of construction that each course must have been completely laid before the next higher course was begun. On the north and west, the lowest course of the temple ranges with the fourth course below the molded crown of the bastion. The builders used stretchers on the north side and headers on the west in courses 4 and 2, while in courses 3 and 1 they alternated the pattern and used headers on the north side and stretchers on the west. In each course an outsized block of irregular shape turned the obtuse angle at the northwest corner, and smaller blocks filled in the triangular space beside the remains of the poros naiskos.[61] The lowermost courses of the temple are thus necessarily contemporary with the raising and enlargement of the Nike bastion. The southern and eastern foundations of the temple, five courses deep instead of four, vary more irregularly in height and were not set perfectly level with the north and west sides until they reached the marble euthynteria. The west end of the temple was exactly aligned with the wall of the bastion and set back only 0.1054 m from the edge (Fig. 112); moreover, on this end the euthynteria of the temple was cut in the same marble blocks as the molded crowning course of the bastion.[62] At

---

[60] On the reconstruction of the western facade, Bohn, *Propylaeen*, 27–28, pl. XVI. On the setting of the stylobate so as to expose the poros foundation, Wrede, *AM* 57 (1932) 81, Abb. 3, 83, Abb. 4, 90; Bundgaard, *Mnesicles*, 174–175, 178. On the anomalies of the entablature: Bundgaard, *Mnesicles*, 73–74 and fig. 42; Mark, *Athena Nike*, 81; cf. Dinsmoor, Jr., *Hesperia* Suppl. 20 (1982) 28–30; *Propylaia* II, 417 and figs. 21:11, 21:7.

[61] On the bonding of the foundations with the bastion facing, see Welter, *AA* (1939) 13–14; Balanos, *ArchEph* (1937) 783–784; Miles, *Hesperia* 49 (1980) 324–325; Giraud, Μελέτη Ἀθηνᾶς Νίκης, 46–47. The system by which the headers and stretchers alternate and interlock with each other on the north and west sides of the bastion is clearly illustrated in Balanos's actual-state plans of the blocks in each of the top four courses, published by Mark, *Athena Nike*, pls. 14–17.

[62] Giraud, Μελέτη Ἀθηνᾶς Νίκης, 46–47 and pl. 13. Dimension of the setback on the bastion crown from Balanos's section, Mark, *Athena Nike*, 152 and pl. 11.

Figure 112. Temple of Athena Nike, view of west facade

the northwest corner, on the other hand, the first three blocks of the bastion crown were cut down to receive the separate blocks of the euthynteria; thus their lowered back sides extended under the edge of the euthynteria and bonded into the topmost course of the poros foundations.[63]

These structural details provide unequivocal evidence for the history of the sanctuary on the bastion. After work had begun on the podium for the southwest wing of the Propylaia, but before Mnesikles was ready to set the western stylobate of the wing, the poros sheathing of the bastion had begun to rise.[64] When the new ashlar facing reached the fourth course below the marble crown, Kallikrates' workmen were prepared to start laying the foundations for the temple, probably no later than ca. 435.[65] By the time construction of the Propylaia was suspended in 432, the marble paving slabs of the classical terrace were in place, sealing beneath them masses of marble building debris from the workshops of the Propylaia. Since the molded crowning course of the pavement included the western euthynteria of the temple, it is almost certainly correct to infer that the lowest course of the marble work had been completely laid, if not the steps of the crepidoma as well. Now, builders do not construct foundations and then begin to design the building to put on top of them, and so we may be certain that by ca. 435 the specifications for the Temple of Athena Nike had been determined in exact detail.

The architectural evidence helps to establish a firm date at which construction of the temple actually began, and one that agrees well with our other information concerning the career of Kallikrates, the architect of the temple. Just as we have seen that Iktinos was commissioned to build

[63] On the bastion crown at the northwest corner, Balanos, *ArchEph* (1937) 783–784; Giraud, *Μελέτη Αθηνάς Νίκης*, 47 and pl. 97:β.

[64] On the timing of the decision, see Bundgaard, *Mnesicles*, 178 and note 354.

[65] In accordance with the commission to which the architect had been appointed by *IG* I³ 35, lines 12–14; see chap. 2, pp. 27–35 above.

the Telesterion at Eleusis in the years around 450,[66] so too Kallikrates had been appointed then to prepare the plans for the Nike temple, whereupon both architects were summoned to the Acropolis in 447 to collaborate on the design of the Parthenon, the project of first priority in the Periklean plan. The dedication of the Parthenon in 438 freed Kallikrates to devote his attention to the Nike temple. The extraordinary architectural similarities between the temple on the Ilissos and the Temple of Athena Nike suggest that they were designed together at about the same time. Construction of the suburban temple no doubt moved forward promptly, and it was certainly completed by the late 430s. The Nike temple, on the other hand, had to await preparation of its virtually artificial site on the bastion of the Acropolis. It probably encountered further delays in the controversy that brought an end to work on the Propylaia, and so its superstructure was not completed until the 420s.

The structural details of the bastion also bear directly on the dating of the documentary records of the sanctuary. The parliamentary process that authorized the temple and appointed its architect must clearly have preceded the beginning of work on its foundations, and so the architectural evidence vitiates all attempts to date the earlier decree for Athena Nike to the 420s. In fact, we saw in an earlier chapter that the stele bearing the two decrees has precisely the correct dimensions to fit into a socket cut in the top of the Z-shaped parapet beside the double anta of the southwest wing. Moreover, the stele was already standing in that position, with the earlier inscription on display, before the anta and columns of the Propylaia received their final polish. Such is the necessary inference from the narrow panel of protective stone still visible on the west face of the double anta, which the masons left undressed rather than risk damage to the stele standing beside it.[67] So the final stonework of the Propylaia provides a firm terminus ante quem both for the earlier inscription pertaining to the cult of Athena Nike and for the beginning of work on the new temple.

There is no way of knowing how much of the temple's stonework was in place by the time work on the Propylaia was abandoned in 432, nor is there any evidence to indicate whether construction of the temple was curtailed at the same time. It is possible that a reduced workforce continued to progress slowly without interruption, as must have happened at times in the case of the Hephaisteion, or it may be that construction was halted completely for a period of years, like the two phases of the Telesterion at Eleusis and the demonstrable interruption in construction of the Erechtheion. In any event, scholars have been inclined to think that passage of the second decree for Athena Nike in 424/3 marked an important epoch in the history of the sanctuary.[68] Its provision for payment of the priestess's salary should be taken together with other evidence for the dedication at that time of votive statuary in the sanctuary.

In 426/5 and 425/4 there is evidence for an unusual number of dedicatory statues to Athena Nike, which implies that the temple and its surrounding bastion were no longer a construction site. First were two golden Nikai, erected by the Athenian state in 426/5, and these statues of precious metal were presumably housed within the temple itself.[69] Another statue of Athena Nike was a thank-offering for the military victories of that year in northwestern Greece: ἣν ἀνέ[θ]εσαν [Ἀθηναῖοι ἀπὸ] Ἀμπρακιωτῶν κα[ὶ τῆ]ς ἐν [Ὀ]λπαις στρατ]ιᾶς καὶ τῶν ἐπαν[αστ]άντ[ων τῶι δήμωι

---

[66] See chap. 6, pp. 174–178 above.

[67] The narrow panel of unpolished stone on the double anta appears in I. M. Shear, *JHS* 119 (1999) pl. 6c; Giraud, *Μελέτη Αθηνάς Νίκης*, pl. 65:β. See also Fig. 5 above.

[68] Earlier scholarship summarized by Mark, *Athena Nike*, 115–122; cf. Dinsmoor, *PAPS* 80 (1939) 124–125; Mattingly, *Historia* 10 (1961) 169–171 = AER, 30–32; Meiggs, *AE*, 496–503; ML 71; chap. 2, pp. 28–29 above.

[69] *IG* I³ 468. These two were part of a series of golden Nikai modeled on the Nike on the hand of Pheidias's statue of Athena in the Parthenon. See D. B. Thompson, *Hesperia* 13 (1944) 173–209; W. E. Thompson, *NC* 10 (1970) 1–6; Mattingly, in Bradeen and McGregor, eds., *Φόρος*, 94–97. The first statues in the series, at least three in number, were authorized by the second Kallias decree of 434/3 (*IG* I³ 52B, line 3). These may have been completed ca. 430, and two of them are possibly described in the fragmentary inventory, *IG* I³ 467; see D. B. Thompson (above) 174; ML, p. 161. There is no record of any addition to the series for nearly five years, until the dedication of the two Nikai in 426/5.

τ]ῶι Κερκυραίων [καὶ ἀπ'] Ἀν[ακτοριῶν] (*IG* II² 403, lines 8–12), "which the Athenians dedicated from the spoils of the Ambrakiots and the army in Olpai and those who revolted against the demos of the Korkyraians and from the Anaktorians."[70] Thucydides describes the victorious campaign of Demosthenes against Ambrakia and Olpai in the winter of 426/5, while the insurrection of the Korkyrian oligarchs ended the following summer. The capture of Anaktorion took place at the very end of the campaigning season, probably in late October of 425,[71] so the sculpture cannot have been finished before the winter of that year. A century later that statue underwent elaborate repair and conservation amid special propitiatory sacrifices, which suggests that it was valuable and much venerated, and some scholars have identified it as a new cult statue for the temple, just then completed in the year of the military victories.[72] A fourth votive statue of Athena Nike commemorated Kleon's famous victory at Sphakteria in August of that same summer, and the demos would also have dedicated this monument in the winter of 425/4.[73] This sudden profusion of votive statuary in the little sanctuary on the bastion is a sure indication that the goddess of victory had begun to smile on Athens's military efforts once again, but it also suggests that her new temple was completed by this time.

The completed Temple of Athena Nike reconfirmed the revolutionary treatment of the Ionic order that had begun a few years earlier with the interior of the Propylaia and had inspired the overall design of the temple on the Ilissos. The component parts of the order, which had been developed in archaic Ionia for the colossal temples at Ephesos, Samos, and Didyma, underwent a total transformation in the Ionic temples at Athens. In the scale of the building, the Temple of Athena Nike was reduced to a miniature version of its Ionic ancestors in the east. The overall dimensions of the little temple, 5.397 × 8.166 m on the stylobate, make it slightly smaller than the Athenian and Siphnian Treasuries at Delphi. It is not altogether impossible that the Athenian architect was influenced by these tiny auxiliary buildings at the Panhellenic sanctuary.[74] The Ionic facade has four columns arranged in prostyle plan with equal axial intercolumniations measuring 1.5485 m, and the front facade is exactly replicated on the rear of the temple to form the same unusual amphiprostyle arrangement that was adopted for the Ilissos temple. Within the framing colonnades, the architect compressed the temple plan even more drastically than in the Ilissos temple. Both pronaos and opisthodomos have been omitted entirely, and the cella consists of a nearly square compartment slightly wider than it is long, with interior dimensions measuring 4.147 × 3.780 m (Fig. 113). In place of the normal door wall, behind the eastern colonnade a pair of rectangular piers is aligned with the antas, the space between them being enclosed originally by metal grilles.

Despite the diminutive scale of the facade, the Ionic columns of the Nike temple have been given the heaviest known proportions of any Ionic temple. With a lower diameter of 0.518 m, the

[70] Cf. Mark, *Athena Nike*, 113–114.
[71] The campaign against Ambrakia and Olpai, Thuc. 3.105–114; the civil strife at Korkyra, Thuc. 3.85.3, 4.2, 4.46 (ending in summer 425); Anaktorion captured, Thuc. 4.49 (at the end of summer and the beginning of winter, 4.50.1). On the date, Gomme, *HCT*, vol. 3, 487, 706.
[72] *IG* II² 403 is a decree of the third quarter of the fourth century responding to the report of a special committee elected by the demos to look into the repair of the statue, lines 6–8. The propitiatory sacrifices to be offered by the priestess, lines 17–20. Possibly a motion to praise the sculptor who conducted the repair, line 30. The statue dedicated in 425/4 identified as the cult statue: originally proposed by Furtwängler, *Masterpieces of Greek Sculpture*, 444–445; see also Dinsmoor, *AAG*³, 185–186, note 4; Dohrn, *Attische Plastik*, 21; Travlos, *PDA*, 149; L. H. Jeffery, in M. J. Fontana et al., eds., Φιλίας χάριν (Rome 1980) vol. 4, 1237–1238; I. B. Romano, "Early Greek Cult Images" (Ph.D. diss., University of Pennsylvania, 1980) 63; argued most fully by P. Schultz, in Palagia, ed., *Art in Athens during the Peloponnesian War*, 151–152. The identification is rejected by Mark, *Athena Nike*, 123–125, and cf. 93–98.
[73] The statue commemorating the victory, Paus. 4.36.6. Kleon's campaign at Pylos, Thuc. 4.27–41. The date of the final victory, Thuc. 4.39; dated about 5 to 10 August 425, Gomme, *HCT*, vol. 4, 478.
[74] Stylobate dimensions from Dinsmoor, *AAG*³, 340; cf. Mark, *Athena Nike*, 72–75. The Siphnian Treasury at Delphi measures 6.04 × 8.41 m: J.-F. Bommelaer, *Guide de Delphes, le site* (Paris 1991) 124. The Athenian Treasury is 6.57 × 9.65 m at the base of the walls: Bommelaer, 133. See also Camp, *Archaeology of Athens*, 90–92; Hurwit, *Athenian Acropolis*, 181–191.

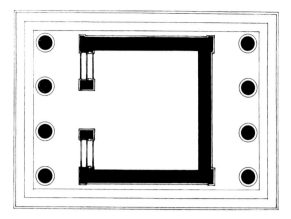

Figure 113. Temple of Athena Nike, restored plan

columns rise to a height of 4.049 m, thus creating a proportion of diameter to height of 7.82. The same proportion on the facade of the Ilissos temple was 8.25, while the interior columns of the Propylaia are 9.93 times their lower diameter in height.[75] In other respects the design of the Ionic columns reveals the close interrelationship between the two temples and the interior columns of the Propylaia (Figs. 110, 114). The column bases of the Nike temple borrowed the tripartite profile of the bases in the Propylaia, with their concave scotia between two half-round tori, of which the upper one is horizontally fluted. But we saw earlier that a closely similar profile was used for the bases of the Ilissos temple, and with a height nearly identical to those of the Nike temple. Likewise, the temple's Ionic capitals share with the Propylaia the volutes set wide apart, with their central eyes outside the lines of the shafts, and the deeply carved egg-and-dart pattern on the echinus. More than that, however, detailed comparison of the two capitals has revealed that many dimensions of the Propylaia capitals have been reduced by almost exactly one half in the design of the capitals for the Nike temple.[76] Many writers have commented on the astonishing similarity between the Ionic capitals of the Ilissos temple and those of the Temple of Athena Nike. Not only are the general proportions of the capitals the same, as well as the detailed forms of the carved decoration, but many of the dimensions are virtually identical. Close analysis of the most minute dimensions has revealed variations that are often measured in only a few millimeters.[77] Yet for all their likeness, the Ionic capitals of the Nike temple exhibit a few tiny details that seem more advanced than the capitals of the Ilissos temple. The darts between the eggs of the echinus terminate at the bottom in double points, like those on the capitals and anthemia of the Erechtheion. The petals of the corner palmettes, still rounded with midribs like those of the Ilissos capitals, have grown more pointed tips, and they have crept noticeably lower on the carved molding of the echinus.

The design of the other decorative moldings in the two temples was frequently identical. In both buildings the distinctive tripartite profile of the Ionic column base, in slightly altered form, was used as a base for the anta and carved along the foot of the exterior walls as a molded toichobate. Earlier in this chapter, we observed the unusual combination of Ionic moldings that formed the anta capitals of the Ilissos temple. An exact replica of this richly decorative profile was borrowed for the anta capitals of the Nike temple. Once again the close interrelationship between the two buildings emerges in the almost identical dimensions of the component moldings and in the detail that on

[75] Dimensions and proportions, Dinsmoor, *AAG*³, 340; cf. the discussion, I. M. Shear, *Hesperia* 32 (1963) 378–379.

[76] As observed by Dinsmoor, *AAG*³, 186, followed by I. M. Shear, *Hesperia* 32 (1963) 380.

[77] On the close similarity of the capitals in the two temples: Puchstein, *Das ionische Capitell*, 14–19; Studniczka, *JdI* 31 (1916) 198–202, 229–230; Dinsmoor, *AAG*³, 185; I. M. Shear, *Hesperia* 32 (1963) 398, 424 (table), for detailed discussion of the capitals; Miles, *Hesperia* 49 (1980) 318–320.

Figure 114. View of Ionic capital and entablature at southeast corner

both buildings the anta capital terminates in a small projecting fillet below the Ionic moldings.[78] On the Nike temple this molding of the anta capitals (without the lower ovolo) was carved along the top of the exterior walls as an epicranitis.

Because the greater part of the Nike temple has survived antiquity and its blocks could be restored to their original positions, modern investigators have been able to observe details of its construction about which we have no evidence for the temple on the Ilissos. Despite the miniature scale of the building, many of its visual features were inflected with the delicate inclinations that had been most fully exploited in the optical refinements of the Parthenon. The risers of the steps are inclined inward, their treads slope slightly downward, and they are further articulated by a narrow rebate along the bottom of the risers.[79] Similar inward inclination is applied to the shafts of the Ionic columns, while the four corner columns lean both inward and toward the center of the facade, like the corner columns of contemporary Doric peripteral temples.[80] In sympathy with the columns, the side walls also incline inward, but the west wall and the front faces of all the antas and piers are perfectly vertical. Possibly because of the small size of the temple, the refinements were limited to inclinations, and no horizontal curvature was applied to steps or stylobate.

[78] I. M. Shear, *Hesperia* 32 (1963) 394–395, pls. 89:a, 90:b.
[79] I. M. Shear, *Hesperia* 32 (1963) 378; Orlandos, *BCH* 71–72 (1947–48) 10–11.
[80] Orlandos, *BCH* 71–72 (1947–48) 23–24; I. M. Shear (note 78 above).

Above the colonnades and the lateral walls, the Ionic entablature is divided almost equally between the epistyle (0.473 m high) and the frieze (0.45 m high) and is crowned by the Ionic geison (0.154 m high), with its projecting drip and plain soffit (Figs. 111, 114). The treatment of the epistyle once again shows a slightly more developed form than the Ilissos temple. Now for the first time the exterior face of the epistyle is divided into three fascias, having been left as a plain band on the Ilissos temple; this detail too the architect of the Nike temple may have borrowed from the interior order of the Propylaia. With the upper half of the entablature the sculptural decoration begins. The frieze displayed an uninterrupted band of sculptural scenes embracing all four sides of the temple. At each end of the building the triangular gable of the pediment was filled with additional sculptural compositions, while elaborate acroteria adorned the apex and corners of the roof. It is possible that the idea of mounting such a rich and sumptuous program of sculptural decoration on so tiny a building may have derived from the archaic Ionic treasuries at Delphi, such as that of the Siphnians, but the scenes themselves, to which we shall turn presently, were thoroughly Athenian.

At the top of the entablature, the geison blocks projected forward from the face of the frieze and carried the sima tiles, which turned upward to form a rain gutter along the eaves of the roof. The profile of the sima has the form of a tall ovolo surmounted by a small cavetto, and the ovolo carried a painted anthemion pattern strikingly similar to that recorded by Stuart and Revett in the pronaos of the Ilissos temple.[81] The ornament on the Nike sima has similar lotus blossoms alternating with palmettes. These are surrounded by oval-shaped tendrils that start as antithetical spirals beneath the palmettes and divide to sprout again as leaves from which the lotus blossoms grow. In both temples the palmettes have eleven rounded petals, and the lotuses have tall, thin, pointed petals, five in number on the Nike sima, but only three as drawn by the British architects. Centered on the ovolo of each lateral tile of the Nike sima was a lion's-head waterspout that allowed drainage of rainwater from the roof of the building. At each end of the temple, the same patterned ovolo sloped up the apex of the pediments as the raking sima, although the molding was not interrupted by waterspouts except at the return of the corners, where the deeper tiles each had two. Enough pieces of the sima and roof tiles have survived to recover the exact unit of measurement as 0.6208 m for the width of the lateral simas and the ordinary pan tiles, while the deeper tiles of the raking sima have a length of 1.1762 m. These dimensions allow each side of the double-pitched marble roof to be restored in ten rows of three ordinary pan tiles rising to the ridge behind the lateral simas, with four of the larger raking simas at each end. The joints where the pan tiles met were capped by eleven rows of four cover tiles, triangular in section, that terminated behind the sima molding without antefixes.[82] Another element of the temple's superstructure has been completely preserved so that the blocks could be replaced in their original positions: the marble ceiling above the colonnades at each end of the building. The ceiling of each porch consists of four rectangular marble slabs equal in thickness to about half the height of the sculptured frieze and set level with its top. The slabs are supported by narrow ceiling beams that span the porches from front to back and find bearing on the inner edge of the epistyle behind the frieze. The entire visible surface of the ceiling was decorated with square coffers arranged in three pairs on each slab and carved into the thickness of the blocks.[83]

This brings us to consideration of the sculptural decoration of the temple, which embellished every available surface of the building above the epistyle. The frieze of the Nike temple has survived in far better condition than that of the temple on the Ilissos. Ten of its original fourteen slabs are

[81] For the profile of the sima tiles, I. M. Shear, *Hesperia* 32 (1963) 385 and pl. 89:d. The anthemion is illustrated in Giraud, Μελέτη Αθηνάς Νίκης, pls. 156, 157; and cf. the anthemion on the Ilissos temple recorded by Stuart and Revett (1762 edition) pl. VIII.

[82] Dimensions of the sima and roof tiles, Giraud, Μελέτη Αθηνάς Νίκης, pl. 223; the roof reconstructed, Giraud, pl. 217.

[83] The ceiling slabs of the porches are drawn in position, Giraud, Μελέτη Αθηνάς Νίκης, pls. 220, 221; and cf. the restored section, pl. 216.

substantially complete, and fragments of at least three others are preserved. The positions that the blocks occupied on the four sides have been established to the satisfaction of many, but not all, scholars.[84] The overall theme of the sculptural program is not in doubt: scenes of violent combat rage along three sides of the frieze, while above the eastern colonnade an assembly of the gods celebrates Athena Nike.[85] Taken as a whole, the program of decoration presents the most vivid depiction we have of the blatant Athenian triumphalism that characterized the last third of the fifth century.

At the center of the east frieze stands a fully armed Athena flanked by two male deities. Her father, Zeus, sits regally enthroned to right, while Poseidon is perched on the rock of Cape Sounion to left, and their wives Hera and Amphitrite stand behind their consorts. In the space between Athena and Zeus, the damaged end of block c preserves the naked left leg of a male figure whose identification has varied depending on the interpretation of the east frieze as a whole. If, as seems most likely, the gods have assembled to glorify the warlike Athena and the military victories that she has bestowed on Athens, then the missing figure may be Ares.[86] But it has also been suggested that the subject should be entirely mythological, the battle scenes from the Trojan War and the east frieze depicting the weighing of the souls of Achilles and Memnon, in which case the missing figure might be restored as Hermes holding the scales to weigh the souls.[87] More recently the assembly has been interpreted as the birth of Athena, with Hephaistos standing between Athena and Zeus on the analogy of the east pediment of the Parthenon.[88] On either side of the central group the divine figures stand at ease: Theseus (?) to the left of Amphitrite, then Leto, Apollo, and Artemis, the three Graces after a heavily damaged figure, followed by Aphrodite, Eros, and Peitho at the southeast corner.[89] On the northern half of the frieze, the two figures beyond Hera may be Herakles and Hebe (or perhaps Hermes and Hygieia),[90] followed by Persephone and Demeter, and the three daughters of Kekrops: Aglauros, Pandrosos, and Herse.[91]

The relatively good state of preservation of the sculpture has not generated unanimity of opinion concerning interpretation of the four friezes, and detailed readings of the iconography have varied wildly. Of the battle friezes, that on the south is clearest. Here we see that the enemy is arrayed in Persian dress and fights with Persian weapons. It has been convincingly shown not only that the scene depicts the Battle of Marathon but that the sculptor probably based his composition on the celebrated painting of that battle in the Stoa Poikile.[92] On the frieze, the Athenian attack moves

[84] The east frieze: (a) southeast corner, Acrop. Mus. inv. 18135; (b) Acrop. Mus. inv. 18136 + 18137; (c) Acrop. Mus. inv. 18138; northeast corner missing. The north frieze: (m) Acrop. Mus. inv. 18140; (r) fragment, Acrop. Mus. inv. 18141; (s) Acrop. Mus. inv. 18142; (h) northwest corner fragment, Acrop. Mus. inv. 18143. The west frieze: (h) northwest corner, Acrop. Mus. inv. 18143; (i) London, BM inv. 421; (k) London, BM inv. 422; (l) southwest corner, Acrop. Mus. inv. 18139. The south frieze: (l) southwest corner, Acrop. Mus. inv. 18139; (f + e) Acrop. Mus. inv. 18144 + 18145; (g) London, BM inv. 424; (o) London, BM inv. 423; (a) southeast corner, Acrop. Mus. inv. 18135. Giraud, Μελέτη Αθηνάς Νίκης, pl. 213, places blocks f + e and block g on the north; pl. 215, he arranges the south frieze: l, o, blank, m, a; and he transposes the order of i and k in the west frieze.
[85] See the extensive bibliography on the temple and its sculptural program assembled by A. F. Stewart, in H. L. Kessler and M. S. Simpson, eds., *Pictorial Narrative in Antiquity and the Middle Ages*, 70–71, note 1. More recent references in Harrison, in D. Buitron-Oliver, ed., *The Interpretation of Architectural Sculpture*, 109–125; Palagia, in Barringer and Hurwit, eds., *Periklean Athens*, 177–192; Knell, *Mythos und Polis*, 140–150; Hurwit, *Athenian Acropolis*, 184–188.
[86] Harrison (note 85 above) 113; also Jeppesen, *ActaArch* 34 (1963) 93; Knell, *Mythos und Polis*, 143.
[87] Felten, *Tektonische Friese*, 123–133, 129.
[88] Palagia, in Barringer and Hurwit, eds., *Periklean Athens*, 188–189.
[89] Identification of the deities on the south half of the east frieze as Harrison, in Buitron-Oliver, ed., *Interpretation of Architectural Sculpture*, 110–111. She identifies figure 11 as Theseus, following Furtwängler, *Masterpieces of Greek Sculpture*, 449, and E. Simon, *Arkhaiognosia* 4 (1985–86) 17–18. Palagia (note 88 above) 187 prefers Dionysos.
[90] Herakles and Hebe: Harrison (note 89 above) 113–114; Hermes and Hygieia: Palagia (note 88 above) 188.
[91] The daughters of Kekrops: Harrison (note 89 above) 114–115; two Horai with their mother (seated): Palagia (note 88 above) 188, following Simon, *Arkhaiognosia* 4 (1985–86) 19.
[92] Harrison, *AJA* 76 (1972) 353–378.

from left to right; but it is the turning point of the battle when the Persian ranks have broken and the confused fighting of the rout begins. At far left (block l) hoplites attack a Persian horseman; the beast rears up, hurling its rider headlong to the ground. Farther on (block f + e) a wounded horse stumbles over Persian corpses, and its rider dismounts in haste to flee the onslaught. In the right half of the frieze, a Persian cavalryman gallops left to defend the fighting retreat (block g), while his comrades on horse and foot alike (blocks o, a) move off at speed to right and the safety of the Persian ships. But they are surrounded, and the Athenian hoplites dart among them lunging and striking with astonishing speed, apparently able to slaughter at will.[93]

At the center of the composition (left end, block g), a pair of dueling combatants is set apart from the turmoil of the rout. The Athenian lunges forward on his right leg with explosive force as he raises his right arm to slash downward with his sword. He swings his shield behind him on his left arm, recklessly exposing his torso, and his himation slips down his thigh to trail on the ground. We recognize at once the unmistakable pose of Harmodios the tyrant-slayer, made famous by Kritias and Nesiotes in the celebrated statues that stood in the Agora. The figure on the frieze has been identified as Kallimachos, the Athenian polemarch who commanded the right wing at the Battle of Marathon.[94] In the sculptor's vivid imagery, the Athenian general impersonates a tyrannicide and strikes a blow for liberty. Herodotos (6.109) also specifically compared Kallimachos to the tyrannicides in Miltiades' speech before the battle: "Kallimachos, it is for you today to choose whether you will enslave Athens or free her, and thereby leave such a memorial for all posterity as was left not even by Harmodios and Aristogeiton." But the image of bold action and heedless daring which the composition evokes has further implications, for we have seen in an earlier chapter that on the friezes of the Hephaisteion the same heroic postures of the tyrannicides were used to depict the hero Theseus, Athens's mythical king, fighting in mythical battles. So on the south frieze of the Nike temple, use of the Harmodios pose to depict the polemarch Kallimachos not only likens his exploit to that of the tyrant-slayer but also assimilates the historical general of the recent past to the archetypal Athenian warrior and military leader that Theseus had become.[95] It is noticeable that his Persian adversary is not yet defeated. He feints and dodges, skillfully handling his lunate shield so as to parry the coming blow, as if in the next instant he will turn the tables on his advancing enemy. The scene may be the sculptor's way of alluding to the sequel, for, according to Herodotos (6.111–115), Kallimachos led the Athenians to break through the Persian lines, only to be killed himself in the moment of victory.

Such a reading of the south frieze is greatly aided by the clearly depicted Persian dress and weapons that provide the necessary specificity to identify the battle. But these attributes are lacking on the other two battle friezes, with the result that the scenes are more enigmatic and difficult to interpret. On the west frieze all the combatants are Greek hoplites, but, like the Athenians on the south frieze, they are not properly equipped for battle. Some wear short chitons or cloaks, most are nude, and their only defensive armor consists of shields and helmets. So the sculptor has made no attempt at all to create a realistic image of hoplite warfare. In fact it is difficult to distinguish the warriors on the two sides from each other. The west frieze actually shows the aftermath of battle. One side has claimed victory and already erected a trophy, visible in the background (block i) as a stripped tree trunk on which a helmet and shield have been hung. In four separate scenes, soldiers attempt to rescue the bodies of fallen comrades, but they come under attack, presumably from the victorious enemy who try to prevent recovery of the dead. As on the south frieze, one feels once again the lightning speed of movement conveyed by the contorted poses of the combatants and the

[93] Cf. the remarks of Stewart, in Kessler and Simpson, eds., *Pictorial Narrative in Antiquity*, 61–62. Cf. Knell, *Mythos und Polis*, 145.

[94] As argued by Harrison, *AJA* 76 (1972) 354–355, and discussed in detail 358–365; followed by Stewart (note 93 above) 63–64.

[95] See chap. 5, pp. 149–152 above; Harrison (note 85 above); and Stewart (note 93 above).

cloaks that flap in the breeze. They attack and defend with reckless abandon as if invulnerable in their heroic nudity.[96]

The only complete block of the north frieze (m) also shows the late stage of a battle as the rout begins. Three hoplites run to the right over a fallen corpse in pursuit of a fleeing enemy warrior, who is caught when he stumbles against a rock and loses his Corinthian helmet. Another assailant in front seizes him by the beard while the man nearest behind him lays a hand on his shoulder. Beyond, two riderless horses gallop off to the right over a fallen shield.[97]

It is plain that the iconography of the battle friezes does not conform to any of the familiar mythological combats in the artistic repertory. This circumstance has taxed the ingenuity of scholars to explain their subject matter. Some have sought to interpret all the battle scenes as mythological, in the belief that it was deemed inappropriate to adorn the temples of the gods with human activities. Thus, on the one hand, all the friezes have been thought to show episodes from the Trojan War[98] or alternatively a local Attic war when King Erechtheus defended Attica against the invading Eleusinians and their Thracian allies.[99] A slightly different strategy has been to read the north and west friezes as a mythical foil to the historical Battle of Marathon on the south side, and here the paired historical and mythical paintings in the Stoa Poikile have been adduced in support of the argument. According to this view, the north frieze showed the capture of the Argive king Eurystheus by the Athenians when they went to the aid of the Herakleidai. On the west side, Theseus and his Athenians recovered the bodies of the Seven against Thebes for proper burial in Attica.[100] Other interpreters of the sculpture have started from the evident presence of warriors in Persian dress on the friezes and concluded that the battles were intended to depict historical military victories. Scenes from the Battle of Plataia have been identified on all three sides of the temple.[101] Alternatively, the south frieze has been seen as a more general allusion to the victories in the Persian Wars, while the battles on the west and north have been attributed to the Peloponnesian War.[102]

E. Harrison's recognition that the south frieze was influenced in both subject and iconography by the Marathon painting in the Stoa Poikile strengthened the notion that the sculptures of the Nike temple commemorated specific historical battles.[103] Others have sought evidence of similar specificity in the west frieze. One suggestion has been a battle in the First Peloponnesian War in which the Athenians, led by Myronides, defeated the Corinthians at Megara in 458.[104] Another has been that the west frieze possibly replicated the painting of the battle at Oinoe that was also displayed in the Stoa Poikile.[105] Plainly, no consensus has evolved concerning the identification of the

[96] Discussion of the west frieze: Harrison, in Buitron-Oliver, ed., *Interpretation of Architectural Sculpture*, 117–119; Palagia, in Barringer and Hurwit, eds., *Periklean Athens*, 185–186; E. G. Pemberton, *AJA* 76 (1972) 303–310; Knell, *Mythos und Polis*, 141.

[97] Felten, *Tektonische Friese*, 126, also Harrison (note 96 above) 199–120, argued that the riderless horses on block m were a chariot team and the car itself was added in paint on the background. The supposed presence of a chariot then led to the conclusion that the north frieze was a mythological battle. The existence of a chariot has been rightly doubted by Palagia (note 96 above) 186. More recently, Harrison's interpretation of block m as the capture of Eurystheus by Iolaos has been revived in detailed, but not altogether convincing, argument by P. Schultz, in Palagia, ed., *Art in Athens during the Peloponnesian War*, 131–147; Knell, *Mythos und Polis*, 142.

[98] Felten, *Tektonische Friese*, 123–133.

[99] Kardara, *ArchEph* (1961) 84–90.

[100] Harrison (note 85 above); followed by Schultz (note 97 above) for the north frieze.

[101] Giraud, Μελέτη Αθηνάς Νίκης, 263, note 27, having divided the blocks with battles against Persians between the north and south friezes (note 84 above), finds that the Battle of Plataia is represented on all three sides of the temple. In this he follows Furtwängler, *Masterpieces of Greek Sculpture*, 446–449.

[102] C. Blümel, *JdI* 65–66 (1950–51) 154; T. Hölscher, *Griechische Historienbilder des 5. und 4. Jahrhunderts vor Chr.* (Würzburg 1973) 91–98, also reads the Persian scenes as generic battles between Greeks and Persians, and the north frieze as a battle between Athenians and Boiotians at Oinophyta.

[103] Note 92 above.

[104] Pemberton, *AJA* 76 (1972) 304–307.

[105] Palagia, in Barringer and Hurwit, eds., *Periklean Athens*, 186.

scenes. But their lack of conformity to the iconography of known mythical battles, taken together with their unusual elements of specificity—Persian dress on the south, the trophy of the west frieze, the captured warrior and riderless horses on the north—all favor the view that the sculptures depict specific historical battles of the recent past, even if we can no longer identify them with certainty; and on the east the gods assemble to celebrate the glorious victories that Athena Nike bestowed on Athens.[106]

If the frieze of the Nike temple illustrates specific exploits of Athenian military prowess, the decoration of the next higher level recedes into the timeless realm of myth. A few sculptural fragments of small scale have been recognized as belonging to pedimental statuary for the Temple of Athena Nike.[107] Most important is a helmeted head of a warlike Athena, turned sharply as if the figure was in violent motion. Together with this belong a kneeling male figure and the torso of another of the same scale.[108] They suggest the restoration, most likely in the eastern pediment, of a Gigantomachy in which Athena brandishes her spear against fallen giants,[109] a scene that had adorned Acropolis temples and other dedications since Archaic times and would form a mythical archetype for the historical battles in the frieze below. None of the surviving fragments shed light on the subject of the western pediment, but a plausible suggestion is the battle of Theseus and the Athenians against the Amazons. A painting of that mythical encounter had been paired with the historical Battle of Marathon in the Stoa Poikile; moreover, scenes of the Amazonomachy occupied the western metopes of the Parthenon and formed a pendant to the Gigantomachy in the eastern metopes. Appropriately, the western pediment of the Nike temple looked out on the Areopagos, where the myth told that the Amazons had made their camp.[110]

The pervasive theme of violent combat leading to triumphant victory was carried to the rooftop of the temple, where acroterion groups in gilded bronze reiterated the basic theme of the program. Evidence for the reconstruction of the statuary comes from the surviving base which crowned the apex of the eastern pediment in two joining blocks. Another single block formed the base for the angle acroterion at the northeast corner.[111] The joining blocks preserve numerous cuttings, arranged more or less symmetrically on the central base, to anchor bronze figures. Close analysis of the shapes and disposition of the cuttings, in comparison with known acroteria from other buildings, has led to several possible conjectural restorations of the central group.[112] That which best accounts for all the preserved cuttings and most appropriately enhances the theme of the sculptural program is a group of three figures. Centered on the base would be a battlefield trophy, like that shown in the west frieze. This would be flanked on either side by two winged Nikai in the act of decorating it with the spoils of victory: a captured shield propped against the foot of the post and a spear on the right

[106] This was also the conclusion of Stewart, in Kessler and Simpson, eds., *Pictorial Narrative in Antiquity*, 55–57. The suggestion of Palagia (note 105 above) 188–189 that the gods of the east frieze are gathered for the birth of Athena is not appropriate for the overarching theme of military victory that pervades the sculptural decoration of the temple. Cf. Stewart (above) 60–63, 67. The sculptures of the Nike temple express in visual imagery the spirit of impending triumph that seized Athens in the mid-420s and has been well described by Schultz, in Palagia, ed., *Art in Athens during the Peloponnesian War*, 150–155.

[107] G. I. Despinis, *ArchDelt* 29 (1974) A′, 1–24.

[108] Head of Athena (Acrop. Mus. inv. 4303): Despinis, *ArchDelt* 29 (1974) A′, 12–13, no. 4, pls. 17, 18; kneeling male figure (Athens, NM, no inv.): Despinis, 2–10, no. 1, pls. 1–5; male torso (Acrop. Mus. inv. 2791): Despinis, 13–14, no. 5, pls. 18, 19.

[109] Despinis, *ArchDelt* 29 (1974) A′, 19–22.

[110] Despinis, *ArchDelt* 29 (1974) A′, 22–24. The Amazons' camp on the Areopagos, first in Aischylos, *Eumenides* 685–690.

[111] Studied in most detail by Schultz, *Hesperia* 70 (2001) 1–47; the central acroterion base illustrated, 7, figs. 3–5; the angle base, 16, figs. 7–9.

[112] Restoration of a single bronze tripod (Schultz, *Hesperia* 70 [2001] 14–15, figs. 12, 13) does not adequately explain all the cuttings, all of which seem to be original. The restoration of a central Nike raised on a high square post and flanked by two additional Nikai (Schultz, 30–38, fig. 20) appears overpowering on the diminutive facade of the temple.

Figure 115. Sanctuary of Athena Nike, parapet relief of Nike

side.[113] The cutting centered on the angle base indicates a simpler composition: single Nikai probably stood at the corners of the roof and gestured toward the central group.

    Unique in the sculptural decoration of Greek temples was the final element in the celebration
of victory that adorned the Temple of Athena Nike . The building's location on the high projecting
salient of the Acropolis severely limited the space around the temple, and the walls of the bastion
fell away precipitously on three sides (see Fig. 3). Thus it was probably planned from the beginning
to enclose it with a protective parapet that was completed with an extraordinary sculptural frieze in
the later years of the fifth century (Figs. 115, 116).[114] On the parapet, the narrative scenes of combat give way to a ritual celebration of victory itself. Although details of the composition are largely
conjectural, it seems that figures of the goddess Athena, seated and with her arms at rest, occupied
the corners on the north and south sides, and the exact center of the west side. On all three sides
the goddess was approached by long processions of winged Nikai, who pause at intervals to erect

[113] Schultz, *Hesperia* 70 (2001) 26–28, fig. 15. Before Schultz's study, P. N. Boulter, *Hesperia* 38 (1969) 133–140,
proposed to restore the central acroterion as a group consisting of Bellerophon on the winged horse Pegasos slaying the
chimera, since such a group seemed to be mentioned as an acroterion in a fragmentary building account from the Acropolis
(*IG* I³ 492). Schultz has shown that this proposal now has to be abandoned.

[114] See generally R. Carpenter, *Sculpture of the Nike Temple Parapet;* M. Jameson, in Osborne and Hornblower, eds.,
Ritual, Finance, Politics, 312–324; E. Simon, in Buitron-Oliver, ed., *Interpretation of Architectural Sculpture,* 127–143; T.
Hölscher, *AM* 112 (1997) 143–163; Knell, *Mythos und Polis,* 148–149; C. Thöne, *Ikonographische Studien zu Nike,* 64–73;
M. Brouskari, "Τὸ θωράκιο τοῦ ναοῦ τῆς Ἀθηνᾶς Νίκης," *ArchEph* 137 (1998), with full bibliography; discussion of the
date, Brouskari, 53–55: the parapet completed by 415.

Figure 116. Sanctuary of Athena Nike, parapet relief of seated Athena and Nike

military trophies or lead cattle to sacrifice.[115] The Nikai move with delicate grace; their voluminous drapery stirs in the breeze, and some at least are shown in the act of sacrificing bulls, apparently with effortless ease, as if performing some fantastic ballet.[116] But the surviving fragments preserve no trace of altars for the sacrifice. Moreover, the male sex of the victims was not appropriate for Athena Nike, who always received "the most beautiful cow" selected from the cattle brought to the Acropolis for the Panathenaic hekatomb.[117] This has led to the suggestion that the sacrifices shown on the parapet were not intended for the goddess herself but were offered in the chthonic rite for the heroes who gave their lives for Athens on the battlefield.[118] Just such sacrifices continued to be offered by the

[115] On the parapet as an allegory of victory, Stewart, in Kessler and Simpson, eds., *Pictorial Narrative in Antiquity*, 58–61.

[116] Acrop. Mus. inv. 985 + 997 (Brouskari [note 114 above] 154–158); Acrop. Mus. inv. 972 (Brouskari, 119–128); Acrop. Mus. inv. 7098 + 7099 (Brouskari, 210–213).

[117] The sacrifice specified: *IG* II² 334, lines 20–21 = *Agora* XVI 75, lines 45–46.

[118] Simon, in Buitron-Oliver, ed., *Interpretation of Architectural Sculpture*, 135–139. Jameson, in Osborne and Hornblower, eds., *Ritual, Finance, Politics*, 312–319, interprets the sacrifices differently. For him they signify the victims offered by armies on the battlefield before the onset of battle. But on the parapet, Athena sits relaxed, having doffed her arms, and the Nikai pirouette before her as they perform the ritual act that every Greek would read as the celebration of victory: the decoration of battlefield trophies. It is difficult to see how anyone would read in these scenes the moments of tense anxiety before the first assault of arms. Jameson asserts (318) "Time in these scenes is compressed. Victory is sought through sacrifice, and victory has been won. We have the powerful action at the beginning and the erection of trophies at the end." Even to the most casual observer, the vivid depiction of the end would seem to contradict Jameson's interpretation of the beginning.

ephebes in the Hellenistic period who sacrificed *enagismata* to the long dead heroes on the great mound at Marathon.[119] On the parapet, the Nikai decorate trophies for both hoplite and naval victories, and one is decked out in Persian spoils.[120] So the parapet presents a visual paean of praise for the glories of Athenian military prowess in wars of distant myth and recent history, and the goddess Athena Nike presides over sacrifices commemorating the heroes who died in these wars.

✦

The two miniature Ionic temples that we have examined in this chapter are monuments of extraordinary interest. Close comparison of the two buildings has served to emphasize their remarkable similarities in the unusual plans, in the way they are placed on their sites, in their treatment of the Ionic order, and in the minute details of the architectural decoration. These similarities greatly strengthen the impression that both temples were the products of nearly contemporary designs, planned in the 430s and influenced in part by the interior Ionic columns of the Propylaia. As we have seen, construction of the Temple of Athena Nike must have gotten started ca. 435, and the temple on the Ilissos possibly somewhat earlier. In the case of the latter, there is no evidence whatever concerning its date of completion. But it is likely enough that the Nike temple became embroiled in the vicissitudes that caused the abandonment of the Propylaia in 432, and its superstructure and sculpture were certainly not finished until the 420s.

Both Ionic temples were monuments that expressed the city's thanks for military victories bestowed upon Athens, and both sanctuaries were the locus of annual sacrifices that perpetuated the act of thanksgiving. If the temple on the Ilissos is correctly attributed to Artemis Agrotera, its construction specifically commemorated the victory at Marathon, and the extravagant annual sacrifices fulfilled the vow made to the goddess before the battle. By contrast, the Athena Nike temple proclaimed generally the triumph of Athenian arms: victories over Persia, victories over Greeks, victories in myth, victories by the goddess herself, and all shown in the sculptural program of the temple. But the wars of recent history are depicted like the exploits of myth, as modern attempts to explain them have revealed. The Athenian hoplites have become a race of heroes. They fight with minimal defensive armor and yet are seemingly invincible in the reckless daring of their attack. But the image of Athenian triumph conveyed by the battle friezes of the Nike temple seems increasingly out of touch with the realities of contemporary warfare, as the long years of the Peloponnesian War dragged on. Sadly, by the time the sculptures of the parapet were complete, the Athenian century was nearing its end.

---

[119] *IG* II² 1006, lines 26–27 (123/2).
[120] Persian: Acrop. Mus. inv. 981 (Brouskari [note 114 above] 149–151, pl. 18); hoplite: Acrop. Mus. inv. 987 (Brouskari, 159–161, pl. 25); Acrop. Mus. inv. 994+ (Brouskari, 171–177, pls. 36–40); naval: no inv., now lost (Brouskari, 218–219).

11

The Periklean Legacy

To the modern student of Athenian history, the events of the last decades of the fifth century appear to unfold with the inexorable logic of a Sophoklean tragedy. The generals who commanded Athenian forces, the orators who harangued the assembly, the men who jockeyed for primacy in the formation of Athenian policy often seem larger than life, but without exception they had fatal flaws, like the heroes of the tragic theater. The Athenian demos, itself a major player in the drama, acted at times like the crazed chorus of *Eumenides*, and we watch with prurient fascination as it lurches toward inevitable disaster at the end of the century. But, unlike a play of Euripides, there was no *deus ex machina* to halt the devastation of the plague, to save the doomed armies at Syracuse, or to stay the turmoil at Athens after the final defeat. The terrified and humiliated city that demolished its fortifications at Spartan command was a vastly different Athens from the proud imperial capital that had set out to build the Parthenon. The foregoing chapters have sought to elucidate the construction of that building and other contemporary temples in accordance with a policy specific to the Periklean age. It may now call for some explanation why such a study should conclude by descending into the troubled years of the Peloponnesian War, especially when the period of Perikles' ascendancy ended with the statesman's death in the autumn of 429. The assorted vicissitudes of the Archidamian War, however, conceal some clues that may shed light on the enduring enigma of Athenian architecture and cult: the relationship of the two temples on the Acropolis that we call the Parthenon and the Erechtheion, after the locution of Pausanias.

One of the most unusual features of the sanctuary of Athena on the Acropolis was the existence of two temples standing side by side, from the late fifth century onward to the end of antiquity.[1] Both buildings always functioned, to the extent that Greek temples functioned at all. Throughout the Classical period, the two temples served as repositories for the sacred treasures of the goddess, and the treasurers catalogued their contents annually at least to the end of the fourth century.[2] In the time of Pausanias, they still housed their original cult statues of the goddess, together with all manner of votive dedications that had accumulated in the six centuries of their service to the cult. This architectural duplication would occasion no surprise if the two buildings celebrated two different aspects of the goddess Athena, with liturgical ritual specific to each temple, or if they distinguished different epithets for the goddess's name, Athena Parthenos and Athena Polias, as the casual parlance of modern writers sometimes seems to imply. But in the Classical period, there was only one cult of

---

[1] For the anomaly of the two temples, see Herington, *Athena Parthenos*, 35–42, but his discussion is confused by his belief in the existence of an early-sixth-century temple on the site of the Parthenon, following Dinsmoor, *AJA* 51 (1947) 109–151, a view which he later partially retracted; see *G&R* 10 Suppl. (1963) 61–62, note 1.

[2] See generally Harris, *Treasures*.

Athena on the Acropolis: she was ἡ θεός, or Athena Polias, as distinct from her more specialized aspects Athena Nike and Athena Hygieia.[3] The goddess had only one priestess of Athena Polias, and she received offerings on only one sacrificial altar called ὁ βωμὸς τῆς Ἀθηνᾶς ὁ μεγάλος, "the great altar of Athena."[4] This altar was not aligned with either classical temple, as was the frequent practice in Greek sanctuaries, but was actually oriented with relation to the ruins of their archaic predecessor that the Persians had sacked. Only one board of officials had custody of the sacred treasures, and in the public documents they have the title οἱ ταμίαι τῶν ἱιερῶν χρεμάτον τῆς Ἀθεναίας, "the treasurers of the sacred properties of Athena."[5] As early as ca. 405/4, they recorded a votive offering dedicated to Athena Polias and kept in the eastern cella of the Parthenon. There too were the twenty-seven silver hydrias belonging to Athena Polias that appear in the inventories year after year throughout the first half of the fourth century. Most significantly, the principal financial reserves of Athens were the property of Athena Polias, and during the Archidamian War she, together with Athena Nike, made regular loans to the Athenian state in support of the war effort.[6] In the official records of the fifth and fourth centuries, Athena Parthenos does not exist, and it is certain that the goddess of the Parthenon was not so named. This curious situation raises at once two related questions that need to be addressed: What was the intended function of the Parthenon? What motivated construction of the Erechtheion?

THE CULT STATUES OF THE ACROPOLIS

In order to explore the functions of the two temples and the relationship between them, we need to consider first the most important offerings dedicated to the goddess in each building. They were, of course, the two cult statues, the two most revered objects in the sanctuary, which between them had an enormous impact on the architecture and topography of the Acropolis. The two images of Athena could hardly have presented more radically different interpretations of the goddess's appearance. In previous chapters, we have considered the details of the iconography in the appropriate contexts, so that here we need do no more than recall their salient features.[7] First is the Ancient Image of Athena

[3] See Herington, *Athena Parthenos*, 8–12; for the goddess's names Polias, Nike, and Hygieia, *IG* II² 334 = *Agora* XVI 75, lines 34, 47. M. Lipka, in Hoepfner, ed., *Kult und Kultbauten*, 37–44, attempts to create a cult of Athena Parthenos on the basis of the invocation φαρθένε, "maiden," in three private dedications (*IG* I³ 728, 745, 850). But Raubitschek, *DAA*, nos. 40 and 79, and Herington, *Athena Parthenos*, 9 and note 5, are surely correct that this is not a cult epithet. The epithet παρθένος never appears in the public records of the cult in the fifth and fourth centuries.

[4] For the priestess of Athena Polias from the genos of the Eteoboutadai: Parker, *Athenian Religion*, 290–293; Lewis, *BSA* 50 (1955) 1–12; Davies, *APF*, 169–173. For the altar, *IG* II² 334 = *Agora* XVI 75, lines 44–45.

[5] The full title appears regularly in the expense accounts of the fifth century and is well preserved in, e.g., *IG* I³ 464, lines 4, 15–16 (433/2); 370, lines 24–25 (417/6), 61–62 (415/4); 375, line 2 (410/9). Well-preserved examples of the title in the inventories of the Pronaos: *IG* I³ 297, line 13 (429/8); 298, line 26 (428/7); 299, line 39 (427/6). Also in the inventories of the Parthenon, e.g., *IG* I³ 354, line 72 (419/8). The building accounts of the Parthenon and Propylaia use a variant of the title, ταμίαι hoὶ τὰ τὲς θεὸς ἐταμίευον, "treasurers who managed the money of the goddess," e.g., *IG* I³ 439, lines 69–70; 449, lines 385–386; 465, line 121. This was shortened in the accounts of the gold and ivory statue to ταμίαι ἐκ πόλεος, "treasurers from the Acropolis," e.g., *IG* I³ 455, line 7. In the fourth-century inventories, the title was frequently abbreviated οἱ ταμίαι τῆς θεὸς, "treasurers of the goddess," e.g., *IG* II² 1407, line 2 (385/4).

[6] The votive to Athena Polias in the Parthenon, *IG* I³ 342, line 16. Record of the silver hydrias is partially preserved in numerous inventories; see the catalogue of Harris, *Treasures*, V.260. Loans from the treasury of the goddess to the Athenian state, *IG* I³ 369, lines 112–117.

[7] The statue is called: ἀρχαῖον ἄγαλμα, *IG* I³ 64A, line 21; ἡ θεός, frequently in the epigraphical sources, e.g., *IG* I³ 7, lines 9, 11; *IG* II² 1424A (Add. p. 802), lines 362–366; τὸ ἕδος: Plut. *Sol.* 12, *Alkib.* 34.1; Xen. *Hell.* 1.4.12; Hesych., s.v. Πραξιεργίδαι. The image was unarmed, with her arm outstretched holding a phiale. The phiale is attested in *IG* II² 1424a, lines 365–366. There has been substantial disagreement as to the appearance of the image and whether she was of the armed Palladion type, seated and unarmed, or standing and unarmed. For earlier scholarship favoring the armed Palladion, L. R.

Polias, called τὸ ἀρχαῖον ἄγαλμα in the inscriptions of the fifth century, and, as is stated in the over-seers' report of 409, the Erechtheion was built specifically to house this statue.[8] Carved of olive wood, the image was so ancient that legend said it had fallen from heaven. Athenians believed that it existed before the union of Attica, and later writers called it one of the oldest cult statues in Greece.[9] Tertullian (*Apologeticus* 16.6) disparaged its primitive form in a rhetorical question which conveys a graphic impression of the statue's appearance: "Et tamen quanto distinguitur a crucis stipite Pallas Attica, et Ceres Pharia, quae sine effigie rudi palo et informe ligno prostant?," "Yet what distinction can you make between the shaft of a cross and the Attic Pallas or Pharian Ceres, each of whom stands there unshaped, a rude pole, a log untrimmed?" Yet this formless wooden image, to later eyes hardly a work of sculpture at all, was the holiest religious relic in Athens for which a new peplos was woven and dedicated at every celebration of the Great Panathenaia.[10] From Tertullian's description, it is a natural inference that the figure stood stiffly upright. In addition to the peplos, she wore a golden aegis with gorgoneion, necklace, and earrings; she had a diadem on her head and a phiale in her outstretched hand.[11] This is the figure that Euripides described in a passage of *Electra* (1254–1257), where Orestes is instructed to seek asylum in Athena's shrine: "When you come to Athens, embrace the holy wooden image of Pallas. The furies will be terrified by the dreadful snakes, and she will prevent them from touching you, as she holds the gorgon-faced circle on her aegis above your head." The Athenian dramatist treats the statue in a lively and sympathetic way, for he imputes to the image itself all of Athena's protective powers. In the poetic imagination of his verses, we see the suppliant clasp the image about the legs, and she stretches out her aegis with its golden gorgoneion like a shield above his head.

For the purposes of the present inquiry, it is interesting to observe how the ancient sources refer to this venerable wooden figure, but in order to isolate the nomenclature of the Classical period, it is important to survey only literature and documents dating to the fifth and fourth centuries. It is also necessary to distinguish passages mentioning the statue itself from general references to the goddess Athena or to her cult and temple. In the Classical period, there were surprisingly few occasions on which literary authors or public inscriptions actually spoke of the cult statue. In the official records of the Acropolis, it was always anonymous: the goddess was Athena Polias, but her image was ἡ θεός. The inventories of the treasurers list the golden ornaments ἣν ἡ θεὸς ἔχει, "which the goddess has (or wears)," and the genos of the Praxiergidai [ἀμ]φιεννύοσιν τὸν πέπλον τὲ[ν θεὸν], "clothe the [goddess] in the peplos."[12] Alternatively, the statue is τὸ ἀρχαῖον ἄγαλμα, "the ancient image," a locution

---

Farnell, *Cults of the Greek States* (Oxford 1896) vol. 1, 334–337; E. Petersen, *Die Burgtempel der Athenaia* (Berlin 1907) 40–60; Petersen, *Klio* 9 (1909) 242–247. For the seated goddess with diadem and phiale, A. Frickenhaus, *AM* 33 (1908) 17–32; Herington, *Athena Parthenos*, 22–26; *LIMC*, vol. 2, s.v. Athena 17, and comments p. 1017; B. S. Ridgway, in J. Neils, ed., *Goddess and Polis* (Princeton 1992) 120–122. Favoring a standing figure with aegis but without weapons: I. B. Romano, "Early Greek Cult Images" (Ph.D. diss., University of Pennsylvania, 1980) 42–53; J. H. Kroll, *Hesperia* Suppl. 20 (1982) 65–76; J. M. Mansfield, "The Robe of Athena and the Panathenaic *Peplos*" (Ph.D. diss., Berkeley, 1985) 135–149.

[8] *IG* I³ 474, line 1. The cult statue is called simply τὸ ἄγαλμα in *IG* I³ 474, line 75, and 475, lines 269–270. Cf. also *IG* I³ 64A, line 21.

[9] Olive wood: schol. Demosth. 22 *Andr.* 13 (45 Dilts). Fallen from heaven (διοπετές, διιπετές): schol. Aristeid. *Panath.* 187.20 (vol. 3, p. 320, Dindorf). Among the oldest statues, dedicated by the *autochthonoi*: Philostratos, *Life of Apollonius* 3.14; Eusebius, *Praep. evang.* 3.8.99b, quoting Plut. *Mor.* frag. 158 (Sandbach); Apollodoros 3.14.6. Before the union of Attica: Paus. 1.26.6. For discussion, see Romano, "Cult Images," 42–57.

[10] Until late in the Hellenistic period, the peplos was woven anew and dedicated on the Acropolis only at the Great Panathenaia in every fourth year. See J. L. Shear, "Polis and Panathenaia," 173–186, and for the change to annual dedication in the second century, 97–103. This discussion argues convincingly against the theory that there were two peploi in the Classical period, one annual and one quadrennial, as postulated by Mansfield, "Robe of Athena," 2–18, 289–296.

[11] The best-preserved text listing the golden jewelry and attributes of the statue is *IG* II² 1424A (Add. p. 802), lines 362–366.

[12] Text of the inventories, note 11 above, and the identical entries, Harris, *Treasures*, 209, VI.20. The prerogatives of the Praxiergidai: *IG* I³ 7, line 11; and cf. Parker, *Athenian Religion*, 307–308. The garments and ornaments of the statue: Mansfield, "Robe of Athena," 139–149. On nomenclature, Herington, *Athena Parthenos*, 6–8.

which emphasizes both the age of the figure and what a delightful gift the dedication was, and how pleasing to the deity. That same word ἄγαλμα was adopted by Herodotos in his account of Kylon and his conspirators who sought asylum at the statue when they failed to capture the Acropolis and establish a tyranny.[13] The fifth-century dramatists use the word βρέτας, which means the wooden image of a deity and suggests its primitive character. The cult statue figures extensively in the action of Aischylos's *Eumenides* and is mentioned once in Aristophanes' *Lysistrata;* but only Euripides, in the passage quoted above, names it "image of Pallas."[14] The only other classical author to mention the statue is Xenephon, who speaks of it as veiled for the celebration of the Plynteria. He calls it τὸ ἕδος τῆς Ἀθηνᾶς, "the cult statue of Athena," an expression that implies by its derivation a seated image but was actually used indiscriminately to describe statues of the gods regardless of pose.[15] Never at this early period is the wooden image called the Polias, and that epithet seems not to have been applied to the statue itself before the second century A.D.[16]

The second cult statue of the Acropolis was one of the most famous masterpieces of classical art, the gold and ivory statue of Athena that Pheidias made for the Parthenon. The colossal scale of the figure, the Olympian beauty of the goddess's features, and the marvelous modeling of her golden robes evoked the wondering admiration of antiquity. She had stood erect for six centuries when Pausanias described her, dressed in peplos and aegis with its ivory gorgoneion, armed with a helmet on her head and shield and spear grounded at her left side. A winged Nike alighted on her outstretched right hand, and a great serpent coiled beside her left foot.[17] Pheidias's statue enjoyed unique notoriety for the removable golden plates of which the drapery was fashioned, and especially for the enormous weight of refined gold bullion that they contained.[18] From the time of its dedication, we have seen that the precious materials of the statue caused allegations of theft and malfeasance to swirl about Pheidias and Perikles. The ensuing scandal drove the sculptor to seek safety in flight and nearly engulfed the statesman.[19] In view of its celebrity in later antiquity, it is somewhat surprising to find that contemporary references to the cult statue of the Parthenon are just as anonymous as those to the Ancient Image. The board of overseers that administered its original construction called it simply τὸ ἄγαλμα or τὸ ἄγαλμα χρυσοῦν, "the statue" or "the golden statue," without further qualification.[20] This same expression also occurs regularly in the inscriptions recording periodic inspections of the statue by the treasurers, and it is possible that Philochoros drew on an epigraphical source when he used the same words to report its dedication in 438.[21] The statue is ἡ θεός when first mentioned in

[13] Cited in note 8 above. The conspiracy of Kylon: Hdt. 5.71.

[14] Aisch. *Eumenides* 80: ἵζου παλαιὸν ἄγκαθεν λαβὼν βρέτας, "sit down and clasp in your arms her ancient image," and cf. *Eumenides* 242, 259, 409, 439–440, 446. Aristoph. *Lys.* 262: κατὰ μὲν ἅγιον ἔχειν βρέτας, "[the women] are in possession of the holy image."

[15] Xen. *Hell.* 1.4.12.

[16] The earliest datable writer to use the term appears to be Plutarch, *De Daedalis Plataeensibus* (*Mor.* frag. 158 Sandbach), quoted by Eusebius, *Praep. evang.* 3.8.99b: [ἄγαλμα] ξύλινον δὲ τὸ τῆς Πολιάδος ὑπὸ τῶν αὐτοχθόνων ἱδρυθέν, ὃ μέχρι νῦν Ἀθηναῖοι διαφυλάττουσιν, "the statue of the Polias is wooden, the one set up by the autochthonoi, which the Athenians keep to this day."

[17] Paus. 1.24.5–7; Pliny, *NH* 36.18. Testimonia conveniently collected: Jahn and Michaelis, *Arx,* 56–61; Overbeck, *Schriftquellen,* 119–125. Reconstructions of the statue's appearance: Schuchhardt, *AntP* 2 (1963) 31–53; Leipen, *Athena Parthenos;* Harrison, *YCS* 30 (1996) 88–52; Lapatin, *Chryselephantine Statuary,* 63–79.

[18] Thuc. 2.13.5 puts the weight of the gold plates at 40 talents; Philochoros, *FGrH* 328 F 121, quoted by schol. Aristoph. *Peace* 605a (Holwerda), says the plates weighed 44 talents; Diod. 12.40.3, citing Ephoros, rounds the figure to 50 talents. Plut. *Mor.* 828B is based on Thucydides; cf. Plut. *Per.* 31.3.

[19] For the attacks on Pheidias and Perikles, see chap. 9, pp. 311–319 above.

[20] *IG* I³ 457, lines 4–5; 458, lines 2–3. For the accounts of the overseers, see chap. 3, pp. 69–77 above.

[21] The fourth-century inspections:, *IG* II² 1407, lines 5–6; 1410, line 7; 1443, lines 10–11; 1468, lines 6–8 = *SEG* 38.136; *SEG* 38.143. Philochoros, *FGrH* 328 F 121. The inventories also record the crown of the Nike ἡ ἐπὶ τῆς χερὸς τὸ ἀγάλματος τὸ χρυσõ, "on the hand of the golden statue," *IG* I³ 342, lines 1–4 (405/4?); *IG* II² 1386, lines 12–14 (401/0). The same entry is listed sixteen times in the fourth century, Harris, *Treasures,* V.94.

literature, in Aristophanes' *Knights* and Thucydides' account of Athenian resources at the outbreak of the war, although to be sure the historian calls it τὸ ἄγαλμα in the next sentence.[22] In the fourth century, Aristotle and Ephoros, as quoted by Diodoros, identified it as τὸ ἄγαλμα τῆς ᾿Αθηνᾶς, while Plato and Aischines refer to the Athena that Pheidias made.[23] On the whole, the classical nomenclature of the two cult statues is extraordinarily similar, the only distinction being their age and the material of which they were made. Particularly interesting is the statement of Isokrates that Pheidias made τὸ τῆς ᾿Αθηνᾶς ἕδος, "the cult statue of Athena," precisely the same words that Xenophon used to describe the Ancient Image.[24] In view of this indistinct mode of reference to the two statues, it is readily understandable how Clement of Alexandria, writing at the end of the second century A.D., could state in confusion that Pheidias had made τὴν ᾿Αθήνησιν Πολιάδα ἐκ χρυσοῦ καὶ ἐλέφαντος, "the Polias at Athens of gold and ivory."[25] The fact is that this most celebrated statue of Athena ever made is nowhere called the "Parthenos" by any author before Pausanias, who twice uses the expression ἡ καλουμένη Παρθένος, "the so-called Parthenos," as if that were some kind of local Athenian nickname.[26] For the Athenian of the Classical period, however, there could be no doubt that the two statues were dedicated to the same goddess: the two ἀγάλματα were ornaments of the same cult.

THE PURPOSE OF THE PARTHENON

In the middle years of the fifth century, the Periklean program for the aggrandizement of the Acropolis called for the erection of a great new temple, and Pheidias's gold and ivory statue was certainly a part of the original conception. The statue was mentioned together with the temple when administrative arrangements were first under discussion around 450. Thereafter its overseers are attested in office as early as 446/5, but it is entirely possible that one earlier board, of which the record is now lost, commenced work the previous year, like the builders of the Parthenon.[27] In chapters 3 and 4, we explored in detail the extraordinary architectural revolution that transpired in the design and construction of that temple. At the time when it was built, the Parthenon was in fact the largest temple in Greece, and that was probably the intention of the builders. It was the only temple on the Greek mainland that had octostyle facades, and in every other way it was the most sophisticated exemplar of the subtleties of the Doric order. But the architects of the Parthenon, for all their innovative genius, adhered closely to traditions that had guided the design of temples on the Acropolis for more than a century. Like its abortive predecessor, the Older Parthenon, the Periklean temple had a most unusual interior plan, for the cella was subdivided into two compartments, the larger eastern one approached through the pronaos at the east end of the temple, and the smaller chamber facing west and entered from the opisthodomos. This anomalous double cella was a direct architectural legacy from the archaic temple destroyed by the Persians, in which the western cella had a more complex tripartite plan. Since that structure in all probability stood on foundations that had been laid down for an earlier archaic temple on the same site, the peculiar plan of the cella recedes backward in time

[22] Aristoph. *Knights* 1169: ὑπὸ τῆς θεοῦ τῇ χειρὶ τηλεφαντίνῃ, "beneath the ivory hand of the goddess." Thuc. 2.13.5.
[23] [Aristot.] *Ath. Pol.* 47.1; Diod. 12.39, 40; Plato, *Hipp. mai.* 290B; Aischin. 3 *Ktes.* 150.
[24] Isokr. 15 *Antid.* 2; cf. Xen. *Hell.* 1.4.12.
[25] Clem. Alex. *Protr.* 4.41.
[26] Paus. 5.11.10, 10.34.8. See Herington, *Athena Parthenos*, 6.
[27] *IG* I³ 32, line 13, mentions works "for the temple and the statue"; see discussion of the passage above, chap. 2, pp. 21–26. The earliest datable fragment of the expense accounts of the statue is *IG* I³ 453. This has the unusual name Exekestos (line 1) in a position appropriate for the secretary of the treasurers, and Exekestos of Athmonon is attested as secretary of the treasurers in Year 2 (446/5) of the Parthenon accounts (*IG* I³ 437, lines 45, 48). Including the treasurer, the name occurs only six times in the fifth century: *LGPN* 143, s.v. Another small fragment of the accounts of the statue, *IG* I³ 454, is not datable and might pertain either to 447/6 or 445/4.

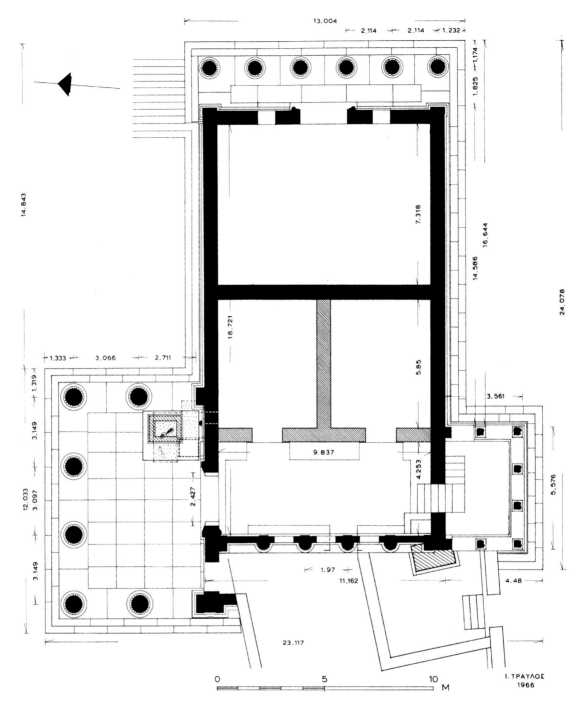

Figure 117. Erechtheion, restored plan

to the early sixth century. Of greater significance is the fact that the interior plan of the archaic temple was even more closely copied in the design of the Erechtheion, for in the most likely restoration of its internal partitions, that building also had a double cella whose western section reproduced the distinctive three compartments of its archaic predecessor (Fig. 117).[28] The plan was unique to the temples of the Acropolis and is found nowhere else among the sanctuaries of classical Greece; it was undoubtedly invented in response to the unusual needs of a building that sheltered jointly the cults of Athena Polias and Poseidon-Erechtheus. But replication of this archaic plan in a temple of the late

[28] For the architectural relation of the Parthenon and the Older Parthenon to the archaic poros temple, see chap. 4, pp. 79–82 above.

fifth century clearly demonstrates that the Erechtheion was, in the event, the direct lineal descendant of the building destroyed by the Persians. Moreover, the overseers' reference to the building as "the temple for the Ancient Image" makes it certain that this most sacred object in Athens resided within its walls from the end of the fifth century onward. So the question arises with still greater urgency: How was the archaic temple related to the Parthenon and why was the Periklean temple designed and begun nearly thirty years before the Erechtheion?

In attempting to answer these questions, one has to concede with all candor that insufficient hard evidence exists to admit of formal proof, and one ventures perforce into quicksands of conjecture. A few certain statements are possible nevertheless. All would agree that the Doric peripteral temple of poros stone that stood on the so-called Dörpfeld Foundations was sacked in the Persian destruction of 480, whereupon portions of its entablature, arranged in their proper order, were built into the northern circuit wall of the Acropolis. This conspicuous reuse of spolia, we have argued, served to memorialize the Persians' destruction of Athena's temple and their subsequent defeat at the hands of the Greek cities. There is, in fact, not the slightest trace of material evidence for the repair or reconstruction of temples, not only on the Acropolis but anywhere in Attica, between the Persian destruction and the beginning of the Periklean buildings. Nor is there any statement in literary or documentary sources to contradict the negative evidence of archaeology. In the Hekatompedon inscriptions of 485, the archaic poros temple is mentioned in the singular with the definite article as *the* temple par excellence on the Acropolis, a landmark familiar to every Athenian.[29] By the 450s, the decree concerning the prerogatives of the Praxiergidai appears to refer to the surviving ruins of the same building as ὁ ἀρχαῖος νεώς, "the Ancient Temple."[30] Not long thereafter, we hear of plans for "works on the Acropolis for the temple and the statue," which must be the earliest reference to the imminent construction of the Parthenon. Once again the building is called *the* temple in the singular with the definite article, as if there were to be no other.[31] It is difficult to escape the impression that, at this stage in the development of the Periklean plans, the Parthenon was conceived as a replacement for the ruined temple, one that would take over all aspects of Athena's cult. Moreover, the great masonry platform erected for its predecessor stood ready to hand a few meters south of the temple site, and that was an eminently appropriate foundation for the new structure. To be sure, the Older Parthenon had felt the Persian flames no less than the archaic temple, and its unfinished column drums had likewise been reused in the fortifications. But thirty years later, Athenian orators could argue that what the Persians had destroyed on the south side of the Acropolis was a construction site and not a temple. The shafts of its columns had scarcely risen above the second drum. The building had never been consecrated; it had no roof, no cult image, no votive offerings. Thus could the arts of persuasion be deployed to counter any lingering opposition.

In preceding chapters we have attempted to reconstruct as full a picture as possible of the Periklean projects for the beautification of Athenian sanctuaries, and we have explored the democratic ideology of imperial Athens that found expression in the sculptural decoration of the temples. In light of the magnitude of these aspirations, it is impossible to believe that the Periklean planners simply failed to accommodate the most sacred relic of Athena's cult, the ancient wooden xoanon of Athena Polias. Are we to suppose that the plan was to build the largest Doric temple in Greece entirely of Pentelic marble and to erect within it a new gold and ivory cult statue of colossal size and exorbitant cost, but the Ancient Image, the central religious artifact of the cult, could remain in some improvised shelter, jerry-built among the ruins of the archaic temple, until the Athenians got around to building a proper temple for it in the late fifth century? It is far more plausible to think that they originally intended to enshrine the ancient cult statue in the "hundred-foot cella" of the

---

[29] *IG* I³ 4A line 16 (restored); 4B, lines 9, 10 (partially restored). Cf. Dinsmoor, *AJA* 51 (1947) 118–127.
[30] *IG* I³ 7, line 6.
[31] *IG* I³ 32, line 13, discussed above, chap. 2, pp. 21–26.

Parthenon, where it would stand beside Pheidias's gold and ivory Athena.[32] Such a striking juxtaposition of two radically different images of the same goddess would have proclaimed the remarkable longevity of the cult, as well as the special piety of which Athenians liked to boast. Moreover, there could be no doubt about the wealth of treasure they lavished upon the city goddess, nor about the luxurious abode in which she had come to reside.

That the architects of the Parthenon conceived the temple as a new home for the wooden xoanon is supported by the evidence of the sculptured frieze. At the midpoint of the east side is a scene depicting the ritual preparations for one of the culminating acts in the liturgy of the Great Panathenaia, the dedication of the peplos (see Fig. 38). Present are the basileus and a girl of the *arrephoroi*, who are shown in the act of folding the sacred robe, while the priestess of Athena Polias directs her acolytes in setting out furniture for the ceremony. The peplos scene implies the presence of the Ancient Image within the cella of the Parthenon.[33] Central to the ritual was the act of clothing the cult statue itself with the new robe in the most literal manifestation of anthropomorphic deity. Whether the frieze shows the new robe being presented at the Parthenon or the old robe folded for storage, its designers cannot have imagined the statue itself standing elsewhere at some undisclosed position on the Acropolis; that notion makes nonsense of the sculptural narrative.

Temples with Ancient Xoana and Modern Aγαλματα

As it happens, several of the oldest sanctuaries of Greece show well-documented examples of precisely the same situation for which the Athenian Acropolis yields only circumstantial evidence, that is to say, early archaic temples later replaced by more splendid structures which displayed new cult statues side by side with the venerable relics of early antiquity. The Argive Heraion provides an exact and nearly contemporary parallel for the scenario that we have postulated at Athens. In the summer of 423, the archaic Temple of Hera burned to the ground, consumed by an accidental fire, whereupon, in rapid response, the Argives erected a new peripteral Doric temple on a lower terrace of the sanctuary.[34] When Pausanias visited this shrine some six centuries later, he saw within its cella no fewer than three images of the goddess, which he described in detail:

> The statue of Hera is seated on a throne; it is of colossal size, made of gold and ivory, and is the work of Polykleitos. On her head is a crown with the Graces and Seasons worked on it in relief, and in one hand she carries a pomegranate, in the other a scepter. . . . By its side is an old image of Hera on a column. But her most ancient image is made of the wood of the wild pear tree; it was dedicated in Tiryns by Peirasos son of Argos, and when the Argives destroyed Tiryns, they brought it to the Heraion. I saw it myself, a small, seated image.[35]

As in the case of the Parthenon, construction of a grand new temple at the Heraion provided an appropriate occasion for the dedication of a new cult statue. Polykleitos's masterpiece, no doubt partly inspired by Pheidias's works in Athens and Olympia, was likewise of colossal scale and fashioned in gold and ivory. It too evoked the praises of later antiquity: Strabo called the statue the most

---

[32] This suggestion was first put forward by A. Furtwängler, *Masterpieces of Greek Sculpture* (London 1895) 426–429, and subsequently rejected by Herington, *Athena Parthenos*, 36 and note 3, largely because of his erroneous belief in Dinsmoor's early archaic temple on the site of the Parthenon.

[33] So argued also by Furtwängler, *Masterpieces*, 427–428. On the duties and prerogatives of the Praxiergidai with respect to the robing and care of the ancient statue, Mansfield, "Robe of Athena," 366–379.

[34] Thuc. 4.133.2–3 reports the destruction of the old temple. For the architecture of the classical temple, C. A. Pfaff, *Argive Heraion*, vol. 1, *The Architecture of the Classical Temple of Hera* (Princeton 2003).

[35] Paus. 2.17.4, 5 and cf. 8.46.3.

beautiful in the world, and Plutarch compared it to the Olympian Zeus.[36] But beside it stood the ancient wooden xoanon of the goddess that had been rescued from the conflagration in the old temple. The small, seated figure that Pausanias saw was so old that one legend attributed its dedication to the founder of the sanctuary.[37] Yet the two statues of Hera, enthroned side by side—modern and ancient, golden and wooden, great and small—cohabited congenially in the same cella.

A similar situation obtained in the sanctuary of Hera on the island of Samos. In a temple inventory of 346/5, the treasurers of the sanctuary devoted twenty-six lines of text to a detailed catalogue describing the "wardrobe of the goddess" (κόσμος τῆς θεοῦ).[38] The inscription lists many items of clothing that have been dedicated to Hera and stored in the temple, but among these certain garments are specifically designated by the phrase τούτους ἡ θεὸς ἔχει, "these the goddess has" or "wears," a locution that plainly identifies clothing draped on the cult statue in a manner closely analogous to the peplos of the Ancient Image at Athens. The outfit of Samian Hera consisted of a μίτρη πάραυλος (lines 18–19), which has been interpreted as a polos or similar headdress;[39] a πρόσλημμα (lines 20–21), probably a purple shoulder wrap with tassels at both ends; and at least six chitons with purple fringes, four of which are described as Lydian (lines 27–29, 31). Clearly to be distinguished from this somewhat overly dressed statue is another entry that reads ἱμάτιον λευκόν, ἡ ὄπισθε θεὸς ἔχει, "a white himation, which the goddess behind wears" (line 27). By this rather elliptical expression, the treasurers evidently differentiated two images of the goddess, one of which stood physically behind the other in the temple. That the figure called simply ἡ θεὸς was the more important of the two is suggested by her more sumptuous costume with multiple vestments, whereas "the goddess behind" wore only a simple white mantle. "The goddess" is surely to be identified with the ancient xoanon of Hera, which a contemporary Samian writer described as nothing more than a "plank" (σανίς) at first that later was made "statue-like" (ἀνδριαντοειδές).[40] The wooden image goes back to the earliest days of the sanctuary at the beginning of the eighth century, and every year at the Tonaia festival the Samians carried it to the seashore, where it was bound with willow branches lest it take flight from the island.[41] "The goddess behind" no doubt described a second cult statue added to the furnishings of the temple in one of its later phases.

The existence of two cult statues within the temple is corroborated by the long and remarkable architectural history of successive temples at the Samian Heraion. The old xoanon stood against the west wall of the tunnel-like, mud-brick structure that formed the first temple of the Geometric period. When the temple was rebuilt in the first half of the seventh century, the cult image continued

[36] Strabo 8.6.10 (p. 372); Plut. *Per.* 2.1. Testimonia in Overbeck, *Antiken Schriftquellen,* 166–167. On the career of Polykleitos, A. H. Borbein, *YCS* 30 (1996) 66–90. On the statue at the Heraion, Lapatin, *Chryselephantine Statuary,* 101–105.

[37] There are conflicting traditions about the oldest xoanon of Hera that Pausanias saw. The *Phoronis,* a poem of about 600, calls it a "tall column," evidently an aniconic image, Clem. Alex. *Strom.* 1.164.2. Demetrios of Argos, *FGrH* 304, probably fourth century, in the second book of his *Argolika,* says that it was made of pear-tree wood by Argos; Clem. Alex. *Protr.* 4.41.5. Plutarch, *De Daedalis Plataeensibus* (*Mor.* frag. 158 Sandbach), quoted by Eusebius, *Praep. evang.* 3.8.99b, reports that Peiras, founder of the sanctuary, cut wood from the pear trees around Tiryns. For discussion of the sources, Donohue, *Xoana,* 196 and note 3.

[38] Michel, *Recueil d'inscriptions grecques,* 832; D. Ohly, *AM* 68 (1953) 46–49; Romano, "Cult Images," 250–271. Cf. Mansfield, "Robe of Athena," 483–484.

[39] The image of Hera on Roman coins wears a polos that has been identified as a μίτρη: R. Fleischer, *Artemis von Ephesos* (Leiden 1973) 207–208. Alternatively, the word can signify a belt or girdle, LSJ[9], s.v. I.2.

[40] Aethlios, *FGrH* 536 F 3, a Samian historian probably of the fifth century, quoted by Clem. Alex. *Protr.* 4.40.3. Cf. the similar descriptions of the image, Callimachus, *Aetia* IV, frag. 100 (Pfeiffer) from Plutarch, *De Daedalis Plateensibus* (*Mor.* frag. 158 Sandbach) = Eusebius, *Praep. evang.* 3.8.

[41] For the traditions on the founding of the sanctuary, especially the local Samian legend that the goddess was born on the island beside the river Imbrasos under a willow tree (λύγος), Paus. 7.4.4. For the Tonaia and the legends behind the festival, Menodotos, *FGrH* 541 F 1, quoted by Athenaeus 15.672A–E. Discussion of the literary testimonia, Romano, "Cult Images," 250–255.

to occupy the same position, although the first base was buried beneath the second.[42] The first half of the sixth century saw the enormous expansion of the temple with the construction of the first great dipteros by the architects Rhoikos and Theodoros. The new building almost completely covered the site of its predecessor; but since the length increased by more than three times, it extended far to the west, and the rear end of the earlier cella fell at the midpoint of the south aisle in the new pronaos. Here the early statue base was still visible, so that the old wooden image stood on the spot it had already occupied for two centuries, although that spot was now in the pronaos rather than the cella of the new temple. At the same time, within the huge cella, a second statue base was erected on a low masonry platform which occupied the exact center of the interior. This base undoubtedly accommodated a new cult statue dedicated together with the temple, so that from the middle of the sixth century onward Hera's temple displayed two images of the goddess, a more recent one in the cella itself, and the old xoanon in the pronaos.[43] Not long after its completion, Rhoikos's temple perished in a fire during the third quarter of the sixth century, whereupon the tyrant Polykrates promptly commenced construction of the second dipteros, similar in plan to the first but of a size that would remain for all time the largest in Greece. In order to create more space between the temple and the great sacrificial altar, the Polykratean building was pushed 41 meters farther to the west, so that its pronaos now rose above the cella of its predecessor. The disposition of the two cult statues in the second dipteros is not absolutely certain, because no foundations for a base have chanced to survive within the cella. Nevertheless, it seems most likely that the sixth-century image was reerected at the center of the cella in the same relative position that it had in Rhoikos's building. Likewise, the ancient wooden statue now took up a position aligned with the great doors at the exact midpoint of the pronaos, where the foundations for a later replacement of its base are still preserved.[44] Thus in the Classical period, when the treasurers compiled the inventory for 346/5, the two statues stood one behind the other on the axis of the temple. It was then perfectly natural to call the venerable old idol ἡ θεός and to refer to the new image as ἡ ὄπισθε θεός.

The practice of dedicating more than one cult statue to the same deity in a single temple was well known to the Athenians, who themselves exhibited three images of Artemis in her temple at Brauron. Evidence for the number of statues comes from inscribed inventories listing the dedications kept in the sanctuary and recorded annually by the epistatai. Numerous fragments of these inscriptions, dating to the mid-fourth century, have come to light on the Acropolis and were thought originally to pertain to Artemis's cult in the city, but the discovery of duplicate texts in the excavations at Brauron now demonstrates that they catalogue the treasures dedicated at the country sanctuary.[45] Many of the items are articles of clothing offered to the goddess by Athenian women. Many of these were regularly labeled with the names of the donor and the archon in whose year the gift was made, since the lists are compiled in the chronological order of donation. Like the similar inventory from the Samian Heraion, the Athenian texts specify that certain garments were actually in use as clothing for the cult statues, and in one of the better-preserved documents, the epistatai were careful to distinguish between three different statues within the space of twenty-two lines.[46] We read first

[42] Ohly, *AM* 68 (1953) 25–26; Romano, "Cult Images," 258.

[43] Ohly, *AM* 68 (1953) 31–33, 45, Anh. 2; Romano, "Cult Images," 258–259.

[44] Ohly, *AM* 68 (1953) 33–34, 35, fig. 3, 45, Anh. 3; Romano, "Cult Images," 259–260.

[45] Linders, *Artemis Brauronia*, 70–73; Romano, "Cult Images," 85–86. The copies of the inventories found on the Acropolis, *IG* II² 1514–1531. Only extracts of the inscriptions from Brauron have been published; see A. Orlandos, *Ergon* (1961) 24–26; G. Daux, *BCH* 86 (1962) 671, 674; J. Papadimitriou, *Scientific American* 208 (1963) 118–120; J. Robert and L. Robert, *REG* 76 (1963) 134–135, no. 91; J. Kondis, *ArchDelt* 22 (1967) Α', 169–170. That all three statues, to be described below, were housed in a single building is argued by Linders, *Artemis Brauronia*, 16–17.

[46] *IG* II² 1514, lines 22–43. Three separate statues are mentioned; see the commentary of Linders, *Artemis Brauronia*, 14–15, essentially following the division of J. Tréheux, *RA* 55 (1964) 1–6. This is a more satisfactory interpretation of the references to the statues than the attempt of Romano, "Cult Images," 88–89, to assign all the references to only two images of the goddess.

of a chiton of Amorgian flax dedicated by Nikolea which is περὶ τῶι ἔδει, "around the statue" (lines 22–23).[47] This is followed shortly by a white himation edged with purple, τοῦτο τὸ λίθινον ἔδος ἀμπέχεται, "this the marble statue wears" (lines 26–28).[48] Then comes a group of four garments donated in 345/4, each of which is described as περὶ τῶι ἔδει τῶι ἀρχαίωι, "around the ancient statue" (lines 34–39). Her outfit consists of two shawls (ἀμπέχονον) dedicated by Theano and Penteteris, respectively: a garment called a ταραντῖνον and one called a διπτέρυγον, a double-winged mantle decorated in a polka-dot pattern.[49] Finally, in lines 41–43 the epistatai listed a chitoniskos that is said to be περὶ τῶι ἀγάλματι τῶι ὀρθῶι, "around the standing statue."[50]

In a much more fragmentary inventory, dating to the decade 420 to 410, τὸ λίθινον ἔδος, "the marble statue," and τὸ ἀρχαῖον ἔδος, "the ancient statue," are juxtaposed to each other in consecutive lines and must certainly describe two different images of the goddess.[51] It is highly likely that "the ancient statue" of the inscription is to be identified as the old wooden xoanon, which Pausanias saw at Brauron and which the Athenians claimed that Iphigenia had carried away from the Taurians.[52] The inventories then differentiate this venerable relic from a newer dedication of a different material by calling the latter "the marble statue." The mention of τὸ ἔδος without further qualification could describe either of these images but is perhaps more likely to be an abbreviated reference to "the ancient statue." Beside these two statues in the same temple stood a third that the epistatai designated τὸ ἄγαλμα τὸ ὀρθόν, "the standing statue." Since that locution seems to emphasize its pose rather than its material, some scholars have argued that the name distinguishes it from the other images, which must have been seated. To be sure, the word ἔδος does not necessarily imply a cult statue in a seated position, for the same term was applied to the gold and ivory Athena in the Parthenon.[53] It seems beyond doubt, however, that the "upright agalma" was so named specifically to differentiate it from the other two images of Artemis in the same temple. In a later inventory "the standing statue" is described by a synonym, τὸ ἄγαλμα τὸ ἑστηκός, and, probably because of the multiple references to its clothing, that nomenclature is abbreviated several times in the same inscription to simply τὸ ἄγαλμα. Like "the ancient statue," "the standing statue" wore an elaborate combination of garments. The inventories list two jackets with sleeves of oriental type (κάνδυς), two chitoniskoi, a himation, and an ἔγκυκλον, possibly some kind of shoulder wrap, all of which are said to be "around the statue."[54] But it detracts not a little from the splendor that we attribute to Greek religious statuary to read that two of Artemis's garments are said to be ῥάκος, "ragged."

These striking examples of multiple cult statues in the temples of Hera at Argos and Samos, and the Temple of Artemis at Brauron encourage the belief that it was the original purpose of the Parthenon to do precisely the same thing. Moreover, this evidence from the other sanctuaries, when combined with the implications of the peplos scene on the Parthenon frieze, leads one to infer that the Ancient Image of Athena was actually installed in the Parthenon. At the Great Panathenaia of

---

[47] The identical entry appears in *IG* II² 1515, lines 14–15; 1516, line 2.

[48] This item is repeated in *IG* II² 1515, lines 18–20 (partly restored); 1516, lines 6–7.

[49] The same dedications are listed in *IG* II² 1516, lines 13–17; 1517, lines 140–143; and with slight differences in wording in 1515, lines 26–31. They are evidently to be restored also in 1524, B II, lines 227–228. On the garments of the cult statues, see Linders, *Artemis Brauronia,* 11–12; Romano, "Cult Images," 89–91; Mansfield, "Robe of Athena," 458–460.

[50] The item is repeated in *IG* II² 1516, lines 19–21; 1517, lines 147–148. Cf. also a different reference to the "standing statue," 1522, line 29.

[51] *IG* I³ 403, lines 12–13 (ca. 416/5), as argued by Tréheux, *RA* 55 (1964) 3–4; Linders, *Artemis Brauronia,* 14; Romano, "Cult Images," 87–88.

[52] Paus. 1.33.1 and cf. 3.16.7–8.

[53] The Brauronian statues seated, Tréheux (note 51 above) and Linders (note 51 above). Pheidias's statue called a ἔδος, Isokr. 15 *Antid.* 2.

[54] "The standing statue" called τὸ ἄγαλμα τὸ ἑστηκός: *IG* II² 1524, B II, line 207; and in adjacent lines referred to in abbreviated form as τὸ ἄγαλμα: lines 202–204, 204–205, 205–206, 214–216, 224. Cf. also *IG* II² 1523, lines 27–29.

438, the "hundred-foot cella" of the new temple was very likely the setting for a ceremony closely analogous to that which the sculptors of the frieze had envisioned. On that occasion the basileus and the clergy of the Acropolis welcomed the goddess to her new home and there performed the ancient ritual, clothing her image in the newly woven robe. For the first time in more than forty years, Athena took up residence in a splendid new temple that was truly suitable to her station. Furthermore, it is logical to assume that the dedication of the peplos was repeated at the great festivals of 434 and 430, and throughout these years the cult statues of the Parthenon would have appeared much as Pausanias described those of the Argive Heraion, with ancient and modern images standing side by side. But if these conclusions are thought to provide a credible explanation of the Parthenon's intended function, then the other riddle of the Acropolis cries out the more urgently for resolution: Why was construction of the Erechtheion begun some fifteen years later and what motivated the decision to build it?

THE WRATH OF THE GODS

If, as we have argued, the Parthenon with its gold and ivory cult statue was the crowning centerpiece of the Periklean building program, the Erechtheion stands in opposition to it. The building's original nomenclature, "the temple in which is the Ancient Image," insists that it was erected specifically to house that most sacred artifact of the cult, and installation there of the old wooden xoanon in the last years of the century left the Parthenon bereft of any religious function thenceforward to the end of antiquity. The Erechtheion was no part of the original plan for the Acropolis, long delayed like the Nike temple, but rather was conceived and inaugurated, as we shall see, by Perikles' political successors in the 420s. Its construction must represent a drastic change of plan motivated by circumstances that were totally unforeseen in the heady days of Perikles' ascendancy. Examination of events at Athens at the beginning of the Archidamian War may help to elucidate this seemingly anomalous decision to build yet another temple for the Ancient Image less than a decade after the completion of the Parthenon sculptures in 432. It will be necessary to consider what impact the wartime conditions exerted on the Athenian people, and how that affected the sanctuary of Athena on the Acropolis.

Thucydides introduces his discussion of the causes of the Peloponnesian War with a statement of dramatically ominous import:

> But the Peloponnesian War was protracted to an immense length, and in the course of it disasters befell Hellas the like of which had never occurred in any equal space of time. . . . There were earthquakes that prevailed over a large part of the earth and were likewise of the greatest violence; eclipses of the sun, which occurred more frequently than is recorded of all former times; there were great droughts also in some quarters and consequent famines; and lastly, the disaster which wrought most harm and destroyed a considerable part of the people, the pestilential plague. For all these fell upon them simultaneously with this war.[55]

The plague broke out at Athens in May of 430, a few days after the second Spartan invasion of Attica[56] and within a couple of months of the Great Panathenaic festival of that year. The epidemic raged through the city for two full years until the summer of 428. Although it never completely died out, there was a brief respite in 428/7 before it resumed with even greater virulence in the winter of

---

[55] Thuc. 1.23.1, 3, translation adapted from Crawley.
[56] Thuc. 2.47.2–3, and for the date, Gomme, *HCT*, vol. 2, 145; cf. Diod. 12.45.4.

427/6.[57] According to Diodoros, the spread of the disease was exacerbated by the unusually heavy rainfall of that winter which destroyed the crops and left swampy pools of stagnant water in the low-lying parts of the city. These festered and putrefied in the scorching heat of the following summer, when the Etesian winds failed to blow and the sick burned with fever.[58] By the time the plague abated in the winter of 426, it had ravaged the population for nearly five years. Of the Athenian military, 4,400 hoplites and 300 cavalrymen died of the disease, and of the general population a number that could not be ascertained, which Diodoros reports to have been in the tens of thousands.[59] Thucydides describes the excruciating symptoms with clinical details that only a survivor could have mustered, while Plutarch conveys the devastating effects on Athenian families. In the family of Perikles alone, not only his sister and both his sons but also most of his relatives and friends died of the disease, before the statesman himself succumbed in the autumn of 429.[60]

In Thucydides' narrative the prolonged duration and exceptional virulence of the plague quite literally ripped asunder the social fabric of the city.[61] So massive was the rate of mortality that families wearied of the endless lamentations for the dead. Corpses lay strewn about the sanctuaries polluting the sacred places, and despairing relatives, overwhelmed by the calamity, abandoned the traditional burial rites. In the cemeteries, some simply flung their family's own dead bodies on the burning pyres of strangers, while others buried their dead as best they could in "shameful graves."[62] These last now stand revealed in graphic detail since recent excavations for the Athens subway system uncovered two mass burial pits in the Kerameikos cemetery. One contained skeletons of 29 adults laid on top of each other in successive layers; the other, an enormous irregular hole 8 meters in diameter, produced 89 skeletons that had been dumped in unceremoniously without any order, but later disturbances in part of the pit suggested to the excavators that the original number of burials was at least 150. The despair that gripped the survivors is vividly illustrated in the paltry number of pots that formed the only funerary offerings for the dead.[63] Even more dire were the religious consequences, for the plague completely undermined the fundamental Athenian beliefs in the efficacy of the pious life and the practice of cult ritual. When beset by disaster, the Greek naturally turned to his gods and sought instruction through divination how to supplicate the appropriate deity. Now, in the throes of devastating sickness, it came as a severe shock to pious Athenians that the gods simply ignored their worshippers' prayers. "Supplications in the temples, or appeals to oracles and the like, were all futile, and finally they desisted from them, overcome by the calamity."[64] Whether or not they worshipped the gods made no difference, for death raged through the city and all about them perished alike. Thus did the Athenian psyche plumb the depths of religious despair.

Distressed as they were by the malignance of the epidemic, the Athenians experienced still other ominous portents in the simultaneous occurrence of natural disasters. As the spring days of 426 heated up into summer, central Greece was shaken by many earthquakes. Thucydides specif-

[57] Thuc. 3.87.1–2. The initial onset of the plague (τὸ δὲ πρότερον καὶ δύο ἔτη) lasted two years. After a short cessation (διοκωχή) in 428/7, it returned a second time at the beginning of winter 427/6 and lasted not less than a year (παρέμεινε δὲ τὸ μὲν ὕστερον οὐκ ἔλασσον ἐνιαυτοῦ), until winter 426/5. Cf. also Thuc. 3.3.1, 13.3.

[58] Diod. 12.58.3–4. The details about the unusual weather in 426 as well as the numbers of the dead are presumably derived from Ephoros. Cf. Gomme, HCT, vol. 2, 148–149.

[59] Thuc. 3.87.3 gives these figures. Diod. 12.58.2 has 4,000 infantry and 400 cavalry. His figures for the losses in the general population are no doubt exaggerated, but cf. Gomme, HCT, vol. 2, 388–389.

[60] Thuc. 2.47–54 for the details of the disease. Plut. Per. 36.6–9 for the losses in Perikles' family; his own death, Thuc. 2.65.6; cf. Plut. Per. 38.1.

[61] See J. D. Mikalson, in K. J. Rigsby, ed., Studies Dow, 217–225, who rightly emphasizes the impact of the plague on the social customs and religious practices of the city.

[62] Thuc. 2.52.4: ἀναισχύντους θήκας. Cf. Mikalson (note 61 above) 218–219.

[63] L. Parlama and N. Stambolidis, eds., Η πόλη κάτω από την πόλη (Athens 2000) 271–273; see also E. Baziotopoulou-Valavani, in M. Stamatopoulou and M. Yeroulanou, eds., Excavating Classical Culture (Oxford 2002) 187–201.

[64] Thuc. 2.47.4; see also 53.4; cf. Mikalson (note 61 above).

ically mentions those in Athens, Boiotia, and the island of Euboia, and he describes in detail the extraordinary tidal wave that devastated the coastal towns of Euboia and Opountian Lokris. At the beginning of the campaigning season, the Peloponnesian armies had advanced to the Isthmus with the intention of invading Attica, as they had in the previous years of the war. But the frequency and violence of the earthquakes caused them to withdraw, and no invasion took place in that year.[65] While the whole of the Greek peninsula is prone to seismic activity, those parts of the country lying along the major faults have generally experienced more frequent and more violent earthquakes. In fact, exceptionally destructive earthquakes have rarely been recorded in Athens and Attica, and their occurrence must have been as unusual in classical antiquity as it has been in subsequent centuries.[66] But the great earthquakes of 426 are now known to be a recognizable horizon in the archaeology of Athens. In the Agora, three large deposits of much broken pottery and several smaller groups were dumped into wells and pits around 425. A mass of broken debris found in a pit behind the Stoa Basileios originated in a public dining place of the kind that served the nine archons and other civic officials.[67] At about the same time, the shattered furnishings of a private house were swept into the shaft of a well on the southeast slope of the Kolonos Agoraios.[68] Both groups were distinguished by an unusually high proportion of figured pottery and black-glazed table ware in relation to coarse ware, and both produced large numbers of pots that could be reassembled whole from the breakage. At the southeast corner of the market square, the kitchens and china cupboards of a commercial tavern sustained heavy damage in the same disaster, and once again the survivors disposed of the wreckage in a nearby well.[69] Thus three contemporary large deposits in widely scattered areas of the public square give evidence of widespread destructions in the middle years of the 420s, and the earthquakes mentioned by Thucydides are the most likely cause.

For the purposes of the present study, even more fascinating evidence comes from the Acropolis, where the great earthquakes of 426 have left their indelible marks on the Parthenon itself. Detailed study of the building's fabric in connection with its restoration has revealed a violent northward shift of the east facade at the northeast corner (Fig. 118).[70] So forceful was the seismic wave that it dislocated the two northernmost columns together with the entablature over the first two intercolumniations. The movement occurred between the second and third drums of the corner column

---

[65] Thuc. 3.87.4, 89.1–5. The phraseology of the list of place names suggests that the epicenter of the earthquakes was at Orchomenos in Boiotia. Cf. Diod. 12.59.1–2 and, for more detail on the wide-ranging destruction in central Greece, Demetrios of Kallatis, *FGrH* 85 F 6, quoted by Strabo 1.3.20 (pp. 60–61). When the Peloponnesian withdrawal occurred, preparations were probably already underway for the next celebration of the Great Panathenaia later in the summer of 426. The date of the withdrawal was presumably mid-May or a little earlier; Gomme, *HCT,* vol. 2, 390 and cf. 70–71.

[66] W. Capelle, *RE* Suppl. 4, s.v. Erdbebenforschung II.2, cols. 349–350. In addition to the earthquake of 426, Thucydides mentions another in 424 that was possibly felt in Athens (4.52.11) and a third in 420 (5.45.4). An earthquake mentioned by Melanthios, *Atthis, FGrH* 326 F 1, quoted by Harpokration, s.v. γρυπάνιον (γ 18 Keaney), may be any one of these or a different one.

[67] Agora deposit H 4:5: S. I. Rotroff and J. H. Oakley, *Debris from a Public Dining Place in the Athenian Agora, Hesperia* Suppl. 25 (Princeton 1992) passim, and, for association with the earthquake of 426, 53–57. A number of small deposits also were closed about the same time and may reflect damage caused by the same disaster: E 19:5 (*Agora* XII, 389; *Agora* XXIII, 331; *Agora* XXX, 362); F 5:3 (*Agora* XII, 389; *Agora* XXX, 362); F 14:2 (*Agora* XII, 389; *Agora* XXX, 362); G 14:6 (*Agora* XII, 391); H 7:1 (*Agora* XII, 392; *Agora* XXX, 363); I 17:1 (*Agora* XII, 393; *Agora* XXIII, 333); M 17:7 (*Agora* XII, 394; *Agora* XXIII, 333; *Agora* XXX, 365); M 18:8 (*Agora* XII, 395; *Agora* XXIII, 334; *Agora* XXX, 365); N 8:3 (*Agora* XII, 395); O 7:10 (*Agora* XII, 396; *Agora* XXX, 365); R 10:6 (*Agora* XII, 398; *Agora* XXX, 366); see Rotroff and Oakley, 56.

[68] Deposit E 13:1 (*Agora* XII, 388; *Agora* XXIII, 331; *Agora* XXX 361); the contents of the well summarized, Rotroff and Oakley, *Debris from a Public Dining Place,* 55–56.

[69] Deposit R 13:4. Full publication of the contents with date of deposit ca. 430: L. Talcott, *Hesperia* 4 (1935) 477–523. The contents summarized: *Agora* XII, 398; *Agora* XXIII, 336; *Agora* XXX, 366, with date of deposit lowered to ca. 425. See Rotroff and Oakley, *Debris from a Public Dining Place,* 56.

[70] M. Korres and Ch. Bouras, Μελέτη ἀποκαταστάσεως τοῦ Παρθενῶνος (Athens 1983) 328–330. The text of Thuc. 3.87.4 places the epicenter of the earthquake at Orchomenos in Boiotia, well to the north of Athens, and that agrees with the northward dislocation in the east facade of the Parthenon.

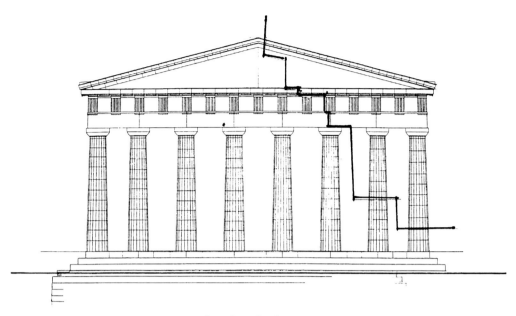

Figure 118. Diagram of earthquake damage to the Parthenon in 426

and between the fifth and sixth drums of the second column so that both shafts have shifted out of alignment by as much as 2½ cm. In the entablature above, the vertical joint of the architrave over the third column has been forced open by more than 2 cm, while at the level of the horizontal cornice the joints above the third intercolumniation have been loosened.[71] The extent of the movement observable in the preserved blocks of the facade makes it certain that the missing block of the pediment above the third intercolumniation would have been at least partially dislodged, and probably the highest parts of the raking cornice as well. The superstructure of the temple obviously sustained still further damage because the existing cornice block above the third column does not belong to the original stonework but is a replacement. The visible face of the block and the details of mutule and guttae differ only imperceptibly from the original carving. But the upper surface is worked with a point instead of a toothed chisel like the blocks on either side; moreover, it is not level but decreases in thickness toward the tympanum wall, a clear indication that the new block was pushed into position from the front when the vertical wall block of the pediment was still in place above it.[72] Still other signs of repair are visible at the north angle of the east pediment, where a third clamp of larger size was inserted to secure the joint between the great corner block of the horizontal cornice and the first normal block. Extra clamps also fastened the base of the acroterion to the adjacent sima only at the northeast corner of the temple.[73] Since the force of the earthquake dislocated so large a part of the facade and evidently damaged irreparably a block of the horizontal cornice, it is unlikely that the pedimental sculpture can have escaped entirely unscathed. Certainly the figure above the third column may have been broken together with the cornice block on which it stood.[74] It is also noticeable

[71] Korres, in Korres and Bouras (note 70 above), 329.

[72] Korres, in Korres and Bouras (note 70 above), 329. The replacement block is the seventh normal cornice block from the north, not counting the great corner block. Korres, in Korres and Bouras (note 70 above) 330, describes in detail how closely the carving approximates the original stonework.

[73] Korres and Bouras (note 70 above) 114–115. Installation of the additional clamp at the north end of the horizontal cornice caused some difficulty. Because the tympanum wall was still in position, it was necessary to cut back a portion of its face at the bottom of the northernmost slab in order to position the larger replacement midway between the two original clamps.

[74] The restoration of the east facade in Orlandos, Παρθ., vol. 1, pls. 4 and 5, shows a gap in the pedimental statuary above the third column from the north.

that the line of movement steps deeper toward the center of the facade in each higher course. This pattern of dislocation suggests that the tympanum wall was wrenched apart at just the point where many modern reconstructions of the sculptural composition place the statue of Athena, fully armed and glorious at her birth. Did the goddess herself crash to the ground and shatter?

Fortunately, it is possible for us to form some notion of the way Athenians reacted to the compounded calamities of 426, for an almost exactly contemporary literary source, written by an eyewitness, refers unmistakably to the events of that year. Euripides' play *Erechtheus* was performed in all probability at the City Dionysia of 422,[75] and although the play has come down to us only in fragments, enough of the text survives to reconstruct the general lines of the story.[76] The play recounts the attack on Athens by Eumolpos, the son of Poseidon, in command of a large force of Thracians. Upon consulting the Delphic oracle, King Erechtheus learns that he must sacrifice one of his daughters if he would successfully defend Athens from impending conquest. His wife, Praxithea, in a stirring patriotic speech, willingly gives her child for the sake of the city; and her two other daughters, loyal to their oaths, join their sister in sacrificing their lives for Athens.[77] In the ensuing battle the Athenians are victorious and Erechtheus strikes down Eumolpos as he flees from the field. But a chasm of the earth opens and swallows up Erechtheus as Poseidon seeks vengeance for the defeat of his son Eumolpos.[78] At the climax of the play, the god wreaks his wrath on the city itself in a great earthquake. In the lyric lines of the chorus, of which only disjointed snatches survive, we can still hear Athenians shrieking in panic:

> Oh, Oh! O earth! Flee… if I might find in any way an ending of my troubles… The city's ground is set dancing by the quake! Poseidon is hurling on the city… Here are troubles… the roof is collapsing!… everything with his Bacchic dancing just now in the palace.[79]

In the Euripidean theater such moments of crisis were easily resolved by the sudden epiphany of the appropriate deity, who straightened out the convolutions into which the mortal characters had twisted the plot and pronounced by divine decree a satisfactory ending to the drama. So in the very next line of *Erechtheus,* the goddess Athena appears as *deus ex machina* and sternly admonishes her fellow Olympian: "I call on you, sea-god Poseidon, to turn your trident away from this country, and not to uproot my land and demolish my delightful city."[80] She charges her citizens to honor the Erechtheid daughters with annual sacrifices and prescribes the details of preliminary sacrifices for them first, prior to raising the spear of war.[81] Then the goddess addresses the widowed queen:

[75] Plut. *Nik.* 9.5, quotes a verse from *Erechtheus* F 369 (without attribution). Such words as these, he says, the Spartans and the Athenians gladly heard the choruses sing when they yearned for peace after a year-long armistice which they had concluded earlier. Thuc. 4.118.12 dates the same armistice to 14 Elaphebolion 423, which was presumably the day after the City Dionysia; see Gomme, *HCT*, vol. 3, 603, and cf. 678–679. The armistice would have been in effect from 14 Elaphebolion 423 to 14 Elaphebolion 422, and production of *Erechtheus* at the Dionysia of 422 is the only date that is consistent with a literal reading of Plutarch's text. See especially W. M. Calder, *GRBS* 10 (1969) 147–156; T. B. L. Webster, *The Tragedies of Euripides* (London 1967) 116, 127–130; P. Carrara, *Euripide: Eretteo* (Florence 1977) 13–17. M. J. Cropp, in C. Collard, M. J. Cropp, and K. H. Lee, eds., *Euripides: Selected Fragmentary Plays*, vol. 1 (Warminster 1995) 155, is more hesitant about the date. C. Austin, *Nova Fragmenta Euripidea* (Berlin 1968) 22, dates the play to 423.
[76] For texts of the fragments, Austin, *Nova Fragmenta*, 23–40; Cropp, in Collard et al., *Fragmentary Plays*, 156–175, and introductory remarks, 148–155.
[77] Praxithea's speech, F 360 (Cropp), [F 50 Austin]. Her daughters are three in number, F 357, F 360.34–37, and they swore that all should perish together, cf. Apollod. 3.15.4; cf. F 370.35–38, 67–68.
[78] The Athenian victory, F 370.5–10, 12–13; Erechtheus dead, F 370.14–22; buried beneath the earth by Poseidon's hand, F 370.59–60.
[79] F 370.45–54, translation adapted from Cropp.
[80] F 370.55–57, translation adapted from Cropp.
[81] F 370.77–86.

For your husband I bid you build a precinct with stone enclosure in the middle of the Acropolis. On account of his killer, Erechtheus will be called august Poseidon and worshipped eponymously by the citizens in cattle sacrifices. And for you, who have restored the foundations of this city, I grant the right to make burnt sacrifices on my altars on behalf of the city, with the title of priestess.[82]

From the first division of the universe and its natural forces among the gods of Greece, Poseidon was not only the lord of the sea, but also quintessentially the "earth-shaker," and he is so named repeatedly in the Homeric poems.[83] He could unleash dark forces from beneath the earth and cause the surface of the ground to roll and toss like the waves of the sea. Great earthquakes are always unexpected, terrifying, often devastating occurrences, to early people among the most awesome manifestations of divine anger in human affairs. No doubt many a superstitious Athenian, like the contemporary dramatist, attributed the unprecedented violence of the earthquake to Poseidon's destructive powers. It will also not have escaped notice that the western pediment of the Parthenon particularly celebrated Athena's humiliating defeat of Poseidon in the contest for the land of Attica, and that was a subject that had never previously been represented in the visual arts. Now, just six years after the completion of the pedimental statuary, the temple itself was nearly shaken to the ground. If our argument is sound, the designers of that temple had planned to uproot the Ancient Image of the goddess from its traditional abode in the archaic temple and install it in the new building. Moreover, it was a building that had arisen amid controversy from the beginning, and which many citizens may have considered to be more a monument to Athenian hubris than a temple to the goddess Athena. It is easy to understand how the terrified Athenians, with their bodies wasted by sickness and their city crashing about their heads, came to the conclusion that the wrath of the gods needed to be assuaged.

Euripides' elaborate presentation of the story of Erechtheus's death provides the foundation myth for the worship of Poseidon-Erechtheus on the Acropolis. The playwright's development of the myth in the immediate aftermath of the plague and earthquakes may have served to explain those devastating disasters and to mitigate the residual anger that Poseidon was thought to harbor against the land.[84] At Athena's express command the city is to institute sacrifices for Poseidon-Erecththeus and to "build a precinct with stone enclosure in the middle of the Acropolis," while the goddess invites Praxithea to become her first priestess. Here is the mythical aition for the construction of that curious double temple that housed jointly the cults of Poseidon-Erechtheus and Athena Polias, and that we call the Erechtheion. Now, in Euripides' telling of the story, it is improbable that the playwright predicted clairvoyantly the building of a temple which the Athenians would undertake only in the later years of the fifth century. The poet was much given to the manipulation of mythology for his own dramatic purposes, and he was far more likely to assimilate to the timeless realm of myth an actual decision previously taken by the Athenian demos, in which case the production of *Erecththeus* in 422 yields a terminus ante quem for the decision to build the temple. Detailed information is available concerning the final phase of construction in the last decade of the century, but no such precise statement attests the date at which building the Erechtheion began. The epigraphical evidence bearing on the chronology of the building has been variously interpreted and needs to be reexamined to see if it is compatible with a date prior to 422 for the work's inception.

---

[82] F 370.90–97.

[83] See W. Burkert, *Greek Religion* (Berkeley 1984) 136–139.

[84] It is noteworthy that Euripides' treatment of the story is unique in the corpus of Attic tragedy, and his play must have been influential in establishing the myth as a part of Athenian patriotic ideology. See Cropp, in Collard et al., *Fragmentary Plays*, 155.

The Date of the Erechtheion

In the absence of any explicit evidence, scholars have found reasons to date the beginning of the building at various times that range from the mid-430s, before the outbreak of the Peloponnesian War,[85] to 421, in the aftermath of the Peace of Nikias.[86] Although the latter date has received wide support, no particularly compelling case has ever been made to urge its acceptance to the exclusion of other solutions. In order to investigate the possibility that work began on the Erechtheion somewhat earlier in the 420s, we need to reconsider a fragmentary inscription which was tentatively associated with the building long ago but has since been reinterpreted or generally disregarded.

IG I³ 132:

```
                    (traces 2 lines)
          ἔδοχσεν τε̑ι βο[λε̑ι καὶ το̑ι δέμοι· – – ἐπρυτάνευε, – – – ἐγραμμά]-
          τευε, Σμίκυθο[ς ἐπεστάτε – – – εἶπε· – – – – – – – – – – – ἀρχιτ]-
     5    έκτονα το̑ νεὸ – – – – – – – – – – – – – – – – – – – – – – – – –
          ιος ἀρχιτέκτ[ον – – – – – – – – – – – – – – – – – – ἀρχιτ – – –]
          ’Αθεναίον μισ[θο̑σαι – – – – – – – – – – – – – – – – – – – – –]
          οσι συνισταμ[ – – – – – – – – – – – – – – – – – – – – – – – – –]
          σιας ηο ἀρχιτέ[κτον – – – – – – – – – – – – – – – – – – – τὲ]-
     10   ν τομὲν καὶ τὲ[ν – – – – – – – – – – – – – – – – – – – – το̑]-
          ν ἔργον, ὅσα δ[ὲ – – – – – – – – – – – – – – – – – ηος – – – –]
          τα καὶ κάλλ[ιστα – – – – – – – – – – – – – – – – – – – – – – –]
          κοσάντον – – – – – – – – – – – – – – – – – – – – – – – – – – –
```

The preserved text consists of thirteen broken lines along the left-hand margin of the stone, no one of which contains more than two or three words. Obviously, the original wording of the text cannot be reconstructed, nor can the fragmentary words be translated so as to yield any sense. But a few interesting observations are possible regarding the content of the document. Lines 3–4 contain the standard prescript for a decree of the boulē and demos.[87] After the opening formula would come the name of the tribe in prytany and the name of the secretary. The name of the presiding officer, a certain Smikythos, is preserved and would be followed by the name of the speaker who made the motion. It is clear from line 5 that the principal subject of the decree is a temple. Since the word "architect," in the accusative, immediately precedes the temple, it is probably the subject of the first infinitive, and it is likely that the initial clause of the text named a specific person and appointed him "architect of the temple." The word is twice repeated in lines 6 and 9, which suggests that the decree went on to specify the architect's various responsibilities. Line 7 appears to refer to the letting out

---

[85] A date for the Erechtheion beginning in the mid-430s was advocated consistently over many years by Dörpfeld: *AM* 22 (1897) 166; *AM* 27 (1902) 401, 416; *AM* 29 (1904) 101–107; *AM* 36 (1911) 41, 42; *JdI* 34 (1919) 13. An attempt to revive this early date has recently been proposed on the basis of the cypress tree contributed to the Temple of Athena τῆς ’Αθηνῶμ μ[εδεόσης] by the islanders of Karpathos (*IG* I³ 1454, lines 9–11). See T. K. Dix and C. A. Anderson, *AJA* 101 (1997) 373. But the tree will have provided one of the major roof timbers of the temple, and the woodwork for the roof of the Erechtheion was not under construction until the last decade of the century. R. Meiggs, *Trees and Timber in the Ancient Mediterranean World* (Oxford 1982) 200–201, assigns the cypress from Karpathos to the Parthenon with much greater probability.

[86] A date after 421, during the Peace of Nikias, has been widely accepted, e.g., by: A. Michaelis, *AM* 14 (1889) 362–364; Paton and Stevens, *Erechtheum,* 454; Dinsmoor, *AAG³,* 188; I. M. Shear, *Hesperia* 32 (1963) 422; Boersma, *Athenian Building Policy,* 82, 88, 182; Travlos, *PDA,* 213; Wycherley, *Stones of Athens,* 146 and note 7; Gruben, *Gr. Tempel⁵,* 209.

[87] The stone preserves the original top and left edge of the stele, together with the first words of eleven lines of text inscribed in the stoichedon style. In the space at the top of the stone there are slight traces of two lines of lettering, but no single letter can actually be deciphered. Not enough of the text survives to determine the original length of the lines.

of contracts, while lines 10–11 may provide for the quarrying and transportation of stone and other works in connection with a construction project. The coincidence of vocabulary, and especially the triple repetition of ἀρχιτέκτον among the remnants of no more than twenty-nine words, strongly suggest that the decree authorized construction of a temple and appointed an architect to prepare the specifications.

The apparent content of the decree suggested to the early investigators of the Erechtheion that it ordered the resumption of work after a period of interruption. Accordingly, they interpreted the document as the decree of Epigenes which had authorized the overseers' report on the condition of the temple in 409/8.[88] But objections were raised immediately that the inscription seemed to be considerably earlier than 409/8 and should thus be dissociated from the Erechtheion.[89] Once divorced from that temple, the decree could be reinterpreted to refer to the beginning of work on the Temple of Athena Nike, and this is the view that was commonly held in the second half of the twentieth century.[90] Plainly, identification of the temple mentioned in the text of the decree depends largely on the date of the inscription, and so it is necessary to review the evidence bearing on that date.

Aside from the character of the lettering, the only piece of internal evidence that may provide a date is the name of the presiding officer, Smikythos (line 4). His is one of the more unusual names in Athenian prosopography, and in fact only ten occurrences of the name are attested in the fifth century. Since five of those, including the epistates of the decree under discussion, all cluster in the period of the Peloponnesian War, it is highly unlikely that more than one man of this name was prominent in Athenian public affairs at the same time.[91] In addition to the man named in our inscription, Smikythos was attacked disparagingly as a supporter of Kleon in Aristophanes' *Knights* (Σμικύθην καὶ κύριον, 969), a play that was produced in January of 424.[92] Smikythos served as secretary of the treasurers of Athena in 424/3, and he is so listed in the inscribed inventory of that year.[93] Another reference to a Smikythos names him as the father of Apolexis of the deme Iphistiadai, who served as one of the overseers in charge of the cult statues in the Hephaisteion during the period 421–415. This man went on to become one of the thirty syngrapheis of 411 and an opponent of Antiphon after the rule of the Four Hundred in 411/10.[94] There is no reason to doubt that his father was the treasurer of 424/3.

Finally, the name Smikythos may be restored as the presiding epistates in a fragmentary and difficult inscription which records the settlement between Athens and Mytilene sometime after the failure of the Lesbian revolt in 427/6: [Σμίκυ]θος ἐπε[στάτει].[95] Two considerations favor this res-

---

[88] So L. D. Caskey, in Paton and Stevens, *Erechtheum*, 280, following Kirchhoff, *IG* I 60, and Michaelis, *AM* 14 (1889) 362. For the decree of Epigenes, *IG* I³ 474, line 5. According to this interpretation, Epigenes' name is restored in line 4 as the orator of the decree.

[89] A. B. West, in Paton and Stevens, *Erechtheum,* 647–648, with date in 427/6; see below.

[90] Dinsmoor, *PAPS* 80 (1939) 124–125; Dinsmoor, *AAG³*, 185–186 and note 4; Mattingly, *Historia* 10 (1961) 170; I. M. Shear, *Hesperia* 32 (1963) 388 and note 97; Travlos, *PDA*, 148–149; Boersma, *Athenian Building Policy,* 179; cf. Gruben, *Gr. Tempel*⁵, 205–206. *IG* I³ 132 is not discussed among the inscriptions pertaining to the Nike temple in Giraud, *Μελέτη Ἀθηνᾶς Νίκης*, 48–52; Mark, *Athena Nike,* 104–114; B. Wesenberg, *JdI* 96 (1981) 50–53.

[91] *LGPN* II, 401, s.v. Σμίκυθος, lists sixty-nine occurrences of the name over the centuries. Of these only ten are datable to the fifth century: (1) sixth/fifth cent.; (6) 490–480; (7) 464; (8) 430–420, the epistates of *IG* I³ 132, line 4; (9) 424; (10) 424/3; (11) ca. 411; (38) 421–415; (64) 427/6; (65) 459. Nos. (8)–(10), (38), and (64) are probably references to the same man; see West, in Paton and Stevens, *Erechtheum,* 647–648.

[92] *LGPN* (9); cf. schol. Aristoph. *Knights* 969a, c (Jones).

[93] *LGPN* (10). The name is partly preserved and can be restored, in three consecutive inventories of the Pronaos: *IG* I³ 301, line 17, ℎοῖς Σμίκυθ[...⁸...]; 302, lines 28, 37, ℎ[οῖς Σμίκυθ]; 303, line 41, ℎοῖς Σμίκ[υθ...⁷...]. The parallel inventories of the Hekatompedon and the Parthenon are not preserved for these years.

[94] *LGPN* (38) and cf. 42, s.v. Ἀπόληξις (1) + (13). Overseer of the Hephaisteion statues, *IG* I³ 472, lines 2–3; syngraphes, Harpokr., s.v. Ἀπόληξις (α 192 Keaney) = Kassel-Austin, *PCG*, vol. 7, 495; Plato, frag. 150. Cf. Thuc. 8.67.1; [Aristot.] *Ath. Pol.* 29. Opponent of Antiphon, Harpokr., s.v. στασιώτης (σ 36 Keaney).

[95] *LGPN* (64); *IG* I³ 66, lines 4–5.

toration: first, the decree was passed when the tribe in prytany was Akamantis (line 3), to which Smikythos and his son belonged in the deme Iphistiadai; and, second, names ending in -θος are extremely rare in Attic prosopography of the fifth century. There are, in fact, so few alternatives as to make it highly probable that the presiding officer in the Mytilene decree was the same man as the Smikythos who presided when construction of a temple was authorized.[96] But that coincidence means that the two decrees were passed at the same meeting of the assembly, because a man could hold the chairmanship of the prytany only one day in his life.[97]

The Mytilene decree has frequently been assigned to the year of the revolt of Lesbos in 427/6, and the text has been restored to reflect events in the fifth year of the Peloponnesian War.[98] Thucydides recounts the dramatic last-minute reprieve of the Mytileneans from total destruction at the hands of the Athenians; and his narrative gives the details of the settlement, including the demilitarization of that city, the confiscation of its lands, and the institution of an Athenian *klerouchia* on the island.[99] The decree clearly referred to some of these matters, for the Athenian *klerouchoi* are mentioned at least twice in the fragmentary lines of the text (lines 17, 25). But the language of the document has about it a tone of amicable diplomacy that seems strangely at odds with the mood at Athens in the summer of 427, when orators railed in high dudgeon, tempers flared in the assembly, and a thousand Mytilenean oligarchs were put to death, if Thucydides' text is to be trusted.[100] By contrast, the treaty preserved in the inscription shows signs of reconciliation between the two parties. According to an attractive restoration of the text, Athens granted a measure of local autonomy to the Mytileneans: ἀπο[δίδοσιν αὐτοῖς τὲν γε̃]ν καὶ αὐτο[νό]μος δοκ[ε̃ι] ε̃ν[αι αὐτὸς ἔχοντας ἅπαντα] τ[ὰ] σφ[έτερα] αὐτõ[ν (lines 10–12),[101] the Athenian demos "restores [to them their land] and resolves that they are to be autonomous [in possession of all] their own property." Legal disputes between private individuals are to be settled on the basis of international agreements in effect before the revolt: κα]τὰ τὰς χσυ[μβο]λὰς hαὶ ε̃σαν [πρὸ τõ (line 16). The decree then goes on to legislate certain matters that are to be transacted between the Athenian settlers and the Mytileneans: πρὶν ἀ[πο]δοθε̃ναι αὐτοῖς [τὲν γὲν hυπὸ τõν στ]ρατεγõν [καὶ] τõν στρατιοτõν (lines 18–19),[102] "before [the land] is to be restored to them by the generals and the soldiers." If these restorations are correct, far from documenting the harsh punishment of Mytilene described by Thucydides, the preserved inscription must record a major reversal of Athenian policy toward the islanders. This, it has been argued, is good evidence for lowering the date of the inscription to 425/4, a year in which the fortunes of Athens had begun to improve. The treaty appears to reflect considerable normalization of relations between Athens and Mytilene and may even have included a formal withdrawal of the

---

[96] In addition to the ten instances of Smikythos cited in note 91 above, only two alternatives are attested in the fifth century. Boethos occurs twice: *LGPN* II, 89, s.v. Βόηθος (1), (2). Phalanthos is found four times: *LGPN* II, 440, s.v. Φάλανθος (1), (2), (3), (5). The following seven names have a single appearance each in the fifth century: Ἄληθος, *LGPN* II, p. 21; Ἄραιθος, p. 48; Ἀρχάγαθος, p. 6; Κλείνοθος, p. 263; Νόθος, p. 342; Τιμόνοθος, p. 432; Φίλαιθος, p. 446. Since all seven of these occur exclusively on sepulchral monuments, none is a viable alternative for the restoration of Smikythos in *IG* I³ 66, lines 4–5. Of the remaining thirty-five names ending in -θος listed in the reverse index, *LGPN* II, 499, all are attested only in the fourth century or in later periods.

[97] [Aristot.] *Ath. Pol.* 44.1.

[98] Date in 427/6: *IG* I² 60; Tod, *GHI*, vol. 1, 63; *ATL* II, D 22, III, 150; *SEG* 10.69; Meritt, *AJP* 75 (1954) 359–368; *IG* I³ 66.

[99] Thuc. 3.49–50.

[100] Thuc. 3.50.1.

[101] The text combines the restoration of Meritt, *AJP* 75 (1954) 362 = *IG* I³ 66 for lines 10–11, with the restoration originally proposed by Tod, *GHI*, vol. 1, 63, and emended by Gomme, *HCT*, vol. 2, 330 (cf. Gomme, in *Robinson Studies*, vol. 2, 335–336) for line 12.

[102] The restoration of *IG* I² 60 as supported by the argumentation of Gomme, in *Robinson Studies*, vol. 2, 335; Gomme, *HCT*, vol. 2, 330–331, against *IG* I³ 66, lines 18–19.

Athenian *klerouchoi* from the island, a possibility which would explain why they were never mentioned again in the later stages of the war.[103]

The chronological considerations that affect the date of the Mytilene decree apply equally to the decree concerning construction of a temple, since Smikythos presided at the assembly that approved both decrees. In order to serve as epistates of the prytany, he was necessarily a councilor for the tribe Akamantis in the boulē of that whole year. The year cannot have been 424/3 because he was then secretary of the treasurers of Athena and could not have been a member of the boulē at the same time. A date in 425/4 for his term of office in the boulē is an attractive alternative. In that year Smikythos provoked the ridicule of Aristophanes in *Knights*, and that date allows two years for the Mytileneans to negotiate a more permanent settlement with Athens that appears to be reflected in the language of the preserved inscription. If that date is accepted, however, the Athenian demos also embarked upon the construction of a new temple in that same year and commissioned an architect to undertake the work. The temple in question was almost certainly on the Acropolis, and in the middle years of the 420s must have been either the Temple of Athena Nike or the Erechtheion.

As long as the two inscriptions were linked inextricably to the year 427/6, it was just possible to identify the temple mentioned by our inscription as the Nike temple. The diminutive size of that building encouraged the belief that it could have been built in the four years between 427/6 and 424/3, when the decree pertaining to the priestess's salary suggested completion of the temple.[104] Several pieces of evidence, however, militate strongly against that identification. The structural relation of the temple foundations to the sheathing walls of the bastion shows beyond doubt that they were laid, probably ca. 435, as work progressed on the Propylaia. By the time that project was abandoned in 432, the marble euthynteria of the Nike temple was certainly in place, and possibly the steps of the crepidoma as well.[105] Obviously, a decree authorizing construction of a temple in 425/4 cannot refer to a building begun ten years earlier. Consequently, our fragmentary inscription, probably also voted in 425/4, which appears to authorize construction of a temple and appointment of its architect, cannot possibly refer to the Temple of Athena Nike.

The decree voted by the demos when Smikythos presided should thus be associated once again with the Erechtheion. The orator who made the motion, however, was not concerned to resume work after a period of interruption, but rather he proposed the commissioning of an architect to design the temple and supervise its construction from the beginning. Many Athenians had probably understood the long sufferings of the plague and the destructive earthquakes of 426 as signs of divine displeasure with the projects of the Periklean builders. In particular the severe damage to the Parthenon provided strong motivation to build a special temple for the Ancient Image that would also accommodate appropriately the sacrifices to appease Poseidon-Erechtheus. That such apparently inexplicable natural occurrences could motivate powerful reactions in human behavior is nowhere more vividly illustrated than by the incident at Syracuse in 413. All was in readiness to evacuate the Athenian camp and withdraw the fleet to a safer position when there occurred an eclipse of the moon. Most of the Athenians took the sign so seriously that they urged the generals

---

[103] The date in 425/4 proposed by Gomme, in *Robinson Studies*, vol. 2, 337–339; Gomme, *HCT*, vol. 2, 330–331. Followed by Mattingly, *Proceedings of the African Classical Association* 7 (1964) 39, note 27; Mattingly, in *Ehrenberg Studies*, 203–204. Cf. P. A. Brunt, in *Ehrenberg Studies*, 82–84, who disagrees with the circumstances postulated by Gomme for the withdrawal of the Athenian *klerouchoi* from Lesbos but does not reject the later date of the inscription. Cf. also P. Gauthier, *REG* 79 (1966) 82–88; Meiggs, *AE*, 261–262, 317.

[104] Dinsmoor, *PAPS* 80 (1939) 124–125, interpreted the two inscriptions, *IG* I³ 132 (there dated in 427/6) and *IG* I³ 36 (424/3), as providing bracketing dates for the construction of the temple, the former a decree authorizing the building and the latter providing a salary for the priestess who had begun to serve in the completed building (the text quoted above, chap. 2, p. 28).

[105] See chap. 10, pp. 344–347 above.

to wait for "thrice nine days," as prescribed by the soothsayers.[106] The decision to delay the departure was made by the general Nikias son of Nikeratos, who Thucydides says was too much given to divination, and the delay led directly to the final naval defeat and disastrous retreat by land in which thousands of men died at the hands of the pursuing Syracusans. It is interesting to speculate that many of those Athenians who urged delay after the lunar eclipse in 413 had possibly reacted similarly to the earthquakes of 426 and may have voted for the new temple when Smikythos presided. It is also well to recall that Nikias was a senior member of the board of generals in the middle years of the 420s, during the worst of the plague and the earthquakes, just as he was the senior commander at Syracuse in 413; and he may well have been personally influential in the decision to build the Erechtheion.[107]

In the winter of 426/5 the plague finally subsided, and some people attributed that occurrence to the purification of the island of Delos that same winter, as reported by Thucydides and Diodoros.[108] Then too the military fortunes of Athens began to improve, and after the Battle of Idomenai the victorious commander Demosthenes dedicated three hundred panoplies "in the Attic sanctuaries."[109] The following campaigning season of 425 brought the most important Athenian victories of the entire Archidamian War. At that moment it appeared that Athens had crossed a significant watershed. The opportunity to thank the gods was at hand, and the dedications to Athena Nike show the demos's grateful response. It was also just the moment to commence construction of a new temple for the Ancient Image of Athena Polias. The motivation was strong, the opportunity was appropriate, and moreover in that same year Athens found the means. Kleon had returned from Pylos with 292 Spartan prisoners. Elated by his military triumph, the assembly boldly enacted the tribute assessment of 425, which increased the tribute payments of the allied cities to a total figure of between 1,460 and 1,500 talents. To be sure, the decree of Thoudippos states expressly that the tribute was raised "in order that the demos may have sufficient money for the war," which implies that the funds were earmarked to defray military expenses.[110] But we have already seen that the principal source of funds for both the Parthenon and the Propylaia was the tribute of the allies, and we need not hesitate to believe that Athens tapped the same source to pay for the Erechtheion, which is a much smaller building and no doubt cost a fraction of the Parthenon. Thus the year 425/4 appears

---

[106] Debate among the Athenian generals on the need to move the camp, Thuc. 7.49.1–4; the eclipse of the moon and the Athenian reaction, Thuc. 7.50.4. On both solar and lunar eclipses recorded by Thucydides, see F. R. Stephenson and L. J. Fatoohi, *Historia* 50 (2001) 245–253.

[107] Nikias son of Nikeratos of Kydantidai: Kirchner, *PA* 10808; Davies, *APF*, 403–404. According to Plut. *Nik.* 2.2, he had been general during Perikles' lifetime, but no specific commands are known or recorded. General in 427/6: Thuc. 3.51; Plut. *Nik.* 6.4; Develin, *Athenian Officials*, 124. General in 426/5: Thuc. 3.91; Diod. 12.65.1–4 (under 424/3); Develin, 126; cf. Fornara, *Generals*, 57–58. General in 425/4: Thuc. 4.27.5–28.5, 42, 53.1, 54; Diod. 12.65.5–9 (under 424/3); Plut. *Nik.* 6.4; Develin, 129; cf. Fornara, 59. General in 424/3: Thuc. 4.119.2; Develin, 132. General in 423/2: Thuc. 4.29.2–5; Diod. 12.72.8–10; Develin, 136.

[108] Thuc. 3.104 mentions the oracle as a result of which the purification of Delos was carried out, but he does not connect it with the cessation of the plague; see, however, Gomme, *HCT*, vol. 2, 414. Diod. 12.58.6–7, presumably with Ephoros as his source, cites the plague as the specific motivation for the purification. Cf. Mikalson, in Rigsby, ed., *Studies Dow*, 221–222, who interprets the motivation differently.

[109] Thuc. 3.114.1.

[110] The decree of Thoudippos, *IG* I³ 71 = ML 69 = *ATL* II, A9. The total figure for the tribute is partly preserved (line 181): [X]ℋℋℋℋℋ<Γ>Δ – –. Line 46 is restored to read: ℎίνα ἔι [τõι δέμοι ἀργύριον ℎικανὸν ἐς τὸμ] πόλ[εμον·]; translation, *ATL* III, 71–73; discussion, 70–89. The basic reconstruction of the text, B. D. Meritt and A. B. West, *The Athenian Assessment of 425 B.C.* (Ann Arbor 1934). See also ML, pp. 192–201; Meiggs, *AE*, 324–339. The total figure probably does not represent the three-fold increase suggested by Wesenberg, *JdI* 96 (1981) 52 and note 102. Plut. *Arist.* 24.3 says that after Perikles' death the tribute was raised little by little, and there is no evidence for the levels of assessment in 430 and 428; cf. Meiggs, *AE*, 325, 331. But the assessment of 425 probably represents a substantial increase.

to be the most propitious moment for the beginning of the new temple, but it cannot be conclusively demonstrated that construction of the Erechtheion actually began in that year.[111]

THE TEMPLE FOR THE ANCIENT IMAGE

When inception of the Erechtheion project is placed in the middle years of the 420s, we encounter the curious paradox of the Periklean legacy. In a burst of triumphalism, Athenians of the midcentury had set out to adorn the Acropolis with magnificent marble buildings that would crown the city as the religious and cultural capitol of the Greek world and, not incidentally, would awe the pilgrim with the wealth and power of the empire which Athena's city ruled. The architects and builders of the Periklean age had risen to the challenge, and they achieved in the Parthenon and Propylaia the two most extraordinary examples of Greek Doric architecture. The sculptors too had lavished upon every available surface of the temple narrative compositions of unprecedented richness and artistry. No Greek deity had ever received so delightful a gift as the ἄγαλμα of gold and ivory that Pheidias fashioned for Athena; it surpassed all previous cult statues in its colossal size and exorbitant cost. Every detail of the Parthenon strove to achieve perfection in a temple for the goddess. And yet in the years following completion of its sculptures in 432, the city had experienced nothing but war and misery and catastrophic sickness, and finally violent earthquakes. It is in this context that the decision to build the Erechtheion becomes readily understandable. From the building's unusual double cella, with its western section subdivided into three compartments, one infers that the charge to the architect was to replicate as closely as possible the archaic temple destroyed by the Persians. On the other hand, the building's disposition on the difficult site to the north of the archaic terrace makes it plain that the architect was not at liberty to raise the new temple on the ruined foundations of its predecessor. And yet the porch of the maidens at the southwest corner reaches out in a seemingly desperate effort to preserve the ancient sanctity of the sacred spot by its physical contact with the earlier structure (Figs. 119, 120). The site of the Erechtheion had been the most sacred place on the Acropolis from primitive times onward. Here were located all those features of the topography which Athenians associated with the mythical foundations of their city and with their perceptions of their own autochthonous identity. It was evidently the designer's intention to incorporate all these features and express them quite literally in the architectural structure of the new temple.

[111] One other inscription might have had some bearing on the beginning of the Erechtheion if only there could be certainty about either its text or its date. *IG* I³ 64 is a fragmentary opisthographic stele, probably datable to the decade 430–420, both sides of which pertain to the Nike temple (lines A 21–22, B 36). Side B has been interpreted as the final expense account for construction of the temple: A. Pogorelski, *AJA* 27 (1923) 314–317; Dinsmoor, *AJA* 27 (1923) 318–321. Side A is a decree stipulating the terms of an open competition for the design of some construction related to the temple (lines A 5–9) and for the judging of the design and the execution of the project (lines A 9–19). All this appears to be under the charge of a board of overseers referred to in lines A 19–21: [ἐπ]ιμελόσθον hοι ἐπιστάται [τõ ἀρχαίο νεõ ἐν hõι κ]α[ὶ] τὸ ἀρχαῖον ἄγαλμα, "[the work] is to be managed by the overseers of the Ancient Temple in which also is the Ancient Image"; the restoration proposed by J. J. E. Hondius, *Novae Inscriptiones Atticae* (Leiden 1925) 79–80. If these overseers are the same as those who styled themselves [ἐ]πιστάται τõ νεõ τõ ἐμ πόλει ἐν hοι τὸ ἀρχαῖον ἄγαλμα when they reported on the state of the Erechtheion in 409 (*IG* I³ 474, line 1), this inscription might be the earliest evidence that construction of the Erechtheion had begun in the 420s. Unfortunately, the restoration remains only a possibility; see the reservations already raised by Paton and Stevens, *Erechtheum,* 454, note 1. The attempt by Mark, *Athena Nike,* 108–110, to deconstruct the text in order to interpret the "Ancient Image" of *IG* I³ 64, line A 21, as the archaic cult statue of Athena Nike contributes nothing. Cf. Meiggs, *AE,* 501.

Figure 119. Erechtheion, east facade from southeast

The foundations of the building rested on the ruins of the Mycenaean palace, seat of the earliest kings of Attica.[112] The eastern cross-wall of the Erechtheion, which separated the higher level of the eastern cella from the lower level of the western, rose on the line of a prehistoric terrace wall and determined the orientation of the temple.[113] That eastern cella belonged to Athena Polias, and here the ancient wooden xoanon was installed, apparently from the outset of construction, while the temple rose round about the cult image.[114] Farther to the west were the "tokens" (μαρτύρια) of the goddess's fateful contest with Poseidon for possession of Attica. Athena's sacred olive tree grew in the adjacent precinct of Pandrosos and marked the western limit beyond which the building could not extend.[115] In light of the recent earthquakes, it is not surprising that Poseidon's "tokens" should receive special veneration in the architecture. Beneath the pavement of the north porch, protected

[112] For the prehistoric remains, L. B. Holland, *AJA* 28 (1924) 142–169. For recent general accounts of the building and its architecture, Camp, *Archaeology of Athens*, 93–100, 253–254; Hurwit, *Athenian Acropolis*, 164–189.

[113] The position of the eastern cross-wall is clearly indicated in the north and south walls of the Erechtheion, but there are no classical foundations on this line. The prehistoric terrace wall that originally supported the classical cross-wall has now disappeared without trace, leaving no cuttings on the bedrock: Holland, *AJA* 28 (1924) 16 and 407, fig. 1; Dinsmoor, *AJA* 36 (1932) 321–322.

[114] The Ancient Image is mentioned three times: (*IG* I³ 474, line 1) ho νεὸς . . . ἐν hõι τὸ ἀρχαῖον ἄγαλμα, the name of the temple; (474, line 75) τõ (τοίχο) πρὸς τõ ἀγάλματος, "on the wall toward the image," that is, the east face of the eastern cross-wall; (475, lines 267–270) καλύμματα . . . ἐπὶ τὲν ὀροφὲν ἐπὶ τὰς σελίδας τὰς ὑπὲρ [τõ] ἀγάλματος, "coffer lids . . . on the ceiling on the beams above the image," that is, the wooden ceiling of the east cella. While it is possible that all three passages refer to the statue proleptically, it is more natural to think that it was already in place: Paton and Stevens, *Erechtheum*, 298–299, 311, 457, the last of which argues erroneously for an archaic predecessor on the same site.

[115] Hdt. 8.55 speaks of μαρτύρια; cf. Paus. 1.26.5, 27.2. Testimonia collected by Jahn and Michaelis, *Arx*, 71. For the precinct of the "tokens," Paton and Stevens, *Erechtheum*, 424–427.

Figure 120. Erechtheion, view of facade from west

by a special crypt, were three deep fissures in the bedrock where legend told that the sea god had driven his trident into the rock of the Acropolis. The trident marks were visible through a well-like opening in the marble altar at floor level, and directly above it an aperture in the ceiling ensured that a spot so struck by divine power should ever afterward be open to the sky.[116] According to the myth, the stroke of the trident had caused a spring of seawater to gush forth, and this was contained in a well within the western cella of the temple.[117] The "tokens" of the contesting deities were linked together by the peculiar design of the north porch, whose colonnade projected nearly 3 meters beyond the exterior western facade of the temple. The anomalous arrangement allowed space for a small doorway at the southwest corner of the porch, which provided the only access to the walled precinct of Pandrosos from outside the temple, while another small doorway in the west facade communicated directly between the Pandroseion and the western cella.[118]

[116] The crypt beneath the north porch and altar above it, Paton and Stevens, *Erechtheum,* 104–110 and fig. 66, 318. The inscriptions refer to the altar of the *thyechoos* ("offering-pourer"): *IG* I³ 474, lines 77–79: ἐν τῆι προστάσει τῆι πρὸς τõ θυρόματος τὸμ βομὸν τõ θ[υ]εχõ, "in the porch before the doorway the altar of the *thyechoos*"; 474, lines 202–208; 476, lines 218–220. Paton and Stevens, *Erechtheum,* 490–491, identify this altar in the inscriptions with the altar of Zeus Hypatos, followed by Hurwit, *Athenian Acropolis,* 204. But Paus. 1.26.5 says that the altar of Zeus Hypatos is πρὸ δὲ τῆς ἐσόδου, "in front of the entrance"; the altar of Poseidon-Erechtheus is ἐσελθοῦσι, "as you go in," which agrees better with the position of the altar of the *thyechoos* in the inscriptions. For the disposition of the various "tokens" and altars in the western section of the building: Dinsmoor, *AJA* 36 (1932) 321, fig. 4; Dinsmoor, *AAG*³, 188, 190.

[117] Paus. 1.26.5; Hdt. 8.55; Apollodoros 3.14.1. The westernmost of the three interior chambers (called τὸ προστõιον in *IG* I³ 474, line 71: see Jeppesen, *Alternative Erechtheion,* 99–107 = *AJA* 87 [1983] 325–333) was completely obliterated by a deep cistern of medieval or Turkish date that destroyed any ancient remains beneath the original pavement of the room; Paton and Stevens, *Erechtheum,* 169–171. Thus the archaeological remains offer no assistance in the identification of the site of Poseidon's "sea."

[118] It is worth noting that the doorway leading to the Pandroseion from the north porch is located directly above the threshold of the early entrance to the precinct of the "tokens" as refurbished in the 470s or 460s. Paton and Stevens, *Erechtheum,* 123 and fig. 72.

In addition to the "tokens" of the divine contest, the western portion of the Erechtheion accommodated several sacrificial altars. That to Poseidon and Erectheus "as you enter the building" (Paus. 1.26.5) was presumably the altar above the trident marks in the north porch. A second received offerings to the hero Boutes, eponymous ancestor of the Eteoboutadai, the clan that controlled the hereditary priesthood of Poseidon-Erechtheus and also provided the priestesses of Athena Polias. This altar and a third dedicated to Hephaistos probably occupied the small inner compartments, divided by walls that rose to half the height of the room.[119] A more curious architectural feature was the little crypt under the floor of the northern chamber that had access, by way of a miniature doorway, to the trident marks below the north porch.[120] Although it is difficult to imagine any realistic function for this installation, it may well have been associated with the sacred household serpent (οἰκουρὸς ὄφις) of which we hear reports from authors of all periods from Herodotos onward. The guardian serpent was said to reside now in the Temple of the Polias, now in the sanctuary of Erechtheus, and in the Classical period it appears that honey cakes were regularly set out for its nourishment.[121] If the creature had any real existence, it may have made its lair beneath the floor of the Erechtheion. In the time of Pausanias, the serpent was thought to represent Erichthonios, the mythical autochthonous ancestor of all Athenians, who was born from the seed of Hephaistos, nurtured by Athena in her temple, and came finally to rest in a tomb in the temenos of the goddess.[122]

One other early monument posed a serious obstacle to normal architectural construction at the southwest corner of the temple. This was the tomb and heroon of Kekrops, first mythical, earthborn king of Attica. The Kekropion was mentioned as a landmark before the Persian Wars in a passage of the Hekatompedon inscriptions; and from references to it in the overseers' report of 409, there can be no doubt that it lay adjacent to the southwest corner of the Erechtheion and partly beneath the caryatid porch.[123] Here the building's foundations stop short of the corner on both the west and south. The lowest four courses formed a visible corner on the interior of the temple, but on the exterior they were cut back obliquely and irregularly so as to avoid making physical contact with a preexisting structure. The gap thus formed in the masonry was bridged by one enormous marble block 4.43 meters in length and corresponding in height to the three upper courses of the west wall. At the southwest corner of the temple the entire weight of the superstructure rests on this block.[124] There is no way of knowing whether the designer of the Erechtheion intended to monumentalize the tomb of Kekrops through the unique iconography of the caryatid porch that rose above it (Fig. 121). When he replaced the normal shafts of columns with statues of young women who bear the entablature on their heads, did he wish to evoke the images of the daughters of Kekrops, those mythical

[119] Paus. 1.26.5; Paton and Stevens, *Erechtheum*, 484; Dinsmoor, *AJA* 36 (1932) 321; Dinsmoor, *AAG*³, 188. A radically different arrangement of the interior was proposed by Travlos, *AAA* 4 (1971) 77–84; his arguments answered by Overbeck, *AAA* 5 (1972) 127–129.

[120] Paton and Stevens, *Erechtheum*, 110, 491, note 1.

[121] The serpent was guardian of the temple: Hdt. 8.41; Aristoph. *Lysist.* 758–759 and schol. 759 (Hangard); Plut. *Them.* 10.1–2; Philostratos, *Imagines* 2.17.6 (p. 366.4 Kayser). It lived in the Temple of the Polias, Eustathios on *Od.* 1.357 (Romana, p. 1422.7); it lived in the Temple of Erechtheus, Hesych., s.v. οἰκουρὸν ὄφιν (ο 270 Latte); fed with honey cakes, Hdt., Plut., and Hesych. (above). Testimonia, Jahn and Michaelis, *Arx*, 70; cf. Mansfield, "Robe of Athena," 213–215. Herodotos (above) is plainly skeptical that the snake actually existed, and nobody ever claims to have seen it.

[122] Paus. 1.24.7 identifies the serpent beside Pheidias's Athena in the Parthenon as Erichthonios. His birth by Hephaistos and Athena and his nurture in the temple, Apollod. 3.14.6; his tomb in the temenos of the goddess, Apollod. 3.14.7; Clem. Alex. *Protrept.* 3.45.1. Cf. Jahn and Michaelis, *Arx*, 72; Mansfield, "Robe of Athena," 213.

[123] The Kekropion in the Hekatompedon inscriptions, *IG* I³ 4, line B 10; at the southwest corner of the building, 474, lines 9, 58–59, 62–63; adjoining the porch of the maidens, 474, lines 83–84. Testimonia and remains, Mansfield, "Robe of Athena," 218–220.

[124] Construction at the southwest corner, Paton and Stevens, *Erechtheum*, 127–137; the great block bridging the gap in the masonry, 58.

Figure 121. Erechtheion, caryatid porch

avatars of all Athenian women? In 409 the overseers described the statues simply as χόραι, "maidens," without offering a more interpretive identification.[125] As early as the 360s, however, the design of the caryatid porch was seen to provide an appropriate model for the facade of a monumental tomb. About that time a close copy of the Athenian building, at almost exactly the same scale, arose in an unlikely corner of the eastern Mediterranean. The quasi-Hellenic Lycian dynast Perikles of Limyra expressed all his would-be Athenian aspirations by replicating the porch of the Erechtheion on the facade of his own tomb and heroon on the acropolis at Limyra.[126] This direct borrowing of the Athenian maidens as the iconographic source for a sepulchral monument suggests that the classical viewer understood the south porch of the temple to be in some sense a monumentalization of the ancient Kekropion. But the chief function of the porch was no doubt always to link the new temple to its archaic predecessor by means of the physical contact that it made with the ruined foundations of the earlier building.

By far the most felicitous idea that inspired the design of the Erechtheion was the architect's decision to use the Ionic order (Figs. 122, 123). That particularly eastern contribution to the vocabulary of Greek architectural form had been developed in the course of the sixth century for the colossal dipteral temples at Ephesos, Samos, and Didyma. The Ionic column itself, with its characteristic spreading capital and tightly coiled volutes, had sprung from iconographic roots among the myriad "sacred trees" and "trees-of-life" that flourished for centuries in the art of the ancient Near

[125] The suggestion of Gruben, *Gr. Tempel*[5], 216, that the caryatids might represent the daughters of Kekrops; they are χόραι in *IG* I[3] 474, lines 83–89. For the origin and earlier use of caryatids as an architectural form, see I. M. Shear, *BCH* 123 (1999) 65–85.

[126] See J. Borchhardt, *Die Bauskulptur des Heroons von Limyra* (Berlin 1976) 27–37, for the reconstruction of the caryatids from the two facades of the monument, and 110–114, for restoration of the architecture. I am grateful to W. A. P. Childs for drawing my attention to this monument.

Figure 122. Erechtheion, east porch from east

East.[127] In the hands of Ionian architects, these marble trees, pulsing with the full bloom of organic life, had grown into mystical forests of a hundred soaring shafts, and in the symbolic language of the architecture they specifically evoked the wooded temenos of the Artemision, the willow trees of Hera, and the sacred laurel grove at the center of Apollo's oracular shrine.[128] So now the Athenian architect applied the same imagery to the Temple of Athena Polias, for the Ionic order of the Erechtheion recalled to the pilgrim the central importance of Athena's sacred olive tree, and it emphasized as well the most primitive, pre-Greek aspects of this mysterious virgin warrior goddess, with her tree, and her snake, and her owl, and her aegis.[129] But on Attic soil the Ionic order took on a decidedly different ethos from its Asiatic antecedents, one that was in part prefigured by the almost miniature scale of the Ionic temple on the Ilissos and the Temple of Athena Nike on the Acropolis. The Ionic columns of the Erechtheion have been reduced in size to just over one-third the dimensions of those of the Artemision,[130] but every molded surface of the entablature or wall-crown has been articulated

---

[127] On the development of Ionic and Aeolic volute capitals and their relation to the Asiatic "tree-of-life" motif, see Y. Shiloh, *The Proto-Aeolic Capital* (Jerusalem 1979) 26–42; P. P. Betancourt, *The Aeolic Style in Architecture* (Princeton 1977); H. L. Mace, "The Archaic Ionic Capital" (Ph.D. diss., University of North Carolina, 1978) 143–149; B. Wesenberg, *Kapitelle und Basen* (Düsseldorf 1971) 63–86; W. Andrae, *Die ionische Säule* (Berlin 1933); J. Braun-Vogelstein, *Die ionische Säule* (Berlin 1921). For briefer accounts of the origin of the Ionic order, Dinsmoor, *AAG*³, 58–63; Gruben, *Gr. Tempel*⁵, 341–348; see also B. A. Barletta, *The Origins of the Greek Architectural Orders* (Cambridge 2001) 84–124.

[128] The wooded temenos at Ephesos: Strabo 14.1.20–22 (pp. 639–640); Tacitus, *Ann.* 3.61; see Gruben, *Gr. Tempel*⁵, 390. The willow tree (λύγος) in the Heraion at Samos: Paus. 7.4.4; Menodotos, *FGrH* 541 F 1 = Athenaeus 15.672A–E; see H. Kyrieleis, *Führer durch das Heraion von Samos* (Athens 1981) 14–18; cf. Romano, "Cult Images," 250–255. The sacred grove at Didyma: Strabo 14.1.5 (p. 634); see K. Tuchelt, *Die archaischen Skulpturen von Didyma* (Berlin 1970) 194–196; K. Tuchelt, *Vorarbeiten zu einer Topographie von Didyma, IstMitt-BH* 9 (Tübingen 1973) 92–94; cf. J. F. Fontenrose, *Didyma* (Berkeley 1988) 30–31, 40.

[129] Cf. Burkert, *Greek Religion*, 139–140.

[130] The height of the columns of the Artemision has been variously estimated depending on the interpretation of Vitruv. 4.1.7: eight lower diameters = 12.60 m (Wesenberg, *Kapitelle und Basen*; Dinsmoor, *AAG*³, 339); twelve lower

Figure 123. Erechtheion, north porch from east

with richly carved Ionic ornament. Wreathes of alternating palmettes and lotus blossoms encircle the top of every shaft, and these are borrowed directly from the similar anthemion on the columns of the Polykratean dipteros at Samos.[131] On the Erechtheion, an endless chain of the same pattern surrounds the entire building at the top of the walls, and this richness of ornament combines with the reduction in scale to produce the celebrated jewel-like quality of the architecture. Despite the peculiar irregularities of the plan and its four external porches, each of which treats the Ionic order in a different way, the architect contrived to canonize for all time the Attic version of Ionic architecture. The Erechtheion became the paradigm that influenced every later Ionic building in the proportions of its columns, or the profiles of its moldings, or the details of its decorative ornament.

In another, completely different, way, the choice of the Ionic order conformed happily to Athenian ideology of the later fifth century. Now for the first time, the central shrine of Athenian religion made manifest in the style of its architecture that ethnic solidarity which Athens had long sought to cultivate with the cities of the Aegean Islands and the Asiatic coast. Ionic architecture was native to those districts, and its use for a major temple on the Athenian Acropolis added verisimilitude to the claim that Athens was the metropolis of the Ionian cities, from which they had been colonized at the

diameters = 18.90 m (Krischen); Gruben, *Gr. Tempel*[5], 388, suggests ±16.18 m, interpreting Vitruvius differently. The heights of the columns of the Erechtheion: east 6.58 m, west 5.61 m, north 7.63 m; Dinsmoor, *AAG*[3], 340.

[131] The columns of the Heraion of Polykrates: G. Gruben, *Die Kapitelle des Heratempels auf Samos* (Diss. Munich 1960); Gruben, *Gr. Tempel*[5], 361, fig. 271.

beginning of the Iron Age. That assertion probably owed much to political myth-makers of the fifth century who hoped to create appropriate ideological underpinnings to justify the empire.[132] In that mythopoeic process, Ion, eponymous ancestor of all Ionians, exchanged his questionable foreign lineage for the divine paternity of Apollo and became the legitimate heir of Erechtheus through his Athenian mother, Kreousa. His four sons gave their names to the Ionian tribes, and in Euripides' version the goddess Athena herself foretold that their descendants would settle the shores of both Europe and Asia.[133] In the late fifth century, Athenian primacy in the settlement of Ionia was widely accepted. Thucydides states as a fact that emigrants from Athens colonized Ionia and the islands, and on two occasions he describes Ionians as descended from Athenians. Herodotos, a native son of Asia, acknowledged that pure Ionians were those of Athenian descent who kept the festival of the Apatouria.[134] And so in these wartime years, when the propaganda of ethnicity had sharply divided Ionians from Dorians and had polarized much of the Greek world, construction of a new Ionic temple for Athena Polias proclaimed to all Hellenic people the natural superiority of the Ionian race and, of course, the equally natural hegemony of Athens.

By the end of the century, a new Ionic temple graced the sanctuary of Athena Polias on the Acropolis, and, as we have seen, it was in different ways just as extraordinary an example of Ionic architecture as the Parthenon had been of Doric. The design of the Parthenon had evolved from an intellectual idea expressed in the precise formal language of the Doric order. Although the architects of the Parthenon had so mastered the vocabulary and syntax of that language that they spoke more eloquently than their peers, the same underlying intellectual idea was common to all Doric temples. Unique to the Erechtheion, on the other hand, was the notion that the formal elements of architecture could be subordinated to the purpose of enclosing within the fabric of a single structure all the holiest places on the Acropolis. Here the natural properties of the Ionic order greatly abetted that purpose, for its proportions and decorative ornaments could be manipulated with effortless flexibility so that each side of the building presented a wholly different countenance to the beholder. But we can read the building's fundamental purpose in the different floor levels of the cella: in the west facade that stops short of the Pandroseion and the north porch that projects beyond it, in the caryatid porch that rests firmly on the old foundation but avoids contact with the Kekropion below, in the marks of the trident enclosed in a special crypt beneath the floor. All these features are intrinsic to the religious function of the temple, and scholarly attempts to explain them as irregularities that arose from frustrated adjustments to an originally symmetrical plan seem to be seriously misconceived.[135] The new Ionic building was indeed "the temple for the Ancient Image," as the overseers entitled it, but more than that, the details of the architecture reveal that it was central in every way to the ritual life of Athena's cult. Here lies the sad irony of the Acropolis. With such consummate skill did the architect apply the rich Ionic ornament to his marble reliquary, so luxuriously did he

[132] For the tradition of Athenian colonization of the Ionian cities: M. B. Sakellariou, *La migration grecque en Ionie* (Athens 1958) 21–24, 29–37; C. Roebuck, *Ionian Trade and Colonization* (New York 1959) 25–31. That the Athenian claim was not widely disseminated or acknowledged until the time of the Delian League: Jacoby, *FGrH* III B (suppl.) I, 32–34; Sakellariou (above); A. J. Graham, *Colony and Mother City in Ancient Greece* (Chicago 1983) 11 and note 2.

[133] Ion son of Xouthos: Philochoros, *FGrH* 328 F 13 = Harpokr., s.v. Βοηδρόμια (β 14 Keaney); Strabo 8.7.1 (p. 383). Xouthos a foreigner of Achaean stock, Eur. *Ion* 57–64. Ion son of Apollo and Kreousa, Eur. *Ion* 8–21; descendant of Erechtheus, 1571–1575. His sons eponyms of the four Ionian tribes, Hdt. 5.66, Eur. *Ion* 1575–1581; they colonized Asia and the islands, Eur. *Ion* 1581–1588. See E. Kearns, *The Heroes of Attica* (London 1989) 109–110, 174–175.

[134] Athenian colonization of Ionia and the islands, Thuc. 1.2.6, 12.4. Ionians described as ἀπ' Ἀθηναίων, Thuc. 2.15.4., 7.57.4. The Apatouria the defining festival of Ionians, Hdt. 1.147.2 and cf. 8.46.2, 9.106.3. Aristoph. *Lysist.* 582 also alludes to Athenian colonization of Ionia and the islands.

[135] See especially the bizarre symmetrical building reconstructed as the original plan by W. Dörpfeld and H. Schleif, *Erechtheion* (Berlin 1942) 82–90, pls. 13–16; but equally Projects "A," "B," and "F" proposed by Dinsmoor, *AJA* 36 (1932) 319–323, figs. 2–4, and *AAG*[3], 190–192, fig. 71.

house the Ancient Image itself, and so successfully did he enshrine the sacred places under the same roof, that the Erechtheion completely displaced the Parthenon as the principal functioning Temple of Athena Polias. Upon completion of the Ionic temple, Iktinos's enduring masterpiece was forever thereafter devoid of function as a religious building. As the inventories of the treasurers vividly attest, the great hundred-foot cella of the Parthenon served thenceforward primarily as a storehouse for Athena's treasures.

✦

The foregoing chapters have sought to explore the numerous monuments that came to be built in the sanctuaries of Athens and Attica, chiefly in the third quarter of the fifth century. We have examined the construction history of ten temples, the Propylaia of the Acropolis, and the Odeion, all of which probably began construction in the same quarter century. Most of the temples seem to have been conceived as thank-offerings to the gods for the victories in the Persian Wars, and most particularly the victory in the Battle of Marathon. Several of them restored earlier temples in the sanctuaries that were destroyed by the Persians or whose construction was interrupted by the invasion. This number includes the three temples on the Acropolis, the Telesterion at Eleusis, the Temple of Poseidon at Sounion, probably the Temple of Nemesis, and possibly the Temple of Athena Pallenis. The mere numbers of religious buildings that arose in this period should be little cause for surprise, for the city had suffered total destruction at the hands of the Persian invaders, and the need for reconstruction was acute.

The biographer Plutarch marveled at the speed of construction: "Each one of them, men thought, would require many successive generations to complete it, but all of them were fully completed in the heyday of a single administration."[136] On the contrary, we have noticed repeatedly evidence for delays in construction or changes in plan. Such delays especially complicated the construction history of the Telesterion at Eleusis, the Hephaisteion, the Propylaia, the Nike temple, and the Erechtheion on the Acropolis. Moreover, some of the buildings were, in fact, never completed, most obviously the Propylaia and the Temple of Nemesis at Rhamnous. Also, the step blocks of the Temple of Athena Pallenis that were moved to the Agora as the Temple of Ares have undressed surfaces on the treads and risers, just like the Temple of Nemesis. The striking exception is the Parthenon, which was indeed completed except for the pediments in ten years. What emerges from our survey is the very clear priority that was accorded to the great temple on the Acropolis. The Parthenon is especially notable for its unusual plan, for its innovative proportional relationships, and for the richness of its sculptural program and architectural detail. We can get some feeling for the revolution which the Parthenon wrought in the design of the Doric order by the immediate borrowing of its innovative features in the smaller Doric temples. The three-sided interior colonnade was introduced into the Hephaisteion and the Temple of Athena Pallenis, and the altered proportions of columns and entablature in all four hexastyle temples.

Another fascinating aspect of the temples is the way that sculptural themes have been employed to memorialize the defeat of the Persians. The Amazonomachy, the Centauromachy, the Trojan War, the battle of the gods and giants, the deeds of Theseus, and the labors of Herakles—these various heroic exploits of ancient story have been assimilated to recent military actions to proclaim the message of Athenian victory. By the 420s, however, when the sculptured friezes of the Athena Nike temple were carved, the Battle of Marathon itself is depicted, and probably other historical engagements. But these are no pictures of real phalanx warfare. The Athenian warriors are themselves

---

[136] Plut. *Per.* 13.1; translation Perrin (Loeb).

heroic in their nudity and armed only with shields and helmets. It is evident that the historical battle
itself has been fully won over into the realm of myth.

What is astonishing to contemplate is the sheer splendor of the architecture. In those few years,
Athenian builders brought the design and construction of Greek religious architecture to a pin-
nacle of perfection that would never be surpassed in later antiquity. Moreover, with the hindsight
of history, the modern student perceives that there are but a few dozen buildings in all the ages of
architecture that can stand beside those on the Acropolis of Athens, and there are fewer still that
have influenced later monuments as much as the Parthenon and the Erechtheion. The two Athenian temples have become icons that proclaim the Hellenic roots of Western civilization, and they
illustrate every history book of art and culture. In the end it may be profitable to ponder how it
came about that a single generation of the Periklean age could contribute so profoundly to the development of religious architecture. What circumstances, we may ask, were necessary to foster such
a remarkable achievement. Certainly economic resources were an essential factor. Athens was the
largest and wealthiest of the city-states of Greece, and in the fifth century her powerful economy was
augmented by the contributions of nearly 250 tributary allies that formed the maritime empire.[137]
But there have been many eras of abundant prosperity that have failed conspicuously to produce
enduring masterpieces of architecture, so the availability of discretionary income is not the sole ingredient. More important perhaps, and more difficult to assess, is the role of artistic vision, and there
can be no doubt that fifth-century Athens was unusually blessed in this respect. The architectural
designs of both the Parthenon and Propylaia reveal that extraordinary quality. Confronted even by
the shattered fragments of the temple's sculpture, we feel the presence of a towering artistic personality. Marble temples, however, were not the works of solitary masters but were assembled by teams
of craftsmen. In the preserved accounts of the Erechtheion, 107 individual workmen are listed by
name.[138] Another vital factor that enabled Athens to erect these splendid monuments was the high
level of technical expertise achieved by these ordinary marble workers, probably from all parts of
Greece. They could carve with flawless precision the complicated geometry of molded profiles, over
dozens of meters in length. They could lift a twelve-ton column drum and align it to the millimeter
on its stylobate. They could polish the face of a marble block to a surface of silken smoothness that
was never equaled later. Indeed, much of the brilliant results we owe to the superior craftsmanship
of the Athenian labor force.

These various factors conspired to render possible the architectural achievement of fifth-century Athens, but perhaps the most important factor of all was the political will. In our attempt
to investigate the parliamentary process by which each of the building projects was approved and
administered, we saw that every decision reflected the sovereign will of the Athenian demos as expressed in the votes of several thousand citizens. And the demos always responded to those speakers
who argued most persuasively for a particular course of action. In later centuries, ancient writers
almost universally attributed the buildings to Perikles and accorded to him administrative oversight
for their construction. But in our analysis of the documents published by the builders themselves
there emerged no trace of an overarching executive authority or managerial position of the kind that
the later sources seem to imply. In fact, the more precisely one seeks to define the role of Perikles in
the building program, the more that figure eludes capture, like some ghostly apparition. What later
authors mistook for the responsibility of public office, however, was the persuasive statecraft of a
consummate politician. Perikles probably confined his activities to the one arena of which he had

---

[137] The inscribed tribute lists bear the names of the allied cities, in later years organized into five districts: Ionian 35,
Hellespontine 45, Thraceward 62, Karian 79, Island 27 = 248 total. See *ATL* II; the information conveniently assembled
in five tables, Meiggs, *AE*, 540–559.
[138] See H. Randall, *AJA* 57 (1953) 203 and table 1.

total mastery, the assembly on the Pnyx, and there it was his enduring achievement to inspire the political will. For it is truly astounding that several thousand Athenians voted on different occasions to build the Parthenon and the Propylaia, the Odeion and the Telesterion, and the other temples of the Periklean age. Several thousand Athenians voted to hire men of artistic genius like Iktinos and Kallikrates, Pheidias and Mnesikles. Several thousand Athenians voted to spend lavishly from the reserve funds for the construction of temples because they had been persuaded that by the aggrandizement of her cults and sanctuaries Athens would enhance the glamour of her image as an imperial capital that was fit to rule the world. Although in the surviving ruins of the buildings we can see only the end result, it is surely correct to view the process by which they came to be built as an outstanding example of Periklean statesmanship.

Endnotes

---

1. The Date of the Naiskos of Athena Nike

The small poros naiskos of Athena Nike, the remains of which lie beneath the floor of the familiar marble Ionic temple, has caused considerable disagreement among scholars with regard to the date of its construction. Shortly after the existence of the structure first came to light, G. Welter (*AA* [1939] 11–12) suggested that it was originally built in the late sixth century and repaired after the Persian Wars. Dinsmoor (*AAG*[3], 151) interpreted the building as a temporary structure erected after 479 to shelter the old wooden image of the goddess. Other scholars have expressed less certainty. Boersma (*Building Policy*, 178, no. 46) cites both possibilities, that the shrine was late archaic and reconstructed or possibly constructed for the first time after the Persian destruction. Travlos (*PDA*, 148) lowered the date of construction to the decade 490–480, but he also thought the naiskos was restored after 479.

A radical revision of the chronology was proposed by J. A. Bundgaard (in *Mélanges G. Daux*, 43–49; also Bundgaard, *Parthenon*, 44–45, 48–53, 168–169), who sought to show that the shrine was not built until the middle years of the fifth century. He argued that the Nike temple decree (*IG* I[3] 35), which authorized Kallikrates to design a temple and altar for the goddess, actually referred to the poros naiskos rather than to the extant Ionic temple. Since he accepted a date at midcentury for the inscription, he accordingly lowered the date of the poros building (cf. chap. 2, pp. 27–35 above). Bundgaard's interpretation of the inscription and his later date for the naiskos were accepted by Romano ("Cult Images," 61–62) and subsequently by both Mark (*Athena Nike*, 58–67, 115–122) and Hurwit (*Athenian Acropolis*, 160–161), although the latter now acknowledges that it may have been "built soon after 480 or closer to 450" (*Acropolis in the Age of Pericles*, 181). In his detailed study for the restoration of the temple that is currently underway, Giraud (Μελέτη Αθηνάς Νίκης, 34–38) returns to the notion that the little poros building and its altar were built in the years immediately following the Persian destruction of the Acropolis, and this date for the naiskos was defended also by I. M. Shear (*JHS* 119 [1999] 120–123).

Travlos (*PDA*, 151, fig. 202:B, C, D) drew attention to the existence of three other diminutive temple-like structures located in different parts of the city. All three resemble closely the naiskos of Athena Nike in scale, design, and materials of construction. Although they yield no independent evidence for the chronology, they provide welcome parallels for the most basic type of sacred structure, so small that it could function only as a shelter for a cult image. (1) At the southeast corner of the precinct of Dionysos: P. Kalligas, *ArchDelt* 18 (1963 [1965]) B′ 1, 16; cf. Travlos, *PDA*, 541, fig. 678. (2) Southwest of the Areopagos: W. Dörpfeld, *AM* 19 (1894) 502; Judeich, *Topographie*[2], 299; Wycherley, *Stones of Athens*, 194–195; cf. Travlos, *PDA*, 275, fig. 351. (3) Inside Gate XIV on the saddle between the Pnyx and the Mouseion: S. Charitonides, *ArchEph* (1979) 164–165; cf. Travlos, *PDA*, 169, fig. 219 (no. 253).

The most elaborate and detailed attempt to support Bundgaard's late date for the naiskos has been mounted by Mark (*Athena Nike*, 58–67, Stage III) and is based on technical details of the architecture.

His argument dwells at length on the lowest foundation block at the southwest corner of the structure (figs. 5, 6, and 8, Block F2). Mark (*Athena Nike*, 58) asserts that this block of Peiraieus limestone "provides the project with a firm *terminus post quem*" because the piece was quarried, he believes, for the Kimonian south fortification wall of the Acropolis and was only subsequently used in the foundations of the naiskos. In its present state the block is 0.03 m wider on its upper surface than on its resting surface; and from this discrepancy Mark concludes not only that it was cut with a batter, but recognizably the same batter that is observable in those portions of the south fortification wall preserving original masonry. Therefore, according to him, the block cannot even have been quarried until after ca. 465 at the earliest and was only later built into the foundations of the naiskos. But the original quarry surface is visible on all sides of F2, only the top having been worked level (Mark, *Athena Nike*, 49–50 and figs. 6, 8). The discrepancy in width between top and bottom cannot be a batter, which would have been applied after the block was set in place in the south wall; rather it means only that the block was left undressed until it was built into the foundation of the naiskos. Thus the block has no evidential value whatever with respect to the chronology of the building. (Cf. the criticism of I. M. Shear, *JHS* 119 [1999] 121–122.)

Aligned on the axis of the naiskos is a small rectangular altar of Aiginetan poros decorated with base and crowning moldings in the cyma reversa profile (Mark, *Athena Nike*, 53–54). Comparison of these profiles with other dated moldings of this type provides the best evidence for the chronology of the altar and the associated naiskos. The development of the cyma reversa molding from the sixth century through the Classical period has been discussed by Shoe, *Greek Mouldings*, 54–57, 84–85, 87–89. Her study has shown that in the sixth century the cyma reversa tended to have rather little horizontal depth in relation to its vertical height, that ratio normally varying between 1:4 and 1:2 (p. 54, note 2), but in the course of the fifth century the molding gradually acquired greater projection, until by the time of the Parthenon the ratio of depth to height was usually between 1:2 and 1:1 (p. 87). Mark (*Athena Nike*, 60–61, fig. 13) compares the base molding of the poros altar with other examples and concludes that "the moldings on the Stage III altar belong rather to the 5th than to the 6th century." But that is not in dispute; the issue is whether the base molding of the altar should be dated just before or after 480, or rather ca. 450. The cyma reversa profile of the altar base has a ratio of depth to height of 1:1.57. By way of comparison, this is set alongside three other examples of base moldings (Mark, *Athena Nike*, fig. 13): (1) a late archaic statue base from Paros with depth to height ratio 1:1.7 (A. Kostoglou-Despini, Προβλήματα τῆς παριανῆς πλαστικῆς [Thessalonike 1979] fig. 4); (2) the toichobate of the Temple of Poseidon at Sounion, with depth to height ratio 1:1.24 (Shoe, pl. XXXVII:3); (3) the sill for the grilles in the opisthodomos of the Parthenon, with depth to height ratio 1:1.28 (Shoe, pl. XXXVII:1).

The closest parallel to the base molding on the altar of Athena Nike, and closer than any of those cited by Mark, is the base molding on the altar of Aphrodite Ourania in the Athenian Agora (see I. M. Shear, *JHS* 119 [1999] 123, fig. 5b). Although Mark was aware of the existence of this example (p. 60, note 57), he failed to make use of its evidence. The altar in the Agora has a base molding that is only slightly larger than that on the Acropolis, but the profile of its cyma reversa is closely analogous; the ratio of depth to height is 1:1.62. Contrary to Mark's assertion that its date is in doubt (*Athena Nike*, p. 60, note 57), the altar of Aphrodite Ourania provides one of the clearest examples of Athenian monuments that were damaged by the Persians in 479 and carefully restored in the third quarter of the fifth century. While the damage and repair to the blocks of the altar plainly signal its pre-Persian date, this is corroborated by the evidence of pottery recovered from stratified layers of fill around and within its base, which pointed to the years around 500 for construction of the monument (preliminary summary of the pottery evidence, Shear, Jr., *Hesperia* 53 [1984] 30, notes 45–47). Thus the comparable examples of the cyma reversa as a base molding span a period of more than half a century, from ca. 500 to the late 440s, and their gradually changing proportions illustrate precisely the development expounded by Shoe. In this sequence, there can be no doubt where the cyma reversa on the altar of Athena Nike belongs. It falls between the altar of Aphrodite Ourania and the Parthenon, but is plainly much closer to the former, and this comparison adds strength to the argument that the little naiskos and its altar were first built in the years just after the Persian Wars. They certainly cannot be associated with the construction that the Nike temple decree (*IG* I³ 35) authorized Kallikrates to undertake.

2. THE DATE OF THE PARTHENON PODIUM

The great solid masonry platform that provides the foundation for the Parthenon rises in fourteen courses of poros blocks at its southwest corner and twenty-two courses at its southeast corner, and thus created an enormous artificial platform on the steeply sloping rock of the Acropolis. Ever since the excavations of 1885 to 1890, which explored the earth filling along the south side of the podium, scholarly attempts to interpret the monument and to ascertain the date of its construction have ignited one of the most contentious disputes of the twentieth century in Athenian archaeology. The same evidence has been rehearsed so frequently and so extensively by so many scholars that only the most cursory summary of their opinions need be included here.

The discovery of broken pieces of archaic sculpture and architectural members in the fill south of the Parthenon not surprisingly reminded the early excavators of the Persian destruction, and Dörpfeld (*AM* 17 [1892] 187–189) accordingly proposed to date the construction of the podium after the Persian Wars, to the period of Kimon, in the second quarter of the fifth century. His later reexamination of the excavation records, however, revealed that the fill that was actually contemporary with the foundation contained no burnt Persian debris and so should be dated prior to 480 (*AM* 27 [1902] 319–416). Dörpfeld then went on to formulate his theory that there had been two predecessors of the Periklean temple: "Parthenon I" was planned in the late sixth century and was to be entirely of poros, of which the crepidoma and a step of Kará limestone were built on the podium before plans were changed in 490 to the marble temple, "Parthenon II," construction of which was interrupted ten years later by the Persian sack, and whose calcined column drums are still visible in the north wall of the citadel (*AM* 17 [1892] 399, 410–412 for the dates). The architectural reconstruction of the Older Parthenon was considerably revised by B. H. Hill (*AJA* 16 [1912] 535–558), who demonstrated that the first step of the crepidoma in Kará limestone is still in situ under the Periklean temple and originally supported a second step and stylobate of marble. The peristyle was designed with 6 × 16 columns around a cella of two compartments entered through the prostyle porches at either end. Hill's reconstruction of the building has stood the test of time and has since been generally accepted.

Publication of the pottery from the excavations south of the Parthenon (B. Graef and E. Langlotz, *Die antiken Vasen von der Akropolis zu Athen*, 2 vols. [1925–33]) enabled Dinsmoor to undertake a detailed analysis of the ceramic material in relation to the stratified layers of fill, as they had been observed by the excavators and recorded in section drawings made by G. Kawerau (Bundgaard, *The Excavation of the Acropolis* [1974], pls. 153:1, 159, 162:1). Dinsmoor's study (*AJA* 38 [1934] 408–448) emphasized the importance of the long wall of polygonal masonry (called S 2 in the literature) that ran nearly parallel to the podium for its full length and extended well beyond it to the east. Dinsmoor interpreted S 2 as a retaining wall contemporary with the podium designed to hold back the deep layers of fill that were dumped in between it and the temple as the foundation was being raised to the appropriate level. Accordingly, the latest pottery from these layers should have been buried while the podium was under construction and should indicate the date at which that construction took place. Unfortunately, of the thousands of pieces of pottery catalogued by Graef and Langlotz, only fifty-six fragments had a sufficiently exact provenience so that they could be assigned with assurance to the layers between S 2 and the podium (Graef and Langlotz, 426, 428, 429), but the latest of these was datable to ca. 490 (Graef and Langlotz, 437–438). This circumstance led Dinsmoor to conclude that the podium was erected in the years immediately following the Battle of Marathon. It was designed to carry the marble Older Parthenon as reconstructed by Hill, and Dörpfeld's putative "poros Parthenon disappears as a myth" (Dinsmoor, *AJA* 38 [1934] 416).

For his part, Dörpfeld took umbrage at Dinsmoor's handling of his theory and stoutly defended his three phases of the Parthenon in an article that appeared the following year (*AJA* 39 [1935] 497–507), but he accepted a date between 490 and 480 for the marble Older Parthenon. The real polemic against the pre-Persian chronology, however, came from W. Kolbe (*JdI* 51 [1936] 1–64), who attacked Dinsmoor's interpretation of both the walls and the stratigraphy south of the Parthenon. For Kolbe, wall S 2, as well as other surviving stretches of masonry in the area, were all temporary ramps and platforms to facilitate the handling and storing of building materials. In his interpretation, construction of the podium began shortly after 480; work on the marble Older Parthenon dates to the 470s; and all the earth fills, even those inside S 2, were deposited between ca. 475 and 445. The alleged fire damage to the marble blocks is illusory, actually caused by algae, and the many unfinished column drums were discarded because of flaws in the stone caused by flecks of mica (Kolbe, *JdI* 51 [1936] 61, 63).

The controversy over the date of the Older Parthenon continued into the second half of the twentieth century, and for a while supporters of the late date espoused by Kolbe were the more numerous. A. Tschira, whose many years of research on the Acropolis were published posthumously in 1972 (*JdI* 87, 158–231), argued for a date between 465 and 460 for the beginning of work on the podium, while he dated the unfinished marble temple between 454 and 449 (pp. 159, 231). In a study primarily concerned to document the curvature of the podium, S. Sinos (*AA* [1974] 157–168) found it no cause for surprise that the whole construction should date to post-Persian times because of the extensive changes that he saw in the plan. At about the same time, Bundgaard (*The Excavation of the Acropolis* [1974], 22) asserted that the unfinished column drums of the older temple had not been entirely removed from its stylobate until 448, preparatory to the enlargement of the foundation for the Periklean building. He went on to state the chronology that he favored more explicitly (*Parthenon and the Mycenaean City on the Heights* [1976], 59–60, 70): construction of the podium began in 458/7 at the earliest, followed directly by the marble Older Parthenon between 457 and 455. All the fill between the podium and the south wall of the Acropolis he dated to the period 457–438. In fact, during the middle years of the twentieth century, one of the few scholars who supported Dinsmoor's interpretation of the stratigraphy south of the Parthenon and accepted a date between 490 and 480 for construction of the podium and the retaining wall S 2 was W. H. Plommer (*JHS* 80 [1960] 137, 139). He also saw no reason to doubt that the podium was designed for the marble Older Parthenon, as reconstructed by Hill, and therefore found "no need to posit an earlier, larger temple of poros" (*JHS* 80 [1960] 135).

In the following years, the same retaining walls and layers of fill, their relation to the podium of the Parthenon and to the south fortification wall of the Acropolis, were subjected again to detailed scrutiny in three separate studies: G. Beckel, in Χαριστήριον Ὀρλάνδος, vol. 4 (1967–68) 329–362; Orlandos, Παρθ., vol. 2 (1977) 40–89; and H. Drerup, *AntK* 24 (1981) 21–38. All three authors reviewed the various theories on both sides of the controversy carefully and objectively. Beckel (p. 362) and Drerup (p. 33) both reached the conclusion, somewhat reluctantly, that construction of the Older Parthenon should more likely be dated to the years between 490 and 480. Orlandos, who concerned himself primarily with the architectural history of the building, avoided expressing a specific opinion about the chronology. From 1970 to the present, there has begun to emerge a general consensus that the unfinished marble Parthenon was begun after the Battle of Marathon and was interrupted by the Persian destruction of the Acropolis in 480. Many scholars who may disagree on other aspects of the archaeological history of the building have now come to support a pre-Persian date for its construction. See, among others, Boersma, *Building Policy* (1970) 38–39; R. Carpenter, *The Architects of the Parthenon* (1970) 28–29, 31, 164; M. Korres, *AM* 108 (1993) 71 (note 37 lists many other authors who favor a pre-Persian date); R. Tölle-Kastenbein, *JdI* 108 (1993) 59–61; Korres, in W. Hoepfner, ed., *Kult und Kultbauten* (1997) 243; R. F. Rhodes, *Architecture and Meaning on the Athenian Acropolis* (1995) 30–32; Hurwit, *Athenian Acropolis* (1999) 130; Gruben, *Gr. Tempel*[5] (2001) 171; M. Steskal, *Der Zerstörungsbefund 480/79 der Athener Akropolis* (2004) 154–155.

This welcome consensus has not always extended to the great poros podium on which the Older Parthenon was being erected at the time of its destruction, for the ghost of Dörpfeld's poros "Parthenon I" continues to rear its head in the scholarship. Since the podium, at its east and west ends, extended 3.146 m beyond the lowest step of the temple and was wider by 2.146 m along its north and south flanks, it is argued that the foundation must have been designed to carry a much larger building than the unfinished marble temple. That plan must have called for a temple of poros stone because it was unthinkable that the lowest step of Kará limestone, which according to Dörpfeld was originally intended to be the stylobate, could have supported a marble colonnade. Of this putative temple, only the foundation platform was ever built, whereupon the plan was changed to a grander building of Pentelic marble after the Athenian victory at Marathon in 490. Scholars have proposed various permutations of the alleged change in plan from

"Parthenon I" to "Parthenon II." See Sinos, *AA* (1974) 166–168; Korres, *AM* 108 (1993) 59–75 and especially 74; Korres, in Hoepfner, ed., *Kult und Kultbauten* (1997) 242–243, accepted by Gruben, *Gr. Tempel*⁵, 171–172; the arguments summarized by Drerup, *AntK* 24 (1981) 24–25; Steskal, *Zerstörungs-befund*, 74–76. Korres (in Hoepfner, ed., *Kult und Kultbauten*) dated construction of the podium to the end of the sixth or the beginning of the fifth century, while a date in the years between 507 and 490 was proposed by Tölle-Kastenbein (*JdI* 108 [1993] 62), although she argued (pp. 63–66) that the platform was built not for the Parthenon but as an open terrace on which a row of small treasury buildings stood.

In light of this tendency to separate the date of the podium from that of the unfinished marble temple, it seems necessary to emphasize that Dinsmoor placed the beginning of construction after 490 not because the unfinished column drums were built into the north wall, and not because many of them had been damaged by fire, but because the latest pottery from the stratified fill between the retaining wall S 2 and the podium was datable to ca. 490. In the analysis of stratigraphy, it is axiomatic that the latest pieces of pottery provide a terminus post quem for the deposit of a given layer of fill. Therefore, if Dinsmoor's interpretation of the ceramic material was correct, all attempts to date construction of the podium to the late sixth century or to the decade 500–490 must be abandoned, and with them of course Dörpfeld's poros "Parthenon I." Possibly for this reason several adherents to these views, as well as scholars who wish to make everything post-Persian, have resorted to a variety of special pleadings that disparage the pottery assemblage and impugn the evidential value of potsherds to provide accurate chronology. See the remarks of Beckel, in Χα-ριστήριον Ὀρλάνδος, vol. 4, 359–361; Tschira, *JdI* 87 (1972) 174; Drerup, *AntK* 24 (1981) 31 and note 74; Tölle-Kastenbein, *AA* (1983) 573–584 and especially 573, note 3; Steskal, *Zerstörungsbefund*, 152–153. It is noticeable, however, that even the most recent writers on these matters have consistently failed to make use of the exhaustive researches of J. D. Beazley into the ordering of black- and red-figured pottery, or the publication of hundreds of contemporary examples from the Agora excavations, many of them found in closely datable closed deposits. At this late date it is disingenuous to assert with Steskal (*Zerstörungsbefund*, 152–153) that "All lines of argument that are based on ceramic evidence must be consistently disregarded." On the contrary, considerably more is now known about the group of pottery that Dinsmoor studied in 1934, and it may be useful to assemble that information in list form.

The main layers of stratified fill between the retaining wall S 2 and the podium of the Parthenon Dinsmoor designated Stratum II. This divided naturally into three parts: IIa, the fill in the V-shaped foundation trench at the foot of the podium; IIb, the main fill behind wall S 2; and IIc, fill overflowing wall S 2 (*AJA* 38 [1934] 417). Of the fifty-six pieces of pottery that could be assigned with assurance to Stratum II, the forty-two listed below are late black figure or red figure, the remainder being too early for consideration (Dinsmoor, *AJA* 38 [1934], 426, 428, 429; Steskal, *Zerstörungsbefund*, 92–93). The catalogue numbers follow the order of Graef and Langlotz (vol. 1, 1925; vol. 2, 1933). References to Beazley's books indicate pieces that he was able to attribute to a specific group or vase painter. References to Moore and Philipides, *Agora* XXIII, cite contemporary examples for comparison. The plaques have been studied most recently by K. Karoglou, *Attic Pinakes: Votive Images in Clay*, BAR International Series 2104 (Oxford 2010).

Late Black Figure
    Stratum IIa or IIb
    (Graef and Langlotz, vol. 1)
      615m: Krater; 14 other frags. of same piece
      716: Column-krater, rim
      798 = *ABV* 119, no. 1: Amphora (?), wall frag., related to Lydos (550–540)
      811: Amphora, wall frag.
      856: Amphora, wall frag.
      1045a: Panathenaic amphora, wall frag.
      1164 = *ABV* 89, no. 4: Loutrophoros, Group of North Slope AP 942; cf. *Agora* XXIII, 375 (550–525)
      1165 = *ABV* 89, no. 5: Loutrophoros, Group of North Slope AP 942; cf. *Agora* XXIII, 375 (550–525)
      1295a: Skyphos; 10 other frags. of same piece (ca. 500?)

1322 = *ABV* 619, no. 62: Skyphos, CHC Group; cf. *Agora* XXIII, 1578–1601 (ca. 500)

1669a: Cup, offset rim and wall

2010: Late cup, rim and wall (500–490)

2028a = *ABV* 643, no. 158: Late cup, Leafless Group, Painter of Oxford 237 (500–490)

2038 = *ABV* 642, no. 130: Late cup, Leafless Group (500–490)

2045 = *ABV* 642, no. 147: Late cup, Leafless Group (500–490)

2046 = *ABV* 635, no. 43: Late eye-cup, Leafless Group (500–490)

2047 = *ABV* 635, no. 45: Late eye-cup, Leafless Group (500–490)

2048 = *ABV* 635, no. 44: Late eye-cup, Leafless Group (500–490)

> For 2028a–2048, cf. *Agora* XXIII, 1761–1765, 1767–1778, 1833–1835, p. 67.

2260: Wall frag., late black figure (500–490?)

2271b, c: Wall frag., black figure (ca. 500?)

2462: Plate frag.

2516: Plaque, natural clay ground, Athena, late black figure; Karoglou, no. 36 (ca. 540–530)

2549: Plaque, Athena seated in temple; Karoglou, no. 102 (ca. 510–500)

2562: Plaque, natural clay ground, racing quadrigas (end 6th cent. [Graef]); Karoglou, no. 81 (ca. 520–510)

Stratum IIb or IIc

914 = *ABV* 666: Panathenaic amphora, 2 frags.

1260: Skyphos, wall frag. (ca. 500?)

1734: Eye-cup, wall frag.

1784: Cup, inner tondo

1994 = *ABV* 654, no. 2: Late cup, Painter of North Slope R. 159 (500–490)

2002: Late cup, wall frag. (500–490)

2515: Plaque, Athena, natural clay ground (ca. 500 [Langlotz, p. vii]); Karoglou, no. 86 (ca. 510–500)

2560 = *ABV* 337, no. 32; joins with Athens, NM AP 165/15124: Plaque, Rycroft Painter, vintage scene; cf. *Agora* XXIII, 187, 195, 196 (510–500); Karoglou, no. 82 (ca. 520–510)

2592: Plaque, white ground, Herakles with quadriga, Athena, Hermes, and Dionysos(?) (early 5th cent. [Graef]); Karoglou, no. 92 (ca. 510–500)

Red Figure

Stratum IIa or IIb

(Graef and Langlotz, vol. 2)

731: Calyx-krater, wall frag. (ca. 490 [Langlotz, p. vi])

1156: Phiale, rim frag.

Stratum IIb or IIc

45 = *ARV*² 62, no. 81: Cup, Oltos, mid- to late (ca. 510)

96 = *ARV*² 105, no. 1: Cup, Group of Acropolis 96 (ca. 510)

99 = *ARV*² 1589, 1699: Cup, kalos name (ca. 510)

114: Cup, "Leagros period" (ca. 510 [Langlotz, p. vii])

238: Cup, foot, dedication by Smikros (ca. 500 [Langlotz, p. vii])

551a = *ARV*² 163, 12: Kantharoid vase, Paseas, Cerberus Painter (ca. 500)

Perusal of the dates that students of Athenian pottery are now able to assign to these fragments reveals that eleven pieces (26.2%) were painted in all likelihood during the first decade of the fifth century, and another seven (16.6%) were made in the years ca. 500. The lower limit of the group is still given by the single red-figured fragment (Langlotz, vol. 2, no. 731), ca. 490, but this should be no cause for surprise in such a tiny sample. In fact, the numerous pieces now datable to the early fifth century provide welcome confirmation that this is the correct terminal date for the deposit. Beazley attributed no fewer than six of these pieces to a large class of late black-figured cups painted by various artists that he called collectively the

Leafless Group. Included in his long lists of cups by these painters are eighteen other examples that were found in fills south of the Parthenon but for which no exact provenience is recorded (*ABV*, 635–647). These, of course, are of no evidential value in determining the date of the podium, but the sheer numbers show the cups of this class were popular dedications on the Acropolis at the beginning of the fifth century. It is of interest that the Agora excavations have produced twenty more cups by the Leafless Group (*Agora* XXIII, 1761–1765, 1767–1768, 1833–1835), of which thirteen came from six of the dumps of debris that resulted from the Persian destruction of the lower city in 479 (Shear, Jr., *Hesperia* 62 [1993] 389). But in these securely dated deposits, the cups by the Leafless Group were enormously outnumbered by the products of another large manufacturer of late black-figured pottery, the Haimon Workshop. As many as seventy-seven pots painted in the manner of the Haimon Painter were found in eleven separate deposits of Persian debris. In striking contrast, among the thousands of catalogued pieces from the Acropolis, Beazley could attribute only three small fragments to the Haimon Group, and these unfortunately without provenience (*ABV* 564, nos. 589–590; 569, no. 673). This is a curious discrepancy in two such large assemblages of pottery that are so obviously close together in both time and space, but it may in part reflect the decade that elapsed between the start of work on the podium of the Parthenon and the destruction of the city by the Persians.

3. THE CONSTRUCTION DATE OF THE HEPHAISTEION

The excavators of the area within and around the temple on the Kolonos Agoraios found that the original earth fillings beneath the floor of the building had been largely removed for the construction of some fifty-three medieval and modern graves (Dinsmoor, *Hesperia* Suppl. 5 [1941] 5, fig. 1). Although fragments of classical pottery were found scattered over much of the bedrock surface of the hill, it could not be specifically associated with the construction of the temple.

One deposit, however, provided much more specific evidence for the temple's date of construction. This was the filling of a rock-cut pit that came to light 33 m to the southwest of the southwest corner of the temple (Agora excavations, deposit C 9:6). The square pit, measuring ca. 3.00 m on a side, had been deliberately excavated in the bedrock to a depth of 1.70 m, whereupon it was filled up with masses of debris from the builders' stone yards. The stratification of the filling showed that the debris had been shoveled in from the north side of the pit, that is, from the side toward the temple. The pit produced great quantities of working chips of Pentelic marble of a quality comparable to that used in the temple. Many pieces retained tooled surfaces identical with the tool marks still observable in the stonework of the building. Of particular interest is a number of large fragments that came from the working of column drums of a size appropriate for the Hephaisteion (Dinsmoor, *Hesperia* Suppl. 5 [1941] 128).

Among the construction debris was a small group of much broken pottery that was undoubtedly all dumped into the pit at the same time. The latest datable pieces of this pottery are of special importance because they provide a terminus ante quem for the beginning of work on the temple. The pottery was fully catalogued and carefully described by L. Talcott as a part of Dinsmoor's publication in 1941 (*Hesperia* Suppl. 5 [1941] 130–149). Since that time, however, the study of classical Athenian pottery has become greatly refined and its dating has become more precise. Most of the pieces originally studied by Talcott have since been incorporated in the series of volumes presenting the definitive publication of pottery from the Agora excavations, and some of the figured pottery has been attributed to specific vase painters. In view of these developments it may be useful to present here a list of the individual pots, together with a reference to their most recent publication and the date there assigned to each. In the following list the numbers preceded by the letter P or L are the Agora inventory numbers; the Roman numerals are volumes in the Agora series, followed by the catalogue number of the pot within the specific volume. The equals symbol (=) indicates that a pot originally described by Talcott has been republished in full. In the lists of figured pottery, "N.A." indicates that piece has not been attributed to a vase painter.

Deposit C 9:6

Black Figure

P 9460 = *Agora* XXIII, 190: Neck-amphora, Swing Painter, *ABV* 310, no. 105 (ca. 540)

P 25375 = *Agora* XXIII, 531: Stand, cf. Manner of Gorgon Painter, Paralipomena 9 (early 6th cent.)

P 9459 = *Agora* XXIII, 661: Hydria, kalpis, N.A. (early 5th cent.)

P 15865 = *Agora* XXIII, 1186: Lekythos, manner of Haimon Painter, *ABV* 542, no. 89 (475–450)

P 9461: Cf. P 24592 (from deposit Q 12: 3): Palmette cup, *Hesperia* 62 (1993) pl. 82:c (500–480)

P 9476: Head vase, *Hesperia* Suppl. 5, 131, N.A. (early 5th cent.)

Red Figure

P15866 = *Agora* XXX, 34: Pelike, N.A. (ca. 470–460)

P9464 = *Agora* XXX, 70: Amphora or pelike, Mykonos Painter, *ARV*² 516, no. 17 (ca. 470–460)

P9465 = *Agora* XXX, 223: Column-krater, Manner of Pig Painter, *ARV*² 566, no. 11 (ca. 470–460)

P8533 = *Agora* XXX, 237: Volute-krater, N.A. (ca. 480)

P9462 = *Agora* XXX, 261: Calyx-krater, Hephaisteion Painter, *ARV*² 298, no. 4 (ca. 470)

P 9483 = *Agora* XXX, 269: Calyx-krater, N.A. (ca. 450)

P 9466 = *Agora* XXX, 614: Oinochoe, N.A. (2nd quarter 5th cent.)

P 9470 = *Agora* XXX, 832: Lekythos, Bowdoin Painter, *ARV*² 681, no. 88 (ca. 480–470)

P 8985 = *Agora* XXX, 1007: Pyxis lid, N.A. (ca. 450)

P 9469 = *Agora* XXX, 1229: Kantharos, Type D (Sotadean), N.A. (ca. 470–460)

P 9467 = *Agora* XXX, 1240: Skyphos, N.A. (2nd quarter 5th cent.)

P 9463 = *Agora* XXX, 1654: Closed, shape uncertain, Pan Painter, *ARV*² 558, no. 140 (ca. 470)

P 9468 = *Agora* XXX, 1683: Plaque, two hoplites in combat, very early red figure, *ARV*² 12, no. 14 (ca. 520); Karoglou, no. 201 (ca. 530–520)

Black Glaze

P 9473: Cf. *Agora* XII, 151: Oinochoe, banded round-mouth (480–450)

P 9471 = *Agora* XII, 640: Kantharos, type D (Sotadean) (ca. 450)

P 9475: Cf. *Agora* XII, 908: Saltcellar, echinus wall (ca. 450)

P 9472 = *Agora* XII, 1236: Lid for ribbon-handled lekanis (ca. 450)

P 8535 = *Agora* XII, 1532: Storage bin (context ca. 450)

P 9474: Cf. *Agora* XII, 1803: Lekane, small (context ca. 470–460)

Ostraka

P 6818 = *Agora* XXV, 98: Dieitrephes Euthoinou, Group M 1 (2nd quarter 5th cent.)

P 9477 = *Agora* XXV, 313: Kallias Kratiou, Group M 1, *Agora* XXV, p. 28 (480s)

P 9478 = *Agora* XXV, 643: Menon Gargettios, Group M 1 (2nd quarter 5th cent.)

P 8534 = *Agora* XXV, 644: Menon Gargettios, Group M 1 (2nd quarter 5th cent.)

P 9481 = *Agora* XXV, 1099: Frag., name uncertain, Group M 1

Inscribed Sherds

P 9482 = *Agora* XXI, C 14: Lekane frag. (2nd quarter 5th cent.)

P 15867 = *Agora* XXI, F 72: Lekythos, foot in two degrees (2nd quarter 5th cent.)

P 15868 = *Agora* XXI, F 73: Olpe, bottom of disc foot (2nd quarter 5th cent.)

P 9479: *Hesperia* Suppl. 5 (1941) 142, no. 34: Cup foot, graffito

P 9480: *Hesperia* Suppl. 5 (1941) 141, no. 32: Cup foot, graffito

Lamps

L 2833 = *Agora* IV, 107: Type 16 variant (ca. 500–480)

L 3961 = *Agora* IV, 142: Type 19 variant (ca. 520, Type 525–480)

L 2834 = *Agora* IV, 167: Type 21 B (context 450, Type 480–415)

Examination of the dates of the pottery reveals at once that, like many such groups of all periods, by far the greater part of the material is substantially earlier than the closing date of the deposit, while a few scattered fragments are nearly a century older than the latest pieces. It is also characteristic that the latest pieces, which determine the closing date, are few in number, only six out of thirty-eight (15.8%). Particularly noticeable is the difference in the state of preservation between the figured pottery and the black-glazed or partly glazed household wares. Both the black and red figure have been reduced to isolated sherds or a few pieces of a single vase, whereas the pots of ordinary tableware are substantially complete. (Cf. *Hesperia* Suppl. 5, fig. 57 [black figure] and 63 [red figure] with 64 [household ware].) This last group also comprises most of the latest pieces, dating ca. 450, and the best preserved of them are vessels of small size that could well have contained a workman's lunch before they broke and were discarded on the building site. A closing date for the deposit in the 450s is also suggested by the two ostraka bearing the name of Menon of Gargettos. Although these individual ballots could have been cast against him at any time in the second quarter of the century, A. E. Raubitschek has argued that his actual ostracism took place, and therefore the most votes were cast against him, in 457 (*Hesperia* 24 [1955] 288–289, citing W. Peek, *Kerameikos* III, 71–72, no. 121; cf. M. Lang, *Agora* XXV, 96). The available evidence thus shows that the pit on the Kolonos Agoraios was filled with debris ca. 450, and that by that time construction of the Hephaisteion was well underway.

4. Interpretations of the Parthenon Frieze

It is not surprising that a work of art as splendid as the Parthenon frieze should have attracted the attention of legions of scholars, who have expended enormous effort and ingenuity to explain its subject matter and meaning in the sculptural program of the temple. What is disconcerting is the discovery that the proposed interpretations of the frieze, together with their many variants, are almost as numerous as the authors who have set out to describe it. Nevertheless, these variations of opinion need to be acknowledged, even if many of them are mutually exclusive. Whatever interpretation one prefers to adopt, however, the subject must be readily legible from afar. It has been shown that the frieze was viewed to best advantage from a position 30 feet outside the stylobate, and from there the line of sight from viewer to sculpture was 60 feet long (R. Stillwell, *Hesperia* 38 [1969] 232–233, fig. 1). In addition, the subject matter must be readily understandable, at least to the ancient viewer, if not also to us.

In recent decades, attempts to explain the frieze have fallen into several broad categories, of which the first approaches the sculpture as mythology. All other sculptural decoration of temples drew on the received mythology of early Greece, and the Parthenon should have done likewise. Such was the argument of C. Kardara (*ArchEph* [1961] 61–158), who interpreted the frieze as the first celebration of the Panathenaia in the reign of the mythical king Kekrops. In her reading, the figures of the peplos scene were the first royal family of Athens. The child Erichthonios (E 35), founder of the festival and dedicator of the Ancient Image of Athena, was shown in the act of handing over the first peplos to Kekrops himself (E 34). At the center of the scene stood the figure of Ge (E 33), goddess of the earth and the true mother of Erichthonios, whose presence emphasized the child's autochthonous birth. The *diphrophoroi* (E 31, 32) represented two of the three daughters of Kekrops. This interpretation, however, is open to the objection that none of the five figures has any attribute to suggest their identification as mythological characters, unlike the twelve Olympians on either side, each of whom is depicted with an attribute specific to the deity. Lacking such vital flags, the man (E 34) appears to wear the priestly costume of a contemporary basileus, while the three women are in no way distinguished from the well-dressed women of the fifth century who lead the procession at the north and south ends of the frieze.

In a more recent mythological interpretation (J. B. Connelly, *AJA* 100 [1996] 53–80), the frieze depicts not only the first celebration of the festival, but more specifically the occasion for its establishment. The victorious Athenians are shown returning from their defeat of Eumolpos, the son of Poseidon, and a large force of Thracians. But in this reading, the central scene of the east frieze, by a curious flashback, shows an episode anterior to the battle, by means of which the Athenian victory was achieved. King Erechtheus (E 34), assisted by his wife, Praxithea (E 33), is shown preparing to sacrifice his youngest daughter (E 35) in accordance with an oracle from Delphi. The cloth handled by the little girl and her father is not the peplos of Athena but a funeral shroud in which the victim will be wrapped prior to her sacrifice. On the left, her two older sisters (E 31, 32) arrive carrying folded shrouds on stools, because they have vowed to join their sister in her patriotic sacrifice for the salvation of the city. So we are presented with a tragic scene in which the Athenian royal family is preparing to indulge in a grisly human sacrifice. It is a lugubrious tale of impending death and mourning, the gloomy spirit of which is in no way conveyed by the sculpture itself and is, in fact, totally at odds with the festive mood that pervades the rest of the frieze. This interpretation of the sculpture is based on the fragments of Euripides' play *Erechtheus*, written more than twenty years after the frieze was designed, and while the story may possibly have been known earlier, there is not a single representation of it in any medium of art either before or after the Parthenon. With no standard iconography to guide the viewer, no sacrificial altar to set the scene, and no sacrificial implements to announce the impending action, it is impossible to decipher this arcane myth from the east frieze of the Parthenon. Moreover, the ancient viewer, approaching the temple from the west end and watching the processional scenes unfold along the north flank, would be totally unprepared for the thematic disjunction that the melancholy sacrifice of the Erechtheids would have caused in the east frieze.

A completely different approach to the interpretation of the frieze was once suggested by J. Boardman (in *Festschrift Brommer*, 39–49; and in *Parthenon-Kongress Basel*, 210–215). He argued that the frieze depicted the procession at a specific historical celebration of the festival, the Great Panathenaia of 490 that took place a few weeks before the Battle of Marathon. As evidence for this theory, Boardman asserted that the portions of the frieze devoted to cavalry and chariotry depicted precisely 192 men, the very number that Herodotos (6.117) reported as the total Athenian casualties in the battle. So the sculpture memorialized the Athenian dead and in fact commemorated their heroization, as we know that they subsequently received the sacrifices offered to heroes. But the count itself was doubtful because it included not only the horsemen and *apobatai*, but also the marshals and grooms. Significantly, however, the charioteers were omitted from the total. More difficult is the notion that any ancient viewer would count the figures in order to decode the message of the sculpture. Even if one could do so accurately, would it be recognized at once that the unarmed, beardless horsemen in festal attire represented the heavily armed hoplites who fought and died at Marathon and were now translated to heroic status? In the face of these problems, the theory found few adherents and was subsequently withdrawn (Boardman, *RA* [1999] 325–330).

By far the majority of scholars has espoused the view that the frieze depicts not a specific or historical celebration of the Panathenaia but rather a generalized and highly idealized version of the great procession. But in this reading of the sculpture, scholars have introduced innumerable variants in the details of interpretation. E. B. Harrison (in *Parthenon-Kongress Basel*, 230–234) suggested that the four sides of the frieze evoke different epochs in the history of the festival. On the west we see the mythical past, and in the central figure (W 15) she recognized the hero Theseus. The south frieze, with its ten ranks of horsemen differentiated by dress, represents democratic Athens of the Periklean present. By contrast, the repeated number four among the marchers and animals of the north frieze recalls the pre-Kleisthenic political order of the archaic city, when the citizenry was divided among the four Ionian tribes. Although the numbers ten and four are surely significant, this rigid evocation of different eras does not account satisfactorily for the ten ranks of horsemen, also on the north frieze, who ride in distinct groups, even if they are more irregularly disposed than on the south (see I. Jenkins, *Frieze*, 97–99). For Harrison, the east frieze shows a timeless moment when the preparations for religious liturgy summon the pantheon of the immortal gods.

A more radical attempt to divide the marchers of the north frieze from those of the south was proposed by E. Simon (*Festivals of Attica*, 61–62). In her reading of the frieze, the north and south flanks depict two separate processions, culminating in two separate sacrifices. The four cows on the north side will be offered to Athena Polias and the four sheep behind them to Pandrosos, in accordance with a regulation quoted from Philochoros (*FGrH* 328 F 10 = Harpokration, s.v. ἐπίβοιον [ε 85 Keaney]) that the sacrifice of a cow to Athena must be accompanied by a ewe for Pandrosos. But the text of Philochoros pertains to the sacrifices of private individuals and says nothing about the great hecatombs offered by the state (cf. Jenkins, *Frieze*, 28–29). Still more problematic is the interpretation of the ten cattle on the south frieze that, according to Simon, are being led for sacrifice to Athena Parthenos, although there is no evidence whatever that a goddess so named was ever the object of cult on the Acropolis. Another scholar who interprets the frieze as a generic representation of the festival procession reads an ideological message in the sculpture (Castriota, *Myth, Ethos*, 184–229). Since processional friezes and chariot races had been used in the sculptural decoration of Ionian temples in Archaic times, the appearance of these subjects on the Parthenon borrowed this iconographical strategy, and it served to reinforce Athens' claim to be the metropolis of all Ionian Greeks, from which the cities of East Greece had been colonized in the remote past. Others have raised issues concerning the physical setting of the scenes and have argued that the whole frieze should be understood to take place in the Agora, including the peplos scene, or, alternatively, that the frieze depicts vignettes of the procession extending from its marshalling in the Kerameikos to the top of the Acropolis (W. Gauer, in *Parthenon-Kongress Basel*, 220–229; Boardman, in *Festschrift Brommer*, 39–49; Boardman, in *Parthenon-Kongress Basel*, 210–215; Boardman, *RA* [1999] 325–326; P. Fehl, *JWI* 24 [1961] 1–44). While most of these writers identify the figures in the peplos scene as idealized mortals representing the clergy of the Acropolis and the basileus, it has been suggested (Jenkins, *Frieze*, 35–38) that they are engaged in a liturgical reenactment of the first presentation of the peplos. In this ritual pageant, the basileus plays the part of Kekrops, his mythical forebear as king; the women are his daughters; and the child who presents him with the robe stands in for Erichthonios.

Inevitably, some investigators have concluded that the subject matter of the Parthenon frieze is not in fact the Panathenaic procession at all, and they have sought to explain the sculptures in other ways. According to one such theory (R. R. Holloway, *ArtB* 48 [1966] 223–226), the frieze represents a kind of symbolic restoration of the votive statues that had once stood on the archaic Acropolis and had been destroyed by the Persians in 480. The women of the east frieze are a reincarnation of the archaic korai, while the cavalry and sacrificial animals stand in for the equestrian and athletic dedications and the animal votives of the Archaic period. After all, the argument goes, the temple itself could be viewed in the same way, as a reconstruction of an earlier building damaged in the Persian sack. So we are presented not with a procession of mortal worshippers, but with a row of symbolically restored statuary. Aside from the fact that there is no parallel for such a subject anywhere in the visual arts, this kind of romantic nostalgia for shattered relics seems utterly foreign to the ethos of fifth-century Athens. In another kind of symbolic interpretation, two scholars have argued that there are close similarities between the Parthenon frieze and the frieze of tribute-bearing subjects that adorns the grand staircase of the Apadana at Persepolis (A. W. Lawrence, *JHS* 71 [1951] 111–119; M. C. Root, *AJA* 89 [1985] 103–120). Although both saw a striking programmatic relationship between the two monuments, they drew opposite ideological inferences from the observation. Lawrence thought the designers of the Parthenon emulated the Persian prototype in order to stress the superiority of Greek democracy over Persian autocracy. Root, on the other hand, read the message differently: imperial Athens that ruled the cities of the Aegean and Asia Minor had now eclipsed the power of the Great King of Persia (criticism of these views: Neils, *Parthenon Frieze*, 182–183).

Another group of scholars compares the sculpture of the Parthenon to the later literary testimonia of all periods concerning the festival procession and laments the discrepancies. Particular criticism is leveled at the preponderant presence of the cavalry, which is not documented by any source, while some still bemoan the absence of the Panathenaic ship, a certain anachronism in the 440s (on its history, see J. L. Shear, "Polis and Panathenaia," 143–155). Having found that the frieze conforms badly to the testimonia, they reject the notion that it depicts the procession itself. Since various scenes seem to illustrate contests and events that took place on different days and in different places, the *anthippasia*, the apobatic races, and the sacrifices on the Acropolis, perhaps it showed different excerpts of the actual festival rather than the great parade on 28 Hekatombaion (L. Beschi, *RendLinc* 39 [1984] 173–195; Beschi, in H. Kyrieleis, ed., *Archaische und klassische griechische Plastik*, 199–224). But it is argued that cattle were led to sacrifice at most religious festivals, and several included elaborate processions. Musicians and *kanephoroi*, bearers of hydrias and trays of offerings, were not specific to the Panathenaia. Other religious celebrations featured athletic competitions and the *anthippasia*; even the apobatic contests may have been performed on other occasions. In this view the frieze presents a potpourri of different festivals, which, taken together, depict a sort of generic medley of Athenian religious life (J. J. Pollitt, in D. Buitron-Oliver, ed., *The Interpretation of Architectural Sculpture in Greece and Rome*, 51–65). This line of thinking has led another scholar to identify specific festivals (B. Wesenberg, *JdI* 110 [1995] 149–178). The *hydriaphoroi* of the north frieze are the porters who carried the tribute of the allies into the theater at the City Dionysia. In the central scene of the east frieze, he sees the annual secret rites of the Arrhephoria, although the little girls have grown to young adults and they carry not stools but trays, a lamp, and a torch. At the same time, in the right half of the scene he sees the quadrennial presentation of the peplos at the Great Panathenaia. In the words of yet another proponent of this theory, the Parthenon frieze is "a distillation of the many processions, athletic and cultural contests, ritual presentations, and sacrifices that characterized Athenian life in the age of Perikles" (Hurwit, *Athenian Acropolis*, 228 = Hurwit, *Acropolis in the Age of Pericles*, 236; the theory rejected by Neils, *Parthenon Frieze*, 183–185).

The idea that the Parthenon frieze depicts a collection of fragments has not found favor in the more recent literature. There has been, in fact, a refreshing tendency to emphasize once again the overarching thematic unity which the processional format provides and, at the same time, to recognize that individual passages allude deftly to the manifold events, contests, and rituals that comprised the Great Panathenaia. Three important recent studies have argued persuasively that the subject of the frieze is not mythology, nor a documentary of historical event, but a highly idealized picture of a contemporary celebration of the festival, which every Athenian would have recognized at once. Most extensive of these works is the book by J. Neils, *The Parthenon Frieze* (2001). The most detailed and succinct summary of the diverse interpretations of the sculpture is given by T. Stevenson, in D. J. Phillips and D. Pritchard, eds., *Sport and Festival in the Ancient Greek World* (2003) 233–280 (see also *AJA* 107 [2003] 629–654). The account of the Parthenon frieze that appears above (chap. 4, pp. 121–135) is greatly indebted to the discussion of the sculpture in J. L. Shear, "Polis and Panathenaia" (2001) 742–761.

EPIGRAPHICAL APPENDIX

IG I³ 435
THE ACCOUNTS OF THE GREAT BRONZE ATHENA, CA. 450

Col. I

(YEAR 1)	[ℾ𐅂ℾℾΔ]	[περιεγένετο τõ λέμματος]	EF
	ΔℾℲℲ[ℲΙΙ]	[ἐς τὸ hύστερον ἔτος]	
	vacat	[*vacat*]	
(YEAR 2)	ℾΜΜΧ𐅂 – –	[hοῖς – – ἐγραμμάτευε]	
5	ΔΔΔℲΙΙΙΙ	[– – ἐπιστάται ἔλαβον]	
	vacat	[παρὰ κολακρετõν σύνπαν·]	
	ℾΧℾℾΔΔ[?]	[λῆμμα περιγενόμενον]	
	ℾℲℲℲΙΙ	[ἐκ τõ προτέρο ἐνιαυτõ·]	
	Hℾ̣ΔΔΔΔℾℲℲℲ – –	[ἀπὸ τούτο ἐς hιερά·]	
10	ΜΜΜΧΧΧΧ	[χαλκõ τάλαντα : – –]	
	ℾΗΗΗℾℲℲ	[τιμὲ τούτο·]	
	ℾΧΗΗΗℾ – –	[καττιτέρο τάλαντα : – –]	
	vacat	[τιμὲ τούτο·]	
		lacuna	
(YEAR 3)		[τιμὲ τούτο?] *vacat*	Z
15		[. . . . .¹⁰. . . . .]ργίαν τ[õι ἔργοι . . . .]	
		[. . . . . . .⁸. . . κ]αὶ οἰκοδομ[ίαν καμίνον·]	
	– – –	[ἄνθρακες] καὶ χσύλα [καύσιμα·]	
	– – –	[μισθοὶ] κατ᾽ ἐμέραν, [μισθοὶ κατὰ]	
		[πρυτ]ανείαν : μισθ[οὶ ἀπόπαχς·]	
20	– – –	[γῆ καὶ τ]ρίχες *vacat*	
		[μισθοὶ] ἐπιστάτ[εσι καὶ γραμ]-	
	– – –	[ματεῖ] καὶ hυπερ[έτει·]	
	– – –	[κεφάλαιον ἀ]να[λόματος]	
		– – – – – – – – – –	

Col. II
at least 12 lines missing

(YEAR 4)	– – –	[ἄνθρακε]ς κ[αὶ χσύλα καύσιμα·]	GH
25		[μισθοὶ] κατ᾽ [ἐμέραν, μισθοὶ κατὰ πρυ]-	
	– – –	[τανεία]ν, μ[ισθοὶ ἀπόπαχς·]	
		[γῆ καὶ] τρίχ[ες·]	
		[μισθοὶ] ἐπ[ιστάτεσι καὶ γραμ]-	
		[ματεῖ κ]αὶ h[υπερέτει·]	
30		[. .⁵. .]λεμ– – – – –	
		[κεφάλ]αιο[ν ἀναλόματος]	

405

[σύνπα]ντο[ς·]

[περιε]γέν[ετ]ο τõ λέ[μματος]

[ἐς τὸ h]ύστ[ερ]ον ἔτο[ς·]

35　　　　　　　　　　　　　　　*vacat*

(YEAR 5)

[hοῖς Κ]αλ[λίστ]ρατος [ἐγραμ]-

[μάτευε] Α[. . .⁶. . .]ς ἐπι[στάται]

[ἔλαβο]ν π[αρὰ κολακ]ρε[τõν σύνπαν·]

[λẽμμα] πε[ριγενόμενον]

40

[ἐκ τõ π]ρο[τέρο ἐνιαυτõ·]

[ἀπὸ τού]τ[ο ἐς hιερά·]

[χαλκõ τάλαντα – – –]

[τιμὲ τούτο·]

[καττιτέρο τάλαντα – – –]

45

[τιμὲ τούτο·]

[. . . . . . .¹⁰. . . . .ρ]γίαν τõι ἔργ]οι　　　　　　Β

[. . . . . . . .¹². . . . . καὶ οἰκο]δομίαν

[καμίνον]　　*vacat*

[ἄνθρακες καὶ χσύλα κ]αύσιμα·

50

[. . . . . .¹⁷. . . . . .]ι·　　*vacat*

[μισθοὶ κατ' ἐμέραν, μι]σθοὶ κατὰ

[πρυτανείαν, μισθοὶ ἀ]πόπαχς·

[γẽ καὶ τρίχες]　　*vacat*

[μισθοὶ ἐπιστάτεσι κ]αὶ γραμ-

55

[ματεῖ καὶ hυπερέτει]　　*vacat*

[ἀργύριον ἄσεμον ἐς] ποικιλί-

[αν τõ ἀγάλματος]　　*vacat*

[κεφάλαιον ἀναλόματ]ος

[σύνπαντος]　　*vacat*

60

[περιεγένετο τõ λέμμ]ατος

[ἐς τὸ hύστερον ἔτος]　　*vacat*

[*vacat*]　　*vacat*

(YEAR 6)

[hοῖς . . . . . . .⁸. . . . . ἐγραμμ]άτευ[ε]

[. . . . . .¹². . . . . . ἐπισ]τάτ[αι]

65

[ἔλαβον παρὰ κολα]κρετ[õν σύνπαν·]　　C

[λẽμμα περιγενό]μενο[ν]

[ἐκ τõ προτέρο ἐν]ιαυτõ·

[ἀπὸ τούτο ἐς hιε]ρά·

[χαλκõ τάλαντα :] Δ Τ Τ Τ Τ Ε[ὐβοικά],

70

[τιμὲ τούτο]　　*vacat*

[καττιτέρο τάλ]αντα : Γ Τ Τ – – – ?

[τιμὲ τούτο]　　*vacat*

[. . . . . .¹⁰. . . . .ρ]γία]ν τõι ἔργο[ι . . . .]

[. . . . . .⁸. . . . . καὶ οἰκο]δομίαν κα[μίνον·]

75　　[. .³⁻⁴. .]Δ Δ ΔΓϜ– – – – – [ἄνθρακες κ]αὶ χσύλα κα[ύσιμα·]

　　　　[ϜΧ]ϜΗΙΙ　　μ[ισθοὶ κατ' ἐμέ]ραν, μισθοὶ κ[ατὰ πρυ]-

　　　　　　　　　τα[νείαν , μισθο]ὶ ἀπόπαχς·

　　　　[Ϝ]ΔΓϜ　　γ[ẽ καὶ τρίχες]　　*vacat*

　　　　[.]ΗΗϜΔ Δ Δ　　ἀ[ργύριον ἄσεμ]ον ἐς ποι[κιλίαν]

80　　[.]ϜΙΙ　　τõ [ἀγάλματος·]

	ΧΡΗΗΗΗ	μ[ισθοὶ ἐπισ]τάτεσι κα[ὶ γραμμα]-
	ΓΔΗΗΙΙ	τ[εῖ καὶ hυπερ]έτει·
	ΜΧΧΗΗΔΓΗΗ– – – –	[κεφάλαιον] ἀναλόματ[ος σύνπαν·]
	ΓΗΗΓΔΔΔ	π[εριεγένετ]ο τõ λέμματ[ος]
85	[. .]Ι	ἐ[ς τὸ hύστερ]ον ἔτος·
		vacat 0.145
		Col. III
		at least 20 lines missing
(YEAR 7)		[γε͂ καὶ τρίχες] *vacat* A
		[μισθοὶ ἐπιστάτε]σι καὶ γρ[αμ]-
		[ματεῖ καὶ hυπερέτ]ει⟦ετει⟧ *vacat*
		[κεφάλαιον ἀν]αλόματος
90		[σύνπαντος] *vacat*
		[περιεγένετ]ο τõ λέμματος
		[ἐς τὸ hύστε]ρον ἔτος·
		[*vacat*] *vacat*
(YEAR 8)		[hοῖς . . .⁵. . .]ς : ἐγραμμάτευε
95		[. . . . .⁹. . . .]ν : ἐπιστάται
		[ἔλαβον πα]ρὰ κολακρετõν
		[σύνπαν] *vacat*
		[λε͂μμα περιγ]εν[όμεν]ον : ἐ[κ τõ]
		[πρ]ο[τέρο ἐνιαυτõ·] X B
100	Γ̣– – –	ἀπὸ το[ύ]το [ἐς hιερά·]
	ΧΗ– – – –ΗΙ	χαλκõ [:] τάλα[ντα : – – –]
	vacat	τιμὲ τούτο·
	ΗΗ– – –	[κα]ττιτέρο : τ[άλαντα – – –]
	ΔΓ– – –	[τιμ]ὲ τούτο·
105	ΗΓ – – – –	[κερõ :] τάλαντα [: – –]
	vacat	[τιμὲ το]ύτ̣[ο·]
	– – –	– – – –
	– – –	– – – –
	– – –	– – – –
110	– – – – – –	[ἄνθρακες καὶ χσ]ύλα καύσιμ[α·] Y
	Μ– – –	[μισθοὶ κατ' ἐμέραν], μισθοὶ κατ[ὰ]
	Η– – –	[πρυτανείαν, μισθ]οὶ ἀπόπαχς·
	Δ– – –	[γε͂ καὶ τρίχες] *vacat*
	Χ[ΓΗΗΗΗ]	[μισθοὶ ἐπιστάτεσ]ι καὶ γραμμ[α]-
115	[ΓΔΗΗΙΙ]	[τεῖ καὶ hυπερέτει·] *vacat*
	– – –	[κεφάλαιον ἀναλόμ]ατος σύνπαν·
	– – –	[περιεγένετο τõ λέμ]ματος
		[ἐς τὸ hύστερον ἔτος] *vacat*
(YEAR 9)		[*vacat*] *vacat*
120		[hοῖς . . . . .⁸. . . . ἐγραμ]μάτευε
		[. . . . . .¹⁰. . . . ἐπιστάτ]αι ἔλαβ[ον]
	– – –	[παρὰ κολακρετõν σύν]παν·
		[λε͂μμα περιγενόμενον ἐ]κ τõ πρ[οτέ]-
		[ρο ἐνιαυτõ] *vacat*

IG I³ 32

The Eleusinian Overseers, ca. 450

[. .]αι̣[. . . . . .²⁸. . . . .]
[hι]εροποιὸς καὶ τ[. . . . . . .¹⁸. . . . .]
[κ]αὶ ἀναλισκοντ[. . . . . . . .¹⁹. . . . .]
[. .] τõ αὐτõ· προσαγό[ν]το[ν δὲ h]ο̣ι πρυτάνες

5   πρὸς τὲν βολὲν τὸς θε[ο]σ[εσ]ίνος hόταν δέ-
οντα̣ι : Θεσπιεὺς [εἶπε· τὰ μὲν] ἄλλα καθάπε-
ρ τε͂[ι β]ο[λ]ε͂ι, ἄ[νδρας δὲ hελέσ]θ̣[αι Ἀ]θεναίο-
ν πέ[ν]τε, τούτ[ος δὲ φέρεν τέττ]αρας ὀβολὸ-
[ς] hέκασ[τ]ον π[α]ρὰ τõν κολ[ακρ]ετõν, hένα δ[ὲ]

10   [τ]ούτον [γρ]αμματε[ύ]ε[ν κατὰ] φσε͂[φ]ον· τούτο-
[ς] δὲ ἐπισ[τε͂]ναι [τ]οῖς χρέμασι τοῖς τοῖν θ-
[ε]οῖν καθάπερ hοι ἐπὶ τοῖς ἐμ πό[λ]ει ἔργ[ο]-
[ι]ς ἐπεστ[ά]το[ν] τõι νεõι καὶ τõι ἀ[γ]άλματι·
[ἐχ]σομοσίαν δὲ μὲ ἔν[α]ι· [τὸς δὲ] hειρεμένο-

15   [ς] προσιόντας πρὸς τὲν βολέν, ἐάν τι ὀφελ-
ό[μ]ενον ε͂[ι] τοῖν θεοῖν, φρά[ζ]εν καὶ ἀ[ν]απρά-
[τ]τεν· ἄρχεν δὲ ἐπ᾽ ἐνιαυτὸ[ν] ὀμόσαντας με-
ταχσὺ τοῖν βομοῖν Ἐλευσῖνι καὶ τὸ λοιπ-
ὸν κατὰ ταὐτὰ hαιρε͂σθαι κ[α]τ᾽ ἐνιαυτὸν τ-

20   ὸς ἄνδ[ρ]ας· ἐπιμελε͂σθαι δὲ καὶ τõν ἐπετε-
ίον hὰ λαμβάνεται τοῖ[ν θ]εοῖν καὶ ἐάν τι
[ἀ]πολολὸς πυνθάνονται [ἀ]νασόι[ζε]ν· τὸς δ-
ὲ λογιστὰς λογίζεσθαι Ἐλευσῖνι μὲν τὰ
Ἐλευσῖνι ἀνελομένα, ἐν ἄστει δὲ τὰ ἐν ἄσ-

25   τει ἀνελομένα ἀνακαλõντας τὸν ἀρχιτέκτονα Κόροιβον καὶ Λυσανίαν ἐν τõι Ἐλευσινίοι, Φαλερõι δὲ ἐν τõι hιερõι hὰ Φαλ-
ερόνδε ἀνέλοται· ἀναλίσκεν δὲ ὅ τι ἂν [μά]-
λιστα δέει μετὰ τõν hιερέον καὶ τε͂ς β[ολ]-

30   ε͂ς βολευομένος τὸ λοιπόν· ἀνα[κ]αλε͂ν δ[ὲ ἀ]-
πὸ τε͂ς ἀ[ρ]χε͂ς ἀρχ[σ]αμένος hὲ Κτε[σ]ί[αι παρ]-
έ[δ]οκε[ν] τὰ χρέματα· γράφσαι δὲ τὸ [φσέφισ]-
μα ἐν στέλει Ἐλευσῖνι κα[ὶ ἐν ἄστει καὶ Φ]-
αλ[ε]ρõι ἐν τõι Ἐλευσιν[ίοι. Λυσανίας εἶπ]-

35   ε· τὰ μὲν ἄλλα καθά[περ Θεσπιεύς· τὲν δὲ ἀρ]-
[ίθμ]εσιν ποιε͂σθα[ι τõν χρεμάτον hõν τõι]
[τα]μίαι παρέδοκ[εν hε βολὲ τὸς ἐπιστάτα]-
[ς καὶ] τὸν ἀρχ[ι]τ[έκτονα . . . . . .¹⁴. . . . .]

IG I³ 395
CLINTON, *ELEUSIS* 23: ELEUSINIAN ACCOUNTS, CA. 450

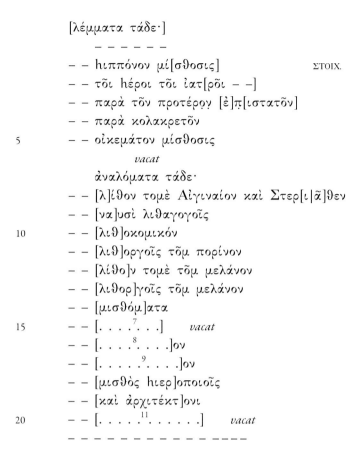

[λέμματα τάδε·]
   – – – – – –
– – ℎιππόνον μί[σθοσις]   ΣΤΟΙΧ.
– – τõι ℎέροι τõι ἰατ[ρõι – –]
– – παρὰ τὸν προτέρο̣ν̣ [ἐ]π̣[ιστατõν]
– – παρὰ κολακρετõν
5 – – οἰκεμάτον μίσθοσις
          vacat
    ἀναλόματα τάδε·
– – [λ]ίθον τομὲ Αἰγιναίον καὶ Στερ[ι|ᾶ]θεν
– – [να]υσὶ λιθαγογοῖς
10 – – [λιθ]οκομικόν
– – [λιθ]οργοῖς τõμ πορίνον
– – [λίθο]ν τομὲ τõμ μελάνον
– – [λιθορ]γοῖς τõμ μελάνον
– – [μισθόμ]ατα
15 – – [. . . . .⁷. . .] *vacat*
– – [. . . . .⁸. . . .]ον
– – [. . . . .⁹. . . .]ον
– – [μισθὸς ℎιερ]οποιοῖς
– – [καὶ ἀρχιτέκτ]ονι
20 – – [. . . . .¹¹. . . . .] *vacat*
  – – – – – – – – – – – – ––––

IG I³ 436–451
THE ACCOUNTS OF THE PARTHENON, 447/6–433/2

YEAR 1   *IG* I³ 436   D

447/6   – – – – – – – – – – – –^{c. 88}– – – – – – – – – – – – – – –ος   *vacat*

         – – – – – – – – – – – –^{c. 88}– – – – – – – – – – – – – –ον   *vacat*

         – – – – – – – – – – – –^{c. 88}– – – – – – – – – – – – –λες   *vacat*

         –*vacat*

5   – – – – – – – – – – – –^{c. 88}– – – – – – – – – – –ναῖος   *vacat*

         –*vacat*

                    Col. I
         V   *lines 7–18 missing*

         [. . .]ΗΗΔΔ   – – –

20   [. . .]ΗⱵ   – – –

                   [. .]εν– – –   R
                   ἀ[ναλ]ό[ματα]

         [.⁴⁻⁵.]ΧΧΧΧⱵΗΗ– –   λιθοτ[όμοις Πεντελε͂θεν]

         [.⁴⁻⁵.]ΗΗΗΗΗΙΙ   λιθαγ[ογίας Πεντελε͂θεν]

25   [.^{c. 5}.]ΔΓΗΗΗΙΙΙ   λιθολκ[ίας πρὸς τὰ ἐργαστέρια]

         [.^{c. 6}.]ΔΗΙΙΙ   τέκτοσ[ι μισθός]

         [.^{c. 6}.]ΗⱵΔΔΔΓΙ– –   ὀνεμάτον

         [.^{c. 6}.]ΗΙΙΙ   hυποργ[οῖς Πεντελε͂θεν hοδοποιο͂σι]

         [.^{c. 6}.] *vacat*   [κ]αταμε[νίον]

30   [ṂṂ. . . .]ΗΗΔΔ– –   [π]εριεγέ[νετο τõ ἐνιαυτõ τούτο]

         [ⱵΔ*Δ*ΣΣΣΣ]   [χ]ρυσõ στ[ατε͂ρες Λαμφσακενοί]

         Δ*Δ*Ⱶ[ΣΣ hέκτε]   [χρυ]σõ σ[τατε͂ρες Κυζικενοί]   F

YEAR 2   *IG* I³ 437

446/5   ἐπὶ τε͂[ς δευτέρας ἀρχε͂ς] he͂ι Ε[. . . .⁸. . . . ἐγραμμάτευε]
         hαλαι[εύς, τε͂ι βολε͂ι Ἀντ]ίδο[ρος πρõτος ἐγραμμάτευε]

35   Στρατ– –
         Σαλαμ[ινοκλε͂ς –]
         τιος Κạ[. . . . .^{c. 27}. . . . . ἐπιστάται]
         καὶ ho[ῖς Ἀντικλε͂ς χσυνεγραμμάτευε καὶ τοῖς προτέ]-
         ροισι[ν ἐπιστάτεσι· τούτοις λέμματα τõ ἐνιαυτõ τάδε·]

40   ṂṂ[. . . .ΗΗΔΔ– –]   [παρέλαβον παρὰ τõν προτέρ]-   S
                            [ον ἐπιστατõ]ν

         ⱵΔ[*ΔΣΣΣΣ]   [χρυσõ στατ]ε͂ρες Λα[μφσακενοί]

         Δ[*ΔⱵΣΣ hέκτε]   [χρυσõ στατ]ε͂ρες Κυ[ζικενοί]

                           [παρὰ ταμιõ]ν hοὶ τ[ὰ τε͂ς θεõ]

45   – – –   [ἐταμίευον], hοῖς Ἐχ[σέκεστος]

                           [ἐγραμμάτε]υε Ἀθμο[νεύς·]

                           [παρὰ ταμιõ]ν hοὶ τὰ [τε͂ς θεõ ἐταμ]-

	– – –	[ίευον, hοῖς] Ἐχσέκ[εστος ἐγραμ]-
		[μάτευε Ἀθμ]ονεύ[ς·]
50		[. . . . . ⁹ . . . .]απο– –
		[. . . . . ⁹ . . . .]νε
		lacuna
	[ΑΓΜΜ]ΜΜ– –	– – – N + W
	[ΜΜΓΧΧ]ΧΧ– –	– – –
	[. . . .]ΓΗ– –	– – –
55	[ΓΜΓΧ]ΧΧΧΓ[ΗΗ]ΗΗ– –	– – –
	[ΜΜ]ΜΜΧΧΧΧΗΔΔΗ– –	– – –
	[ΜΜ]ΓΧΗΗΗΗΓΔΔ– –	– – –
	[ΜΓ]ΧΧΧΧΗΓΔΔΔ– –	– – –
	vacat	[περιεγένετο τõ ἐνιαυτõ τούτο]
60	ΓΔΔΣ[Σ]ΣΣ	[χρυσõ στατε̃ρες Λαμφσακενοί]
	ΔΔΓ[ΣΣ hέκτε]	[χρυσõ στατε̃ρες Κυζικενοί]
		vacat

Year 3   *IG* I³ 438

445/4	ἐπι τε̃ς [τρίτες ἀρχε̃ς hε̃ι – – ἐγραμμάτευε – –]
	[. . .]εύς, [τε̃ι βολε̃ι – – – πρõτος ἐγραμμάτευε]
65	[. . . .]Π– –
	lacuna

Col. II

Year 4   *IG* I³ 439

ca. 21 lines missing

444/3	– – – – –	παρ[ὰ τõν προτέρον ἐπιστατõν]	J
	[ΓΔΔΣΣΣ]Σ	χρυσõ [στατε̃ρες Λαμφσακενοί]	
	[ΔΔΓΣΣ h]έκτε	χρυσõ στα[τε̃ρες Κυζικενοί]	
		παρὰ ταμιõν [hοὶ τὰ τε̃ς θεõ]	
70	[ΓΜΜΜ]ΜΓΓΗΗΗΔΔΗ	ἐταμίευον, hο[ῖς – – –]	
		ἐγραμμάτευ[ε – – –]	
		παρὰ hελλε[νοταμιõν, hοῖς]	
	[ΜΜΜΓ]ΧΧΓΗΓΔΔΓΙΙΙΙΙ	Στρόμβιχο[ς ἐγραμμάτευε]	
		Χολλείδε[ς]	
75		παρὰ χσεν[οδικõν, hοῖς – –]	
	[. . . .]ΧΧΗΔΔΔΔΓΗΗ	ἐγραμμά[τευε – –]	
	[ΓΜΜΜ]Μ	παρὰ τρ[ιεροποιõν]	
		lacuna 4 lines	
82	– – – – –	πα[ρὰ – – –]	G
		π– – – – – –	
		α– – – – – –	
85		ο– – – – – –	
		ἀναλ[όματα]	
		lacuna 18 lines	
105		[. . .]Ει[.]Ε– – – – – –	I

                                                    [.]ος ἐπιστ[ατ– – –]

                                                    πεύκινα κ– – – – –

[. . .^{c.8}. . .]ΔΗΗΙΙΙΙ   περιεγέν[ετο τõ ἐνιαυτõ τούτο]   T

[𝈒ΔΔΣΣΣΣ]   χρυσõ στα[τε̃ρες Λαμφσακενοί]

110   [ΔΔ𝈒ΣΣ hέ]κτε   χρυσõ στα̣[τε̃ρες Κυζικενοί]

                                                               vacat

YEAR 5   *IG* I³ 440

443/2   [ἐπὶ τε̃ς πέμπτες ἀρχε̃]ς he̅ι Τιμόθε[ος ἐγραμμάτευε – –]

        [– –, τε̃ι βολε̃ι –]ος προ̃τος ἐ[γραμμάτευε – – – –]

        [. . . . . ¹⁷. . . . .]ος Ἰφιστι̣[άδες – – –]

115   [. . . .⁷. . . . ἐπιστάται κ]αὶ hοῖς Ἀν[τικλε̃ς χσυνεγραμμά]-

        [τευε – – – · τούτοις] λέμματα τ[õ ἐνιαυτõ τούτο τάδε·]

        [. . . .^{c.8}. . . . ΔΗΗΙΙΙΙ]   παρὰ το̃ν [προτέρον ἐπιστατõν]

        [𝈒ΔΔΣΣΣΣ]   χρυσõ στ̣[ατε̃ρες Λαμφσακενοί]

        [ΔΔ𝈒ΣΣ hέκτε]   χρυσõ στ[ατε̃ρες Κυζικενοί]

120   – – – – – – –   [π]αρὰ ταμ[ιõν – – – – –]

                                                    [κ]αὶ ἐγ βα[λανείον]

        – – – – – – –   [π]αρὰ ταμι[õν hοὶ τὰ τε̃ς θεõ ἐταμίευον]

                                                    [ho]ῖς Ἀνδρ[– – ἐγραμμάτευε – –]

        – – – – –   [παρ]ὰ hελλ[ενοταμιõν, hοῖς Σοφίας]

125   [Ἐλ]ευσίνι[ος ἐγραμμάτευε]

        – – – – –   [π]αρὰ χσε[νοδικõν]

        – – – – –   [π]αρὰ τειχ[οποιõν]

                                                               vacat

                                                          Col. III

                              – – – – – – – – – – – –ντι   D

                              – – – – – – – – – – – –τον

                                      lacuna 6 lines

136   [– – – – – – – – κατα]λεπτε-   E

          – – – – – – – – – – – – – *vacat*

          – – – – – – – – – – – – –τος

          – – – – – – – – – – – – – *vacat*

140   – – – – – – – – – – – –ο τίμε

          [– – – – – – – –τι]μὲ τοῦτο

                                      lacuna 7 lines

                              – – – – – – – – – – – –ν τὲν   A

150   [– – – – – –ἐς τὸν] νεόν

          – – – – – – – – – – – he̅ι

          – – – – – – – – – – – –ι

          [– – – – – σταθμὸν –]ΔΓ

                                      lacuna

Year 6 *IG* I³ 441

442/1

160   [. . . . . ²² . . . .]ι κιόνον   M
            [. . . . . ²¹ . . . .]τοῖς χσυλίνοις
            [. . . . . ²¹ . . . .]\ιτο
            [. . . . . ²¹ . . . .]ν τὸ hυπὸ πόλει
            [. . . . . ²⁰ . . . .]νοις hυποργοῖς

165 [ᴹᴹ– –]   [περιεγένετο τõ ἐνιαυτõ] τούτο
    [ℙΔΔΣΣΣΣ]   [χρυσõ στατε͂ρες Λαμφσακ]ενοί
    [ΔΔℙ ΣΣ hέκτε]   [χρυσõ στατε͂ρες Κυζικενο]ί
               vacat

Col. IV
reverse side of stele

Year 7 *IG*³ 442

441/40 ἐ[πὶ τε͂ς heβδόμες ἀρχε͂ς he͂ι – – ἐγραμμάτευε]   D
    Φ[– – –, τε͂ι βολε͂ι – – – πρõτος ἐγραμμάτευε]
170 Χα– –
    Τε[ιθράσιος ἐπιστάται hοῖς Ἀντικλε͂ς χσυνεγραμμάτευε·]
    το[ύτοις λέμματα τõ ἐνιαυτõ τούτο τάδε·]
    ᴹᴹ– – – – –   [παρὰ τõν προτέρον ἐπιστατõν]
175 ℙΔ[ΔΣΣΣΣ]   [χρυσõ στατε͂ρες Λαμφσακενοί]
    ΔΔℙ[ΣΣ hέκτε]   [χρυσõ στατε͂ρες Κυζικενοί]
            [παρὰ ταμιõν hοὶ τὰ τε͂ς θεõ]
    MM– – – –   [ἐταμίευον, hοῖς Φυρόμαχος]
            [ἐγραμμάτευε – – – –]
            [παρὰ hελλενοταμιõν, hοῖς]
180 MM[M– – –]   [– – – – – – ἐγραμμάτευε]
            [. . . ᶜ· ⁶ . .τιος]
          lacuna 16 lines
    – – – –   [περιεγένετο τõ ἐνιαυτõ τούτο]
    [ℙΔΔΣΣΣΣ]   [χρυσõ στατε͂ρες Λαμφσακενοί]
200 ΔΔ[ℙΣΣ hέκτε]   [χρυσõ στατε͂ρες Κυζικενοί]   H
               vacat

Year 8 *IG* I³ 443

440/39 ἐπὶ τ[ε͂ς ὀγδόες ἀρχε͂ς he͂ι – – – ἐγραμμάτευε]
    Προβ[αλίσιος, τε͂ι βολε͂ι Ἐπιχαρῖνος Περαιεὺς πρõτος]
    ἐγρα[μμάτευε – – – – – – – – – – – – – – – –]
205 Χσυ[πεταιόν – – – – – – – – – – – – – – –]
          lacuna 21 lines
         [μισ]θομάτ[ον – – ?]   K
         [το]ῖς θυρόμασι – – –
         [. .]ις καὶ τε͂ς hιερᾶ[ς – –]
230   [ἐπι]σκευε͂ς καὶ hομ– – –
    – – – –   [κατ]αμενίον
    – – – –   [περι]εγένετο τõ ἐγ[ιαυτõ τούτο]

[𐅄ΔΔΣΣΣΣ]	[χρυσ]ō στατε̃ρες Λαμφσ[ακενοί]
[ΔΔΓΣΣ ℎέκτε]	[χρυσ]ō στατε̃ρες Κυζ[ικενοί]

235   *vacat*

Col. V

YEAR 9   *IG* I³ 444

439/8   [ἐπὶ τε̃ς ἐνάτες ἀρχε̃ς ℎε̃ι – – – ἐγραμμάτευε – –]ιος,   U
        [τε̃ι βολε̃ι – – – πρõτος ἐγραμμάτευε – – – – Περγ]ασε̃θεν

     -
     -

240   [ἐπιστάται ℎοῖς Ἀντικλε̃ς χσυνεγραμμάτευε·]
        [τούτοις λέμματα τõ ἐνιαυτõ τούτο τάδε·]

- - - - -	[παρὰ τõν προτέρον ἐπιστ]ατõν
[𐅄ΔΔΣΣΣΣ]	[χρυσõ στατε̃ρες Λαμφσακ]ενοί
[ΔΔΓΣΣ ℎέκτε]	[χρυσõ στατε̃ρες Κυζικε]νοί
245	[παρὰ ταμιõν ℎοὶ τὰ τε̃ς θ]εõ ἐταμίευον,
- - - - -	[ℎοῖς . .⁵. . ἐγραμμάτευ]ε Λακιάδες
	[παρὰ ℎελλενοταμιõν, ℎοῖ]ς Ἐργόφιλος
- - - - -	[ἐγραμμάτευε Ἀναφλύστι]ος
	[παρὰ ταμιõν ℎεφαιστικõ] ἀπὸ Λαυρε[ίο]
250	- - - - - [. . . . . . . .¹⁴. . . . . . τõμ π]έντε μερ[õν]

                     - - - - - - - - - - - - -
                     - - - - - - - - - - ετ - - -

                     lacuna 12 lines

265   [ἀναλόματα]

- - - - -	ἐλέ[φας ἐονέθε· – – ?]	L
	τιμὲ τούτ[ο]	
- - - - -	τõν ἄλλον ὀν[εμάτον]	
- - - - -	χσυλοργίας	
270 - - - - -	λιθοτόμοις Πε[ντελε̃θεν]	
- - - - -	λιθαγογίας Πε[ντελε̃θεν]	
- - - - -	λιθολκίας πρὸ[ς τὰ ἐργαστέρια]	
- - - - -	λιθοργ[ί]ας καὶ [ῥαβδόσεος τõν κιόνον]	
	χρυσοχοῖς μισ[θὸς – – ?]	
275	τὰ ἔργα τὰ ἀργυ[ρᾶ – – ?]	
	[ἅ]εχει ἀργυρίο [σταθμόν – –]	
- - - - -	[μ]ισθομάτο[ν]	
- - - - -	[ℎυ]πορ[γοῖς]	
- - - -	[περιεγένετο τõ ἐνιαυτõ τούτο]	
280 [𐅄ΔΔΣΣΣΣ]	[χρυσõ στατε̃ρες Λαμφσακενοί]	
[ΔΔΓΣΣ ℎέκτε]	[χρυσõ στατε̃ρ]ες Κυζι[κενοί]	G

                            vacat

YEAR 10   *IG* I³ 445

438/7   [ἐπὶ τε̃ς δεκάτες ἀρχε̃ς ℎε̃ι . . .⁶. . .]φιλος ἐγρ[αμμάτευε]
        [– –, τε̃ι βολε̃ι – – – – – – – πρõ]τος ἐγρα[μμάτευε]
285   - - - - - - - - - - - - - - - - - -γεσίας Τ- -

```
- - - - - - - - - - - - - - -ύδες ηαλ[αιεὺς]
[ἐπιστάται ηοῖς Ἀτικλῆς χσυνεγρ]αμμάτευ[ε·]
[τούτοις λέμματα τõ ἐνιαυτõ τούτο τ]άδε·
```

	- - - - -	[παρὰ τõν προτ]έρον ἐπι[στατõν]	
290	[𐅈ΔΔΣΣΣΣ]	[χρυσõ στατῆρε]ς Λαμφ[σακενοί]	
	[ΔΔ𐅄ΣΣ ηέκτε]	[χρυσõ στατῆρε]ς Κυζικ[ενοί]	
		[παρὰ ηελλενοτα]μιõν, η[οῖς - - -]	
	- - - - -	[ἐγραμμάτευε Ῥαμ]νόσιο[ς]	
	- - - - -	[παρὰ ταμιõν ηεφαι]στικ[õ ἀπὸ Λαυρείο]	
295		[- - - - τ]õν π[έντε μερõν]	
		χ[ρυσίο πραθέντος σ]ταθμ[ὸν - -]	B
	- - - - -	τιμὲ [τούτο]	
	- - - - -	χσύλον [πραθέντο]ν τιμ[έ]	
	- - - - -	παρ᾽ Εὐφέρ[ο, παρὰ Πλε]ισ[τίο]	
300	- - - - -	παρὰ Σαύρονο[ς - -]	
		[ἀναλ]όματα	
	- - - - -	[ὀ]νεμάτον	
	- - - - -	[μι]σθομάτον	
	- - - - -	[λιθ]οτόμοις Πεντε[λῆθεν καὶ πελεκετῆσι]	
305		[τõν λ]ίθον τõν ἐς τὰ [ἐναιέτια]	
		[ηοδοποι]οῖς καὶ λίθ[ος ἐπὶ τὰ κύκλα]	
		[ἀνατιθῆ]σ[ι] τὸς ἐς τὰ [ἐναιέτια]	
	- - - - -	[λιθαγογίας Π]εντελῆ[θεν]	
	- - - - -	[λιθολκίας ἐς] τὰ ἐργα[στέρια]	
310	- - - - -	[ἀγαλματοποιοῖ]ς ἐνα[ιετίον μισθός]	
		- - - - - - - -οχ- - - - -	
		lacuna	

Col. VI

YEAR 11   *IG* I³ 446

437/6	[τοῖς ἐπιστάτεσι η]οῖς Ἀντ[ικλῆς χσυ]νεγραμμάτευ[ε]	P O
	[ἐπὶ τῆς ηενδεκάτες] βολῆς ηῆι Πειθιάδες πρõτος ἐγρα[μ]-	
	[μάτευεν ἐπ᾽ Εὐθυμέν]ος ἄρχον[τος] Ἀθεναίοισιν *vacat*	
315	[λέμματα τõ ἐνιαυτõ] τούτο τάδε *vacat*	
		[περιγε]νόμενομ μὲν ἐκ τῆς	
	- - - - -	[προτέρ]ας ἀρχῆς	
	[𐅈ΔΔΣΣΣΣ]	[χρυσõ σ]τατῆρες Λαμφσακενοί	
	[ΔΔ𐅄ΣΣ ηέκτε]	[χρυσõ σ]τατῆρες Κυζικενοί	
320	- - - - -	[ἐλέφαντος πραθέ]ντος	
		[σταθμὸν . . . .⁹. . . . .] τιμὲ τούτο	
	- - - - -	[. . . .¹¹. . . . . παρέλ]αβον ἐς τὰ ἐργα-	
		[στέρια παρὰ . . .⁶. . .]οντος	
	- - - -	[χσύλον πραθέντον τρ]οχõν κυκλιαίον	
325		[τιμέ τούτον] *vacat*	
	- - - -	[. . . . . .¹⁵. . . . . . . κ]αττιτέρο τιμέ	C
		- - - - - *vacat*	
		[ἀναλόματα] *vacat*	
```
```

	[ὀνεμάτον] *vacat*	
330 – – – – –	[μισθομάτον] *vacat*	
	[λιθοτόμοι]ς Πεντελε͂θεν καὶ πελεκ-	
– – – – –	[ετε͂σι τὸν λ]ίθον [τ]ὸν ἐς τὰ ἐναιέτια	
	[hοδοποιο͂ι]ς καὶ [λί]θος ἀνατιθε͂σι ἐπὶ	
– – – – –	[τὰ κύκλα Πε]ντελ[ε͂]σι τὸς [ἐ]ς τὰ ἐναιέτια	
335 – – – – –	[λιθαγογία]ς Πεντελε͂θεν	
– – – – –	[λιθολκίας] ἐς τὰ ἐργαστέρια	
	[. . . . .]ϝον– – –	
– – – – –	[ἀγαλματοποιο͂ις ἐναιετ]ίο[ν] μισθός	
– – – – –	[καταμενίον] *vacat*	
340 – – – – –	[περιεγένετο τὸ] ἐνι[αυτο͂ τ]ούτο	R
[⋮ΔΔΣΣΣΣ]	[χρυσο͂ στατε͂]ρες Λαμφ[σακε]νοί	
[ΔΔⲦΣΣ hέκτε]	[χρυσο͂ στατε͂]ρες Κυζικ[εν]οί	
	vacat	

YEAR 12   *IG* I³ 447

436/5	[τοῖς ἐπιστάτεσι hοῖς Ἀντικλε͂ς ἐ]γραμμάτευε [ἐπὶ] τε͂ς [δο]-	F
345	δεκάτες βολε͂ς hε͂ι . . . . . .¹³ . . . . .] προ͂τος ἐγρ[αμμ]άτευ[ε]	
	[ἐπὶ Λυσιμάχο ἄρχοντος Ἀθεναίοι]ς λέμματα το͂ [ἐνι]αυτο͂ τά[δε·]	
– – – –	[περιγενόμενο]ν ἐκ το͂ προτέρ[ο ἐνι]αυτο͂	
[⋮ΔΔΣΣΣΣ]	[χρυσο͂ στατέρ]ες Λαμφσακεν[οί]	
[ΔΔⲦΣΣ hέκτε]	[χρυσο͂ στα]τέρες Κυζικενο[ί]	
350	[παρὰ πρακ]τόρον hιερο͂ν ho[. . .⁵. .]ενδαιος	
	[. . . . .⁹. . . .]ν τοῖν ἀδυνάτοιν [– – ?] *vacat*	
	[ἀναλόματα]	
– – – – –	[ὀνεμάτ]ον	
– – – –	[μισθομά]τον	
355 – – – – –	[λιθοτ]όμ[οις Πεντελε͂θεν]	Q
– – – – –	[λιθα]γογία[ς Πεντελε͂θεν]	
	[hοδο]ποιο͂ις καὶ τὸλ λίθο[ς ἀνατιθε͂σι]	
– – – –	[ἐπὶ τ]ὰ κύκλα [Πεντελ]ε͂σι τὸς [ἐς τὰ ἐναιέτια]	
– – – – –	[λιθολ]κίας ἐς τὰ ἐργαστέρια	
360 – – – – –	[ἀγαλ]ματοποιο͂ις ἐναιετίο[ν μισθός]	
– – – – –	[καταμενίον]	
– – – – –	[περιε]γέ[νετο] τὸ ἐνιαυτ[ο͂ τούτο]	
[⋮ΔΔΣΣΣΣ]	[χρυσο͂] στα[τε͂ρ]ες Λαμ[φσακενοί]	
[ΔΔⲦΣΣ hέκτε]	[χρυσο͂] στατε͂ρες Κυζικ[ενοί]	
365	*vacat*	

YEAR 13   *IG* I³ 448

435/4	[τοῖς ἐπιστάτεσι hοῖς Ἀντικλ]ε͂ς ἐγραμμάτε[υε ἐπὶ τε͂ς τρίτες]	
	[καὶ δεκάτες βολε͂ς hε͂ι . . . .]ι[. . .]ο[ς προ͂τος ἐγραμμάτευε κτλ.]	
	lacuna	
	[ἀγαλματοποιο͂ις ἐναιετίον μισθ]ός	N
	lacuna	

Col. VII
right side of stele

YEAR 14   *IG* I³ 449

434/3		τοῖς ἐπιστάτεσι hοῖς	D
370		Ἀντικλῆς ἐγραμμάτευ[ε]	
		ἐπὶ τῆς τετάρτες καὶ δε-	
		κάτες βολῆς hῆι Μετα-	
		γένες πρῶτος ἐγραμμ-	
		άτευε ἐπὶ Κράτετος ἄρχ-	
375		οντος Ἀθεναίοισιν	
		λέμματα τõ ἐνιαυτõ	
		τούτο ταδε·	
	XHHH	περιγενόμενομ	
	HℾΔΔ	μὲν ἐκ τõ προτέρο	
380		____ ἐνιαυτõ	
	ℾ̣ΔΔ	χρυσõ στατῆρες	
	[ΣΣΣΣ]	[Λαμφσ]ακενοί	
	ΔΔℾΣΣ	[χρυσõ] στατῆρες	F
	hέκτε :	____ Κ[υζικεν]οί	
385		πα[ρὰ ταμι] õν [hοὶ τὰ]	
	MMℾ :	τῆς θεõ [ἐτ]αμίευ[ον]	
		hοῖς Κράτες ἐγρ[α]-	
		____ μμάτευε Λαμπτρε[ύς]	
	XHHH	χρυσίο πραθέ[ντος]	
390	ℾΔΔΗ⊦	σταθμὸν ℾΔΔΔ[Δ]ℾ[⊦⊦⊦]	
		____ τιμὲ τούτο	
	XHHH	ἐλέφαντος [πρα]θ[έν]-	
	ℾIIII	τος σταθμὸ[ν Τ]ΤΤ	
		____ ℾΔ : τιμὲ τ[ούτο]	
395		ἀ ν α λ ό μ α [τ] α	
	[. . .]HH :	ὀνεμάτο[ν]	
	– – ⊦⊦⊦ :	_____	
		____ μισθομ[άτον]	
	Xℾ̣[HH]	[h]υπορ[γοῖς Πεντελῆ]-	A
	HHΔ[Δ]	[σι καὶ λίθος ἀνατιθ]-	
400	ℾ⊦II	____ ῆ[σι ἐπὶ τὰ κύκλα]	
	Mℾ̣XHH	ἀγ[αλματοπο]ιοῖς	H
	HℾΔΔΔ	ἐνα[ιετίον μι]σθός	
	ΔH⊦	_____	
	[X]ℾHHH	καταμ[ενίο]ις	
	[. .]ΔH⊦!		
	– – –	[περ]ιε[γέν]ετο	
405	– – –	[τõ ἐνιαυτ]õ τού[το]	
	[ℾ̣ΔΔ]	[χρυσõ στατῆρες]	
	[ΣΣΣΣ]	[Λαμφσακενοί]	
	[ΔΔℾΣΣ]	[χρυσõ στατῆρες]	
	[hέκτε :]	[Κυζικενοί]	

Col. VIII

left side of stele

YEAR 15   *IG* I³ 450

                                              vacat 0.057
433/2

410   [τ]οῖς ἐπιστάτεσι ho-   F
       [ῖ]ς Ἀντικλε͂ς ἐγραμ-
       μάτευε : ἐπὶ τε͂ς πέμ[π]-
       τες καὶ δεκάτες βολ-
       ε͂ς hε͂ι Κριτιάδες προ͂-
415   τος ἐγραμμάτευε ᵛ ᵛ
       ἐπὶ Ἀφσεύδος ἄρχον-
       [τ]ος Ἀθεναίοις : λέμμ-
       [ατ]α το͂ ἐνιαυτο͂ τάδε·
       – – –   [πε]ριγενόμενο-
420   – – –   [μ μὲν] ἐκ το͂ προτ-
                    [έρο ἐνιαυτο͂]
       – – – – – – – – – – – –

IG I³ 451

       reverse of stele, uncertain location   X
              – – – – –
              – –ΑΡΑΔ
              – –ΣΤΕΚ
              – –[.]ΥΛΟ
425   – –[. .]Ο[.]
              – – – – –

IG I³ 453–46
THE GOLD AND IVORY STATUE, 446/5?–438

IG I³ 453

446/5 ?   *vacat* 0.19

[– – – – – – – .] Ἐχσέκ[εστος – –]   ΣΤΟΙΧ.

[– – – – – – – .] ατι|– –

[– – – – – – – .]ς βου– – – –

– – – – – – – – μίαι ἔ[σαν ?– –]

                        vacat 0.085

5   [λῆμμα παρὰ ταμιõ]ν

        – – – – – – – – – –

IG I³ 454

447/6 or 445/4   – – – – – – – – – – –

[. . . . . .¹⁵. . . . . .] Ε– – – – –   ΣΤΟΙΧ.

[. . . . . .¹⁴. . . . .]ρινο– – – –

                        vacat

[παρὰ ταμιõν ἐκ π]όλεος h[οῖς – –]

5   [. . .⁶. . . ἐγραμμά]τευε· τα[μίαι – –]

[. . . . .⁸. . . . ἐκ Κερα]μέον Λ– – – – –

[. . . . . . . .¹³. . . . . Π]ρασιε[ὺς – – – –]

[ἀναλόματα]   *vacat*

[. . . . . . . .¹⁷. . . . . . .] – – – – –

        – – – – – – – – – – –

IG I³ 455

445/4 or 444/3   [. . . . . .¹⁷. . . . .] Κι[.]   ΣΤΟΙΧ.

[. . . . . .¹¹. . . γρα]μματεύ-

[οντος ἐπιστάτ]εσι χρυσõ

[. . . . . . .⁹. . . .]ο[.] ἐπὶ τῆς βολ-

5   ῆς ἒ[ι Ἱ]ππόνικος Ἀλοπεκῆ-

θεμ πρõτος ἐγραμμάτευε·

λ ῆ μ μ α παρὰ ταμιõν ἐκ πόλεος

ΔΔΔ   [hοῖ]ς Δεινία[ς] Εὐάγος

ΤΤΤ   Φ[ι]λαίδες ἐ[γραμμά]τευε,

10   ΧΧ𐅈   ταμ[ί]αι δὲ Φ[ιλ]όνεος Ἰδο-

HHH   μεν[έ]ος Κεφισ[ι]εύς, Ἀρίσ-   (I)

𐅂Γ𐅄   τυλλος Ἐλ[λεσπο]ντίο Ἐρχι-   (II)

[𐅂]𐅄ΙΙ   εύ[ς], Γλαυκ[ίας Αἰ]σχίνο

Κυ[δ]αθεναιεύ[ς], Δεμοχάρες   (III)

15   Σι[μ]ύλο Πο[τά]μιος, Τεισί-   (IV)

μα[χ]ος Τει[σίο] Κεφαλῆθεν,   (V)

Χάρισος [. . . .]νθίο Ἀχαρν(εύς),   (VI)

Δ[ί]ογχις Χσενοκλέος Φλυ-   (VII)

                              ἔθεν, Διο[ν]ύσιος Εὐκλεί[δο]
20   Περαιεύς, Χαιρελεί[δες]   (VIII)
                              Χαριξένο Ἀφιδνα[. . .⁷. . .]   (IX)
                              αρινος Ἐπιχαρ[. . . .⁹. . . .]   (X)
                                   vacat
        [ἀ ν α] λ όματ[α]
25   χρ[υσίον ἐονέθε]
                  στ[αθμόν – – – –]
   ΔΔΔΤ   τ[ιμὲ τούτο]
   ΤΤΤΧ   – – – – – –
   [.]ΗΗ[.]   – – – – – –

IG I³ 456

443/2 or 441/0   [θε]ο[ί ⋮   Ἀθενᾶ ⋮ Τύχε·]
                  [Η]𐅄Δ   [– – – ἐγραμ]-
                  – – – – –   [μάτευε ἀγάλμα]-
                            [τος ἐπιστάτεσι]

                            – – – – –

IG I³ 457

442/1   θεοί [Ἀθεναία ?]
                  ἐπὶ Ἀρρε[νεί]δο [γρ]-   ΣΤΟΙΧ. 14
                  αμματεύον[τ]ο[ς ἐπ]-
                  ιστάτεσι ἀ[γάλμα]-
5   τος ⋮ χρυσõ ἐπὶ [τẽς]
        ΔΔ   βολẽς hẽ[ι] Ἀρ[χέστ]-
        ΓΤ   ρατο[ς ἐγραμμάτε]-
                  υε ⋮ πρ[õτος . . .⁶. . .]
                  [.]σαν [. . .⁷. . . hοῖ]-
10   σι ⋮ Φιλο[. . .⁶. . . ἐγ]-
                  ραμμάτε[υε Ἀφιδν]-
                  αῖο[ς ⋮ . . . .⁸. . . . Κυ]-
                  δαθ[εναιε]ύς ⋮ Μ[. . .]   (III)
                  ος ⋮ Μ[ελιτε]ύς ⋮ Λύκο   (VII)
15   ς ⋮ Κ[. . .⁶. . .], Διερχ[σ]-
                  ις Μ[α]ρα[θ]όνιος ⋮ Ἀ[ν]-   (IX)
                  τίφι[λος ⋮] Ἀναφλύ[σ]-   (X)
                  τιο[ς ⋮ Κ]λυτίας ⋮ Πε[ρ]-
                  γασẽθεν, Πετραῖ[ο]-   (I)
20   ς ⋮ Θαλίαρχος ⋮ λẽμ[μ]-
                  α παρὰ [τ]αμιõν vacat
                                   vacat
   [.]ṬΤ ⋮ ἐλέφ[αν]τος ⋮ τιμ[έ]
   [.]ΧΧΧΗΗ – – – – – – – –

                  – – – – – – – – – – – – –

IG I³ 458

440/39		Κιχέσιππος ἐγ[ρ]-	a ΣΤΟΙΧ. 13
		αμμάτευε : ἀγάλ[μ]-	
		ατος : ἐπιστάτε[σ]-	
		ι : Μυρρινόσιος : λ-	
5		ῦμμα : παρὰ ταμιõ-	
	Ͱ	ν : hοῖς Δεμόστρα-	
		τος : ἐγραμμάτευ-	
		ε : Χσυπεταόν : ταμ-	
		ίαι : Κτεσίον : Στ[ρ]-	
10		οσίας : Ἀντιφάτ[ε]-	
		ς : Μένανδρος : Θ[υμ]-	
		οχάρες : Σμόκορ[δ]-	
		ος : Φειδελείδ[ες.]	
		vacat	
15	⋻ΔΔΔ :	χρυσίον : ἐονέθ- ᵛ	
	ΓΤΤΧ :	ε : σταθμόν : ΓΤΧ⋻Ͱ	
	ΧΧΧ⋻ :	τιμὲ τούτο ΔΓͰͰͰ	
	Ͱ⋻ͰͰ :	ΙΙΙΙΙ *vacat*	
		vacat	
20	ΤΤ⋻Ͱ	ἐλέφας ἐονέθε	
	ͰΔΔΔ	*vacat*	
	ΔͰͰͰ	*vacat*	
		lacuna	
		vacat b	
439/8		ἀναλόμ[ατα ᵛ χρυσ]-	
25	[. .]ΔΤ	ίον : ἐον[έθε *vacat*]	
	[. .]ͰΔ	χρυσίο[ν ἄσεμον, σ]-	
	[Δ]ΔΔΓ	ταθμόν [: – – –]	
	[Ͱ]Ͱι	ΔΔΔΔͰ – – – –	
		Κροίσ[ειοι στατῦ]-	
30		ρες : ͰΔ– – –	
		τιμὲ τ[ούτοιν ἀμφ]-	
		οτέ[ροιν *vacat*]	
	[.]ΤΧΧ	*vacat*	
	[. .] . .	– – – – – –	

IG I³ 459

440/39		θεοί : Ἀθενᾶ : Τύχε·
		Κιχέσιππος : ἐγραμμά-
		τευε : ἀγάλματος : ἐπι-
		στάτεσι : Μυρρινόσιος
5		λῦμμα : παρὰ *vacat*
		vacat

IG I³ 460

438   ἐπιστά[ται – – – – – – –]
           τάδε ἔλ[αβον – – – – ἀργ]-
           ύριον *vacat* [*vacat*   ]
           ⱵΗΗ – – – – – – – – – – –
5   Ⱶ𐅄Δ – – – – – – – – – – –
           χρυσι[ο – – – – – – – – –]
           ετο : ΗΗ – – – – – – – –
           Κάλλα[ισχρος – – – – – ἀνέ]-
           θεκεν – – – – – – – – – –
10   ἀναλό[ματα – – – – – – – –]
           [.] Ḥ – – – – – – – – – – –
           Ⱶ𐅄Δ – – – – – – – – – – –
           ἀπεργα[σία – – – – – – – –]
           ⱵΗΗⱵΔΔ – – – – – – – –
15   κατάβλ[εμα – – – – – – – –]
           𐅄𐅄𐅄 – – – – – – – – – –
           ΗΗΗ – – – – – – – – – – –
           χρυσιο [– – – – – – – – ἀγά]-
           [λ]ματι π– – – – – – – – –

IG I³ 462–466
The Accounts of the Propylaia, 437/6–433/2

Year 1   *IG* I³ 462

obverse of stele
above columns I–II

437/6   [θεοί : ᾿Αθεναία : Τύχε?]   C + D

[. . . . . ᾿ἐπιστάτ]αι Π[ρο]πυλαίο ἐργασ[ίας]
          c.22

[ℎοῖς – – – ἐγραμμάτευε – – – ε]ύς, ἐπ᾽ Ε[ὐ]θυμένος ἄρχο[ντος]

[᾿Αθεναίοισιν ἐπὶ τ ͂ες βολ ͂ες ℎ ͂ει Πε]ιθ[ι]άδε[ς] πρ ͂οτος ἐγραμ[μάτε]-

5   [υε : ἐπιστάται – – – – – – : Τ]ιμογέν[ες ᾿Ικ]αριεύς : Δ[. . . . . . .]
                                                            5

          – – – – – – – – – –ς ᾿Επ[ι]χα[ρι. . .] ᾿Αμφιτρο[π ͂εθεν]

[τούτοις λέμματα τ ͂ο ἐνιαυτ ͂ο τούτ]ο τάδε·

Col. I
7 lines missing

15   [παρὰ ℎελλενοταμι ͂ον ℎοῖς – –]   B + P

– – –   [. .]υλος [ἐγραμμάτευε – – – τ ͂ο]

                 χσυμμ[αχικ ͂ο φόρο μν ͂α ἀπὸ τ ͂ο ταλάντο]

                 κεράμο [τ ͂ο ἀπὸ τ ͂ον – –]

– – –   ον καθα[ιρεθέντον – – –]

20   οντον ε– – – – – –

                 πιδο κα– – – – – –

– – –   χσύλον [πραθέντον τιμέ]

– – –   πινάκο[ν] τι[μέ– – –]

– – –   οἰκίας ℎειρ ͂α[ς μίσθοσις]

25   παρὰ Πλ[ε]ιστίο – – –

– – –   σκυτ ͂ον [π]εριτμ[εμάτον τιμέ]

                 παρὰ Σ[αύ]ρονος – – – –

– – –   [.]θεντ[. . .]ολεο– – –

                 [ἀ ν α λ ό μ α]τ α

30   – – –   [. . . . .]ν
                         8

     – – –   – – – –

     – – –   [. . . . . ἀπὸ Σκιρά]δος   E
                           c.12

     – – –   [. . . . .]ισιείας
                                  c.20

                 – – – – – – – – – – – – – – vacat   T

35   – – –   [. . . . . ἐ]γ δεμ[. . .] vacat
                         10

     – – –   [. . . . .] ᾿Ελευσ[ινό]θεν
                       10

     – – –   [. . . . .] Πεντε[λ ͂εθ]εν
                       10

     – – –   [. . . . . ἐ]χς ᾿Ακτ ͂ε[ς] vacat
                       9

     – – –   [. . . . . ἀ]πὸ Σκιρ[άδ]ος
                       9

40   – – –   [. . . . . ἐ]κ τ ͂ε[ς . . . . ι]σιείας
                       9

                 – – – – – – – – – – – – vacat

                 – – – – – – – – – – – – ν

lacuna, 5 lines vacant

– – –   ℎυποργ[οῖς – – – – – –]

$\quad\quad\quad\quad\quad\quad\quad$ hυποργ[οῖς Πεντελε͂θεν hοδο]ποιο[ῖς] $\quad\quad$ M + N + O
50 $\quad\quad\quad\quad\quad$ καὶ λίθ[ος ἀνατιθε͂σι ἐπὶ τὰ] κύκ[λα]
$\quad\quad\quad\quad\quad\quad\quad$ καταμε[νίον]
$\quad\quad\quad\quad\quad\quad\quad$ μισθομά[τον ἐς τὲν ἀκρόπολιν]
$\quad\quad\quad\quad\quad\quad\quad$ ἄνευ τõν [ἐς τὰ Προπύλαια?]
$\quad\quad\quad\quad\quad\quad\quad$ παρέ[δ]ομ[εν τοῖς νέοις ἐπιστάτεσι]
$\quad\quad\quad\quad\quad\quad\quad\quad\quad\quad$ *vacat*

Year 1, uncertain location $\quad\quad\quad\quad\quad\quad\quad\quad\quad\quad\quad\quad\quad$ X

$\quad\quad\quad\quad\quad\quad$ – – –
55 $\quad\quad\quad$ [. . .]ΧႲΗΗ – –
$\quad\quad\quad\quad$ [. . .]ΧΧႲΗΗ – –
$\quad\quad\quad\quad$ [. . .]ᖵΔΔΔႷᖷ – –
$\quad\quad\quad\quad$ [. . .]ᖵΔΔႷᖷᖷᛁᛁ
$\quad\quad\quad\quad$ [. . .]ႲΗΗΗΔΔΔ – –
60 $\quad\quad\quad$ [. . .⁵. .] *vacat*

YEAR 2 $\quad\quad$ *IG* I³ 463

436/5 $\quad$ [ἐπὶ τε͂ς δευτέρας] ἀρχε͂ς [hε͂ι – – –] $\quad\quad\quad\quad\quad\quad$ N + O
$\quad\quad\quad$ [. . . . .¹¹. . . . . ἐπὶ τε͂]ς βολε͂[ς hε͂ι – – –]
$\quad\quad\quad$ [πρõτος ἐγραμμάτε]υε : ἐ[πιστάται – – –]
$\quad\quad\quad$ [. . . . . . .¹⁶⁻¹⁷. .]ε[. .ᶜ⁵.]σται – – – – – –
65 $\quad\quad$ [. . . . . . . .¹⁴. . . . .?Λευκον]οεύς, Βλ[επ– – – – – –]
$\quad\quad\quad$ [. . . . . .¹⁹. . . . . . .] τούτοις λ[έμματα τõ ἐνιαυτõ τάδε·]
$\quad\quad\quad\quad\quad\quad\quad\quad$ [π]αρὰ [τõν προτέρον ἐπιστατõν hοῖς]
$\quad\quad\quad\quad\quad\quad\quad\quad$ [– – – ἐγραμμάτευε – – –]
$\quad\quad\quad\quad\quad\quad\quad\quad\quad$ *lacuna*
$\quad\quad\quad\quad\quad\quad\quad\quad$ [παρὰ ταμιõν] οἳ τὰ [τε͂ς θεõ ἐταμίευον] $\quad\quad$ J
70 $\quad\quad\quad\quad\quad\quad\quad$ [οἷς . .⁵. . ἐ]γραμ[μάτευε – – –]
$\quad\quad\quad\quad\quad\quad\quad$ [παρὰ ἑλλε]νοταμ[ιõν hοῖς – – – –]
$\quad\quad\quad\quad\quad\quad\quad$ [ἐγραμμάτ]ευε Αἰχ[σονεὺς τõ χρυμμαχικõ]
$\quad\quad\quad\quad\quad\quad\quad$ [φόρο μνᾶ ἀ]πὸ τõ τα[λάντο]
$\quad\quad\quad\quad\quad\quad\quad\quad$ *vacat* 0.045

$\quad\quad\quad\quad\quad\quad\quad\quad\quad\quad$ *Col. II*

$\quad\quad$ ḢΔΔΔᖷᖷ $\quad\quad\quad\quad$ [οἰκί]ας hειρᾶς μί[σθοσις] $\quad\quad$ C + D + L
75 $\quad$ ႷᖷᛁⲤ $\quad\quad\quad\quad\quad$ [πινά]κον τιμέ
$\quad\quad\quad\quad\quad\quad$ [ἀ ν α λ ό] μ α τ α
$\quad$ ΧΧΧΧႲΗḢ[Η]ᖵΔᖷᖷ $\quad$ [ὀνε]μάτον
$\quad$ ΜᖵΧႲ[Η]ΗΔΔႷᛁⲤ $\quad\quad$ [. . .⁵. .]
$\quad$ ᖵΧ[Χ]ႲΗΗΗΗΔႷᖷ–– $\quad$ – – –
80 $\quad$ [. .]ΧႲΗΗΗΗ $\quad\quad\quad$ – – –
$\quad$ [. .⁴⁻⁵. .]ᖷᖷᖷ $\quad\quad\quad$ – – –
$\quad\quad\quad\quad\quad\quad\quad$ *lacuna*
$\quad$ – – $\quad\quad\quad\quad\quad$ [.]ι – – – $\quad\quad\quad\quad\quad$ S + H
$\quad$ – – $\quad\quad\quad\quad\quad$ λιθο– $\quad\quad$ –
$\quad$ – – $\quad\quad\quad\quad\quad$ λιθοτό[μοις – – –]

85 – –   λιθοτόμοι[ς – –]

    – –   λιθοτόμοι[ς – –]

                                 vacat

    – –   [λιθ]αγογ[ίας – –]

                                 lacuna

                                 traces of letters

90   [μι]σθομάτ[ον – –]   Q

                                 lacuna

    Μ[Μ – – – –]   [παρέδομεν – – –]   E

                                 1 line vacat

YEAR 3   *IG* I³ 464

435/4   ἐ[πὶ τῆς τρίτες ἀρχῆς hῆι Ἐπικλῆς ἐγραμμάτευε]

        Θ[ορίκιος ἐπὶ τῆς βολῆς hῆι – – – πρῶτος]

        ἐγ[ραμμάτευε· ἐπιστάται – – – – – – – –]

95   ΔΙ– – – – – – – – – – – –

        Ἀγ[αφλύστιος? τούτοις λέμματα τῶ ἐνιαυτῶ τάδε·]

        ΜΜ– – – –   [παρὰ τῶν προτέρον ἐπιστατῶν]

                         – – – – – – – – – – – – – – – – –

        ΜΜ– – – –   – – – – – – – – – – – – – – – – –

100   Δ– – – – – –   – – – – – – – – – – – – – – – – –

        – –   – – – – – – – – – – – – – – – – –

                         lacuna

                         [παρὰ ταμιῶν hεφαιστικῶ ἀπὸ Λαυρείο]   FI

        – – –   [. . . . . . .ᶜ·¹⁴. . . . . .] τῶμ π[έντε μερῶν]

105   [ἀπὸ τῆς στρατι]ᾶς τῆς με[τ]ὰ Γ[λαύκονος?]

        [παρὰ hελλενοτ]αμιῶν ἀπὸ στ[ρατ]ιᾶς :

        [τῆς μετὰ? Προ]τέο : παρὰ Δεμ[ο]χάρος

        [. . . . .ᶜ·¹¹. . . .]ασίππο Φλυέος

        [παρὰ hελλενοτα]μιῶν hοῖς Θοινίλος

110   [ἐγραμμάτευεν Ἀ]χαρνεύς : τῶ χσυμ-

        [μαχικῶ φόρο μνᾶ ἀπὸ τ]ῶ ταλάντο

        [. . . . . . .ᶜ·¹⁷. . . . .]ς παρὰ

        – – – – – – – – – – – – – – – – –

        reverse of stele

        Col. III

YEAR 4   *IG* I³ 465

434/3   [θεοί : Ἀ]θεναία [: Τύχε·]   D + C

        [ἐπὶ τῆς τετ]άρτες ἀρχῆς hῆι Διογέ[νες ἐγρ[αμμάτευε]

115   [. . . . .⁹. . . .] ἐπὶ τῆς βολῆς hῆι Μετα[γένες] πρ[ῶτος ἐγραμ]-

        [μάτευε : ἐπι]στάται : Ἀρί[στυλ]λος Μ[ελιτεύ]ς, Μ[. . . .⁸. . . .]

        [. . . .⁸. . . .]ς, Δίκτυς Κο[ι]λεύ[ς], Τιμ[όστρατος] Κε[. . . .⁷. . . .]

        [. . . .⁸. . . . Θ]οραιεύς· τούτοις λ[έμματα τ]ῶ ἐνια[υτῶ τάδε·]

        – – – – ΗΗΗΔΓΗΗΗ   παρὰ τῶμ πρ[οτέρον ἐ]πιστατ[ῶν hοῖς]

120 Ἐπικλε͂ς ἐγρα[μμάτευ]ε Θορίκ[ιος]
– – – παρὰ ταμιο͂ν ηο[ὶ τὰ τε͂]ς θεο͂ ἐτα[μίευον]
      ηοῖς Κράτες ἐγρα[μμά]τε[υ]ε Λαμπ[τρεύς]
      [π]αρὰ ηελλενοταμ[ιο͂ν η]οῖς Προτόγ[ικος]
– – – [ἐγραμ]μάτευε Κερ[αμε]ύς, το͂ χσυμ[μαχ]-
125   [ικο͂ φόρο μ]νᾶ ἀπὸ το͂ [τα]λάντο
      [παρὰ ταμ]ιο͂ν ηεφα[ισ]τικο͂ ἀπὸ Λ[αυ]ρ[είο]
– – – [. . . . .⁸. . . . .]ο[.]το[. . τ]ο͂μ πέντε μ[ε]ρο͂[ν]
      [παρὰ ηελλενοταμιο͂ν ἀ]πὸ στρατιᾶς τε͂[ς]
      [μετὰ . . .⁶. . . παρὰ . .ᶜ⁴.]σίππο Ἀγρυλε͂θε[ν]
130   – – – – – – – – – – πα]ρὰ Τιμοσθένο[ς]
            lacuna
      – – – – – – – – – –vac.   AE
      [– – – – – – – – – – Πε]ντελε͂σι
      – – – – – – – – vac.
      – – – – – – – –vac.
135   [μισθομάτο]ν
      [ἐς τὲν ἀκρό]πολιν ἄνευ τ[ο͂ν ἐς τὰ Π]ροπύλαια
      [παρέδομ]εν τοῖς νέοι[ς ἐπισ]τάτεσι
            vacat 0.13

U *Year 4, uncertain location*

      – –   – – – – – –
      Χ– –   – – – – – – – –
140   ╒ΗΗ– –   – – – – – – –

            Col. IV

YEAR 5   *IG* I³ 466

433/2   [. .⁵. .] Μαραθ[ονίο – – –]   B
– – –   [παρ]ὰ ταμιο͂ν – – – – – –
            Μελιτέος κ– – – – – –
– – –   παρὰ ηελλε[ονταμιο͂ν ἀπὸ στρατιᾶς τε͂ς]
145   μετ᾽ Ἀρχενα[ύτο – – – – – – –]
            οἰκίας ηιερ[ᾶς μίσθοσις]
            κυάνο πι– – – – – – –
            Κο[. . .]τε– – – – – – –
            [ἀ ν α λ] ό μ α [τ α]
150   [λ]ιθοτ[όμοις – – –]
            [λ]ιθαγ[ογίας – – –]
            [λ]ιθοτ[όμοις – – –]
            [λ]ιθα[γογίας – – –]
            [λι]θ– – – – – – –
155   [τέ]κ[τοσι? – – –]
                  lacuna

Fragments of uncertain location

YEAR 2

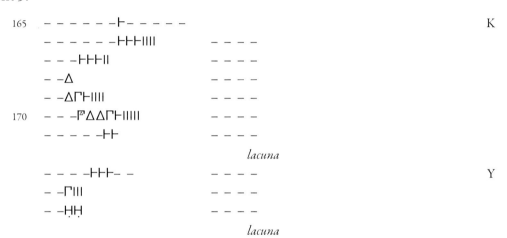

		Col. II?	G
	Γ– –	– – – –	
	ΧΓ– –	– – – –	
	ΧΧΧ– –	– – – –	
	ΓΜΓ– –	– – – –	
160	ΧΧΧ– –	– – – –	
		– – – –	
	ΧΧΓΗ– –	– – – –	
		– – – –	
	ΧΧΗΗ– –	– – – –	

YEAR 5?

165	– – – – – –Ͱ– – – – –		K
	– – – – – –ͰͰͰIIII	– – – –	
	– – –ͰͰͰII	– – – –	
	– –Δ	– – – –	
	– –ΔΓͰIIII	– – – –	
170	– – –ΓΔΔΓͰIIIII	– – – –	
	– – – – –ͰͰ	– – – –	
		lacuna	
	– – – –ͰͰͰ– –	– – – –	Y
	– –ΓIII	– – – –	
	– –ḤḤ	– – – –	
		lacuna	

CHRONOLOGICAL TABLE

ca. 460	Column trophy at Marathon
	Marathon painting in Stoa Poikile
460–450	Great bronze Athena constructed
ca. 450	Hephaisteion, construction begun
	Temple of Athena Nike authorized; construction postponed
	Telesterion at Eleusis, construction begun, work of Iktinos
	Odeion, construction begun
447	Telesterion, work suspended
	Parthenon, construction begun
446	Gold and ivory statue under construction
446/5	Odeion complete for Great Panathenaia
450–440	Hephaisteion, exterior peristyle built
445–440	Temple of Poseidon at Sounion built
438	Parthenon, architecture complete
	Gold and ivory statue dedicated
440–430	Temple of Athena Sounias built
	Telesterion construction resumed, work of Koroibos
438–430	Hephaisteion, cella altered for interior colonnades
	Temple of Athena Pallenis built, stonework unfinished
437	Propylaia, construction begun
436–434	Bastion of Athena Nike raised
435–430	Temple on the Ilissos River built
ca. 434	Temple of Athena Nike, construction begun
432	Parthenon, pediment sculptures complete
	Propylaia, construction suspended, stonework unfinished
430–420	Temple of Nemesis at Rhamnous built, stonework unfinished
	Cult statue of Nemesis dedicated
426	Parthenon damaged by earthquake
ca. 425	Hephaisteion friezes, pediments, and roof complete
425	Statues of Athena Nike dedicated
425/4	Erechtheion, construction begun
424/3	Temple of Athena Nike complete
ca. 420	Telesterion, construction continued under Metagenes
421–415	Hephaisteion, cult statues constructed
413	Erechtheion, construction suspended
409–405	Erechtheion, construction resumed and completed
408/7	Telesterion, construction unfinished, lantern of Xenokles still to be built

BIBLIOGRAPHY

Multiple publications by a single author are listed in chronological order. Abbreviations of periodicals and series are those used by the *American Journal of Archaeology* (www.ajaonline.org/submissions/abbreviations).

Abatino, G., *La colonna del tempio di Hera Lacinia* (Naples 1901).

Abramson, H., "A Hero Shrine for Phrontis at Sounion?" *CSCA* 12 (1979) 1–19.

Accame, S., "Il decreto di Callia nella storia della finanza ateniese," *RivFil,* n.s., 13 (1935) 468–496.

———, "Note per la storia della Pentecontaetia," *RivFil,* n.s., 33 (1955) 146–174.

Aleshire, S. B., and S. D. Lambert, "Making the Peplos for Athena: A New Edition of *IG* II², 1060 + *IG* II², 1036," *ZPE* 142 (2003) 65–86.

Alexandri, O., "Ἐφορεία κλασσικών αρχαιοτήτων Ἀττικής," *ArchDelt* 29 (1974) Β′ 1, Χρον. 31–181.

Allen, T. W., and E. E. Sikes, *The Homeric Hymns* (London 1904).

Amandry, R., *Fouilles de Delphes* II.5: *La colonne des Naxiens et le portique des Athéniens* (Paris 1953).

———, "Notes de topographie et d'architecture delphique X: Le 'socle marathonien' et le trésor des athéniens," *BCH* 122 (1998) 75–90.

Ameling, W., "Plutarch, Perikles 12–14," *Historia* 34 (1985) 47–63.

———, "Zu einem neuen Datum des Phidiasprozesses," *Klio* 68 (1986) 63–66.

Amiet, P., *Art of the Ancient Near East* (New York 1980).

Anderson, W. D., *Music and Musicians in Ancient Greece* (Ithaca, NY, 1994).

Andrae, W., *Die ionische Säule: Bauform oder Symbol?* (Berlin 1933).

Andrewes, A., "The Opposition to Perikles," *JHS* 98 (1978) 1–8.

Andronicos, M., *Vergina: The Royal Tombs and the Ancient City* (Athens 1984).

Antonaccio, C., *An Archaeology of Ancestors: Tomb Cult and Hero Cult in Early Greece* (Lanham, MD, 1995).

Austin, C., *Nova Fragmenta Euripidea in Papyris Reperta* (Berlin 1968).

Badian, E., *From Plataea to Potidaea* (Baltimore 1993).

Balanos, N., "Ἡ νέα ἀναστήλωσις τοῦ ναοῦ τῆς Ἀθηνᾶς Νίκης (1935–1939)," *ArchEph* (1937) pt. 3 [1956] 776–807.

Bammer, A., and U. Muss, *Das Artemision von Ephesos* (Mainz 1996).

Bancroft, S., "Problems Concerning the Archaic Acropolis at Athens" (Ph.D. diss., Princeton University, 1979).

Bannier, W., "Zu attischen Inschriften XV," *PhilWoch* 47 (1927) 667–671.

Barber, E. J. W., "The Peplos of Athena," in J. Neils, ed., *Goddess and Polis: The Panathenaic Festival in Ancient Athens* (Princeton 1992) 103–117.

———, *Women's Work: The First 20,000 Years; Women, Cloth, and Society in Early Times* (New York 1994).

Barletta, B. A., *The Origins of the Greek Architectural Orders* (Cambridge 2001).

———, "In Defense of the Ionic Frieze of the Parthenon," *AJA* 113 (2009) 547–568.

Barrett, A. A., and M. Vickers, "Columns *in antis* in the Temple on the Ilissus," *BSA* 70 (1975) 11–16.

Barron, J. P., "New Light on Old Walls: The Murals of the Theseion," *JHS* 92 (1972) 20–45.

———, "The Liberation of Greece," in *CAH*², vol. 4 (1988) 592–622.

Bates, W. N., "Notes on the Old Temple of Athena on the Acropolis," *HSCP* 12 (1901) 319–326.

Baziotopoulou-Valavani, E., "A Mass Burial from the Cemetery of Kerameikos," in M. Stamatopoulou and
    M. Yeroulanou, eds., *Excavating Classical Culture: Recent Archaeological Discoveries in Greece* (Oxford
    2002) 187–201.

Beazley, J. D., *The Development of Attic Black-Figure* (Berkeley 1951).

Beckel, G., "Akropolisfragen," in Χαριστήριον εἰς Ἀναστάσιον Κ. Ὀρλάνδον, vol. 4 (Athens 1967–68) 329–362.

Berger, E., *Die Geburt der Athena in Ostgiebel des Parthenon* (Basel 1974).

———, "Parthenon-Studien: Zweiter Zwischenbericht," *AntK* 20 (1977) 124–141.

———, *Der Parthenon in Basel: Dokumentation zu den Metopen* (Mainz 1986).

Berger, E., and M. Gisler-Huwiler, *Der Parthenon in Basel: Dokumentation zum Fries* (Mainz 1996).

Beschi, L., "Contributi di topografia ateniese," *ASAtene*, n.s., 29–30 (1967–68) 511–536.

———, "Il fregio del Partenone: Una proposta di lettura," *RendLinc* 39 (1984) 173–195.

———, "Η ζωφόρος του Παρθενώνα· Μιά νέα πρόταση ερμηνείαι," in H. Kyrieleis, ed., *Archaische und klassische
    griechische Plastik* (Mainz 1986) 199–224.

———, "I Tirreni di Lemno a Brauron e il tempietto ionico dell'Ilisso," *RivIstArch* 57 (2002) 7–36.

Betancourt, P. P., *The Aeolic Style in Architecture: A Survey of Its Development in Palestine, the Halikarnassos
    Peninsula, and Greece* (Princeton 1977).

Beyer, I., "Die Position der Peplosfigur Wegner im Parthenon-Ostgiebel," *AM* 89 (1974) 123–149.

Bieber, M., "The Entrances and Exits of Actors and Chorus in Greek Plays," *AJA* 58 (1954) 277–284.

Binder, J., "Acropolis Acroterion Fragments," in U. Höckmann and A. Krug, eds., *Festschrift für Frank Brom-
    mer* (Mainz 1977) 29–31.

———, "The West Pediment of the Parthenon: Poseidon," in K. J. Rigsby, ed., *Studies Presented to Sterling
    Dow on His Eightieth Birthday, GRBS* Monograph 10 (Durham, NC, 1984) 15–22.

Blegen, C. W., *Troy and the Trojans* (London 1963).

Blegen, C. W., and M. Rawson, *The Palace of Nestor at Pylos in Western Messenia*, vol. 1, *The Buildings and
    Their Contents* (Princeton 1966).

Blouet, A., *Expédition scientifique de Morée*, vol. 3 (Paris 1838).

Blümel, C., *Griechische Bildhauerarbeit, JdI-EH* 11 (Berlin 1927).

———, "Der Fries des Tempels der Athena Nike in der attischen Kunst des fünften Jahrhunderts vor Christus,"
    JdI 65–66 (1950–51) 135–165.

———, *Greek Sculptors at Work,* 2nd ed. (London 1969).

Boardman, J., "The Parthenon Frieze—Another View," in U. Höckmann and A. Krug, eds., *Festschrift für
    Frank Brommer* (Mainz 1977) 39–49.

———, "Herakles, Theseus and Amazons," in D. Kurtz and B. Sparkes, eds., *The Eye of Greece: Studies in the
    Art of Athens* (Cambridge 1982) 1–28.

———, "The Parthenon Frieze," in E. Berger, ed., *Parthenon-Kongress Basel* (Mainz 1984) 210–215.

———, "Notes on the Parthenon East Frieze," in M. Schmidt, ed., *Kanon: Festschrift Ernst Berger* (Basel 1988)
    9–14.

———, "The Naked Truth," *OJA* 10 (1991) 119–121.

———, "The Parthenon Frieze, A Closer Look," *RA* (1999) 305–330.

Boardman, J., and D. Finn, *The Parthenon and Its Sculptures* (London 1985).

Bockelberg, S. von, "Die Friese des Hephaisteions," *AntP* 18 (1979) 23–50.

Boegehold, A. L., "Perikles' Citizenship Law of 451/0 B.C.," in A. L. Boegehold and A. C. Scafuro, eds., *Athe-
    nian Identity and Civic Ideology* (Baltimore 1994) 57–66.

Boersma, J. S., "On the Political Background of the Hephaisteion," *BABesch* 39 (1964) 101–106.

———, *Athenian Building Policy from 561/0 to 405/4 B.C.* (Groningen 1970).

Bogaert, R., "Le cours de statère de Cyzique aux Ve et IVe siècles avant J.-C.," *AntCl* 32 (1963) 85–119.

Bohn, R., "Bericht über die Ausgrabungen auf der Akropolis zu Athen im Frühjahr 1880," *AM* 5 (1880)
    259–267.

———, *Die Propylaeen der Akropolis zu Athen* (Berlin and Stuttgart 1882).

Bol, P. C., "Die Giebelskulpturen des Schatzhauses von Megara," *AM* 89 (1974) 65–74.

Bommelaer, J.-F., *Guide de Delphes, le site* (Paris 1991).

Bonner, R., and G. Smith, *The Administration of Justice from Homer to Aristotle*, 2 vols. (Chicago 1930–38).

Borbein, A. H., "Polykleitos," *YCS* 30 (1996) 66–90.

Borchhardt, J., *Die Bauskulptur des Heroons von Limyra: Das Grabmal des lykischen Königs Perikles*, IstForsch 32 (Berlin 1976).

Bothmer, D. von, *Amazons in Greek Art* (Oxford 1957).

Boucharlat, R., "Suse et la Susianne à l'époque achéménide: Donnés archéologiques," in H. Sancisi-Weerdenburg and A. Kuhrt, eds., *Centre and Periphery: Proceedings of the Groningen 1986 Achaemenid History Workshop*, Achaemenid History 4 (Leiden 1990) 149–175.

Boulter, P. N., "The Akroteria of the Nike Temple," *Hesperia* 38 (1969) 133–140.

Bouras, C., Ἡ ἀναστήλωσις τῆς στοᾶς τῆς Βραυρῶνος (Athens 1967).

Bowie, T., and D. Thimme, eds., *The Carrey Drawings of the Parthenon Sculptures* (Bloomington, IN, 1971).

Brandau, B., *Troia: Eine Stadt und ihr Mythos* (Bergisch Gladbach 1997).

Braun-Vogelstein, J. V., *Die ionische Säule* (Berlin and Leipzig 1921).

Briant, P., "Le nomadisme du Grand Roi," *IrAnt* 23 (1988) 253–272.

Brinkmann, V., "Archaische Formelemente in der Zeit der frühen Klassik," in P. C. Bol, ed., *Geschichte der antiken Bildhauerkunst I* (Mainz 2002) 271–280.

Brommer, F., *Die Skulpturen der Parthenon-Giebel* (Mainz 1963).

———, *Die Metopen des Parthenon* (Mainz 1967).

———, *Vasenlisten zur griechischen Heldensage*, 3rd ed. (Marburg 1973).

———, *Der Parthenonfries* (Mainz 1977).

———, *Hephaistos: Der Schmiedegott in der antiken Kunst* (Mainz 1978).

———, *The Sculptures of the Parthenon* (London 1979).

Broneer, O., "The Tent of Xerxes and the Greek Theater," *CPCA* 1, no. 12 (1944) 305–311.

———, *Isthmia* I: *The Temple of Poseidon* (Princeton 1971).

Brouskari, M. S., *The Acropolis Museum: A Descriptive Catalog* (Athens 1974).

———, "Τὸ θωράκιο τοῦ ναοῦ τῆς Ἀθηνᾶς Νίκης," *ArchEph* 137 (1998) 1–268.

Brückner, A., "Das Reich des Pallas," *AM* 16 (1891) 200–234.

———, "Ein Athenischer Theseus in Berlin und Wien," *ÖJh* 13 (1910) 50–62.

Brunt, P. A., "Athenian Settlements Abroad in the Fifth Century B.C.," in E. Badian, ed., *Ancient Society and Institutions: Studies Presented to Victor Ehrenberg on His 75th Birthday* (Oxford 1966) 71–92.

Bugh, G. R., *The Horsemen of Athens* (Princeton 1988).

Bundgaard, J. A., *Mnesicles, A Greek Architect at Work* (Copenhagen 1957).

———, *The Excavation of the Athenian Acropolis 1882–1890: The Original Drawings,* 2 vols. (Copenhagen 1974).

———, "Le sujet de *IG* I², 24," in *Mélanges helléniques offerts à Georges Daux* (Paris 1974) 43–49.

———, *Parthenon and the Mycenaean City on the Heights* (Copenhagen 1976).

Burford, A., "Heavy Transport in Classical Greece," *Economic History Review* 13 (1960) 1–18.

———, "The Economics of Greek Temple Building," *PCPS* 191 (1965) 21–32.

———, *The Greek Temple Builders at Epidauros: A Social and Economic Study of Building in the Asklepian Sanctuary, during the Fourth and Early Third Centuries B.C.* (Liverpool 1969).

Burkert, W., *Homo Necans: The Anthropology of Ancient Greek Sacrificial Ritual and Myth,* trans. P. Bing (Berkeley 1983).

———, *Greek Religion: Archaic and Classical,* trans. J. Raffan (Cambridge, MA, 1984).

Burn, A. R., *Persia and the Greeks,* 2nd ed. (London 1984).

Busolt, G., *Griechische Geschichte bis zur Schlacht bei Chaeroneia*, 2nd ed., 3 vols. (Gotha 1893–1904).

Butz, P. A., "The 'Hekatompedon Inscription' at Athens: Site, Text, and Stoichedon Style" (Ph.D. diss., University of Southern California, 1995).

Calder, W. M., "The Date of Euripides' *Erectheus*," *GRBS* 10 (1969) 147–156.

Camp, J. M., *The Athenian Agora: Excavations in the Heart of Classical Athens* (New York 1986).

———, *The Archaeology of Athens* (New Haven 2001).

Carpenter, J. R., "The Propylon in Greek and Hellenistic Architecture" (Ph.D. diss., University of Pennsylvania, 1970).

Carpenter, R., *The Sculpture of the Nike Temple Parapet* (Cambridge, MA, 1929).

———, "The Lost Statues of the East Pediment of the Parthenon," *Hesperia* 2 (1933) 1–88.

———, "The Unfinished Colossus on Mt. Pendeli," *AJA* 72 (1968) 279–280.

———, *The Architects of the Parthenon* (Baltimore 1970).

Carrara, P., *Euripide: Eretteo* (Florence 1977).

Casson, S., *The Technique of Early Greek Sculpture* (Oxford 1933).

Castriota, D., *Myth, Ethos, and Actuality: Official Art in Fifth-Century B.C. Athens* (Madison, WI, 1992).

Cavaignac, E., *Études sur l'histoire financière d'Athènes au Ve siècle* (Paris 1908).

———, *Le trésor sacré d'Éleusis* (Versailles 1908).

Cavanaugh, M. B., *Eleusis and Athens: Documents in Finance, Religion, and Politics in the Fifth Century B.C.* (Atlanta 1996).

Chambers, M. H., R. Gallucci, and P. Spanos, "Athens' Alliance with Egesta in the Year of Antiphon," *ZPE* 83 (1990) 38–57.

Charitonides, S., "Ἀνασκαφὴ παρὰ τὸν Ἅγιον Δημήτριον τὸν Λουμπαρδιάρην ἐν Ἀθήναις," *ArchEph* (1979) 161–187.

Childs, W. A. P., "In Defense of an Early Date for the Frieze of the Temple on the Ilissos," *AM* 100 (1985) 207–251.

———, "Herodotos, Archaic Chronology, and the Temple of Apollo at Delphi," *JdI* 108 (1993) 399–441.

———, "The Date of the Old Temple of Athena on the Athenian Acropolis," in W. D. E. Coulson et al., eds., *The Archaeology of Athens and Attica under the Democracy* (Oxford 1994) 1–6.

Choremi-Spetsieri, A., "Η οδός των Τριπόδων και τα χορηγικά μνημεία στην αρχαία Αθήνα," in W. D. E. Coulson et al., eds., *The Archaeology of Athens and Attica under the Democracy* (Oxford 1994) 31–42.

Clairmont, C. W., "The Lekythos of Myrrhine," in G. Kopke and M. B. Moore, eds., *Studies in Classical Art and Archaeology: A Tribute to Peter von Blanckenhagen* (Locust Valley, NY, 1979) 103–110.

———, "Girl or Boy?" *AA* (1989) 496–497.

Clarke, J. T., F. H. Bacon, and R. Koldewey, *Investigations at Assos* (Cambridge, MA, 1902).

Clinton, K., "Inscriptions from Eleusis," *ArchEph* (1971) [1972] 81–136.

———, *The Sacred Officials of the Eleusinian Mysteries,* TAPS 64, pt. 3 (Philadelphia 1974).

———, "The Date of the Classical Telesterion," in *Φίλια ἐπὴ εἰς Γεώργιαν Ε. Μυλωνᾶν,* vol. 2 (Athens 1987) 254–262.

———, "The Treasury of the Two Goddesses and Eleusinian Construction in the Classical Period," in *Πρακτικά του XII διεθνούς συνέδριον κλασικής αρχαιολογίας,* vol. 4 (Athens 1988) 33–36.

———, *Myth and Cult: The Iconography of the Eleusinian Mysteries* (Stockholm 1992).

———, *Eleusis, the Inscriptions on Stone: Documents of the Sanctuary of the Two Goddesses and Public Documents of the Deme,* vol. 1A (Athens 2005).

Cohen, B., "Paragone: Sculpture Versus Painting—Kaineus and the Kleophrades Painter," in W. G. Moon, ed., *Ancient Greek Art and Iconography* (Madison, WI, 1983) 171–192.

Cohen, E. E., *Ancient Athenian Maritime Courts* (Princeton 1973).

Colini, A. M., "Aedes Veiovis inter Arcem et Capitolium," *BullComm* 70 (1942) 5–56.

Collard, C., M. J. Cropp, and K. H. Lee, eds., *Euripides: Selected Fragmentary Plays,* vol. 1 (Warminster 1995).

Collignon, M., *Le Parthénon* (Paris 1914).

Connelly, J. B., "Parthenon and *Parthenoi:* A Mythological Interpretation of the Parthenon Frieze," *AJA* 100 (1996) 53–80.

Connor, W. R., *Theopompos and Fifth-Century Athens* (Washington, DC, 1968).

Conticello de' Spagnolis, M., *Il tempio dei Dioscuri nel Circo Flaminio* (Rome 1984).

Conwell, D. H., "The Athenian Long Walls: Chronology, Topography and Remains" (Ph.D. diss., University of Pennsylvania, 1992).

Cook, A. B., *Zeus: A Study in Ancient Religion,* 3 vols. (Cambridge 1914–40).

Corso, A., *Monumenti Periclei: Saggio critico sulla attività edilizia di Pericle*, Istituto Veneto di Scienze, Lettere ed Arti, *Memorie*, Classe di scienze morali, lettere ed arti 40, fasc. 1 (Venice 1986).

———, "Vitruvius and Attic Monuments," *BSA* 92 (1997) 373–400.

Coulton, J. J., "Towards Understanding Doric Design: Stylobate and Intercolumniations," *BSA* 69 (1974) 61–86.

———, *The Architectural Development of the Greek Stoa* (Oxford 1976).

———, *Greek Architects at Work: Problems of Structure and Design* (London 1977).

———, "Doric Capitals: A Proportional Analysis," *BSA* 74 (1979) 81–153.

———, "The Parthenon and Periklean Doric," in E. Berger, ed., *Parthenon-Kongress Basel* (Mainz 1984) 40–44.

Courby, F., *Exploration archéologique de Délos* XII: *Les temples d'Apollon* (Paris 1931).

Crosby, M., "The Leases of the Laureion Mines," *Hesperia* 19 (1950) 189–312.

Crowther, N. B., "The Apobates Reconsidered (Demosthenes lxi 23–9)," *JHS* 111 (1991) 174–176.

Curtius, E., and F. Adler, eds., *Olympia*: *Die Ergebnisse der von dem deutschen Reich veranstalteten Ausgrabung* II: *Die Baudenkmäler*, 2 vols. (Berlin 1892); V: *Die Inschriften* (Berlin 1896).

Danner, P., "Die Maße der Akrotere im Verhältnis zur Architektur in der griechischen Baukunst der archaischen und klassischen Zeit," *ÖJh* 58 (1988) 41–51.

Daux, G., "Deux stèles d'Acharnes," in Χαριστήριον εἰς Ἀναστάσιον Κ. Ὀρλάνδον, vol. 1 (Athens 1965) 78–90.

Davies, J. K., *Athenian Propertied Families,* 600–300 B.C. (Oxford 1971).

———, "Rebuilding a Temple," in D. J. Mattingly and J. Salmon, eds., *Economics beyond Agriculture in the Classical World* (London 2001) 209–229.

Davison, C. C., *Pheidias: The Sculptures and Ancient Sources*, *BICS* Suppl. 105, 3 vols. (London 2009).

Davison, J. A., "Notes on the Panathenaea," *JHS* 78 (1958) 23–42; repr. in J. A. Davison, *From Archilochus to Pindar: Papers on Greek Literature of the Archaic Period* (London 1968) 28–69.

———, "Addenda to 'Notes on the Panathenaea,'" *JHS* 82 (1962) 141–142.

de la Coste-Messelière, P., "Nouvelles remarques sur les frises Siphniennes," *BCH* 68–69 (1944–45) 5–35.

——— *Fouilles de Delphes* IV.4: *Sculptures du trésor des Athéniens* (Paris 1957).

Delcourt, M., *Héphaistos ou la légende du magicien* (Paris 1957).

Delivorrias, A., "Eine klassische Kora-Statue vom Metroon am Ilissos," *AntP* 9 (1969) 7–14.

———, "Poseidon-Tempel auf Kap Sunion: Neue Fragmente der Friesdekoration," *AM* 84 (1969) 127–142.

———, Συμβολὴ στὴ μελέτη τοῦ ἔργου τοῦ Ἀγορακρίτου (Athens 1971).

———, *Attische Giebelskulpturen und Akrotere des fünften Jahrhunderts* (Tübingen 1974).

———, "Τὰ γλυπτὰ τῶν ἀετωμάτων τοῦ ναοῦ τῆς Ἀθηνᾶς Νίκης," *ArchDelt* 29 Α′ (1974) 1–24.

———, "Zur Akroterkomposition des Parthenon," in E. Berger, ed., *Parthenon-Kongress Basel* (Mainz 1984) 289–292.

———, "Zum Athener Brauronion," in W. Hoepfner, ed., *Kult und Kultbauten auf der Akropolis* (Berlin 1997) 209–217.

———, "Athena Sunias—Eine Vermutung," *AA* (1999) 173–181.

Develin, R., "From Panathenaia to Panathenaia," *ZPE* 57 (1984) 133–138.

———, *Athenian Officials, 684–321 B.C.* (Cambridge 1989).

Dinsmoor, W. B., "Attic Building Accounts," *AJA* 17 (1913) 53–80.

———, "Attic Building Accounts, III: The Propylaea," *AJA* 17 (1913) 371–398.

———, "Attic Building Accounts," *AJA* 25 (1921) 233–247.

———, "Structural Iron in Greek Architecture," *AJA* 26 (1922) 148–158.

———, "The Inscriptions of Athena Nike," *AJA* 27 (1923) 318–321.

———, "Supplementary Excavation at the Entrance to the Acropolis, 1928," *AJA* 33 (1929) 101–102.

———, *The Archons of Athens in the Hellenistic Age* (Cambridge, MA, 1931).

———, "The Burning of the Opisthodomos," *AJA* 36 (1932) 143–172, 307–326.

———, "The Date of the Older Parthenon," *AJA* 38 (1934) 408–448.

———, "The Final Account of the Athena Parthenos," *ArchEph* (1937) pt. 2, 507–511.

———, "Archaeology and Astronomy," *PAPS* 80 (1939) 95–173.

———, "The Tribal Cycles of the Treasurers of Athena," in *Athenian Studies Presented to William Scott Ferguson, HSCP* Suppl. 1 (Cambridge, MA, and Oxford, 1940) 157–182.

———, "The Temple of Ares at Athens," *Hesperia* 9 (1940) 1–52.

Dinsmoor, W. B., *Observations on the Hephaisteion, Hesperia* Suppl. 5 (Athens 1941).

———, "The Hekatompedon on the Athenian Acropolis," *AJA* 51 (1947) 109–151.

———, *The Architecture of Ancient Greece*, 3rd ed. (London 1950).

———, "The Athenian Theater of the Fifth Century," in G. E. Mylonas, ed., *Studies Presented to David Moore Robinson on His Seventieth Birthday* (Saint Louis, MO, 1951) vol. 1, 309–330.

———, "Rhamnountine Fantasies," *Hesperia* 30 (1961) 179–204.

———, "Two Monuments on the Athenian Acropolis," in Χαριστήριον εἰς ᾿Αναστάσιον Κ. ᾿Ορλάνδον, vol. 4 (Athens 1967–68) 145–155.

Dinsmoor, W. B., and W. B. Dinsmoor, Jr., *The Propylaia to the Athenian Akropolis*, vol. 2, *The Classical Building* (Princeton 2004).

Dinsmoor, W. B., Jr., *Sounion* (Athens 1971).

———, "New Fragments of the Parthenon in the Athenian Agora," *Hesperia* 43 (1974) 132–155.

———, "The Temple of Poseidon: A Missing Sima and Other Matters," *AJA* 78 (1974) 211–238.

———, "The Roof of the Hephaisteion," *AJA* 80 (1976) 223–246.

———, *The Propylaia to the Athenian Akropolis*, vol. 1, *The Predecessors* (Princeton 1980).

———, "Anchoring Two Floating Temples," *Hesperia* 51 (1982) 410–452.

———, "The Asymmetry of the Pinakotheke—For the Last Time?" in *Studies in Athenian Architecture, Sculpture, and Topography Presented to Homer A. Thompson, Hesperia* Suppl. 20 (Princeton 1982) 18–33.

Dix, T. K., and C. A. Anderson, "The Eteocarpathian Decree (*IG* I³, 1454) and the Construction Date of the Erechtheion," *AJA* 101 (1997) 373.

Djordjevitch, M., "Pheidias's Athena Promachos Reconsidered," *AJA* 98 (1994) 323.

Dörig, J., "Sunionfriesplatte 13," *AM* 73 (1958) 88–93.

———, *Le frise est de l'Héphaisteion* (Mainz 1985).

Dörpfeld, W., "Untersuchungen am Parthenon," *AM* 6 (1881) 283–302.

———, "Der Tempel von Sunion," *AM* 9 (1884) 324–337.

———, "Die Propyläen der Akropolis von Athen II: Über die Gestalt des Südwestflügels," *AM* 10 (1885) 131–144.

———, "Die ältere Parthenon," *AM* 17 (1892) 158–189.

———, "Die Ausgrabungen am Westabhange der Akropolis, I," *AM* 19 (1894) 496–509.

———, "Der alte Athena-Tempel auf der Akropolis, V," *AM* 22 (1897) 159–178.

———, "Funde," *AM* 22 (1897) 225–228.

———, "Die Zeit des älteren Parthenon," *AM* 27 (1902) 379–416.

———, "Der ursprüngliche Plan des Erechtheion," *AM* 29 (1904) 101–107.

———, "Zu den Bauwerken Athens," *AM* 36 (1911) 39–72.

———, "Das Hekatompedon in Athen," *JdI* 34 (1919) 1–40.

———, "Parthenon I, II, III," *AJA* 39 (1935) 497–507.

Dörpfeld, W., and H. Schleif, *Erechtheion* (Berlin 1942).

Dohrn, T., *Attische Plastik vom Tode des Phidias bis zum Wirken der grossen Meister des IV. Jahrhunderts v. Chr.* (Krefeld 1957).

Donnay, G., "Les comptes de l'Athéna chryséléphantine du Parthénon," *BCH* 91 (1967) 50–86.

———, "La date du procès de Phidias," *AntCl* 37 (1968) 19–36.

Donohue, A. A., *Xoana and the Origins of Greek Sculpture* (Atlanta 1988).

Dontas, G., "Α΄ ἐφορεία κλασσικῶν ἀρχαιοτήτων," *ArchDelt* 25 (1970) Β΄ 1, 24–30.

———, "The True Aglaurion," *Hesperia* 52 (1983) 48–63.

Dover, K. J., "The Freedom of the Intellectual in Greek Society," *Talanta* 7 (1975) 24–54.

Drachmann, A. G., *The Mechanical Technology of Greek and Roman Antiquity* (Copenhagen 1963).

Drerup, H., "Parthenon und Vorparthenon—zum Stand der Kontroverse," *AntK* 24 (1981) 21–38.

Dugas, C., "La mission de Triptolème d'après l'imagerie athénienne," *MÉFRA* 62 (1950) 6–31.

Dworakowska, A., *Quarries in Ancient Greece,* Biblioteca Antiqua 14 (Warsaw 1975).

Dyson, R. H., "Problems of Protohistoric Iran as Seen from Hasanlu," *JNES* 24 (1965) 193–217.

———, "The Architecture of Hasanlu: Periods I to IV," *AJA* 81 (1977) 548–552.

———, "The Question of Balconies at Hasanlu," in K. DeVries, ed., *From Athens to Gordion: The Papers of a Memorial Symposium for Rodney S. Young* (Philadelphia 1980) 149–157.

Eddy, S. K., "The Value of the Cyzicene Stater at Athens in the Fifth Century," *ANSMN* 16 (1970) 13–22.

———, "Some Irregular Amounts of Athenian Tribute," *AJP* 94 (1973) 47–70.

———, "The Gold in the Athena Parthenos," *AJA* 81 (1977) 107–111.

Edmonson, C. N., "Brauronian Artemis in Athens," *AJA* 72 (1968) 164–165.

Eickstedt, K.-V. von, "Bemerkungen zur Ikonographie des Frieses vom Ilissos-Temple," in W. D. E. Coulson et al., eds., *The Archaeology of Athens and Attica under the Democracy* (Oxford 1994) 105–111.

Eiteljorg, H., *The Entrance to the Athenian Acropolis before Mnesicles* (Dubuque, IA, 1993 [1995]).

Elderkin, G. W., *Problems in Periclean Buildings* (Princeton 1912).

Fabricius, E., "Die Skulpturen von Tempel in Sounion," *AM* 9 (1884) 338–353.

Farnell, L. R., *The Cults of the Greek States,* 5 vols. (Oxford 1896–1909).

Feaver, D. D., "Historical Development in the Priesthoods of Athens," *YCS* 15 (1957) 123–158.

Fehl, P., "The Rocks on the Parthenon Frieze," *JWarb* 24 (1961) 1–44.

Felten, F., *Griechische tektonische Friese archaischer und klassischer Zeit* (Waldsassen-Bayern, 1984).

Felten, F., and K. Hoffelner, "Die Relieffriese des Poseidontempels in Sounion," *AM* 102 (1987) 169–184.

Ferrari, G., "The Ilioupersis in Athens," *HSCP* 100 (2000) 119–150.

———, "The Ancient Temple on the Acropolis at Athens," *AJA* 106 (2002) 11–35.

Fleischer, R., *Artemis von Ephesos und verwandte Kultstatuen aus Anatolien und Syrien,* ÉPRO 35 (Leiden 1973).

Fontenrose, J., *Didyma: Apollo's Oracle, Cult, and Companions* (Berkeley 1988).

Forbes, R. J., *Studies in Ancient Technology,* vol. 8, *Metallurgy in Antiquity,* pt. 1, 2nd ed. (Leiden 1971).

Fornara, C. W., "The Date of the Callias Decrees," *GRBS* 11 (1970) 185–196.

———, *The Athenian Board of Generals from 501–404, Historia* Einzelschriften 16 (Wiesbaden 1971).

Fornara, C. W., and L. J. Samons, *Athens from Cleisthenes to Perikles* (Berkeley 1991).

Foucart, P., *Les mystères d'Éleusis* (Paris 1914).

Francis, E. D., and M. Vickers, "The Oenoe Painting in the Stoa Poikile and Herodotos' Account of Marathon," *BSA* 80 (1985) 99–113.

Franco, F., "Le assimetrie della Pinacoteca dei Propilei," *ASAtene* 13–14 (1930–31) 9–25.

Francotte, H., *L'industrie dans la Grèce ancienne,* 2 vols. (Brussels 1900–1901).

Fraser, P. M., and E. Matthews, *A Lexicon of Greek Personal Names,* vol. 1, *The Aegean Islands, Cyprus, Cyrenaica* (Oxford 1987).

Frazer, J. G., *Pausanias's Description of Greece,* 5 vols. (London 1898; repr. New York 1965).

Frickenhaus, A., "Das Athenabild des alten Tempels in Athen," *AM* 33 (1908) 17–32.

Fritz, K. von, "Ὅπερ σαφεστάτη πίστις: Thukydides I 35,5," in O. Hiltbrunner et al., eds., *Thesaurismata: Festschrift für Ida Kopp zum 70. Geburtstag* (Munich 1954) 25–37; repr. in K. von Fritz, *Schriften zur griechischen und römischen Verfassungsgeschichte und Verfassungstheorie* (Berlin 1976) 169–176.

Frost, F., "Pericles and Dracontides," *JHS* 84 (1964) 69–72.

———, "Pericles, Thucydides Son of Melesias, and Athenian Politics before the War," *Historia* 13 (1964) 385–399.

Furtwängler, A., "Zu den Skulpturen von Sunion," *AM* 7 (1882) 396–397.

———, *Meisterwerke der griechischen Plastik* (Leipzig 1893).

———, *Masterpieces of Greek Sculpture,* E. Sellers, ed. (London 1895).

———, "Zu den Tempeln der Akropolis von Athen," *Sitzungsberichte der philosophisch-philologischen und der historischen Classe der k. b. Akademie der Wissenschaften zu München* 1 (1898) 349–390.

———, *Aegina das Heiligtum der Aphaia* (Munich 1906).

Gall, H. von, "Das persische Königzelt und die Hallenarchitektur in Iran und Griechenland," in U. Höchmann and A. Krug, eds., *Festschrift für Frank Brommer* (Mainz 1977) 119–132.

———, "Das Zelt des Xerxes und seine Rolle als persischer Raumtyp in Griechenland," *Gymnasium* 86 (1979) 444–462.

Gardner, P., *A History of Ancient Coinage, 700–300 B.C.* (Oxford 1918).

Garland, R. J., "Religious Authority in Archaic and Classical Athens," *BSA* 79 (1984) 75–123.

———, *Introducing New Gods: The Politics of Athenian Religion* (London 1992).

Gasparri, C., "Lo stadio Panatenaico," *ASAtene* 52–53 (1974–75) 313–392.

Gauer, W., *Weihgeschenke aus den Perserkriegen, IstMitt-BH* 2 (Tübingen 1968).

———, "Was geschieht mit dem Peplos?" in E. Berger, ed., *Parthenon-Kongress Basel* (Mainz 1984) 220–229.

Gauthier, P., "Les cléruques de Lesbos et la colonisation Athénienne au Ve siècle," *REG* 79 (1966) 64–88.

Geissler, P., *Chronologie der altattischen Komödie* (Zurich 1969).

Gell, W., *The Itinerary of Greece: Containing One Hundred Routes in Attica, Boeotia, Phocis, Locris, and Thessaly* (London 1827).

Gerding, H., "The Erechtheion and the Panathenaic Procession," *AJA* 110 (2006) 389–401.

Ghirshman, R., "L'Apadana de Suse," *IrAnt* 3 (1963) 148–154.

Gildersleeve, B. L., *Syntax of Classical Greek from Homer to Demosthenes*, 2 vols. (New York 1900–1911).

Gill, D. W. J., "The Decision to Build the Temple of Athena Nike (*IG* I³, 35)," *Historia* 50 (2001) 257–278.

Giovannini, A., "Le Parthénon, le trésor d'Athéna et le tribut des alliés," *Historia* 39 (1990) 129–148.

———, "La participation des alliés au financement du Parthénon: *Aparchè* ou tribut?" *Historia* 46 (1997) 145–157.

Giraud, D., Μελέτη αποκαταστάσεως του ναού της Αθηνάς Νίκης, 2 vols. (Athens 1994).

Goette, H. R., "Die Steinbrüche von Sounion im Agrileza-Tal," *AM* 106 (1991) 201–222.

———, "Athena Pallenis und ihre Beziehungen zur Akropolis von Athen," in W. Hoepfner, ed., *Kult und Kultbauten auf der Akropolis* (Berlin 1997) 116–131.

———, "Ὁ δῆμος της Παλλήνης· Ἐπιγραφές από την περιοχή του ναού της Ἀθηνᾶς Παλληνίδος," *Horos* 10–12 (1992–98) 105–118.

———, Ὁ ἀξιόλογος δῆμος Σούνιον: *Landeskundliche Studien in Südost-Attika* (Rahden/Westf., 2000).

Gomme, A. W., "*IG* I², 60 and Thucydides III 50.2," in G. E. Mylonas, ed., *Studies Presented to David Moore Robinson*, vol. 2 (Saint Louis, MO, 1953) 334–339.

———, "Thucydides ii 13, 3," *Historia* 2 (1953/54) 1–21.

———, "Thucydides ii 13, 3: An Answer to Professor Meritt," *Historia* 3 (1954/55) 333–338.

Gomme, A. W., et al., *A Historical Commentary on Thucydides*, 5 vols. (Oxford 1945–81).

Goodwin, W. W., *Syntax of the Moods and Tenses of the Greek Verb* (London 1889).

Goodyear, W. H., *Greek Refinements: Studies in Temperamental Architecture* (New Haven 1912).

Gow, A. S. F., and D. L. Page, *The Greek Anthology*, 2 vols. (Cambridge 1968).

Graef, B., and E. Langlotz, *Die antiken Vasen von der Akropolis zu Athen*, 2 vols. (Berlin 1925–33).

Graham, A. J., *Colony and Mother City in Ancient Greece,* 2nd ed. (Chicago 1983).

Graindor, P., "L'architecte Kallikratès et le mur est de l'Acropole," *RA* 19 (1924) 174–178.

Gropengiesser, H., *Die pflanzlichen Akrotere klassischer Tempel* (Mainz 1961).

Gruben, G., *Die Kapitelle des Heratempels auf Samos* (diss. Munich 1960).

———, "Naxos und Delos: Studien zur archaischen Architektur der Kykladen," *JdI* 112 (1997) 261–416.

———, *Griechische Tempel und Heiligtümer,* 5th ed. (Munich 2001).

Guépin, J., "Le cours de Cyzicène," *AntCl* 34 (1965) 199–203.

Guthrie, W. K. C., *The Greeks and Their Gods* (Boston 1955).

Habicht, C., "Falsche Urkunden zur Geschichte Athens im Zeitalter der Perserkriege," *Hermes* 89 (1961) 1–35.

Hall, E., *Inventing the Barbarian: Greek Self-Definition through Tragedy* (Oxford 1989).

Hampe, R., "Neue Funde aus Olympia," *Die Antike* 15 (1939) 39–44.

Hampe, R., and U. Jantzen, "Getriebene Bleche," in *Bericht über die Ausgrabungen in Olympia*, vol. 1, *Herbst 1936–Frühjahr 1937* (Berlin 1937) 85–94.

Hansen, M. H., *Eisangelia: The Sovereignty of the People's Court in Athens in the Fourth Century B.C. and the Impeachment of Generals and Politicians,* Odense University Classical Studies 6 (Odense 1975).

Harper, P. O., J. Aruz, and F. Tallon, eds., *The Royal City of Susa: Ancient Near Eastern Treasures in the Louvre* (New York 1992).

Harris, D., *The Treasures of the Parthenon and Erechtheion* (Oxford 1995).

Harrison, E. B., *The Athenian Agora* XI: *Archaic and Archaistic Sculpture* (Princeton 1965).

———, "The Composition of the Amazonomachy on the Shield of Athena Parthenos," *Hesperia* 35 (1966) 107–133.

———, "Athena and Athens in the East Pediment of the Parthenon," *AJA* 71 (1967) 27–58.

———, "U and Her Neighbors in the West Pediment of the Parthenon," in D. Fraser et al., eds., *Essays in the History of Art Presented to Rudolf Wittkower* (London 1967) 1–9.

———, "The South Frieze of the Nike Temple and the Marathon Painting in the Painted Stoa," *AJA* 76 (1972) 353–378.

———, "Alkamanes' Sculptures for the Hephaisteion: Part I, The Cult Statues," *AJA* 81 (1977) 137–178; "Part II, The Base," 265–287; "Part III, Iconography and Style," 411–426.

———, "Apollo's Cloak," in G. Kopke and M. B. Moore, eds., *Studies in Classical Art and Archaeology: A Tribute to Peter Heinrich von Blanckenhagen* (Locust Valley, NY, 1979) 91–98.

———, "The Iconography of the Eponymous Heroes on the Parthenon and in the Agora," in O. Mørkholm and N. M. Waggoner, eds., *Greek Numismatics and Archaeology: Essays in Honor of Margaret Thompson* (Wetteren 1979) 71–85.

———, "Motifs of the City-Siege on the Shield of Athena Parthenos," *AJA* 85 (1981) 281–317.

———, "Time in the Parthenon Frieze," in E. Berger, ed., *Parthenon-Kongress Basel* (Mainz 1984) 230–234.

———, "Hellenic Identity and Athenian Identity in the Fifth Century B.C.," in S. J. Barnes and W. S. Melion, eds., *Cultural Differentiation and Cultural Identity in the Visual Arts,* Studies in the History of Art 27 (Washington, DC, 1989) 41–61.

———, "Pheidias," *YCS* 30 (1996) 16–65.

———, "The Web of History: A Conservative Reading of the Parthenon Frieze," in J. Neils, ed., *Worshipping Athena: Panathenaia and Parthenon* (Madison, WI, 1996) 198–214.

———, "The Glories of the Athenians: Observations on the Program of the Frieze of the Temple of Athena Nike," in D. Buitron-Oliver, ed., *The Interpretation of Architectural Sculpture in Greece and Rome,* Studies in the History of Art 49 (Washington, DC, 1997) 109–125.

Hartog, F., *The Mirror of Herodotos: The Representation of the Other in the Writing of History,* trans. J. Lloyd (Berkeley 1988).

Hellström, P., "The Asymmetry of the Propylaia—Once More," *OpAth* 11 (1975) 87–92.

———, "The Planned Function of the Mnesiklean Propylaia," *OpAth* 17 (1988) 107–121.

Henry, A. S., *Honours and Privileges in Athenian Decrees: The Principal Formulae of Athenian Decrees,* Subsidia Epigraphica 10 (Hildesheim 1983).

Henry, M. M., *Prisoner of History: Aspasia of Miletus and Her Biographical Tradition* (Oxford 1995).

Herbig, R., "Untersuchungen am dorischen Peripteral-Tempel auf Kap Sunion," *AM* 66 (1941) 87–133.

Herington, C. J., *Athena Parthenos and Athena Polias: A Study in the Religion of Periclean Athens* (Manchester 1955).

———, "Athena in Athenian Literature and Cult," in G. T. W. Hooker, ed., *Parthenos and Parthenon, G&R* 10 Suppl. (Oxford 1963) 61–73.

Hignett, C., *A History of the Athenian Constitution to the End of the Fifth Century B.C.* (Oxford 1952).

———, *Xerxes' Invasion of Greece* (Oxford 1963).

Hill, B. H., "The Older Parthenon," *AJA* 16 (1912) 535–558.

Hill, G., "The East Frieze of the Parthenon," *CR* 8 (1894) 225–226.

Hill, I. T., *The Ancient City of Athens* (London 1953).

Hodge, A. T., and R. A. Tomlinson, "Some Notes on the Temple of Nemesis at Rhamnous," *AJA* 73 (1969) 185–192.

Hölscher, T., *Victoria Romana* (Mainz 1967).

———, *Griechische Historienbilder des 5. und 4. Jahrhunderts vor Chr.* (Würzburg 1973).

———, "Ritual und Bildsprache: Zur Deutung der Reliefs an der Brüstung um des Heiligtum der Athena Nike in Athen," *AM* 112 (1997) 143–163.

Hoepfner, W., "Propyläen und Nike-Tempel," in W. Hoepfner, ed., *Kult und Kultbauten auf der Akropolis* (Berlin 1997) 160–177.

Holland, L. B., "Erechtheum Papers, I–IV," *AJA* 28 (1924) 1–23, 142–169, 402–434.

Holloway, R. R., "The Archaic Acropolis and the Parthenon Frieze," *ArtB* 48 (1966) 223–226.

Hondius, J. J. E., *Novae Inscriptiones Atticae* (Leiden 1925).

Hoorn, G. van, *Choes and Anthesteria* (Leiden 1951).

Hopper, R. J., "The Attic Silver Mines in the Fourth Century B.C.," *BSA* 48 (1953) 200–254.

———, "The Mines and Miners of Ancient Athens," *G&R* 8 (1961) 138–151.

Hornblower, S., *A Commentary on Thucydides*, 3 vols. (Oxford 1991–2008).

Hose, M., "Kratinos und der Bau des Perikleischen Odeions," *Philologus* 137 (1993) 3–11.

Hurwit, J. M., *The Athenian Acropolis: History, Mythology, and Archaeology from the Neolithic Era to the Present* (Cambridge 1999).

———, *The Acropolis in the Age of Pericles* (Cambridge 2004).

Iakovidis, S. E., Ἡ Μυκηναϊκὴ Ἀκρόπολις τῶν Ἀθηνῶν (Athens 1962).

Immerwahr, H. R., *Attic Script: A Survey* (Oxford 1990).

Jahn, O., and A. Michaelis, *Arx Athenarum a Pausania Descripta* (Bonn 1901; repr. Chicago 1976).

Jameson, M., "The Ritual of the Athena Nike Parapet," in R. Osborne and S. Hornblower, eds., *Ritual, Finance, Politics: Athenian Democratic Accounts Presented to David Lewis* (Oxford 1994) 312–324.

Jeffery, L. H., "The Battle of Oenoe in the Stoa Poikile," *BSA* 60 (1965) 41–57.

———, "Some Nikai-Statues at Olympia in the Late Fifth Century B.C.," in M. J. Fontana et al., eds., Φιλίας χάριν: *Miscellanea di studi classici in onore di Eugenio Manni* (Rome 1980) vol. 4, 1233–1239.

———, *The Local Scripts of Archaic Greece*, 2nd ed. (Oxford 1990).

Jenkins, I., "The Ambiguity of Greek Textiles," *Arethusa* 18 (1985) 109–132.

———, "The Composition of the So-Called Eponymous Heroes on the East Frieze of the Parthenon," *AJA* 89 (1985) 121–127.

———, *The Parthenon Frieze* (London 1994).

Jeppesen, K., "The Pedimental Compositions of the Parthenon: A Critical Survey," *ActaArch* 24 (1953) 103–125.

———, *Paradeigmata: Three Mid-Fourth Century Main Works of Hellenic Architecture, Reconsidered* (Aarhus 1958).

———, "Bild und Mythus an den Parthenon," *ActaArch* 34 (1963) 1–96.

———, "Where Was the So-Called Erechtheion?" *AJA* 83 (1979) 381–394.

———, "Evidence for the Restoration of the East Pediment Reconsidered in the Light of Recent Achievements," in E. Berger, ed., *Parthenon-Kongress Basel* (Mainz 1984) 267–277.

———, *The Theory of the Alternative Erechtheion* (Aarhus 1987).

Jones, J. E., "The Laurion Silver Mines: A Review of Recent Researches and Results," *G&R* 29 (1982) 169–183.

Jordan, B., *The Athenian Navy in the Classical Period,* University of California Publications in Classical Studies 13 (Berkeley 1975).

———, *Servants of the Gods: A Study in the Religion, History and Literature of Fifth-Century Athens,* Hypomnemata 55 (Göttingen 1979).

Judeich, W., *Topographie von Athen,* 2nd ed. (Munich 1931).

Kagan, D., *The Outbreak of the Peloponnesian War* (Ithaca, NY, 1969).

Kahil, L., *Les enlèvements et le retour d'Hélène dans les textes et les documents figurés* (Paris 1955).

———, "Le 'cratérisque' d'Artémis et le Brauronion de l'Acropole," *Hesperia* 50 (1981) 253–263.

Kallet-Marx, L., "Did Tribute Fund the Parthenon?" *ClAnt* 8 (1989) 252–266.

———, "The Kallias Decree, Thucydides, and the Outbreak of the Peloponnesian War," *CQ* 39 (1989) 94–113.

———, *Money, Expense, and Naval Power in Thucydides' History* (Berkeley 1993).

Kalligas, P., "Ἐργασίαι τακτοποιήσεως καὶ διαμορφώσεως Ἱεροῦ Διονύσου Ἐλευθερέως τῆς νοτίου κλιτύος Ἀκροπόλεως," *ArchDelt* 18 (1963 [1965]) Β' 1, 12–18.

——, "Ἡ περιοχή του ιερού και του θεάτρου του Διονύσου στην Αθήνα," in W. D. E. Coulson et al., eds., *The Archaeology of Athens and Attica under the Democracy* (Oxford 1994) 25–30.

Kallipolitis, V. G., "Der Kouros von Sounion im Athener Nationalmuseum nach der neuen Wiederherstellung," *AntW* 4.2 (1973) 47–51.

Kalpaxis, T., *Hemiteles: Akzidentelle Unfertigkeit und "Bossen-Stil" in der griechischen Baukunst* (Mainz 1986).

Karatheodori, K., "Περὶ τῶν καμπυλῶν τοῦ στυλοβάτου τοῦ Παρθενῶνος καὶ περὶ τῆς ἀποστάσεως τῶν κιόνων αὐτου," *ArchEph* (1937) 120–124.

Kardara, C., "Γλαυκῶπις· ὁ ἀρχαῖος ναὸς καὶ τὸ θέμα τῆς ζωφόρου τοῦ Παρθενῶνος," *ArchEph* (1961) 61–158.

Karoglou, K., *Attic Pinakes: Votive Images in Clay,* BAR International Series 2104 (Oxford 2010).

Karusu, S., "Ein Akroter klassischer Zeit," *AM* 77 (1962) 178–190.

Kassel, R., and C. Austin, *Poetae Comici Graeci*, 8 vols. (Berlin and New York 1983–2001).

Kastriotes, P., "Τὸ Ὠδεῖον τοῦ Περικλέους καὶ ἀνασκαφαὶ κατὰ τὴν ΒΑ γωνίαν τῆς Ἀκροπόλεως," *ArchEph* (1914) 143–166.

——, "Το Ὠδεῖον τοῦ Περικλέους καὶ ἀνασκαφαὶ κατὰ τὴν ΜΑ γωνίαν τῆς Ἀκροπόλεως," *Prakt* (1914) 81–124.

——, "Ἀνασκαφαὶ Ὠδείου τοῦ Περικλέους," *Prakt* (1915) 55–58.

——, "Τὸ Ὠδεῖον τοῦ Περικλέους," *ArchEph* (1915) 145–155.

——, "Περίκλειον Ὠδεῖον," *ArchEph* (1918) 109–110.

——, "Τὸ Ὠδεῖον τοῦ Περικλέους," *Prakt* (1919) 27–31.

——, "Τὸ Ὠδεῖον τοῦ Περικλέους," *ArchDelt* 5 (1919) parart., 1–14.

——, "Περίκλειον Ὠδεῖον," *ArchEph* (1922) 25–38.

——, "Ἀνασκαφαὶ τοῦ ἐν Ἀθήναις Ὠδείου τοῦ Περικλέους," *Prakt* (1925) 21–24.

——, "Ἀνασκαφαὶ ἐν τῷ Ὠδείῳ τοῦ Περικλέους," *Prakt* (1926) 98–103.

——, "Ἀνασκαφαὶ ἐν τῷ Ὠδείῳ τοῦ Περικλέους," *Prakt* (1927) 23–27.

——, "Τὸ Περίκλειον Ὠδεῖον," *Prakt* (1928) 34–40.

——, "Ἀνασκαφαὶ ἐν τῷ Ὠδείῳ τοῦ Περικλέους κατὰ τὸ ἔτος 1929," *Prakt* (1929) 52–57.

Kavvadias, P., "Περὶ τοῦ ναοῦ τῆς Ἀπτέρου Νίκης," *ArchEph* (1897) 174–194.

Kavvadias, P., and G. Kawerau, Ἡ ἀνασκαφὴ τῆς Ἀκροπόλεως ἀπὸ τοῦ 1885 μέχρι τοῦ 1890 (Athens 1906).

Kearns, E., *The Heroes of Attica, BICS* Suppl. 57 (London 1989).

Kenner, H., "Zur Archäologie des Dionysostheaters in Athen," *ÖJh* 57 (1986–87) 55–91.

Kent, R. G., *Old Persian: Grammar, Texts, Lexicon,* 2nd ed. (New Haven 1953).

Kerényi, C., *Eleusis: Archetypal Image of Mother and Daughter*, trans. R. Manheim (London 1967).

Kienast, D., "Der innenpolitische Kampf in Athen von der Rückkehr des Thukydides bis zu Perikles' Tod," *Gymnasium* 60 (1953) 210–229.

Kirchner, J. E., *Prosopographia Attica,* 2 vols. (Berlin 1901–3; repr. 1966).

Klein, R., "Die innenpolitische Gegnerschaft gegen Perikles," in G. Wirth, ed., *Perikles und seine Zeit* (Darmstadt 1979) 494–533.

Kleiss, W., "Zur Entwicklung der achaemenidischen Palast-architektur," *IrAnt* 15 (1980) 199–211.

Knell, H., *Die Darstellung der Götterversammlung in der attischen Kunst des VI. und V. Jahrhunderts v. Chr.: Eine Untersuchung zur Entwicklungsgeschichte des "Daseinsbildes"* (diss. Freiburg 1965).

——, "Vier attische Tempel klassischer Zeit: Zum Problem der Baumeisterzuschreibung," *AA* (1973) 94–114.

——, *Perikleische Baukunst* (Darmstadt 1979).

——, *Mythos und Polis: Bildprogramme griechisches Bauskulptur* (Darmstadt 1990).

Koch, H., *Studien zum Theseustempel in Athen* (Berlin 1955).

Koch, M., "La courbure du stylobate du Parthénon," *ActaArch* 34 (1963) 231.

Koepp, F., "Die Herstellung der Tempel nach den Perserkriegen," *JdI* 5 (1890) 268–277.

Körte, A., "Zur Athena-Nike Inschrift," *Hermes* 45 (1910) 623–627.

——, "Die Attischen Xenodikai," *Hermes* 68 (1933) 238–242.

Köster, A, "Das Altar des Athena-Niketempels," *JdI* 21 (1906) 129–147.

Kokkou, A., "Τὸ κιονόκρανον τοῦ ναοῦ τῆς Σουνιάδος ᾿Αθηνᾶς Ε.Μ. 4478 καὶ ἡ συλλογὴ τοῦ Καντακουζηνοῦ," *ArchEph* (1974) 102–112.

Kolbe, W., "Die Neugestaltung der Akropolis nach den Perserkriegen," *JdI* 51 (1936) 1–64.

Kondis, J., "᾿Αρτεμις Βραυρωνία," *ArchDelt* 22 (1967) Α′, 156–206.

Korres, M. E., "Α′ εφορεία προιστορικών και κλασικών αρχαιοτήτων Ακροπόλεως," *ArchDelt* 35 (1980) Β′ 1, 9–21.

———, "Wilhelm Dörpfelds Forschungen zum Vorparthenon und Parthenon," *AM* 108 (1993) 59–78.

———, "The Architecture of the Parthenon," in P. Tournikiotis, ed., *The Parthenon and Its Impact in Modern Times* (Athens 1994) 54–97.

———, "The History of the Acropolis Monuments," in R. Economakis, ed., *Acropolis Restoration, the CCAM Interventions* (London 1994) 34–51.

———, "The Ancient Quarries on Mount Pentelikon," in Y. Maniatis, N. Herz, and Y. Basiakos, eds., *The Study of Marble and Other Stones Used in Antiquity* (London 1995) 1–5.

———, *From Pentelicon to the Parthenon* (Athens 1995).

———, "Die Athena-Tempel auf der Akropolis," in W. Hoepfner, ed., *Kult und Kultbauten auf der Akropolis* (Berlin 1997) 218–243.

———, "Some Remarks on the Structural Relations between the Propylaea and the NW Building of the Athenian Acropolis," in W. Hoepfner, ed., *Kult und Kultbauten auf der Akropolis* (Berlin 1997) 244–245.

———, "Από τον Σταυρό στην αρχαία Αγορά," *Horos* 10–12 (1992–98) 83–104.

———, "On the North Acropolis Wall," in M. Stamatopoulou and M. Yeroulanou, eds., *Excavating Classical Culture: Recent Archaeological Discoveries in Greece* (Oxford 2002) 179–186.

Korres, M. E., and Ch. Bouras, *Μελέτη ἀποκαταστάσεως τοῦ Παρθενῶνος*, vol. 1 (Athens 1983).

Kotsidu, H., *Die musischen Agone der Panathenäen in archaischer und klassischer Zeit: Eine historisch-archäologische Untersuchung* (Munich 1991).

Kourouniotes, K., ᾿Ελευσινιακά, vol. 1 (Athens 1932).

———, "᾿Ανασκαφαὶ ᾿Ελευσῖνος 1934," *ArchDelt* 15 (1933–35) parart., 1–48.

———, ᾿Ελευσίς, ὁδηγὸς τῶν ἀνασκαφῶν καὶ τοῦ μουσείου (Athens 1934).

Kourouniotes, K., and J. N. Travlos, "Τελεστήριον καὶ ναὸς τῆς Δήμητρος," *ArchDelt* 15 (1933–35) 54–114.

———, "Συμβολὴ εἰς τὴν οἰκοδομικὴν ἱστορίαν τοῦ ᾿Ελευσινιακοῦ Τελεστηρίου," *ArchDelt* 16 (1935–36) 1–42.

Krefter, F., *Persepolis Rekonstruktionen: Der Wiederaufbau des Frauenpalastes, Rekonstruktionen der Paläste, Modell von Persepolis*, Teheraner Forschungen 3 (Berlin 1971).

Krentz, P., "The Ostracism of Thoukydides, Son of Melesias," *Historia* 33 (1984) 499–504.

Kroll, J. H., "The Ancient Image of Athena Polias," in *Studies in Athenian Architecture, Sculpture, and Topography Presented to Homer A. Thompson, Hesperia* Suppl. 20 (Princeton 1982) 65–76.

———, *The Athenian Agora* XXVI: *The Greek Coins* (Princeton 1993).

Kron, U., *Die zehn attischen Phylenheroen, AM-BH* 5 (Berlin 1976).

———, "Die Phylenheroen am Parthenonfries," in E. Berger, ed., *Parthenon-Kongress Basel* (Mainz 1984) 235–244.

Krug, A., "Der Fries des Tempels am Ilissos," *AntP* 18 (1979) 7–21.

Krumme, M., "Das Heiligtum der 'Athena beim Palladion' in Athen," *AA* (1993) 213–227.

Kyle, D., *Athletics in Ancient Athens, Mnemosyne* Suppl. 95 (Leiden 1987).

Kyrieleis, H., *Führer durch das Heraion von Samos* (Athens 1981).

Labarbe, J., "La distribution de blé de 445–444 à Athènes et ses incidences démographiques," in H. J. Diesner, ed., *Sozialökonomische Verhältnisse im alten Orient und im klassischen Altertum* (Berlin 1961) 191–207.

Lalonde, G. V., M. K. Langdon, and M. B. Walbank, *The Athenian Agora* XIX: *Inscriptions: Horoi, Poletai Records, Leases of Public Lands* (Princeton 1991).

Lambrinoudakis, B. K., ᾿Οικοδομικά προγράμματά στην ᾿Αθήνα ἀπό το 479 ἕως το 431π. Χ. (Athens 1986).

Lang, M., *The Athenian Agora* XXV: *The Ostraka* (Princeton 1990).

Langdon, M. K., and L. V. Watrous, "The Farm of Timesios: Rock-Cut Inscriptions in South Attica," *Hesperia* 46 (1977) 162–177.

Lange, K., "Tempelskulpturen von Sunion," *AM* 6 (1881) 233–237.

Lapatin, K. D. S., *Chryselephantine Statuary in the Ancient Mediterranean World* (Oxford 2001).

Lauenstein, D., *Die Mysterien von Eleusis* (Stuttgart 1987).

Lawrence, A. W., "The Acropolis and Persepolis," *JHS* 71 (1951) 111–119.

———, *Greek Architecture*, 5th ed., revised by R. A. Tomlinson (New Haven 1996).

Leipen, N., *Athena Parthenos: A Reconstruction* (Toronto 1971).

Lendle, O., "Philochorus über den Prozess des Phidias," *Hermes* 83 (1955) 284–303.

Lepsius, G. R., *Griechische Marmorstudien* (Berlin 1890).

Leroux, G., *Exploration archéologique de Délos* II: *La salle hypostyle* (Paris 1909).

———, *Les origines de l'édifice hypostyle en Grèce et chez les romains* (Paris 1913).

Lethaby, W. R., *Greek Buildings Represented by Fragments in the British Museum* (London 1908).

Leventi, I., "Der Fries des Poseidon-Tempels in Sounion," *AntP* 30 (2008) 7–54.

———, "Interpretations of the Ionic Frieze of the Temple of Poseidon at Sounion," in P. Schultz and R. von den Hoff, eds., *Structure, Image, Ornament: Architectural Sculpture in the Greek World* (Oxford 2009) 121–132.

Lewis, D. M., "Notes on Attic Inscriptions (I)," *BSA* 49 (1954) 39–49.

———, "Notes on Attic Inscriptions (II)," *BSA* 50 (1955) 1–36.

———, "Double Representation in the Strategeia," *JHS* 81 (1961) 118–123.

———, "New Evidence for the Gold–Silver Ratio," in C. M. Kraay and G. K. Jenkins, eds., *Essays in Greek Coinage Presented to Stanley Robinson* (Oxford 1968) 105–110.

———, "The Athenian Coinage Decree," in I. Carradice, ed., *Coinage and Administration in the Athenian and Persian Empires* (Oxford 1987) 53–63.

———, "Chronological Notes," in *CAH*², vol. 5 (1992) 499–505.

Linders, T., *Studies in the Treasure Records of Artemis Brauronia Found in Athens* (Stockholm 1972).

———, *The Treasurers of the Other Gods in Athens and Their Functions* (Meisenheim am Glan 1975).

Linfert, A., "Die Götterversammlung in Parthenon-Ostfries und das attische Kultsystem unter Perikles," *AM* 94 (1979) 41–47.

———, "Athenen des Phidias," *AM* 97 (1982) 57–77.

Lipka, M., "Anmerkungen zu den Weihinschriften der Athena Parthenos und zur Hekatompedon-Inschrift," in W. Hoepfner, ed., *Kult und Kultbauten auf der Akropolis* (Berlin 1997) 37–44.

Lloyd-Jones, H., *The Justice of Zeus*, 2nd ed. (Berkeley 1983).

Loraux, N., *The Invention of Athens: The Funeral Oration in the Classical City* (Cambridge, MA, 1986).

Lundgreen, B., "A Methodological Inquiry: The Great Bronze Athena," *JHS* 117 (1997) 190–197.

Luschey, H., "Iran und der Westen von Kyros bis Khosrow," *AMIran* 1 (1968) 15–37.

Maaß, M., *Die Prohedrie des Dionysostheaters in Athen* (Munich 1972).

MacDowell, D., *The Law in Classical Athens* (Ithaca, NY, 1978).

———, ed., *Andokides On the Mysteries* (Oxford 1962).

Mace, H. L., "The Archaic Ionic Capital: Studies in Formal and Stylistic Development" (Ph.D. diss., University of North Carolina, 1978).

Macridy, T., "Un tumulus macédonien à Langaza," *JdI* 26 (1911) 193–215.

Maier, F. G., *Griechische Mauerbauinschriften* (Heidelberg 1959).

Mallwitz, A., *Olympia und seine Bauten* (Darmstadt 1972).

Mallwitz, A., and W. Schiering, *Die Werkstatt des Pheidias in Olympia*, *OlForsch* 5 (Berlin 1964).

Malten, L., "Hephaistos," *JdI* 27 (1912) 232–264.

Mansfeld, J., "The Chronology of Anaxagoras' Athenian Period and the Date of His Trial, Part II: The Plot against Pericles and His Associates," *Mnemosyne*, ser. 4, 33 (1980) 17–95.

Mansfield, J. M., "The Robe of Athena and the Panathenaic *Peplos*" (Ph.D. diss., University of Calfornia, Berkeley, 1985).

Mark, I. S., "The Gods on the East Frieze of the Parthenon," *Hesperia* 53 (1984) 289–342.

———, *The Sanctuary of Athena Nike in Athens: Architectural Stages and Chronology*, *Hesperia* Suppl. 26 (Princeton 1993).

————, "Levels Taken on the Nike Bastion," *Hesperia* 64 (1995) 383–388.

Marsden, E. W., *Greek and Roman Artillery: Technical Treatises* (Oxford 1971).

Martin, R., *Manuel d'architecture grecque*, vol. 1, *Matériaux et techniques* (Paris 1965).

Mattingly, H. B., "The Athenian Coinage Decree," *Historia* 10 (1961) 148–188 = Mattingly, *AER*, 5–52.

————, "The Financial Decrees of Kallias (*IG* I², 91/92)," *Proceedings of the African Classical Association* 7 (1964) 35–55.

————, "The Peace of Kallias," *Historia* 14 (1965) 273–281 = Mattingly, *AER*, 107–116.

————, "Periclean Imperialism," in E. Badian, ed., *Ancient Society and Institutions: Studies Presented to Victor Ehrenberg on His 75th Birthday* (Oxford 1966) 193–223 = Mattingly, *AER*, 147–170.

————, "Athens and the Western Greeks: C. 500–413 B.C.," in *Atti del I convegno del Centro Internazionale di Studi Numismatici* (Naples 1967) 201–222 = Mattingly, *AER*, 259–280.

————, "Athenian Finance in the Peloponnesian War," *BCH* 92 (1968) 450–485 = Mattingly, *AER*, 215–257.

————, "Athens and Eleusis: Some New Ideas," in D. W. Bradeen and M. F. McGregor, eds., Φόρος: *Tribute to Benjamin Dean Meritt* (Locust Valley, NY, 1974) 90–103 = Mattingly, *AER*, 325–345.

————, "The Athena Nike Temple Reconsidered," *AJA* 86 (1982) 381–385 = Mattingly, *AER*, 461–471.

————, review of D. Lewis, ed., *Inscriptiones Graecae* I³, fasc. 1, *Decreta et Tabulae Magistratuum*, in *AJP* 105 (1984) 340–357.

————, "The Athenian Coinage Decree and the Assertion of Empire," in I. Carradice, ed., *Coinage and Administration in the Athenian and Persian Empires* (Oxford 1987) 65–71 = Mattingly, *AER*, 477–486.

————, "Some Fifth-Century Epigraphic Hands," *ZPE* 83 (1990) 110–122 = Mattingly, *AER*, 505–517.

————, *The Athenian Empire Restored: Epigraphical and Historical Studies* (Ann Arbor 1996).

————, "The Athena Nike Dossier: *IG* I³ 35/36 and 64 A–B," *CQ* 50 (2000) 604–606.

————, "The Athenian Decree for Chalcis (*IG* I³ 40)," *CQ* 52 (2002) 377–379.

————, "Two Fifth-Century Attic Epigraphic Texts Revisited," *ZPE* 162 (2007) 107–110.

Mattusch, C. C., "Bronze- and Ironworking in the Area of the Athenian Agora," *Hesperia* 46 (1977) 340–379.

————, *Greek Bronze Statuary: From the Beginnings through the Fifth Century B.C.* (Ithaca, NY, 1988).

Mavrikios, A. D., "Aesthetic Analysis Concerning the Curvature of the Parthenon," *AJA* 69 (1965) 264–268.

McAllister, M. H., "The Temple of Ares at Athens," *Hesperia* 28 (1959) 1–64.

Meiggs, R., "A Note on Athenian Imperialism," *CR* 63 (1949) 9–12.

————, "The Crisis of Athenian Imperialism," *HSCP* 67 (1963) 1–36.

————, "The Dating of Fifth-Century Attic Inscriptions," *JHS* 86 (1966) 86–98.

————, *The Athenian Empire* (Oxford 1972).

————, *Trees and Timber in the Ancient Mediterranean World* (Oxford 1982).

Meiggs, R., and D. Lewis, *A Selection of Greek Historical Inscriptions*, 2nd ed. (Oxford 1988).

Meinel, R., *Das Odeion: Untersuchungen an überdachten antiken Theatergebäuden* (Frankfurt am Main 1980).

Meritt, B. D., "Fragments of Attic Building Accounts," *AJA* 36 (1932) 472–476.

————, "Greek Inscriptions," *Hesperia* 5 (1936) 355–441.

————, "Greek Inscriptions," *Hesperia* 7 (1938) 77–146.

————, "Greek Inscriptions," *Hesperia* 8 (1939) 48–82.

————, "Attic Inscriptions of the Fifth Century," *Hesperia* 14 (1945) 61–147.

————, "The Athenian Covenant with Mytilene," *AJP* 75 (1954) 359–368.

————, "The Tribute Quota List of 454/3," *Hesperia* 41 (1972) 403–417.

Meritt, B. D., and G. R. Davidson, "The Treaty between Athens and Haliai," *AJP* 56 (1935) 65–71.

Meritt, B. D., and H. T. Wade-Gery, "Athenian Resources in 449 and 431 B.C.," *Hesperia* 26 (1957) 163–197.

————, "The Dating of Documents to the Mid-Fifth Century I," *JHS* 82 (1962) 67–74; II, *JHS* 83 (1963) 100–117.

Meritt, B. D., H. T. Wade-Gery, and M. F. McGregor, *The Athenian Tribute Lists*, 4 vols. (Cambridge, MA, and Princeton 1939–53).

Meritt, B. D., and A. B. West, *The Athenian Assessment of 425 B.C.* (Ann Arbor 1934).

Meritt, L. S., "Athenian Ionic Capitals from the Athenian Agora," *Hesperia* 65 (1996) 121–174.

Meyer, E., *Geschichte des Altertums,* 3rd ed., 5 vols. (Stuttgart 1910–31).

Michaelis, A., "Die Zeit des Neubaus des Poliastempels in Athen," *AM* 14 (1889) 349–366.

Michel, C., *Recueil d'inscriptions grecques*, 2 vols. (Brussels 1900–27).

Mikalson, J. D., "Religion and the Plague in Athens," in K. J. Rigsby, ed., *Studies Presented to Sterling Dow on His Eightieth Birthday, GRBS* Monograph 10 (1984) 217–225.

Milchhoefer, A., *Untersuchungen über die Demenordnung des Kleisthenes* (Berlin 1892).

Miles, M. M., "The Date of the Temple on the Ilissos River," *Hesperia* 49 (1980) 309–325.

——, "A Reconstruction of the Temple of Nemesis at Rhamnous," *Hesperia* 58 (1989) 133–249.

Miller, M. C., *Athens and Persia in the Fifth Century B.C.: A Study in Cultural Receptivity* (Cambridge 1997).

Möbius, H., "Zu Ilissosfries und Nikebalustrade," *AM* 53 (1928) 1–8.

——, "Das Metroon in Agrai und sein Fries," *AM* 60–61 (1935–36) 234–268.

——, *Die Ornamente der griechischen Grabstelen klassischer und nachklassischer Zeit* (Munich 1968).

Moore, M., and M. Z. P. Philippides, *The Athenian Agora* XXIII: *Attic Black-Figured Pottery* (Princeton 1986).

Morgan, C. H., "The Sculptures of the Hephaisteion, I–II," *Hesperia* 31 (1962) 210–219, 221–235; III–IV, *Hesperia* 32 (1963) 98–108.

Morrison, J. S., and J. F. Coates, *The Athenian Trireme* (Cambridge 1986).

Müller, K., *Tiryns: Die Ergebnisse der Ausgrabungen des Instituts*, vol. 3, *Die Architektur der Burg und des Palastes* (Augsburg 1930).

Mylonas, G. E., *The Hymn to Demeter and Her Sanctuary at Eleusis* (Saint Louis, MO, 1942).

——, *Eleusis and the Eleusinian Mysteries* (Princeton 1961).

——, *Mycenae and the Mycenaean World* (Princeton 1966).

Nagy, B., "Athenian Officials on the Parthenon Frieze," *AJA* 96 (1992) 55–69.

Neer, R., *Style and Politics in Athenian Vase Painting: The Craft of Democracy, ca. 530–460 B.C.* (Cambridge 2002).

——, "The Athenian Treasury at Delphi and the Material of Politics," *ClAnt* 23 (2004) 63–93.

Neils, J., "Reconfiguring the Gods on the Parthenon Frieze," *ArtB* 81 (1999) 6–20.

——, *The Parthenon Frieze* (Cambridge 2001).

——, ed., *Goddess and Polis: The Panathenaic Festival in Ancient Athens* (Princeton 1992).

Neils, J., and P. Schultz, "Erechtheus and the Apobates Race on the Parthenon Frieze (North XI–XII)," *AJA* 116 (2012) 195–207.

Nik, G., "Die Athena Parthenos: Ein griechisches Kultbild," in W. Hoepfner, ed., *Kult und Kultbauten auf der Akropolis* (Berlin 1997) 22–24.

Nilsson, M. P., *Greek Popular Religion* (New York 1940).

Noack, F., *Eleusis, die baugeschichtliche Entwicklung des Heiligtumes* (Berlin 1927).

Noble, J. V., *The Techniques of Painted Attic Pottery* (London 1988).

Nylander, C., *Ionians in Pasargadae: Studies in Old Persian Architecture* (Uppsala 1970).

——, "Foreign Craftsmen in Achaemenian Persia," in *The Memorial Volume of the Vth International Congress of Iranian Art and* Archaeology, vol. 1 (Tehran 1972) 311–318.

——, "Anatolians in Susa—and Persepolis(?)," in *Monumentum H. S. Nyberg,* vol. 3, Acta Iranica, ser. 2, no. 6 (Tehran and Leiden 1975) 317–323.

Ohly, D., "Die Göttin und ihre Basis," *AM* 68 (1953) 25–50.

Oikonomides, A. L., "A New Commentary on the Statues Represented on Athenian Coins," in F. W. Imhoof-Blumer and P. Gardner, *Ancient Coins Illustrating Lost Masterpieces of Greek Art*, new ed. (Chicago 1964).

Olsen, E. C., "An Interpretation of the Hephaisteion Reliefs," *AJA* 42 (1938) 276–287.

Orlandos, A. K., "Τὸ ἀέτωμα τοῦ ἐν Σουνίῳ ναοῦ τοῦ Ποσειδῶνος," *ArchDelt* 1 (1915) 1–27.

——, "Τοῦ ἐν Σουνίῳ ναοῦ τοῦ Ποσειδῶνος τοῖχοι καὶ ὀροφή," *ArchEph* (1917) 213–226.

——, "Ἀνασκαφαὶ τοῦ ἐν Ἀθήναις Ὠδείου τοῦ Περικλέους," *Prakt* (1931) 25–36.

——, "Nouvelles observations sur la construction du temple d'Athéna Niké," *BCH* 71–72 (1947–48) 1–38.

——, "Ἡ γραπτὴ ἀρχιτεκτονικὴ διακόσμησις τοῦ ἐν Σουνίῳ ναοῦ τοῦ Ποσειδῶνος," *ArchEph* (1953–54) pt. 3, 1–18.

————, Τὰ ὑλικὰ δομῆς τῶν ἀρχαίων Ἑλλήνων, 2 vols. (Athens 1955, 1958).

————, Ἡ ἀρχιτεκτονικὴ τοῦ Παρθενῶνος, 3 vols. (Athens 1976–78).

Orlandos, A. K., and J. N. Travlos, Λέξικον ἀρχαίων ἀρχιτεκτονικῶν ὅρων (Athens 1986).

Osborne, M. J., and S. G. Byrne, *A Lexicon of Greek Personal Names*, vol. 2, *Attica* (Oxford 1994).

Osborne, R., *Demos: The Discovery of Classical Attika* (Cambridge 1985).

————, "The Viewing and Obscuring of the Parthenon Frieze," *JHS* 107 (1987) 98–105.

Ostwald, M., *Autonomia* (Chico, CA, 1982).

Overbeck, J., *Die antiken Schriftquellen zur Geschichte der bildenden Künste bei den Griechen* (Leipzig 1868; repr. Hildesheim 1959).

Overbeck, J. C., "Some Notes on the Interior Arrangement of the Erechtheum," *AAA* 5 (1972) 127–129.

Page, D. L., ed., *Poetae Melici Graeci* (Oxford 1962).

Palagia, O., *The Pediments of the Parthenon*, Monumenta Graeca et Romana 7 (Leiden 1993).

————, "Interpretations of Two Athenian Friezes: The Temple on the Ilissos and the Temple of Athena Nike," in J. M. Barringer and J. M. Hurwit, eds., *Periklean Athens and Its Legacy: Problems and Perspectives* (Austin, TX, 2005) 177–192.

Papachristodoulou, I., "Β' Ἐφορεία κλασσικῶν ἀρχαιοτήτων," *ArchDelt* 28 (1973) Β' 1, Χρον. 46–51.

Papadimitriou, J., "Ἀττικὰ I," *ArchEph* (1948–49) 146–153.

————, "The Sanctuary of Artemis at Brauron," *Scientific American* 208, no. 6 (June 1963) 110–120.

Papaioannou, A. A., "Ἡ ἐπιγραφή τοῦ Κοροίβου," in Φίλια Ἔπη: *Studies Presented to George Mylonas*, vol. 3 (Athens 1989) 231–244.

Papathanasopoulos, G., "Σούνιον Ἱρόν· Συμβολή στήν ἐξέταση τῶν Κούρων τοῦ ἱεροῦ καί στή διερεύνηση τοῦ προβλήματος τῆς παλαιοτέρας ὑπαίθριας λατρείας στό Σούνιο" (Ph.D. diss., University of Athens, 1983).

Pareti, L., "Il processo di Fidia ed un papiro di Ginevra," *RM* 24 (1909) 271–316; repr. in L. Pareti, *Studi minori di storia antica*, vol. 2, *Storia greca* (Rome 1961) 133–177.

Parker, R., *Athenian Religion: A History* (Oxford 1996).

————, *Polytheism and Society* (Oxford 2005).

Parlama, L., and N. Stambolides, eds., Η πόλη κάτω από την πόλη· Ευρήματα από τις ανασκαφές του Μητροπολιτικού Σιδηροδρόμου των Αθηνών [English edition: *The City beneath the City*] (Athens 2000).

Paton, J. M., G. P. Stevens, et al., *The Erechtheum* (Cambridge, MA, 1927).

Patterson, C., *Pericles' Citizenship Law of 451–50 B.C.* (New York 1981).

Pearson, A. C., *The Fragments of Sophocles*, 2 vols. (Cambridge 1917).

Peek, W., *Kerameikos: Ergebnisse der Ausgrabungen*, vol. 3, *Inschriften, Ostraka, Fluchtafeln* (Berlin 1941).

————, "Attische Inschriften," *AM* 67 (1942 [1951]) 1–218.

Pemberton, E. G., "The East and West Friezes of the Athena Nike Temple," *AJA* 76 (1972) 303–310.

————, "The Gods of the East Frieze of the Parthenon," *AJA* 80 (1976) 113–124.

Penrose, F. C., *An Investigation of the Principles of Athenian Architecture*, 2nd ed. (London 1888).

Perrot, J., "Survey of Excavations in Iran during 1968–69: Suse et Susiane," *Iran* 8 (1970) 190–194.

————, "Survey of Excavations in Iran, 1969–70: Mission de Suse," *Iran* 9 (1971) 178–181.

————, "Survey of Excavations in Iran during 1970–71: Suse et Susiane," *Iran* 10 (1972) 181–183.

Perrot, J., M. Kervran, D. Ladiray, J. Trichet, D. Stronach, M. Roaf, F. Vallat, and J. Yoyotte, "Recherches dans le secteur est du tépé de l'Apadana en 1973–1974," *Cahiers de la Délégation Archéologique Française en Iran (DAFI)* 4 (1974).

Pesely, G. E., "Hagnon," *Athenaeum*, n.s., 67 (1989) 191–209.

Petersen, E., *Die Burgtempel der Athenaia* (Berlin 1907).

————, "Hekatompedon," *Klio* 9 (1909) 229–247.

Petrakos, B. K., *A Concise Guide to Rhamnous* (Athens 1983).

————, Ο δῆμος τοῦ Ῥαμνοῦντος, vol. 1, Τοπογραφία (Athens 1999).

Pfaff, C. A., *The Argive Heraion*, vol. 1, *The Architecture of the Classical Temple of Hera* (Princeton 2003).

Philios, D., "Ἔκθεσις περὶ τῶν ἐν Ἐλευσῖνι ἀνασκαφῶν," *Prakt* (1884) 64–87.

————, "Ἐπιγραφαὶ ἐξ Ἐλευσῖνος," *ArchEph* (1890) 117–132.

————, "Ἐλευσινιακὰ μελετήματα," *JIAN* 7 (1904) 11–59.

———, Ἐλευσίς, Μυστήρια, ἐρείπια καὶ μουσεῖον αὐτῆς (Athens 1906).

Phillips, D. J., "Men Named Thoukydides and the General of 440/39 B.C. (Thuc. 1.117.2)," *Historia* 40 (1991) 385–395.

Picard, C., "L'architecte Coroibos et le Télesterion d'Éleusis," *CRAI* (1933) 8–21.

Pick, B., "Mitteilungen aus dem Kerameikos V: Die Promachos des Phidias und die Kerameikos-Lampen," *AM* 56 (1931) 59–74.

Pickard-Cambridge, A. W., *The Dramatic Festivals of Athens*, 2nd ed., revised by J. Gould and D. M. Lewis (Oxford 1968).

Picón, C. A., "The Ilissos Temple Reconsidered," *AJA* 82 (1978) 47–81.

Piérart, M., "Les εὔθυνοι Athéniens," *AntCl* 40 (1971) 526–573.

Platonos-Giota, M., "Το Ιερό της Αθηνάς Παλληνίδος," *Archaiologia* 65 (Dec. 1997) 92–97.

Plommer, W. H., "Three Attic Temples," *BSA* 45 (1950) 66–112.

———, "The Archaic Acropolis: Some Problems," *JHS* 80 (1960) 127–159.

———, "The Temple of Poseidon on Cape Sunium: Some Further Questions," *BSA* 55 (1960) 218–233.

———, "Sunium: Another Time Round," *BSA* 71 (1976) 113–115.

Podes, S., "The Introduction of Jury Pay by Pericles: Some Mainly Chronological Considerations," *Athenaeum* 82 (1994) 95–110.

Podlecki, A. J., *Perikles and His Circle* (London 1998).

Pogorelski, A., "The New Athenian Stele with Decree and Accounts," *AJA* 27 (1923) 314–317.

Pollitt, J. J., *The Ancient View of Greek Art: Criticism, History, and Terminology* (New Haven 1974).

———, "The Meaning of the Parthenon Frieze," in D. Buitron-Oliver, ed., *The Interpretation of Architectural Sculpture in Greece and Rome,* Studies in the History of Art 49 (Washington, DC, 1997) 51–65.

Prandi, L., "I processi contro Fidia, Aspasia, Anassagora e l'opposizione a Pericle," *Aevum* 51 (1977) 10–26.

Praschniker, C., "Die Akroterien des Parthenon," *ÖJh* 13 (1910) 5–39.

———, *Parthenonstudien* (Augsburg and Vienna 1928).

———, "Neue Parthenonstudien," *ÖJh* 41 (1954) 5–54.

Premerstein, A. von, "Untersuchungen zur Geschichte des Kaisers Marcus II," *Klio* 12 (1912) 139–178.

Price, M., and N. Waggoner, *Archaic Greek Coinage: The Asyut Hoard* (London 1975).

Pritchett, W. K., *Studies in Ancient Greek Topography,* vol. 1 (Berkeley 1965).

———, *The Greek State at War*, 5 vols. (Berkeley 1976–91).

Puchstein, O., *Das ionische Capitell,* Programm zum Winckelmannsfeste der Archaeologischen Gesellschaft zu Berlin 47 (Berlin 1887).

Radt, S., ed., *Tragicorum Graecorum Fragmenta*, vol. 3, *Aeschylus* (Göttingen 1985).

Raepsaet, G., "Transport de tambours de colonnes du Pentélique à Éleusis au IVe siècle avant notre ère," *AntCl* 53 (1984) 101–136.

Rahn, P. J., "Funeral Memorials of the First Priestess of Athena Nike," *BSA* 81 (1986) 195–207.

Randall, R. H., "The Erechtheum Workmen," *AJA* 57 (1953) 199–210.

Raubitschek, A. E., "A New Fragment of A.T.L., D 8," *AJP* 61 (1940) 475–479.

———, "Greek Inscriptions," *Hesperia* 12 (1943) 12–88.

———, *Dedications from the Athenian Akropolis* (Cambridge, MA, 1949).

———, "Menon, Son of Menekleides," *Hesperia* 24 (1955) 286–289.

———, "The Covenant of Plataea," *TAPA* 91 (1960) 178–183.

———, "Herodotus and the Inscriptions," *BICS* 8 (1961) 59–61.

Raubitschek, A. E., and I. K Raubitschek, "The Mission of Triptolemos," in *Studies in Athenian Architecture, Sculpture, and Topography Presented to Homer A. Thompson, Hesperia* Suppl. 20 (Princeton 1982) 109–117.

Reber, K., "Das Hephaisteion in Athen—ein Monument für die Demokratie," *JdI* 113 (1998) 31–48.

Reisch, E., "Athena Hephaisteia," *ÖJh* 1 (1898) 55–93.

Rhodes, P. J., *The Athenian Boule* (Oxford 1972).

———, *A Commentary on the Aristotelian Athenaion Politeia* (Oxford 1981).

———, "After the Three-Bar Sigma Controversy: The History of Athenian Imperialism Reassessed," *CQ* 58 (2008) 500–506.

Rhodes, P. J., and R. Osborne, *Greek Historical Inscriptions, 404–323 B.C.* (Oxford 2003).

Rhodes, R. F., *Architecture and Meaning on the Athenian Acropolis* (Cambridge 1995).

Rhodes, R. F., and J. J. Dobbins, "The Sanctuary of Artemis Brauronia on the Athenian Acropolis," *Hesperia* 48 (1979) 325–341.

Rhomaios, K., Ὁ μακεδόνικος τάφος τῆς Βεργίνας (Athens 1951).

Richardson, N. J., *The Homeric Hymn to Demeter* (Oxford 1974).

Richter, G. M. A., *Kouroi: Archaic Greek Youths*, 3rd ed. (New York 1970).

Ridgway, B. S., *The Archaic Style in Greek Sculpture* (Princeton 1977).

———, *Fifth Century Styles in Greek Sculpture* (Princeton 1981).

———, "Images of Athena on the Akropolis," in J. Neils, ed., *Goddess and Polis: The Panathenaic Festival in Ancient Athens* (Princeton 1992) 119–142.

Riemann, H., *Zum griechischen Peripteraltempel: Seine Planidee und ihre Entwicklung bis zum Ende des 5. Jhds.* (Düren 1935).

———, "Der peisistratidische Athenatempel auf der Akropolis zu Athen," *MittdAI* 3 (1950) 7–39.

Roaf, M. D., "Sculptures and Sculptors at Persepolis," *Iran* 21 (1983) 1–164.

Robert, J., and L. Robert, "Bulletin épigraphique," *REG* 76 (1963) 121–192.

Robert, L., *Études épigraphiques et philologiques* (Paris 1938).

Roberts, J. T., *Accountability in Athenian Government* (Madison, WI, 1982).

Robertson, D. S., *A Handbook of Greek and Roman Architecture,* 2nd ed. (Cambridge 1945).

Robertson, M., and A. Frantz, *The Parthenon Frieze* (London 1975).

Robertson, N. D., "The True Nature of the 'Delian League,' 478–461," *AJAH* 5 (1980) 64–96, 110–133.

———, *Festivals and Legends: The Formation of Greek Cities in the Light of Public Ritual* (Toronto 1992).

———, "Athena's Shrines and Festivals," in J. Neils, ed., *Worshipping Athena* (Madison, WI, 1996) 27–77.

Robinson, E. S. G., "The Athenian Currency Decree and the Coinages of the Allies," in *Commemorative Studies in Honor of Theodore Leslie Shear, Hesperia* Suppl. 8 (Athens 1949) 324–340.

———, "The Beginnings of Achaemenid Coinage," *NC* 18 (1958) 187–193.

Robkin, A. L. H., "The Odeion of Perikles: Some Observations on Its History, Form, and Functions" (Ph.D. diss., University of Washington, 1976).

———, "The Odeion of Perikles: The Date of Its Construction and the Periklean Building Program," *AncW* 2 (1979) 3–12.

———, "The Tent of Xerxes and the Odeion of Themistokles: Some Speculations," *AncW* 3 (1980) 44–46.

Roccos, L. J., "The Kanephoros and Her Festival Mantle in Greek Art," *AJA* 99 (1995) 641–666.

Rodríguez-Almeida, E., "Un frammento di una nuova pianta marmorea di Roma," *JRA* 1 (1988) 120–131.

Roebuck, C., *Ionian Trade and Colonization* (New York 1959).

Romano, I. B., "Early Greek Cult Images" (Ph.D. diss., University of Pennsylvania, 1980).

Root, M. C., "The Parthenon Frieze and the Apadana Reliefs at Persepolis: Reassessing a Programmatic Relationship," *AJA* 89 (1985) 103–120.

Rosivach, V. J., *The System of Public Sacrifice in Fourth-Century Athens* (Atlanta 1994).

Ross, L., E. Schaubert, and C. Hansen, *Der Tempel der Nike Apteros* (Berlin 1839).

Rotroff, S. I., "The Parthenon Frieze and the Sacrifice to Athena," *AJA* 81 (1977) 379–382.

Rotroff, S. I., and J. H. Oakley, *Debris from a Public Dining Place in the Athenian Agora, Hesperia* Suppl. 25 (Princeton 1992).

Rubensohn, O., review of K. Kourouniotis, Ἐλευσινιακά, in *Gnomon* 9 (1933) 421–437.

———, "Das Weihehaus von Eleusis und sein Allerheiligstes," *JdI* 70 (1955) 1–49.

Rumpf, A., and A. Mallwitz, "Zwei Säulenbasen," *AM* 76 (1961) 15–20.

Sakellariou, M. B., *La migration grecque en Ionie* (Athens 1958).

Salmon, J., "Temples the Measure of Men: Public Building in the Greek Economy," in D. J. Mattingly and J. Salmon, eds., *Economics beyond Agriculture in the Classical World* (London 2001) 195–208.

Samons, L. J., "Athenian Finance and the Treasury of Athena," *Historia* 42 (1993) 129–138.

———, "The 'Kallias Decrees' (*IG* I³, 52) and the Inventories of Athena's Treasure in the Parthenon," *CQ* 46 (1996) 91–102.

———, "A Note on the Parthenon Inventories and the Date of *IG* I³, 52B," *ZPE* 118 (1997) 179–182.

———, *Empire of the Owl: Athenian Imperial Finance, Historia* Einzelschriften 142 (Stuttgart 2000).

Sardmann, W., *Eleusinische Übergabeurkunden* (diss. Marburg 1914).

Sauer, B., *Das sogenannte Theseion* (Berlin 1899).

Schäfer, T., "Diphroi und Peplos auf dem Ostfries des Parthenon: Zur Kultpraxis bei den Panathenäen in klassischer Zeit," *AM* 102 (1987) 185–212.

Schafter, D., "Musical Victories in Early Classical Vase Paintings," *AJA* 95 (1991) 333–334.

Schaps, D. M., *Economic Rights of Women in Ancient Greece* (Edinburgh 1979).

Schefold, K., *Myth and Legend in Early Greek Art* (New York 1966).

———, "Die Gestaltung des Raumes in der frühen iranischen und griechischen Kunst," *AMIran* 1 (1968) 49–62.

———, *Gods and Heroes in Late Archaic Greek Art* (Cambridge 1992).

Schelp, J., *Das Kanoun: Der griechische Opferkorb* (Würzburg 1975).

Schlaifer, R., "The Cult of Athena Pallenis," *HSCP* 54 (1943) 35–67.

Schleif, H., "Der Nikepyrgos und Mnesikles," *JdI* 48 (1933) 177–184.

Schmidt, E., *Persepolis*, vol. 1, *Structures, Reliefs, Inscriptions* (Chicago 1953).

———, *Persepolis*, vol. 2, *Contents of the Treasury and Other Discoveries* (Chicago 1957).

Schmitt Pantel, P., *La cité au banquet: Histoire des repas publics dans les cités grecques* (Rome 1992).

Schneider, R. von, "Marmorreliefs in Berlin," *JdI* 18 (1903) 91–93.

Schrader, H., *Die archaischen Marmorbildwerke der Akropolis* (Frankfurt am Main 1939).

Schuchhardt, W.-H., "Athena Parthenos," *AntP* 2 (1963) 31–53.

———, "Zur Basis der Athena Parthenos," in *Wandlungen: Studien zur antiken und neueren Kunst Ernst Homann-Wedeking gewidmet* (Waldsassen-Bayern 1975) 120–130.

Schultz, P., "The Akroteria of the Temple of Athena Nike," *Hesperia* 70 (2001) 1–47.

———, "The North Frieze of the Temple of Athena Nike," in O. Palagia, ed., *Art in Athens during the Peloponnesian War* (Cambridge 2009) 128–167.

Schwarze, J., *Die Beurteilung des Perikles durch die attische Komödie und ihre historische und historiographische Bedeutung* (Munich 1971).

Schweitzer, B., "Prolegomena zur Kunst des Parthenon-Meisters I," *JdI* 53 (1938) 1–89.

———, "Pheidias der Parthenonmeister," *JdI* 55 (1940) 170–241.

———, "Mnesikles und die perikleische Planung des Westaufganges zur Akropolis," in S. Morenz, ed., *Aus Antike und Orient: Festschrift Wilhelm Schubart zum 75. Geburtstag* (Leipzig 1950) 116–125.

Sealy, R., "P. Strassburg 84 Verso," *Hermes* 86 (1958) 440–446.

———, "Theopompos and Athenian Lies," *JHS* 80 (1960) 194–195.

———, "Ephialtes," *CP* 59 (1964) 11–22.

Segre, M., "La legge ateniese sull'unificazione della moneta," *Clara Rhodos* 9 (1938) 149–178.

Shapiro, H. A., *Art and Cult under the Tyrants in Athens* (Mainz 1989; 2nd ed. 1998).

———, "*Mousikoi Agones:* Music and Poetry at the Panathenaia," in J. Neils, ed., *Goddess and Polis: The Panathenaic Festival in Ancient Athens* (Princeton 1992) 53–75.

———, *Art and Cult under the Tyrants in Athens: Supplement* (Mainz 1995).

Shear, I. M., "Kallikrates," *Hesperia* 32 (1963) 375–424.

———, "Maidens in Greek Architecture: The Origin of the Caryatids," *BCH* 123 (1999) 65–85.

———, "The Western Approach to the Athenian Akropolis," *JHS* 119 (1999) 86–127.

Shear, J. L., "Polis and Panathenaia: The History and Development of Athena's Festival" (Ph.D. diss., University of Pennsylvania, 2001).

———, "Prizes from Athens: The List of Panathenaic Prizes and the Sacred Oil," *ZPE* 142 (2003) 87–108.

Shear, T. L., "The Campaign of 1936," *Hesperia* 6 (1937) 333–381.

Shear, T. L., Jr., "The Athenian Agora: Excavations of 1970," *Hesperia* 40 (1971) 241–279.

———, "The Athenian Agora: Excavations of 1973–1974," *Hesperia* 44 (1975) 331–374.

———, "Athens: From City-State to Provincial Town," *Hesperia* 50 (1981) 356–377.

Shear, T. L., Jr., "The Demolished Temple at Eleusis," in *Studies in Athenian Architecture, Sculpture, and Topography Presented to Homer A. Thompson, Hesperia* Suppl. 20 (Princeton 1982) 128–140.

———, "The Athenian Agora: Excavations of 1980–1982," *Hesperia* 53 (1984) 1–57.

———, "The Persian Destruction of Athens: Evidence from Agora Deposits," *Hesperia* 62 (1993) 383–482.

———, "Ἰσονόμους τ' Ἀθήνας ἐποιησάτην: The Agora and the Democracy," in W. D. E. Coulson et al., eds., *The Archaeology of Athens and Attica under the Democracy* (Oxford 1994) 225–248.

———, "Bouleuterion, Metroon, and the Archives at Athens," in M. H. Hansen and K. Raaflaub, eds., *Studies in the Ancient Greek Polis, Historia* Einzelschriften 95 (Stuttgart 1995) 157–190.

———, "The Athenian Agora: Excavations of 1989–1993," *Hesperia* 66 (1997) 495–548.

Shefton, B. B., "Herakles and Theseus on a Red-Figured Louterion," *Hesperia* 31 (1962) 330–368.

Shiloh, Y., *The Proto-Aeolic Capital and Israelite Ashlar Masonry* (Jerusalem 1979).

Shoe, L. T., *Profiles of Greek Mouldings* (Cambridge, MA, 1936).

———, "Dark Stone in Greek Architecture," in *Commemorative Studies in Honor of Theodore Leslie Shear, Hesperia* Suppl. 8 (Athens 1949) 341–352.

Siewert, P., *Der Eid von Plataiai* (Munich 1972).

Simon, E., "Die Wiedergewinnung der Helena," *AntK* 7 (1964) 91–95.

———, "Versuch einer Deutung der Südmetopen des Parthenon," *JdI* 90 (1975) 100–120.

———, "Die Mittelgruppe im Westgiebel des Parthenon," in H. A. Cahn and E. Simon, eds., *Tainia: Roland Hampe zum 70. Geburtstag* (Mainz 1980) 238–255.

———, "Die Mittelszene in Ostfries des Parthenon," *AM* 97 (1982) 127–144.

———, *Festivals of Attica: An Archaeological Commentary* (Madison, WI, 1983).

———, "Τὰ γλυπτά του ναού και του θωρακείου της Αθηνάς Νίκης," *Arkhaiognosia* 4 (1985–86) 11–28.

———, "An Interpretation of the Nike Temple Parapet," in D. Buitron-Oliver, ed., *The Interpretation of Architectural Sculpture in Greece and Rome*, Studies in the History of Art 49 (Washington, DC, 1997) 127–143.

Sinn, U., "Sunion," *AntW* 23 (1992) 175–190.

Sinos, S., "Zur Kurvatur des Parthenonstereobats," *AA* (1974) 157–168.

Skias, A. N., "Ἀνασκαφαὶ παρὰ τὸν Ἰλισόν," *Prakt* (1897) 73–85.

Smaltz, B., "Der Parthenos des Phidias: Zwischen Kult und Repräsentanz," in W. Hoepfner, ed., *Kult und Kultbauten auf der Akropolis* (Berlin 1997) 25–30.

Smith, A. H., *The Sculptures of the Parthenon* (London 1910).

Smyth, H. W., *Greek Grammar* (Cambridge, MA, 1956).

Sokolowski, F., *Lois sacrées de cités grecques* (Paris 1969).

Solon, L. V., *Polychromy; Architectural and Structural, Theory and Practice* (New York 1924).

Sommerstein, A. H., ed., *The Comedies of Aristophanes,* vol. 2, *Knights* (Warminster 1981).

Spaeth, B. S., "Athenians and Eleusinians in the West Pediment of the Parthenon," *Hesperia* 60 (1991) 331–362.

Sparkes, B. A., and L. Talcott, *The Athenian Agora* XII: *Black and Plain Pottery of the 6th, 5th and 4th Centuries B.C.* (Princeton 1970).

Stadter, P. A., *A Commentary on Plutarch's Pericles* (Chapel Hill, NC, 1989).

Stähler, K., "Zur Rekonstruktion und Datierung des Gigantomachiegiebels von der Akropolis," in *Antike und Universalgeschichte: Festschrift Hans Erich Stier* (Münster 1972) 88–112.

———, "Der Zeus aus dem Gigantomachiegiebel der Akropolis?" *Boreas* 1 (1978) 28–31.

Stais, B., "Ἀνασκαφαὶ ἐν Σουνίῳ," *ArchEph* (1900) 113–150.

———, "Σουνίου ἀνασκαφαί," *ArchEph* (1917) 168–213.

Stanton, G. R., "Some Attic Inscriptions," *BSA* 79 (1984) 289–306.

———, "Some Attic Inscriptions," *BSA* 80 (1985) 259, pl. 23.

Ste. Croix, G. E. M. de, *The Origins of the Peloponnesian War* (London 1972).

Stephenson, F. R., and L. J. Fatoohi, "The Eclipses Recorded by Thucydides," *Historia* 50 (2001) 245–253.

Steskal, M., *Der Zerstörungsbefund 480/79 der Athener Akropolis: Eine Fallstudie zum etablierten Chronologie-gerüst* (Hamburg 2004).

Stève, M.-J., "Inscriptions des Achéménides à Suse (suite)," *StIr* 3 (1974) 135–169.

Stevens, G. P., "Concerning the Curvature of the Steps of the Parthenon," *AJA* 38 (1934) 533–542.

———, "The Periclean Entrance Court of the Acropolis of Athens," *Hesperia* 5 (1936) 443–520.

———, *The Setting of the Periclean Parthenon, Hesperia* Suppl. 3 (Athens 1940).

———, "The Sills of the Grilles of the Pronaos and Opisthodomos of the Parthenon," *Hesperia* 11 (1942) 354–364.

———, "The Curve of the North Stylobate of the Parthenon," *Hesperia* 12 (1943) 135–143.

———, "Architectural Studies Concerning the Acropolis of Athens," *Hesperia* 15 (1946) 73–106.

Stevens, G. P., and A. E. Raubitschek, "The Pedestal of the Athena Promachos," *Hesperia* 15 (1946) 107–114.

Stevenson, T., "Cavalry Uniforms on the Parthenon Frieze?" *AJA* 107 (2003) 629–654.

———, "The Parthenon Frieze as an Idealized, Contemporary Panathenaic Festival," in D. J. Phillips and D. Pritchard, eds., *Sport and Festival in the Ancient Greek World* (Swansea 2003) 233–280.

Stewart, A. F., "History, Myth and Allegory in the Program of the Temple of Athena Nike, Athens," in H. L. Kessler and M. S. Simpson, eds., *Pictorial Narrative in Antiquity and the Middle Ages*, Studies in the History of Art 16 (Washington, DC, 1985).

Stillwell, R., "The Siting of Classical Greek Temples," *JSAH* 13 (1954) 3–8.

———, "The Panathenaic Frieze," *Hesperia* 38 (1969) 231–241.

Stronach, D., *Pasargadae: A Report on the Excavations Conducted by the British Institute of Persian Studies from 1961 to 1963* (Oxford 1978).

———, "The Apadana: A Signature of the Line of Darius I," in J.-L. Huot, M. Yon, and Y. Calvet, eds., *De l'Indus aux Balkans: Recueil à la mémoire de Jean Deshayes* (Paris 1985) 433–445.

———, "The Royal Garden at Pasargadae: Evolution and Legacy," in L. de Meyer and E. Haerinck, eds., *Archaeologia Iranica et Orientalis: Miscellanea in Honorem Louis Vanden Berghe* (Ghent 1989) 475–502.

———, "The Garden as a Political Statement: Some Case Studies from the Near East in the First Millennium B.C.," *Bulletin of the Asia Institute*, n.s., 4 (1990) 171–182.

Stronach, D., and M. Roaf, "Excavations at Tepe Nush-i Jan, Part 1: A Third Interim Report," *Iran* 16 (1978) 1–11.

Stroud, R. S., *The Athenian Empire on Stone,* David Lewis Lecture, Oxford, May 24, 2006 (Athens 2006).

Stuart, J., and N. Revett, *The Antiquities of Athens*, 3 vols. (London 1762–94).

Studniczka, F., "Zu den Friesplatten vom ionischen Tempel am Ilissos," *JdI* 31 (1916) 169–230.

———, "Neues über die Parthenonmetopen," *Neue Jahrbücher für Wissenschaft und Jugendbildung* 5 (1929) 637–652.

Svoronos, J. N., "Ελευσινιακα," *JIAN* 8 (1905) 131–160.

———, "La Tholos d'Athènes," *NZ* 55 (1922) 119–149.

———, *Les monnaies d'Athènes* (Munich 1923–26).

Talcott, L., "Attic Black-Glazed Stamped Ware and Other Pottery from a Fifth Century Well," *Hesperia* 4 (1935) 477–523.

Tanoulas, T., "The Pre-Mnesiclean Cistern on the Athenian Acropolis," *AM* 107 (1992) 129–160.

———, "Structural Relations between the Propylaea and the NW Building of the Athenian Acropolis," *AM* 107 (1992) 199–215.

Tataki, A. B., *Sounion: The Temple of Poseidon* (Athens 1994).

Thöne, C., *Ikonographische Studien zu Nike im 5. Jahrhundert v. Chr.* (Heidelberg 1999).

Thompson, D. B., "The Golden Nikai Reconsidered," *Hesperia* 13 (1944) 173–209.

Thompson, H. A., "Buildings on the West Side of the Agora," *Hesperia* 6 (1937) 1–266.

———, "The Pedimental Sculpture of the Hephaisteion," *Hesperia* 18 (1949) 230–268.

———, "Itinerant Temples of Attica," *AJA* 66 (1962) 200.

———, "The Sculptural Adornment of the Hephaisteion," *AJA* 66 (1962) 339–347.

———, "A Colossal Moulding in Athens," in Χαριστήριον εἰς Ἀναστάσιον Κ. Ὀρλάνδον, vol. 1 (Athens 1965) 314–323.

———, "Activity in the Athenian Agora 1960–1965," *Hesperia* 35 (1966) 37–54.

Thompson, H. A., and R. E. Wycherley, *The Athenian Agora* XIV: *The Agora of Athens* (Princeton 1972).

Thompson, W. E., "The Value of the Kyzikene Stater," *NC* 3 (1963) 1–4.

———, "Gold and Silver Ratios at Athens during the Fifth Century," *NC* 4 (1964) 103–123.

———, "The Date of the Athenian Gold Coinage," *AJP* 86 (1965) 159–174.

———, "The Chronology of 432/1," *Hermes* 96 (1968) 216–232.

———, "The Golden Nikai and the Coinage of Athens," *NC* 10 (1970) 1–6.

———, "A Rubric in the Propylaia Accounts," *CQ*, n.s., 20 (1970) 39–40.

Tiberi, C., *Mnesicle, l'architetto dei Propilei* (Rome 1964).

Tod, M. N., *A Selection of Greek Historical Inscriptions*, 2nd ed., 2 vols. (Oxford 1946–48).

———, "A New Eleusinian Title?" *AJP* 77 (1956) 52–54.

Tölle-Kastenbein, R., "Das Hekatompedon auf der Athener Akropolis," *JdI* 108 (1993) 43–75.

Tomlinson, R. A., "The Sequence of Construction of Mnesikles' Propylaia," *BSA* 85 (1990) 405–413.

Townsend, R. F., "Aspects of Athenian Architectural Activity in the Second Half of the Fourth Century B.C." (Ph.D. diss., University of North Carolina, 1982).

Tracy, S. V., "Hands in Fifth-Century B.C. Attic Inscriptions," in K. J. Rigsby, ed., *Studies Presented to Sterling Dow on His Eightieth Birthday, GRBS* Monograph 10 (Durham, NC, 1984) 277–282.

Traill, J. S., *The Political Organization of Attica: A Study of the Demes, Trittyes, and Phylai and Their Representation in the Athenian Council, Hesperia* Suppl. 14 (Princeton 1975).

Travlos, J. N., "The Topography of Eleusis," *Hesperia* 18 (1949) 138–147.

———, "Τὸ Ἀνάκτορον τῆς Ἐλευσῖνος," *ArchEph* (1950–51) 1–16.

———, "Ἡ παλαιοχριστιανικὴ βασιλικὴ τοῦ Διονυσιακοῦ θεάτρου," *ArchEph* (1953–54) B', 301–316.

———, "Τὸ γυμνάσιον τοῦ Κυνοσάργους," *AAA* 3 (1970) 6–14.

———, "Ἡ ἐσωτερικὴ διάταξις τοῦ Ἐρεχθείου," *AAA* 4 (1971) 77–84.

———, *Pictorial Dictionary of Ancient Athens* (London 1972).

———, *Bildlexikon zur Topographie des antiken Attika* (Tübingen 1988).

Tréheux, J., "Sur le nombre des statues cultuelles du Brauronion et la date de l'Artemis Brauronia de Praxitèle," *RA* 55 (1964) 1–6.

Tschira, A., "Die unfertigen Säulentrommeln auf der Akropolis von Athen," *JdI* 55 (1940) 242–261.

———, "Untersuchungen im süden des Parthenon," *JdI* 87 (1972) 158–231.

Tuchelt, K., *Die archaischen Skulpturen von Didyma*, IstForsch 27 (Berlin 1970).

———, *Vorarbeiten zu einer Topographie von Didyma: Eine Untersuchung der inschriftlichen und archäologischen Zeugnisse, IstMitt-BH* 9 (Tübingen 1973).

Vallat, F., "Deux nouvelles 'chartes de fondation' d'un palais de Darius Ier à Suse," *Syria* 48 (1971) 53–59.

———, "Deux inscriptions élémites de Darius Ier (DSf et DSz)," *StIr* 1 (1972) 3–13.

Vallois, R., "La réforme administrative des sanctuaires éleusiniens," *REA* 35 (1933) 195–200.

Vallois, R., and G. Poulsen, *Exploration archéologique de Délos* III: *Nouvelles récherches sur la salle hypostyle* (Paris 1914).

Vanderpool, E., "News Letter from Greece," *AJA* 63 (1959) 279–283.

———, "A Monument to the Battle of Marathon," *Hesperia* 35 (1966) 93–106.

———, "The Marble Trophy from Marathon in the British Museum," *Hesperia* 36 (1967) 108–110.

———, "Three Prize Vases," *ArchDelt* 24 (1969 [1971]) 1–5.

———, "The Date of the Pre-Persian City-Wall of Athens," in D. W. Bradeen and M. F. McGregor, eds., *Φόρος: Tribute to Benjamin Dean Meritt* (Locust Valley, NY, 1974) 156–160.

———, "Victories in the Anthippasia," *Hesperia* 43 (1974) 311–313.

Vanhove, D., "À propos d'un chariot servant à transporter le marbre," *AntCl* 56 (1987) 284–289.

Vian, F., *La guerre des géants: Le mythe avant l'époque hellénistique* (Paris 1952).

von den Hoff, R., "Herakles, Theseus, and the Athenian Treasury at Delphi," in P. Schultz and R. von den Hoff, eds., *Structure, Image, Ornament: Architectural Sculpture in the Greek World* (Oxford 2009) 96–104.

Wace, A. J. B., *Mycenae, an Archaeological History and Guide* (Princeton 1949).

Wade-Gery, H. T., *Essays in Greek History* (Oxford 1958).

Wade-Gery, H. T., and B. D. Meritt, "The Decrees of Kallias," *Hesperia* 16 (1947) 279–286.

Waele, J. A. K. E. de, *The Propylaia of the Akropolis in Athens: The Project of Mnesikles,* Publications of the Netherlands Institute at Athens 1 (Amsterdam 1990).

Walbank, M. B., "Criteria for the Dating of Fifth-Century Attic Inscriptions," in D. W. Bradeen and M. F. MacGregor, eds., Φόρος: *Tribute to Benjamin Dean Meritt* (Locust Valley, NY, 1974) 161–169.

———, "Leases of Sacred Properties in Attica, Parts I–IV," *Hesperia* 52 (1983) 100–135, 177–231.

———, "Two Notes on Leases of Sacred Property in Attica," *ZPE* 116 (1997) 39–40.

Walker, H. J., "The Early Development of the Theseus Myth," *RhM* 138 (1995) 1–33.

Wallace, P. W., "Psyttaleia and the Trophies of the Battle of Salamis," *AJA* 73 (1969) 293–303.

———, "The Tomb of Themistokles in the Peiraieus," *Hesperia* 41 (1972) 451–462.

Walser, G., *Die Völkerschaften auf den Reliefs von Persepolis* (Berlin 1966).

———, *Persepolis: Die Königspfalz des Darius* (Tübingen 1980).

Walsh, J., "The Authenticity and Dates of the Peace of Callias and the Congress Decree," *Chiron* 11 (1981) 31–63.

Watrous, L. V., "The Sculptural Program of the Siphnian Treasury at Delphi," *AJA* 86 (1982) 159–172.

Webster, T. B. L., *The Tragedies of Euripides* (London 1967).

Weickert, C., *Studien zur Kunstgeschichte des 5. Jahrhunderts v. Chr.,* pt. 2, Ἔργα Περικλέους, *AbhBerl* (1950) no. 1.

Weidauer, L., "Eumolpus und Athen: Eine ikonographische Studie," *AA* (1985) 195–210.

Weller, C. H., "The Pre-Periclean Propylon of the Acropolis at Athens," *AJA* 8 (1904) 35–70.

Welter, G., "Vom Nikepyrgos," *AM* 48 (1923) 190–201.

———, *Aigina* (Berlin 1938).

———, "Vom Nikepyrgos," *AA* (1939) 1–22.

Wesenberg, B., *Kapitelle und Basen: Beobachtungen zur Entstehung der griechischen Säulenformen* (Düsseldorf 1971).

———, "Zur Baugeschichte des Niketempels," *JdI* 96 (1981) 28–54.

———, "Panathenäische Peplosdedikation und Arrhephorie," *JdI* 110 (1995) 149–178.

West, M. L., *Ancient Greek Music* (Oxford 1992).

West, W. C., "Greek Public Monuments of the Persian Wars" (Ph.D. diss., University of North Carolina, 1965).

———, "The Trophies of the Persian Wars," *CP* 64 (1969) 7–19.

———, "Saviors of Greece," *GRBS* 11 (1970) 271–282.

Wickens, J. M., "The Archaeology and History of Cave Use in Attica" (Ph.D. diss., Indiana University, 1986).

Wiegand, T., *Die archaische Poros-Architektur der Akropolis zu Athen* (Kassel and Leipzig 1904).

Wiencke, M. I., "The Date of the Parthenon Frieze," *AJA* 67 (1963) 219.

Wilkins, J., *Euripides Heraclidae with Introduction and Commentary* (Oxford 1993).

Wiseman, J., "An Unfinished Colossus on Mt. Penteli," *AJA* 72 (1968) 75–76.

Woodford, S., "More Light on Old Walls," *JHS* 94 (1974) 158–165.

Woodward, A. M., "The Golden Nikai of Athena," *ArchEph* (1937) pt. 1, 159–170.

Wrede, W., "Mnesikles und der Nikepyrgos," *AM* 57 (1932) 74–91.

Wright, J. C., "The Mycenaean Entrance System at the West End of the Akropolis of Athens," *Hesperia* 63 (1994) 323–360.

———, "Note," *Hesperia* 64 (1995) 389.

Wyatt, W. F., and C. N. Edmonson, "The Ceiling of the Hephaisteion," *AJA* 88 (1984) 135–167.

Wycherley, R. E., *The Athenian Agora* III: *Literary and Epigraphical Testimonia* (Princeton 1957).

———, "The Temple of Hephaistos," *JHS* 79 (1959) 153–156.

———, "The Scene of Plato's *Phaidros*," *Phoenix* 17 (1963) 88–98.

———, "'Addendum' to D. M. Lewis and A. M. Woodward, 'A Transfer from Eleusis,'" *BSA* 70 (1975) 188–189.

———, *The Stones of Athens* (Princeton 1978).

Young, T. C., "Thoughts on the Architecture of Hasanlu IV," *IrAnt* 6 (1966) 48–71.

————, *Excavations at Godin Tepe: First Progress Report* (Toronto 1969).

Young, T. C., "The Godin Project: Godin Tepe," *Iran* 12 (1974) 207–211.

————, "Architectural Developments in Iron Age Western Iran," *Bulletin of the Canadian Society for Mesopotamian Studies* 27 (1994) 25–32.

Young, T. C., and L. D. Levine, *Excavations of the Godin Project: Second Progress Report* (Toronto 1974).

Zorides, P., "Ἡ σπηλιά τῶν Νυμφῶν τῆς Πεντέλης," *ArchEph* (1977) Χρόν., 4–11.

Zuntz, G., *The Political Plays of Euripides* (Manchester 1955).

SUBJECT INDEX

Page references in italics indicate illustrations. For citations of ancient texts and inscriptions, please consult the separate index locorum.

Academy, 156, 159, 204n27

Achilles Painter, 16

Acropolis: cult statues on, 360–63, 360–61n7, 362n18, 365–66 (*see also* Athena statue, gold and ivory); fortifications, 8, 77, 77n179; as fortified castle vs. religious precinct, 273; geomorphology of, 157–58; landscaping, 310; plans for, *3*, 22–26, 22n50, 25n63; variations in the pace of work on, 11; views of, *2*, *275*. *See also specific buildings and statues*

Aghia Marina quarries, 263–64

Aghia Triada, 258n114

Aghios Ioannes o Theologos, 254

Agorakritos, 262–63

Agrai, 329–30, 330n3, 339–41, 341n50; Metroon, 339. *See also* Ilissos temple

Agrileza quarries, 231–32

Aiantis (IX) tribe, 70

Aigeis (II) tribe, 70

Aigeus, King, 128, 155, 242

Aigina, Temple of Aphaia, 95n41, 95n44, 230, 234, 280–81, 283n35

Aiginetan poros stone, 170–71, 176, 178–79, 187, 394

Akamantis (V) tribe, 324, 378–79

Alexander the Great, 215–19, 226–27

Alkamenes, 43, 250, 281n23

Alkibiades, 293, 316n174

Alkimachos, 212, 214

Amandry, P., 7

Amazons, defeated by Theseus and Athenians, 15–17, 108–9, 117–20, 355. *See also* Mikon

Ambrakia campaign, 348

Amphipolis (Thrace), 318

Anaktoron, in Eleusinian sanctuary, 162–63, 182–83, 187, 193, 195; location of, 166–68, 191; roofing of, 180

Anaxagoras, 317–18, 318n183

Antikles, 45–49, 47n28, 47n30, 67

apadanas (audience halls for Persian kings), 219n87; Apadana at Persepolis, 220, 220nn92–93, 222–23; Apadana at Susa, 192, 192n122, 194–95, 219–20, 222–23

Apatouria, festival of, 388, 388n134

Aphaia, Temple of (Aigina), 230, 234, 280–81, 283n35

apobatic contest, 123–24, *124*, 124n135, 157n51, 403–4

Apollo, divine paternity of, 388

Apollo, gilded tripod dedicated to (Delphi), 8

Apollo, Temple of (Bassai), 239

Apollo, Temple of (Corinth), 96n48

Apollo, Temple of (Delos), 83n16

Apollo, Temple of (Delphi), 10

Apollo, Temple of (Selinous), 84n

Apollo statue, colossal bronze (Delphi), 8

apotheosis, 131–32

Archenautes, 304, 324

Archestratos, 323–24

Archidamian War, 226, 304, 323, 360, 380

Areopagos, 21, 251, 355

Ares, Temple of, *2*, 229, 250–51, 250n82, 258n109, 389. *See also* Athena Pallenis, Temple of

Ares and Athena Areia, sanctuary of (Acharnai), 251

Argive Heraion, 366–67, 367n37, 369–70

Argos, 10

Ariobarzanes I Philoromaios, 203n17, 205–6, 206n36

Ariobarzanes II Philopator, 206–7, 206n36

Aristion, 206, 206n35

Aristokleides, 213–14, 214n74

Arreneides, 70

arrhephoroi, 132–34, 132n160, 134n164, 158, 404

Artaxerxes I, 221

Artemis, Temple of (Brauron), 368–69, 368nn45–46

Artemis, Temple of (Ephesos), 193

Artemis, Temple of (Korkyra), 84n

Artemis Agrotera, *2*, 339–41, 358. *See also* Ilissos temple

Artemis Brauronia, Temple/sanctuary of, 282–83, 312

Artemis Hekate (Epipyrgidia), 281, 281n23

Index Locorum